FROM 1859 TO 1992

1891 — Mary Whiton Calkins
Establishes a psychology laboratory at Wellesley and later becomes the first woman president of the American Psychology Association.

1892 — Edward Titchener
Earns his doctorate and moves to the United States, where he continues his work with the structuralist technique of introspective analysis at Cornell.

1894 — Margaret Floy Washburn
First woman to receive a Ph.D. in psychology and later writes several important textbooks on comparative psychology.

1898 — Edward Thorndike
One of the pioneers in animal learning who develops the "law of effect" as a result of research on trial and error learning of animals using his puzzle box.

1913 — John Watson
Publishes his article "Psychology as the Behaviorist Views It," in which he describes his program on behaviorism.

1906 — Ivan Pavlov
Publishes his learning research on the salivation response in dogs, which later became known as classical conditioning.

1905 — Alfred Binet
Develops the first intelligence test in France. Lewis Terman later published the Stanford-Binet Intelligence Scale, which becomes the world's foremost intelligence test.

1900 — Sigmund Freud
Publishes Interpretation of Dreams and presents his ideas on psychoanalysis, which later became a very influential form of psychotherapy and theory of personality.

1945 — Karen Horney
Criticizes Freud's psychosexual theories and later becomes known for her theories of personality development.

1946 — Solomon Asch
Demonstrates crucial factors in impression formation and later studies the effects of group pressure on independence and conformity.

1950 — Erik Erikson
Publishes Childhood and Society, which revises Freud's psychoanalytic theory and extends it across the life span.

1954 — Abraham Maslow
Helps found the school of humanistic psychology and later develops an influential theory of motivation.

1957 — Leon Festinger
Proposes the theory of cognitive dissonance and later becomes a prominent figure in social psychology.

1954 — Kenneth B. Clark
Research with his wife Mamie is cited by the U. S. Supreme Court in a decision to overturn racial discrimination in schools. He later becomes the first African American president of the American Psychological Association.

1954 — Gordon Allport
Writes The Nature of Prejudice, and is widely known for his trait theory of personality.

1980 — David Hubel & Torsten Wiesel
Win the Nobel Prize for their work identifying cortical cells that respond to specific events in the visual field.

1987 — Anne Anastasi
Author of the classic text on psychological testing, as well as numerous articles on psychological testing and assessment and is awarded the National Medal of Science.

1992 — Eleanor Gibson
Awarded the National Medal of Science for her lifetime of research on topics such as depth perception and basic processes involved with reading.

PSYCHOLOGY IN ACTION

Sixth Edition

Karen Huffman

Palomar College

JOHN WILEY & SONS, INC.

New York | Chichester | Weinheim | Brisbane | Singapore | Toronto

Acquisitions Editor	Ellen Schatz
Developmental Editor	Johnna Barto/Harriett Prentiss
Editorial Assistant	Lilli DeGrasse
Marketing Manager	Kevin Molloy
Senior Production Editor	Sandra Russell
Senior Designer	Kevin Murphy
Interior Design	Lee Goldstein/Norm Chrisitansen
Cover Design	Suzanne Noli
Illustration Editor	Sandra Rigby
Photo Editors	Sara Wight/Hilary Newman
Production Management Services	Hermitage Publishing Services
Photo Researcher	Mary Ann Price
Cover Image	*"Lightbulb IV", 1992, by Paul Giovanopoulos*

This book was typeset in 10/12 Fairfield LH Medium by Hermitage Publishing Services and printed and bound by R.R. Donnelley (Willard). The cover was printed by Lehigh Press, Inc.

The paper in this book was manufactured by a mill whose forest management programs include sustained yield harvesting of its timberlands. Sustained yield harvesting principles ensure that the number of trees cut each year does not exceed the amount of new growth.

This book is printed on acid-free paper. ♾

Library of Congress Cataloging-in-Publication Data:

Huffman, Karen.
    Psychology in action/Karen Huffman.—6th ed.
        p. cm.
    Includes bibliographical references and indexes.
    ISBN 0-471-39495-5 (cloth: alk. paper)
      1. Psychology. I. Title.
  BF121 .H78 2001
  150—dc21   2001017673

Printed in the United States of America.

10 9 8 7 6 5 4 3 2 1

Brief Contents

Contents

Preface

The art of progress is to preserve order amid change and to preserve change amid order.

ALFRED NORTH WHITEHEAD

Almost 20 years have passed since we first began planning and writing this text. The preface for the first edition talked about our dreams and values for an introductory psychology text. We asked: "Why are texts so cluttered and explanations so confusing?" "Do texts have to be either condescendingly easy or overly difficult and encyclopedic?" We sought to create a text that was comprehensive and comprehensible, scientific yet practical, and classic in foundation — yet contemporary in application. Our fundamental dreams, values, and goals have remained constant. But everything else has changed.

In the last 20 years, research in psychology has exploded, and nowhere is this "information explosion" more acute than in introductory psychology. How can we possibly introduce students to all the essential, classic material in psychology, as well as all the exciting new research, without creating a twenty-volume encyclopedia? How can students read, remember, and master all the old and new material when the number of hours and weeks of instruction are the same as they were 20 years ago?

To complicate things even further, college students and college life have dramatically changed. In the past, the typical college student was 18–22 years of age, a recent high school graduate, and seeking a four-year degree. Today, a "typical" college campus includes students who are non-native speakers, immigrants, first generation college students, visiting students from other cultures, full and part-time workers, full and part-time students, high school students seeking extended studies, recent high school graduates, college graduates requiring new skills or careers, returning older students, and general interest students searching for new interests, hobbies, and second careers.

How can we "preserve order amid change" when both our information and our students' needs are ever increasing? The theme for this edition, *"Eureka (Aha!): Discovering the Joy of Learning,"* reflects our response to this question. Rather than struggling with an information explosion, we can *use psychological tools to learn psychology.* With our discoveries in learning, memory, motivation, stress management, and other areas, the science of psychology is uniquely qualified to help students perfect their learning skills. *Psychology in Action's* numerous pedagogical aids, such as Visual Summaries, Tools for Student Success, SQ4R method, Try This Yourself, Interim Check and Reviews, Running Glossary, and so on, also help the reader understand and master chapter content. We believe that just as teaching is an art with skills and habits that can be perfected, so too is learning.

NEW TO THIS EDITION

The first significant change to this Sixth Edition is in the authorship. My coauthors, Mark and Judy Vernoy, have chosen other career paths, but their dreams and values remain. From the beginning, we have shared our love and excitement for the field — and hoped our readers would develop a similar appreciation that they would carry with them long after completing the course and reading our text. Writing for the first time as a solo author, I continue *Psychology in Action's* ongoing commitment to the needs of both students and teachers, while also including the latest psychological research and the most effective pedagogical aids. I hope the delight and excitement I have found as a single author are apparent in the chapters that follow.

Psychology in Action, Sixth Edition, strives to increase the reader's "aha" experiences. Numerous pedagogical aids that were successful in earlier editions remain and others were added. Recognizing that change is essential to progress, I also incorporated six major revisions:

1. **Increased emphasis on neuroscience, behavior genetics, evolutionary psychology, cognitive psychology, and positive psychology.** Reviewers and colleagues have agreed that these areas dominate contemporary psychology, and are therefore important to emphasize. Rather than creating new chapters or segregating this information in special boxes, it is *integrated* throughout the text (Table 1).

2. **Significant updating and revision of seven chapters.** Each chapter of the text contains hundreds of 2000 and 2001 citations and discussion of the latest research, and Chapters 1, 2, 3, 4, 6, 7, and 8 have been completely rewritten to reflect current research. For example, Chapter 1 has been reorganized and renamed *"Introduction and Research Methods"* to increase the emphasis on research methods. Chapter 2, *Neuroscience and Biological Foundations*, has been significantly updated, renamed, and reorganized to include the latest and most important neuroscience research. Similarly, Chapters 3, 4, 6, 7, and 8 have been significantly reorganized and updated to reflect recent changes in neuroscience, evolutionary psychology, and the cognitive perspective. They are also organized to reflect the way most instructors teach these important topics.

3. **Rearrangement of chapter order.** In response to reviewer and student suggestions, I placed Stress and Health Psychology (Chapter 3) immediately following Neuroscience and Biological Foundations (Chapter 2). This allows the reader an opportunity to see how biological research and scientific methods can be applied to everyday life before continuing with the Sensation and Perception chapter (Chapter 4).

4. **Streamlining and updating to achieve greater depth of understanding.** The American Association for the Advancement of Science (AAAS) and the National Research Council have advised all scientists to teach for depth of understanding rather than breadth of coverage. Adopting this goal, we have streamlined the Sixth Edition, resulting in fewer pages, but with increased coverage of the latest areas of research. Significant rewriting and the book's new design allowed more effective use of space in the margins and the body of the text, without cutting important topics. As an author and a lifelong student of psychology, I naturally believe that *all* the details of this field are important, fascinating, and intrinsically useful. However, I also recognize that if we are to teach for understanding rather than "coverage" we need to focus on the most important concepts. In deciding which material could be omitted or shortened, I relied heavily upon the advice of users and reviewers.

5. **Expanded, *integrated* coverage of "Gender and Cultural Diversity."** This has been a recognized strength of *Psychology in Action* from its First Edition, and the Sixth Edition has increased this emphasis. As always, I believe psychology is global and our readership is worldwide. We are all citizens of a growing global economy, and this edition strives to increase student awareness and appreciation of both similarities and differences between genders and cultures.

6. **Innovative and expanded technology.** Exciting new online resources can by used by the instructor who teaches online courses or as an addition to more traditional lecture courses. These resources include practice quizzes, graded quizzes, demonstrations, simulations, Critical Thinking/Active Learning exercises, and additional features.

As a user of *Psychology in Action,* you have guaranteed access to John Wiley & Sons student resource Web site *http://www.wiley.com/college/huffman.* Each chapter of the text contains specific website icons ( ) located near topics that have important website resources. The site also includes special online student tutorial quizzes and practice tests, active learning exercises, links to psychology related topics, Internet activities, as well as other valuable features and activities. Check us out!

T A B L E   1 .   SAMPLE HIGHLIGHTS FROM THE SIXTH EDITION

Neuroscience *(in addition to the expanded and general updating in Chapter 2)*	• Rewiring, repairing, and transplanting brains and spinal cords (pp. 74, 75) • Neuroplasticity, neurogenesis, and stem cell research (pp. 74, 75) • The myth of the neglected right brain (pp. 73–76) • The mapping of the human genome (pp. 79, 80) • Phantom pain and phantom limbs (p. 122) • Addictive drugs as the brain's "evil tutor" (pp. 186) • Neuroscience and learning (pp. 227, 228) • Brain scans of learning (pp. 228) • Neuronal and synaptic changes in memory (pp. 250, 251) • Where is memory stored? (pp. 252, 253) • Traumatic brain injury and Alzheimer's disease (pp. 261, 262) • Biological influences on intelligence, including brain size, speed, and efficiency (pp. 307, 308) • Brain changes with fetal alcohol syndrome (FAS) (pp. 325, 326) • Brain and emotion (pp. 429–431) • Biological aspects of personality (pp. 476–477) • Biological contributors to mental disorders (pp. 499, 501, 502, 509, 510, 517) • Biomedical therapies (pp. 527–532) • Biology of aggression (pp. 365, 592–593)
Behavioral Genetics *(in addition to the expanded and general updating in Chapter 2)*	• Basic principles and recent research (pp. 77–80) • Methods for studying (pp. 77, 78) • Genetic mutant "smart mice" (p. 251) • Genetic influences on intelligence (pp. 308, 309) • The Bell Curve debate (pp. 310–312) • Nature versus nurture controversy (pp. 318, 319) • Theories of language development (pp. 334) • Attachment and imprinting (pp. 335, 336) • Nature versus nurture sex and gender differences (pp. 379–381, 384–386) • Genetic influences on obesity (p. 415) • Genetic contributions to personality (pp. 477, 478) • The role of genetics and environment in mental disorders, such as schizophrenia (pp. 509, 510) • Genetic contributors to aggression (pp. 365, 592)
Evolutionary Psychology *(in addition to the expanded and general updating in Chapter 2)*	• Basic principles such as natural selection (pp. 76–82) • The evolution of sex differences (pp. 81, 82) • Evolutionary advantages of sensory adaptation (pp. 120, 121) • Evolutionary/circadian theory of sleep (p. 168) • Classical conditioning and biological preparedness (pp. 229, 230) • Operant conditioning and instinctive drift (p. 230) • Evolution and emotions (pp. 432–434) • Animal personalities (p. 458)

- Evolution and attraction (pp. 395, 575–576)
- Evolution and aggression (p. 592)
- Evolution and altruism (p. 596)

Cognitive Psychology (*in addition to the expanded and general updating in Chapters 7 and 8*)

- Bottom-up and top-down processing (pp. 118, 138)
- Cognitive view of dreams (pp. 170, 171)
- Stereotype threat and intelligence tests (pp. 310–312)
- Age-related memory problems (pp. 347, 348)
- Intellectual processes of resilient children (p. 367)
- Social/cognitive approaches to personality (pp. 474–476)
- Cognitive processes in mental disorders (pp. 498, 499, 502)
- Cognitive therapy (pp. 537, 541)
- Attitude change and cognitive processing (pp. 569–570)
- Cognitive processes in prejudice (pp. 572, 573, 574)

Positive Psychology

- Alternative routes to alternate states (pp. 188–191)
- Altruism and helping behaviors (pp. 596–597)
- Benefits of androgyny (pp. 386, 387)
- Creativity (pp. 288, 289)
- Effectiveness of therapy (pp. 553–555)
- Emotional intelligence (p. 436)
- Ethical research (pp. 23–26)
- Hardiness (p. 107)
- High achievers (pp. 419–421)
- Improving memory (pp. 267–270)
- Improving physical health (pp. 90–95, 104–112, 129, 191)
- Love and interpersonal attraction (pp. 335–337, 575–581)
- Moral behavior (pp. 356–357)
- Multiple intelligences (pp. 297–301)
- Overcoming prejudice and discrimination (pp. 369, 370, 573–575)
- Overcoming sleep disorders (p. 173)
- Positive aspects of aging (pp. 330, 331, 369, 370)
- Promoting secure attachment (pp. 336–337)
- Reducing aggression (pp. 594–595)
- Resilient children (p. 367)
- The "tricky business" of punishment (pp. 215–217)
- Wellness (pp. 90–112, 129, 191)

SPECIAL AND CONTINUING FEATURES

Tools for Student Success

To help students become more efficient and successful, this Sixth Edition includes a special feature called, "Tools for Student Success." In Chapter 1, there is a special end-of-chapter segment that includes tips for active reading, time management, and improving course grades, as well as important resources for college success.

In addition, several *student success sections* (identified with a light bulb icon 💡) are sprinkled throughout the text. For example, Chapters 3, 6, 7, 8, 12, and 15 all include strategies for improving learning strategies, memory, test performance, and overall achievement.

Research Highlights

In response to the "information explosion" in psychology mentioned previously, I carefully surveyed the literature and provide one or more expanded Research Highlights in each chapter. These recent, high interest topics are explored in enough detail to fully explain the topic, yet remain brief enough to maintain full reader attention.

- Chapter 1: An elegant study of therapeutic touch (p. 24)
- Chapter 2: Rewiring, Repairing, and Transplanting Brains and Spinal Cords (pp. 75-76)
- Chapter 2: Breakthrough—The Human Genome is Mapped! (p.80)
- Chapter 3: Procrastination, Performance, and Health (p. 103)
- Chapter 4: Tracking Down the Gene for Deafness. (p. 130)
- Chapter 5: Addictive Drugs as the Brain's "Evil Tutor" (p. 186)
- Chapter 6: Scanning the Brain for Learning (p. 228)
- Chapter 7: Looking for Memory in All the Right Places (pp. 252–253)
- Chapter 8: Language and the Brain (p. 295)
- Chapter 9: Romantic Love and Attachment. (p.337)
- Chapter 10: Children Who Survive Despite the Odds (p. 367)
- Chapter 11: The Art and Science of Flirting (p. 388)
- Chapter 12: Are Abused Children More Alert to Negative Emotions? (p. 441)
- Chapter 13: Do Animals Have Personality? (p. 458)
- Chapter 14: Alcohol Problems and Comorbidity (p. 518)
- Chapter 15: Therapy in the Electronic Age (p. 555)
- Chapter 16: America's Anger Epidemic (pp. 594–595)

Visual Summaries

In addition to the Tools for Student Success, each chapter of the text ends with a unique study tool that visually summarizes and organizes the main concepts. This Visual Summary is a two-page spread that can be used both as an overview "to get the big picture" before reading the chapter and as a quick review after completing the reading. Students, readers, reviewers, and adopters are all very excited by this feature. They report finding it "extremely helpful" and "the best study tool ever invented!"

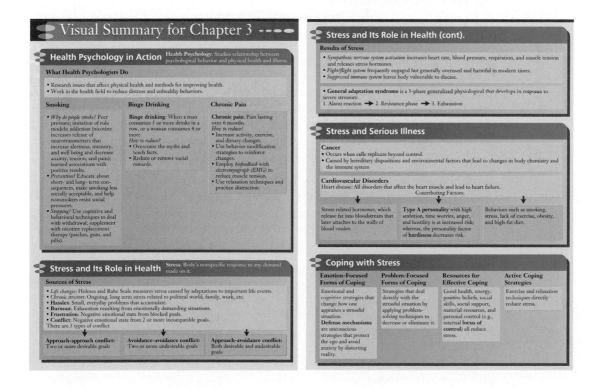

Focus on Critical Thinking and Active Learning

I hear and I forget. I see and I remember. I do and I understand. Chinese Proverb

Since ancient times, folk wisdom and philosophy have told us that the best learning takes place when the student is a critically thinking, active participant in the process. I have carefully designed this text to help students experiment, test, and apply psychological principles, develop the ability to think critically, work through problems logically, and make connections with the real world–in short, to become active learners.

To promote both critical thinking and active learning, I include "Try This Yourself" activities in every chapter. These high-interest and simple-to-do experiments, demonstrations, and self-tests give students an opportunity to apply basic principles and concepts. In Chapter 14, for example, one "Try This Yourself" activity debunks myths about mental illness and another presents a checklist for recognizing serious depression. In addition to "Try This Yourself" activities, each chapter also presents an in-depth "Critical Thinking/Active Learning Exercise" based on chapter content and devoted to developing specific critical thinking skills. For example, the Active Learning Exercise in Chapter 16 asks readers, "Would you have followed Milgram's experimenters?" and aims to develop independent thinking as a critical thinking skill.

Student and reader comments indicate that both the "Try This Yourself" and "Critical Thinking/Active Learning Exercises" are enjoyable and educational. One student wrote, "I looked forward to the "Try This Yourself sections because they were a fun, quick, and an easy way to try out the ideas in the chapter." Another student wrote: "The 'Try This Yourself' feature was always interesting to do. I especially liked the one about culture and the 'proper' ways to ride an elevator. My friends and I still have fun going into an elevator and facing toward the people instead of away from them." As for the "Critical Thinking/Active Learning Exercises," one student wrote that they "made me really think about what I was studying and how it pertained to my life." Another student said they were "not only useful in this course, but could be applied to other courses and daily life as well."

SQ4R Learning Activities

To further encourage active learning, the text is designed to include the SQ4R (Survey, Question, Read, Recite, Review, and "wRite") method of learning:

Survey and Question

Each chapter begins with four survey techniques: learning objectives, a chapter outline, a vignette that introduces essential concepts, and an introductory paragraph that previews content and organization. In addition to listing the core learning objectives on the chapter opening page, these learning objectives are repeated in the margin at the place in the chapter where they are discussed.

Read

Each chapter has been carefully evaluated for clarity, conciseness, and student reading level. To further facilitate in-depth comprehension of psychology's scientific methods, each chapter contains one or more Research Highlights presenting a more in-depth coverage of recent research. These boxed highlights provide stimulating, but nonintrusive, enrichment of the general text material.

Recite and Review

To encourage recitation and review, the text offers a short interim review and multiple-choice, fill-in, and short answer questions after each major section. These "Check and Review" sections provide another opportunity for active participation. To further encourage reviewing, each chapter concludes with a two page "Visual Summary" that visually organizes and connects essential concepts throughout the text. Each chapter concludes with a list of important terms, topically organized and with page references.

wRite

As part of the fourth R to the SQ4R method, this book is also designed to incorporate writing as a way of improving student retention. In addition to the writing students do in the survey, question, and review sections, note taking is encouraged in the margin of each page, which have been kept as clear as possible. The Instructor's Manual, which accompanies this text, also describes a special "marginal marking" technique that can be easily taught to students. The accompanying Student Study Guide discusses the SQ4R method in more detail.

Numerous Learning Aids

In addition to the SQ4R techniques, *Psychology in Action* incorporates other learning aids that are known to increase comprehension and retention:

- *Key terms.* Important terms are put in **boldface** type and immediately defined in the text.

- *Running glossary.* Key terms also appear with their definitions and a phonetic pronunciation in the margin of each page near where they are first introduced. Calling out and defining key terms in the margin not only increases overall comprehension, it also provides a useful review tool.

- *End-of-text glossary.* All key terms are also gathered in a complete, cumulative glossary at the end of the text.

- *Summary tables.* To increase student insight and "aha" experiences, we include numerous summary tables, some containing important illustrations, such as the table on drug actions and neurotransmitters in Chapter 5. The tables that compare classical and operant conditioning in Chapter 6 and contrasting theories of memory in Chapter 7 also serve as important educational tools.

- *Study tips.* In addition to the Tools for Student Success discussed earlier, we also include specific short study tips that students have found very useful. For example, the study tip in Chapter 9 (pp. 333-334) helps clarify *overgeneralization* and *overextension*. The study tip on positive and negative symptoms of schizophrenia in Chapter 14 (p. 508) incorporates earlier concepts of positive and negative reinforcement found in Chapter 6 (p. 211).

- *Timeline.* The grouping of famous contributors to psychology on the text's front endpapers provides a visual organizer and overview of the history of psychology.

Emphasis on the Science of Psychology

> *The pursuit of scientific understanding is among the noblest of all human goals. Like the pursuit of great art or the preservation of a beautiful wilderness, it is good in and of itself.*
>
> RANDY GALLISTEL [cited in Loftus, E. (1999, January),
> Higher intolerance. *APS Observer,* 12(1), 3, 20.]

It is important to recognize that a century of psychological research has advanced tremendously our understanding of human behavior. Therefore, in preparing this Sixth Edition, I have tried to enhance students' appreciation of psychology as an empirical study of human experience and demonstrate the advantages of the scientific method over speculation and "common" sense.

Chapter 1 sets the stage with a thorough discussion of the scientific method, bias in research, and types of correlation, but every chapter includes extended research examples that demonstrate the scientific nature of psychology. In addition, all biological figures have been reviewed and when necessary redrawn to clarify difficult concepts, such as neurotransmitter reuptake at the synapse.

SUPPLEMENTS

Psychology in Action Sixth Edition, is accompanied by a host of ancillary materials designed to facilitate the theme of this edition, "Eureka (Aha!): Discovering the Joy of Learning." Ordering information and policies may be obtained by contacting your local Wiley sales representative.

Instructor's Supplements

Computerized Test Bank

Wendy J. Hunter, Ph.D., prepared the Computerized Test Bank, a multiplatform CD-ROM, that fully supports graphics, prints tests, student answer sheets and answer keys. The software's advanced features allow you to create an exam to your exact specifications, within an easy-to-use interface. The test generation program has nearly 2,000 test items which include approximately 10 essay questions for each chapter (with suggested answers) and a variety of multiple-choice questions. Each multiple-choice question has been linked to the student learning objective it pertains to, coded "Factual" or "Applied," the correct answer indicated, and page referenced to its source in the text. Also included are several "humorous questions" that can be inserted in tests to reduce test anxiety. In addition, the Computerized Test Bank includes questions from the Student Study Guide and the main text's "review questions." These can be easily added to the test to reinforce student efforts or simply for the professor's reference.

Instructor's Resource Guide (available in hard copy and electronic format — Microsoft Word files)

Prepared by Kathleen Weatherford, Trident Technical College, this comprehensive resource includes for each text chapter: an outline, student learning objectives, outline/lecture organizer (page referenced to text), lecture lead-ins, supplemental lectures ("hot" topics), key terms (page referenced to text), chapter summary/lecture organizer, discussion questions, suggested films and videos, activities section, three active learning/critical thinking exercises, and a writing project. This edition also includes a Cross-Cultural Focus (either an activity or a brief lecture) and numerous Active Learning Exercises specifically created for use with any size class.

Transparency Acetates

One hundred full-color overhead transparencies are created from text illustrations, resized with bold type for use in large lecture halls.

Videos

Please contact your Wiley sales representative for information on Videos that are available to adopters of the text, such as Roger Bingham's series on the brain, and many other titles.

Student's Supplements

Student Study and Review Guide (Sixth Edition)

Prepared by Karen Huffman and Richard Hosey, this valuable resource offers students an easy way to review the textbook material and ensures that they know it. For each textbook chapter students have numerous tools that help them master the material, including: chapter outline, learning objectives, key terms, key term crossword puzzles, matching exercises, fill-in exercises, an additional Active Learning Exercise, and two Sample Tests (20 items each) with answers.

Take Note! Art Booklet

A student supplement with all of the transparency acetate images printed in a black-and-white lay-flat booklet. Images are the same size and quality as the transparency acetates. This supplement allows students to take notes and keep up with their instructor more easily during class.

Media Package: Web Site

An exciting new Web site has been created expressly for the Sixth Edition that will include both student and instructor materials. All of the assets can be accessed directly from the Web site.

The media package includes the following supplementary material: multimedia mini-modules to enhance teaching of complex topics such as conditioning; HTML-based exercises, homework assignments, and more; self-tests; Web Links; and In the News articles and discussion questions prepared by Jon Iuzzini, Texas A&M University. The package also includes additional free downloads, such as the following:

- *PowerPoint Files.* Prepared by Paul J. Wellman, Texas A&M, two sets of files will be available for both student and instructor use: art slides and lecture note slides. Students will be able to access the Power Point files on the Web, and instructors will have the files on the Instructor's Resource CD-Rom, as well as, on the Web.

- *Vocabulary Flash Cards.* Prepared by Marvin W. Lee, Shenandoah University, the vocabulary flash cards comprise an interactive module that allows students to test their knowledge of vocabulary terms. Students will also be able to take self-tests and monitor their progress.

- *Simulations.* These exciting and new interactive modules will help students understand introductory but complex concepts that are featured in the text. Each interactive simulation will include summaries and thought-provoking questions to help support the student's understanding of the module.

- *Online Guide.* Prepared by Paul J. Wellman, this guide offers information about how to use the Web for research, and how to best find the information you are seeking.

WebCT

In addition to the Web site, we also offer a WebCT course prepared by John Conklin, Camosun College, a Web course management system in the highly customizable WebCT format. The course includes: chapter overviews, chapter reviews for each section, assignments, Web links, discussion questions, self-tests, quiz questions and test questions, as well as all standard features of WebCT, such as bulletin board, calendar, e-mail and chat. A brief Instructor's Manual will be available (in electronic format only) to assist you in your use of this course.

Blackboard

Due to its popularity, we also offer a Web course management system in the popular Blackboard format. The course includes: chapter overviews, chapter reviews for each section, homework assignments, Web links, discussion questions, self-tests, quiz questions and test questions, as well as all standard features of Blackboard.

ACKNOWLEDGMENTS

The writing of this text has been a group effort involving the input and support of our families, friends, and colleagues. To each person we offer our sincere thanks. A special note of appreciation goes to Jay Alperson, Bill Barnard, Haydn Davis, Ann Haney, Herb Harari, Terry Humphrey, Teresa Jacob, Kandis Mutter, Bob Miller, Harriett Prentiss, Jeanne Riddell, Sabine Schoen, and Kate Townsend-Merino.

To the reviewers, focus group, and telesession participants who gave their time and constructive criticism, we offer our sincere appreciation. We are deeply indebted to the following individuals and trust that they will recognize their contributions throughout the text.

Student Reviewers

To help us verify that our book successfully shaped active learning, we asked introductory psychology students about their experience studying from *Psychology in Action*. Their reactions confirmed our belief that the book is an effective learning tool. We are grateful to the following students who took the time to share their honest opinions with us:

Idalia S. Carrillo, *University of Texas at San Antonio*

Sarah Dedford, *Delta College (Michigan)*

Laural Didham, *Cleveland State University*

Danyce French, *Northampton Community College (Pennsylvania)*

Stephanie Renae Reid, *Purdue University – Calumet*

Betsy Schoenbeck, *University of Missouri at Columbia*

Sabrina Walkup, *Trident Technical College (South Carolina)*

Reviewers for Psychology in Action (Sixth Edition)

L. Joseph Achor
Baylor University

M. June Allard
Worcester State College

Jeffrey S. Anastasi
Francis Marion University

Susan Anderson
University of South Alabama

Marilyn Andrews
Hartnell College

Susan Barnett
*Northwestern State University
(Louisiana)*

Dan Bellack
Trident Technical College

Daniel Bitran
College of Holy Cross

John Bouseman
Hillsborough Community College

John P. Broida
University of Southern Maine

Lawrence Burns
Grand Valley State University

David Cohen
California State University, Bakersfield

Anne E. Cook
University of Massachusetts

Amy Cota-McKinley
The University of Tennessee – Knoxville

Robert E. DeLong
Liberty University

Tami Eggleston
McKendree College

A. Jeanette Engles
Southeastern Oklahoma State University

Kathleen A. Flannery
Saint Anselm College

Joseph Hardy
Harrisburg Area Community College

John J. Hummel
Valdosta State University

Nancy Jackson
Johnson & Wales University

Charles Johnston
William Rainey Harper College

Guadalupe Vasquez King
Milwaukee Area Technical College

Norman E. Kinney
Southeast Missouri State University

Richard A. Lambe
Providence College

Sherri B. Lantinga
Dordt College

Elise Lindenmuth
York College

David G. McDonald
University of Missouri, Columbia

Juan S. Mercado
McLennan Community College

Michelle Merwin
University of Tennessee, Martin

Mitchell Metzger
Penn State Shenango

Ron Mossler
LA Valley College

Susan Nolan
Seton Hall University

Lillian Range
University of Southern Mississippi

George A. Raymond
Providence College

Celia Reaves
Monroe Community College

Kathleen R. Rogers
Purdue University North Central

Harvey Richard Schiffman
Rutgers University

Michael B. Sewall
Mohawk Valley Community College

Royce Simpson
Campbellsville University

Emily G. Soltano
Worcester State College

Kevin Sumrall
Montgomery College

Todd Zakrajsek
Southern Oregon University

Focus Group and Telesession Participants

Brian Bate, Cuyahoga Community College; Hugh Bateman, Jones Junior College; Ronald Boykin, Salisbury State University; Jack Brennecke, Mount San Antonio College; Ethel Canty, University of Texas — Brownsville; Joseph Ferrari, Cazenovia College; Allan Fingaret, Rhode Island College; Richard Fry, Youngstown State University; Roger Harnish, Rochester Institute of Technology; Richard Harris, Kansas State University; Tracy B. Henley, Mississippi State University; Roger Hock, New England College; Melvyn King, State University of New York at Cortland; Jack Kirschenbaum, Fullerton College;

Cynthia McDaniel, Northern Kentucky University; Deborah McDonald, New Mexico State University; Henry Morlock, State University of New York at Plattsburgh; Kenneth Murdoff, Lane Community College; William Overman, University of North Carolina at Wilmington; Steve Platt, Northern Michigan University; Janet Proctor, Purdue University; Dean Schroeder, Laramie Community College; Michael Schuller, Fresno City College; Alan Schultz, Prince George Community College; Peggy Skinner, South Plains College; Charles Slem, California Polytechnic State University — San Luis Obispo; Eugene Smith, Western Illinois University; David Thomas, Oklahoma State University; Cynthia Viera, Phoenix College; Matthew Westra, Longview Community College

Reviewers of Previous Editions

Joyce Allen, Lakeland College; Worthon Allen, Utah State University; Emir Andrews, Memorial University of Newfoundland; Richard Anglin, Oklahoma City Community College; Susan Anzivino, University of Maine at Farmington; Ronald Baenninger, Temple University; Peter Bankart, Wabash College; Patricia Barker, Schenectady County Community College; Donald Baughman, University of Wisconsin — Stout; Tamara Beauboeuf, University of Houston – Downtown; Daniel Bellack, College of Charleston; Dan Bellack, Trident Technical College; Terry Blumenthal, Wake Forest University; Theodore N. Bosack, Providence College; Linda Bosmajian, Hood College; David Burdick, Richard Stockton College; Lawrence Burns, Grand Valley State University; Bernado J. Carducci, Indiana University Southeast; Michael Caruso, University of Toledo; Charles S. Carver, University of Miami; Marion Cheney, Brevard Community College; Meg Clark, California State Polytechnic University — Pomona; Dennis Cogan, Texas Tech University; Michael Connor, California State University — Long Beach; Kathryn Jennings Cooper, Salt Lake Community College; Steve S. Cooper, Glendale Community College; Mark Covey, University of Idaho; William Curtis, Camden County College; Nat DeAnda, Los Medanos College; Patricia Decker, DeVry Institute, Kansas City, Linda Scott DeRosier, Rocky Mountain College; Grace Dyrud, Augsburg College; Thomas Eckle, Modesto Junior College; James A. Eison, Southeast Missouri State University; Eric Fiazi, Los Angeles City College; Sandra Fiske, Onondaga Community College; Pamela Flynn, Community College of Philadelphia; William F. Ford, Bucks City Community College; Harris Friedman, Edison Community College; Paul Fuller, Muskegon Community College; Frederick Gault, Western Michigan University; Russell G. Geen, University of Missouri, Columbia; Leah Geiger, Charles County Community College; Joseph Giacobbe, Adirondack Community College; Robert Glassman, Lake Forest College; Patricia Marks Greenfield, University of California — Los Angeles; David A. Griese, SUNY Farmingdale; Frances Grossman, Boston University; Sam Hagan, Edison County Community College; Sylvia Haith, Forsyth Technical College; Frederick Halper, Essex County Community College; George Hampton, University of Houston — Downtown; Algea Harrison, Oakland University; Mike Hawkins, Louisiana State University; Ed Headrick, Abilene Christian University; Linda Heath, Loyola University of Chicago; Sidney Hochman, Nassau Community College; Debra Hollister, Valencia Community College; Kathryn Jennings, College of the Redwoods; James Johnson, Illinois State University; Dennis Jowaisis, Oklahoma City Community College; Richard D. Honey, Transylvania University; Seth Kalichman, University of South Carolina; Paul S. Kaplan, SUNY Stony Brook & Suffolk Community College; Bruno Kappes, University of Alaska; Jada Kearns, Valencia Community College; Kevin Keating, Broward Community College; Marsha Laswell, California State Polytechnic University — Pomona; Fred Leavitt, (CSU–Hayward) Bogazici University, Turkey; Christopher LeGrow, Marshall University; Judith LeMaster, Scripps College; Allan A. Lippert, Manatee Community College; Thomas Linton, Coppin State College; Virginia Otis Locke, University of Idaho; Maria Lopez-Trevino, Mount San Jacinto College; Kathleen Malley-Morrison, Boston University; Tom Marsh, Pitt Community College; John Mastenbrook, Del Mar College; Edward McCrary III, El Camino Community College; Yancy McDougal, University of South Carolina — Spartanburg; Nancy Meck, University of Kansas Medical Center; Gary Melville, Trident Technical College; Mitchell Metzger, Penn State University; David Miller, Daytona Beach Community College; Michael Miller, College of St. Scholastica; Phil Mohan, University of Idaho; Melinda Jo Muzi, City College of Philadelphia; Kathleen Navarre,

Delta College; John Near, Elgin Community College; Steve Neighbors, Santa Barbara City College; Leslie Neumann, Forsyth Technical Community College; Sarah O'Dowd, Community College of Rhode Island; Joseph J. Palladino, University of Southern Indiana; Linda Palm, Edison Community College; Carol S. Perrino, Morgan State University; Richard S. Perroto, Queensborough Community College; Larry Pervin, Rutgers University, New Brunswick; Valerie Pinhas, Nassau Community College; Leslee Pollina, Southeast Missouri State University; Howard R. Pollio, University of Tennessee — Knoxville; Christopher Potter, Harrisburg Community College; Derrick Proctor, Andrews University; Antonio Puete, University of North Carolina — Wilmington; Joan S. Rabin, Towson State University; Michael J. Reich, University of Wisconsin—River Falls; Edward Rinalducci, University of Central Florida; Leonard S. Romney, Rockland Community College; Thomas E. Rudy, University of Pittsburgh; Carol D. Ryff, University of Wisconsin — Madison; Neil Salkind, University of Kansas—Lawrence; Richard J. Sanders, University of North Carolina—Wilmington; Harvey Schiffman, Rutgers University; Steve Schneider, Pima College; Michael Scozzaro, State University of New York at Buffalo; Tizrah Schutzengel, Bergen Community College; Lawrence Scott, Bunker Hill Community College; Hyacinth Sealy, Morgan State University; Fred Shima, California State University—Dominquez Hills; Nancy Simpson, Trident Technical College; Art Skibbe, Appalachian State University; Larry Smith, Daytona Beach Junior College; John Spores, Purdue University-North Central; Debra Steckler, Mary Washington College; Michael J. Strube, Washington University; R. Bruce Tallon, Niagara College, Ontario, Canada; Debra Terrell, University of North Carolina; Ronald Testa, Plymouth State College; Cynthia Viera, Phoenix College; Lori Van Wallendael, University of North Carolina; John T. Vogel, Baldwin Wallace College; Benjamin Wallace, Cleveland State University; Jeff Walper, Delaware Technical and Community College; Mary Wellman, Rhode Island College; Paul J. Wellman, Texas A & M University; Lisa Weyandt, Central Washington University; I. Eugene White, Salisbury State College; Delos D. Wickens, Colorado State University—Fort Collins; Fred Whitford, Montana State University; Charles Wiechert, San Antonio College; John R. Williams, Westchester Community College; Bonnie S. Wright, St. Olaf College; Brian T. Yates, American University; Mary Lou Zanich, Indiana University of Pennsylvania

Special thanks also go to the staff at John Wiley & Sons. This project benefited from the wisdom and insight of Johnna Barto, Sandra Russell, Jennifer Mullin, and the staff of Hermitage Publishing Services. In particular, I would like to thank my psychology editor (and friend), Ellen Schatz, for her dedication to making the Sixth Edition the best ever. Her patience, guidance, and ongoing commitment to excellence greatly improved the project. Our developmental editor, Harriett Prentiss, has also been an essential contributor throughout four editions of this text. Her careful attention, long hours of rewriting, thoughtful feedback, and necessary criticism were invaluable.

I also would like to extend my appreciation to Walter Lonner and his fellow cross-cultural specialists who conducted an intensive workshop at Western Washington University on "Making basic texts in psychology more culture-inclusive and culture-sensitive." My attendance at this workshop greatly increased my knowledge and exposure to the field of cultural psychology. Following this workshop, I consulted further with Patricia Marks Greenfield, and her expertise in this field and specific suggestions were indispensable.

Finally, I would like to express my continuing appreciation to my students. They taught me what students want to know and inspired me to revise the book. In addition, two individuals deserve special recognition for their research assistance, Chris Wagner and Sandy Harvey. My warm appreciation is also extended to Kandis Mutter and Richard Hosey. They provided careful editing of this text, library research, and a unique sense of what should and should not go into an introduction to psychology text. I sincerely appreciate their contributions. If you have suggestions or comments, please feel free to contact me at my email address: Karen Huffman (khuffman@palomar.edu).

Critical Thinking/ Active Learning

This text's focus on active learning naturally contributes to the development of critical thinking. I believe that an active learner is by definition also a critical thinker. Critical thinking has many meanings and some books dedicate entire chapters to defining the term. The word *critical* comes from the Greek word kritikos, which means to question, makes sense of, be able to analyze. Thinking is the cognitive activity involved in making sense of the world around us. Critical thinking, therefore, is defined as thinking about and evaluating our thoughts, feelings, and behavior so that we can clarify and improve them (adapted from Chaffee, 1988, p. 29).

Critical thinking is a process. As a process — something you do — you can do it better. You can develop your critical thinking skills. Each chapter of *Psychology in Action* (and corresponding chapters in the Student Study and Review Guide and Instructor's Resource Guide) includes a specific Active Learning Exercise devoted to improving one or more of the components of critical thinking. To learn more about each of these components, study the following three lists. They present the affective (emotional), cognitive (thinking), and behavioral (action) components of critical thinking. You will no doubt find that you already employ some of these skills. You will also no doubt recognize areas you could strengthen through practice.

I. Affective Components — the emotional foundation that either enables or limits critical thinking

- *Valuing truth above self-interest.* Critical thinkers hold themselves and those they agree with to the same intellectual standards to which they hold their opponents.

- *Accepting change.* Critical thinkers remain open to the need for adjustment and adaptation throughout the life cycle. Because critical thinkers fully trust the processes of reasoned inquiry, they are willing to use these skills to examine even their most deeply held values and beliefs, and to modify these beliefs when evidence and experience contradict them.

- *Emphathizing.* Critical thinkers appreciate and try to understand others' thoughts, feelings, and behaviors. Noncritical thinkers view everything and everyone in relation to the self.

- *Welcoming divergent views.* Critical thinkers value examining issues from every angle and know that it is especially important to explore and understand positions with which they disagree.

- *Tolerating ambiguity.* Although formal education often trains us to look for a single "right" answer, critical thinkers recognize that many issues are complex and subtle, and that complex issues may not have a "right" answer. They recognize and value qualifiers such as "probably," "highly likely," and "not very likely."

- *Recognizing personal biases.* Critical thinkers use their highest intellectual skills to detect personal biases and self-deceptive reasoning so they can design realistic plans for self-correction.

II. Cognitive Components — the thought processes actually involved in critical thinking

- *Thinking independently.* Critical thinking is independent thinking. Critical thinkers do not passively accept the beliefs of others and are not easily manipulated.

- *Defining problems accurately.* A critical thinker identifies the issues in clear and concrete terms, to prevent confusion and lay the foundation for gathering relevant information.

- *Analyzing data for value and content.* By carefully evaluating the nature of evidence and the credibility of the source, critical thinkers recognize illegitimate appeals to emotion, unsupported assumptions, and faulty logic. This enables them to discount sources of information that lack a record of honesty, contradict themselves on key questions, or have a vested interest in selling a product or idea.

- *Employing a variety of thinking processes in problem solving.* Among these thinking processes are inductive logic — reasoning that moves from the specific to the general; deductive logic — reasoning that moves from the general to the specific; dialogical thinking — thinking that involves an extended verbal exchange between differing points of view or frames of reference; and dialectical thinking — thinking that tests the strengths and weaknesses of opposing points of view.

- *Synthesizing.* Critical thinkers recognize that comprehension and understanding result from combining various elements into meaningful patterns.

- *Resisting overgeneralization.* Overgeneralization is the temptation to apply a fact or experience to situations that are only superficially similar.

- *Employing metacognition.* Metacognition, also known as reflective or recursive thinking, involves reviewing and analyzing your own mental processes — thinking about your own thinking.

III. Behavioral Components — the actions necessary for critical thinking

- *Delaying judgment until adequate data is available.* A critical thinker does not make snap judgments.

- *Employing precise terms.* Precise terms help critical thinkers identify issues clearly and concretely so they can be objectively defined and empirically tested.

- *Gathering data.* Collecting up-to-date, relevant information on all sides of an issue is a priority before making decisions.

- *Distinguishing fact from opinion.* Facts are statements that can be proven true. Opinions are statements that express how a person feels about an issue or what someone thinks is true.

- *Encouraging critical dialogue.* Critical thinkers are active questioners who challenge existing facts and opinions and welcome questions in return. Socratic questioning is an important type of critical dialogue in which the questioner deeply probes the meaning, justification, or logical strength of a claim, position, or line of reasoning.

- *Listening actively.* Critical thinkers fully engage their thinking skills when listening to another.

- *Modifying judgments in light of new information.* Critical thinkers are willing to abandon or modify their judgments if later evidence or experience contradicts them.

- ***Applying knowledge to new situations.*** When critical thinkers master a new skill or experience an insight, they transfer this information to new contexts. Noncritical thinkers can often provide correct answers, repeat definitions, and carry out calculations, yet be unable to transfer their knowledge to new situations because of a basic lack of understanding.

> A great many people think they are thinking when they are merely rearranging their prejudices.
>
> WILLIAM JAMES

From One Student to Another

Deborah Vicino
Montgomery College
Rockville, MD

Just this past year I decided to go back to school after many years working on and off as a bookkeeper. I wanted a change and a better salary and decided to pursue nursing. I am a 46-year-old woman who, needless to say, was very apprehensive about the thought of actually studying again after 25 or so years. To put it more bluntly, I was down right scared.

To start off my first semester back, I only signed up for two classes so that I could ease myself into this study thing. One of the two was "Introduction to Psychology." As soon as I opened up the text *Psychology in Action* and the accompanying study guide, I knew I could do this.

Most people, I believe, don't bother to read the Preface of a book, but I strongly recommend that you start right there. It put my mind at ease and let me know that this is a student friendly book. It explained all of the features and aids that were available to me throughout the chapters and also gave an in-depth discussion of a study method of learning called SQ4R. Since I needed all the help and suggestions I could get, I applied this tool from the beginning and it works. I got an "A" in this course.

The opening vignette in each chapter caught my attention and piqued my curiosity, which made me actually want to read on. I liked the "breaks in the action" with the Check and Review sections, which I always completed. This was the recite and review part of the SQ4R method. The Visual Summary at the end of each chapter was invaluable in reviewing for an upcoming test. When I read through it, if there were any concepts that I couldn't remember or just wanted to refresh my memory, I would go back to that section in the chapter and review.

The Study Guide was my favorite and most useful tool. Completing it might seem like a lot of work, but once you get in the habit, you will be glad that you did. I answered all of the questions going back and forth to the text. Then I would take the practice tests. I put the answers to these questions on a blank piece of notebook paper then checked them against the key. If I answered any questions incorrectly, I then went back and reviewed and saved this answer sheet. Just before a test in class, I would take the practice test again (this is why I didn't want my answers written in the Study Guide). After checking my answers again, if I found any to be incorrect, I would compare it to the previous test. If I answered any questions incorrectly on both tests, a red flag would shoot up in my brain, and I would go back and review. After this I really knew the material.

I am not what you would call a person who loves computers. I am being dragged kicking and screaming into the computer age, but I did make use of the on-line tools that were made available to me. I did have some problems getting into the Electronic Study Guide site, but the publisher's representative, John Swift, was so helpful to me. He walked me through it every step of the way and stuck with me until some kinks in the system could be worked out to make sure I could in fact get into the site and navigate successfully through it. I always took the tests that were offered here and enjoyed browsing around looking at case studies and other things that made this course come to life.

The importance of going to classes cannot be emphasized enough. I know it's tempting to skip some classes, even when your attendance is mandatory, but you will miss so much. My professor, Dr. Leonard Rosenbaum, truly demonstrated his passion for psychology through his lectures and lively class discussions. He was always ready to heighten our understanding with in-depth explanations and real-life examples.

The way this book it written made me feel like someone was sitting with me in my living room just having a discussion. It is a book that I will surely keep on my shelf. I have a daughter going off to college soon. If the school she will be attending is not using this text for the psychology course that she will have to take, I'm going to send it to her. That way she will have a supplemental tool that will help her really understand concepts that can be confusing if not presented in such an easy-to-comprehend fashion.

Thanks *Psychology in Action* for helping to ease my fears about returning to college after all these years, and the assurance that I can do this. The things that you have taught me will help me in my future nursing career and have already helped me in life. And the study skills that you taught me will be used in the many courses yet to come.

PSYCHOLOGY IN ACTION

Sixth Edition

Karen Huffman

Palomar College

JOHN WILEY & SONS, INC.

New York | Chichester | Weinheim | Brisbane | Singapore | Toronto

1 Introduction and Research Methods

LEARNING OBJECTIVES

Alongside the outline is a list of four to six questions that represent general questions you should be asking yourself as you read the chapter. For reinforcement, they are repeated in the margins at the place where they are discussed. These questions are an important part of the SQ4R method described in the Preface and the Student Study and Review Guide that accompanies this text.

CHAPTER OUTLINE

Each chapter begins with an outline of major topics and subtopics that will be discussed. The major topics are boldfaced. Under each are approximately three to five subtopics. This pattern of headings is repeated within the chapter itself. The chapter outline and the corresponding headings give you a mental scaffold upon which to build and arrange the new information you are learning.

Imagine that you are Emily Rosa, a 9-year-old looking for a topic for your school's annual science fair. Like most fourth-graders, you turn to your parents for ideas. It so happens that your mom and stepfather have frequently discussed the controversial practice of therapeutic touch (TT) — an alternative nursing technique designed to treat many medical conditions by manipulating "human energy fields." Although acknowledging that massage or actual touch can

Emily Rosa

help patients, your parents are highly skeptical that TT practitioners can cure illness by simply waving their hands above the patient's body. You've heard your parents complain that TT practitioners charge up to $70 an hour for their treatment, despite the lack of corroborating scientific evidence. Suddenly, it hits you! Why not design a science fair project that tests TT?

As it turns out, your simple but elegant scientific study so completely debunks TT that you're invited to publish your findings in the highly respected Journal of the American Medical Association (JAMA). As the youngest researcher to ever publish in a major medical journal, you are recognized by the Guinness Book of World Records, receive a $1,000 check from the Skeptics Society, and are invited to appear on several nationally televised news broadcasts.

Although this sounds like a fourth-grader's fantasy, the story is true. Nine-year-old Emily Rosa (almost) single-handedly debunked an entire medical treatment employed by over 100,000 trained practitioners. As JAMA editor George Lundberg stated in a television interview, "Age doesn't matter. It's good science that matters, and this is good science" (Lemonick, 1998).

Now, think of yourself as Dr. Antonio Damasio, distinguished professor and head of the Department of Neurology at the University of Iowa College of Medicine in Iowa City.

You are introduced to a tall, slender, and extremely pleasant young female patient, referred to as "S." Tests show that she has normal healthy sensory perceptions, language abilities, and intelligence. Shortly after being introduced, S hugs and touches you repeatedly. You discover that this same cheerful, touching behavior pervades all

Antonio R. Damasio

areas of her life. She makes friends and romantic attachments easily and is eager to interact with almost anyone. By all reports, S lives in an extremely pleasant world dominated by positive emotions.

So what's "wrong" with S? Can you diagnose her? The real Dr. Damasio discovered that a very small part of S's brain, the amygdala, is damaged, and she can't, therefore, recognize or respond to fear in a person's face. As a result, "she has not learned the telltale signs that announce possible danger and possible unpleasantness, especially as they show up in the face of another person…" (Damasio, 1999, p. 66).

Finally, imagine yourself as a highly respected research psychologist. The U.S. government asks you and your colleagues to develop better techniques for predicting violent behavior in convicted criminals. They also seek your help in two other areas. Do herbal products such as Ginkgo biloba improve memory? Do smaller classes result in greater student achievement, and, if so, for what type of student? The government offers lucrative contracts, but do you have the psychological training to answer these questions?

The stories of Emily Rosa and S are true. And the research questions in the third case are similarly real. They are taken from a recent national research initiative, known as Psychological Science in the Public Interest (PSPI). Recognizing that psychological research is a critical resource in our society, the PSPI commissions panels of psychologists to study issues of national concern and strong public interest (Ceci & Bjork, 2000; Swets, Dawes, & Monahan, 2000).

OPENING VIGNETTE

Every chapter begins with a short opening story that sets the stage for the chapter. These vignettes introduce interesting real-world examples and applications of the theories covered.

INTRODUCTORY PARAGRAPH

Following the vignette is a paragraph of commentary that presents the major topics to be discussed in the chapter, reinforcing and setting the stage for the material that follows.

What is psychology? What are its goals and main career specialties?

RUNNING GLOSSARY

Key terms and concepts are bold-faced in the text the first time they appear. They are also printed again in the margin and defined in a "running glossary." The running glossary provides a helpful way of reviewing key ideas before tests. If you want to check the meaning of a term from another chapter, use the end-of-book glossary

Psychology *The scientific study of behavior and mental processes*

Critical Thinking *The process of objectively evaluating, comparing, analyzing, and synthesizing information. Critical thinking has three components: affective skills (e.g., empathy and tolerance for ambiguity), cognitive abilities (e.g., independent thinking and synthesizing), and behavioral traits (e.g., delaying judgment and applying knowledge to new situations).*

Welcome to the world of psychology. As a new traveler in this territory, you may be expecting a tour focusing on abnormal behavior and psychotherapy. But as the introductory stories show, psychology is much more than mental disorders and their treatment. In the upcoming chapters, we will introduce you to a broad range of topics in psychology. As your tour guides, we take our responsibilities seriously and promise to make your journey exciting, intellectually stimulating, rewarding, and practical. So let's get started!

In this introductory chapter, we begin by defining **psychology** and examining its goals. Then we look at types of psychological research and the problems and ethics involved. Along the way, we also discuss career opportunities in psychology. We conclude with a look at psychology's past and present. To help you get the most out of psychology and this textbook, we also offer a special section, *Tools for Student Success*, at the end of this chapter.

UNDERSTANDING PSYCHOLOGY

What Is Psychology?

We began this chapter with three stories that demonstrate psychology's scientific foundation. Emily's skepticism and empirical approach, Dr. Damasio's careful observation and treatment of his patient, and the research goals of PSPI exemplify that, at its core, **psychology** is a science — the *scientific* study of behavior and mental processes. Psychologists value *empirical evidence,* information acquired by direct observation and measurement using systematic scientific methods. By taking an empirical approach, psychologists can be reasonably confident that the results of their studies are not contaminated by factors unrelated to the behavior being studied.

Our introductory examples also demonstrate another core value of psychology, that of **critical thinking,** the process of objectively evaluating, comparing, analyzing, and synthesizing information. Learning to think critically is one of the most important and lasting benefits of a college education.

Each chapter of this text contains a "Critical Thinking/Active Learning Exercise" designed to help you improve your critical thinking skills while you master specific chapter material. You'll also find "Try This Yourself" activities sprinkled throughout the text that further boost your critical thinking. Would you like to try one right now? Answer true or false for each statement in the following "Try This Yourself."

TRY THIS
Yourself

TRY THIS YOURSELF ACTIVITIES

In each chapter you will find several opportunities to apply what you are learning. These "Try This Yourself" sections are clearly identified with a special heading shown above. These activities are brief and fun to do. Research shows that actively involving yourself in learning increases comprehension and retention.

_____ 1. Most people only use about 10 percent of their brain.

_____ 2. Brain activity almost stops during sleep.

_____ 3. Police departments often use psychics to help solve crimes.

_____ 4. Punishment is the most effective way to permanently change behavior.

_____ 5. Eyewitness testimony is often unreliable.

_____ 6. Most adults go through a stormy midlife crisis in middle age.

_____ 7. Polygraph ("lie detector") tests can accurately identify attempts to deceive.

_____ 8. People who threaten suicide seldom actually commit suicide.

_____ 9. People with schizophrenia have two or more distinct personalities.

_____ 10. Males are naturally more aggressive than females.

Answers: 1. False (Chapter 2). 2. False (Chapter 5). 3. False (Chapter 5). 4. False (Chapter 6). 5. True (Chapter 7). 6. False (Chapter 10). 7. False (Chapter 12). 8. False (Chapter 14). 9. False (Chapter 14). 10. It depends on how you define *aggression.* (Chapters 11 and 16).

How did you do? If you're like most of our students, you probably missed several questions. One reason may be that your "common sense" led you astray. Dealing with human behavior every day, you may think you already know about psychology — after all, it's "just common sense." In addition, the media may have misled you. Many "pop psychology" findings publicized in the popular press are in fact bogus — they do not follow from *scientifically* collected data. The belief that people use only "10 percent of our brains" is an example of this type of misinformation. Furthermore, the media and public often fail to differentiate *scientific* psychology from *pseudopsychologies,* which give the appearance of science but are actually false. (*Pseudo* means "false.") Pseudopsychologies include claims made by psychics (who supposedly help police locate missing children and communicate with the dead), palmistry (reading people's character from the markings on the palms of their hands), psychometry (the ability to determine facts about an object by handling it), psychokinesis (the movement of objects by purely mental means), and astrology (the study of how the positions of the stars and planets influence people's personalities and affairs).

For some, pseudopsychologies are mere entertainment, but about half of all Americans say they believe in them and report spending thousands of dollars and valuable time on useless calls to psychic hotlines and horoscope readings. It's important to recognize that after thousands of experiments, no one has ever produced a *single,* reproducible, scientifically valid demonstration of *any* pseudopsychology (Druckman & Swets, 1988; Kelly, 1998, 1999; Milton & Wiseman, 1999). In fact, James Randi ("The Amazing Randi") is a famous magician who has dedicated his life to educating the public about fraudulent pseudopsychologists, and for many years has offered $1.1 million to "anyone who proves a genuine psychic power under proper observing conditions" (Randi, 1997; Opinion Archive, 2001). Although some have tried, the money has never been collected. If you would like

Beware of the pseudopsychologist. Only scientific psychological research enables us to reliably understand and predict behavior. Pseudopsychologists, such as astrologers and psychics, make many claims that do not meet scientific or critical thinking standards.

The "Amazing Randi." World-renowned magician, James Randi, has offered $1.1 million dollars for scientific proof of any ESP or paranormal phenomena. After many years, the offer still stands.

Nature–Nurture Controversy *The long-standing dispute over the relative contributions of nature (heredity) and nurture (environment) to the development of behavior and mental processes*

Interaction *A process in which multiple factors mutually influence the outcome — as in the interaction between heredity and environment*

Basic Research *Research conducted to study theoretical questions without trying to solve a specific problem*

more information about James Randi (and his million dollar offer), visit his website at http://www.randi.org.

Goals of Psychology: To Describe, Explain, Predict, and Change Behavior and Mental Processes

In contrast to pseudopsychologies, which rely upon self-report, anecdotal evidence, and opinions, true psychology bases its findings on scientific research and critical thinking. Psychology has four basic goals: to describe, explain, predict, and change behavior and mental processes through the use of scientific methods.

1. *Description.* Description tells "what" occurred. In some studies, psychologists attempt to *describe,* or name and classify, particular behaviors by making careful scientific observations. Description is usually the first step in understanding behavior. For example, if someone says, "Boys are more aggressive than girls," what does that mean? The speaker's definition of *aggression* may differ from yours. Science requires specificity.

2. *Explanation.* An explanation tells "why" a behavior occurred. In other words, *explaining* a behavior or mental process depends on discovering and understanding its causes. One of the most enduring debates in science is the **nature–nurture controversy** (Collins, 2000; McCrae et al., 2000). To what extent are behavior and mental processes *explained* by biological and genetic factors (the nature side) or by environment and learning (the nurture side)? As you will see throughout the text, however, psychology (like all sciences) generally avoids "either-or" positions and focuses instead on **interactions.** Today, almost all scientists agree that nature and nurture *interact* to produce most psychological traits and even most physical traits. For example, research on aggression suggests numerous interacting causes or explanations, including culture and learning, as well as genes, instincts, and higher levels of testosterone (Anderson & Dill, 2000; Gay, 1999; Pahlavan, Bonnet, & Duda, 2000; Zillman & Weaver, 1999).

3. *Prediction.* Once psychologists meet the goals of description and explanation (answering the "whats" and "whys"), they move on to the higher-level goal of *prediction,* specifying the conditions under which a behavior or event is likely to occur. For instance, knowing that alcohol leads to increased aggression (Goodwin, 2000), we can predict that more fights will erupt at sports matches where alcohol is sold than at those where alcohol isn't sold.

4. *Change.* For some people, "change" as a goal of psychology brings to mind evil politicians or cult leaders "brainwashing" unknowing victims. However, to psychologists, *change* means applying psychological knowledge to prevent unwanted outcomes or bring about desired goals. In almost all cases, change as a goal of psychology is positive. Psychologists help people improve their work environment, stop addictive behaviors, become less depressed, improve their family relationships, and so on. Furthermore, as you know from personal experience, it is very difficult (if not impossible) to change someone against her or his will. (*Question:* Do you know how many psychologists it takes to change a lightbulb? *Answer:* None. The lightbulb has to want to change itself.)

Basic Versus Applied Research

To meet these four goals psychologists use two major forms of research – basic and applied. **Basic research** is usually conducted in universities or in research laboratories to explore new theories and advance general scientific understanding. Discoveries linking aggression to testosterone, instincts, genes, substance abuse, culture, and learning came primarily from basic research. Because basic research almost always leads to later applications of the findings, it may not have any immediate real-world uses. It is primarily conducted for the sheer joy of learning — knowledge for its own sake.

Basic research meets the first three goals of psychology (description, explanation, and prediction). When we want to apply the fourth goal of psychology, to change existing real-world problems, scientists conduct **applied research.** As you can see in Figure 1.1, applied research in *human factors* has generated important safety and design improvements in automobiles, airplanes, and even stovetop burner arrangements.

Basic and Applied Research. During the 2000 Presidential election, the U.S. watched while politicians heatedly debated the "butterfly ballot" in Palm Beach, Florida. Basic research on general cognitive processes and applied research on ballot design might have prevented this problem (Baron, Roediger, & Anderson, 2000).

Applied Research *Research that uses the principles and discoveries of psychology for practical purposes, to solve real-world problems*

Keep in mind that basic and applied research often interact, with one leading to the other. For example, once basic research identifies specific factors that contribute to aggression, psychologists may conduct applied research to address problems related to aggressive behavior. For example, knowing that alcohol is linked to aggression, some sports stadiums now limit the sale of alcohol during the final quarter of football and the last two innings of baseball.

Careers in Psychology: What Psychologists Do

Knowing what psychology is and understanding its four major goals, would you consider a career in the field? Many students think of psychologists only as therapists,

(a) Spatial Correspondence

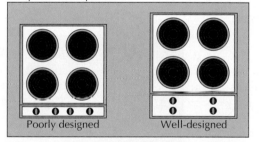

(b) Visibility

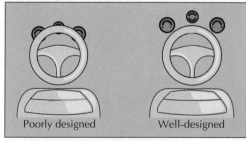

(c) Shape Indicates Function

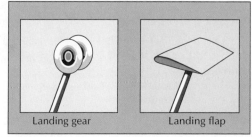

···· **ILLUSTRATIONS**
Don't skip over the photos, figures, and tables. They visually reinforce important concepts and often contain material that may appear on exams.

WEBSITE ICONS
Topics which have important website resources are marked with a special web icon as seen here. The student resource website at http:www.wiley.com/college/huffman includes online tutorial quizzes, practice tests, active learning exercises, internet links to psychology related topics, additional "check and review" questions, and other valuable features that will be updated regularly. Visit this site often.

Figure 1.1 *Human factors design and the real world.* Well-designed appliances and machinery are easily understood and operated. (a) The controls for stovetops should be arranged in a pattern that corresponds to the placement of the burners. (b) In an automobile, gauges for fuel, oil, and speed should be easily visible to the driver. (c) Controls and knobs are easier and safer to use if their shape corresponds to their function.

TABLE 1.1 SAMPLE SPECIALTIES IN PSYCHOLOGY

Biopsychology/behavior neuroscience	Investigates the relationship between biology and and mental processes, including how physical and chemical processes affect the structure and function of the brain and nervous system
Clinical psychology	Specializes in the evaluation, diagnosis, and treatment of mental and behavioral disorders
Cognitive psychology	Examines "higher" mental processes, including thought, memory, intelligence, creativity, and language
Counseling psychology	Overlaps with clinical psychology but generally works with adjustment problems that are less severe, including marital, behavioral, or academic
Developmental psychology	Studies the course of human growth and development from conception until death
Educational and school psychology	Studies the process of education and works to promote the intellectual, social, and emotional development of children in the school environment
Experimental psychology	Examines processes such as learning, conditioning, motivation, emotion, sensation, and perception in humans and other animals (The term *experimental psychologist* is somewhat misleading because psychologists working in almost all areas of specialization also conduct experiments.)
Gender and/or cultural psychology	Investigates how males and females and different cultures differ from one another and how they are similar.
Industrial/organizational psychology	Applies the principles of psychology to the workplace, including personnel selection and evaluation, leadership, job satisfaction, employee motivation, and group processes within the organization
Social psychology	Investigates the role of social forces and interpersonal behavior, including aggression, prejudice, love, helping, conformity, and attitudes

Neuroscientist Candace Pert (and others) discovered the body's natural painkillers, called endorphins (Chapter 2).

Psychologists often wear many hats. Dan Bellack teaches full-time at Trident Technical College, serves as Department Chair, and also works with faculty on teaching improvement.

For most people, this is the role they commonly associate with psychology — that of clinical or counseling psychologist.

Dr. Louis Herman's research with dolphins has provided important insight into both animal and human behavior.

but there are numerous career paths in psychology. Although many psychologists are employed as full-time therapists, a large percentage also work in academic, business, industrial, and government settings (Table 1.1).

Note that Table 1.1 is divided into several career specialties and that psychologists typically wear more than one hat. For example, your instructor may be an experimental psychologist by training but devote his or her entire professional life to teaching. On the other hand, this same experimental psychologist might teach, conduct research, and serve as an industrial consultant all at the same time. Similarly, a clinical psychologist might teach college courses while also being a full-time therapist.

What is the difference between a psychiatrist and a clinical or counseling psychologist? The joke answer would be "about $100 an hour." The serious answer is that psychiatrists are medical doctors. They have M.D. degrees with a specialization in psychiatry and are licensed to prescribe medications and drugs. In contrast, most clinical and counseling psychologists have received Ph.D., Psy.D., or Ed.D. degrees after intense study of human behavior and methods of therapy. Many clinical and counseling psychologists work with psychiatrists in a team approach to therapy.

Because of its diversity, psychology is currently one of the most popular career choices, and the U.S. Department of Labor expects that employment opportunities for psychologists will continue at least through the year 2005. To get an idea of the relative number of psychologists working in different fields of psychology, see Figure 1.2.

In this text, we will introduce many psychological fields of study and career options that may interest you. For example, Chapter 2 explores the world of neuroscience, and you may decide you would like the work of a neuroscientist/biopsychologist. Similarly, Chapter 3 discusses health psychology and the work of health psychologists, whereas Chapters 14 and 15 examine problems in mental health and how therapists treat them. If you find a particular area of interest, ask your instructor and campus career counselors for further career guidance. We also encourage you to explore the APA home page (http://www.apa.org) or the APS home page (http://www.psychologicalscience.org). Psychology is always looking "for a few good men" — and women.

> **NARRATIVE QUESTIONS**
> *These embedded, narrative questions model for you the process of active learning and the questioning goal for the SQ4R method. This helps focus your reading and increases comprehension.*

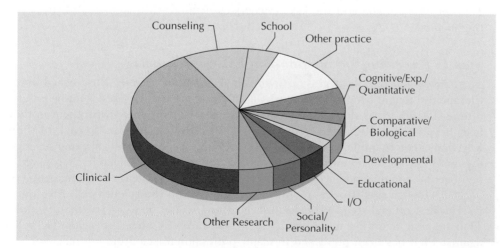

Figure 1.2 *Percentage of psychology degrees awarded by subfield.* Note that this is just a small sampling of the numerous specialty areas in psychology. The percentages shown here are based on data from the *American Psychological Association* (APA), the largest professional psychological organization. The other major organization is the *American Psychological Society* (APS). Source: *Graduate Studies in Psychology, 2000.*

Check & Review

UNDERSTANDING PSYCHOLOGY

Psychology is the scientific study of behavior and mental processes. It emphasizes the empirical approach and the value of **critical thinking.** Psychology is not the same as common sense, "pop psychology," or pseudopsychology. The goals of psychology are to *describe, explain, predict,* and *change* behavior and mental processes. To meet these goals, psychologists conduct either **basic research**, which studies theoretical issues, or **applied research**, which seeks to solve specific real-world problems.

There are many opportunities for a career in psychology. Some professional areas are grouped under the heading of basic research, including experimental, biopsychology or neuroscience, cognitive, gender and cultural, developmental, and social psychology. Applied areas include clinical, counseling, industrial/organizational, educational, and school psychology.

Questions

1. Psychology is the _____ study of _____ and _____.
2. What is the definition of *critical thinking*?
3. List and describe the four goals of psychology.
4. Name the subfield of psychology that studies each of the following topics:
   _____ a. The brain and nervous system
   _____ b. Growth and development from conception to death
   _____ c. Thinking, memory, and intelligence
   _____ d. Evaluation, diagnosis, and treatment of mental and behavioral disorders
   _____ e. Application of psychological principles to the workplace

Answers to Questions can be found in Appendix B.

CHECK & REVIEW

Each major section of a chapter concludes with an interim summary and four to six self-test questions that allow you to stop and check your understanding of the important concepts just discussed. These review questions give you feedback on whether you have fully mastered the major concepts in that section. Use these questions to review for exams, too. Answers for all questions are in Appendix B in the back of the text.

What is the scientific method?

DOING RESEARCH IN PSYCHOLOGY

Because psychology involves studying behavior and mental processes scientifically, psychologists approach research in the same way as scientists in biology, chemistry, or any other scientific field. First, they conduct an investigation and methodically collect data. They then piece together their findings, bit by bit, until they come to an objective conclusion. Throughout the entire process, psychologists follow standardized scientific procedures so that others — laypeople as well as scientists — can understand, interpret, and repeat their research. In this section, we will examine the *scientific method* in general, specific types of psychological research, and various research and ethical problems.

The Scientific Method: A Way of Discovering

Scientific investigations generally involve six basic steps, as summarized in Figure 1.3. Let's look at some of the key concepts associated with each step of the *scientific method.*

Step 1: Reviewing the Literature of Existing Theories

Most research actually begins with informal questions. Emily Rosa asked about therapeutic touch. Students often ask about study methods for tests. Young parents often ask what to do about their small child who wants to sleep with them in their bed. If you asked 20 people, you might get 20 different answers to each of these questions. For example, one of the most popular beliefs about sleeping arrangements in our Western culture is that "children who regularly sleep in their parents' bed become too dependent on their parents and will never learn to sleep alone."

Let's look at this "theory" more closely. How would you scientifically investigate it? The first official step in the scientific method would be to *review the literature.* That is, as a scientific researcher, you would carefully check this popular belief against what has been published in major professional, scientific journals (such as *Psychological Science, Journal of Cross Cultural Psychology,* and others). Scientific

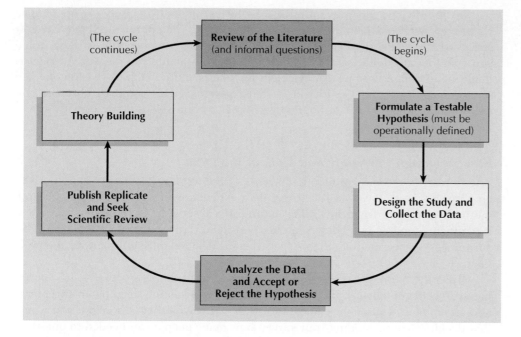

Figure 1.3 *The six steps of the scientific method.* A scientific investigation consists of six carefully planned steps, beginning with a review of the existing theories and ending with a return to theory building. Note that the steps are arranged in a circle to symbolize the circular, cumulative nature of science. One scientific study generally leads to additional and refined hypotheses, further studies and clarification of the results, and additions to the overall scientific knowledge base, known as *theories.*

researchers do *not* rely on reports in the popular media (such as the *New York Times* or *Psychology Today*).

During this review, you might find several studies about children's sleeping arrangements, including cross-cultural studies noting that the "family bed," where the entire family sleeps in one bed, is a common arrangement in many parts of the world. In these cultures, shared sleeping arrangements are considered important to a child's social and emotional development (see Morelli, Rogoff, Oppenheim, & Goldsmith, 1999). You might also find *scientific* theories explaining why sleeping with parents may or may not be a good idea. (See Chapter 9 for a further discussion of theories of attachment.) Unlike casual, informal theories, scientific theories represent accumulated scientific knowledge developed from previous research and empirical observation. Contrary to common belief, theories are *not* just guesses or hunches or beliefs. A *scientific* **theory** is an interrelated set of concepts that explains a body of data.

Theory *A system of interrelated, accumulated research findings used to explain a set of observations and generate testable hypotheses*

Step 2: *Formulate a Testable Hypothesis*

As you just saw with the sleeping arrangement example, theories can come from many sources, including an investigator's personal observations, empirical findings from previous studies, or extensions from previous studies. Once the review of literature is completed, the researcher is in a position to begin testing the original theory or a revised theory based on findings from the literature. A cardinal rule of a scientific theory is that it must make testable *predictions* about *observable* behavior. That is, the theory must make predictions that can be objectively tested.

To test a theory, the researcher formulates a "testable hypothesis." A **hypothesis** is a specific prediction about how one variable is related to another. The *variables* in any given hypothesis are simply the factors that can vary or change. To test the theory about sleeping arrangements, a researcher might formulate this hypothesis: "Children who sleep with their parents on a regular basis will be more attached to their parents." Alternatively, such children "will be overly dependent." A hypothesis may or may not be correct; it is merely a possible explanation for a behavior that can be verified through scientific testing.

Hypothesis *A statement of a predicted relationship between two or more variables*

Operational Definition *A precise description of how the variables in a study will be observed and measured; for example, drug abuse might be defined as "the number of missed work days due to excessive use of an addictive substance"*

To be fully *testable*, a hypothesis must be formulated precisely (as opposed to vaguely or loosely), and the variables under study must be **operationally defined**, or stated in observable, measurable terms. With our previous hypothesis, how would you operationally define *sleeping arrangements*? What could you measure? One way might be to define *sleeping arrangements* as "one or more children sharing one bed for the majority of nights with one or more parents." This could be observed and measured as "the number of hours a week that a child sleeps alone or with one or more parents or caregivers."

Step 3: Design the Study and Collect the Data

The third step in the scientific method is to figure out how to put the hypothesis to an empirical test. As you will learn in the next section, there are various research methods to choose from, including naturalistic observation, case studies, surveys, experiments, and so on. The researcher considers the relative advantages and disadvantages of each method, then selects the one deemed most appropriate and practical.

Once the method is chosen, the researcher decides how to collect *data,* or the measurements of behaviors. For example, if you were testing sleeping arrangements and attachment, you might choose to use the survey method. To begin, you would first decide when to conduct your survey, how many people you needed to question, and where you would get your subjects or *participants* (the people or animals that are systematically observed and tested in a study.) In your sleeping and attachment survey, you might decide to mail 500 questionnaires to parents asking about their child's sleeping habits and attachment behaviors. Questions might include the following: "How many hours a day does your child sleep alone or with one or more parents?" "Does the child cry when you leave him or her in the care of another trusted adult?" "How does your child respond when you return after a brief (30-minute) separation?"

Step 4: Analyze the Data and Accept or Reject the Hypothesis

After the observations and measurements have been collected, the "raw data" must be analyzed so that you can decide whether they support or reject your initial hypothesis. To do such an analysis, researchers rely on *statistics,* mathematical methods used to organize, summarize, and interpret numerical data. Statistics play a vital role in the scientific method. If you are interested in learning more about statistical analysis, see Appendix A at the back of this book.

Step 5: Publish, Replicate, and Seek Scientific Review

To advance in any scientific discipline, researchers must share their work with one another and with the general public. Thus, the fifth step in the scientific method begins when the researcher writes up the study and its results and submits it to scientific journals for *publication.* Most journals ask other psychologists to critically evaluate material that is submitted for publication. On the basis of these peer reviews, the study may then be accepted for publication.

Throughout this text, you'll see *citations,* authors' names and publication dates, at the end of many sentences, like this: (Andreasen, 2000). This tells you that the material comes from reputable sources and is as up-to-date as possible. Complete publication information (title of article or chapter, author, journal name or book title, date, and page numbers) is provided in the References section at the back of this book. We hope you use these references as a starting point for research projects, for additional information on a topic of interest, and to "check up on us." As a critical thinker, never take the word of any one author or authors. Check their sources.

Once a study is published, other scientists interested in that topic attempt to replicate, or repeat, the study. *Replication* increases scientific confidence if the findings are the same. If not, researchers look for explanations and conduct further studies. As responsible scientists, psychologists almost never accept a theory on the basis of a single study; they wait for replication. The more times a study is replicated by other researchers using different participants in varied settings, the greater confidence psychologists have in the findings.

What if some replications find contradictory results? If the study can't be replicated or the findings are questionable, it is publicly criticized in follow-up journal articles. Also, researchers can average or combine the results of all such studies and reach conclusions about the overall weight of the evidence. Using a popular statistical technique, called **meta-analysis**, researchers can combine and analyze data from many studies, instead of assessing each study's results separately. For example, researchers Daniel Voyer, Susan Voyer, and M. P. Bryden (1995) used meta-analysis of almost 50 years of research on gender differences in spatial abilities. They found that males do better than females on some, but not all, tests of spatial ability. This meta-analysis also found that the differences have decreased in recent years, possibly owing to changes in educational practices. As you can see, with time the process of *scientific review* gradually discloses flaws and gradually weeds out erroneous findings.

Meta-analysis *A statistical procedure for combining and analyzing data from many studies*

Step 6: Theory Building — The Cycle Continues

In steps 1 through 5, the researcher reviews the literature, formulates a hypothesis, conducts the research, analyzes the data, and publishes the findings so they can be replicated and reviewed. Now, the fun begins. In addition to explaining existing research findings, a good theory also generates *new* hypotheses and suggests new methods of inquiry. Thus, the research cycle continues. As Figure 1.3 shows, the scientific method is *circular* and *cumulative*.

Be forewarned. This ongoing, continually circular nature of theory building often frustrates students. In every chapter, you will encounter numerous and sometimes conflicting hypotheses and theories about behavior and mental processes. You will be tempted to ask, "Which theory is right?" But remember that theories are never absolute. As we mentioned in the earlier discussion of the nature–nurture controversy, the "correct" answer is almost always *interactionism*. In this case, many theories contribute to the full understanding of complex concepts. (Do you want to hear a corny joke about psychology's lack of absolute answers? *Question:* Why are there no "true/false" tests in psychology? *Answer:* Because all the answers are "maybe/it depends.")

Experiments: Looking for the Causes

Now that you have a good basic understanding of the scientific method, we can examine two major types of psychological research — experimental research and nonexperimental studies. As Table 1.2 shows, both types of research have distinct advantages and disadvantages. We will discuss each approach separately, but keep in mind that most psychologists use several methods to study a single problem. In fact, when multiple methods are used and the findings are mutually supportive, scientists have an especially strong foundation for concluding that one variable does affect another in a particular way.

We begin our discussion with the single most powerful research method, the **experiment**, where an experimenter manipulates and controls the variables to determine cause and effect. Only through an experiment can researchers isolate a single factor and examine the effect of that factor alone on a particular behavior (Ray,

How do psychologists conduct experiments?

Experiment *A carefully controlled scientific procedure conducted to determine whether certain variables manipulated by the experimenter have a causal effect on other variables*

TABLE 1.2 BASIC METHODS OF PSYCHOLOGICAL RESEARCH

Method	Basic Purpose	Advantages	Disadvantages
Experiment: manipulation and control of variables	Identify cause and effect	Allows researchers precise control over variables and to identify cause and effect	Ethical concerns, practical limitations, artificiality of lab conditions, uncontrolled variables may confound results, researcher and participant biases
Nonexperimental/ descriptive studies: naturalistic observation, surveys, case studies	Observe and record behavior and mental processes	Minimizes artificiality, easier to collect data	Little or no control over variables, researcher and participant biases, can't explain why certain behaviors occur
Nonexperimental/correlational studies: statistical analyses of relationships between variables	Identify relationships and how well one variable predicts another	Helps clarify relationships between variables that can't be examined by other methods and allows prediction	Does not allow researchers to identify cause and effect relationships

2000). For example, in studying for an upcoming test, you probably use several methods — reading lecture notes, rereading highlighted sections of your textbook, and repeating key terms with their definitions over and over. Using multiple methods, however, makes it impossible to determine which study methods are effective or ineffective. The only way to discover which method is most effective is to isolate each one in an experiment. In fact, several experiments have been conducted to determine effective learning and study techniques (Son & Metcalfe, 2000). If you're interested in the results of this research or want to develop better study habits, refer to "Tools for Student Success" at the end of this chapter and in other special sections throughout the text identified with this icon 🔑 .

An experiment has several critical components: independent variables, dependent variables, and experimental controls:

Independent and Dependent Variables

If a researcher chooses to use an experiment to test a hypothesis, he or she must then decide which variables to manipulate and which to examine for possible changes. The variables in an experiment are either independent or dependent. An **independent variable** (IV) (sometimes called the *treatment variable* or the *intervention variable*) is a factor that is selected and manipulated by the experimenter. It is hypothesized to have some effect on the dependent variable, and the experiment is conducted to verify this effect. In contrast, a **dependent variable** (DV) (or *outcome variable*) is a measurable behavior exhibited by the participant in the experiment. Because the IV is free to be selected and varied by the experimenter, it is called *independent*. The DV is called *dependent* because it is assumed to *depend* (at least is part) on manipulations of the IV.

For example, if you were designing an experiment to discover whether watching violence on television causes aggressiveness in viewers, you might randomly assign

Independent Variable (IV) *In an experiment, a variable that is manipulated by the experimenter to determine its causal effect on the dependent variable*

Dependent Variable (DV) *The variable that is observed and measured for change in an experiment; thought to be affected by (or dependent on) the manipulation of the independent variable*

groups of children to watch violent or nonviolent television programs (the IV) for one hour. Afterward, you could put a large plastic doll in front of each child and record the number of times the child hits, kicks, or punches the plastic doll in one hour (the DV).

Establishing a Control Group and One or More Experimental Groups

In addition to IVs and DVs, each experiment must have one control group and one or more *experimental conditions,* or ways of treating the subject/participants. Having at least two groups allows the performance of one group to be compared with that of another.

In the simplest experimental design, the researcher *randomly assigns* one group of participants to the *experimental group* and the other participants to the *control group* (Dehue, 2000). In the violence on TV and aggression example, one group, the **experimental group**, is exposed to the IV — in this case violent TV programs. The **control group** members would be treated exactly the same way as those in the experimental group, except that they would be assigned to a zero, or *control condition,* which means they are not exposed to any amount of the IV. They would watch a nonviolent TV program for the same amount of time.

We also could design the experiment with more than two *comparison groups* by using different levels of the independent variable. If one group watches 6 hours of violent TV whereas the comparison group watches 2 hours of violent TV and the control group watches no violent TV, then any observable difference in the DV (aggression) is logically caused by the IV.

While creating both control and comparison groups, experimenters also take care that all **extraneous variables** (those that are not being directly manipulated or measured) are held constant (the same). For example, time of day, heating, and lighting would need to be kept constant for all participants so that they do not affect participants' responses.

Experimental Safeguards

Every experiment is designed to answer essentially the same question: Does the IV *cause* the predicted change in the DV? To answer this question, the experimenter must establish several safeguards. In addition to the previously mentioned controls within the experiment itself (e.g., operational definitions, having a control group, and holding extraneous variables constant), a good scientific experiment also protects against potential sources of error from both the researcher and the participant. As we discuss these potential problems (and their possible solutions), you may want to refer several times to the summary in Table 1.3.

Experimental Group *In a controlled experiment, the group of participants that receives the independent variable*

Control Group *In a controlled experiment, the group of participants that receives a zero level of the independent variable and that is used to assess the effects of the independent variable or treatment*

Extraneous Variables *Variables that are not directly related to the hypothesis under study and that the experimenter does not actively attempt to control (e.g., time of day and heating of room).*

TABLE 1.3 POTENTIAL RESEARCH PROBLEMS AND SOLUTIONS

	Problem	Solution
Researcher	Experimenter bias	Blind observers, single-blind and double-blind studies, placebos
	Ethnocentrism	Cross-cultural sampling
Participant	Sample bias	Random/representative sampling, random assignment
	Participant bias	Anonymity, confidentiality, deception (as well as single- and double-blind studies and placebos)

Researcher Problems

Researchers must guard against two particular problems — *experimenter bias* and *ethnocentrism*.

1. *Experimenter bias.* Experimenters, like everyone else, have their own personal beliefs and expectancies. The danger in research, however, is that these personal matters may produce a *self-fulfilling prophecy*: The researchers find what they expect to find. In collecting data, they may *inadvertently* give subtle cues or treat participants differently in accordance with their expectations. For example, an experimenter may breathe a sigh of relief when a participant gives a response supporting the researcher's hypothesis. This tendency of experimenters to influence the results in the expected direction is called **experimenter bias**.

Experimenter Bias *The tendency of experimenters to influence the results of a research study in the expected direction*

Experimenters can prevent bias in several ways. One technique is to set up objective methods for recording data and enlist "blind observers" (neutral people other than the researcher) to collect the data without knowing what the researcher has predicted. In addition, researchers can arrange the experiment so that *either* the observer or the participant is unaware of which group received the experimental treatment. This is called a *single-blind study*. When *both* the experimenter and the participants are unaware, it is known as a **double-blind study**.

Double-Blind Study *A study in which neither the participant nor the experimenter knows which treatment is being given to the participant or to which group the participant has been assigned*

In a typical double-blind experiment testing a new drug, both the experimenter administering the drug and the participants taking the drug are unaware (or "blind") as to who is receiving a **placebo**, a fake pill or injection, and who is receiving the drug itself. Researchers use placebos because they have found that the mere act of taking a pill or receiving an injection can change the behavior of a participant. (The term *placebo* comes from the Latin verb *placere*, "to please.") Thus, to ensure that a particular effect is indeed due to the drug being tested and not to the *placebo effect*, control participants must be treated exactly as the experimental participants, even if this means faking the motions of giving them drugs or medications.

Placebo [pluh-SEE-bo] *An inactive substance or fake treatment used as a control technique, usually in drug research, or given by a medical practitioner to a patient*

2. *Ethnocentrism.* Researchers cannot assume that just because a certain behavior is typical in their own culture, it is typical in all cultures. One way to avoid this type of **ethnocentrism** is to have two researchers, one from one culture and one from another, conduct the same research study two times, once with their own culture and once with at least one other culture. When using this kind of *cross-cultural sampling*, differences due to ethnocentrism can be isolated from actual differences in behavior between the two cultures.

Ethnocentrism *The belief that behavior in one's culture is typical of all cultures; also, viewing one's own ethnic group (or culture) as central and "correct" and then judging the rest of the world according to this standard*

Participant Problems

In addition to potential problems from the researcher, there are also several possibilities for error associated with participants, which can be grouped under the larger categories of *sample bias* and *participant bias*.

1. *Sample bias.* A *sample* is a group of research participants selected to represent a larger group, or *population*. When we do research, we obviously cannot measure the entire population, so we select and test a limited sample. However, using such a small group requires that the sample be reasonably similar to the composition of the population at large. If systematic differences exist among the groups being studied, known as **sample bias**, experimental results may not truly reflect the influence of the independent variable.

Sample Bias *The tendency for the sample of participants in a research study to be atypical of a larger population*

For example, much research has been done on heart disease. The research, however, has been conducted almost exclusively with men. Doctors apply findings from this research to the treatment of all their patients, both men and women, with no regard for the male sample bias in the studies. Because the purpose of conducting experiments is to apply, or generalize, the results to a wide population, it is extremely important that the sample represents the general population.

To safeguard against sample bias, research psychologists use random/representative sampling and random assignment:

- *Random/representative sampling.* Obviously, psychologists want their research findings to be applicable to more people than just those who took part in the study. For instance, critics have suggested that much psychological literature is biased because it is based primarily on white participants (see Robert Guthrie's 1998 book, *Even the Rat was White*). One way to ensure less bias and more relevance is to select participants who constitute a representative sample of the entire population of interest. Proper *random sampling* will likely produce a *representative,* unbiased sample.

- *Random assignment.* To ensure the validity of the results, participants must also be assigned to experimental groups using a chance, or *random,* system, such as a coin toss or drawing numbers out of a hat. This procedure of **random assignment** ensures that each participant is equally likely to be assigned to any particular group and that differences among the participants will be spread out across all experimental conditions.

2. Participant bias. In addition to problems with initial sampling of participants, bias can also occur when participants try to present themselves in a good light (the *social desirability response*) or deliberately attempt to mislead the researcher. They may also be less than truthful when asked embarrassing questions or placed in awkward experimental conditions.

Researchers attempt to control for this type of participant bias by offering anonymous participation and other guarantees for privacy and confidentiality. Also, as mentioned above, single- and double-blind studies and placebos offer additional safeguards. If participants don't know which group they're in, or whether they're receiving the real drug or the "fake one," they won't try to overly please or deliberately mislead the experimenter.

Finally, one of the most effective, but controversial, ways to prevent participant bias is *deception.* Just like the unsuspecting subjects on the popular TV program *Candid Camera,* research participants will behave more naturally when they don't know they are part of a research project. However, many researchers consider the use of deception unethical — a topic we discuss in a later section.

Random Assignment *Occurs when participant's chances of being assigned to each group in an experiment are equal, thereby ensuring that any later differences between people in the experimental and control conditions must be the result of the treatment*

Check & Review

SCIENTIFIC METHOD AND EXPERIMENTS

The scientific method consists of six carefully planned steps: (1) reviewing the literature for existing **theories**, (2) formulating a testable hypothesis, (3) designing the study and collecting the data, (4) analyzing the data and accepting or rejecting the **hypothesis**, (5) publishing followed by replication and scientific review, and (6) building further theory. The steps are arranged in a circle to show the circular, cumulative nature of science.

The experimental method is the only research method that can be used to identify cause-and-effect relationships. **Independent variables** (IVs) are the factors the experimenter manipulates, and **dependent variables** (DVs) are measurable behaviors of the participants. Experimental controls include having one control group and one or more experimental groups, and holding **extraneous variables** constant.

To safeguard against the researcher problem of **experimenter bias**, researchers employ blind observers, single-blind and **double-blind studies**, and **placebos**. To control for **ethnocentrism**, they use cross-cultural sampling. In addition, to offset participant problems with **sample bias**, researchers use random/representative sampling and **random assignment**. To control for participant bias, they rely on many of the same controls in place to prevent experimenter bias, such as double-blind studies. They also attempt to ensure anonymity and confidentiality and sometimes use deception.

Questions

1. What are the six steps of the scientific method?

2. Why is an experiment the only way we can determine the cause of behavior?

3. If researchers gave participants varying amounts of a new "memory" drug and then gave them a story to read and measured their scores on a quiz, the _____ would be the IV, and the _____ would be the DV. (a) response to the drug, amount of the drug; (b) experimental group, control group; (c) exposure to the drug, quiz scores; (d) researcher variables, extraneous variables.

4. What are the two primary sources of problems for both researchers and participants? What are the solutions?

Nonexperimental Studies: Naturalistic Observation, Surveys, Case Studies, and Correlational Studies

> What are the advantages and disadvantages of nonexperimental studies?

Does drinking alcohol during pregnancy cause birth defects? Can stress cause cancer? Does smoking marijuana diminish motivation? Both the public and the scientific community would like answers to all these questions. However, only after performing carefully controlled experiments can we legitimately say that "A" *causes* "B."

But how could you experimentally discover if alcohol causes birth defects? You would need to administer large doses of disguised alcoholic drinks to pregnant women (the experimental group) while giving the same disguised drink without alcohol to another group of pregnant women (the control group). At the end of the pregnancy, you would carefully examine the newborns for increased levels of birth defects! Obviously, this kind of experiment could never be done on humans. It is *always* unethical to assign people to undergo research that may prove harmful. (Ethical problems associated with animal research are discussed in an upcoming section.)

When experiments cannot be used to determine cause and effect, scientists must rely on nonexperimental studies, such as naturalistic observation, surveys, individual case studies, and correlational studies. What distinguishes these nonexperimental methods is that the researcher cannot manipulate the variables under study. This lack of control means that none of these methods can be used to determine the *causes* of behavior. Nonetheless, nonexperimental studies are valuable for describing specifics about behavior, determining relationships between variables, and predicting behavior.

In this section, we will discuss four major nonexperimental methods: *naturalistic observation, surveys, case studies,* and *correlational studies.* As we discuss each of these methods, keep in mind that most of the problems and safeguards discussed with the experimental method also apply to the nonexperimental methods.

Naturalistic Observation

Naturalistic Observation *The systematic recording of observable behavior in the participant's natural state or habitat with little or no experimenter intervention*

When using **naturalistic observation**, researchers systematically measure and record observable behavior of participants as it occurs in the real world, without interfering in any way. The purpose of most naturalistic observation is to gather descriptive information. Because of the popularity of researchers like Jane Goodall, most people picture naturalistic observation occurring in jungles, but supermarkets, libraries, subways, airports, museums, classrooms, assembly lines, and other settings also lend themselves to naturalistic observation.

Recall from the introductory vignette that the PSPI (2000) initiative is commissioning a review of studies asking, "Do smaller classes result in greater student achievement? If so, for what type of student?" A researcher who wanted to study these questions might not want to begin the investigation by bringing students and teachers into a controlled experimental laboratory setting. She or he might first go to several classrooms and observe how children and teachers behave in their natural setting.

In naturalistic observation, the researcher does not manipulate or control anything in the situation. In fact, the observer tries to be as unobtrusive as possible, to become, as they say, "like a fly on the wall." If participants know someone is watching, their behavior becomes unnatural. For example, have you ever been driving down the street, singing along with the radio, only to stop in the middle of a phrase as you realize that the person in the next car is watching you? The same type of thing normally happens when participants in scientific studies realize they are being observed. The researcher might conceal him- or herself in the background, stand behind a one-way mirror, or observe from a distance while the participants are (hopefully) unaware that they are being observed.

The chief advantage of using naturalistic observation is that researchers can obtain data about a truly natural behavior rather than about a behavior that is a reaction to an artificial experimental situation. If Jane Goodall had observed chimpanzees in a lab (or zoo), their behavior would probably be quite different from their behavior in their natural habitat. On the other hand, naturalistic observation can be difficult and time-consuming, and the lack of control by the researcher makes it difficult to conduct observations for behavior that occurs infrequently.

Naturalistic observation. Studying behavior in its natural environment allows behavior to unfold naturally (without interference).

Surveys

Surveys, tests, questionnaires, and interviews (we will refer to them all as "surveys") are similar techniques for sampling a wide variety of behaviors and attitudes. They range from personality inventories that probe the makeup of individuals to public opinion surveys such as the well-known Gallup and Harris Polls.

The survey technique was used in a study conducted by S. Plous, who wanted a portrait of animal rights activists in the United States. At a big animal rights rally in Washington, D.C., in June 1990, he surveyed 574 people. After asking them whether they considered themselves animal rights activists (402 did) or nonactivists (172), he asked what they felt should be the agenda of the animal rights movement. Table 1.4 (Plous, 1991, 1998) shows a portion of the survey results. Just over half the activists felt that the single highest priority of the animal rights movement should be banning use of animals in research, whereas only one-quarter of the nonactivists agreed.

Surveys are typically used to determine general opinions, attitudes, feelings, or behaviors related to a specific issue, such as voting preferences prior to state or national elections. One problem with surveys is that they rely on self-reported data, and not all participants are completely honest. In addition, survey techniques cannot, of course, be used to explain *causes* of behavior. But they can be helpful in predicting behavior. Plous, for example, could not pinpoint the causes of the activists' beliefs, but the results of his survey might be used to predict the attitudes and goals of some animal rights activists in the United States. As a critical thinker, can you see why his results are limited? Because he administered his survey only to participants at an animal rights rally, he lacked a *random/representative sampling*.

Survey *Nonexperimental research technique that assesses behaviors and attitudes of a sample or population*

TRY THIS
Yourself

Why not conduct your own sample survey? Station yourself at a conspicuous spot on campus, in your dorm, or some other place. Ask random passersby whether they consider themselves animal rights activists or nonactivists. Then read them the question in Table 1.4 and ask them to indicate their response next to the appropriate item. How do your survey results compare with those of Plous?

TABLE 1.4 WHAT SHOULD THE ANIMAL RIGHTS MOVEMENT FOCUS ON MOST?

The Treatment of:	Activists[a]	Nonactivists
Animals used in research	54	26
Animals used for food	24	8
Animals used for clothing or fashion	12	22
Animals in the wild	5	30
Animals used in sports or entertainment	4	14
Animals used in education	1	0

[a] Figures indicate the percentage of respondents giving each answer.

Case Studies

What if a researcher wants to investigate photophobia, fear of light? Most people are not afraid of light, so it would be next to impossible to gather enough participants to conduct an experiment or to use surveys or naturalistic observation. In the case of such rare disorders, researchers try to find someone who has the problem and study him or her intensively. Such an in-depth study of a single research participant is called a **case study**.

In a case study, many aspects of a person's life are examined in detail to allow full description of the person's problem behavior and evaluation of any treatment. Dr. Damasio's (1999) study of patient "S," mentioned in this chapter's opening vignette, provides an excellent example of a case study. Damasio and his colleagues began with comprehensive evaluations of the patient's physical and mental health, intelligence, and personality. Results showed that S was in good health with normal sensory perception, language ability, and intelligence. She also had remarkable artistic and drafting skills. Her one problem was that she could not identify facial expressions of fear. She easily recognized other emotions and could mimic them with her own facial muscles. And, interestingly, she could draw finely detailed faces showing all emotions — except fear.

After extensive neurological tests and extensive interviews, Damasio and his staff discovered that S's inability to recognize fear in someone's face resulted from damage to her amygdala. They also found that S does not experience fear in the same way as others. She intellectually knows "what fear is supposed to be, what should cause it, and even what one may do in situations of fear, but little or none of that intellectual baggage, so to speak, is of any use to her in the real world" (Damasio, 1999, p. 66). Her inability to recognize fear in herself and others has led to poor social judgments and serious problems in social interactions.

At this time, there is no "happy ending" for S and others with similar damage, but case studies like this may eventually provide valuable clues that will lead to successful treatment. Keep in mind, however, that case studies have their research limits, including lack of generalizability, biased and inaccurate recall among participants, and so on.

Case Study *An in-depth study of a single research participant*

Correlational Studies

Nonexperimental researchers sometimes want to determine the degree of relationship, or *correlation,* between two variables, so they turn to **correlational studies.** As the name implies, when any two variables are *correlated,* they are "related," and a change in one variable is accompanied by a concurrent change in the other.

Using the correlational method, researchers begin with their topic of interest, such as alcohol consumption during pregnancy. Then they select a group for study. In our previous example of drinking alcohol during pregnancy, the group under investigation would be pregnant women. After selecting the group, the variables of interest are measured for each participant in the study. In this case, the researchers might survey or interview the selected group of women about the amount and timing of any alcohol use during their pregnancies.

After the data are collected, the researchers analyze their results using a statistical formula that results in a *correlation coefficient,* a numerical value that indicates the degree and direction of the relationship between the two variables. (Note that there is an important distinction between correlational studies and correlation as a mathematical procedure. *Correlational studies* are a type of research methodology in which researchers set out to identify relationships between variables, whereas *correlation coefficients* are statistical procedures used in correlational studies, as well as with surveys and other research designs.)

A correlation coefficient can vary between 0 and +1.00 and 0 and −1.00. A perfect correlation (+1.00 or −1.00) would allow us to make completely accurate predictions. The sign (+ or −) tells whether the two variables vary in the same or opposite direction (Figure 1.4). The number indicates the relative strength. Thus, a correlation of −.45 or +.45 is higher (and more predictive) than a lower number like −.20 or +.20.

The Value of Correlations

Understanding correlational studies and correlation coefficients may be difficult, but it's worth the effort. Correlations help us make reliable and valuable predictions. For example, correlational studies have repeatedly found high correlation coefficients between birth defects and a pregnant mother's use of alcohol, and between car accidents and the driver's use of cellular phones. This information enables us to reliably predict our relative risks and make informed decisions about our lives and

Correlational Study *A form of research that studies relationships between variables without the ability to infer causal relationships; correlational studies describe how strongly two variables are related and whether they are positively, negatively, or not at all (zero) correlated*

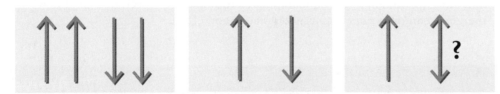

Figure 1.4 *Three types of possible correlation.* (a) ***Positive correlation.*** If both variables vary in the same direction — both go up or both go down — the relationship is described as positive. For instance, salary and years of education are *positively correlated.* As the number of years of education goes up, there is a concurrent upward movement in salary. Similarly, as the number of drunk drivers goes down, the number of car accidents also goes down. (b) ***Negative correlation.*** When two variables vary in the opposite direction — as one goes up, the other goes down — the relationship is negative. For example, the number of absences from class and scores on exams are *negatively correlated.* Students who miss a lot of class miss important information and tend to get lower grades on exams. (c) ***Zero correlation.*** Variables that are not at all related have a *zero correlation.* As one variable goes up, the other variable can go up or down because there is no relationship between the two. Shoe size and intelligence, for example, are not related. They have a zero correlation.

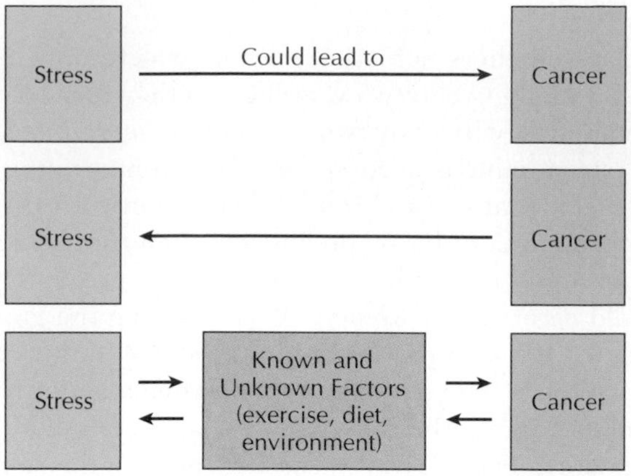

Figure 1.5 *Correlation is not causation.* Research has found a strong correlation between stress and cancer (Chapter 3). However, this correlation does not tell us whether stress causes cancer, cancer causes stress, or whether other known and unknown factors could contribute to both stress and cancer.

behavior. If you would like additional information about correlations, see Appendix A at the back of the book.

Before we leave this topic, it's important to caution you that *correlation does not imply causation.* This is a logic error commonly associated with correlational studies. Although a high correlation allows us to predict one variable from another, it does not tell us whether a cause–effect relationship exists between the two variables. For example, what if we said we there was a substantial positive correlation between the size of young children's feet and how fast they read? Would this mean that having small feet *causes* a child to be a slow reader? Obviously not! Nor do increases in reading speed *cause* increases in foot size. Instead, both are caused by a third variable — an increase in children's age. Although we can safely *predict* that as a child's foot size increases, his or her reading speed will also increase, this *correlation does not imply causation.*

We use this extreme example to make an important point about an all too common public reaction to research findings. People read media reports about *relationships* between stress and cancer or between family dynamics and homosexuality and then jump to the conclusion that "stress causes cancer" or that "withdrawn fathers and overly protective mothers cause their son's homosexuality." But they fail to realize that a third factor, perhaps genetics, may cause greater susceptibility to both cancer and increased rates of homosexuality (Chapters 3 and 11).

Once again, as Figure 1.5 shows, a correlation between two variables does not mean that one variable *causes* another. Correlational studies do sometimes point to *possible* causes, like the correlation between alcohol and birth defects. However, only the experimental method manipulates the IV under controlled conditions and therefore can draw conclusions about cause and effect.

CRITICAL THINKING/ACTIVE LEARNING EXERCISES

Each chapter contains a special critical thinking/active learning exercise that provides important insight into the chapter material and improves your basic critical thinking skills.

critical thinking   *Active Learning*

Becoming a Better Consumer of Scientific Research

The news media, advertisers, politicians, teachers, close friends, and other individuals frequently use research findings in their attempts to change your attitudes and behavior. How can you tell whether their information is accurate and worthwhile?

The following exercise will improve your ability to critically evaluate sources of information. It is based on the concepts you learned in the previous discussion of psychological research techniques. Read each "research" report and decide what the primary problem or research limitation is. In the space provided, make one of the following marks:

CC = The report is misleading because correlation data are used to suggest causation.

CG = The report is inconclusive because there was no control group.

EB = The results of the research were unfairly influenced by experimenter bias.

SB = The results of the research are questionable because of sample bias.

_____ 1. A clinical psychologist strongly believes that touching is an important adjunct to successful therapy. For two months, he touches half his patients (Group A) and refrains from touching the other half (Group B). He then reports a noticeable improvement in Group A.

_____ 2. A newspaper reports that violent crime corresponds to phases of the moon. The reporter concludes that the gravitational pull of the moon controls human behavior.

_____ 3. A researcher interested in women's attitudes toward premarital sex sends out a lengthy survey to subscribers of *Vogue* and *Cosmopolitan* magazines.

_____ 4. An experimenter is interested in studying the effects of alcohol on driving ability. Prior to testing on an experimental driving course, Group A consumes 2 ounces of alcohol, Group B consumes 4 ounces of alcohol, and Group C consumes 6 ounces of alcohol. After the test drive, the researcher reports that alcohol consumption adversely affects driving ability.

_____ 5. After reading a scientific journal that reports higher divorce rates among couples living together before marriage, a college student decides to move out of the apartment she shares with her boyfriend.

_____ 6. A theater owner reports increased beverage sales following the brief flashing of a subliminal message to "Drink Coca-Cola" during the film showing.

Answers: 1. EB; 2. CC; 3. SB; 4. CG; 5. CC; 6. CG

Ethical Problems: Protecting the Rights of Others

The APA, the largest professional organization of psychologists, recognizes the importance of maintaining high ethical standards in research, therapy, and all other areas of professional psychology. The preamble to their publication *Ethical Principles of Psychologists and Code of Conduct* (1992) admonishes psychologists to maintain their competence, to retain objectivity in applying their skills, and to preserve the dignity and best interests of their clients, colleagues, students, research participants, and society. In this section, we will discuss three important areas of ethical concern: human participants, animal rights, and clients in therapy.

What are the major research and ethical issues and biases?

Respecting the Rights of Human Participants

The APA has developed guidelines regulating research with human participants. These are the key issues:

- **Informed consent and voluntary participation.** One of the chief principles set forth in the APA document is that an investigator should obtain the participant's **informed consent** before initiating an experiment. The researcher should fully inform the participant as to the nature of the study, including significant factors that might influence a person's willingness to participate, such as physical risks, discomfort, or unpleasant emotional experiences. The researcher must also explain that participants are free to decline to participate or to withdraw from the research at any time.

Informed Consent *A participant's agreement to take part in a study after being told what to expect*

- **The use of deception.** Participation in research should be voluntary and informed, but what if you're studying topics like persuasion techniques or attitude change? If participants know the true purpose behind some studies, they will almost certainly not respond naturally. Therefore, APA acknowledges the need for some *deception research*. When using deception, researchers are expected to follow strict guidelines, including **debriefing** participants at the end of the experiment. Debriefing involves explaining the reasons for conducting the research and clearing up any misconceptions or concerns on the part of the participant.

Debriefing *A necessary and important aspect of deception research in which the participants are informed after the research about the purpose of the study, the nature of the anticipated results, and any deceptions used*

RESEARCH HIGHLIGHT

An Elegant Study of Therapeutic Touch

Nine-year-old Emily Rosa, the child in our opening story, is a wonderful model of critical thinking and the scientific approach to everyday life. Therapeutic touch (TT) practitioners claim to heal or alleviate medical problems by passing their hands over the patient's body, supposedly realigning energy fields until they're "in balance" (Scheiber & Selby, 2000). This realignment reportedly stems disease and allows the patient's body to heal itself (Quinn & Strelkauskas, 1993). But rather than asking TT practitioners or their patients if their energy manipulations actually heal or relieve pain, Emily asked a more important question. She wanted to know whether *human energy fields* (HEF) even exist.

As you can see in Figure 1.6, Emily set up a small screen and then asked 21 TT practitioners to stick their hands, palms up, through the screen. The researcher (Emily) then held her hand over either the left or right hand of the practitioner — decided by a flip of coin. In 10 to 20 separate trials, the TT practitioners had to say which of his or her hands was nearer to the researcher's hand. Each participant was allowed to make any desired "mental preparations" ahead of time and to take as much time as necessary to make each determination. When the results were analyzed, the TT practitioners performed no better than chance (Rosa, Rosa, Sarner, & Barrett, 1998)!

Not only did Emily's research bring her personal recognition and science fair honors but it also demonstrated the importance of scientifically analyzing therapeutic claims. This fourth-grader's "simple" study demonstrated that 21 practitioners failed to even *detect* her energy field — much less modify it. As our earlier discussion of the goals of psychology and the scientific method explained, therapeutic techniques must meet basic scientific standards. Given the lack of scientific support for TT's most fundamental claim, members of the medical and scientific community now question its continued use.

Needless to say, TT practitioners and supporters dispute the findings of Emily's study (Gorman, 1999). They say the research arrangement was unnatural, that

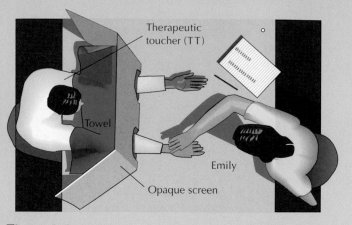

Figure 1.6 *Emily's clever design*. Nine-year-old Emily Rosa designed a clever scientific experiment to test whether therapeutic touch practitioners could sense her presence. The practitioners placed their hands through the holes in a screen. Then Emily tossed a coin and held one of her hands over the practitioner's left or right hand to see if they could detect her "energy field." They couldn't.

"our hands are moving, not stationary. You don't just walk into a room and perform — it's a whole process" (Lemonick, 1998, p. 67). TT practitioners who fully believe in their work can contact the James Randi Educational Foundation. As mentioned earlier, Randi offers $1.1 million to anyone who can demonstrate proof of any HEF or other pseudopsychology under scientifically controlled conditions. Despite extensive recruiting efforts, only one TT practitioner has attempted the test. She failed (Rosa, Rosa, Sarner, & Barrett, 1998).

- **Confidentiality.** All information acquired about people during a study must be held confidential and not published in such a way that individual rights to privacy are compromised.

- **Students as research participants.** If research participation is a course requirement or an opportunity for extra credit, the student must be given the choice of an alternative activity of equal value.

Respecting the Rights of Animal Participants

Most psychological research involves the use of human participants, but in some cases animals are used. For example, researchers sometimes study behavior continuously over months or years (longer than people are willing to participate), and occasionally they want to control aspects of life that people will not let them control and that would be unethical to control (such as who mates with whom or serious food restrictions). The relative simplicity of some animals' nervous systems also provides important advantages for research.

Keep in mind that the amount of animal research in psychology is relatively small. Only about 7 to 8 percent of all psychological research is done on animals, and 90 percent of that is done with rats and mice (American Psychological Association, 1984). In addition, most animal research involves naturalistic observation or learning experiments using rewards rather than punishments (Burgdorf, Knutson, & Panksepp, 2000; Neuringer, Deiss, & Olson, 2000). Furthermore, in all institutions where animal research is conducted, animal care committees are established to ensure proper treatment of research animals, to review projects, and to set guidelines that are in accordance with the APA standards for the care and treatment of research animals.

Finally, keep in mind that animal research has benefited both humans and other animals in many ways. Without animals in medical research, how would we test new drugs, surgical procedures, and methods for relieving pain? In psychology, research on learning in rats and pigeons led to the development of programmed learning materials, and teaching sign language to chimps and gorillas has led to a better understanding of the structure of human language. Animal research is also pursued for its potential benefit to animals themselves. As a result of psychological research, more natural environments have been created for zoo animals, successful breeding techniques have been developed for endangered species, and more effective training techniques have been developed for pets and wild animals in captivity. Despite the benefits of animal research, the use of animals in psychological research continues to be a controversial and ethical problem. While the controversy continues, psychologists take great care in the handling of research animals and actively search for new and better ways to protect them (Guidelines for the Treatment, 2000; Miller, 1991).

Is animal research ethical? Opinions are sharply divided on this question.

Respecting the Rights of Clients

Ethics are important in therapy, as well as in research. Successful psychotherapy requires that clients reveal their innermost thoughts and feelings during the course of treatment. It follows, then, that clients must trust their therapists. This places a burden of responsibility on therapists to maintain the highest of ethical standards and uphold this trust.

Therapists are expected to conduct themselves in a moral and professional manner. They should remain objective while becoming sufficiently involved with the client's problems to know how to best help them. They should encourage their clients to become involved not only in deciding the type of treatment but also in the treatment process itself. Therapists are also expected to evaluate their clients' progress and report that progress to them.

All personal information and therapy records must be kept confidential, with records available only to authorized persons and with the client's permission. Such confidentiality can become an ethical issue when a client reveals something that might affect or possibly injure another person. For example, if you were a therapist, what would you do if a client revealed plans to commit murder? Would you alert the police or uphold your client's trust?

In cases of serious threat to others, the public's right to safety ethically outweighs the client's right to privacy. In fact, a therapist is legally required to break confidentiality if a client threatens violence to self or others, in cases involving suspected or actual child or elderly abuse, and in some other limited situations. In general, however, a counselor's primary obligation is to protect client disclosures (Corey, 2001).

A Final Note on Ethical Issues

After discussing ways research can be flawed and ethics can be violated, you may be unnecessarily concerned. Remember that guidelines exist to protect the rights of humans, animals, and therapy clients. Most importantly, a *human subjects committee* or *institutional review board* must first approve all research using human participants conducted at a college, university, or any reputable institution. This group ensures that every proposed study provides for informed consent, participants' confidentiality, and safe procedures. Similar committees also exist to oversee and protect the rights of animal participants.

Any member of APA who disregards these principles may be censured or expelled from the organization. Clinicians who violate ethical guidelines for working with clients risk severe sanctions and can permanently lose their license to practice. In addition, both researchers and clinicians are held professionally and legally responsible by their institutions, as well as by local and state agencies.

Check & Review

NONEXPERIMENTAL STUDIES/RESEARCH AND ETHICAL PROBLEMS

Unlike experiments, nonexperimental methods cannot determine the causes of behavior, but they can describe specifics, determine relationships, and help with prediction. **Naturalistic observation** is used to study and describe behavior in its natural habitat. **Surveys** use interviews or questionnaires to obtain information on a sample of participants. Individual **case studies** are in-depth studies of a participant.

Correlational studies examine how strongly two variables are related (+1.00 to −1.00) and whether the relationship is positively, negatively, or not at all (zero) correlated. Correlational studies and the correlation coefficient provide important research findings and valuable predictions. However, it is important to remember that *correlation does not imply causation.*

Psychologists are expected to maintain high ethical standards in their relations with human and animal research participants, as well as with clients in therapy. The APA has published guidelines detailing these ethical standards.

Questions

1. What is the major difference between naturalistic observations, surveys, and case studies?

2. Maria is thinking of running for student body president, but she wonders whether her campaign should emphasize campus security, improved parking facilities, or increased health services. Which scientific method of research would you recommend she use to determine the focus of her campaign? (a) case study; (b) naturalistic observation; (c) an experiment; (d) a survey.

3. Which of the following correlation coefficients indicates the strongest relationship? (a) +.78; (b) −.84; (c) +.35; (d) 00.

4. A participant's agreement to take part in a study after being told what to expect is known as _____ (a) participant observer; (b) placebo effect; (c) informed consent; (d) debriefing.

Answers to Questions can be found in Appendix B.

Who are the important contributors to psychology's past, and what are the primary perspectives that guide modern psychology?

PERSPECTIVES IN PSYCHOLOGY

People have always been interested in human nature. Before psychology became a separate scientific discipline, the study of why people act as they do and how one person is different from another fell within the realm of philosophy. It was not until the first psychological laboratory was founded in 1879 that psychology as a science officially began. As interest in the new field grew, psychologists took various approaches to their research. Eventually, the different approaches and beliefs regarding the study of behavior came to be grouped into *schools of psychology*. In the next few pages, we will first explore those schools in psychology's past and then briefly summarize the seven major approaches or *perspectives* in modern psychology.

Psychology's Past: Important Pioneers

As you can see in Table 1.5, the early pioneers and approaches to psychology are grouped into six major schools: experimental psychology, structuralism, functionalism, psychoanalytic, behaviorism, and Gestalt.

TABLE 1.5 PSYCHOLOGY'S PAST — MAJOR SCHOOLS OF PSYCHOLOGY

School	Prominent Figures	Major Emphases	Study Techniques
Experimental psychology (1870s–1880s)	Wilhelm Wundt	Thought processes	Trained introspection
Structuralism (1890s)	Titchener	Thought processes, structure of the mind, and identification of the elements of thought	Trained introspection
Functionalism (1890s)	William James John Dewey	Applying psychological findings to practical situations and the function of mental processes in adapting to the environment	Introspection Experimental method Comparative method (humans and animals)
Psychoanalytic/ psychodynamic (1895–present)	Sigmund Freud Carl Jung Alfred Adler Karen Horney	Unconscious determinants of behavior, effect of early life experiences on later personality development	Individual case studies of patients
Behaviorism (1906–present)	Ivan Pavlov Edward Thorndike John B. Watson B. F. Skinner	Objective, observable behavior, stimulus–response, and effect of the environment on overt behavior	Experiments, primarily on learning and often done with animals
Gestalt psychology (1910s)	Max Wertheimer Wolfgang Kohler Kurt Koffka	Organization and context in the perception of meaningful wholes	Sensation and perception experiments

"Well, you don't look like an experimental psychologist to me."

Experimental Psychology

Wilhelm Wundt is generally known as the founder of experimental psychology. He established the first psychological laboratory at the University of Leipzig, Germany, in 1879, and wrote what is often considered the most important book in the history of psychology, *Principles of Physiological Psychology.*

In this laboratory, Wundt and his followers undertook the study of psychology, which to them consisted of the study of experience. They went about this study by trying to break down conscious experiences into basic elements. Their chief method was termed *introspection,* monitoring and reporting on the contents of consciousness. If you were one of Wundt's participants trained in introspection, you might be presented with the sound of a clicking metronome. You would focus solely on the clicks and report only your immediate reactions to them — your basic sensations and feelings.

Structuralism

Edward Titchener, one of Wundt's followers, brought Wundt's ideas to the United States. Titchener established a psychological laboratory and coined the term *structuralism* to embody Wundt's ideas. Like Wundt, structuralists believed that, just as the elements hydrogen and oxygen combine to form the compound water, the "elements" of conscious experience combine to form the "compounds" of the mind. They sought to identify the elements of thought through introspection and then determine how these elements combined to form the whole of experience. Thus, their study focused on the investigation of thought processes and the structure of the mind.

Functionalism

Structuralists inaugurated psychology as a science and established the importance of studying mental processes. However, psychologists, especially those in the United States, became impatient with structuralism. They felt it was limited to only one area of behavior (e.g., introspection) and had few practical applications. These

American psychologists, feeling the need for application of psychological findings to practical situations, began a new school of psychology known as *functionalism,* which stressed the importance of how behavior *functions* to allow people and animals to adapt to their environment.

By the end of the nineteenth century, Charles Darwin's theory of evolution was beginning to have a significant impact on psychology (Segerstrale, 2000). Of particular interest was his idea of the "survival of the fittest," which stressed the function of superior biological structures in adapting organisms to their environment. It was this idea that led several American psychologists to investigate the function of mental processes in adapting the individual to the environment — thus the name *functionalism.* Darwin's theory of evolution also suggested the possibility that mental processes of animals and people might be part of a continuum. Therefore, *functionalists* studied mental processes of both animals and humans to test their theories. Many then applied their research findings to practical situations.

William James was the leading force in the functionalist school. In keeping with structuralism, he viewed psychology as the study of consciousness, but James did not believe consciousness could be separated into distinct elements. He felt that mental activities form a unit of experience — that they are continually changing, while remaining interrelated, one thought flowing into another in a continuous "stream of consciousness."

Functionalism had a great impact on the development of psychology. It expanded the scope of psychology to include research on emotions and observable behaviors, initiated the psychological testing movement, changed the course of modern education, and extended psychology's influence to diverse areas in industry.

William James (1842–1910). James was a leading force in the Functionalist school of psychology, which stressed the adaptive and practical functions of human behavior.

Psychoanalytic

During the late 1800s and early 1900s, while functionalism was prominent in the United States, the *psychoanalytic* school was forming in Europe (Gay, 2000). Its founder, Sigmund Freud, was an Austrian physician who was fascinated by the way the mind influences behavior. After encountering several patients with ongoing physical complaints that seemed to have no physiological basis, Freud assumed that their complaints must be psychological. Further studies of these patients convinced Freud that such problems are caused by conflicts between what people believe to be acceptable behavior and their unacceptable motives, which are primarily of a sexual or aggressive nature. Freud believed these motives, the driving forces behind behavior, were hidden in the *unconscious,* the part of the mind that is outside of our awareness. Freud developed psychoanalytic theory to explain these conflicts and to provide a basis for a system of therapy known as *psychoanalysis.*

Sigmund Freud (1856–1939). Freud founded the Psychoanalytic perspective, an influential theory of personality, and a type of therapy known as psychoanalysis.

Isn't there a lot of criticism of Freud? Freud's nonscientific approach and emphasis on sexual and aggressive impulses have caused a great deal of controversy over the years. Even some of Freud's most ardent followers, Carl Jung, Alfred Adler, Karen Horney, and Erik Erikson, later broke away from their mentor — in large part because they wanted less emphasis on sex and aggression and more on social motives and relationships. Some also objected to possible sexist bias in his writings and theories. These early followers and their theories are now referred to as *neo-Freudians* (*neo* means "new" or "recent").

Today, there are few strictly Freudian psychoanalysts left, but the broad features of his theory remain in the modern approach known as *psychodynamic.* Although psychodynamic psychologists are making increasing use of experimental methods, their primary method is the analysis of case studies, because their primary goal is to interpret complex meanings hypothesized to underlie people's actions.

In sum, the original psychoanalytic approach has had a profound impact on psychotherapy, psychiatry, and modern psychodynamic psychologists. Freud is generally credited with expanding the impact of psychology throughout the world.

Ivan Pavlov (1849–1936). Pavlov earned Russia's first Nobel prize in 1904 for his study of digestion, but his lasting contribution to psychology was his accidental discovery of classical conditioning

B. F. Skinner (1904–1990). Skinner was a prominent figure in Behaviorism and one of the most influential psychologists of the twentieth century.

Behaviorism

In the early 1900s, another major school of thought appeared that dramatically shaped the course of psychology. Whereas structuralism, functionalism, and the psychoanalytic school looked at nonobservable mental forces, *behaviorism* emphasized objective, observable behaviors. Behaviorist John B. Watson strongly objected to the method of "introspection," the study of mental processes, and the influence of unconscious forces. Because he believed all behavior could be viewed as a response to a *stimulus* (an object or event, either internal or external, that stimulates or causes an organism to respond), Watson adopted Russian physiologist Ivan Pavlov's concept of conditioning to explain behavior as a result of *stimulus and response*. In Pavlov's famous experiment teaching a dog to salivate to the sound of a bell, the bell is the stimulus and the salivation is the response.

Because animals are ideal subjects for studying objective, overt behaviors, the majority of early behaviorist research was done with animals or with techniques developed through animal research. Using dogs, rats, pigeons, and other animals, behaviorists such as John Watson in the early 1900s and, more recently, B. F. Skinner focused primarily on learning — on how behaviors are acquired. They formulated a number of basic principles about learning that are explained in Chapter 6.

It sounds like behaviorists are interested only in animals. Aren't any of them interested in humans? Yes, behaviorists *are* interested in people. One of the most well-known behaviorists, B. F. Skinner, was convinced that we could use behaviorist approaches to actually "shape" human behavior and thereby change the present negative course (as he perceived it) of humankind. He did considerable writing and lecturing to convince others of this position. Behaviorists have been most successful in treating people with overt (observable, behavioral) problems, such as phobias (irrational fears) and alcoholism (Chapters 14 and 15).

Gestalt Psychology

Another early influence on psychology was the school of *Gestalt psychology*, founded by a group of German psychologists headed by Max Wertheimer in the early 1900s. Unlike behaviorism, Gestalt psychology assigned an important role to mental activities, which they believed organized sensations into meaningful perceptions.

Although Wundt and the structuralists were also interested in perception, the underlying philosophy of the Gestaltists was quite different. Gestaltists rejected the notion that experiences can be broken down into elements. Rather, they insisted that experience can be studied only as a whole — that the whole experience is qualitatively different from the sum of the distinct elements of that experience (*Gestalt* means roughly "organized whole" or "pattern" in German). As you will note in upcoming chapters, Gestalt psychology remains an important contributor to modern studies of sensation, perception, personality, and a type of psychotherapy.

Women and Minorities

Before leaving the topic of "psychology's past," we need to explore the contributions of women and minorities. During the late 1800s and early 1900s, most colleges and universities provided little opportunity for women and minorities, either as students or faculty. Despite these early limitations, both women and minorities have made important contributions to psychology.

One of the first women to be recognized in the field was Mary Calkins. Calkins performed valuable research on memory and in 1905 served as the first female president of the APA. Her achievements are particularly noteworthy, considering the significant discrimination against women in those times. Even after completing all the requirements for a Ph.D. at Harvard and being described by William James as his brightest student, the university refused to grant the degree to a woman. The first woman to receive a Ph.D. in psychology was Margaret Floy Washburn (in 1894), who wrote several influential books and served as the second female president of APA.

Francis Cecil Sumner, without benefit of a formal high school education, became the first African American to earn a Ph.D. in psychology from Clark University in 1920. He translated over 3,000 articles from German, French, and Spanish and founded one of the country's leading psychology departments. One of Sumner's students at Clark University, Kenneth B. Clark, later (in 1971) became the first African American to be elected APA president. Along with his wife, Mamie, Kenneth Clark documented the harmful effects of prejudice. Their research had a direct effect on the Supreme Court's ultimate ruling against racial segregation in the schools.

Sumner and Clark, Calkins and Washburn, along with other important minorities and women, made important and lasting contributions to the developing science of psychology. In recent years, several programs have been developed to encourage people of color and women to pursue graduate degrees in psychology.

Mary Calkins (1863–1930). Calkins was the first woman president of the American Psychological Association, established a psychology laboratory at Wellesley College, and conducted important research on memory.

Kenneth Clark (1914 –). Clark was the first African-American president of the American Psychological Association. He and his wife, Mamie, also conducted research on prejudice that was cited in 1964 by the Supreme Court.

Psychology's Present: Seven Perspectives

In modern psychology, early schools like structuralism have almost entirely disappeared, whereas viewpoints like functionalism, psychoanalytic, and Gestalt have blended into newer, broader perspectives. In addition, rather than "schools of psychology," most psychologists today talk about different "perspectives." By this, they mean approaches that influence the topics psychologists study, how they conduct their research, and what information they consider important. Many modern psychologists also recognize the value of using several perspectives and that no one view has all the answers; this is referred to as an *eclectic approach*.

The rest of this book focuses on the current era in psychology, with occasional references to the history we've just described. Today, seven perspectives dominate: biopsychology or neuroscience, cognitive, behavioral, sociocultural, evolutionary, humanistic, and psychodynamic. Table 1.6 previews the major figures and emphases of these perspectives. The upcoming chapters provide detailed descriptions.

A Final Note

One final note as you begin your study of psychology: You will learn a great deal about psychological functioning, but take care that you don't overestimate your expertise. Once friends and acquaintances know that you're taking a course in psychology, they may ask you to interpret their dreams, help them to discipline their children, or even offer your opinion on whether they should break up their relationships. It is a good idea, therefore, to remember that the ideas, philosophies, and even experimental findings of the science of psychology are continually being revised. As David L. Cole, a recipient of the APA Distinguished Teaching in Psychology Award, stated, "Undergraduate psychology can, and I believe should, seek to liberate the student from ignorance, but also the arrogance of believing we know more about ourselves and others than we really do" (1982).

At the same time, psychological findings and ideas developed through careful research and study can make important contributions to our lives. As Albert Einstein once said, "One thing I have learned in a long life: that all our science, measured against reality, is primitive and childlike — and yet, it is the most precious thing we have."

TABLE 1.6 PSYCHOLOGY'S PRESENT — SEVEN MAJOR PERSPECTIVES

Perspectives	Prominent Figures	Major Emphases
Psychoanalytic/psychody-namic (1895–present)	Sigmund Freud Carl Jung Alfred Adler Karen Horney	Unconscious determinants of behavior, effect of early life experiences on later personality development
Behaviorism (1906–present)	Ivan Pavlov Edward Thorndike John B. Watson B. F. Skinner	Objective, observable behavior; stimulus–response; and effect of the environment on overt behavior
Humanistic psychology (1950s–present)	Carl Rogers Abraham Maslow	Self-concept, free will, and human nature as naturally positive and growth-seeking
Cognitive psychology (1950s–present)	Jean Piaget Albert Ellis Albert Bandura Robert Sternberg Howard Gardener	Conscious thought, perception, and information processing
Neuroscience/biopsychology (1950s–present)	Johannes Müller Karl Lashley David Hubel James Olds Roger Sperry Candace Pert	Genetics and physiological processes occurring in the brain and nervous system
Evolutionary psychology (1980s–present)	Charles Darwin Konrad Lorenz E. O. Wilson David Buss	Natural selection, adaptation, and evolution of behavior patterns
Sociocultural psychology (1980s–present)	John Berry Patricia Greenfield Richard Brislin	Social interaction and the cultural determinants of behavior

GENDER & CULTURAL DIVERSITY

Are There Cultural Universals?

Psychology is a broad field with numerous subdisciplines and professions. Until recently, most psychologists worked and conducted research primarily in Europe and North America. Given this "one-sided" research, psychology's findings may not apply equally to people in other countries, or to minorities and women in Europe and North America, for that matter (Matsumoto, 2000; Shiraev & Levy, 2000). However, modern psychology, in particular *cultural psychology*, is working to correct this imbalance. Key research from cross-cultural and multiethnic studies is integrated throughout the text, and each chapter includes a "Gender and Cultural Diversity" section with a special icon in the margin that looks like this: ✳

In this first gender and cultural diversity discussion, we explore a central question in cultural psychology: Are there *cultural universals*? That is, are there aspects of human behavior and mental processes that are true and *pancultural* or *universal* for all people of all cultures?

For many "universalists," emotions and facial recognition of emotions provide the clearest example of a possible cultural universal. Numerous studies conducted over many years with people from very different cultures suggests that everyone can easily identify facial expressions for at least six basic emotions: happiness, surprise, anger, sadness, fear, and disgust. All humans supposedly have this capacity whether they are shown the face of a child or an adult, a Western or non-Western person (Ekman, 1993; Ekman & Friesen, 1971; Hejmadi, Davidson, & Rozin, 2000; Matsumoto, 1992, 2000). Moreover, nonhuman primates and congenitally blind infants also display similarly recognizable facial signals. In other words, across cultures (and some species), a frown is recognized as a sign of displeasure, and a smile, as a sign of pleasure (Figure 1.7).

Critics of the universalist position emphasize problems with these studies. For example, how do you label and study the emotion described by Japanese as *hagaii* (feeling helpless anguish mixed with frustration). Particularly, if the Western psychologist has no experience with these emotions and no English equivalent words? Other critics argue that *if* cultural universals exist, it is because they are biological and innate — and they should be labeled as such. However, equating biology with

Figure 1.7 *Do you recognize these emotions?* The recognition and display of facial expressions of emotion may be true "culture universals."

universality has its own problem. Behaviors or mental processes that are universal may be so because of culture-constant learning rather than biological destiny (Matsumoto, 2000). For example, *if* we found that certain gender roles were expressed the same in all cultures, it might reflect shared cultural training beginning at birth and not an "anatomy is destiny" position.

As we discussed earlier, scientists avoid the tendency to compartmentalize behaviors into "either-or" categories. Like the nature–nurture controversy, the answer once again is an *interaction*. Emotions and their recognition may be both biological and culturally universal. As a beginning student in psychology, you will encounter numerous areas of conflict, with well-respected arguments and opponents on each side. Your job is to adopt an open-minded, critical-thinking approach to each of these debates.

In addition to building your critical thinking skills, hearing arguments from both sides also will develop your understanding and appreciation for diversity, both intellectual and cultural. It might even improve your personal and business interactions. Richard Brislin (1993) told the story of a Japanese businessman who was asked to give a speech to a Fortune 500 company in New York. He was aware that Americans typically begin speeches by telling an amusing story or a couple of jokes. In contrast, Japanese typically begin speeches by apologizing for the "inadequate" talk they are about to give. This savvy businessman began his speech: "I realize that Americans often begin by making a joke. In Japan, we frequently begin with an apology. I'll compromise by apologizing for not having a joke" (p. 9). By appreciating cultural diversity, we can, like the Japanese businessman, learn to interact successfully in other cultures.

Check & Review

SCHOOLS OF PSYCHOLOGY

Among the early schools of psychology, the experimentalists focused on the study of experience and the use of introspection, whereas the structuralists sought to identify elements of consciousness and how those elements formed the structure of the mind. Functionalists studied how mental processes help the individual adapt to the environment. A later pioneer in psychology, Sigmund Freud developed psychoanalytic theory to explain psychological problems developed from unconscious conflicts. Behaviorism emphasizes observable behaviors and stimulus–response rela-

tionships. The Gestalt school studied organizing principles of perceptual processes.

Seven major perspectives guide modern psychology: biopsychology or neuroscience, cognitive, behavioral, sociocultural, evolutionary, humanistic, and psychodynamic. These seven perspectives permeate the field of psychology and will be discussed in great detail in later chapters.

Questions

1. The _____ school of psychology originated the method of introspection to examine thoughts and feelings.

2. _____ investigated the function of mental processes in adapting to the environment, and many applied their findings to real-world situations.

3. Why is Freud's theory so controversial?

4. Which of the following terms do not belong together? (a) structuralism, observable behavior; (b) behaviorism, stimulus–response; (c) psychoanalytic, unconscious conflict; (d) Gestalt; whole.

Answers to Questions can be found in Appendix B.

TOOLS FOR STUDENT SUCCESS

Congratulations! The fact that you are reading this section is an important first step to succeeding in college. We recognize that "student success skills" have a bad reputation and that many people reject such help because they think it's only for "nerds" or "problem students." But would these same individuals assume they could become top-notch musicians or athletes without mastering the "tools" of those trades? All students (even those who seem to get A's without much effort) can improve their "student tools."

In the next few pages, we offer specific, well-documented tips and strategies guaranteed to make you a more efficient and successful college student. You'll learn about active reading, time management, and improving your grades. Finally, we'll point you toward some important resources for college success. We will revisit these topics as appropriate throughout the book, specifically as related to issues such as learning, memory, thinking, motivation, and stress. The icon will help you identify these passages.

TOOLS FOR STUDENT SUCCESS

This special feature in chapter 1 includes tips for overall college success, as well as success in this course. In addition, the "tool" icon identifies additional sections in chapters 6, 7, 8, 12 which address other strategies for dealing with test anxiety, improving memory, performance and overall achievement.

ACTIVE READING   How to Study (and Master) This Text

Have you ever read several pages of a text and then found you couldn't recall a single detail? Or have you read and believed you understood the text yet done poorly on an exam? Such problems generally reflect a lack of *active reading*. There are a number of ways to actively read a text. Let's begin with Step One.

STEP ONE *Familiarizing Yourself with the General Text*

Your textbook is the major tool for success in any course. Most instructors rely on it to present basic course material, reserving class time for clarifying and elaborating on important topics. You can be a more successful student (and test taker) if you take full advantage of all the special features offered in *Psychology in Action*. Here's how to use these features:

- *Preface.* If you have not already read the preface, do it now. It is a road map for the rest of the text.

- *Table of Contents.* Scan the table of contents for a bird's-eye view of what you will study in this course. Get the big picture from the chapter titles and the major topics within each chapter.

- *Individual Chapters.* Each chapter of *Psychology in Action* contains numerous learning aids to help you master the material. There are chapter outlines, learning objectives, introductory vignettes, running glossaries, Check and Review (summaries and self-test questions), visual summaries, and more. These learning aids are highlighted and explained in the margin of Chapter 1.

- *Appendixes.* Two appendixes, A, *Statistics, and B, Answers to Review Questions and Activities*, present important information. The statistics appendix further discusses some of the concepts introduced in Chapter 1. It also explains how to read and interpret the graphs and tables found throughout the text. Appendix B contains answers to the Check and Review questions, Try This Yourself feature, and various other activities found in the chapters.

- *Glossary.* There are two glossaries in this text. A running glossary appears in the margins of each chapter to define key terms and concepts when they are first introduced. There is also an end-of-book glossary that gathers all the terms from the running chapter glossaries in one place. Use the end-of-book glossary to review terms from other chapters.

- *References.* As you read each chapter, you will see references cited in parentheses, not in footnotes, as is common in other disciplines. For example, *(Ventner et al.,*

Visual Summary for Chapter 1

Understanding Psychology

Psychology is the *scientific* study of behavior and mental processes. It values empierical evidence and **critical thinking,** unlike pseudopsychologies, which use nonscientific and nonverifiable methods.

Goals of Psychology

Describe, explain, predict, and change behavior and mental processes.

Careers or Specialties

Various areas, including biopsychology, clinical, cognitive, counseling, developmental, educational and school, experimental, gender and/or cultural, industrial/organizational, and social.

Types of Research

Basic research studies theoretical questions.
Applied research attempts to answer real-world problems.

Doing Research in Psychology

The Scientific Method

Six *basic steps*: 1) Review the literature, 2) Formulate the **hypothesis**, 3)Design the study and collect data, 4) Analyze the data and accept or reject the hypothesis, 5) Publish, replicate, and undergo scientific review, 6) Continue **theory** building.

Experimental Research

Distinguishing feature: establishes cause and effect.

Components:
- **Independent variables** (what the experimenter manipulates)
- **Dependent variables** (what the experimenter measures)
- Experimental controls (including **control group, experimental group, extraneous variables)**

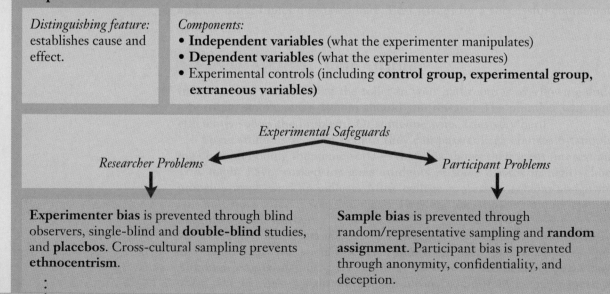

Experimental Safeguards

Researcher Problems

Participant Problems

Experimenter bias is prevented through blind observers, single-blind and **double-blind** studies, and **placebos.** Cross-cultural sampling prevents **ethnocentrism.**

Sample bias is prevented through random/representative sampling and **random assignment.** Participant bias is prevented through anonymity, confidentiality, and deception.

VISUAL SUMMARY

At the end of each chapter, the entire chapter is summariezed in a visual format. This unique study tool visually summarizes and organizes the main concepts of each chapter in a clear, two-page layout that serves as a quick review after completing your reading. Relationships between topics can be clearly seen and understood.

Doing Research in Psychology (cont).

Nonexperimental Studies

Distinguishing feature: Describes specifics about behavior, determines relationships between variables, and helps with prediction.

Methods

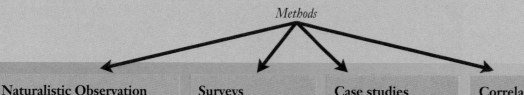

Naturalistic Observation
Systematic recording of observable behavior in the participant's natural habitat with little or no experimenter intervention.

Surveys
Assesses behaviors and attitudes of a sample or population.

Case studies
In-depth study of a single research participant.

Correlational Studies
Statistical analyses of relationships between variables.

Ethical Problems

Human research participants have rights, including **informed consent** and voluntary participation, limited use of deception, **debriefing**, and confidentiality. Rights of animal participants and clients in therapy are protected through careful adherence to APA standards.

Perspectives in Psychology

Psychology's Past

- *Experimental psychology*: Studied experience through introspection.
- *Structuralism*: Focused on thought processes and the structure of the mind through introspection.
- *Functionalism*: Emphasized the function of mental processes in adapting to the environment and application of psychology to practical situations.
- *Psychoanalytic/Psychodynamic*: Emphasized unconscious processes and early life experiences.
- *Behaviorism*: Studied objective, observable behavior, and the effect of the environment.
- *Gestalt psychology*: Emphasized organization, context, and meaningful wholes.

Psychology's Present

- *Psychoanalytic/Psychodynamic*: Emphasizes unconscious processes and early life experiences.
- *Behaviorism*: Studies objective, observable, environmental influences.
- *Humanistic*: Focuses on self-concept, free will, and human nature as positive growth-seeking.
- *Cognitive*: Emphasizes conscious thought, perception, and information processing.
- *Neuroscience/Biopsychology*: Studies natural selection, adaptation, and evolution of behavior patterns.
- *Sociocultural*: Focuses on social interaction and cultural determinants of behavior.

2 Neuroscience and Biological Foundations

In 1848, when the Rutland and Burlington Railroad was laying new track through Vermont, 25-year-old Phineas P. Gage was a foreman in charge of blasting through the rocky terrain. Blasting a boulder into smaller, more easily removed rocks was a dangerous job, but not very complicated. First, a hole was drilled into the boulder and partially filled with blasting powder. Then a fuse was run into the blasting powder that was carefully tamped down, and the hole was filled with sand. The sand was tamped again with a metal rod to remove any air pockets that might diminish the blast, the fuse was lit, and everyone ran for cover.

Gage had done this hundreds of times, but on September 13, 1848, he failed to notice that his assistant had not yet put sand into the hole. So when Gage put down the tamping rod, it scraped against the rock and created sparks that ignited the blasting powder. But instead of shattering the boulder, the blast turned the iron rod into a missile. The 13-pound metal rod, $1\frac{1}{4}$ inches in diameter and $3\frac{1}{2}$ feet long, rocketed out of the hole and shot through Gage's head. Entering under his left cheekbone, the rod slammed through his brain, exiting out the top of his skull into the air, and eventually landing 60 to 80 feet away. Portions of his brain's frontal lobes littered the ground and smeared the tamping iron. This should have been the end of the story, but it wasn't.

Gage was stunned and his extremities shook convulsively. But in just a few minutes, he was able to talk to his men, and he even walked with little or no assistance up a flight of stairs before receiving medical treatment $1\frac{1}{2}$ hours later. Although his mind was "clear" and Gage insisted he would be back at work in a day or two, the attending physician, John Harlow, doubted that he would recover and the town cabinetmaker even measured Gage so there would be a coffin "in readiness to use" (Harlow, 1848, 1868; Macmillan, 1986, 2000).

Gage did survive physically, but not psychologically. A serious personality transformation had occurred. Before the accident, Gage was "the most efficient and capable foreman," "a shrewd, smart business man," and very energetic and persistent in executing all his plans. After the accident, Gage "frequently changed what he proposed doing, and was, among

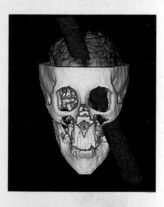

other things, fitful, capricious, impatient of advice, obstinate, and lacking in deference to his fellows" (Macmillan, 2000, p. 13). In the words of his friends and acquaintances, "Gage was no longer Gage" (Harlow, 1868). Following months of recuperation, Gage attempted to return to work but was refused his old job. The damage to his brain had changed him too profoundly.

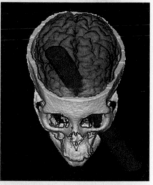

According to historical records by his physician, Gage never again held a job equal to that of foreman. He supported himself with odd jobs and traveled around New England, exhibiting himself and the tamping iron, and for a time he did the same at Barnum Museum. He even lived in Chile for 7 years before ill health forced a return to the United States. Near the end of his life, Gage experienced numerous epileptic seizures of increasing severity and frequency. Despite the massive damage to his frontal lobes caused by the tamping iron, Phineas Gage lived on for another $11\frac{1}{2}$ years, eventually dying from the epileptic seizures.

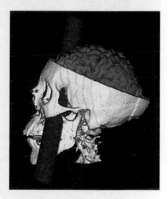

How did Gage physically survive? What accounts for his radical change in personality? If the tamping iron had traveled through the brain at a slightly different angle, Gage would have immediately died. But as you can see in the photos above, the rod entered and exited the front part of the brain, a section unnecessary for physical survival but intimately involved in motivation, emotion, and a host of other cognitive activities.

Neuroscience *An interdisciplinary field studying how biological processes, especially activity in the brain and nervous system, relate to behavior*

Neuroscience and you. All behavior and mental processes require a complex interaction between the brain, nervous system, and body.

How is the nervous system organized?

Central Nervous System (CNS) *The brain and spinal cord.*

Phineas Gage's injury and "recovery" is a classic example from the field of **neuroscience** and *biopsychology*, the scientific study of the *biology* of behavior and mental processes. Most beginning psychology students expect to study only abnormal behavior and are surprised by the amount of biology. Obviously, the brain is critical to survival, but have you thought about how it is also responsible for all your thoughts, fears, loves, and other behavior and mental processes? Your brain and nervous system control everything you do, feel, see, or think. *You are your brain.*

To help you fully understand and appreciate the wonders of your brain and nervous system, this chapter provides a basic overview and lays the foundation for the biological processes discussed throughout the text. We begin with a brief overview of the nervous system. Then we examine the *neuron,* or nerve cell, and the way neurons communicate with one another to produce thinking, feeling, and behavior. The bulk of the chapter explores the brain itself. We conclude with a look at heredity and evolutionary processes.

BIOLOGICAL FOUNDATIONS

One of the many advantages of taking this psychology course is learning about yourself and how you learn. As you'll discover in Chapter 7, when you are introduced to a large set of new terms and concepts, the best way to master this material (and get it "permanently" stored in long-term memory) is through *organization.* A broad overview showing the "big picture" helps you organize and file specific details. Just as you would use a large globe of the world that shows all the continents to learn about individual countries, you need a "map" of the entire nervous system before studying the individual parts. Thus, we begin with this broad overview, followed by a close examination of the neuron itself, communication between neurons, and chemical messengers in the nervous system.

An Overview of the Nervous System: The Central Nervous System and Peripheral Nervous System

Have you heard the expression "Information is power?" Nowhere is this truer than in the human body. Without information we could not survive. Our brain and bodies must take in information from the outside world, decide what to do with the information, and then follow through. Just as the circulatory system handles blood, our nervous system handles information.

To fully comprehend the intricacies of the nervous system, it helps to know the names of its major parts and how they are interrelated. Take a look at Figure 2.1. The nervous system has two major divisions, the *Central Nervous System* (CNS), which processes and organizes information, and the *Peripheral Nervous System* (PNS), which serves primarily as a relay system getting information to and from the CNS.

Central Nervous System (CNS)

The **central nervous system (CNS)** consists of the *brain* and the *spinal cord,* both of which are surrounded by a protective bony structure — the skull and spinal column. Unlike neurons in the PNS that can regenerate and require less protection, serious damage to cells in the CNS is usually permanent. However, the brain may not be as "hard wired" as we once believed. As you will discover throughout this chapter and the text, the brain changes with learning and experience. In response to environmental demands (and some injuries), the brain can reorganize its functions, rewire itself with new connections, possibly reroute neurons around damaged areas, and even generate new brain cells (Begley, 2000; Gage, 2000; Kempermann & Gage, 1999; Taub, Crago, & Uswatte, 1998; Taub & Uswatte, 2000; Travis, 2000; Vogel, 2000).

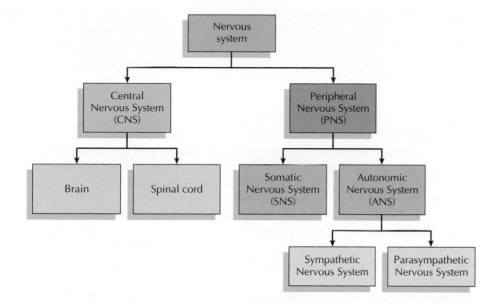

Figure 2.1 *The nervous system.* Note how the nervous system is divided and subdivided into various subsystems according to their differing functions. Review this diagram often as you study upcoming sections.

Because of its central importance for psychology and behavior, the brain is the major subject of this chapter, but the spinal cord is also important. Beginning at the base of the brain and continuing down the back, the spinal cord contains nerve fibers that link the brain to other parts of the body. These fibers relay incoming sensory information to the brain and send messages from the brain to muscles and glands.

The spinal cord is also responsible for one of our simplest behavior patterns-the *reflex arc,* which occurs when a stimulus provokes an automatic response. Have you ever noticed that you automatically jerk your hand away from a hot pan *before* your brain has a chance to respond? Reflexes occur within the spinal cord, without any help from the brain (Figure 2.2). It is only later, when the spinal cord transfers the

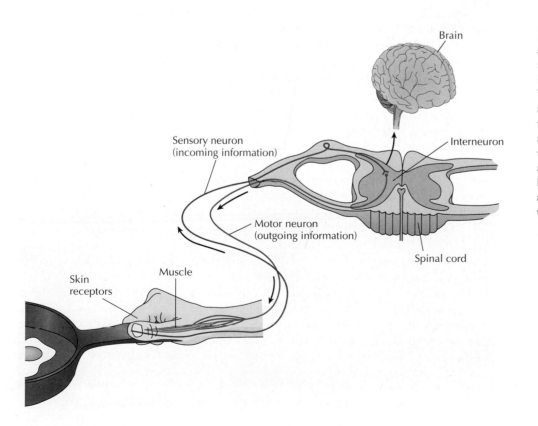

Figure 2.2 *The workings of the spinal cord* In a simple reflex arc, a sensory receptor initiates a neural impulse that travels to the spinal cord. The signal then travels back to the appropriate muscle, which then contracts. Action is automatic and immediate in a reflex because the signal only travels as far as the spinal cord before action is initiated, not all the way to the brain. The brain is later "notified" of the action when the spinal cord sends along the message.

sensory information to the brain, that you actually experience the sensation called *pain*. If the top of your spinal cord were severed, you would not feel pain — or pleasure. As you will discover in Chapter 4, the brain receives and interprets sensory messages, while the independently operating spinal cord allows us to react automatically and protect ourselves.

Peripheral Nervous System (PNS)

The **peripheral nervous system (PNS)** is just what it sounds like — the part that involves nerves *peripheral* to (or outside of) the brain and spinal cord. The chief function of the PNS is to carry information to and from the CNS. It links the brain and spinal cord to the body's sense receptors, muscles, and glands.

The PNS is subdivided into the somatic nervous system and the autonomic nervous system. The **somatic nervous system (SNS)** (also called the skeletal nervous system) consists of all the nerves that connect to sensory receptors and control skeletal muscles. The name comes from the term soma, which means "body," and the somatic nervous system plays a key role in communication throughout the entire *body*. In a kind of "two way street," the somatic nervous system first carries sensory information to the CNS, and then carries messages from the CNS to skeletal muscles. When you hear a question from your instructor and then raise your hand to volunteer an answer, it is chiefly due to your *somatic nervous system.*

Although the somatic system can help you respond to your college instructor's questions, it cannot make your pupils dilate or your heartbeat respond to the attractive classmate sitting beside you. For this, you need the other subdivision of the PNS known as the **autonomic** (or self-governing) **nervous system (ANS).** The ANS is responsible for *involuntary* tasks, such as heart rate, digestion, pupil dilation, and breathing. One function of the ANS is to maintain *homeostasis*, the body's steady state of normal functioning. It does this by regulating the endocrine glands, the heart muscle, and the smooth muscles of the blood vessels and internal organs

The autonomic nervous system is itself further divided into two branches, the **sympathetic** and **parasympathetic.** These tend to work in opposition to each other to regulate the functioning of such target organs as the heart, the intestines, and the lungs (Figure 2.3). A convenient, if somewhat oversimplified, distinction is that the sympathetic branch arouses the body for action (often called the "fight or flight" response), whereas the parasympathetic branch relaxes it. It's important to note, however, that these two systems are not an either/or arrangement. Like two children

Peripheral Nervous System (PNS)   *All nerves and neurons outside the brain and spinal cord. Its major function is to connect the CNS to the rest of the body.*

Somatic Nervous System (SNS) *A subdivision of the peripheral nervous system (PNS) that connects to sensory receptors and controls skeletal muscles.*

Autonomic Nervous System (ANS)   *Subdivision of the peripheral nervous system (PNS) that controls involuntary functions, such as heart rate and digestion. It is further subdivided into the sympathetic nervous system, which arouses, and the parasympathetic nervous system, which calms.*

Sympathetic Nervous System *Subdivision of the autonomic nervous system (ANS) responsible for arousing the body and mobilizing its energy during times of stress; also called the "fight or flight" system.*

Parasympathetic Nervous System *Subdivision of the autonomic nervous system (ANS) responsible for calming the body and conserving energy.*

The fight-or-flight response of the sympathetic nervous system is activated in both of these animals.

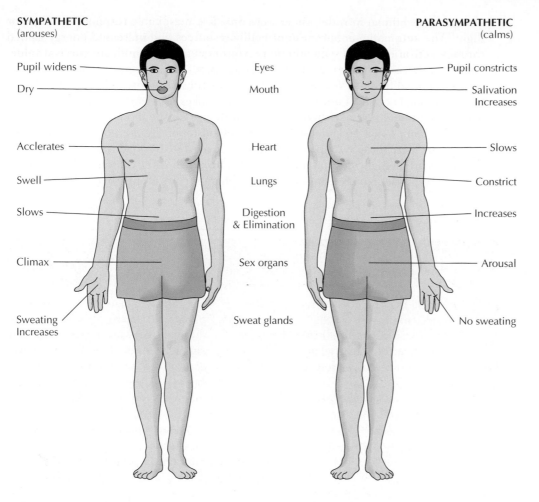

SYMPATHETIC
(arouses)

Pupil widens — Eyes

Dry — Mouth

Acclerates — Heart

Swell — Lungs

Slows — Digestion & Elimination

Climax — Sex organs

Sweating Increases — Sweat glands

PARASYMPATHETIC
(calms)

Eyes — Pupil constricts

Mouth — Salivation Increases

Heart — Slows

Lungs — Constrict

Digestion & Elimination — Increases

Sex organs — Arousal

Sweat glands — No sweating

Figure 2.3 *Actions of the autonomic nervous system (ANS).* This figure illustrates the chief functions of the parasympathetic and sympathetic branches of the ANS.

on a teeter-totter, one will be up while the other is down, but they essentially balance each other out. If either one of them truly took over, you would die. Your heart would either slow down and stop (parasympathetic complete dominance), or speed out of control and stop (sympathetic system complete dominance).

The *parasympathetic nervous system* dominates when you are in a relaxed, low-stress physical and mental state — when you calmly smell the roses in your garden. Its major task is to conserve energy by slowing your heart rate, lowering your blood pressure, and increasing your digestive and eliminative processes. It is definitely healthier to have the parasympathetic system dominant.

During stressful times, either mental or physical, the *sympathetic nervous system* dominates. If you noticed a dangerous snake coiled around the base of the rose bush, your sympathetic nervous system would increase your heart rate, respiration, and blood pressure, stop your digestive and eliminative processes, and cause several hormones, such as epinephrine and cortisol to be released into the bloodstream. The net result of sympathetic activation is to get more oxygenated blood and energy to the skeletal muscles, thus allowing you to cope with the stress-to "fight or flight." (Study tip: One way to differentiate the two subdivisions of the ANS is to imagine yourself jumping out of an airplane. When you initially jump, your *sympathetic* nervous system would be in charge. When your "para" chute opens, your "para"sympathetic nervous system also "opens" to help calm you and return normal functioning.)

Can you see how the fight-flight system provides an adaptive, evolutionary advantage? At the beginning of human evolution, when we faced a dangerous bear or aggressive human intruder, there were only two reasonable responses — fight or flight! The automatic mobilization of bodily resources and increased energy gained through activation of the sympathetic nervous system had significant survival value. Today, we have the same autonomic responses as our ancient ancestors, but our world is quite different. Now when we face stressful situations, we rarely respond by taking physical action. If our boss yells at us or makes unreasonable demands, we've learned not to fight or take flight. We have little use for the increased heart rate and stress hormones that are released into the bloodstream by the autonomic nervous system. In fact, the physiological changes caused by stress-activated sympathetic responses are actually detrimental to our health. We'll discuss stress and the fight-or-flight response in more detail in the next chapter (Stress and Health Psychology).

Check & Review

AN OVERVIEW OF THE NERVOUS SYSTEM

Neuroscience is an interdisciplinary field that studies how biological processes, especially activity in the brain and nervous system, relate to behavior. The **central nervous system** is composed of the brain and the spinal cord. The spinal cord is the communications link between the brain and the rest of the body below the neck. It is involved in all voluntary and reflex responses of the body below the neck.

The **peripheral nervous system** includes all nerves going to and from the brain and spinal cord. Its two major subdivisions are the **somatic nervous system** and the **autonomic nervous system**.

The somatic nervous system includes all nerves carrying incoming sensory information and outgoing motor information to and from the sense organs and skeletal muscles. The autonomic nervous system includes the nerves outside the brain and spinal cord that maintain normal functioning of glands, heart muscle, and the smooth muscle of blood vessels and internal organs.

The autonomic nervous system is further divided into two branches, the **parasympathetic** and the **sympathetic**, which tend to work in opposition to one another. The parasympathetic nervous system normally dominates when a person is relaxed. The sympathetic nervous system dominates when a person is under physical or mental stress. It mobilizes the body for fight or flight by increasing heart rate and blood pressure and slowing digestive processes.

Questions

1. The nervous system is separated into two major divisions: the _____ nervous system, which consists of the brain and spinal cord, and the _____ nervous system, which consists of all the nerves going to and from the brain and spinal cord.

2. The autonomic nervous system is subdivided into two branches called the _____ and _____ systems. (a) automatic, semiautomatic; (b) somatic, peripheral; (c) afferent, efferent; (d) sympathetic, parasympathetic

3. If you are startled by the sound of a loud explosion, the _____ nervous system will become dominant. (a) peripheral; (b) somatic; (c) parasympathetic; (d) sympathetic

4. What is the major difference between the sympathetic and parasympathetic nervous systems?

Answers to Questions can be found in Appendix B.

Neurons as the Basic Building Blocks: We Are Our Neurons

What are neurons, and how do they convey information throughout the body?

Neuron *Individual nerve cell responsible for processing, storing, and transmitting information throughout the body.*

Your brain and the rest of your nervous system essentially consist of **neurons**, individual cells that communicate information throughout the body, as well as within the brain. Each neuron is a tiny information processing system with thousands of connections for receiving and sending signals to other neurons. Although nobody knows for sure, one well-educated guess is that a human has 100 billion to 150 billion neurons, about the same number as there are stars in our galaxy.

Neurons are held in place and supported by **glial cells** (from the Greek for "glue"). They surround neurons, control their supply of chemicals, perform clean-up tasks, and even insulate one neuron from another so their neural messages do not get scrambled. Although glial cells greatly outnumber neurons and interact in ways that make information transfer and the brain more efficient, they are only supporting players. The "star" is the neuron. Most neuroscientists believe that all behavior — every move you make, every thought you have, and every heartbeat — ultimately depends on what happens at the level of the neuron.

Basic Parts of a Neuron

Just as no two people are alike, no two neurons are exactly alike, although most share three basic features: dendrites, the cell body, and an axon (Figure 2.4). Information from other cells normally enters the neuron via numerous dendrites, passes through the cell body, and is transmitted to other cells by the axon.

Dendrites look like leafless branches of a tree; in fact, the word *dendrite* means "little tree" in Greek. Dendrites act like antennas, receiving electrochemical information from other neurons and transmitting it to the cell body. Current research suggests that dendrites not only send information to the cell body but also relay information from the cell body back down to the ends of the dendrites, which modifies the dendrites' responses to further signals (Sejnowski, 1997). Each neuron may have hundreds or thousands of dendrites.

From the many dendrites, information flows into the cell body and then to the axon. The **cell body**, or *soma*, contains the biochemical machinery that keeps the neuron alive. The **axon** (from the Greek word for "axle") is a long, tubelike structure specialized for carrying information away from the cell body, toward other neurons or to muscles and glands. The **myelin sheath**, a white, fatty coating derived from glial cells, surrounds the axons of some neurons, helping to insulate and speed neural messages. (Study tip: To remember how information travels through the neuron, think of the three parts in reverse alphabetical order: *dendrite, cell body, axon*.)

How Neurons Communicate: An Electrical and Chemical Language

The basic function of neurons is to transmit information throughout the nervous system. Neurons "speak" to each other or, in some cases, to muscles or glands, in a

Glial Cells *Nervous system cells that provide structural, nutritional, and other support for the neuron; also called* glia *or* neuroglia.

Dendrites *Branching neuron structures that receive neural impulses from other neurons and convey impulses toward the cell body*

Cell Body *The part of the neuron that contains the cell nucleus, as well as other structures that help the neuron carry out its functions.*

Axon *A long, tubelike structure that conveys impulses away from the neuron's cell body toward other neurons or to muscles or glands*

Myelin [MY-uh-lin] Sheath *A layer of fatty insulation wrapped around the axon of some neurons, which increases the rate at which nerve impulses travel along the axon.*

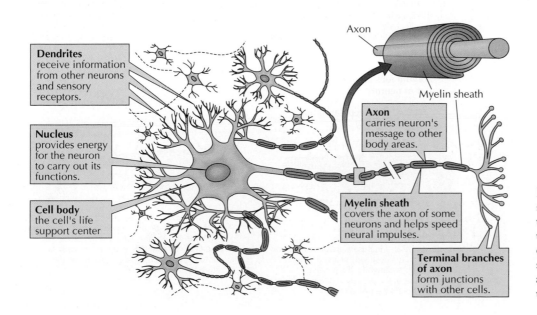

Dendrites
receive information from other neurons and sensory receptors.

Nucleus
provides energy for the neuron to carry out its functions.

Cell body
the cell's life support center

Axon

Myelin sheath

Axon
carries neuron's message to other body areas.

Myelin sheath
covers the axon of some neurons and helps speed neural impulses.

Terminal branches of axon
form junctions with other cells.

Figure 2.4 *The structure of a neuron.* Information enters the neuron through the dendrites, is integrated in the cell body, and then transmitted to other neurons via the axon. The myelin sheath is a fatty insulation wrapping around the axon that greatly increases the speed of the neural impulse.

type of electrical and chemical language. We begin our discussion by looking at communication *within* the neuron itself. Then we explore how communication occurs *between* neurons.

Action Potential *A neural impulse that carries information along the axon of a neuron. The action potential is generated when positively charged ions move in and out of channels in the axon's membrane.*

Action Potential — How a Neuron "Talks" to Itself

The process of neural communication begins within the neuron itself, when messages are received by the dendrites and cell body. These messages are passed along the axon in the form of a neural impulse or **action potential** (Figure 2.5).

Because the neural impulse that travels down the axon is chemical, the axon does not transmit it in the same way a wire conducts an electrical current. The movement down the axon actually results from a change in the permeability of the cell membrane. Picture the axon as a tube of membranous tissue filled with chemicals. This tube is floating in a sea of still more chemicals. The chemicals both inside and outside the tube are *ions,* molecules that carry an electrical charge, either positive or negative.

When the neuron is inactive, or *resting,* it is said to be *polarized.* That is, the fluid inside has mostly negatively charged ions, whereas the fluid outside the axon is the "polar opposite" — primarily positive. When the neuron is activated by sufficient stimulation from other neurons or sensory receptors, the electrical potential between the inside and the outside of the cell changes. A sudden inflow of positive ions *depolarizes* that first, small section of the axon, so that it becomes "overly positive." This change then causes nearby ion channels to open and also become depolarized, and then the next channel, and the next. In short, a chemical chain reaction occurs. The neural impulse (or action potential) travels down the axon, one section at a time, until it reaches the end of the axon.

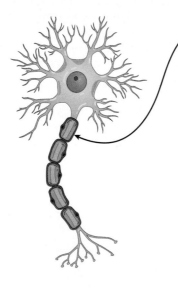

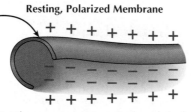

Resting, Polarized Membrane

1. When an axon is in its *resting* (or *polarized*) state, there is a balance between the number of positively charged ions on the outside of the cell membrane and the negatively charged ions on the inside.

Sodium ions pumped out of neuron

Depolarization

3. This depolarization produces an imbalance of ions in the adjacent section on the axon membrane. Pores in this neighboring area now open, and more positively charged sodium ions flow in. Meanwhile, the positively charged ions in the previous section sre being "pumped" out if the first section.

Depolarization (sodium ions flow in)

2. An *action potential* begins when a small section of the axon adjacent to the cell body is adequately stimulated by an incoming message. Pores (or channels) in the membrane at the stimulated area open and allow positively charged sodium ions to move inside the cell membrane. This movement causes a *depolarization* at that spot on the membrane.

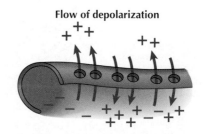

Flow of depolarization

4. As the action potential continues down the axon, neighboring sections open and the process is repeated. Note that the first section has now completely recharged and is beginning the return to the resting state.

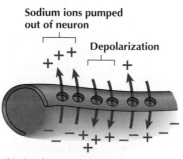

Figure 2.5 *The action potential — How a neuron "talks" to itself.*

How fast does a neural impulse travel? Actually, a nerve impulse moves slowly, much more slowly than electricity through a wire. Because electricity travels by a purely physical process, it can move through a wire at 97 percent of the speed of light, approximately 300 million meters per second. A neural impulse, on the other hand, travels along a bare axon at only about 10 meters per second.

Some axons, however, are enveloped in fatty insulation, the myelin sheath, which greatly increases the speed of an action potential. The myelin blankets the axon, with the exception of periodic *nodes,* points at which the myelin is very thin or absent (see again Figure 2.4). In a myelinated axon, the speed of the nerve impulse increases because the action potential jumps from node to node rather than traveling point by point along the entire axon. An action potential in a myelinated axon moves about 10 times faster than in a bare axon, at over 100 meters per second. The importance of the myelin sheath becomes apparent when it is destroyed in certain diseases such as multiple sclerosis. The greatly slowed rate of conduction of action potentials affects the person's movement and coordination.

It is important to remember that once the action potential is started, it continues. There's no such thing as a "partial" action potential. Similar to the firing of a bullet from a gun, the action potential fires either completely or not at all. This is referred to as the *all-or-none law.* Immediately after a neuron fires, it enters a brief *refractory period* where it cannot fire again. During the refractory period, the neuron *repolarizes:* The resting balance is restored with negative ions inside and positive ions outside. Now the neuron is free to fire again.

Neurotransmitters — How Neurons "Talk" to One Another

Now that you understand the basic structure of the neuron and how the neuron communicates with itself (by passing electrochemical messages along its length), we can examine how neurons communicate with other neurons, which is primarily through neurotransmitters.

Communication between one neuron and the next begins at the junction between neurons, known as the **synapse**. This synaptic juncture includes the axon terminal of the sending neuron, the tiny space between neurons (the *synaptic gap*), and the covering membrane of the receiving neuron (Figure 2.6). When the action potential reaches the knoblike terminals at the axon's end, it causes tiny sacs, called *synaptic vesicles,* to open and release a few thousand molecules of a chemical substance known as a **neurotransmitter**. These molecules then flow across the synaptic gap. If the adjacent, receiving neuron receives sufficient neurotransmitter stimulation, a follow-up action potential is initiated along its membrane and communication is "successful."

Although communication is said to be successful when the neurotransmitter reaches its target cell, it is important to note that action potentials do not always occur in the receiving neuron. Neurotransmitters have either an *excitatory* or *inhibitory* effect on their target cells.

Think of the case of a sculptor welding the final touches on to her masterpiece. As the heat soaks through her glove, she almost drops the very expensive part. However, this excitation is counteracted by inhibition, supplied by her brain. Recognizing that dropping the piece would be a very costly mistake, her brain sends information to the spinal cord inhibiting the withdrawal reflex. When neurotransmitters are excitatory, they make the target neuron more likely to fire an action potential; when they are inhibitory, they make the target neuron less likely to fire. In short, neurotransmitters carry one of two messages — "fire" or "don't fire."

Both types of messages are critical to your survival. Just as driving a car requires both an accelerator and brakes, your body needs both "on" and "off" neural switches. Your nervous system manages an amazing balancing act between *overexcitation,* leading to seizures, and *underexcitation,* leading to coma and death. In fact, poisons, such as strychnine, works by disabling many inhibitory messages, with the resulting overexcitation causing uncontrollable convulsions that can be fatal.

Synapse [SIN-aps] *The junction between the axon tip of the sending neuron and the dendrite or cell body of the receiving neuron; during an action potential, chemicals called neurotransmitters are released and flow across the synaptic gap*

Neurotransmitter *Chemicals manufactured and released by neurons that alter activity in other neurons.*

Figure 2.6 *Neurotransmitters —
How neurons "talk" to one another.*
(a) In this schematic view of a synapse,
neurotransmitter chemicals are stored
in small synaptic vesicles at the end of
the axon. When action potentials reach
the axon terminal, they stimulate the
release of neurotransmitter molecules
into the synaptic gap. The neurotransmitter chemicals then travel across the
synaptic gap, and bind to receptor sites
on the dendrites or cell body of the
receiving neuron. (b) If the receiving
neuron is sufficiently stimulated, a new
action potential is generated and communication is successful.

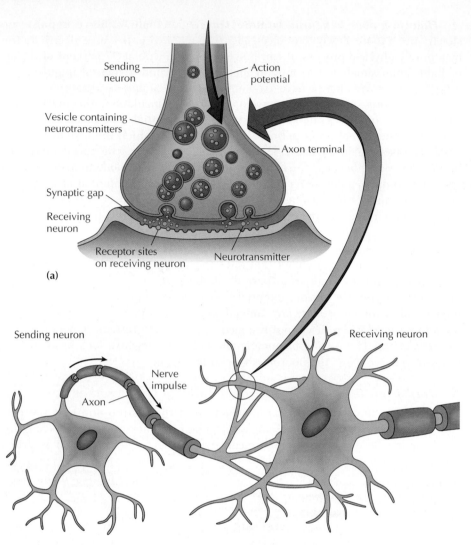

Chemical Messengers in the Nervous System: Neurotransmitters, Endorphins, and Hormones

Our brains and nervous systems would be lifeless without communication. The
major chemical messengers responsible for communication are the *neurotransmitters*, *endorphins*, and *hormones*.

Neurotransmitters

Researchers have discovered hundreds of substances known or suspected to be neurotransmitters. Some neurotransmitters regulate the actions of glands and muscles;
others promote sleep or stimulate mental and physical alertness; others affect learning and memory; and still others affect motivation, emotions, and psychological disorders, including schizophrenia and depression. Table 2.1 lists a few of the better-
understood neurotransmitters and their known or suspected effects.

Neurotransmitters and Disease

One of the many advantages of studying your brain and its neurotransmitters is an
increased understanding of your own or others' medical problems and their treatment. For example, do you remember why actor Michael J. Fox retired from his popular TV sitcom, *Spin City*? It was because of muscle tremors and movement problems related to a poorly understood condition called *Parkinson's disease* (PD). As
Table 2.1 shows, the neurotransmitter *dopamine* is a suspected factor in PD, and its

TABLE 2.1 HOW NEUROTRANSMITTERS AFFECT US

Neurotransmitter	Known or Suspected Effects
Serotonin	Affects mood, sleep, appetite, sensory perception, temperature regulation, pain suppression, impulsivity, and aggression; may play a role in some psychological disorders, such as depression
Acetylcholine (ACh)	Affects muscle action, cognitive functioning, memory, REM (rapid-eye-movement) sleep, emotion. Suspected role in Alzheimer's disease
Dopamine (DA)	Affects movement, attention, memory, learning, and emotion. Plays a role in both schizophrenia and Parkinson's disease.
Norepinephrine (NE) (or noradrenaline)	Affects learning, memory, dreaming, emotion, waking from sleep, eating, alertness, wakefulness, reactions to stress
Epinephrine (or adrenaline)	Affects emotional arousal, memory storage, and metabolism of glucose necessary for energy release
GABA (gamma aminobutyric acid)	Neural inhibition in the central nervous system; Tranquilizing drugs act on GABA to decrease anxiety

symptoms are reduced with L-dopa (levodopa), a drug that increases dopamine levels in the brain (Brundin et al., 2000; Diederich & Goetz, 2000).

Interestingly, when some Parkinson's patients are adjusting to L-dopa and higher levels of dopamine, they may experience symptoms that mimic schizophrenia, a serious psychological disorder that disrupts thought processes and produces delusions and hallucination. As you will see in Chapter 15, excessively high levels of *dopamine* are a suspected contributor to some forms of *schizophrenia*, and when patients take antipsychotic drugs that suppress dopamine, their symptoms are sometimes reduced or even eliminated (Laruelle, Abi-Dargham, Gil, Kegeles, & Innis, 1999; Reynolds, 1999). In sum, *decreased* levels of dopamine are associated with Parkinson's disease, whereas *increased* levels are related to some forms of schizophrenia.

Another neurotransmitter, *serotonin* (Table 2.1), may also be involved in the depression that often accompanies Parkinson's disease. Although some researchers believe Parkinson's patients become depressed in reaction to the motor disabilities of the disorder, others think the depression is directly related to lower levels of serotonin (Schapira, 1999). As Chapter 15 discusses, certain forms of depression are indeed related to lowered levels of serotonin. And popular antidepressant drugs, like *Prozac* and *Zoloft*, work by boosting levels of available serotonin (Margolis & Swartz, 2001; Tauscher et al., 1999; Wegerer et al., 1999). Even without medication, serotonin levels increase after successful psychotherapy for depression (Bransfod, 2000). (Recall from Chapter 1 that scientific research is "circular and cumulative" and that basic and applied research often overlap. Research with Parkinson's disease demonstrates these principles.)

Neurotransmitters, Poisons, and Mind-Altering Drugs

An understanding of neurotransmitters explains not only the origin of certain diseases and their pharmaceutical drug treatments but also how poisons, such as snake venom, and mind-altering drugs, such as nicotine, alcohol, caffeine, and cocaine, affect the brain (see also Chapter 5).

Why study neurotransmitters? Actor Michael J. Fox suffers from Parkinson's disease, which involves a decrease in cells that produce dopamine. In this photo, he is testifying before a U.S. subcommittee to urge increased funding for research on Parkinson's and other medical conditions.

Figure 2.7 *Receptor sites.* (a) Receptor sites on the dendrite recognize neurotransmitters because of their three-dimensional shape. (b) Molecules without the correct shape will not fit the receptors and therefore will not stimulate the dendrite. (c) Some *agonist* drugs, like nicotine, are similar enough in structure to a certain neurotransmitter (in this case, acetylcholine) that they mimic its effects on the receiving neuron. (d) Some *antagonist* drugs, like curare, block the action of neurotransmitters (again, acetylcholine) by filling a receptor site and thus not allowing the neurotransmitter to stimulate the receptor.

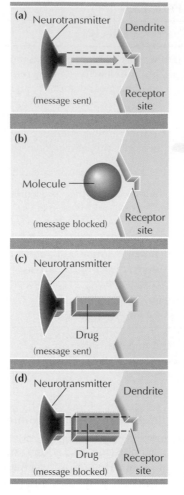

Most poisons and drugs act at the synapse by replacing, decreasing, or enhancing the amount of neurotransmitter. Given that transmission of messages *between* neurons is chemical, many chemicals that we ingest can significantly affect neurotransmission. They can do this because their molecules have shapes similar to various neurotransmitters.

Neurotransmitters communicate with other neurons by binding to receptor sites in much the same way that a key fits into a lock. Just as different keys have distinct three-dimensional shapes, various chemical molecules, including neurotransmitters, have distinguishing three-dimensional characteristics. If a neurotransmitter has the proper shape, it will bind to the receptor site (Figure 2.7a and 2.7b) and thereby influence the firing of the receiving cell.

Some drugs, called *agonists* (from the Greek *agon,* meaning "contest, struggle"), mimic or enhance the action of neurotransmitters (Figure 2.7c). For example, both the poison in the black widow spider and the nicotine in cigarettes have a molecular shape similar enough to the neurotransmitter *acetylcholine* (*ACh*) that they can mimic its effect, including increasing the heart rate. Amphetamines have a similar excitatory effect by mimicking the neurotransmitter *norepinephrine.*

In contrast, *antagonist* drugs (from the Greek word meaning "a member of the opposing team"), work by opposing or blocking neurotransmitters (Figure 2.7d). Most snake venom and some poisons, like the lethal drug *curare* that South American hunters use, act as antagonists to ACh. Because ACh is vital in muscle action, blocking it paralyzes muscles, including those involved in breathing, which can be fatal.

Neurotransmitters, poisons, and drugs. Most poisons and psychoactive drugs work by replacing, decreasing, or increasing the amount of certain neurotransmitters. The neurotransmitter acetylcholine (ACh) is responsible for muscular contraction, including the muscles responsible for breathing. The poison curare blocks the action of ACh and South American hunters sometimes apply it to the tips of blowgun darts or arrows to paralyze their prey. In contrast, nicotine in cigarettes increases the effects of ACh and smokers experience increased heart and respiration rates.

Endorphins

In addition to neurotransmitters, the body also has chemical messengers called *endogenous opioid peptides*, more commonly known as **endorphins**. These chemicals produce effects similar to those of opium-based drugs such as morphine — they reduce pain and promote pleasure. (Some endorphins work as neurotransmitters, but most act as *neuromodulators* that increase or decrease [modulate] the effects of neurotransmitters.)

Endorphins were discovered in the early 1970s, when Candace Pert and Soloman Snyder (1973) were doing research on morphine, a pain-relieving and mood-elevating opiate derived from opium, which is made from poppies. They found that the morphine was taken up by specialized receptors in areas of the brain linked with mood and pain sensations.

But why would the brain have special receptors for morphine — a powerfully addicting drug? Pert and Snyder reasoned that the brain must have its own internally produced, or *endogenous*, morphinelike chemicals. They later confirmed that such chemicals do exist and named them *endorphins* (a contraction of *endogenous* [self-produced] and *morphine*). The brain evidently produces its own naturally occurring chemical messengers that elevate mood and reduce pain, as well as affect memory, learning, blood pressure, appetite, and sexual activity (Chapters 3, 4, 11, and 12). Endorphins also help explain why soldiers and athletes continue to fight or play the game despite horrific injuries.

Hormones

The neural system communicates through the production and circulation of *neurotransmitters, endorphins,* and **hormones**. On receiving signals from the brain, glands within the **endocrine system** release these chemicals into the bloodstream, which circulates them throughout the body. Like neurotransmitters, hormones affect the nervous system, and sometimes the same chemical functions as both a hormone and a neurotransmitter. But unlike neurotransmitters that are released immediately adjacent to the cells they are to excite or inhibit, hormones are released into the blood, thus taking more time to diffuse throughout the body.

The nervous system and the endocrine system work hand in hand to direct our behavior and maintain our body's normal functioning. This interplay between the two systems is most evident in the fight-or-flight response of the sympathetic branch of the ANS, discussed earlier. The major functions of many endocrine glands, including the pituitary, the thyroid, the adrenals, and the pancreas (Figure 2.8), is to help the ANS respond to emergencies and maintain *homeostasis*, establishing a balance and normal functioning of bodily processes.

In times of emergency, chemical messengers travel along two paths — the ANS and the pituitary gland. The pituitary gland is sometimes referred to as the "master gland" because it releases a large variety of hormones throughout the body, which stimulate action in the other endocrine glands. In response to stressful situations, the pituitary sends messages to the adrenal glands (organs that are right above the kidneys). The adrenal glands then release *cortisol*, which boosts energy and blood sugar levels, *epinephrine* (commonly called *adrenaline*), and *norepinephrine*. When these adrenal hormones are released into your system, they activate the sympathetic branch of the ANS — thus preparing your body for "fight or flight."

Hormones produced by the endocrine system also help preserve *homeostasis* (or balance). They accomplish this by maintaining the tissue and blood levels of certain chemicals within a specific range. For example, sugar is a chemical that the body needs to function normally. But if too much sugar enters the bloodstream, the pancreas (an endocrine gland) secretes the hormone *insulin* to lower the blood sugar level to a more normal, safer level. When the insulin level is extremely low, as in people with diabetes, blood sugar levels may be three or more times higher than normal.

Endorphins [en-DOR-fins] *Chemical substances in the nervous system that are similar in structure and action to opiates and are involved in pain control, pleasure, and memory*

Hormones *Chemicals manufactured by endocrine glands and circulated in the bloodstream to produce bodily changes or maintain normal bodily functions*

Endocrine [EN-doh-krin] System *A system of glands located throughout the body that secrete hormones into the bloodstream*

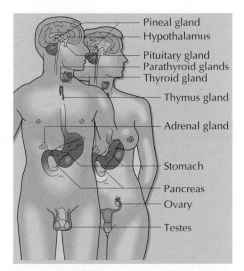

Figure 2.8 *The endocrine system.* The major endocrine glands are shown along with some internal organs to help you locate the glands.

Abnormally high levels of blood sugar can lead to dangerous changes in body tissues, including diabetes-related blindness.

Hormones also influence our growth, reproduction, moods, and response to stress. As you will see in a later section of this chapter, the amount of sex hormone (testosterone) present during prenatal development even determines whether the fetus develops a penis and scrotum or a clitoris and labia. The "sex hormones" are discussed further in Chapter 11, whereas *melatonin*, discovered somewhat recently, is explored in Chapter 5.

Before closing, we want to emphasize that our discussion of neurotransmitters, endorphins, and hormones is greatly simplified. Diseases like Parkinson's, schizophrenia, depression, and diabetes are complex and involve interacting, multiple causes and treatment. Similarly, neurotransmitters, endorphins, and hormones all play multiple, overlapping roles. However, even this limited coverage gives you a foundation for understanding the brain and nervous system — topics in our upcoming section.

Check & Review

NEURONS, NEURAL COMMUNICATION, AND CHEMICAL MESSENGERS

Neurons are cells that transmit information throughout the body. They have three main parts: **dendrites**, which receive information from other neurons; the **cell body**, which provides nourishment and "decides" whether the axon should fire; and the **axon**, which sends along the neural information. **Glial cells** support and provide nutrients for neurons in the central nervous system (CNS).

The axon is specialized for transmitting neural impulses, or **action potentials**. During times when no action potential is moving down the axon, the axon is at rest. The neuron is activated, and an action potential occurs, when the charge within the neuron becomes more positive than the charge outside the cell's membrane. Action potentials travel more quickly down myelinated axons because the **myelin sheath** serves as insulation.

Information is transferred from one neuron to another at synapses by chemicals called **neurotransmitters**. Neurotransmitters bind to receptor sites much as a key fits into a lock, and their effects can be *excitatory* or *inhibitory*. Most psychoactive drugs affect the nervous system by acting directly on receptor sites for specific neurotransmitters or by increasing or decreasing the amount of neurotransmitter that crosses the **synapse**.

In addition to neurotransmitters, there are two other important chemical messengers — endorphins and hormones. Neuromodulators (such as **endorphins**) — increase or decrease the effects of neurotransmitters. **Hormones** are released from glands in the **endocrine system** directly into the bloodstream. They regulate levels of critical chemicals in the body.

Questions

1. Draw and label the three major parts of a neuron and the myelin sheath.

2. An impulse travels through the structures of the neuron in the following order: (a) cell body, axon, dendrites; (b) cell body, dendrites, axon; (c) dendrites, cell body, axon; (d) axon, cell body, dendrites

3. Chemical messengers that are released by axons and stimulate dendrites are called _____. (a) chemical messengers; (b) neurotransmitters; (c) synaptic transmitters; (d) neuromessengers

4. Explain how neurotransmitters, endorphins, and hormones carry messages throughout the body.

Answers to Questions can be found in Appendix B.

A TOUR THROUGH THE BRAIN

Having covered basic, biological foundations (neurons, neurotransmitters, divisions of the neural system, and hormones), we come now to the "main event" of neuroscience — the brain itself. We began this chapter with the tale of Phineas Gage and his horrible brain injury because it emphasized the vital importance of this relatively tiny three-pound organ that sits atop your shoulders. Who would you be without your brain? Without its lower-level structures, you would not be alive. Without your cortex, you would not be capable of thinking, speaking, or perceiving. And as we saw with Phineas Gage, when the cortex is damaged, we lose much of what we define as "self."

We begin our study of the brain with a look at the tools neural cartographers have used to study and map it. Then we start our exploration of the brain at the lower end, where the spinal cord joins the brainstem, and move upward toward the cerebral cortex. Note as we move from the brainstem to the cortex that the functions of brain structures change from regulating "lower," basic functions like survival to controlling "higher," more complex mental processes such as thinking.

Tools for Exploration: Mapping the Brain

The earliest explorers of the brain dissected the brains of deceased humans and conducted experiments on other animals using *lesioning techniques* (systematically destroying brain tissue to study the effects on behavior and mental processes) (Table 2.2). By the mid-1800s, this early research had produced a basic map of the peripheral nervous system and some areas of the brain. Early researchers also relied on clinical observations and case studies of living people. Tragic accidents, as in the case of Phineas Gage, and diseases or other brain disorders also offered valuable insights into brain functioning. The story of Phineas Gage might have ended with his death were it not for his doctor, John Harlow (1848), who wrote a detailed account of the accident. Years later, when he learned of Gage's death, he also petitioned Phineas's family to exhume the body and allow him to keep Phineas Gage's skull as a medical record. Today, both the skull and the tamping iron that had been buried with Gage are on display at Harvard University's Warren Anatomical Medical Museum.

Modern researchers still use dissection, lesioning, clinical observation, and case studies, but they also employ other techniques such as electrical recording and electrical brain stimulation. *Electrodes* (tiny electrified disks or wires) pasted to the skin or skull translate brain waves (electrical energy from the brain) to produce wavy lines on a moving piece of paper; this report is called an *electroencephalogram* (*electro-* means "electrical," *encephalon* means "brain," and *gram* means "record"). The electroencephalograph (EEG) is a major research tool for studying changes in brain waves during sleep and dreaming. For even more precise information, researchers can use *electrical stimulation of the brain* (ESB). Electrodes are inserted into the brain to record the naturally occurring electrical activity of neurons or to stimulate certain areas with weak electrical currents.

In recent years, advances in brain science have led to exciting, new techniques, including various types of brain-imaging scans (see again Table 2.2). Most of these methods are relatively *noninvasive*. That is, they are performed without breaking the skin or entering the body. They can be used both in clinical settings to examine suspected brain damage and disease, and in laboratory settings to study brain function during ordinary activities like sleeping, eating, reading, speaking, and so on (Goldman, Nahas, & George, 2000; Robertson et al., 2000). For example, computed tomography (CT) scans (a computer-enhanced series of X-rays of the brain) have been used to look for abnormalities in brain structures among people suffering from mental illness, whereas positron emission tomography (PET) scans map actual *activity* in the brain and can be used to pinpoint brain areas that handle various activities, such as singing or fist clenching, and even areas responsible for different emotions (Craik et al., 1999; Mayberg et al., 1999).

It is important to note that each method has its particular strengths and weaknesses, but all provide invaluable insights and information. We'll discuss findings from these research tools in upcoming chapters on sleep and dreaming (Chapter 5), memory (Chapter 7), thinking and intelligence (Chapter 8), and abnormal behavior and its treatment (Chapters 14 and 15).

Lower-Level Brain Structures: The Oldest Parts of the Brain

Brain size and complexity vary significantly from species to species. Lower species such as fish and reptiles have smaller, less complex brains than do higher species

What are the best tools for studying the brain?

What are the lower-level structures of the brain, and what are their roles in behavior and mental processes?

TABLE 2.2 TOOLS FOR STUDYING THE BRAIN

Method	Description	Sample Results
Brain dissection	Careful cutting and study of a cadaver brain to reveal structural details	Brain dissections of Alzheimer's disease victims often show identifiable changes in various parts of the brain (Chapter 7).
Ablation/lesions	Surgically removing parts of the brain (ablation), or destroying specific areas of the brain (lesioning), is followed by observation for changes in behavior or mental processes.	Lesioning specific parts of the rat's hypothalamus greatly affects its eating behavior (Chapter 12).
Clinical observations/ case studies	Observing and recording changes in personality, behavior, or sensory capacity associated with brain diseases or injuries	Damage to one side of the brain often causes numbness or paralysis on the body's opposite side; also Phineas Gage's injury and subsequent changes.
Electrical recordings	Using electrodes attached to a person or animal's skin or scalp, brain activity is recorded to produce an electroencephalogram.	Reveals areas of the brain most active during a particular task or changes in mental states, like sleeping, and hypnosis (Chapter 5); also traces abnormal brain waves caused by brain malfunctions, like epilepsy or tumors
Electrical stimulation of the brain (ESB)	Using an electrode, a weak electric current stimulates specific areas or structures of the brain.	Penfield (1958) mapped the surface of the brain and found that different areas have different functions.

Brain dissection. Structures of the brain can be examined by dissecting the brains of deceased people who donated their bodies for scientific study.

Electroencephalograph (EEG). Electrodes are attached to the patient's scalp, and the brain's electrical activity is displayed on a computer monitor or recorded on a paper chart.

(Table continues)

TABLE 2.2 CONTINUED

Method	Description	Sample Results
Brain imaging	Studies intact, living brains by taking pictures	Reveals various brain structures, their functions, and changes associated with disease or injury
Types of images: • CT (computed tomography) scan	A computer that creates cross-sectional pictures of the brain reads X-rays directed through the brain at different angles; least expensive type of imaging and widely used in research	Reveals the effects of strokes, injuries, tumors, and other brain disorders
• PET (positron emission tomography) scan	Radioactive form of glucose is injected into the bloodstream; scanner records amount of glucose used in particularly active areas of the brain and produces computer-constructed picture of the brain	Originally designed to detect abnormalities, also used to identify brain areas active during ordinary activities (reading, singing, etc.)
• MRI (magnetic resonance imaging) scan	A high-frequency magnetic field is passed through the brain by means of electromagnets.	Produces high-resolution three-dimensional pictures of the brain useful for identifying abnormalities and mapping brain structures and function
• fMRI (functional magnetic resonance imaging) scan	A newer, faster version of the MRI that detects blood flow by picking up magnetic signals from blood that has given up its oxygen to activate brain cells	Indicates which areas of the brain are active or inactive during ordinary activities or responses (like reading or talking); also, shows changes associated with disorders

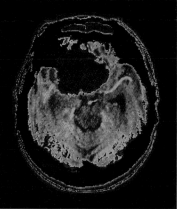

This false color CT scan used X rays to locate a brain tumor. The tumor is the deep purple mass at the top left.

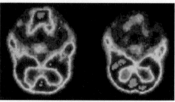

PET scans and brain functions. In these two scans, the left one shows brain activity when the eyes are open, whereas the one on the right is with the eyes closed. Note the increased activity, red and yellow, in the occipital lobe (the top of the photo) when the eyes are open.

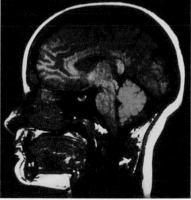

Magnetic resonance imaging (MRI). Note the fissures and internal structures of the cerebral cortex, as well as the cerebellum and the brain stem. The throat, nasal airways, and cerebrospinal fluid surrounding the brain are dark.

such as cats and dogs. The most complex brains belong to whales, dolphins, and higher primates such as chimps, gorillas, and humans. The billions of neurons that make up the human brain control much of what we think, feel, and do.

As we begin our tour of the brain, keep in mind that certain brain structures are specialized to perform certain tasks, a process known as **localization of function**. Don't, however, exaggerate the differences. Most parts of the brain perform integrating, overlapping functions. Figure 2.9 shows the major structures of the brain. You should refer to it as you read.

Localization of Function *Specialization of various parts of the brain for particular functions*

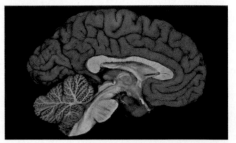

Corpus callosum
Thick band of axons connecting the two hemispheres of the cerebral cortex

Cerebral cortex
Divided into two hemispheres and responsible for higher mental functions

Amygdala
Part of the limbic system and involved in emotion

Thalamus
Relays sensory messages to cortex

Pons
Involved with respiration, movement, waking, sleep, and dreaming

Hypothalamus
Responsible for regulating emotions and drives like hunger, thirst, sex, and aggression

Reticular formation
Helps screen incoming sensory information and arouses the cortex

Cerebellum
Coordinates smooth movement, balance, and some perception and cognition

Medulla
Responsible for breathing, heartbeat, and other vital life functions

Spinal cord
Responsible for transmitting information between brain and rest of body; handles simple reflexes

Brain stem
(Pons, Reticular Formation and Medulla)

Figure 2.9 *The human brain.* If your brain were sliced down the center, lengthwise, it would look like the top right photo. Although you wouldn't be alive to read this, the drawing on the lower half of the page would depict what the inside surface of the left half of your brain would look like. It highlights key structures and some of their principal functions. As you read about each of these structures, you may find it helpful to keep this drawing in mind or to refer back to it as necessary.

The Brainstem

You are sleeping. Your eyes dart back and forth as you begin your last dream of the night. Your heart rate, blood pressure, and respiration increase as the dream gets more exciting. But then your dream is shattered by a buzzing alarm clock. All your automatic behaviors and survival responses in this scenario have been either controlled by or influenced by parts of the brainstem. The **brainstem** looks like its name. The lower-end "stem" is a continuation of the spinal cord, and the higher end lies deep within the brain. Three structures generally are associated with the brainstem — the pons, the medulla, and the reticular formation.

Messages to and from upper-level brain structures pass through two major structures in the brainstem — the pons and medulla. The **pons**, located in the upper portion of the brainstem, is involved in respiration, movement, sleeping, waking, and dreaming (among other things). The **medulla** is below the pons, at the bottom of the brainstem and just above the spinal cord. Its functions are similar to those of the pons. Because the medulla is essentially an extension of the spinal cord, many nerve fibers pass through it carrying information to and from the brain. The medulla also contains many nerve fibers that control automatic bodily functions such as respiration and heart rate. Damage to the medulla can lead to failure of bodily functions and death. This is the area of the brain that was damaged when Senator Robert Kennedy was assassinated in 1968.

Running through the core of the brainstem and extending upward is the **reticular** (netlike) **formation** (RF). This dense, finger-shaped network of neurons filters incoming sensory information and arouses the higher centers of the brain when something happens that demands their attention. Basically, without your RF, you would not be alert or perhaps even conscious. Damage to this area can cause a coma.

Brainstem *An area at the base of the brain in front of the cerebellum that is responsible for automatic, survival functions*

Pons *A structure at the top of the brainstem that is involved in respiration, movement, waking, sleep, and dreaming*

Medulla [muh-DUL-uh] *A structure at the base of the brainstem responsible for automatic body functions such as breathing and heart rate*

Reticular Formation (RF) *A diffuse set of neurons in the core of the brainstem that screens incoming information and arouses the cortex*

The Cerebellum

The **cerebellum** ("little brain") is located at the base of the brain behind the brainstem. (Some say it looks like a cauliflower.) In evolutionary terms, it is a very old structure responsible for maintaining smooth movement and coordinating motor activity. Although the actual commands for movement come from higher brain centers in the cortex, the cerebellum coordinates the muscles so that movement is smooth and precise. The cerebellum is also involved with the sense of balance. In fact, roadside tests for drunken driving are essentially testing the cerebellum, because it is one of the first structures depressed by alcohol.

Research suggests that the cerebellum does much more than just coordinate movement and maintain physical balance. It may also have a role in perception and cognition. Using magnetic resonance imaging (MRI), researchers have documented that parts of the cerebellum are very active during perceptual and cognitive activities that require the processing of sensory data (Luft, Skalej, Stefanou, Klose, & Voight, 1998).

The cerebellum at work. Can you see why the cerebellum might be important to this construction worker? It is responsible for coordinating movement and maintaining posture and balance.

Cerebellum [sehr-uh-BELL-um] *Structure at the base of the brain, behind the brainstem, responsible for maintaining smooth movement, balance, and some aspects of perception and cognition*

The Thalamus

Thalamus [THAL-uh-muss] *A brain structure at the top of the brainstem that relays sensory messages to the cerebral cortex*

The **thalamus** lies at the top of the brainstem. Resembling two little footballs, one on each side of the brain, connected by a thin group of nerve fibers, it serves as the major sensory relay center for the brain. Like an air traffic control center that receives information from all aircraft, and then directs them to the appropriate landing or take off areas, the thalamus receives input from nearly all the sensory systems and then directs this information to the appropriate cortical areas. For example, while reading this page, your thalamus sends incoming visual signals to the visual area of your cortex. When your ears receive sound, the information is transferred to the auditory (or hearing) area of your cortex.

The thalamus plays an active role in integrating information from various senses and may be involved in learning and memory (Crosson, 1999). Injury to the thalamus can cause deafness, blindness, or loss of any other sense (except smell). This suggests that some analysis of sensory messages may occur here. Because the thalamus is the major sensory relay area to the cerebral cortex, damage or abnormalities also might cause the cortex to misinterpret or not receive vital sensory information. Other research using brain-imaging techniques links abnormalities in the thalamus to schizophrenia (Andreasen, 1999, 2000; Hazlett et al., 2000; Omori et al., 2000). Schizophrenia is a serious psychological disorder characterized by problems with sensory filtering and perception (Chapter 14). Can you see how a defective thalamus might produce characteristics of schizophrenia, such as hallucinations and delusion?

The Hypothalamus

Hypothalamus [hi-poh-THAL-uh-muss] *A small brain structure beneath the thalamus that maintains homeostasis and regulates emotions and drives, such as hunger, thirst, sex, and aggression*

Beneath the thalamus lies the **hypothalamus** (*hypo-* means "under"). Although no larger than a kidney bean, it has been called the "master control center" for emotions and many basic motives such as hunger, thirst, sex, and aggression (Fulton, Woodside, & Shizgal; Meston & Frohlich, 2000). Its general function is *homeostasis,* including temperature control, which it accomplishes by regulating the endocrine system. Hanging down from the hypothalamus, the *pituitary gland* is usually considered the master endocrine gland because it releases hormones that activate the other endocrine glands. The hypothalamus influences the pituitary through direct neural connections and by releasing its own hormones into the blood supply of the pituitary.

Despite its relatively small size, the hypothalamus influences important aspects of behavior either *directly,* by generating some behaviors itself, or *indirectly* by controlling parts of the autonomic nervous system (ANS) and endocrine system. An example of its direct effects are found when animals exhibit increased or decreased eating and drinking patterns depending on what area of the hypothalamus is affected (Chapter 12). The indirect effects of the hypothalamus are seen in the interaction of stress and the ANS (Chapter 3).

The Limbic System

Limbic System *An interconnected group of lower-level brain structures involved with the arousal and regulation of emotion, motivation, memory, and many other aspects of behavior and mental processes*

The **limbic system** is an interconnected group of structures located roughly along the border between the cerebral cortex and the lower-level brain structures (hence the term *limbic,* which means "edge" or "border"). The limbic system includes the *fornix,* the *hippocampus,* the *amygdala,* and the *septum* (Figure 2.10). Scientists disagree about which structures should be included in the limbic system, and many also include the hypothalamus, parts of the thalamus, and parts of the cerebral cortex.

Recent research studying the fornix and hippocampus suggests that they, along with the amygdala, are involved in the formation of new and short-term memories

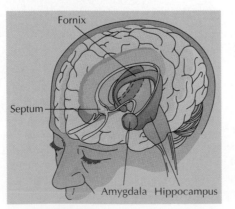

Figure 2.10 *The major brain structures associated with the limbic system.*

(Chin, 2000; Giovagnoli, 2001; McGaugh, 2000). However, the major focus of interest in the limbic system, and particularly the **amygdala**, has been its production and regulation of emotional behavior, particularly aggression and fear. Research on cats and rats shows that stimulating the amygdala increases aggressive behavior, and research on the human amygdala demonstrates its role in aggression and violence, as well as, the learning and expression of fear and the ability to recognize fear in the faces of others (Adolphs, Tranel, & Damasio, 1998; Cahill, Vazdarjanova, & Setlow, 2000; Davidson, Putnam, & Larson, 2000; Schmolck & Squire, 2001).

Perhaps one of the best-known functions of the limbic system is its role in pleasure or reward. James Olds and Peter Milner (1954) were the first to note that electrically stimulating certain areas of the limbic system caused a "pleasure" response in rats. The feeling was apparently so rewarding that the rats would cross electrified grids, swim through water (which they normally avoid), and press a lever thousands of times until they collapsed from exhaustion — just to have their brains stimulated. Follow-up studies found somewhat similar responses in other animals and even among human volunteers (Blum, Cull, Braverman, & Comings, 1996; Wise & Rompre, 1989). Modern research suggests that brain stimulation activates neurotransmitters or neuromodulators rather than discrete "pleasure centers."

Keep in mind that even though limbic system structures and neurotransmitters are instrumental in emotional behavior, emotion in humans is also tempered by the cerebral cortex, especially the frontal lobes. As the case of Phineas Gage shows, damage to the frontal lobes, which have neural connections to the amygdala and other parts of the limbic system, can permanently impair social and emotional behavior. This is yet another example of the inseparable interconnectivity of the entire brain.

Amygdala [uh-MIG-dull-uh] *An almond-shaped lower-level brain structure that is part of the limbic system and is involved in emotion*

Check & Review

TOOLS FOR EXPLORATION AND LOWER-LEVEL BRAIN STRUCTURES

Researchers study the brain through dissection of brains of cadavers, lesion techniques (which involve destroying part of an animal's brain to study resultant changes in behavior), and direct observation or case studies. Electrical recording techniques involve implanting electrodes into the brain or on its surface to study the brain's electrical activity. Computed tomography (CT), positron emission tomography (PET), magnetic resonance imaging (MRI), and functional magnetic resonance imaging (fMRI) scans are sophisticated techniques for studying intact, living brains.

The most important lower-level brain structures are the brainstem, cerebellum, thalamus, hypothalamus, and limbic system. The **brainstem** controls automatic functions such as heartbeat and breathing; the cerebellum contributes to balance, muscle coordination, and some higher mental operations. Parts of the brain stem (the **pons** and **medulla**) are involved in sleeping, waking, dreaming, and control of automatic bodily functions, whereas the **reticular formation** screens incoming information and arouses the cortex. The **cerebellum** maintains smooth movement, balance, and some aspects of perception and cognition. The **thalamus** is the major incoming sensory relay area of the brain. The **hypothalamus** is involved in emotion and in drives associated with survival, such as regulation of body temperature, thirst, hunger, sex, and aggression.

The **limbic system** is a group of brain structures (including the **amygdala**) involved with emotional behavior and memory.

Questions

1. What is the difference between electrical recording and electrical stimulation of the brain?

2. The four major techniques used for scanning the brain are _____, _____, _____, and _____.

3. Roadside test for drunk driving primarily test responses of the _____.

4. What is the major sensory relay area for the brain? (a) hypothalamus; (b) thalamus; (c) cortex; (d) hindbrain

Answers to Questions can be found in Appendix B.

The Cerebral Cortex: The Center of "Higher" Processes

Above the lower-level brain structures, such as the brainstem, thalamus, and limbic system, lie the two *cerebral hemispheres,* the outer surface of which is called the

How does the cortex control behavior and mental processes?

Figure 2.11 *Information crossover.* Information from left side of the body crosses over to the right brain.

Cerebral Cortex *The bumpy, convoluted area on the outside surface of the two cerebral hemispheres that regulates most complex behavior, including receiving sensations, motor control, and higher mental processes*

Frontal Lobes *Cortical lobes in front of the brain, which govern motor control, speech production, and higher functions, such as thinking, personality, emotion, and memory*

cerebral cortex. (The word *cortex* means "bark," and the cerebral cortex surrounds most of the brain like the bark on a tree.) In general, the right hemisphere is in charge of the left side of the body, whereas the left hemisphere controls the right side of the body (Figure 2.11). We will later discuss how the two hemispheres have somewhat different tasks and special functions.

If you were able to open your skull and look inside at your own brain, you would note that the two hemispheres take up most of the room. They balloon out and cover most of the lower-level structures from view. The hemispheres together are slightly larger than two clenched fists. The thin surface layer of the cerebral hemispheres (the cortex) contains approximately 30 billion neurons and nine times as many glial cells. If the cortex of both hemispheres were spread out, they would cover an area almost the size of a standard newspaper page and be about a quarter of an inch thick. How does all this material fit inside our skull? Imagine crumpling the newspaper sheet into a loose ball. You would retain the same surface area but in a much smaller space. The cortex contains numerous "wrinkles" (called *convolutions*), which allow it to hold billions of neurons in the restricted space of the skull.

Each of the two cerebral hemispheres is divided into four areas, or *lobes*: frontal (behind your forehead), parietal (at the top and to the rear of your skull), temporal (in the "temple" region above your ears), and occipital (at the back of your head). Divisions of these lobes are marked by prominent folds, which provide convenient geographic landmarks (Figure 2.12). Like the lower-level brain parts discussed earlier, each lobe specializes in somewhat different tasks — another example of *localization of function*. At the same time, some functions overlap between lobes. As we describe each lobe and its functions, you may want to refer frequently to Figure 2.12.

The Frontal Lobes

By far the largest of the cortical lobes, the **frontal lobes** are located at the top front portion of the two brain hemispheres — right behind your forehead. The frontal lobes receive and coordinate messages from the other three lobes of the cortex and are responsible for at least three additional major functions:

1. *Motor control.* At the very back of the frontal lobes lies the *motor cortex*, which sends messages to the various muscles and glands in the body. All neural signals that instigate voluntary movement originate here. For instance, when you reach out to

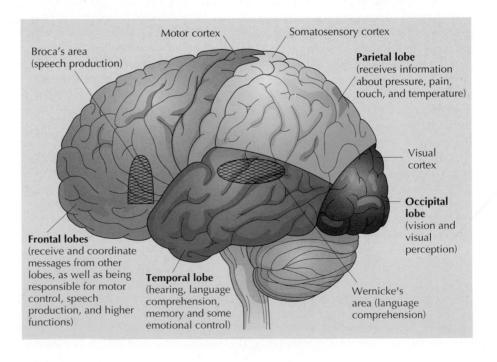

Figure 2.12 *The cerebral cortex.* This is a view of the left hemisphere with its four lobes, the frontal, parietal, temporal, and occipital, along with their major functions.

choose a candy bar from a vending machine, it is the motor control area of the frontal lobes that guides your hand in pulling the proper lever.

2. Speech production. In the *left* frontal lobe, on the surface of the brain near the bottom of the motor control area, lies *Broca's area*, which is known to play a crucial role in speech production. In 1865, French physician Paul Broca was the first to note that patients with damage to this area had great difficulty speaking but could comprehend written or spoken language. This type of aphasia (or impaired language ability) has come to be known as *Broca's aphasia*.

3. Higher functions. Most functions that distinguish humans from other animals, such as thinking, personality, emotion, and memory, are controlled primarily by the frontal lobes. Abnormalities in the frontal lobes are often observed in patients with schizophrenia (Chapter 14). And as we discovered in the story of Phineas Gage, damage to the frontal lobe affects motivation, drives, creativity, self-awareness, initiative, and the ability to plan ahead. Damage in this area also affects emotional behavior.

Using advanced research techniques, Hanna Damasio and her colleagues (1994) constructed computer images of Gage's brain, which showed the tamping iron most likely destroyed frontal lobe areas governing emotional control, social behavior, and decision-making. As Gage's case and other research indicates, what makes us uniquely human and what makes up our individual personalities is regulated by our frontal lobes.

A recent case reminiscent of Phineas Gage's experience also suggests that a person's short-term or "working memory" (Chapter 7) is located in the very front of the frontal lobes. In 1998, a construction worker named Travis Bogumill was accidentally shot in the head with a nail gun. The nail entered the right side of his brain near the rear of the frontal lobe. Like Gage, Bogumill was able to walk and talk after the accident. The nail was removed and, so far, Bogumill seems to be doing well. The only damage seems to be an impaired ability to perform complex mathematical problems in his head. Before the accident, Bogumill was able to easily multiply two-digit numbers in his head. After the accident, he was barely able to multiply two-digit numbers with a paper and pencil. This case supports other experimental research that shows that the frontal lobes and the working memory are responsible for reasoning, problem solving, mathematical calculation, and thinking about future rewards or actions (Giovagnoli, 2001; Hazlett, 2000; Koechlin, Basso, Pietrini, Panzer, & Grafman, 1999; O'Doherty, Kringelbach, Rolls, Hornak, & Andrews, 2001).

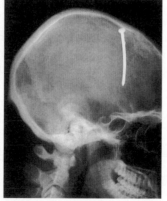

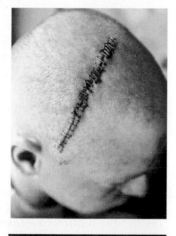

A modern day Phineas Gage? Construction worker Travis Bogumill was accidentally shot in the head with a nail gun. Like Phineas Gage, he was able to walk and talk immediately after the accident but also suffered some damage to his frontal lobes. The x-ray in the bottom photo shows the 3¼ inch nail that was removed from his brain.

Parietal Lobes

At the top of the brain just behind the frontal lobes are the **parietal lobes**, the seat of body sensations and much of our memory about the environment. At the front of the parietal lobes is the *somatosensory cortex*, which receives information about pressure, pain, touch, and temperature. When you step on a sharp nail, you quickly (and reflexively) withdraw your foot because the messages travel directly to and from your spinal cord. However, you don't experience "pain" until the neural messages reach the parietal lobes of the brain.

Parietal [puh-RYE-uh-tuhl] Lobes *Cortical lobes at the top of the brain where bodily sensations are interpreted.*

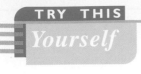

Would you like a quick way to understand both your motor cortex and your sensory cortex?

1. *Motor cortex.* Try wiggling each of your fingers one at a time. Now try wiggling each of your toes. Note on Figure 2.13 how the area of your motor cortex is much larger for your fingers than for your toes, which correlates with your greater sensitivity and precise control in your fingers.
2. *Somatosensory cortex.* Ask a friend to close his or her eyes. Using a random number of fingers (one to four), press down on the skin of your friend's back for 1 or 2 seconds and ask your friend to report how many fingers you are using. Now repeat the same procedure on the palm or back of your friend's hand. Your friend should be much better at guessing when you're pressing on his or her hand than on his or her back. Again as in Figure 2.13, the area of the somatosensory cortex is much larger for the hands than for the back, which reflects more sensitivity and higher accuracy in detecting the finger pressure on the hand.

As you can see in Figure 2.13, the more sensitive a body part is, the greater the area of sensory cortex devoted to it. Note how the face and hands receive the largest share of cortical tissue. These areas are much more sensitive than the rest of the body and require more precise control. Note also that the greater the area of motor cortex, the finer the motor control.

The Temporal Lobes

Temporal Lobes *Cortical lobes above the ears involved in audition (hearing), language comprehension, memory, and some emotional control*

The **temporal lobes** (Latin for "pertaining to the temples") are found on the sides of the brain right above your ears. Their major functions are auditory perception (hearing), language comprehension, memory, and some emotional control. An area called the *auditory cortex* (which processes sound) is located at the top front of each temporal lobe. Incoming sensory information from the ears is processed in this area and then sent to the parietal lobes, where it is combined with visual and other body sensation information.

An area of the *left* temporal lobe, *Wernicke's area*, is involved in language comprehension. About a decade after Broca's discovery, German neurologist Carl Wernicke noted that patients with damage in this area could not understand what they read or heard, but they could speak quickly and easily. However, their speech was often unintelligible because it contained made-up words, like *chipecke*, sound substitutions (*girl* became *curl*), and word substitutions (*bread* became *cake*). This syndrome is now referred to as *Wernicke's aphasia.* (Study tip: Remember that *Broca's area* in the left frontal lobes is responsible for *speech* production, whereas *Wernicke's area* in the left temporal lobe is involved in *language* comprehension.)

David Hubel and Thorsten Wiesel received the Nobel Prize for their work in mapping visual areas in the occipital cortex of the brain.

Occipital [ahk-SIP-uh-tuhl] Lobes *Cortical lobes at the back of the brain responsible for vision and visual perception*

Occipital Lobes

As the name implies, the **occipital lobes** (Latin for *oh,* "in back of," and *caput,* "head") are located at the lower back of the brain. Among other things, the occipital lobes are responsible for vision and visual perception. Damage to the occipital lobe can produce blindness, even though the eyes and their neural connection to the brain are perfectly healthy. The occipital lobes are also involved in shape, color, and motion perception.

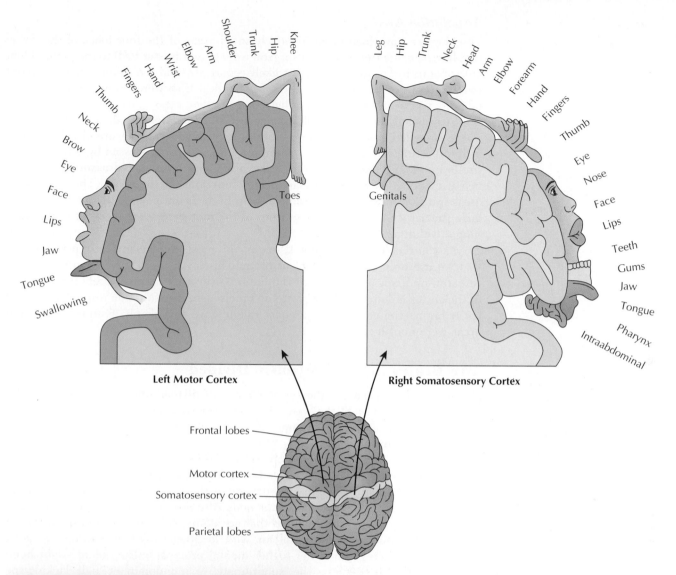

Left Motor Cortex

Right Somatosensory Cortex

Frontal lobes

Motor cortex

Somatosensory cortex

Parietal lobes

The motor and somatosensory cortex. This fanciful representation of a human suggests the overriding importance of the hands and the mouth by the amount of cortex that is dedicated to them.

Figure 2.13 *Body representation on the motor cortex and somatosensory cortex.* This drawing represents a vertical cross-section taken from the left hemisphere's motor cortex and right hemisphere's somatosensory cortex. The amount of cortex devoted to a specific body part is depicted by the oddly shaped human figures draped around the outside edge of the cortex. (These figures are sometimes referred to as the "motor homunculus" and "somatosensory homunculus.") Note the disproportionate size of the hands and faces on each of these figures. The larger sizes reflect the larger cortical area necessary for the precise motor control and greater sensitivity of the hands and face.

Association Areas

Thus far, we have focused on relatively small areas of the four lobes of the cortex that have specific functions. If a surgeon were to administer ESB to the parietal lobe area of your brain, you would most likely report physical sensations, such as feeling touch, pressure, and so on. On the other hand, if ESB were applied to your occipital lobe, you would see flashes of light or color.

Surprisingly, most areas of your cortex, if stimulated, produce nothing at all. These so-called quiet sections are not dormant, however. They are clearly involved in interpreting, integrating, and acting on information processed by other parts of the brain. Thus, these collective "quiet areas" are aptly called **association areas** because they *associate* various areas and functions of the brain. The association areas in the frontal lobe, for example, help in decision making and planning. Similarly, the association area right in front of the motor cortex is involved in the planning of voluntary movement.

As you recall from Chapter 1, one of the most popular myths in psychology is that we use only 10 percent of our brain. This myth might have begun with early research on association areas of the brain. Given that approximately three-fourths of the cortex is "uncommitted" (with no precise, specific function responsive to electrical brain stimulation), researchers might have mistakenly assumed that these areas were nonfunctional.

Association Areas *So-called quiet areas in the cerebral cortex involved in interpreting, integrating, and acting on information processed by other parts of the brain*

Two Brains in One? A House Divided

We mentioned earlier that the cerebral cortex is divided into two hemispheres that control opposite sides of the body. Each hemisphere also has separate areas of specialization. (This is another example of *localization of function*, yet it is technically referred to as **lateralization**.)

By the mid-1800s, early researchers had discovered that the left and right hemispheres carry out different tasks. In addition to mapping the brain and nervous system, they also noted that injury to one side of the brain produced paralysis or loss of sensation on the opposite side of the body. Also around this same time, case studies like Phineas Gage's documented that accidents, strokes, and tumors in the left hemisphere generally led to problems with language, reading, writing, speaking, arithmetic reasoning, and other higher mental processes. The "silent" right hemisphere came to be viewed as the "subordinate" or "nondominant" half, lacking special functions or abilities.

How do the left and right hemispheres of the brain affect behavior and mental processes?

Lateralization *Specialization of the left and right hemispheres of the brain for particular operations*

Split-Brain Research

In the 1960s, this portrayal of the left and right hemispheres as dominant and subordinate players began to change as a result of landmark research with **split-brain** patients.

The two cerebral hemispheres are normally connected at several places, but the primary connection between the left and right halves is a thick, ribbonlike band of nerve fibers under the cortex called the **corpus callosum**. (See Figure 2.9 on page 62.) In some cases of *severe* epilepsy, surgeons cut the corpus callosum to stop the spread of epileptic seizures from the cortex of one hemisphere to the other. Given that brain surgery is a radical and permanent procedure, such an operation is always a last resort and is performed only when patients' conditions have not responded to other forms of treatment. However, the results are generally successful — epileptic seizures are reduced and sometimes disappear entirely.

Split-brain patients also provide an unintended, dramatic side benefit to scientific research. Because this operation cuts the only direct communication link between the two hemispheres, it reveals what each half of the brain can do when it is quite literally cut off from the other. Although relatively few split-brain operations have been

Split-Brain *A surgical separation of the brain's two hemispheres used medically to treat severe epilepsy; split-brain patients provide data on the functions of the two hemispheres*

Corpus Callosum [CORE-puss] [cah-LOH-suhm] *Bundle of nerve fibers connecting the brain's left and right hemispheres.*

conducted since 1961, the resulting research has profoundly improved our understanding of how the two halves of the brain function. In fact, in 1981 Roger Sperry received a Nobel Prize in physiology/medicine for his split-brain research.

How do these patients function after the split-brain surgery? The surgery does create a few unusual responses. For example, one split-brain patient reported that when he dressed himself, he sometimes pulled his pants down with his left hand and up with his right (Gazzaniga, 2000). However, patients generally show very few outward changes in their behavior, other than fewer epileptic seizures. If you met and talked with a split-brain patient, you probably wouldn't even know he or she had had the operation. In fact, one famous psychologist, Karl Lashley, joked that the only function of the corpus callosum seemed to be to keep the two hemispheres from sagging (Gazzaniga, 1995).

The subtle changes in split-brain patients normally appear with simple but specialized testing. For example, when a split-brain patient is asked to stare straight ahead while a photo of a fork is flashed to his left visual field, he cannot name it, although he can point to a similar photo with his left hand. Can you explain why?

To answer this question, you need to understand two major points about your brain. First, as you know, the left hemisphere receives and sends messages from and to the right side of the body, and vice versa. However, vision is different. Your eyes connect to your brain in such a way that, when you look straight ahead, the left half of your field of vision sends an image through both eyes to your right hemisphere (Figure 2.14). Likewise, the right side of your visual field is transmitted to your left hemisphere.

Assuming you don't have a split-brain, if information were presented only to your right hemisphere, it would be quickly sent to your left hemisphere — where the language center could name it. However, when the corpus callosum is split and experimenters present an image to only the left visual field, information cannot be transferred from the right hemisphere to the left. Thus, the patient cannot say what he saw, but he can point to a photo of the same object with his left hand. (Figure 2.15 offers a further example of split-brain testing.)

Keep in mind that split-brain surgery is a last resort medical treatment, which reduces the severity of epileptic seizures and generally has few effects on everyday functioning. An unexpected benefit of this surgery is that it has allowed researchers to demon-

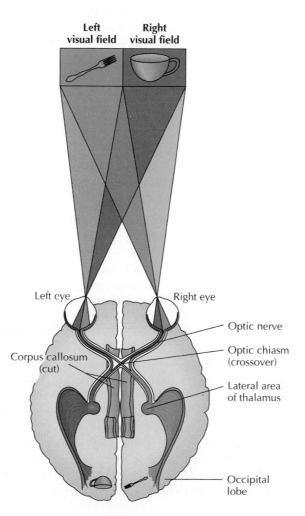

Figure 2.14 *Crisscrossing of visual information.* Imagine this as a drawing of your brain, and that you are being asked to stare straight ahead. Note how visual images from the left half of each eye connect only to the left half of your brain; whereas, images from the right half of each eye connect to the right half. The information received by either hemisphere is normally transmitted across your corpus callosum to the other side. When the corpus callosum is cut, however, the "split-brain" patient does not receive the shared information.

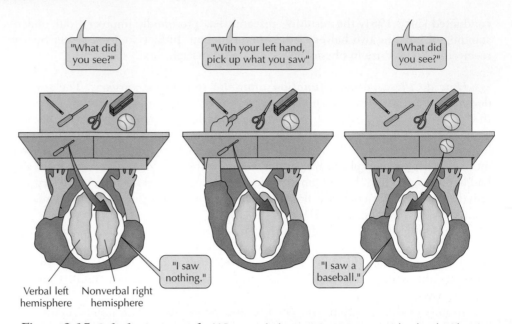

Figure 2.15 *Split-brain research.* When a split-brain patient stares straight ahead and a picture of a screw driver is flashed only to the left visual field, the information goes only to the nonverbal right hemisphere, and he cannot name what he saw. However, when asked to "pick up what you saw," his left hand can touch the items hidden behind the screen and easily identify the screwdriver. This shows that the right hemisphere received the photo image of the screwdriver, but the patient could not name it because the information did not travel across the severed corpus callosum to the left hemisphere where language is stored. Note when the image of a baseball is presented to the left hemisphere, the patient easily names it. Can you see why split-brain research is so important to brain researchers interested in studying the various functions of the two hemispheres?

strate the functional specialization of each hemisphere (Schiffer, Zaidel, Bogen, & Chasan-Taber, 1998).

Hemispheric Specialization

Dozens of studies on split-brain patients, and newer research on people whose brains are intact, have documented several differences between the two brain hemispheres (summarized in Figure 2.16) (Franz, Waldie, & Smith, 2000; Gazzaniga, 1970, 1995, 2000; Robertson et al., 2000; Zaidel, 1985, 1998). In general, for roughly 95 percent of all adults, the left hemisphere is specialized not only for language functions (speaking, reading, writing, and understanding language) but also for analytical functions, such as mathematics (Dehaene, Spelke, Pinel, Stanescu, & Tsivkin, 1999). In contrast, the right hemisphere is specialized primarily for nonverbal abilities, including art and musical abilities and perceptual and spatiomanipulative skills, such as maneuvering through space, drawing or building geometric designs, working jigsaw puzzles, building model cars, painting pictures, and recognizing faces (Springer & Deutsch, 1998). However, recent research with fMRI imaging suggests that the right hemisphere may also contribute to complex language comprehension (Robertson et al., 2000).

In another study, a team of researchers led by Fredric Schiffer (1998) at McLean Hospital in Massachusetts reported that different aspects of personality appear in the different hemispheres. In one patient, the right hemisphere seemed more disturbed by childhood memories of being bullied than did the left. In another patient, the right hemisphere seemed to regard the patient more positively, while also feeling more negative emotions such as loneliness and sadness (Schiffer, Zaidel, Bogen, & Chasan-Taber, 1998).

Is this left and right brain specialization reversed in left-handed people? Not necessarily. About 68 percent of left-handers (people who use their left hands to write, hammer a nail, and throw a ball) and 97 percent of right-handers have their language areas on the left hemisphere. This suggests that even though the right side of the brain is dominant for movement in left-handers, other types of skills are often localized in the same brain areas as for right-handers.

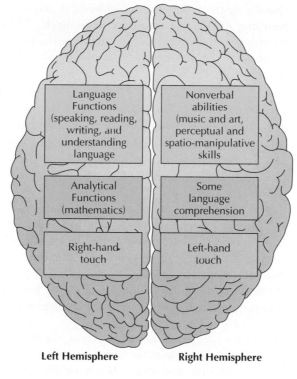

Left Hemisphere   **Right Hemisphere**

Figure 2.16 *Functions of the left and right hemispheres.* The left hemisphere specializes in verbal and analytical functions, whereas the right hemisphere focuses on nonverbal abilities, such as spatiomanipulative skills, art and musical abilities, and visual recognition tasks.

Although lefthanders are generally penalized for living in a right-handed world, there may be some benefits to being left-handed. For example, history shows that a disproportionate number of lefties have achieved greatness in art, music, sports, mathematics, and architecture, including Leonardo da Vinci, Michelangelo, Picasso, and M. C. Escher. Because the right hemisphere is superior at imagery and

Would you like a demonstration of the specialized functions of your own two hemispheres? Some research suggests that the eyes tend to move to the right when a mental task involves the left hemisphere and to the left when the task involves the right hemisphere (see Kinsbourne, 1972). Read the following questions to a friend and record whether his or her eyes move to the right or to the left as he or she ponders the answers. Try to keep the monitoring of your friend's eye movements as natural as possible.

1. Define the word *neuroscience*.
2. What is a function of the corpus callosum?
3. What structure of the brain is located right above pituitary gland?

4. If you are on top of the brain and traveling straight down, what is directly below the parietal lobes?

The first two questions involve language skills and the left hemisphere, which should produce more eye movement to the right. Questions 3 and 4 require spatial reasoning and the right hemisphere, which should elicit more eye movement to the left.

Try the same test on at least four other friends or family members. You'll note two major points: (1) cerebral lateralization is a matter of degree — not all or nothing, and (2) individual differences do exist, especially among left-handers.

visualizing three-dimensional objects, it may help to use the left hand for drawing, painting, or drafting (Springer & Deutsch, 1998). Moreover, left-handers tend to recover better from strokes that damage the language areas in the brain, which may be because the nonspeech hemisphere in left-handers is better able to compensate (Geschwind, 1979).

The Myth of the "Neglected Right Brain"

Courses and books directed at "right-brain thinking" and "drawing on the right side of the brain" often promise to increase your intuition, creativity, and artistic abilities by waking up your neglected and underused right brain (e.g. Bragdon & Gamon, 1999; Edwards, 1999). This myth of the neglected right brain arose from popularized accounts of split-brain patients and exaggerated claims and unwarranted conclusions about differences between the left and right hemispheres.

The fact is that the two hemispheres work together in a coordinated, integrated way, with each making important contributions. If you are a married student with small children, you can easily understand this principle. Just as you and your partner often "specialize" in different jobs (one giving the kids their baths, the other washing the dinner dishes), the hemispheres also divide their workload. However, both parents and both hemispheres are generally aware of what the other "half" is doing.

In our tour of the nervous system, the principles of *localization of function* and *specialization* are common — dendrites receive information, the occipital lobe specializes in vision, and so on. However, it's important to remember that all parts of the brain and nervous system play overlapping and synchronized roles.

Check & Review

THE CEREBRAL CORTEX AND HEMISPHERIC SPECIALIZATION

The left and right cerebral hemispheres of the brain take up most of the room inside the skull. The outer covering of the hemispheres, the **cerebral cortex**, is divided into four lobes. The **frontal lobes** control movement and speech and are involved with self-awareness and planning ahead. The **parietal lobes** are the receiving area for sensory information. The **temporal lobes** are concerned with hearing and language. The occipital lobes are dedicated to vision and visual information processing.

The two hemispheres of the brain are linked by the **corpus callosum**, through which they communicate and coordinate. However, **split-brain** research shows that each hemisphere does perform somewhat separate functions. In most people, the left hemisphere is dominant in verbal skills, such as speaking and writing, and also for analytical tasks. The right hemisphere appears to excel at nonverbal tasks, such as spatio-manipulative skills, art and music, and visual recognition.

Recent research shows the brain can reorganize and change its structure and function throughout the lifespan (**neuro-plasticity**), and create new nerve cells (**neurogenesis**) from stem cells.

Questions

1. The bumpy, convoluted area making up the outside surface of the brain is the _____.

2. You are giving a speech. Name the cortical lobes involved in the following behaviors:

   a. Identifying faces in the audience

   b. Hearing questions from the audience

   c. Remembering where your car is parked when you're ready to go home

   d. Noticing that your new shoes are too tight and hurting your feet

3. The case of Phineas Gage suggests that the _____ lobes regulate our personality and are largely responsible for much of what makes us uniquely human. (a) frontal; (b) temporal; (c) parietal; (d) occipital

4. Although the left and right hemispheres of the brain are specialized, they are normally in close communication through the _____. (a) reciprocating circuits; (b) thalamus; (c) corpus callosum; (d) cerebellum

Answers to Questions can be found in Appendix B.

Understanding Central Nervous System Anatomy and Function

Being able to define a term or concept doesn't necessarily mean you fully comprehend it. The following exercise will help clarify your understanding of brain terminology and function. It also provides a model for the types of questions that lead to critical thinking.

Situation #1
A neurosurgeon is about to perform brain surgery. The surgeon stimulates (touches with an electrode) a tiny portion of the patient's brain, and the patient's right finger moves. After noting the reaction, the surgeon stimulates a portion of the brain a short distance away and the patient's right thumb moves.

Questions to Answer

1. What section of the brain has been stimulated? In which lobe of the brain is this section found?

2. Which hemisphere of the brain is being stimulated?

3. During this stimulation, would the patient experience pain? Why or why not?

Situation #2
The scene: An emergency room in a hospital. Two doctors are talking about a car crash victim who has just been wheeled in.

First Doctor: "Good grief! The whole cerebral cortex is severely damaged; we'll have to remove the entire area."

Second Doctor: "We can't do that. If we remove all that tissue, the patient will die in a matter of minutes."

First Doctor: "Where did you get your medical training — watching *General Hospital*? The patient won't die if we remove his whole cerebral cortex."

Second Doctor: "I resent your tone and insinuation. I went to one of the finest medical schools, and I'm telling you the patient will die if we remove his whole cerebral cortex."

Questions to Answer

1. If the whole cerebral cortex is removed, will the patient die? Explain your answer.

2. If the patient is kept alive without a cerebral cortex, what kinds of behaviors or responses would be possible? What changes would you expect in personality, memories, and emotions?

3. What behaviors could be expected with only the subcortex, medulla, and spinal cord intact? What if only the medulla and spinal cord were functioning? Only the spinal cord?

4. If a patient could be kept alive without a cerebral cortex, would life be worth living? How much of your brain would have to be removed before you would rather die?

RESEARCH HIGHLIGHT

Rewiring, Repairing, and Transplanting Brains and Spinal Cords

In 1989, President George Bush signed a resolution declaring the 1990s the "Decade of the Brain." The decade is over. What did we learn during those 10 years? Was it worth the thousands of research hours and millions of research dollars? You be the judge.

Imagine being completely paralyzed and unable to speak. Each year, thousands of people suffer serious brain and spinal cord injuries, and until recently, these injuries were considered permanent and beyond medical help. Scientists have long believed that after the first 2 or 3 years of life humans and most animals lack the capacity to repair or replace damaged neurons in the brain or spinal cord. Though nerves in the peripheral nervous system sometimes repair and regenerate themselves, it was accepted doctrine that this could not occur in the central nervous system.

Thanks in part to the "Decade of the Brain," this dogma has been overturned — the human brain is capable of lifelong *neuroplasticity* and *neurogenesis*. Let's begin with neuroplasticity. Rather than being a solid fixed organ, your brain is capable of changing its structure and function in response to changing environmental conditions (Beatty,

2001; Hata & Stryker, 1994; Tierney, Varga, Hosey, Grafman, & Braun, 2001). This process is termed **neuroplasticity**. Although the basic brain organization (cerebellum, cortex, and so on) is irreversibly established well before birth, the details are subject to revision. As you're learning a new sport or foreign language, for example, your brain changes and "rewires" itself. New synapses form and others disappear. Some dendrites grow longer and sprout new branches, whereas others are "pruned" away. This is what makes our brains so wonderfully adaptive (Begley, 2000; Hyman, 1999).

Remarkably, this rewiring has even helped "remodel" the brain following

Neuroplasticity *The brain's ability to reorganize and change its structure and function throughout the life span*

strokes. For example, psychologist Edward Taub and his colleagues (1998, 2000) have had success with constraint-induced (CI) movement therapy in stroke patients. Immobilizing the unaffected ("good") arm (or leg) of the patient has restored function in some patients as long as 21 years after their strokes. Rather than coddling the affected arm, Taub requires rigorous and repetitive exercise, which he believes causes intact parts of the brain to take over for the stroke-damaged areas. In effect, Taub "recruits" intact brain cells.

Other scientists researching Alzheimer's disease suggest "rerouting" neurons around damaged areas of the brain (Begley, 2000). This treatment would be analogous to an electrician's wiring a shunt around the damaged part of an electrical circuit. Obviously, there are limits to neuroplasticity. Even with the best "rewiring," most of us will never become another Tiger Woods or Albert Einstein. However, the fact that our brains continually reorganize themselves throughout our lives has enormous implications.

Perhaps the most dazzling find of the Decade of the Brain is **neurogenesis** — the production of nerve cells. Until very recently, it was believed that we are born with all the neurons we'll ever have. Life was a slow process of dying neurons and increasing loss of brain tissue. Today, however, we know that 80-year-olds have just as

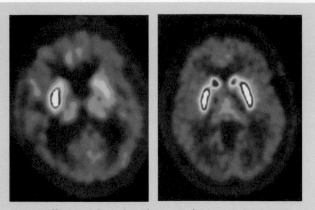

many neurons as 20-year-olds. Although we do lose hundreds of cells each day, our brains also replenish themselves with *new* cells that originate deep within the brain and migrate to become part of the brain's circuitry (Fuchs & Segre, 2000; Gage, 2000; Gould, Reeves, Graziano, & Gross, 1999; Kempermann & Gage, 1999; Vogel, 2000).

Even more exciting is the fact that the source of these newly created cells is neural **stem cells** — rare, precursor ("immature") cells that can grow and develop into any type of cell depending on the chemical signals they receive as they grow. Until now, physicians have used stem cells for bone marrow transplants, but many more clinical applications have already begun. For example, clinical trials using stem cells to repopulate or replace cells devastated by injury or disease have helped patients suffering from strokes, Alzheimer's, Parkinson's, epilepsy, stress, and depression (Diederich & Goetz, 2000; Park, 2000; Travis, 2000).

Stem cell research and Parkinson's disease. A fetal graft implanted in the brain of a Parkinson's patient ten years ago still produces significant levels of dopamine (the brain scan on the left). Note, however, that the activity of this area of the brain is still below that of the normal brain on the right.

Does this mean that people paralyzed from spinal cord injuries might be able to walk again? At this point, neurogenesis in the brain and spinal cord is minimal, but one possible bridge might be *transplanting* embryonic stem cells in the damaged area of the spinal cord. In research with rats, researchers have transplanted mouse embryonic stem cells into a damaged rat spinal cord (McDonald et al., 1999). When the damaged spinal cord was viewed several weeks later, the implanted cells had survived and spread throughout the injured spinal cord area. More importantly, the transplant-rats also showed some movement in previously paralyzed parts of their bodies. Medical researchers have also begun human trials using nerve grafts to repair damaged spinal cords (Barker & Dunnett, 1999; Saltus, 2000).

Although it is unwise to raise false hopes, we are making remarkable breakthroughs in neuroscience. The rewiring, repairing, and transplanting we discussed in

this section are just a small part of what was discovered in the last 10 years. It has been said the Decade of the Brain represents the human brain's first big step toward understanding itself. Can you imagine what the next step (or the next decade) might bring?

Can adult brains grow new neurons? Neuroscientists once believed that each of us was born with all the brain cells we would ever have, but Fred Gage and others have shown that neurons are renewed throughout our life span.

Is paralysis permanent? Findings from the "Decade of the Brain" may provide hope for actor Christopher Reeve who was paralyzed in a horse riding accident and for people with other serious medical conditions.

Neurogenesis [nue-roh-JEN-uh-sis] *The division of nonneuronal cells to produce neurons*

Stem Cell *Precursor (immature) cells that give birth to new specialized cells; a stem cell holds all the information it needs to make bone, blood, brain — any part of a human body — and can also copy itself to maintain a stock of stem cells*

GENETICS AND EVOLUTION

We began this chapter with a look at the smallest part of the nervous system — the neuron — and then toured the structures of the brain. Now, we go backward in time to the moment of your own conception to see how *behavioral genetics* helps to explain your present adult being. Then we close this section and chapter by going even further back in history to look at the role of *evolution*.

Behavioral Genetics: How Much Can We Blame Our Parents?

A relatively new field called **behavioral genetics** has greatly increased our understanding of the relative contributions of genetic and environmental influences on behavior. As we discussed in Chapter 1, one of the oldest debates in psychology is the nature–nurture controversy. Throughout this text, you will find numerous examples of how both nature and nurture contribute to various behaviors and mental processes, such as intelligence (Chapter 8), prenatal development (Chapter 9), and mental disorders (Chapter 14). To provide a foundation for these upcoming discussions, we will explore a few basic principles of genetics and the methods used to study behavioral genetics.

Basic Principles of Genetics

Every cell in your body contains lifelong *messages* from your parents — and you thought it was just their phone calls that bothered you! At the moment of your conception, your mother contributed one set of 23 **chromosomes** and another set of 23 came from your father. Each of these 46 chromosomes is composed of double-stranded molecules of DNA *(deoxyribonucleic acid)*, which, in turn, are made up of thousands of **genes** (Figure 2.17). Genes, the basic units of heredity, are themselves composed of small segments of DNA. We share many of the same genes with other animals and even insects and plants. But it's the genes we share with other humans that set us apart from gorillas, spiders, and tomatoes.

Have you ever wondered why some children have blond hair if both parents have brown hair? It depends on the particular combinations of gene types inherited by the child. For most characteristics, the child inherits two genes, one from each parent. If the inherited gene is *dominant,* the trait encoded in the gene will always be expressed. If the gene is *recessive,* the trait for that gene will be expressed only if the other gene in the pair is also a recessive gene. Because many people have single recessive genes that are not expressed, two brown-eyed parents, who both have recessive genes for blond hair, could produce a blond haired child.

Methods for Studying Behavioral Genetics

Beyond hair and eye color or vision, how much are you shaped by your genetic inheritance? Or by your environment? To answer these questions, researchers generally rely on four methods:

1. *Twin studies.* Because each of us receives a different combination of genes, each person is truly biologically unique. The only exception to this genetic uniqueness occurs with *identical (monozygotic) twins,* which result when a fertilized ovum divides and forms two identical separate cells. These cells go on to produce two complete individuals with identical genetic information. *Fraternal (dizygotic) twins,* on the other hand, result from the fertilization of two separate eggs by different

How are heredity and evolution linked to human behavior?

Behavioral Genetics *A new field that combines genetics and psychology to study genetic and environmental influences on behavior*

Chromosome *Threadlike strands of DNA (deoxyribonucleic acid) molecules that carry genetic information*

Gene *A segment of DNA (deoxyribonucleic acid) that occupies a specific place on a particular chromosome and carries the code for hereditary transmission*

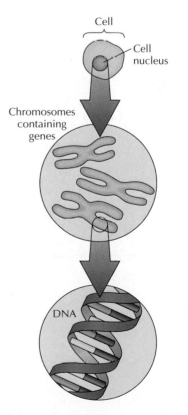

Figure 2.17 DNA, *genes, chromosomes, cell.*

TRY THIS
Yourself

Can you curl your tongue lengthwise? This "ability" is one of the few traits that depends on only one dominant gene. You can increase your understanding of dominant versus recessive genes by doing a simple observation. If you can curl your tongue, one or both of your biological parents must also be able to curl his or her tongue — because this is a dominant trait. Conversely, if you cannot curl your tongue, both of your biological parents cannot curl their tongues.

sperm. These two "womb mates" are genetically no more alike than brothers and sisters born at different times.

The study of identical and fraternal twins offers a unique opportunity to evaluate the relative contributions of genetic and environmental forces in development (Segal & Bouchard, 2000). Identical twins who are separated at birth and reared apart are particularly important because they provide a limited form of control for the relative contributions of nature and nurture.

2. *Adoption studies.* Aside from studies of identical twins who may be adopted and reared apart, adoption studies compare two groups of relatives — biological parents and siblings ("blood relatives") and adoptive parents and siblings. If adopted children resemble their biological parents (and siblings), even though they were not raised in that family, then genetic factors probably had the greatest influence. On the other hand, if adopted children resemble their adoptive family, even though they do not share similar genes, then environmental factors may predominate.

3. *Family studies.* Researchers can also limit their studies to only blood relatives to see how much heredity has an influence. In these studies, the family history is explored in great detail. If a specific trait is inherited, there should be trait similarity among biological/blood relatives. Moreover, relatives who share more genes, like siblings, should exhibit more similarity than cousins. However, correlation does not prove causation! Remember that families share not only genes but also environments. Family studies can provide useful insights about the *possible* impact of heredity, but they can't be used to establish cause-and-effect relationships.

4. *Genetic abnormalities.* One type of research that can provide definitive evidence is the study of genetic abnormalities. For example, an extra twenty-first chromosome fragment almost always causes a condition called Down syndrome. People with Down syndrome often have distinctive round faces, with small folds of skin across the inner edge of the eyes, and impaired psychomotor and physical development, as well as mental retardation. Other disorders like Alzheimer's disease, involving brain deterioration and memory loss, and schizophrenia, a severe mental disorder characterized by loss of contact with reality, are suspected to be caused by abnormalities in several genes or chromosomes (Bailer et al., 2000; Berretini, 2000). We will discuss these disorders in detail in upcoming chapters.

Findings from these four methods have allowed behavior geneticists to estimate the **heritability** of various traits. That is, the extent to which differences among individuals on psychological dimensions, such as intelligence and personality, are determined by genetic factors, as opposed to differences in environment. If genetics contributed *nothing* to the trait, it would have a heritability estimate of zero percent. If a trait were *completely* due to genetics, we would say it had a heritability estimate of 100 percent.

There are two important points to remember about heritability:

1. *Heritability estimates do not apply to individuals.* When people hear media reports that intelligence, musical abilities, or athletic talents are 30 to 50 percent inherited, they often mistakenly assume that this applies to them as individuals. Thus, if intelligence is 50 percent inherited, they believe that 50 percent is due to their parents and 50 percent to the environment. However, estimates of *heritability* are mathematical computations of the proportion of total variance in a trait that is explained by genetic variation within a *group*. In other words, these statistics *describe groups, not individuals*. Height, for example, has one of the highest heritability estimates — around 90 percent (Plomin, 1990). However, any one individual's personal height may be very different from his or her parents' or other blood relatives' height. We each inherit a unique combination of genes (unless we are identical twins). It is impossible to predict your individual height from a heritability estimate. You can estimate only for the group as a whole.

2. *Genes and environment are inseparable.* As first discussed in Chapter 1 (and throughout upcoming chapters), nature and nurture interact — they play off each other and are inseparable (Casti, 2000; Gottlieb, 2000; Maccoby, 2000). Imagine your inherited genes as analogous to water, sugar, salt, flour, eggs, baking powder, and oil. When you mix these ingredients and pour them on a hot griddle (one environment), you get pancakes. Add more oil (a different combination of genes) and a waffle iron (a different environment), and you get waffles. With another set of ingredients and environments (different pans and an oven), you can have crepes, muffins, or cakes. How can you separate the effects of ingredients and cooking methods? You can't. Nature and nurture interact.

> With a good heredity, nature deals you a fine hand at cards; and with a good environment, you learn to play the hand well.
>
> Walter C. Alvarez

"Virtual Twins" Julie (left) and Sara. Traditionally, biological twins have been "the gold standard" for genetic studies, but psychologist Nancy Segal has recently studied "virtual twins" (pairs of unrelated siblings of the same age, one or both adopted, who have been raised together since infancy). Segal suggests these twins provide unique information because they share a common family environment but no common genes.

Heritability *The proportion of observed variance in a particular trait (such as intelligence) that can be attributed to inherited genetic factors in contrast to environmental ones*

RESEARCH HIGHLIGHT

Breakthrough — The Human Genome is Mapped!

Since the 1980s, an exciting, ambitious, multibillion dollar international scientific effort called the *Human Genome Project (HGP)*, led by Francis Collins, and the *International Human Genome Sequencing Consortium (IHGSC)*, led by Craig Venter, have been creating "the human book of life." Working with new, high-tech methods, these two research teams set out to map all of the estimated 100,000 genes on the human chromosome. (The full set of genes for any organism is known as the *genome*—the total DNA blueprint of heritable traits contained in every cell of the body.)

On February 12, 2001, the journals *Science* and *Nature* published the breakthrough news that the mapping was complete, and that humans have only about 30,000 genes, which compares to around 19,000 for the roundworm and 13,000 for the fruit fly (International Human Genome, 2001; Venter et al., 2001). Although humans seem to have fewer genes than originally thought, their genes appear to be far more complex, and the completion of the analyses of the human genome is considered one of the most significant landmarks of all time, comparable to landing a man on the moon or splitting the atom. Francis Collins, leader of the HGP, described the genome as a "book of life" with three volumes:

> "It's a history book—a narrative of the journey of our species through time. It's a shop manual, with an incredibly detailed blueprint for building every human cell. And it's a transformational textbook of medicine, with insights that will give healthcare providers immense new powers to treat, prevent, and cure disease" (cited in Sherrid, p. 48).

Cracking the genetic code. J. Craig Venter and Francis Collins, lead researchers for the Human Genome Project, received joint credit for mapping the human genome. Their work is considered a monumental milestone in genetic research. Can you explain why?

This enormous research venture has already produced important findings on genetic contributors to disease (Jegalian & Lahn, 2001; Lemonick, 2000; Seppa, 2000).

Evolutionary Psychology: Darwin Explains Behavior and Mental Processes

If you've traveled in many countries or taken courses in anthropology, your initial focus may have been on all the strange and unusual practices of other cultures. But over time, you also undoubtedly noted that people the world over seem to eat, work, play with their friends, care for their children, and fight with their enemies in remarkably similar ways. How do we explain this?

Evolutionary Psychology *A branch of psychology that studies evolutionary principles, like natural selection and genetic mutations, which affect adaptation to the environment and help explain commonalities in behavior*

Natural Selection *The driving mechanism behind evolution that allows individuals with genetically influenced traits that are adaptive in a particular environment to stay alive and produce offspring*

Evolutionary psychology suggests that many behavioral commonalities, from eating to fighting with our enemies, emerged and remain in human populations because they helped our ancestors (and ourselves) survive. This perspective is based on the writings of Charles Darwin (1859) who suggested that natural forces select traits that are adaptive to the organism's survival. This process of **natural selection** occurs when one particular genetic trait gives a person a reproductive advantage over others. Although some people mistakenly believe that natural selection means "survival of the fittest," what really matters is *reproduction* — the survival of the genome. Because of natural selection, the fastest or otherwise most fit organisms will be more likely than the less fit to live long enough to mate and thus pass on their genes to the next generation.

Imagine that you are camping alone in a remote area and see a large grizzly bear approaching. According to the principles of *natural selection*, your chances for survival depend on how quickly and smartly you respond to the threat. But what if your child and a group of strangers and their children are also camping in the same spot? Whom do you protect? Most parents would "naturally" choose to help their own child. Why? Why does this feel so "natural" and automatic? According to evolutionary psychologists, natural selection favors animals whose concern for kin is proportional to their degree of biological relatedness. Thus, most people will devote more resources, protection, love and concern to close relatives. This helps ensure their "genetic survival."

In addition to natural selection, *genetic mutations* also help explain behavior. Given that each of us inherits over 100,000 genes, the probability is quite high that everyone carries at least one gene that has *mutated*, or changed from the original. The vast majority of mutated genes have no effect on behavior whatsoever. But, on occasion, a mutated gene will change an individual's behavior. It might cause someone to be more social, more risk taking, more shy, more careful. If the gene gives the person reproductive advantage, he or she will be more likely to pass on the gene to future generations. Another common misunderstanding is that evolution translates into continuing, long-term improvement. A genetic mutation can produce a population that is perfectly adapted to a current environment, but which may later perish if the environment changes.

Social and cultural factors can also affect evolution, as evidenced when the social or cultural factors influence the mating behavior of the people in a population (Segerstrale, 2000). For example, as explained in Chapter 16, the concept of beauty is culturally influenced. Therefore, those who best fit their culture's concept of beauty may find it easier to acquire mates and have more offspring, to whom they pass on their physical and behavioral traits. Similarly, in cultures that arrange marriages according to social class or religious factors, different traits may be selected and passed along to succeeding generations.

Evolutionary psychology is one of the seven major perspectives in modern psychology (Chapter 1, Introduction and Research Methods), and we will revisit this field many times throughout this text. For example, in Chapter 3 (Stress and Health Psychology), we examine the role of stress over the course of evolution, and Chapter 9 (Life Span Development I) explores the role of evolution in infant reflexes, language development, and attachment. In Chapter 11 (Gender and Human Sexuality), we look at modern controversies surrounding evolution and gender role development and supposed differences in sexual behavior. Chapter 12 (Motivation and Emotion) discusses the role of evolution in drives toward novelty and exploration and the universal recognition of facial expressions of emotion. Evidence of evolution in our helping and aggressive behaviors is discussed in Chapter 16 (Social Psychology).

In the following section, we explore biological differences between women and men that may have evolved from different gender-related adaptations.

Evolution in Action? Similar behaviors in humans and other animals may suggest common evolutionary influences.

GENDER & CULTURAL DIVERSITY

The Evolution of Sex Differences

Because of the way our species evolved, modern men and women have many abilities that helped our ancestors adapt to their environment and hence to survive and reproduce. For example, Figures 2.18 and 2.19 show that men tend to score higher on tests of mathematical reasoning and spatial relationships, whereas women score higher on tests involving mathematical calculation and tasks requiring perceptual speed. Men also tend to be more accurate in target-directed motor skills, whereas women tend to be more efficient in skills requiring fine motor coordination. What accounts for these differences?

One possible answer from evolutionary psychologists is that ancient societies typically assigned men the task of "hunters" and women as "gatherers." The man's superiority on many spatial tasks and target-directed motor skills, for example, may have evolved from the adaptive demands of hunting. Similarly, activities such as gathering, child-rearing, and domestic tool construction and manipulation may have contributed to the woman's language superiority (Farber, 2000; Joseph, 2000; Silverman & Phillips, 1998). Some critics, however, suggest that evolution progresses much too slowly to account for this type of behavioral adaptation. Furthermore, evolutionary

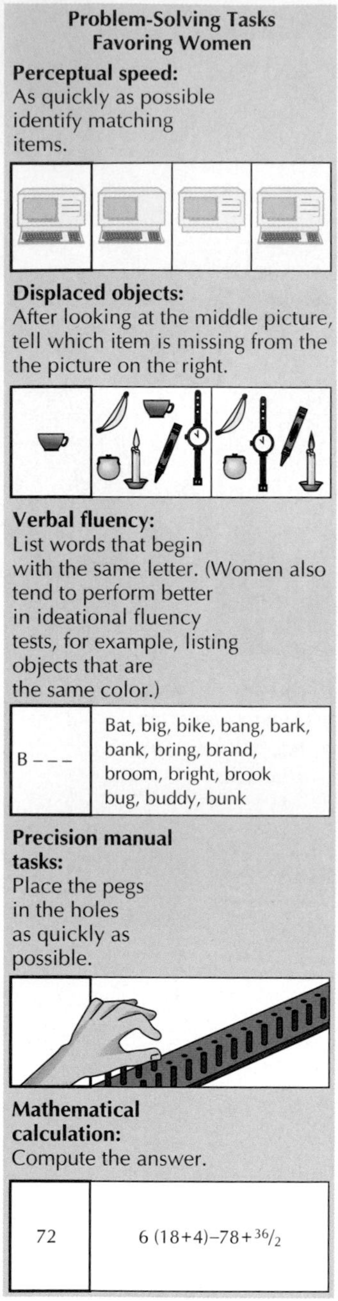

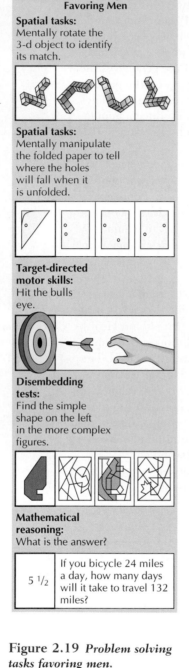

Figure 2.18 *Problem solving tasks favoring women.*

Figure 2.19 *Problem solving tasks favoring men.*

explanations of sex differences are highly speculative and obviously difficult to test scientifically (Eagly & Wood, 1999).

A less controversial explanation of sex differences comes from well-established knowledge of hormonal effects. All women and men produce both estrogens and androgens (the principal classes of female and male hormones). It is the relative proportion of these hormones that accounts for sex differences. Even before birth, development of genital anatomy is largely due to the presence or absence of *testosterone* (one of the androgens secreted by the testes). Although genetic sex is determined at the moment of conception — an XX pairing produces a female zygote and an XY pairing produces a male — during the first 6 to 8 weeks after conception, the genital areas of both male and female embryos are essentially the same. Once the sex glands begin to produce differing levels of hormonal secretions (androgens and estrogens), their genital organs *differentiate*.

In some cases, however, endocrine disorders can lead to overproduction or underproduction of these hormones during prenatal development. In general, males exposed prenatally to abnormally low levels of androgens exhibit more femalelike behavior than other males. Conversely, females exposed prenatally to abnormally high levels of androgens tend to show more malelike behavior compared with other females.

For example, studies of girls with *congenital adrenal hyperplasia* (CAH), a rare genetic disorder with an excess amount of *androgens*, grow up to be more "tomboyish" and aggressive than nonaffected girls (Leveroni & Berenbaum, 1998). Moreover, girls with CAH tend to outperform nonaffected girls on cognitive tests of spatial ability on which males are known to excel, such as the mental rotation task shown in Figure 2.19 (Hampson, Rouet, & Altman, 1998; Nass & Baker, 1991). Although physiological effects resulting from CAH — the development of male genitals and the overproduction of androgens — can be surgically or medically corrected, the hormonal influence on brain development appears irreversible.

In addition to possible sex differences due to prental hormonal influences, there also may be differences in the anatomical structure of men and women's brains (Boone, 2000; Castle, 2000; Dorion et al., 2000; Amunts, Jaencke, Mohlberg, Steinmetz, & Zilles, 2000). For example, Mark Lumley and Kevin Sielky (2000) found an interesting gender difference in a disorder known as *alexithymia,* which involves difficulty identifying and describing feelings. The disorder seems to reflect deficiencies in right hemisphere function or interhemispheric transfer, but only for men. For women, poorer short-term memory is a better predictor. In another study, Ruben Gur and his colleagues (1999) found that women have a greater percentage of their brains dedicated to gray matter (neuron cell bodies) than do men. Considering that there is very little or no difference between men and women in overall intelligence, the increased percentage of gray matter might just be an evolutionary adaptation to the smaller cranial size in women. Most women (and their brains) tend to be smaller than most men. Thus, some of the structural differences between male and female brains might reflect adaptations to differences in skull size (De Vries & Boyle, 1998).

Evolutionary psychology research emphasizes heredity and early biological processes in determining gender differences in cognitive behavior, but keep in mind that almost all sex differences are *correlational*. The mechanisms involved in the actual *cause* of certain human behaviors have yet to be determined. Furthermore, it is important to remember that all known variations *between* the two sexes are much smaller than differences *within* each sex. Finally, to repeat a theme discussed throughout this text, it is extremely difficult to separate the effects of biology (nature) from those of the environment (nurture) (Gottlieb, 2000; Maccoby, 2000).

Check & Review

GENETICS AND EVOLUTIONARY PSYCHOLOGY

Genes are strings of chemicals that hold the code for certain traits that are passed on from parent to child, and they can be dominant or recessive. Genes are found on long strands of DNA molecules called **chromosomes. Behavioral geneticists** use twin studies, adoption studies, family studies, and genetic abnormalities to explore genetic contributions to behavior and make estimates of **heritability.**

Evolutionary psychology is the branch of psychology that looks at evolutionary changes related to behavior. Sev-eral different processes, including **natural selection**, mutations, and social and cultural factors can affect evolution.

Questions

1. Evolutionary psychology is the branch of psychology that looks at
   a. How fossil discoveries affect behavior
   b. The relationship between genes and the environment
   c. The relationship between evolutionary changes and behavior
   d. The effect of culture change on behavior

2. What are the four chief methods used to study behavioral genetics?

3. According to evolutionary theorists, why are people more likely to help their family members than strangers?

4. How would evolutionary psychology explain why men tend to score higher on mathematical reasoning, spatial relationships, and target directed motor skills, whereas women score higher on mathematical calculation, tasks requiring perceptual speed, and fine motor coordination?

Answers to Questions can be found in Appendix B.

KEY TERMS

neuroscience (p. 46)
Biological Foundations
action potential (p. 52)
autonomic nervous system (ANS) (p. 48)
axon (p. 51)
cell body (p. 51)
central nervous system (CNS) (p. 46)
dendrites (p. 51)
endocrine [EN-dohe-krin] system (p. 57)
endorphins [en-DOR-fins] (p. 57)
glial cells (p. 51)
hormones (p. 57)
myelin [MY-uh-lin] sheath (p. 51)
neuron (p. 50)
neurotransmitter (p. 53)
parasympathetic nervous system (p. 48)
peripheral nervous system (PNS) (p. 48)

somatic nervous system (SNS) (p. 48)
sympathetic nervous system (p. 48)
synapse [SIN-aps] (p. 53)
A Tour Through the Brain
amygdala [uh-MIG-dull-uh] (p. 65)
association areas (p. 70)
brainstem (p. 63)
cerebellum [sehr-uh-BELL-um] (p. 63)
cerebral cortex (p. 66)
corpus callosum [CORE-puss] [cah-Loh-suhm] (p. 70)
frontal lobes (p. 66)
hypothalamus [hi po THAL-uh-muss] (p. 64)
lateralization (p. 70)
limbic system (p. 64)
localization of function (p. 62)
medulla [muh-DUL-uh] (p. 63)
neurogenesis [nue-roe-JEN-uh-sis] (p. 76)
neuroplasticity (p. 76)

occipital [ahk-SIP-uh-tuhl] lobes (p. 68)
parietal [puh-RYE-uh-tuhl] lobes (p. 67)
pons (p. 63)
reticular formation (RF) (p. 63)
split brain (p. 70)
stem cell (p. 76)
temporal lobes (p. 68)
thalamus [THAL-uh-muss] (p. 64)
Genetics and Evolution
behavioral genetics (p. 77)
chromosome (p. 77)
evolutionary psychology (p. 80)
gene (p. 77)
heritability (p. 79)
natural selection (p. 80)

Visual Summary for Chapter 2 ----

Biological Foundations

An Overview of the Nervous System

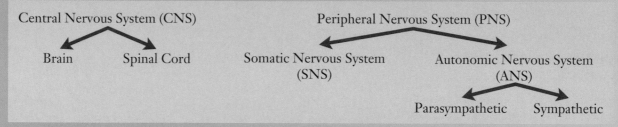

Neurons as the Basic Building Blocks

Neurons: Individual nerve cells that transmit information throughout the body.
Glial cells: Provide structural, nutritional, and other support for neurons.

Key Features of a Neuron

- **Dendrites**: Receive information and send impulses to cell body.
- **Cell body**: Integrates incoming information and nourishes neuron.
- **Axon**: Carries information from cell body to other neurons.
(**Myelin Sheath**: Fatty insulation around some axons that speeds up action potential.)

How Neurons Communicate

- Communication *within the neuron* is through the **action potential**, a neural impulse that carries information along the axon.
- Communication *between neurons* occurs when an action potential reaches the axon terminal and stimulates the release of **neurotransmitters** into the **synapse**.

Chemical Messengers in the Nervous System

Three key chemical messengers:
1) **Neurotransmitters**: Chemicals manufactured and released by neurons that alter activity in other neurons, which thereby affects behavior and mental processes.
2) **Endorphins**: Chemicals that produce effects similar to those of opium based drugs like morphine.
3) **Hormones**: Chemicals released from the endocrine system into the bloodstream, which affect the nervous system.

A Tour Through the Brain

Tools for Exploration

Methods include brain dissection, ablation, lesioning, clinical observation, case studies, electrical recordings, electrical stimulation of the brain (ESB), brain imaging (such as CT, PET, MRI, fMRI).

A Tour Through the Brain (cont).

Lower-Level Brain Structures

Brain Stem

Group of structures including the **pons** (breathing, sleeping, waking, dreaming, etc.), **medulla** (breathing, heart rate, etc.), and **reticular formation** (screening incoming information and arousing the cortex).

Cerebellum

Responsible for smooth movement, balance, and aspects of perception and cognition.

Thalamus

Relays sensory messages to the cortex.

Hypothalamus

Maintains homeostasis and controls emotions and motives like hunger, thirst, sex, and aggression.

Limbic System

Group of interconnected structures responsible for arousal and regulation of emotion, motivation, memory, and learning. The **amygdala** is the structure most involved with emotion.

The Cerebral Cortex
The cerebral cortex is responsible for all higher mental processes and is divided into four lobes:

Frontal Lobes

Motor control, speech production, and higher functions (thinking, personality, emotion, and memory).

Parietal Lobes

Sensory processing (pressure, pain, touch, and temperature).

Temporal Lobes

Audition, language comprehension, memory, and some emotional control.

Occipital Lobes

Vision and visual perception.

(**Association areas**: Remaining areas of the cortex that interpret, integrate, and act on information from other parts of the brain.)

Two Brains in One
Splitting the **corpus callosum**, which transfers neural impulses between the brain's left and right hemispheres, is a treatment for some forms of epilepsy. **Split-brain research** on these patients shows:

Left hemisphere specializes in verbal and analytical functions.

Right hemisphere governs nonverbal abilities (spatio-manipulative skills, art, music, and visual recognition).

The brain can reorganize and change its structure and function throughout the lifespan (**neuroplasticity**), and create new nerve cells (**neurogenesis**) from **stem cells** (immature cells that produce specialized cells).

Genetics and Evolution

Behavioral Genetics

Each of the 46 human **chromosomes** is composed of DNA, which is made up of **genes**.

Genetics studies are done with twins, adopted children, families, and genetic abnormalities. Such studies allow estimates of **heritability**.

The Human Genome Project (HGP) and the International Human Genome Sequencing Consortium (IHGSC) have mapped all the genes on the human chromosome.

Evolutionary Psychology

Studies evolutionary principles, like **natural selection** and genetic mutations, which affect adaptation to the environment and help explain commonalities in behavior.

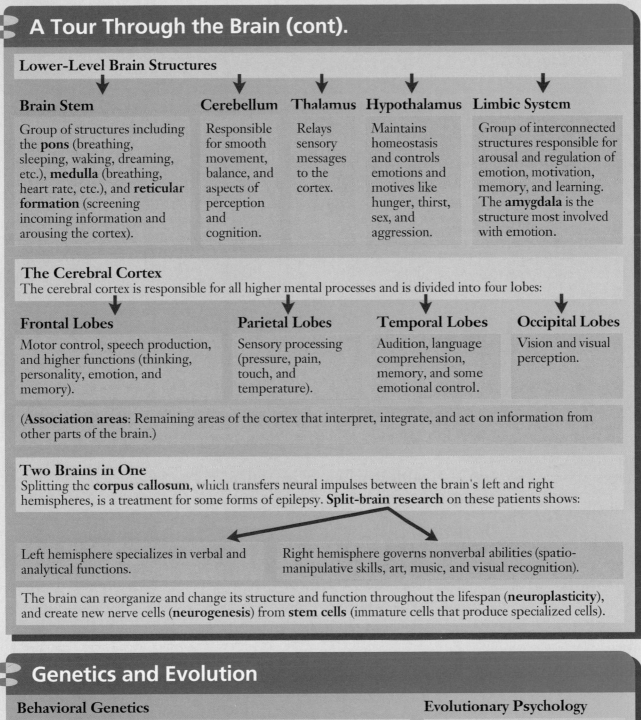

3

Stress and Health Psychology

College Life Stress Inventory

Copy the "stress rating" number into the last column for any event you have experienced in the last year. Then add up the ratings for your total stress score.

Event	Stress Rating	Your Items
1. Being raped	100	_____
2. Finding out that you are HIV-positive	100	_____
3. Being accused of rape	98	_____
4. Death of a close friend	97	_____
5. Death of a close family member	97	_____
6. Contracting a sexually transmitted disease (other than AIDS)	94	_____
7. Concerns about being pregnant	91	_____
8. Finals week	90	_____
9. Concerns about your partner being pregnant	90	_____
10. Oversleeping for an exam	89	_____
11. Flunking a class	89	_____
12. Having a boyfriend or girlfriend cheat on you	85	_____
13. Ending a steady dating relationship	85	_____
14. Serious illness in a close friend or family member	85	_____
15. Financial difficulties	84	_____
16. Writing a major term paper	83	_____
17. Being caught cheating on a test	83	_____
18. Drunk driving	82	_____
19. Sense of overload in school or work	82	_____
20. Two exams in one day	80	_____
21. Cheating on your boyfriend or girlfriend	77	_____
22. Getting married	76	_____
23. Negative consequences of drinking or drug use	75	_____
24. Depression or crisis in your best friend	73	_____
24. Difficulties with parents	73	_____
25. Talking in front of a class	72	_____
26. Lack of sleep	69	_____
27. Change in housing situation (hassles, moves)	69	_____
28. Competing or performing in public	69	_____
29. Getting in a physical fight	66	_____
30. Difficulties with a roommate	66	_____
31. Job changes (applying, new job, work hassles)	65	_____
32. Declaring a major or concerns about future plans	65	_____
33. A class you hate	62	_____
34. Drinking or use of drugs	61	_____
35. Confrontations with professors	60	_____
36. Starting a new semester	58	_____
37. Going on a first date	57	_____
38. Registration	55	_____
39. Maintaining a steady dating relationship	55	_____
40. Commuting to campus or work, or both	54	_____
41. Peer pressures	53	_____
42. Being away from home for the first time	53	_____
43. Getting sick	52	_____
44. Concerns about your appearance	52	_____
45. Getting straight A's	51	_____
46. A difficult class that you love	48	_____
47. Making new friends; getting along with friends	47	_____
48. Fraternity or sorority rush	47	_____
49. Falling asleep in class	40	_____
50. Attending an athletic event (e.g., football game)	20	_____
Total		_____

From Renner & Mackin, 1998.

Marriage as a stressor? Getting married is normally a very happy occasion; nevertheless the changes it brings can be stressful.

How did you do? Were you surprised that getting married or getting straight A's could be considered stressful? Michael Renner and Scott Mackin (1998) developed this scale on the basis of their research with college students, and they found that scores ranged between a low of 182 and a high of 2,571, with an average of 1,247. What was your total score? If you are a "typical" college student, 18 to 22 years of age, living on campus, and away from home for the first time, this scale may provide an accurate assessment of important stressors in your life. However, as an older returning student, a young student living at home, or a married person with small children, you have different stressors (such as divorce, unemployment, child care) and this scale would be inappropriate.

We use this scale as an introduction to the complex and fascinating world of health psychology. The topics of health and stress are a part of everyday conversation, with most people assuming that everyone shares the same definitions and life experiences. As you have just found with the college stress inventory, however, stress is highly individual. Stress is also a normal part of all our lives, but when it is chronic or severe, it can damage our health.

The well-established relationship between stress and physical illness takes us into a broader discussion of the psychology of health. In the first part of this chapter, we explore this field and three important health issues: smoking, binge drinking, and chronic pain. After that, we examine the numerous causes and results of stress, the role of stress in cancer and heart disease, and how people cope with stress. We end the chapter with specific tips to help you stay healthy.

HEALTH PSYCHOLOGY IN ACTION

Throughout most of history, the relationship between mind and physical health had been a widely accepted fact. However, in the late 1800s, the discovery of physiological causes for infectious diseases such as typhoid and syphilis led scientists to intensify the search for physiological causes of disease. As a result, medicine and public health made marked advances. Over the last century, life expectancy for Americans of all races and genders has steadily increased, and for those born in 1997 it is an all-time high of 76.5 years (National Center for Health Statistics, 2001).

> What is health psychology? Can health psychologists help with problems related to smoking, binge drinking, and chronic pain?

Interestingly, the major causes of death have shifted from contagious diseases (pneumonia, influenza, tuberculosis, measles, and typhoid fever) to noncontagious diseases (cancer, heart and cardiovascular disease, chronic lung disease) (National Center for Health Statistics, 2001). Can you see how today's key health problems are strongly related to behavior and lifestyle? Scientists and medical experts are now reemphasizing the close relationship between psychological behavior and physical health and illness, with an emphasis on wellness and the prevention of illness. This is the heart (and definition) of **health psychology** (Baum & Posluszny, 2001).

Health Psychology *The study of the relationship between psychological behavior and physical health and illness, with an emphasis on wellness and the prevention of illness.*

What Health Psychologists Do: Research and Practice

Health psychologists study how people's lifestyles and activities, emotional reactions, ways of interpreting events, and personality characteristics influence their physical health and well-being. Some health psychologists are involved primarily in research, whereas others work directly with physicians and other health professionals to implement research findings.

As researchers, they have been particularly interested in the relationship between stress and the immune system. A normally functioning immune system helps detect and defend against disease, and a suppressed immune system leaves the body susceptible to any number of diseases. Today we know that stress plays a role in suppressing the immune system and may make us more vulnerable to a host of modern illnesses and disease, including cancer, heart disease, AIDS (acquired immunodeficiency syndrome, and even the common cold (Cohen et al., 1998, 1999; Kiecolt-Glaser & Glaser, 2001; Leserman et al., 2000; Pratt et al., 1996). Until the 1970s, however, most experts believed the immune system was completely independent of the other body systems. As you will see in a later section, the scientific view of stress and the immune system has changed dramatically in the last few years.

As practitioners, health psychologists can work as independent clinicians or as consultants alongside physicians, physical and occupational therapists, and other health care workers. Their goal is to reduce psychological distress or unhealthy behaviors. They also help patients and families make critical decisions and prepare psychologically for surgery or other treatment.

In addition to their work as researchers and practitioners, health psychologists also educate the general public about health *maintenance*. They provide information about the effects of stress, smoking, alcohol, lack of exercise, and other health issues. In addition, health psychologists help people cope with chronic problems, such as pain, diabetes, and high blood pressure, as well as unhealthful behaviors, such as lack of assertiveness and anger expression (Davidson, MacGregor, Stuhr, Dixon, & MacLean, 2000; Haerenstam, Theorell, & Kaijser, 2000; Lepore, Ragan, & Jones, 2000). To illustrate the work of health psychologists, we begin this chapter discussing two of the most prevalent (and preventable) health problems in the United States — smoking and binge drinking.

Smoking: Hazardous to Your Health

A custom loathsome to the eye, hateful to the nose, harmful to the brain, dangerous to the lungs, and in the black, stinking fume thereof, nearest resembling the horrible Stygian smoke of the pit that is bottomless.

This is what King James I wrote about smoking in 1604, shortly after Sir Walter Raleigh introduced tobacco to England from the Americas. Today, nearly 400 years later, many people would agree with the king's tirade against the practice.

According to the latest U.S. Public Health Service report, tobacco is the single most preventable cause of death and disease in the United States (Fiore, 2000). Smoking is a major risk factor for coronary heart disease and lung cancer and contributes to cancers of the mouth, larynx, throat, esophagus, bladder, and pancreas (Centers for Disease Control, 2001). Smoking also contributes to chronic bronchitis, emphysema, and ulcer disease. Moreover, smoking shortens life (Burns, 2000). This is true for both the smoker and those who breathe secondhand smoke.

What about all the new antismoking laws? Do they help? Ironically, the antismoking laws passed in the 1990s may have made quitting smoking even more difficult for some. First, the fact that smokers have to leave smoke-free environments and group together outdoors on the hottest summer days and the worst winter days to satisfy their habit creates a strong social bond: Together they will suffer the tyranny of nonsmoking laws. Cigarette companies play to this group loyalty (and the individual's "independence" and "perseverance") by showing smokers sitting high up on the ledges of office buildings and on the wings of airplanes in flight "going to any lengths" to have a cigarette. Second, when people cannot smoke in offices, on airplanes, in restaurants, or other public places, the interval between nicotine doses increases, which increases the severity of the withdrawal symptoms (Palfai, Monti, Ostafin, & Hutchinson, 2000). In effect, the smoker gets repeated previews of just how unpleasant quitting is going to be — and who wouldn't rather avoid something unpleasant?

Smoker's unite? Due to increased restrictions, many people are forced to go outside to smoke. Ironically, this may forge stronger bonds between smokers and make them even more resistant to quitting.

Most people know that smoking is bad for their health and that the more they smoke, the more at risk they are. It is therefore not surprising that most health psychologists and medical professionals are concerned with preventing smoking in the first place and getting those who already smoke to stop.

Smoking Prevention

The first puff on a cigarette is rarely pleasant. Why, then, do people ever start smoking? The answer is complex. First, smoking usually starts when people are young. The European School Survey Project on Alcohol and Other Drugs (ESPAD) (2001) reported that tobacco smoking was well established by the mid-teens in most European countries and showed few signs of diminishing since the previous ESPAD survey in 1995. A similar survey of U.S. middle schools, grades 6 to 8, found that one in eight students were experimenting with some form of tobacco, such as cigarettes, cigars, and chewing tobacco (Kaufman, 2000). There are many reasons people begin to smoke at such a young age, but peer pressure and imitation of role models (such as celebrities) are particularly strong factors. Young smokers want to look mature and be accepted by their social peers.

Secondly, regardless of the age at which a person begins smoking, once he or she begins to smoke, there is a biological need to continue because of the addictive effects of nicotine. The evidence clearly shows that nicotine is a powerful addictive drug, comparable to heroin, cocaine, and alcohol (Balfour & Ridley, 2000; Pahlavan, Bonnet, & Duda, 2000; Pich et al., 1997). In fact, when we inhale smoke, it takes only seconds for the nicotine to reach the brain, where it increases the release of the neurotransmitters acetylcholine and norepinephrine. Acetylcholine and norepinephrine, in turn, increase alertness, concentration, memory, and feelings of pleasure (McGaughy, Decker, & Sarter, 1999; Picciotto, 1998; Quattrocki, Baird, & Yurgelun-Todd, 2000). Several recent research projects have also indicated that nicotine stimulates the release of dopamine, the neurotransmitter most closely related to reward centers in the brain (Noble, 2000; Carboni, Bortone, Giua, & DiChiara, 2000). These neurotransmitters also decrease the symptoms of nicotine withdrawal, anxiety, tension, and pain, which come after a short period without tobacco.

Finally, social pressures and physical addiction combine to create additional benefits (Lazev, Herzog, & Brandon, 1999). For example, smokers learn to associate smoking with pleasant things, such as good food, friends, sex, and, not least, the high that nicotine gives them, so their smoking is rewarded. When smokers are deprived of cigarettes, they go through physical withdrawal with extremely unpleasant symptoms. When they get their next puff, the nicotine relieves the symptoms, so smoking is rewarded. It follows that the best way to reduce the number of smokers is to prevent people from taking their first puff.

Smoking as a "pediatric disease." Because many smokers take up the habit as adolescents or preteens, health psychologists recommend that anti-smoking programs begin in elementary school.

If most people begin smoking during adolescence, shouldn't prevention be aimed at this group? Prevention programs for teens face a tough uphill battle. For adolescents, the long-term health disadvantages of heart disease and cancer seem totally irrelevant, whereas smoking itself provides immediate short-term rewards from peers and the addictive, reinforcing properties of nicotine. Many smoking prevention programs therefore focus on immediate short-term problems with smoking, such as bad breath and interference with athletic performance.

Through films and discussion groups, teens also are educated about peer pressure and the media's influence on smoking, given opportunities to role-play refusal skills, taught general social and personal skills needed in decision making, and given strategies for coping with the stresses of adolescence and daily life (Worden, Flynn, Solomon, & Secker-Walker, 1996). Unfortunately, the research shows that the effect of psychosocial prevention programs is small (Baum & Posluszny, 1999). To have even a modest effect, these programs must begin early and continue for many years (Eckhardt, Woodruff, & Elder, 1997).

To reduce the health risk and help fight peer pressure, many schools ban smoking in college buildings and offer more smoke-free dormitories. Another possible deterrent to the college smoking trend results from expensive legal battles and settlements by the tobacco industry and the fact that these expenses are passed on to consumers in the form of higher prices for cigarettes. This increase, added to state and local taxes, brings the cost to over $4 per pack in most states. For a student who smokes a pack of cigarettes a day, the annual cost is nearly $1,500 — more than twice the cost of textbooks for an entire academic year.

Stopping Smoking

> To cease smoking is the easiest thing I ever did; I ought to know, for I have done it a thousand times.
>
> Mark Twain

Unfortunately, Mark Twain was never able to quit for very long, and many ex-smokers say that stopping smoking was the most difficult thing they ever did. Although some people find the easiest way for them to cope with the physical withdrawal from nicotine is to suddenly and completely stop, the success rate for this "cold turkey" approach is extremely low. Even with medical aids, such as patches, gum, or pills, it is still very difficult to quit (Killen et al., 2000; Patten, 2000). Any program designed to help smokers break their habit must combat the social rewards of smoking as well as the physical addiction to nicotine.

Sometimes the best approach is a combination of cognitive and behavioral techniques and nicotine replacement therapy. Cognitively, smokers can learn to identify stimuli or situations that make them feel like smoking and then change or avoid them (Brandon, Collins, Juliano, & Lazev, 2000). They can also refocus their attention on something other than smoking or remind themselves of the benefits of not smoking (Taylor, Harris, Singleton, Moolchan, & Heishman, 2000). Behaviorally, they might cope with the urge to smoke by chewing gum, exercising, or chewing on a toothpick after a meal instead of lighting a cigarette.

No program to quit smoking will work without a tremendous amount of personal motivation, but the payoffs can be just as tremendous: a more enjoyable and longer life. (See Wetter et al., 1998, for the Agency for Health Care Policy and Research's "Smoking Cessation Clinical Practice Guidelines.")

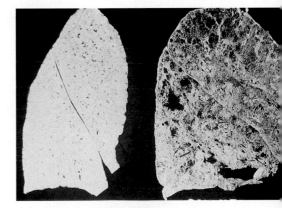

A hidden cost of smoking. Would people continue to smoke if they could see what it does to their lungs? Compare the healthy tissue of the lung of a nonsmoker on the left to the blackened, unhealthy lung of the smoker on the right.

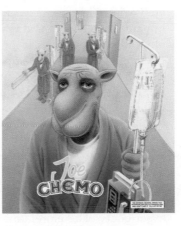

Antismoking ads. Because Joe Camel was once a popular icon that reportedly encouraged young children to smoke, antismoking activists created a "Joe Chemo" image to advertise the dangers of smoking.

Check & Review

WHAT HEALTH PSYCHOLOGISTS DO AND SMOKING

Health psychology is the study of the relationship between psychological behavior and physical health and illness, with an emphasis on wellness and the prevention of illness. As researchers, health psychologists study psychological issues that affect physical health and find ways to help patients cope with medical procedures and health problems. As practitioners, health psychologists work with patients alongside health care professionals to help reduce psychological distress and unhealthy behaviors and educate the general public about health risks and health maintenance.

Because smoking is the single most preventable cause of death and disease in the United States, prevention and cessation of smoking are of primary importance to all health practitioners, including health psychologists. Smoking prevention programs involve educating the public about short- and long-term consequences of smoking, trying to make smoking less socially acceptable, and helping nonsmokers resist social pressures to smoke. Most approaches to help people quit smoking

Health psychology in action. Your lifestyle and behavioral risk factors have a significant impact on your health and life expectancy (Gorman, 2001).

include cognitive and behavioral techniques to aid smokers in their withdrawal and nicotine replacement therapy (using patches, gum, and pills).

Questions

1. What is health psychology?
2. Since the late 1800s, major causes of death have shifted from _____ to _____ diseases.
3. Knowing smoking is very dangerous, why do many people find it so difficult to stop?
4. If you are mounting a campaign to prevent young people from taking up smoking, you are likely to get the best results if you emphasize the _____. (a) serious, unhealthy, long-term effects of tobacco use; (b) number of adults who die from smoking; (c) value of having a relatively healthy retirement; (d) short-term detrimental effects of tobacco use.

Answers to Questions can be found in Appendix B.

Binge Drinking: A Growing Social Problem

Were you surprised by news reports of two freshmen at Massachusetts Institute of Technology who died from alcohol poisoning after binge drinking at fraternity parties? One of the students had a blood alcohol level of .5888 percent — the equivalent of more than 20 beers in 1 hour and over seven times the legal driving limit in most states. Unlike smoking, alcohol and other drugs can kill directly and immediately when they are taken in large amounts over a short period of time. They also impair the judgment and reaction times of the user, thus contributing to thousands of deaths and injuries from automobile accidents, rapes, and other assaults. (See Chapter 5 to review the short- and long-term health risks of alcohol.)

Binge drinking occurs when a man consumes five or more drinks in a row or a woman consumes four or more drinks at a time (Weingardt et al., 1998). Approximately 5.1 million Americans between the ages of 12 and 20 years are binge drinkers, and the greatest majority are college students (Wechsler, Lee, Kuo, & Lee, 2000). Binge drinking is a serious health problem for all college-age students, those who drink and those who don't.

What can be done about college binge drinking? Stopping students from binge drinking is very difficult. Students seem to think of it as part of the "college experience." Therefore, any real attack on binge drinking must approach the prob-

Binge drinking can be fatal. *On many college campuses, it is a tradition to "drink your age" on your 21st birthday. Following this tradition, Bradley McCue, a University of Michigan Junior, drank 21 shots of alcohol plus three more to break his friends' record. He died on the morning of his 21st birthday from alcohol poisoning. For more information, contact www.BRAD.org.*

lem from many different directions. First, it is important to overcome the myths about college drinking and teach the facts. But just learning the facts does not stop people from drinking. The social rewards also must be reduced or removed.

So what are these misconceptions, and how do we reduce the social rewards? Henry Wechsler (1998), the first author of *The Harvard School of Public Health College Alcohol Study,* suggests the following:

- **Students who binge tend to think that they are just average or moderate drinkers.** We must make it clear to these students that binge drinking is not the norm. It is not normal or healthy to drink four or five drinks at a sitting, let alone to do that frequently.

- **Many students believe that binge drinking is harmless to the drinker and to college society.** But binge drinkers risk AIDS from unprotected sex and can be the victims or perpetrators of assault, rape, and car accident injuries.

- **Many students think that it's okay to binge-drink because the college administration looks the other way.** College administrations must enforce antidrinking rules and make a greater effort to help students who abuse alcohol. Strict penalties might help repeat offenders.

- **Members of fraternities and sororities seem to think that drinking is part of the Greek life.** College communities therefore have a responsibility to work with these organizations so that drinking is not central to social events.

- **When students see alumni drinking at tailgate parties and hear their stories of partying until dawn, they think that drinking is what alumni expect them to do at college.** Any alcohol-control measures directed at students must also apply to visiting alumni. Sporting events should be alcohol free, and colleges should avoid alcohol-related sports promotions.

GENDER & CULTURAL DIVERSITY

Binge Drinking Around the World

After reading the above section on binge drinking, you may think it is a problem unique to college students in the United States. Unfortunately, binge drinking is a worldwide problem.

- The European School Survey Project (2001) found an overall increase in binge drinking since 1995, especially in Britain, Denmark, Ireland, and Poland. More than 30 percent of school children in those countries reported binge drinking three or more times in the last month.

- In Mexico, a study of drinking patterns at 16 religious fiestas and 13 nonreligious fiestas in the community of Santa María Atzompa found that nearly all the men qualified as binge drinkers at every fiesta. Furthermore, the binge drinking contributed to several outbreaks of violence at the fiestas (Perez, 2000).

- A study in Spain and South America found that young men who reported binge drinking were more likely than others to behave aggressively toward people outside their family (Orpinas, 1999).

- Scientists in Denmark compared the drinking patterns of 56,970 men and women who prefer drinking beer, wine, or spirits (Gronbaek, Tjonneland, Johansen, Stripp, & Overvad, 2000). Results showed that beer drinkers were the least likely of the different types of drinkers to binge, whereas wine drinkers were the most likely to binge.

Alcohol is a global problem. Like the Octoberfest in Munich, Germany, many cultures use alcohol as a common part of holiday celebrations.

- Research on alcohol consumption in Russia shows that 44 percent of men are binge drinkers (Bobak, McKee, Rose, & Marmot, 1999).

- The lower rate of binge drinking in Japan has been linked to a genetic mutation that makes it difficult for many Japanese, and other Asians, to metabolize alcohol. Nearly half of the Japanese population is sensitive to alcohol owing to this genetic mutation. Research shows that Japanese who do not carry the mutation are much more likely to be binge drinkers than those who do not carry the mutation (Takeshita & Morimoto, 1999; Tu & Israel, 1995).

Chronic Pain: The Role of Psychologists in Helping Patients Cope

Chronic Pain *Continuous or recurrent pain over a period of 6 months or more.*

Pain is the most common reason why people seek medical attention. It is the major symptom reported in over 80 percent of all visits to physicians (Turk, 1994). Although we try to avoid pain, it is necessary for our survival. Pain alerts us to dangerous or harmful situations, and pain forces us to rest and recover from injury (Watkins & Maier, 2000). But **chronic pain**, pain that continues long past the healing of a wound or pain that is associated with a chronic disease, does not serve a useful function.

Although psychological factors rarely are the source of chronic pain, they can encourage and intensify it, and increase the related anguish and disability (Affleck, Tennen, & Apter, 2001; Fruehwald, Loffler, Eher, Saletu, & Baumhackl, 2001; Snow-Turek, Norris, & Tan, 1996). To treat chronic pain, health psychologist use specific treatment methods, such as behavior modification, biofeedback, and relaxation.

Behavior Modification

Chronic pain is a serious problem with no simple solution. For example, exercise is known to produce an increase in *endorphins,* naturally produced chemicals that attach themselves to nerve cells in the brain and block the perception of pain (Chapter 2). However, chronic pain patients tend to decrease their activity and exercise. In addition, well-meaning family members often ask chronic pain sufferers, "How are you feeling?" "Is the pain any better today?" Unfortunately, talking about pain focuses attention on it and increases its intensity (Harvey & McGuire, 2000). Furthermore, as the pain increases, anxiety increases, the anxiety itself then increases the pain, which further increases the anxiety, which further increases the pain!

To counteract these hidden personal and family problems and negative cycles, health psychologists may begin a behavior modification program for both the patient with chronic pain and his or her family. The effectiveness of such programs for treating chronic pain was first shown in the late 1970s (Cairns & Pasino, 1977). Researchers established individualized pain management programs, monitored each patient's adherence, and congratulated those who followed through with their pain treatment programs (daily exercise, use of relaxation techniques, and so on). Compared with a control group, patients who used these techniques experienced substantially reduced pain. Today, many pain control programs incorporate similar techniques for rewarding "well behaviors" (Kole-Snijders et al., 1999).

Biofeedback

In *biofeedback,* information about physiological functions, such as heart rate or blood pressure, is monitored, and the feedback helps the individual learn to control these functions. Such feedback about physiological processes helps reduce some types of chronic pain. Most biofeedback with chronic pain patients is done with the *electromyograph* (EMG). This device measures muscle tension by recording electrical activity in the skin. The EMG is most helpful when the pain involves extreme muscle tension, such as tension headache and lower back pain. Electrodes are attached to the site of the pain, and the patient is instructed to relax. When sufficient relaxation is achieved, the machine signals with a tone or a light. The signal serves as feedback to the patient.

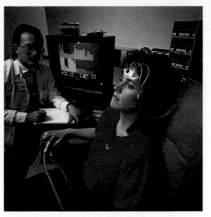

Pain control through biofeedback. Using an electromyograph (EMG), muscular tension is recorded and the patient is taught specific relaxation techniques that reduce tension and help relieve chronic pain.

Research shows that biofeedback is sometimes as effective as more expensive and lengthy forms of treatment (Newton-John, Spence, & Schotte, 1995). The reason for its success seems to be that it teaches patients to recognize patterns of emotional arousal and conflict that affect their physiological responses. This self-awareness, in turn, enables them to learn self-regulation skills that help control their pain (McKee, 1991).

Relaxation Techniques

Because the pain always seems to be there, chronic pain sufferers tend to talk and think about their pain whenever they're not thoroughly engrossed in an activity. Watching TV shows or films, attending parties, or any activity that diverts attention from the pain seems to reduce discomfort. Attention might also be diverted with special *relaxation techniques* like those that are taught in so-called "natural childbirth" classes. These techniques focus the birthing mother's attention on breathing and relaxing the muscles, which helps distract her attention from the fear and pain of the birthing process. Similar techniques also can be helpful to chronic pain sufferers. Remember, though, that these techniques do not eliminate the pain; they merely allow the person to ignore it for a time. (Later in this chapter, you'll learn a relaxation technique that can be used for chronic pain and for everyday stress.)

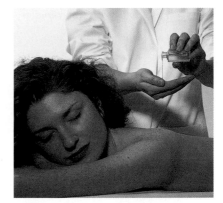

Relaxation techniques. Massage is a healthy way to reduce stress and tension related pain.

Check & Review

BINGE DRINKING AND CHRONIC PAIN

Binge drinking is a serious problem that can lead to rape or assault, to death from alcohol poisoning, or automobile and other accidents. It occurs when a man has five or more drinks in a row and a woman has four or more. To reduce binge drinking, we must overcome the myths about drinking and teach the facts. We also must reduce or remove the social rewards.

Chronic pain is continuous or recurrent pain that persists over a period of six months or more.

Although psychological factors rarely are the source of chronic pain, they can encourage and intensify it. Increased activity, exercise, and dietary changes help to reduce chronic pain. Health psychologists also use behavior modification, biofeedback, and relaxation techniques to treat chronic pain.

Questions

1. What is binge drinking?

2. What are the 5 misconceptions about binge drinking, and how can we remove the social reinforcers?

3. Continuous or recurrent pain over a period of 6 months or more is known as _____.

4. An increase in activity and exercise levels benefits patients with pain because exercise increases the release of (a) endorphins; (b) insulin; (c) acetylcholine; (d) norepinephrine.

Answers to Questions can be found in Appendix B.

STRESS AND ITS ROLE IN HEALTH

What is stress, and what are its major sources and results?

Stress *A nonspecific response of the body to any demand made on it; the arousal, both physical and mental, to situations or events that we perceive as threatening or challenging.*

Eustress *Pleasant, desirable stress*

Distress *Unpleasant, objectionable stress*

Hans Selye (1974), a physiologist renowned for his research and writing in the area of stress since the 1930s, defines **stress** as the nonspecific response of the body to any demand made on it. When you play two nonstop tennis matches in the middle of a heat wave, your body responds with a fast heartbeat, rapid breathing, and an outpouring of perspiration. When you find out 10 minutes before class starts that the term paper you just started is due today rather than next Friday, your body has the same physiological stress response to a very different stressor. Stress reactions can occur to either internal, cognitive stimuli or external, environmental stimuli (Baum & Posluszny, 1999).

The body is nearly always in some state of stress, whether pleasant or unpleasant, mild or severe. *Anything* placing a demand on the body can cause stress. When stress is beneficial, such as moderate exercise, it is called **eustress** and when it is objectionable, as from chronic illness, it is called **distress** (Selye, 1974). The total absence of stress would mean the total absence of external stimulation, which would eventually lead to death. Because health psychology has been chiefly concerned with the negative effects of stress, we will adhere to convention and use the word "stress" to refer primarily to harmful or unpleasant stress (Selye's *distress*), even though there are some forms of beneficial *eustress*.

Sources of Stress: From Major Life Changes to Minor Hassles

Although stress is pervasive in our lives, some things cause more stress than others. The major sources of stress are life changes, chronic stressors, hassles, burnout, frustration, and conflict.

THE FAR SIDE® BY GARY LARSON

© 1985 FarWorks, Inc. All Rights Reserved/Dist. by Creators Syndicate

"The fuel light's on, Frank! We're all going to die! ... Wait, wait. ... Oh, my mistake— that's the intercom light."

Life Changes

The College Life Stress Inventory that you took at the beginning of the chapter is designed especially for college students. It is based on an earlier inventory developed for adults past college age by Thomas Holmes and Richard Rahe (1967) — the Social Readjustment Rating Scale (SRRS). The SRRS measures stress related to *life changes* brought about by major events, such as marriage, the death of a family member, moving to a new home, and getting (or losing) a job.

Such major changes disrupt our lives and cause more stress than normal. Holmes and Rahe believed that change, of any kind, that required some adjustment in behavior or lifestyle caused stress. Moreover, they believed that exposure to numerous stressful events within a short period of time could have a detrimental effect on health. Keep in mind, however, that Holmes and Rahe use the scientific definition of *stress*. Therefore, change can be anguishing, as with the loss of a parent or divorce, but it can also be joyous, as in the case of a marriage, or emotionally neutral, as with a change in work hours. The point is that all change causes stress. And too much stress can exceed the body's ability to cope, leading to moderate or serious illness.

In recent years, Mark Miller and Richard Rahe updated the original Holmes and Rahe SRRS. As you can see in Table 3.1, this scale is very similar to the one at the beginning of the chapter, but it is designed for older adults outside of college. These items are ranked according to their relative importance in contributing to health problems. Each event is assigned a numerical rating expressed in *life change units* (LCUs). To score yourself on this scale, add up the LCUs for all life events you have experienced during the last year and compare your score with the following standards: 0–150 = No significant problems, 150–199 = Mild life crisis (33 percent chance of illness), 200–299 = Moderate life crisis (50 percent chance of illness), 300 and above Major life crisis (80 percent chance of illness).

The SRRS scale is an easy and popular way to measure stress, and cross-cultural studies have shown that most people rank the magnitude of stressful events in similar ways (McAndrew, Akande, Turner, & Sharma, 1998). However, the SRRS is not foolproof. First, it only shows a *correlation* between stress and illness, and as you recall from Chapter 1, *correlation does not prove causation*. Like results on all correlational studies, stress could cause subsequent illnesses, but they could also be caused by other (yet unknown) factors.

In addition, as noted earlier, stress varies according to the individual. Any one event may be perceived as a stressful ordeal, a neutral occurrence, or an exciting opportunity. It depends on your personal interpretation and appraisal (Whelan & Kirkby, 2000). You might find moving to another state a terrible sacrifice and a tremendous stressor, whereas your friend might see the move as a wonderful opportunity and experience little or no stress. Furthermore, different people have differing abilities to deal with change, perhaps because of good coping skills, general physical health, healthier lifestyles, or even genetic predisposition.

Chronic Stressors

Not all stressful situations are single, short-term events such as a death or a birth. A bad marriage, poor working conditions, or an intolerable political climate can be *chronic stressors*. Even the stress of chronic aircraft noise is associated with measurable hormonal and cardiac changes (Evans et al., 1995). Our social lives also can be chronically stressful, because making and maintaining friendships involves considerable thought and energy (Griffith, Dubow, & Ippolito, 2000).

Perhaps the largest source of chronic stress is work. People often experience stress associated with keeping or changing jobs or with job performance (Steptoe, Cropley, & Joekes, 2000). However, the most stressful jobs are those that make great demands on performance and concentration but allow little creativity or opportunity for advancement (Parasuraman & Purohit, 2000). Assembly-line work ranks very high in this category.

Chronic stress? Although assembly line work might seem stress-free, the lack of creativity and little opportunity for advancement make this a highly stressful job.

TABLE 3.1 SOCIAL READJUSTMENT RATING SCALE

Life Events	Life Change Units
Death of spouse	100
Divorce	73
Marital separation	65
Jail term	63
Death of a close family member	63
Personal injury or illness	53
Marriage	50
Fired at work	47
Marital reconciliation	45
Retirement	45
Change in health of family member	44
Pregnancy	40
Sex difficulties	39
Gain of a new family member	39
Business readjustment	39
Change in financial state	38
Death of a close friend	37
Change to different line of work	36
Change in number of arguments with spouse	35
Mortgage or loan for major purchase	31
Foreclosure on mortgage or loan	30
Change in responsibilities at work	29
Son or daughter leaving home	29
Trouble with in-laws	29
Outstanding personal achievement	28
Spouse begins or stops work	26
Begin or end school	26
Change in living conditions	25
Revision of personal habits	24
Trouble with boss	23
Change in work hours or conditions	20
Change in residence	20
Change in schools	20
Change in recreation	19
Change in church activities	19
Change in social activities	18
Mortgage or loan for lesser purchase (car, major appliance)	17
Change in sleeping habits	16
Change in number of family get-togethers	15
Change in eating habits	15
Vacation	13
Christmas	12
Minor violations of the law	11

Source: Holmes & Rahe (1967).

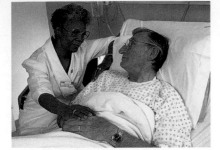

Is nursing a stressful career? People who think of their profession as a "calling" may lose their idealism when faced with the ongoing stresses and emotional turmoil. Over time they may suffer a type of mental and physical exhaustion known as "burn out."

Hassles *Little problems of daily living that are not significant in themselves but that accumulate and sometimes become a major source of stress*

Burnout *A state of physical, emotional, and mental exhaustion attributable to long-term involvement in emotionally demanding situations*

Researchers have documented that stress at work can also cause serious stress at home not only for workers but for other family members as well. And, of course, in our private lives, divorce, child and spouse abuse, alcoholism, and money problems can place severe stress on all members of a family (Grunberg, Moore, Anderson-Connolly, & Greenberg, 1999; Thompson & Kaslow, 2000; Tien, Sandler, & Zautra, 2000).

Hassles and Burnout

In addition to chronic stressors, a great deal of daily stress is in the form of **hassles**, little problems of daily living that are not significant in themselves but that pile up to become a major source of stress (Repetti, 1993). Some hassles tend to be shared by all: time pressures (getting to work or school on time, finding a parking place, fighting traffic jams), problems with family and coworkers (equitable sharing of work, scheduling conflicts, gossip), and financial concerns (competing demands for available funds, increasing prices). But our reactions to hassles may vary. For example, compared to women, men tend to have more impairment of their immune system and an increased heart rate in response to hassles (Delahanty et al., 2000; Scanlan, Vitaliano, Ochs, Savage, & Borson, 1998).

Some authorities believe hassles can be more significant than major life events in creating stress (Lazarus, 1999; Tien, Sandler, & Zautra, 2000). For example, divorce is extremely stressful, but it may so be because of the increased number of hassles — change in finances, child-care arrangements, longer working hours, and so on. Similarly, a move is a stressful life change, but preparing to move or having your house up for sale for an extended period of time can be more stressful than the actual move itself.

Persistent hassles in your work situation can lead to a form of physical, mental, and emotional exhaustion known as **burnout**. Although the term has become an overused buzzword, health psychologists use it to describe a specific syndrome that develops most commonly in idealistic people who are exposed to chronically stressful and emotionally draining professions (Alexander & Hegarty, 2000; Melamed et al., 1999). People who tend to think of their job as a "calling" tend to enter their careers with a high sense of motivation and commitment. But over

TRY THIS

Kanner and others developed a *Hassles Scale* to assess those everyday events on the job, at school, and in interpersonal relations that annoy, frustrate, and anger us (Kanner, Coyne, Schaefer, & Lazarus, 1981). Write down the top 10 hassles you most commonly experience and then compare your answers to the following list:

The 10 Most Common Hassles for College Students

		Percentage of Times Checked
1.	Troubling thoughts about the future	76.6
2.	Not getting enough sleep	72.5
3.	Wasting time	71.1
4.	Inconsiderate smokers	70.7
5.	Physical appearance	69.9
6.	Too many things to do	69.2
7.	Misplacing or losing things	67.0
8.	Not enough time to do the things you need to do	66.3
9.	Concerns about meeting high standards	64.0
10.	Being lonely	60.8

Source: Kanner, A. D., Coyne, J. C., Schaefer, C., & Lazarus, R. S. (1981). Comparison of two modes of stress measurement: Daily hassles and uplifts versus major life events. *Journal of Behavioral Medicine, 4,* 1–39.

time, some become emotionally drained and disillusioned and feel a loss of personal accomplishment — they "burn out." The result may be increased absences from work, a sharp downturn in productivity, and an increased risk of physical problems. Police officers, nurses, social workers, and teachers are particularly vulnerable.

Frustration

Frustration is a negative emotional state generally associated with a blocked goal such as not being accepted for admission to your first-choice college. The more motivated we are, the more frustration we experience when our goals are blocked. After getting stuck in traffic and missing an important appointment, we may become very frustrated. On the other hand, if the same traffic jam causes us to be five minutes late to a painful medical appointment, we may experience little or no frustration.

Frustration *An unpleasant state of tension, anxiety, and heightened sympathetic activity resulting from a blocked goal*

Conflicts

A final source of stress is **conflict,** which arises when people are forced to make a choice between at least two incompatible alternatives. The amount of stress produced by a conflict depends on the complexity of the conflict itself, and the difficulty involved in resolving it. There are three basic types of conflict: *approach–approach, avoidance–avoidance,* and *approach–avoidance.*

Conflict *A negative emotional state caused by having to choose between two or more incompatible goals or impulses*

In an **approach–approach conflict,** a person must choose between two or more *favorable* alternatives. Thus, no matter what choice is made, the result will be desirable. At first it might seem that this type of conflict shouldn't create any stress, but consider this example. Suppose you have to choose between two summer jobs. One job is at a resort where you will meet interesting people and have a good time; the other will provide you with valuable experience and look impressive on your résumé. No matter which job you choose, you will benefit in some way. In fact, you would like to take both jobs, but you can't. The requirement to choose is the source of stress.

Approach–Approach Conflict *Conflict in which a person must choose between two or more alternatives that will lead to desirable results*

An **avoidance–avoidance conflict** involves making a choice between two or more unpleasant alternatives that will lead to negative results, no matter which choice is made. In the book (and film) *Sophie's Choice,* Sophie and her two children are sent to a German concentration camp. A soldier demands that she give up (apparently to be killed) either her daughter or her son, or they both will be killed. Obviously, neither alternative is acceptable; both will have tragic results. Although this is an extreme example, avoidance–avoidance conflicts can lead to intense stress.

Avoidance–Avoidance Conflict *Conflict in which a person must choose between two or more alternatives that will both lead to undesirable results*

An **approach–avoidance conflict** occurs when a person must choose between alternatives that will have both desirable and undesirable results. We have all been faced with such decisions as "I want to spend more time in a close relationship, but that means I won't be able to see as much of my old friends." This conflict thus leads to a great deal of ambivalence. In an approach–avoidance conflict, we experience both good and bad results from any alternative we choose.

Approach–Avoidance Conflict *Conflict in which a person must make a choice that will lead to both desirable and undesirable results*

The longer any conflict exists or the more important the decision, the more stress a person will experience. Generally, the approach–approach conflict is the easiest to resolve and produces the least stress. The avoidance–avoidance conflict, on the other hand, is usually the most difficult because all choices lead to unpleasant results. Approach–avoidance conflicts are somewhat less stressful than avoidance–avoidance conflicts and are usually moderately difficult to resolve.

TRY THIS
Yourself

One thing that seems to increase the hassles and frustration in our lives is the fact that technology is constantly changing. In their book *TechnoStress: Coping with technology @WORK @HOME @PLAY,* Michelle Weil and Larry Rosen (1997) discuss how emerging technologies can add stress to our lives.

Do any of the following situations sound familiar to you? Buying a new VCR that is (still!) impossible to program? Coming across yet another bug in your new word processing program that dumps your entire term paper? Playing endless phone tag with a professor whom you want to write a recommendation for you? Never getting your e-mail cleaned up because of endless ads and dumb jokes? Being stranded on the freeway because the computer that controls your car's engine malfunctions? These are examples of technostress.

Just as some handle generalized stress differently, people handle technostress in different ways. Weil and Rosen identify three techno-types. You can readily categorize yourself by answering the questions in the following techno-type quiz:

1. Suppose that for your birthday someone gives you a new electronic kitchen appliance (a coffeemaker, for example) that is completely computerized. Which of the following best describes how you would feel when you open the package?
   a. Thrilled, excited, and eager. Can't wait to give it a try.
   b. Hesitant and wondering if you really need it. The way you do it now works just fine. Maybe you'll just put it away for now.
   c. Upset, worried, or nervous. Unsure of your ability to use it correctly. Considering how you can return it for something a bit more practical.
2. When you want to record a TV show that airs while you are at work, what do you do?
   a. Quickly, confidently, and easily program the VCR to record the show.
   b. Ask your son, daughter, or spouse to set the VCR, or find the manual and try to figure out how to do it. You

know it's possible but are unsure that you'll be able to make it work.
   c. Squelch the thought, unless there is someone in the house to do it for you. After all, aren't VCRs just for playing rented movies?
3. Your friend calls and tells you that he just bought a new state-of-the-art, souped-up multimedia computer system and wants you to come see it. What's your response?
   a. Drop all your plans for the weekend, run right over, and play with the new toy for 8 hours.
   b. Murmur words of congratulations and promise to get over to see it as soon as your schedule clears.
   c. Pretend to listen, adding appropriately placed *oh*'s and *uh-huh*'s while clearly evading the request.

How did you do? If you answered *a* to two or three of the questions, chances are that you are what is called an *eager adopter.* If you mostly answered *B,* you, like most people, are most probably a *hesitant "prove it."* If you felt that *c* was the answer for you, you are a *resister.*

According to Weil and Rosen, eager adopters love technology. They make up only 10 to 15 percent of the population, but they consider technology fun and are the first to buy the latest gadget. Hesitant "prove its" account for one-half to two-thirds of the population, and they do not think technology is fun. They take a wait-and-see attitude, but once they are convinced that a new technology will make their life easier or is necessary, they will try to adopt it. Finally, the resisters avoid technology because they feel inadequate.

If you are an eager adopter, you are probably not stressed by technology. If you are one of the other types, consider this advice to relieve technostress: First, evaluate each new technology on its usefulness for you and your lifestyle. If something is useful, try to use it in the least stressful manner. Second, recognize that technology is here to stay, and you can learn to cope with technostress just as you do with other types of stress.

Check & Review

SOURCES OF STRESS

Stress is the body's arousal, both physical and mental, to situations or events that we perceive as threatening or challenging. A situation or event, either pleasant or unpleasant, that triggers arousal and causes stress is known as a stressor.

The major sources of stress are life changes, chronic stressors, hassles, burnout, frustration, and conflicts. Chronic stressors are ongoing events such as poor working conditions. **Hassles** are little everyday life problems that pile up to cause major stress. Persistent hassles and a loss of initial idealism in your work situation can lead to a form of physical, mental, and emotional exhaustion known as **burnout**. **Frustration** has to do with blocked goals, whereas **conflict** involves two or more competing goals. Conflicts can be classified as **approach–approach**, **avoidance– avoidance**, or **approach–avoidance**.

Questions

1. John was planning to ask Susan to marry him. When he saw Susan kissing another man at a party, he was quite upset. In this situation, John's seeing Susan kissing another man is _____, and it illustrates _____. (a) a stressor, distress; (b) eustress, a stressor; (c) distress, a stressor; (d) a stressor, eustress.

2. The Social Readjustment Rating Scale constructed by Holmes and Rahe measures the stress situation in a person's life on the basis of _____. (a) life changes; (b) stress tolerance; (c) daily hassles; (d) the balance between eustress and distress.

3. Frustration is a negative emotional state that is generally associated with _____, whereas _____ is a negative emotional state caused by an inability to choose between two or more incompatible goals or impulses.

4. Give an example for each of the 3 types of conflict: approach–approach, approach–avoidance, and avoidance–avoidance.

Answers to Questions can be found in Appendix B.

Results of Stress: How the Body Responds

When stressed either mentally or physically, your body undergoes several major and minor physiological changes, some of which we have already mentioned. The most significant changes are controlled by the autonomic nervous system (Chapter 2) and are particularly important because they can lower the body's resistance to disease.

Physiological Effects of Stress

Under normal, everyday low-stress conditions, the parasympathetic part of the autonomic nervous system tends to lower heart rate and blood pressure, while increasing muscle movement in the stomach and intestines. This allows the body to conserve energy, absorb nutrients, and maintain normal functioning. Under stressful conditions, the sympathetic part of the autonomic nervous system is dominant. It increases heart rate, blood pressure, respiration, and muscle tension; decreases the movement of stomach muscles; constricts blood vessels; and releases hormones such as epinephrine (adrenaline) and cortisol. These hormones in turn release fats and glucose into the bloodstream for energy.

Fight or Flight

There is a good reason for all this sympathetic activity. At the beginning of human evolutionary history, the autonomic nervous system served as the fight-or-flight system. Back then, when a person was under extreme stress — when she was confronted by a bear or he found big, strong strangers hunting in his territory — there were only two reasonable alternatives: fight or flight. Our ancestors, when faced with such stressors, needed the physiological boosts supplied by their sympathetic nervous system.

Today we have the same autonomic responses of our ancient ancestors, but our world is quite different. When we encounter stressful situations, we rarely jump into action. If we hear from our boss that we're being fired or that the stock market just dropped another 20 percent, we cannot "fight or flee." We have little need for the

Stress in ancient times. The automatic, "fight or flight" response was adaptive and necessary for early human survival. However, in modern society it occurs as a response to situations in which we cannot fight or flee, and is often detrimental to our health.

increased heart rate, blood pressure, and hormone levels produced by our autonomic nervous system. In fact, we are taught not to fight or to flee but to stay calm and resolve stressful situations rationally. When we comply with these cultural rules, we are left with all the arousal but no outlet for the physical changes caused by stressors. Thus, in modern times, the fight/flight response of the autonomic nervous system is less helpful than to our ancestors. It might even be maladaptive and dangerous (Arnsten, 1998).

Stress causes physiological changes that in the long run can be detrimental to health. Hans Selye, who was mentioned earlier in the chapter, described a generalized physiological reaction to severe stressors that he called the **general adaptation syndrome** (GAS) (1936). Figure 3.1 shows the three phases of this reaction. In the initial phase, called the *alarm reaction*, the body reacts to the stressor by activating the sympathetic nervous system (with increases in heart rate, blood pressure, secretion of hormones, and so on). The body has abundant energy and is alert and ready to deal with the stressor but is in a lowered state of resistance to illness.

If the stressor remains, the body enters the *resistance phase*. Now the alarm reaction subsides and the body adapts to the stressor, with resistance to illness increasing above normal levels. However, this adaptation and resistance phase is very taxing, and long-term exposure to the stressor may eventually lead to the *exhaustion phase* if the resistance is not successful. During this final stage, the signs of the alarm reaction reappear, resistance to illness decreases, all adaptation energy becomes depleted, and our susceptibility to illness increases. In severe cases, long-term exposure to stressors can be life threatening because we become vulnerable to serious illness such as heart attacks, stroke, and cancer.

General Adaptation Syndrome *As described by Hans Selye, a generalized physiological reaction to severe stressors consisting of three phases: the alarm reaction, the resistance phase, and the exhaustion phase*

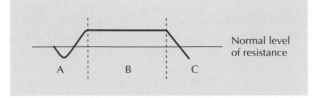

Figure 3.1 *The general adaptation syndrome (GAS).* According to Hans Selye, when the body is exposed to severe, prolonged stress, it goes through three phases. During the initial phase, the alarm reaction (A), the body is in a lowered state of resistance to illness. If the stress continues, the body enters the resistance phase (B), when it is in a heightened state of resistance. After prolonged exposure to stress, the body enters the exhaustion phase (C), when resistance to illness decreases. Eventually this can lead to death.

Stress and the Immune System

A relatively new field, **psychoneuroimmunology**, studies the interactions of psychological factors (*psycho-*), the nervous and endocrine systems (*neuro-*), and the immune system (*immunology*). This interdisciplinary research has shown that the sympathetic nervous system is *directly* linked to virtually every part of the immune system and that physiological changes caused by stress (such as bereavement, surgery, sleep deprivation, or divorce) can suppress immune system functioning (De Moranville et al., 2000; Leonard, 2000; Miller & Cohen, 2001). Normal functioning of the immune system includes detecting and defending against disease. Therefore, a suppressed immune system leaves the body susceptible to illness. Changes in immune function have been linked to high levels of such stress-related hormones as epinephrine, norepinephrine, and cortisol in the bloodstream. Apparently, increases in these hormones often precede suppressed immune system function and the appearance of disease.

But how does something psychological, like bereavement, affect the cells of the immune system? Psychological factors do not directly affect cells of the immune system. Rather, a psychological stressor (such as death of a loved one) activates the autonomic fight-or-flight response. Autonomic functioning mobilizes the body's energy resources for immediate survival by releasing hormones, such as cortisol, that put all the body's long-term processes — tissue repair, immunity, digestion, reproduction — on hold, thus making more energy available to the brain and muscles. If the emergency lasts only a few minutes, this is a good solution to the fight–flight problem, and immune functioning soon resumes. But when a person is under prolonged stress, such as a difficult final exam schedule or a bad marriage that lasts for years, he or she is constantly in a state of heightened autonomic activation and may have reduced immune system response for an extended period.

Does this mean that I might get a cold or the flu just because I've been under a lot of stress? Sheldon Cohen and his colleagues (1998, 1999) have conducted studies that show stress does indeed have a small to moderate effect both on becoming infected with the cold virus and on exhibiting full-blown cold symptoms. It seems that stress suppresses the body's defenses that normally prevent the cold virus from multiplying and spreading throughout the body.

Psychoneuroimmunology [sye-koh-NEW-roh-IM-you-NOLL-oh-gee] *An interdisciplinary field that studies the effects of psychological factors on the immune system*

RESEARCH HIGHLIGHT

Procrastination, Performance, and Health

If your professor assigned a term paper for this class, have you already started working on it? Or are you putting it off until the last minute? Have you ever wondered if working continuously on a term paper from the first day of class until the paper is due might ultimately be more stressful than putting off the paper until the last minute?

To answer this question, Dianne Tice and Roy Baumeister (1997) at Case Western Reserve University assigned a term paper in their health psychology class at the beginning of the semester. Throughout the semester, they carefully monitored the stress, health, and procrastination levels of 44 student volunteers from the class. After the term papers were submitted at the end of the course, Tice and Baumeister found that procrastinators suffered significantly more stress and developed more health problems than nonprocrastinators. They

were also more likely to turn in their papers late and earn lower grades on those papers.

In the Tools for Student Success section in Chapter 1, you learned that research shows that spacing out your studying rather than cramming the night before produces higher scores on exams. Now you have additional research showing that distributed work also produces better grades on term papers — as well as less stress. The bottom line is this: *Don't procrastinate.* It can be hazardous to your health, as well as your grades.

Check & Review

RESULTS OF STRESS

When stressed, the body undergoes physiological changes. The sympathetic branch of the autonomic nervous system is activated, increasing heart rate and blood pressure. This sympathetic activation is beneficial if people need to fight or flee, but in today's world, it generally has negative consequences.

Hans Selye described a generalized physiological reaction to severe stressors, which he called the **general adaptation** syndrome (GAS). It has three phases: the alarm reaction, the resistance phase, and the exhaustion phase. Prolonged stress can suppress the immune system, which can render the body susceptible to a number of diseases.

Questions

1. How does the autonomic nervous system respond to stress?

2. The GAS consists of three phases: the _____ reaction, the _____ phase, and the _____ phase.

3. As Michael watches his instructor pass out papers, he suddenly realizes this is the first major exam and he is totally unprepared. Which phase of the GAS is the most likely experiencing? (a) resistance; (b) alarm; (c) exhaustion; (d) phaseout.

4. Why do students tend to get sick with a cold or flu during midterms or finals?

STRESS AND SERIOUS ILLNESS

How is stress related to serious illnesses like cancer and coronary heart disease?

We now know that many diseases far more serious than the common cold are either caused by or made worse by stress. Some of these are heart disease, cancer, rheumatoid arthritis, bursitis, migraine headache, asthma, and gastrointestinal conditions such as ulcers and colitis (Kiecolt-Glaser & Glaser, 2001; Matuszek, 2000; Sapolsky, 1999; Wu et al., 2000). In this section, we will explore how stress is related to two of our main killers — *cancer* and *coronary heart disease*.

Cancer: A Variety of Causes — Even Stress

The word *cancer* is frightening to nearly everyone, and for good reason: Cancer is among the leading causes of death for adults in the U.S. It occurs when a particular type of primitive body cell begins rapidly dividing, and then forms a tumor that invades healthy tissue. Unless destroyed or removed, the tumor eventually damages organs and causes death. To date, over 100 types of cancer have been identified. They appear to be caused by an interaction between environmental factors and inherited predispositions.

To understand how the environment contributes to cancer, it helps to know what normally happens to cancerous cells. Whenever cancer cells start to multiply, the immune system checks the uncontrolled growth by attacking the abnormal cells (see the accompanying photograph). This goes on constantly, with abnormal cells arising, and, in a healthy person, the immune system keeping cancer cells in check.

Something different happens when the body is stressed. As you read earlier, the stress response involves the release of adrenal hormones that suppress immune system functioning. The compromised immune system is less able to resist infection and cancer development. An experimental animal study found that stress inhibited immune system defenses against cancer and promoted tumor growth (Wu et al., 2000). Other research with humans suggests that stress can also directly affect lymphocytes, the main immune system cells that control cancer (Goebel & Mills, 2000).

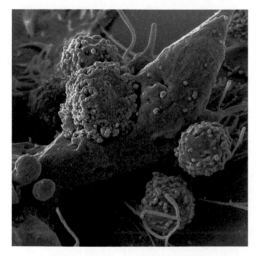

White blood cells and the immune system. The round structure near the left center of this photomicrograph is a T-lymphocyte, a type of white blood cell produced by the immune system. It has just killed a cancer cell, the sweet potato-shaped structure.

The good news is that we can substantially reduce our risk of cancer by making changes that reduce our stress level and enhance our immune system. For example, even mild sleep deprivation can affect the immune system. When researchers interrupted the sleep of 23 men and then measured their *natural killer cells* (a type of immune system cell), they found the killer cells were 28 percent below average (Irwin et al., 1994). Can you see how staying up late studying for an exam (or partying) can decrease the effectiveness of your immune system? Fortunately, these researchers also found that a normal night's sleep after the deprivation returned the killer cells to their normal levels.

Cardiovascular Disorders: The Leading Cause of Death in the United States

Cardiovascular disorders are the cause of over half of all deaths in the United States (Centers for Disease Control, 2001). Understandably, then, health psychologists are concerned because stress is a major contributor to these deaths. *Heart disease* is a general term for all disorders that eventually affect the heart muscle and lead to heart failure. *Coronary heart disease* results from *atherosclerosis*, a thickening of the walls of the coronary arteries that reduces or blocks the blood supply to the heart. Atherosclerosis causes *angina* (chest pain due to insufficient blood supply to the heart) or *heart attack* (death of heart muscle tissue). Controllable factors that contribute to heart disease include stress, smoking, certain personality characteristics, obesity, a high-fat diet, and lack of exercise (American Heart Association, 2000; Tennant, 1999).

How does stress contribute to heart disease? Recall that one of the major autonomic nervous system fight–flight reactions is the release of epinephrine and cortisol into the bloodstream. These hormones increase heart rate and release fat from the body's stores to give muscles a quickly available source of energy.

If no physical action is taken (and this is most likely the case in our modern lives), the fat released into the bloodstream is not burned as fuel and may become fatty deposits on the walls of blood vessels (Figure 3.2). These fatty deposits are a major cause of blood supply blockage that causes heart attacks. In other words, if stress causes blocked arteries and blocked arteries cause heart attacks, then people who are continually under a lot of stress are prone to heart attacks.

Personality Types

The effects of stress on heart disease may be amplified if an individual tends to be hard driving, competitive, ambitious, impatient, and hostile. People with such

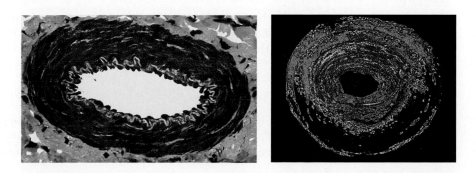

Figure 3.2 *Fatty deposits in arteries.* One major cause of heart disease is the blockage of arteries that supply blood to the heart. The artery at the left is normal; the one on the right is almost completely blocked. Reducing stress, exercising, and eating a low-fat diet can help prevent the buildup of fatty deposits in the arteries.

Type A Personality *Set of behavior characteristics that includes intense ambition, competition, drive, constant preoccupation with responsibilities, exaggerated time urgency, and a cynical, hostile outlook*

Type B Personality *Set of behavior characteristics consistent with a calm, patient, relaxed attitude toward life*

Type A personalities are chronically on edge, tend to talk rapidly, feel intense time urgency, and are preoccupied with responsibilities. The antithesis of the Type A personality is Type B. People with a **Type B personality** have a laid-back, calm, relaxed attitude toward life.

Two cardiologists, Meyer Friedman and Ray Rosenman (1959) were the first to identify and describe the Type A personality. The story goes that in the mid-1950s, an upholsterer who was recovering the waiting room chairs in Friedman's office noticed an odd wear pattern. He mentioned to Friedman that all the chairs looked like new except for the front edges, which were badly worn, as if all the patients sat only on the edges of the chairs. Initially, this didn't seem too important to Friedman. However, this chronic sense of time urgency and being literally "on the edge of your seat" was later believed to be a possible contributing factor to heart disease and the hallmark of the Type A personality.

Initial research into Type A behavior suggested Friedman and Rosenman were right, but more recent research has been less supportive. When researchers examined the relationship between characteristics of the Type A behavior pattern and heart disease, they found that the critical component and strongest predictor of heart disease was *hostility* (Fredrikson, Wik, & Fischer, 1999; Miller, Smith, Turner, Guijarro, & Hallet, 1996).

Actually, *cynical* hostility appears to be the most important factor in the Type A relationship to heart disease. Having a negative attitude toward the world means cynical people always expect problems. They are constantly alert and "on watch," trying to foresee problems and possibly avert them. This attitude produces a nearly constant state of stress, which translates physiologically into higher blood pressure, heart rate, and production of stress-related hormones. In addition, because of their hostile, suspicious, argumentative, and competitive style, these people tend to have more interpersonal conflicts (Friedman, Hawley, and Tucker, 1994). Constant interpersonal conflicts can lead to a loss of social support and heightened autonomic activation, which can then lead to increased risk of cardiovascular disease (Sher, 2000; Tennant, 1999).

Can people with a Type A personality change their behavior? Health psychologists have developed two types of behavior modification to help people with Type A personality — the *shotgun approach* and the *target behavior approach*. The *shotgun approach* aims to change all the behaviors that relate to the Type A personality. Friedman and his colleagues (1986) use the shotgun approach in their Recurrent Coronary Prevention Program. The program provides individual counseling, dietary advice, exercise, drugs, and group therapy to eliminate or modify Type A behaviors. Type A's are specifically encouraged to slow down and perform tasks incompatible with their personalities. For example, they might try to listen to other people without interrupting or stand in the longest supermarket line on purpose. The major criticism of the shotgun approach is that it eliminates desirable (ambitiousness and drive) as well as undesirable Type A traits (cynicism and hostility).

The alternative approach, the *target behavior approach*, focuses on only those Type A behaviors that are likely to cause heart disease — namely, cynical hostility. By modifying target behaviors, the person will likely reduce his or her risk of heart disease.

Hardiness

In addition to Type A and Type B personalities, there may be other personality patterns that affect the way we respond to stress. Have you ever wondered how some people survive in the face of great stress (repeated personal tragedies, demanding jobs, and even a poor home life) but others do not? Suzanne Kobasa was among the first to study this question (Kobasa, 1979, Pengilly & Dowd, 2000). Examining male executives with high levels of stress, she found that some people are more resistant to stress than others because of a personality factor called **hardiness**, a resilient type of optimism that comes from three distinctive attitudes:

1. *Commitment.* Hardy people feel a strong sense of commitment to both their work and personal life. They also make intentional commitments to purposeful activity and problem solving.

2. *Control.* These people also see themselves not as victims of whatever life brings but as personally in control.

3. *Challenge.* Finally, hardy people look at change as an opportunity for growth and improvement — not as a threat. Hardy people welcome challenges.

The important lesson from this research is that hardiness is a *learned behavior* — not luck or genetics. If you're not one of the *hardy* souls, you can develop the trait. The next time you face a bad stressor, such as four exams in one week, try using the 3 C's: "I am fully *committed* to my college education." "I can *control* the number of tests by taking one or two of them earlier than scheduled, or I can rearrange my work schedule." "I welcome this *challenge* as a final motivation to enroll in those reading improvement and college success courses I've always planned to take."

Before we go on, it's also important to note that Type A personality and lack of hardiness are not the only controllable risk factors associated with heart disease. Smoking, obesity, and lack of exercise are very important factors. Smoking restricts blood circulation, and obesity stresses the heart by causing it to pump more blood to the excess body tissue. A high-fat diet, especially one high in cholesterol, contributes to the fatty deposits that clog blood vessels. Lack of exercise contributes to weight gain and prevents the body from obtaining important exercise benefits, including strengthening heart muscle, increasing heart efficiency, and releasing hormones such as serotonin that alleviate stress and promote well-being.

Hardiness *A resilient personality characteristic based on three qualities: a commitment to personal goals, control over life, and viewing change as a challenge rather than a threat.*

Check & Review

STRESS AND SERIOUS ILLNESS

Cancer appears to result from an interaction of heredity, environmental insults (such as smoking), and immune system deficiency. Stress may be an importnat cause of decreased immunity. During times of stress, the body may be less able to check cancerous tissue growth because the immune system is suppressed.

The leading cause of death in the United States is heart disease. Risk factors in heart disease include smoking, stress, obesity, a high-fat diet, lack of exercise, and **Type A personality** (if it includes cynical hostil-ity). The two main approaches to modifying Type A behavior are the shotgun approach and the target behavior approach. People with psychological **hardiness** are less vulnerable to stress because of three distinctive personality characteristics — commitment, control, and challenge.

Questions

1. Stress can contribute to heart disease by releasing the hormones _____ and _____, which increase the level of fat in the blood.

2. Which of the following is *not* among the characteristics associated with Type A personality? (a) time urgency; (b) patience; (c) competition; (d) hostility.

3. The two major approaches to modifying Type A behavior are the _____ approach and the _____ approach. Which one do you think would work best for you, and why?

4. Explain how the three characteristics of the hardy personality help reduce stress.

Answers to Questions can be found in Appendix B.

COPING WITH STRESS

> What techniques and resources are available to help people cope with stress?

It would be helpful if we could avoid all negative stressful situations, but this is impossible. Everyone encounters pressure at work, long lines at the bank, and the death of a family member. Because we can't escape stress, we need to learn how to effectively cope with it. Lazarus and Folkman (1984) defined *coping* as "constantly changing cognitive and behavioral efforts to manage specific external and/or internal demands that are appraised as taxing or exceeding the resource of the person." In simpler terms, coping is an attempt to manage stress in some effective way. It is not one single act but a process that allows us to deal with various stressors. The coping process can focus on the emotional effects of the stressor or on solving the problem causing the stress.

Emotion-Focused Forms of Coping: Reappraising the Situation

Emotion-Focused Forms of Coping *Coping strategies based on changing one's perceptions of stressful situations*

Emotion-focused forms of coping are emotional or cognitive strategies that change how we view a stressful situation. Suppose you are refused a highly desirable job or rejected by a desired lover. You might reappraise the situation and decide that the job or lover might not have been the right match for you or that you weren't really qualified or ready for that specific job or relationship.

One of the most common forms of emotion-focused coping is the use of **defense mechanisms**, unconscious strategies that protect the ego and avoid anxiety by distorting reality (Chapter 13). The use of defense mechanisms reduces anxiety and often helps us cope with unavoidable stress. For instance, *fantasizing* about what you will do once you graduate from college can motivate you to study for exams.

Defense Mechanisms *Unconscious strategies used to distort reality and relieve anxiety and guilt*

On the other hand, defense mechanisms can sometimes be destructive. You might decide you didn't get the job or the lover because you didn't have the right "connections" or "the perfect body." This is known as *rationalization*, fabricating excuses when frustrated in attaining particular goals. Not seeing the situation more clearly and realistically might prevent you from developing skills or qualities that could get you a desirable job or lover in the future.

In sum, emotion-focused forms of coping that are accurate reappraisals of stressful situations and do not distort reality may alleviate stress in some situations (Burke & Greenglass, 2000; Gold & Friedman, 2000). Many times, however, it is necessary and more effective to confront the stressor directly.

Problem-Focused Forms of Coping: Putting Problem-Solving Skills to Work

Problem-Focused Forms of Coping *Coping strategies based on using problem-solving strategies to decrease or eliminate the source of stress*

Problem-focused forms of coping deal directly with the situation or the stressor to eventually decrease or eliminate it (Bond & Bunce, 2000). Generally, these approaches are the same as problem-solving strategies discussed in Chapter 8. Thus, the better a person is at solving problems, the more likely he or she will develop effective strategies. These strategies include identifying the stressful problem, generating possible solutions, selecting the appropriate solution, and applying the solution to the problem — thus eliminating the stress.

To illustrate the difference between the two forms of coping, let's suppose that you are flying to Denver to be in your best friend's wedding. You have an exam that lets out at 10:00 and your plane leaves at noon; the wedding is at 4:00. It will be tight, but you can make it. Unfortunately, on the way to the airport, the taxi has a flat tire. You can cognitively evaluate the situation and tell yourself that because this is your best friend, he'll understand that you did everything you could to be there; it wasn't your fault that the taxi had a flat (emotion-focused approach). Or, you could ask the driver to immediately call for another taxi to come and take you to the airport (problem-centered approach).

In general, the better a person is at solving problems, the more likely he or she will develop effective problem-focused coping strategies, including identifying the stressful problem, generating possible solutions, selecting the appropriate solution, and applying the solution to the problem.

Can people use both forms of coping strategies at once? Yes, most stressful situations are complex, and people often combine problem-focused and emotion-focused coping strategies. Furthermore, as you know from your own life, stressful situations change and the type of strategy we use depends not only on the stressor but also the changing nature of the stressor. In some situations, we may first need to use an emotion-focused strategy, which allows a step back from an especially overwhelming problem. Then, later on, when we have our emotional strength and our feet on the ground, we can reappraise the situation and use the problem-solving approach to look for solutions.

---

critical thinking ▸▸▸▸▸▸▸▸▸▸▸▸▸▸▸▸▸ Active Learning

Is Your Job Stressful?

An important component of critical thinking is the ability to *define problems accurately*. By carefully identifying the problem in clear and concrete terms, critical thinkers prevent confusion and lay the foundation for gathering relevant information. Health psychologists (and industrial/organizational psychologists) have studied numerous factors in job-related stress. Their findings suggest that one way to prevent these stresses is to gather lots of information before making a career decision.

If you would like to apply this to your own career plans, start by identifying what you like and do not like about your current (and past) jobs. With this information in hand, you are then prepared to research jobs that will better suit your interests, needs, and abilities and avoid the stress caused by jobs failing to meet this criteria. To help your analysis, answer yes or no to these questions:

1. Is there a sufficient amount of laughter and sociability in your workplace?

2. Does your boss notice and appreciate your work?

3. Is your boss understanding and friendly?

4. Are you embarrassed by the physical conditions of your workplace?

5. Do you feel safe and comfortable in your place of work?

6. Do you like the location of your job?

7. If you won the lottery and were guaranteed a lifetime income, would you feel truly sad if you also had to quit your job?

8. Do you watch the clock, daydream, take long lunches, and leave work as soon as possible?

9. Do you frequently feel stressed and overwhelmed by the demands of your job?

10. Compared to others with your qualifications, are you being paid what you are worth?

11. Are promotions made in a fair and just manner?

12. Given the demands of your job, are you fairly compensated for your work?

Now score your answers. Give yourself one point for each answer that matches the following: 1. No; 2. No; 3. No; 4. Yes; 5. No; 6. No; 7. No; 8. Yes; 9. Yes; 10. No; 11. No; 12. No.

The questions you just answered are based on four factors that research shows are conducive to increased job satisfaction and reduced stress: supportive colleagues, supportive working conditions, mentally challenging work, and equitable rewards (Robbins, 1996). Your total score reveals your overall level of dissatisfaction, whereas a look at specific questions can help identify which of these four factors is most important to your job satisfaction — and most lacking in your current job.

Supportive colleagues (items 1, 2, 3): For most employees, work fills important social needs. Therefore, having friendly and supportive colleagues and superiors leads to increased satisfaction.

Supportive working conditions (items 4, 5, 6): Not surprisingly, studies find most employees prefer working in safe, clean, and relatively modern facilities. They also prefer jobs close to home.

Mentally challenging work (items 7, 8, 9): Jobs with too little challenge create boredom and apathy, whereas too much challenge creates frustration and feelings of failure.

Equitable rewards (items 10, 11, 12): Employees want pay and promotions based on job demands, individual skill levels, and community pay standards.

Coping with stress. Exercise and friends are important resources for effective stress reduction. "I get by with a little help from my friends." John Lennon and Paul McCartney, Sgt. Pepper's Lonely Hearts Club Band, 1967.

work out tension that has built up in muscles. Third, exercise increases strength, flexibility, and stamina for encountering future stressors and increases the efficiency of the cardiovascular system. The best exercise for all these purposes is aerobic exercise — regular strenuous activity that heightens cardiovascular functioning, such as brisk walking, jogging, bicycling, swimming, dancing, and so on.

Relaxation

One of the most effective means of dealing with physical stress reactions is to make a conscious decision to relax during the stressful situation (Matuszek, 2000; Robert-McComb, 2001). There are a variety of relaxation techniques. Earlier, we discussed the use of biofeedback with chronic pain, but it is also extremely helpful in teaching people to relax and manage their stress. Progressive relaxation is also very helpful in reducing or relieving the muscular tension commonly associated with stress. Using this technique, patients first tense and then relax specific muscles, such as in the neck, shoulders, and arms. This technique teaches people to recognize the feel of tense and relaxed muscles.

A Final Note

You are the one who is ultimately responsible for your own health and well-being. Although doctors, nurses, and other health professionals are there for you if you become ill, it is best to do all you can to prevent disease in the first place. By minimizing the harmful effects of stress in our lives, we help our bodies stay well and fight off disease.

TRY THIS Yourself

You can use the following progressive relaxation technique anytime and anywhere you feel stressed, such as while waiting for an exam to begin. Here's how:

1. Sit in a comfortable position, with your head supported.
2. Start breathing slowly and deeply.
3. Let your entire body go limp — let go of all tension. Try to visualize your body getting more and more relaxed.
4. Systematically tense and release each part of your body, beginning with your toes. Focus your attention on your toes and try to visualize what they are doing. Curl them tightly, while counting to 10, then release them and feel the difference between the tense state and the relaxed state. Next, tense your feet to the count of 10, then relax them and feel the difference between the two states. Continue with your calves, thighs, buttocks, abdomen, back muscles, shoulders, upper arms, forearms, hands and fingers, neck, jaws, facial muscles, and forehead.

Try practicing progressive relaxation twice a day for about 15 minutes. You will be surprised at how quickly you can learn to relax — even in the most stressful situations.

Check & Review

COPING WITH STRESS

The two major forms of coping with stress are **emotion-focused** and **problem-focused**. Emotion-focused coping change how we view stressful situations. Problem-focused coping deal directly with the situation or the factor causing the stress so as to decrease or eliminate it. The ability to cope with a stressor also depends on the resources available to a person. Resources include health and energy, positive beliefs, social skills, social support, material resources, and personal control. Exercise and relaxation are active methods people can use to cope with stress.

Questions

1. Which form of coping is being used in the following reactions to forgetting your best friend's birthday? (a) "I can't be expected to remember everyone's birthday"; (b) "I'd better put Cindy's birthday on my calendar so this won't happen again."

2. What are two common defense mechanisms, and why should people avoid using them?

3. People with a(n) _____ locus of control are better able to cope with stress.

4. What are the six major resources for coping with stress? Which resource is most helpful for you? Least helpful?

Answers to Questions can be found in Appendix B.

KEY TERMS

Health Psychology in Action
health psychology (p. 88)
Stress and Its Role in Health
approach–approach conflict (p. 99)
approach–avoidance conflict (p. 99)
avoidance–avoidance conflict (p. 99)
burnout (p. 98)
chronic pain (p. 94)
conflict (p. 99)
distress (p. 96)

eustress (p. 96)
frustration (p. 99)
general adaptation syndrome (GAS)
    (p. 102)
hassles (p. 98)
psychoneuroimmunology [sye-ko-NEW-ro-IM-you-NOLL-oh-gee] (p. 103)
stress (p. 96)
Stress and Serious Illness
hardiness (p. 107)

Type A personality (p. 106)
Type B personality (p. 106)
Coping with Stress
defense mechanisms (p. 108)
emotion-focused forms of coping
    (p. 108)
locus of control (p. 111)
problem-focused forms of coping
    (p. 108)

Visual Summary for Chapter 3 ----

Health Psychology in Action

Health Psychology: Studies relationship between psychological behavior and physical health and illness.

What Health Psychologists Do

- Research issues that affect physical health and methods for improving health.
- Work in the health field to reduce distress and unhealthy behaviors.

Smoking

- *Why do people smoke?* Peer pressure; imitation of role models; addiction (nicotine increases release of neurotransmitters that increase alertness, memory, and well being and decrease anxiety, tension, and pain); learned associations with positive results.
- *Prevention?* Educate about short- and long- term consequences, make smoking less socially acceptable, and help nonsmokers resist social pressures.
- *Stopping?* Use cognitive and behavioral techniques to deal with withdrawal; supplement with nicotine replacement therapy (patches, gum, and pills).

Binge Drinking

Binge drinking: When a man consumes 5 or more drinks in a row, or a woman consumes 4 or more.
How to reduce?
- Overcome the myths and teach facts.
- Reduce or remove social rewards.

Chronic Pain

Chronic pain: Pain lasting over 6 months.
How to reduce?
- Increase activity, exercise, and dietary changes.
- Use behavior modification strategies to reinforce changes.
- Employ *biofeedback* with *electromyograph (EMG)* to reduce muscle tension.
- Use relaxation techniques and practice distraction.

Stress and Its Role in Health

Stress: Body's nonspecific response to any demand made on it.

Sources of Stress

- *Life changes*: Holmes and Rahe Scale measures stress caused by adaptations to important life events.
- *Chronic stressors*: Ongoing, long term stress related to political world, family, work, etc.
- **Hassles**: Small, everyday problems that accumulate.
- **Burnout**: Exhaustion resulting from emotionally demanding situations.
- **Frustration**: Negative emotional state from blocked goals.
- **Conflict**: Negative emotional state from 2 or more incompatible goals.

There are 3 types of conflict

↓ | ↓ | ↓

Approach-approach conflict: Two or more desirable goals

Avoidance-avoidance conflict: Two or more undesirable goals

Approach-avoidance conflict: Both desirable and undesirable goals

Stress and Its Role in Health (cont).

Results of Stress

- *Sympathetic nervous system activation* increases heart rate, blood pressure, respiration, and muscle tension and releases stress hormones.
- *Fight/flight system* frequently engaged but generally overused and harmful in modern times.
- *Suppressed immune system* leaves body vulnerable to disease.

- **General adaptation syndrome** is a 3-phase generalized physiological that develops in response to severe stressors:

1. Alarm reaction ➡ 2. Resistance phase ➡ 3. Exhaustion

Stress and Serious Illness

Cancer
- Occurs when cells replicate beyond control.
- Caused by hereditary dispositions and environmental factors that lead to changes in body chemistry and the immune system

Cardiovascular Disorders
Heart disease: All disorders that affect the heart muscle and lead to heart failure.

Contributing Factors:

⬇ | ⬇ | ⬇

Stress related hormones, which release fat into bloodstream that later attaches to the walls of blood vessels.	**Type A personality** with high ambition, time worries, anger, and hostility is at increased risk; whereas, the personality factor of **hardiness** decreases risk.	Behaviors such as smoking, stress, lack of exercise, obesity, and high-fat diet.

Coping with Stress

Emotion-Focused Forms of Coping	Problem-Focused Forms of Coping	Resources for Effective Coping	Active Coping Strategies
Emotional and cognitive strategies that change how one appraises a stressful situation. **Defense mechanisms** are unconscious strategies that protect the ego and avoid anxiety by distorting reality.	Strategies that deal directly with the stressful situation by applying problem-solving techniques to decrease or eliminate it.	Good health, energy, positive beliefs, social skills, social support, material resources, and personal control (e.g., internal **locus of control**) all reduce stress.	Exercise and relaxation techniques directly reduce stress.

4

Sensation and Perception

I have just touched my dog. He was rolling on the grass, with pleasure in every muscle and limb. I wanted to catch a picture of him in my fingers, and I touched him as lightly as I would cobwebs. ... He pressed close to me, as if he were fain to crowd himself into my hand. He loved it with his tail, with his paw, with his tongue. If he could speak, I believe he would say with me that paradise is attained by touch. [pp. 3–4]

Thus Helen Keller began her book The World I Live In. Her world was totally different from that of most people: She couldn't see it or hear it because she was blind and deaf, but she was as capable and as appreciative of life — if not more so — as any person with all five senses. This was because she made the most of the senses she did have. Excerpts from her book describe how she used these senses:

Through the sense of touch I know the faces of friends, the illimitable variety of straight and curved lines, all surfaces, the exuberance of the soil, the delicate shapes of flowers, the noble forms of trees, and the range of mighty winds. Besides objects, surfaces, and atmospherical changes, I perceive countless vibrations. ... Footsteps, I discover, vary tactually according to the age, the sex, and the manners of the walker. ... When a carpenter works in the house or in the barn near by, I know by the slanting, up-and-down, toothed vibration, and the ringing concussion of blow upon blow, that he is sawing or hammering...

In the evening quiet there are fewer vibrations than in the daytime, and then I rely more largely upon smell. ... Sometimes, when there is no wind, the odors are so grouped that I know the character of the country and can place a hayfield, a country store, a garden, a barn, a grove of pines, a farmhouse with the windows open. ... I know by smell the kind of house we enter. I have recognized an old-fashioned country house because it has several layers of odors, left by a succession of families, of plants, perfumes, and draperies. [pp. 43–44, 46, 68–69]

Helen Keller wasn't born deaf and blind. When she was 19 months old, she suffered a fever that left her without sight or hearing and thus virtually isolated from the world. Keller's parents realized they had to find help for their daughter, and after diligently searching, they found Anne Sullivan, a young teacher who was able to break through Keller's barrier of isolation by taking advantage of her sense of touch. One day, Sullivan took Keller to the pumphouse and, as Sullivan (1902) wrote,

I made Helen hold her mug under the spout while I pumped. As the cold water gushed forth, filling the mug, I spelled "w-a-t-e-r" in Helen's free hand. The word coming so close upon the sensation of cold water rushing over her hand seemed to startle her. She dropped the mug and stood as one transfixed. A new light came into her face. [p. 257]

That one moment, brought on by the sensation of cold water on her hand, was the impetus for a lifetime of learning about, understanding, and appreciating the world through her remaining senses. In 1904, Helen Keller graduated cum laude from Radcliffe College and went on to become a famous author and lecturer, inspiring physically limited people throughout the world.

Sensation *The process of receiving, translating, and transmitting raw sensory data from the external and internal environments to the brain*

Perception *The process of selecting, organizing, and interpreting sensory data into usable mental representations of the world*

Bottom-Up Processing *Information processing that begins "at the bottom" with raw sensory data that feed "up" to the brain; perceptual analysis that emphasizes characteristics of the stimulus itself rather than internal, cognitive processes*

Top-Down Processing *Information processing that starts "at the top" with the observer's thoughts, expectations, and knowledge and works down; perceptual analysis that emphasizes the perceiver's internal, cognitive processes rather than being driven by characteristics of the outside stimuli*

The story of Helen Keller has been told and retold as an example of how people can overcome sensory deficiencies by using their other senses to the optimum. It also provides a wonderful introduction to the two major topics of this chapter: **sensation,** the process of receiving, converting, and transmitting information from the outside world (outside the brain, not necessarily outside the body), and **perception,** the process of selecting, organizing, and interpreting raw sensory data into useful mental representations of the world.

As you can see in Figure 4.1, the basic function of sensation is *detection* of sensory stimuli, whereas perception generally involves *interpretation* of the same stimuli. Like the central nervous system (CNS) and peripheral nervous system (PNS), the basic functions of sensation and perception are somewhat different. But also like the CNS and PNS, the boundary between these two processes is not precise — there is considerable overlap.

We begin this chapter discussing how we receive sensory information and work our way upward to the top levels of perceptual processing. Psychologists refer to this type of information processing as **bottom-up processing,** taking sensory data in through the sensory receptors and sending it "upward" to the brain for analysis. In contrast, **top-down processing** begins with "higher," "top"-level processing involving thoughts, previous experiences, expectations, language, and cultural background and works down to the sensory level. When first learning to read, you used *bottom-up processing.* You initially learned that certain arrangements of lines and "squiggles" represented specific letters. Only later did you realize that these letters joined together to make up words. After years of experience and language training, you quickly perceive the words in this sentence before the individual letters — *top-down processing.* Although top-down processing is far superior for reading, both bottom-up and top-down processing are important to perception.

Our opening discussion of sensation covers not only what are commonly known as the five senses — vision, hearing, taste, smell, and touch — but also those senses that provide the brain with data from inside the body: the *vestibular sense* (the sense of balance) and *kinesthesis* (the sense of bodily position and movement). After we've covered sensation, we will study perception, where the focus is on how we select, organize, and interpret sensory data. In that section, you discover how we decide what to pay attention to, how we perceive distance, how we see different colors, and whether there is any scientific evidence to support subliminal perception and extrasensory perception (ESP).

(a)

(b)

What do you see — sensation or perception? (*a*) *When you stare at this drawing (known as the Necker cube), which area is the top, front, or back of the cube? In the process of sensation, your visual sensory system detects a collection of lines, angles, patterns of color, and so on. But at the perceptual level, you interpret these lines as a geometric shape called a cube. If you stare at it long enough, your perception/interpretation will change. (*b*) Now look at this drawing of a woman. Do you see a young woman looking back over her right shoulder or an older woman with her chin down on her chest? Although basic sensory input stays the same, your brain's attempt to interpret ambiguous stimuli creates a type of perceptual dance, shifting from one interpretation to another (Gaetz, Weinberg, Rzempoluck, & Jantzen, 1998).*

EXPERIENCING SENSATIONS

To experience sensations, we must have both a means of detecting stimuli and a means of converting them into a language the brain can understand. Let's take a closer look at how our sensory organs accomplish both tasks.

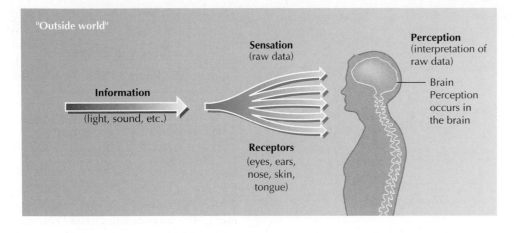

Figure 4.1 *Sensation and perception.* Sensation is the detection and conversion of raw data from the senses. Perception is the interpretation of these raw sensory data by the brain.

Processing: Detection and Conversion

Our eyes, ears, skin, and other sense organs all contain special cells called *receptors*, which receive and process sensory information from the environment. For each sense, these specialized cells respond to a distinct stimulus, such as sound waves or odor molecules.

Through a process called **transduction**, the receptors convert the stimulus into neural impulses, which are sent to the brain. In hearing, for example, tiny receptor cells in the inner ear convert mechanical vibrations (from sound waves) into electrochemical signals. These signals are carried by neurons to the brain. Each type of sensory receptor is designed to detect a wide variety of stimuli and a wide range of stimulation. However, also built into our sensory systems are structures that purposefully reduce the amount of stimuli we receive.

Why would we want to reduce the amount of sensory information we receive? Can you imagine what would happen if you did not have some natural filtering of stimuli? You would constantly hear blood rushing through your veins and continually feel your clothes brushing against your skin. Some level of filtering is needed so the brain is not overwhelmed with unnecessary information. It needs to be free to respond to those stimuli that have meaning for survival. Each of our senses is therefore custom-designed to respond to only a select range of potential sensory information.

All species have evolved selective receptors that suppress or amplify information to allow survival. For example, hawks have an acute sense of vision but a poor sense of smell. Similarly, we humans cannot sense many stimuli, such as ultraviolet light, microwaves, the ultrasonic sound of a dog whistle, or infrared heat patterns from warm-blooded animals (which rattlesnakes can). However, we can see a candle burning 30 miles away on a dark, clear night, hear the tick of a watch at 20 feet under quiet conditions, smell one drop of perfume in a six-room apartment, and taste 1 teaspoon of sugar dissolved in 2 gallons of water.

In the process of **sensory reduction**, we not only filter incoming sensations, we also analyze the sensations sent through before a neural impulse is finally sent to the cortex of the brain. If cells in the reticular formation within the brainstem (Chapter 2) decide the information is important, it is passed on to the cerebral cortex. This explains why parents of a newborn can sleep through passing sirens and blaring stereos yet awaken to the slightest whimper of their baby.

How does the brain differentiate between various incoming sensations, such as sounds and smells? It depends on the number and type of sensory cells that are activated, on the precise nerve that is stimulated, and ultimately on the part of the brain that the nerve stimulates. Through a process known as **coding**, sounds and smells are interpreted as distinct sensations not because of the envi-

How do our sensory organs gather sensory information and convert it into signals the brain can understand?

Transduction *The process by which a stimulus to a receptor is converted into neural impulses*

Sensory Reduction *The process of filtering and analyzing incoming sensations that occurs before a neural impulse is sent to the cortex*

Coding *The three-part process that converts a particular sensory input into a specific sensation*

Figure 4.2 *Sensory areas of the brain.* Neural impulses travel from the sensory receptors to various parts of the brain.

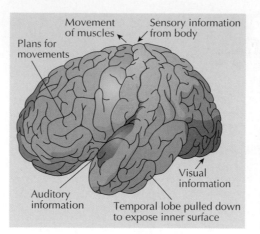

Movement of muscles
Sensory information from body
Plans for movements
Visual information
Auditory information
Temporal lobe pulled down to expose inner surface

Psychophysics *The branch of psychology that studies the relation between attributes of the physical world and our psychological experience of them*

Absolute Threshold *The smallest magnitude of a certain stimulus energy that can be detected*

Difference Threshold *The smallest magnitude of difference in stimulus energy that a person can detect; also called the just noticeable difference*

Sensory Adaptation *A sensory phenomenon in which the perceived intensity of a repeated stimulus decreases over time*

ronmental stimuli that activate them but because their respective neural impulses travel by different routes and arrive at different parts of the brain. Figure 4.2 illustrates the parts of the brain involved in sensory reception.

Thresholds: Testing the Limits and Changes

How do we know that humans can hear a watch ticking at 20 feet or smell one drop of perfume in a six-room apartment? The answer comes from research in **psychophysics**, an area of psychology that examines how physical stimuli (such as sound and smell) are related to an individual's psychological reactions to those stimuli. Using knowledge from both physics and psychology, psychophysicists study how the strength or intensity of a stimulus affects an observer.

Suppose you are the parent of a school-age daughter who, like Helen Keller, has just suffered from a serious illness accompanied by high fever. During her period of recovery, you notice that she does not seem to hear as well as before her illness, so you take her to a hearing specialist.

In a test for hearing loss, the specialist uses a tone generator that produces sounds of differing pitches and intensities. Your daughter listens to the sounds over earphones and is asked to indicate the earliest point at which she can hear a tone. She thereby indicates her **absolute threshold**, or the smallest magnitude of sound she can detect. To test your daughter's **difference threshold**, or *just noticeable difference* (JND), the examiner presents a small change in volume and asks the child to respond when she notices a difference. By noting your daughter's thresholds and comparing them with thresholds of people with normal hearing, the specialist can determine whether your daughter has a hearing loss and, if so, the extent of the loss.

Sensory thresholds exist not only for hearing but also for vision, taste, smell, and the skin senses. In fact, much of the research done in all areas of sensation originally began with the study of various thresholds.

Do people's thresholds vary? People with sensory impairments obviously have thresholds that differ from the norm. But even among individuals with no sensory difficulties, there is a considerable range in sensitivities. Moreover, the sensitivity of an individual can vary from moment to moment, depending on his or her physiological state. Lack of food and certain drugs, for example, can change a person's normal threshold.

Adaptation: Weakening the Response

Your friends have invited you to come by to visit their beautiful new baby daughter. As they greet you at their front door, you are overwhelmed by the odor of a nearby diaper pail and even the baby herself. You wonder what's wrong. Why don't they do something about the smell? The answer is **sensory adaptation**: When a constant stimulus is presented for a length of time, sensation often fades or disappears. Receptors higher up in the sensory system get "tired" and actually fire less frequently.

Sensory adaptation makes sense from an evolutionary perspective. Basically, we can't afford to waste attention and time on unchanging, normally unimportant stimuli. "Turning down the volume" on repetitive information helps the brain cope with an overwhelming amount of sensory stimuli and allows time to pay attention to *change*.

This helps your friends with their smelly baby, and if you stay long enough, your senses also will adapt — fortunately. Sometimes this adaptation, however, can be dangerous, as when we stop paying attention to that gas leak we noticed in the kitchen.

Although some senses adapt quickly, like smell and touch, we never completely adapt to visual stimuli or extremely intense stimuli, such as the odor of ammonia, the heat of the desert sun, or the pain of a burned hand. Again, from an evolutionary perspective, these limitations on sensory adaptation aid survival. They remind us to avoid strong odors and heat and to do something about the damaged tissue, such as put some ice on that burned hand.

If we don't adapt to pain, how do athletes keep playing despite painful injuries? In certain situations, the body releases natural painkillers called *endorphins* (see Chapter 2). Endorphins act in the same way as morphine to relieve pain by inhibiting pain perception. Both pleasant (the "runner's high," sexual activity) and unpleasant stimuli (injuries, fighting) can release endorphins. Pain relief through endorphins may also be the secret behind *acupuncture*, the ancient Chinese technique of gently twisting thin needles placed in the skin.

In addition to endorphin release, one of the most accepted explanations of pain perception is the **gate-control theory**, first proposed by Ronald Melzack and Patrick Wall (1965). According to this theory, the experience of pain depends partly on whether the neural message gets past a "gatekeeper" in the spinal cord that either blocks pain signals or allows them to pass on to the brain. Normally, the gate is kept shut, either by impulses coming down from the brain itself or by messages coming into the spinal cord from large-diameter fibers that conduct most sensory signals, such as touch and pressure. However, when body tissue is damaged, impulses from smaller pain fibers open the gate.

Gate-Control Theory of Pain *The idea that pain sensations are processed and altered by mechanisms within the spinal cord*

The gate-control theory helps explain why touch and pressure, such as rubbing your banged elbow, can reduce pain: The large fibers carry competing pressure messages. Messages from the brain itself can also control the pain gate, thus explaining how athletes and soldiers can carry on despite excruciating pain. When we are soothed by endorphins or distracted by competition or fear, our experience of pain can be greatly diminished. On the other hand, when we get anxious or dwell on our pain by talking about it constantly, we can intensify it (Sullivan, Tripp, & Santor, 1998).

Research also suggests that the pain gate may be chemically controlled, that a neurotransmitter called *substance P* opens the pain gate, and that endorphins close it (Cesaro & Ollat, 1997; Liu, Mantyh, & Basbaum, 1997). Other research finds that the brain not only responds to incoming signals from sensory nerves but also is capable of *generating* pain (and other sensations) entirely on its own (Melzack, 1999; Vertosick, 2000). Have you heard of *tinnitus*, the ringing-in-the-ears sensation

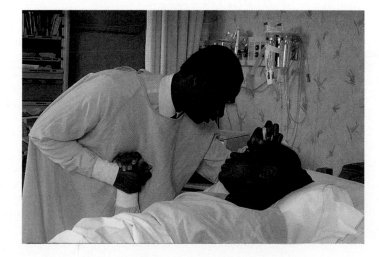

Childbirth and the gate-control theory of pain. Modern childbirth classes teach women to focus their attention away from the pain during childbirth, and the partner (or "labor coach) is encouraged to talk to her and gently massage the back and neck muscles. Can you see how the gate-control theory explains the effectiveness of these techniques?

that sometimes accompanies hearing loss? In the absence of normal sensory input, nerve cells send conflicting messages ("static") to the brain, and in this case the brain interprets the static as "ringing." A similar process happens with the strange phenomenon of *phantom pain*, wherein people continue to feel pain (and itching or tickling) long after a limb is amputated. The brain interprets the static as pain because it arises in the area of the spinal cord responsible for pain signaling (Vertosick, 2000).

Each of the sensory principles we've discussed thus far — reduction, transduction, coding, thresholds, and adaptation — applies to all the senses. Yet the way in which each sense is processed is uniquely different, as we shall see in the remainder of the chapter.

Check & Review

EXPERIENCING SENSATIONS

Sensation refers to the process of receiving, converting, and transmitting information from the outside world, whereas **perception** is the process of selecting, organizing, and interpreting raw sensory data into useful mental representations of the world.

Sensory processing includes transduction, reduction, and coding. **Transduction** converts stimuli into neural impulses that are sent to the brain, and we cope with the vast quantities of sensory stimuli through the process of **sensory reduction**. Each sensory system is specialized to **code** its stimuli into unique sets of neural impulses that the brain interprets as light, sound, touch, and so on.

The **absolute threshold** is the smallest magnitude of a stimulus we can detect. The **difference threshold** is the smallest change in a stimulus that we can detect. The process of **sensory adaptation** decreases our sensitivity to constant, unchanging stimuli.

Questions

1. The key functions of sensation and perception are, respectively, (a) stimulation and transduction; (b) transmission and coding; (b) reduction, and transduction; (c) detection and interpretation; (d) interpretation and transmission.

2. If a researcher were testing to determine the dimmest light a person could perceive, the researcher would be measuring the _____.

3. Why can't you smell your own perfume or aftershave after a few minutes?

4. The _____ theory of pain helps explain why it sometimes helps to rub or massage an injured thumb. (a) sensory adaptation; (b) gate-control; (c) just noticeable difference; (d) Lamaze.

Answers to Review Questions can be found in Appendix B.

HOW WE SEE AND HEAR

How do our eyes and ears enable us to see and hear?

While on a long train trip, Helen Keller's aunt improvised a doll for 6-year-old Helen out of a few towels. It had no nose, no mouth, no ears, and no eyes — nothing to indicate a face. Helen found this disturbing. Most disturbing, though, was the lack of eyes. In fact, it agitated her so much that she was not content until she found some beads and her aunt attached them for eyes. Uncomprehending as she was of the myriad sensations our eyes bring us, Helen still seemed to know the importance of having eyes.

Vision: The Eyes Have It

To fully appreciate the marvels of sight, we first need to examine the properties of light, because without it, we wouldn't be able to see. We will then examine the structure and function of the eye, and finally, the way in which visual input is processed.

What does a butterfly see? The flower on the right was photographed under ultraviolet light. Because butterflies have ultraviolet receptors, this may be what it's like to see like a butterfly.

Waves of Light

Light is a form of electromagnetic energy that moves in waves similar to the movement of waves in the ocean. There are many different types of electromagnetic waves, from short X-rays to long radio waves. Together they form the *electromagnetic spectrum* (Figure 4.3). Most wavelengths are invisible to the human eye; only a small part of the spectrum, known as the *visible spectrum*, can be detected by our visual receptors.

As Table 4.1 shows, light waves vary in length, height, and range — each with a distinct effect on vision. The **wavelength**, the distance between the crest of one wave and the crest of the next, determines its **frequency** (in vision, its **hue** or color). Longer wavelengths produce reddish colors, whereas shorter wavelengths produce bluish colors. The **amplitude**, or height, of a light wave determines its *intensity* (in vision, its *brightness*). Higher waves produce brighter colors, and smaller waves produce dimmer colors. The range of waves — that is, the mixture of length and amplitude — determines its *complexity* (in vision, its *saturation*). The wider range produces more saturated (more varied and complex) color, whereas a narrow range produces less saturated color (less complex and varied; may be a single pure color).

Eye Anatomy and Function

The eye is uniquely designed to capture light and focus it on receptors at the back of the eyeball. The receptors, in turn, convert light energy into neural signals to be interpreted by the brain. Several structures in the eye are involved in the process. We will trace the path of light through these structures — the cornea, pupil, lens, and retina. As we do, please refer to Figure 4.4.

Wavelength *The length of a light or sound wave, measured from the crest of one wave to the crest of the next*

Hue *The visual dimension seen as a particular color; determined by the length of a light wave*

Frequency *How often a light or sound wave cycles — that is, the number of complete wavelengths that pass a point in a given time (e.g., per second)*

Amplitude *The height of a light or sound wave; pertaining to light, it refers to brightness*

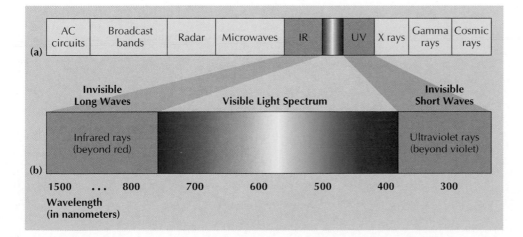

Figure 4.3 *The electromagnetic spectrum.* (a) Gamma radiation and X radiation have short wavelengths, visible light has medium wavelengths, and TV, radio, and AC (alternating current) circuits have long wavelengths. (b) The human eye can see only visible light, a small part of the full spectrum. Visible light with a short wavelength is perceived as blue, visible light with a medium wavelength is green or yellow, and visible light with a long wavelength is red.

TABLE 4.1 PROPERTIES OF VISION AND HEARING

Physical properties	**Wavelength:** The distance between successive peaks.	**Wave Amplitude:** The height from peak to trough.	**Range of Wavelengths:** The mixture of waves.
	Long wavelength/low frequency	*Low amplitude/low intensity*	*Low range/low complexity*
	Short wavelength/ high frequency	*High amplitude/ high intensity*	*High range/high complexity*
VISION (Light Waves)	**Hue:** Short wave lengths produce higher frequency and bluish colors; long wavelengths produce lower frequency and reddish colors.	**Brightness:** Great amplitude produces more intensity and bright colors; small amplitude produces less intensity and dim colors.	**Saturation:** Wider range produces more complex color; narrow range produces less complex color.
AUDITION (Sound Waves)	**Pitch:** Shorter wavelengths produce higher frequency and high pitched sounds; long wavelengths produce lower frequency and low-pitched sounds.	**Loudness:** Great amplitude produces loud sounds; small amplitude produces soft sounds.	**Timbre:** Pure tones produce only one frequency; complex tones produce multiple frequencies.

Light waves first enter the eye through a tough, transparent shield called the *cornea*, which is attached to the white, opaque outer wall of the eye. Light passes from the cornea through the *pupil*, an adjustable opening controlled by the *iris* (the colored part of the eye), and then on through the *lens*, a transparent elastic structure. Light waves eventually end up at the back of the eyeball on the *retina*, a group

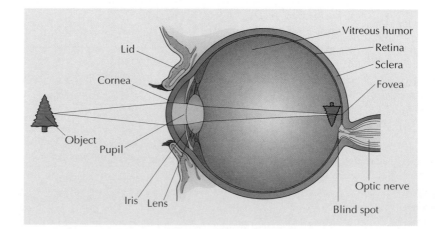

Figure 4.4 *The anatomy of the eye.* Note the path of light waves as they travel from the outside world, enter the eye at the cornea, and pass through the pupil and lens to the retina. In the retina, light waves are transduced (or changed) into neural impulses that move along the optic nerve upward to the brain.

of light receptors, where they are transduced into neural messages and then carried by the *optic nerve* to the brain.

Now that we have the big picture of eye anatomy, and how light information enters and travels to the brain, let's examine how the main structures function.

Cornea and Lens

The cornea protects the eye and does part of the focusing of incoming light rays. The lens further bends incoming rays of light to focus them on the retina. The focus is adjustable, like in a camera. But unlike a camera lens, which changes the focus for objects at different distances by moving relative to the film plane, the lens of the eye work by changing their shape. The lens become more or less curved to focus light from objects located at varying distances. This focusing process is known as **accommodation**. When you look at a faraway object, your lens accommodates by thinning and flattening to focus; when your glance shifts back to a near object, such as the book you're reading, your lens accommodates by thickening and curving.

Small abnormalities in the eye sometimes interfere with accommodation (Figure 4.5). If you have normal vision, your lens focuses the image of any object — near or far — on the retina at the back of your eye. If you are **nearsighted**, however, your eyeball is deeper than normal in relation to its lens, or your cornea may be too sharply curved. The light rays are focused at a point in front of the retina, and at the retina, the image is blurred. The opposite occurs if you are **farsighted**. Your eyeball is shorter than normal and the light is focused on a point beyond the retina, leading to an inability to focus on objects at close range. Nearsightedness *(myopia)* and farsightedness *(hyperopia)* can occur at any age; however, at about age 40, most people find that they need reading glasses. This is because the lenses start to lose elasticity and the ability to accommodate for near vision *(presbyopia)*. Both nearsightedness and farsightedness are easily remedied with corrective lenses. Advances in laser surgery now make it possible to change the shape of the cornea to correct some visual acuity problems.

Retina

Ultimately, incoming light waves end up on the **retina**. This is an area at the back of the eye that contains blood vessels and a network of neurons that transmit neural information to the occipital lobes of the brain. The retina also contains special light-sensitive cells called **rods** and **cones**, so named for their distinctive shapes (Figure 4.6). There are about 6 million cones and 120 million rods tightly packed together at the back of the retina (Carlson, 1998).

The rods, besides being much more numerous, are also more sensitive to light than the cones. They enable us to see in dim light. This greater sensitivity, however, is achieved at the expense of fine detail and and color vision — the job of the cones.

Cones become more numerous toward the center of the retina, and in the center is the *fovea*, a tiny pit filled with cones, responsible for our sharpest vision. Cones function better in bright light and diminish in function as the light dims. Cones enable us not only to see things in fine detail but also to see in color. All cones are sensitive to many wavelengths, but each is maximally sensitive to one color — red, green, or blue. You may have noticed that it is impossible to see the color and fine detail of a flower in near-dark conditions, when only the rods are functioning.

In normal vision, an image is focused on the retina.

In nearsightedness (myopia), the image is focused in front of the retina.

In farsightedness (hyperopia), the image is focused behind the retina.

Figure 4.5 *Normal vision, nearsightedness, and farsightedness.*

Accommodation *The process by which the lens changes shape to focus light on the retina; the lens thins and flattens to focus on distant objects and thickens and bulges to focus on a nearby object*

Nearsightedness (Myopia) *A visual acuity problem that occurs when the cornea and lens focus an image in front of the retina*

Farsightedness (Hyperopia) *A visual acuity problem that results when the cornea and lens focus an image behind the retina*

Retina *The light-sensitive inner surface of the back of the eye, which contains the receptor rods and cones plus other neurons that help in processing visual information*

Rods *Visual receptors in the retina that detect black, white, and gray and are responsible for peripheral vision; they are most sensitive in dim light*

Cones *Visual receptors concentrated near the center of the retina that are responsible for color vision and fine detail; they are most sensitive in brightly lit conditions*

Figure 4.6 *Structures of the retina.* (a) The retina of the eye is a complicated structure with many different types of cells. The most important are the rods and cones. (b) In this photomicrograph, the two large yellow cone-shaped objects are retinal cones, and the long reddish rod-shaped objects are the retinal rods. The bipolar cells are located directly above the rods and cones.

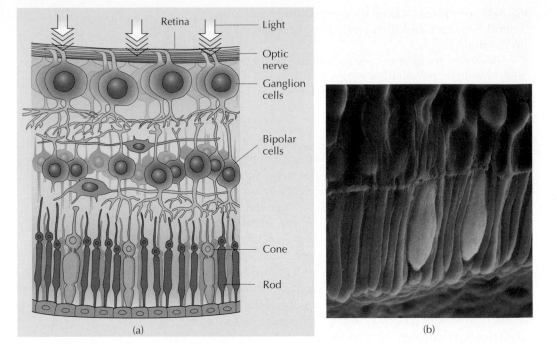

(a)

(b)

Near the fovea lies an area that has no visual receptors at all and absolutely no vision. This aptly named "blind spot" is where blood vessels and nerve pathways enter and exit the eyeball. Normally, we are unaware of our blind spot because our eyes are always moving. We fill in the information missing from the blind spot with information from adjacent areas on the retina or with images from the other eye.

When the brightness level suddenly changes, how do the rods "take over" from the cones, and vice versa? Think back to the last time you walked into a dark movie theater on a sunny afternoon. You were momentarily blinded. This happens because in bright light, the pigment inside the rods is bleached and they are temporarily nonfunctional. Going from a very light to a very dark setting requires a rapid shift from cones to rods. During the changeover, there is a second or two before the rods are functional enough for you to see. They continue to adjust for 20 to 30 minutes, until your maximum light sensitivity is reached. This process is known as **dark adaptation**. The visual adjustment that takes place when you leave the theater and go back into the sunlight — *light adaptation* — takes about 7 to 10 minutes and is the work of the cones. This adaptation process is particularly important to remember when driving your car from a brightly lit garage into a dark night.

Dark Adaptation *The process by which rods and cones adjust to allow vision in dim light*

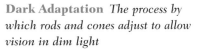

To experience your blind spot, hold the book about 1 foot in front of you, close your right eye, and stare at the X below with your left eye. Very slowly, move the book closer to you. You should see the worm disappear and the apple become whole.

Hearing: A Sound Sensation

In this section, we examine **audition**, the sense of hearing, which we use nearly as much as our sense of vision. In fact, Helen Keller said she "found deafness to be a much greater handicap than blindness. ... Blindness cuts people off from things. Deafness cuts people off from people." What is it about hearing that makes it so important? In discussing vision, we talked first about waves of light, then about the anatomy of the eye, and, finally, about problems with vision. We'll follow the same pattern with audition, starting here with waves of sound.

Audition *The sense of hearing*

Waves of Sound

Sound is the movement of air molecules in a particular wave pattern. The waves produced are called *sound waves*. They result from rapid changes in air pressure caused by vibrating objects, such as vocal cords or guitar strings.

Like light waves, sound waves vary in three basic ways (see again Table 4.1):

1. **Length** Wavelengths in hearing correspond to **pitch** (wavelengths of light correspond to hue or color). Sounds of different frequencies are perceived as high or low. For instance, the faster a person's vocal cords vibrate (the more waves per second), the higher the pitch of the person's voice.

Pitch *The highness or lowness of tones or sounds, depending on their frequency*

2. **Height** The amplitude (or height) of the sound wave determines *loudness*, which is measured in units termed *decibels* (the height of light waves determines *brightness*). Figure 4.7 gives decibel ratings for various sounds.

3. **Range** The range (or mixture) of sound waves determines *timbre*, or complexity of tone. Timbre is the quality of sound that allows us to know whether a note is being played by a violin, trumpet, or oboe.

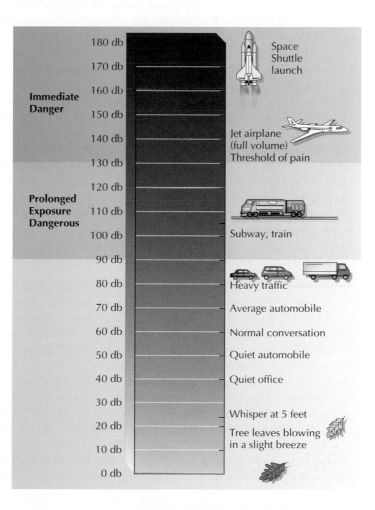

Figure 4.7 *Loudness*. The loudness of a sound is measured in decibels. This figure lists some familiar sounds and their decibel levels. One decibel is the faintest sound a normal person can hear. Normal conversation takes place at about 60 decibels. Constant noise above about 90 decibels can cause permanent nerve damage to the ear.

Figure 4.8 *Anatomy of the ear.* Sound waves enter the outer ear, are amplified and concentrated in the middle ear, and are transduced in the inner ear.

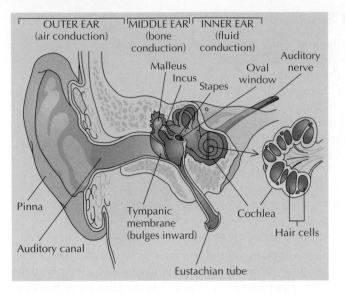

Cochlea [KOK-lee-uh] *The three-chambered, snail-shaped structure in the inner ear that contains the receptors for hearing*

Place Theory *Theory that explains how we hear higher-pitched sounds; different high-pitched sounds bend the basilar membrane hair cells at different locations in the cochlea*

Frequency Theory *Theory that explains how we hear lower-pitched sounds; hair cells on the basilar membrane of the cochlea bend and fire action potentials at the same rate as the frequency of the low sound*

Ear Anatomy and Function

The ear has three major sections: the *outer ear*, the *middle ear*, and the *inner ear*. The outer ear gathers and delivers sound waves to the middle ear, which amplifies and concentrates the sounds. The inner ear contains the receptor cells that ultimately transduce the mechanical energy created by sounds into neural impulses. As we trace the path of sound waves through the ear, it will help to refer to Figure 4.8.

Sound waves are gathered and funneled into the outer ear by the *pinna*, the external, visible part of the ear that we automatically envision when we think of an ear. The pinna channels the sound waves into the *auditory canal*, a tubelike structure that focuses the sound. At the end of the auditory canal is a thin, tautly stretched membrane known as the *eardrum*, or *tympanic membrane*. As sound waves hit the eardrum, it vibrates. The vibrating eardrum causes the three tiniest bones in the body, the *malleus* (hammer), the *incus* (anvil), and the *stapes* (stirrup), to vibrate. (Together, these three bones are referred to as the *ossicles*.) The stapes presses on a membrane, known as the *oval window*, and causes it to vibrate.

The movement of the oval window creates waves in the fluid that fills the **cochlea**, a snail-shaped structure that contains the *basilar membrane*, on which are located the receptors for hearing. The hearing receptors are known as *hair cells*, and they do in fact resemble hairs. As the waves travel through the cochlear fluid, the hair cells bend from side to side. It is at this point that the mechanical energy of the wave is transduced into electrochemical impulses that are carried by the *auditory nerve* to the brain.

Pitch and Loudness

We hear different pitch and loudness levels by a combination of mechanisms, depending on the frequency of the sound. First, let's discuss how we hear various pitches of sounds. It seems that we hear high-pitched sounds according to the place along the *basilar membrane* that is most stimulated. When we hear a particular sound, it causes the eardrum, the ossicles, and the oval window to vibrate, which in turn produces a "traveling wave" through the fluid in the cochlea. This wave causes some bending of hair cells all along the basilar membrane, but there is a single point where the hair cells are maximally bent for each distinct pitch. This localized maximal bending is described by the **place theory**, which explains how we hear higher-pitched sounds.

How we hear lower-pitched sounds is explained by the **frequency theory**. According to this theory, we hear a particular low sound because it causes hair cells along the basilar membrane to bend and fire action potentials at the same rate as the frequency of that low sound. For example, a sound with a frequency of 90 hertz would produce 90 action potentials per second in the auditory nerve.

How we detect loudness levels also differs according to the frequency of the sounds. When a sound has a high pitch, we hear it as louder because the neurons fire at a faster rate. Louder sounds produce more intense vibrations, which result in a greater bending of the hair cells, a greater release of neurotransmitters, and consequently a higher firing rate of action potentials. However, there must be an alternate explanation for the perception of the loudness of low sounds, because as just described, rate of firing explains how we hear the pitch of a low sound. Most researchers think that the loudness of lower-pitched sounds is detected by the number of axons that are firing at any one time.

Is it true that loud music can damage your hearing? Yes. There are basically two types of deafness: (1) *conduction deafness*, or middle-ear deafness, which results from problems with the mechanical system that conducts sound waves to the inner ear, and (2) *nerve deafness*, or inner-ear deafness which involves damage to the cochlea, hair cells, or auditory nerve. Disease and biological changes associated with aging can cause nerve deafness. But the most common (and preventable) cause of nerve deafness is continuous exposure to loud sounds that damages the hair cells. If a noise is loud (150 decibels or more), such as stereos or headphones at full blast, jackhammers, or a jet airplane engine, even brief exposure can cause permanent deafness. Daily exposure to approximately 85 decibels (such as heavy traffic or motorcycles) can also lead to permanent hearing loss. Obviously, if you cannot avoid such loud noises, earplugs will help reduce the damage. Pay attention to any change in your normal hearing threshold or if you experience *tinnitus*, a whistling or ringing sensation in your ears. These are often the first signs of hearing loss.

Because damage to the nerve or receptor cells is almost always irreversible, the only treatment for nerve deafness is a small electronic device called a *cochlear implant*. If the auditory nerve is intact, the implant bypasses hair cells and directly stimulates the nerve. At present, a cochlear implant produces only a crude approximation of hearing, but the technology is improving. The best bet is to protect your sense of hearing. That means avoiding exceptionally loud noises (rock concerts, jackhammers, stereo headphones at full blast), wearing earplugs when such situations cannot be avoided, and paying attention to bodily warnings. These warnings include a change in your normal hearing threshold and tinnitus.

Loud noise and nerve deafness. Members of the Red Hot Chili Peppers (and their audience) are potential victims of noise-induced nerve deafness, which is irreversible.

RESEARCH HIGHLIGHT

Tracking Down the Genes for Deafness

Some people suffer hearing loss because of disease (as in Helen Keller's case), accident, or exposure to extremely loud noise. Others are born with a gene that causes deafness. Researchers trying to track down these genes have generally taken one of two approaches. One approach uses animals, such as mice, which have certain known genetic mutations that are naturally occurring or are experimentally induced by the researchers (Self et al., 1998; Wang et al., 1998). The second

approach is to study the genetics of human families that have a large percentage of members who are born deaf or become deaf later in life (Denoyelle et al., 1997; Lynch et al., 1997).

Together, the two approaches have located several human deafness gene mutations (Pennisi, 1997). These genes are responsible for producing a type of protein called *myosin*, which is, in turn, instrumental in the development of the auditory hair cells. The mutation alters the structure of the hair cells, causing the person to be deaf at birth or to go deaf several years after birth. But problems with myosin cannot be the only cause of genetic deafness. It is suspected that many more genetic mutations will be discovered in the next few years.

Check & Review

HOW WE SEE AND HEAR

Light is a form of energy that is part of the electromagnetic spectrum. The **wavelength** of a light determines its **hue**, or color; the **amplitude**, or the height, of a light wave, determines its *intensity*. The range of light waves determines its *complexity*. The function of the eye is to capture light and focus it on visual receptors that convert light energy to neural impulses. Light enters through the pupil and lens to the retina, and then travels along the optic nerve to the brain. Cells in the **retina** called **rods** are specialized for night vision, whereas **cones** are specialized for color and fine detail.

The sense of hearing is known as **audition**. We hear sound via sound waves, which result from rapid changes in air pressure caused by vibrating objects. The wavelength of these sound waves is sensed as the **pitch** of the sound, whereas the amplitude of the waves is perceived as *loudness*. The range of sound waves is sensed as *timbre*, the purity or complexity of the tone. The outer ear conducts sound waves to the middle ear, which in turn conducts vibrations to the inner ear, where hair cells in the **cochlea** transduce mechanical energy into neural impulses. The neural message is then carried along the auditory nerve to the brain.

Questions

1. Trace the path of light as it enters the eye and leaves to go to the brain.
2. The lens of the eye focuses by _____ and _____. The focusing process is known as _____.
3. Trace the path of sound as it enters the ear and leaves to go to the brain.
4. Explain how place theory differs from frequency theory.

Answers to Questions can be found in Appendix B.

OUR OTHER SENSES

How do our other senses enable us to experience the world?

Vision and audition may be the most prominent of our senses, but the others — taste, smell, and the body senses — are also important for gathering information about our environment. The enjoyment of a summer's day comes not only from the visual and auditory beauty of the world but also from the taste of a fresh garden tomato, the smell of honeysuckle, and the feel of a warm, gentle breeze.

Smell and Taste: Sensing Chemicals

Smell and taste are sometimes referred to as the *chemical senses* because they both involve *chemoreceptors* that are sensitive to certain chemical molecules rather than to electromagnetic or mechanical energy. Smell and taste receptors also are located near each other and often interact so closely that we have difficulty separating the sensations. Have you ever noticed how food seems bland when your nose is blocked by a cold and you cannot smell your food?

Olfaction

The sense of smell, or **olfaction**, results from stimulation of receptor cells in the nose (Figure 4.9). These receptors are embedded in a mucus-coated membrane called the *olfactory epithelium*. The olfactory receptors are actually modified neurons, with branched dendrites extending out into the epithelium. When chemical molecules in the air passing through the nose come in contact with the dendrites, they initiate a neural impulse. The impulse travels along the neuron's axon directly to the *olfactory bulb*, a structure just below the frontal lobes where most olfactory information is processed before being sent to other parts of the brain.

Figuring out how we distinguish different odors is complicated for many reasons, not least that we have over 1,000 types of receptors, and we can detect over 10,000 distinct smells (floral, musky, rotten, fruity, and so on). According to one prominent theory, each odor fits into only one type of olfactory receptor cell, like a key into a lock. This theory is, in fact, called the *lock-and-key theory of olfaction*. Another theory proposes that each olfactory receptor is sensitive to only part of a molecule's structure, and distinct odors activate unique combinations of receptor types (Malnic, Hirono, & Buck, 1999).

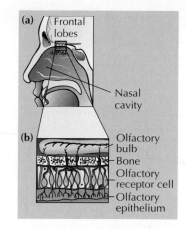

Figure 4.9 *Anatomy of the olfactory system.* (a) The nasal cavity showing the location of olfactory receptors. (b) All olfactory receptors that are sensitive to the same odor send their axons to the same area of the olfactory bulb.

Olfaction *The sense of smell*

GENDER & CULTURAL DIVERSITY

Do Some People Smell Better Than Others?

No, we are not asking if some people smell like roses and others smell like rotten eggs. The question relates to differences in olfactory sensitivity between people. Research has shown that women and younger adults are better at identifying smells, smokers have a dulled sense of smell, and up to 35 percent of people have some form of *anosmia* (odor blindness) (Frye, Schwartz, & Doty, 1990; Gilbert & Wyslocki, 1987; Segal et al., 1995).

Interestingly, some research also finds possible ethnicity differences in smell sensitivity. Using international data from the 1986 National Geographic Smell Survey, C. E. Barber (1997) was able to compare the olfactory sensitivity of several different groups. He compared men to women, young to old, and African to American respondents on one particular odor — androstenone, which is produced by bacteria on the human body and is a component of sweat. Survey respondents included 19,219 Americans and 3,204 Africans of both genders and many different ages.

Barber's research supported earlier findings of increased sensitivity among women and young adults, but African respondents (both men and women) were better than their American counterparts at detecting androstenone. There are many possibilities for the differences in sensitivity, including the environment. Because this was survey research, no one cause can be accurately determined, and the findings of this one study on androstenone cannot be generalized to other odors without further research.

Pheromones [FARE-oh-mones]
Airborne chemicals released from one individual that affect another individual's behavior, including recognition of family members, aggression, territorial marking, and sexual mating

Does smell affect sexual attraction? People have always been interested in increasing their sexual attractiveness. One popular means has been the use of perfumes and, today, aftershave lotions and men's cologne. Is there any scientific basis to such practices? One line of research has focused on **pheromones** — chemical odors we give off that are thought to affect the behavior of others, including their sexual behavior.

Pheromones have been found in a number of animal species and are used to mark trails to food, define territory, and increase sexual arousal and mating behaviors. Although some research supports the idea that pheromones increase sexual behaviors in humans (Cutler, 1999; Cutler, Friedmann, & McCoy, 1998), other findings question the results (Wysocki & Preti, 1998). Despite what the perfume ads might suggest, human sexuality is much more complex than that of other animals (Chapter 11).

Nonetheless, human pheromones may explain several interesting phenomena other than sex. For example, researchers have documented an olfactory linkage behind the common belief that women who live together (in an apartment, military barracks, or sorority) eventually develop synchronized menstrual cycles (Stern & McClintock, 1998). Also, mothers and their babies can recognize each other solely on the basis of smell just a few hours after birth. Will other human pheromone phenomena be discovered? Only further study will tell.

Gustation

Gustation *The sense of taste*

In modern times, **gustation** (the sense of taste) may be the least critical of our senses. In our primate past, however, it probably contributed to our survival. The major function of taste is to provide information about substances that are entering our digestive tract so that we can screen out those that may be harmful. This function is aided by the sense of smell.

When the sense of smell is eliminated, the enormous variety of tastes can be reduced to four: sweet, sour, salty, and bitter. Like smell receptors in the lock-and-key theory, taste receptors respond differentially to the varying shapes of food and liquid molecules. The major taste receptors (or *taste buds*) are clustered within little bumps called *papillae*. You can see these papillae on the surface of your tongue (Figure 4.10).

Why are children so picky about food? In young people, taste buds die and are replaced about every 7 days. As we age, however, the buds are replaced more slowly, so taste diminishes. Thus, children, who have abundant taste buds, often dislike foods with strong or unusual tastes (such as liver and spinach), but as they grow older and lose taste buds, they may come to like these foods.

Some pickiness is related to learning. Many food and taste preferences result from childhood experiences and cultural influences. For example, many Japanese children eat raw fish and some Chinese children eat chicken feet as part of their normal diet, whereas American children might consider these foods "yucky." Likewise, most American children love cheese, which children in some other cultures find repulsive.

Pickiness also relates to the fact that the sense of taste enables humans and animals to discriminate between foods that are safe to eat and foods that are poisonous. Because many plants that taste bitter contain toxic chemicals, an animal is more likely to survive if it avoids bitter-tasting plants (Guinard et al., 1996). On the other hand, humans and animals have a preference for sweet foods that are generally nonpoisonous and are good sources of energy.

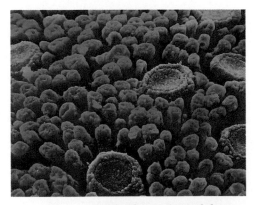

Figure 4.10 *The surface of the human tongue magnified 47 times.* When liquids enter the mouth or food is chewed and dissolved, the fluid runs over the papillae (the lavender circular areas) and into the pores to the taste buds, which contain the receptors for taste. This is why we should chew our food slowly and completely if we want maximum taste satisfaction.

The Body Senses: More Than Just Touch

Imagine for a moment that you are an Olympic skier and you're anxiously awaiting the starting signal that will begin your once-in-a-lifetime race for the gold medal in the giant slalom. What senses will you need to manage the subtle and ever-changing balance adjustments required for Olympic-level skiing? How will you make your skis carve the cleanest, shortest, fastest line from start to finish? What will enable your arms, legs, and trunk to work in perfect harmony so that you can record the shortest time and win the gold? The senses that will allow you to do all this, and much more, are the body senses. The *body senses* tell the brain how the body is oriented, where and how the body is moving, the things it touches or is touched by, and so on. These senses include the skin senses, the vestibular sense, and the kinesthetic sense.

The Skin Senses

The skin senses are extremely vital. Skin not only protects the internal organs but also provides the brain with basic survival information. With nerve endings in the various layers of skin, our skin senses tell us when a pot is dangerously hot, when the weather is freezing cold, and when we have been hurt. Researchers have "mapped" the skin by applying probes to all areas of the body. Mapping shows there are three basic skin sensations: touch (or pressure), temperature, and pain. Receptors for these sensations occur in various concentrations and depths in the skin. For example, touch (pressure) receptors are maximally concentrated on the face and fingers and least in the back and legs. As your hands move over objects, pressure receptors register the indentations created in the skin, allowing perception of texture, and people who are blind learn to read the raised dots that constitute Braille.

The relationship between the types of receptors and the different sensations is not clear. It used to be thought that each receptor responded to only one type of stimulation, but we now know that some receptors respond to more than one. For example, pressure receptors also respond to certain sound waves. And itching, tickling, and vibrating sensations seem to be produced by light stimulation of both pressure and pain receptors.

In conducting studies on temperature receptors, researchers have found that the average square centimeter of skin contains about six cold spots where only cold can be sensed, and one or two warm spots where only warmth can be felt. Interestingly, we don't seem to have separate "hot" receptors. Instead, our cold receptors detect not only coolness but also extreme temperatures — both hot and cold (Craig & Bushnell, 1994). See Figure 4.11.

The Vestibular Sense

The *vestibular sense* is the sense of body orientation and position with respect to gravity and three-dimensional space (in other words, it is the sense of balance). Even the most routine activities — riding a bike, walking, or even sitting up — would be impossible without this sense. The vestibular apparatus is located in the inner ear and is composed of the vestibular sacs and the semicircular canals.

The **semicircular canals** provide the brain with balance information, particularly information about the rotation of the head. As the head moves, liquid in the canals moves and bends hair cell receptors. At the end of the semicircular canals are the *vestibular sacs*, which contain hair cells sensitive to the specific angle of the head — straight up and down or tilted. Information from the semicircular canals and the vestibular sacs is converted to neural impulses that are then carried to the appropriate section of the brain.

What causes motion sickness? Information from the vestibular sense is used by the eye muscles to maintain visual fixation and sometimes by the body to change body orientation. If the vestibular sense gets overloaded or becomes confused by boat, airplane, or automobile motion, the result is often dizziness and

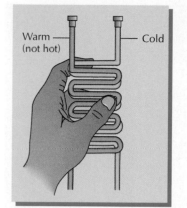

Warm (not hot) — Cold

Figure 4.11 *How do we experience "hot?"* Researchers use an instrument called a "heat grill" — two pipes twisted together, one containing warm water and the other cold. If you grasp both pipes, you experience intense heat because both warm and cold receptors are activated simultaneously. We do not have separate "hot" receptors.

Semicircular Canals *Three arching structures in the inner ear that contain hair receptors that respond to head movements to provide information on balance*

How do they do it? Without her finely tuned vestibular and kinesthetic senses to maintain her balance and coordination, US gymnast Amy Chow would be on her way to the hospital rather than the Olympics.

Kinesthesis *The sensory system that provides information on body posture and orientation*

nausea. Random versus expected movements also are more likely to produce motion sickness. Thus, automobile drivers are better prepared than passengers for upcoming movement and are less likely to feel sick (Rolnick & Lubow, 1991). Motion sickness seems to vary with age: Infants are generally immune, children between ages 2 and 12 years have the highest susceptibility, and the incidence declines in adulthood.

The Kinesthetic Sense

Kinesthesis (from the Greek word for "motion") is the sense that provides the brain with information about bodily posture and orientation, as well as bodily movement. Unlike the receptors for sight, hearing, smell, taste, and balance, which are clumped together in one organ or area, kinesthetic receptors are found throughout the muscles, joints, and tendons of the body. As we sit, walk, bend, lift, turn, and so on, our kinesthetic receptors respond by sending messages to the brain. They tell which muscles are being contracted and which relaxed, how our body weight is distributed, where our arms and legs are in relation to the rest of our body. Without these sensations, we would literally have to watch every step we make.

We rely on kinesthesis constantly yet seldom acknowledge it, because this sense is rarely disturbed in our everyday lives. In one study, an experimenter intentionally disturbed participants' wrist tendon receptors by producing certain vibrations. Participants reported sensations of having multiple forearms and impossible positions of their arms (Craske, 1977). But we don't have to go through experimental procedures to appreciate our kinesthetic sense. All we have to do is observe children learning new skills and remember when we were just learning to ride a bike or catch a football. During the learning process, we consciously move certain body parts and certain muscles, but gradually we learn to operate on "automatic pilot." Our kinesthetic sense needs training in recognizing how various postures and movements should feel.

Check & Review

OUR OTHER SENSES

The sense of smell (**olfaction**) and the sense of taste (**gustation**) are called the chemical senses and are closely interrelated. The receptors for olfaction are at the top of the nasal cavity. According to the lock-and-key theory, we can smell different odors because each three-dimensional odor molecule fits into only one type of receptor. The receptors for gustation are located on the tongue, and are sensitive to four basic tastes: salty, sweet, sour, and bitter.

The body senses are the skin senses, the vestibular sense, and the **kinesthetic** sense. The skin senses detect pressure, temperature, and pain. They protect the internal organs and provide basic survival information. The vestibular apparatus is located in the inner ear. The kinesthetic sense provides the brain with information about body posture and orientation, as well as body movement. The kinesthetic receptors are spread throughout the body in muscles, joints, and tendons.

Questions

1. The _____ theory of olfaction suggests that we cannot smell carbon monoxide because of the shape of the carbon monoxide molecule. (a) chemoreceptor; (b) lock-and-key; (c) geometric; (d) multidimensional.

2. The weightlessness experienced by space travelers as a result of zero gravity has its greatest effect on the _____ senses. (a) visceral; (b) reticular; (c) somasthetic; (d) vestibular.

3. Receptors located in the muscles, joints, and tendons of the body provide _____ information to maintain bodily posture, orientation, and movement.

4. The skin senses include _____. (a) pressure; (b) pain; (c) warmth and cold; (d) all of these

Answers to Questions can be found in Appendix B.

PERCEPTION

At this point, we are ready to move from sensation and the major senses to perception. Keep in mind, however, that the boundary between the two is ambiguous. Look, for example, at Figure 4.12a. What do you see? Most people see splotches of light and dark, but they perceive no real pattern. If you stare long enough, your brain will try to organize the picture into recognizable shapes or objects, as it does when you lie on your back outdoors and gaze at the clouds on a summer's day. Have you seen the image in the photo yet? If not, try rotating the picture (so that the caption is at the top left). Now do you see it? If you still can't, turn the page and look at Figure 4.12b. Before you *perceived* the cow, you *sensed* only light and dark splotches. Only when you could select relevant splotches and organize them into a meaningful pattern were you able to interpret them as the face of a cow.

Normally, our perceptions agree with our sensations, but there are times when they do not. This results in an **illusion**. Illusions are false impressions of the physical world that can be produced by actual physical distortions, as in desert mirages, or by errors in the perceptual process, as in the illusions shown in Figures 4.13 and 4.14. Besides being amusing, illusions provide psychologists with a tool for studying the normal process of perception (e.g., Humphreys and Muller, 2000; Kramer, Hahn, Irwin, & Theeuwes, 2000). (Be careful not to confuse *illusion* with *hallucination* or *delusion* [Chapters 5 and 14]. *Hallucinations* are sensory perceptions that occur without an external stimulus, as in seeing "pulsating flowers" after using LSD [lysergic acid diethylamide] and other hallucinogenic drugs. *Delusions* refer to false beliefs, often of persecution or grandeur, which also may accompany drug or psychotic experiences.)

Illusion *A false impression of the environment*

Perception consists of three basic processes: selection, organization, and interpretation of incoming sensations. We will examine how each process contributes to our perception of the world.

Selection: Extracting Important Messages

The first step in perception is *selection*: choosing where to direct our attention. Three major factors are involved in the decision to pay attention to some stimuli in our environment and not to others: selective attention, feature detectors, and habituation.

How do we decide what to pay attention to in our environment?

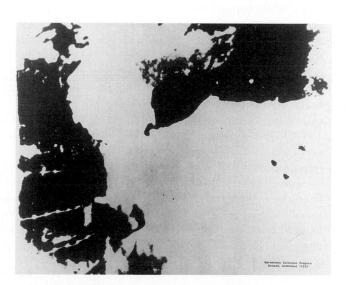

Optometric Extension Program
Duncan, Oklahoma 73533

Figure 4.12a *What is it?*

Figure 4.12b *It's a cow!* Now go back to Figure 4.12a and you will easily perceive a cow.

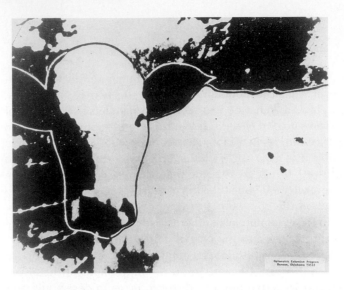

Figure 4.13 *The horizontal–vertical illusion.* Which is longer, the horizontal or the vertical line? People living in areas where they can see long straight lines on the ground, such as roads and shadows of telephone poles, perceive the horizontal line as shorter because of the foreshortening effect.

Selective Attention *The process whereby the brain sorts out, and only attends to, the important messages from the senses*

Feature Detectors *Specialized cells in the brain that respond only to certain sensory information*

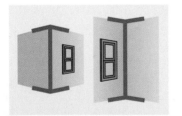

Figure 4.14 *The Müller–Lyer illusion.* Which vertical line is longer? Both are actually the same length, but people who live in urban environments normally see the vertical line on the right as longer than the line on the left. This is because they are used to making size and distance judgments from perspective cues created by right angles and horizontal and vertical lines of buildings and streets.

Selective Attention

As you sit reading this chapter, you may be ignoring sounds from another room or the discomfort of the chair you're sitting on. In almost every situation, there is an excess of sensory information, but the brain manages to sort out the important messages and discard the rest (Folk & Remington, 1998; Kramer, Hahn, Irwin, & Theeuwes, 2000). When you are in a group of people, surrounded by various conversations, you can still select and attend to the voices of people you find interesting. This process is known as **selective attention**.

Feature Detectors

The second major factor in selection is the presence of specialized cells in the brain called **feature detectors** (or *feature analyzers*) that respond only to certain sensory information. In 1959, researchers discovered specialized nerve cells in the optic nerve of a frog, which they called "bug detectors" because they respond only to moving bugs (Lettvin, Maturana, McCulloch, & Pitts, 1959), and in the early 1960s, researchers found feature detectors in cats that respond to specific lines and angles (Hubel, 1963; Hubel & Wiesel, 1965, 1979). Similar studies with humans have found feature detectors in the temporal and frontal lobes that respond maximally to faces, and damage to these areas can produce a condition called *prosopagnosia* (*prospon* means "face" and *agnosia* means "failure to know") (O'Scalaidhe, Wilson, & Goldman-Rakic, 1997). Interestingly, people with this disorder can recognize that they are looking at a face, but cannot say whose face it is — even if it belongs to a relative or friend or is their own, reflected in a mirror.

Certain basic mechanisms for perceptual selection are thus built into the brain, but a certain amount of interaction with the environment is apparently necessary for feature detector cells to develop normally (Crair, Gillespie, & Stryker, 1998). One well-known study demonstrated that kittens raised in a cylinder with vertically or horizontally striped walls develop severe behavioral and neurological impairments (Blakemore & Cooper, 1970) (Figure 4.15). When "horizontal cats" — those raised with only horizontal lines in their environment — were removed from the cylinder and allowed to roam, they could easily jump onto horizontal surfaces but had great difficulty negotiating objects with vertical lines, such as chair legs. The reverse was true for the "vertical cats": They could easily avoid table and chair legs but never attempted to jump onto horizontal structures. Examination of the visual cortex of these cats revealed that because of their restricted environment, they had failed to develop their potential feature detectors for either vertical or horizontal lines.

Habituation

Another physiological factor important in selecting sensory data is **habituation**, the tendency to ignore environmental factors that remain constant. The brain seems "prewired" to pay more attention to changes in the environment than to stimuli that remain constant. For example, when you buy a new CD, you initially listen carefully to all the songs. Over time, your attention declines and you can play the entire CD and not really notice it. This may not matter with CDs — we can always replace them when we become bored. But this same habituation phenomenon also applies to your friends and love life — and people aren't as easily replaced. Attention and compliments from a stranger are almost always more exciting and "valuable" than from long-time friends and lovers. Unfortunately, some people leave good relationships not realizing that they will soon *habituate* to the new person. (This knowledge is another payoff for studying psychology!)

How does habituation differ from sensory adaptation? Good question. Habituation is a perceptual process that occurs in the brain, whereas sensory adaptation occurs when sensory receptors (in the skin, eyes, ears, and so on) actually decrease the number of sensory messages they send to the brain. This is another example of bottom-up versus top-down processing. Sensory adaptation occurs when you first put on your shoes in the morning. Pressure/touch receptors in your feet send multiple messages to your brain, but with time they *adapt* and send fewer messages. You also habituate and your brain "chooses to ignore" the fact that you're wearing shoes. You only notice when something changes — when you break a buckle or shoelace or get a blister from new shoes.

When given a wide variety of stimuli to choose from, we automatically select stimuli that are *intense, novel, moving, contrasting,* and *repetitious.* Parents and teachers often use these same attention-getting principles, but advertisers and politicians have spent millions of dollars developing them to a fine art. The next time you're watching TV, notice the commercial and political ads. Are they louder or brighter than the regular program (intensity)? Do they use talking dogs, singing frogs, or politicians playing saxophones (novelty)? Is the promoted product or candidate set in *favorable* contrast to the competition? No need to ask about repetition. This is the foundation of all commercial and political ads. Surprisingly, obnoxious advertising does not always deter people from buying the advertised product (or candidate). For sheer volume of sales, the question of whether you like the ad is irrelevant. If they get your attention, that's all that matters.

Figure 4.15 *Nature versus nurture.* Kittens reared in a vertical world failed to develop their "innate" ability to detect horizontal lines or objects, whereas the reverse is true for kittens restricted to only horizontal lines. This is because brain cells sensitive to these features deteriorated during the critical (and irreversible) period in visual development.

Habituation *The tendency of the brain to ignore environmental factors that remain constant*

Check & Review

SELECTION

The selection process allows us to choose which of the billions of separate sensory messages will eventually be processed. **Selective attention** allows us to direct our attention to the most important aspect of the environment at any one time.

Feature detectors are specialized cells in the brain that distinguish between different sensory inputs. The selection process is very sensitive to changes in the environment. We **habituate** to unchanging stimuli and pay attention when stimuli change in intensity, novelty, location, and so on.

Questions

1. Explain how *illusions* differ from *delusions* and *hallucinations.*
2. Specialized cells in the brain called _____ respond only to certain types of sensory information.

Organization: Form, Constancies, Depth, and Color

Having selected incoming information, we must organize it into patterns and principles that will help us understand the world. In other words, raw sensory data are like the parts of a watch — they must be assembled in a meaningful way before they are useful. We organize sensory data in terms of *form, constancy, depth,* and *color.*

Form Perception

Look at the first drawing in Figure 4.16. What do you see? Can you draw a similar object on a piece of paper? This is known as an "impossible figure," yet it clearly exists — on this page. The second part of the figure shows a painting by M. C. Escher, a Dutch painter who created striking examples of perceptual distortion. Although drawn to represent three-dimensional objects or situations, the parts don't assemble into logical wholes. Like the illusions studied earlier, impossible figures also help us understand perceptual principles — in this case, the principle of *form organization.*

Gestalt psychologists were among the first to study how the brain organizes sensory impressions. The German word *gestalt* means "whole" or "pattern." Accordingly, Gestaltists emphasized the importance of organization and patterning in enabling us to perceive the whole stimulus rather than perceiving its discrete parts as separate entities. The Gestaltists proposed laws of organization that specify how people perceive form. The most fundamental Gestalt principle or law of organization is that we tend to distinguish between **figure and ground**.

> How do we organize stimuli in order to perceive form, constancies, depth, and color?

Figure and Ground *A Gestalt law of perceptual organization stating that our perceptions consist of two aspects: the figure, which stands out and has a definite contour or shape, and the ground, which is less distinct*

Figure 4.16 *Can you explain these "impossible figures?"* When you first glance at figure (a) and the famous painting by M.C. Escher in (b), you detect specific features of the stimuli and judge them as sensible (an example of *bottom-up* processing). But as you try to sort and organize the different elements into a stable, well-organized whole, you realize they don't add up — they're illogical or "impossible" (an example of *top-down processing*).

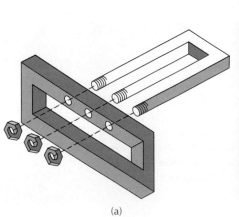

(a)   (b)

For example, while you are reading this material, your eyes are receiving sensations of black lines and white paper, but your brain is organizing these sensations into letters and words that are perceived against a backdrop of white pages. The letters constitute the figure and the pages constitute the ground. The discrepancy between figure and ground is sometimes so vague that we have difficulty perceiving which is which, as can be seen in Figure 4.17. This is known as a *reversible figure*. The figure and ground and other basic Gestalt principles are summarized in Figure 4.18. Although these examples are all visual, each law applies to other modes of perception as well.

Figure 4.18 *Basic Gestalt principles of organization.* Figure–ground, proximity, continuity, closure, and similarity are shown here, but the Gestalt principle of contiguity cannot be shown because it involves nearness in time, not visual nearness. Top photo: Maria Martinez (1881(?)–1980), black-on-black jar. Jerry Jacka photography, Museum of New Mexico. Center cartoon: B. Kliban. "July" page from the 1977 Cat Calendar published by Workman Publishing. Copyright Judith Kamman Kliban. Bottom photo: Alexander Calder. The Hostess (1928), Wire construction, $11^1/_2 \times 4^1/_2 \times 11^7/_8$, The Museum of Modern Art, New York. Gift of Edward M. M. Marburg. Photograph © 1997 The Museum of Modern Art, New York.

Figure 4.17 *Figure and ground.* What do you see? A vase or two faces looking at one another? Your answer depends on whether your perceptual expectations cause you to see the vase as figure or as ground.

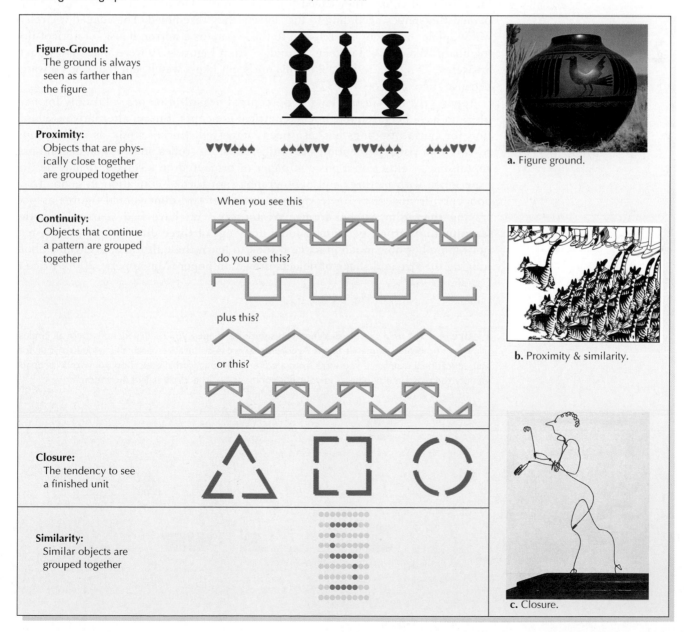

Figure-Ground:
The ground is always seen as farther than the figure

Proximity:
Objects that are physically close together are grouped together

Continuity:
Objects that continue a pattern are grouped together

When you see this

do you see this?

plus this?

or this?

Closure:
The tendency to see a finished unit

Similarity:
Similar objects are grouped together

a. Figure ground.

b. Proximity & similarity.

c. Closure.

GENDER & CULTURAL DIVERSITY

Are the Gestalt Laws Universally True?

Are the Gestalt laws of perception universally true for all people? The Gestalt psychologists conducted most of their work with formally educated people from urban European cultures, but A. R. Luria (1976) wondered whether their laws held true for all participants, regardless of their type of education and cultural setting. In what is now a classic study, Luria recruited a wide range of participants living in what was then the USSR, including Ichkeri women from remote villages (with no formal education), collective farm activists (who were semiliterate), and female students in a teachers' school (with years of formal education).

Luria found that when presented with the stimuli shown in Figure 4.19, the formally trained female students were the only ones who identified the shapes by their categorical names. That is, whether circles were made of solid lines, incomplete lines, or solid colors, they called them all circles. However, the other two groups named the shapes according to the objects they resembled. They called a circle a watch, plate, or moon, and referred to the square as a mirror, house, or apricot-drying board. When asked if items 12 and 13 from Figure 4.19 were alike, one woman answered, "No, they're not alike. This one's not like a watch, but that one's a watch because there are dots" (p. 37).

Apparently, the Gestalt laws of perceptual organization are valid only for people who have been schooled in geometrical concepts. But an alternative explanation for Luria's findings has also been suggested. Luria's study, as well as most research on visual perception and optical illusions, relies on two-dimensional presentations — either on a piece of paper or projected on a screen. It may be that experience with pictures and photographs (not formal education in geometrical concepts) is necessary for learning to interpret two-dimensional figures as portraying three-dimensional forms. Westerners who have had years of practice learning to interpret two-dimensional drawings of three-dimensional objects may not remember how much practice it took to learn the cultural conventions about judging the size and shape of objects drawn on paper (Matsumoto, 2000; Price & Crapo, 1999).

Figure 4.19 *Luria's stimuli.* When you see these shapes, you readily identify them as circles, triangles, and other geometric forms. According to cross-cultural research, this is due to your formal educational training. If you were from a culture without formal education, you would probably identify them as familiar objects in your environment — "the circle is like the moon."

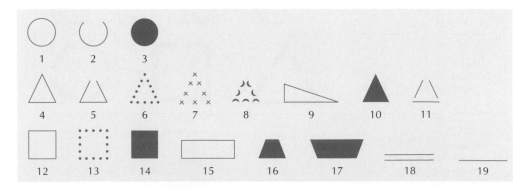

Perceptual Constancies

Now that we've seen how form perception contributes to organization, let's examine perceptual constancies. As noted earlier with sensory adaptation and habituation, we are particularly alert to change. However, we also manage to perceive a great deal of consistency in the environment. Without **perceptual constancy** our world would be totally chaotic. Things would seem to grow as we got closer to them, to change shape as our viewing angle changed, and to change color as light levels changed. The four best-known constancies are visual:

Perceptual Constancy *The tendency for the environment to be perceived as remaining the same even with changes in sensory input*

1. Size constancy. Most perceptual constancies are based on prior experience and learning. For example, preschoolers express wonder at the fact that the car parked down the street is only "this high" (as they show about 2 inches between their fingers), whereas the car they are standing next to is taller than they are. Their size judgment is mistaken because they haven't yet had the experiences necessary for learning size constancy. According to this principle, the perceived size of an object remains the same even though the size of its retinal image changes.

Anthropologist Colin Turnbull (1961) provided a now classic example of an adult who had never developed a sense of size constancy. While studying the Twa people living in the dense rain forest of the Congo River valley in Africa, Turnbull took a native named Kenge for a Jeep ride to the African plains. Kenge had lived his entire life in an area so dense with foliage that he had never seen distances farther than about 100 yards. Now he was suddenly able to see for almost 70 miles. Lacking perceptual experience with such wide-open spaces, Kenge had great difficulty judging sizes. When he first saw a herd of water buffalo in the distance, he thought they were insects. When Turnbull insisted they were buffalo that were very far away, Kenge was insulted and asked, "Do you think that I am ignorant?" To Kenge's surprise, as they drove toward the "insects," the creatures seemed to grow into buffalo. He concluded that witchcraft was being used to fool him, and after Turnbull showed him a lake so large that its opposite shore couldn't be seen, he asked to be taken back to his rain forest.

2. Shape constancy. Other constancies also develop through individual experience. When you look at a chair directly from the front or the back, it has a rectangular shape. When you look at it directly from the side, it has an h shape. Yet you still perceive the chair as having a single shape because your brain remembers past experiences with objects that only seemed to change shape as you moved but actually remained constant. This is known as *shape constancy.*

An ophthalmologist named Adelbert Ames demonstrated the power of shape and size constancies by creating what is now known as the Ames room (see photographs on next page). On examining this photograph, you might conclude that the person on the left is a midget and the person on the right is a giant. In actuality, both people are normal size. This illusion is based on the unusual construction of the room. As can be seen in the diagram in Figure 4.20, perspective tricks the observer into perceiving the room as square when it is actually shaped like a trapezoid. The illusion is so strong that when a person walks from the left corner to the right, the observer perceives the person to be "growing," even though that is not possible.

If we know the truth of this illusion, why does it still work? Our brain has had a lifetime of interaction with normally constructed rooms, and our desire to perceive the room according to our experience is so powerful that we overrule the

The Ames room illusion. In the left photo, the woman on the right appears much taller than the boy on the left, but when they reverse positions (the right photo) the boy is taller. For an explanation of how this is possible, see Figure 4.20.

truth. This is not a breakdown in perception but rather a result of trying to apply the standard perceptual processes of shape and size constancy to an unusual situation.

3. *Color constancy* and 4. *Brightness constancy.* Other forms of constancy that add stability to our world are *color constancy* and *brightness constancy*. These enable us to perceive things as retaining the same color or brightness levels even though the amount of light may vary. For example, if you place a piece of gray paper in bright sunlight and a piece of white paper in shade, you will still perceive the white as lighter and the gray as darker. This is true regardless of the amount of reflected light actually coming from their surfaces. If you know an object from prior experience, you expect it will be the same color and the same relative brightness in bright light as in low light. That is, you expect it to be its "right" color.

As is the case with shape and size constancy, color constancy and brightness constancy are learned as a result of experience with familiar objects. If an object is unfamiliar, we determine its color and brightness by the actual wavelength of reflected light in combination with the color and brightness of the background.

Figure 4.20 *Explanation for the Ames room illusion.* To the viewer peering through the peephole, the room appears perfectly normal. However, in this specially constructed room, the trapezoidal shape and sloping ceilings and floors provide misleading depth cues. Because the brain assumes the two people are the same distance away, it compensates for the differences in retinal size by making the person on the left appear much smaller.

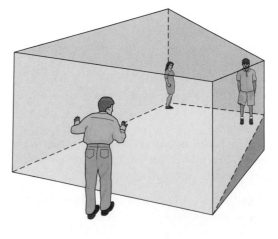

Check & Review

ORGANIZATION — FORM AND CONSTANCIES

The Gestalt psychologists set forth laws explaining how people perceive form. The most fundamental principle is the distinction between **figure and ground**. Other principles include proximity, continuity, closure, contiguity, and similarity. Through the **perceptual constancies** of size, shape, color, and brightness, we are able to perceive a stable environment, even though the actual sensory information we receive may be constantly changing.

These constancies are based on our prior experiences and learning.

Questions

1. Name the Gestalt principle that is being described: (a) You see a black line on the concrete and realize that it is a single trail of ants. (b) You can read a sentence on a bulletin board even if someone is standing in front of a few words. (c) You see a circle even though part of its curve is erased in three spots.

2. The principle of _____ is at work when, as your brother walks away from you, you don't perceive him to be shrinking.

3. The principle of _____ allows us to see a white blouse as white both in sunlight and in shade.

4. As a flock of Canadian geese flies overhead in its familiar V formation, the geese are seen as _____ and the sky as _____. (a) continuity, a closure; (b) a sensation, perception; (c) figure; ground; (d) ground, figure

Answers to Questions can be found in Appendix B.

Depth Perception

The role of experience and learning in organizing perceptions is particularly clear in depth perception. **Depth perception** allows us to accurately estimate the distance of perceived objects and thereby perceive the world in three dimensions. It is possible to judge the distance of objects with nearly all senses. For example, if a person enters a dark room and walks toward you, his or her voice and footsteps get louder, and body smells grow stronger, and you may even be able to feel the slight movement of air from his or her approaching movement. However, in most cases, we rely most heavily on vision to perceive distance. When you add the ability to accurately perceive distance to the ability to judge the height and width of an object, you are able to perceive the world in three dimensions. But no matter which sense you use to perceive the three-dimensional world, perception of depth is primarily learned.

Take the classic example of a patient known as S. B., blind since the age of 10 months, whose sight was restored at age 52. Following the operation that removed cataracts from both eyes, S. B. had great difficulty learning to use his newly acquired vision for judging distance and depth. On one occasion, he was found trying to crawl out of the window of his hospital room. He thought he would be able to lower himself by his hands to the ground below, even though the window was on the fourth floor.

Didn't S. B. have some inborn depth and distance perception? The answer is not clear. As you know (Chapter 1), one of the most enduring debates in psychology (and other sciences) is the question of "nature versus nurture," inborn versus learned. In this case, naturists argue that depth perception is inborn, whereas nurturists insist it is learned. Today, most scientists think there is some truth in both viewpoints.

Evidence for the innate position comes from a set of interesting experiments with an apparatus called the *visual cliff* (Figure 4.21). The apparatus consists of a tabletop with a slightly raised platform across the middle. On one side of the platform the tabletop is clear glass, with the red-and-white-checked pattern running down the side of the table and onto the floor several feet below the glass, simulating a steep cliff.

Depth Perception *By organizing perception in three-dimensions — even though the images that strike the retina are two-dimensional — we can perceive distance*

At first sight. In this love story, Val Kilmer stars as blind masseur who undergoes experimental surgery to have his sight restored. To the audience's surprise, Kilmer is not completely happy as a sighted person.

Figure 4.21 *The visual cliff.* Crawling infants generally refuse to move across this glass surface designed to look like the edge of an elevated platform—even when their mothers stood on the opposite side and coaxed them. This suggests they are able to perceive depth.

Binocular Cues *Visual input from two eyes that allows perception of depth or distance*

Monocular Cues *Visual input from a single eye alone that contributes to perception of depth or distance*

Retinal Disparity *A binocular cue to distance in which the separation of the eyes causes different images to fall on each retina*

Convergence *A binocular depth cue in which the closer the object, the more the eyes converge, or turn inward*

When an infant is placed on the platform and is coaxed by his or her mother to crawl to one side of the table, the infant will readily move to the "shallow" side but will hesitate or refuse to move to the "deep" side (Gibson & Walk, 1960). This reaction is given as evidence of innate depth perception — the infant's hesitation is attributed to fear of the apparent cliff.

Although some have argued that by the time infants are crawling and old enough to be tested they may have *learned* to perceive depth, research with babies at 2 months of age will show a change in heart rate when placed on the deep side of the cliff, but not on the shallow side (Banks & Salapatek, 1983). Similar research with baby chickens, goats, and lambs — animals that walk almost immediately after birth — supports the hypothesis that some depth perception is inborn, as these animals hesitate in stepping onto the steep side.

Once again, the nature–nurture debate continues. However, we all recognize that in our three-dimensional world, the ability to perceive depth and distance is essential. But how do we perceive a three-dimensional world with a two-dimensional receptor system? One mechanism is the interaction of both eyes to produce **binocular cues**; the other involves **monocular cues**, which work with each eye separately.

1. Binocular cues. One of the most important cues for depth perception comes from **retinal disparity**. Because our eyes are about $2^{1}/_{2}$ inches apart, each retina receives a slightly different view of the world. You can demonstrate this for yourself by pointing at some distant object across the room with your arm extended straight in front of you. Holding your pointing finger steady, close your left eye and then your right. You will notice that your finger seems to jump from one position to another as you change eyes, because of retinal disparity. The brain fuses the different images received by the two eyes into one overall visual image (Figure 4.22). Such *stereoscopic vision* provides important cues to depth.

As we move closer and closer to an object, a second binocular (and neuromuscular) cue, **convergence**, helps us judge depth. The closer the object, the more our eyes are turned inward, toward our noses (Figure 4.23). Hold your index finger at arm's length in front of you and watch it as you bring it closer and closer until it is right in front of your nose. The amount of strain in your eye muscles created by the convergence, or turning inward of the eyes, is used as a cue by your brain to interpret distance.

Knowing how convergence operates might help you improve your performance in athletic endeavors. Allen Souchek (1986) found that depth perception is better when looking directly at an object, rather than out of the corner of your eye. Thus, if you turn your body or your head so that you look straight at your tennis opponent or the pitcher, you will more accurately judge the distance of the ball and thereby more likely swing at the right time.

2. Monocular cues. Retinal disparity (see page 145) and convergence are inadequate in judging distances longer than the length of a football field. According to R. L. Gregory (1969), "we are effectively one-eyed for distances greater than perhaps

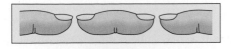

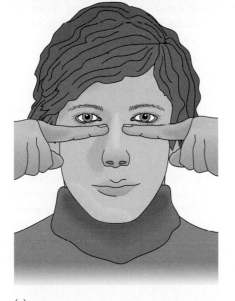

(a)

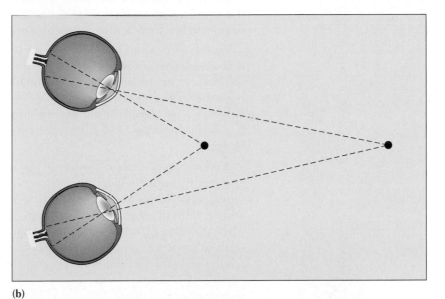

(b)

(c)

Figure 4.22 *Retinal disparity.* (a) Stare at your two index fingers a few inches in front of your eyes with their tips a half inch apart. Do you see the "floating finger?" Move it further away and the "finger" will shrink. Move it closer and it will enlarge. (b) Because of retinal disparity, objects at different distances (such as the "floating finger") project their images on different parts of the retina. Far objects project on the retinal area near the nose, whereas near objects project farther out, closer to the ears. (c) "Magic Eye" images take advantage of retinal disparity. Patiently stare at this image while focusing your eyes beyond it. Most people eventually see the three-dimensional image. © Magic Eye 1983 N. E. Thing Enterprises, Inc. Reproduced with permission of Andrews and McMeel. All rights reserved.

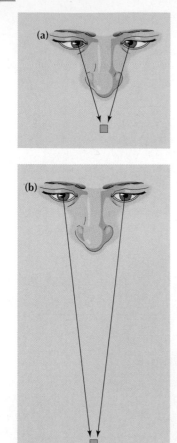

Figure 4.23 *Convergence.* (a) Your eyes turn in to view close objects and (b) turn out to view distant objects.

100 meters" (p. 67). Luckily, we have several monocular cues available separately to each eye. Artists use these same monocular cues to create an illusion of depth on a flat canvas, a three-dimensional world on a two-dimensional surface. Figure 4.24 demonstrates six different monocular cues.

Two additional monocular cues — ones that cannot be used by artists — are *accommodation* of the lens of the eye and *motion parallax.* As you learned earlier in the chapter, *accommodation* refers to changes in the shape of the lens of the eye in response to the distance of the object being focused. For near objects, the lens bulges; for far objects, it flattens. Information from the muscles that move the lens is sent to the brain, which interprets the signal and perceives the distance of the object.

Motion parallax (also known as *relative motion*) refers to the fact that when an observer is moving, objects at various distances move at different speeds across the retinal field. Close objects appear to whiz by, farther objects seem to move slowly, and very distant objects appear to remain stationary. This effect can easily be seen when traveling by car or train. Telephone poles and fences next to the road or track seem to move by very rapidly, houses and trees in the midground seem to move by relatively slowly, and the mountains in the distance seem not to move at all.

Color Perception

We humans may be able to discriminate among 7 million different hues. Is such color perception inborn and culturally universal? Research on many cultures with many different languages suggests that we all seem to see essentially the same colored world (Davies, 1998). Furthermore, studies of infants old enough to focus and move their eyes show that they are able to see color nearly as well as adults (Teller, Peeples, & Sekel, 1978; Werner & Wooten, 1979).

Figure 4.24 *Monocular depth cues.* Several monocular depth cues can be seen in this photograph. (a) *Linear perspective* results when parallel lines converge in the distance. (b) *Interposition* results when a close object obscures part of a distant object. (c) *Relative size* is the result of close objects projecting a larger retinal image than distant objects. (d) *Texture gradient* results from the change in perceived texture as the background recedes into the distance. (e) *Aerial perspective* means that faraway objects look fuzzy and blurred compared with near objects because of intervening particles of dust or haze in the atmosphere. (f) *Light and shadow* means that brighter objects are perceived as closer, whereas darker objects are perceived as farther away.

(a) Perspective   (b) Interposition

(c) Relative size

(d) Texture gradient

Although we know color is produced by different wavelengths of light, the actual way in which we perceive color is a matter of scientific debate. Traditionally, there have been two theories of color vision, the trichromatic (three-color) theory and the opponent-process theory. The **trichromatic theory** (from the Greek *tri-*, "three," and *chroma*, "color") was first proposed by Thomas Young in the early nineteenth century and was later refined by Hermann von Helmholtz and others. It states that there are three "color systems," as they called them — one system that is maximally sensitive to blue, another maximally sensitive to green, and another maximally sensitive to red (Young, 1802). The proponents of this theory demonstrated that mixing lights of these three colors could yield the full spectrum of colors we perceive. Unfortunately, this theory has two major flaws. One is that it doesn't explain defects in color vision; the other is that it doesn't explain *color aftereffects*, a phenomenon you can experience in the Try This Yourself feature on this page.

The **opponent-process theory**, proposed by Ewald Hering later in the nineteenth century, also proposes three color systems, but with the stipulation that each is sensitive to two opposing colors — blue and yellow, red and green, black and white — in an "on–off" fashion. In other words, each color receptor responds either to blue or yellow or to red or green, with the black-or-white system responding to differences in brightness levels. This theory makes a lot of sense because when different colored lights are combined, people are unable to see reddish greens and bluish yellows; in fact, when red and green lights or blue and yellow lights are mixed in equal amounts, we see white. The opponent-process theory adequately explains color vision defects, because most people who have a color weakness are unable to see either red and green or blue and yellow.

Are you color-blind? Figure 4.25 provides one type of test. Actually, most color vision defects are weaknesses — color confusion rather than color blindness. Many people who have some color blindness are not even aware of it.

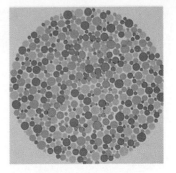

Figure 4.25 *Color-deficient vision.* People who suffer red–green deficiency have trouble perceiving the number within the design.

Trichromatic Theory *The theory first proposed by Thomas Young stating that color perception results from mixing three distinct color systems — red, green, and blue*

Opponent-Process Theory *The theory first proposed by Ewald Hering that color perception is based on three systems of color opposites — blue–yellow, red–green, and black–white*

TRY THIS *Yourself*

The opponent-process theory also accounts for the phenomenon of color aftereffects — images that are perceived after staring at a particular colored pattern for a period of time. Try staring at the color-distorted American flag for several minutes. Then stare at a plain sheet of white paper. You should get interesting color aftereffects — red in place of green, blue in place of yellow, and white in place of black, a "genuine" American flag.

What happened? As you stared at the figure, the green stripes stimulated only the green channel of the red–green opponent color cells. Several minutes of continuous stimulation fatigued the green channel, whereas the nonstimulated red channel was not fatigued. When you looked at the blank piece of paper, the white stimulated both the red and the green channels equally. Under normal viewing conditions, the red and green channels would have canceled each other out and you would have seen white. However, because the green channel was fatigued, the red channel fired at a higher rate and you therefore saw a red color aftereffect.

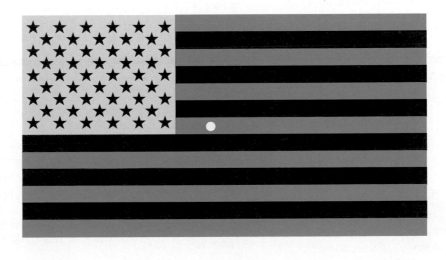

Two Correct Theories

Judging from the discussion so far, it would seem the opponent-process theory is the correct one. Actually, however, both theories are correct. In 1964, George Wald demonstrated that there are indeed three different types of cones in the retina, each with its own type of photopigment. One type of pigment is sensitive to blue light, one is sensitive to green light, and the third is sensitive to red light.

At nearly the same time that Wald was doing his research on cones, R. L. DeValois (1965) was studying electrophysiological recording of cells in the optic nerve and optic pathways to the brain. DeValois discovered cells that respond to color in an opponent fashion in the thalamus. Thus, it appears that both theories have been correct all along. Color is processed in a trichromatic fashion at the level of the retina (in the cones) and in an opponent fashion at the level of the optic nerve and the thalamus (in the brain).

Check & Review

ORGANIZATION — DEPTH AND COLOR

Depth perception allows us to accurately estimate the distance of perceived objects and thereby perceive the world in three dimensions. But how do we perceive a three-dimensional world with two-dimensional receptors called eyes? There are two major types of cues: **binocular cues**, which require two eyes, and monocular cues, which require only one eye. The binocular cues are **retinal disparity** and **convergence**. **Monocular cues** include linear perspective, aerial perspective, texture gradients, interposition, light and shadow, relative size, accommodation, and motion parallax.

Color perception is explained by a combination of two color theories. The **trichromatic theory** proposes three color systems maximally sensitive to blue, green, and red. The **opponent-process theory** also proposes three color systems but holds that each is sensitive to two opposing colors — blue and yellow, red and green, and black and white — and that they operate in an on–off fashion. The trichromatic system operates at the level of the retina, whereas the opponent-process system occurs in the brain.

Questions

1. The visual cliff is an apparatus designed to study _____ in young organisms. (a) color discrimination; (b) shape constancy; (c) depth perception; (d) monocular vision.

2. Since Jolly Roger, the pirate, lost one eye in a fight, he can no longer use _____ as a cue for the perception of depth and distance. (a) accommodation; (b) retinal disparity; (c) motion parallax; (d) aerial perspective.

3. After staring at a bright red rectangle for a period of time, a phenomenon known as _____ occurs, which means that if you look away and at a white background, you will see a _____.

4. Explain how the trichromatic theory of color perception differs from the opponent-process theory.

Answers to Questions can be found in Appendix B.

Interpretation: Explaining Our Perceptions

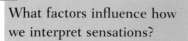

What factors influence how we interpret sensations?

After selectively sorting through incoming sensory information and organizing it into patterns, the brain uses this information to explain and make judgments about the external world. This final stage of perception — interpretation — is influenced by several factors, including perceptual adaptation, perceptual set, individual motivation, and frame of reference.

1. *Perceptual adaptation.* What would it be like if your visual field was inverted and reversed? You would certainly have trouble getting around. Things that you expected to be on your right would be on your left, and things you expected to be above your head would be below your head. Do you think you could ever *adapt* to this distorted world?

To answer such a question, psychologist George Stratton (1897) wore special lenses for 8 days. For the first few days, Stratton had a great deal of difficulty navigating in this environment and coping with everyday tasks. But by the third day, his experience had begun to change and he noted:

> Walking through the narrow spaces between pieces of furniture required much less care than hitherto. I could watch my hands as they wrote, without hesitating or becoming embarrassed thereby.

By the fifth day, Stratton had almost completely adjusted to his strange perceptual environment. His expectations of how the world should be arranged had changed.

2. *Perceptual set.* Our previous experiences, assumptions, and expectations also affect how we interpret and perceive the world. If a car backfires, runners at a track meet may jump the gun. People who believe that extraterrestrials occasionally visit the earth may interpret a weather balloon or an odd-shaped cloud as a spaceship. These mental predispositions, or **perceptual sets**, prepare us in a certain way and greatly influence our perception — in other words, we largely see what we expect to see. Studies that used the famous reversible figure of the young/old woman that you saw on page 118 found that when people are led to expect either a young woman or an old woman generally see the one they expect (Leeper, 1935). Perceptual set also explains why labels such as *mental patient*, *nerd*, *fag*, or *bitch* can lead to painful and dangerous forms of prejudice and discrimination (see Chapters 11, 14, and 16).

3. *Individual motivation.* How we interpret what we perceive is also influenced by our personal interests and needs. Stephan, Berscheid, and Walster (1971) found that sexually aroused men judged photographs of women as more attractive than did nonaroused males, and this reaction was particularly strong when the men believed they would actually have dates with the women.

4. *Frame of reference.* Our perceptions of people, objects, or situations are also affected by their frame of reference, or context. A man might judge a woman's photograph attractive when seen by itself, but he might judge it unattractive if it is seen next to a photo of a Miss America.

What if the world were upside down? The student on the right is wearing inverting lenses that literally turn the world upside down–the sky is down, the ground is up. The one on the left is wearing displacement goggles that shift the apparent location of objects 40 degrees to the left. Both have difficulty shaking hands. However, the human brain adapts to this type of distortion relatively quickly, and eventually the upside down world would appear normal.

Perceptual Set *A readiness to perceive in a particular manner, based on expectations*

Perceptual set. Do you notice anything unusual in this photo? What happens when you turn the book upside down? Despite the distortion, most people see the first photo as normal because of perceptual set.

Can we be influenced by subliminal messages, and do some people have ESP?

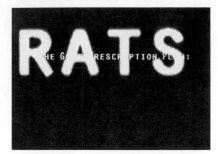

Subliminal ads and politics? During the 2000 Presidential campaign, Republicans allegedly used subliminal ads (the word "RATS") to create negative perceptions of Democrat drug prescription plans.

Subliminal *Pertaining to any stimulus presented below the threshold of conscious awareness*

Subliminal Perception and ESP: Are They for Real?

Does *subliminal perception* really exist? Can people really send and receive messages about the world by using *extrasensory perception* (ESP)? What are the facts?

Subliminal Perception

Several years ago, it was popular to believe that movie theaters were manipulating consumers by subliminally presenting messages like "Eat popcorn" and "Drink Coca-Cola." Similarly, record companies were supposedly embedding subliminal messages in rock music that encouraged violence and sex in listeners. The words on the movie screen and the messages in the music were allegedly presented so quickly that they were below the threshold for awareness. The public was both fascinated and outraged. Politicians rushed to pass laws against the "invisible sell" and the "moral corruption" of our youth. Were they right to be concerned?

There are two major issues surrounding *subliminal perception*. First, is it possible to perceive something without conscious awareness? The answer is clearly yes. Scientific research on **subliminal** (literally, "below the threshold") stimuli demonstrates that information processing does occur even when we are not aware of it (Bargh, 1999; Dimberg, Thunberg, & Elmehed, 2000; Greenwald & Banaji, 1995).

Experimental studies commonly use an instrument called a *tachistoscope* to flash images too quickly for conscious recognition but slowly enough to be registered. For example, in one study the experimenter flashed one of two pictures subliminally (either a happy or angry face) followed by a neutral face. They found this subliminal presentation evoked matching unconscious facial expressions in the participant's own facial muscles (Dimberg, Thunberg, & Elmehed, 2000). As you will discover in Chapter 12, the fact that participants were unaware of the subliminal stimuli, as well as their own matching facial response, raises questions regarding our own emotional states. (For example, do we unconsciously become a little more "up" or "down" if we're exposed to good-natured, pleasant people or depressed and angry people?) This study also demonstrates that at least some behaviors can be influenced by subliminal stimuli.

Although subliminal perception *does* occur, the second — and more important — question is "Does it lead to *subliminal persuasion*?" The answer to this question is less clear. Subliminal stimuli are basically *weak* stimuli. At best, they have a modest (if any) effect on consumer behavior and absolutely *no effect* on the minds of youth listening to rock music or citizens' voting behavior (Begg, Needham, & Bookbinder, 1993; Trappey, 1996). If you're wondering about buying subliminal tapes promising to help you lose weight or relieve stress, save your money. Blank "placebo" tapes appear to be just as "effective" as subliminal tapes.

In sum, there is evidence that subliminal perception occurs, but the effect on actual behavior is uncertain. When it comes to commercials and self-help tapes, advertisers are better off using the loudest, clearest, and most attention getting stim-

Zits

uli, and your money and time for self-improvement are better spent on the old-fashioned methods of exercise and diet.

Extrasensory Perception

Extrasensory perception (ESP) is the alleged ability to perceive things that cannot be perceived with the normal five senses. People who claim to have ESP, so-called *psychics*, profess to be able to read other people's minds (*telepathy*), perceive objects or events that are inaccessible to their normal senses (*clairvoyance*), predict the future (*precognition*), or move or affect objects without touching them (*psychokinesis*). Popular tabloids arc filled with accounts of psychics claiming to be able to find lost children, talk to the dead, or even predict the stock market (Jaroff, 2001; McDonald, 2001).

Scientific investigations of ESP began in the early 1900s with Joseph B. Rhine. Many of these early experiments, as well as those done by subsequent ESP researchers, involved Zener cards, a deck of 25 cards that bear five different symbols — a plus sign, a square, a star, a circle, and wavy lines. When experimenters want to study telepathy, for instance, they ask a "sender" to concentrate on a card; then they ask a "receiver" to try to "read the mind" of the sender. By chance alone, the receiver will guess the symbols on about five of the 25 cards correctly. A participant who consistently scores above "chance" is credited with having ESP.

Using Zener cards, Rhine apparently found a few people who scored somewhat better than chance, but his methodology has been severely criticized, particularly in the area of experimental control. In many early experiments, for example, the Zener cards were so cheaply printed that a faint outline of the symbol could be seen from the back. Also, because experimenters knew which cards were correct, they could unknowingly give participants cues through subtle facial gestures.

The most important criticism of both experimental and casual claims of ESP is their lack of stability and replicability — a core requirement for scientific acceptance. Findings in ESP are notoriously "fragile" (Hyman, 1996). A meta-analysis of 30 studies using scientific controls, such as double-blind procedures and maximum security and accuracy in recordkeeping, reported absolutely no evidence of ESP (Milton & Wiseman, 1999). As one critic pointed out, positive ESP results usually mean "Error Some Place" (Marks, 1990).

If ESP is so unreliable, why do so many people believe in it? Our fast-paced technological world and rapid scientific progress lead many people to believe that virtually anything is possible, and *possible* is often translated as *probable*. Because ESP is by nature subjective and extraordinary, people tend to accept it as an explanation for out-of-the-ordinary experiences. Moreover, as mentioned earlier in the chapter, people's motivations and interests can influence their perceptions. Often, both research participants and researchers are strongly motivated to believe in ESP. They *selectively attend* to things they want to see or hear. In addition, people generally have difficulty processing and evaluating complex scientific information. In the case of psychic abilities, it is hard to distin-

Extrasensory Perception *Perceptual, or "psychic," abilities that supposedly go beyond the known senses, including telepathy, clairvoyance, precognition, and psychokinesis*

ESP and pizza. Can you label the supposed psychic ability of this pizza delivery person?

guish chance and coincidental events from the multitude of experiences in daily life.

But the most important underlying reason for why people believe in ESP is that they want to. A quick glance at children's fairy tales, comic books, and popular movies finds an abundance of superhuman characters and violations of the laws of physics. It seems that release from natural law is one of the most common and satisfying human fantasies. When it comes to ESP, people eagerly engage in a process known as "the willing suspension of disbelief." We seem to have a hard time accepting our finiteness, and a belief in psychic phenomena offers an increased feeling of power and control.

A Final Note

In this chapter, we have seen that a number of internal and external factors can affect sensation as well as all three stages of perception — selection, organization, and interpretation. In upcoming chapters, we will continue our study of perception by examining how incoming sensory information is processed and retrieved in the different types of memory (Chapter 7), how perception develops in infants (Chapter 9), and how we perceive ourselves and others (Chapter 16).

Helen Keller recognized how crucial sensation and perception are to our lives. She learned to "see" and "hear" with her sense of touch and often recognized visitors by their smell or by vibrations from their walk. Despite the heightened sensitivity of her functioning senses, however, Keller professed a lifelong yearning to experience a normal sensory world. She gave this advice to those whose senses are "normal":

> I who am blind can give one hint to those who see: use your eyes as if tomorrow you would be stricken blind. And the same method can be applied to the other senses. Hear the music of voices, the song of a bird, the mighty strains of an orchestra as if you would be stricken deaf tomorrow. Touch each object as if tomorrow your tactile sense would fail. Smell the perfume of flowers, taste with relish each morsel as if tomorrow you could never smell and taste again. Make the most of every sense; glory in all the facets of pleasure and beauty that the world reveals to you through the several means of contact which nature provides. [1962, p. 23]

Check & Review

INTERPRETATION, SUBLIMINAL PERCEPTION, AND ESP

Interpretation, the final stage of perception, can be influenced by perceptual adaptation, **perceptual set,** and individual motivation and frame of reference. **Subliminal** (below the threshold) messages can be perceived without our knowing awareness. However, there is little or no evidence of subliminal persuasion. **Extrasensory perception** (ESP) is the supposed ability to perceive things that go beyond the normal senses. ESP research has produced "fragile" results, and critics condemn its lack of experimental control and replicability.

Questions

1. George Stratton's research is important because it demonstrated _____. (a) the role of learning in perception; (b) innate factors in human perception; (c) the difference between sensation and perception; (d) the ability of the retina to invert images.

2. Experiments on subliminal perception have _____. (a) supported the existence of the phenomenon but it has little or no effect on persuasion; (b) shown that subliminal perception occurs only among children and some adolescents; (c) shown that subliminal messages affect only people who are highly suggestible; (d) failed to support the phenomenon.

3. The supposed ability to read other people's minds is called _____, perceiving objects or events that are inaccessible to the normal senses is known as _____, predicting the future is called _____, and moving or affecting objects without touching them is known as _____.

4. A major criticism of studies that indicate the existence of ESP is that they _____.

Answers to Questions can be found in Appendix B.

Problems with Believing in Extrasensory Perception

The subject of extrasensory perception (ESP) often generates not only great interest but also strong emotional responses. And when individuals feel strongly about an issue, they sometimes fail to recognize the faulty reasoning underlying their beliefs. Belief in ESP is particularly associated with illogical, noncritical thinking. This exercise gives you a chance to practice your critical thinking skills as they apply to ESP. Begin by studying the following types of faulty reasoning:

1. *Fallacy of positive instances:* Noting and remembering events that confirm personal expectations and beliefs (the "hits") and ignoring nonsupportive evidence (the "misses"). Remembering the time the palmist said you would receive a call in the middle of the night (a "hit") but ignoring that she also said that you had three children (a "miss").

2. *Innumeracy:* Failing to recognize chance occurrences for what they are owing to a lack of training in statistics and probabilities. Unusual events are misperceived as statistically impossible (such as predicting a president's illness), and extraordinary explanations, such as ESP, are seen as the logical alternative.

3. *Willingness to suspend disbelief:* Refusing to engage one's normal critical thinking skills because of a personal need for power and control. Although few people would attribute a foreign country's acquisition of top-secret information to ESP, some of these same individuals would willingly believe that a psychic could help them find their lost child.

4. *The "vividness" problem:* Human information processing and memory storage and retrieval are often based on the initial "vividness" of the information. Sincere personal testimonials, theatrical demonstrations, and detailed anecdotes easily capture our attention and tend to be remembered better than rational, scientific descriptions of events. This is the heart of most stories about extraterrestrial visitations.

Now decide which type of faulty reasoning *best* describes each of the following. Although more than one type may be applicable, enter only one number beside each report. Comparing your answers with your classmates' and friends' answers will further sharpen your critical thinking skills.

_____ John hadn't thought of Paula, his old high school sweetheart, for years. Yet one morning he woke up thinking about her. He was wondering what she looked like and whether she was married now, when suddenly the phone rang. For some strange reason, he felt sure the call was from Paula. He was right. John now cites this call as evidence for his personal experience with extrasensory perception.

_____ A psychic visits a class in introductory psychology. He predicts that out of this class of 23 students, 2 individuals will have birthdays on the same day. When a tally of birthdays is taken, his prediction is supported and many students leave class believing that the existence of ESP has been supported.

_____ A National League baseball player dreams of hitting a bases-loaded triple. Two months later, during the final game of the World Series, he gets this exact triple and wins the game. He informs the media of his earlier dream and the possibility that ESP exists.

_____ A mother is sitting alone in her office at work and suddenly sees a vivid image of her home on fire. She immediately calls home and awakens the sitter, who excitedly reports smoke coming under the door. The sitter successfully extinguishes the fire, and the mother later attributes her visual images to ESP.

KEY TERMS

bottom-up processing (p. 118)
perception (p. 118)
sensation (p. 118)
top-down processing (p. 118)
Experiencing Sensations
absolute threshold (p. 120)
coding (p. 119)
difference threshold (p. 120)
gate-control theory of pain (p. 121)
psychophysics (p. 120)
sensory adaptation (p. 120)
sensory reduction (p. 119)
transduction (p. 119)
How We See and Hear
accommodation (p. 125)
amplitude (p. 123)
audition (p. 127)
cochlea (p. 128)

cones (p. 125)
dark adaptation (p. 126)
farsightedness (hyperopia) (p. 125)
frequency (p. 123)
frequency theory (p. 128)
hue (p. 123)
nearsightedness (myopia) (p. 125)
pitch (p. 127)
place theory (p. 128)
retina (p. 125)
rods (p. 125)
wavelength (p. 123)
Our Other Senses
gustation (p. 132)
kinesthesis (p. 134)
olfaction (p. 131)
pheromones [FARE-oh-mones] (p. 132)
semicircular canals (p. 133)

Perception
binocular cues (p. 144)
convergence (p. 144)
depth perception (p. 143)
extrasensory perception (ESP) (p. 151)
feature detectors (p. 136)
figure and ground (p. 138)
habituation (p. 137)
illusion (p. 135)
monocular cues (p. 144)
opponent-process theory (p. 147)
perceptual constancy (p. 141)
perceptual set (p. 149)
retinal disparity (p. 144)
selective attention (p. 136)
subliminal (p. 150)
trichromatic theory (p. 147)

Visual Summary for Chapter 4

Experiencing Sensations

Sensation: Input of sensory information
Perception: Brain's interpretation of sensory input.

Processing

To process sensations, we need:
- **Receptors**: Body cells that detect and respond to stimulus energy.
- **Transduction**: A process of converting receptor energy into neural impulses the brain can understand.
- **Sensory reduction**: Filtering and analyzing of sensations before messages are sent to the brain.
- **Coding**: A three-part process that converts sensory input into specific sensations (sight, sound, touch, etc.).

Thresholds

Absolute threshold: Smallest *magnitude* of a stimulus we can detect

Difference threshold: Smallest *change* in a stimulus we can detect

Adaptation

Sensory adaptation: Decreased sensory response to continuous stimulation.

How We See and Hear

Vision

Light is a form of energy and part of the *electromagnetic spectrum*. Light waves vary in:

1) *Length* (the **wavelength** of a light determines **frequency**, which creates **hue**, or color)
2) *Height* (the **amplitude** determines intensity or brightness)
3) *Range* (the mixture of length and amplitude determines complexity or saturation)

Eye anatomy and function

The eye captures light and focuses it on visual receptors, which convert light energy to neural impulses sent along to the brain.

Parts of the Eye
- *Cornea*: Clear bulge at front of eye, where light enters.
- *Pupil*: Hole through which light passes into eye.
- *Iris*: Colored muscles that surround pupil.
- *Lens*: Elastic structure that bulges and flattens to focus an image on retina (a process called **accommodation**).
- **Retina**: Contains visual receptor cells, called **rods** (for night vision) and **cones** (for color vision and fine detail).

Hearing

Audition (or hearing) occurs via *sound waves*, which result from rapid changes in air pressure caused by vibrating objects. Sound waves vary in:

1) *Length* (the wavelength of a sound determines frequency, which corresponds to **pitch**)
2) *Height* (the amplitude of a sound determines loudness)
3) *Range* (the mixture of a sound wave determines timbre)

Ear anatomy and function

Outer ear conducts sound waves to *eardrum*, which vibrates tiny bones of middle ear that conduct sound vibrations to oval window. Movement of the oval window creates waves in **cochlea**, which contains *hair cells* (receptors for hearing) that convert sound energy to neural impulses sent along to the brain.

Our Other Senses

Smell and Taste

Olfaction (sense of smell) receptors are in the *olfactory epithelium* at the top of the nasal cavity. *Lock-and-key theory*: We smell different odors because each 3-D odor molecule fits only into one type of receptor.

Gustation (sense of taste) receptors are taste buds clustered within *papillae* of tongue. Four basic tastes: salty, sweet, sour, and bitter.

The Body Senses

Skin senses detect touch (pressure), temperature, and pain.

Vestibular sense (or sense of balance) results from receptors in inner ear.

Kinethesis (body posture, orientation, and body movement) results from receptors in muscles, joints, and tendons.

Perception

Selection

Three major factors:
1) **Selective attention**: The brain sorts out and only attends to most important sensory messages.
2) **Feature detectors**: Specialized brain cells that only respond to specific sensory information.
3) **Habituation**: Tendency of brain to ignore environmental factors that remain constant.

Organization

Four general attributes:
1) **Form**: Gestalt psychologists explain that we perceive form by looking at **figure and ground**, *reversible figure*, *proximity*, *continuity*, *closure*, *contiguity*, and *similarity*.
2) **Constancy**: Even though actual sensory data may be constantly changing, we perceive the world as stable due to *size constancy*, *shape constancy*, *color constancy*, and *brightness constancy*.
3) **Depth**: **Binocular** (2 eyes) **cues** involve **retinal disparity** and **convergence**. **Monocular** (one eye) **cues** include *linear perspective*, *interposition*, *relative size*, *texture gradient*, *aerial perspective*, *light and shadow*, *accomodation*, and *motion parallax*.
4) **Color**: Color perception is a combination of two theories: **trichromatic theory**, which says we have 3 color systems maximally sensitive to blue, green, and red. And **opponent-process theory**, which says we have 3 color systems but each is sensitive to two opposing colors (blue and yellow, red and green, black and white).

Interpretation

Four major factors:
1) *Perceptual adaptation*: The brain adapts to changed environment.
2) *Perceptual set*: A readiness to perceive in a particular manner based on expectations.
3) *Individual motivation*: Based on personal interests and needs and context.
4) *Frame of reference*: Based on context of situation.

Subliminal Perception and ESP

Subliminal stimuli occur below the threshold of our conscious awareness, but have a weak effect (if any) on behavior.

Extrasensory perception (ESP) is the supposed ability to perceive things through unknown senses, but research results are "fragile," lack experimental control, and are nonreplicable.

5

States of Consciousness

On September 4, 1974, an Eastern Airlines flight from Charleston, South Carolina, to Charlotte, North Carolina, crashed, killing the pilot, Captain James Reeves, all of his flight crew, and 68 passengers. The week before, Captain Reeves's hectic work schedule was filled with long flights, erratic start times, and work shifts that began anywhere from early morning to late night. Approximately 30 minutes before the crash, Captain Reeves checked in with the Charlotte control

tower. Sounding tired and depressed, Reeves complained, "Rest. That's what I need is rest. I don't need all of this [expletive] flying" (cited in Coren, 1996, p. 227).

In October 1996, President Bill Clinton signed into law a bill adding an extra 20 years to a criminal's prison sentence if a certain drug was used to incapacitate the criminal's victim. This was the first time in U.S. history that using a drug was considered a weapon and classified as a crime. What is the drug? Rohypnol — also known as the "date rape drug." Colorless, odorless, and tasteless when dissolved in liquid, Rohypnol can easily be slipped into any drink. Unsuspecting victims have reported waking up naked in fraternity houses, on beaches, or in the homes of their dates, with no recall of the previous several hours (Tattersall, 2000). In addition to the horror of rape and the possibility of sexually

transmitted diseases and pregnancy, Rohypnol can also lead to respiratory depression and death.

On March 13, 2000, Time magazine declared, "Americans are in love with Ecstasy" (Barnes, Graft, Reaves, & Shannon, 2000, p. 66). Once used for therapeutic purposes and then by elite club hoppers, Ecstasy, known scientifically as MDMA, is now flooding college dorms, rave parties, and high school campuses. Why? According to users, "it's fun." College students describe melting into "cuddle puddles," groups of writhing individuals massaging and embracing one another on the dance floor. They report that their skin feels "tremblingly alive when caressed." According to 23-year-old, "Katrina," "A guy touching your skin with a cold drink. It's delicious."

What do these three stories have in common? All the situations involve an altered state of consciousness: a fatigued pilot surrendering to much-needed sleep, unsuspecting dates slipping into unconsciousness and amnesia, and party-goers seeking out "cuddle puddles."

Consciousness *An organism's aware-ness of its own self and surroundings (Damasio, 1999). Consciousness is always about something. It concerns perceptions (of objects and events), thoughts (including verbal thought and mental images, such as dreams and daydreams), feelings, and actions (Far-thing, 1992).*

Alternate States of Conscious-ness *A mental state other than ordi-nary waking consciousness, found dur-ing sleep, dreaming, psychoactive drug use, hypnosis, and so on; distinct changes typically occur in perception, emotion, memory, time sense, thinking, self-control, and suggestibility*

How can we define and describe *consciousness*?

What do we mean by "altered consciousness?" And when does a change in consciousness become dangerous? In this chapter, we begin with a general look at the definition and description of **consciousness**, an organism's awareness of its own self and its surroundings (Damasio, 1999). Next, we examine changes in everyday, waking consciousness, known as *altered* or **alternate states of conscious-ness** (ASCs). ASCs include sleep and dreaming, chemically induced changes from psychoactive drugs, daydreaming, fantasies, hypnosis, and meditation. The chapter concludes by exploring why humans throughout history and across cultures have sought alternate states of consciousness.

UNDERSTANDING CONSCIOUSNESS

How Do We Define It? The Participant as the Inquirer

Our definition of *consciousness* is fairly simple and currently popular: an organism's awareness of its own self and surroundings. We could have chosen another, because psychologists have many definitions of consciousness. The problem is that the term is difficult to *scientifically* study and define. What, for example, do we mean by "awareness"? What would it be like to be "unaware"? How can we study the contents of our consciousness when the only tool of discovery is the object itself? How can the mind's awareness study itself? Consciousness is a fundamental concept in the field of psychology, yet it eludes simple definition (Damasio, 1999).

In the late nineteenth century, when psychology first became a scientific disci-pline separate from philosophy, it defined itself as "the study of human conscious-ness." But such a nebulous area of study eventually led to great dissatisfaction within the field. One group, the behaviorists, led by John Watson, believed that *behavior,* not consciousness, was the proper focus of the new science. In fact, he declared that "the time seems to have come when psychology must discard all ref-erences to consciousness; when it need no longer delude itself into thinking that it is making mental states the object of observation" (1913, p. 164).

In recent years, psychology has renewed its original interest in consciousness thanks to research in cognitive and cultural psychology. Also, advances in scien-tific technology, such as the electroencephalograph (EEG) and positron emission tomography (PET), allow scientific study of brain activity during various states of consciousness. Many neuroscientists believe consciousness will ultimately be linked to patterns of neural activity in the brain, although the precise location or functioning of this "seat of consciousness" has not yet been discovered (Johnson, 2000).

How Do We Describe It? A Flowing Stream with Varying Depths

Consciousness may be easier to *describe* than to define. The first American psychol-ogist, William James, likened consciousness to a stream that's constantly changing yet always the same. It meanders and flows, sometimes where the person wills and sometimes not. Through the process of *selective attention* (Chapter 4), we control our consciousness by deliberate concentration and full attention. For example, at the present moment you are (we hope) fully awake and concentrating on the words on this page. At times, however, your control may weaken, and the stream of your consciousness may drift to thoughts of a computer you want to buy, your job, or that attractive classmate sitting nearby.

TABLE 5.1 LEVELS OF CONSCIOUSNESS

High level of awareness	Controlled processes	High level of awareness, focused attention required	
Middle level of awareness	Automatic processes	Awareness, but minimal attention required	
	Daydreaming	Low level of awareness and conscious effort, somewhere between active consciousness and dreaming while asleep	
Minimal or no awareness	Unconscious mind (Freudian)	Reservoir of unacceptable thoughts, feelings, and memories that are too painful or anxiety provoking to be admitted to consciousness	
	Unconscious (biologically based)	Lowest level of awareness due to head injuries, disease, anesthesia during surgery, or coma	

Levels of Consciousness. Consciousness is not an all-or-nothing phenomenon. Instead, it exists along a continuum, with highly focused awareness at one extreme and minimal or no awareness at the other.

In line with James's metaphor, modern researchers have found that the "stream of consciousness" also varies in depth. Consciousness is not an all-or-nothing phenomenon — we are not simply conscious or unconscious. Instead, consciousness exists along a continuum, ranging from high awareness and sharp, focused alertness at one extreme, to middle levels of awareness such as daydreaming, to unconsciousness and coma at the other extreme (Table 5.1).

Controlled Processes *Mental activities found at one extreme of the continuum of awareness; they require focused attention and generally interfere with other ongoing activities*

Automatic Processes *Mental activities requiring minimal attention; other ongoing activities are generally not affected*

Table 5.1 portrays Freud's concept of the unconscious mind as one step up from true, biological unconsciousness. Freud believed that this lowest level of awareness (the "unconscious") was a reservoir containing thoughts and emotions too embarrassing or threatening to be allowed into conscious awareness. (Freudian theory is discussed more fully in Chapter 13, and we'll cover daydreaming later in this chapter.)

Controlled Versus Automatic Processes

When you're working at a demanding task or learning something new, like how to drive a car, consciousness is at the high end of the continuum. **Controlled processes**, like these, demand focused attention and generally interfere with other ongoing activities. Have you ever been so absorbed during an exam that you completely forgot your surroundings until the instructor announced, "Time is up," and asked for your paper? This type of focused attention is the hallmark of controlled processes.

In contrast, **automatic processes** require minimal attention and generally do not interfere with other ongoing activities. Have you ever wondered why it was so difficult to learn to drive a car, yet now you can listen to the radio, think about your classes, and talk to fellow passengers all while driving? Learning a new task requires complete concentration and *controlled processing,* but once that task is well learned, you can relax and rely on your *automatic processes* (Fanz, Waldie, & Smith, 2000).

Automatic processes are generally helpful. However, there are times when we are on "automatic pilot" and don't want to be. Consider the problems of Novelist Colin Wilson (1967):

> When I learned to type, I had to do it painfully and with much nervous wear and tear. But at a certain stage a miracle occurred, and this complicated operation was "learned" by a useful robot that I conceal in my subconscious mind. Now I only have to think about what I want to say; my robot secretary does the typing. He is really very useful. He also drives the car for me, speaks French (not very well), and occasionally gives lectures at American universities. [My robot] is most annoying when I am tired, because then he tends to take over most of my functions without even asking me. I have even caught him making love to my wife. [p. 98]

Check & Review

UNDERSTANDING CONSCIOUSNESS

Most of our lives are spent in normal, waking **consciousness**, an organism's awareness of its own self and surroundings. However, we also spend considerable time in various **alternate states of consciousness** (ASCs), such as sleep and dreaming, daydreams, sexual fantasies, chemically induced changes from psychoactive drugs, hypnosis, and meditation.

Consciousness has always been difficult to study and define. William James described it as a "flowing stream." Modern researchers emphasize that consciousness exists along a continuum. **Controlled processes**, which require focused attention, are at the highest level of awareness. **Automatic processes**, which require minimal attention, are found in the middle of the continuum. Unconsciousness and coma are at the lowest level of awareness.

Questions

1. _____ is (are) best defined as our awareness of our environments and ourselves. (a) Alternate states of consciousness (ASCs); (b) Consciousness; (c) States of consciousness; (d) Selective attention

2. Why were early psychologists reluctant to study consciousness?

3. Controlled processes require _____ attention, whereas automatic processes need _____ attention.

4. As you read this text, you will likely do best if you _____ . (a) are in an alternate state of consciousness; (b) employ automatic processing; (c) let your stream of consciousness take charge; (d) employ controlled processing

Answers to Questions can be found in Appendix B.

SLEEP AND DREAMS

Having explored the definition and description of everyday, waking consciousness, we now turn to sleep and dreaming — the major forms of ASCs. Although each of us spends almost one-third of our life sleeping and dreaming, these ASCs are widely misunderstood.

The Power of Circadian Rhythms: Sleep and the 24-Hour Cycle

Sleep has always been a welcome but mysterious and sometimes elusive guest in our lives. The ancient Greeks believed the god Morpheus granted — or refused — sleep to mortals. In other words, sleep was a gift.

To understand sleep, you first need to understand that sleep is an integral part of biological, circadian rhythms (Siegel, 2000). Each day, our planet cycles from light to dark and back again. Most animals have adapted to this change by develop-

Before reading on, test your personal knowledge of sleep and dreaming by reviewing the common myths below.

- **Myth:** *Everyone needs 8 hours of sleep a night to maintain sound mental and physical health.*
  Although most of us average 7.6 hours of sleep a night, some people get by on an incredible 15 to 30 minutes, whereas others need as much as 11 hours (Doghramji, 2000; Maas, 1999). Moreover, in the past 25 years, Americans have reduced their sleep time 20 percent and have added 1 month per year to our average work/commute time (National Sleep Foundation, 2000).
- **Myth:** *It is easy to learn complicated things, like a foreign language, while asleep.*
  Although some learning can occur during the lighter stages (1 and 2) of sleep, the processing and retention of this material is minimal (Aarons, 1976; Ogilvie, Wilkinson, & Allison, 1989). Wakeful learning is much more effective and efficient.
- **Myth:** *Some people never dream.*
  In rare cases, adults with certain brain injuries or disorders do not dream (Solms, 1997), but otherwise, adults regularly dream. Even people who firmly believe they never dream report

dreams if they are repeatedly awakened during an overnight study in a sleep laboratory. Children also dream regularly. For example, between ages 3 and 8, they dream approximately 20 to 28 percent of their sleep time (Foulkes, 1982, 1993). Apparently, almost everyone dreams, but some people don't remember their dreams.
- **Myth:** *Dreams last only a few seconds.*
  Research shows that dreams seem to occur in "real time;" that is, a dream that seemed to last 20 minutes probably did last approximately 20 minutes (Dement & Wolpert, 1958).
- **Myth:** *When people experience genital arousal during sleep, it means they are having a sexual dream.*
  When sleepers are awakened during this time, they are no more likely to report sexual dreams than at other times (Rechtschaffen & Siegel, 2000).
- **Myth:** *Dreaming of dying can be fatal.*
  This is a good opportunity to exercise your critical thinking skills. Take time to critically evaluate this common belief. Where did this myth come from? Has anyone ever personally experienced and recounted a fatal dream? How would we scientifically prove or disprove this belief?

Circadian [ser-KAY-dee-an] Rhythms *Biological changes that occur on a 24-hour cycle (circa = about, and dies = day)*

ing a 24-hour cycle of activities, or **circadian rhythms** — in Latin, *circa* means "about" and *dies* means "day."

Although nocturnal animals, such as rats, sleep most of the day and stay awake at night, humans and most other animals are awake during the light times of the 24-hour period and asleep during the dark periods. For humans, circadian rhythms influence not only sleep and waking but also fluctuations in blood pressure, pulse rate, body temperature, blood sugar level, and cell growth (Siegel, 2000).

What controls these circadian rhythms and associated changes like sleep? Recent research suggests that these changes are automatically regulated by structures in the brain called *biological clocks*. The "clock" is not a single mechanism but a complex set of interrelated physiological operations that may be dictated by our genetic inheritance (Bower, 2000; Dunlap, 1998). The biological "overseer" of this complex set of operations seems to be a group of cells in the hypothalamus, thalamus, and a tiny structure at the base of the brain (the suprachiasmatic nucleus) that are sensitive to the light and dark cycles of day and night (Rechtschaffen & Siegel, 2000).

Disrupted Circadian Rhythms and Sleep Deprivation

Changes in circadian rhythms help explain problems that arise from late-night study sessions and changing work shifts. In addition to meeting the demands of college life, many students also work full or part time and often on rotating shifts. Between studying and working, their sleep cycle changes frequently. Studies show that disruptions in circadian rhythms generally lead to increased fatigue, decreased concentration, sleep disorders, and other health problems (Boiven, Czeisler, & Waterhouse, 1997; Rechtschaffen & Siegel, 2000).

As a student, you may be comforted to know that others share your own complaints. Less comforting is the knowledge that physicians, nurses, police, and other workers also tend to work under less than optimal conditions. In fact, more than 20 percent of employees in the United States (primarily in the fields of health care, data processing, and transportation) have work schedules that change from day to day or week to week (Maas, 1999).

Although some people seem to function well despite these changes, studies do show that shift workers are generally less productive and more accident-prone while on the job (Dement & Vaughan, 1999; Lenne, Triggs, & Redman, 1998; National Sleep Foundation, 2000). In a major review of Japanese near-collision train incidents, 82 percent took place between midnight and morning (Charland, 1992).

Some of the worst recent disasters — including the Union Carbide chemical accident in Bhopal, India, the nuclear power plant disaster in Chernobyl, and the Alaskan oil spill from the *Exxon Valdez* — occurred during the night shift. And, as described in the chapter opener, official investigations of airline crashes often cite pilot shift work as a possible contributing factor. Although it's true that catastrophic accidents can be traced to unusual coincidences, a case could be made that the workers most directly involved were working against the circadian cycle and oriented toward sleep when full alertness was required.

Not only can rotating work schedules disrupt circadian cycles but so can flying across several time zones. Have you ever taken a long airline flight and felt fatigued, sluggish, and irritable for the first few days after arriving? If so, you experienced symptoms of *jet lag*. Like rotating shift work, jet lag correlates with decreased alertness, decreased mental agility, exacerbation of psychiatric disorders, and overall reduced efficiency (Iyer, 2001; Maas, 1999).

Is it true that jet lag is worse when you fly long distances eastward rather than westward? Transcontinental flights in either direction disrupt our circadian cycles, but traveling westward is easier because our bodies adjust more easily to *phase advances* (accelerations of circadian rhythms). Conversely, traveling eastward is harder because our bodies have trouble adjusting to *phase delays* (decelerations of circadian rhythms).

Why our bodies react differently to phase advances and phase delays is somewhat of a mystery. Scientists can only cite research with young adults isolated without daylight or clocks where participants generally move to a 25-hour day (a phase advance) (Moore, 1997). Studies also show that phase advances are less troublesome for women, night owls, extroverted people, and younger people (Kiester, 1997). But again, the reasons are not clear.

Disruptions in circadian cycles due to shift work and jet lag can have serious effects, but what about long-term sleep deprivation? History shows that over 2,000 years ago, during Roman times and in the Middle Ages, sleep deprivation was a form of torture. Today, armies use loud, blaring music and noise to disrupt their enemy's sleep.

Exploring the scientific effects of severe sleep loss is limited by obvious ethical concerns. We do know that after about 72 hours, research participants unwillingly slip into brief, repeated periods of "microsleep," lasting a few seconds at a time. To

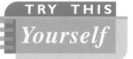

Are you sleep deprived? Take the following two-part test and find out.

Part 1 A typical task used by sleep deprivation researchers is to ask people to trace a star using their nondominant hand while watching their hand in a mirror. Set up a small mirror next to the text and see if you can copy the star below. The task is difficult, and sleep-deprived people typically make many errors when tested at the low point in their circadian cycle.

Sleep deprivation. Insufficient sleep can seriously affect your college grades—as well as your physical health, motor skills, and overall mood.

Part 2 Now give yourself one point each time you answer yes to the following questions:

Do you often fall asleep...
watching TV?
during boring meetings or lectures or in warm rooms?
after heavy meals or after a small amount of alcohol?
while relaxing after dinner?
within five minutes of getting into bed?

In the morning, do you generally...
need an alarm clock to wake up at the right time?

struggle to get out of bed?
hit the snooze bar several times to get more sleep?

During the day, do you...
feel tired, irritable, and stressed out?
have trouble concentrating and remembering?
feel slow when it comes to critical thinking, problem solving, and being creative?
feel drowsy while driving?
need a nap to get through the day?
have dark circles around your eyes?

According to Cornell University psychologist James Maas (1999), if you answered yes to three or more items, you probably are not getting enough sleep.

Source: Quiz adapted and reprinted from Maas, 1999 with permission.

complicate things, sleep deprivation increases stress, making it difficult to identify what is cause and what is effect.

Despite these problems, sleep researchers have documented several hazards related to sleep deprivation — mood alterations, reduced concentration and motivation, increased irritability, lapses in attention, reduced motor skills, and increased cortisol levels (a sign of stress) (Lenne, Triggs, & Redman, 1998; Pilcher & Huffcutt, 1996; Rechtschaffen & Siegel, 2000). Experiments with severe sleep deprivation in rats show even more serious side effects and sometimes death (Rechtschaffen, 1997; Rechtschaffen & Bergmann, 1995). But perhaps the greatest danger associated with sleep deprivation comes from pilots and other workers whose lapses in attention cost many lives (McCartt, Rohrbaugh, Hammer, & Fuller, 2000; Siegel, 2000).

It is interesting to note, however, that many physiological functions are not significantly disrupted by periods of sleep deprivation (Walsh & Lindblom, 1997). In fact, in 1965, a 17-year-old student named Randy Gardner, who wanted to earn a place in the *Guinness Book of World Records,* stayed awake for 264 consecutive hours. He did become irritable and had to remain active to stay awake, but he did not become incoherent or psychotic (Coren, 1996; Spinweber, 1993). Afterward, Randy slept a mere 14 hours and then returned to his usual 8-hour sleep cycle (Dement, 1992).

Stages of Sleep: How Scientists Study Sleep

Sleep is an important component of our circadian rhythms. Each night, we go through four to five cycles of distinct sleep stages, each with a rhythm of its own and corresponding changes in brain and behavior. How do we know this? How can scientists study private mental events like sleep? Surveys and interviews can provide some information about the nature of sleep, but perhaps the most important tool for sleep researchers is the EEG.

As we move from a waking state to deep sleep, our brains show complex and predictable changes in electrical activity. The EEG records these brain wave changes by means of small disklike electrodes placed on the scalp. The electrodes pick up electrical changes in the nerve cells of the cerebral cortex. The changes are then amplified and recorded on a long roll of paper or computer monitor. These recordings, or electroencephalograms, allow researchers to observe the brain's activity while its owner is asleep. Sleep researchers also use other recording devices, such as those seen in Figure 5.1.

Cycling Through the Stages of Sleep

Perhaps the best way to appreciate the methods and findings of sleep researchers is to pretend for a moment that you are a participant in a sleep experiment. When you

Figure 5.1 *How sleep is studied.* Researchers in a sleep laboratory use sophisticated equipment to record physiological changes during sleep. Electroencephalograph (EEG) electrodes are taped to the scalp to measure brain wave activity. Electromyograph (EMG) electrodes are applied to the chin and mouth to measure muscular activity. Electrooculograph (EOG) electrodes are taped near the eyes to record eye movements. Other devices not shown in this photo record heart rate, respiration rate, and genital arousal.

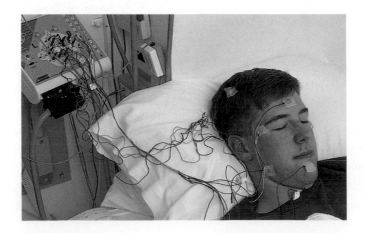

arrive at the sleep lab, you are assigned one of several "bedrooms." The researcher hooks you up to various physiological recording devices, such as the EEG, EMG, and electrooculograph (EOG). If you are like other participants, you probably need a night or two to adapt to the equipment and return to a normal mode of sleeping.

Once adapted, you are ready for the researchers to monitor your typical night's sleep. As your eyes close and you begin to relax, the researcher in the next room notices that your EEG recordings have moved from the wave pattern associated with normal wakefulness, *beta waves*, to the slower *alpha waves*, which indicate drowsy relaxation (Figure 5.2). During this relaxed, "presleep" state, you may experience a *hypnogogic state*, which is characterized by feelings of floating, weightlessness, visual images (such as flashing lights or colors), or swift, jerky movements and a corresponding feeling of slipping or falling. Hypnogogic experiences are sometimes incorporated into fragmented dreams and remembered in the morning. They may also explain reported accounts of alien abduction. These alleged encounters typically occur while the victim is falling asleep, and many reports mention "strange flashes of light" and "floating off the bed."

As you continue relaxing, your brain's electrical activity slows even further. You are now in *Stage 1* sleep; your breathing becomes more regular, your heart rate slows, and your blood pressure decreases. At this stage, you could still be readily awakened. No one wakens you, though, so you relax more deeply and slide gently into *Stage 2* sleep. This stage is noted on your electroencephalograph by occasional short bursts of rapid, high-amplitude brain waves known as *sleep spindles*. During Stage 2 sleep, you become progressively more relaxed and less responsive to the external environment. Even deeper levels of sleep follow Stage 2 — *Stages 3 and 4*. As shown in Figure 5.3, these stages are marked by the appearance of slow, high-amplitude *delta waves*. It is very hard to awaken you in the deepest stages of sleep, even by shouting and shaking. (Can you see why it is difficult to learn foreign languages or other material from tapes while sound asleep [Wyatt & Bootzin, 1994]?) Stage 4 sleep is also the time when children are most likely to wet the bed and when sleepwalking occurs.

In about an hour, you progress through all four stages of sleep. Then the sequence begins to reverse itself (see again Figure 5.3). Although we don't necessarily go through all sleep stages in this sequence, during the course of a night people usually complete four to five cycles of light to deep sleep and back. Each cycle lasts about 90 minutes.

Figure 5.3 also shows an interesting phenomenon that occurs at the end of the first cycle. You go back through Stage 3, and then to Stage 2, but instead of reentering the calm, relaxed Stage 1, something totally different happens. Quite

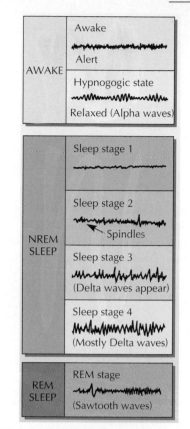

Figure 5.2 *Electroencephalograph patterns during sleep.* As you move from being awake to deeply asleep, your brain waves decrease in frequency (cycles per second) and increase in amplitude (height). Note how the REM (rapid-eye-movement) sleep waves most closely resemble the pattern in the "presleep," hypnogogic state. The brain is more aroused during REM sleep than it is in the lightest level of non-REM sleep, Stage 1.

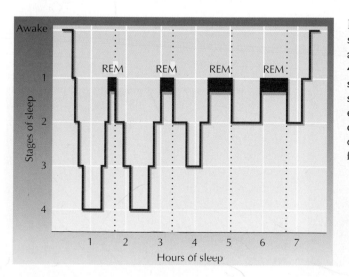

Figure 5.3 *Stages in a typical night's sleep.* During a normal night's sleep, the sleeper moves in and out of various stages of sleep. Starting off alert, the sleeper gradually shifts downward into Stage 1, then Stages 2, 3, and 4. The sleep cycle then reverses. At the peak of the return trip, the sleeper spends some time in REM (rapid-eye-movement) sleep and then the cycle starts downward again. As the night continues, the sleeper repeats the general cycle four to five times. (The dashed lines indicate the boundaries of each cycle.) Note that the periods of Stage 4 and then Stage 3 sleep diminish during the night, whereas REM periods increase in duration. *Source:* Adapted from Julien, 2000, with permission.

abruptly, your scalp recordings display a pattern of small-amplitude, fast wave activity similar in many ways to an awake, vigilant person's brain waves. Your breathing and pulse rates become fast and irregular, and your genitals very likely show signs of arousal (an erection or vaginal lubrication). Although your brain and body are giving many signs of active arousal, your musculature is deeply relaxed and unresponsive. This stage is often referred to as paradoxical sleep because it is in some ways the deepest sleep and in other ways the lightest. (The term *paradoxical* means "apparently self-contradictory.")

REM Sleep

Rapid-Eye-Movement (REM) Sleep *A stage of sleep marked by rapid eye movements, high-frequency brain waves, and dreaming*

During the paradoxical sleep stage, rapid eye movements occur under your closed lids. Thus, another — and more common — name for paradoxical sleep is **rapid-eye-movement (REM) sleep**. REM sleep often signals that dreaming is taking place. When researchers awaken participants to ask them whether they have been dreaming, REM awakenings produce dream recall about 80 to 90 percent of the time, whereas the other stages of sleep are accompanied by dream recall a smaller percentage of the time (Rechtschaffen & Siegel, 2000; Squier & Domhoff, 1998). The muscle "paralysis" that occurs during REM sleep may have evolved so that humans will not act out their dreams by running, fighting, or injuring themselves (Pressman & Orr, 1997).

What is the purpose of REM sleep? Although the exact function of REM sleep is unknown, we do know that it is the primary time for dreaming. At the same time, memory circuits of the brain are activated by self-generated brain waves primarily during REM sleep. This indicates that REM sleep may play an important role in consolidating new memories (Kavanau, 2000; Squier & Domhoff, 1998). It also plays a role in learning, because animals increase their REM sleep following learning sessions (Hennevin, Hars, Matio, & Bloch 1995). Further evidence of the importance of REM sleep in complex brain functions comes from the fact that it occurs only in mammals of higher intelligence and is absent in nonmammals such as reptiles (Rechtschaffen & Siegel, 2000). There is general agreement that it serves an important biological need. When researchers selectively deprive sleepers of REM sleep (by waking them each time they enter the state), most people experience *REM rebound*. That is, they try to "catch up" on REM sleep on subsequent occasions by spending more time than usual in this state (Dement & Vaughan, 1999).

Non-REM Sleep

Although REM sleep is important to our biological functioning, the need for non-REM sleep may be even greater. When people are deprived of *total* sleep, rather than

The sleep cycle in cats. During non-REM (non–rapid-eye-movement) sleep, cats often sleep in an upright position. With the onset of REM sleep, postural muscles are deeply relaxed so the cat rolls over on its side.

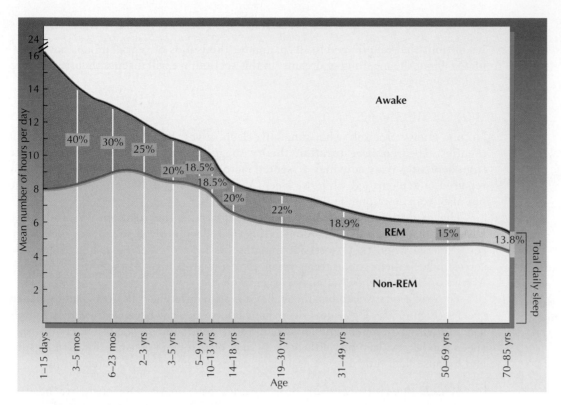

Figure 5.4 *Sleep and dreaming over the life span.* Notice that as you get older, the overall amount of sleep and the proportion of REM (rapid-eye-movement) sleep both decrease. The most dramatic changes occur during the first 2 to 3 years of life. As an infant, you spent almost 8 hours a day in REM sleep, but age 70, you spend less than an hour.

just REM sleep, and then allowed their recovery sleep, their first uninterrupted night has a greater proportion of non-REM sleep (Borbely, 1982). It seems that nature's first need is for non-REM sleep. As you may remember from Figure 5.3, when you initially begin to sleep, you spend more time in Stage 1 sleep through Stage 4 sleep (non-REM). After this need has been satisfied, the latter parts of the night are devoted to more REM sleep.

The idea that nature first satisfies its need for non-REM sleep before going on to REM sleep is also supported by studies showing that adults who are "short sleepers" (5 or fewer hours each night) spend less time in REM sleep than do "long sleepers" (9 or more hours each night). Similarly, infants get more sleep and have a higher percentage of REM sleep than do adults (Figure 5.4). Apparently, the greater the total amount of sleep, the greater the percentage of REM sleep.

Check & Review

CIRCADIAN RHYTHMS AND STAGES OF SLEEP

Circadian rhythms affect our sleep and waking cycle so that disruptions due to shift work and jet lag can cause serious problems.

A typical night's sleep consists of four to five 90-minute cycles. The cycle begins in Stage 1 and then moves through Stages 2, 3, and 4. After reaching the deepest level of sleep, the cycle reverses up to the **REM** (rapid-eye-movement) state, in which the person often is dreaming.

Questions

1. Biological rhythms that occur on a daily basis are called _____ rhythms. (a) circuitous; (b) chronobiology; (c) calendrical; (d) circadian

2. Jet lag results from _____. (a) sleep deprivation; (b) disruption of the circadian rhythms; (c) the effect of light on the pineal gland; (d) disruption of brain wave patterns that occur at high altitudes.

3. The machine that measures the voltage (or brain waves) that the brain produces is the _____.

4. Just before sleep, brain waves move from _____ waves, indicating normal wakefulness, to _____ waves associated with drowsy relaxation. (a) beta, alpha; (b) theta, delta; (c) alpha, beta; (d) sigma, chi

Answers to Questions can be found in Appendix B.

Theories of Sleep and Dreaming: What Are the Functions?

It's obvious that we all need to sleep, and for thousands of years humans have speculated about the meaning of dreams. In this section, we will discuss theories of sleep and dreaming.

Why Do We Sleep?

No one knows precisely what functions sleep serves, but there are two prominent theories. The **repair/restoration theory** suggests that sleep helps us recuperate from depleting, daily activities. Essential factors in our brain or body are apparently repaired or replenished while we sleep. We recover not only from physical fatigue but also from emotional and intellectual demands.

The **evolutionary/circadian theory** emphasizes the relationship of sleep to basic circadian rhythms. According to this view, sleep evolved so animals could conserve energy when they were not foraging for food or seeking mates. Sleep also serves to keep them still at times when predators are active (Hirshkowitz, Moore, & Minhoto, 1997; Rechtschaffen & Siegel, 2000).

The evolutionary/circadian theory helps explain differences in sleep patterns across species (Figure 5.5). Opossums sleep many hours each day because they are relatively safe in their environment and are able to easily find food and shelter. In comparison, sheep and horses sleep very little because their diets require constant foraging for food and because their only defense against predators is vigilance and running away.

Which theory is correct? Both theories have merit. Obviously, we need to repair and restore ourselves after a busy day. But bears don't hibernate all winter simply to recover from a busy summer. Like humans and other animals, they also need to conserve energy when the environment is hostile. It may be that sleep initially served to conserve energy and keep us out of trouble, and over time it has evolved to allow for repair and restoration.

Is there a known biological cause for sleep? Some researchers have looked for a specific neurotransmitter. But the answer is not that simple. For example, the neurotransmitter acetylcholine plays a complicated role in arousal. Have you ever noticed how coffee, tea, or colas wake you up when you're feeling tired? The caffeine in these drinks increases arousal by blocking the chemical that inhibits acetylcholine (Rainnie, Grunze, McCarley, & Greene, 1994). In other words, by inhibiting an inhibitor, the net effect is increased arousal. Both acetylcholine and other neurotransmitters, such as serotonin and norepinephrine, affect sleep (Hobson &

Repair/Restoration Theory *The theory that sleep serves a recuperative function, allowing organisms to repair or replenish key factors in the brain or body that are depleted during daytime activities*

Evolutionary/Circadian Theory *The theory that sleep is a part of circadian rhythms and evolved as a means of conserving energy and protecting individuals from predators*

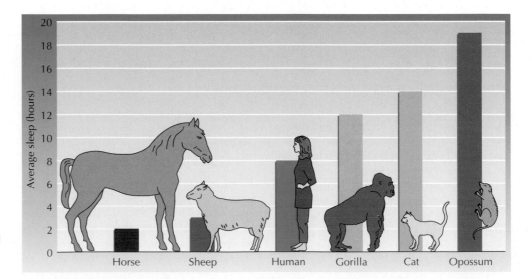

Figure 5.5 *Average daily hours of sleep for different mammals.* According to the evolutionary/circadian theory of sleep, animals that sleep the longest are least threatened by the environment and can easily find food and shelter. Note how the opossum and cat spend longer hours in sleep than the horse and sheep, presumably because of differences in diet and the number of predators.

Silvestri, 1999). In addition, pathways within the brain that contribute to arousal use histamine as their neurotransmitter, which helps explain why allergy sufferers feel drowsy when they take antihistamine drugs (Lin, Hou, Sakai, & Jouvet, 1996). In short, no single neurotransmitter serves as a "sleeping pill."

Other researchers are studying the role of the brain in sleep. Many areas have been identified as having a role in producing or maintaining sleep, including the ventrolateral preoptic nucleus (VPN), the pons, the ascending reticular activating system (ARAS), the basal forebrain, the medulla, the thalamus, the hypothalamus, and the limbic system (Hobson & Silvestri, 1999; Rechtschaffen & Siegel, 2000). But there seems to be no single "Morpheus area" for sleep as there is a Broca's area for language (Chapter 2).

Why Do We Dream?

What do we dream about? Is there special meaning or information in our dreams? Why do we have bad dreams? Why do we dream at all? These questions have long fascinated writers and poets, as well as psychologists. This section begins with a look at gender and cultural diversity in dream content, followed by a discussion of the three major theoretical explanations for why we dream: psychoanalytic/psychodynamic, biological, and cognitive. We then examine nightmares and other sleep disorders.

Throughout the ages, humans have wondered about dreams. A Chinese Taoist of the third century B.C. spoke of the interplay of reality and dreams: "Suddenly I woke up and I was indeed Chuang Tzu. Did Chuang Tzu dream he was a butterfly? Or did the butterfly dream he was Chuang Tzu?"

GENDER & CULTURAL DIVERSITY

Variations and Similarities in Dreams

Research comparing men and women and their dream content generally finds that dreams reflect life events important to the dreamer. Although men and women tend to share many common dream themes, women are more likely to dream of children, family and familiar people, household objects, and indoor events. Men, on the other hand, more often dream about strangers, violence, weapons, sexual activity, achievement, and outdoor events (Domhoff, 1996; Hall et al., 1982; Murray, 1995). However, recent evidence suggests that as gender differences and stereotypes lessen, segregation of dream content by gender becomes less distinct (Bursik, 1998).

Likewise, researchers have found strong similarities and differences in dream content between cultures. For example, dreams involving basic human needs and fears (like sex, aggression, and death) seem to be found in all cultures. Children often dream about large, threatening, wild animals. People of all ages dream of falling, being chased, and being unable to do something they need to do. Dreams also typically include more misfortune than good fortune, and the dreamer is more often the victim of aggression than the cause of it (Domhoff, 1996, 1999; Hall & Van De Castle, 1996).

Yet there are also cultural differences. The Yir Yoront, an Australian hunting and gathering group, generally prefer marriage between a man and his mother's brother's daughter (Schneider & Sharp, 1969). Therefore, it is not uncommon (or surprising) that young, single men in the group often report recurrent dreams of aggression from their mother's brother (their future father-in-law) (Price & Crapo, 1999). Similarly, Americans often report embarrassing dreams of being naked in public, but these dreams are rare in cultures where few clothes are worn.

Interestingly, how people interpret dreams and their cultural value also varies across cultures (Matsumoto, 2000; Price & Crapo, 1999). The Iroquois of North America believe that one's spirit uses dreams to communicate unconscious wishes to the conscious mind (Wallace, 1958). They often share their dreams with religious leaders, who help them interpret and cope with their underlying psychic needs to prevent illness and even death. On the other hand, the Maya of Central America

Dream images. *Have you ever had a dream like this? How would you interpret this dream according to the theories discussed in the text?*

Manifest Content *The surface content of a dream, containing dream symbols that distort and disguise the true meaning of the dream, according to Freudian dream theory*

Latent Content *The true, unconscious meaning of a dream, according to Freudian dream theory*

Activation–Synthesis Hypothesis *The idea that dreams are by-products of random stimulation of brain cells; the brain attempts to combine (or synthesize) this spontaneous activity into coherent patterns, known as dreams*

shared their dreams and interpretations at communal gatherings as an important means of teaching cultural folk wisdom (Tedlock, 1992).

The Psychoanalytic/Psychodynamic View One of the oldest and most scientifically controversial explanations for why we dream is Freud's *psychoanalytic view.* His original theory suggested that dreams are disguised symbols of repressed desires and anxieties and that someone trained in dream interpretation must decipher the true meaning of the dream (Chapter 15). In one of his first books, *The Interpretation of Dreams* (1900), Freud argued that dreams are "the royal road to the unconscious." Dreaming is a special state where forbidden and personally unacceptable desires rise to the surface of consciousness. (As a critical thinker, do you notice the close similarity between Freudian theory and the Iroquois concept of dreaming? Some historians believe that Freud borrowed many concepts from the Iroquois — without giving appropriate credit.)

According to Freud, dreams sometimes offer direct insight into the unconscious, as when a lonely person dreams of romance or an angry child dreams of getting even with the class bully. More often, though, the dream content is so threatening and anxiety-producing that it must be couched in symbols. A journey, for example, is often a symbol for death, horseback riding and dancing are symbols for sexual intercourse, and a cigar or a gun might represent a penis. Freud referred to these symbols (the journey, horseback riding, or the gun) as the **manifest content** (or the story line) of the dream and the underlying, true meaning (death, sex, penis) as the **latent content**.

How correct is Freud's theory? Modern psychodynamic theorists believe that latent content can be a wish, a fear, or anything that is emotionally important to the dreamer, but traditional Freudian ideas about how and why dreams happen have little or no scientific support (Fisher & Greenberg, 1996). After being confronted about the symbolic nature of his beloved cigars, Freud himself supposedly remarked, "Sometimes, a cigar is just a cigar."

The biological view. According to the **activation–synthesis hypothesis**, dreams are a by-product of random stimulation of brain cells and have no direct psychological meaning (Hobson, 1988, 1999). On the basis of research conducted on the brain activity of cats during REM sleep, Alan Hobson and Robert McCarley (1977) proposed that specific neurons in the brain stem fire spontaneously during REM sleep and that the cortex struggles to "synthesize" or make sense out of this random stimulation by manufacturing dreams.

Have you ever dreamed that you were trying to run away from a frightening situation but found that you cannot move? The activation–synthesis hypothesis might explain this dream as random stimulation of the amygdala and paralysis of major postural muscles during REM sleep. The amygdala is a specific brain area linked to strong emotions, especially fear, and research shows high activity in the amygdala during REM sleep (Rechtschaffen & Siegel, 2000). If the amygdala is randomly stimulated and the sleeper experiences fear, the brain may attempt to send messages telling the muscles to move, but there would be no movement, owing to the paralysis. The dreamer then struggles to make sense out of this limited, conflicting information by manufacturing a dream about running away and being unable to move.

This is *not* to say that dreams are totally meaningless. Hobson (1988, 1999) suggests that even if dreams begin with more-or-less random activity in various brain areas, the dreamer's interpretation of this activity depends on his or her personality, motivations, memories, and life experiences.

The Cognitive View. According to the cognitive view, dreams are an extension of everyday life — a form of thinking during sleep. Rather than seeing dreams as mysterious messages from the unconscious or the result of random brain stimulation, dreams are simply another type of *information processing*: They help us sift and sort our everyday experiences and thoughts. The brain periodically shuts out sensory input so it can process, assimilate, and update information — a type of *mental housecleaning* similar to disk defragmentation on your computer.

critical thinking ▶▶▶▶▶▶▶▶▶▶▶▶▶▶▶▶▶ *Active Learning*

Interpreting Your Dreams

Television, movies, and other popular media often portray dreams as highly significant and easily interpreted. However, scientists are deeply divided about the meaning of dreams and their relative importance. These differences in scientific opinion provide an excellent opportunity for you to practice the critical thinking skill of *tolerance for ambiguity*.

To improve your tolerance for ambiguity (and learn a little more about your own dreams), begin by briefly jotting down a recent and vivid dream. This should be at least three or four paragraphs in length. Now analyze your dream using the following perspectives:

1. According to the psychoanalytic/psychodynamic view, what might be the forbidden, unconscious fears, drives or desires represented by your dream? Can you identify the manifest content versus the latent content?

2. How would the biological view, the activation–synthesis hypothesis, explain your dream? Can you identify a specific thought that might have been stimulated and then led to this particular dream?

3. Psychologists from the cognitive perspective believe dream analysis provides important information processing, helps us make needed changes in our life, and even suggests solutions to real-life problems. Do you agree or disagree? Does your dream provide an insight that increases your self-understanding?

Having analyzed your dream from each perspective, can you see how difficult it is to find the one right answer? Higher-level critical thinkers recognize that competing theories are akin to the story of the four blind men who are each exploring separate parts of an elephant. By listening to their description of the trunk, tail, leg, and so on, critical thinkers can synthesize the information and develop a greater understanding. But no one part — or single theory — reveals the whole picture.

As we discovered earlier, REM sleep increases following stress and intense learning periods, and other research reports strong similarities between dream content and waking thoughts, fears, and concerns (Domhoff, 1996, 1999; Hill, Diemer, & Heaton, 1997). For example, college students often report "examination-anxiety" dreams: You can't find your classroom, you're running out of time, your pen or pencil won't work, or you've completely forgotten a scheduled exam and show up totally unprepared (Van de Castle, 1995). (Sound familiar?)

In Sum. The psychoanalytic/psychodynamic, biological, and cognitive views of dreaming offer three perspectives, but numerous questions remain. How, for example, could a complex phenomenon like dreaming have evolved if it requires *expert* interpretation? Can the "random firing" of brain cells explain complicated, storylike dreams or recurrent dreams? How would they explain why human fetuses show REM patterns? Is the fetus working out suppressed wishes and anxieties in the womb? What does it have to dream about in response to random brain activity? Or could it be sifting and sorting its "waking" experiences? And how is it that the same dream can often be explained by many theories? To see this for yourself, try the Critical Thinking/Active Learning Exercise on this page.

Check & Review

THEORIES OF SLEEP AND DREAMING

The exact function of sleep is not known, but according to the **repair/restoration theory**, it is thought to be necessary for its restorative value, both physically and psychologically. According to **evolutionary/circadian theory**, it also has adaptive value. Sleep seems to be controlled by several neurotransmitters and by various areas of the brain.

Three major theories attempt to explain why we dream: The psychoanalytic/psychodynamic view says dreams are disguised symbols of repressed anxieties and desires. The biological (**activation–synthesis hypothesis**) perspective argues that dreams are simple by-products of random stimulation of brain cells. The cognitive view suggests that dreams are an important part of information processing of everyday experiences.

Questions

1. How does the repair/restoration theory of sleep differ from the evolutionary/circadian theory?

& Comings, 1996). In the past 30 years, a growing body of research has also suggested a biological predisposition toward alcohol/drug dependence (Fehr et al., 2000; Kendler, Gardner, & Prescott, 1997).

Once drug use is established, it is more likely to continue because removal or withholding of the drug leads to painful withdrawal symptoms. For example, someone who quits opiates after long-term use usually experiences physical symptoms such as rapid breathing, perspiration, tremors, and muscle twitches.

RESEARCH HIGHLIGHT

Addictive Drugs as the Brain's "Evil Tutor"

Have you ever wondered why alcoholics and other addicts continue to take drugs that are clearly destroying their lives? One explanation may be that the brain "learns" to be addicted. Scientists have long known that various neurotransmitters are key to all forms of normal learning. Now evidence suggests that addictive drugs (acting on certain neurotransmitters) teach the brain to want more and more of the destructive substances — whatever the cost. Drugs become the brain's "evil tutor" (Wickelgren, 1998, p. 2045.)

How does this happen? The neurotransmitter dopamine has been a primary focus of drug abuse research because of its well-known effect on a part of the brain's reward system known as the *nucleus accumbens* (Blum et al., 2000; DiChiara, 1997; Giros, Jaber, Jones, Wrightman, & Caron, 1996). Nicotine and amphetamines, for example, stimulate the release of dopamine, and cocaine blocks its uptake. Drugs that increase dopamine activity are most likely to result in physical dependence.

Recently, however, evidence points to the importance of another neurotransmitter, glutamate. Although surges in dopamine caused by drug use appear to activate the brain's reward system, glutamate may explain compulsive drug taking. Even after the initial effects of a drug disappear, glutamate-induced learning encourages the addict to want more and more of the drug and directs the body to get it. Glutamate apparently creates lasting memories of drug use by changing the nature of "conversations" between neurons. Changes in neuronal connections

"That is not one of the seven habits of highly effective people."

result whenever we learn something or store it in memory. But in this case, glutamate "teaches" the brain to be addicted.

Glutamate's lesson is rarely forgotten. Even when users are highly motivated to end the vicious cycle of drug abuse, glutamate related changes in the brain keep them "hooked." In addition to the well-known intense cravings and pain of withdrawal, the addicted brain also creates cravings at the mere sight of drug-related items. When 13 cocaine addicts and 5 controls watched films of people using both neutral objects and drug-associated items (such as glass pipes and razor blades), the addicts reported significant cravings. During this same time, positron emission tomography (PET) scans of the addicts' brains showed significant neural activity in brain regions known to release glutamate

(Grant et al., 1996). Apparently, activating the glutamate system — through drug use or some reminder of the drug — creates strong cravings, which helps explain the common problem of drug relapse.

As a critical thinker, are you wondering how this new research might help with drug abuse and relapse? Recalling earlier information about agonists and antagonists: What about developing and trying a glutamate antagonist? The good news is that this exact method seems to work. When shown drug-related objects, long-term drug addicts who received a glutamate antagonist reported a significant reduction in cravings and less drug-seeking behavior (Herman & O'Brien, 1997). Drugs that interfere with glutamate transmission are also being tested for the treatment of general drug abuse (Wickelgren, 1998).

The brain produces chemicals closely resembling opiates (endorphins) and contains special receptor sites for them (Chapter 2). As regular opiate use overloads the endorphin receptor sites, the brain soon stops producing these substances. When the drugs are no longer taken, neither opiates nor endorphins are available for regulating pain and discomfort, and the user experiences excruciating pains of withdrawal. Problems with withdrawal symptoms are also the primary reason people fail in their efforts to stop smoking (Chapter 3).

A Concluding Note

Before we go on, we'd like to offer a brief warning about our presentation on drugs. Every attempt has been made to be as factual as possible, but space is obviously limited and information can quickly become dated. With all drug consumption, both prescription and "recreational," the consumer must assume responsibility for maintaining a complete and up-to-date drug education.

This warning is particularly important for illicit street drugs and **designer drugs**, illicitly manufactured variations on known recreational drugs. One of the best-known designer drugs is Ecstasy, the common name for MDMA, which possesses stimulant and hallucinogenic properties (Abadinsky, 2001). As discussed in the chapter opener, Ecstasy users report feeling warm, friendly, sensual, and alert. Keep in mind, however, that studies show the drug also causes heart arrhythmias, high blood pressure, and its long-term effects on the human brain are unknown (Burgess, O'Donohoe, & Gill, 2000).

Street and designer drugs are particularly dangerous for two reasons. First, they lack scientific study on their potential side effects, interaction with other drugs, and long-term risks. Second, there are no truth-in-packaging laws to protect illicit drug buyers from unscrupulous practices. Sellers often substitute unknown, cheaper, and possibly even more dangerous substances for the ones they claim to be selling. When you add in the risk of contracting deadly infectious diseases such as AIDS and hepatitis from sharing nonsterile needles, the dangers of drug use go far beyond the particular drug itself (Doweiko, 1999).

Designer Drugs *Illicitly manufactured variations on known recreational drugs*

Check & Review

DRUGS AND CONSCIOUSNESS

Psychoactive drugs change conscious awareness or perception. *Drug abuse* refers to drug taking that causes emotional or physical harm to the individual or others, whereas *addiction* is a broad term referring to a person's feeling of compulsion to use a specific drug. Psychoactive drug use can lead to psychological dependence or physical dependence or both. **Psychological dependence** is a desire or craving to achieve the effects produced by a drug. **Physical dependence** is a change in bodily processes due to continued drug use that results in **withdrawal** symptoms when the drug is withheld. **Tolerance** is a physiological process whereby the user needs larger and more frequent doses of a drug to produce the desired effect.

The major categories of psychoactive drugs are **depressants**, **stimulants**, **opiates**, and **hallucinogens**. Depressant drugs slow the central nervous system, whereas stimulants activate it. Opiates numb the senses and relieve pain, whereas hallucinogens produce sensory or perceptual distortions.

Drugs act primarily by changing the effect of neurotransmitters in the brain. Drugs that act as **agonists** mimic neurotransmitters, whereas **antagonists** oppose or block normal neurotransmitter functioning. There are many reasons for drug use and abuse, which fall into the two main categories of environment and biology.

Questions

1. Drugs that change behavior, mental processes, and conscious experience are called _____. (a) addictive; (b) hallucinogenic; (c) psychoactive; (d) mind altering

2. Drug-taking that causes emotional or physical harm to the drug user or others is known as _____. (a) addiction; (b) physical dependence; (c) psychological dependence; (d) drug abuse

3. How does physical dependence differ from psychological dependence?

4. Describe four ways psychoactive drugs act on neurotransmitters.

Answers to Questions can be found in Appendix B.

ADDITIONAL ROUTES TO ALTERNATE STATES

How do alternate states of consciousness, like hypnosis, affect consciousness?

As we have discovered thus far in this chapter, ASCs may be reached through everyday activities such as sleep and dreaming or through the chemical means of drugs. In this section, we explore several additional routes for changing consciousness: daydreams and fantasies, hypnosis, and meditation.

Daydreams and Fantasies: A Mild Form of ASC

In the mildest forms of altered consciousness, *daydreaming* and *fantasies,* attention shifts away from the external world to focus internally on memories, desires, and expectations. Scientists have found that during a typical 24-hour period, we spend as much as one-third of our waking hours daydreaming. And, over 95 percent of both men and women say they have had sexual fantasies. Men's sexual fantasies tend to have more visual images and explicit sexual behaviors, whereas women's fantasies include more touching and romance within a committed and caring relationship (Leitenberg & Henning, 1995; Renaud & Byers, 1999).

Can daydreams and sexual fantasies be dangerous? Daydreaming while sitting in a lecture or driving a car may be counterproductive and potentially dangerous, but under other circumstances, it can be helpful. Most people daydream during quiet, private moments when outside events are boring or automated, such as while waiting at bus stops or washing dishes. It appears that our consciousness responds to an unchanging external world by turning inward and creating more interesting thoughts and images. Daydreaming not only helps us escape and cope with boring tasks and difficult situations but also seems to allow mental and physical relaxation, improve intellectual functioning, and release creative abilities (Klinger, 1987).

Sexual fantasies also serve many purposes. They entertain and excite with no risk of embarrassment, pregnancy, or sexually transmitted diseases (Allgeier & Allgeier, 2000). Many sexual fantasies involve having sex with unavailable or multiple partners — behaviors we would not consider in real life. Such fantasies may lead to feelings of guilt, but thinking about something is not the same as doing it. This lack of distinction between thought and behavior may explain the negativism and uncertainty surrounding both daydreams and fantasies. However, just as parents accept that children often think about hitting others but do not accept the actual behavior, we can accept our daydreams about running away to Tahiti with a sexy stranger without the fear of actually doing it.

Hypnosis: Myths and Therapeutic Uses

"Relax ... your body is so tired ... your eyelids are so very heavy ... your muscles are becoming more and more relaxed ... your breathing is becoming deeper and deeper ... relax ... your eyes are closing and your whole body feels like lead ... let go ... relax." These are the types of suggestions most hypnotists use to begin hypnosis. Once hypnotized, some people can be convinced they are standing at the edge of the ocean listening to the sound of waves and feeling the ocean mist on their faces. Invited to eat a delicious apple that is actually an onion, the hypnotized person may relish the flavor. Told they are watching a very funny or sad movie, they may begin to laugh or cry at their self-created visions.

Hypnosis *An alternate state of heightened suggestibility characterized by relaxation and intense focus*

What is hypnosis? Scientific research has removed much of the mystery surrounding **hypnosis.** It is defined as an ASC characterized by one or more of the following: (1) narrowed, highly focused attention (the participant is able to "tune out" competing sensory stimuli); (2) increased use of imagination and hallucinations (in the case of visual hallucinations, a person may see things that aren't there or not see things that are); (3) a passive and receptive attitude; (4) decreased responsiveness to pain; (5) heightened suggestibility (a willingness to respond to proposed changes in perception — "this onion is an apple") (Barber, 2000; Hilgard, 1986, 1992; Spiegel, 1999).

Hypnotism has been well researched, yet several myths and controversies persist. We'll try to clear up some of the confusion in the following section.

Stage hypnosis. Many people mistakenly believe that people can be hypnotized against their will. Stage hypnotists generally use eager volunteers who want to be hypnotized and willingly cooperate.

Five Common Myths and Controversies

1. Forced hypnosis. One of the most common misconceptions is that people can be hypnotized against their will. But hypnosis requires the person to make a conscious decision to relinquish control of his or her consciousness to someone else, so it is virtually impossible to hypnotize someone who is unwilling. As a matter of fact, about 8 to 9 percent of people cannot be hypnotized even when they are willing and trying very hard to cooperate. And the notion that people can be hypnotically brainwashed and turned into mindless robots is false. The best potential subjects are able to focus attention, are open to new experience, and are capable of imaginative involvement or fantasy (Barber, 2000; Ligett, 2000).

2. Unethical behavior. A related myth is that hypnosis can make a person behave immorally or take dangerous risks against his or her will. Generally, people will not go against their strongest and most basic values. Participants retain the ability to control their behavior during hypnosis. They are aware of their surroundings and can refuse to comply with the hypnotist's suggestions (Kirsch & Lynn, 1995).

3. Exceptional memory. Another myth is that hypnotized people can recall things they otherwise could not. Some research has found that recall memory for some information is occasionally improved under hypnosis because the participant is able to relax and focus intently. However, the number of errors also increases! Furthermore, when pressed to recreate details, hypnotized participants have more difficulty separating fact and fantasy and are more willing to guess (Perry, Orne, London, & Orne, 1996). As you will see in Chapter 6, all memory is ultimately a *reconstruction* rather than a *reproduction*. Therefore, because memory is normally filled with fabrication and distortion, hypnosis generally increases the potential for error (Baker, 1998; Perry, 1997). Consequently, a growing number of judges and state bar associations ban the use of hypnosis and the testimony of hypnotized individuals from the courtroom (Brown, Scheflin, & Hammond, 1997; McConkey, 1995).

4. Superhuman strength. It is also a misconception that under hypnosis, people can perform acts of special, superhuman strength. When nonhypnotized people are simply asked to try their hardest on tests of physical strength, they can generally do anything that a hypnotized person can (Druckman & Bjork, 1994).

5. Fakery. Are hypnosis participants faking it and simply playing along with the hypnotist? Or are they actually in a special state of consciousness that changes normal awareness and perception? Although most participants are not consciously faking hypnosis, some researchers believe the effects result from a blend of conformity, relaxation, obedience, suggestion, and role playing (Baker, 1996, 1998; Kirsch & Lynn, 1995; Lynn, 1997). According to this relaxation/*role-playing theory,* hypnosis is a normal mental state in which deeply relaxed, suggestible people allow the hypnotist to direct their fantasies and behavior.

In contrast, the *altered-state theorists* believe that hypnotic effects result from a special altered state of consciousness (Bowers & Woody, 1996; Hilgard, 1978, 1992). They doubt that relaxation, role playing, and suggestion explain instances in which patients endure complex surgeries without drug-induced anesthesia. As in

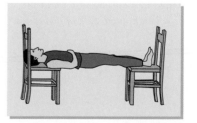

You can recreate a favorite trick that stage hypnotists promote as evidence of superhuman strength under hypnosis. Simply arrange two chairs as shown in the picture. You will see that hypnosis is not necessary — all that is needed is a highly motivated volunteer willing to stiffen his or her body.

other controversial areas of psychology, there is a group of "unified" theorists here; they suggest that hypnosis is a combination of both relaxation/role playing and a unique alternate state of consciousness.

Therapeutic Uses

From the 1700s to modern times, hypnosis has been used (and abused) by entertainers and quacks, while also being employed as a respected clinical tool by physicians, dentists, and therapists. This curious dual existence began with Franz Anton Mesmer (1734–1815). Mesmer believed that all living bodies were filled with magnetic energy and claimed to use this "knowledge" to cure diseases. After lulling his patients into a deep state of relaxation and making them believe completely in his curative powers, Mesmer passed magnets over their bodies and told them their problems would go away. For some people, it worked — hence the term *mesmerized*.

Mesmer's theories were eventually discredited, but James Braid, a Scottish physician, later put people in this same trancelike state for surgery. Around the same time, however, powerful and reliable anesthetic drugs were discovered, and interest in Braid's technique dwindled. It was Braid who coined the term *hypnosis* in 1843, from the Greek word for sleep.

Today, hypnosis is frequently used in both medical and psychotherapy settings (Spiegel, 1999). Even with available anesthetics, it is occasionally used in surgery and for the treatment of chronic pain and severe burns (Chaves, 2000; Horton-ausknecht, Mitzdorf, & Melchart, 2000).

Hypnosis has found its best use, however, in medical areas in which patients have a high degree of anxiety, fear, and misinformation, such as dentistry and obstetrics. Because pain is strongly affected by tension and anxiety, any technique that helps the patient relax is medically useful.

In psychotherapy, hypnosis can help patients relax, remember painful memories, and reduce anxiety. It has had modest success in the treatment of phobias and in efforts to lose weight, stop smoking, and improve study habits (Ahijevych, Yerardi, & Nedilsky, 2000; Gemignani et al., 2000).

Many athletes use self-hypnosis techniques (mental imagery and focused attention) to improve performance. Long-distance runner Steve Ortiz, for example, mentally relives all his best races before a big meet. He says that by the time the race actually begins, "I'm almost in a state of self-hypnosis. I'm just floating along" (cited in Kiester, 1984, p. 23).

Meditation: A "Higher" State of Consciousness?

Meditation *A group of techniques designed to focus attention and produce a heightened state of awareness*

Meditation refers to a group of techniques designed to focus attention and produce a heightened state of awareness. Success in meditation requires controlling the mind's natural tendency to wander.

Some meditation techniques involve body movements and postures, as in t'ai chi and hatha yoga. In other techniques, the meditator remains motionless, attending to a single focal point — gazing at a stimulus (such as a candle flame), observing the breath, or silently repeating a mantra. (A mantra is a special sound, word, or phrase used for mind concentration or spiritual worship.)

Meditation has only recently gained acceptance and popularity in the United States, primarily for its value in promoting relaxation and reducing anxiety. It has, however, been practiced in some parts of the world for centuries. Some believe meditation offers a higher and more enlightened form of consciousness, superior to all other levels, and that it allows meditators to have remarkable control over bodily processes (Epstein, 1998; Flora, 2000).

With sophisticated electronic equipment, researchers have verified that meditation can produce dramatic changes in basic physiological processes such as brain

You can enjoy many of the experiences and benefits of meditation with a relaxation technique developed by Herbert Benson (1977):

1. Pick a focus word or short phrase that is calming and rooted in your personal value system (such as *love*; *peace*; *one*; *shalom*; *Hail, Mary, full of grace*).
2. Sit quietly in a comfortable position, close your eyes, and relax your muscles.
3. Focusing on your breathing, breathe through your nose, and as you breathe out, say your focus word or phrase silently to yourself. Continue for 10 to 20 minutes. You may open your eyes to check the time, but do not use an alarm. When you have finished, sit quietly for several minutes, at first with closed eyes and later with opened eyes.
4. Maintain a passive attitude throughout the exercise — permit relaxation to occur at its own pace. When distracting thoughts occur, ignore them and gently return to your repetition.
5. Practice the technique once or twice daily, but not within 2 hours after a meal — the digestive processes seem to interfere with a successful relaxation response.

waves, heart rate, oxygen consumption, and sweat gland activity. For the one in four Americans who suffers from high blood pressure, it may be useful to know that meditation has proven somewhat successful in reducing stress and lowering blood pressure (Andresen, 2000).

What does it feel like when you meditate? In the beginning stages of meditation, people often report a mellow type of relaxation, followed by a mild euphoria. With long practice, some advanced meditators report experiences of profound rapture and joy or strong hallucinations (Smith, 1982). A particularly vivid description is provided by Gopi Khrishna (1999):

> Suddenly, with a roar like that of a waterfall, I felt a stream of liquid light entering my brain through the spinal cord. The illumination grew brighter and brighter, the roaring louder. I experienced a rocking sensation and then felt myself slipping out of my body, entirely enveloped in a halo of light. I felt the point of consciousness that was myself growing wider, surrounded by waves of light. [pp. 4–5]

GENDER & CULTURAL DIVERSITY

Consciousness Across Cultures

Throughout recorded history, people have sought ways to alter consciousness. As early as 2500 B.C., the Sumerians recorded their reactions to the drug opium with a symbol that archeologists translate as "joy" or "rejoicing," and the oldest known code of laws, from Hammurabi of Babylonia (ca. 1792–1750 B.C.), regulated the sale of wine.

In a survey of 488 societies in all parts of the world, 90 percent were found to practice institutionally recognized methods of changing consciousness (Bourguignon, 1973). These methods include taking drugs, ritualistic fasting, dancing, chanting, and inducing a trance. Such historical and cultural commonalities have

Alternate routes to alternate states. *Meditation, drugs, and childhood experiences with swings are common ways of changing consciousness*

led some researchers to suggest that there is a basic, inborn human need to experience nonordinary reality (Barr, 1999; Weil & Rosen, 1993).

Why Are People So Interested in Altering Their Consciousness?

Studies of *kava*, a drink made from the dried roots of a South Pacific Island plant, offer three possible answers to this question ("Hawaii high," 1998; Merlin, Lebot, & Lindstrom, 1992). Though other cultures use different substances or means, most attempts to achieve ASC serve the same functions as kava does for the Pacific Islanders:

1. ***Sacred rituals.*** Many cultures seek an alternate state of consciousness (ASC) as a pathway to spiritual enlightenment. The earliest use of kava was as a means of communicating with the gods. The islanders believed that the voices of their ancestors could be heard in the nonordinary reality induced by the kava. Similarly, tobacco has always been an integral part of Native American religions (Robicsek, 1992). It serves as a ritual fumigant, a goodwill offering, a sacrifice, and a sacrament. In addition to drug use, individuals in many cultures voluntarily undergo long fasts, isolation, chanting, whirling, and sensory deprivation in search of spiritual enlightenment.

2. ***Social interactions.*** ASCs are also an integral part of most cultures' social functions. Pacific Islanders often exchange large, elaborately decorated kava plants at festivals and weddings, and political meetings often start with a ritual cup of kava. In small amounts, the drink relaxes the muscles and produces a mild euphoria while leaving the mind alert ("Hawaii high," 1998). Thus, kava is favored both for celebrations and as a means of reducing the frictions of village life (Sahelian, 1998). In comparison, have you noticed how often champagne is used to celebrate weddings, births, and New Year's Eve? In our North American culture, alcohol is a prominent feature of many social interactions.

3. ***Individual rewards.*** In addition to spiritual and social functions, many ASCs are desirable on an individual level because they provide pleasure and escape from anxiety or stress. In New Guinea and Fiji, people commonly visit kava bars after work for a relaxing cup of kava. The stresses of the day are replaced with a sense of well-being. In Western societies, alcohol serves a similar purpose.

Alcohol or kava? *Americans often use alcohol, like the Pacific Islanders use kava, to celebrate special occasions.*

Check & Review

ADDITIONAL ROUTES TO ALTERNATE STATES

Daydreaming and sexual fantasies are common forms of mild alternate states of consciousness (ASCs). They serve many functions — primarily positive. **Hypnosis** is an alternate state of heightened suggestibility characterized by relaxation and intense focus. Hypnosis has been used to reduce pain and increase concentration and as an adjunct to psychotherapy. **Meditation** is a group of techniques designed to focus attention and produce heightened aware-ness. Meditation can produce dramatic changes in physiological processes, including heart rate and respiration.

Although the study of consciousness has waxed and waned among psychologists, the public has historically been very interested — particularly in ASCs. Among peoples of all cultures, ASCs (1) are part of sacred rituals, (2) serve social interaction needs, and (3) provide individual rewards.

Questions

1. Why do some people feel guilty or negative about daydreaming and sexual fantasies?

2. Why is it almost impossible to hypnotize an unwilling participant?

3. _____ is a group of techniques designed to focus attention and produce a heightened state of awareness. (a) Hypnosis; (b) Scientology; (c) Parapsychology; (d) Meditation

4. List three major functions served by ASCs in all cultures.

Answers to Questions can be found in Appendix B.

KEY TERMS

alternate states of consciousness (ASCs) (p. 158)
consciousness (p. 158)
Understanding Consciousness
automatic processes (p. 160)
controlled processes (p. 160)
Sleep and Dreams
activation–synthesis hypothesis (p. 170)
circadian [ser-KAY dee-an] rhythms (p. 162)
evolutionary/circadian theory (p. 168)
insomnia (p. 172)
latent content (p. 170)

manifest content (p. 170)
narcolepsy [NAR co-lep-see] (p. 174)
nightmares (p. 174)
night terrors (p. 174)
rapid-eye-movement (REM) sleep (p. 166)
repair/restoration theory (p. 168)
sleep apnea (p. 173)
Drugs That Influence Consciousness
agonist (p. 183)
antagonist (p. 183)
depressants (p. 177)
designer drugs (p. 187)
drug abuse (p. 176)

hallucinogens [hal LU-sin-o-jenz] (p. 181)
opiates (p. 181)
physical dependence (p. 176)
psychoactive drugs (p. 175)
psychological dependence (p. 176)
stimulants (p. 179)
tolerance (p. 176)
withdrawal (p. 176)
Additional Routes to Alternate States
hypnosis (p. 188)
meditation (p. 190)

Visual Summary for Chapter 5 ----

Understanding Consciousness

Consciousness: An organism's awareness of its own self and surroundings. **Alternate states of consciousness (ASCs)**: Mental states other than ordinary waking consciousness found in sleep, dreaming, drug use, hypnosis, and so on.

A Continuum of Awareness

- Top: **Controlled processes** requiring focused attention

- Middle: **Automatic processes** requiring minimal attention

- Lowest: Minimal or no awareness

Examples

→ Taking an exam

→ Brushing your teeth
Daydreams and fantasies

→ Unconsciousness and coma

Sleep and Dreams

- *Sleep as a Biological Rhythm:* 24-hour cycles **(Circadian rhythms)** affect our sleep and waking cycle. Disruptions due to shift work, jet lag and sleep deprevation can cause serious problems.
- *Stages of Sleep:* Typical night's sleep has four to five 90-minute cycles. Non-REM cycle begins in Stage 1 and then moves through Stages 2, 3, and 4. After reaching deepest level, cycle reverses up to REM state.

non-REM Sleep – (Stages 1–4)

Function: Required for basic biological functioning.

REM Sleep (paradoxical sleep)

Function: Important for memory, learning, and basic biological functioning. Rapid eye movement often signals dreaming.

Theories of Sleep

1) **Repair/Restoration:** Allows recuperation from physical, emotional, and intellectual fatigue.
2) **Evolutionary/Circadian:** Sleep is part of circadian cycle, and evolved to conserve energy and protect from predators.

Theories of Dreaming

1) Psychoanalytic/psychodynamic view: Dreams are disguised symbols **(manifest and latent content)** of repressed desires and anxieties.
2) Biological view: Random stimulation of brain cells **(activation-synthesis hypothesis)**.
3) Cognitive view: Dreams help sift and sort everyday experiences (information processing theory).

Sleep and Dreaming (cont).

Sleep Disorders

Insomnia
Repeated difficulty falling or staying asleep or awakening too early.

Sleep Apnea
Temporary stopping of breathing during sleep; causing snoring and poor quality sleep.

Narcolepsy
Sudden and irresistible onsets of sleep during waking hours.

Nightmares
Bad dreams generally during REM sleep.

Night Terrors
Abrupt awakenings and panic during non-REM sleep.

Drugs and Consciousness

Psychoactive drugs: Chemicals that change conscious awareness or perception.

Important Terminology

Drug abuse: Drug taking that causes emotional or physical harm to the individual or others.
Addiction: Broad term referring to feelings of compulsion.
Psychological dependence: Desire or craving to achieve effects produced by a drug.
Physical dependence: Change in bodily processes due to continued drug use that results in withdrawal symptoms when the drug is withheld.
Tolerance: Larger and more frequent doses of drug are needed to produce desired effect.

Four Major Categories of Drugs

1) **Depressants** or "downers" (alcohol and barbiturates) slow down central nervous system (CNS).
2) **Stimulants** or "uppers" (caffeine, nicotine, and cocaine) activate CNS.
3) **Opiates** (heroin or morphine) numb senses and relieve pain.
4) **Hallucinogens** or psychedelics (LSD or marijuana) produce sensory or perceptual distortions.

Explaining Drug Use

"How?" Drugs that act as **agonists** mimic neurotransmitters, while **antagonists** oppose or block normal neurotransmitter functioning.

"Why?" Environmental factors (such as positive portrayals and positive emotions) and biological factors (such as stimulation of brain's reward system, genetics, and prevention of withdrawal symptoms).

Additional Routes to Alternate States

Daydreaming and Sexual Fantasies: Common forms of mild ASCs that serve mostly positive functions.

Hypnosis: Alternate state of heightened suggestibility characterized by relaxation and intense focus.

Myths and Controversies: 1) Forced hypnosis, 2) Unethical behavior, 3) Exceptional memories, 4) Superhuman strength, and 5) Fakery.

Uses: Reduce pain and anxiety, increase concentration, and as an adjunct to psychotherapy.

Meditation: Group of techniques designed to focus attention and produce a heightened awareness.

Uses: Can produce dramatic changes in physiological processes, including heart rate and respiration.

Consciousness Across Cultures: ASCs among peoples of all cultures 1) are part of sacred rituals, 2) serve social interaction needs, and 3) provide individual rewards.

6

Learning

Core Learning Objectives

As you read Chapter 6, keep the following questions in mind and answer them in your own words:

► What is classical conditioning, and how can I apply it in everyday life?

► What is operant conditioning, and how can I apply it in everyday life?

► How and when do we learn according to cognitive-social theory?

► What neurological changes take place during and after learning? What are the evolutionary advantages to learning?

During the 2000 presidential debates, George W. Bush mentioned the case of James Byrd and the death penalty conviction of his murderers as evidence of how Texas dealt with this particular "hate crime." Sadly, a follow-up national poll of likely voters found that many people did not know about (or could no longer remember) the brutal murder of James Byrd that happened only 2 years before.

Do you remember what happened on Sunday morning, June 28, 1998? James Byrd, a disabled 49-year-old African American, was hitchhiking home along Martin Luther King Boulevard in Jasper, Texas, when three young white men pulled up and offered him a ride. But they had no intention of taking him home. Instead, they chained Mr. Byrd by his

James Byrd

ankles to the back of their rusted 1982 pickup and dragged him along an old logging road outside of town until his head and right arm ripped from his body.

The three men who committed this grisly murder were quickly captured and brought to justice. Two were sentenced to death and the third was given life imprisonment without the possibility of parole. During the trial, jurors recoiled in horror as they viewed photographs of Byrd's dismembered body. They seemed almost as stunned by the horrific tattoos on the body of one of his murderers (see the photo to the right).

John William "Bill" King. King was sentenced to death for the murder of James Byrd. Note the tattoos on his arm, which include a Satanic image of the Virgin Mary holding a horned baby Jesus, Nazi and racist prison gang insignias, Ku Klux Klan symbols, and the figure of a lynched Black man (Galloway, 1999).

The swift arrest and conviction of James Byrd's murderers brought a measure of comfort to his family, the residents of Jasper, and the nation as a whole.

But now as time has passed and the media spotlight has faded, we're left wondering what turns three young men into such callous, hate-filled monsters. Moreover, how do we explain the Imperial Wizard of the Ku Klux Klan who placed a KKK sticker on James Byrd's grave in March 2000? Despite the nation's collective outrage over this savage murder, hate crimes targeting groups solely on the basis of ethnicity, sexual orientation, gender, or religious preference continue to occur. Why? Where does such hatred come from? Is racism learned?

Learning *A relatively permanent change in behavior or behavioral potential as a result of practice or experience*

I n the everyday sense, *learning* usually refers to classroom activities, such as math and reading, or motor skills, like riding a bike or playing the piano. But to psychologists, **learning** is much broader. It is formally defined as a relatively permanent change in behavior or behavioral potential as a result of practice or experience. Unlike that of fish, birds, and other animals that are driven primarily by innate, *instinctual* drives, human behavior results chiefly from learning. Our behavior is flexible and adaptive, rather than genetically programmed. Tragedies like the murder of James Byrd show us the dark side of human learning, but the very fact that racism and hatred are *learned* offers great hope. What is learned can be unlearned (or at least suppressed). Unlike salmon that are born with a predetermined, unchangeable instinct that drives them upstream to mate and die, humans are flexible and can learn new, more adaptive behaviors.

In this chapter, we will discover how we learn hatred, racism, phobias, and superstitions, as well as love and generosity. Much of this chapter focuses on the most basic form of learning called *conditioning*, which is the process of learning associations between environmental stimuli and behavioral responses. We begin with two types of conditioning — classical and operant conditioning. (As you're reading through this section, it may help you organize and learn the material to repeatedly review the summary table provided in Table 6.1.) We also look at cognitive-social learning, and along the way, we discuss how learning theories and concepts can be used to improve your life. We conclude with an exploration of the neurological changes that take place during and after learning and then the evolutionary perspective.

CLASSICAL CONDITIONING

Have you ever noticed that when you are hungry and see a large slice of chocolate cake or a juicy steak, your mouth starts to water? It seems natural that your mouth should water if you put food into it, but why do you salivate at just the sight of the food?

What is classical conditioning, and how can I apply it in everyday life?

Understanding Classical Conditioning: Pavlov's and Watson's Contributions

The answer to this question was accidentally discovered in the Leningrad laboratory of Ivan Pavlov (1849–1936). Pavlov was a Russian physiologist who was awarded the Nobel Prize for his work on the role of saliva in digestion. One of Pavlov's experiments involved salivary responses in dogs, where he attached a glass funnel to the experimental dogs' salivary glands to collect and measure the output (Figure 6.1). Pavlov wanted to determine whether dry food required more saliva than moist food and if nonfood objects required varying amounts of saliva, depending on how hard it was to spit them out.

Pavlov's (Accidental) Discovery

In the course of Pavlov's research, one of his students noticed that many dogs began to salivate at the sight of the food, the food dish, the smell of the food, or even the person who delivered the food — long *before* food was placed in their mouth. (This is the important, *accidental* part of the discovery, which might have gone unnoticed if the collection tubes had not been in place.) Although this "unscheduled" salivation interfered with Pavlov's research design and irritated him, it was also intriguing. Salivation is a *reflex response*, a largely, involuntary, automatic response to an external stimulus. Why were his dogs reflexively salivat-

TABLE 6.1 AN OVERVIEW OF CLASSICAL AND OPERANT CONDITIONING

	Classical Conditioning	Operant Conditioning
Other Names	Respondent conditioning Pavlovian conditioning	Instrumental conditioning Law of effect (Thorndike) Skinnerian conditioning
Pioneers	Ivan Pavlov John B. Watson	Edward Thorndike B. F. Skinner
Example	Sound of bell (CS) begins to produce salivation	Baby cries and parents pick up baby
Major Terms	Unconditioned stimulus (UCS) Conditioned stimulus (CS) Unconditioned response (UCR) Conditioned response (CR) Conditioned emotional response (CER)	Reinforcers (primary and secondary) Reinforcement (positive and negative) Punishment (positive and negative) Shaping Reinforcement schedules (continuous and partial)
Shared Terms	Extinction Spontaneous recovery Generalization Discrimination	Extinction Spontaneous recovery Generalization Discrimination
Major Differences	Involuntary (subject is passive)	Voluntary (subject is active)
Behavior Order	CS must come *before* the UCS	Reinforcement comes *after* the behavior

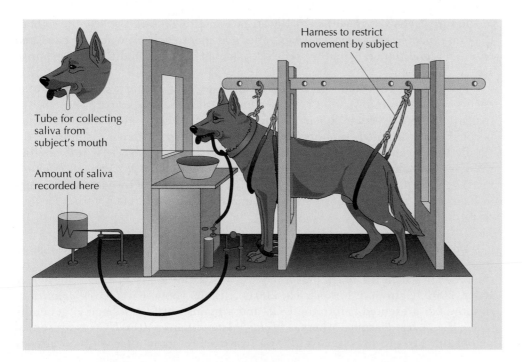

Harness to restrict movement by subject

Tube for collecting saliva from subject's mouth

Amount of saliva recorded here

Figure 6.1 *Pavlov's original classical conditioning apparatus.* During Pavlov's initial experiments, a tube was inserted into the dog's salivary gland to collect and measure the salivation produced under different experimental conditions.

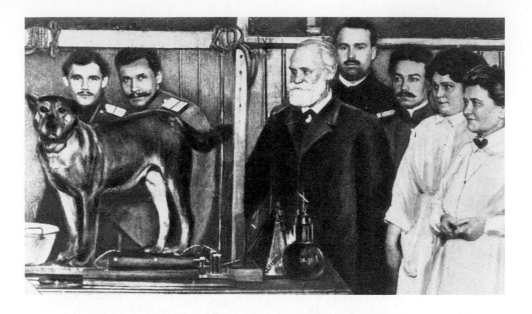

Ivan Pavlov (1849–1936), his assistants, and his famous "salivating dog." In 1903, Pavlov published the results from his first "conditioned reflex" (classical conditioning) study. Pavlov's dogs learned to salivate to many experimental stimuli, including a metronome, tuning fork, and bell. They also learned to salivate at the mere sight of the experimenter and the harness—unintentional conditioning!

Classical Conditioning *A basic form of learning in which an organism involuntarily learns to associate stimuli; a previously neutral stimulus is paired with an unconditioned stimulus to elicit a conditioned response that is identical or very similar to the unconditioned response (also known as respondent or Pavlovian conditioning)*

Unconditioned Stimulus (UCS) *Any stimulus that causes a reflex or emotional response without any learning or conditioning required*

Unconditioned Response (UCR) *The reflex response evoked by a stimulus without any learning required*

Conditioned Stimulus (CS) *A previously neutral stimulus that, through conditioning, now causes a classically conditioned response*

Conditioned Response (CR) *A learned response to a previously neutral stimulus that has been associated with the stimulus through repeated pairings*

ing *before* the food was even presented? Why did they salivate to extraneous stimuli other than food?

Pavlov's scientific training helped him appreciate the significance of what had at first seemed annoying. A reflex (salivation) that occurred *before* the appropriate stimulus (food) was presented is clearly not inborn and biological. It had to have been acquired through experience — through *learning*. The type of learning that Pavlov described came to be known as **classical conditioning** (as in first [*classical*] learning [*conditioning*]). Classical conditioning (also known as *respondent* or *Pavlovian conditioning*) occurs when a previously neutral stimulus elicits a response through association with a stimulus that already elicits a similar or related response.

To understand this definition, you need to learn four basic terms describing each element of the classical conditioning process: *unconditioned stimulus* (UCS), *unconditioned response* (UCR), *conditioned stimulus* (CS), and *conditioned response* (CR).

Before Pavlov's dogs *learned* to salivate at something extraneous like the sight of the experimenter, the original salivary reflex was inborn and biological. It consisted of an **unconditioned stimulus** (UCS), food, and an **unconditioned response** (UCR), salivation.

Pavlov's discovery (and great contribution to psychology) was that learning occurs when a *neutral stimulus* (NS) (a stimulus that does not evoke a response) is regularly paired with an unconditioned stimulus. The neutral stimulus then becomes a **conditioned stimulus** (CS), which elicits a **conditioned response** (CR). (Study tip: If you're finding this confusing, note that *conditioning* is just another word for *learning*. When you see words like *unconditioned response*, mentally rearrange and think "unlearned response." It also helps to read through the diagram in Figure 6.2, which provides a visual organizer and detailed example from Pavlov's research.)

Does the neutral stimulus always come first? Researchers have investigated four different ways to pair stimuli (Table 6.2) and found that both the timing and the order in which the NS is presented are very important (Chromiak, Barber, & Kyler, 2000; Church & Kirkpatrick, 2001). Results show that *delayed conditioning* (the NS presented before the UCS and remains until UCR begins) generally yields the fastest learning; whereas *backward conditioning* (the UCS is presented before the NS) is least effective. If you heard a fire alarm *after* you had already

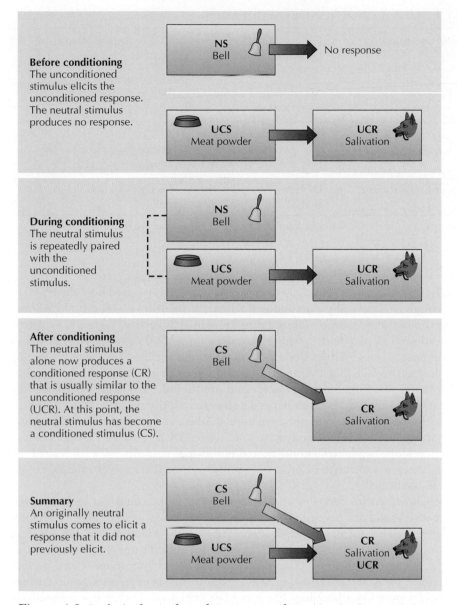

Figure 6.2 *Pavlov's classical conditioning paradigm.* Use this figure to help you visualize and organize the three major phases of classical conditioning and their associated key terms.

abandoned a building (backward conditioning), would you have the same association as if you heard the alarm first? No, because the sound of the fire alarm is the signal of the upcoming event (the fire), and hearing it afterward would lack real significance.

Watson's Contribution to Classical Conditioning

At this point, you may be wondering what dogs salivating to the sound of a bell has to do with your life — other than explaining why you salivate at the sight of delicious food. In fact, classical conditioning has been shown to be the most basic and fundamental way that all animals, including humans, learn most new responses, emotions, and attitudes. Your love for your parents (or significant other), the hatred and racism that led to the murder of James Byrd, and your drooling at the sight of chocolate cake are largely the result of classical conditioning.

TABLE 6.2 CONDITIONING SEQUENCES

Delayed conditioning	NS presented before UCS and remains until UCR begins	Bell presented with food until dog begins to salivate
Simultaneous conditioning	NS presented at the same time as UCS	Bell and food presented simultaneously
Trace conditioning	NS presented and then taken away, or ends before UCS presented	Bell rung, but food presented only once the sound stops
Backward conditioning	UCS presented before NS	Food presented before the bell

NS = neutral stimulus; UCR = unconditioned response; UCS = unconditioned stimulus.

Conditioned Emotional Response (CER) *Any classically conditioned emotional response to a previously neutral stimulus*

In one of the most famous (and controversial) psychological studies, John Watson and Rosalie Rayner (1920, 2000) experimentally demonstrated how the emotion of fear could be classically conditioned. Albert, a healthy 11-month-old normal child, was brought to Watson's lab at Johns Hopkins University (Figure 6.3). Albert was first allowed to play with a white laboratory rat to find out if he was afraid of rats. Like most infants, "Little Albert" was curious and reached for the rat, showing no fear. Using the fact that infants are naturally frightened (UCR) by loud noises (UCS), Watson stood behind Albert and again put the rat (NS) near him. When the infant reached for the rat, Watson banged a steel bar of Albert's crib with a hammer. As you might imagine, the loud noise frightened Albert and made him cry. The white rat (NS) was paired with the immediate loud noise (UCS) only seven times before the white rat alone produced a **conditioned emotional response** (CER), fear of the rat. Thus, Watson and Rayner's original hypothesis that fears are classically conditioned was confirmed.

For obvious reasons, Watson and Rayner's experiment could not be performed today because it violates several ethical guidelines for scientific research (Chapter 1). Moreover, shortly after the experiment, Albert was adopted, and Watson and Rayner simply ended their experiment. They did not attempt to extinguish (remove) Albert's fear even though they believed that a CER could endure for a long period. This disregard for Albert's well-being is a serious criticism of Watson and Rayner's study. Their research methodology has also been criticized. Rather than objectively measuring Albert's fear, Watson and Rayner only subjectively evaluated it, which raises doubt about the degree of fear conditioned (Paul & Blumenthal, 1989).

Despite such criticisms, John B. Watson made important and lasting contributions to psychology. At the time he was conducting research, psychology's early

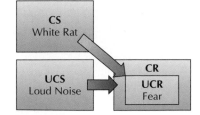

Figure 6.3 *Watson and Rayner.* This diagram shows how Little Albert's fear of rats was conditioned using a loud noise. In the photo, Watson and Rayner are shown with Little Albert who's crying from the loud noise.

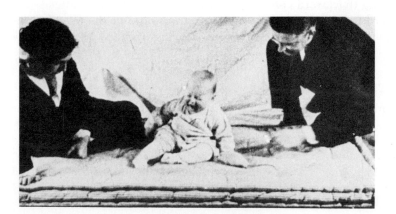

founders were defining the field as the *scientific study of the mind* (Chapter 1). Watson criticized psychology's study of subjective mental processes, insisting that it was "unscientific and a dead end." Instead, he focused on strictly observable behaviors and founded the new school or approach known as *behaviorism*, which believes that human behavior, though biologically influenced, is almost completely the result of conditioning and learning. His study of Little Albert has had legendary significance for many psychologists. He showed us that many of our likes, dislikes, prejudices, and fears are conditioned emotional responses.

Historical note: Shortly after the Little Albert experiment, Watson was fired from his academic position and no other university would hire him, despite his international fame as a scientist. His firing resulted from his scandalous and highly publicized affair with his graduate student Rosalie Rayner and divorce from his wife. Watson later married Rayner and became an influential advertising executive. He is credited with many successful ad campaigns based on classical conditioning, including ones for Johnson & Johnson baby powder, Maxwell House coffee, and Lucky Strike cigarettes (Angelo, 1998; Buckley, 1982, 1989; Hunt, 1993).

Check & Review

UNDERSTANDING CLASSICAL CONDITIONING

In **classical conditioning**, the type of learning investigated by Pavlov and Watson, an originally *neutral stimulus* (NS) is paired with an **unconditioned stimulus** (UCS) that causes a particular reflex or **unconditioned response** (UCR). After several pairings, the neutral stimulus becomes a **conditioned stimulus** (CS) that alone will produce a **conditioned response** (CR) or **conditioned emotional response** (CER) that is the same as the original reflex response.

There are four conditioning sequences: delayed conditioning, simultaneous conditioning, trace conditioning, and backward conditioning. Delayed conditioning is the most effective, and backward conditioning is the least effective.

Pavlov's work laid a foundation for Watson's insistence that psychology must be an objective science, studying only overt behavior, without considering internal, mental activity. Watson called this position *behaviorism*, demonstrated in his famous "Little Albert" study, that emotional responses can be classically conditioned.

Questions

1. Eli's grandma gives him a Tootsie roll every time she visits. When Eli sees his grandma arriving, his mouth begins to water. In this example the conditioned stimulus (CS) is _____ . (a) hunger; (b) Grandma; (c) the Tootsie roll; (d) the watering mouth

2. After conditioning, the _____ elicits the _____ .

3. In John Watson's demonstration of classical conditioning with little Albert, the unconditioned STIMULUS was _____ . (a) symptoms of fear; (b) a rat; (c) a bath towel; (d) a loud noise

4. A Vietnam War veteran experiences an intense emotional reaction to a clap of thunder. His emotional response is an example of a(n) _____ . (a) CS; (b) UCS; (c) CER; (d) UCR

Answers to Questions can be found in Appendix B.

Principles of Classical Conditioning: Fine-Tuning the Process

Now that you understand the basics of classical conditioning and how they explain CERs, we can build on this foundation. In this section, we will discuss five important principles of classical conditioning: *stimulus generalization*, *stimulus discrimination*, *extinction*, *spontaneous recovery*, and *higher-order conditioning*.

Generalization and Discrimination

Remember Pavlov's experiment conditioning dogs to salivate at the sound of a low-pitched tone? Pavlov and his students later demonstrated that the dogs also would salivate to higher-pitched tones. When objects or sounds that are similar to the originally conditioned stimulus (low-pitched tone) trigger the conditioned response (salivation), it is called **stimulus generalization**. The more the stimulus resembles

Stimulus Generalization *The occurrence of a learned response not only to the original stimulus but also to other similar stimuli*

Figure 6.4 *The process of extinction.* In this hypothetical graph from a typical experiment demonstrating extinction, note how the response rate decreases over time and with additional extinction trials.

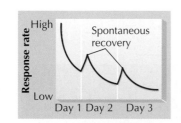

Figure 6.5 *Spontaneous recovery.* A hypothetical graph from a standard extinction experiment, but note that on occasion the extinguished response will "spontaneously reappear."

Stimulus Discrimination *The occurrence of a learned response to a specific stimulus but not to other, similar stimuli*

Extinction *The gradual suppression of a behavior or a response that occurs when a conditioned stimulus is repeatedly presented without the unconditioned stimulus with which it had been previously associated*

Spontaneous Recovery *The reappearance of a previously extinguished response after a period of time without exposure to the conditioned stimulus*

Higher-Order Conditioning *In classical conditioning, a procedure in which a neutral stimulus (NS) becomes a conditioned stimulus (CS) through association with an already established conditioned stimulus. A NS is paired with a previous CS$_1$, which then becomes a CS$_2$ and produces the same CR as CS$_1$*

the conditioned stimulus, the stronger the conditioned response (Hovland, 1937). Stimulus generalization also occurred in Watson's experiment with Albert. After conditioning, Albert feared rats, as well as a white rabbit, a white glove, cotton balls, and even a white beard on a Santa Claus mask.

Would Little Albert still be afraid of a Santa Claus mask as he grew older? Probably not. Through the process of **stimulus discrimination**, he would eventually learn to recognize differences between rats and other stimuli. Although stimulus generalization seems to naturally follow from initial classical conditioning, organisms only learn to distinguish (or *discriminate*) between an original CS and similar stimuli if they have enough experience with both. Just as you learn to discriminate between the sound of your cellular phone and the ringing of others, when Pavlov repeatedly presented food following a high-pitched tone, but not with a low-pitched tone, the dog gradually learned to distinguish between the two tones. Thus, both Little Albert and Pavlov's dog produced conditioned responses only to specific stimuli — *stimulus discrimination*.

Extinction and Spontaneous Recovery

Classical conditioning, like all learning, is only *relatively* permanent. Most behaviors that are learned through classical conditioning can be suppressed. The process is called **extinction**. Extinction occurs when the UCS is repeatedly withheld whenever the CS is presented, which weakens the previous association. For instance, when Pavlov sounded the tone again and again without presenting food, the dog's salivation gradually declined. Similarly, if you have a classically conditioned fear of the sound of a dentist's drill and later start to work as a dental assistant, your fear would gradually diminish (Figure 6.4).

Does extinction cause us to "unlearn" a classical conditioned response? No, extinction is not *unlearning* (Bouton, 1994). A behavior becomes extinct when the response rate decreases and the person or animal no longer responds to the stimulus. It does not mean the person or animal has "erased" the previous learned connection between the stimulus and the response. In fact, if the stimulus is reintroduced, the conditioning is much faster the second time. Furthermore, Pavlov found that if he allowed several hours to pass after the extinction procedure and then presented the tone again, the salivation would spontaneously reappear. The reappearance of a conditioned response after extinction, referred to as **spontaneous recovery**, helps explain why you suddenly feel excited at the sight of your old high school sweetheart. Even though years have passed (and extinction has occurred), some people (who haven't read this book and studied this phenomenon) might mislabel this excitement as "lasting love." You, on the other hand, would recognize it as possible *spontaneous recovery* (Figure 6.5).

Higher-Order Conditioning

Children are not born salivating to McDonald's golden arches. However, you've probably heard them begging to eat at a McDonald's restaurant after seeing this symbol. How did this happen? In Pavlov's original study, the NS was paired with a UCS. It was later learned that pairing a second, new stimulus with the already conditioned stimulus could make it also become a CS. This is known as **higher-order conditioning**.

If you wanted to demonstrate higher-order conditioning in Pavlov's dogs, you would first condition the dogs to salivate to the sound of the bell. Then you would pair the flash of light to the ringing of the bell. Eventually, the dog would salivate to the flash of light alone (Figure 6.6a,b). In a similar fashion, children first learn to pair up the general McDonald's restaurant with food, and later learn that two golden arches are a symbol for McDonald's (Figure 6.6c,d). Their salivation and begging to eat at the restaurant are a classic case of higher-order conditioning (and successful advertising).

Classical Conditioning in Real Life: From Prejudice to Advertisements

As you might expect, advertisers, politicians, film producers, music artists, and others have used classical conditioning to manipulate our purchases, votes, emotions, and motivation. It has also been used to our benefit (Woods & Ramsay, 2000). Let's examine several examples, good and bad, from everyday life.

Prejudice

In a classic study in the 1930s, Kenneth Clark and Mamie P. Clark (1939) studied children's reactions to black dolls and to white dolls. They found that given a choice, both black and white children preferred the white dolls. When asked which doll was good and which was bad, both groups of children also responded that the white doll was good and nice and that the black doll was bad, dirty, and ugly. The Clarks reasoned that the children, as well as many others in the United States, had *learned* to associate inferior qualities with darker skin and positive qualities with light skin. The Clark study played a pivotal role in the famous *Brown v. Board of Education of Topeka* ruling in 1954 that segregation of public facilities was unconstitutional. (This was also the first time social science research was formally cited in a U.S. Supreme Court case to support a legal argument.)

Figure 6.6 *How children learn to salivate for McDonald's.* As you can see in the top two boxes (a and b), *higher-order conditioning* is a two-stage process. In the first stage, a neutral stimulus (such as a bell) is paired with an unconditioned stimulus (such as meat powder) until it becomes a conditioned stimulus that elicits a conditioned response (salivation). During the second stage (higher order conditioning), a different neutral stimulus (such as a flashing light) is paired with the bell until it also becomes a conditioned stimulus. Now examine the bottom two boxes (c and d). Can you see how the same two-stage type of higher-order conditioning helps explain why children become so excited (and salivate) when they see the golden arches.

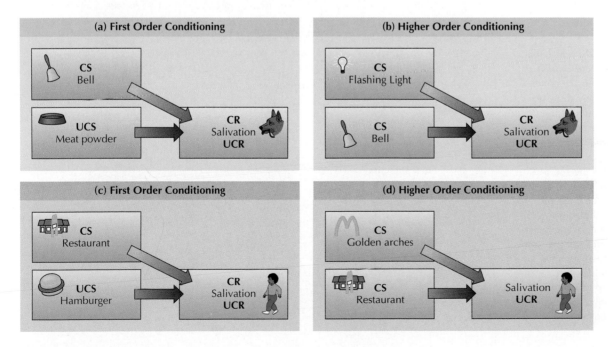

If you're thinking this 1930 study no longer applies, follow-up research in the late 1980s found that 65 percent of the African American children and 74 percent of the white children still preferred the white doll (Powell-Hopson & Hopson, 1988). The Clark study provided important insights into the negative effects of prejudice on the victims — African American children. But what about the white children who also strongly preferred the white doll? Was their preference also due to classical conditioning? And did a similar type of classical conditioning contribute to the vicious murder of James Byrd? Although we can't be sure how the hatred and racism that took James Byrd's life originally started, prejudice of many types (racism, ageism, sexism, homophobia, and religious intolerance) can be classically conditioned, as Figure 6.7 shows.

Phobias

Do you know someone who "freaks out" at the sight of a cockroach? At some time during childhood, this person probably was conditioned to associate the NS (cockroach) with a UCS (perhaps seeing a parent flinch at the sight of a cockroach) until

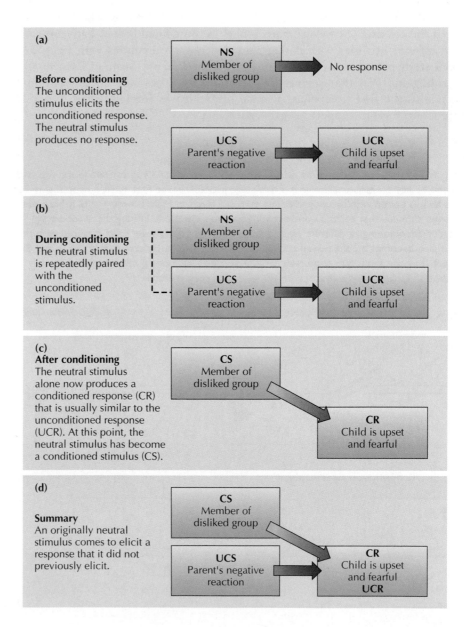

Figure 6.7 *How prejudice may be acquired through classical conditioning.* (a) Before children are conditioned to be prejudiced, they show no response to a member of different group. (b) Given that children are naturally upset and fearful when they see their parents upset, they can learn to be upset and fearful (UCR) if the see their parents respond negatively (UCS) to a member of a disliked group (NS). (c) After several pairings of the person from this group with their parents' negative reactions, the sight of the other person becomes a conditioned stimulus (CS), and being upset and fearful becomes the conditioned response (CR). (d) A previously unbiased child has now learned to be prejudiced.

(a)
Before conditioning
The unconditioned stimulus elicits the unconditioned response. The neutral stimulus produces no response.

NS
Member of disliked group → No response

UCS
Parent's negative reaction → UCR
Child is upset and fearful

(b)
During conditioning
The neutral stimulus is repeatedly paired with the unconditioned stimulus.

NS
Member of disliked group

UCS
Parent's negative reaction → UCR
Child is upset and fearful

(c)
After conditioning
The neutral stimulus alone now produces a conditioned response (CR) that is usually similar to the unconditioned response (UCR). At this point, the neutral stimulus has become a conditioned stimulus (CS).

CS
Member of disliked group → CR
Child is upset and fearful

(d)
Summary
An originally neutral stimulus comes to elicit a response that it did not previously elicit.

CS
Member of disliked group

UCS
Parent's negative reaction → CR
Child is upset and fearful
UCR

a CR (fear at the sight of a cockroach) was conditioned. Researchers have found that classically conditioned emotional responses explain most *phobias*, exaggerated and irrational fears of a specific object or situation (Evans & Rilling, 2000; Schneider et al., 1999). The good news is that extreme fear of cockroaches, hypodermic needles, spiders, closets, and even snakes can be effectively treated with *behavior modification* (Chapter 15).

Medical Treatments

Examples of classical conditioning are also found in the medical field. For example, a program conducted by several hospitals in California gives an *emetic* (a nausea-producing drug) to their alcohol-addicted patients. But before the nausea begins, the patient gargles with his or her preferred alcoholic beverage to maximize the taste and odor cues paired with nausea. During conditioning, the smell and taste of various alcoholic drinks (NS) are paired with nausea (UCS), making the patient vomit or feel sick (UCR). Afterward, just the smell or taste of alcohol (CS) makes the person sick (CR). Some patients have found this treatment successful, but not all (Chapter 15).

Although nausea is deliberately produced in this treatment for alcoholism, it is an unfortunate, unintended side effect of some cancer treatment. The nausea and vomiting produced by chemotherapy often generalize to other environmental cues, such as the hospital room color or odor (Stockhorst et al., 2000). Using their knowledge of classical conditioning to change associations, therapists can now help cancer patients control their nausea and vomiting response.

Advertising

Beginning with John B. Watson in the 1920s, advertisers have employed numerous classical conditioning principles to market their products. For example, TV commercials, magazine ads, and business promotions often pair their products or company logo (NS) with pleasant images, such as attractive models and celebrities (UCS) that automatically trigger favorable responses (UCR). Advertisers hope that after repeated viewings, their products (CS) alone will elicit those same favorable responses (CR) and that we will buy their products or use their services. Researchers caution that these ads also help produce visual stimuli that trigger conditioned responses such as urges to smoke or drink alcohol, which makes addiction recovery more difficult (Dols, Willems, van den Hout, & Bittoun, 2000; Foltin & Haney, 2000).

Classical conditioning in action. Have you ever wondered why politicians kiss babies? It's because they hope to become a favorable conditioned stimulus. They hope that by pairing themselves with positive stimuli (like babies or the American flag) you will have a favorable predisposition to vote for them (a conditioned emotional response).

TRY THIS *Yourself*

If you'd like to see how classical conditioning affects your own life, try this:

1. Look through a popular magazine and find several advertisements. What images are used as the unconditioned stimulus (UCS)? Note how you react to these images.

2. While watching a movie or a favorite TV show, note what sounds and images are used as conditioned stimuli. (Hint: certain types of music are used to set the stage for happy stories, sad events, and fearful situations.) What are your conditioned emotional responses (CERs)?

3. Read the words below and pay attention to your emotional response. Your reactions — positive, negative, or neutral — are a result of your own personal classical conditioning history. Can you trace back to the UCS?

   father final exams spinach
   Santa Claus beer mother

Check & Review

PRINCIPLES AND APPLICATIONS OF CLASSICAL CONDITIONING

In classical conditioning, **stimulus generalization** occurs when stimuli similar to the original conditioned stimulus (CS) elicit the conditioned response (CR). **Stimulus discrimination** takes place when only the CS elicits the CR. **Extinction** occurs when the unconditioned stimulus (UCS) is repeatedly withheld and the association between the CS and the UCS is broken. **Spontaneous recovery** happens when a CR that had been extinguished reappears with no prompting. In **higher-order conditioning**, the neutral stimulus (NS) is paired with a CS to which the participant has already been conditioned, rather than with a UCS.

Classical conditioning has many applications in everyday life. Through classical conditioning, we can learn negative attitudes toward groups of people — and unlearn those attitudes. It is also used in behavior modification programs, some medical treatments, and to help patients change associations and reduce undesirable conditioned behavior. In addition, classical conditioning is the basis for a great deal of advertising.

Questions

1. Like most college students, your heart rate and blood pressure greatly increase when the fire alarm sounds. If the fire alarm system was malfunctioning and rang every half hour, by the end of the day, your heart rate and blood pressure would no longer increase. Why?

2. A baby is bitten by a dog and then is afraid of all small animals. This is an example of (a) stimulus discrimination; (b) extinction; (c) reinforcement; (d) stimulus generalization.

3. When a conditioned stimulus is used to reinforce the learning of a second conditioned stimulus, _____ has occurred.

4. If you wanted to use higher order conditioning to get little Albert to fear Barbie dolls, you would present a Barbie doll with _____. (a) the loud noise; (b) the original unconditioned response; (c) the white rat; (d) the original conditioned response

Answers to Questions can be found in Appendix B.

OPERANT CONDITIONING

What is operant conditioning, and how can I apply it in everyday life?

Operant Conditioning *Learning based on consequences; behavior is strengthened if followed by reinforcement and diminished if followed by punishment*

Consequences are the heart of **operant conditioning** (also called *instrumental conditioning* or *Skinnerian conditioning*). In classical conditioning, the consequences of an animal or person's behavior are irrelevant. Pavlov's dog still got the meat powder whether it salivated or not. However, in operant conditioning the *consequences* of an organism's behavior are all important. Whether behavior is reinforced or punished (consequences) determines whether the response will occur again. Stated in a different way, behaviors that are reinforced are more likely to be repeated, whereas those that are punished are less likely to be repeated. If you receive praise and an A on your term paper, you will be more likely to write another term paper, and the reverse is true if you receive an F and critical comments.

Classical and operant conditioning also tend to differ in the types of responses they generate. In classical conditioning, the organism's response is *passive* and *involuntary*. It "happens to" the organism when a UCS follows a CS. In operant conditioning, the organism's response is *active* and *voluntary*. The learner "operates" on the environment and produces effects. These effects (or consequences), in turn, influence whether the behavior will occur again.

It's important to mention that these distinctions between classical and operant condition are *generally* true — but not *always* true. Technically speaking, classical conditioning does sometimes influence voluntary behavior, and operant conditioning can influence involuntary, reflexive behavior. Furthermore, both forms of conditioning often interact to produce and maintain behavior. But for most purposes, the distinction holds, and it's easier simply to remember that classical conditioning is passive and operant conditioning is active.

In the sections that follow, we will examine the historical contributions of Thorndike and Skinner, the general principles of operant conditioning, and several interesting applications of operant conditioning to real life.

Understanding Operant Conditioning: Thorndike and Skinner

Edward Thorndike (1874–1949), the pioneer of operant conditioning, was among the first to examine how voluntary behaviors are influenced by their consequences. In one of his famous experiments, he put a cat inside a specially built *puzzle box* (Figure 6.8). The only way the cat could get out was by pulling on a rope or stepping on a pedal, whereupon the door would open and the cat could get out to eat. Eventually, through trial-and-error, the cat would accidentally pull on the rope or step on the pedal that opened the door. With each additional trial, the cat's actions became more purposeful and it soon learned to open the door immediately.

Thorndike concluded that the frequency of a behavior is modified by its consequences. He is credited with developing the *law of effect*: the probability of a action being repeated *strengthens* if it is followed by a pleasant or satisfying consequence. In short, rewarded behavior is more likely to reoccur (Thorndike, 1911). Thorndike's law of effect was a first step in understanding how active, *voluntary* behaviors can be modified by their consequences.

B. F. Skinner (1904–1990) extended Thorndike's law of effect to more complex forms of behaviors. As a strict behaviorist, however, Skinner avoided terms like *pleasant*, *desired*, and *voluntary* because they make assumptions about what an organism feels and wants and because they imply that behavior is due to conscious choice or intention. He argued that to understand behavior, we should consider only observable, external or environmental stimuli and responses. We should look outside the learner, not inside.

To test his theories, Skinner conducted systematic research. The typical Skinner experiment used an animal, usually a pigeon or a rat, and an apparatus that has come to be called a *Skinner box*. Skinner trained a rat to push a lever to receive a food pellet. The rat got a pellet each time it pushed the lever, and the number of responses made by the rat was recorded. Skinner used this basic experimental design to demonstrate a number of operant conditioning principles that are discussed in the next section.

Principles of Operant Conditioning: How It All Works

There are several important principles that you need to understand about operant conditioning. We begin with factors involved in *strengthening a response*, including primary and secondary reinforcers, positive and negative punishment, schedules of reinforcement, and shaping. We then explore those principles that *weaken a response*, including positive and negative punishment. We conclude this section with a look at the pros and cons of punishment and with a review of terms that are shared between classical and operant conditioning.

As we discuss these concepts, keep in mind that the effects or consequences of behavior result from either reinforcement or punishment. Specifically, **reinforcement** is any procedure that results in an increase in a response. Conversely, **punishment** is any procedure that results in a decrease in a response. The distinction between reinforcement and punishment is critical to understanding operant conditioning and applying its principles to your life.

Strengthening a Response

Earlier, we said that Skinner was a strict behaviorist who insisted that scientific observation be limited to that which can be observed. Therefore, instead of using words like *rewards* (which focuses on feelings), Skinner talked about reinforcers and reinforcement in terms of "strengthening the response." Thus, reinforcement (and punishment) are always defined *after the fact*. If the rate of response increases *after* a supposed reinforcer is presented, then we can say the behavior has been *rein-*

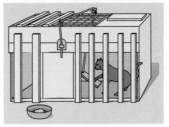

Figure 6.8 *Thorndike box.* This is a typical Thorndike box that was used in Edward Thorndike's trial-and-error experiments with cats. When a cat stepped on a pedal inside the box, the door latch was released and a weight attached to the door pulled it open so the cat could exit. (From Thorndike, 1898).

Reinforcement *Any action or event that increases the probability that a response will be repeated*

Punishment *Any action or event that decreases the likelihood that a response will be repeated*

B. F. Skinner and a typical Skinner box. The rat in the box has been conditioned to receive a pellet of food as reinforcement for bar pressing.

TABLE 6.3 HOW REINFORCEMENT STRENGTHENS AND INCREASES BEHAVIORS

Positive Reinforcement (+; adds to and strengthens behavior)	Type of Reinforcer	Negative Reinforcement (−; takes away and strengthens behavior	Type of Reinforcer
You're hungry and eat a delicious hamburger.	Primary	The hamburger takes away your hunger pains.	Primary
Your boyfriend/girlfriend hugs you.	Primary	You take an aspirin for your headache, which takes away the pain.	Primary
You receive $200 as a bonus.	Secondary	After high sales, your boss says you won't have to work on weekends.	Secondary
You receive a good grade on your psychology exam.	Secondary	Professor says you won't have to take the final exam because you did so well on your unit exam.	Secondary

forced. This may seem complicated, but the distinction is important. For example, men may buy women candy and flowers, believing that "all women love these things." However, some women hate candy (imagine that!), and some are allergic to flowers. Even avid candy and flower lovers aren't interested after a heavy meal or if they already have a lot of flowers. In both of these cases, the men were attempting to reinforce the women's feelings for them, but the women's reactions suggest that this is not what happened. Skinner would advise the men to watch the organisms' responses, *not* what they think the women should like or do.

As Table 6.3 shows, reinforcers can be grouped into two major classes:

1. *Primary and secondary reinforcers.* One of the chief methods for strengthening a response is with primary and secondary reinforcers. Through his research, Skinner found that food was an effective reinforcer for responses in rats but that humans responded according to primary or secondary reinforcers. Reinforcers such as food, water, and sex are called **primary reinforcers** because they normally satisfy an unlearned biological need. Reinforcers such as money, praise, attention, and material possessions that have no intrinsic value are called **secondary reinforcers**; the only power they have to reinforce behavior results from their learned value. A baby, for example, would find milk much more reinforcing than a hundred-dollar bill. Needless to say, by the time this baby has grown to adolescence, he or she will have learned to prefer the money. Among Westerners, money may be the most widely used secondary reinforcer because of its learned association with desirable commodities.

2. *Positive and negative reinforcement.* Adding or taking away relevant stimuli can also strengthen behavior. Suppose you tickle your baby and he smiles at you. His smile increases (or strengthens) the likelihood that you will tickle him again in the future. The smile itself is a *positive reinforcer*. The *process* whereby he "adds" his smile to the transaction and increases the likelihood that you will repeat the same tickling behavior is called **positive reinforcement**. On the other hand, suppose your baby is upset and crying, so you hug him and he stops crying. In this case, the removal of crying is a *negative reinforcer*, and the *process* is called **negative reinforcement** because it increases (or strengthens) the likelihood that you will hug him

Primary Reinforcers *Stimuli that increase the probability of a response because they satisfy a biological need, such as food, water, and sex*

Secondary Reinforcers *Stimuli that increase the probability of a response because of their learned value, such as money and material possessions*

Positive Reinforcement *The process of adding or presenting a stimulus that increases the likelihood of that response occurring again*

Negative Reinforcement *The process of taking away or removing a stimulus that increases the likelihood of that response occurring again*

again in the future when he cries. Both responses to your behavior have been reinforced, and your behavioral tendencies have been strengthened.

(As a critical thinker, you may be wondering what's happening for the baby in this example. Assuming he likes being tickled, his smiling behavior will increase when he learns that his smile causes the parent to tickle him — *positive reinforcement*. In the second case, the baby learns that crying brings hugs from his parents, so his crying also will increase — *positive reinforcement*. Although this may seem like a potential problem, the baby soon will learn to talk and develop "better" ways to communicate.)

How can I keep from thinking of negative reinforcement as punishment? It is difficult to think of the word *negative* and not consider it as punishment. But it's important to remember that these two terms are actually completely opposite procedures. Reinforcement (either positive or negative) *strengthens a behavior*, whereas punishment *weakens a behavior*.

Our students also find it less confusing to think of positive and negative reinforcement in the mathematical sense (as shown in Table 6.3) rather than as personal values of good and bad. Personal values can get confusing because what's good for one person is bad for another. Again, this is why Skinner insisted we must only look at the response. Instead of "good" or "bad," think of positive reinforcement as something being added (+) that increases the likelihood that the behavior will increase. If your boss compliments you on a job well done, the compliment is added (+) as a consequence to the good job you did, and your behavior is likely to increase. Similarly, if your baby awakens you in the morning and you bring her to bed with you and she stops crying, the taking away of the noise (–) is reinforcing, and your placing of the baby in your bed is likely to increase.

Researchers who study negative reinforcement have generally used two kinds of learning procedures: *escape learning* and *avoidance learning*. In a typical escape learning study, the animal learns that a response will end some kind of aversive (unpleasant) stimulus. For example, a rat might learn to escape a mild electric shock on the bottom of a cage by running to an area of the cage that is not electrified. This escape response leads to the removal of the aversive stimulus, so it is strengthened through negative reinforcement. In avoidance learning, the response the animal learns *prevents* the negative situation from occurring. The experimenter gives a signal (such as a light) that shock is forthcoming. In this case, the rat might learn to avoid the shock by running to the safe area of the cage as soon as the light comes on. Table 6.4 summarizes these concepts and offers additional (human) examples.

When I make myself study before I let myself go to the movies, is this escape learning? No, but it is an excellent strategy. You're actually using the **Premack principle**, named after psychologist David Premack, who suggested using any naturally occurring, high-frequency response to reinforce low-frequency responses. Rec-

Premack principle *Using a response that has a high probability of occurrence to reinforce a response that has a lower probability of occurrence*

T A B L E 6.4 ESCAPE LEARNING AND AVOIDANCE LEARNING

Escape Learning	Avoidance Learning
A negative reinforcement that eliminates an aversive state of affairs that already exists	A negative reinforcement that prevents an expected aversive event from happening
Example: A parent begins to scold her child and the child runs from the room to escape; the child is negatively reinforced because the scolding stops when the child leaves the room	Example: A parent gets angry when a teenager comes home late, so the teen avoids the aversive confrontation by waiting until the parent is asleep to return home

ognizing that you love to go to movies, you intuitively tied your less-desirable, low-frequency activities (studying) to high-frequency behavior (going to the movies). You can use the Premack principle in other aspects of your college life, such as making yourself write 4 pages on your term paper or reading 20 pages before you allow yourself to call a friend or have a snack.

Should I use the Premack principle every time I want to go to the movies or just occasionally? The answer is complex and depends on your most desired outcome. To make this decision, you need to understand various *schedules of reinforcement,* or rules that determine when a response will be rewarded and when it will not (Purdy, Markham, Schwartz, & Gordon, 2001).

Schedules of Reinforcement

The term *schedule of reinforcement* refers to the rate or interval at which responses are reinforced (Gallistel & Gibbon, 2000). Although there are numerous schedules of reinforcement, they can be grouped into two types: *continuous* or *partial.* When Skinner was training his animals, he found that learning was most rapid if the response is reinforced each time it occurs — a procedure called **continuous reinforcement.** However, real life seldom provides continuous reinforcement. You do not get an A each time you write a paper or a date each time you ask, but your behavior persists because your efforts are occasionally rewarded. Most everyday behavior is rewarded on a **partial (or intermittent) schedule of reinforcement,** which involves reinforcing only some responses, not all of them.

It is important to remember that continuous reinforcement leads to faster learning than does partial reinforcement. For example, if you are rewarded every time you blast an alien starship in a video game (*continuous reinforcement*), you will learn how to play faster than if you are rewarded for every third or fourth hit (*partial reinforcement*). However, although a continuous schedule of reinforcement leads to faster initial learning, it is *not* an efficient system for maintaining long-term behaviors. Imagine having to reward your children every morning for getting up, brushing their teeth, making their beds, dressing, and so on. You simply cannot reward someone constantly for every appropriate response. It is therefore important to move to a partial schedule of reinforcement once a task is well learned.

Why? Because under partial schedules, behavior is more resistant to extinction. Have you noticed that people spend long hours pushing buttons and pulling levers

Continuous Reinforcement *Reinforcement in which every correct response is reinforced*

Partial (Intermittent) Reinforcement Schedule *Reinforcement in which some, but not all, correct responses are reinforced*

Continuous or partial reinforcement. *Gumball machines provide continuous reinforcement, whereas roulette and other gambling games provide partial reinforcement.*

on slot machines in hopes of winning the jackpot? This high response rate and the compulsion to keep gambling in spite of significant losses are evidence of the strong resistance to extinction with partial schedules of reinforcement.

Four Forms of Partial Schedules of Reinforcement

Partial schedules of reinforcement are based on the number of responses between reinforcements (*ratio schedules*), or on the interval of time between reinforced responses (*interval schedules*). In addition, each type can be *fixed* or *variable*. There are, thus, four partial schedules of reinforcement: **fixed ratio**, **variable ratio**, **fixed interval**, and **variable interval**. Table 6.5 defines these terms and provides examples.

How do I know which schedule to choose? The type of partial schedule selected depends on the type of behavior being studied and on the speed of learning desired (Neuringer, Deiss, & Olson, 2000). For example, suppose you want to teach your dog to sit. Initially you reinforce your dog with a cookie every time he sits (continuous reinforcement). To save on your cookie bill and to make his training more resistant to extinction, you eventually switch to one of the partial reinforcement schedules, such as the *fixed ratio* schedule. You would then give your dog a cookie after he sat a certain number of times. The dog must make a fixed number of

Fixed Ratio Schedule *A partial schedule of reinforcement in which a participant must make a certain number of responses before being reinforced*

Variable Ratio Schedule *A schedule of reinforcement in which the participant is reinforced, on the average, for making a specific number of responses but the number of required responses between reinforcement is varied*

Fixed Interval Schedule *A schedule of reinforcement in which a participant is reinforced for the first response after a specific period of time has elapsed*

Variable Interval Schedule *A schedule of reinforcement in which the participant is reinforced for the first response after a period of time has elapsed; this period of time varies from one reinforcement to the next*

TABLE 6.5 FOUR FORMS OF PARTIAL SCHEDULES OF REINFORCEMENT

	Definitions	Response Rates	Examples
Fixed ratio (FR)	Reinforced after a fixed number of responses	Produces a high rate of response but a brief dropoff just after reinforcement	In a laboratory, a rat receives a food pellet after pressing the bar 7 times Parents pay a child $10 after he washes 2 cars
Fixed interval (FI)	Reinforced for the first response after a specified time has elapsed	Responses tend to increase as the time for the next reinforcer is near but drop off after reinformencement and during interval	Rat's behavior is reinforced with a food pellet each time it presses a bar after 20 seconds has elapsed. You get a weekly paycheck
Variable ratio (VR)	Reinforced on an average number of responses, but the number varies	High response rates, no pause after reinforcement, and very resistant to extinction	Slot machines designed to pay out after an average number of responses (maybe every 10 times), but any one machine may pay out on the first response, then seventh, then the twentieth
Variable interval (VI)	Reinforced on a variable time interval	Relatively low, but steady rates because the animal or person cannot predict when reward will come	Rat's behavior reinforced with a food pellet after a response and a variable, unpredictable interval of time In a class with pop quizzes, you study at a slow but steady rate because you can't anticipate the next quiz

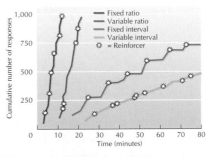

Figure 6.9 *Which is the best schedule of reinforcement?* Each of the different schedules produces its own unique pattern of response, and the best schedule depends on the specific task — see Table 6.5. Note that the "stars" on the lines represent the delivery of a reinforcer. (Adapted from Skinner, 1961.)

Operant conditioning in action. Momoko, a five-year-old female monkey, is famous in Japan for her water-skiing, deep-sea diving, and other amazing abilities. Can you imagine how her trainers undoubtedly used shaping to teach this type of behavior?

Shaping *A procedure in which reinforcement is delivered for successive approximations of the desired response*

responses before he receives the reinforcement. As you can see in Figure 6.9, a fixed ratio leads to the highest overall response rate, but each of the four types of partial schedules has different advantages and disadvantages (Table 6.5).

Shaping

Each of the principles discussed above are important for maintaining behavior, but how do you teach something like playing the piano or a foreign language to someone who's never seen a piano or been exposed to another language? **Shaping** teaches a desired response by reinforcing, a series of successive steps leading to the final goal response. It is especially effective for teaching complex or novel behaviors. Skinner believed that shaping explains a wide variety of skills and abilities that each of us possess, from eating with a fork, to playing a musical instrument, to driving a stick-shift car.

Parents, athletic coaches, teachers, and animal trainers all use shaping techniques. For example, if you want to shape a child to make his bed, you could begin by reinforcing when he first gets the sheets and pillows on the bed. Over time, you would stop reinforcing that level of behavior and only reinforce when he gets the bedspread on the bed and tucked over the pillows. Again, after a little time, you would stop reinforcing until he gets the bedspread on, tucked over the pillows, and straight. Each step in shaping, then, moves slightly beyond the previously learned behavior, allowing the person to link the new step to the behavior previously learned.

Weakening a Response

Now that you understand how to *strengthen* a response, we will examine ways to *weaken* undesirable behaviors. Like reinforcement, punishment affects behavior, but it has the opposite effect: it *decreases* the strength of the response — that is, the likelihood that a behavior will be repeated again. Just as with reinforcement, there are two kinds of punishment, *positive* and *negative* (Skinner, 1953; Gordon, 1989). Also as with reinforcement, remember to think in mathematical terms of adding and taking away, rather than good and bad (Table 6.6).

Positive punishment is the addition of a stimulus that decreases (or weakens) the likelihood of the response occurring again. If your dog digs a hole every time he sees a gopher mound, and you shout at him to decrease the digging, you are applying positive punishment. **Negative punishment** is the taking away of a stimulus that decreases (or weakens) the likelihood of the response occurring again. Parents use negative punishment when they take the car keys away from a teen who doesn't come home on time. Notice, as with reinforcement, that the concept is defined in terms of its effect (consequences) on behavior. Also, in both positive and negative punishment, the behavior has been punished and the behavioral tendencies have been weakened.

Positive Punishment *The process of adding or presenting a stimulus that decreases the likelihood of that response occurring again*

Negative Punishment *The process of taking away or removing a stimulus that decreases the likelihood of that response occurring again*

TABLE 6.6 HOW PUNISHMENT WEAKENS AND DECREASES BEHAVIORS

Positive Punishment (+; adds to and weakens the behavior)	Negative Punishment (−; takes away and weakens the behavior)
You have to run 4 extra laps in your gym class because you were late.	You aren't allowed to join the gym class because you were late.
Your teacher asks you to give an oral report after you mention an interesting article in the school newspaper.	Your teacher reassigns you to another group because you were talking too much to your friend.
Your boss complains about your performance.	Your boss takes away your overtime pay because you finished all the work ahead of schedule.

The "Tricky Business" of Punishment

When we discuss punishment, our students tend to think only of disciplinary procedures used by parents, teachers, and other authority figures. But from the psychological perspective (and the previous definitions), punishment is much more than parents giving a child a time-out for misbehaving or teachers giving demerits. Any process that adds or takes away something that causes the behavior to decrease is punishment. By this definition, if parents ignore all the A's on their child's report card and ask repeated questions about the B's and C's, they may unintentionally punish and weaken the likelihood of future A's. Dog owners who yell at their dogs for coming to them after being called several times are actually punishing the desired behavior — coming when called. Similarly, college administrators who take away "leftover" money from a department's budget because it wasn't spent by the end of the year are punishing desired behavior — saving money. (Yes, we did add this last example as a "subtle" message to our college administrators.)

As you can see, punishment is a tricky business. But an advantage of studying psychology is that you understand how positive and negative punishment (and positive and negative reinforcement) operate, and you can use this knowledge to become a better parent, teacher, and authority figure, as well as a better friend and lover. Punishment encompasses more than discipline, a difficult concept because of the way we use the terms *punish* and *discipline* in everyday language. To help you become a better disciplinarian, we offer the following general discussion and specific suggestions.

First of all, it's important to acknowledge that punishment plays a significant and unavoidable role in our social world. In his book *Walden Two* (1948), Skinner described a utopian world where reinforcers almost completely replaced punishment. Unfortunately, in our real world, reinforcement is not enough. Dangerous criminals must be stopped and possibly removed from society. Parents must stop their child from running into the street and their teenagers from drinking and driving. And teachers must stop disruptive students in the classroom and bullies on the playground.

There is a need for punishment at times, but it brings problems (Larzelere & Johnson, 2000; MacMillan, 2000). To be effective, punishment should be immediate and consistent. However, in the real world, this is extremely hard to do, and during the delay the behavior is likely to be reinforced on a partial schedule, which makes it highly resistant to extinction. Think about gambling. For almost everyone, it should be a *punishing* situation — on most occasions, you lose far more money than you win. However, the fact that you occasionally win keeps you "hanging in there." Furthermore, even when punishment immediately follows the misbehavior, the recipient may learn what *not* do but doesn't learn what he or she *should* do. Imagine trying to teach a child the word *dog* by only saying *"No!"* each time she said *dog* when it was inappropriate. The child (and you) would soon become very frustrated. It's much more efficient to teach someone by giving him or her clear examples of correct behavior. Punishment has several other serious side effects, as Table 6.7 shows.

Shared Terms for Both Classical and Operant Conditioning

In our earlier discussion of the principles of classical conditioning, you learned about *stimulus generalization*, *stimulus discrimination*, *extinction*, and *spontaneous recovery*. As you may have noticed in Table 6.1 at the beginning of the chapter, these same terms also are used in operant conditioning, and your previous learning will help you here. For example, just as 11-month-old Albert generalized his fear of rats to rabbits and Santa Claus masks, operantly conditioned responses also generalize. After learning the word for *Daddy* (through operant conditioning), children often use this same word for all adult men. This would be a form of *stimulus generalization* (and potential embarrassment to the parents). After parents explain the distinction, the child learns to differentiate (stimulus discrimination) and only call one man Daddy.

In both classical and operant conditioning, *extinction* occurs when the original source of the learning is removed. In classical conditioning, the CR (Albert's fear of the rat) is extinguished if the CS (the rat) is repeatedly presented without the UCS (the loud noise). In operant conditioning, if the reinforcement (the rat's food pellets) is removed, the response (bar pressing) will gradually decline. Following extinction in either classical or operant conditioning, you also sometimes have

TRY THIS
Yourself

Now that you have completed your study of both reinforcement and punishment, check your understanding by filling in your own personal examples in the bottom box in the following figure:

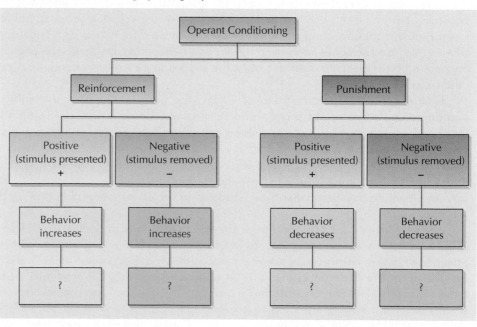

TABLE 6.7 SIDE EFFECTS OF PUNISHMENT

1. *Passive aggressiveness.* Punishment often leads to frustration in the animal or person being punished, which can lead to anger and eventually aggression. But most of us have learned from experience that retaliatory aggression toward a punisher (especially one who is bigger and more powerful) is usually followed by more punishment. We therefore tend to control our impulse toward open aggression and instead resort to more subtle techniques, such as, showing up late or forgetting to mail a letter for someone. This is known as *passive aggressiveness* (McIlduff & Coghlan, 2000; Stormshak, Bierman, McMahon, & Lengua, 2000).

2. *Increased aggression.* Because punishment often produces a decrease in undesired behavior, at least for the moment, the punisher is in effect rewarded for applying punishment. Thus, a vicious circle may be established in which both people are actually being reinforced for inappropriate behavior — the punisher for punishing and the recipient for being fearful and submissive. This side effect partially explains the escalation of violence in spousal, child, and elder abuse despite immense pain and suffering (Larzelere & Johnson, 1999). In addition to fear and submissiveness, the recipient might also become depressed and/or respond with his or her own aggression.

3. *Avoidance behavior.* People and animals do not like to be punished, so they try to avoid the punisher. If every time you come home your parents or spouse starts yelling at you, you will delay coming home or find another place to go.

4. *Modeling.* Have you ever seen a parent spank or hit a child for hitting another child? The punishing parent may unintentionally serve as a "model" for the same behavior he or she is attempting to stop.

5. *Only temporary suppression of behavior.* Do you notice that car drivers quickly slow down when they see a police car but quickly resume their previous speed once the police officer is out of sight? Punishment generally suppresses the behavior only during the presence of the punishing person or circumstances.

6 *Learned helplessness.* Why do some people stay in abusive homes or marital situations? Research shows that if you repeatedly fail in your attempts to control your environment, you acquire a general sense of powerlessness or *learned helplessness* and may make no further attempts to escape (Alloy & Clements, 1998; Seligman, 1975).

spontaneous recovery. Just as the classically conditioned fear of rats may spontaneously return, the operantly conditioned bar pressing behaviors may reoccur.

One final comparison: In classical conditioning, we talked about *higher-order conditioning,* wherein a neutral stimulus (NS) is paired with a conditioned stimulus (CS), which is another stimulus that already produces a learned response. We said that if you wanted to demonstrate higher-order conditioning in Pavlov's dogs, you would first condition the dogs to salivate to the sound of the bell. Then you would pair the flash of light to the ringing of the bell. Eventually, the dog would salivate only to the flash of light.

A similar process, with a different name, also occurs in operant conditioning. If a rat learns that bar pressing produces food *only* when a light is flashing, the rat will soon learn to respond only when the light is flashing. The light has become a **discriminative stimulus**, which signals whether a response will pay off or not. We depend on discriminative stimuli many times every day. We pick up the phone only when it rings. We look for the *Women* or *Men* signs on bathroom doors. And children quickly learn to ask Grandma for toys.

Discriminative Stimulus *A cue that signals when a particular response is likely to be followed by a certain type of consequence*

After studying these basic operant conditioning principles, can you effectively apply them in your own life? The best method seems to be a combination of the major principles: Reinforce appropriate behavior, extinguish inappropriate behavior, and save punishment for the most extreme cases (such as a 2-year-old running into the street). Also, remember that you have grown up in a culture that considers reinforcement "bribery" and, ironically, stresses punishment. We encourage you to explore the technique of reinforcement — you'll find it very rewarding! Here are some further guidelines:

1. *Feedback.* When using both reinforcement and punishment, be sure to provide immediate and clear feedback to the person or animal whose behavior you wish to change. When using punishment, it is particularly important to make clear the desired response, because punishment is merely an indication that the response is undesirable. In other words, give the participant an alternative response to the punished one.

2. *Timing.* Reinforcers and punishers should be presented as close in time to the response as possible. The old policy of "wait till Father gets home" is obviously inappropriate for many reasons. In this case, it is because the delayed punishment is no longer associated with the inappropriate response. The same is true for reinforcement. If you're trying to lose weight, don't say you'll buy yourself a new wardrobe when you lose 30 pounds; reward yourself with a small treat (like a new blouse or shirt) after every few pounds.

3. *Consistency* To be effective, both reinforcement and punishment must be consistent. Have you ever seen a child screaming for candy in a supermarket? Parents often begin by saying "No," but when the child gets louder and throws a complete temper tantrum sometimes they give in and buy the candy. Although the parents are momentarily relieved (*negatively reinforced*) when the screaming stops, can you see how they're creating bigger problems in the long run? First, the child is being *positively reinforced* for the screaming and temper tantrum — and this behavior will increase. To make matters worse, the parents' inconsistency (saying "no" and then occasionally giving in) places candy begging on a *partial schedule of reinforcement,* which is highly resistant to extinction. Like a gambler who continues playing despite the odds, the child will continue the temper tantrums in hopes of the occasional payoff. Because effective punishment requires constant surveillance and *consistent* responses, it's almost impossible to be a "good punisher." It's best (and easiest) to use consistent reinforcement for good behavior and extinction for bad behavior. Praise the child for happy and cooperative behavior in the supermarket, and extinguish the temper tantrum by consistently refusing the request and ignoring the tantrum.

4. *Order of presentation.* As a teenager, did you ever promise to wash the family car or mow the grass on Saturday if they would just let you use the car on Friday night? Did your parents ever make you come home much earlier than your friends because they knew "that all teenagers get into trouble after midnight?" Can you see why the reward of using the car must come *after* the car wash or lawn mowing, and why punishment that comes *before* the behavior may create frustration and resentment? Both reinforcement and punishment should come *after* the behavior, never *before.*

Operant Conditioning in Real Life: Reinforcements Real and Accidental

Operant conditioning has many interesting applications in real life. Here we talk about *prejudice*, *biofeedback*, and *superstitious behavior*.

Prejudice

Recall the opening story and the three men who murdered James Byrd. What might have reinforced such a behavior? Could it have been attention, notoriety — something else? As you discovered earlier, people can learn prejudice through classical conditioning. They also learn prejudice through operant conditioning. For example, because demeaning others gains attention and sometimes approval from others, as well as increases one's self-esteem (at the expense of the victim), prejudice and discrimination are positively reinforced (Fein & Spencer, 1997). People also may have a single negative experience with a specific member of a group that they then generalize and apply to all members of the group (Vidmar, 1997) — an example of stimulus generalization.

But the men who killed James Byrd were sentenced to death or life imprisonment. Why would people do anything that they know could bring the death penalty? Punishment does suppress behavior, but as mentioned before, to be effective it must be consistent and immediate. Unfortunately, this seldom happens. To make matters worse, when punishment is inconsistent and the criminal gets away with one or more crimes, that behavior is put on a *partial (intermittent) schedule of reinforcement*. It is thus more likely to reoccur and more resistant to *extinction*.

Biofeedback

In **biofeedback** (short for *biological feedback*, sometimes called *neurofeedback*), information about some biological function, such as heart rate, is conveyed to the individual through some type of signal. Sit quietly for a moment and try to determine your blood pressure. Is it high or low? Is it different from a few minutes ago? You can't tell, can you? Therefore, it is impossible for you to learn to control your blood pressure consciously. But if you were hooked up to a monitor that recorded, amplified, and displayed this information to you (biofeedback), you could learn to control it (Figure 6.10).

Researchers have successfully used biofeedback techniques to treat hypertension and anxiety by lowering blood pressure and muscle tension (Lal et al., 1998; Nakao et al., 1997; Sarkar, Rathee, & Neera, 1999); epilepsy by changing brain wave patterns (Sterman, 1996); urinary incontinence by better pelvic muscle control

Biofeedback *A procedure for electronically recording, amplifying, and feeding back information about internal bodily changes that would normally be imperceptible (such as blood pressure); aids voluntary regulation of these changes*

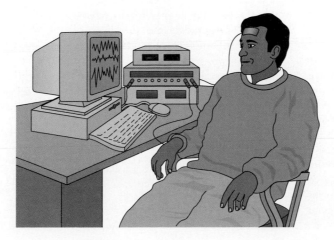

Figure 6.10 *Biofeedback.* In biofeedback training, internal bodily processes (like blood pressure or muscle tension) are electronically recorded, amplified, and then reported back to the patient through headphones, signal lights, or other means. This information helps the person learn to control bodily processes not normally under voluntary control.

Superstition in everyday life. *Bingo players, like many other people, engage in special rituals and carry lucky charms, which they superstitiously believe will bring them good luck.*

(Sherman, Davis, & Wong, 1997); and headache by redirecting blood flow (Marcus, Scharff, & Turk, 1995; Kropp et al., 1997).

Biofeedback demonstrates several operant conditioning principles. Something is added (feedback) that increases the likelihood that the behavior will be repeated — *positive reinforcement*. The biofeedback itself is a *secondary reinforcer* because of the learned value of the relief from pain or other aversive stimuli (*primary reinforcer*). Finally, biofeedback involves *shaping*. The person watches a monitor screen (or other instrument) that provides graphs or numbers indicating their blood pressure (or other bodily states). Like a mirror, the biofeedback reflects back the results of the various strategies the participant uses to gain control. Through trial and error, the participant gets progressively better at lowering heart rate (or making other desired changes). Biofeedback techniques are limited, however, and so far, most successful when used in conjunction with other techniques, especially for pain control and stress management.

Superstitious Behavior

B. F. Skinner (1948, 1992) conducted a fascinating experiment to show how accidental reinforcement could lead to *superstitious behaviors*. He set the feeding mechanism on the cages of eight pigeons to feed them once every 15 seconds. No matter what the birds did, they were reinforced at 15-second intervals. Six of the pigeons acquired behaviors that they repeated over and over, even though the behaviors were not necessary to receive the food. For example, one pigeon kept turning in counterclockwise circles, and another kept making jerking movements with its head.

Why did the pigeons engage in such repetitive and unnecessary behavior? Recall that a *reinforcer* increases the probability that a response just performed will be repeated. Although Skinner was not using the food to reinforce any particular behavior, the pigeons associated the food with whatever behavior they were engaged in when the food was originally dropped into the cage. Thus, if the bird was circling counterclockwise when the food was presented, it would repeat that motion to receive more food.

Many people believe in superstitions and follow specific rituals (Table 6.8). Professional and Olympic-level athletes sometimes carry lucky charms or perform a particular ritual before every competition. Phil Esposito, a hockey player with the Boston Bruins and the New York Rangers for 18 years, always wore the same black

critical thinking

Active Learning

Using Learning Principles to Succeed in College

Psychological theory and research have taught us that an active approach to learning is rewarded by better grades. Active learning means using the SQ4R (Survey, Question, Read, Recite, Review, and Write) study techniques discussed in the Tools for Student Success (pages 35–40). An active learner rises above old, easy patterns of behavior and applies new knowledge to everyday situations. When you transfer ideas or concepts you learn from class to

your personal life, your insight grows. Now that you have studied the principles of learning, use the following questions to help you apply your new knowledge to achieve your education goals and have an enjoyable college experience:

1. How can you positively reinforce yourself for studying, completing assignments, and attending class?

2. How might participating in club and campus activities reinforce your education commitment?

3. Compare the difference in the effort you spend studying for an exam when you get a high grade compared with your study effort when you get a low grade. How could you apply the Premack principle to your advantage in this situation?

4. When you take exams, are you anxious? How might this be a classically conditioned response? How could you use the principle of extinction to weaken this response?

TABLE 6.8 COMMON WESTERN SUPERSTITIONS

Behavior	Superstition
Wedding plans: *Why do brides wear something old and something borrowed?*	The something old is usually clothing that belongs to an older woman who is happily married. Thus, the bride will supposedly transfer that good fortune to herself. Something borrowed is often a relative's jewelry. This item should be golden, because gold represents the sun, which was once thought to be the source of life.
Spilling salt: *Why do some people throw a pinch of salt over their left shoulder?*	Years ago, people believed good spirits lived on the right side of the body and bad spirits on the left. When a man spilled salt, he believed his guardian spirit had caused the accident to warn him of evil nearby. At the time, salt was scarce and precious. Therefore, to bribe the spirits who were planning to harm him, he would quickly throw a pinch of salt over his left shoulder.
Boasting, making a prediction, or speaking of good fortune: *Why do some people knock on wood?*	Down through the ages, people have believed that trees were homes of gods, who were kind and generous if approached in the right way. A person who wanted to ask a favor of the tree god would touch the bark. After the favor was granted, the person would return to knock on the tree as a sign of thanks.

turtleneck and drove through the same tollbooth on his way to a game. In the locker room, he put on all his clothes in the same order and laid out his equipment in exactly the same way he had for every other game. All this because once when he had behaved that way years before, he had been the team's high scorer. Alas, the power of accidental reinforcement.

Check & Review

OPERANT CONDITIONING

In **operant conditioning**, people or animals learn by the *consequences* of their responses. Whether behavior is reinforced or punished (consequences) determines whether the response will occur again. Thorndike and Skinner are the two major contributors to operant conditioning. Thorndike's *law of effect* states rewarded behavior is more likely to recur. Skinner extended Thorndike's work to more complex behaviors but emphasized only external, observable behaviors.

Operant conditioning involves several important terms and principles. **Reinforcement** is any procedure that results in an increase in a response, whereas **punishment** is any procedure that results in a decrease. To strengthen a response, we use **primary reinforcers**, which satisfy an unlearned biological need (e.g., sex, thirst), and **secondary reinforcers**, which have learned value (e.g., money). **Positive reinforcement** (adding something) and **negative reinforcement** (taking something away) increase the likelihood the response will occur again. *Escape learning* and *avoid-*

ance learning are two of the learning procedures used to study negative reinforcement. According to the **Premack principle**, activities or behaviors that are more common or probable in one's life will act as reinforcers for activities that are less probable.

Continuous reinforcement rewards each correct response, whereas a **partial (intermittent) schedule** reinforces for some, not all, designated responses. The four partial reinforcement schedules are **variable ratio**, **variable interval**, **fixed ratio**, and **fixed interval**. Partial reinforcement schedules reinforce for some, but not all, responses. Complex behaviors can be trained through **shaping**, which refers to reinforcing successive approximations to the desired behavior.

To weaken a response, we use punishment, which decreases the likelihood of responding. **Positive punishment**

(adding something) and **negative punishment** (taking something away) decrease the likelihood the response will occur again. Although some punishment is essential in social relations, it has serious side effects. To be effective, punishment must be immediate, consistent, and moderate.

Operant conditioning has several applications in real life. It helps explain prejudice, which is sometimes learned through positive reinforcement and stimulus generalization. **Biofeedback**, another application, is the feeding back of biological information, such as heart rate or blood pressure, which a person uses to control normally automatic functions of the body. The third major application, superstitions, involves behaviors that are continually repeated because they are believed to cause desired effects. In reality the behaviors are only accidentally related.

Questions

1. Define operant conditioning and explain how it differs from classical conditioning.

2. Negative punishment _____ and negative reinforcement _____ the likelihood the response will continue. (a) decreases, decreases; (b) increases, decreases; (c) decreases, increases; (d) increases, increases

3. Partial reinforcements schedules make responses more _____ to extinction.

4. Marshall wears the same necklace to every exam. Explain how his superstitious behavior might have developed.

Answers to Questions can be found in Appendix B.

COGNITIVE-SOCIAL LEARNING

How and when do we learn according to cognitive-social theory?

Cognitive-Social Theory *A theory of learning that emphasizes the role of thought and social learning in behavior*

So far, we have examined learning processes that involve associations between a stimulus and an observable behavior. Some behaviorists believe almost all learning can be explained in such stimulus–response terms, but other psychologists feel there is more to learning than can be explained solely by operant and classical conditioning. **Cognitive-social theory** (also called *cognitive-social learning* or *cognitive-behavioral theory*) incorporates concepts of conditioning but emphasizes thought processes, or cognitions, and social learning. According to this view, people (as well as, rats, pigeons, and other animals) have attitudes, beliefs, expectations, motivations, and emotions that affect learning. Furthermore, both humans and nonhuman animals are capable of learning new behaviors through observation and imitation. We begin with a look at the *cognitive* part of cognitive-social theory, followed by an examination of the *social* aspects of learning.

Insight and Latent Learning: Where are the Reinforcers?

As you'll discover throughout this text, cognitive factors play a large role in human behavior and mental processes. Given that these factors are covered in several other chapters (e.g., Learning, Memory, Thinking/Language/Intelligence), our discussion here is limited to the classic research of Wolfgang Köhler and Edward Tolman and their studies of *insight* and *latent learning*.

Köhler's Study of Insight

Although early behaviorists likened the mind to a "black box," whose workings could not be observed directly, German psychologist Wolfgang Köhler wanted to look inside the box. He believed there was more to learning — especially learning to solve a complex problem — than responding to stimuli in a trial-and-error fashion. In several experiments conducted during World War I, Köhler posed several different types of problems to chimpanzees and apes to see how they learned to solve them. For example, in one experiment, he placed a banana just outside the reach of a caged chimpanzee. To reach the banana, the chimp would have to use a stick placed near the cage to extend its reach. The chimp did not solve this problem in the random trial-and-error fashion of Thorndike's cats or Skinner's rats and pigeons. Köhler noticed that he seemed to sit and think about the situation for a while. Then, in a flash of **insight** (a sudden understanding), the chimp picked up the stick and maneuvered the banana within its grasp (Kohler, 1925).

Another of Köhler's chimps, an intelligent fellow named Sultan, was put in a similar situation. But this time there were two sticks available to him and the banana was placed even farther away, too far to reach with a single stick. Sultan seemingly lost interest in the banana, but continued to play with the sticks. When he later discovered that the two sticks could be interlocked, he instantly used the now longer stick to pull the banana within grasp. Köhler designated this type of learning *insight learning,* because some internal mental event that we can only describe as "insight" went on between the presentation of the banana and the use of the stick to retrieve it.

Tolman's Study of Latent Learning

Although previous researchers suggested that rats learned mazes through trial-and-error and rewards, Edward C. Tolman (1898–1956) believed they underestimated the rat's cognitive processes and cognitive learning. He noted that rats placed in experimental mazes seemed to pause at certain intersections—almost as if they were *deciding* which route to take. When allowed to roam aimlessly in a maze with no food reward at the end, the rats also seemed to develop a **cognitive map,** or mental representation of the maze.

To test the idea of cognitive learning, Tolman allowed one group of rats to explore a maze in an aimless fashion with no reinforcement, a second group was always reinforced with food whenever they reached the end of the maze, and a third group was not rewarded initially (during the first 10 days of the trial), but starting on day 11 they found food at the end of the maze. As expected from simple operant conditioning, the first and third groups were slow to learn the maze; whereas the second group that had reinforcement showed fast, steady improvement. Also as expected, when the third group started receiving reinforcement (on the 11th day), the rats' learning of the maze quickly matched the performance of the group that had been reinforced every time (Tolman & Honzik, 1930). For Tolman, this was significant. It proved that the nonreinforced rats had been learning during their aimless wandering, but that their hidden, **latent learning** only showed up when there was a reason to display it (the food reward).

Cognitive learning is not limited to rats. If a new log is placed in its territory, a chipmunk will explore it for a time, but soon move on if no food is found. When a predator comes into the same territory, the chipmunk heads directly for and hides beneath the log. Similarly, as a child you may have casually ridden a bike around your neighborhood with no particular reason or destination in mind, and only demontrated your hidden knowledge of the area when your dad was searching for the closest mailbox. The fact that Tolman's nonreinforced rats quickly caught up to the reinforced ones, that the chipmunk knew about the hiding place under the log, that you knew the location of the mailbox, and recent experimental evidence (Burgdorf, Knutson, & Panksepp, 2000) all provide clear evidece of latent learning and the existence of internal, cognitive maps.

Is this insight? *Grande, one of Wolfgang Köhler's chimps, has just solved the problem of how to get the banana. Is this insight or trial and error?*

Insight *A sudden flash of understanding that occurs during problem solving*

Cognitive Map *A mental image of a three-dimensional space that person or animal has navigated*

Latent Learning *Learning that occurs in the absence of a reward and remains hidden until there is some incentive to demonstrate it.*

Observational Learning: Watching the Consequences of Others' Behavior

In addition to cognitive processes (such as insight and latent learning), observation and imitation also play important roles in learning. When you want to know how to act at a party, what do you do? If you want to learn how to give a speech, what is the best way? We learn these behaviors by observing others — thus the name *observational learning* (or *social learning*). When we learn by imitating someone, it is called *modeling*.

Albert Bandura (born in 1925) and others have demonstrated the importance of observation and modeling. In one experiment, one of three groups of children viewed a film of an adult acting aggressively toward a Bobo doll (hitting, punching, and kicking) (Bandura & Walters, 1963). Later, the children were given the opportunity to play in the same room with the same toys. The children who had seen the film were much more aggressive with the toys than were children who had not seen it. They had learned how to act in a particular situation by observing another person in that situation.

According to Bandura, four processes are involved in learning through observation; we must

1. Attend (or pay attention) to the model
2. Remember the modeled behavior
3. Be able to put into practice what was observed (for instance, we wouldn't be able to imitate someone riding a bike if we were paralyzed)
4. Decide whether we want to repeat the modeled behavior, on the basis of whether the model was reinforced or punished and/or on the basis of our esteem for the model

We can see these processes at work when we apply them to the children in Bandura's experiment. They paid attention to and remembered the aggressive behavior of the models, and were able to physically perform the modeled behaviors. Most of the children also decided to imitate the observed behaviors.

Applications of Cognitive-Social Learning: We See, We Do?

We use cognitive-social learning in many ways in our everyday lives, yet two of the most powerful areas of learning are frequently overlooked: **prejudice** and **media influences**.

Bandura's classic Bobo doll study. This child watched while an adult hit the Bobo doll and then imitated the behavior.

Prejudice

Did the three men who murdered James Byrd learn some of their hatred and prejudice through observational learning? Family and friends of Bill King say that he was pleasant and quiet until he began serving an 8-year prison sentence for burglary (Galloway, 1999). It's also interesting to speculate what King might have learned from an uncle who was convicted of murdering a gay traveling salesman a number of years earlier, or what he might have observed during his active membership with the KKK (Associated Press, 1999).

In addition to what we learn from family, friends, and group memberships, the media also encourage some types of prejudice. Experimental and correlational research clearly show that when children watch TV, go to movies, and read books and magazines that portray minorities and women in demeaning and stereotypical roles, they learn to expect these behaviors and to accept them as "natural." Exposure of this kind initiates and reinforces the learning of prejudice (Dovidio, Brigham, Johnson, & Gaertner, 1995).

Media Influences

Observational learning also can teach us what to buy. Because most of us are well aware of the media's influence on children's food and toy preferences, let's consider adult behavior. For instance, when a TV commercial shows children enjoying a particular cereal and beaming at their mom in gratitude (and Mom is smiling back), the parents in the audience learn that they will be rewarded with happy children for buying a particular brand or will be punished (with children who won't eat) for buying a different brand. In other words, the consumer is rewarded vicariously and the purchasing behavior is reinforced (Solomon & Englis, 1994).

Unfortunately, both children and adults also may be learning violence through observational learning and the media. Correlational evidence from more than 50 studies indicates that observing violent behavior is related to performing violent behavior (Huesmann & Moise, 1996). As a critical thinker, you may be automatically noting that correlation is not causation. However, over 100 *experimental* studies have shown a causal link between observing violence and later performing it (Primavera & Herron, 1996).

What about video games? How do they affect behavior? Researchers are just beginning to study these questions. For example, psychologists Craig Anderson and Karen Dill (2000) have found that students who played more violent video games in junior high and high school also engage in more aggressive behaviors. Furthermore, when these researchers experimentally assigned 210 students to first play either a violent or a nonviolent video game and later allowed them to punish their opponent with a loud sound blast, those who played the violent game punished the opponent not only for a longer period of time but also with greater intensity. The researchers hypothesize that video games are more likely to model aggressive behavior because, unlike TV and other media, they are interactive, engrossing, and require the player to identify with the aggressor.

Video games and aggression. According to research, these young boys identify with the aggressor and may be more likely to imitate this behavior (Anderson & Dill, 2000). What do you think? Do video games affect your behavior or that of your friends?

GENDER & CULTURAL DIVERSITY

Scaffolding as a Teaching Technique in Different Cultures

Learning in the real world is often a combination of classical conditioning, operant conditioning, and observational learning. This is especially evident in informal situations in which an individual acquires new skills under the supervision of a master

Scaffolding as a form of learning. *This young Zinacanteco girl is learning to weave through the process of scaffolding.*

teacher. The ideal process used by teachers in these situations is known as *scaffolding* (Wood, Bruner, & Ross, 1976).

Scaffolding enables a student to accomplish tasks that would be impossible without the greater skill and knowledge of the teacher. In most cases, scaffolding is a combination of shaping and modeling, where the teacher selectively reinforces successes of the student and models more difficult parts of the task. Patricia Marks Greenfield (1984) has described two very different examples of scaffolding from two diverse cultures, language learning in Los Angeles and learning to weave in Zinacantán, Mexico. Although the cultures, tasks, and ages of the learners are quite different, the scaffolding process is very similar.

The Los Angeles study focused on the process by which children learn the meaning of adult-initiated offers, such as "Do you want a cookie?" or "Do you want to go for a ride?" Greenfield defines a successful offer in terms of its organizational structure: The offer must be presented to the child; the child must acknowledge the offer; and some object, action, or information must be transmitted from the adult to the child. Therefore, in a successful offer of a piggyback ride, the mother makes a verbal offer, the child acknowledges the offer in some way (by indicating he or she wants it), and the mother gives the child the ride.

When the child's verbal skills are not developed enough to comprehend a verbal offer, the mother uses a scaffolding process. She uses nonverbal cues as the scaffold and models the correct verbal response. In this way, the mother shapes the response of the child capable of making a verbal response and models appropriate behavior for the child who has not yet acquired the necessary verbal skills. Thus, it is through the scaffolding process that mothers help children learn verbal and nonverbal language involved in accepting offers of things they want.

Weaving, of course, is not as universal as language, but the scaffolding process is similar. Weaving is an important part of the culture of the Zinacantecos, who live in the highlands of southern Mexico. Greenfield videotaped 14 girls at different levels of learning to weave. The weaving skills of the girls varied considerably, but the researchers were unable to distinguish between the final products of the girls because of the widespread use of scaffolding. The inexperienced girls were constantly monitored by experienced teachers. Each girl was allowed to complete what she was able to do with ease, whereas a more experienced teacher took over during the more difficult parts. Thus, no matter what the skill level of the novice weaver, she was able to produce a final product equal to the other weavers because of the scaffolding process. The experienced weaver created the scaffold by reinforcing correct weaving technique and modeling more difficult technique. For the first-time weavers, the teachers took over 53 percent of the time, during which the new weavers watched the teacher approximately 87 percent of the time. Although both the tasks and the cultures are different, the scaffolding processes are similar. First, the scaffold is adapted to the skill level of the learner so that learners are able to accomplish tasks they cannot accomplish on their own. Second, the amount of scaffolding and intervention by the parent or teacher decrease as the skill level of the learner increases. Third, scaffolding always involves a combination of shaping and modeling. Finally, in both situations the teachers appear oblivious of their teaching methods or of the fact that they are teaching at all. Most of the Zinacanteco women believe that girls learn to weave by themselves, and it is a common belief in Western culture that children learn to talk by themselves.

Check & Review

COGNITIVE-SOCIAL LEARNING

Cognitive-social theory incorporates concepts of conditioning but emphasizes thought processes, or cognitions, and social learning. According to this perspective, people learn through insight, latent learning, observation, and modeling.

Wolfgang Köhler, in working with chimpanzees, demonstrated that learning could occur with a sudden flash of **insight**. Tolman demonstrated that **latent learning** takes place in the absence of reward and remains hidden until some future time when it can be retrieved as needed. A **cognitive map** is a mental image of an area that a person or animal has navigated.

According to Albert Bandura, observational learning is the process of learning how to do something by watching others and performing the same behavior in the future. To imitate the behavior of others, we must pay attention, remember, be able to reproduce the behavior, and be motivated by some reinforcement.

Cognitive-social theory helps explain prejudice and media influences. People often learn their prejudices by imitating and modeling the behavior they see in friends, family, and the media. The media affect our purchasing behaviors as well as our aggressive tendencies. Video games may have a particularly strong influence.

Questions

1. _____ were influential in early studies of cognitive learning. (a) William James and Ivan Pavlov; (b) B. F. Skinner and Edward Thorndike; (c) Wolfgang Köhler and Edward Tolman; (d) Albert Bandura and R. H. Walters.

2. Learning that occurs in the absence of a reward and remains hidden until some future time when it can be retrieved is called _____.

3. Mental images of an area that a person or animal has navigated are known as _____.

4. Bandura's observational learning studies focused on how _____. (a) rats learn cognitive maps through exploration; (b) children learn aggressive behaviors by observing aggressive models; (c) cats learn problem solving through trial-and-error; (d) chimpanzees learn problem solving through reasoning

Answers to Questions can be found in Appendix B.

NEUROSCIENCE AND EVOLUTION

As you recall, learning is defined as *a relatively permanent change in behavior as a result of practice or experience*. For this change in behavior to persist over time, lasting biological changes must occur within the organism. In this section, we will examine the neurological changes that occur during and after learning. We also will explore the evolutionary advantages of learning.

What neurological changes take place during and after learning? What are the evolutionary advantages to learning?

Neuroscience and Learning: Changes in the Biochemistry and the Brain

Research conducted on humans and other animals indicates that learning involves at least two important biological changes:

1. *Biochemistry.* Neurological research confirms that learning results in alterations in synaptic transmission at specific sites. Because millions of neurons may be activated during an instance of classical conditioning in humans, researchers often use a small sea snail called *Aplysia.* This particular animal has fewer neurons than any vertebrate, and their neurons are often large (up to 1 mm in diameter) and therefore easier to study.

When disturbed by a squirt of water, the Aplysia will protectively withdraw its gill. If the squirt continues, the gill withdrawal diminishes (the snail "habituates" – see Chapter 4). During classical conditioning experiments, the snail repeatedly receives a small electric shock just after being squirted. The Aplysia learns to associate the squirt with the coming shock, and the withdrawal response to the squirt alone becomes stronger. Kandel and his colleagues have shown that this type of learning in the Aplysia coincides with an increase or decrease in the release of specific neurotransmitters by presynaptic and postsynaptic neurons (Bailey & Kandel, 1995; Kandel & Schwartz, 1982; Martinez & Derrick, 1996).

2. *The Brain's Role in Learning.* What happens within the brain when something is learned? An impressive series of experiments focused on changes within a structure at the base of the brain known as the cerebellum (Krupa, Thompson, & Thompson, 1993; Steinmetz, 1998; Thompson, 1989, 1992). Studying classical conditioning of blinking in rabbits, they presented first a tone (CS) and then a puff of air (UCS) to the cornea of the rabbit's eye. At first the rabbit would blink at the air puff but not at the tone. After repeated pairings, classical conditioning occurred, and the rabbit blinked at the tone also. The researchers' who recorded activity in various brain cells' found that when a microscopic spot in the cerebellum was destroyed, the rabbit continued to blink in response to the puff of air but not the tone. This research tells us that the cerebellum is involved in some types of classical conditioning. It does *not* mean that the cerebellum is the key to all learning. Other forms of learning create different pathways and involve additional areas of the brain — as you will discover in the following Research Highlight.

RESEARCH HIGHLIGHT

Scanning the Brain for Learning

Researchers have long used PET and fMRI brain scans to study various structures in the brain (Chapter 2). Now they're also using this highly sophisticated technology to scan for learning activity. In Norway, Kenneth Hugdahl (1998) paired a tone (NS) with a shock to the wrist (UCS) and used PET scans to determine which brain areas were activated during the acquisition of a conditioned response. He recorded significant brain activation in certain right hemisphere frontal lobe areas. In another study, participants were presented with either neutral words (no conditioning) or with threat-related words (higher-order conditioning) (Maddock & Buonocore, 1997). When the fMRI images were compared for the two different conditions, researchers found that the threat words activated a different part of the cerebral cortex than the neutral words.

In addition to these studies, other research has shown that classical conditioning activates other areas of the brain, including the thalamus, hippocampus, hypothalamus, amygdala, and cortex (Furmark, Fischer, Wik, Larsson, & Fredrikson, 1997; Schreurs, Shi, Pineda, & Buck, 2000; Steinmetz, 2000). As you can see, learning involves complex processes and numerous brain structures that are not yet well understood (Purdy, Markham, Schwartz, & Gordon, 2001).

Evolution and Learning: Biological Preparedness and Instinctive Drift

So far, we have emphasized the learned aspects of behavior, but humans and other animals also are born with certain biological abilities that help ensure their survival. When your fingers touch a hot object, you immediately pull your hand away. When a foreign object approaches your eye, you automatically blink. These simple *reflexes* involve making a specific automatic reaction to a particular stimulus. In addition to reflexes, many species also have a second set of adaptive responses called *instincts,* or species-specific behaviors. For example, the weaverbird is known to tie a particular grass knot to hold its nest together. But even when these birds are raised in total isolation for several generations, they will still tie the same knot.

Although these inborn, innate abilities are important to our evolutionary survival, they are inadequate for coping with a constantly changing environment. Reflexively withdrawing your fingers from a hot object is certainly to your advantage. But what if you saw a sign showing that the hot object was an unusual door handle, which would allow you to escape a burning building? There are numerous important stimuli in the environment that require a flexible approach to unusual stimuli. Only through learning are we are able to react to spoken words, to written symbols, and other important environmental stimuli. From an evolutionary perspective, *learning* is an adaptation that enables organisms to survive and prosper in a constantly changing world. In this section, we will explore several evolutionary advantages to learning, as well as the limits imposed by an organism's biological heritage.

Taste aversion. *Coyotes find sheep a readily available source of food, but if they are conditioned to develop a taste aversion to sheep, they will avoid them and seek other food.*

Classical Conditioning and Biological Preparedness

Years ago, a former student, named Rebecca, was unwrapping her favorite candy bar as she walked to class. After taking the first horrible bite, she stopped eating and looked questioningly at the candy, which was making small movements in her hand. The sight of the small, wriggling maggots filling the candy bar left an immediate and permanent impact. Are you surprised that many years later she still feels nauseous just thinking about this candy bar? Rebecca's response is called a *taste aversion,* and it may have an evolutionary purpose.

Several interesting studies have been done with taste aversion and its link to **biological preparedness,** the idea that an organism is innately predisposed to form associations between certain stimuli and responses. Garcia and his colleagues (1966) produced taste aversion in lab rats by pairing flavored water (NS) and a drug (UCS) that produced gastrointestinal distress (UCR). After being conditioned and recovering from the illness, the rats refused to drink the flavored water (CS) because of the conditioned taste aversion. But, remarkably, Garcia discovered that only certain neutral stimuli could produce the nausea. Pairings of a noise (NS) or a shock (NS) with the nausea-producing drug (UCS) produced no taste aversion. This finding called into question Pavlov's belief that any NS could be conditioned. Garcia suggested that when we are sick to our stomachs, we have a natural, evolutionary tendency to attribute it to food or drink. Being *biologically prepared* to quickly associate nausea with food or drink is adaptive because it helps us avoid that food or drink in the future (Elkins, 1991; Kalat, 1985; Schafe et al., 2000).

Garcia's findings on taste aversion are important for two reasons: First, identifying exceptions to classical conditioning led to a better understanding of biological preparedness. And second, he and his colleagues used their basic research to help solve an economic problem for western ranchers. Coyotes were killing sheep, and the ranchers wanted to kill all coyotes. But this "solution" would have created a

Biological Preparedness *The idea that an organism is innately predisposed to form associations between certain stimuli and responses*

larger ecological problem because coyotes eat rabbits and small rodents. In a form of applied research, Garcia and his colleagues used classical conditioning to teach the coyotes not to eat sheep (Gustavson & Garcia, 1974). The researchers began by lacing freshly killed sheep with a chemical that causes extreme nausea and vomiting in coyotes that eat the tainted meat. The conditioning worked so well that the coyotes would run away from the mere sight and smell of sheep. This research has since been applied many times in the wild and in the laboratory with coyotes and with wolves (Gustavson, Kelly, Sweeney, & Garcia, 1976; Ziegler, Gustavson, Holzer, & Gruber, 1983).

Operant Conditioning and Instinctive Drift

Just as later research found that biological preparedness affects classical conditioning, researchers also have found that an animal's natural behavior pattern can interfere with operant conditioning. For example, the Brelands (1961) tried to teach a chicken to play baseball. Through shaping and reinforcement, the chicken first learned to pull a loop that activated a swinging bat, and then learned to actually hit the ball. But instead of running to first base, it would chase the ball as through it were food. Regardless of the lack of reinforcement for chasing the ball, the chicken's natural behavior took precedence. This biological constraint is known as **instinctive drift,** when an animal's learned responses tend to shift (or *drift*) toward innate response patterns.

Instinctive Drift *A biological constraint that occurs when an animal's learned responses shifts (or drifts) toward innate response patterns*

Although animals can be operantly conditioned to perform a variety of novel behaviors (like hitting a baseball), these studies show that reinforcement alone does not determine behavior. Rather, there is a biological tendency in species to favor natural inborn behaviors. Learning theorists initially believed that the fundamental laws of conditioning would apply to almost all species and all behaviors, but recent findings have identified several limits (such as biological preparedness and instinctive drift) that limit the generality of conditioning principles. As you discovered in Chapter 1, scientific inquiry is a constantly changing and evolving process.

A Final Note

We began this chapter with the story of James Byrd because prejudice is a worthy (but unusual) topic for a learning chapter and his story deserved retelling. Although the death of James Byrd shocked many Americans into facing the terrible hatred and racism that still exists in our country, unfortunately his death (like others) is too quickly forgotten. As you have discovered in this chapter, however, little (if anything) about prejudice is biologically driven. It is *learned*. The good news is that *what we learn we can change* — through retraining, counseling, and self-reflection.

Those who won't forget. *Ross Byrd, left, and Renee Mullins, children of murder victim James Byrd, leaving the Jasper County Courthouse after John "Bill" King was convicted of capital murder.*

Check & Review

NEUROSCIENCE AND EVOLUTION

Learning and conditioning produce relatively permanent changes in biochemistry and various parts of the brain. But not all behaviors are learned. At least some behavior is *innate*, or inborn, in the form of either reflexes or instincts. It appears that all animals are programmed to engage in certain innate behaviors that have evolutionary survival benefits.

Through **biological preparedness** an organism is innately predisposed to form associations between certain stimuli and responses. Taste aversions are classically conditioned associations of food to illness that are rapidly learned, often in a single pairing, and reflect a protective survival mechanism for a species. Findings on **instinctive drift** show there are biological constraints on operant conditioning.

Questions

1. Research on classical conditioning of the eyeblink response in rabbits shows that the _____ is an important brain structure for learning. (a) hippocampus; (b) brainstem; (c) corpus callosum; (d) cerebellum.

2. How did Garcia condition a taste aversion in coyotes?

3. What is biological preparedness?

4. _____ occurs when an animal's learned responses tend to shift toward innate response patterns.

Answers to Questions can be found in Appendix B.

KEY TERMS

learning (p. 198)
Classical Conditioning
classical conditioning (p. 200)
conditioned emotional response (CER) (p. 202)
conditioned response (CR) (p. 200)
conditioned stimulus (CS) (p. 200)
extinction (p. 204)
higher-order conditioning (p. 204)
spontaneous recovery (p. 204)
stimulus discrimination (p. 204)
stimulus generalization (p. 203)
unconditioned response (UCR) (p. 200)
unconditioned stimulus (UCS) (p. 200)

Operant Conditioning
biofeedback (p. 219)
continuous reinforcement (p. 212)
discriminative stimulus (p. 217)
fixed interval schedule (p. 213)
fixed ratio schedule (p. 213)
negative punishment (p. 214)
negative reinforcement (p. 210)
operant conditioning (p. 208)
partial (intermittent) reinforcement schedule (p. 212)
positive punishment (p. 214)
positive reinforcement (p. 210)
Premack principle (p. 211)
primary reinforcers (p. 210)
punishment (p. 209)

reinforcement (p. 209)
secondary reinforcers (p. 210)
shaping (p. 214)
variable interval schedule (p. 213)
variable ratio schedule (p. 213)
Cognitive-Social Learning
cognitive map (p. 223)
cognitive-social theory (p. 222)
insight (p. 223)
latent learning (p. 223)
Neuroscience and Evolution
biological preparedness (p. 229)
instinctive drift (p. 230)

Visual Summary for Chapter 6 ----

Classical Conditioning

Understanding Classical Conditioning

Pioneers: Pavlov and Watson
Process: Involuntary
  1) Before conditioning, originally **neutral stimulus (NS)** causes no relevant response, while **unconditioned stimulus (UCS)** causes **unconditioned response (UCR)**.
  2) During conditioning, NS is paired with UCS that elicits the UCR.
  3) After conditioning, previous NS becomes **conditioned stimulus (CS)**, which now causes a **conditioned response (CR)** or **conditioned emotional response (CER)**.

Principles of Classical Conditioning

- **Stimulus generalization**: Stimuli similar to original CS elicit CR.
- **Stimulus discrimination**: Only the CS elicits the CR.
- **Extinction**: Gradual suppression of a learned behavior by repeatedly presenting the CS without the UCS.
- **Spontaneous recovery**: Voluntary reappearance of a previously extinguished CR.
- **Higher order conditioning**: The NS is paired with the CS to which the organism has already been conditioned.

Classical Conditioning in Real Life

- *Prejudice*: Negative perceptions of others that are acquired through classical conditioning processes.
- *Phobias*: Irrational fears that are developed through association of a feared object with the UCS.
- *Medical treatments*: Using nausea producing drugs, alcoholics learn to pair alcohol (CS) with nausea (CR).
- *Advertising*: Products (NS) are repeatedly paired with pleasant images (UCS) until they become a CS.

Operant Conditioning

Understanding Operant Conditioning

Pioneers: Thorndike and Skinner
Process: Voluntary
  People or animals learn through consequences of their behavior. When responses are reinforced, they are likely to increase; when punished, they are likely to decrease.

Principles of Operant Conditioning

- *Strengthening a response occurs through*:
  1) Primary and secondary reinforcers: **Primary reinforcers**, like food, satisfy a biological need, whereas the value of **secondary reinforcers**, like money, is learned.
  2) Positive and negative reinforcement: **Positive reinforcement** is adding something that increases the likelihood of the response, whereas **negative reinforcement** involves taking away something that increases the likelihood of the response.

Additional concepts:

In a **continuous schedule of reinforcement** every correct response is reinforced, whereas in a **partial (or intermittent) schedule** only some responses are reinforced. Partial schedules include **fixed ratio**, **variable ratio**, **fixed interval**, and **variable interval**.

Shaping involves reinforcement for successive approximations of the desired response.

Operant Conditioning (cont).

• *Weakening a response* occurs through:
   1) **Positive punishment** is adding something that decreases the likelihood of the reponse.
   2) **Negative punishment** involves taking away something that decreases the likelihood of the response.

Operant Conditioning in Real Life

• *Prejudice*: Negative perceptions of others that are acquired through operant conditioning processes.

• *Biofeedback*: "Feeding back" biological information (heart rate or blood pressure) to learn to control normally automatic body functions.

• *Superstitious behavior*: Develops from accidental rewarding of specific behaviors.

Cognitive-Social Learning

Insight and Latent Learning

• *Kohler*: Learning can occur with a sudden flash of understanding (**insight**).
• *Tolman*: Learning can happen without reinforcement and remain hidden until needed (**latent learning**). After navigating their environments people and animals create **cognitive maps**.

Cognitive-Social Learning

• *Bandura*: Learning occurs by observing others who serve as models.

Applications

• *Prejudice*: Learned by imitating and modeling prejudiced behavior of others.
• *Media influences*: Consumerism and aggressive behaviors are learned through watching media models.

Neuroscience and Evolution

Learning and conditioning produce relatively permanent changes in neural connections and various parts of the brain. Evolutionary theorists believe some behavior is unlearned (e.g., reflexes or instincts), and that learning and conditioning are further adaptations that enable organisms to survive and prosper in a constantly changing world.

7 Memory

My fellow Americans,

I have recently been told that I am one of the millions of Americans who will be afflicted with Alzheimer's disease. Upon learning this news, Nancy and I had to decide whether as private citizens we would keep this a private matter or whether we would make this news known in a public way. In the past, Nancy suffered from breast cancer and I had my cancer surgeries. We found through our open disclosures we were able to raise public awareness. We were happy that as a result, many more people underwent testing.

Ronald Reagan

They were treated in early stages and able to return to normal, healthy lives.

So now we feel it is important to share with you. In opening our hearts, we hope this might promote greater awareness of this condition. Perhaps it will encourage a clearer understanding of the individuals and families who are affected by it.

Thank you, my friends. May God always bless you.

Sincerely,
Ronald Reagan

So wrote Ronald Reagan, fortieth president of the United States, in an open letter to the people of the United States dated November 1994, weeks after being diagnosed with Alzheimer's disease.

In 1953, a patient referred to as H. M. had portions of his temporal lobes surgically removed in an attempt to control severe epileptic seizures. The surgery was successful in reducing the severity and number of seizures, but his long-term memory processes were profoundly disrupted. Today, almost 50 years after the operation, H. M. still can't recognize the room where he lives, the people who care for him, or the scientists who have studied him for decades. He spends his days in an always-unfamiliar nursing home, often reading the same books and magazines over and over, each time as though it were the first. He thinks he is much younger than he is, and no longer recognizes a photograph of his own face. He cannot recognize the names or faces of people who became famous after the mid-1950s. He remembers Ronald Reagan as an actor, but not as president of the United States. Like Rip van Winkle (the fictional character who slept for 20 years and awakened to a vastly changed world), H. M. becomes more confused with each passing year. He remains trapped in his own personal time warp.

Former President Ronald Reagan and H. M. both suffer from biological (or organic) causes of memory failure, but these are not the only reasons for trouble. Consider the following psychologically induced memory problem:

At the age of 14, Elizabeth's mother drowned. The details surrounding the death were always rather vague for Elizabeth, but she did remember her mother's tip-toed visit the evening before her death, the quick hug and whispered "I love you." At a family reunion some 30 years later, a relative told Elizabeth that she had been the one to find her mother's drowned body. Despite her initial shock and denial, over the next few days the memories slowly started coming back:

> I could see myself, a thin, dark-haired girl, looking into the flickering blue-and-white pool. My mother, dressed in her nightgown, is floating face down. I start screaming. I remember the police cars, their lights flashing, and the stretcher with the clean, white blanket tucked in around the edges of the body. The memory had been there all along, but I just couldn't reach it"

Loftus & Ketcham, 1994, p. 45   Elizabeth Loftus

Imagine being a former president of the United States. What would it be like to discover you will slowly and inevitably lose your memory to Alzheimer's disease? Would you prefer to be H. M. — existing only in the present moment, unable to learn and form new memories? Can you imagine why a child might forget the details surrounding her mother's drowning? But what if the relative was wrong? Could Elizabeth create a *false memory* of finding her mother's body?

In this chapter, you will discover several amazing stories, facts, and theories about memory and learn how to use this information in your everyday life. Along the way, you will learn that our memory is *not* a gigantic library or storehouse of facts available for later retrieval. It is also *not* a video recorder or movie camera that accurately records and stores our everyday experiences. It is a highly selective and constructive process subject to serious errors and distortion.

On the other hand, our memories are also highly functional and biologically well adapted for everyday life. Every moment of the day, we rather automatically filter and sort through a barrage of information and then select, retain, and recover information essential to our survival. In striking contrast to the memory deficits described above, there are also people with exceptional memories. Rajan Mahadevan, for example, earned a place in the *Guinness Book of World Records* by reciting the first 31,811 digits of pi. His exceptional memory is apparently based on elaborate memory devices, which we will discuss near the end of this chapter (Thompson, Cowan, & Frieman, 1993).

We begin with a brief overview of the three most popular theories and models that help explain "What is memory?" Next, we discuss several factors and theories that help answer "Why do we forget?" We then explore both common and unusual problems with memory, including amnesia, brain traumas, repressed memories, and eyewitness testimony. We conclude with a summary of the research and examine some techniques that help improve memory.

WHAT IS MEMORY?

Memory *An internal record or representation of some prior event or experience; also a set of mental processes that receives, encodes, stores, organizes, alters, and retrieves information over time*

What are the three major approaches that help explain memory?

Memory is most often defined as "an internal record or representation of some prior event or experience" (Purdy, Markham, Schwartz, & Gordon, 2001, p. 9). Remember, however, that this internal record is fallible. It may be composed of less detail (or more) than the actual event or experience. Recognizing the problems and frailties of memory, we have sprinkled memory improvement suggestions throughout this chapter. Our first tip: *organization*. When you want to learn and remember a large amount of information, you must organize it into meaningful patterns or categories. To provide an example, we have summarized and organized the first section of this chapter to create Table 7.1. Like a map that helps you plan your trip, note how this overview gives you "the big picture" and helps you master and remember the important details.

Each of the approaches shown in Table 7.1 and discussed in the upcoming section offers a slightly different but overlapping perspective on the way memory operates and is organized. They also offer you, the reader, a greater understanding of how your memory works — and when it fails. (Specific techniques for improving memory are summarized at the end of the chapter.) Let's begin with the first major approach.

Traditional Three-Stage Memory Model: The Need for Differing Storage Times

Since the late 1960s, one of the most widely used models in memory research has been the *traditional three-stage memory model* or the *three-box model* (Atkinson &

TABLE 7.1 AN OVERVIEW OF THREE COMMON MEMORY MODELS

Traditional three-stage memory model	This model suggests humans need to store information for different lengths of time. The first stage, *sensory memory*, holds information just long enough to select items worthy of further processing. The second stage, *short-term memory* (STM), allows time for brief sorting and organizing of information to send on to relatively permanent storage. The third stage, *long-term memory* (LTM), is a relatively permanent storehouse of all our memories.
Encoding, storage, and retrieval approach	Memory is seen as a *process*, with a variety of control mechanisms operating at each point in the process. At the beginning of the process (*encoding*), we select certain incoming environmental stimuli and translate (encode) them into neural messages the brain can understand. During storage, we select and organize specific information to save in "files" for permanent storage. At the final point in the process (*retrieval*), we search these files and bring back the necessary data.
Biological approach	This approach explains memory by looking at biological changes in the synapses that occur during encoding and storage and at where memories are located when retrieval is required.

Shiffrin, 1968; Healy & McNamara, 1996). According to this model, we need different storage "boxes" or stages to house information for various lengths of time. The first stage holds information for exceedingly short intervals, the second retains information for approximately 30 seconds or less (unless renewed), and the third stage provides relatively permanent storage. Because information must pass through each of these stages to get to the next, they are often depicted as three boxes with directional arrows indicating the flow of information (Figure 7.1). Each of these three

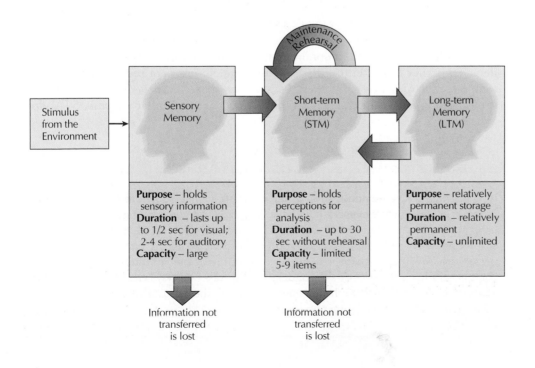

Figure 7.1 *Traditional three-stage memory model.* Each "box" represents a separate memory system that differs in duration, capacity, and function. When information is not transferred from sensory memory or short-term memory, it is assumed to be lost. Information stored in long-term memory can be retrieved and sent back to short-term memory for use.

Figure 7.2 *Experiments with sensory memory.* When George Sperling flashed an arrangement of letters like these for $^1/_{20}$ of a second, most people could only recall 4 or 5 (of 12). But when instructed to report the top, middle, or bottom row, depending on whether they heard a high, medium, or low tone, they reported almost all the letters correctly. Apparently, all 12 letters are held in sensory memory right after viewing them, but only those that are immediately attended to (with the tone) are noted and processed.

Sensory Memory *The first stage of memory in which a relatively exact image of each sensory experience is held briefly until it can be further processed; its capacity is relatively large, but its duration is restricted to a few seconds*

Short-Term Memory (STM) *The second stage of memory that contains information a person is consciously thinking about or working with; its capacity is limited to five to nine items and its duration is about 30 seconds*

stages (*sensory*, *short-term*, and *long-term*) has a somewhat different purpose, duration, and capacity.

Sensory Memory

Everything we see, hear, touch, taste, and smell must first enter our **sensory memory**, a very brief storage of sensory information. The *purpose* of sensory memory is to retain a relatively exact image of each sensory experience just long enough to locate and focus on relevant bits of information and transfer them on to the next stage of memory. The *duration* of sensory memory varies according to the specific sense. For visual information, known as *iconic memory*, the visual icon (or image) lasts about one-half of a second. Auditory information (what we hear) is held in sensory memory about the same length of time as visual information, one-quarter of a second, but a weaker "echo," or *echoic memory*, can last up to 2 to 4 seconds (Lu, Williamson, & Kaufman, 1992; Neisser, 1967).

How can such brief sensory messages be measured in a laboratory? One of the earliest researchers, George Sperling (1960), designed a clever experiment that briefly showed people visual arrays of 12 letters arranged in rows (Figure 7.2). Sperling rapidly flashed this three-letter–by–four-letter matrix on a screen. Immediately after the letters flashed off, he asked the participants to recall the letters. Participants generally recalled only 4 or 5 letters but insisted they had seen more letters before the memory slipped away. To test this possibility, Sperling devised a "partial report" experiment. Rather than reporting everything from the display, he asked participants to report the first row of letters if they heard a high tone, the second row if they heard a medium tone, and the third row when they heard a low tone. Whatever row or column the participants were asked to recall, they were able to name the letters without any trouble, which indicates that they had memory access to all letters in the matrix for at least a few thousandths of a second. This suggests, then, that all objects in the visual field are available in sensory memory if they can be attended to quickly.

From this and other studies, early researchers assumed that sensory memory had an unlimited capacity. However, later research suggests that sensory memory does have its limits and that the stored images are fuzzier than was once thought (Best, 1999). Bear in mind, too, that all senses — taste, touch, smell, and hearing, as well as vision — have a sensory memory.

Short-Term Memory

Just as sensory memory maintains environmental stimuli only long enough to decide whether to send it on, the second stage, **short-term memory** (STM), only temporarily stores and processes the sensory image until it decides whether to send it along to the third stage. Although they share a similar *purpose*, STM does

TRY THIS Yourself

If you'd like a simple demonstration of the duration of visual, *iconic memory*, hold your hand about 12 inches in front of you. Stare at it for a few seconds and then close your eyes. Note how the image, or *icon*, of your hand lingers for a fraction of a second. To appreciate (and remember) *echoic memory*, think about times when someone interrupted while you were deeply absorbed in a task. Did you sometimes ask "What?" yet find you could still answer their question without a repeat? Now you know why. If we divert our attention from the absorbing task quickly enough, we can "hear again" the echo of what was said.

not store *duplicates* of sensory information but rather an end product of perceptual analyses. When your sensory memory registers the sound of your professor's voice, it holds the actual auditory information for a few seconds. If you decide the voice needs further processing, you send it along to STM. While being transferred from sensory memory, the voice is converted into a larger, more inclusive type of message capable of being analyzed and interpreted during short-term memory. If your STM decides the information is important (or may be on a test), it organizes and sends this information along to relatively permanent storage, called long-term memory (LTM).

The *duration* and *capacity* of STM are relatively limited. STM holds a restricted amount of new information, five to nine items, for up to 30 seconds, by most estimates, although some researchers extend the time to a few minutes (Best, 1999; Kareev, 2000). As with sensory memory, information in STM either is transferred quickly into the next stage (LTM) or it decays and is lost.

How can I increase the duration and capacity of my STM? Look back to the memory model in Figure 7.1 and note the looping arrow at the top labeled "maintenance rehearsal." You can extend STM almost indefinitely by consciously repeating the information over and over again, a process called **maintenance rehearsal**. You are using maintenance rehearsal when you look up a phone number and repeat it over and over until you dial the number. It is like juggling a set of plates; the plates stay in perfect shape as long as you keep juggling them. Once you stop, however, the plates fall and are destroyed (or the memory is lost).

To extend the *capacity* of STM, you can use **chunking**, a process of grouping separate pieces of information into units (or *chunks*) (Glassman, 1999; Miller, 1956). Have you noticed that numbers on credit cards, your Social Security identification, and telephone number are all grouped into three or four units separated by hyphens? This is because most people find it easier to remember numbers in chunks like *(760) 744–1129* rather than as a string of single digits. Similarly, in reading-improvement courses, students are taught to chunk groups of words into phrases so that fewer eye movements are required and the brain can process the phrases as units rather than as individual words.

Expert chess players also use chunking to organize the information on a game board into meaningful patterns or units. Researchers have found that novice players who look at a standard chessboard with the pieces arranged in a typical play position can remember the positions of only a few pieces. Expert chess players generally remember all the positions (Chase & Simon, 1973; Gobert, 1998). To the expert players, these seemingly randomly arranged pieces form meaningful patterns. Just as you group the letters of this sentence into meaningful words and remember them long enough to understand the meaning, expert chess players group the chess pieces into patterns (or chunks) that can be easily recalled.

If I have room for five to nine units or chunks, why doesn't chunking help me remember even three or four names during introductions? The limited capacity and brief duration of STM both work against you in this situation. Instead of concentrating on the name of someone you meet for the first time, you sometimes use all your short-term memory capacity wondering how you look and thinking about what to say. You might even fill STM space worrying about the fact that you have already forgotten his or her name! People who are good at remembering names repeat the name of each person out loud or silently to keep it entered in STM (maintenance rehearsal). They also make sure that other thoughts don't intrude until they have tested their ability to remember the name. Note that maintenance rehearsal keeps the name available only while you're actively rehearsing. If you want to really learn that name, you will need to transfer it into long-term memory.

Short-term memory and maintenance rehearsal. When you look up a telephone number, you can rehearse it over and over to keep it in short-term memory; however, you might not remember the number after you dial unless you stored it in long-term memory.

Maintenance Rehearsal *The process of repeating the contents of short-term memory over and over to maintain it in short-term memory*

Chunking *The process of grouping information into units to store more information in short-term memory*

Chess as a type of chunking. World-class chess players such as Garry Kasparov are able to remember groups of pieces by chunking them into meaningful patterns.

Problems with short-term memory?
When being introduced to several peo-
ple at a party, you will be more apt to
remember the person's name if you
repeat it several times, and focus solely
on the person rather than other inter-
fering factors.

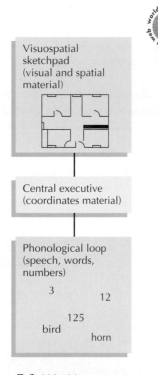

Figure 7.3 Working memory as a
central executive. According to this
model, working memory serves as a
central executive that coordinates the
visuospatial sketchpad and the phonological loop.

Long-Term Memory (LTM) *The*
third stage of memory that functions as
storage of information for long periods
of time; its capacity is limitless and its
duration is relatively permanent

Short-Term Memory as a "Working Memory"

Most current researchers (Baddeley, 1992, 2000; Cantor & Engle, 1993) prefer to
think of STM as a three-part *working memory* (Figure 7.3):

1. *Visuospatial sketchpad.* This component is the visual workspace that allows us
to temporarily hold and manipulate visual images and spatial information (Best,
1999; Friedman & Miyake, 2000). Mentally rearranging the furniture in your home
requires activation of the visuospatial sketchpad.

2. *Central executive.* This component works as a supervisor that integrates and
manages information from the phonological loop and the visuospatial sketchpad, as
well as other material retrieved from LTM. It also coordinates material used during
reasoning and decision making. When you mentally weigh the pros and cons of different movies to view, you are using the central executive.

3. *Phonological rehearsal loop.* This is the component responsible for holding and
manipulating material related to speech, words, and numbers (Best, 1999; Gathercole & Pickering, 2000; Jiang et al., 2000). Suppose you're a waitperson (without a
notepad) and you have the following orders from a table of diners: "I want the breakfast special with two scrambled eggs, orange juice, and coffee." "Give me the ham,
very well done, with the stack of pancakes, and nothing to drink." "I'll have oatmeal
without the raisins, dry toast, coffee, and grapefruit juice." Thanks to your phonological loop, and your use of maintenance rehearsal, you can keep these directions
in working memory until you reach the kitchen and pass them along to the chef.

Long-Term Memory

The *purpose* of the third stage, **long-term memory** (LTM), is to serve as a storehouse
for information that must be kept for long periods of time. Once information is transferred from STM, it is organized and integrated with other information in LTM. It
remains there until we need to retrieve it. Then it is sent back to STM for our use.

Compared to the sensory memory and short-term memory, long-term memory
has unlimited *capacity* and *duration* (Klatzky, 1984). Although it may seem that
lots of information gets lost in your long-term memory storehouse, your problem
is more likely a result of poor organization. During the transfer of information
from STM to LTM, incoming information is "tagged" or filed, hopefully in the

appropriate place. If information is improperly stored, it creates major delays and problems during retrieval. The better you label and arrange things (whether it's your CD collection, your bills, or your memory), the more likely they will be accurately stored and readily available for retrieval. Organization is the key.

Admittedly, organization takes time and work. But you'll be happy to know that some memory organization and filing actually goes on while you sleep. Researchers have found that recent additions to LTM are partially reviewed, improved, and systematically catalogued during REM (rapid-eye-movement) sleep (Hennevin, Hars, Maho, & Bloch, 1995). Other research shows that sleep itself improves memory (Koulack, 1997; Plihal & Born, 1999).

What about tapes suggesting you can learn new skills like foreign languages while you sleep? Do they work? In one early study, participants' brain waves were recorded while they listened to tapes as they slept. Afterward, they were asked questions about the information they heard. Participants who listened to the tapes while in a drowsy state could answer 50 percent of the questions. Listeners in a transition state between drowsiness and light sleep could answer 5 percent of the questions. Listeners who were fully asleep did not remember any information (Simon & Emmons, 1956).

Learning a foreign language or anything else requires proper transfer and storage of information, which demands an alert, attentive mind. Even being slightly drowsy affects your ability to process and store information, thus the importance of staying alert while studying. It's easy to begin nodding off when you're reading a long textbook assignment. But if you're doing *active reading* (see Tools for Student Success at the end of Chapter 1), you'll stay alert and be more likely to remember what you read.

Encoding, Storage, and Retrieval: The Processes of Memory

The traditional three-stage memory model remains the leading approach because it offers a convenient way to organize the major findings of memory. However, later research has helped clarify several missing elements. The second approach adds to the three-stage model a focus on the memory *process* — how information is changed as it moves through the following operations: *encoding*, *storage*, and *retrieval*. Each of these three processes represents a different function that is somewhat analogous to those of a computer (Figure 7.4).

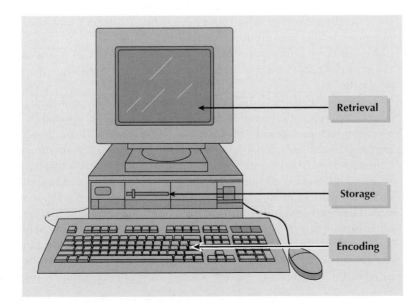

Figure 7.4 *Memory as a computer.* The encoding, storage, and retrieval model uses a computer metaphor to explain the three basic functions of our memory system. Similar to a computer, incoming information is first *encoded* (typed on a keyboard and translated into computer language), stored on a disk or the hard drive, and later retrieved and brought to the computer screen to be used.

Human and computers. Even in jokes, our memory system is thought of in computer terms

"I forgot to make a back-up copy of my brain, so everything I learned last semester was lost."

Encoding *The process of translating information into neural codes (language) that will be retained in memory*

Storage *The process of retaining neural coded information over time*

Retrieval *The process of recovering information from memory storage*

How do you remember the date of your next exam in psychology, the five items you need to buy at the grocery store, or your first romantic kiss? To remember any piece of information, you must first get it into your brain (**encoding**), then you must retain it (**storage**), and later you will need to recover it (**retrieval**). To input data into a computer, you begin by typing letters and numbers on the keyboard, which the computer translates into its own electronic language. In a similar fashion, your brain *encodes* sensory information (sound, visual image, and other senses) into a neural code (language) it can understand and use. Once information is encoded, it must be *stored*. Whereas computer memories are stored on a disk or hard drive, your human memories are stored in the brain. Finally, to retrieve information from either the computer or brain, you must search and locate the appropriate "files" and then bring the information up on the computer monitor or to your conscious awareness where it can be used.

Parallel Distributed Processing Approach

Like all analogies, this "memory as computer" model has its limits. Human memories are often fuzzy and fragile compared to the literal, "hard" data stored on a computer disk or hard drive. Critics of both the traditional three-stage model and the encoding, storage, and retrieval approach suggest that the human brain does not operate like a computer. A computer processes instructions and data *sequentially*; units of information follow one after another in a logical, orderly fashion. Human memory, however, occurs *simultaneously*, through the action of multiple networks.

Parallel Distributed Processing Approach *A model of memory in which knowledge is represented as connections among interacting processing units, distributed in a vast network, and all operating in parallel*

Because of these differences between computers and humans, some cognitive scientists prefer the **parallel distributed processing approach** (PDP), or *connectionist model*, of memory (McClelland, 1995; Sartori & Umilta, 2000). As the name implies, instead of recognizing patterns as a sequence of information bits (like a computer), our brain and memory processes perform multiple, *parallel* operations all at one time. In addition, memory is spread out, or *distributed*, throughout an entire network of processing units (nodes in the network). If you're swimming in the ocean and see a large fin nearby, your brain does not conduct a complete search of all fish with fins before urging you to begin a rush to the beach. Instead, you conduct a mental *parallel* search, noting the color of the fish, the fin, and the potential danger all at the same time. Because the processes are parallel, you can quickly process the information — and possibly avoid being eaten by the shark!

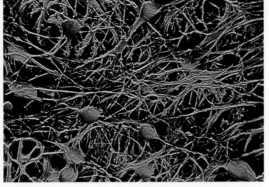

Parallel distributing processing (**PDP**). *According to PDP research, our memory system is like a telephone company simultaneously directing and processing a multitude of calls.*

The PDP model of how memory works represents the most recent shift in theories of memory. As we just noted, survival in our environment requires instantaneous information processing. The PDP model allows a faster response time, and it also seems consistent with neurological information of brain activity (Chapter 2) and the parallel processing used when we recognize patterns (Chapter 4). Therefore, the PDP approach may soon become the standard model for explaining memory.

Check & Review

THREE-STAGE MEMORY MODEL AND ENCODING, STORAGE, AND RETRIEVAL

The traditional three-stage memory model proposes that information must pass through each of three stages before being stored: *sensory memory*, *short-term memory*, and *long-term memory*. **Sensory memory** preserves a brief replica of sensory information. It has a large capacity and information lasts between 2 to 4 seconds. Selected information is sent to short-term memory. **Short-term memory** (STM), also called *working memory*, involves memory for current thoughts. Short-term memory can hold five to nine items for about 30 seconds before they are forgotten. Information can be stored longer than 30 seconds through **maintenance rehearsal**, and the capacity of STM can be increased with **chunking**. **Long-term memory** (LTM) is relatively permanent memory storage with an unlimited capacity.

The encoding, storage, and retrieval approach sees memory as a *process*. It uses similarities between human memory and a computer. Like typing on a keyboard, **encoding** translates information into neural codes that match the brain's language. **Storage** retains neural coded information over time, like saving material on the computer's hard drive or a disk. **Retrieval** gets information out of LTM storage and sends it to STM to be used, whereas the computer retrieves information and displays it on the monitor.

The **parallel distributed processing** (PDP), or *connectionist*, model explains that contents of our memory are represented as a vast number of interconnected units and modules distributed throughout a huge network, all operating in parallel — simultaneously.

Questions

1. According to the three-stage memory model, information must first enter _____, then transfer to _____ and then to _____ to be retained in our memory system.
   (a) sensory memory; short-term memory; permanent memory;
   (b) short-term memory; sensory memory; long-term memory;
   (c) sensory memory; short-term memory; long-term memory;
   (d) working memory; short-term memory; permanent memory

2. Maintenance rehearsal allows us to keep information in _____ memory longer than the typical 30 seconds.
   (a) short-term; (b) long-term; (c) sensory; (d) permanent

3. Explain how the encoding, storage, and retrieval approach to human memory is analogous to the workings of a computer.

4. How does the PDP approach explain memory?

Answers to Questions can be found in Appendix B.

Integrating the Two Major Approaches: Three-Stage Memory Model Meets Encoding, Storage, and Retrieval

Memory researchers continue to debate the merits and limits of the several models of memory. Given the durability of the *three-stage memory model* and the additional information provided by the *encoding*, *storage*, and *retrieval* approach, most psychologists currently emphasize an integration of these two models (Figure 7.5). In this section, we will show how an integration of the two major memory models provides a convenient way to organize the major findings on memory, as well as providing a good accounting for those findings. Let's start with encoding.

Integrating Encoding with the Three-Stage Memory Model

When we encode information, we are translating or recording it into a form the brain can recognize and use. As you can see in Figure 7.5, we first encode information when we transfer it from sensory memory to STM. We also perform a second type of encoding during the transfer from STM to LTM.

Although we cannot directly observe or measure how encoding occurs, the best guess is that storage codes are primarily *verbal* or *sensory*. To remember your most romantic kiss, you encode (or translate the experience) into a verbal description, "It was a wonderful, exciting moment that happened as we were..." But how would you encode the sight of his or her face, the sound of his or her laughter, or the smell of his or her skin? Sometimes words are inadequate, so we encode sensory impressions — smells, sounds, and visual images. There is truth to the saying that a picture (or smell or sound) is worth a thousand words. Finally, some memories are also encoded according to movement or action. This so-called "muscle" or kinesthetic memory explains why you also have a memory of how it felt to kiss this person. Driving a stick shift car, using a spoon or chopsticks to eat, or typing on a keyboard all seem to be coded verbally and pictorially, but they also involve your muscle memory.

Research findings related to encoding and the three-stage model can be integrated and grouped under two major strategies: *organization* and *rehearsal*:

1. Organization. As we discovered earlier, organization is one of the most important elements in memory. It is particularly important during encoding. Two of the

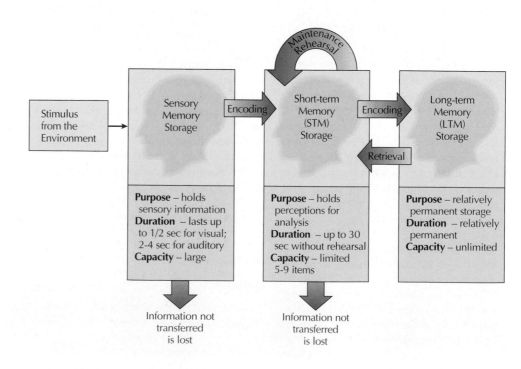

Figure 7.5 *The "Integrated Model"* This diagram shows how the traditional three-stage memory model can be incorporated with the encoding, storage, and retrieval approach. Note that encoding and storage take place, to some degree, in all three stages, whereas retrieval occurs only from long-term memory to short-term memory.

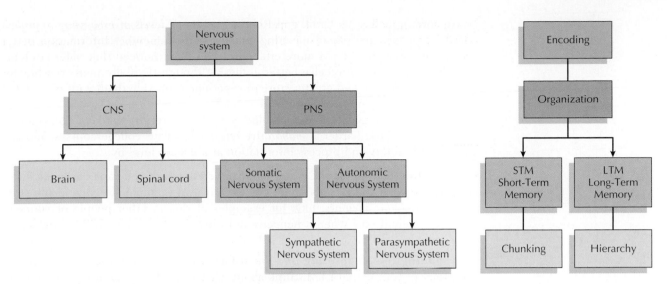

Figure 7.6 *Hierachies are a natural part of LTM.* Just as the diagram of the nervous system helped organize the material in Chapter 2, a similar diagram of the current information on memory helps you order and arrange the various terms. Encoding, storage, and retrieval in LTM are all improved through the use of hierarchies.

most important forms of organization during encoding are *chunking* for STM and *hierarchies* for LTM. To extend the capacity of short-term memory (5 9 units), we discussed how to organize the information into chunks. To encode information for LTM, we need to organize these chunks into *hierarchies*, arranging a number of elements of information into a few broad concepts that are further divided and subdivided.

Do you recall how Chapter 2 organized the large body of information about the nervous system into a hierarchy with smaller and smaller units or chunks? Look at Figure 7.6. Note how the hierarchy for the nervous system is similar to our newly created hierarchy for the current information. Can you see how arranging the information into such hierarchies helps make them more understandable and *memorable*? This is the reason we use so many hierarchies throughout this text (in the form of diagrams and tables). If you want to improve your memory in this and other courses, study these carefully.

Better yet, try making your own hierarchies when studying for exams. Although this may sound difficult, keep in mind that you already possess all the basic skills. Think back to the first day you walked around your college campus. You probably felt overwhelmed by all the buildings, sidewalks, and parking lots, and needed a map just to find your classes. After being on campus for a while, however, the map was discarded because you "naturally" organized all the information into personally meaningful chunks (science building, library, cafeteria) that were further organized into an overall personal hierarchy. Try using these same skills to arrange the large assortment of facts and concepts required for a typical college exam.

2. Rehearsal. Because information is normally kept in STM for only about 30 seconds, encoding is very important. As we learned earlier, if you need to hold information longer than 30 seconds, you can do a type of juggling act called *maintenance rehearsal*, where you simply keep repeating it over and over. This type of *shallow processing* is normally enough for some information that you don't need in long-term storage. But if you've ever tried simple maintenance rehearsal to study for exams, you unfortunately discovered that it doesn't work. Storage in LTM requires *deep processing*, or **elaborative rehearsal**, in which new information is actively reviewed and related to information already in LTM.

Elaborative Rehearsal *An encoding technique of associating new information with already stored knowledge in long-term memory; (also known as deeper levels of processing)*

According to Fergus Craik and Robert Lockhart's *levels-of-processing approach* (1972), a deeper analysis of meaning enables us to remember information better because we store it in LTM more efficiently. Have you noticed that older students in college classes often receive better grades? Although there are many reasons for this, their longer life and greater store of experiences provide them with more LTM information available for elaborative rehearsal.

If you're a younger student or an older student just returning to college, you may have to work a little harder at *elaborative rehearsal* in your college courses. You can improve this ability and process information at a deeper level by

- *Generating new, personal examples of the concept.* If you can't easily tag information to what you already know, create your own example. To encode and store the term *echoic memory*, look for examples of this in other people or yourself. Make a mental note when it happens and store the example with the term *echoic memory.*

- *Expanding (or elaborating on) the information.* To store the term *long-term memory* in your actual LTM, think about what it would be like if you could store information for only 30 seconds. Picture the life of H. M. (the man introduced in the opening vignette). The more you elaborate on the term, the more likely you are to remember it.

- *Actively exploring and questioning new information.* Think about the term *iconic memory.* Ask yourself, "Why did they use this term?" Look up the term *icon* in the dictionary and you'll learn that *icon* is from the Greek word for image or likeness.

- *Trying to find meaningfulness.* When you meet people at a party, don't just maintenance-rehearse their name. Ask about their favorite TV shows, their career plans, political beliefs, or anything else that requires deeper analysis. You'll be much more likely to remember their name.

Integrating Storage with the Three-Stage Memory Model

As we discovered earlier, both sensory memory and STM store a very limited amount of information for a brief period of time. Our most important and valuable storehouse is that of LTM. Given that LTM is virtually unlimited in duration and capacity, we obviously collect a vast amount of information over a lifetime. How do we store it? Once again, organization is the key. As you can see in Figure 7.7 and Table 7.2, LTM appears to be composed of several interacting systems and subsystems — the brain's built-in *hierarchy.* At the top of the hierarchy, you can see that LTM is

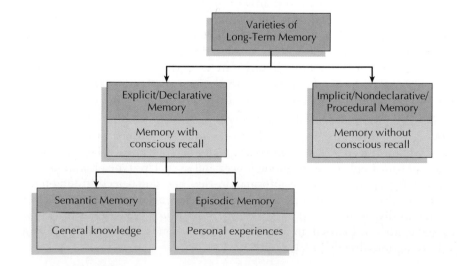

Figure 7.7 *A Hierarchy for Long-Term Memory.* Taking time to study and memorize the separate systems and subsystems for long-term memory can improve your understanding and mastery of this material because it involves *elaborative rehearsal* or a *deeper level of processing.*

TABLE 7.2 LONG-TERM MEMORY (LTM)

Categories and Subcategories	Definition	Examples
Explicit (declarative) memory	Memory with awareness	Explicit memories of life events and facts
Semantic memory	General knowledge of rules, facts, and events; personal encyclopedia of information	Add *s* to make plurals. There are 3 feet in a yard. There are 12 months in a year.
Episodic memory	Personally experienced events; a cumulative record of the episodes of a person's life	Your high school graduation The birth of your first child
Implicit (nondeclarative or procedural) memory	Memory without awareness	Implicit memories of skills and procedures
Procedural memory	How to perform skills, operations, and actions; memories of perfected motor skills	How to drive a car How to brush your teeth How to ride a bike

divided into two major systems — *explicit/declarative memory* and *implicit/nondeclarative memory.*

1. *Explict/declarative memory* *Explicit memory* refers to intentional learning or conscious knowledge. It is *memory with awareness.* Remembering your Social Security number, your first kiss, the name of your first-grade teacher, and the name of your current psychology professor are all examples of explicit memories. This type of memory is sometimes referred to as *declarative memory,* because, if asked, you consciously know the information and can "declare" it. When people think of memory, they often are referring to declarative memory (Best, 1999; Hayne, Boniface, & Barr, 2000).

Explit/declarative memory can be further subdivided into two parts — *semantic memory* and *episodic memory.* **Semantic memory** is memory for general knowledge, rules, events, objective facts, and information. It is our internal mental dictionary or encyclopedia of stored knowledge. If you read and remember terms like *semantic, episodic, explicit/declarative,* and *implicit/nondeclarative,* it is because you have stored them in your semantic memory. Our **episodic memory** is somewhat like a mental diary (Best, 1999; Tulving, 1985). It records the episodes in our life — our first day in school, the people we have known, the places we have visited, and all the personal experiences we have had throughout our lifetime.

2. *Implicit/nondeclarative/procedural memory* *Implicit memory* refers to unintentional learning or unconscious knowledge. It is *memory without awareness.* It consists of motor skills, habits, and simple classically conditioned responses (Squire, Knowlton, & Musen, 1993). This type of memory is also sometimes called *nondeclarative memory* because it includes procedures involved in well-perfected skills and habits outside our conscious awareness, such as driving a car or eating with utensils (Best, 1999; Fernandez-Ruiz & Diaz, 1999).

Explicit/Declarative Memory *The subsystem within long-term memory that stores facts, information, and personal life experiences (also called explicit memory or declarative memory)*

Semantic Memory *The subpart of explicit/declarative memory that stores general knowledge; a mental enclyclopedia or dictionary*

Episodic Memory *The subpart of explicit/declarative memory that stores memories of personally experienced events; a mental diary of a person's life*

Implicit/Nondeclarative Procedural Memory *The subsystem within long-term memory that consists of skills acquired through repetitive practice, habits, and simple classically conditioned responses (also called implicit memory, nondeclarative memory, or procedural memory*

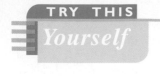

One way to remember each of these various systems and subsystems is to encode them in your long-term memory (LTM) using *elaborative rehearsal* or a *deeper level of processing*. Our chapter opening incident included the story of former President Ronald Reagan's unfortunate experiences with Alzheimer's disease and the story of H. M. Try your hand at elaborative rehearsal by filling in the following blanks with the name of the correct subdivision of LTM.

1. When President Reagan couldn't remember the events and experiences surrounding his acting role in the film *Prisoners of War,* he was experiencing the fading of his _____ memory.
2. Later, it became apparent that Reagan's _____ memory was failing when he couldn't remember facts, such as the names of influential friends, like his secretary of state (Reagan & Reagan, 2000).
3. Most recently, Reagan's _____ memory has been affected, which makes everyday skills such as dressing and eating difficult.
4. After his operation, H. M. could not tell the researchers the day of the week, the year, or even about his last meal. His _____ memory was lacking.
5. Because his _____ memory remained intact, H. M. could acquire new manual or problem-solving skills, such as playing tennis.
6. When tested under specialized conditions that do not require conscious remembering, H. M. can approach or even match the performance of normal participants. This suggests that his _____ memory is intact.

Answers: *1. episodic; 2. semantic; 3. procedural; 4. declarative; 5. procedural; 6. implicit/nondeclarative.*

Priming *The process by which an earlier encounter with a stimulus (such as a word or picture) increases the likelihood of that stimulus or a related stimulus being remembered at a later time*

Associated with implicit/nondeclarative/procedural memory is a phenomenon known as **priming**, where prior presentation of information subsequently makes it easier to recall related items — even when we have no conscious memory of the original information (Toth & Reingold, 1996). In a typical priming research experiment, the researcher flashes a word or symbol on a computer screen so briefly that it is not consciously perceived. When participants are later exposed to a group of unrelated stimuli and asked whether they recognize any item, they are more likely to identify the previously flashed stimuli — even though they deny having seen it before. This indicates that *priming* has taken place.

Integrating Retrieval with the Three-Stage Memory Model

So far, we've discussed how encoding and storage can be integrated with the three-stage memory model. In this section, we will examine *retrieval*, the process of accessing stored information, and how it also can be integrated with the three-stage model. To do this, we examine four related areas of research: retrieval cues, recognition, recall, and the encoding specificity principle.

Retrieval Cue *A clue or prompt that helps stimulate recall and retrieval of a stored piece of information from long-term memory*

A **retrieval cue** is a stimulus that can begin a retrieval process from LTM (Klatzky, 1984). There are basically two types of retrieval cues—either specific or general. When you retrieve a memory using a specific cue, it is called **recognition**. When you use a general cue, it is called **recall**.

Recognition *Process of matching a specific retrieval cue to an appropriate item in long-term memory*

Recall *Process of using a very general retrieval cue to search the contents of long-term memory*

If you pick out a particular face you have previously seen from a police lineup, you use *recognition* to check the specific cue (the face) against your LTM contents to see if something matches (Figure 7.8). If, on the other hand, you remember someone's name from a description of that person (a general cue), you are using *recall*, which is a much more difficult task (Bransford, 1979). During recall, you use a general cue to generate a list of material associated with that cue and then search through LTM to find something that matches the cue (Best, 1999, p. 143). This

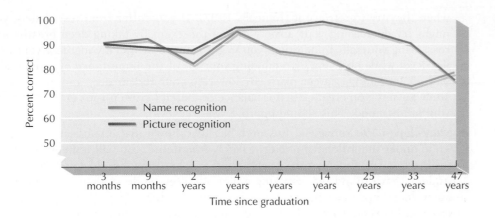

Figure 7.8 *Recognition memory.*
Results from a study of recognition
memory in which participants were
asked to identify pictures of their high
school classmates. As you can see, both
name recognition and picture recognition remain high, whereas recall memory
would be expected to drop significantly
over time.

general cue often isn't enough to locate a single piece of information because the
list of possible matches is often quite large. Therefore, the more specific the cue,
the more likely you are to retrieve the needed information from your memory.

Most essay tests require *recall*. The questions provide only relatively general
cues that ask you to dredge up and organize your memories on a particular topic. In
contrast, multiple-choice questions primarily require *recognition*. Because you are
given specific alternatives to match with your memories, recognition is easier and
usually leads to more success in retrieving memories. (Tip for student success:
While students are taking a test, most professors permit questions regarding clarification on difficult items. Their answers may provide additional retrieval cues.)

*If retrieval is so difficult, why do we remember questions that we got wrong
on an exam, even when we're trying to forget?* Research has shown that interrupted tasks are better recalled than completed tasks, a phenomenon known as the
Zeigarnik effect (House, & McIntosh, 2000; Munroe & Gauvain, 2001; Zeigarnik,
1927). Your frustration over the incorrect items creates a type of arousal that apparently facilitates retrieval. One of the best ways to prevent this unwanted retrieval is
to complete the task by looking up the correct answer immediately after the exam.
This will also improve your later performance on similar questions.

One of the best ways to improve retrieval is to recreate the original learning conditions. The ease of retrieval depends on the match between the way information is
encoded and later retrieved; this is known as the **encoding specificity principle**
(Tulving & Thompson, 1973). Three important research findings are related to this
principle that may help improve your academic success:

- *Context and retrieval.* Have you noticed that you do better on a test when you
  take it in the same seat and classroom where you originally studied the material?
  This happens because the location is a retrieval cue to the material you studied.
  Godden and Baddeley (1975) demonstrated how context affects learning and
  memory in a clever study some years ago. They had underwater divers learn a list
  of 40 words either on land or underwater. The divers had better recall for lists they
  had encoded underwater when they were underwater at retrieval; conversely, lists
  encoded above water were better recalled above water. This can be one reason
  why we feel confident about material while studying at home yet still have trouble recalling it at school later.

- *Mood congruence.* Have you ever become so anxious during an exam that you
  had trouble remembering material you thought you knew well? When you are sad,
  do you tend to think of the same things as when you were sad in the past? When
  you are angry, do you tend to remember other situations that made you angry? The
  idea that a given mood tends to evoke memories that are consistent with that
  mood is called *mood congruence.*

  Research shows that people remember something better if their emotional
  states are the same at the time when they learn something and during the time

Zeigarnik Effect *Process whereby
interrupted tasks are better recalled
than completed tasks*

Encoding Specificity Principle
*Retrieval of information is improved
when conditions of recovery are similar
to the conditions when information
was encoded*

when they try to retrieve it (Kenealy, 1997). If you suffer from test anxiety, you might try decreasing your anxiety during the exam by taking deep breaths and reassuring yourself. In addition, you might want to artificially increase your anxiety level while studying by reminding yourself of the importance of good grades or your long-range career plans. By lowering your test anxiety and upping your study anxiety, you create a better balance or match between your exam mood and your study mood. This should improve your retrieval.

- **State-dependent retrieval.** Research has also shown that if you learn something while under the influence of a drug, such as caffeine, you will remember it more easily when you take that drug again than at other times (Baddeley, 1998). Some students have found that drinking a cup of coffee while studying and before an exam does improve their performance. However, this study does *not* mean that you should drink alcohol as you study and then again during exams! In fact, alcohol and most other drugs impair memory, as well as create serious health and social problems (Chapter 5).

Biological Perspective: Memory's Effect on the Brain and Nervous System

Our two previous models of memory emphasize how information is processed into memories. In this section, we will focus our attention on the biological aspects of memory. It is obvious that something physical must happen in the brain and nervous system when we learn something new. (How else could we later recall and use this information?) In this section, we will first look at neuronal and synaptic changes that occur with memory. Then we will discuss hormonal influences on memory. Finally, in the Research Highlight we explore the anatomy of memory — where memory is located in the brain.

Neuronal and Synaptic Changes in Memory

One of the earliest researchers to study the biochemistry of memory was Donald Hebb (1949, 1955, 1966). After measuring the electrical activity of the brain during learning, Hebb suggested that neurons fire in *reverberating circuits* — that is, a set of neurons fires over and over during the STM process. Structural changes in the synapses from the reverberating circuits do not happen instantaneously. They take time. Before short-term memories can be converted into long-term memories, they must go through a general process called **consolidation**. The consolidation period can be compared to writing your name in freshly poured cement. When the cement dries and sets, your name is there to stay. In the meantime, until the cement is set, it is vulnerable to damage. This can explain why people suffering head injuries, such as a concussion from a traffic accident, often have trouble remembering the events just before the injury. The "cement" for those potential long-term memories was still wet and not fully consolidated.

Consolidation *A hypothetical process explaining the gradual conversion of information into long-term memories*

The research by Hebb and others has suggested a two-stage model for memory consolidation (McGaugh, 2000). The first stage involves STM and the reverberating circuits. During the second stage, information from STM is transferred to LTM where a permanent change occurs in the nervous system.

What causes this change? As you recall from Chapters 2 and 6, learning modifies the brain's neural networks. As a response is learned, specific neural pathways are established that become progressively more excitable and responsive. While you are learning to play tennis, for example, the repeated practice builds neural "pathways" that make it easier and easier to get the ball over the net. This prolonged strengthening of potential neural firing is called **long-term potentiation** (LTP). There are at least two ways that LTP can happen:

Long-Term Potentiation *A long-lasting increase in the strength of synaptic responsiveness believed to be a biological mechanism for learning and memory*

1. *Repeated stimulation of a synapse can strengthen the synapse by stimulating the dendrites to grow more spines* (Barinaga, 1999). This then would result in more synapses, more receptor sites, and more sensitivity. These structural changes were first demonstrated when rats placed in enriched environments grew more sprouts on their dendrites compared with those of rats raised in deprived environments (Rosenzweig, Benet, & Diamond, 1972).

2. *The ability of a particular neuron to release its neurotransmitters can be increased or decreased.* Support comes from *Aplysia*, sea slugs, which can be classically conditioned to reflexively withdraw their gills when squirted with water. After the conditioning occurs, the slugs release more neurotransmitters at certain synapses, and these synapses become more efficient at transmitting signals (see Chapter 6). Further evidence comes from researchers at Princeton University who have created mice with an added gene with additional receptors for a neurotransmitter named NMDA (N-methyl-D-aspartate). These genetic mutant "smart mice" performed significantly better on memory tasks than normal mice did (Tang et al, 1999; Tsien et al., 2000). In fact, they were so far superior that the researchers named them Doogie after the boy genius on the TV show *Doogie Howser, M.D.*

Obviously, it is difficult to generalize from sea slugs and mice. However, research on LTP in humans also has been widely supportive (Kikusui, Aoyagi, & Kaneko, 2000; Sutherland & McNaughton, 2000). Furthermore, research shows that drugs that block LTP interfere with learning and memory (Maren, 1999). As you may have noticed, people often have trouble remembering events of a previous evening after a night of heavy drinking.

Improving memory through genetic engineering. Scientists have created mice with an added gene, which so improved their memory they were named "Doogie" after the boy genius on the television show, Doogie Howser, M.D. This "Doogie" mouse stands on an object used in one of their standard learning and memory tests.

Hormonal Changes and Memory

In addition to neuronal changes with memory, emotion also has a significant effect on memory (Cahill & McGaugh, 1998; McGaugh, 1992, 2000). When stressed or excited, we naturally produce hormones that arouse the body — the inner part of the adrenal glands sends out two hormones, epinephrine and norepinephrine. Can you see why heightened emotions might enhance memory? To survive, an animal or a person must remember exactly how they got into a dangerous situation and how they got out of it. The naturally produced surge of hormones apparently alerts our brains to "pay attention and remember!"

The power of hormones on memory can be seen in the common phenomenon known as *flashbulb memories* — a vivid image of circumstances associated with surprising or strongly emotional events (Brown & Kulik, 1977). Do you remember the moment of your high school graduation or your first romantic kiss? Is this memory so clear that it seems like a flashbulb went off, capturing every detail of the event in your

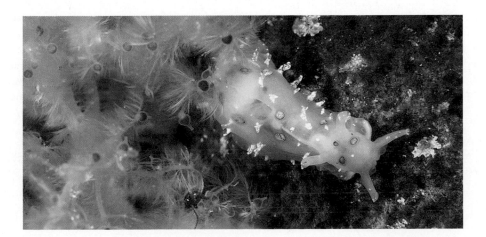

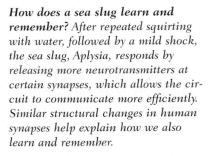

How does a sea slug learn and remember? After repeated squirting with water, followed by a mild shock, the sea slug, Aplysia, responds by releasing more neurotransmitters at certain synapses, which allows the circuit to communicate more efficiently. Similar structural changes in human synapses help explain how we also learn and remember.

Flashbulb Memories. Can you recognize the unintended benefit of studying psychology? You gain greater appreciation for Gary Larson cartoons!

THE FAR SIDE® By GARY LARSON

© 1993 FarWorks, Inc. All Rights Reserved/Dist. by Creators Syndicate

More facts of nature: All forest animals, to this very day, remember exactly where they were and what they were doing when they heard that Bambi's mother had been shot.

memory? Assassinations (JFK, Bobby Kennedy, Martin Luther King, Jr.), disasters (*Challenger* explosion, Mount St. Helens's eruption, the Oklahoma City bombing), and tragic events involving famous figures (the death of Princess Diana) have lasting effects on memory. We secrete fight-or-flight hormones when we initially hear of the event and replay these events in our minds again and again, which makes for stronger memories.

Despite their intensity, flashbulb memories are not as accurate as you might think (Schmolck, Buffalo, & Squire, 2000). For example, in a study of flashbulb memories after the space shuttle *Challenger* explosion, Jeffrey Gutkin (1989) reported significant memory changes over a 3-year period following the disaster. Thus, not even flashbulb memories are immune to alteration. It is also important to note the limits to "hormonally induced memory." If you've ever become so anxious that you "blanked out" during an exam or while giving a speech, you understand that emotions can also interfere with both the formation and retrieval of memories.

RESEARCH HIGHLIGHT

Looking for Memory in All the Right Places

So far, our discussion has focused on the formation of memories as a result of neural changes or hormonal influences. But where is memory stored? What parts of the brain are involved? One of the first scientists to explore this idea was Karl Lashley (1890–1958). Believing that memory was *localized*, or stored in a specific brain area, Lashley began with a standard learning maze experiment for rats. Once the maze was learned, he surgically removed tiny portions of the rats' cortex and then retested their memory of the maze. After 3 decades of frustrating research, Lashley found that rats were still able to run the maze regardless of

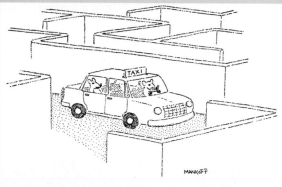

©2001 The New Yorker Collection. Robert Mankoff from cartoonbank.com. All Rights Reserved.

the area of cortex he removed (Lashley, 1929, 1950). Lashley joked, "I sometimes feel in reviewing the evidence on localization of the memory trace, the necessary conclusion is that learning is not possible" (1950, p. 477). Failing to locate a single brain site for memory, Lashley ulti-

mately decided memories were not localized. Instead, they were *distributed* throughout the cortex. Later research suggests that Lashley was both right and wrong: Memory tends to be localized *and* distributed throughout the brain — not just the cortex.

Since Lashley's time, the brain structures involved in long-term memory (LTM) have been under investigation for many years. Today, research techniques are so advanced that we can experimentally induce and measure memory-related brain changes as they occur — on-the-spot reporting! For example, James Brewer and his colleagues (1998) used functional magnetic resonance imaging (fMRI) to locate areas of the brain responsible for encoding memories of pictures. They showed 96 pictures of indoor and outdoor scenes to participants while scanning their brains, then later tested them on their ability to recall those pictures. Brewer and his colleagues identified the right prefrontal cortex and the parahippocampal cortex as the most active during the encoding of the pictures.

Keep in mind, however, that several brain regions are involved in memory (Figure 7.9). For example, some researchers believe memories are *consolidated* in the hippocampal region of the brain and then sent on to be stored in other areas (Gluck & Myers, 1997). This helps explains why H. M. (described in this chapter's introductory incident) found it impossible to form new memories. This area was removed as part of his temporal lobe surgery.

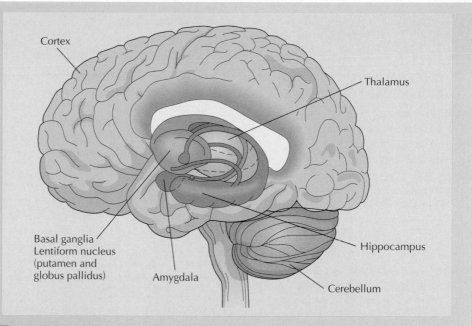

Figure 7.9 *Brain and memory formation.* Damage to any one of these areas can affect encoding, storage, and retrieval of memories.

Brain Area	Known or Suspected Relationship to Memory	Sources
Amygdala	Emotional memory and memory consolidation	McCaugh, 2000; Spanis, Bianchin, Izquierdo, & McGaugh, 1999
Basal Ganglia and Cerebellum	Creation and storage of implicit/nondeclarative memories (such as skills, habits, and simple classical conditioned responses)	Baddeley et al., 2000; Hazeltine, Grafton, & Ivry, 1997; Jog, Kubota, Connolly, Hillegaart, & Graybiel, 1999; Steinmetz, 1998
Hippocampal Formation (Hippocampus and Surrounding Area)	Memory recognition; explicit, spatial, episodic memory; and consolidation of declarative long-term memory	Chou et al., 1990; Eichenbaum. 1999; Fernandez et al., 1999
Thalamus	Formation of new memories and working memory	Bloom & Lazerson, 1988; Johnson & Ojemann, 2001; Manoach et al., 2000).
Cortical Areas: Motor, Parahippocampal, and Prefrontal Cortex; Regions of Occipital and Temporal Lobes	Encoding of explicit/declarative memories; storage of episodic and semantic memories; skill learning; priming	Abel et al., 2000; Gabrieli, Brewer, & Poldrack, 1998; Romo, Brody, Hernandez & Lemus, 1999; Wagner et al., 1998

Check & Review

INTEGRATION MODEL AND BIOLOGICAL PERSPECTIVE

Most psychologists currently emphasize an integration of the traditional *three-stage memory model* and the *encoding, storage, and retrieval approach*.

We first encode information when we transfer it from sensory memory to short-term memory, and then again during the transfer from STM to LTM. Organization and rehearsal are important to successful encoding. To improve encoding during STM, we can use the organizational method of *chunking* or the rehearsal key of *maintenance rehearsal*. During LTM, we can use the organizational strategy of creating *hierarchies* and the rehearsal key of *elaborative rehearsal*.

Storage in LTM is divided into two major systems—**explicit/declarative** and **implicit/nondeclarative/procedural** memory. Explit/declarative memory can be further subdivided into two parts—**semantic** and **episodic** memory.

Retrieval from LTM relies on **retrieval cues** (**recognition** and **recall**) and the **encoding specificity principle.**

The biological perspective of memory focuses on changes in neurons and hormones, as well as on searching for the locations of memory in the brain. Hebb's original idea that memory traces consist of specific neural circuits is supported by research on **long-term potentiation** (**LTP**). When we are stressed or excited, we naturally produce hormones that may enhance memory. Memory tends to be localized *and* distributed throughout the brain — not just in the cortex.

Questions

1. What is the difference between semantic and episodic memory?

2. Taking a multiple-choice test requires _____, whereas essay tests involve _____.

3. Circuits of neurons that fire over and over during STM are called _____. (a) reverberating circuits; (b) coding sequences; (c) electrically active units; (d) consolidation pathways.

4. Describe the two processes involved in LTP.

Answers to Questions can be found in Appendix B.

WHY DO WE FORGET?

What causes forgetting? How do we prevent forgetting of important information?

Memory is what makes you wonder what you've forgotten.

Anonymous

It may surprise you to learn that forgetting is essential to the proper functioning of memory. Think about what your life would be like if you couldn't forget. Your LTM would be filled with meaningless data, such as what you ate for breakfast every morning of your life. Although you might enjoy reliving the intense joy of previous happy experiences, think of the incredible pain and sorrow you would continuously endure if you couldn't escape through forgetting. Forgetting unnecessary or painful information, then, is essential to our lives. But what about those times when forgetting is an inconvenience or even dangerous? What causes forgetting? How can we prevent forgetting of important information?

Research Findings: Factors Explaining Forgetting

These questions have been important issues in psychology ever since Hermann Ebbinghaus, a pioneer memory researcher who often used himself as his only subject, first introduced the experimental study of learning and forgetting in 1885. To measure memory performance, he calculated how long it took for him to learn a list of *nonsense syllables.* For his trials, Ebbinghaus chose three-letter nonsense syllables such as *SIB* and *RAL* because they were equally difficult to learn. Furthermore, nonsense syllables don't have the meanings and associations that words do, thus avoiding the complications of previous learning.

After Ebbinghaus memorized lists of nonsense syllables until he knew them perfectly, he retested his memory at regular intervals. He found that 1 hour after he knew a list perfectly, he remembered only 44 percent of the syllables. A day later, he recalled 35 percent, and a week later only 21 percent. Figure 7.10 presents his famous, and depressing, "forgetting curve."

Do we forget everything this fast? If you were to forget textbook materials and lecture notes this rapidly, you would be able to pass a test only if you took it immediately after studying the material. An hour later, you would fail the test because you would remember less than half of what you had studied. Keep in mind, however, that the forgetting curve in Figure 7.10 applies to meaningless nonsense syllables. Meaningful material is much less likely to be forgotten. The material you study for a test can be retained much longer if you make an effort to make it meaningful. But meaningful or not, you will still forget some of what you have studied.

On a more cheerful note, after some time passed and he had forgotten the list, Ebbinghaus also calculated the time it took to relearn the same list. He found that relearning a list took less time than the initial learning period; this is known as **relearning** (or the *savings method*). Ebbinghaus's research suggests that we often retain some memory for things we have learned, even when we seem to have forgotten them completely. This finding should be encouraging to you if you studied a foreign language years ago but are no longer proficient in recalling or recognizing the vocabulary. You could expect to relearn the material more rapidly the second time.

Since Ebbinghaus's original research, scientists have discovered numerous factors that contribute to forgetting — which may have important implications for your life as a student. Two of the most important are the *serial position effect* and *spacing of practice*:

1. Serial position effect. When study participants are given lists of words to learn and are allowed to recall them in any order they choose, they remember the words at the beginning (*primacy effect*) and the end of the list (*recency effect*) better than those in the middle, which are quite often forgotten (Jones & Roediger, 1995) (Figure 7.11). The general term, including both the primacy effect and recency effect, is known as the **serial position effect**.

The reasons for this effect are complex, but it does help explain why material at the beginning and end of a chapter is better remembered than that in the middle, or why you remember the first people you meet at a party and the last. It also has interesting applications for your employment success. If a potential employer calls to set up an interview, you can increase their memory for you and your application by asking to be either the first or last candidate.

2. Spacing of practice. Despite their best intentions, students often study in ways that encourage forgetting. In addition to studying in noisy places where attention is easily diverted and interference is maximized, they often try to memorize too much at one time by "cramming" the night before an exam. As the Tools for Student Success section in Chapter 1 emphasized, the single most important key to improving grades may be *distributed study*. **Distributed practice** refers to spacing your learning periods, with rest periods between sessions. Cramming is called **massed practice** because the time spent learning is massed into long, unbroken intervals. John Donovan and David Radosevich (1999) compared 63 separate

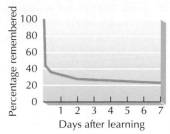

Figure 7.10 *Ebbinghaus's forgetting curve.* This graph dramatizes how rapidly nonsense syllables are forgotten, especially in the first few hours after learning.

Relearning *Learning material a second time, which usually takes less time than original learning (also called the savings method)*

Serial Position Effect *The phenomenon of remembering the material at the beginning and the end of a list better than the material in the middle*

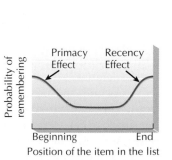

Figure 7.11 *The serial position effect.* If you try to recall a list of similar items, you'll tend to remember the first and last items best.

Distributed Practice *A learning technique in which practice sessions are interspersed with rest periods*

Massed Practice *A learning technique in which time spent learning is massed into long, unbroken intervals (also known as cramming)*

Massed versus distributed practice. *Cramming for an examination is an attempt to learn too much at one time and is therefore less effective than spacing out study time into several sessions.*

studies and found that distributed practice produced superior memory and learning compared with massed practice. Unfortunately, research shows that most students study right before the test (Taraban, Maki, & Rynearson, 1999).

GENDER & CULTURAL DIVERSITY

Cultural Differences in Memory and Forgetting

How do you remember the dates for all your quizzes, exams, and assignments in college? What memory aids do you use if you need to buy 15 items at the supermarket? Most people from industrialized societies rely on written shopping lists, calendars, books, notepads, or computers to store information and prevent forgetting. Can you imagine living in a culture without these aids? What would it be like if you had to rely solely on your memory to store and retrieve all your past, current, and future information? Would you develop better memory skills if you didn't have the ability to write things down? Do people raised in preliterate societies with rich oral traditions develop better memory skills than do people raised in literate societies?

Ross and Millson (1970) designed a cross-cultural study to answer these questions. They compared American and Ghanaian college students' abilities to remember stories that were read aloud. Students listened to the stories without taking notes and without being told they would be tested. Two weeks later, all students were asked to write down as much as they could remember. As you might expect, the Ghanaian students had better recall than the Americans. Their superior performance was attributed to their culture's long oral tradition, which requires developing greater skill in encoding oral information (Matsumoto, 2000).

Does this mean that cultures with an oral tradition have better memories? Recall from Chapter 1 that a core requirement for scientific research is *replica-*

Culture and memory. In many societies, tribal leaders pass down vital information through stories related orally. Because of this rich oral tradition, children living in these cultures have better memories for information related through stories than do other children

tion and the generation of related hypotheses and studies. In this case, when other researchers tested nonliterate African participants with lists of words instead of stories, they did *not* perform better (Cole, Gray, Glick, & Sharp, 1971). However, when both educated Africans and uneducated Africans were compared for memory of lists of words, the educated Africans performed very well (Scribner, 1979). This suggests that formal schooling helps develop memory strategies for things like lists of words, which preliterate participants may see as unrelated and meaningless.

Wagner (1982) conducted a study with Moroccan and Mexican urban and rural children that helps explain the effect of formal schooling. Participants were presented with seven cards placed facedown in front of them, one at a time. They were then shown a card and asked to point out which of the seven cards was its duplicate. Everyone, regardless of culture or amount of schooling, was able to recall the latest cards presented (the *recency effect*). However, the amount of schooling significantly affected overall recall and the ability to recall the earliest cards presented (*primacy effect*).

Wagner suggests that the primacy effect depends on *rehearsal* — the silent repetition of things you're trying to remember — and that this strategy is strongly related to schooling. As a child in a typical classroom, you were expected to memorize letters, numbers, multiplication tables, and a host of other basic facts. This type of formal schooling provides years of practice in memorization and in applying these skills in test situations. According to Wagner, memory has two parts: a "hardware" section that does not change across cultures and a "software" part that develops particular strategies for remembering, which are learned.

In summary, research indicates that the "software" (or programming) part of memory is affected by culture. In cultures in which communication relies on oral tradition, people develop good strategies for remembering orally presented stories. In cultures in which formal schooling is the rule, people learn memory strategies that help them remember lists of items. From these studies, we can conclude that across cultures, people tend to remember information that matters to them, and they develop memory skills to match the demands of their environment.

Theories of Forgetting: Why We Don't Remember Everything

Five major theories have been offered to explain why forgetting occurs: *decay, interference, motivated forgetting, encoding failure*, and *retrieval failure*. Each theory focuses on a different stage of the memory process or on a particular type of problem in processing information. (Study tip: If you want to remember the five theories, think of how forgetting involves memories that grow "dimmer," and note that the first letters of each theory has almost the same spelling — *D-I-M-E-R*.)

Decay Theory

Decay theory is based on the commonsense assumption that memory, like all biological processes, deteriorates as time passes. If memory is processed and stored in a physical form — for example, in a network of neurons — the fidelity of the representation could be expected to decrease over time. It is well documented that skills and memory are degraded if they are not used for a long period of time (Arthur, Bennett, Stanush, & McNelly, 1998). However, experimental support for decay theory is difficult to obtain. As we discovered in Chapter 3 when we discussed extrasensory perception, how do you prove something does *not* exist?

Interference Theory

Perhaps the most widely accepted theory, known as *interference theory*, suggests forgetting is caused by one memory competing with or trying to replace another memory (Anderson, Bjork, & Bjork, 1994; Conway & Pleydell-Pearce, 2000; Parkes & White 2000). Interference is particularly strong among memories for similar events or having similar retrieval cues.

There are two types of interference, *retroactive* and *proactive* (Figure 7.12). When new information leads to forgetting of previous material, it is called **retroactive interference** (acting backward in time). Learning your new phone number causes forgetting of your old phone number. Conversely, when old information leads to forgetting of new information, it is called **proactive interference** (acting forward in time). Old information (like the Spanish you learned in high school) may interfere with your ability to learn and remember your new college course in French.

Proactive Interference *Forgetting in which old information interferes with remembering new information; forward-acting memory interference*

Retroactive Interference *Forgetting in which new information interferes with remembering old information; backward-acting interference*

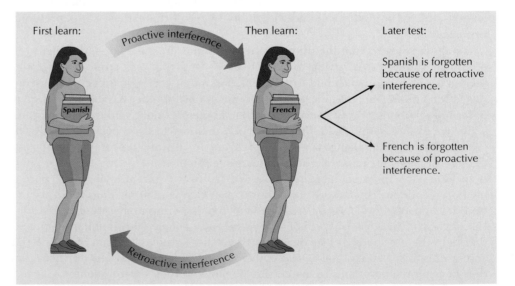

First learn:

Proactive interference

Then learn:

Later test:

Spanish is forgotten because of retroactive interference.

Spanish

French

French is forgotten because of proactive interference.

Retroactive interference

Figure 7.12 *Types of interference.* (a) Retroactive (backward) interference occurs when new information causes forgetting of old material (*new interferes with the old*), and (b) proactive (forward-acting) interference occurs when old information causes forgetting of new material (*old interferes with the new*).

Motivated Forgetting Theory

A third theory of forgetting focuses on our sometimes unconscious wish to forget something unpleasant. According to the *motivated forgetting theory*, we forget for a reason, which leads to inhibition of retrieval. Forgetting the name of an instructor who gave you a low grade, your dental appointment, or that embarrassing speech you made in eighth grade are all examples of motivated forgetting.

People obviously try to inhibit unpleasant or anxiety-producing thoughts or feelings. According to Freudian theory (Chapter 13), when they do this consciously, telling themselves not to worry about an upcoming final exam, it is called *suppression*. When they do it unconsciously, it is called *repression*. Sigmund Freud claimed that people repressed painful memories to avoid anxiety. If this is the case, appropriate therapy might overcome the repressive mechanisms and cause the repressed memory to be recovered. Memories of child abuse, sexual assault, war atrocities, and so on may create such painful experiences that the individual is highly motivated to forget them. The controversy surrounding repressed memories is discussed later in this chapter.

Encoding Failure

Whose head is on a U.S. penny? What is written at the top of a penny? Despite having seen a real penny thousands of times in your life, most of us have difficulty recognizing the details (Figure 7.13). Although the U.S. penny has eight distinguishing characteristics (Lincoln's head, the date it was minted, which way Lincoln is facing, and so on), the average person can only remember three (Nickerson & Adams, 1979). This is a great example of *encoding failure*. Unless we are coin collectors, we have likely never encoded the details of a penny. Our sensory memory certainly received the information and passed it along (encoded it) to STM. But during STM, we probably decided there was no need to remember the precise details of the penny, so we did not encode it and pass it on for storage in LTM.

Retrieval Failure Theory

Anyone who has ever "blanked out" during an exam or a conversation only to remember the "forgotten" information later has had a firsthand experience with the *retrieval failure* (or *cue-dependent*) *theory of forgetting*. According to this theory, memories stored in LTM are never really forgotten; they are just momentarily inaccessible as a result of such things as interference, faulty cues, or emotional states.

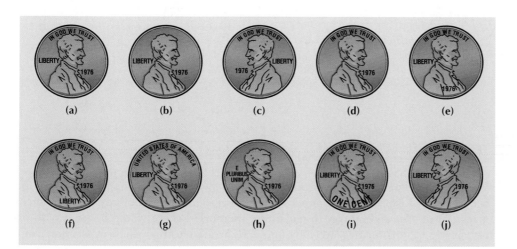

Figure 7.13 *Encoding failure.* Can you identify a drawing of a real penny among fakes?

As you might imagine, it is difficult to distinguish retrieval failure from encoding failure. In fact, most memory failures are probably due to poor encoding, rather than retrieval failure (Howe & O'Sullivan, 1997). An experiment designed to find out why parents are so poor at reporting when and if their children received vaccinations illustrates this point. In this experiment, parents were asked immediately after their child's medical visit if the child had a vaccination during that visit (Lee et al., 1999). The same parents were asked the same question 10 weeks later. The researchers found that the parents were equally bad on both surveys. It appears that the reason for the forgetting is poor encoding, not retrieval failure. Retrieval failure would have caused the 10-week memories to be much worse than the immediate memories.

One of the most common experiences of retrieval *failure* is the **tip-of-the-tongue (TOT) phenomenon** — the feeling that at any second, a word or event you are trying to remember will pop out from the "tip of your tongue" (Brown & McNeill, 1966; Read & Bruce, 1982). Even though you can't say the word, you can often tell how many syllables it has, the beginning and ending letters, or what it rhymes with.

Tip-of-the-Tongue Phenomenon
A retrieval failure that involves a sensation of knowing that specific information is stored in long-term memory but of being temporarily unable to retrieve it

Check & Review

WHY DO WE FORGET?

Hermann Ebbinghaus was one of the first researchers to extensively study forgetting. His famous "curve of forgetting" shows that it occurs most rapidly immediately after learning. However, Ebbinghaus also showed that **relearning** usually takes less time than original learning. Two important factors in forgetting are the **serial position effect** (in which material at the beginning and end of the list is remembered better than material in the middle) and spacing of practice (in which **distributed practice** is found to be superior to **massed practice**).

The decay theory of forgetting simply states that memory, like all biological processes, deteriorates as time passes. The interference theory of forgetting suggests memories are forgotten because of either proactive or retroactive interference.

Proactive interference occurs when old information interferes with newly learned information. **Retroactive interference** occurs when new information interferes with previously learned information. The motivated forgetting theory states that people forget things that are painful, threatening, or embarrassing. Some material is forgotten because it was never encoded from short-term memory to long-term memory (LTM). Other forgetting occurs because of retrieval failure; information stored in LTM is not forgotten but may at times be inaccessible.

Questions

1. When taking an exam, students often do better with items taken from the first and last of the chapters covered by the exam. This demonstrates the (a) superiority of distributed practice; (b) Zeigarnik effect; (c) state-dependent effect; (d) serial position effect.

2. How would you study for a test using distributed practice? Using massed practice?

3. Which theory of forgetting is being described in each of the following examples?
   a. You are very nervous about having to introduce all the people at a party, and you forget a good friend's name.
   b. You meet a friend you haven't seen for 25 years and you cannot remember his name.
   c. You were molested as a child and have completely forgotten the incident.

Answers to Questions can be found in Appendix B.

PROBLEMS WITH MEMORY

What are the key memory problems?

What happens when people abruptly lose all memory of their past in cases of amnesia, or slowly lose it with Alzheimer's? Imagine a total loss of memory. With no memories of the past and no way to make new memories, there would be no way to use our previous skills or to learn new ones. We wouldn't know each other, nor would we know ourselves. In fact, our very survival would be in question. In this section, we will discuss the serious personal and social issues associated with memory problems. We begin with organically caused problems (including injury, disease, and amnesia). We then discuss problems with the constructive nature of memory — how we sometimes alter, distort, and create our personal memories.

Organic Causes: Injury and Disease

Some memory problems are the result of injury and disease (organic pathology). When people are in serious accidents or suffer strokes or other events that cause trauma to the brain, memory loss or deterioration can occur. Disease also can alter the physiology of the brain and nervous system and thereby affect memory processes. As we explore organic causes of memory problems, we will focus our attention on *brain injury* and *Alzheimer's disease*.

The Injured Brain

Have you ever wondered why health professionals are so insistent about participants' always wearing a helmet during most sports activities? *Traumatic brain injury* happens when the skull makes a sudden collision with another object. The compression, twisting, and distortion of the brain inside the skull often cause serious and sometimes permanent damage to the brain. The frontal and temporal lobes often take the heaviest hit because they directly impact against the bony ridges inside the skull. In the United States, traumatic brain injury is the leading cause of neurological disorders among Americans ages 15 to 25. These injuries most commonly result from car accidents, falls, blows, and gunshot wounds

What happens to our memory when we have a serious head injury or trauma? Forgetting as a result of brain injury or trauma is called *amnesia*. In **retrograde amnesia**, the patient loses memory for events that occurred *before* the accident yet has no trouble remembering things that happened afterward. Conversely, **anterograde amnesia** is a loss of memory for events that occur *after* an accident. Anterograde amnesia may result from a surgical injury or from diseases, such as chronic alcoholism. H. M. (the man introduced at the start of this chapter) suffers from both forms of amnesia. He has trouble remembering events that happened the last several years before the operation (*retrograde amnesia*). Also, for years after the operation, he thought the year was 1953 and that he was only 27 (*anterograde amnesia*). In most cases, retrograde amnesia is temporary and most patients recover slowly over time. Unfortunately, anterograde amnesia is usually permanent — as is the case with H. M.

Retrograde Amnesia *Difficulty in remembering previously learned material*

Anterograde Amnesia *The inability to form new memories*

Alzheimer's Disease

Alzheimer's disease (AD) is a progressive mental deterioration that occurs most commonly in old age. The most noticeable early symptoms are disturbances in memory, beginning with typical incidents of forgetfulness that everyone experiences from time to time. With AD, the forgetfulness progresses until, in the final stages, the person fails to recognize loved ones, needs total nursing care, and ultimately, dies. Not all types of memory are affected equally. One of the major differences between normal memory loss and memory loss due to AD is the latter's extreme decrease in episodic declarative memory (Collette, Van der Linden, & Salmon, 1999; Salmon, Butters, & Chan, 1999).

Autopsies of the brain of people with AD show unusual *tangles* (structures formed from degenerating cell bodies) and *plaques* (structures formed from degenerating axons and dendrites). Hereditary AD runs in families and generally strikes its victims between the ages of 45 and 55. Some experts believe the cause of AD is primarily genetic, but others think genetic makeup may make some people more sus-

Alzheimer's [ALLS-high-merz] Disease *A progressive mental deterioration that occurs most commonly in old age and is characterized by severe memory loss*

The effect of Alzheimer's disease on the brain. Note the high amount of red and yellow color (signs of brain activity) in the positron emission tomography scans of the normal brain on the left, and the reduced activity in the brain of the Alzheimer's disease patient on the right. The loss is most significant in the temporal and parietal lobes, which indicates that these areas are particularly important for storing memories.

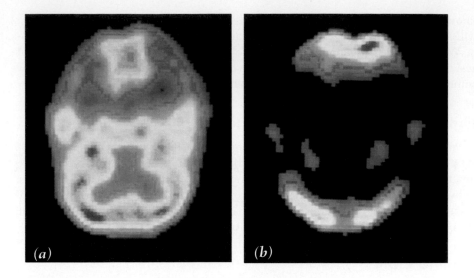

ceptible to environmental triggers (Cowley, 2000; Mattila et al., 1998; Vickers et al., 2000).

Constructive Processes: How We Create and Distort Our Own Memories

Now that we've discussed organic causes of memory problems, you may want to try this short memory test before we continue discussing additional sources of errors in memory:

> Below is a series of words. Take a moment to carefully read through the entire list, then cover it and write down all the words you can recall in 2 minutes. Now, compare your recalled words with the original list.

Bed	Awake	Tired	Dream	Wake	Snooze	Snore
Rest	Blanket	Doze	Slumber	Nap	Peace	Yawn
Drowsy	Nurse	Sick	Lawyer	Medicine	Health	Hospital
Dentist	Physician	Patient	Stethoscope	Curse	Clinic	Surgeon

> **Number of correctly recalled words:**
> 21 to 28 words = excellent memory
> 16 to 20 words = better than most
> 12 to 15 words = average
> 8 to 11 words = below average
> 7 or fewer = you might need a nap

How did you do? Do you have a good or excellent memory? Did you recall seeing the words *sleep* and *doctor*? If so, you have constructed a false memory. Look back over the list. These words were not there, yet over 65 percent of students will believe they saw these words. Why? The answers are found throughout this chapter. As we form new memories and sort through the old, we fill in missing pieces, we make "corrections," and rearrange information to make it logically consistent. Thus, the memory that we eventually retrieve is affected not just by the actual direct experiences we have had with the stimulus but also by our guesses and inferences about its meaning as well. You falsely remembered *sleep* and *doctor* because they were logically consistent. As we mentioned at the opening, memory is *not* a faithful duplicate of an event; it is a **constructive process** where we actively shape and build on information as it is encoded and retrieved.

When we encode information, we *construct* a mental representation (not an exact recording). Think about a recent, important lecture from your psychology instructor that you (hopefully) encoded for storage in LTM. You obviously did not record a word-for-word copy of the lecture. You summarized, augmented, and tied it in with related memories you have in LTM. Similarly, when we retrieve information, we *reconstruct* the previously *constructed* memories, thus introducing another set of potential errors. If you need to retrieve the stored lecture from your LTM, you repeat the general ideas or facts that were said, while leaving out seemingly unimportant elements or misremembering the details.

Why isn't the original version stored in long-term memory? General constructive processes that occur during encoding and retrieval and alter the original version as well include three more specific types of construction errors: *source amnesia*, the *sleeper effect*, and the *misinformation effect*:

1. Source amnesia. We sometimes imagine or dream about something and later aren't sure whether it really happened. You might mistakenly recall that you heard the lecture information from a friend during shared study times or read it in the text, rather than from your psychology professor. This is known as **source amnesia**, which occurs when the true source of the memory is forgotten (Leichtman & Ceci, 1995).

2. Sleeper effect. Because of source amnesia, we also tend to confuse reliable information with the unreliable. This is particularly true with the passage of time. Research on the **sleeper effect** finds that when we first hear something from an unreliable source we tend to disregard that information in favor of a more reliable source. However, over time, the source of the information is forgotten and the unreliable information is no longer discounted (Underwood & Pezdek, 1998). This sleeper effect can be a significant problem when reliable and unreliable information are intermixed. As a critical thinker, can you see why advertisers of shoddy services or products might benefit from "channel surfing?" What happens to the LTM of the television viewer who skips from news programs to cable talk shows to infomercials? Can you see how a movie star who offers an opinion about a weight-loss diet might later be remembered as a dietary expert?

3. Misinformation effect. Have you ever heard a story about your sibling or a friend and then later confused it as your own? As we discovered in the earlier discussion of flashbulb memories, people often misremember details about their own experiences and those of others. This type of incorporating other, outside information into your own memory is known as the **misinformation effect.**

As a critical thinker, see if you can identify *source amnesia* and the *misinformation effect* in this childhood memory experienced by the famous cognitive and developmental psychologist Jean Piaget (1951):

> One of my first memories would date, if it were true, from my second year. I can still see, most clearly, the following scene, in which I believed until I was about fifteen. I was sitting in my pram, which my nurse was pushing in the Champs-Élysées, when a man tried to kidnap me. I was held in by the strap fastened round me while my nurse bravely tried to stand between the thief and me. She received various scratches, and I can still see vaguely those on her face. Then a crowd gathered, a policeman with a short cloak and a white baton came up, and the man took to his heels. I can still see the whole scene, and can even place it near the tube station. When I was about fifteen, my parents received a letter from my former nurse saying that she had been converted to the Salvation Army. She wanted to confess her past faults, and in particular to return the watch she had been given as a reward on this

Constructive Process *The active organizing and shaping of information as we encode and retrieve it, which can result in errors and distortions*

Source Amnesia *Attributing to a wrong source an event that we have experienced, heard about, read about, or imagined (also called source confusion or source misattribution)*

Sleeper Effect *The tendency to initially discount information from an unreliable source but later consider it more trustworthy because the source is forgotten*

Misinformation Effect *A memory error that results from incorporating outside information into one's own memory of an event (also known as suggestibility)*

occasion. She had made up the whole story, faking the scratches. I, therefore, must have heard, as a child, the account of this story, which my parents believed, and projected it into the past in the form of a visual memory, which was a memory of a memory, but false. [pp. 187–188].

How did you do? Did you identify *source amnesia* when Piaget falsely attributed his memory to his own experience rather than to his nursemaid's made-up story? Did you note how he incorporated her faked scratches into his own memory of actually seeing the scratches at the time of the "attempted kidnapping?" This would be part of the *misinformation effect*. Because Piaget's parents probably trusted the nursemaid and considered her information reliable, the *sleeper effect* was not a factor in this false memory.

Eyewitness Testimony and Repressed Memories: Serious Memory Problems

Misremembering the source for a new weight-loss product and Piaget's memory of being saved by a kind nursemaid may be relatively harmless memory problems. But what if the police had mistakenly arrested and convicted an innocent man because of Piaget's nursemaid's false claim? In this section, we will discuss two areas of memory problems that have profound legal and social implications: *eyewitness testimony* and *repressed memories*.

Eyewitness Testimony

You know the old saying "Seeing is believing." But can we really trust what we see — or *think* we see? In the past, one of the best forms of trial evidence a lawyer could have was an eyewitness, yet numerous research studies have identified several problems with eyewitness testimony (Bidrose & Goodman, 2000; Johnson & Seifert, 1994; Loftus, 2000; Wells et al., 2000).

In one eyewitness study, participants were shown a film of a car driving through the countryside. Members of one group were asked to estimate how fast the car was going when it passed the barn. Participants in the other group who saw the same film were also asked to estimate the car's speed, but a barn was not mentioned. When all participants were later asked if they saw a barn in the film, six times as many in the group given the misinformation about the barn reported having seen it, even though it never appeared in the film (Loftus, 1982).

It is impossible to determine how often eyewitnesses are mistaken in their recollections of events, but experimental evidence indicates that the error rate might be disturbingly high. For example, in an experiment at the University of Nebraska, participants watched people committing a staged crime. About an hour later, they were asked to pick out suspects from mug shots, and a week later, from a lineup. None of the participants in the staged crime appeared in the mug shots or lineups, yet 20 percent of the eyewitnesses identified innocent people in the mug shots, and 8 percent identified innocent people in the lineup (Brown, Deffenbacher, & Sturgill, 1977).

How could the research participants have been so mistaken? Several properties of memory could combine to create the type of mistaken identity that occurred at the lineup stage. First, we know that seeing a mug shot would lead to familiarity, which might lead to false recognition during the later lineup. Next, we know that memory is constructive, so the participants might have constructed an inaccurate memory of the crime situation using memories instilled by the mug shots.

These problems are so well established and important that judges now allow expert testimony on the unreliability of eyewitness testimony and routinely instruct jurors on its limits (Durham & Dane, 1999; Ramirez, Zemba, & Geiselman, 1996). If you serve as a member of a jury or listen to accounts of crimes in the news, remind yourself of these problems. Also keep in mind that research participants in eyewitness studies generally report their inaccurate memories with great self-assurance and strong conviction (Migueles & Garcia-Bajos, 1999). Eyewitnesses to actual crimes may similarly identify — with equally high confidence — an innocent person.

Repressed Memories

Do you recall the opening story of Elizabeth, who suddenly remembered a childhood scene of finding her mother's drowned body? This is a true story of Elizabeth Loftus, one of the leading experts in repressed memory research. The recovery of the memory, although painful, also brought great relief. "I started putting everything into place. Maybe that's why I'm such a workaholic." It also seemed to explain why she had always been fascinated by the topic of memory and had spent so many years on its research.

After all this resolution and relief, however, her brother called to say there had been a mistake! The relative who told Elizabeth that she had been the one to discover her mother's body later remembered it had actually been Aunt Pearl, not Elizabeth Loftus. Other relatives also confirmed that it was Aunt Pearl. Even though Loftus is an expert on memory distortions and false memories, she was not immune to the problems of memory construction.

As we've seen throughout this chapter, our memories are frequently faulty, and researchers have demonstrated that it is relatively easy to create false memories (Blagrove & Akehurst, 2000; Human & Kleinknecht, 1999; Loftus, 1993, 1997, 2000). Seeing the words *sleep* and *doctor* in the previous list, Piaget's kidnapping memory, the eyewitness participants who later recalled a nonexistent barn, and Loftus's memory of finding her mother's body are all examples of false memories.

So what about repressed memories? Can people recover true childhood memories? *Repression*, which was mentioned earlier as a part of motivated forgetting, is the supposed unconscious coping mechanism by which anxiety-provoking thoughts are prevented from reaching consciousness. Therefore, thoughts or memories that are extremely frightening to a person, such as memories of childhood sexual abuse, might be repressed. According to some therapists, these memories exist in a hidden corner of the person's brain, but they're normally inaccessible because of the pain they would causes if brought to conscious awareness (Bertram & Widener, 1999). In most cases, therapy would be necessary to unlock these hidden memories (Davies, 1996).

As you might imagine, this is a complex and controversial topic in psychology. No one doubts that some memories are forgotten and later recovered. When cued by a remark or experience, many people recover memories of long-forgotten events — a childhood trip to Disneyland, the move from one house to another, or details surrounding a painful event. What is questioned is the concept of *repressed memories* of painful experiences (*especially childhood sexual abuse*), and their storage in the unconscious mind (Loftus & Polage, 1999). Critics suggest that most people who have witnessed or experienced a violent crime, or are adult survivors of childhood sexual abuse, have intense, persistent memories. They have trouble forgetting, not remembering.

Some critics also wonder whether therapists retrieve actual memories or inadvertently create false memories. Just as a scientist's *experimenter bias* might unintentionally influence participants' responses (Chapter 1), clinicians who sincerely believe their client may have been abused as a child may unintentionally influence their client's recall of information. If the clinician mentions possible abuse, the client's own constructive processes may lead him or her to create a false memory.

Remember how Loftus used her relative's suggestion that she found her mother's body to create her own detailed false memory? As a critical thinker, can you see how clients might respond similarly to their therapists' suggestions? Even though the clinician suggests only the possibility of abuse, the client might start to think about movies and books portraying other people's experiences and incorporate this information into his or her own memory (the *misinformation effect*), might forget where they heard these stories (*source amnesia*), and over time might forget these originally unreliable sources and see them as reliable (the *sleeper effect*).

Thus, the question "Are recovered memories true or false?" may be impossible to answer. As we've noted before, research clearly demonstrates that *all* our memories are imperfect constructions during encoding and reconstructions during retrieval. Attempting to label some memories as "true" and others as "false" may be misleading and oversimplifying.

The so-called repressed memory debate, however, has grown increasingly bitter, and research on both sides is hotly contested (Lindsay, 1998). This is not just an "academic debate." It has serious implications because civil lawsuits and criminal prosecutions are sometimes based on recovered memories of childhood sexual abuse, and family bonds are sometimes irreparably damaged by false accusations. It is dangerous to trust memory — recovered or repressed — to provide accurate recollections of the past. Researchers are currently seeking more information about the mechanisms underlying delayed remembering. (For more information about this research and the continuing controversy, call or write the American Psychological Association in Washington, D.C. Ask for the pamphlet "Questions and Answers about Memories of Childhood Abuse." Also check the *Psychology in Action* website.)

We will return to this hotly debated issue of repressed memories in Chapter 14. In the meantime, it is important to remember that child sexual abuse is a fact, not

critical thinking

Active Learning

Exploring Your Memories

Reflective thinking is the ability to review and analyze your own mental processes — to "think about thinking." Reflective thinking is an important component of critical thinking. It allows you to objectively examine your thoughts and cognitive strategies and evaluate their appropriateness and accuracy. In the context of this chapter, we could employ reflective thinking to evaluate the processes used in recalling memories.

To practice reflective thinking:

1. Take out a sheet of paper and write down all you can remember about the first day of your introductory psychology course. What did you do from the minute you entered the room that day? What did the professor say or do?

Write down only the things you can remember in vivid detail, not those you "think" you remember.

2. Now compare your memories with your classmates'. Are your memories exactly the same? Are some personal and some shared? Do you remember only the ordinary first-day happenings, or do you remember any unusual occurrences? Do you remember any feelings or emotions? What do you remember that your classmates do not? Do additional memories come flooding back when triggered by others' recollections?

3. Take time to reflect on how your memories were stored and organized in your brain, on the basis of comparisons you made in the previous item. Most

people do not remember things in vivid detail. Most often, memories are more general, allowing you to fill in the details according to how you "think" the memory should have been rather than providing all the details for you. Is this true in your case?

4. Finally, try to recall an older memory, a vivid memory from your childhood. Write down as much detail as you can and then try to evaluate which part of that memory is likely to be factual and which part is reconstructed. You may find it necessary to ask your parents or old friends to verify the accuracy of these memories. But it is unlikely that even your most vivid childhood memories are a perfectly accurate representation of the past.

a disputed issue, and we must be careful not to ridicule or condemn people who recover true memories of abuse. In the same spirit, we must protect the innocent from wrongful accusations that come from false memories. We look forward to a time when we can justly balance the rights of the victim with those of the accused.

Check & Review

PROBLEMS WITH MEMORY

Some memory problems are the result of injury and disease (organic pathology). Forgetting as a result of serious brain injuries or trauma is called *amnesia*. In **retrograde amnesia**, memory for events that occurred *before* the accident is lost. In **anterograde amnesia**, memory for events that occur *after* an accident is lost. **Alzheimer's disease** is a progressive mental deterioration and severe memory loss occurring most commonly in old age.

Memories are not exact duplicates. We actively shape and build on information as it is encoded, stored, and retrieved. There are three major errors that occur during the constructive processes of memory: **source amnesia,** the **sleeper effect** and the **misinformation effect.** Two areas of memory problems that have profound legal and social implications are *eyewitness testimony* and *repressed memories*.

Questions

1. Forgetting that results from brain damage or trauma is called _____.

2. Ralph couldn't remember anything that happened to him between the time he fell through the floor of his tree house and found himself in the hospital. His lack of memory for the interval between the events is called _____ amnesia. (a) retroactive; (b) proactive; (c) anterograde; (d) retrograde

3. Explain the difference between source amnesia, the sleeper effect, and the misinformation effect.

4. Why is eyewitness testimony not considered reliable in a court of law?

Answers to Questions can be found in Appendix B.

IMPROVING MEMORY

After reading about all the problems and dangers associated with memory, you'll be glad to know that our memories are normally quite accurate and serve us well in most situations. Our memories have evolved to encode, store, and retrieve information vital to our survival. While working to secure our food and shelter, we constantly search and monitor our potentially dangerous environment. Even while sleeping, we process and store important memories.

Evolutionarily speaking, our memories are adaptive and quite remarkable. However, when faced with tasks like remembering precise details in a college text, the faces and names of potential clients, or where we left our house keys, our brains are simply not well equipped. The beauty of the human brain is that we can recognize such limits and develop appropriate coping mechanisms. Just as our ancestors domesticated wild horses and cattle to overcome the physical limits of the human body, we can develop ways to improve our memory for fine detail. The field of psychology provides numerous helpful theories and concepts for improving memory, and concrete suggestions are sprinkled throughout this text. In this section, we will briefly summarize the most effective memory enhancement techniques. Then we close with a discussion of the "seven sins of forgetting," a topic with further tips for improving memory.

How can we improve our memory?

Specific Tips: Using Memory Research to Remember More

Everyone can improve his or her memory. The harder you work at it, the better your memory will become. Below, we have summarized key points from the chapter that you can put into practice to improve your memory. (You might also recognize several points that were presented earlier in Tools for Student Success in Chapter 1.)

- *Pay attention and reduce interference.* If you really want to remember something, you must pay attention to it. So when you're in class, focus on the instructor and sit away from people who might distract you. When you study, choose a place with a minimum of distractions. Also, try to avoid studying topics that are closely related (such as French and Spanish) on the same night or even within the same academic year.

- *Use rehearsal techniques.* Remember that the duration of STM is about 30 seconds, so to lengthen this time use *maintenance rehearsal*. To effectively encode memory into LTM, use *elaborative rehearsal*, which involves thinking about the material and relating it to other information that has already been stored. Hopefully, you've noticed that we formally define each key term immediately in the text, in the margin, and in the glossary at the back of the book. We also give a brief explanation and one or two examples for each of these terms. When you're studying this text, use these tools to help your elaborative rehearsal, while also making up your own examples. The more elaborate the encoding of information, the more memorable it will be.

- *Improve your organization.* This may be most important key to a good memory. Because the capacity of STM is around seven items, you can expand the capacity of STM by *chunking* (organizing) information into seven or fewer groups. To improve your LTM, create *hierarchies* that organize the material in meaningful patterns. The tables in this book and the visual summaries at the end of each chapter are examples of hierarchies that help you organize chapter material. Be sure to study them carefully — and make up your own whenever possible.

- *Counteract the serial position effect.* Because we tend to remember information that occurs at the beginning or end of a sequence, spend extra time with the information in the middle. When reading or reviewing the text, start at different places — sometimes at the second section, sometimes at the fourth.

- *Manage your time.* Study on a regular basis and avoid cramming. *Distributed* (spaced) learning sessions are more efficient than *massed practice* (cramming). In other words, five separate half-hour sessions tend to produce better consolidation and retention than one session of $2\frac{1}{2}$ hours. When you learn something new, take the time to associate it with what you already know. By doing this, you'll be cataloguing the new information so that you can retrieve it easily. Also, get plenty of sleep, for two reasons: (1) we don't remember information acquired when we're drowsy as well as we do when we're alert and (2) during REM sleep we process and store most of the new information we acquired when awake.

- *Use the encoding specificity principle.* When we form memories, we store them with links to the way we thought about it at the time. Therefore, the closer the retrieval cues are to the original encoding situation the better the retrieval. Because you encode a lot of material during class time, avoid "early takes" or makeup exams generally scheduled in other classrooms. The *context* will be different and your retrieval may suffer. Similarly, when you take a test, try to remain calm and reinstate the psychological and physiological state that you were in when you originally learned the material. According to the *mood congruence* effect, you will recall more if the mood of your test taking matches the mood of the original learning. Also, according to the *state-dependent memory* research, if you normally drink a cup of coffee while studying, you might want to have a cup of coffee before your exam. (Remember: Caffeine is the only drug that could be recommended as a possible study aid.)

- *Employ self-monitoring and overlearning.* Whenever you are studying a text, you should periodically test your understanding of the material. This is why we build in the Check & Review sections throughout each chapter. Stopping to read these reviews and completing the short quiz section will provide personal feedback on your mastery of the material. Even when you are studying a single sentence, you need to monitor your understanding. Poor readers tend to read at the same speed for both easy and difficult material. Good readers tend to recognize when they are having difficulty and they slow down or repeat difficult sentences.

  When you finish reading a chapter or prepare to end a study session, do an additional monitoring of your understanding. If you evaluate your learning only immediately after reading the material, you will overestimate your understanding (because the information is still in STM). If you delay making your judgment (for at least a few minutes), your evaluation will be more accurate (Weaver & Kelemen, 1997). The best way to ensure your full understanding of material (and success on an exam) is through *overlearning* — studying information even after you think you already know it. Don't just study until you *think* you know it; work hard until you *know* you know it!

- *Use mnemonic devices.* We saved this technique for last. **Mnemonic devices** (derived from the Greek word for "memory") are memory aids (or tricks) based on encoding items in a special way. As we mentioned at the beginning of the chapter, some memory experts use these mnemonics to perform amazing feats of recall. However, our experience as educators has been that simple mnemonics can be helpful with shopping lists and some academic tasks, but spending too much time on mnemonics may be more trouble than it's worth. Our students do better with the well-researched principles discussed in the chapter and reviewed above.

  If you would like to try some of the most popular mnemonic techniques, they are listed below:

  - The *method of loci* was developed by early Greek and Roman orators to keep track of the parts of their long speeches. *Loci* is the Latin word for "physical places." Orators would imagine the parts of their speeches attached to places inside a building or, if they were outside, in a courtyard. For example, if an opening point in a speech was the concept of *justice*, they might visualize a courtroom placed in the first corner of their garden to remind them of this point. As they mentally walked around their garden during their speech, they would encounter each of the points to be made in their appropriate order.

  - To use the *peg-word* mnemonic, you first need to memorize a set of 10 visual images that you can use as pegs or markers on which to hang ideas. The easiest system of peg-words is to learn 10 items that rhyme with the numbers they stand for (e.g., *one in a bun, two in a shoe, three in a tree,* and so on). When you can mentally produce the peg-word image for each number, you are ready to use the images as pegs to hold the items of any list. Try it with items you might want to buy on your next trip to the grocery store: milk, eggs, bread, and razor blades. Visualize the first item (milk) with a bun, the second (eggs) with a shoe, and so on. Imagine a soggy bun in a bowl of milk. Imagine a giant shoe stepping on a carton of eggs, slices of bread hanging on a tree, and a giant razor blade as a door, complete with doorknob.

  - The *substitute word* method is useful for when you are learning many new and complicated terms. For example, to remember some of the terms associated

Mnemonic [nih-MON-ik] Device
A memory-improvement technique based on encoding items in a special way

with the brain, break the word to be remembered into parts or use words that sound similar that can be visualized. The word *occipital* can be converted into *ox*, *sip it*, *tall*. Then create a vivid image. (You might visualize an ox on stilts sipping something through a straw.) Try a similar strategy with *parietal* (*pear*, *eye*, *it all*).

- The *method of word associations* is a mnemonic device that creates verbal associations for items to be learned. If you're taking a physics course and must remember the colors of the spectrum, think of a man's name: *Roy G. Biv* (Red, Orange, Yellow, Green, Blue, Indigo, Violet). Or, to recall the names of the Great Lakes for a geography course, think of *HOMES on a great lake* (Huron, Ontario, Michigan, Erie, Superior).

Seven Sins: Final Thoughts on Memory Improvement

Daniel Schacter (1999) from Harvard University wrote an interesting article entitled "The Seven Sins of Memory: Insights from Psychology and Cognitive Neuroscience." The first three sins are types of *forgetting*, the second three involve memory *distortions*, and the last sin is *persistence*. A brief discussion of these seven sins helps summarize the chapter (a form of *elaborative rehearsal*), as well as providing additional tips for memory improvement.

Three Sins of Forgetting

People forget because of three sins: *transience*, *absentmindedness*, and *blocking*. *Transience* means that not all memories are permanent. Even memories that are well encoded at the beginning may eventually be lost. Memory is especially likely to be lost if it is not used over time — "use it or lose it." Using information stored in your LTM creates interconnections and associations with other memories, builds better retrieval cues, and helps prevent storage decay.

Memories are also forgotten because we did not pay attention or take the time to encode the memory well in the first place. *Absentmindedness* at the time of encoding is a significant source of memory loss. You sit in your psychology class, but your mind wanders to other topics during the lecture. If you want to remember the lecture, you have to keep your mind and your attention focused on the lecture. Sit in the front of the room, ask questions, participate in the discussions, and look directly at the instructor. If you do not encode the memory, you cannot retrieve it at a later date.

Blocking occurs when something has been well encoded and retained in memory but cannot be retrieved. Although blocking normally has negative connotations, there are times when it is very helpful. Being unable to retrieve undesirable memories of abuse or the details surrounding the death of a loved one might allow people to better cope with tragedies and unpleasant life events. Elizabeth Loftus's inability to remember the details of her mother's death may be an example of blocking.

Three Sins of Distortion

Our memories are also faulty because of the three sins of distortion — *misattribution*, *suggestibility*, and *bias*. When we incorrectly identify the time, place, or person responsible for a memory, we've committed the sin of *misattribution*. This can happen in several ways:

- We can correctly remember an item or event from our past and misattribute it to an incorrect source.

- We may believe what we're writing or saying is our own creative idea, when in fact we've unintentionally "borrowed" material from others.
- We can recall a real event but believe that it is a fantasy.
- We can recall a fantasy event as real.

(Study tip: Recall that *misattribution* is another term for *source amnesia*, which we discussed earlier as a problem with LTM. To help your *elaborative rehearsal* and retention of this material, think about how it helps explain faulty eyewitness testimony, former President Reagan's confusion over his acting roles and actual historical events, some forms of plagiarism, as well as some cases of false memories.)

Suggestibility is the sin of incorporating information suggested by someone else into our own memory. This can easily happen because of misleading questions, comments, or direct suggestions — particularly at the time of retrieval. A witness can falsely remember a suspect's face after being questioned in a leading manner, and a therapist's comment about "possible signs of sexual assault" may later become a client's false memory. Therefore, it is important for parents, police, and therapists not to attempt to clarify memories with leading questions, comments, or suggestions during recall. (Study tip: Note that *suggestibility* is just another term for the *misinformation effect* discussed earlier as a problem with LTM.)

Memory *bias* occurs when current knowledge and beliefs distort our memory of the past. Most people believe that their beliefs and attitudes have not changed much over time, yet during a divorce, couples tend to only remember the bad things about their marriage. In contrast, couples celebrating their fiftieth wedding anniversary seem to remember "always being in love."

Final Sin of Persistence

And finally, sometimes our memories are better than we would like. Traumatic and extremely emotional events can cause memories to persist even when we would like to forget. This sin of *persistence* is especially noticeable in patients with post-traumatic stress disorder (PTSD). PTSD occurs when a person is exposed to an extremely emotional event or a life-threatening event that evokes extreme horror or helplessness (Chapter 14). This results in nightmares, flashbacks, and an inability to forget the event. The extreme emotional memory that accompanies PTSD may lead to impaired social and mental functioning. (Study tip: Can you see that *persistence* is just another form of *mood congruence* discussed earlier as part of the *encod-*

Memory problems. According to the "sin of persistence," some memories persevere even when they cause tremendous pain and suffering.

ing specificity principle? Persistence may reflect the fact that we tend to remember more negative memories when we're depressed than when we're happy.)

Some of these "seven sins of memory," such as persistence, may be evolutionary adaptations that have helped humans survive. Whatever the reason for these "sins," knowing about them can help us. As we have seen throughout this chapter, our memories are remarkable — yet highly fickle. Recognizing these limits will make us better jurors in the courtroom or consumers of daily news reports when we assess accounts of "eyewitness testimony" and "repressed memories." Knowing the frailties of memory might similarly improve our skills as students, teachers, friends, and, perhaps most importantly, as critical thinkers.

An intellectual is someone whose mind watches itself.

Albert Camus

Check & Review

IMPROVING MEMORY

This chapter offers concrete strategies for improving memory. These include paying attention and reducing interference, using rehearsal techniques (both maintenance and elaborative rehearsal), improving your organization (by chunking and creating hierarchies), counteracting the serial position effect, managing your time, using the encoding specificity principle, employing self-monitoring and overlearning, and using **mnemonic devices**.

According to Daniel Schacter, there are seven sins that affect memory and forgetting. The first three sins are types of *forgetting*, the second three involve memory *distortions*, and the last sin is *persistence*.

Questions

1. How can maintenance rehearsal and elaborative rehearsal improve your memory?

2. Explain how you can overcome the serial position effect while studying.

3. The best way to ensure your full understanding of material (and success on an exam) is through _____.

4. Which mnemonic device is being described in each of the following situations?

   a. You remember items to bring to a meeting by visualizing them in association with a previously learned sequence.

   b. You remember a speech for your communications class by forming visual images of the parts of your speech and associating them with areas in the classroom.

   c. You remember errands you need to run by making up the rhyme "First go to the store, then get books galore. Get my ring and then some gas, and the cleaners at the last."

   d. You remember a new acquaintance's name, Paul Barrington, by linking it to words that can be visualized: *pall-bearing town*.

Answers to Questions can be found in Appendix B.

KEY TERMS

semantic memory (p. 247)
sensory memory (p. 238)
short-term memory (STM) (p. 238)
storage (p. 242)
Ziegarnik effect (p. 249)

Why Do We Forget?
distributed practice (p. 255)
massed practice (p. 255)
proactive interference (p. 258)

relearning (p. 255)
retroactive interference (p. 258)
serial position effect (p. 255)
tip-of-the-tongue phenomenon (TOT)
  (p. 260)

Problems With Memory
Alzheimer's [ALLS-hi-merz] disease
  (AD) (p. 261)
anterograde amnesia (p. 261)

constructive processes (p. 263)
misinformation effect (p. 263)
retrograde amnesia (p. 261)
sleeper effect (p. 263)
source amnesia (p. 263)

Improving Memory
mnemonic [nih-MON-ik] device
  (p. 269)

Visual Summary for Chapter 7 ••••

What is Memory?
The capacity to preserve and recover information, which gives history to our lives.

Traditional Three-Stage Memory Model

Sensory Memory: Holds information just long enough to select items worthy of further processing and sends along to STM.

→

Short-Term Memory (STM): Allows time for brief sorting and organizing of selected information, which is then passed along to LTM.

→ ←

Long-Term Memory (LTM): Relatively permanent storage of all memories.

Encoding, Storage, and Retrieval Approach

Encoding: Specific incoming environmental stimuli are translated into neural messages the brain can understand.

→

Storage: Certain information is selected and organized to save in "files" for permanent storage.

←

Retrieval: Stored files are searched and information recovered.

Integrating the Two Major Approaches

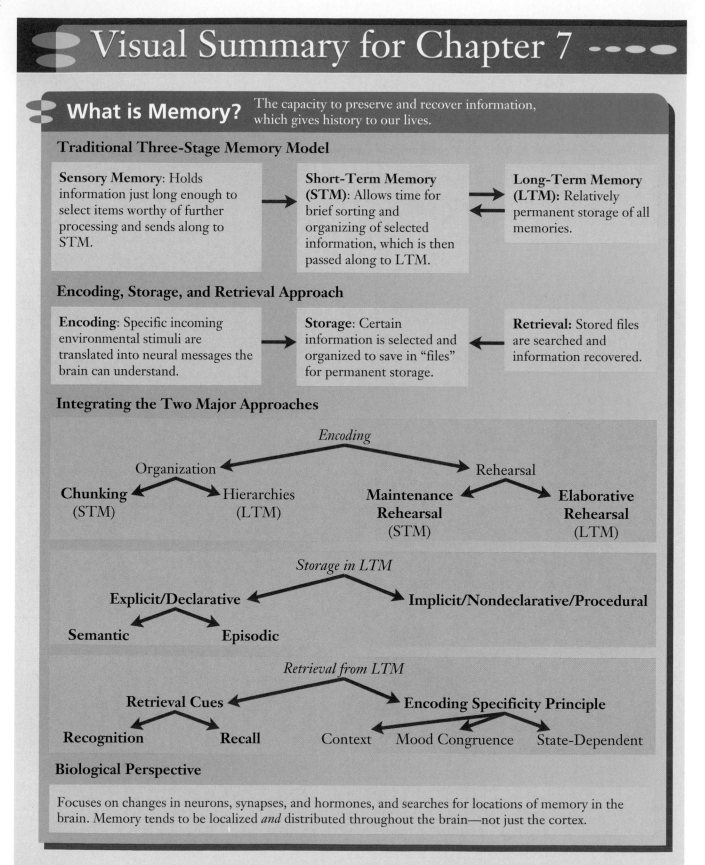

Encoding

Organization ← → Rehearsal

Chunking (STM) ← → Hierarchies (LTM)

Maintenance Rehearsal (STM) ← → **Elaborative Rehearsal** (LTM)

Storage in LTM

Explicit/Declarative ← → **Implicit/Nondeclarative/Procedural**

Semantic ← → **Episodic**

Retrieval from LTM

Retrieval Cues ← → **Encoding Specificity Principle**

Recognition ← → **Recall**

Context ← Mood Congruence → State-Dependent

Biological Perspective

Focuses on changes in neurons, synapses, and hormones, and searches for locations of memory in the brain. Memory tends to be localized *and* distributed throughout the brain—not just the cortex.

Why Do We Forget?

Research Findings

- Ebbinghaus: Found that forgetting occurs most rapidly immediately after learning, but **relearning** usually takes less time than original learning.
- **Serial position effect**: Material at the beginning and end of the list is remembered better than material in the middle.
- Spacing of practice: **Distributed practice** is better than **massed practice**.

Theories of Forgetting

Decay	Memory deteriorates over time.
Interference	Memories forgotten due to **proactive interference** (old information interferes with new) or **retroactive interference** (new information interferes with old).
Motivated Forgetting	Painful, threatening, or embarrassing memories are forgotten.
Encoding Failure	Material from STM to LTM was never successfully encoded.
Retrieval Failure	Information is not forgotten, just temporarily inaccessible.

Problems with Memory

Organic Causes

- *Brain injuries or trauma*: **Retrograde amnesia**, memory is lost for events that occurred before the accident , **Anterograde amnesia** memory is lost for events that occur after an accident.
- *Disease*: **Alzheimer's disease** is a progressive mental deterioration and severe memory loss occurring most commonly in old age.

Constructive Processes

Memory is a **constuctive process** that can have at least 3 major errors:
1) **Source amnesia** where we attribute memories to a wrong source.
2) **Sleeper effect** where we confuse reliable information with unreliable.
3) **Misinformation effect** where we incorporate outside information as our own.

Improving Memory

Specific Tips

- Pay attention and reduce interference.
- Use rehearsal techniques (maintenance for STM and elaborative for LTM).
- Improve organization (chunking for STM and hierarchies for LTM).
- Counteract the serial position effect.
- Time management (distributed versus massed practice).
- Use the encoding specificity principle (including context, mood congruence, and state-dependent retrieval).
- Employ self-monitoring and overlearning.
- Use **mnemonic devices** (method of loci, peg-word, substitute word , and method of word associations).

8

Thinking, Language, and Intelligence

Core Learning Objectives

As you read Chapter 8, keep the following questions in mind and answer them in your own words:

► What is thinking, and how does the brain do it?
► What are the building blocks of thought?
► How do we solve problems?
► What is creativity, and how is it measured?
► What is language, and how is it related to thinking?
► What is intelligence, and how is it measured?
► How do biology, genetics, and the environment influence intelligence?

Are you familiar with this very popular TV game show? Contestants must correctly answer 15 questions to win $1,000,000. After hearing each question, players can answer on their own or elect to use one of their limited number of lifeline helpers: polling the audience, asking a friend over the phone, or having the possible answers narrowed from four to two. They can also choose to quit at any time and walk away with their current winnings.

Were you watching the program when John Carpenter had successfully answered the $500,000 question and was one correct answer away from the million dollars? With only one lifeline remaining and the pressure mounting, the game show host, Regis Philbin, asked the $1,000,000 question: "Which of these U.S. presidents appeared on the television series Laugh-In? (a) Lyndon Johnson, (b) Richard Nixon, (c) Jimmy Carter, (d) Gerald Ford." While using his final remaining lifeline to call his father, John surprised everyone by announcing that he didn't need help from his father; he wanted to call him only so that his father would be on the line while he announced his final answer — Richard Nixon. With this answer, John Carpenter became the first contestant to win $1,000,000. Although the million-dollar question may seem easy, John also answered very difficult questions and even earned the title of "fastest finger" (honoring how quickly he answered the questions). Do you consider John Carpenter intelligent?

What about the famous case of the "wild child" known as Genie? From the age of 20 months until authorities rescued her at age 13 years, Genie had been kept locked in a tiny, windowless room in solitary confinement. By day, she was kept naked and tied to a chair with nothing to do and no one to talk to. At night, she was put in a kind of straitjacket and "caged" in a covered crib. Genie's abusive father forbade anyone to speak to her for the entire 13 years and refused to have a radio or TV in the home. If Genie made any noise, her father would beat her while he barked and growled like a dog. After she was discovered at age 13, linguists and psychologists worked with her intensively for many years, but she never progressed much beyond sentences like "Genie, go" (Curtiss, 1977; Rymer, 1993). With her limited language skills, would you say Genie is intelligent?

What about Thomas, a child who attended school for only 3 months? Despite his lack of formal education and progressive deafness throughout his life, Thomas patented over 1,000 inventions — more than any other single individual in history. His insatiable curiosity led him to study fields ranging from metallurgy to plastics, and long hours of tinkering produced momentous discoveries, including the phonograph, the kinetoscope for motion pictures, and the carbon transmitter for telephones. He has been called the "greatest inventor in American history" (Israel, 1998), yet some have said he was a "technologist rather than a scientist, adding little to original scientific knowledge" (Baldwin, 2001). Did you recognize this as the story of Thomas Edison, the famous inventor of the light bulb? Would you consider him intelligent?

Who Wants To Be A Millionaire? *John Carpenter was the first contestant to win the million dollars. He's pictured here with the show's host, Regis Philbin.*

Thomas Edison with his most famous invention — the light bulb.

I nventing the light bulb or winning a million dollars in a competitive game show obviously requires a large repertoire of thinking processes and intellectual agility. But doesn't Genie's survival also require some form of intelligence? To be intelligent, you must be aware and possess the capacity to learn. But awareness requires thinking, or the mental processing of information. And to express this thinking and intelligence, you need language.

The three topics of this chapter — thinking, language, and intelligence — are often studied together under the larger umbrella of **cognition**, the mental activities of acquiring, storing, retrieving, and using knowledge. In a real sense, we discuss cognition throughout the text, because psychology is "the scientific study of behavior and *mental processes*." In this chapter, however, we will explore cognitive processes in some depth — we will "think about our thinking."

Cognition *The mental activities involved in acquiring, storing, retrieving, and using knowledge*

THINKING

What is thinking and how does the brain do it?

The term *thinking* has several meanings. For example, unsuccessful contestants on the *Who Wants To Be a Millionaire?* game might complain that they "needed more time to think of the right answer," that their particular question was confusing, or that they simply "couldn't think." As you can see, *thinking* involves problem solving and judgment, as well as long-term memory (LTM). Every time you use information and mentally act on it by forming ideas, reasoning, solving problems, drawing conclusions, expressing thoughts, and comprehending the thoughts of others, you are thinking. We begin this section by exploring how our brains perform the basic (but seemingly magical) act of thinking. Next, we examine the building blocks of thought, images, and concepts. Then, we discuss the mental processes and barriers to problem solving and creativity.

The Thinking Brain: Making Connections

Thought processes are distributed throughout the brain in networks of neurons, much like a tightly interwoven galaxy of shooting stars. Like other psychological functions, however, thought processes are also localized. In some instances, especially during problem solving or decision making, our brains are active in a special processing area — the prefrontal cortex. It associates complex ideas, makes plans, forms and initiates attention, and allocates our attention as well. This is also the area involved in multitasking behavior, such as washing the dishes while also talking to your family or friends and simultaneously listening for the doorbell (Koechlin, Basso, Pietrini, Panzer, & Grafman, 1999).

The prefrontal cortex also links to other areas of the brain to synthesize information from several senses, as well as to the limbic system, which is the center of our emotions. As you recall from Chapter 2, Phineas Gage, the railroad foreman whose brain was pierced by an iron rod, suffered damage to his prefrontal cortex. Like Gage, patients with damage to this region can solve problems, manipulate information in working memory, and generally have little trouble recalling events from the recent or distant past. However, they do have difficulty controlling their emotions and in making connections between their feelings and thoughts (Damasio, 1999). Interestingly, when other areas of the prefrontal cortex are damaged, the person may experience little or no emotion, and they also have significant problems in thinking and decision making (Bechara, Damasio, Damasio, & Lee, 1999; Damasio, 1994). In sum, whether it is because of links to emotion or the processing of complex ideas, regions of the prefrontal cortex may be the part of the brain most actively involved with thought.

Cognitive Building Blocks: The Foundation of Thought

Thinking involves three basic building blocks — *mental images*, *concepts*, and *language*. When you're thinking about your sweetheart, you may have a mental image of him or her in your mind. You might also think in terms of concepts or categories, such as *woman, man, strong, happy*. And you may have in mind linguistic statements such as "I wish I could be with him or her right now instead of reading this text." (Study tip: Keep in mind the *law of effect* from Chapter 6 — *rewarded behaviors are more likely to recur*. If you want to improve your study habits, use "time with your sweetheart" as reinforcement *after* you finish studying.) In this section, we will discuss the role of images and concepts in thinking. Language will be considered in a later section.

What are the building blocks of thought?

Mental imagery. Can you imagine what this mountain climber is visualizing in his "mind's eye?" Constant use of mental imagery is critical to his success.

Mental Images

Stop for a moment and think about a warm, sandy ocean beach. Do you see tall palms swaying in the wind? Can you smell the salty ocean water and hear the laughter of the children playing in the surf? What you've just created in your mind's eye is a **mental image**, a mental representation of a sensory experience. As you noticed, mental imagery is not limited to the visual sense — you also experience auditory, olfactory, tactile, motor, and gustatory imagery (McKellar, 1972).

Where is this mental image located? According to research, we all have a fixed-size mental space (similar to the screen of a computer monitor) where we mentally

Mental Images *The mind's representation of a sensory experience, including visual, auditory, gustatory, motor, olfactory, and tactile elements (e.g., visualizing a train and hearing its whistle)*

TRY THIS *Yourself*

Look at the four geometrical patterns below. Can you see why the two forms in (a) are the same but the two forms in (b) are different? Solution to this problem requires mental manipulation of the patterns. (Those of you who are familiar with the computer game *Tetris* might find this puzzle rather simple. Others might want to turn to Appendix B for an explanation of the answer.)

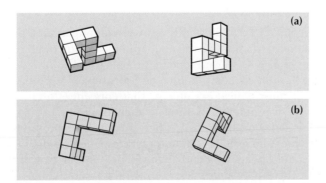

(a)

(b)

visualize and manipulate our sensory images (Brewer & Pani, 1996; Kosslyn, 1987). In fact, some of our most creative moments come when we're forming mental images and manipulating them. Albert Einstein said that his first insight into relativity theory occurred when he pictured a beam of light and imagined himself chasing after it at its own speed.

Concepts

Concept *A mental category that groups objects, events, activities, or ideas that share similar characteristics (e.g., the concept of river groups together the Nile, the Amazon, and the Mississippi because they share the common characteristic of being a large stream of water that empties into an ocean or lake)*

In addition to mental images, our thinking also involves **concepts** — mental representations of a group or category. We form concepts by grouping objects, events, activities, or ideas that share similar characteristics (Smith, 1995). Our mental concept of *car* represents a large group of objects that share similar characteristics (vehicles with four wheels, seating space for at least one person, and a generally predictable shape). We also form concepts for ideas, such as *honesty*, *intelligence*, or *pornography*. These ideas, however, are often our own individual constructions that may or may not be shared by others. Therefore, it's generally harder to communicate about honesty than about a car.

Concepts are an essential part of thinking and communication because they simplify and organize information. Imagine being Genie, the "wild child" described at the beginning of the chapter. If you had been confined to a small, windowless room your entire life, how would you process the world around you without the use of concepts? Normally, when you see a new object or encounter a new situation, you relate it to your existing conceptual structure and categorize it according to where it fits. For example, if you see a rectangular box with moving pictures and sound and people are staring at it, you safely assume it is a TV set. Even though you've never encountered this specific brand before, you understand the concept of *TV set*. But if you were Genie, how would you process a TV set, a telephone, or even a bathroom? Without concepts, each object, event, and activity would be one of a kind. Can you see why she might have had difficulty adjusting to this world and learning language?

How do we learn concepts? There are at least three major methods: *artificial concepts*, *natural concepts*, and *hierarchies*:

1. Artificial concepts. Some of our concepts arise out of logical rules or definitions. For example, consider the concept of *triangle*, a geometric figure with three sides and three angles. Using this definition, we would group together and classify all three-sided geometric forms as triangles. If any of the defining features were missing, we would not include the object in the concept of triangle. These concepts are called *artificial* (or *formal*) because the rules for inclusion are so sharply defined. Artificial concepts are often found in the sciences and other academic disciplines. As we will see in the upcoming discussion of language, for example, psychologists (and other scientists) have created specific rules for what is labeled "language" and what is labeled "communication."

Prototype *A typical, highly representative example that serves as a model on which other examples are based or judged (e.g., baseball is a prototype of the concept of sports)*

2. Natural concepts. In real life, however, we seldom use such precise, logical definitions. For example, when we see a small animal, we don't immediately turn to our *artificial concept* of *bird* — warm-blooded animals that fly, have wings, and lay eggs. Instead, we use *natural concepts*, known as **prototypes**. A prototype is essentially a "best example" or most typical example of that concept (Rosch, 1973). Most of us have a model bird, or prototype, in mind — such as a robin or a sparrow — that captures for us the essence of "birdness." When we develop a prototype in our mind, we abstract out the most important common features from the definition — most birds have wings, fly, and lay eggs — and then choose one or two prototypes (robin or sparrow) that fit these characteristics.

Prototypes provide a mental shortcut that helps us quickly and efficiently classify information. However, when confronted with a new item, like *penguin*, we cannot use our prototype robin. In this case, we need time to review our artificial concept (the definition of *bird*). Because the penguin doesn't fly, it takes longer to classify. For most of us, our prototype robin is a "birdier bird."

3. *Hierarchies.* When an object fits into more than one category (for example, a bird is also an animal), we tend to organize these concepts into successive ranks, or *hierarchies*, with specific concepts grouped as subcategories within broader concepts. Note in Figure 8.1 (a) how the top (superordinate) category of *animals* is very broad and includes lots of members, the midlevel categories of *bird* and *dog*, are more specific but still rather general, and the lowest (subordinate) categories of *parakeet* and *poodle* are the most specific.

Interestingly, research shows that we first learn and most commonly use the middle categories, which are called *basic-level* concepts (Rosch, 1978). For example, children tend to learn *bird* or *dog* before they learn superordinate concepts like *animals* or subordinate concepts like *parakeet* and *poodle*. Even when we as adults are shown a picture of a parakeet, we first classify it as a bird before thinking of the concepts of *animal* or *parakeet*.

As you learned in Chapter 6, organization and hierarchies are essential to efficient encoding and storage in LTM. If children did not build a mental hierarchy of *animal*, *bird*, and *parakeet*, they would have a terrible time trying to label or memorize the definition of each. You may have a similar problem if you attempted to simply memorize a long list of chapter Key Terms. It's much easier to master a large amount of material when it's organized into a hierarchy. This is one of the main reasons we include so many tables throughout this text and the visual summaries at the end of each chapter. It is even better if you develop your own hierarchies. For example, to help you master the material in this section, you could create a hierarchy similar to Figure 8.1b.

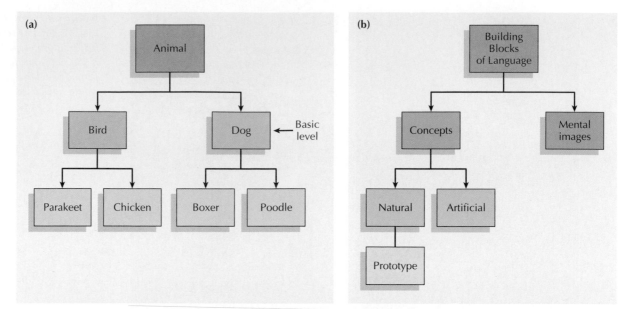

Figure 8.1 *Can hierarchies improve both thinking and exam scores?* (a) When we think, we naturally organize concepts according to superordinate and subordinate classes. We organize *concepts*, like *animals* or *birds*, with the most general concept at the top and the most specific at the bottom, and research shows we use the middle, *basic level* when initially categorizing objects and later add the upper and lower levels. Although they may look complicated, hierarchies significantly reduce the time and effort necessary for learning. For example, when you learn that all animals have mitochondria in their cells, you don't have to relearn that fact each time you learn a new animal species. (b) Hierarchies can be generated from almost any set of interrelated facts and can be used to provide a similar savings in time and effort. For example, instead of focusing on and attempting to memorize the key terms of *concepts*, *mental images*, and *prototype*, you should begin by making a hierarchy of how these terms are interrelated. Once you have this "big picture," it speeds up your mastery of the material, which translates into better exam scores.

Check & Review

THE THINKING BRAIN AND COGNITIVE BUILDING BLOCKS

Cognition, or thinking, is defined as mental activities involved in acquiring, storing, retrieving, and using knowledge. Thought processes are distributed throughout the brain in neural networks. Almost the entire cerebral cortex is activated when thinking involves forming mental representations. During problem solving and decision making, our thoughts are localized for special processing within the frontal lobes.

The prefrontal cortex links to other areas of the brain to synthesize information from several senses. It is also connected to the limbic system. Without connecting thoughts to feelings, solving problems and making decisions would be difficult.

The three basic building blocks of cognition are mental images, concepts, and language. **Mental images** are mental representations of a sensory experience, including visual, auditory, gustatory, motor, olfactory, or tactile elements. **Concepts** are mental categories that group objects, events, activities, or ideas that share similar characteristics. (Language is discussed in a later section.)

There are three ways we learn concepts: (1) *Artificial concepts* are formed by logical, specific rules or characteristics. (2) *Natural concepts* are formed by experience in everyday life. When we are confronted with a new item, we compare it with the **prototype** (most typical) of that concept. (3) Concepts are generally organized into *hierarchies*. We most frequently use the middle, basic-level concepts, when first learning material.

Questions

1. All of the following are examples of concepts EXCEPT _____. (a) trees; (b) tools; (c) blue; (d) umbrellas

2. How do we learn concepts?

3. When asked to describe the shape and color of an apple, you probably rely on a _____.

4. For most psychologists, language is a formal _____, whereas the public generally uses fuzzy _____. (a) definition, descriptions; (b) artificial concept, natural concepts; (c) mental image, concepts; (d) superordinate concept, basic-level concepts

Answers to Questions can be found in Appendix B.

Solving Problems: Three Steps to the Goal

Several years ago in Los Angeles, a 12-foot-high tractor-trailer rig tried to pass under a bridge 11 feet 6 inches high. As you might expect, the truck got stuck, unable to move forward or back, thus causing a huge traffic jam. After hours of towing, tugging, and pushing, the police and transportation workers were stumped. About this time, a young boy happened upon the scene and asked, "Why don't you let some air out of the tires?" It was a simple, creative suggestion — and it worked.

Our everyday lives are filled with problems, some easier to solve than others. For example, figuring a way to make coffee without a filter is much easier than rescuing 118 Russian navy seamen trapped inside a submarine at the bottom of the Barents Sea. In all cases, though, problem solving requires moving from a *given state* (the problem) to a *goal state* (the solution), a process that usually involves three steps (Bourne, Dominowski, & Loftus, 1979).

Step 1: *Preparation.* Using the introductory story of the *Millionaire* contestants, there are at least three separate components to successful preparation:

- *Identifying given facts.* Contestants probably watched every program and carefully memorized the rules for the game.

- *Separating relevant from irrelevant facts.* Contestants might have tried to identify patterns in the questions. For example, if they noticed that many questions focused on historical facts and rarely on great literature, they might have reviewed history because it was relevant and didn't spend much time on facts about great literature.

- *Defining the ultimate goal.* This part of the preparation stage was easy for the contestants: They all wanted to win as much money as possible and they hoped for the full million dollars! But defining the goal isn't always this easy. The adults in the "stuck truck" problem thought the goal was to pull or push the truck from under the bridge. Only when the child defined the goal as freeing the truck did a solution present itself. Solving a problem often depends on how broadly we define the goal.

Step 2: *Production.* During the *production step*, the problem solver produces possible solutions, called *hypotheses*. There are at least two major approaches to generating hypotheses — *algorithms* and *heuristics*:

- An **algorithm** is a step-by-step procedure that, if appropriate to the problem, will always produce the solution. Math problems are ideal for demonstrating algorithms: An algorithm for solving the problem 2×10 is $2 + 2 + 2 + 2 + 2 + 2 + 2 + 2 + 2 + 2$. Algorithms will eventually lead to the correct answer, but for complex problems they may take a long time. Given the limited time allowed for finding solutions during the *Millionaire* game show, the contestants were unlikely to use algorithms. However, they are an excellent way to balance your checkbook or compute your grade point average. Computers are especially well suited for algorithms because they can quickly perform millions of calculations and logical operations in a step-by-step solution to a problem.

- A **heuristic** is a simple rule of thumb, or educated guess, resulting from watching others or developed from direct experience with similar problems. *Millionaire* contestants who decide to quit and protect their previous winnings might have watched previous contestants and developed a heuristic called "quit while you're ahead." Unlike algorithms, which generally require a lot of time, heuristics provide shortcuts to solutions because they examine only the options most likely to produce a solution. However, heuristics are error prone and do not guarantee a solution — they work most of the time, but not always.

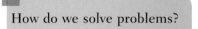

How do we solve problems?

A failure of problem solving? On August 12, 2000, the Russian nuclear submarine "Kursk" sank as a result of a torpedo room explosion and all 118 men perished. Would faster or better problem solving have saved them?

Algorithm *A problem-solving strategy that guarantees a solution if correctly applied; it involves a step-by-step procedure, and as such, is particularly suited to use by a computer for math problems*

Heuristic *Problem-solving strategies, or rules of thumb, used as shortcuts to complex solutions, which generally, but not always, lead to a solution.*

TRY THIS Yourself

Practice your newfound understanding of the steps in solving problems with this classic thinking problem (Bartlett, 1958). Your task is to determine the numerals 0 through 9 that are represented by letters, with each letter representing a separate, distinct number. You get one hint before you start: D = 5.

D O N A L D
+ G E R A L D
R O B E R T

Did you try solving this problem with an algorithm? If so, you probably wasted a lot of time. There are 362,880 possible com-binations of letters and numbers. At the rate of one combination per minute, 8 hours per day, 5 days a week, 52 weeks a year, it would take nearly 3 years to try all the possible combinations.

A heuristic approach is much easier and quicker. If you successfully solved the problem, you probably used the "creating subgoals" heuristic. You employed previous knowledge of arithmetic to set subgoals, such as determining what number T rep-resents (if D = 5, then D + D = 10, so T = 0, with a carryover of 1 into the tens col-umn). The complete answer is at the end of the next Check & Review section.

Several heuristics are particularly helpful in college, including (1) *means–end analysis*, (2) *working backward*, and (3) *creating subgoals* (Table 8.1). Successful college students seem to be particularly good at breaking down a solution into subgoals. When you're faced with a heavy schedule of exams and term papers, try creating subgoals to make the problem more man-ageable and increase the likelihood of reaching the overarching solution — a college degree.

Step 3: *Evaluation.* Once the hypotheses are generated, they must be evaluated to see if they meet the criteria defined in step 1. If one or more of the hypotheses meet the criteria, the problem is solved. If not, then you must return to the production stage and produce more possible solutions. Keep in mind, however, that "action must follow solution." Once the little boy solved the "stuck truck" problem, some-one had to follow through and actually let some air out of the tires. Similarly, once you use the "means–end analysis" heuristic (Table 8.1) to solve your problem (get-ting an A in your psychology course), you must follow through and implement the necessary solution — more and improved study time.

Barriers to Problem Solving

Do you find that you can solve some problems easily yet seem to have a mental block when it comes to others? You're not alone; we all encounter barriers that prevent us from effectively solving problems. Three of the most common barriers are *mental sets*, *functional fixedness*, and *confirmation bias*:

1. Mental sets. Like the police and transportation workers who were trying to pull or shove the truck that was stuck under the bridge, have you ever persisted in attack-ing problems using the same or similar solutions that have worked in the past? This is known as a **mental set**. Although pulling and shoving obviously works sometimes, in this instance the old solution created a mental barrier to new, and possibly more effective, solutions (such as deflating the tires). The habit (or *mental set*) of working arithmetic problems from the right (ones) column to the left also explains why most people fail to see the solution to the DONALD + GERALD problem. Similarly, men-tal sets block some college students from using the SQ4R (Survey, Question, Read,

Mental Set *A mental barrier to prob-lem solving that occurs when people apply only methods that have worked in the past rather than trying innova-tive ones*

TABLE 8.1 PROBLEM-SOLVING HEURISTICS

Problem-Solving Heuristics	Description	Example
Means–end analysis	The problem solver determines what measure would reduce the difference between the given state and the goal. Once the means to reach the goal are determined, the problem is solved.	You want an A in your psychology course. You ask your professor for suggestions, you interview several A students to compare and contrast their study habits, you assess your own study habits, and then determine the specific means (the number of hours and which study techniques) required to meet your end goal of an A.
Working backward	An approach that starts with the solution, a known condition, and works backward through the problem. Once the search has revealed the steps to be taken, the problem is solved.	Deciding you want to be an experimental psychologist, you ask your psychology professor and career counselor to recommend courses, graduate and undergraduate colleges and universities, areas to emphasize, and so on. Then you write the recommended college(s) requesting information on their admission policies and standards. You then plan your current college courses accordingly and work hard to meet (or exceed) the admission standards.
Creating subgoals	Large, complex problems are broken down into a series of small subgoals. These subgoals then serve as a series of stepping-stones that can be taken one at a time to reach the original large goal.	To write a successful college term paper, you choose a topic, go to the library and Internet to locate information related to the topic, organize the information, write an outline, write the paper, review the paper, rewrite, rewrite again, and submit the final paper on or before the due date.

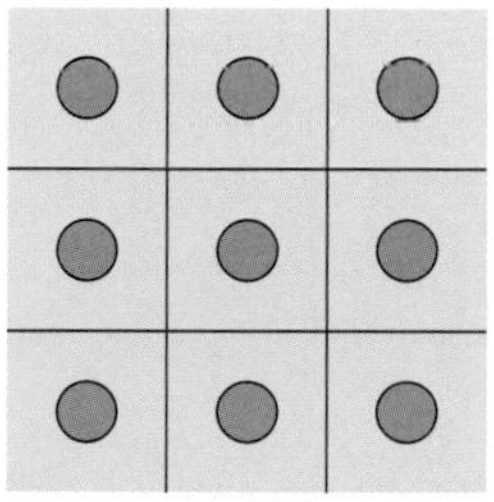

Figure 8.2 The nine-dot problem. Draw no more than four lines that run through all nine dots on this page without lifting your pencil from the paper. (See Figure 8.3, page 286, for the solution.)

Figure 8.4 Overcoming functional fixedness. Can you use these supplies to mount the candle on a wall so that it can be lit in a normal way?

Functional Fixedness *A barrier to problem solving that occurs when people are unable to recognize novel uses for an object because they are so familiar with its common use*

Recite, Review, and wRite) method or other study techniques described in the Tools for Student Success at the end of Chapter 1. Their reliance on past study habits blocks them from considering newer and more efficient strategies. If we try to be flexible in our thinking, we can offset the natural tendency toward mental sets. To practice your flexibility, try the nine-dot problem in Figure 8.2.

2. Functional fixedness. The tendency to view objects as functioning only in the usual or customary way is known as **functional fixedness**. Suppose you wanted to make coffee in your automatic coffee maker but were out of filters. Would you dig through the trash looking for an old, dirty filter without thinking of using paper towels? What if you were given the objects shown in Figure 8.4 and asked to mount the candle on the wall so that it could be easily lit in the normal fashion, with no danger of toppling (Duncker, 1945)? How would you do this? Think about it before you read on.

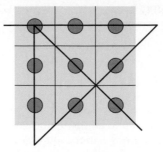

Figure 8.3 *Solution to the nine-dot problem.* People find this puzzle difficult because they see the arrangement of dots as a square. This *mental set* limits possible solutions because they "naturally" assume they can't go out of the boundaries of the square.

Figure 8.5 *The solution to the candle problem in Figure 8.4.* Use the tacks to mount the matchbox tray to the wall. Stand the candle on the tray and light the candle.

The solution is to empty the box, use the tacks to attach it to the wall, light the candle, drop some melted wax on the bottom of the box, then set the candle in the dripped wax (Figure 8.5). In the original test, research participants had a much more difficult time solving the problem when the box was filled with matches than when it was presented with the matches separately. In the former situation, the participants saw the box as only a container for matches and overlooked it as a useful item in itself. When you use a table knife instead of a screwdriver to tighten a screw, you have overcome functional fixedness.

3. *Confirmation bias.* Have you noticed how politicians frequently accept opinion polls that support their political views and ignore those that don't? Have you caught yourself agreeing with psychological theories that support your personal biases and discounting conflicting theories? This inclination to seek out evidence that confirms our own hypotheses, while at the same time discounting or overlooking contradictory evidence is known as **confirmation bias** (Nickerson, 1998). This phenomenon was first demonstrated by British researcher Peter Wason (1968) with the following test:

Confirmation Bias *The tendency to seek out and pay attention to information that confirms existing positions or beliefs while at the same time ignoring contradictory information*

| Can you guess the rule? | 2 | 4 | 6 |

Wason asked participants to guess the rule that applied to this same three-numbered set. Before submitting their rule, participants were also asked to generate additional sets of numbers that conformed to their hypothesized rule. The participants generated sets, such as (4, 6, 8) or (1, 3, 5). These sets reflected their commonly shared (but unspoken) guess that the rule was "numbers increasing by two." (Is this the same rule you generated?)

Each time the participants presented their list of numbers, Wason assured them their set of numbers conformed to the rule. However, when Wason later informed them that the rule "numbers increasing by 2" was incorrect, they were very frustrated. The actual rule was "numbers in increasing order of magnitude." (Did you guess the correct rule?) The barrier to solving this problem was that participants searched only for confirming information and failed to look for evidence that would disprove their hypothesis. If they had proposed a series, such as 1, 3, 4 instead, they would have discovered that their initial hypothesis was incorrect and they could have easily discovered the correct rule.

Solving Problems in College Life

Critical thinking requires adaptive, flexible approaches to thinking and problem solving. Given that your success in college requires overcoming a number of problems in both school and life, the following exercise offers practice in critical thinking, new insights into common college-related problems, and a quick review of terms and concepts discussed in this section of the chapter.

Before you begin, you may want to review the major problem-solving approaches we discussed — *algorithms* (step-by-step procedures that guarantee solu-tions) and *heuristics* (generating possible solutions based on previous knowledge and experience). See Table 8.1 for three specific heuristics: *means–end analysis*, *working backward*, and *creating subgoals*.

Below, you will find two problems. For each problem, answer the following questions:

1. What was your first step in approaching the problem?

2. Which problem-solving approach did you select and why?

3. Did you consider potential obstacles, such as mental sets, functional fixed-ness, and confirmation bias during the problem-solving process?

Problem 1 It is the end of the semester and you have a paper due Friday. Thursday afternoon, after studying for an exam, you turn on your computer to print your paper and can't find the file on your computer. How will you find the file?

Problem 2 The financial aid office has refused to give you your student loan until you verify how much money you made last year. You need to find your pay stubs to verify income.

If I leave an especially difficult problem alone for a while and return to it later, I sometimes find the answer just pops into my mind. Why is that? Some problems require a period of **incubation**, or time out, to allow the facts and possibil-ities to come into better focus. Wolfgang Kohler (1925) observed incubation in his chimpanzee Sultan. As described in Chapter 6, Sultan was presented with a banana that was out of reach and only two sticks at his disposal. Initially, the chimp was stumped. After a few weeks' incubation, however, the solution came to him in a flash of "insight." He fitted the two sticks together and successfully reached the banana.

Incubation *A period of time during which active searching for a problem's solution is set aside; this is sometimes necessary for a successful solution of the problem*

Check & Review

SOLVING PROBLEMS

Problem solving entails three steps: *prepa-ration*, *production*, and *evaluation*. During the preparation stage, we identify given facts, separate relevant from irrelevant facts, and define the ultimate goal.

During the production stage, we generate possible situations, called hypotheses. We typically generate hypotheses by using **algo-rithms** and **heuristics**. Algorithms, as problem-solving strategies, are guaranteed to lead to a solution eventually, but they are not practical in many situations. Heuristics, or simplified rules of thumb that are based on experience, are much faster but do not guarantee a solution. Three common heuris-tics are *means–end analysis*, *working back-ward*, and *creating subgoals*.

The evaluation step in problem solving involves judging the hypotheses generated during step two (production stage) against the criteria established in step one (prepa-ration stage).

Three major barriers to successful problem solving are **mental sets**, **func-tional fixedness**, and **confirmation bias**. Some problems require a period of **incubation**, or time out, before a solution is apparent.

Questions

1. List and describe the three stages of problem solving.

2. Rosa is shopping in a new supermarket and wants to find a specific type of mustard. Which problem-solving strat-egy would be most efficient? (a) algo-rithm; (b) heuristic; (c) instinct; (d) mental set.

3. Before a new product arrives in the store, a manufacturer goes through several stages, including designing, building, testing a prototype, setting up a production line, and so on. This approach is called (a) working back-ward; (b) means–end analysis; (c) diver-gent thinking; (d) creating subgoals.

4. What are three barriers to problem solving, and how might incubation be useful in overcoming these obstacles?

Answers to Questions can be found in Appendix B.

Solution to the DONALD + GERALD = ROBERT problem:

```
    5 2 6 4 8 5
+   1 9 7 4 8 5
  -------------
    7 2 3 9 7 0
```

Creativity: Finding Unique Solutions

What is creativity, and how is it measured?

Creativity *The generation of ideas that are original, novel, and useful*

Divergent Thinking *Thinking that produces many alternatives or ideas; a major element of creativity (e.g., finding as many uses as possible for a paper clip)*

Convergent Thinking *Conventional thinking; thinking directed toward a single correct answer (e.g., standard academic tests generally require convergent thinking)*

Are you a creative person? Like most students, you may think of only painters, dancers, and composers as creative and may fail to recognize examples of your own creativity. Even when doing ordinary tasks, such as taking notes in class, you are being somewhat creative — unless you're copying the lecture verbatim. Similarly, if you've ever tightened a screw with a penny or used a magazine to splint a broken arm, you've found creative solutions to problems. All of us, to a greater or lesser degree, exhibit a certain amount of creativity in some aspects of life. Whether a solution or performance is considered creative often depends on its need and usefulness at the time (Weisberg, 1993). Definitions of creativity vary among psychologists and between cultures, but it is generally agreed that **creativity** is the ability to produce valued outcomes in a novel way (Bink & Marsh, 2000; Boden, 2000).

Measuring Creativity

Creative thought is associated with three special characteristics: *originality, fluency,* and *flexibility*. As you can see in Table 8.2, Thomas Edison's invention of the ligh bulb offers a prime example of each of these characteristics. In addition to the three characteristics of creativity, there is a distinct type of thinking that is related to creativity, called **divergent thinking**, where many possibilities are developed from a single starting point (Baer, 1994). The opposite of divergent thinking is **convergent thinking**, or *conventional thinking*. In this case, lines of thinking converge (come together) on the answer, and we select a single correct solution from among several alternatives. You used convergence in the DONALD + GERALD problem to find the one correct number represented by each letter.

Divergent thinking is the type of thinking most often associated with creativity and is thus the focus of most tests of creativity. In the *Unusual Uses Test*, the person is asked to think of as many uses as possible for an object (such as "How many ways can you use a brick?"). In the *Anagrams Test*, people are asked to reorder the letters in a word to make as many new words as possible. A type of anagram test is found in the following six groups of letters. Try rearranging these letters in these words to make new words, and then decide what they share in common. (Answers are listed after the Check & Review for this section.)

1. grevenidt _____
2. neleecitlgn _____
3. ytliibxilef _____
4. ptoyropet _____
5. yvitcearti _____
6. niubcaiotn _____

TABLE 8.2 THREE ELEMENTS OF CREATIVE THINKING

	Explanations	Thomas Edison Examples
Originality	Seeing unique or different solutions to a problem	After noting that electricity passing through a conductor produced a glowing red or white heat, Edison imagined capturing this light for practical uses.
Fluency	Generating a large number of possible solutions	Edison tried literally hundreds of different materials to find one that would heat to the point of glowing white heat without burning up.
Flexibility	Shifting with ease from one type of problem-solving strategy to another	When he couldn't find a long-lasting material, he thought of heating it in a vacuum — thereby creating the first lightbulb.

TABLE 8.3 RESOURCES OF CREATIVE PEOPLE

Intellectual Ability	Knowledge	Thinking Style	Personality	Motivation	Environment
Enough intelligence to see problems in a new light	Sufficient basic knowledge of the problem to effectively evaluate possible solutions	Pursue their own novel ideas and can distinguish between the worthy and worthless	Willing to grow and change, take risks, and work to overcome obstacles	Sufficient motivation to accomplish the task; internal rather than external motivation is best	Creative people need to work in an environment that supports creativity

Researching Creativity

Some researchers view creativity as a special talent or ability and therefore look for common personality traits among people they define as creative (Guilford, 1967; Jausovec & Jausovec, 2000). Other researchers explain the distinction between creative and noncreative people in terms of cognitive processes. That is, creative and noncreative people differ in life experiences, how they encode information, how they store it, and in what information they generate to solve problems (Bink & Marsh, 2000; Cooper, 2000; Jacoby, Levy, & Steinbach, 1992).

According to Sternberg and Lubart's *investment theory* (1992, 1999), creative people are willing to "buy low and sell high" in the realm of ideas. They buy low by championing ideas that they feel have potential but that most people think are worthless or worth very little. Once their creative ideas are supported and highly valued, they "sell high" and move on to another unpopular but promising idea.

Investment theory also suggests that creativity requires the coming together of six different but interrelated resources: intellectual ability, knowledge, thinking style, personality, motivation, and environment (Goertz, 2000; Sternberg & Lubart, 1999). These resources are summarized in Table 8.3. One way to improve your personal creativity is to study this list and then strengthen yourself in those areas that you think need improvement.

TRY THIS
Yourself

Do you want to test your creativity? Try the following. (See Figure 8.6 for the solution.)

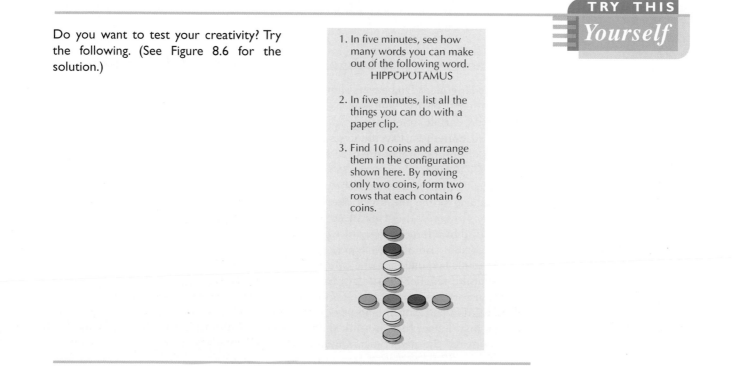

1. In five minutes, see how many words you can make out of the following word. HIPPOPOTAMUS

2. In five minutes, list all the things you can do with a paper clip.

3. Find 10 coins and arrange them in the configuration shown here. By moving only two coins, form two rows that each contain 6 coins.

Check & Review

CREATIVITY

Creativity is the generation of ideas that are original, novel, and useful. Creative thinking involves *originality*, *fluency*, and *flexibility*. **Divergent thinking**, trying to generate as many solutions as possible, is a special type of thinking involved in creativity. In contrast, **convergent thinking**, or conventional thinking, works toward a single solution to a problem and is not related to creativity.

The investment theory of creativity proposes that creative people "buy low" by pursuing promising but unpopular ideas and "sell high" by developing the ideas until they are widely accepted. It also proposes that creativity depends on six specific resources: intellectual ability, knowledge, thinking style, personality, motivation, and environment.

Questions

1. Which of the following items would MOST likely appear on a test measuring creativity? (a) How long is the Ohio River? (b) What are the primary colors? (c) List all the uses of a pot. (d) Who was the first governor of New York?

2. Identify the type of thinking for each of these examples.
   a. You create numerous excuses ("reasons") for not studying.
   b. On a test, you must select one correct answer for each question.
   c. You make a list of ways to save money.

3. According to investment theory, what are the six resources necessary for creativity?

4. As a music teacher, you would like your students to create their own songs. Should you offer a prize as an incentive for the most creative song? Why or why not?

Answers to Questions can be found in Appendix B.

Solutions to the Anagrams Test
1. divergent
2. intelligence
3. flexibility
4. prototype
5. creativity
6. incubation

The answers are key terms found in this chapter.

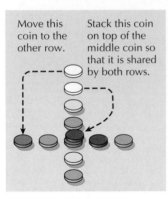

Move this coin to the other row.

Stack this coin on top of the middle coin so that it is shared by both rows.

Figure 8.6 *Coin problem solution.* Stack one coin on top of the middle coin so that it shares both the row and the column.

What is language, and how is it related to thinking?

LANGUAGE

Any discussion of human thought processes must include a discussion of language. As mentioned earlier, language (along with mental images and concepts) is a foundation or building block of thinking. Language enables us to mentally manipulate symbols, thereby expanding our thinking. Most importantly, whether it's spoken, written, or signed, language allows us to communicate our thoughts, ideas, and feelings.

Characteristics of Language: Structure and Production

What is language? Do beavers slapping their tails, birds singing their songs, and ants laying their trails use language? Not according to a strict scientific definition. As we discussed earlier, scientists develop precise definitions and restrictions for certain **artificial concepts.** Psychologists, linguists, and other scientists define *language* as a form of communication whereby we put together sounds and symbols according to specified rules.

Beavers, birds, and ants obviously communicate. Even amoebae seem to send and receive crude messages chemically by discharging small amounts of carbon dioxide. However, this type of communication is believed to be simple, ritualistic, and bound by a limited repertoire of sounds or movements that are performed whenever a certain stimulus evokes them. In short, it is *instinctive* behavior.

Human language, on the other hand, is largely *learned* — passed on from parent to child, teacher to student, friend to friend. Despite the complexity of communication patterns among some nonhuman animals, these patterns differ significantly from human patterns of language. For example, because animal call systems are primarily instinctive, they are inflexible — each call almost always has the same form and conveys the same meaning. In contrast, once the rules of a language are learned, humans use them in creative and complex ways to convey their thoughts and feelings to others.

Building Blocks of Language

To produce language, we first build words using *phonemes* and *morphemes*. Then we string words into sentences using rules of *grammar* (*syntax* and *semantics*) (Table 8.4):

1. *Phonemes.* The basic building blocks of language are sounds of speech called **phonemes**. These basic speech sounds make up every language. The English language has about 40 or so phonemes. Each one has distinctive features, such as variations in sound (like the letter *a* in *am* and *ape*) or unvoiced versus voiced components (when we say *s*, we simply hiss; when we say *z*, we do the same but add the voice).

2. *Morphemes.* Phonemes are combined to form the second building block of language, morphemes. **Morphemes** are the smallest *meaningful* units of language. Morphemes are divided into two types: (a) *content morphemes*, which hold the basic meaning of a word, such as *cat*, and (b) *function morphemes*, which are prefixes and suffixes, such as *un-*, *dis-*, *-able*, and *-ing*. Function morphemes add additional meaning to the word.

3. *Grammar.* Phonemes, morphemes, words, and phrases are joined together by the third building block of language, the rules of **grammar**. Grammatical rules govern how to combine phonemes into morphemes and words, how to use various classes of words (nouns, verbs, etc.) and their inflections (plurals, verb tenses, etc.), and how to choose and order words to form meaningful sentences. Grammar is made up of two components, syntax and semantics.

- **Syntax.** The grammatical rules for ordering words in sentences are known as rules of **syntax**. By the time we are able to read, our syntactical sense is so

Phoneme [FOE-neem] *The most basic unit of speech; an individual speech sound*

Morpheme [MOR-feem] *The smallest meaningful unit of language, formed from a combination of phonemes*

Grammar *The rules of a language that specify how phonemes, morphemes, words, and phrases should be combined to meaningfully express thoughts*

Syntax *The grammatical rules that specify in what order the words and phrases should be arranged in a sentence to convey meaning*

TABLE 8.4 BUILDING BLOCKS OF LANGUAGE

Blocks	Description	Example
Phonemes	The smallest units of sound that make up every language	*p* in pansy; *ng* in sting
Morphemes	The smallest units that carry meaning; they are created by combining phonemes (*Function morphemes* are prefixes and suffixes. *Content morphemes* are root words.)	*unthinkable = un•think•able* (prefix = *un*, root word = *think*, suffix = *able*)
Grammar	A system of rules (syntax and semantics) used to generate acceptable language that enables us to communicate with and understand others	*I enjoy my psychology class.* versus *I my class psychology enjoy.*
Syntax	A system of rules for putting words in order	*I am happy.* versus *Happy I am.*
Semantics	A system of using words to create meaning	*I went out on a limb for you.* versus *Humans have several limbs.*

highly developed that even a sentence composed of nonsense words sounds as if it makes sense, as long as it follows proper syntax, as in Lewis Carroll's poem, "Jabberwocky":

'Twas brillig, and the slithy toves

Did gyre and gimble in the wabe...

The word arrangement follows the rules of English syntax so well that we feel we know what Carroll is talking about.

Syntax varies from language to language. In English, for example, the verb is usually the second element in a sentence ("He *has driven* to New York"). But in German, the main verb often comes at the very end of a sentence (German word order would be "He *has* to New York *driven*"). English speakers always put the adjective before the noun ("my *precious* love"), but Italian, speakers sometimes place the adjective before and sometimes after, depending on the intended meaning: *Una carrisima amore* means "a very dear, precious love," whereas *un' amore carrisima* means "a very expensive love," one that costs a lot to keep kindled!

- *Semantics.* The choosing of words according to the meaning we want to convey is known as **semantics**. When we add *-ed* to the word *walk*, it refers to walking in the past. If we want to refer to a baby sheep, we use the word *lamb*, not the word *limb*, which means something entirely different. Actually, *limb* has several meanings, so we must depend on context to know whether the speaker is referring to an arm or a leg or to one of the larger branches of a tree. Then there is the expression "to go out on a limb," which means not that someone literally climbs a tree but rather that someone takes a risk. Meaning thus depends on many factors, including word choice, context, and whether the intent is literal or figurative, to name just a few.

Semantics *Meaning or the study of meaning derived from morphemes, words, and sentences*

How do children learn such complex rules? The linguist Noam Chomsky (1957, 1965) proposed that humans are born with an innate mental grammar, an ability to put words together in a meaningful way. Chomsky also proposed that every sentence we generate has two grammatical structures, a *surface structure* and a *deep structure*. The surface structure consists of the words that are spoken or written (or signed). *Deep structure* refers to the underlying meaning of the sentence. For example, the sentence "Terry made the coffee" can be rewritten as "The coffee was made by Terry." Although the surface structure changed, the deep structure remains the same.

As it turns out, both children and adults tend to focus on and remember the deep structure of a sentence rather than its surface structure. In a study by Sachs (1967), participants read a passage and were interrupted at various intervals and asked whether a certain sentence had appeared earlier in the passage. In some cases, the sentences were repeated verbatim, but in others, either the meaning or the syntax was slightly changed. When tested immediately, participants recognized changes in the sentence, but when tested after some time had elapsed, they noticed only when the meaning had changed. Thus, we tend to remember the meaning of sentences, though we might not remember the exact words used to convey that meaning. As a critical thinker, can you see why this might be to our evolutionary advantage and part of a child's built-in innate capacity?

Language and Thought: A Complex Interaction

Our cognitive processes and language are intricately related. Does the fact that you speak English versus Spanish — or Chinese versus Swahili — mean that you reason, think, and perceive the world differently? According to linguist Benjamin

Whorf (1956), the language that a person speaks largely determines the nature of that person's thoughts. Whorf's *linguistic relativity* hypothesis suggests that our vocabulary determines how we perceive and categorize the world around us. As proof, Whorf offered a now classic example: Because Eskimos [Inuits] have many words to describe different kinds of snow (*apikak* for "first snow falling," *pukak* for "snow for drinking water," and so on), their richer vocabulary supposedly enables them to perceive and think about snow differently from English speakers, who have only one word — *snow*. People who speak different languages have different conceptions of the world around them.

Whorf's hypothesis is certainly intriguing, but most research does not support it. For one thing, he apparently exaggerated the number of Inuit words for snow (Pullum, 1991) and ignored the fact that English speakers have terms like *slush*, *sleet*, *hard pack*, *powder*, and so on. More importantly, Eleanor Rosch (1973) found counterevidence for Whorf's hypothesis when she experimentally tested his ideas with the Dani tribe in New Guinea. Although the Dani language has only two color names, one indicating cool, dark colors and the other warm, bright colors, Rosch found that the Dani could discriminate among color hues just as well as people speaking languages with multiple names for colors. In other words, although it may be easier to express a particular idea in one language than in another, language does not necessarily determine how or what we think.

Whorf apparently went too far with his theory that language *determines* thought, but there is no doubt that language *influences* thought (Lillard, 1998). For example, what happens when people speak two or more languages? Studies have found that people who are bilingual report feeling a different sense of self, depending on the language they are using (Matsumoto, 2000). When using Chinese, they found they tended to behave in ways appropriate to Chinese cultural norms, but when speaking English, they tended to adopt Western norms.

The influence of language on thought is also readily apparent in our word choice. For example, when companies want to alter workers' perceptions, they don't *fire* employees; rather, employees are *outplaced*, *dehired*, or *nonrenewed*. Similarly, the military uses terms like *preemptive strike* to cover the fact that they attacked first and *tactical redeployment* to refer to a retreat of troops. Our choice of words also has had some embarrassing and financial consequences for North American businesses. When Pepsi-Cola used its "Come alive with Pepsi" slogan in Japan, they later learned that it translated as "Pepsi brings your dead ancestors back from the grave." Words evoke different images and value judgments. Our words, therefore, *influence* not only our thinking but also the thinking of those who hear them.

Animals and Language: Can We Talk to the Animals?

Heated controversies exist over whether animals use language or can be taught to use language. Without question, animals communicate. Most species send warnings, signal sexual interest, share location of food sources, and so on. The question is this: Are animals capable of mastering the rich complexity of human language?

One of the earliest attempts to answer this question came from psychologists Winthrop and Luella Kellogg (1933), who raised a baby chimpanzee for several years alongside their son of about the same age. Although the chimp learned a few rudimentary, communicative gestures, she never uttered sounds that resembled language. Other early animal language researchers concluded, however, that the Kelloggs probably failed simply because apes do not have the necessary anatomical structure to vocalize that humans do.

Subsequent studies focused on teaching apes nonvocal languages. One of the most successful was a study by Beatrice and Allen Gardner (1969), who recognized the manual dexterity of chimpanzees and their ability to imitate gestures. The Gardners used American Sign Language (ASL), a language used by many deaf

Is Koko using language? Researcher Francine (Penny) Patterson taught a gorilla named Koko to communicate through American Sign Language. At first she rewarded Koko with pieces of fruit if she made any sign that remotely resembled the correct one. Gradually, she reinforced only those gestures that were formed correctly. Today Koko reportedly knows over 600 signs and continues to learn new ones.

people, with a chimp named Washoe. Their success story speaks for itself. By the time Washoe was 4 years old, she had learned 132 signs and was able to combine them into simple sentences such as: "Hurry, gimme toothbrush" and "Please tickle more."

Since the Gardners' success with Washoe, several other language projects have been conducted with apes (Itakura, 1992; Savage-Rumbaugh, 1990). David Premack (1976) taught a chimp named Sarah to "read" and "write" by arranging plastic symbols on a magnetic board. She learned not only to use the plastic symbols but also to follow certain grammatical rules in communicating with her trainers.

Another well-known study was conducted with a chimp named Lana. She learned to push symbols on a computer to get things she wanted, such as food, a drink, a tickle from her trainers, and her curtains opened (Rumbaugh et al., 1974). And, of course, there is the famous gorilla Koko. Researcher Penny Patterson (1981) reportedly taught Koko over 600 signs in ASL.

A number of language studies have also been done with dolphins. Communication with dolphins is by means of hand signals or audible commands. The commands may be spoken by trainers or generated by computer and transmitted through an underwater speaker system. In one typical study, dolphins were given commands made up of two- to five-word sentences, such as "Big ball — square — return," which meant they should go get the big ball, put it in the floating square, and return to the trainer (Herman, Richards, & Woltz, 1984).

The interesting part of this experiment was that the commands varied in syntax and content, both of which altered meaning. For example, the next command might be "Square — big ball — return," which meant the dolphin should go to the square first, then get the big ball, then return to the trainer with the ball. Or the command might refer to one of the other objects floating in the pool, thereby changing its content: "Triangle — little ball — square," which required the dolphin to discriminate among various shapes and various sizes of balls to carry out the command. The study demonstrated that dolphins could carry out a great variety of commands that varied in both content and syntax.

Evaluating Animal Language Studies

Although these ape and dolphin studies seem impressive, psychologists nevertheless do not agree on the interpretation of the findings. Most psychologists believe that nonhuman animals communicate at some level, but compared with humans, animals express a severely limited repertoire of ideas. The average length of sentences produced and understood by humans is also significantly greater than the two- to five-word sentences used by other animals. Moreover, critics claim that apes and dolphins are unable to learn the rules of grammar and syntax that humans use to convey subtle differences in meaning. They question whether animals can use language in ways that are considered creative or unique and point out that they do not express the concept of time (*tomorrow, last week*), request information (*How do birds fly?*), comment on the feelings of others (*Penny is sad*), express similarities (*That cloud looks like a tree*), or propose possibilities (*The cat might sit on my lap*) (Jackendoff, 1994).

Finally, some critics raise the issue of operant conditioning (Chapter 6). They claim that animals do not have a conceptual understanding of the complex signs and symbols of language; those who do engage in simple human language are merely imitating symbols to receive rewards. In short, animals are not really trying to communicate but are simply performing operantly conditioned responses (Jackendoff, 1994; Savage-Rumbaugh, 1990; Terrace, 1979).

RESEARCH HIGHLIGHT

Language and the Brain

In some respects, the brain appears naturally "prewired" to learn language. At birth, the language areas of the temporal cortex are larger in the left than the right hemisphere, and the neurons in the left hemisphere are sensitive to speech sounds. Our neurological understanding of language is just beginning to unfold, but a number of studies provide insight into language and its development.

Functional magnetic resonance imaging (fMRI) studies, for example, indicate that areas of the brain may be organized differently depending on the age at which language is learned. When bilingual individuals learn both languages in childhood, a single region of *Broca's area* is used to produce complex sentences. But when people learn a second language during adolescence, two different regions of *Broca's area* are used (Kim et al., 1997), and the right hemisphere seems to be used more than if the language is learned during childhood (Barinaga, 2000). Finally, recent information suggests that two separate areas of the brain

are involved in the processing and production of language. *Broca's area* is involved in both speech production and language production, whereas the *supramarginal gyrus* (located in the parietal lobe) combines word meaning with the production of words (Crosson et al., 2001; Grodzinsky, 2000).

Although the brain may seem prepared to learn language, cognitive neuroscientists, linguists, and psychologists debate whether language is inborn and if we have sensitive periods for language acquisition (Plomin & Dale, 2000; Ramus, Hauser, Miller, Morris, & Mehler, 2000). (The *sensitive period hypothesis* suggests that humans most easily learn language between birth and puberty, the time when the brain is becoming increasingly specialized. If learning does not occur during this special time, it may be impossible to later "catch up.")

Genie's case provides an excellent example of the importance of sensitive periods for language development. When first discovered at age 13, she was almost completely silent. Because her father severely punished her for making any vocal sounds, Genie did not sob when she cried nor speak when in a fit of rage. She under-

stood only a few "word phrases" such as *stopit* and *nomore* (Rymer, 1993). After 8 months of training, Genie had a vocabulary of more than 200 words and was putting together 2-word sentences. However, her language development did not continue in the usual explosive pattern of normal children. According to last reports, Genie's adult language skills are limited to those of a typical 2- or 3-year-old (Harris, 1995). This is a conversation between Genie and her foster mother, when Genie was 18:

GENIE: At school is washing car.
MOTHER: Whose car did you wash?
GENIE: People car.
MOTHER: How many cars did you wash?
GENIE: Two car. [Curtiss, 1977, p. 28]

Despite years of intensive training, brain scans showed that Genie's left hemisphere remained virtually unresponsive. This suggests that her isolation during critical language-learning years may have failed to trigger innate brain mechanisms, and the cortical tissue normally committed to language may have functionally atrophied.

On the other hand, proponents of animal language are quick to point out that chimpanzees and gorillas can use language creatively and have even coined some words of their own. For example, Washoe called a refrigerator "open eat drink" and a swan a "water bird" (Gardner & Gardner, 1971). Koko signed "finger bracelet" to describe a ring and "eye hat" to describe a mask (Patterson & Linden, 1981). Proponents also argue that, as demonstrated by the dolphin studies, animals can be taught to understand basic rules of sentence structure.

Still, the fact remains that the gap between language as spoken and understood by humans and that generated and understood by other animals is considerable. All the evidence seems to suggest that animals can learn language at a rudimentary level, but that this language is less complex, creative, and rule-laden than any language used by humans. (As a critical thinker, have you ever thought about an opposite approach to animal language research? Why don't humans learn animal language? Could humans be taught to comprehend and use chimpanzee communication systems, for example?)

Check & Review

LANGUAGE

Human language is a creative form of communication consisting of symbols put together according to a set of rules. The three building blocks of language are **phonemes**, **morphemes**, and **grammar**. Phonemes are the basic speech sounds; they are combined to form morphemes, the smallest meaningful units of language. Phonemes, morphemes, words, and phrases are put together by rules of grammar (**syntax** and **semantics**). *Syntax* refers to the grammatical rules for ordering words in sentences; *semantics* refers to meaning in language.

Noam Chomsky believes that humans are born with an ability to put words together in a meaningful way. Also, according to Chomsky, every sentence has both a *surface structure* (the words themselves) and a *deep structure* (the actual meaning).

According to Benjamin Whorf's *linguistic relativity hypothesis*, language shapes thought. Generally, Whorf's hypothesis is not supported. However, our choice of vocabulary can influence our mental imagery and social perceptions.

The most successful animal language studies have been done with apes using American Sign Language. Dolphins have also been taught to comprehend sentences that vary in syntax and meaning. Some psychologists believe that animals can truly learn human language, but others suggest that the animals are merely responding to rewards.

Questions

1. The basic speech sounds /ch/ and /v/ are known as _____; the smallest meaningful units of language, such as *book*, *pre-*, and *-ing*, are known as _____.

2. Explain what Chomsky meant by the terms *surface* and *deep* structure.

3. What is Whorf's *linguistic relativity hypothesis*?

4. Human language differs from the communication of other animals in that it is (a) used more creatively to express thoughts and ideas; (b) the expression of an innate capability; (c) essential for thought; (d) composed of sounds.

Answers to Questions can be found in Appendix B.

INTELLIGENCE

What is intelligence, and how can it be measured?

Millions of people watched when John Carpenter faced his final challenge on *Who Wants To Be A Millionaire?* As the studio lights glared down, he sat poised ready to answer the questions. Does this game show test for intelligence? Are Genie and Thomas Edison intelligent? What is intelligence? Are there different types of intelligence?

The Nature of Intelligence: Is it Real?

Intelligence *The general capacity to profit from experience, to acquire knowledge, and adapt to changes in the environment*

The term **intelligence** is commonly defined in psychology as the general capacity to profit from experience, to acquire knowledge, and adapt to changes in the environment. Although we use the term *intelligence* in our everyday conversation and assume we all share the same definition, we don't. Even among psychologists there is considerable debate over its definition and appropriate methods for measurement. However, there is one area of agreement — it is not a *thing*. It has no mass and it occupies no space. When people talk about intelligence as though it were a concrete, tangible object, they commit an error in reasoning, known as *reification*. Like consciousness, learning, memory, or personality, intelligence is nothing more than a useful *hypothethical, abstract construct*. As you will see later, it is estimated, rather arbitrarily, by scores on intelligence tests. Practically speaking, intelligence is what intelligence tests measure.

Intelligence is also socially constructed, and its definition varies according to the characteristics and skills valued in that culture (Sternberg & Kaufman, 1998). In fact, many languages have no word that corresponds to our notion of intelligence. The closest Mandarin word is a Chinese character meaning "good brain and talented" (Matsumoto, 2000), which is commonly associated with traits like imitation, effort, and social responsibility (Keats, 1982).

Because of the difficulty in identifying and defining intelligence, it remains a complex and controversial topic. For most Western psychologists, modern research on intelligence has centered on two unresolved questions:

- What is the basis for intelligence? Does it depend more on nature or nurture?
- What are the properties of intelligence? Is it a single general ability or several distinct kinds of abilities (intelligences)?

We will discuss several theories that attempt to answer these questions, beginning with Charles Spearman's early theory of *general intelligence*.

Intelligence as a Single Ability

In the early years of intelligence testing, psychologists viewed intelligence as innate, a broad mental ability that included all the cognitive functions. Charles Spearman (1923) proposed that intelligence is a single factor, which he termed *general intelligence* (g). He based his theory on his observation that high scores on separate tests of mental abilities, such as spatial and reasoning ability, tend to correlate with each other. Thus, Spearman believed g underlies all intellectual behavior, including reasoning, solving problems, and performing well in all areas of cognition. On the basis of Spearman's work, standardized tests were widely used in the military, schools, and business to measure this general intelligence (Lubinski & Dawis, 1992).

Intelligence as Multiple Abilities

About a decade later, L. L. Thurstone (1938) proposed seven primary mental abilities: verbal comprehension, word fluency, numerical fluency, spatial visualization, associative memory, perceptual speed, and reasoning. He felt that Spearman's g had little, if any value. Naturally, at the time, Thurstone's view was rather radical. Many years later, J. P. Guilford (1967) expanded on this number and proposed that as many as 120 factors were involved in the structure of the intellect.

Intelligence Again as a Single Ability

About the same time that Guilford was working, Raymond Cattell (1963, 1971) reanalyzed Thurstone's data and argued against the idea of multiple intelligences. He proposed that a single g does exist, but that there are two types of g:

1. **Fluid intelligence** (gf) refers to reasoning abilities, memory, and speed of information processing. If you were asked to solve analogies or remember a long set of numbers, you would be relying on your fluid intelligence. Being relatively independent of education and experience, it reflects an inherited predisposition, and like other biological capacities it declines with advancing age (Burns, Nettelbeck, & Cooper, 2000; Schaie, 1993, 1994).

2. **Crystallized intelligence** (gc) refers to knowledge and skills gained through experience and education (Facon & Facon-Bollengier, 1999). You would rely on your crystallized intelligence if you were asked to explain the President's social security policy or the difference between a "bear" or "bull" stock market. Crystallized intelligence tends to increase over the life span, which explains why physicians, teachers, musicians, politicians, and people in many other occupations can continue working well into old age.

Recent findings show increased frontal lobe activity during very complex tasks, which helps support the idea of g (Duncan & Owen, 2000). Recall from Chapter 1, however, that correlation does not necessarily imply causation and that other explanations are equally possible. Moreover, other studies find that more intelligent people are likely to show less, not more frontal lobe activation, possibly because tasks are not as challenging to them as to those less intelligent (Haier et al., 1993; Sternberg, 1999). All in all, the debate concerning g continues.

Fluid Intelligence *Aspects of intelligence, including reasoning abilities, memory, and speed of information processing, that tend to decline slowly as people age*

Crystallized Intelligence *Knowledge and skills gained through experience and education that tend to increase over the life span*

Multiple intelligences. *Most psychologists agree that there are many forms of intelligence.*

Paul Greengard, Arvid Carlsson, and Eric R. Kandel

Condoleezza Rice

Oprah Winfrey

Gao Xingjian

Celine Dion

Ricky Martin

Venus and Serena Williams

Julie Payette

A Return to Multiple Intelligences

Many contemporary cognitive theorists see a relationship among diverse mental abilities and point out that some people excel in specific areas of intelligence more than in other areas. So perhaps, as suggested by Thurstone and Guilford, mental abilities actually are distinct from one another.

Gardner's theory of multiple intelligences. One cognitive theorist, Howard Gardner, has proposed a *theory of multiple intelligences* (Figure 8.7). Using his own stringent criteria, Gardner (1983, 1998) has identified the eight distinct intelligences shown in Table 8.5. According to Gardner (1991), people come to know their world through these eight intelligences. Also, people have different *profiles of intelligence* because they are stronger in some areas than others, and they use their intelligences differently to learn new material, perform tasks, and solve problems.

Gardner's theory has wide-reaching implications for intelligence testing and for education. Gardner (1986) maintains that intelligence testing should consist of assessing a person's strengths rather than coming up with a single "IQ score." He also challenges our education system to present material in a variety of learning modes rather than the traditional linguistic and logical–mathematical and to develop multiple means of assessment rather than the traditional paper-and-pencil method.

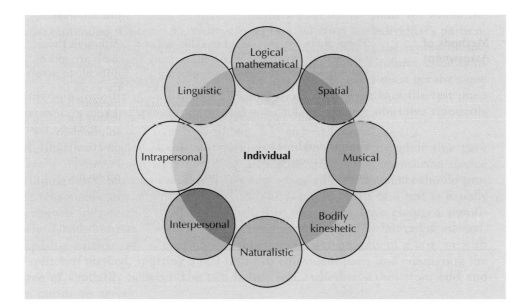

Figure 8.7 *Gardner's Theory of Multiple Intelligences.* Howard Gardner believes there are independent forms of intelligence and that the value of these intelligences may change according to culture.

TABLE 8.5 GARDNER'S MULTIPLE INTELLIGENCES

Linguistic:	**Spatial:**	**Bodily–kinesthetic:**	**Intrapersonal:**	**Logical–mathematical:**	**Musical:**	**Interpersonal:**	**Naturalistic:**
language, such as speaking, reading a book, writing a story	mental maps, such as figuring out how to pack multiple presents in a box or how to draw a floor plan	body movement, such as (dancing, hitting a baseball, or skiing)	understanding oneself, such as setting achievable goals or recognizing self-defeating emotions	problem solving or scientific analysis, such as following a logical proof or solving a mathematical problem	musical skills, such as singing a song or playing the piano	social skills, such as talking with other people	Being attuned to nature, such as noticing seasonal patterns or using environmentally safe products

Visual Summary for Chapter 8

Thinking

The Thinking Brain

Thought processes are distributed throughout the brain, but during problem solving and decision making, they are localized in the prefrontal cortex, which is directly connected to the emotional area of the brain—the limbic system. Without this connection, thinking and emotions are disrupted.

Cognitive Building Blocks

1) **Mental images**: Mind's representation of a sensory experience.

2) **Concepts**: Mental representations of a group or category that share similar characteristics. How do we learn concepts? They arise out of logical rules and definitions (artificial concepts), we create natural categories or concepts (**prototypes**), and we organize them into successive ranks (hierarchies).

3) Language: Method of communication.

Solving Problems

Step 1: Preparation	*Step 2: Production*	*Step 2: Evaluation*
• Identify given facts • Separate relevant facts • Define ultimate goal	Create hypotheses using **algorithms** and **heuristics** (means-end analysis, working backward, creating subgoals).	Judge the hypotheses from Step 2 against criteria from Step 1.

Barriers to problems solving: **Mental sets**, **functional fixedness**, and **confirmation bias**. **Incubation**, or time out, may help overcome these barriers.

Creativity

- *Elements of creativity*: Originality, fluency, and flexibility.
- *Measuring creativity*: Assess **divergent thinking** versus **convergent thinking**.
- *Researching creativity*: Investment theory finds creativity is a combination of intellectual ability, knowledge, thinking style, personality, motivation, and environment.

Language

Human language is a creative form of communication consisting of symbols put together according to a set of rules.

Characteristics of Language

Language is produced from words using **phonemes** (basic speech sounds) and **morphemes** (the smallest meaningful units of a language). The words are strung together into sentences using rules of **grammar**—**syntax** (the grammatical rules for ordering words) and **semantics** (meaning in language). Chomsky believes humans have an innate ability to put words together in a meaningful way, and that every sentence has both a *surface structure* (the words themselves) and a *deep structure* (the actual meaning).

Language (cont).

Language and Thought

According to Whorf's *linguistic relativity hypothesis*, language shapes thought. This theory is generally not supported, but choice of vocabulary can influence mental imagery and social perceptions.

Animals and Language

Apes, dolphins, and other animals have been taught to communicate with humans. Whether they are demonstrating creative language, or merely responding to rewards, is a topic of ongoing debate.

Intelligence

The Nature of Intelligence

Intelligence is the general capacity to profit from experience, to acquire knowledge, and adapt to environmental changes.

Competing theories and definitions:
- Spearman→Intelligence is "g," a general intelligence.
- Thurstone→Intelligence is seven distinct mental abilities.
- Guiliford→Intelligence is composed of 120 or more separate abilities.
- Cattell→Intelligence is two types of "g" (**fluid intelligence** and **crystallized intelligence**).
- Gardner→There are eight types of intelligence.
- Sternberg→Triarchic theory of intelligence (analytical, creative, and practical).

Test Construction

Elements of a useful test:
1) **Standardization**: Test is given to many people to establish norms and identical administrative procedures are used.
2) **Reliability**: The scores are stable over time.
3) **Validity**: The test measures what it is intended to measure.

Assessing Intelligence

Intelligence quotient (IQ) tests do not, and are not intended to, measure overall intelligence. Instead, they are designed to measure verbal and quantitative abilities needed for school success.

- *Stanford–Binet* measures verbal abilities of children ages 3 to 16.
- *Wechsler* measures verbal and nonverbal abilities of three distinct age levels.
- IQs of 70 and below are identified as mentally retarded, whereas IQs of 135 and above are identified as gifted.

Explaining Differences in Intelligence

- Neuroscientists ask: 1) Does a bigger brain mean greater intelligence? Not necessarily. 2) Is a faster brain more intelligent? A qualified yes. 3) Does a smart brain work harder? No, the smarter brain is more efficient.
- The Minnesota Study of Twins Reared Apart found heredity and environment are important, inseparable factors in intellectual development.

9

Life Span Development I

On April 13, 1997, Tiger Woods won the Masters Championship golf tournament in Augusta, Georgia. What makes this noteworthy? Consider that he was the youngest golfer ever to win the Masters and that he won with the lowest score (270) and by the largest margin ever (12 strokes). This accomplishment was also a first for a player of African or Asian heritage at the Masters — a tournament that had its first African American player only two decades earlier (Lace, 1999; Rosaforte, 2000).

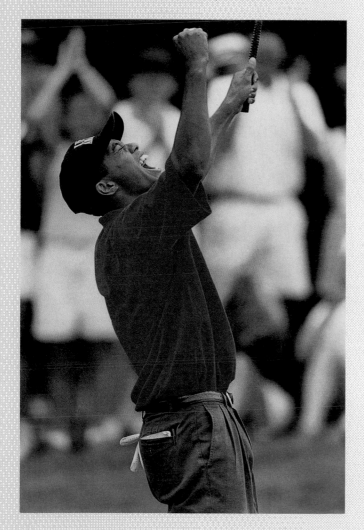

On October 29, 1998, John Glenn spent nine days in the space shuttle Discovery. What makes this exceptional? Consider that he is the oldest human to travel in space and that 36 years earlier, in 1962, he was the first U.S. astronaut to orbit the earth. Moreover, in the years between these two historic flights, he served four terms as a senator from Ohio (Cole, 2000).

Developmental Psychology *The branch of psychology that describes, explains, predicts, and sometimes aims to modify age-related behaviors from conception to death; this field emphasizes maturation, early experiences, and various stages in development*

The accomplishments of Tiger Woods and John Glenn illustrate not only our need to rethink stereotypes about youth, minorities, and older adults but also the importance of understanding how people grow and develop throughout the entire life span. In this chapter and the next, we will explore the field of **developmental psychology**, the study of age-related changes in behavior and abilities throughout the life span, from conception to death (Table 9.1).

To emphasize that development is an ongoing, lifelong *process*, we will take a topical approach (as opposed to a chronological approach, which arbitrarily divides study into two periods, childhood–adolescence and adulthood). Thus, in this chapter, we will trace physical, language, social–emotional, and cognitive development — one at a time — from conception to death.

Then, in the next chapter, we will explore moral development, personality development, and special issues related to death and dying, again, one topic at a time. The topical approach allows us to see how any one aspect of development affects an individual over the entire life span.

STUDYING DEVELOPMENT

How is research in developmental psychology different from research in other areas of psychology?

Maturation *Biological growth processes that enable orderly changes in behavior, relatively uninfluenced by the environment*

In all fields of psychology, certain theoretical issues seem to guide the basic direction of research. First, we look at what those issues are in human development, and then we will look at how developmental psychologists do research.

Theoretical Issues: Ongoing Debates

The three most important issues or questions in human development are *nature versus nurture, continuity versus stages,* and *stability versus change.*

1. *Nature or nurture.* The issue of "nature versus nurture" has been with us since the beginning of psychology. Even the ancient Greeks had the same debate — Plato arguing for innate knowledge and abilities, and Aristotle, for learning through the five senses. Early philosophers proposed that at birth our minds are a tabula rasa (or blank slate) and that the environment determines what messages are written on the slate.

According to the nature position, human behavior and development are governed by automatic, genetically predetermined signals in a process known as **maturation**. Just as a flower unfolds in accord with its genetic blueprint, we humans crawl before

TABLE 9.1 LIFE SPAN DEVELOPMENT

Stage	Approximate Age
Prenatal	Conception to birth
Infancy	Birth to 18 months
Early childhood	18 months to 6 years
Middle childhood	6–12 years
Adolescence	12–20 years
Young adulthood	20–45 years
Middle adulthood	45–60 years
Later adulthood	60 years to death

we walk and walk before we run. Furthermore, there is an optimal period shortly after birth, one of several **critical periods**, when an organism's exposure to certain stimuli or experiences produces proper development.

Naturists would therefore say that Tiger Woods's achievements primarily reflect his innate athletic abilities. They would point out that Tiger shot 48 for nine holes at age three, was featured in Golf Digest at age five, and won the Optimist International Junior tournament six times before age 15. On the other side of the debate, those who hold an extreme nurturist position would argue that development occurs by learning through observation and experience. Nurturists would point to the close teaching and strong encouragement from his father and other family members as the major contributors to Tiger's exceptional accomplishments.

2. Continuity or stages. Continuity proponents say development is continuous, with new abilities, skills, and knowledge gradually added at a relatively uniform pace. The continuity model, then, suggests that adult thinking and intelligence differ quantitatively from a child's. We simply have more math skills or verbal skills, for example. Stage theorists, on the other hand, believe development occurs at different rates, alternating between periods of little change and periods of abrupt, rapid change. In this chapter and the next, we will discuss several stage theories: Piaget's theory of cognitive development, Erikson's psychosocial theory of personality development, and Kohlberg's theory of moral development.

3. Stability or change. Have you generally maintained your personal characteristics as you matured from infant to adult (stability)? Or does your current personality bear little resemblance to the personality you displayed during infancy (change)? Psychologists who emphasize stability in development hold that measurements of personality taken during childhood are important predictors of adult personality (Caspi, 2000; McCrae et al., 2000). Of course, psychologists who emphasize change disagree.

Which of these positions is more correct? Most psychologists do not take a hard line either way. Rather, they prefer an *interactionist perspective*. In the *nature or nurture* debate, for example, psychologists generally believe that development emerges from each individual's unique genetic predisposition and from individual experiences in the environment (Gottlieb, 2000; Maccoby, 2000). Similarly, the *continuity versus stage* question is not a matter of "either-or." Physical development and motor skills, for example, are believed to be primarily continuous in nature, whereas cognitive skills usually develop in discrete stages. Finally, research on *stability versus change* also shows that the answer is somewhere in the middle: Some traits are stable, whereas others vary greatly across the life span.

We will return to these three questions several times in this chapter and the next. Now we turn our attention to another aspect of studying development — how developmental psychologists collect their information.

Research Methods: Two Basic Approaches

To study development, psychologists use either a *cross-sectional* or *longitudinal* method. The **cross-sectional method** examines individuals of various ages (20, 40, 60, and 80 years) at one point in time — and gives information about age differences. The **longitudinal method** follows a single individual or group of individuals (for example, only 20-year-olds) over an extended period of time and gives information about age changes (Figure 9.1).

Imagine you are a developmental psychologist interested in studying intelligence in adults. Which method would you choose — cross-sectional or longitudinal? Before you decide, note the different research results shown in Figure 9.2.

Critical Period *A period of special sensitivity to specific types of learning that shapes the capacity for future development*

Cross-Sectional Method *A technique of data collection that measures individuals of various ages at one point in time and gives information about age differences*

Longitudinal Method *A data collection technique that measures a single individual or group of individuals over an extended period and gives information about age changes*

Figure 9.1 *Cross-sectional versus longitudinal research.* Note that cross-sectional research uses different participants and is interested in age-related differences, whereas longitudinal research studies the same participants over time to find age-related changes.

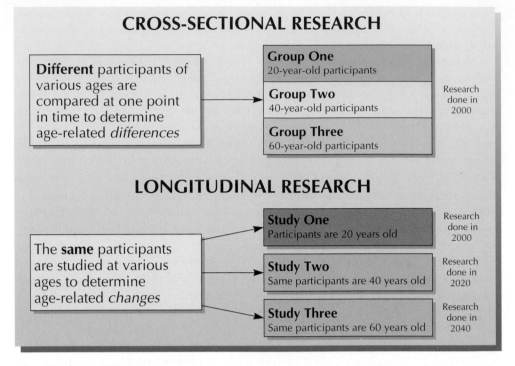

CROSS-SECTIONAL RESEARCH

Different participants of various ages are compared at one point in time to determine age-related *differences*

Group One 20-year-old participants	
Group Two 40-year-old participants	Research done in 2000
Group Three 60-year-old participants	

LONGITUDINAL RESEARCH

The **same** participants are studied at various ages to determine age-related *changes*

Study One Participants are 20 years old	Research done in 2000
Study Two Same participants are 40 years old	Research done in 2020
Study Three Same participants are 60 years old	Research done in 2040

Researchers suggest that the different results may reflect a central problem with cross-sectional studies. They often confuse genuine age differences with *cohort effects*, differences that result from specific histories of the age group studied (Elder, 1998). The decline in intelligence found in cross-sectional research might reflect early educational experiences rather than a true effect of aging. We cannot tell. Age effects and cohort effects are hopelessly tangled.

Longitudinal studies also have their limits. They are expensive in terms of time and money, and their results are restricted in *generalizability*. Because participants often drop out or move away during the extended test period, the experimenter may end up with a self-selected sample that differs from the general population in important ways. As you can see in Table 9.2, each method of research has its own strengths and weaknesses. Keep these differences in mind when you read the findings of developmental research.

Before leaving the topic of research, let's examine the unique contributions cultural psychologists have made to the field of developmental studies.

Figure 9.2 Cross-sectional studies have historically shown that intelligence reaches its peak in early adulthood and then gradually declines. Longitudinal studies have found that a marked decline in intelligence does not begin until about age 60 (Schaie, 1994). How would you explain the differences? (Adapted from Schaie, 1994, with permission.)

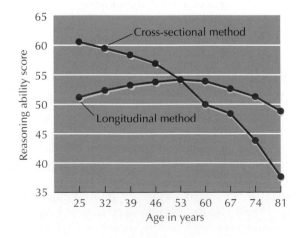

TABLE 9.2 ADVANTAGES AND DISADVANTAGES OF CROSS-SECTIONAL AND LONGITUDINAL RESEARCH DESIGNS

	Cross-Sectional	Longitudinal
Advantages	Gives information about age differences Quick Less expensive Typically larger sample	Gives information about age changes Increased reliability More in-depth information per participant
Disadvantages	Cohort effects Restricted generalizability (measures behaviors at only one point in time)	More expensive Time consuming Restricted generalizability (typically smaller sample and dropouts over time)

GENDER & CULTURAL DIVERSITY

Cultural Psychology's Guidelines for Developmental Research

How would you answer the following question: "If you wanted to predict how a human child anywhere in the world was going to grow up, what his or her behavior was going to be like as an adult, and you could have only one fact about that child, what fact would you choose to have?"

According to cultural psychologists like Patricia Greenfield (1994, 2000), the answer to this question should be "culture." Yet developmental psychology has traditionally studied people (children, adolescents, and adults) with little attention to the sociocultural context (Brislin, 2000; Valsiner, 2000). In recent times, however, psychologists are paying increasing attention to the following points:

1. ***Culture may be the most important determinant of development.*** If a child grows up in an individualistic/independent culture (such as North America or most of western Europe), we can predict this child will probably be competitive and question authority as an adult. Were this same child reared in a collectivist/interdependent culture (common in Africa, Asia, and Latin America), she or he would most likely grow up to be cooperative and respectful of elders (Delgado-Gaitan, 1994; Segall, Dasen, Berry, & Portinga, 1990).

2. ***Human development, like most areas of psychology, cannot be studied outside its sociocultural context.*** In parts of Korea, most teenagers see a strict, authoritarian style of parenting as a sign of love and concern (Kim & Choi, 1995). Korean American and Korean Canadian teenagers, however, see the same behavior as a sign of rejection. Thus, rather than studying specific behaviors, such as "authoritarian parenting styles," researchers in child development suggest that children should be studied only within their *developmental niche* (Harkness & Super, 1996). A developmental niche has three components: the physical and social contexts in which the child lives, the culturally determined rearing and educational practices, and the psychological characteristics of the parents (Bugental & Johnston, 2000).

3. ***Each culture's ethnotheories are important determinants of behavior.*** Within every culture, people have a prevailing set of ideas and beliefs that attempts to explain the world around them (an *ethnotheory*) (Rosenthal & Roer-Strier, 2001). In the area of child development, for example, cultures have specific ethnotheories about how children should be trained. As a critical thinker, you can anticipate that

TRY THIS
Yourself

If you would like a personal demonstration of the invisibility of culture, try this simple experiment: The next time you walk into an elevator, don't turn around. Remain facing the rear wall. Watch how others respond when you don't turn around, or if you stand right next to them rather than walk to the other side of the elevator. Our North American culture has rules that prescribe the "proper" way to ride in an elevator, and people become very uncomfortable when these rules are violated.

differing ethnotheories can lead to problems between cultures. Even the very idea of "critical thinking" is part of our North American ethnotheory regarding education. And it, too, can produce culture clashes.

Concha Delgado-Gaitan (1994) has found that Mexican immigrants from a rural background have a difficult time adjusting to North American schools, which teach children to question authority and think for themselves. In their culture of origin, these children are trained to respect their elders, be good listeners, and participate in conversation only when solicited. Children who argue with adults are reminded not to be *malcriados* (naughty or disrespectful).

4. ***Culture is largely invisible to its participants.*** Culture consists of ideals, values, and assumptions that are widely shared among a given group and that guide specific behaviors (Brislin, 2000). Precisely because these ideals and values are widely shared, they are seldom discussed or directly examined. We take our culture for granted, operating within it, although being almost unaware of it.

Cultural influences on development. *How might these two groups differ in their physical, social–emotional, cognitive, and personality development?*

Check & Review

STUDYING DEVELOPMENT

Developmental psychology is concerned with describing, explaining, predicting, and sometimes modifying age-related behaviors across the entire life span. Three important research issues are *nature or nurture, continuity or stages,* and *stability or change.*

Researchers in developmental psychology generally do **cross-sectional** (different participants of various ages at one point in time) or **longitudinal studies** (same participants over an extended period). Each method has advantages and disadvantages.

Cultural psychologists suggest that developmental researchers keep the following points in mind:

• Culture is the most important determinant of development.
• Human development cannot be studied outside its sociocultural context.
• Each culture's ethnotheories are important determinants of behavior.
• Culture is largely invisible to its participants.

Questions

1. Briefly define *developmental psychology.*

2. What three major questions are studied in developmental psychology?
3. Differences in age groups that reflect factors unique to a specific age group are called _____ effects. (a) generational; (b) social–environmental; (c) operational; (d) cohort
4. _____ studies are the most time-efficient method, whereas _____ studies provide the most in-depth information per participant. (a) Correlational, experimental; (b) Fast-track, follow-up; (c) Cross-sectional, longitudinal; (d) Cohort-sequential, cohort-intensive

Answers to Questions can be found in Appendix B.

PHYSICAL DEVELOPMENT

Perhaps the most obvious aspects of development are physical growth and changes in body proportions and size. In this section, we will look at two separate periods of life: prenatal and early childhood (characterized by rapid change) and adolescence and adulthood (a time of both dramatic and gradual physical change).

Prenatal and Early Childhood: A Time of Rapid Change

Do you remember being a young child and feeling it would "take forever to grow up?" Contrary to a child's sense of time, the early years of development are a time of rapid and unparalleled change. In fact, if you continued to develop at the same rapid rate that marks the first 2 years of life, you would weigh several tons and be over 12 feet tall as an adult! Thankfully, physical development slows, yet it is important to note that change continues until the very moment of death.

Prenatal Physical Development

Your prenatal development began at *conception*, when your mother's egg, or ovum, united with your father's *sperm* cell. At that-time, you were a single cell barely $1/175$ of an inch in diameter — smaller than the period at the end of this sentence (Figure 9.3).

What are the major physical changes that occur throughout the life span?

(a)

(b)

Figure 9.3 *The moment of conception.* (a) Note the large number of sperm surrounding the ovum. (b) Although a "joint effort" is required to break through the outer coating, only one sperm will actually fertilize the egg.

Germinal Period *The first stage of pregnancy (conception to 2 weeks) characterized by rapid cell division*

Embryonic Period *The second stage of pregnancy (from uterine implantation through the eighth week), characterized by development of major body organs and systems*

This new cell, called a *zygote*, then began a process of rapid cell division that resulted in a multimillion-celled infant (you) some 9 months later.

The vast changes that occur during the 9 months of a full-term pregnancy are usually divided into three stages (Figure 9.4). The **germinal period** begins with fertilization and ends with implantation of the rapidly dividing mass of cells (the zygote) in the wall of the uterus. The outer portion of the zygote forms part of the placenta and umbilical cord, whereas the inner portion becomes the *embryo*. The **embryonic period**, the second stage, begins after implantation and lasts through

(a)

Figure 9.4 *(a) From ovulation to implantation.* After discharge from either the left or right ovary (number 1 on the diagram), the ovum travels to the opening of the fallopian tube. If fertilization occurs (2), it normally takes place in the first third of the fallopian tube. The fertilized ovum is referred to as a *zygote*. When the zygote reaches the uterus, it implants itself in the wall of the uterus (3) and begins to grow tendril-like structures that intertwine with the rich supply of blood vessels located there. After *implantation,* the organism is known as an *embryo*. *(b) Embryonic period.* This stage occurs from implantation to 8 weeks. At 8 weeks, the major organ systems have become well differentiated. Note that at this stage, the head grows at a faster rate than other parts of the body. *(c) Fetal stage.* This is the period from the end of the second month to birth. At four months all the actual body parts and organs are established. The fetal stage is primarily a time for increased growth and "fine detailing."

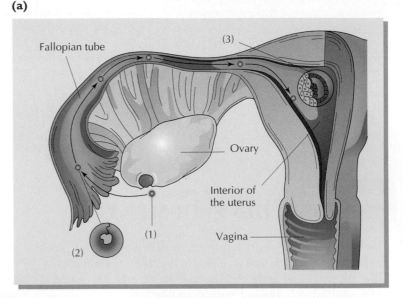

Fallopian tube · (3) · Ovary · Interior of the uterus · Vagina · (1) · (2)

(b)

(c)

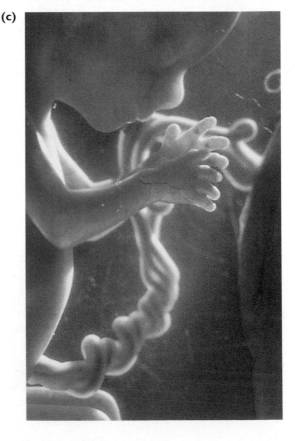

the eighth week. During this time, the embryo's major organ systems begin to develop. The final stage is the **fetal period**, from the end of the second month until birth. During this period, the *fetus* continues to grow and the organs begin to function. Prenatal growth, as well as growth the first few years after birth, is *proximodistal* (near to far), with the head and upper body developing before the lower body.

Hazards to Prenatal Development

During pregnancy, the placenta (connected to the embryo and fetus by the umbilical cord) serves as the link for food and excretion of wastes, and it screens out some, but not all, harmful substances. Environmental hazards such as X-rays or toxic waste, drugs, and diseases such as rubella can cross the *placental barrier* (Table 9.3, page 326). These influences generally have their most devastating effect during the first 3 months of pregnancy — making this a *critical period* in development.

The pregnant mother obviously plays a primary role in prenatal development, because her health directly influences the child she is carrying. Furthermore, almost everything she ingests can cross the placental barrier (a better term might be *placental sieve*). However, the father also plays a role — other than just fertilization. Environmentally, the father's smoking may pollute the air the mother breathes, and genetically, he may transmit heritable diseases. In addition, recent research suggests alcohol, opiates, cocaine, various gases, lead, pesticides, and industrial chemicals can all damage sperm (Pollard, 2000; Raloff, 1999).

Perhaps the most important, and generally avoidable, danger to the developing fetus comes from drugs — both legal and illegal (Abadinsky, 2001; Butler, Joel, & Jeffries, 2000; Pollard, 2000). Nicotine and alcohol are two major **teratogens**, environmental substances that can cause birth defects. Mothers who smoke tobacco have significantly higher rates of premature births, low-birth-weight infants, and fetal deaths (American Cancer Society, 2000; Day, Richardson, Goldschmidt, & Cornelius, 2000; Windham, Hopkins, Fenster, & Swan, 2000). Smoking during pregnancy has also been linked to lower IQ scores for children (Bower, 1999).

Alcohol also readily crosses the placenta, affects fetal development, and can result in a neurotoxic syndrome called **fetal alcohol syndrome** (FAS). Prenatal exposure to alcohol can cause facial abnormalities and stunted growth. But the most disabling features of FAS are neurobehavioral problems, ranging from hyperactivity and learning disabilities to mental retardation, depression, and psychoses. Recent research suggests that these problems may be due to widespread neuron death and reduced brain mass caused by alcohol's effect on two important brain neurotransmitters, glutamate and GABA (gamma aminobutyric acid) (Ikonomidou et al., 2000).

Early Childhood Physical Development

Although Shakespeare described newborns as capable of only "mewling and puking in the nurse's arms," they are actually capable of much more. In this section, we will explore three areas of change in early childhood: *brain, motor,* and *sensory/perceptual development.*

1. *Brain development.* The brain and other parts of the nervous system grow faster than any other part of the body during both prenatal development and the first 2 years of life. A newborn's brain is one-fourth its full adult size and will grow to about 75 percent of its adult weight and size by the age of 2 years. At age 5 years, the child's brain is nine-tenths its full adult weight (Figure 9.5, page 327).

It is generally believed that the newborn's brain contains most of the neurons it will ever have. Further brain development and learning occur primarily because

Why start life under a cloud?

Fetal Period *The third, and final, stage of prenatal development (eight weeks to birth), characterized by rapid weight gain in the fetus and the fine detailing of body organs and systems*

Teratogen [TER-ah-toh-jen] *An external, environmental agent that can cross the placental barrier and disrupt development, causing minor or severe birth defects; the term comes from the Greek word teras, meaning "malformation"*

Fetal Alcohol Syndrome (FAS) *A combination of birth defects, including organ deformities and mental, motor, and/or growth retardation, that results from maternal alcohol abuse*

TABLE 9.3 SAMPLE ENVIRONMENTAL CONDITIONS THAT ENDANGER THE CHILD

Maternal Factors	Possible Effects on Embryo, Fetus, Newborn, or Young Child
Malnutrition	Low birth weight, malformations, less-developed brain, greater vulnerability to disease
Stress exposure	Low birth weight, hyperactivity, irritability, feeding difficulties
Exposure to X-rays	Malformations, cancer
Legal and illegal drugs	
Thalidomide	Hearing defects, deformed limbs, death
Androgens	Masculinization of female fetus
Diethylstilbestrol	Uterine and vaginal abnormalities in female fetus, possible carcinogenesis in male and female fetus, infertility
Analgesics	Respiratory depression
Aspirin in large doses	Respiratory depression
Tetracycline	Inhibition of bone growth, discolored teeth
Streptomycin	Hearing loss
Narcotics	Growth deficiency, withdrawal syndrome, central nervous system and respiratory depression, death
Nicotine	Low birth weight, increased fetal heart rate, premature birth, increased risk of spontaneous abortion, fetal death
Alcohol	Fetal alcohol syndrome (growth deficiency, developmental lag, mental retardation); increased risk of spontaneous abortion, fetal death, attention deficits in childhood
Cocaine	Increased risk of spontaneous abortion, withdrawal syndrome, erratic emotions in infants
Marijuana	Increased tremors and startles among newborns and poorer verbal and memory development at 4 years of age
Diseases	
German measles (rubella)	Blindness, deafness, mental retardation, heart malformation
Herpes, AIDS (acquired immunodeficiency syndrome), other STDs (sexually transmitted diseases)	Brain infection, death, spontaneous abortion, premature birth, mental retardation
Toxoplasmosis	Miscarriage, mental retardation, low birth weight, malformations

Fetal alcohol syndrome. This child was born with fetal alcohol syndrome (FAS). Note the wide-set eyes and thin upper lip. These subtle facial abnormalities, as well as defective limbs and heart, result from the mother's heavy alcohol consumption during pregnancy. Many children with FAS are also below average in intelligence.

Sources: Abadinsky, 2001; Butler, Joel, & Jeffries, 2000; Doweiko, 1999; Rybacki & Long, 1999; Watson, Mednick, Huttunen, & Wang, 1999.

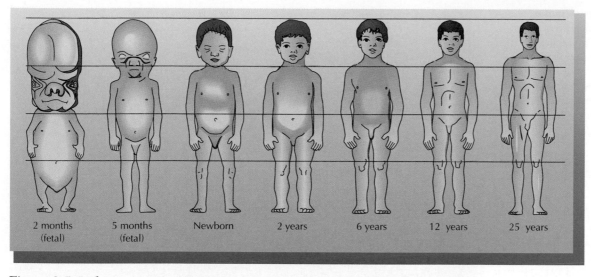

| 2 months (fetal) | 5 months (fetal) | Newborn | 2 years | 6 years | 12 years | 25 years |

Figure 9.5 *Body proportions.* Notice how body proportions change as we grow older. At birth, an infant's head is one-fourth their body's size, whereas in adulthood, the head is one-eighth.

neurons grow in size and because the number of axons and dendrites, as well as the extent of their connections, increases (DiPietro, 2000). The brain reaches its full adult weight by about age 16, but *myelination*, the accumulation of fatty tissue coating the axons of nerve cells, continues until early adulthood. Given that myelin increases the speed of neural impulses, the speed of information processing shows a corresponding increase (Chapter 2). In addition, synaptic connections in the frontal lobes and other parts of the brain continue growing and changing throughout the entire life span (Chapters 2 and 7).

2. Motor development. Compared to the hidden, internal changes in brain development, the orderly emergence of active movement skills, known as *motor development*, is easily observed and measured. The newborn's first motor abilities are limited to *reflexes*, involuntary responses to stimulation. For example, the rooting reflex occurs when something touches a baby's cheek: The infant will automatically turn its head, open its mouth, and root for a nipple.

In addition to simple reflexes, the infant soon begins to show voluntary control over movements of various body parts. As you can see in Figure 9.6, page 328, a helpless newborn that cannot even lift her head is soon transformed into an active toddler capable of crawling, walking, and climbing.

3. Sensory and perceptual development. At birth, a newborn can smell most odors and distinguish between sweet, salty, and bitter tastes. Breastfed newborns also recognize and show preference for the odor and taste of their mother's milk over another mother's (DiPietro, 2000). The newborn's sense of touch and pain is also highly developed, as evidenced by reactions to heel pricks for blood testing and circumcision (Williamson, 1997).

The sense of vision, however, is poorly developed. At birth, a newborn is estimated to have vision between 20/200 and 20/600 (Haith & Benson, 1998). If you have normal 20/20 vision, you can imagine what the infant's visual life is like. The level of detail you see at 200 or 600 feet is what they see at 20 feet. Within the first few months, vision quickly improves, and by six months, it is 20/100 or better. At 2 years, visual acuity reaches a near-adult level of 20/20 (Courage & Adams, 1990).

One of the most interesting findings in infant sensory and perceptual research concerns hearing. Not only can the newborn hear quite well at birth (Matlin & Foley,

Maturation and motor development. Some Hopi Indian infants spend a great portion of their first year of life being carried in a cradleboard, rather than crawling and walking freely on the ground. Yet by age one, their motor skills are very similar to those of infants who have not been restrained in this fashion (Dennis & Dennis, 1940).

Figure 9.6 *Milestones in motor development.* In the typical progression of motor abilities, "chin up" occurs at age 2.2 months and walking up stairs at 17.1 months. However, no two children are exactly alike; all follow their own individual timetable for physical development. (Adapted from Frankenburg et al., 1992, with permission.)

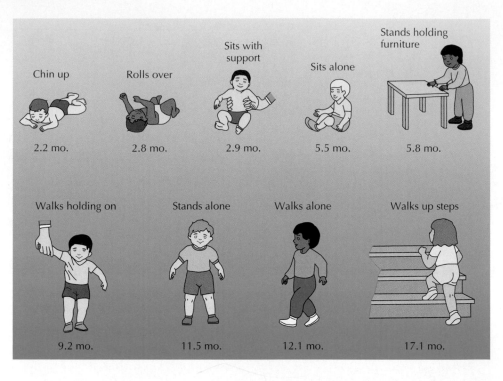

1997) but also, during the last few months in the womb, the fetus can apparently hear sounds outside the mother's body (Vaughan, 1996). This raises the interesting possibility of fetal learning, and some doctors have advocated special stimulation for the fetus as a way of increasing intelligence, creativity, and general alertness (e.g., Van de Carr & Lehrer, 1997). Devices such as the "pregaphone" have been specially designed to help eager parents talk to their babies before birth (Figure 9.7).

Studies on possible fetal learning have found that newborn infants easily recognize their own mother's voice over that of a stranger. They also show preferences for children's stories (such as *The Cat in the Hat* or *The King, the Mice, and the Cheese*) that were read to them while they were still in the womb (DeCasper & Fifer, 1980; DeCasper & Spence, 1986; Trotter, 1987). On the other hand, some experts caution that too much or the wrong kind of stimulation before birth can be stressful for both the mother and fetus (Diamond & Hopson, 1998). They suggest that the fetus gets what it needs without any special stimulation.

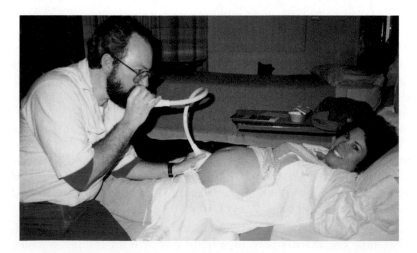

Figure 9.7 *Can a fetus learn before birth?* This father apparently thinks so. He is using a special device called a "pregaphone" to talk to his baby.

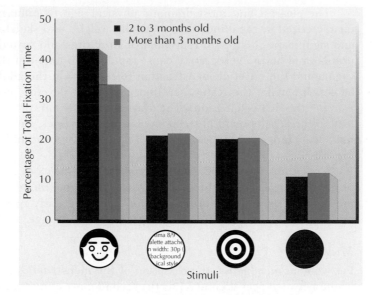

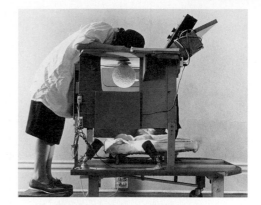

Figure 9.8 *Fantz's "looking chamber."* Using this specially designed testing apparatus, Fantz and his colleagues measured the length of time infants stared at various stimuli. They found that infants preferred complex rather than simple patterns and pictures of faces rather than nonfaces.

How can scientists measure perceptual abilities and preferences in such young babies? Newborns and infants obviously cannot talk or follow directions, so researchers have had to create ingenious experiments to evaluate their perceptual skills. One of the earliest experimenters, Robert Fantz (1956, 1963), designed a "looking chamber" in which infants lie on their backs and look at visual stimuli (Figure 9.8).

Researchers also use newborns' heart rate and innate abilities, such as the sucking reflex, to study how they learn and how their perceptual abilities develop. To study the sense of smell, researchers measure changes in the newborns' heart rates when different odors are presented. Presumably, if they can smell one odor but not the other, their heart rate will change in the presence of the first but not the second. From research such as this, we now know that the senses develop very early in life.

Adolescence and Adulthood: A Time of Both Dramatic and Gradual Change

Whereas the adolescent years are marked by dramatic changes in appearance and physical capacity, middle age and later adulthood are times of gradual physical changes. We begin with a look at adolescence.

Adolescence

Think back for a moment to your teen years. Were you concerned about the physical changes you were going through? Did you worry about how you differed from your classmates? Changes in height and weight, breast development and menstruation for girls, and a deepening voice and beard growth for boys are important milestones for adolescents. **Puberty**, the period of life when a person becomes capable of reproduction, is a major physical milestone for everyone. It is a clear biological signal of the end of childhood.

Although commonly associated with puberty, *adolescence* is the loosely defined psychological period of development between childhood and adulthood. In the United States, it roughly corresponds to the teenage years. It is important to recognize that adolescence, like childhood, is not a universal concept. Some nonindustrialized countries have no need for such a slow transition, and children simply assume adult responsibilities as soon as possible.

Puberty *The period in life when sex organs mature and sexual reproduction becomes possible; puberty generally begins for girls around ages 10 to 12, and for boys, about 2 years later*

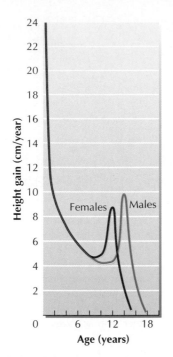

Figure 9.9 *Adolescent growth spurt.* Note the gender differences in height gain during puberty. Most girls are about 2 years ahead of boys in their growth spurt and therefore are taller than most boys between the ages of 10 and 14.

The clearest and most dramatic physical sign of puberty is the *growth spurt,* characterized by rapid increases in height, weight, and skeletal growth (Figure 9.9), and significant changes in reproductive structures and sexual characteristics. Maturation and hormone secretion cause rapid development of the ovaries, uterus, and vagina and the onset of menstruation (*menarche*) in the adolescent female. In the adolescent male, the testes, scrotum, and penis develop, and he undergoes *spermarche* (the first ejaculation). The ovaries and testes in turn produce hormones that lead to the development of *secondary sex characteristics,* such as the growth of pubic hair, deepening of the voice, growth of facial hair, growth of breasts, and so on (Figure 9.10).

Once the large and obvious pubertal changes have occurred, further age-related physical changes are less dramatic. Other than some modest increase in height and muscular development during the late teens and early twenties, most individuals experience only minor physical changes until middle age.

Middle Age

For women, *menopause,* the cessation of the menstrual cycle, which occurs somewhere between ages 45 and 55, is the second most important life milestone in physical development. The decreased production of estrogen (the dominant female hormone) produces certain physical changes. However, the popular belief that menopause (or "the change of life") causes serious psychological mood swings, loss of sexual interest, and depression is *not* supported by current research (Morrison & Tweedy, 2000; Stewart & Ostrove, 1998).

Beginning in middle adulthood, men experience a gradual decline in the production of sperm and testosterone (the dominant male hormone), although they may remain capable of reproduction into their eighties or nineties. Physical changes such as unexpected weight gain, decline in sexual responsiveness, loss of muscle strength, and graying or loss of hair may lead some men (and women as well) to feel depressed and to question their life progress. They often see these alterations as a biological signal of aging and mortality (Powell, 1998). Such physical and psychological changes in men are known as the *male climacteric.*

Figure 9.10 *Secondary sex characteristics.* Complex physical changes in puberty result primarily from hormones secreted from the ovaries and testes, the pituitary gland in the brain, and adrenal glands near the kidneys.

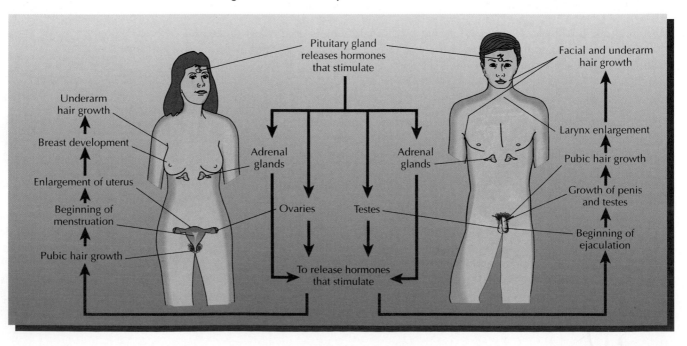

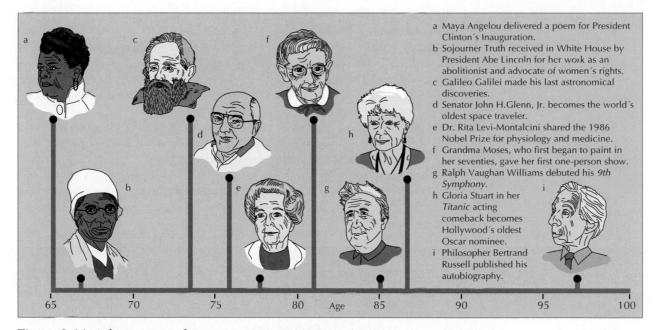

a Maya Angelou delivered a poem for President Clinton´s Inauguration.
b Sojourner Truth received in White House by President Abe Lincoln for her work as an abolitionist and advocate of women´s rights.
c Galileo Galilei made his last astronomical discoveries.
d Senator John H.Glenn, Jr. becomes the world´s oldest space traveler.
e Dr. Rita Levi-Montalcini shared the 1986 Nobel Prize for physiology and medicine.
f Grandma Moses, who first began to paint in her seventies, gave her first one-person show.
g Ralph Vaughan Williams debuted his *9th Symphony*.
h Gloria Stuart in her *Titanic* acting comeback becomes Hollywood´s oldest Oscar nominee.
i Philosopher Bertrand Russell published his autobiography.

Figure 9.11 *Achievement in later years.* Note the high level of productivity among some of the world's most famous figures late in their lifetime.

Late Adulthood

After middle age, most physical changes in development are gradual and occur in the heart and arteries and sensory receptors. For example, cardiac output (the volume of blood pumped by the heart each minute) decreases, whereas blood pressure increases due to the thickening and stiffening of arterial walls. Visual acuity and depth perception decline, hearing acuity lessens, especially for high-frequency sounds, and smell sensitivity decreases (Atchley & Kramer, 2000; Medina, 1996).

This all sounds depressing. Can anything be done about it? Television, magazines, movies, and advertisements generally portray aging as a time of graying hair, balding pates, sagging parts, poor vision and hearing, and, of course, no sex life. Recent research, however, shows that getting old may be better than we think. For example, a group of Dutch scientists (Lamberts, van den Beld, & van der Lely, 1997) believe the loss of muscle strength and physical frailty commonly seen in people as they age is neither inevitable nor irreversible. Their research suggests that hormone replacement treatment for both men and women can greatly offset the effects of osteoporosis, heart disease, Alzheimer's disease, and several other age-related diseases. Scientists do caution, however, that hormone replacement therapy is still controversial and that more studies are needed on long-term risks and benefits.

What about people who have inherited genetic tendencies toward Alzheimer's disease and other serious diseases of old age? There's good news on this front, too. Scientists Caleb Finch and Rudolf Tanzi (1997) have found that genes have a "relatively minor effect" on our well-being in later years. They discovered that lifestyle and environmental factors (like exercise and good nutrition) "may profoundly influence the outcomes of aging." As we discovered in the chapter opener's description of John Glenn, for many individuals the later years of life are their most productive (Figure 9.11).

If we set aside contributions from *secondary aging* (changes resulting from disease, disuse, or neglect), we are left with studies of *primary aging* (gradual, inevitable age-related changes in physical and mental processes). There are two

Use it or lose it? *Research shows exercise may be the most important factor in maintaining mental and physical abilities throughout the life span.*

main theories explaining primary aging and death — programmed theory and damage theory (Cristofalo, 1996; Medina, 1996; Wallace, 1997).

According to the *programmed theory,* aging is genetically controlled. Once the ovum is fertilized, the program for aging and death is set and begins to run. Researcher Leonard Hayflick (1977, 1996) found that human cells seem to have a built-in life span. After about 50 doublings of laboratory-cultured cells, they cease to divide — they have reached the *Hayflick limit.*

The other explanation of primary aging is *damage theory,* which proposes that an accumulation of damage to cells and organs over the years ultimately causes death. Whichever theory is correct, human beings appear to have a maximum life span of about 110 to 120 years. Although we can try to control secondary aging in an attempt to reach that maximum, so far we have no means to postpone primary aging.

Check & Review

PHYSICAL DEVELOPMENT

The prenatal period of development consists of three major stages: the **germinal**, **embryonic**, and **fetal**. Fetal development can be affected by environmental influences. Poor prenatal nutrition is a leading cause of birth defects, and most prescription and over-the-counter drugs are potentially **teratogenic** (capable of producing birth defects). Doctors advise pregnant women to avoid all unnecessary drugs, especially nicotine and alcohol.

During the prenatal period and the first year of life, the brain and nervous system grow faster than any other part of the body. Early motor development (crawling, standing, and walking) is largely the result of maturation. The sensory and perceptual abilities of newborns are relatively well developed.

At **puberty**, the adolescent becomes capable of reproduction and experiences a sharp increase in height, weight, and skeletal growth because of the pubertal growth spurt. Both men and women experience bodily changes in middle age. Many changes in women are related to the hormonal effects of menopause; similar psychological changes in men are called the male climacteric.

Although many of the changes associated with physical aging (such as decreases in cardiac output and visual acuity) are the result of primary aging, others are the result of abuse, disuse, and disease — secondary aging. Physical aging may be genetically built in from the moment of conception (programmed theory), or it may result from the body's inability to repair damage (damage theory).

Questions

1. What are the three stages of prenatal development?

2. Teratogens are _____ that can cause birth defects. (a) DNA fragments; (b) environmental agents; (c) recessive genes; (d) dominant genes

3. The period of life when an individual first becomes capable of reproduction is known as _____. (a) the age of fertility; (b) adolescence; (c) puberty; (d) the adolescent climacteric

4. What is the difference between primary and secondary aging?

Answers to Questions can be found in Appendix B.

LANGUAGE DEVELOPMENT

How do children develop language?

From birth, the child has a multitude of ways to communicate. Through such nonverbal means as facial expressions, eye contact, and body gestures, babies only hours old begin to "teach" their parents and caregivers when and how they want to be held, fed, and played with. As early as the late 1800s, Charles Darwin proposed that most emotional expressions, such as smiles, frowns, and looks of disgust, are universal and innate (Figure 9.12). Darwin's contention is supported by the fact that children who are born blind and deaf exhibit the same facial expressions for emotions that sighted and hearing children do.

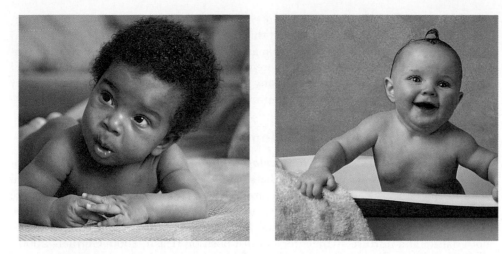

Figure 9.12 *Early nonverbal communication.* Can you identify these emotions? Infants as young as 2.5 months at age can express several basic emotions, including interest, joy, anger, and sadness.

Stages of Language Development: From Crying to Talking

Eventually, children also communicate verbally. The first, *prelinguistic stage* begins with the newborn baby's reflexive cry. Within a short time, crying becomes more purposeful. At least three distinct patterns have been identified: the basic hunger cry, the anger cry, and the pain cry (Wolff, 1969). Although many child-care texts suggest that each of these cries can be easily identified and responded to by the primary caregivers, most parents find that they must learn through a process of trial and error what actions will satisfy their child.

At about age 2 to 3 months, babies begin **cooing**, producing vowel-like sounds ("ooooh" and "aaaah"). Around ages 4 to 5 months they start **babbling**, adding consonants to their vowels ("bahbahbah" and "dahdahdah"). Some parents mark babbling as the beginning of language and consider their child's vocalizations as "words," even though the child typically does not associate a "word" with a specific object or person, and despite the fact that all children the world over babble in the same fashion.

The true *linguistic stage* begins toward the end of the first year of life, when babbling begins to sound more like the language of the child's home and when the child seems to understand that sound is related to meaning. At the beginning of this stage, the child is generally limited to a single-utterance vocabulary such as "mama," "go," "juice," or "up." Children manage to get a lot of mileage out of these singular utterances: "Mama" can be used to mean, "I want you to come and get me," "I'm hurt," and "I don't like this stranger." However, their vocabulary more than doubles once they begin to express themselves by joining words into short phrases such as "Go bye-bye," "Daddy milk," and "No night-night!"

At this age, children sometimes overextend the words they use. **Overextension** is using words to include objects that do not fit the word's meaning. For example, having learned the word *doggie,* a child often overextends the word to include all small, furry animals (e.g., kittens, bunnies).

Around age 2 years, most children are creating short but intelligible sentences by linking several words. However, they leave out nonessential, connecting words: "Me want cookie;" "Grandma go bye-bye?" This pattern is called **telegraphic speech** because, like telegrams of days gone by, children's speech includes only words directly relevant to meaning, and nothing more.

While increasing their vocabulary at a phenomenal rate during these early years, children are also acquiring a wide variety of rules for grammar, such as adding -*ed* to indicate the past tense and *s* to form plurals. They also make mistakes, however, because they **overgeneralize**, or *overuse* the basic rules of grammar. This results in novel sentences like "I goed to the zoo" and "Two mans." (Study tip: If you're hav-

Cooing *Vowel-like sounds infants produce beginning around age 2 to 3 months*

Babbling *Vowel/consonant combinations that infants begin to produce at about age 4 to 6 months*

Overextension *A child's tendency to define a word too broadly, to include objects that do not fit the word's meaning*

Telegraphic Speech *The two- or three-word sentences of young children that contain only the most necessary words*

Overgeneralize *A common error in language acquisition where the child overuses the basic rules of grammar; the rules for past tense and plurals are extended to irregular forms (e.g., they may say mans instead of men.)*

ing difficulty differentiating between *overextension* and *overgeneralization,* remember the *g* in *overgeneralize* as a cue that this term applies to problems with grammar.)

By age 5 years most children have mastered the basic rules of grammar and typically use about 2,000 words. (Many foreign-language instructors consider this level of mastery adequate for getting by in any given culture.) Past this point, vocabulary and grammar acquisition gradually improve throughout the entire life span.

Theories of Language Development: Nature Versus Nurture

What motivates children to develop language? Some theorists believe language capability is innate, whereas others claim it is learned through imitation and reinforcement (the nature-versus-nurture controversy again). Although there are staunch supporters of both sides, most psychologists find neither of these extreme positions satisfactory. Most believe that language acquisition is a combination of both nature and nurture — the interactionist position (Casti, 2000; Gottlieb, 2000).

According to the nativist position, language acquisition is primarily a matter of maturation. The most famous advocate of this viewpoint, Noam Chomsky (1968, 1980), suggests that children are born "prewired" to learn language. They possess a type of **language acquisition device** (LAD) that needs only minimal exposure to adult speech to unlock its potential. The LAD enables the child to analyze language and unconsciously extract the basic rules of grammar.

To support his viewpoint, Chomsky points to the fact that children all over the world go through similar stages in language development at about the same age and in a pattern that parallels motor development. He also cites the facts that babbling is the same in all cultures and that deaf babies babble just like hearing babies.

Although the nativist position enjoys considerable support, it fails to adequately explain individual differences. Why does one child learn rules for English, for example, whereas another learns rules for Spanish? The "nurturists" can explain individual differences and distinct languages. From their perspective, children learn language through a complex system of rewards, punishments, and imitation. Any vocalization attempt ("mah" or "dah") from the young infant is quickly rewarded with smiles and other forms of encouragement. When the infant later babbles "mama" or "dada," proud parents respond even more enthusiastically. (As a critical thinker, can you see how these parents are unknowingly using a type of *shaping* — a term we discussed in Chapter 6?)

Language Acquisition Device (LAD) *In Noam Chomsky's view, the child's inborn brain capacity to analyze language and unconsciously understand essential grammatical rules*

Check & Review

LANGUAGE DEVELOPMENT

Children go through two stages in their acquisition of language: prelinguistic (crying, **cooing, babbling**) and linguistic (which includes single utterances, **telegraphic speech**, and the acquisition of rules of grammar).

Nativists believe that language is an inborn capacity and develops primarily by maturation. Noam Chomsky suggests that humans possess a **language acquisition device** (LAD) that needs only minimal environmental input. Nurturists empha-size the role of the environment and suggest that language development results from rewards, punishments, and imitating models.

Questions

1. How is "cooing" different from "babbling"?

2. Children make errors like "mouses" and "goed" versus "mice" and "went" because they _____ the rules of grammar. (a) ignore; (b) haven't learned;
(c) overextend; (d) overgeneralize

3. Noam Chomsky believes we possess an inborn ability to learn language known as a _____. (a) telegraphic understanding device (TUD); (b) language acquisition device (LAD); (c) language and grammar translator (LGT); (d) overgeneralized neural net (ONN)

4. Compare and contrast the nature versus the nurture position on language development.

Answers to Questions can be found in Appendix B.

SOCIAL–EMOTIONAL DEVELOPMENT

The poet John Donne wrote, "No man is an island, entire of itself." In addition to physical and language development, developmental psychologists are very interested in social–emotional development. That is, they study how human beings become *entire* with the help of other human beings. Two of the most important topics in social–emotional development are those of *attachment* and *parenting styles*.

Attachment: The Importance of Early Bonds

An infant arrives in the world with a multitude of behaviors that encourage a strong bond of attachment with primary caregivers. **Attachment** can be defined as an active, intense, enduring emotional relationship that is specific to two people. Although most research has focused on the attachment between mother and child, fathers, grandparents, and other caretakers may also form attachment bonds with an infant.

Attachment *An active, intense, emotional relationship between two people that endures over time*

In studying attachment behavior, researchers are often divided along the lines of the now-familiar nature-versus-nurture debate. Those who advocate the innate or biological position cite John Bowlby's work (1969, 1989, 2000). He proposed that newborn infants are biologically equipped with verbal and nonverbal behaviors (such as crying, clinging, smiling) and with "following" behaviors (such as crawling and walking after the caregiver) that serve to elicit certain instinctive nurturing responses from the caregiver. The biological argument for attachment is also supported by Konrad Lorenz's (1937) studies of **imprinting**. Lorenz's studies demonstrated how baby geese attach to, and then follow, the first large moving object they see during a certain critical period in their development.

Imprinting *An innate or instinctual form of learning in which the young of certain species follow and become attached to large moving objects (usually their mothers)*

Feeding or Contact Comfort?

According to Freud, infants become attached to the caregiver that provides oral pleasure (Chapter 13). But is there scientific evidence to support Freud's claim? In what is now a classic experiment, Harry Harlow and Robert Zimmerman (1959) set out to experimentally investigate the variables that might affect attachment. They started by creating two types of wire-framed *surrogate* (substitute) "mother" monkeys: one covered by soft terry cloth and one left uncovered. The infant monkeys were fed by either the cloth or the wire mother and had access to both mothers (Figure 9.13).

Harlow and Zimmerman found those monkeys who were "reared" by a cloth mother spent significant amounts of time clinging to the soft material of their surrogate mother. They also developed greater emotional security and curiosity than did monkeys assigned to the wire mother. Monkeys who were given free choice of both mothers also showed strong attachment behaviors toward the cloth mother — even when the wire-framed mother provided all food!

Further evidence of the importance of contact comfort came from later research by Harlow and Harlow (1966), in which monkey babies were exposed to various forms of rejection. Some of the "mothers" contained metal spikes that would suddenly protrude from the cloth covering and push the babies away; others had air jets that would sometimes blow the babies away. Nevertheless, the infant monkeys waited until the rejection was over and then clung to the cloth mother as tightly as before.

On the basis of these and related findings, Harlow concluded that what he called *contact comfort,* the pleasurable tactile sensations provided by a soft and cuddly "parent," is a powerful contributor to attachment. The satisfaction of other physical needs, such as food, is not enough.

Figure 9.13 *Contact comfort and attachment.* Harlow and Zimmerman found that infant monkeys spent more time on the terry-cloth-covered "mother," even when it was the wire "mother" that provided food. They concluded that contact comfort, rather than feeding, was the most important determinant of a monkey's attachment to its caregiver.

Imprinting and attachment. These ducklings are following scientist Konrad Lorenz because they instinctually form a strong attachment to the first large moving object they see. Usually it is the mother duck, but in this case it was Lorenz.

Is contact comfort similarly important between human mothers and infants? Several studies suggest that it may be. Touching and massaging premature infants, for example, produce significant physical and emotional benefits (de Roiste & Bushnell, 1996; Drummond, 1998). Touch elicits positive emotions and attention from almost all babies (Pelaez-Nogueras, Gewirtz, Field, & Cigales, 1996). Mothers around the world tend to kiss, nuzzle, nurse, comfort, clean, and respond to their children with lots of physical contact.

Japanese mothers and their children are rarely separated during the first months of life. They touch their infants to communicate with them, breast-feed, carry them around on their backs, and take baths with them. Japanese infants do not even sleep in separate beds (Matsumoto, 2000). Mayan children sleep alongside their mothers for several years. If a new baby comes along, the older child moves to a bed in the same room or shares a bed with another family member (Morelli, Oppenheim, Rogoff, & Goldsmith, 1992).

In short, attachment seems to depend, at least in part, on the hugging, cuddling, and caresses babies naturally receive from their mothers. We use the word *mother* because almost all research in this area has focused on mothers and their infants. However, research also shows the same results apply to fathers and other caregivers (Lopez, Melendez, & Rice, 2000; Peters & Day, 2000; van IJzendoorn & De Wolff, 1997).

What happens if a child does not form an attachment? Researchers have investigated this question in two ways: They have looked at children and adults who spent their early years in institutions without the stimulation and love of a regular caregiver or who lived at home but were physically isolated under abusive conditions (Zeanah, 2000).

Infants raised in impersonal or abusive surroundings suffer from a number of problems. They seldom cry, coo, or babble; they become rigid when picked up; and they have few language skills. As for their social–emotional development, they tend to form shallow or anxious relationships. Some appear forlorn, withdrawn, and uninterested in their caretakers, whereas others seem insatiable in their need for affection (Zeanah, 2000). They also tend to show intellectual, physical, and perceptual retardation; increased susceptibility to infection; and neurotic "rocking" and isolation behaviors; in some cases, they die from lack of attachment (Belsky & Cassidy, 1994; Bowlby, 1973, 1982, 2000; Spitz & Wolf, 1946).

Levels of Attachment

Although most children are never exposed to extreme institutional conditions, Mary Ainsworth and her colleagues (1967, 1978) have found significant differences in the typical level of attachment between infants and their mothers. Moreover, *level of attachment* affects long-term behaviors. Using a method called the *strange situation procedure,* a researcher observes infants in the presence or absence of their mother and a stranger. Ainsworth found that children could be divided into three groups: *securely attached, avoidant,* and *anxious/ambivalent.*

Is contact comfort biological? When nestled next to a hen or held in a person's cupped hands, chicks will almost immediately "relax" and close their eyes.

1. *Securely attached* (65%). When exposed to the stranger, the infant seeks closeness and contact with the mother, uses the mother as a safe base from which to explore, shows moderate distress on separation, and is happy when the mother returns.

2. *Avoidant* (25%). The infant does not seek closeness or contact with the mother, treats the mother much like a stranger, and rarely cries when the mother leaves the room.

3. *Anxious/Ambivalent* (10%). The infant becomes very upset as the mother leaves the room and when she returns seeks close contact, then squirms angrily to get away.

Ainsworth found that infants with a secure attachment style have caregivers that are sensitive and responsive to their signals of distress, happiness, and fatigue (Ainsworth et al., 1967, 1978; van IJzendoorn & DeWolff, 1997). On the other hand, avoidant infants had caregivers that were aloof and distant, and anxious/ambivalent infants had inconsistent caregivers that alternated between strong affection and indifference.

Can you see why infants who are securely attached generally develop feelings of emotional security and trust in others? Or why avoidant infants learn to avoid others and suppress their attachment needs, whereas anxious/ambivalent infants tend to be temperamental and anxious that others will not return their affection? It is not surprising that follow-up studies found securely attached children were the most sociable, enthusiastic, cooperative, persistent, curious, and competent (Goldberg, 2000; Jacobsen & Hofmann, 1997).

RESEARCH HIGHLIGHT

Romantic Love and Attachment

If you've been around young children, you've probably noticed how often they share toys and discoveries with a parent and seem much happier when a parent is near. You've probably also thought how cute and sweet it is when infants and parents coo and share baby talk with each other. But have you noticed that these very same behaviors often occur between you and your adult romantic partner?

Intrigued by these parallels, several researchers have studied the relationship between an infant's attachment to a parent figure and an adult's love for a romantic partner (Bachman & Zakahi, 2000; Klohnen & Bera, 1998). In one study, Cindy Hazan and Phillip Shaver (1987, 1994) discovered that adults who had an avoidant pattern in infancy are uncomfortable with intimacy as adults. They find it hard to trust others, difficult to self-disclose, and rarely report finding "true love" (Cooper, Shaver, & Collins, 1998; Fraley & Shaver, 1997). Anxious/ambivalent adults also have difficulty with intimate relationships, but unlike avoidants, they tend to be obsessed with their romantic partners, fearing their intense love will not be reciprocated. Individuals who are securely attached as infants easily become close to others, expect intimate relationships to endure, and perceive others as generally trustworthy.

Would you like to test your own attachment style? Thinking of your current and past romantic relationships, place a check next to those statements that best describe your feelings.

1. I find it relatively easy to get close to others and am comfortable depending on them and having them depend on me. I don't often worry about being abandoned or about someone getting too close.
2. I am somewhat uncomfortable being close. I find it difficult to trust partners completely or to allow myself to depend on them. I am nervous when anyone gets close, and love partners often want me to be more intimate than is comfortable for me.
3. I find that others are reluctant to get as close as I would like. I often worry that my partner doesn't really love me or won't stay with me. I want to merge completely with another person, and this desire sometimes scares people away.

According to research, 55 percent of adults agree with item 1 (*secure attachment*), 25 percent choose number 2 (*avoidant attachment*), and 20 percent choose item 3 (*anxious/ambivalent attachment*) (adapted from Fraley & Shaver, 1997; Hazan & Shaver, 1987; Shaver & Hazan, 1994). Note that the percentages for these adult attachment styles are roughly equivalent to the percentages for infant–parent attachment.

What your responses to this test may mean is that avoidant and anxious/ambivalent adults have developed intimacy patterns

The importance of attachment. Researchers have found that the degree and quality of attachments you formed as an infant may carry over to your adult romantic relationships.

from their early childhood experiences that frustrate, if not destroy, adult love relationships. The avoidant lover may block intimacy by being emotionally aloof and distant, whereas the anxious/ambivalent lover may smother intimacy by being possessive and emotionally demanding.

As you may expect, the securely attached lover has intimacy patterns that foster long-term relationships and is the most desired partner by the majority of adults, regardless of their own attachment styles (Klohnen & Bera, 1998; Pietromonaco & Carnelley, 1994). Studies of adult attachment are significant because they suggest our earliest bonding experiences may have lasting effects. Bowlby (1979), in fact, believed attachment behaviors "characterize human beings from the cradle to the grave" (p. 129).

Friendship and attachment. These 50-year-old women have remained close friends since kindergarten. Despite heavy schedules, they get together at least once a year for a "summer reunion."

Evaluating Attachment Theories

Although Hazan and Shaver's research and similar studies are consistent with infant attachment theory, the results are correlational rather than experimental. And as you know from Chapter 1, it is always risky to infer causation from correlation. Accordingly, the relationship between romantic love style and early infant attachment is subject to several alternative causal explanations. Further research is necessary before we fully understand the link between infant attachment and adult intimate relationships.

Also, be aware that early attachment experiences may predict the future but do not determine it. Despite the significance of the initial infant–parent attachment bond, we are capable of learning new social skills and different attitudes toward relationships in our later interactions with peers, close friends, lovers, and spouses. Unlike diamonds, attachment styles are not necessarily forever.

Parenting Styles: Their Effect on Development

How much of our personality comes from the way our parents treat us as we are growing up? Researchers since the 1920s have studied the effects of different methods of child rearing on children's behavior, development, and mental health. Recent studies done by Diana Baumrind (1980, 1995) found that parenting styles could be reliably divided into three broad patterns: *authoritarian*, *permissive*, and *authoritative*.

1. *Authoritarian*. These parents value unquestioning obedience and mature responsibility from their children, while remaining aloof and detached. An authoritarian parent might say, "Don't ask questions. Just do it my way or else." Children of authoritarian parents are easily upset, moody, aggressive, and generally have poor communication skills.

2. *Permissive*. Permissive parents come in two styles: (a) *permissive-indifferent*, the parent who sets few limits and provides little in the way of attention, interest, or emotional support, and (b) *permissive-indulgent*, the parent who is highly involved but places few demands or controls on the child. Children of permissive-indifferent parents have poor self-control (becoming demanding and disobedient) and poor social skills. Children of permissive-indulgent parents often fail to learn respect for others and tend to be impulsive, immature, and out of control.

3. *Authoritative*. These parents are caring and sensitive toward their children, but they also set firm limits and enforce them, while encouraging increasing responsibility. As you might expect, children do best under the authoritative parents. They become self-reliant, self-controlled, and high achieving. They also seem more content, friendly, and socially competent in their dealings with others (Baumrind, 1995; Parke & Buriel, 1998).

Evaluating Baumrind's Research

Before you conclude that the authoritative pattern is the only way to raise successful children, you should know that many children raised in the other styles also become caring, cooperative adults. Criticism of Baumrind's findings generally falls into three areas: *child temperament*, *child expectations*, and *parental warmth*:

1. *Child temperament*. Results may reflect the child's unique temperament and reactions to parental efforts rather than the parenting style per se (Clarke-Stewart, Fitzpatrick, Allhusen, & Goldberg, 2000; McCrae et al., 2000). That is, the parents of mature and competent children may have developed the authoritative style because of the child's behavior rather than vice versa.

2. Child expectations. Cultural research suggests that a child's expectations of how parents should behave also plays an important role in parenting styles (Brislin, 2000; Valsiner, 2000). As we discovered at the beginning of this chapter, adolescents in Korea expect strong parental control and interpret it as a sign of love and deep concern. Adolescents in North America, however, would interpret the same behavior as a sign of parental hostility and rejection.

3. Parental warmth. Cross-cultural studies suggest that the most important variable in parenting styles and child development might be the degree of warmth versus rejection parents feel toward their children. On the basis of analyses of over 100 societies, Rohner (1986) concluded that universally, parental rejection adversely affects a child. The neglect and indifference shown by rejecting parents tend to produce hostile, aggressive children who have a difficult time establishing and maintaining close relationships. These children are also more likely to develop psychological problems that require professional intervention (Brook, Richter, and Whiteman, 2000; Giancola, 2000).

Are fathers important? Although overlooked in the past, the father's role in a child's development is now a topic of active research.

Do fathers differ from mothers in their parenting style? Until recently, the father's role in discipline and child care was largely ignored. But as more fathers have begun to take an active role in child rearing, there has been a corresponding increase in research. From these studies, we now know that fathers are absorbed with, excited about, and responsive to their newborns and that there are few differences in the way children form attachments to either parent (Biller, 1993; Lamb, 1996). After infancy, the father becomes increasingly involved with his children, yet he still spends less overall time in direct child care than the mother does (Demo, 1992; Hewlett, 1992). But fathers are just as responsive, nurturing, and competent as mothers when they do assume child-care responsibilities.

Check & Review

SOCIAL–EMOTIONAL DEVELOPMENT

Nativists believe that **attachment** is innate, whereas nurturists believe it is learned. The Harlow and Zimmerman experiments with monkeys raised by cloth or wire surrogate mothers found that contact comfort might be the most important factor in attachment.

Infants who fail to form attachments may suffer serious effects. When attachments are formed, they may differ in level or degree. Research on securely attached, avoidant, and anxious/ambivalent children found significant differences in behaviors that may persist into adulthood.

Parenting styles fall into three major categories: authoritarian, permissive, and authoritative. Critics suggest that a child's unique temperament, their expectations of parents, and the degree of warmth versus rejection from parents may be the three most important variables in parenting styles.

Questions

1. According to Harlow and Zimmerman's research with cloth and wire surrogate mothers, _____ is the most important variable for attachment. (a) availability of food; (b) contact comfort; (c) caregiver and infant bonding; (d) imprinting

2. List the three types of attachment reported by Mary Ainsworth.

3. Using Hazan and Shaver's research on adult attachment styles, match the following adults with their probable type of infant attachment:

____ 1. Mary is nervous around attractive partners and complains that lovers often want her to be more intimate than she finds comfortable.

____ 2. Bob complains that lovers are often reluctant to get as close as he would like.

____ 3. Rashelle finds it relatively easy to get close to others and seldom worries about being abandoned.

(a) avoidant; (b) secure; (c) anxious/ambivalent

4. Briefly summarize Baumrind's three parenting styles.

Answers to Questions can be found in Appendix B.

COGNITIVE DEVELOPMENT

The following fan letter was written to Shari Lewis (1963), a children's television performer, about her puppet Lamb Chop:

> Dear Shari:
>
> All my friends say Lamb Chop isn't really a little girl that talks. She is just a puppet you made out of a sock. I don't care even if it's true. I like the way Lamb Chop talks. If I send you one of my socks will you teach it how to talk and send it back?
>
> Randi

<div class="margin-note">

How does cognition, or the way we think about the world, change during the life cycle?

</div>

Randi's understanding of fantasy and reality is certainly different from an adult's. Just as a child's body and physical abilities change, his or her way of knowing and perceiving the world also grows and changes. This seems intuitively obvious, but early psychologists — with one exception — focused on physical, emotional, language, and personality development. The one major exception was Jean Piaget (pronounced Pee-ahzhay).

Piaget demonstrated that a child's intellect is fundamentally different from an adult's (Flavell, 1999; Papert, 1999). He showed that an infant begins at a cognitively "primitive" level and that intellectual growth progresses in distinct stages, motivated by an innate need to know. Piaget's theory, developed in the 1920s and 1930s, has proven so comprehensive and insightful that it remains the major force in the cognitive area of developmental psychology today.

To appreciate Piaget's contributions, we need to consider three major concepts: schemas, assimilation, and accommodation. **Schemas** are the most basic units of intellect. They act as patterns that organize our interactions with the environment, like architect's drawings or builder's blueprints.

<div class="margin-note">

Schema *Cognitive structures or patterns consisting of a number of organized ideas that grow and differentiate with experience*

</div>

In the first few weeks of life, for example, the infant apparently has several schemas based on the innate reflexes of sucking, grasping, and so on. These schemas are primarily motor and may be little more than stimulus-and-response mechanisms — the nipple is presented and the baby sucks. Soon, however, other schemas emerge. The infant develops a more detailed schema for eating solid food, a different schema for the concepts of "mother" and "father," and so on. It is important to recognize that schemas, our tools for learning about the world, are enlarged and changed throughout our lives (Leahy and Harris, 1997). For example, a computer user previously accustomed to DOS (disk operating system, a text-based format) would need to develop new schemas in order to work with Windows (a graphic user interface).

Assimilation and accommodation are the two major processes by which schemas grow and change over time. **Assimilation** is the process of taking in new information that easily fits into an existing schema. For instance, infants use their sucking schema not only in sucking nipples but also in sucking blankets or fingers.

<div class="margin-note">

Assimilation *The process of responding to a new situation in the same manner that is used in a familiar situation*

Accommodation *The process of adjusting existing ways of thinking (reworking schemas) to encompass new information, ideas, or objects*

</div>

Accommodation occurs when new information or stimuli cannot be assimilated and new schemas are developed or when old schemas are changed to adapt to the new features. An infant's first attempt to eat solid food with a spoon is a good example of accommodation. When the spoon first enters her mouth, the child attempts to assimilate it by using the previously successful sucking schema — shaping lips and tongue around the spoon as around a nipple. After repeated trials, she accommodates by adjusting her lips and tongue in a way that moves the food off the spoon and into her mouth.

Study the "impossible figure" below. Now take out a piece of paper and try to draw the same figure (without tracing!). Students with artistic training generally find it relatively easy to reproduce, whereas the rest of us find it "impossible." This is because we lack the necessary artistic *schema* and cannot *assimilate* what we see. With practice and training, we could *accommodate* the new information and easily draw the figure.

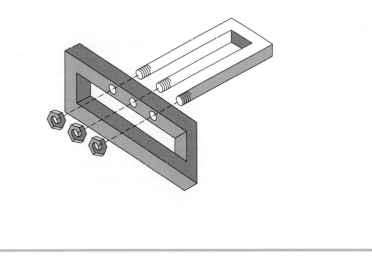

Stages of Cognitive Development: Birth to Adolescence

As a result of assimilation, accommodation, and the corresponding changes in schemas, a child's cognitive abilities undergo an orderly series of increasingly complex changes. When enough changes have occurred, the individual experiences a large developmental shift in his or her point of view. Piaget called these developmental shifts cognitive stages in development (Table 9.4).

According to Piaget, all children go through the same four cognitive stages at approximately the same age, regardless of the culture in which they live. No stage can be skipped, because skills acquired at earlier stages are essential to mastery at later stages. Let's take a closer look at these four stages: sensorimotor, preoperational, concrete operational, and formal operational.

The Sensorimotor Stage

During the **sensorimotor stage**, lasting from birth until "significant" language acquisition (about age 2 years), children explore the world and develop their schemas primarily through their senses and motor activities — hence the term *sensorimotor*.

One important concept acquired during this stage is **object permanence**. At birth and for the next 3 or 4 months, children lack object permanence. They seem to have no schemas for objects that disappear from their vision — out of sight is truly out of mind (Figure 9.14).

Preoperational Stage

During the **preoperational stage** (roughly ages 2 to 7 years), language advances significantly, and the child begins to think *symbolically* — using symbols, such as

Sensorimotor Stage *The first of Piaget's stages (birth to approximately age two years), in which cognitive development takes place by exploring the world via sensory perceptions and motor skills*

Object Permanence *A Piagetian term for an infant's understanding that objects (or people) continue to exist even when they cannot be directly seen, heard, or touched*

Preoperational Stage *The second of Piaget's stages (roughly ages 2 to 7 years), characterized by the ability to employ significant language and to think symbolically, but the child lacks operations (reversible mental processes), and thinking is egocentric and animistic*

Can you guess this child's stage of cognitive development? Can you see why this stage is called "sensorimotor"?

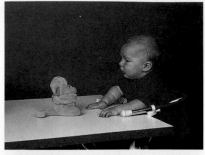

Figure 9.14 *Object permanence.* According to Piaget, young infants lack *object permanence* — an understanding that objects continue to exist even when they cannot directly be seen, heard, or touched. The baby in these pictures seems to believe the toy no longer exists once it is blocked by the screen.

Egocentrism *The inability to consider another's point of view, which Piaget considered a hallmark of the preoperational stage*

TABLE 9.4 PIAGET'S FOUR STAGES OF COGNITIVE DEVELOPMENT

Birth to 2 years	***Sensorimotor*** Abilities: Uses senses and motor skills to explore and develop cognitively. Limits: Beginning of stage lacks *object permanence* (understanding things continue to exist even when not seen, heard, or felt).
Ages 2–7 years	***Preoperational*** Abilities: Has significant language and thinks symbolically. Limits: • Cannot perform "operations." • *Egocentric* thinking (inability to consider another's point of view). • *Animistic* thinking (believing all things are living).
Ages 7–11 years	***Concrete Operational*** Abilities: • Can perform "operation" on concrete objects. • Understands *conservation* (realizing thoughts and changes in shape or appearance can be reversed). Limits: Cannot think abstractly and hypothetically.
Ages 11 years and up	***Formal Operational*** Abilities: Can think abstractly and hypothetically. Limits: *Adolescent egocentrism* at the beginning of this stage, with related problems of the *personal fable* and *imaginary audience*.

words, to represent concepts. On the other hand, there are also three major "problems" or limits to the child's thinking:

1. *Cannot perform operations.* Piaget labeled this period "preoperational" because the child lacks *operations*, reversible mental processes. For instance, if a preoperational boy who has a brother is asked, "Do you have a brother?" He will easily respond, "Yes." However, when asked, "Does your brother have a brother?" he will answer, "No!" To understand that his brother has a brother, he must be able to *reverse* the concept of "having a brother."

2. *Egocentric thinking.* Children at this stage have difficulty understanding that there are points of view other than their own. **Egocentrism** refers to the preoperational child's limited ability to distinguish between his or her own perspective and someone else's. The preschooler who moves in front of you to get a better view of the TV or repeatedly asks questions while you are talking on the telephone is demonstrating egocentrism. They assume that others see, hear, feel, and think exactly as they do. Consider the following telephone conversation between a 3-year-old, who is at home, and her mother, who is at work:

Mother: Emma is that you?

Emma: (Nods silently).

Mother: Emma, is Daddy there? Can I speak to him?

Emma: (Twice nods silently).

Egocentric preoperational children fail to understand that the phone caller cannot see their nodding head.

3. *Animistic thinking.* Children in the preoperational stage believe that objects such as the sun, trees, clouds, and bars of soap have motives, feelings, and intentions (for example, "dark clouds are angry" and "soap sinks to the bottom of the bathtub because it is tired"). *Animism* refers to the belief that all things are living (or animated). Our earlier example of Randi's letter asking puppeteer Shari Lewis to teach her sock to talk like Lamb Chop is also an example of animistic thinking.

Can't preoperational children be taught how to use operations and to avoid egocentric and animistic thinking? Although some researchers have reported success in accelerating the preoperational stage, Piaget did not believe in pushing children ahead of their own developmental schedule. He believed children should be allowed to grow at their own pace, with minimal adult interference (Elkind, 1981, 2000, 2001). In fact, Piaget thought Americans were particularly guilty of pushing children, calling American childhood the "Great American Kid Race."

Concrete Operational Stage

Between the approximate ages of 7 and 11 years, children are in the **concrete operational stage**. During this stage many important thinking skills emerge. Unlike the preoperational stage, concrete operational children are able to perform operations on *concrete* objects. Because they understand the concept of *reversibility*, they recognize that certain physical attributes (such as volume) remain unchanged although the outward appearance is altered, a process known as **conservation**.

If you know children in the preoperational or concrete operational stages, you may enjoy testing their grasp of conservation by trying some of the experiments shown in Table 9.5, page 344. The equipment is easily obtained, and you will find their responses fascinating. Keep in mind that this should be done as a game. Do not allow the child to feel that he or she is failing a test or making a mistake.

Formal Operational Stage

The final period in Piaget's theory is the **formal operational stage**, which typically begins around age 11 years. In this stage, children begin to apply their operations to abstract concepts, in addition to concrete objects. They also become capable of hypothetical thinking ("What if?"), which allows systematic formulation and testing of concepts.

Adolescents considering part-time jobs, for example, may think about possible conflicts with school and friends, the number of hours they want to work, and the kind of work they are qualified for before they start filling out applications. Formal operational thinking also allows the adolescent to construct a well-reasoned argument based on hypothetical concepts and logical processes. Consider the following argument:

1. If you hit a glass with a feather, the glass will break.

2. You hit the glass with a feather.

What is the logical conclusion? The correct answer, "The glass will break," is contrary to fact and direct experience. Therefore, the child in the concrete operational stage would have difficulty with this task, whereas the formal operational thinker understands that this problem is about abstractions that need not correspond to the real world.

Problems with Early Formal Operational Thinking

Along with the benefits of this cognitive style come several problems. Adolescents in the early stages of the formal operational period demonstrate a type of *egocentrism* different from that of the preoperational child. Although adolescents do recognize that others have unique thoughts and perspectives, they often fail to differentiate between what others are thinking and their own thoughts. This *adolescent egocentrism* has two characteristics that may affect social interactions as well as problem solving:

Test for conservation. *Using Piaget's research method, a child is first shown two equal-sized glasses filled with the same amount of water. The child then pours one of the glasses of water into a taller, thinner glass, and is asked if they both still contain the same amount of water. A preoperational child will say the taller glass has "more" because he or she lacks the cognitive ability known as conservation*

Concrete Operational Stage *The third of Piaget's stages of cognitive development (roughly ages 7 to 11 years); the child can perform mental operations on concrete objects and understands reversibility and conservation*

Conservation *The ability to recognize that a given quantity, weight, or volume remains constant despite changes in shape, length, or position*

Formal Operational Stage *Piaget's fourth stage of cognitive development (around age 11 years and beyond), characterized by abstract and hypothetical thinking*

TABLE 9.5 ADDITIONAL TESTS FOR CONSERVATION

Type of Conservation	Step 1 of Experiment	Experimenter then . . .	Child is asked conservation question	Average age at which concept is grasped
Length	Center two sticks of equal length. Child agrees that they are of equal length.	. . . moves stick over.	*Which stick is longer?* Preconserving child will say that one of the sticks is longer. Conserving child will say that they are both the same length.	6–7
Substance amount	Center two identical clay balls. Child acknowledges that the two have equal amounts of clay.	. . . rolls out one of the balls.	*Do the two pieces have the same amount of clay?* Preconserving child will say that the long piece has more clay. Conserving child will say that the two pieces have the same amount of clay.	6–7
Area	Center two identical sheets of cardboard with wooden blocks placed on them in identical positions. Child acknowledges that the same amount of space is left open on each piece of cardboard.	. . . scatters the blocks on one piece of cardboard.	*Do the two pieces of cardboard have the same amount of open space?* Preconserving child will say that the cardboard with scattered blocks has less open space. Conserving child will say that both pieces have the same amount of open space.	8–10
Volume	Center two balls of clay in two identical glasses with an equal amount of water. Child acknowledges that they displace equal amounts of water.	. . . changes the shape of one of the balls.	*Do the two pieces of clay displace the same amount of water?* Preconserving child will say that the longer piece displaces more water. Conserving child will say that both pieces displace the same amount of water.	10–12

This is a sample of experiments used to test Piaget's different types of convervation. Try them with children of various ages. Do they fit the stages as described by Piaget?

1. Personal fable. As a result of their unique form of egocentrism, adolescents may conclude they alone are having certain insights or difficulties and that no one else could understand or sympathize. David Elkind (1967, 2000, 2001) described this as the formation of a *personal fable,* an intense investment in their own thoughts and feelings, and a belief that these thoughts are unique. One student in our class remembered being very upset in junior high when her mother tried to comfort her over the loss of an important relationship. "I felt like she couldn't possibly know how it felt — no one could. I couldn't believe that anyone had ever suffered like this or that things would ever get better."

Several forms of risk taking, such as engaging in sexual intercourse without contraception, driving dangerously, and experimenting with drugs, also seem to arise from the personal fable (Coley & Chase-Lansdale, 1998; Greene, Rubin, Hale, & Walters, 1996). The adolescent has a sense of uniqueness, invulnerability, and immortality. They recognize the dangers of these activities, but the rules don't seem to apply to them.

2. Imaginary audience. In early adolescence, people tend to believe they are the center of others' thoughts and attentions, instead of considering that everyone is equally wrapped up in his or her own concerns and plans. In other words, adolescents picture all eyes focused on their behaviors. Elkind referred to this as the *imaginary audience.* This may explain what seems like extreme forms of self-consciousness and concern for physical appearance ("Everyone knows I don't know the answer"; "They're noticing how fat I am and this awful haircut").

If the imaginary audience results from an inability to differentiate the self from others, the personal fable is a product of differentiating too much. Thankfully, these two forms of adolescent egocentrism tend to decrease during later stages of the formal operational period.

Assessing Piaget's Theory: Criticisms and Contributions

As influential as Piaget's account of cognitive development has been, it has received significant criticisms. Let's look briefly at two major areas of concern: underestimated abilities and underestimated genetic and cultural influences.

Personal fable in action? *Can you see how this type of risk-taking behavior may reflect the personal fable — an adolescent's tendency to believe he or she is unique and special and that dangers don't apply to them?*

---

critical thinking

Applying Your Knowledge of Piaget

One of the most important behavioral components in critical thinking is applying what you learn to new situations. If you can use new knowledge in different contexts, you have mastered it. Demonstrate your understanding of Piaget's theories by applying what you have learned to the following situations.

A young mother is encouraging her son to try another bite of chicken and rice, which he clearly doesn't like. The child is quietly whining, until the mother spreads the food around to cool it. He then becomes hysterical. What upset the child? Identify the cognitive stage of the child.

Last month Janie's mom could easily substitute a stuffed toy animal for a noisy toy, and Janie would continue happily playing. Now she cries and reaches for the noisy toy even when it is out of sight. What cognitive changes have occurred? Identify Janie's cognitive stage of development.

Tom is deeply upset when his parents forbid him to ride motorcycles. He refuses to believe this is risky behavior. Explain Tom's refusal from a Piagetian perspective, and label his stage of cognitive development.

An aunt gives her two nephews three cookies and tells them to share. The older child takes two cookies for himself and offers his brother the other cookie broken in half. Both children are happy with this arrangement. Label each child's stage of cognitive development.

Answers appear in Appendix B.

Contrary to Piaget's belief, children in the preoperational stage are not completely egocentric. They can occasionally take the perspective of another — like the children in this photo.

Underestimated Abilities

Research shows that Piaget may have underestimated young children's cognitive development. For example, researchers report that very young infants have a basic concept of how objects move, are aware that objects continue to exist even when screened from view, can recognize speech sounds, and even understand the concept of addition (Haith & Benson, 1998).

Research on infant imitation of facial expression also raises questions about Piaget's estimates of early infant cognition. In a series of well-known studies, Meltzoff and Moore (1977, 1985, 1994) found that newborns could imitate such facial movements as tongue protrusion, mouth opening, and lip pursing (Figure 9.15). At age 9 months, infants will imitate facial actions a full day after seeing them (Heimann & Meltzoff, 1996).

Underestimated Genetic and Cultural Influences

Piaget's model, like other stage theories, has also been criticized for not sufficiently taking into account genetic and cultural differences (Matusov & Hayes, 2000; Matsumoto, 2000; Plomin & Rutter, 1998). During Piaget's time, the genetic influences on cognitive abilities were poorly understood, but as you know from earlier chapters and discussions in this text, there has been rapid explosion of information in this field in the last few years. In addition, formal education and specific cultural experiences can also significantly affect cognitive development. Consider the following example from a researcher attempting to test the formal operational skills of a farmer in Liberia (Scribner, 1977):

> Researcher: All Kpelle men are rice farmers. Mr. Smith is not a rice farmer. Is he a Kpelle man?
>
> Kpelle farmer: I don't know the man. I have not laid eyes on the man myself.

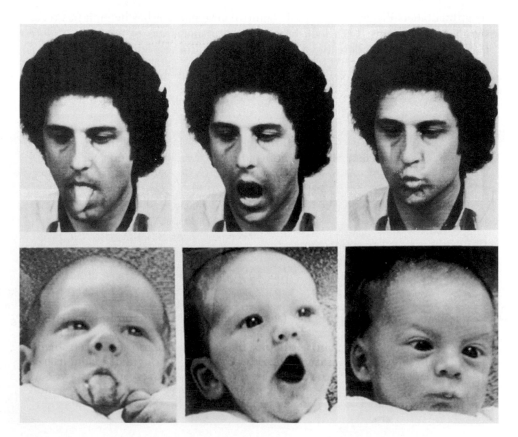

Figure 9.15 *Infant imitation.* When an adult models a facial expression, even very young infants will respond with a similar expression. Is this true imitation or a simple stimulus–response reflex?

Instead of reasoning in the "logical" way of Piaget's formal operational stage, the Kpelle farmer reasoned according to his specific cultural and educational training, which apparently emphasized personal knowledge. Not knowing Mr. Smith, the Kpelle farmer did not feel qualified to comment on him. Thus, Piaget's theory may have underestimated the effect of culture on a person's cognitive functioning.

Despite criticisms, Piaget's contributions to psychology are enormous. As one scholar put it, "assessing the impact of Piaget on developmental psychology is like assessing the impact of Shakespeare on English literature or Aristotle on philosophy — impossible" (cited in Beilin, 1992, p. 191).

Information Processing: A Computer Model of Cognition

An alternative to Piaget's theory of cognitive development is the *information processing model,* which compares the workings of the mind to a computer and studies how information is received, encoded, stored, organized, retrieved, and used by people of different ages. This model offers important insights into two major areas of cognition: attention and memory.

Attention

Attention refers to focusing awareness on a narrowed range of stimuli. Infants pay attention to their environment for only short periods of time. Even toddlers, who can pay attention for longer periods, are easily distracted. When watching TV, for example, 2-year-olds talk more to other people, play more with toys, and look around the room more than 4-year-olds do. As children get older, their attention spans improve and they learn to discriminate between what is and what is not important to concentrate on at any given time (Bjorklund, 1995).

Memory

After children attend to information and take it into their information processing system, they must remember it. Attention determines what information enters the "computer," whereas memory determines what information is saved.

Like attention, memory skills also improve gradually throughout childhood and adolescence (Hayne, Boniface, & Barr, 2000; Richards, 1997). Two-year-olds can repeat back about two digits immediately after hearing them, but 10-year-olds can repeat about six. Improvement comes as children acquire strategies during the school years for storing and retrieving information. For example, they learn to rehearse or repeat information over and over, to use mnemonics (like "i before e except after c"), and to organize their information in ways that facilitate retrieval (Chapter 7).

As people grow older, their use of information processing strategies and overall memory continue to change. Recall from Chapter 8 that *fluid intelligence* (requiring speed or rapid learning) tends to decrease with age, whereas *crystallized intelligence* (knowledge and information gained over the life span) continues to increase until advanced old age. Despite concerns about "keeping up with 18-year-olds," older returning students often do as well as or better than their younger counterparts in college classes. This superior performance in older adult students is due in part to their generally greater academic motivation, but it also reflects the importance of prior knowledge. Cognitive psychologists have demonstrated that the more people know, the easier it is for them to lay down new memories (Chi & Glaser, 1985; Leahy & Harris, 1997). Older students, for instance, generally find this chapter on development easier to master than do younger students. Their interactions with children and greater knowledge about life changes create a framework on which to hang new information.

Age and intelligence. Although many people believe intelligence declines with age, research suggests that this is largely a myth.

In summary, the more you know, the more you learn. Thus, having a college degree and stimulating occupation may help you stay mentally sharp in your later years (Mayr & Kliegl, 2000; Powell, 1998).

Haven't studies also shown decreases in older adults' memory capabilities? As mentioned at the beginning of the chapter, this may reflect problems with cross-sectional versus longitudinal research. In addition, earlier studies often asked participants to memorize simple lists of words or paired association tasks, which older people often find meaningless and uninteresting. When the information is meaningful, an older person's rich web of existing knowledge helps him or her remember it (Graf, 1990).

The public and most researchers have long thought aging is accompanied by widespread death of neurons in the brain. Although this decline does happen with degenerative disorders like Alzheimer's disease, this is no longer believed to be a part of normal aging (Chapter 2). It is also important to remember that age-related memory problems are not on a continuum with Alzheimer's disease (Wilson et al., 2000). That is, normal forgetfulness "does not reflect a predisposition" for serious dementia.

Aging does seem to take its toll on *speed* of information processing, however (Miller & Vernon, 1997). Recall from Chapter 7 that decreased speed of processing may reflect problems with *encoding* (putting information into long-term storage) and *retrieval* (getting information out of storage) (Finkel & Pedersen, 2000; Mayr & Kliegl, 2000). If memory is like a filing system, older people may have more filing cabinets, and it may take them longer to initially file and later retrieve information.

In summary, many psychologists have criticized earlier studies of memory deficits in the elderly. Although mental speed declines with age, general information processing and much of memory ability is largely unaffected by the aging process (Baltes, Staudinger, & Lindenberger, 1999; D'Esposito & Weksler, 2000). Contrary to popular stereotypes of frail and forgetful elderly, growing old, for most of us, will probably be better than expected — and, of course, far better than the alternative!

Check & Review

COGNITIVE DEVELOPMENT

Jean Piaget's theories of cognitive development are based on the concept of **schemas**, mental patterns or blueprints used to interpret the world. Sometimes existing schemas can be used "as is" and information is **assimilated**; on other occasions, existing schemas must be modified, which calls for **accommodation**.

According to Piaget, cognitive development occurs in an invariant sequence of four stages: **sensorimotor** (birth to 2 years), **preoperational** (between 2 and 7 years), **concrete operational** (between 7 and 11 years), and **formal operational** (age 11 years and up).

In the sensorimotor stage, children acquire **object permanence**. During the preoperational stage, children are better equipped to use symbols, but their thinking is limited by their lack of operations, **egocentrism**, and animism.

In the concrete operational stage, children learn to perform operations (to think about concrete things while not actually doing them). They understand the principles of conservation and reversibility. During the formal operational stage, the adolescent is able to think abstractly and deal with hypothetical situations but again is prone to egotism.

Although Piaget has been criticized for underestimating abilities and genetic and cultural influences, he remains one of the most respected psychologists in modern times.

Psychologists who explain cognitive development in terms of the information processing model have found this model especially useful in explaining attention and memory changes across the life span. In contrast to pessimistic early studies, recent research is much more encouraging about age-related changes in information processing.

Questions

1. _____ was one of the first scientists to prove that a child's cognitive processes are fundamentally different from an adult's. (a) Baumrind; (b) Beck; (c) Piaget; (d) Elkind

2. _____ occurs when existing schemas are used to interpret new information, whereas _____ involves changes and adaptations of the schemas. (a) adaptation; accommodation; (b) adaptation; reversibility; (c) egocentrism; postschematization; (d) assimilation; accommodation

3. Match the Piagetian stage with the relevant concept:

____ 1. Egocentrism, animism
____ 2. Object permanence
____ 3. Abstract and hypothetical thinking
____ 4. Conservation, reversibility
____ 5. Personal fable, imaginary audience

a. Sensorimotor
b. Preoperational
c. Concrete operational
d. Formal operational

4. How does the information processing model explain some memory problems in older adults?

Answers to Questions can be found in Appendix B.

KEY TERMS

developmental psychology (p. 318)
Studying Development
critical period (p. 319)
cross-sectional method (p. 319)
longitudinal method (p. 319)
maturation (p. 318)
Physical Development
embryonic period (p. 324)
fetal alcohol syndrome (FAS) (p. 325)
fetal period (p. 325)
germinal period (p. 324)
puberty (p. 329)
teratogen [TER-ah-toe-jen] (p. 325)

Language Development
babbling (p. 333)
cooing (p. 333)
language acquisition device (LAD) (p. 334)
overextension (p. 333)
overgeneralize (p. 333)
telegraphic speech (p. 333)
Social–Emotional Development
attachment (p. 335)
imprinting (p. 335)
Cognitive Development
accommodation (p. 340)

assimilation (p. 340)
concrete operational stage (p. 343)
conservation (p. 343)
egocentrism (p. 342)
formal operational stage (p. 343)
object permanence (p. 341)
preoperational stage (p. 341)
schema (p. 340)
sensorimotor stage (p. 341)

Visual Summary for Chapter 9

Studying Development

Developmental Psychology: concerned with describing, explaining, predicting, and modifying age-related behaviors from conception to death.

Theoretical Issues

Research Methods

Key Issues:
- Nature vs. Nurture
- Continuity vs. Stages
- Stability vs. Change

Cross–sectional: Different participants, various ages, one point in time. Major problem: cohort effects (a given generation may be affected by specific cultural/historical events).

Longitudinal: Same participants, extended period. Major problem: expensive, time consuming

Physical Development

Prenatal and Newborn

Three Major Stages: **germinal, embryonic,** and **fetal. Teratogens:** Environmental agents capable of producing birth defects.

Newborn and Early Childhood

Sensory and perceptual abilities are relatively well developed in newborns. Motor development comes with **maturation**.

Adolescence

Adolescence: Psychological period between childhood and adulthood.

Puberty: When sex organs become capable of reproduction.

Secondary sex characteristics: Hormonally induced changes (pubic hair, breasts, beards).

Adulthood

Menopause: Cessation of menstruation. Male climacteric: Physical and psychological changes in midlife. Primary aging: Inevitable, biological changes with age. Secondary aging: Accelerated aging due to disease, disuse, or abuse. Explanations of primary aging: *Programmed theory* (genetically built-in) and *wear-and-tear theory* (body's inability to repair damage).

Language Development

Stages

- *Prelinguistic:* Crying → **cooing** (vowel sounds) → **babbling** (vowel/consonant combinations).
- *Linguistic:* One-word utterances → **telegraphic speech** (omits unnecessary, connecting words) → grammatical speech.
- Problems: **Overextension** (e.g., "bunnies" called "dogs") and **overgeneralization** (e.g., "foots," "goed").

Theories

- *Nature:* Language results from maturation. Chomsky's innate **language acquisition device (LAD)**.
- *Nurture:* Environment and rewards/punishments explain language.

Social-Emotional Development

Attachment

- Infant attachment: **Imprinting:** Attaching to first large moving object. Harlow's experiments found "contact comfort" very important to **attachment**. Infants who do not attach may suffer serious, lasting effects.
- Adult attachment: Patterns of infant attachment (secure, avoidant, and anxious/ambivalent) may carry over into adult romantic attachments.

Parenting Styles

There are three major categories (authoritarian, permissive, and authoritative), but critics suggest that a child's unique temperament, expectations of parents, and degree of warmth versus rejection from parents may be the most important determinants of parenting styles.

Cognitive Development

Piaget's Major Concepts:

- **Schema:** Cognitive structure for organizing ideas.
- **Assimilation:** Adding new information to an existing schema.
- **Accommodation:** Revising schemas to account for new information.

Four Stages	Abilities	Limits
Sensorimotor (Birth to 2 years)	Uses senses and motor skills to explore and develop cognitively.	Beginning of stage infant lacks **object permanence** (understanding things continue to exist even when not seen, heard, or felt).
Preoperational (Ages 2 to 7)	Has significant language and thinks symbolically.	• Cannot perform "operations." • **Egocentric** thinking (inability to consider another's point of view). • Animistic thinking (believing all things are living).
Concrete Operational (Ages 7 to 11)	• Can perform "operations" on concrete objects. • Understands **conservation** (realizing changes in shape or appearance can be reversed).	Cannot think abstractly and hypothetically.
Formal Operational (11 and up)	Can think abstractly and hypothetically.	Adolescent egocentrism at the beginning of this stage, with related problems of the *personal fable* and *imaginary audience*.

Information Processing Model: Process of taking in, remembering or forgetting, and using information. Major concepts: The mind is like a computer. Focuses on quantitative changes vs. Piaget's qualitative changes.

10 Life Span Development II

I n Europe, a woman was near death from a special kind of cancer. There was one drug that doctors thought might save her. It was a form of radium that a druggist in the same town had recently discovered. The drug was expensive to make, but the druggist was charging 10 times what the drug cost him to make. He paid $200 for the radium and charged $2,000 for a small dose of the drug.

The sick woman's husband, Heinz, went to everyone he knew to borrow the money, but he could get together only about $1,000, which is half of what it cost. He told the druggist that his wife was dying and asked him to sell it cheaper or let him pay later. But the druggist said, "No, I discovered the drug, and I'm going to make money from it." So Heinz got desperate and broke into the man's store to steal the drug for his wife. Kohlberg, 1964, pp. 18–19

Was Heinz morally right to steal the drug? What do you consider moral behavior? Is morality "in the eye of the beholder," and everyone simply argues for his or her own self-interest? Or are there universal truths and principles? Whatever your answer, your ability to think, reason, and respond to Heinz's dilemma demonstrates another type of development that is very important to psychology: moral development.

As we discussed in Chapter 9, developmental psychology is devoted to the study of age-related changes in behavior and abilities from conception to death. Chapter 9 explored life span changes in physical development, language development, social–emotional development, and cognitive development. In this chapter, we continue our study with moral development, personality development, and special issues related to bereavement and death.

MORAL DEVELOPMENT

Developmental psychologists have traditionally examined morality from a developmental stage perspective. That is, they study how moral thoughts, feelings, and behaviors change over the life span (Eisenberg, 2000).

How does morality change over the life span?

Kohlberg's Research

One of the most influential researchers in moral development was Lawrence Kohlberg (1927–1987). He presented what he called "moral stories" like the Heinz dilemma to people of all ages, and on the basis of his findings, he developed a model of moral development (1964, 1984).

What is the right answer to Heinz's dilemma? Kohlberg was interested not in whether participants judged Heinz right or wrong but in the reasons they gave for their decision. On the basis of participants' responses, Kohlberg proposed three broad levels in the evolution of moral reasoning, each composed of two distinct stages (Table 10.1). Individuals at each stage and level may or may not support Heinz's stealing of the drug, but for different reasons.

Like Piaget's stages of cognitive development (Chapter 9), Kohlberg believed his stages of moral development were *universal* and *invariant*. That is, they supposedly exist in all cultures, and everyone goes through each of the stages in a predictable fashion. The age trends that are noticed tend to be rather broad:

Preconventional Level *Lawrence Kohlberg's first level of moral development, characterized by moral judgments based on fear of punishment or desire for pleasure*

1. *Preconventional level* (stages 1 and 2 — birth to adolescence). At this level, moral judgment is *self-centered*. What is right is what one can get away with or what is personally satisfying. This level is called *preconventional* because children have not accepted society's (conventional) rule-making processes.

"DON'T YOU REALIZE, JASON, THAT WHEN YOU THROW FURNITURE OUT THE WINDOW AND TIE YOUR SISTER TO A TREE, YOU MAKE MOMMY AND DADDY VERY SAD?"

© Sidney Harris

TABLE 10.1 KOHLBERG'S STAGES OF MORAL DEVELOPMENT

Name of Stage	Moral Reasoning	Heinz's Dilemma Responses	
		Pro	Con
Preconventional level			
Stage 1: punishment—obedience orientation	Morality is what you can get away with	If you let your wife die, you will get in trouble. You'll be blamed for not spending the money to save her and there'll be an investigation of you and the druggist for your wife's death.	You shouldn't steal the drug, because you'll be caught and sent to jail. If you do get away, your conscience would bother you thinking how the police will catch up with you at any minute.
Stage 2: instrumental—exchange orientation	Obey rules to obtain rewards or favors	If you do happen to get caught, you could give the drug back and you wouldn't get much of a sentence. It wouldn't bother you much to serve, a little jail term if you had your wife when you got out.	You may not get much of a jail term if you steal the drug, but your wife will probably die before you get out, so it won't do you much good. If your wife dies, you shouldn't blame yourself; it isn't your fault she has cancer.
Conventional level			
Stage 3: good child orientation	Obey rules to get approval	No one will think you're bad if you steal the drug, but your family will think you're an inhuman husband if you don't. If you let your wife die, you'll never be able to look anybody in the face again.	It isn't just the druggist who will think you're a criminal; everyone else will, too. After you steal it, you'll feel bad thinking how you've brought dishonor on your family and yourself, and you won't be able to face anyone again.
Stage 4: law-and-order orientation	Obey laws because they maintain the social order	If you have any sense of honor, you won't let your wife die just because you're afraid to do the only thing that will save her. You'll always feel guilty that you caused her death if you don't do your duty to her.	You're desperate and you may not know you're doing wrong when you steal the drug. But you'll know you did wrong after you're sent to jail. You'll always feel guilty for breaking the law.
Postconventional level			
Stage 5: social-contract orientation	Moral reasoning reflects belief in democratically accepted laws	You'll lose other people's respect, not gain it, if you don't steal. If you let your wife die, it would be out of fear, not out of reasoning it out. So you'd lose self-respect and probably the respect of others, too.	You would lose your standing and respect in the community and violate the law. You'd lose respect for yourself if you're carried away by emotion and forget the long-range point of view.
Stage 6: universal ethics orientation	Moral reasoning reflects individual conscience	If you don't steal the drug and let your wife die, you'll always condemn yourself for it afterward. You wouldn't be blamed and you would have lived up to the outside rule of the law, but you wouldn't have lived up to your own standards of conscience.	If you stole the drug, you wouldn't be blamed by other people, but you'd condemn yourself because you wouldn't have lived up to your own conscience and standards of honesty.

Sources: Kohlberg (1966, 1969), Rest, Turiel, & Kohlberg (1969).

- During stage 1 (punishment-and-obedience orientation), the child conforms to rules made by authority figures so he or she can avoid punishment. Interestingly, goodness or badness also depends on the magnitude of the consequences. Thus, a 5-year-old will often say that *accidentally* breaking 15 cups is "badder" and should receive more punishment than *intentionally* breaking 1 cup.

- During stage 2 (instrumental-exchange orientation), moral reasoning reflects some concern for others, but it is ultimately motivated by the hope of benefit in return. "You scratch my back and I'll scratch yours" is the guiding philosophy.

Conventional Level *Lawrence Kohlberg's second level of moral development, where moral judgments are based on compliance with the rules and values of society*

2. *Conventional level* (stages 3 and 4 — adolescence and young adulthood). During this time, moral reasoning advances from being self-centered to *other-centered*. The individual accepts and internalizes *conventional* societal values.

- At stage 3 ("good child" orientation) the primary moral concern is with being nice and gaining approval. People are also judged by their intentions and motives — "His heart was in the right place."

- During stage 4 (law-and-order orientation), rules and laws are valued because they maintain a social order that is worth preserving. Stage 4 individuals understand that if everyone violated laws, even with good intentions, there would be chaos. Thus, doing one's duty and respecting law and order are highly valued. According to Kohlberg, stage 4 is the highest level attained by most adolescents and adults.

Postconventional Level *Lawrence Kohlberg's highest level of moral development, which occurs when individuals develop personal standards for right and wrong*

3. *Postconventional level* (stages 5 and 6 — adulthood). This level advances beyond conventional societal rules that suggest authority and laws must be obeyed automatically. Instead, morality is guided by higher principles of human conduct, such as those described in the U.S. Constitution or the Ten Commandments.

- During stage 5 (social-contract orientation), individuals appreciate the underlying purposes served by laws. Furthermore, they believe laws should be derived from a democratic consensus so that they express the will of the majority or maximize social welfare.

- At stage 6 (universal-ethics orientation), "right" is determined by universal ethical principles that *all* religions or moral authorities might view as compelling or fair, such as nonviolence, human dignity, freedom, and equality. Thus, Mohandas Gandhi, Martin Luther King, Jr., and Nelson Mandela intentionally violated laws that they considered unjust because they did not treat all people equally. Few individuals actually achieve stage 6 (about 1 or 2 percent of those tested worldwide), and Kohlberg found it difficult to separate stages 5 and 6. Thus, in time, he combined the stages (Kohlberg, 1981).

Moral Behavior

Are the people who achieve higher stages on Kohlberg's scale really more moral than others, or do they just "talk a good game"? Although we might assume that moral reasoning would lead to moral behavior, there is considerable debate over whether Kohlberg's stages accurately predict an individual's actions. Some studies show a positive correlation between higher stages of reasoning and higher levels of moral behavior (Bond, Felter, & Ross, 2000; Borba, 2001; Rest, Narvaez, Bebeau, & Thoma, 1999), but others have found that the pressures of the situation are better predictors of moral behavior (Bandura, 1986, 1991; Bruggeman & Hart, 1996).

In addition to the questionable relationship between moral reasoning and behavior, Kohlberg's model has also been criticized as politically biased (favoring liberals over conservatives), culturally biased (favoring Western ideals of what is morally "advanced"), and gender biased (favoring males over females). The last two points are the focus of our next section.

GENDER & CULTURAL DIVERSITY

Insights into Morality

Recall from Chapter 9 two of the basic questions that guide developmental researchers: "nature or nurture?" and "continuity or stages?" Cross-cultural research on morality confirms that children in different cultures do conform to Kohlberg's model and generally progress sequentially from his first level, the preconventional, to his second, the conventional (Snarey, 1985, 1995; Rest, Narvaez, Bebeau, & Thoma, 1999). Thus, the *nature* and *stage* sides of these two basic questions seem to be supported by cross-cultural studies.

At the same time, cultural *differences* suggest that nurture, or culture, also determines morality. For example, cross-cultural comparisons of responses to Heinz's moral dilemma show that Europeans and Americans tend to consider whether they like or identify with the victim in questions of morality. In contrast, Hindu Indians consider social responsibility and personal concerns two separate issues (Miller & Bersoff, 1998). Researchers suggest that the difference reflects the Indians' broader sense of social responsibility.

In India, Papua New Guinea, China, and Israeli kibbutzim, rather than choosing between the rights of the individual and the rights of society (as the top levels of Kohlberg's model require), most people seek a compromise solution that accommodates both interests (Killen & Hart, 1999; Miller & Bersoff, 1998). Thus, Kohlberg's standard for judging the highest level of morality (the postconventional) may be more applicable to cultures that value individualism over community and interpersonal relationships.

Researcher Carol Gilligan has also criticized Kohlberg's gender bias (Mandel & Midler, 2000). Initially, Gilligan believed male and female values reflected two basic approaches to moral reasoning — *justice* versus *caring* (Gilligan, 1977, 1990, 1993; Hoffman, 2000). In the **justice perspective**, the person is seen as standing alone, and the focus is on the rights of the individual. The **care perspective**, on the other hand, stresses concern for others, and the person is viewed in terms of his or her relationship with others. Gilligan suggested Kohlberg emphasizes the justice perspective and underplays the care perspective in his studies of moral development.

In the case of Heinz, for example, arguing that Heinz should steal the drug because saving a life is more important than obeying laws is demonstrating a justice orientation, according to Gilligan. On the other hand, arguing that Heinz should steal the drug because he has an obligation to help someone he loves reflects a care orientation, in Gilligan's view.

Recent research supports Gilligan's idea that people have at least two forms of moral reasoning, but most studies have found few if any gender differences in level or type of moral reasoning (Hoffman, 2000; Jaffee & Hyde, 2000; Wark & Krebs, 1996). Both sexes typically use both care and justice orientations. Gilligan has therefore modified her initial position: Each of us has within ourselves two "voices" of morality — and both voices are valid (Gilligan & Attanucci, 1988).

Justice Perspective *Carol Gilligan's term for an approach to moral reasoning that emphasizes individual rights and views people as differentiated and standing alone*

Care Perspective *Carol Gilligan's term for an approach to moral reasoning that emphasizes interpersonal responsibility and interconnectedness with others*

Gilligan versus Kohlberg. *According to Carol Gilligan, women score "lower" on Lawrence Kohlberg's stages of moral development because they are socialized to assume more responsibility for the care of others.*

Check & Review

MORAL DEVELOPMENT

According to Lawrence Kohlberg, morality progresses through three levels, and each level consists of two stages. At the **preconventional level**, morality is self-centered. What is right is what one can get away with (Stage 1) or what is personally satisfying (Stage 2). **Conventional level** morality is based on a need for approval (Stage 3) and obedience to laws because they maintain the social order (Stage 4). **Postconventional level** morality comes from adhering to the social contract (Stage 5) and the individual's own principles and universal values (Stage 6).

Kohlberg's theory has been criticized for being politically, culturally, and gender biased. Carol Gilligan has suggested that women tend to take a **care perspective** in their moral reasoning, whereas men favor a **justice perspective**. Research shows that in real-life situations, not hypothetical situations, both sexes typically use both the justice and care orientations.

Questions

1. According to Kohlberg's theory of morality, self-interest and avoiding punishment are characteristic of the _____ level, personal standards or universal principles characterize the _____ level, and gaining approval or following the rules describes the _____ level.

2. Calvin would like to wear baggy, torn jeans and a nose ring, but he is concerned that others will disapprove. Calvin is at Kohlberg's _____ level of morality. (a) conformity; (b) approval seeking; (c) conventional; (d) preconventional

3. Five-year-old Tyler believes "bad things are what you get punished for." Tyler is at Kohlberg's _____ level of morality. (a) concrete; (b) preconventional; (c) postconventional; (d) punishment-oriented

4. How is Kohlberg's theory culturally and gender biased?

Answers to Questions can be found in Appendix B.

PERSONALITY DEVELOPMENT OVER THE LIFE SPAN

How does personality change from infancy to old age?

What were you like as an infant? Do your parents say you were an "easy" baby or a "difficult" baby? Are these early differences in personality related to later adult traits? In this section, we explore Stella Thomas and Alexander Chess's temperament theory and Erik Erikson's psychosocial theory.

Thomas and Chess's Temperament Theory: A Biological Look at Personality Development

From the moment you were born, you differed from other infants in characteristic ways. As an infant, did you lie quietly and seem oblivious to loud noises? Or did you tend to kick and scream and respond immediately to every sound? Did you respond warmly to people, or did you fuss, fret, and withdraw? Your answers to these questions would help determine what developmental psychologists call **temperament**, the basic, natural disposition of an individual.

Temperament *A basic, inborn disposition that appears shortly after birth and characterizes an individual's style of approaching people and situations*

As you might imagine, there is considerable controversy over the essential dimensions of temperament. One of the earliest and most influential theories came from the work of psychiatrists Stella Thomas and Alexander Chess (Thomas & Chess, 1977, 1987, 1991). Thomas and Chess found that approximately 65 percent of the babies they observed could be reliably separated into three categories:

1. *Easy children.* These were children who were happy most of the time, relaxed and agreeable, and adjusted easily to new situations (approximately 40 percent).

2. *Difficult children.* These were children who were moody, easily frustrated, tense, and overreactive to most situations (approximately 10 percent).

3. *Slow-to-warm-up children.* These were children who showed mild responses, were somewhat shy and withdrawn, and needed time to adjust to new experiences or people (approximately 15 percent).

Follow-up studies found that certain aspects of an infant's basic temperamental styles tend to be consistent and enduring throughout early childhood and even adulthood (Caspi, 2000; Kagan, 1995, 1998; McCrae et al., 2000). That is not to say every shy, cautious infant ends up a shy adult. Many events take place between infancy and adulthood that shape an individual's development.

One of the most influential factors in early personality development is *goodness of fit* between a child's nature and the social and environmental setting (Eccles et al., 1999; Solomon, 2000; Thompson, 1998). For example, a slow-to-warm-up child does best if allowed time to adjust to new situations, whereas a difficult child thrives in a structured, understanding environment but not in an inconsistent, intolerant home. Alexander Thomas, the pioneer of temperament research, thinks parents should work with their child's temperament, rather than trying to change it. Goodness of fit is another example of how nature and nurture interact (Gottlieb, 2000; Maccoby, 2000).

Erikson's Psychosocial Theory: The Eight Stages of Life

Erik Erikson (1902–1994) used Freud's notion of inborn biological forces as the basis for his theory of personality. But unlike Freud, Erikson continued his stage theory beyond adolescence all the way to mature adulthood (65 and older) (see Table 10.2, page 360). Erikson believed that Freud underestimated the power of social and cultural influences on human behavior and developed his theory, called **psychosocial stages** of development, in contrast to Freud's *psychosexual stages* (Chapter 13). Erikson identified eight stages in life, each characterized by a specific conflict or tension that the person must resolve.

Psychosocial Stages *Erik Erikson's theory that individuals pass through eight developmental stages and that adult personality reflects how the distinct challenges or crises at each stage are resolved*

Erikson's First Stage

In Erikson's first stage (birth to approximately 12 months), the major tension is *trust versus mistrust.* When and how the infant's needs are met determine whether the infant decides the world is a good and satisfying place to live or a source of pain, frustration, and uncertainty.

Stages 2 to 4

The second stage, *autonomy versus shame and doubt* (ages 1 to 3 years), is a time for developing self-awareness and independence. During the "terrible twos," toddlers continually assert their wills — "no, no" and "me, me." Parents who handle these beginning attempts at independence with patience and good-humored encouragement help their toddlers develop a sense of autonomy. Conversely, if the parents are ridiculing, impatient, or controlling, the child develops feelings of shame and doubt.

During the third stage, *initiative versus guilt* (ages 3 to 6 years), the major conflict is between a child's desire to initiate activities and the guilt that comes from unwanted or unexpected consequences. If loving adults provide an environment that encourages the ever-increasing need for independence and opportunities for interaction with other children, the child will predominantly develop feelings of power and initiative rather than guilt and doubt.

TABLE 10.2   ERIKSON'S EIGHT STAGES

	Approximate Age	Psychosocial Crisis	Description
 *Erikson's first stage*	Infancy (0–1)	Trust versus mistrust	Infants learn to trust that their needs will be met by the world, especially by the mother; if not, mistrust develops.
	Early childhood (1–3)	Autonomy versus shame and doubt	Children learn to exercise will, to make choices, to control themselves; if not, they become uncertain and doubt that they can do things by themselves.
	Play age (3–6)	Initiative versus guilt	Children learn to initiate activities and enjoy their accomplishments, acquiring direction and purpose; if they are not allowed initiative, they feel guilty for their attempts at independence.
 *Erikson's second stage*	School age (6–12)	Industry versus inferiority	Children develop a sense of industry and curiosity and are eager to learn; if not, they feel inferior and lose interest in the tasks before them.
	Adolescence (12–20)	Identity versus role confusion	Adolescents come to see themselves as unique and integrated persons with an ideology; if not, they become confused about what they want out of life.
 *Erikson's sixth stage*	Young adulthood (20–30)	Intimacy versus isolation	Young people become able to commit themselves to another person; if not, they develop a sense of isolation and feel they have no one in the world but themselves.
	Adulthood (30–65)	Generativity versus stagnation	Adults are willing to have and care for children, to devote themselves to their work and the common good; if not, they become self-centered and inactive.
 *Erikson's eighth stage*	Mature (65+)	Ego integrity versus despair	Older people enter a period of reflection, becoming assured that their lives have been meaningful, and they grow ready to face death with acceptance and dignity; if not, they despair for their unaccomplished goals, failures, and ill-spent lives.

Source: Adapted from Clarke-Stewart, A., Friedman, S., and Koch, J., 1985. *Child development: A topical approach.* Copyright © 1985 by John Wiley & Sons, Inc. Reprinted by permission of John Wiley & Sons, Inc.

During the fourth stage, *industry versus inferiority* (age 6 years through puberty), children develop a sense of industry, or competency, as they begin to practice skills they will use for a lifetime in productive work. How the external world reacts to a child's successes and failures determines whether she or he develops feelings of competency and industriousness or feelings of insecurity and inferiority.

Stages 5 and 6

Erikson's fifth stage is the period of *identity versus role confusion*. Erikson believed each individual's personal identity develops from a period of serious questioning and intense soul searching. During this **identity crisis**, adolescents attempt to discover who they are, what their skills are, and what kinds of roles they are best suited to play for the rest of their lives. Failure to resolve the identity crisis may be related to a lack of stable identity, delinquency, or difficulty in maintaining close personal relationships in later life.

Once a firm sense of identity is established, Erikson believes the individual (now in young adulthood) is ready to meet the challenges of *intimacy versus isolation*, stage 6 of development. If close bonds are formed, a basic feeling of intimacy with others will result. If not, the individual may avoid interpersonal commitments and experience feelings of isolation. Erikson's model for stages 5 and 6 suggests that if we are to have close, loving relationships with others, we must first learn who we are and how to be independent.

Identity Crisis *According to Erik Erikson, a period of inner conflict during which an individual examines his or her life and values and makes decisions about life roles*

Erikson's Last Two Stages

In the seventh stage, *generativity versus stagnation (middle age)*, the individual expands feelings of love and concern beyond the immediate family group to include all of society. If this expansion and effort do not occur, an individual stagnates, becoming concerned with only material possessions and personal well-being.

In the final years of life, adults enter the period of *ego integrity versus despair*, stage 8. Those who have been successful in resolving their earlier psychosocial crises will tend to look back on their lives with feelings of accomplishment and satisfaction. Those who resolved their earlier crises in a negative way or who lived fruitless, self-centered lives may deeply regret lost opportunities or become despondent because they realize it is too late to start over.

critical thinking

Active Learning

Applying Erikson's Stages to Your Own Life

Two important components of critical thinking are applying knowledge to new situations and clarifying personal values. Can you see evidence of Erik Erikson's stages in your friends and family? Perhaps more importantly, can you see how these stages apply to your own life? Answering the following questions will improve your understanding of Erikson's theory and help develop your critical thinking.

1. What Eriksonian stage are you now in? Does the description of that stage seem valid to you?

2. How have you resolved the crises you have already gone through? Is your personality affected by a negative resolution at one of the earlier stages?

3. If you found it difficult to identify your current stage, it may be because you are a woman or were raised in a collectivist culture. How might gender and culture affect the development and resolution of various Eriksonian stages?

(Study tip: If you're having difficulty remembering Erikson's eight stages, try this mnemonic device based on the peg-word system from Chapter 7: *One is a bun, trust no one. Two is a shoe, shame on you. Three is a tree, I feel so guilty. Four is a door, I feel inferior. Five is a hive, I'm a busy bee working on my identity. Six are sticks, pick them up alone, I am working on my isolation. Seven is heaven, filled with stagnation? Eight is a gate, is it too late for integrity?* This study tip was adapted from one developed by Professor Eggleston of McKendree College in Illinois.)

Evaluating Erikson's Theory

Many psychologists agree with Erikson's general idea that psychosocial conflicts, which are based on interpersonal and environmental interactions, do contribute to personality development (Bugental & Goodnow, 1998; Friedman & Coles, 1999). However, Erikson also has his critics. The labels Erikson uses to describe the eight stages may not be entirely appropriate cross-culturally. For example, in individualistic cultures, *autonomy* is highly preferable to *shame and doubt*, but in collectivist cultures, the preferred resolution might be *dependence* or *merging relations* (Matsumoto, 2000). In addition, it is difficult to squeeze an entire lifetime of development into one comprehensive theory.

Despite their limits, Erikson's stages have greatly contributed to the study of North American and European psychosocial development. Moreover, Erikson was among the first theorists to suggest that development continues past adolescence, and his theory encouraged further research.

Myths of Development

Until recently, most psychologists characterized adolescence as a time of *storm and stress* — great emotional turbulence and psychological strain. Research within the last 20 years, however, has found that storm and stress is largely a myth: Adolescence is no stormier than any other life transition. And, contrary to Erikson's predicted need for psychological separation from parents in order to establish identity, most teenagers of both sexes remain close to their parents and admire them (Diener & Diener, 1996; Lerner & Galambos, 1998).

Numerous other beliefs about age-related crises have not been supported by research either. For example, the popular idea of a *midlife crisis* began largely as the result of Gail Sheehy's national best seller *Passages* (1976). Sheehy drew on the theories of Daniel Levinson (1977, 1996) and psychiatrist Roger Gould (1975), as well as her own interviews, and reported a "predictable crisis" at about age 35 for women and 40 for men. Although middle age is typically a time of reexamining one's values and lifetime goals (Smart & Peterson, 1997), Sheehy's book led many people to automatically expect a midlife crisis with drastic changes in personality and behavior. Research suggests that a severe reaction or crisis may actually be quite rare and not typical of what most people experience during middle age (Benazzi, 2000; McCrae & Costa, 1990; Stewart & Ostrove, 1998).

It is also a myth that when the last child leaves home, most parents experience an *empty nest syndrome* — a painful separation and time of depression for the mother, the father, or both parents. Again, however, research suggests that the empty nest syndrome may be an exaggeration of the pain experienced by a few individuals and an effort to downplay positive reactions (White & Rogers, 1997; Whyte, 1992). For example, one major benefit of the empty nest is an increase in marital satisfaction (Figure 10.1). Furthermore, parent–child relationships do continue once the child leaves home. As one mother said, "The empty nest is surrounded by telephone wires" (Troll, Miller, & Atchley, 1979).

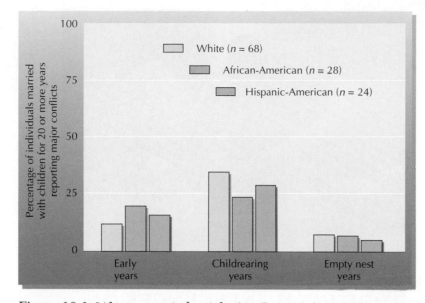

Figure 10.1 *Life span marital satisfaction.* Do you believe children make a marriage happy or that parents experience a depressing empty nest syndrome when they later leave home? Research shows that the highest levels of conflict actually occur during the childbearing years and that the lowest levels are before children are born and after they leave home (Mackey & O'Brien, 1998, p. 132).

Check & Review

PERSONALITY DEVELOPMENT OVER THE LIFE SPAN

Stella Thomas and Alexander Chess emphasize the genetic component of certain traits (such as sociability) and the fact that babies often exhibit differences in **temperament** shortly after birth.

Erik Erikson expanded on Freud's ideas to develop eight **psychosocial stages** of development that cover the entire life span. The four stages that occur during childhood are trust versus mistrust, autonomy versus shame and doubt, initiative versus guilt, and industry versus inferiority.

Erikson believes the major psychosocial **identity crisis of** adolescence is the search for identity versus role confusion. During young adulthood, the individual's task is to establish intimacy over isolation, and during middle adulthood, the person must deal with generativity versus stagnation. At the end of life, the older adult must establish ego integrity or face overwhelm-

ing despair at the realization of lost opportunities.

Research shows that adolescent storm and stress, the midlife crisis, and the empty nest syndrome may be exaggerated accounts of a few people's experiences and not that of most people.

Questions

1. An infant's inborn disposition is known as _____. (a) personality; (b) reflexes; (c) temperament; (d) traits

2. Briefly describe Thomas and Chess's temperament theory.

3. Erikson suggests that problems in adulthood are sometimes related to unsuccessful resolution of one of his eight stages. For each of the following individuals, identify the most likely "problem" stage:

   a. Marcos has trouble keeping friends and jobs because he continually asks

   for guarantees and reassurance of his worth.

   b. Ann has attended several colleges without picking a major, has taken several vocational training programs, and has had numerous jobs over the last 10 years.

   c. Teresa is reluctant to apply for a promotion even though her coworkers have encouraged her to do so. She worries that she will be taking jobs from others and questions her worth.

   d. George continually obsesses over the value of his life. He regrets that he never married or had children and feels very lonely.

4. Discuss the text's three common myths of development.

Answers to Questions can be found in Appendix B.

Families and personality. Does this remind you of your own family? How did your father, mother, and siblings affect your own personality development?

ADDITIONAL INFLUENCES ON DEVELOPMENT

Theorists like Erikson and Thomas and Chess offer important insights into general personality development. But what about family violence, teen pregnancy, divorce, and occupational choice? How do they influence development? We will explore these questions in the next section.

Families: Their Effect on Personality

Our families exert an enormous influence on our development, but not always for the best. Family violence, teen pregnancy, and divorce — the topics we discuss in this section — can have long-lasting, damaging effects on individual development.

Family Violence

Families can be warm and loving, but they can also be cruel and abusive. It is difficult to measure family violence because it usually occurs in private, and out of shame, powerlessness, or fear of reprisal, victims are reluctant to report it. Nevertheless, every year millions of domestic violence, child abuse, and elderly abuse cases are reported to police and service agencies (Fantuzzo & Mohr, 1999; McCloskey & Bailey, 2000; Wolfe, 1999).

What causes family violence? Violence occurs more often in families experiencing marital conflict, substance abuse, mental disorders, and economic stress (Melchert, 2000; Niehoff, 1999; Reppucci, Woolard, & Fried, 1999). It is important to remember that abuse and violence occur at all socioeconomic levels. However, abuse and violence occur more frequently in families disrupted by unemployment or other financial distress.

In addition to financial problems, many parents are socially isolated and lack good communication and parenting skills. Their anxiety and frustration may explode into spouse, child, and elderly abuse. In fact, one of the clearest identifiers of abuse potential is *impulsivity*. Parents who abuse their children, their spouses, or elderly parents seem to lack impulse control, especially when stressed. They also respond to stress with more intense emotions and greater arousal (Cicchetti & Toth, 1998). This impulsivity is related not only to psychosocial factors like economic stress and social isolation but also to possible biological influences.

Biologically, three regions of the brain are closely related to the expression and control of aggression: the amygdala, the prefrontal cortex, and the hypothalamus (see Chapter 2 to review these regions). Interestingly, head injuries, strokes, dementia, schizophrenia, alcoholism, and abuse of stimulant drugs have all been linked to these three areas and to aggressive outbursts (Niehoff, 1999). Research also suggests that low levels of the neurotransmitter serotonin are associated with irritability, hypersensitivity to provocation, and impulsive rage (Oguendo & Mann, 2000; Volavka, 1999).

Is there anything that can be done to reduce this type of aggression? Treatment with antianxiety and serotonin-enhancing drugs like fluoxetine (Prozac) may lower the risk of some forms of impulsive violence. However, given the correlation between spousal, child, sibling, and elder abuse, and because violence affects other family members who are not victims or perpetrators, treatment generally includes the entire family (Briggs & Hawkins, 1999; Emery & Laumann-Billings, 1998).

Most professionals advocate two general approaches in dealing with family violence. *Primary programs* attempt to identify "vulnerable" families and prevent abuse by teaching parenting and marital skills, stress management, and impulse control. These programs also publicize the signs of abuse and encourage people to report suspected cases. *Secondary programs* attempt to rehabilitate families after abuse has occurred. They work to improve social services, establish self-help groups such as Parents Anonymous and AMAC (Adults Molested as Children), and provide individual and group psychotherapy for both victims and the abusers.

Teen Pregnancy

Another factor that may affect development is becoming a parent and starting a family at too early an age. The United States has one of the highest rates of teen pregnancy among major industrialized nations (Meschke, Bartholomae, & Zentall, 2000; Miller & Coyl, 2000). Ironically, today's rate is actually much lower than it has been throughout much of the twentieth century. For example, between 1960 and 1985, the rate of U.S. teen births was 89.1 per 1,000, compared to 52.3 per 1,000 in the mid-1990s (Ventura, Martin, Curtin, & Mathews, 1999).

With this decline, why is everyone so worried about teen pregnancies? Although the total rate has declined substantially, the percentage of *unwed teen births* has soared (Endersbe, 2000; Henshaw, 1998). The higher nonmarital rate is important because single-parent families headed by women are at great risk of poverty.

Pregnancy during adolescence also carries with it considerable health risk for both the mother and child (Chapter 9), decreased chances of marital success, and lower education achievement (Endersbe, 2000; Fullerton, 1997; Roye & Balk, 1997). Pregnancy, in fact, is the most common reason for dropping out of high school. In view of these facts, is it any wonder that teen mothers also report one of the highest levels of depression (Figure 10.2)?

What can be done to reduce the number of teen pregnancies? Comprehensive *health-oriented services* seem to be the most promising avenue for decreasing the rate of pregnancy among high-risk teenagers (Coley & Chase-Lansdale, 1998). The Johns Hopkins Pregnancy Prevention Program, for example, provides complete medical care, contraceptive services, social services (such as counseling), and parenting education. This approach postponed the age of sexual activity onset, increased contraception use, reduced the frequency of sex, and reduced the actual pregnancy rate in the experimental group by 30 percent. During the same period, pregnancy rates in a comparison school rose by 58 percent (Hardy & Zabin, 1991).

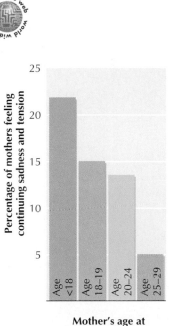

Figure 10.2 *Maternal age and satisfaction.* Note that the age of the mother directly relates to the percentage of reported feelings of sadness and tension.

The Teen Outreach Program is another success story. This program aims to enhance social development among adolescents through structured volunteer community service and classroom discussions of life choices, careers, and relationships (Allen, Philiber, Herrling, & Kupermine, 1997). Research shows that many teen pregnancies are due to poverty and the resulting perception that life options and choices are limited (Brewster, Billy, & Grady, 1993; Luker, 1996).

Most research and social programs (like the two described here) focus on economics: how money (or the lack of it) affects teen pregnancies. But researchers Rebekah Coley & Lindsay Chase-Lansdale (1998) suggest we should also be exploring the psychological consequences of early parenting. If adolescence is a time for solidifying identity and developing autonomy from parents, what happens with teen parents? What are the effects on a teen mother if she lives with her mother? What happens to the life span development of the "early" grandparents? What about the teen father? How does early fatherhood affect his course of development? And what about the child who is being raised by a teen mother or teen father or grandparent? How does this affect his or her development? Answers to these questions rest with the next generation of researchers (perhaps some of you who are reading this text).

The Impact of Divorce

> After years of advising other people on their personal problems, I was stunned by my own divorce. I only wish I had someone to write to for advice.
>
> Ann Landers

Although there has been a modest decline in the divorce rate since the 1970s, nearly one-half of marriages end in divorce in the United States (Hetherington, Bridges, & Insa-bella, 1998). Divorce has serious implications for both adult and child development (Lengua, Wolchik, Sandler, & West, 2000; Lopez, Melendez, & Rice, 2000). Both spouses generally experience emotional as well as practical difficulties and are at high risk for depression and physical health problems (Carbone, 2000; Davies & Cummings, 1998).

Some individuals appear to adapt well in the early stages of divorce but show effects at a later time (Hetherington & Stanley-Hagan, 1999; Wallerstein & Lewis, 1998; Whiteside & Becker, 2000). However, many problems assumed to be due to divorce are actually present before marital disruption (Carrere, Buehlman, Gottman, Coan, & Ruckstuhl, 2000; Sigelman, 1999). Thus, for some, divorce can be life enhancing. In a "healthy" divorce, ex-spouses must accomplish three tasks: *let go*, *develop new social ties*, and, when children are involved, *redefine parental roles* (Everett & Everett, 1994).

In addition to stresses on the divorcing couple, some research shows that children suffer both short-term and long-lasting effects. Compared with children in continuously intact two-parent families, children of divorce generally exhibit more behavioral problems, poorer self-concepts, more psychological problems, lower academic achievement, and more social difficulties (Hetherington & Stanley-Hagan, 1999; Melchert, 2000; Tein, Sandler, & Zautra, 2000; Wallerstein & Lewis, 1998). On the other hand, other research finds that children's psychological development is not affected by parental separation per se. Instead, it is related to mother's income, education, ethnicity, childrearing beliefs, depressive symptoms, and behavior (Clarke-Stewart, Vandell, McCartney, Owen, & Booth, 2000). Other researchers have suggested that children may also do better in homes without the constant tension and fighting of an unhappy, intact home (Emery, 1999).

Whether children become "winners" or "losers" in a divorce depends on the (1) individual attributes of the child, (2) qualities of the custodial family, (3) continued

TRY THIS
Yourself

If you want to estimate your personal chances for a happy marriage, consider the following points. Your chances for a successful marriage increase each time you answer *true*.

1. You and your partner are out of your teens and have known each other for at least 6 months.
2. Both sets of parents support the marriage, and neither set is divorced.
3. Neither you nor your partner is pregnant at the time of marriage.
4. You and your partner finished college and have a good income.
5. Both you and your partner think of one

another as your best friend, and you both like one another as a person.
6. You were engaged before getting married and did not cohabit.
7. You agree on how to handle housework and child care.
8. You and your partner are religious and believe that marriage is sacred.
9. During conflicts, you and your partner communicate in an open, straightforward way and accept negative feedback without becoming overly defensive.

Source: Adapted from Gottman, 1998; Lauer & Lauer, 1992; Sigelman, 1999.

---

involvement with noncustodial parents, and (4) resources and support systems available to the child and parents (Carbone, 2000; Gottman, 1998; Hetherington & Stanley-Hagan, 1999). If you or your parents are currently considering or going through divorce, you might want to keep these four factors in mind when making legal and other decisions about children.

Resilience A term referring to a child's good developmental outcome, sustained competence under stress, and recovery from trauma despite high-risk status

RESEARCH HIGHLIGHT

Children Who Survive Despite the Odds

Children fortunate enough to grow up with days filled with play and discovery, nights that provide rest and security, and dedicated, loving parents usually turn out fine. But what about those who are raised in violent, impoverished, or neglectful situations? As we saw in the previous discussion of family violence, teen pregnancy, and divorce, a troubled childhood creates significantly higher risk of serious physical, emotional, and behavioral problems. There are exceptions to this rule, however. Some offspring of wonderful, loving parents have serious problems, and some children growing up amid major stressors are remarkably well adjusted.

What is it about children living in harsh circumstances that helps them survive and prosper — despite the odds? The answer holds great interest for both parents and society. Such *resilient* children can teach us

better ways to reduce risk, promote competence, and shift the course of development in more positive directions (Luthar, 1999; Masten, 1998). **Resilience** refers to good developmental outcomes, sustained competence under stress, and recovery from trauma despite high-risk status (Werner, 1995).

Resilience has been studied throughout the world in a variety of situations, including poverty, natural disasters, war, and family violence (e.g., Luthar, 1999; Taylor & Wang, 2000; Werner, 1995, 1999; Wright & Masten, 1997). Two researchers — Ann Masten at the University of Minnesota and Douglas Coatsworth at the University of Miami (1998) — identified several traits of the resilient child and the environmental circumstances that might account for the resilient child's success.

Most children who do well have (1) good intellectual functioning; (2) relationships with caring adults; and, as they grow older, (3) the ability to regulate their attention, emotions, and behavior. These traits

obviously overlap. Good intellectual functioning, for example, may help resilient children solve problems or protect themselves from adverse conditions as well as attract the interest of teachers who serve as nurturing adults. Their greater intellectual skills also may help them learn from their experiences and from the caring adults, so in later life they have better self-regulation skills.

In times of growing concern about homelessness, poverty, abuse, teen pregnancy, violence, and divorce, studies of successful children can be very important. On the other hand, there is no such thing as an invulnerable child. Masten and Coatsworth remind us that "if we allow the prevalence of known risk factors for development to rise while resources for children fall, we can expect the competence of individual children and the human capital of the nation to suffer" (Masten & Coatsworth, 1998, p. 216).

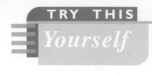

TRY THIS
Yourself

Did you grow up in a "high-risk" environment? Are you a resilient child? A 30-year longitudinal study of resilience (Werner, 1993, 1999) identified several environmental factors of high-risk children. Place a check mark by each risk factor that applies to your childhood:

____   Born into chronic poverty
____   Stressful fetal or birth conditions (e.g., prenatal hazards, low birth weight)
____   Chronic discord in the family environment
____   Parents divorced
____   Mental illness in one or both parents

Two-thirds of the high-risk children who had experienced four or more of these factors by age 2 years later developed serious adjustment problems. But one-third of the children who also experienced four or more such risk factors were resilient. They developed into competent, confident, and caring adults.

Occupational Choices: The Effect of Work and Careers

Most working adults spend more time on the job than with their families. Erikson emphasized the importance of generativity to adult development — the need to accomplish something with one's life. Most people channel their accomplishment needs into their work.

How can I find a rewarding career that suits my personality and interests? Choosing an occupation is one of the most important decisions in our lives, and the task is becoming ever more complex as career options increase as a result of specialization. The *Dictionary of Occupational Titles*, a government publication, currently lists more than 200,000 job categories. One way to learn more about job categories and potential careers is to visit your college career center. Career counselors may suggest that you take vocational interest tests. (You can also try the online version of several vocational interest inventories — http://www.keirsey.com/cgi-bin/newkts.cgi).

Too often, career choices are made on the basis of income. Nearly 74 percent of college freshmen surveyed by the Higher Education Research Institute said that being "very well off financially" was "very important" or "essential." Seventy-one percent felt the same way about raising a family ("This year's freshmen," 1995). These young people no doubt expect to combine both family and work roles and "live the good life," but many will have to work long hours just to keep up with the rate of inflation. Given the decline in construction and many high-paying manufacturing jobs (which on the average pay three times the minimum wage), a college education is more important than ever in obtaining higher paying and more satisfying occupations.

Although they are still able to work, the large majority of men and women in the United States choose to retire sometime in their sixties. Like the midlife crisis and empty nest syndrome, the loss of self-esteem and depression that is commonly assumed to accompany retirement may be largely a myth. Life satisfaction after retirement appears to be most strongly related to good health, control over one's life, and participation in community services and social activities (Voltz, 2000; Whitbourne, 2000).

Although most researchers believe a fulfilling old age comes from remaining active and involved as long as possible, the **activity theory of aging**, some believe

Activity Theory *A theory of aging that suggests successful adjustment is fostered by a full and active commitment to life*

Disengagement versus activity.
Although disengagement theory suggests that older people naturally disengage and withdraw from life, activity theory argues that everyone should remain active and involved throughout the entire life span.

successful aging is a natural and graceful withdrawal from life, the **disengagement theory** (Achenbaum & Bengtson, 1994; Voltz, 2000).

Although disengagement theory has been seriously questioned, it has stimulated important research. For example, studies have found that *selective* disengagement is one key to living fully throughout our entire adult life span (Carstensen, 1995; Schulz & Heckhausen, 1996). Beginning in early adulthood, we realize we cannot care deeply about 50 friends or work our best at 10 different pursuits. We must establish priorities. Gradually divesting ourselves of superfluous relationships and activities to focus on the most meaningful may be a healthy response at any age.

Disengagement Theory *A theory of aging suggesting that both the individual and society gradually and naturally pull away from each other in preparation for death*

GENDER & CULTURAL DIVERSITY

Cultural Differences in Ageism

As discussed in Chapter 9, physical decline is part of later life and causes emotional stress — although much less than most people think. A greater stress for the elderly, at least in the United States, is the **ageism** they encounter. In a society in which the old are seen as wise elders or keepers of valued traditions, the stress of aging is less than in a society in which they are seen as mentally slow and socially useless. In cultures like that in the United States in which youth, speed, and progress are strongly emphasized, a loss or decline in any of these qualities is deeply feared and denied (Powell, 1998).

Aren't there also cultures that honor their elderly? Yes, there are. In Japan, China, and in the United States, among African Americans and most tribes of Native Americans, the elderly are generally revered. Aging parents are respected for their wisdom and experience, are deferred to in family matters, and are expected to live with their children until they die (Klass, 2000; Martire, Stephens,

Ageism *Prejudice against people based on their age*

& Townsend, 2000). In Korea, for example, over 80 percent of the elderly are cared for by family members (Yoo & Sung, 1997). However, as these cultures become more urbanized and Westernized, often there is a corresponding decline in respect for the elderly.

Ageism in the United States

Between the extremes of being held in high or low esteem, there is considerable difference in the status and treatment of different subgroups of the elderly. In the United States, for example, studies show that older men have more social status, income, and sexual partners than do older women. Elderly women, on the other hand, have more friends and are more involved in family relationships but have lower status and income. Contrary to popular stereotype of the "rich old woman," elderly females represent one of the lowest income levels in North America (U.S. Bureau of the Census, 2001).

It is also interesting to look at ethnic differences in aging in the United States. Ethnic minority elderly, especially African Americans and Latinos, face problems related to both ageism and racism. They are more likely to become ill but less likely to receive treatment, and they are overrepresented among the elderly poor living below the poverty line (Contrada et al., 2000; Harrison & Gardiner, 1999; Markides, 1995).

Other research, however, reports that African Americans are more likely than Anglo-Americans to regard elderly persons with respect (Mui, 1992). Also, compared with whites, other ethnic groups often have a greater sense of community and may have stronger bonds of attachment, owing to their shared traits and experiences with prejudice. Ethnicity itself may therefore provide some benefits. "In addition to shielding them from majority attitudes, ethnicity provides the ethnic elderly with a source of esteem" (Fry, 1985, p. 233).

Elder respect. *Native Americans generally revere and respect the elder members of their tribe. How would aging be different if being old was an honor and blessing versus a dreaded process?*

Check & Review

ADDITIONAL INFLUENCES ON DEVELOPMENT

Family violence, teenage pregnancy, and divorce almost always have a negative effect on a child's development. **Resilient** children who survive abusive and stress-filled childhoods usually have good intellectual functioning; a relationship with a caring adult; and the ability to regulate their attention, emotions, and behavior.

The kind of work you do and the occupational choices you make can play a critical role in your life. One theory of successful aging, **activity theory**, says people should remain active and involved through-out the entire life span. The other major theory, **disengagement theory**, says the elderly naturally and gracefully withdraw from life because they welcome the relief from roles they can no longer fulfill. **Ageism** is an important stressor for the elderly, but in some cultures, the aged are revered.

Questions

1. Efforts to identify and prevent family violence are called _____ programs. (a) directive; (b) redirective; (c) primary; (d) secondary

2. The _____ theory of aging suggests that you should remain active and involved until death, whereas the _____ theory suggests that you should naturally and gracefully withdraw from life.

3. _____ is prejudice against people based on their age. (a) Ethnocentrism; (b) Elder abuse; (c) Ageism; (d) Disengagement

4. Explain how ethnicity may help the elderly overcome some problems of aging.

Answers to Questions can be found in Appendix B.

BEREAVEMENT AND DEATH

In this section, we will look at the four stages of grief and attitudes toward death and dying. We will then explore death itself as a final developmental crisis.
Are there predictable stages for grief and dying?

Grief: Lessons in Survival

> What do I do now that you're gone? Well, when there's nothing else going on, which is quite often, I sit in a corner and I cry until I am too numbed to feel. Paralyzed motionless for a while, nothing moving inside or out. Then I think how much I miss you. Then I feel fear, pain, loneliness, desolation. Then I cry until I am too numbed to feel. Interesting pastime.
>
> PETER McWILLIAMS, *HOW TO SURVIVE THE LOSS OF A LOVE*

Have you ever felt like this? If so, you are not alone. Bereavement and grief are an inevitable part of all our lives. Feelings of desolation, loneliness, and heartache, accompanied by painful memories, are common reactions to loss, disaster, or misfortune. Ironically, such painful emotions may serve a useful function. Evolutionary psychologists suggest that bereavement and grief may be adaptive mechanisms for both social animals and humans: The pain may motivate parents and children or mates to search for one another. Obvious signs of distress may also be adaptive because they bring the group to the aid of the bereaved individual.

What does it mean if someone seems emotionless after an important loss?
Grieving is a complicated and personal process. Just as there is no right way to die, there is no right way to grieve (Koppel, 2000). People who restrain their grief may be following the rules for emotional display that prevail in their cultural group. Moreover, outward signs of strong emotion may be the most obvious expression of grief, but this is only one of four stages in the "normal" grieving process: numbness, yearning, disorganization/despair, and resolution (James & Friedman, 1998; Parkes, 1972, 1991).

In the initial phase of grief, *numbness*, bereaved individuals often seem dazed and may feel little emotion other than numbness or emptiness. They also may deny the death, insisting that a mistake has been made.

Next, individuals enter a stage of *yearning*, intense longing for the loved one, and pangs of guilt, anger, and resentment. The bereaved may also experience illusions: They "see" the deceased person in his or her favorite chair or in the face of a stranger, they have vivid dreams in which the deceased is still alive, or they feel the

Grieving. Individuals vary in their emotional reactions to loss. There is no right or wrong way to grieve.

"presence" of the dead person. They also experience strong guilt feelings ("If only I had gotten her to a doctor sooner"; "I should have been more loving") and anger or resentment ("Why wasn't he more careful?"; "It isn't fair that I'm the one left behind").

Once the powerful feelings of yearning subside, the individual enters the *disorganization/despair* phase. Life seems to lose its meaning. The mourner feels listless, apathetic, and submissive. As time goes by, however, the survivor gradually begins to accept the loss both intellectually (the loss makes sense) and emotionally (memories are both pleasurable as well as painful). This acceptance, combined with building a new self-identity ("I am a single mother"; "We are no longer a couple"), characterizes the final state of grief — the *resolution or reorganization* stage.

Grief is obviously not the same for everyone. People vary in the stages of grief that they experience and the length of time for "recovery" (Davis, Nolen-Hoeksema, & Larson, 1998; Koppel, 2000). You can help people who are grieving by accepting their individual differences and recognizing that there is no perfect response. Simply say "I'm sorry," and then let the person talk if he or she wishes. Your quiet presence and caring is generally the best type of support.

When it comes to dealing with your own losses and grief, psychologists offer several techniques that you may find helpful (Holland, 1998; Napolitane, 1997; Wartik, 1996):

1. *Recognize the loss and allow yourself to grieve.* Despite feelings of acute loneliness, remember that loss is a part of everyone's life and accept comfort from others. Take care of yourself by avoiding unnecessary stress, getting plenty of rest, and giving yourself permission to enjoy life whenever possible.

2. *Set up a daily activity schedule.* One of the best ways to offset the lethargy and depression of grief is to force yourself to fill your time with useful activities (studying, washing your car, doing the laundry, and so on).

3. *Seek help.* Recognize that professional counseling may be necessary in cases of extreme or prolonged numbness, anger, guilt, or depression. (You will learn more about depression and therapy in Chapters 14 and 15.)

Attitudes Toward Death and Dying: Cultural and Age Variations

Cultures around the world interpret and respond to death in widely different ways: "Funerals are the occasion for avoiding people or holding parties, for fighting or having sexual orgies, for weeping or laughing, in a thousand combinations" (Metcalf & Huntington, 1991, p. 62).

Similarly, subcultures within the United States also have different responses to death. Irish Americans are likely to believe the dead deserve a good send-off — a wake with food, drink, and jokes. On the other hand, African Americans traditionally regard funerals as a time for serious grief, demonstrated in some congregations by wailing and singing spirituals (Barley, 1997; Wartik, 1996). Most Japanese Americans, however, try to restrain their grief and smile so as not to burden others with their pain and to avoid the shame associated with losing emotional control (Cook & Dworkin, 1992).

Attitudes toward death and dying also vary with age. As adults, we understand death in terms of three basic concepts: (1) *permanence* — once a living thing dies, it cannot be brought back to life; (2) *universality* — all living things eventually die; (3) *nonfunctionality* — all living functions, including thought, movement, and vital signs, end at death.

Research shows that permanence, the notion that death cannot be reversed, is the first and most easily understood concept. Preschoolers seem to accept the fact that the dead person cannot get up again, perhaps because of their experiences with dead butterflies and beetles found while playing outside (Furman, 1990).

Understanding of universality comes slightly later, and by the age of 7 years, most children have mastered nonfunctionality and have an adultlike understanding of death. Although parents may fear that discussing death with young children will make them unduly anxious, children who are offered open, honest discussions of death have an easier time accepting it (Aspinall, 1996; Kastenbaum, 1999).

The Death Experience: Our Final Developmental Crisis

Have you thought about your own death? Would you like to die suddenly and alone, or would you prefer to know ahead of time so you could plan your funeral and spend time saying good-bye to your family and friends? If you find thinking about these questions uncomfortable, it may be because most people in Western societies deny death. Unfortunately, avoiding thoughts and discussion of death and associating aging with death contribute to ageism (Atchley, 1997).

During the Middle Ages (from about the fifth century), people were expected to recognize when death was approaching so they could bid their farewells and die with dignity surrounded by loved ones (Aries, 1981). In recent times, Western societies have moved death out of the home and put it into the hospital and funeral parlor. Rather than personally caring for our dying family and friends, we have shifted responsibility to "experts" — physicians and morticians. We have made death a medical failure, rather than a natural part of the life cycle.

This avoidance of death and dying may be changing, though. Since the late 1990s, right-to-die and death-with-dignity advocates have been working to bring death out in the open, and mental health professionals have suggested that understanding the psychological processes of death and dying may play a significant role in good adjustment.

Confronting our own death is the last major crisis we face in life. What is it like? Is there a "best" way to prepare to die? Is there such a thing as a "good death"? After spending hundreds of hours at the bedsides of the terminally ill, Elisabeth Kübler-Ross developed her stage theory of the psychological processes surrounding death (1983, 1997, 1999).

On the basis of extensive interviews with patients, Kübler-Ross proposed that most people go through five sequential stages when facing death: *denial* of the terminal condition ("This can't be true; it's a mistake!"), *anger* ("Why me? It isn't fair!"), *bargaining* ("God, if you let me live, I'll dedicate my life to you!"), *depression* ("I'm losing everyone and everything I hold dear"), and finally *acceptance* ("I know that death is inevitable and my time is near").

Evaluating Kübler-Ross's Theory

Critics of the stage theory of dying stress that each person's death is a unique experience and that emotions and reactions depend on the individual's personality, life situation, age, and so on (Dunn, 2000; Kastenbaum, 1999). Others worry that popularizing stage theory will cause further avoidance and stereotyping of the dying ("He's just in the anger stage right now"). In response, Kübler-Ross (1983, 1997, 1999) agrees that not all people go through the same stages in the same way and regrets that anyone would use her theory as a model for a "good death."

In spite of the potential abuses, Kübler-Ross's theory has given us valuable insights and spurred research into a long-neglected topic. **Thanatology**, the study of death and dying, has become a major topic in human development. Thanks in part to thanatology research, the dying are being helped to die with dignity by the hospice movement, which has created special facilities and trained staff and volunteers to provide loving support for the terminally ill and their families (Smith & Smith, 1997).

Healthy children will not fear life, if their parents have integrity enough not to fear death…

Erik Erikson

Thanatology [THAN-uh-tall-uh-gee] *The study of death and dying. The term comes from thanatos, the Greek name for a mythical personification of death, and was borrowed by Freud to represent the death instinct*

Check & Review

BEREAVEMENT AND DEATH

Attitudes toward death and dying vary greatly across cultures and among age groups. Although adults understand the *permanence*, *universality*, and *nonfunctionality* of death, children often don't master these concepts until around age 7 years. Grief is a natural and painful reaction to a loss. For most people, grief consists of four major stages — *numbness*, *yearning*, *disorganization/despair*, and *resolution*. Elisabeth Kübler-Ross's theory of the five-stage process of dying (*denial*, *anger*, *bargaining*, *depression*, and *acceptance*) offers important insights into the last major crisis we face in life. The study of death and dying, **thanatology**, has become an important topic in human development.

Questions

1. Explain how an adult's understanding of death differs from a preschool child's.

2. Grieving people generally begin with the _____ stage and end with the _____ stage. (a) numbness, bargaining; (b) grief, anger; (c) yearning, acceptance; (d) numbness, resolution

3. Match the following statements with Elisabeth Kübler-Ross's five-stage theory of death and dying:

     _____ a. "I understand that I'm dying, but if I could just have a little more time…"

     _____ b. "I refuse to believe the doctors. I want a fourth opinion."

     _____ c. "I know my time is near. I'd better make plans for my spouse and children."

     _____ d. "Why me? I've been a good person."

     _____ e. "I'm losing everything. I'll never see my children again. Life is so hard."

4. The study of death and dying is known as _____ (a) gerontology; (b) ageism; (c) mortality; (d) thanatology

Answers to Questions can be found in Appendix B.

KEY TERMS

Moral Development
care perspective (p. 357)
conventional level (p. 356)
justice perspective (p. 357)
postconventional level (p. 356)
preconventional level (p. 354)
Personality Development Over the Life Span

identity crisis (p. 361)
psychosocial stages (p. 359)
temperament (p. 358)
Additional Influences on Development
activity theory (p. 368)
ageism (p. 369)
disengagement theory (p. 369)

resilience (p. 367)
Bereavement and Death
thanatology [THAN-uh-tall-uh-gee] (p. 374)

Visual Summary for Chapter 10

Moral Development

Kohlberg's Three Levels and Six Stages

Preconventional Morality

Stage 1: *Punishment-obedience orientation.* Morality is what you can get away with.

↓

Stage 2: *Instrumental-exchange orientation.* Obeys rules to obtain rewards or favors.

Conventional Morality

Stage 3: *Good-child orientation.* Obeys rules to get approval.

↓

Stage 4: *Law-and-order orientation.* Obeys laws because they maintain the social order.

Postconventional Morality

Stage 5: *Social-contract orientation.* Moral reasoning reflects belief in democratically established laws.

↓

Stage 6: *Universal ethics orientation.* Moral reasoning reflects individual conscience.

Criticisms of Kohlberg's theory: Politically, culturally, and gender biased. Gilligan says women take a **care perspective** in their moral reasoning and men a **justice perspective.** In fact, research shows both sexes typically use both perspectives.

Personality Development Over the Life Span

Thomas & Chess'
Temperament Theory

Temperament: Basic, inborn disposition. Three temperament styles: easy, difficult, and slow-to-warm-up. Styles seem consistent and enduring.

Erikson's
Eight **Psychosocial Stages**

Childhood: Trust vs. mistrust, autonomy vs. shame and doubt, initiative vs. guilt, industry vs. inferiority.
Adolescence: Identity vs. role confusion.
Young Adulthood: Intimacy vs. isolation.
Middle Adulthood: Generativity vs. stagnation.
Older Adult: Ego integrity vs. despair.

Additional Influences on Personality Development

Families

- Family violence, teenage pregnancies, and divorce can damage personality development.
- **Resilience** helps some children survive an abusive or stress-filled childhood.

Occupational Choices

Occupational choice is critically important because most people channel their accomplishment needs into their work.

Aging

Ageism: Prejudice against people based on their age. Two major theories of aging:

activity theory (should remain active).   →   **disengagement theory** (should gracefully withdraw).

Bereavement and Death

Grief

Grief: A natural and painful reaction to a loss, consists of four major stages:

1) numbness → 2) yearning → 3) disorganization and despair → 4) resolution

Attitudes

Attitudes toward death and dying vary greatly across cultures and among age groups. Children generally don't fully understand the permanence, universality, and nonfunctionality of death until around age seven.

Death Experience

- Kübler-Ross proposes a five-stage process of dying (denial, anger, bargaining, depression, and acceptance).
- **Thanatology:** Study of death and dying.

11 Gender and Human Sexuality

I t was an unusual circumcision. The identical twin boys were already 8 months old when their parents took them to the doctor to be circumcised. For many years in the United States, most male babies have had the foreskin of their penis removed during their first week of life, when it is assumed they will experience less pain. The most common procedure is cutting or pinching off the foreskin tissue. In this case, however, the doctor used an electrocautery device, which is used to burn off moles or small skin growths. The electrical current used for the first twin was too high, and the entire penis was accidentally ablated, or removed. (The parents did not let the physician try to circumcise the other twin.)

In anguish over the tragic accident, the parents sought advice from medical experts. Following discussions with John Money and other specialists at John Hopkins University, the parents and doctors made an unusual decision — the twin with the destroyed penis would be raised as a girl.

The first step in the reassignment process occurred at age 17 months, when the child's name was changed — Bruce became "Brenda" (Colapinto, 2000). Brenda was dressed in pink pants and frilly blouses and "her" hair was allowed to grow long. At 21 months, plastic surgery was performed to create external female genital structures. Further plastic surgery to create a vagina was planned for the beginning of adolescence, when the child's physical growth would be nearly complete. At this time she would also begin to take female hormones to complete the boy-to-girl transformation.

According to John Money (Money & Ehrhardt, 1972), the children's mother was surprised and pleased by the striking differences that developed in her two children. The case of "John/Joan" (pseudonyms) was reported in the medical literature as an unqualified success. By age three, the "female" twin wore nightgowns and dresses almost exclusively and liked bracelets and hair ribbons. During the preschool years, the girl reportedly preferred playing with "girl-type" toys and asked for a doll and carriage for Christmas. Her brother

asked for a garage with cars, gas pumps, and tools. By age 6, the brother was accustomed to defending his sister if he thought someone was threatening her. The daughter copied the mother in tidying and cleaning up the kitchen, whereas the boy did not. The mother agreed that she encouraged her daughter when she helped with the housework and expected the boy to be uninterested.

What first looked like a success was, in fact, a dismal failure. Follow-up studies report that the child never really adjusted to her assigned gender (Diamond & Sigmundson, 1997). In spite of being raised from infancy as a girl, she did not feel like a girl and avoided most female activities and interests. By age 14, she was so unhappy that she contemplated suicide. The father then tearfully explained what had happened earlier. For the child, "All of a sudden everything clicked. For the first time things made sense, and I understood who and what I was" (Thompson, 1997, p. 83).

Questions

1. Match the following dimensions of gender with their appropriate meaning:

_____ Chromosomal sex

_____ Gender identity

_____ Gonadal sex

_____ Gender role

_____ Hormonal sex

_____ Secondary sex characteristics

_____ External genitals

_____ Sexual orientation

_____ Internal accessory organs

a. Ovaries and testes

b. XX and XY

c. Estrogens and androgens

d. One's perception of oneself as male or female

e. Breasts, beards, menstruation

f. Uterus, vagina, prostate gland, vas deferens

g. Labia majora, clitoris, penis, scrotum

h. Homosexual, bisexual, heterosexual

i. Differing societal expectations for appropriate male and female behavior

2. Individuals who have the genitals and secondary sex characteristics of one sex but feel as if they belong to the other sex are known as _____. (a) transvestites; (b) heterosexuals; (c) gays or lesbians; (d) transsexuals

3. Briefly summarize the two major theories of gender role development.

4. A combination of both male and female personality traits is called _____. (a) heterosexuality; (b) homosexuality; (c) transsexualism; (d) androgyny

Answers to Questions can be found in Appendix B.

RESEARCH HIGHLIGHT

The Art and Science of Flirting

Pretend for the moment that you are watching a man (Tom) and woman (Kaleesha) at a singles bar. As Tom approaches the table, Kaleesha sits up straighter, smiles, and touches her hair. Tom asks her to dance, and Kaleesha quickly nods and stands up while smoothing her skirt. During the dance, she smiles and sometimes glances at him from under her lashes. When the dance finishes, Kaleesha waits for Tom to escort her back to her chair. She motions him to sit in the adjacent chair and they engage in a lively conversation. Kaleesha allows her leg to graze his briefly. When Tom reaches for popcorn from the basket in front of Kaleesha, she playfully pulls it away. This surprises Tom and he frowns at Kaleesha. She quickly turns away and starts talking to her friends. Despite his repeated attempts to talk to her, Kaleesha ignores him.

What happened? Did you recognize Kaleesha's sexual signals? Did you understand why she turned away at the end? If so, you are skilled in the art and science of flirting. If not, you may be very interested in the work of Monica Moore at the Uni-

versity of Missouri (1998). As a scientist interested in describing and understanding flirting and the role it plays in human courtship, Moore has observed and recorded many scenes — in singles bars and shopping malls — like the one with Tom and Kaleesha. Although she prefers the term *nonverbal courtship signaling*, what Moore and her colleagues have spent thousands of hours secretly observing is flirting behavior.

From these naturalistic observations, we know a great deal more about what works and doesn't work in courtship. First of all, though both men and women flirt, women generally initiate a courtship. The woman signals her interest with glances that may be brief and darting, or direct and sustained. Often she smiles at the same time she gestures with her hands — often with an open or extended palm. Primping (adjusting clothing or patting hair) is also common. A flirting woman will also make herself more noticeable by sitting straighter, with stomach pulled in and breasts pushed out.

Once contact is made and the couple is dancing or sitting at a table, the woman increases the level of flirting. She orients her body toward his, whispers in his ear, and frequently nods and smiles in response to his conversation. Most significant, she touches the man or allows the man to touch her. Like Kaleesha with Tom, allowing her leg to graze his is a powerful indication of her interest.

Women also use play behaviors to flirt. They tease, mock-hit, and tell jokes, not only to inject humor but also to test the man's receptivity to humor. As in the case of Tom's reaction to the popcorn tease, when a man doesn't appreciate the playfulness, a woman often uses rejection signals to cool or end the relationship. Other studies confirm Moore's description of women's nonverbal sexual signaling (Lott, 2000).

Now that you know what to look for, watch for flirting behavior in others — or perhaps in your own life. According to Moore and other researchers, flirting may be the single most important thing a woman can do to increase her attractiveness. Because the burden of making the first approach is usually the man's, men are understandably cautious and welcome a woman who clearly signals her interest.

Two cautions are in order, however. First, signaling interest does not mean that the woman is ready to have sex with the man. She flirts because she wants to get to know the man better; later, she'll decide whether she wants to develop a relationship (Allgeier & Allgeier, 2000). Second, Moore reminds women to "use their enhanced flirting skills only when genuinely interested" (1997, p. 69). Being aware of sexual signals can benefit both men and women, but flirting should be reserved for times when you genuinely want to attract or keep the attention of a particular partner.

THE STUDY OF HUMAN SEXUALITY

Sex is used and abused in many ways: as a theme in literature, movies, and music; to satisfy sexual desires; to gain love and acceptance from partners and peer groups; as a way of expressing love or commitment in a relationship; as a way of ending relationships through affairs with others; to dominate or hurt others; and, perhaps most conspicuously, to sell products.

People have probably always been interested in understanding their sexuality, but cultural forces have often suppressed and controlled this interest. During the nineteenth century, for example, polite society avoided mention of all parts of the body covered by clothing. The breast of chickens became known as "white meat," female patients were examined by male doctors in totally dark rooms, and some

How do scientists study a sensitive topic like sex?

TRY THIS
Yourself

Before we begin our study of human sexuality, try this quiz. The answers are at the bottom, and expanded explanations are found throughout this chapter.

Which of the following statements are true and which are false?

1. The breakfast cereal Kellogg's Corn Flakes was originally developed to discourage masturbation.
2. Nocturnal emissions and masturbation are signs of abnormal sexual adjustment.
3. The American Academy of Pediatrics (AAP) no longer recommends routine circumcision for male babies.
4. The American Psychiatric Association and the American Psychological Association (APA) consider homosexuality a type of mental illness.
5. Sexual skill and satisfaction are learned behaviors that can be increased through education and training.
6. If you're HIV positive (have human immunodeficiency virus) you cannot infect someone else; only if you have AIDS (acquired immunodeficiency syndrome) can you spread the disease.
7. Women cannot be raped against their will.

Answers: 1. T   2. F   3. T   4. F   5. T
6. F   7. F

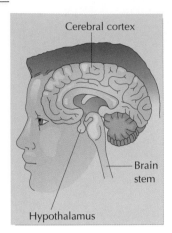

Figure 11.4 *The hypothalamus and sexual orientation.* Researcher Simon LeVay found that an area of the hypothalamus was smaller among gay men compared to the same area in men he assumed were heterosexual.

Hate crimes. The vicious beating and muder of Mattew Shepard in 1998 is a tragic reminder of the costs of sexual prejudice.

Sexual Prejudice *Negative attitudes toward an individual because of her or his sexual orientation*

- *"By default" myth.* Gays and lesbians were unable to attract partners of the other sex or had unhappy heterosexual experiences.

- *Poor parenting theory.* Sons become gay because of domineering mothers and weak fathers, whereas daughters become lesbians because their fathers were their primary role model.

- *Modeling theory.* Children raised by gay and lesbian parents usually end up adopting their parents' sexual orientation.

It is important to remember that all of these popular beliefs have been shown to be *false* and that the causes of sexual orientation are still unknown. At this point, however, most studies suggest that genetics and biology play the dominant role in sexual orientation (Bailey, Dunne, Martin, 2000; Hamer & Copeland, 1999; Hershberger, 1997; LeVay, 1996; Williams et al., 2000).

For example, a genetic predisposition toward homosexuality is supported by studies on identical male and female twins, fraternal twins, and adopted siblings (Kirk, Bailey, Dunne, & Martin, 2000; Pillard & Bailey, 1995). These studies found that if one identical twin was gay, about 48 to 65 percent of the time so was the second twin. (Note that if the cause were totally genetic, the percentage would be 100.) The rate for fraternal twins was 26 to 30 percent and 6 to 11 percent for adopted brothers or sisters. Estimates of homosexuality in the general population run between 2 and 10 percent.

Some researchers have also hypothesized that prenatal hormone levels affect fetal brain development and sexual orientation. Animal experiments have found that administering male hormones prenatally can cause female sheep to engage in the mounting behavior associated with male sheep (Bagermihl, 1999). Because it is obviously unethical to experiment with human fetuses, we cannot come to any meaningful conclusions about the effect of hormones on fetal development. Furthermore, no well-controlled study has ever found a difference in adult hormone levels between heterosexuals and gays and lesbians (Banks & Gartrell, 1995; Le Vay, 1996).

The possibility of structural brain differences received support (and wide media attention) when Simon LeVay (1991, 1996) found that the front part of the hypothalamus (Figure 11.4) was smaller among gay men than among those he assumed were heterosexuals. Because we know the hypothalamus influences sexual behavior, LeVay's findings may help explain differences in sexual orientation. However, it is impossible to determine whether the brain differences were a cause or result of sexual orientation.

Although the origin of sexual orientation remains a mystery, the fact of being gay or lesbian brings certain difficulties and challenges. Gays and lesbians endure verbal and physical attacks; disrupted family and peer relationships; and high rates of anxiety, depression, and suicide (Fone, 2000; Herek, 2000; Lock & Steiner, 1999; Rottnek, 1999). Some of the hostility supposedly stems from an irrational fear of homosexuality in oneself or others, which Martin Weinberg labeled *homophobia* in the late 1960s. However, this term is too limited and not scientifically acceptable: It implies that antigay attitudes are limited to individual irrationality and pathology. Psychologist Gregory Herek (2000) proposes the term **sexual prejudice** instead, to emphasize multiple causes and to allow researchers to draw on the rich scientific research on prejudice (Chapter 16).

Despite the acknowledgment in 1973 by both the American Psychiatric Association and the American Psychological Association that homosexuality is not a mental illness, it continues to be a divisive societal issue in the United States. Seeing *sexual prejudice* as a socially reinforced phenomenon rather than an individual pathology, coupled with political action by gays and lesbians, may help fight discrimination and hate crimes.

3.

4.

5.

Fighting back against sexual prejudice. These protesters are working to increase public awareness of and acceptance of different sexual orientations.

Check & Review

SEXUAL BEHAVIOR

William Masters and Virginia Johnson identified a four-stage **sexual response cycle** during sexual activity — *excitement*, *plateau*, *orgasm*, and *resolution*. There are numerous similarities and differences between the sexes in this cycle, but differences are the focus of most research. According to the *evolutionary perspective*, men engage in more sexual behaviors with more sexual partners because it helps the species survive. The *social role approach* suggests this difference results from traditional cultural divisions of labor.

Although researchers have identified several myths concerning the causes of homosexuality, the origins remain a puzzle. In recent studies, the genetic and biological explanation has gained the strongest sup-

port. Despite increased understanding, sexual orientation remains a divisive issue in the United States.

Questions

1. Briefly describe the four stages of Masters and Johnson's sexual response cycle.

2. How do the evolutionary and social role perspectives explain male and female differences in sexual behavior?

3. The genetic influence on sexual orientation has been supported by research reporting that_____.

   a. among identical twins, if one brother is gay, the other brother has a 52 percent chance of also being gay

   b. gay men have fewer chromosomal pairs than straight men, whereas

lesbians have larger areas of the hypothalamus than straight women

   c. among adoptive pairs of brothers, if one brother is gay, the other brother has an increased chance of also being gay

   d. parenting style influences adult sexual orientation for men but not for women

4. A homosexual orientation appears to be the result of_____.

   a. seduction during childhood or adolescence by an older homosexual

   b. a family background that includes a dominant mother and a passive, detached father

   c. a hormonal imbalance

   d. unknown factors

Answers to Questions can be found in Appendix B.

SEXUAL PROBLEMS

When we are functioning well sexually, we tend to take this part of our lives for granted. But what happens when things don't go smoothly? What causes normal sexual functioning to stop for some people and never begin for others? What are the major diseases that can be spread through sexual behavior? We will explore these questions in the following section.

What factors contribute to sexual dysfunction and sexually transmitted diseases?

K

Se
an

ge
ge
ge
se
se

Visual Summary for Chapter 11

Sex and Gender

Definitions

Sex: Biological dimensions of maleness or femaleness, and physical activities (such as intercourse).

Gender: Psychological and sociocultural meanings of maleness and femaleness.

Gender Role Development

Gender role: Social expectations for appropriate male and female behavior.
Two major theories:

Social learning (reward, punishment, and imitation).

Cognitive Developmental (active thinking processes).

Sex and Gender Differences

Sex differences: Physical differences (like height) and brain differences (function and structure).

Gender differences: Females tend to score somewhat higher in verbal skills. Males score somewhat higher in math and are more physically aggressive.

Androgyny: Combination of masculine and feminine personality traits.

Study of Human Sexuality

Havelock Ellis

Based his research on personal diaries.

Kinsey & Colleagues

Popularized the use of surveys and interviews.

Masters and Johnson

Used direct observation and measurement of human sexual response.

Cultural Studies

Provide insight into universalities and variations in sexual behavior across cultures.

Sexual Behavior

Sexual Arousal and Response

Masters and Johnson's **sexual response cycle: excitement, plateau, orgasm,** and **resolution.** There are numerous similarities of the sexes in this cycle, but differences are the focus of most research. According to the *evolutionary perspective*, males engage in more sexual behaviors with more sexual partners because it helps the species survive. The *social role approach* suggests this difference results from traditional cultural divisions of labor.

Sexual Orientation

Two major theories

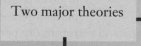

Genetic/biological (genetic, prenatal biasing of the brain, and brain differences).

Psychosocial ("disturbed family," inability to attract opposite sex, and seduction—all unsupported by research).

Sexual Problems

Sexual Dysfunctions

Possible causes:

Biological: Anxiety blocks arousal. Parasympathetic nervous system must dominate for sexual arousal to occur, whereas sympathetic nervous system must dominate for orgasm to happen.

Psychological:

- Negative gender role training
- Unrealistic **sexual scripts**
- **Double standard** encourages male sexuality but discourages female's
- **Performance anxiety**, fearing one will not meet partner's sex expectations

Treatment: Masters and Johnson emphasize couple's relationship, combined physiological and psychosocial factors, cognitions, and specific behavioral techniques.

Sexually Transmitted Infections (STIs)

Most publicized STI is **AIDS.** AIDS transmitted only through sexual contact or exposure to infected bodily fluids, but irrational fears of contagion persist. An estimated one million in the U.S. are **HIV positive** and therefore carriers.

12

Motivation and Emotion

hen Wilt Chamberlain died in October 1999, he left a hole in the heart of his many fans and in the world of professional sports. His list of awards was impressive: 2 NBA championships, scoring the most points in a season (4,029), setting the record for career rebounds (23,924), 7 straight scoring titles, 11 rebound titles, and setting an NBA record by scoring 100 points in a single game against the New York Knicks (Rosenblatt, 1999).

But perhaps his most important accomplishments were leading the league in assists and never fouling out of a game. These feats speak volumes. In a world of professional sports where players attack their opponents, teammates, fans, and referees, Wilt Chamberlain made a graceful difference. He almost never got into a fight. When opposing players tripped and fell, he picked them up. He was over 7 feet tall and dominated the game, but not once did he foul out. Chamberlain appreciated the importance of civility and sportsmanship. This "gentle giant" is missed.

Bobby Knight

Coach Bobby Knight is another well-known sports figure with an impressive list of accomplishments. Knight was one of the most successful coaches in college basketball, but his success was based on intimidation and boorish behavior. Obscenity-filled shouting matches and frequent temper tantrums were used to psychologically terrorize his players as well as college administrators, who continued to give him "just one more chance."

What a contrast. Chamberlain controlled his strength and temper, supported his teammates, and respected his opponents, whereas Knight bullied and abused his players, opponents, coaches, referees, administrators, reporters, and anyone else who just happened to be there (Walton, 2000). Indiana University imposed a "zero tolerance" on Coach Knight's behavior in May 2000. But a few months later, Knight allegedly grabbed and twisted the arm of a student and cursed him for not calling him "Mr. Knight" or "Coach Knight" (Leo, 2000). Apparently, this was the last straw. Indiana University fired Coach Knight on September 10, 2000.

Wilt Chamberlain

hat motivated Chamberlain to rise to the top of the extremely competitive sports world? Why did Coach Knight continue to explode, despite promises to control his temper and the risk to his coaching position? What makes him so angry? Research in *motivation* and *emotion* attempts to answer such "what" and "why" questions and to explain emotional states such as anger.

Motivation refers to the process of activating, maintaining, and directing behavior toward a particular goal. **Emotion**, on the other hand, refers to subjective feelings or affective responses. In other words, motivation energizes and directs behavior, whereas emotion is the "feeling" response.

Motivation and emotion overlap. If you saw your loved one in the arms of another, you might experience a wide variety of emotions (jealousy, fear, sadness, and anger), and differing motives may determine how you act in the situation. Your desire for revenge might lead you to look for another partner, whereas your need for love and belonging might motivate you to look for ways to explain the behavior and protect your relationship. There is considerable overlap not only between motivation and emotion but also among motivation, emotion, and most areas of psychology. Moreover, recent advances in neuroscience and cognitive science have made the study of motivation and emotion one of the hot topics in science today (Cacioppo & Gardner, 1999; Damasio, 1999). In this chapter, we will discuss some of the most recent and exciting findings, as well as classic studies in the field.

Motivation *Factors within an individual (such as needs, desires, and interests) that activate, maintain, and direct behavior toward a goal*

Emotion *An individual's feelings or affective responses that include cognitions (thoughts, beliefs, and expectations), physiological arousal (heart pounding), and behavioral expressions (frowns, smiles, running, and so on)*

UNDERSTANDING MOTIVATION

Research in motivation attempts to answer the "why" questions about human and animal behavior. Why do you spend hours playing a new computer game instead of studying for a major exam? Why do salmon swim upstream to spawn? Human behavior comes from many different motives, some of which have been discussed already. For example, the sleep motive and the need for alternate states of consciousness were covered in Chapter 5, and sexual motivation was discussed in Chapter 11. Aggression, altruism, and interpersonal attraction will be discussed in Chapters 16. Here, we will focus on three basic motives: hunger and eating, arousal, and achievement. We will also look at the major biological and psychological theories that best explain general motivation — or why we do what we do.

Why do we feel hungry, search for stimulation, and need to achieve?

Hunger and Eating: The Interaction of Both Internal and External Factors

What causes hunger? Is it your growling stomach? Or is it the sight of a juicy hamburger or the smell of a freshly baked cinnamon roll? Although hunger is obviously an internal, biological need, external, environmental forces also heavily influence it. Let's examine some of the major players in hunger.

The Stomach

Walter B. Cannon and A. L. Washburn (1912) conducted one of the earliest experiments exploring the internal factors in hunger. In this study, Washburn swallowed a balloon and then inflated it in his stomach. His stomach contractions and subjective reports of hunger feelings were then simultaneously recorded (Figure 12.1). Because each time Washburn reported having stomach pangs (or "growling") the

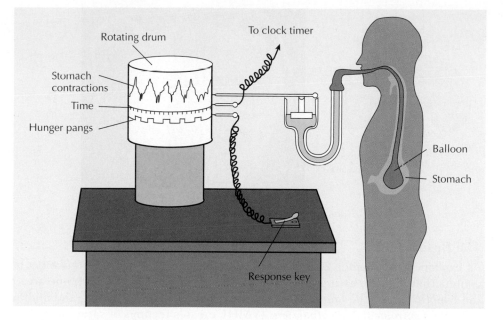

Figure 12.1 *Cannon and Washburn's technique for measuring hunger.* As a participant in his own study, Washburn swallowed a special balloon designed to detect stomach movement. His stomach movements were automatically recorded on graph paper attached to a rotating drum. At the same time, whenever Washburn experienced "hunger pangs," he would press a key that made a recording on the same graph paper. The two recordings (stomach movements and hunger sensations) were then compard. Finding that Washburn's stomach contractions occurred at the same time as his feelings of hunger led these early researchers to conclude that stomach movements caused hunger. Later research altered this conclusion.

balloon also contracted, the researchers concluded that stomach movement caused the sensation of hunger.

What do you think was wrong with this study? As you learned in Chapter 1, researchers must always control for the possibility of *extraneous variables*, factors that contribute irrelevant data and confuse the results. In this case, it was later found that an empty stomach is relatively inactive and that the stomach contractions experienced by Washburn were an experimental artifact — something resulting from the presence of the balloon. Washburn's stomach had been tricked into thinking it was full and was responding by trying to digest the balloon. Sensory input from the stomach is not essential for feeling hungry, as dieters have learned when they try to "trick" their stomachs into feeling full by eating large quantities of carrots and celery and drinking lots of water.

Does this mean there is no connection between the stomach and feeling hungry? Not necessarily. Specialized pressure receptors in the stomach walls do signal fullness or a feeling of emptiness (Woods, Schwartz, Baskin, & Seeley, 2000). However, animals and humans without stomachs continue to experience hunger and satiety (a feeling of fullness), so other factors must be involved.

Blood Chemistry

Research suggests that the level of glucose (sugar) in the blood may be a central factor in hunger (Woods, Schwartz, Baskin, & Seeley, 2000). When you've just finished a meal, your glucose level is high and you lose interest in food. Early research suggested low glucose does contribute to hunger, but people with diabetes can have high glucose levels and still be hungry. How could that be explained? Because it is not the *level* of glucose that affects feelings of hunger or satiety but the *uptake* of glucose (Franken, 1998).

Thus, in addition to glucose, the body needs *insulin* (a hormone secreted by the pancreas) to uptake or extract glucose from the blood. In nondiabetic people, both glucose and insulin are normally available after food is eaten and hunger feelings are satisfied. When diabetics take insulin, their cells can then use the glucose from food, and they stop feeling hungry.

Figure 12.2 *How the brain affects eating.* (a) This diagram shows a rat's brain with the front half cut away. Note the positions of the ventromedial hypothalamus (VMH) and the lateral hypothalamus (LH). (b) The ventromedial area of the hypothalamus of the rat on the left was destroyed, which led to a tripling of body weight. Compare his size to that of the normal rat on the right.

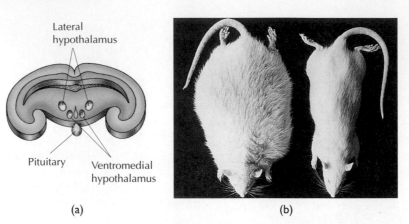

(a)   (b)

The Brain

As explained in Chapter 2, a part of the brain known as the *hypothalamus* has centers that regulate eating, drinking, and body temperature. In fact, one area of the hypothalamus, the *lateral hypothalamus* (LH), stimulates eating and another area, the *ventromedial hypothalamus* (VMH), creates feelings of satiation and signals the animal to stop eating. When the VMH area is destroyed in rats, they overeat to the point of extreme obesity (Figure 12.2). When the LH area is destroyed, animals may starve to death if they are not force-fed. (In time, LH-damaged rats will resume eating, but their weight stays well below normal.) Humans with tumors in the LH or VMH area show similar extreme weight loss or gain.

But the LH and VMH areas are not simple on–off switches for eating. For example, lesions to the VMH make animals picky eaters — they reject food that doesn't taste good. Lesions also increase the secretion of insulin, which may in turn cause overeating (Challem, Berkson, Smith, & Berkson, 2000). Lesions to the VMH may also raise the **set point**, or natural weight level. A higher set point may increase hunger, making the animal eat more (Woods, Seeley, Porte, & Schwartz, 1998). In contrast, when the LH is lesioned, the animal experiences a decrease in hunger and a lowered set point.

In sum, internal factors such as structures in the hypothalamus (the LH and VMH), blood chemistry (glucose and insulin), and signals from the stomach all seem to play important roles in hunger and eating. Other internal factors have also been researched, including other areas of the brain, genetics, and the presence or absence of certain neurotransmitters (DeFalco et al., 2001; Tai, Lau, Ho, Fak, & Tan, 2000; Woods, Schwartz, Baskin, & Seeley, 2000).

Cultural Factors

One of the most important *external* influences on when, what, where, and why we eat is cultural conditioning (Rozin, 1996). North Americans, for example, tend to eat their evening meal around 6 P.M., whereas people in Spain and South America tend to eat around 10 P.M. When it comes to *what* we eat, have you ever eaten rat, dog, or horsemeat? If you are a typical North American, this might sound repulsive to you, yet most Hindus would feel a similar revulsion at the thought of eating meat from cows.

Hunger is a complex psychological motive controlled by interacting internal and external factors. For instance, although innate biological factors may explain the basic need to eat (babies will reflexively turn and nurse when the nipple is placed near their mouth), learning through classical conditioning may be a major factor in

Set Point *An organism's personal homeostatic level for a particular body weight that results from factors such as early feeding experiences and heredity*

specific, goal-oriented eating and drinking behaviors (Hall, Arnold, & Myers, 2000). Similarly, we are born with internal biological preferences for sweet and high-fat foods, but the manufacture and wide availability of snack foods in our external world exploit this inborn preference.

Is there any way to counteract these internal and external factors and successfully lose weight? Most cases of obesity result from consuming more calories than the body can metabolize, or burn up. Therefore, the safest and most reliable way to lose weight is to follow a sensible diet and to exercise regularly (Migliore, 2000; Wadden et al., 1997).

At the same time, weight is more than a simple function of caloric intake and energy expenditure. We all know some people who can eat anything they want and still not add pounds. Research suggests that these "naturally" thin people may be faster at digesting food or have a higher metabolic rate or lower set point (Bouchard, 1996, 1997; Migliore, 2000). Adoption and twin studies also suggest that each of these factors may result from inherited genes. Adoptive children of all weights (ranging from very thin to very obese) tend to resemble their biological parents more than their adoptive parents in body size (Hewitt, 1997). The causes of obesity are complex. Simplistic answers, like willpower or genetics, are appealing, but obesity occurs for a variety of reasons, including many that are outside an individual's control (Hill & Peters, 1998; Woods, Schwartz, Baskin, & Seeley, 2000).

Before we leave this topic, the role of biology in weight regulation should be put in perspective. Obesity is a major cause of morbidity (disease) and mortality (death) (American Heart Association, 2000). Overstating the role of genetics and biology may discourage lifestyle changes that could ultimately improve health. On the other hand, vast numbers of individuals operate on destructive cycles of diets and relapses, followed by guilt, depression, and new rounds of dieting. Recent research finds this type of "yo-yo dieting" can also significantly increase the risk of gallstones (Horowitz, 1999; U.S. Department of Public Health, 2000). According to Brownell and Rodin (1994b), "dieting clearly has costs and, for some, has the potential for benefit... Hence, it is important to distinguish dieting in individuals who are not overweight from those whose weight increases medical or psychosocial risks" (p.781).

Anorexia Nervosa and Bulimia Nervosa

Two serious eating disorders that demonstrate the potential dangers of dieting are **anorexia nervosa** (self-starvation and extreme weight loss) and **bulimia nervosa** (intense, recurring episodes of binge eating followed by purging through vomiting or taking laxatives). Contrary to myth, these eating disorders are not restricted to females from upper-middle-class backgrounds. They are found in all socioeconomic levels, and a few men also develop eating disorders, although the incidence is rare compared with that for women (Brooks, Taylor, Hardy, & Lass, 2000; Hewitt, Coren, & Steel, 2001).

Anorexia nervosa is characterized by an overwhelming fear of becoming obese, disturbed body image, and the use of dangerous measures to lose weight. The fear of fatness does not diminish even with radical and obvious weight loss, and the body image is so distorted that even a skeletal body is perceived as fat. Many people with anorexia nervosa not only refuse to eat but also take up extreme exercise regimens — hours of cycling or running or constant walking. The extreme malnutrition often leads to bone fractures and osteoporosis. Menstruation in women often ceases, and brain computed tomography (CT) scans show enlarged ventricles (cavities) and widened grooves. Such signs generally indicate loss of brain tissue (Wentz, Gillberg, Gillberg, & Rastam, 2000). A sig-

Anorexia Nervosa *An eating disorder, seen mostly in adolescent and young adult females, in which a severe loss of weight results from an obsessive fear of obesity and self-imposed starvation*

Bulimia Nervosa *An eating disorder in which enormous quantities of food are consumed (binges), followed by purging through vomiting or taking laxatives*

nificant percentage of individuals with anorexia nervosa ultimately die of the disorder (Gordon, 2000).

Occasionally the person suffering from anorexia nervosa succumbs to the desire to eat and gorges on food, then vomits or takes laxatives. This type of bingeing and purging is also characteristic of bulimia nervosa, which is much more common than anorexia nervosa (Greeno, Wing, & Shiffman, 2000). Individuals suffering from bulimia nervosa are not just impulsive eaters; they also show impulsivity in other areas, sometimes by petty shoplifting or alcohol abuse (Dansky, Brewerton, & Kilpatrick, 2000; Narduzzi & Jackson, 2000). The vomiting associated with bulimia nervosa causes eroded tooth enamel and tooth loss, severe damage to the throat and stomach, cardiac arrhythmias, metabolic deficiencies, and serious digestive disorders.

What causes anorexia nervosa and bulimia nervosa? There are almost as many causes as there are victims. Some theories focus on physical causes such as hypothalamic disorders, low levels of various neurotransmitters, and genetic or hormonal disorders. Other theories emphasize psychological or social factors, such as a need for perfectionism, a perceived loss of control, destructive thought patterns, depression, dysfunctional families, distorted body image, and sexual abuse (Gordon, 2000; Richter, 2001; Robert-McComb, 2001; Wade, Bulik, Sullivan, Neale, & Kendler, 2000).

Culture and Eating Disorders

Culture and the media also play important roles in eating disorders (Anastasio, Rose, & Chapman, 1999; Davis, Dionne, & Shuster, 2001). A number of cross-cultural studies have found important differences in perceptions and stereotypes about eating, thinness, and obesity. For instance, Asian and African Americans report fewer eating and dieting disorders and greater body satisfaction than do European Americans (Akan & Grilo, 1995), and Mexican students report less concern about their own weight and more acceptance of fat people than do North American students (Crandall & Martinez, 1996).

Although social pressures for thinness certainly contribute to the development of eating disorders, it is interesting to note that anorexia nervosa has also been found in nonindustrialized areas like the Caribbean island of Curaçao (Riva, Marachi, & Molinari, 2000). On that island, being overweight is socially acceptable and the average woman is considerably heavier than women in North America are, yet some women still have anorexia nervosa. This research suggests that both culture and biology help explain eating disorders. Regardless of the causes, it is important to recognize the symptoms of anorexia and bulimia (Table 12.1) and seek therapy if the symptoms apply to you. There is no question that both disorders are serious and require treatment.

Arousal: The Need for Stimulation

Another biological motive that influences us is *arousal*, which refers to a general state of alertness and mental and physical activation. Although the hunger motive obviously affects behavior, we are less likely to recognize that all living organisms also need a certain degree of stimulation. According to the *arousal motive* theory, there is an ideal or optimal level of arousal that organisms are motivated to achieve and maintain.

The need for sensory stimulation begins shortly after birth. For example, infants show a marked preference for complex versus simple visual stimuli. Adults also pay more attention, and for a longer period of time, to complex and changing stimuli. Similarly, research with monkeys shows they will perform various tasks for the sim-

TABLE 12.1 *DSM-IV-TR*[A] SYMPTOMS OF ANOREXIA NERVOSA AND BULIMIA NERVOSA

Symptoms of Anorexia Nervosa
- Body weight below 85% of normal for one's height and age
- Intense fear of becoming fat or gaining weight, even though underweight
- Disturbance in one's body image or perceived weight
- Self-evaluation is unduly influenced by body weight
- Denial of seriousness of abnormally low body weight
- Absence of menstrual periods
- Purging behavior (vomiting or misuse of laxatives or diuretics)

Symptoms of Bulimia Nervosa
- Normal or above-normal weight
- Recurring binge eating
- Eating within an hour or two an amount of food that is much larger than most people would consume
- Feeling a lack of control over eating
- Purging behavior (vomiting or misuse of laxatives or diuretics)
- Excessive exercise to prevent weight gain
- Fasting to prevent weight gain
- Self-evaluation is unduly influenced by body weight

The extreme thinness of popular television stars like Lara Flynn Boyle may contribute to anorexia and bulimia.

[a] *DSM-IV-TR = Diagnostic and Statistical Manual of Mental Disorders,* fourth edition, revised.

ple "reward" of a brief look around the laboratory (Butler, 1954). As can be seen in Figure 12.3, they will also learn to open latches for the sheer pleasure of curiosity and manipulation (Harlow, Harlow, & Meyer, 1950).

When arousal is too low or too high, performance is diminished, as shown in Figure 12.4. This inverted U-shape curve, so-named because the graph looks like an upside-down letter *U,* also demonstrates that performance is maximized when arousal is at an "optimum" level. Have you noticed this effect while taking exams? When underaroused, your mind wanders, causing you to make careless errors (like

(a)

(b)

Figure 12.3 *Arousal-seeking behavior.* (a) Monkeys will work very hard at opening latches for the sheer pleasure of satisfying their curiosity. (b) The arousal motive is also seen in young children, who are fascinated by ordinary household objects.

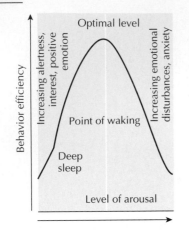

Figure 12.4 *Optimal level of arousal.* Our need for stimulation (the arousal motive) suggests that behavior efficiency increases as we move from deep sleep to increased alertness. However, there is a point at which we become too aroused and performance declines.

filling in the space for option A on a multiple-choice exam when you meant to fill in B). When overaroused, you may become so anxious that you can't remember what you studied. (This kind of forgetting is explained in part by the fact that overarousal seems to interfere with retrieving information from long-term memory [LTM].)

If you do become overly aroused on exam day, you may want to take a class in study skills or test anxiety. You can also try these basic study tips:

Step 1: *Prepare in advance.* Improve your reading, note taking, and study skills by reviewing and practicing the advice in Tools for Student Success in Chapter 1. The single most important cure for test anxiety is advance preparation and *hard work.* If you are well prepared, you will feel calmer and more in control.

- Read your textbook using the SQ4R (Survey, Question, Read, Recite, Review, and wRite) method.
- Practice good time management and distribute your study time; don't cram the night before.
- Actively listen during lectures and take detailed, and summarizing notes.
- Follow the general strategies for test taking mentioned in Chapter 1.

Step 2: *Learn to cope with the anxiety.* As you just learned, performance is best at a moderate level of arousal. A few butterflies before and during exams are okay and to be expected, but too much anxiety can interfere with concentration and cripple your performance. To achieve the right balance of arousal, try the following:

- Replace anxiety with relaxed feelings. Practice the relaxation response described in Chapter 3, on page 112.
- Desensitize yourself to the test situation. See Chapter 15, page 546.
- Exercise regularly. This is a great stress reliever and promotes deeper and more restful sleep.

Sensation Seeking

Each of us is motivated to achieve an optimal level of arousal, but how do we explain people who seem to have an extreme need for stimulation? What motivates people who hang-glide over deep canyons or go whitewater rafting down dangerous rivers? According to research, these "high sensation seekers" may be biologically "prewired" to need a higher level of stimulation (Zuckerman, 1979, 2000).

TRY THIS
Yourself

Before we continue, circle the choice, A or B, that *best* describes you in each of the following items:

1. A I would like a job that requires a lot of traveling.
    B I would prefer a job in one location.
2. A I am invigorated by a brisk, cold day.
    B I can't wait to get indoors on a cold day.
3. A I get bored seeing the same old faces.
    B I like the comfortable familiarity of everyday friends.
4. A I would prefer living in an ideal society where everyone is safe, secure, and happy.
    B I would have preferred living in the unsettled days of our history.
5. A I sometimes like to do things that are a little frightening.
    B A sensible person avoids activities that are dangerous.
6. A I would not like to be hypnotized.
    B I would like to have the experience of being hypnotized.
7. A The most important goal of life is to live it to the fullest and experience as much as possible.
    B The most important goal of life is to find peace and happiness.

8. A I would like to try parachute jumping.

   B I would never want to try jumping out of a plane, with or without a parachute.

9. A I enter cold water gradually, giving myself time to get used to it.

   B I like to dive or jump right into the ocean or a cold pool.

10. A When I go on a vacation, I prefer the comfort of a good room and bed.

    B When I go on a vacation, I prefer the change of camping out.

11. A I prefer people who are emotionally expressive even if they are a bit unstable.

    B I prefer people who are calm and even-tempered.

12. A A good painting should shock or jolt the senses.

    B A good painting should convey a feeling of peace and security.

13. A People who ride motorcycles must have some kind of unconscious need to hurt themselves.

    B I would like to drive or ride on a motorcycle.

Scoring

Count 1 point for each of the following items that you have circled: 1A, 2A, 3A, 4B, 5A, 6B, 7A, 8A, 9B, 10B, 11A, 12A, 13B. Add up your total and compare it with the norms below:

0–3: very low need for sensation seeking
4–5: low
6–9: average
10–11: high
12–13: very high

Source: Zuckerman, M. (1978, February). The search for high sensation, *Psychology Today*, pp. 38–46. Copyright © 1978 by the American Psychological Association. Reprinted by permission.

High sensation-seeking? *Would you be willing to try bungee jumping? If not, are you a low sensation-seeker on Zuckerman's scale?*

Research based on longer versions of Zuckerman's scale suggest four distinct factors that characterize sensation seeking (Franken, 1998; Johnson & Cropsey, 2000): (1) thrill and adventure seeking (skydiving, driving fast, or trying to beat a train), (2) experience seeking (travel, unusual friends, drug experimentation), (3) disinhibition ("letting loose"), and (4) susceptibility to boredom (lower tolerance for repetition and sameness).

If you scored very high or very low on this test, you might have problems in relationships with individuals who score toward the other extreme. Zuckerman warns that this is true not just between partners or spouses but also between parent and child and therapist and patient. There might also be job difficulties for a high-sensation seeker with a routine clerical or assembly line job or a low-sensation seeker with a highly challenging and variable occupation.

Achievement: The Need for Success

Do you wonder what motivated Wilt Chamberlain to achieve such success in basketball or why Coach Bobby Knight drove his players so mercilessly? What about someone like Thomas Edison? Inventing the lightbulb would have been achievement enough for any person, but Edison also received patents for the microphone, the phonograph, and over a thousand other inventions. Even as a child, he spent hours doing experiments and figuring out how things work. What drove Edison?

The key to understanding Wilt Chamberlain, Bobby Knight, and Thomas Edison lies in what psychologist Henry Murray (1938) identified as a high need for achievement (nAch), or **achievement motivation**, a desire for significant accomplishment. Before you continue reading, complete the Critical Thinking/Active Learning exercise that follows this section. It gives you an opportunity to test your own need for achievement.

Achievement Motivation *The need for success, for doing better than others, and for mastering challenging tasks; the desire to excel, especially in competition with others*

Characteristics of Achievers

How do individuals with a high nAch differ from other people? Researchers have identified several distinguishing traits in these people (McClelland, 1958, 1987, 1993; Mueller & Dweck, 1998; Wigfield & Eccles, 2000).

1. *Preference for moderately difficult tasks.* People high in nAch avoid tasks that are too easy because they offer little challenge or satisfaction. They also avoid extremely difficult tasks because the probability of success is too low. In a ring-toss game, for instance, they often stand at an intermediate distance from the target.

2. *Competitiveness.* High achievement–oriented people are more attracted to careers and tasks that involve competition and an opportunity to excel.

3. *Preference for clear goals with competent feedback.* High achievement–oriented people tend to prefer tasks with a clear outcome and situations in which they can receive feedback on their performance. They also prefer criticism from a harsh but competent evaluator to one who is friendlier but less competent.

4. *Responsibility.* People with high nAch prefer being personally responsible for a project. When they are directly responsible, they can feel satisfied when the task is well done.

5. *Persistence.* High achievement–oriented people are more likely to persist at a task when it becomes difficult. When participants were given an unsolvable task, 47 percent of the high-nAch individuals persisted until time was called. On the other hand, only 2 percent of those who were low on achievement motivation persisted.

6. *More accomplished.* People who have high nAch scores do achieve more than others. They do better on exams, earn better grades in high school and college, and excel in their chosen professions.

What causes some people to be more achievement oriented than others? Achievement orientation appears to be largely learned in early childhood, primarily through interactions with parents. Highly motivated children tend to have parents who encourage independence and frequently reward successes (Maehr & Urdan, 1999). The culture that we are born and raised in also affects achievement needs (Lubinski & Benbow, 2000). Events and themes in children's literature, for example, often contain subtle messages about what the culture values. In North American and Western European cultures, many children's stories are about persistence and the value of hard work. A study by Richard de Charms and Gerald Moeller (1962) found a significant correlation between the achievement themes in children's literature and the actual industrial accomplishments of various countries. Conversely, can you see how gambling and the lottery — both based on luck of the draw — might lower a person's nAch?

Intrinsic and Extrinsic Motivation and Achievement

Having some understanding of the characteristics of high achievers, let's look at two forms of motivation that affect achievement — *intrinsic* and *extrinsic*. **Intrinsic motivation** comes from within the individual. The person engages in an activity for its own sake or for internal satisfaction, with no ulterior purpose or need for an external reward. Some researchers believe this self-motivation comes from an innate need (e.g., Ryan & Deci, 2000). In contrast, **extrinsic motivation** stems from obvious external rewards or avoidance of punishment and is learned through interaction with the environment. Participation in sports and hobbies, like swimming or playing a guitar, is usually intrinsically motivated. Working at a boring job and going to the dentist come from extrinsic motivation. In most people's mind, "play" is intrinsic and "work" is extrinsic.

What do you think would happen if you were suddenly given extrinsic rewards (money, praise, or other incentives) for your current "play" activities? Studies have

*A **prime example of intrinsic motivation.** Vincent van Gogh only sold one painting during his entire lifetime, yet he was one of the most prolific nineteenth century artists. How would you explain his motivtion?*

Intrinsic Motivation *Motivation that comes from personal enjoyment of a task or activity, rather than from external rewards or fear of punishment*

Extrinsic Motivation *Motivation based on obvious external rewards or threats of punishment, rather than on factors within the individual or the behavior itself*

critical thinking ▶▶▶▶▶▶▶▶▶▶▶▶▶▶▶▶ Active Learning

Measuring Your Own Need for Achievement

Are you interested in measuring your own need for achievement? If so, try the following:

Test 1

On the basis of how you feel in *most* situations, answer the following questions honestly with a yes or no:

1. If offered a choice of tasks, would you pick one that is moderately difficult rather than one that is very difficult or easy?

2. Do you enjoy tasks more if you compete against others?

3. Do you prefer tasks that have clear, defineable goals and measurable outcomes?

4. Do you like receiving feedback about how well you are doing when you are working on a project?

5. Would you rather receive criticism from a harsh but competent evaluator than from one who is friendlier but less competent?

6. Do you prefer tasks where you are personally responsible for the outcome?

7. When working on a difficult task, do you persist even when you encounter roadblocks?

8. Do you typically receive high performance evaluations (e.g., receiving top honors or special recognition in sports, clubs, and other activities)?

Test 2

The Thematic Apperception Test (TAT) consists of a series of ambiguous pictures such as the one shown in Figure 12.5. The TAT is one of the most common methods for measuring achievement motivation. Look closely at the two women in the figure and write a short story answering the following questions:

1. What is happening in this picture, and what led up to it?

2. Who are the people in this picture, and how do they feel?

3. What is going to happen in the next few moments, and in a few weeks?

Scoring

Test 1: Give yourself 1 point for each time you answered yes to the eight questions. On the basis of the characteristics of achievers discussed in the text, people with a higher number of yes answers tend to be high in achievement motivation.

Test 2: Give yourself 1 point each time any of the following is mentioned: (1) defining a problem, (2) solving a problem, (3) obstructions to solving a problem, (4) techniques that can help overcome the

Figure 12.5 *Measuring achievement.* This card is one of several from the Thematic Apperception Test (TAT). The strength of an individual's need for achievement is measured by the stories he or she tells about the TAT photos.

problem, (5) anticipation of success or resolution of the problem. The higher your score on this test, the higher your overall need for achievement.

The higher your score on both tests, the higher your overall need for achievement. Compare your scores with those of your friends and classmates.

---

found that people who are paid or rewarded for something they had previously done for the sheer fun of it often lose enjoyment and interest in the task (Hennessey & Amabile, 1998; Kohn, 2000). One of the earliest experiments to demonstrate this effect involved preschool children who liked to draw (Lepper, Greene, & Nisbett, 1973). The children were all given artist's paper and felt-tipped pens, and one group was promised a "Good Player" certificate with a gold seal and ribbon for their drawings. A second group was asked to draw and then received an unexpected reward when they were done. A third group received no promise of a certificate and no reward was given. A few weeks later, these same children were placed in a situation in which they could draw if they wanted to, and the amount of time they spent drawing was recorded.

What do you think happened? As Figure 12.6 shows, offers of a "Good Player" certificate greatly undermined the children's subsequent interest in drawing.

3. *Emphasize intrinsic reasons for behaviors.* Rather than thinking about whom you'll impress with good grades or all the great jobs you'll get when you finish college, focus instead on personally satisfying, intrinsic reasons. Think about how exciting it is to learn new things or the value of becoming an educated person and a critical thinker.

Obviously, not all college classes or all aspects of our lives can be intrinsically interesting. Nor should they be. We all have to do many worthwhile things that are obviously extrinsically motivated — going to the dentist, cleaning the house, and studying for exams. It's a good idea, therefore, to save your external reinforcers for the times you're having trouble motivating yourself to do an undesirable task, and avoid "wasting" rewards on well-established intrinsic activities. In other words, "Don't sweat the intrinsic stuff" and "Save rewards for a rainy day."

Check & Review

UNDERSTANDING MOTIVATION

Motivation is the study of the "whys" of behavior, whereas **emotion** is the study of feelings. Because motivated behaviors are often closely related to emotions, these two topics are frequently studied together. A wide variety of motives are discussed throughout this text. In this chapter, we focus on hunger, arousal, and **achievement motivation.**

Both internal (stomach, blood chemistry, the brain) and external (cultural conditioning) factors affect hunger and eating. A large number of people have eating disorders. Obesity seems to result from biological factors, such as the individual's genetic inheritance, and from psychological factors. **Anorexia nervosa** (extreme weight loss due to self-imposed starvation) and **bulimia nervosa** (excessive consumption of food followed by purging) are both related to an intense fear of obesity.

According to the arousal motive, people seek an optimal level of arousal that maximizes their performance. There are, however, individual differences in this need. According to Zuckerman, high-sensation seekers are biologically "prewired" to need a higher level of stimulation, whereas the reverse is true for low-sensation seekers. Achievement involves the need for success, for doing better than others, and for mastering challenging tasks. Research with **intrinsic** versus **extrinsic motivation** shows that extrinsic rewards can lower interest and achievement motivation.

Questions

1. Compare and contrast motivation and emotion.

2. What are the major internal and external factors that control hunger and eating behavior?

3. The _____ motive causes us to look for a certain amount of novelty and complexity from our environment for no apparent reason. (a) sensory; (b) social; (c) drive; (d) arousal

4. _____ refers to the desire to perform an act for its own sake, whereas _____ refers to the desire to perform an act because of external rewards or the avoidance of punishment. (a) Personal motivation, external motivation; (b) Internal drive, external drive; (c) Intrinsic motivation, extrinsic motivation; (d) Individual drive, social drive

Answers to Questions can be found in Appendix B.

GENERAL THEORIES OF MOTIVATION

Are we motivated by biological or by psychosocial factors? Or both?

Think back to the introductory stories about Wilt Chamberlain and Bobby Knight while reading the following section. See if you can identify which theory best explains both of their behaviors. We will explore four separate theories that fall into two general categories — biological or psychosocial (Table 12.2).

Biological Theories: Looking for Internal "Whys" of Behavior

Many theories of motivation are biologically based — that is, they look for inborn processes that control and direct behavior. Among these biologically oriented theories are *instinct* and *drive* theories.

TABLE 12.2 FIVE THEORIES OF MOTIVATION

Theory	View
Biological Theories	
Instinct	Motivation results from behaviors that are unlearned, uniform in expression, and universal in a species.
Drive-reduction	Motivation begins with a physiological need (a lack or deficiency) that elicits a psychological energy (drive) directed toward behavior that will satisfy the original need.
Psychosocial Theories	
Incentive	Motivation results from environmental stimuli that "pull" the organisms in certain directions.
Cognitive	Motivation reflects thought processes (such as attributions and expectancies) in goal-directed behaviors.
Interactionism	
Maslow's hierarchy of needs	Lower motives (such as physiological and safety needs) must be satisfied before advancing to higher needs (such as belonging and self-esteem).

What motivates this behavior? Which theory best explains this man's love for and collection of banana paraphernalia?

Instinct Theories

In the earliest days of psychology, researchers like William McDougall (1908) proposed that humans had numerous "instincts," such as repulsion, curiosity, and self-assertiveness. Other researchers later added their favorite "instincts," and by the 1920s, the list became so long it was virtually meaningless. One early researcher found listings for over 10,000 human instincts (Bernard, 1924).

In addition to producing a never-ending list, the label *instinct* led to circular explanations. Have you ever heard someone say that men are just naturally or instinctually aggressive, or that all women have a maternal instinct? When asked for evidence of these instincts, the person (like the researchers did in McDougall's time) most likely points to examples of male aggression or female nurturing. Thus, the explanation of the behavior is the behavior: "They act that way because they naturally act that way." Circular reasoning, however, is not acceptable to science.

In recent years, a branch of biology called *sociobiology* has revived the case for **instincts**. These are rigid and fixed motor response patterns that are not learned, are characteristic of a species, and have an inherited, genetic foundation established in the course of evolution. Instinctual behaviors are obvious in many animals: birds build nests and salmon swim upstream to spawn. But sociobiologists such as Edward O. Wilson (1975, 1978) believe humans also have instincts, like competition or aggression, which are genetically transmitted from one generation to another.

Instincts *Behavioral patterns that are (1) unlearned, (2) always expressed in the same way, and (3) universal in a species*

Drive-Reduction Theory *The theory that motivation begins with a physiological need (a lack or deficiency) that elicits a psychological energy or drive directed toward behavior that will satisfy the original need; once the need is met, a state of balance (homeostasis) is restored and motivation decreases*

Drive-Reduction Theory

In the 1930s, the concepts of drive and drive reduction began to replace the theory of instincts. According to **drive-reduction theory** (Hull, 1952; Spence, 1951), all living organisms have certain biological *needs* (such as food, water, and oxygen) that must be met if they are to survive. When these needs are unmet, a state of tension (known as a *drive*) is created, and the organism is motivated to reduce it. When we are deprived of food, our biological need creates a state of tension, in this case the hunger *drive*, and we are motivated to find food.

Instincts? Nurturing of the young are instinctual behaviors for many species.

Figure 12.8 *Drive-reduction theory.* Homeostasis, the body's natural tendency to maintain a state of internal balance, is the foundation of drive-reduction theory. When you need food or water, for example, the imbalance creates a drive that motivates you to search for food or water. When the balance is restored, your motivation (to seek food or water) is also decreased.

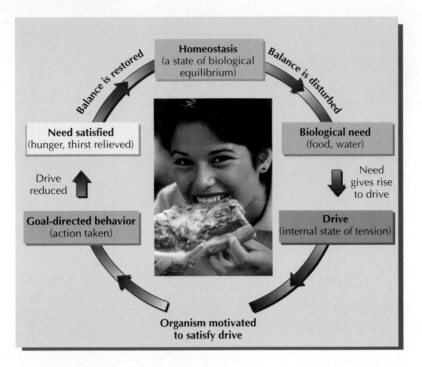

Drive-reduction theory is based largely on the biological concept of *homeostasis* — a state of balance or stability in the body's internal environment. Body temperature, blood sugar, oxygen level, and water balance are all normally maintained in a state of equilibrium (Chapter 2). When this balance is disrupted, a need arises (a drive is created), and we are motivated to restore homeostasis. Drive-reduction theory and homeostasis are summarized in Figure 12.8.

Psychosocial Theories: Incentives and Cognitions

Instinct and drive-reduction theories explain some motivations but not all. Why, for example, do we continue to eat after our biological need is completely satisfied? Or why does someone work overtime when his or her salary is sufficient to meet all basic biological needs? These questions are better answered by psychosocial theories that emphasize incentives and cognition.

Incentive Theory

Incentive Theory *The theory that motivation results from environmental stimuli that "pull" the organism in certain directions, as opposed to internal needs that drive or "push" the organism*

Although drive theory says internal factors *push* people in certain directions, **incentive theory** says external stimuli *pull* people (Bolles, 1970, 1975; Pfaffmann, 1982). Certain characteristics of external stimuli motivate an individual to act to obtain desirable goals or avoid undesirable events. People initially eat because their hunger "pushes" them, but they continue to eat because the sight of apple pie or ice cream "pulls" them. Many *incentives* drew Wilt Chamberlain to basketball, including fame, status, large financial rewards, and the simple joy of playing the game. But cognitive factors might have provided even more compelling motivation.

Cognitive Theories

If you receive a high grade in your psychology course, you can interpret that grade in several ways: You earned it because you really studied; you "lucked out"; the textbook was exceptionally interesting and helpful (our preferred interpretation!). According to the cognitive perspective, motivation is directly affected by *attribu-*

tions, or how we interpret or think about our own and others' actions. Researchers have found that people who attribute their successes to personal ability and effort tend to work harder toward their goals than people who attribute their successes to luck (Weiner, 1972, 1982).

Expectancies are also important to motivation (Higgins, 1997). Your anticipated grade on a test affects your willingness to study — "If I can get an A in the course, then I will study very hard" — just as your expectancies regarding promotions at work affect your willingness to work overtime for no pay.

Interactionism: Maslow's Hierarchy of Needs

As we've seen throughout this text, research in psychology generally emphasizes either biological or psychosocial factors (nature or nurture), but in the final analysis, *interactionism* almost always wins. Theories of motivation are no exception. One researcher who recognized this interactionism and developed a theory that accounts for both biological and psychosocial needs in motivation was Abraham Maslow (1954, 1970, 1999). Maslow believed that we all have numerous needs that compete for fulfillment but that some needs are more important than others. For example, your need for a good grade in psychology may compete with demands from other classes, but your need for food and shelter is more important than how you do in college.

As Figure 12.9 shows, Maslow's **hierarchy of needs** *prioritizes* needs, with survival needs at the bottom and social, spiritual needs at the top. Maslow's theory is usually depicted as a pyramid to emphasize that human motivation rests on a foundation of basic biological needs that must be satisfied for survival before higher-level needs can be addressed. As a humanistic psychologist, Maslow also believed that we all have a compelling need to "move up" — to grow, improve ourselves, and ultimately become "self-actualized." (We'll revisit Maslow and other humanistic perspectives in the next chapter.)

Hierarchy of Needs *Maslow's theory of motivation, that some motives (such as physiological and safety needs) have to be satisfied before an individual can attend to higher needs (such as belonging and self-actualiztion)*

Figure 12.9 *Maslow's hierarchy of needs.* According to Maslow, basic physical necessities must be satisfied before higher-growth needs can be addressed.

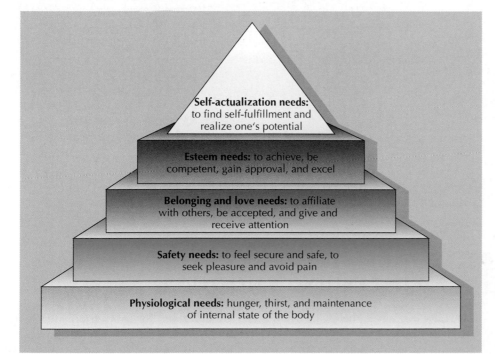

Self-actualization needs: to find self-fulfillment and realize one's potential

Esteem needs: to achieve, be competent, gain approval, and excel

Belonging and love needs: to affiliate with others, be accepted, and give and receive attention

Safety needs: to feel secure and safe, to seek pleasure and avoid pain

Physiological needs: hunger, thirst, and maintenance of internal state of the body

Maslow's hierarchy of needs seems intuitively correct — a starving person would first look for food, then worry about safety, then seek love and friendship, and so on. This prioritizing and the concept of *self-actualization* are important contributions to the study of motivation (Leclerk, Lefrancois, Dube, Hebert, & Gaulin, 1998; Rowan, 1998). But critics argue that parts of Maslow's theory are poorly researched. People sometimes seek to satisfy higher-level needs even when lower-level needs have not been met (Geller, 1982; Neher, 1991; Williams & Page, 1989).

In some nonindustrialized societies, for example, people may be living in a war zone, subsisting on very little food, and suffering from injury and disease (in other words, not fulfilling Maslow's two most basic needs), yet still seek strong social ties and high self-esteem. During the famine and war in Somalia, many parents sacrificed their own lives to carry starving children hundreds of miles to food distribution centers, and parents at the centers often banded together to share the limited supplies. Because Maslow argued that each individual's own lower needs must be at least partially met before higher needs can influence behavior, these examples "stand Maslow's need hierarchy on its head" (Neher, 1991, p. 97). Although we're normally motivated to fulfill basic needs first, in certain circumstances we can bypass these lower stages and pursue higher-level needs.

Check & Review

GENERAL THEORIES OF MOTIVATION

There are three approaches to explaining motivation: biological (including **instinct theory** and **drive-reduction theory**) psychosocial (including **incentive** and cognitive), and interactionist (Maslow's **hierarchy of needs**).

Instinct theories emphasize inborn, genetic components in motivation. Drive-reduction theory suggests that internal tensions (produced by the body's demand for homeostasis) "push" the organism toward satisfying basic needs. According to **incentive** theory, motivation results from the "pull" of external environmental stimuli. Cognitive theories emphasize the importance of attributions and expectations. Maslow's hierarchy of needs or motives incorporates both biological and psychosocial theories. He believed that basic survival needs must be satisfied before a person can attempt to satisfy higher needs. Critics question the importance of sequentially working upward through these steps.

Questions

1. Define *instinct* and *homeostasis*.
2. Match the following examples with their appropriate theory of motivation: (a) instinct; (b) drive-reduction; (c) incentive; (d) cognitive; (e) Maslow's hierarchy of needs
   _____ i. Joining a club because you want to be accepted by others
   _____ ii. Two animals fighting because of their inherited, evolutionary desire for survival
   _____ iii. Eating to reduce hunger
   _____ iv. Studying hard for an exam because you expect that studying will result in a good grade
   _____ v. Eating because the pie looks so delicious
3. _____ theories emphasize the importance of attributions and expectancies in motivated behaviors. (a) Attribution; (b) Motivational; (c) Achievement; (d) Cognitive
4. According to _____ theory, basic survival and security needs must be satisfied before one can move on to such higher needs as self-actualization. (a) evolutionary; (b) instinct; (c) Maslow's; (d) Weiner's

Answers to Questions can be found in Appendix B.

UNDERSTANDING EMOTION

What major concepts do I need to know in order to understand emotion?

We have reviewed the major theoretical explanations for motivation and specific motives like hunger, eating, arousal, and achievement. But as we mentioned at the beginning of this chapter, motivation is inextricably linked to emotion. In this section, we will explore the three basic components of all emotions and then look at controversies surrounding the polygraph (or "lie detector") test and the concept of emotional intelligence (EQ).

Components of Emotion: Three Basic Ingredients

Emotions play an important role in our lives. They color our dreams, memories, and perceptions, and when they are disturbed they contribute significantly to psychological disorders. But what do we mean by the term *emotion*? In everyday usage, we describe emotions in terms of feeling states — Wilt Chamberlain "felt thrilled" when he set the NBA record against the New York Knicks, Bobby Knight frequently "felt angry" when coaching, and you "feel happy" watching a good basketball game. Psychologists define and study emotions according to their three basic components (cognitive, physiological, and behavioral).

The Cognitive Component

Our thoughts, beliefs, and expectations help determine the type and intensity of our emotional responses. Or, as Shakespeare wrote in *Hamlet*, "There is nothing either good or bad, but thinking makes it so." Consequently, emotional reactions are very individual: What you experience as intensely pleasurable may be boring or aversive for another.

To study the cognitive component of emotions, psychologists typically use self-report techniques such as paper-and-pencil tests, surveys, and interviews. But our cognitions or thoughts about our own and others' emotions are typically difficult to describe and scientifically measure. Individuals differ in their ability to monitor and report on their emotional states. In addition, some people may lie or hide their feelings because of social expectations or as an attempt to please the experimenter. Furthermore, it is often impractical or unethical to artificially create emotions in a laboratory. How can we ethically create strong emotions like anger in a research participant just to study his or her emotional reactions? Finally, memories of emotions are not foolproof. You may remember that trip to Yellowstone as the "best family camping trip ever," whereas your brother or sister may remember it as the "worst." Our individual needs, experiences, and personal interpretations all affect the accuracy of our memories (Chapter 7).

The Physiological Component

Internal physical changes occur in our bodies whenever we experience an emotion. Imagine walking alone on a dark street in a dangerous part of town. You suddenly see someone jump from behind a stack of boxes and start running toward you. How do you respond? Like most of us, you would undoubtedly interpret the situation as threatening and would run. Your predominant emotion, fear, would involve several physiological reactions, including increased heart rate and blood pressure, dilated pupils, perspiration, dry mouth, rapid or irregular breathing, increased blood sugar, trembling, decreased gastrointestinal motility, and piloerection (goose bumps). Such physiological reactions are controlled by certain brain structures and by the autonomic branch of the nervous system (ANS).

The brain. The brain's reticular formation, limbic system, and cerebral cortex play important roles in emotion (Chapter 2). Each of these structures plays a complex and interwoven role. There is some evidence that emotional reactions, such as Coach Knight's anger at his players, begin with the brainstem's reticular formation, which is responsible for general arousal and motor control (Davidson, 1999; Rosenzweig, Leiman, & Breedlove, 1999).

Situated above the reticular formation, limbic structures (in particular, the *hypothalamus* and *amygdala*) (Figure 12.10) are also involved in recognizing and

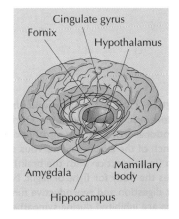

Figure 12.10 *Brain areas involved in emotion.* The limbic system consists of several subcortical structures that form a border (or limbus) around the brainstem. (The red structure in the center is the thalamus.)

Visual Summary for Chapter 12

Understanding Motivation

Motivation: study of the "whys" of behavior, **emotion:** study of feelings.

Hunger and Eating

- Both *internal* (stomach, blood chemistry, brain) and *external* (cultural conditioning) factors.
- Eating disorders due to combination of both biological and psychological factors:

| 1) **Obesity:** Being significantly above the recommended weight level. | 2) **Anorexia nervosa:** Extreme weight loss due to self-imposed starvation. | 3) **Bulimia nervosa:** Excessive consumption of food followed by purging. |

Arousal

Arousal motive: People seek *optimal level* of *arousal* that maximizes their performance. High sensation seekers are biologically "prewired" to need a higher level of stimulation.

Achievement

Achievement motivation: Need for success, doing better than others, and mastering challenging tasks. **Intrinsic** vs. **extrinsic motivation** research shows extrinsic rewards can lower interest and achievement motivation.

General Theories of Motivation

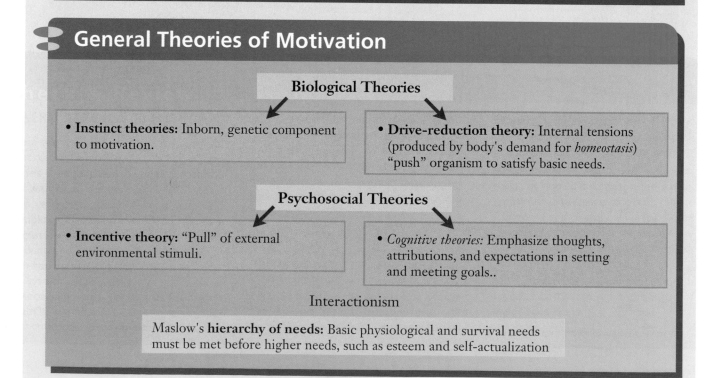

Biological Theories

- **Instinct theories:** Inborn, genetic component to motivation.

- **Drive-reduction theory:** Internal tensions (produced by body's demand for *homeostasis*) "push" organism to satisfy basic needs.

Psychosocial Theories

- **Incentive theory:** "Pull" of external environmental stimuli.

- *Cognitive theories:* Emphasize thoughts, attributions, and expectations in setting and meeting goals..

Interactionism

Maslow's **hierarchy of needs:** Basic physiological and survival needs must be met before higher needs, such as esteem and self-actualization

Understanding Emotion

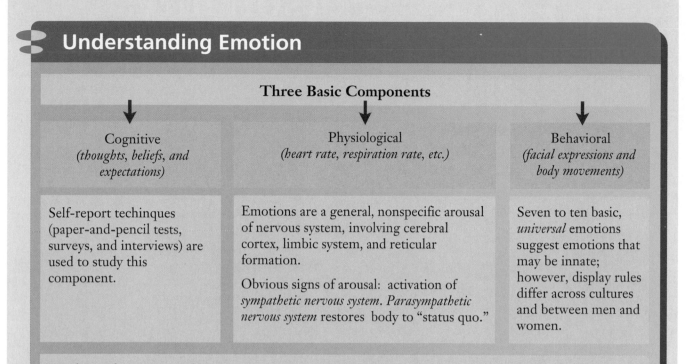

Three Basic Components

Cognitive
(thoughts, beliefs, and expectations)

Self-report techinques (paper-and-pencil tests, surveys, and interviews) are used to study this component.

Physiological
(heart rate, respiration rate, etc.)

Emotions are a general, nonspecific arousal of nervous system, involving cerebral cortex, limbic system, and reticular formation.

Obvious signs of arousal: activation of *sympathetic nervous system. Parasympathetic nervous system* restores body to "status quo."

Behavioral
(facial expressions and body movements)

Seven to ten basic, *universal* emotions suggest emotions that may be innate; however, display rules differ across cultures and between men and women.

- **Polygraph**: Measures changes in emotional arousal but is not valid for measuring guilt or innocence.
- **Emotional intelligence (EQ)**: Knowing and managing emotions, empathizing, and maintaining satisfying relationships.

General Theories of Emotion

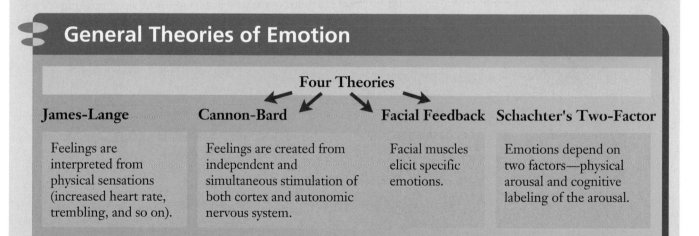

Four Theories

James-Lange

Feelings are interpreted from physical sensations (increased heart rate, trembling, and so on).

Cannon-Bard

Feelings are created from independent and simultaneous stimulation of both cortex and autonomic nervous system.

Facial Feedback

Facial muscles elicit specific emotions.

Schachter's Two-Factor

Emotions depend on two factors—physical arousal and cognitive labeling of the arousal.

13 Personality

Consider the following personality description. How well does it describe you?

You have a strong need for other people to like you and admire you. You have a tendency to be critical of yourself. You have a great deal of unused capacity that you have not turned to your advantage. Although you have some personality weaknesses, you are generally able to compensate for them. You pride yourself on being an independent thinker and do not accept other opinions without satisfactory proof. Disciplined and self-controlled outside, you tend to be worried and insecure inside. At times, you have serious doubts whether you have made the right decision or done the right thing.

Adapted from Ulrich, Stachnik, & Stainton, 1963
What do you think? Does this sound like you? When this same personality description was given to research par-

ticipants and they were told that it was written specifically for them on the basis of previous psychological tests, a high percentage reported that the description was "very accurate." Surprisingly, even when participants were informed that this was a made-up assessment based on generalized information, most still believed the description fit them better than a bona fide personality profile developed from scientifically designed tests (Hyman, 1981). You may be even more surprised to find that about 78 percent of women and 70 percent of men read newspaper horoscopes, and many of them believe these horoscopes are so correct that they were written especially for them (Halpern, 1998).

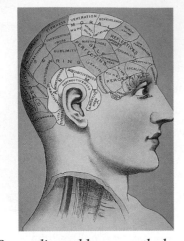

Personality and bumps on the head?
Franz Gall, founder of phrenology, believed that personality could be measured by reading bumps on the skull. Note that terms like sublimity *(ability to squelch natural impulses, especially sexual) and* ideality *(ability to live by high ideals) probably reflect personality traits important in the 1800s. Can you imagine what traits might be measured if we still believed in phrenology? Would we create terms like* suppressity *(withholding of natural impulses, especially sexual) and* computericity *(ability to live in the Information Age)?*

Personality *An individual's relatively stable and enduring pattern of thoughts, feelings, and actions*

How do psychologists measure personality?

Back in the 1800s, if you wanted to have your personality assessed, you would go to a *phrenologist*. This highly respected person would carefully measure your skull, examine the bumps on your head, and then give you a psychological profile of your unique qualities and characteristics. Phrenologists used a *phrenology* chart to determine which personality traits were associated with bumps on different areas of the skull. Today, some people consult fortune-tellers, horoscope columns in the newspaper, tarot cards, and even fortune cookies in Chinese restaurants.

Why are so many people attracted to such nonscientific methods? For one thing, we think these fortune-tellers and pseudotests have somehow tapped into our unique selves. Actually, however, the traits they supposedly reveal are generalizations shared by almost everyone. Furthermore, the traits are generally positive and flattering — or at least neutral. (Would we like tests revealing that we are "irritable, selfish, and emotionally unstable"?) In this chapter, rather than these nonscientific methods, we will focus on research based methods used by psychologists to assess personality.

Before we begin, we need to define *personality*. For most people, "personality" is a relatively simple, everyday concept, as in "He's got a great (or lousy) personality." But for psychologists, personality is an inherently complicated topic, and there are numerous definitions. One of the most widely accepted models defines **personality** as an individual's unique and relatively stable pattern of thoughts; feelings, and actions. Personality describes you as a *person*: how you are different from other people and what patterns of behavior are typical of you. You might qualify as an "extrovert," for example, if you are talkative and outgoing most of the time, or as "conscientious" if you are responsible and self-disciplined most of the time.

Unlike pseudopsychologies presented in supermarket tabloids and newspaper horoscopes, personality theorists focus on empirical studies — the *science* of personality. In line with the basic goals of psychology presented in Chapter 1, they seek to (1) *describe* individual differences in personality, (2) *explain* how those differences come about, and (3) *predict* individual behavior based on personality findings. Before describing, explaining, or predicting personality, we must *assess* or measure it. Therefore, the first topic of this chapter is personality assessment. We then discuss four major theories: trait, psychoanalytic/psychodynamic, humanistic, social/cognitive, and biological.

PERSONALITY ASSESSMENT

Throughout history, people have sought information about their own and others' personalities. Modern research has produced various methods for assessing personality, which are used by clinical and counseling psychologists, psychiatrists, and other helping professionals in the diagnosis of patients and to assess progress in therapy. Personality assessment is also used for educational and vocational counseling and by industries and businesses to aid in hiring decisions.

How We Measure Personality: Do You See What I See?

Like a detective solving a mystery, modern psychologists typically use numerous methods and a complete *battery* (or series) of tests to fully *assess* personality. This assortment of measures can be grouped in a few broad categories: *interviews*, *observations*, *objective tests*, and *projective tests*.

Interviews

We all use informal "interviews" to get to know other people. When first meeting someone, we ask about their jobs, college major, family, and hobbies or interests. Psychologists also use interviews — both *structured* and *unstructured*. Unstructured interviews are often used for job and college selection and for diagnosing psychological problems. In an unstructured format, interviewers get impressions and pursue hunches or let a person expand on information that promises to disclose personality characteristics. The interviewee has a chance to explain unique qualifications in his or her own words. Structured interviews, on the other hand, ask specific questions and follow a set of procedures so that the person being evaluated can be evaluated more objectively. The results of a structured interview are often charted on a rating scale to standardize the evaluations and make comparisons easier.

Observation

In addition to structured and unstructured interviews, psychologists also use direct behavioral observation to assess personality. Most of us enjoy "people watching," but observation as an assessment procedure is a very sophisticated technique. The psychologist looks for examples of specific behaviors and follows a careful set of evaluation guidelines. For instance, a psychologist might arrange to observe a troubled client's interactions with his or her family. Does the client become agitated by the presence of certain family members and not others? Does he or she become passive and withdrawn when asked a direct question? Through careful observation, the psychologist gains valuable insights into the client's personality.

Objective Tests

Objective personality tests, or *inventories*, are standardized questionnaires that require written responses, typically to multiple-choice or true–false items. Answers to these questions help people to describe themselves — to "self-report." They are considered "objective" tests because they have a limited number of possible responses to items and empirical standards for constructing test items and scoring. Given that objective tests can be administered to a large number of people in a relatively short period of time and evaluated in a standardized fashion, they are by far the most widely used method for assessing personality.

You have been introduced to several self-report personality tests in this textbook. There was the androgyny scale in Chapter 11, for example, and the sensation – seeking scale in Chapter 12. Later in this chapter, we discuss the locus of control scale. The complete versions of these tests measure one specific personality trait and are used primarily in research. Often, however, psychologists in clinical, counseling, and industrial settings are interested in assessing a range of personality traits all at once. To do this, they generally use *multitrait* (or *multiphasic*) inventories.

Many multitrait tests have been developed, including the Sixteen Personality Factors Questionnaire (16PF) discussed later. The most widely researched and clinically used multitrait test is the **Minnesota Multiphasic Personality Inventory** (MMPI) — or its revision, the MMPI-2 (Butcher, 2000; Butcher & Rouse, 1996). The test consists of over 500 statements that participants respond to with *True*, *False*, or *Cannot say*. The following are examples of the kinds of statements found on the MMPI:

> My stomach frequently bothers me.
>
> I have enemies that really wish to harm me.
>
> I sometimes hear things that other people can't hear.
>
> I would like to be a mechanic.
>
> I have never indulged in any unusual sex practices.

Why are some of these questions about really unusual, abnormal behavior? Although there are many "normal" questions on the full MMPI, the test is designed primarily for clinical and counseling psychologists to diagnose psychological disor-

Minnesota Multiphasic Personality Inventory *The most widely researched and clinically used self-report personality test (called the MMPI; the revised version is called the MMPI-2)*

TABLE 13.1 SUBSCALES OF THE MMPI-2[A]

Name of Subscale	Typical Interpretations of High Scores
Clinical Scales	
1. Hypochondriasis	Numerous physical complaints
2. Depression	Seriously depressed and pessimistic
3. Hysteria	Suggestible, immature, self-centered, demanding
4. Psychopathic deviancy	Rebellious, nonconformist
5. Masculinity/femininity	Interests like those of other sex
6. Paranoia	Suspicious and resentful of others
7. Psychasthenia	Fearful, agitated, brooding
8. Schizophrenia	Withdrawn, reclusive, bizarre thinking
9. Mania	Distractible, impulsive, dramatic
10. Social introversion	Shy, introverted, self-effacing
Validity Scales	
1. L (lie)	Denial of common problems, "saintliness," presenting a false picture
2. F (confusion)	Validity of profile is doubtful
3. K (defensiveness)	Minimizes social and emotional complaints
4. ? (cannot say)	Number of items left unanswered

ders. Table 13.1 shows how MMPI test items are grouped into 10 *clinical scales*, each measuring a different disorder. Depressed people, for example, tend to score higher on one group of questions, whereas people with schizophrenia score higher on a different group. Each group of items is called a *scale*. There are also four *validity scales* designed to reflect the extent to which respondents distort their answers, do not understand the items, or are being uncooperative. Research has found that the validity scales effectively detect "pseudopatients" who were asked to fake psychological disturbances or try to appear more psychologically healthy (Bagby, Rogers, & Buis 1994).

Are these tests the same as career inventories? Personality tests, like the MMPI, are often confused with other self-report tests called *vocational interest tests* that help people make career decisions. For example, the *Strong Vocational Interest Blank* asks whether you would rather write, illustrate, print, or sell a book or whether you'd prefer the work of a salesperson or teacher. This self-report test compares the things you like to do to the responses of people in various occupational groups.

Given your vocational interest test profile, along with your scores on *aptitude tests* (which measure potential abilities) and *achievement tests* (which measure what you have already learned), a counselor can help you identify the types of jobs that best suit you. Most colleges have career counseling centers where you can take vocational interest tests to guide you in your career decisions.

Projective Techniques

Unlike objective tests, **projective tests** use ambiguous, unstructured stimuli, such as inkblots, which can be perceived in many ways. As the name implies, *projective* tests supposedly allow each person to *project* his or her own unconscious conflicts, psychological defenses, motives, and personality traits onto the test materials. Because respondents are unable (or unwilling) to express their true feelings if asked directly, the ambiguous stimuli reportedly provide an indirect, "psychological x-ray" of important unconscious processes. Two of the most widely used projective tests are the *Rorschach Inkblot Test* and the *Thematic Apperception Test* (TAT).

Projective Tests *Psychological tests using ambiguous stimuli, such as inkblots or drawings; the ambiguity of the stimuli reportedly allows the test taker to project his or her true, unconscious conflicts, motives, psychological defenses, and personality traits onto the test material*

The most widely used projective test is the **Rorschach Inkblot Test**, introduced in 1921 by Swiss psychiatrist Hermann Rorschach. It consists of ten inkblots originally developed by spilling ink on paper and folding the paper in half (Figure 13.1). You report what you see in each card and the clinician records your responses verbatim while also observing your gestures and reactions. The clinician later interprets your answers as indications of your unconscious feelings and conflicts. If you report seeing a bear in one of the inkblots, for example, the interpretation might be that you have a strong degree of emotional control (Meloy, Acklin, Gacono, Murray, & Peterson, 1997).

Created by personality researcher Henry Murray in 1938, the **Thematic Apperception Test (TAT)** is another of the most frequently used projective tests. It consists of a series of black-and-white ambiguous pictures, such as Figure 13.2. As mentioned in Chapter 12, the TAT is frequently used to measure achievement motivation, as well as for personality assessment. If you were taking this test, you would be asked to create a story about the picture, including what the characters are feeling and how the story turns out. As with the Rorschach, your responses reportedly reflect your unconscious needs and conflicts. For example, a person who sees a picture of a young girl looking at mannequins in a store window might create a story with angry references to the girl's parents. The clinician might infer that the test taker has hidden resentments toward his or her own parents (Davison & Neale, 2001).

Rorschach [ROAR-shock] Inkblot Test *A projective test that presents a set of 10 cards with symmetrical abstract patterns, known as inkblots, and respondents describe what they "see" in the image; their response is thought to be a projection of unconscious processes*

Thematic Apperception Test (TAT) *A projective test that shows a series of ambiguous black-and-white pictures and asks the test taker to create a story related to each; the responses presumably reflect a projection of unconscious processes*

Are Personality Measurements Accurate? Evaluating the Methods

What do you think of these interpretations of the projective tests? Do they accurately reflect true personality? Let's evaluate each of the various methods of personality assessment, beginning with interviews and observations:

- *Interviews and observations.* Both of these methods can provide valuable insights to personality, but they are time consuming and therefore expensive. Furthermore, just as football fans can dis-

Figure 13.2 *The Thematic Apperception Test (TAT).* Like the Rorschach, the TAT is a projective test designed to reveal unconscious parts of the personality. Participants are asked to talk about what led up to the pictured situation, what is happening now, and how the story will end. (Reproduced with permission.)

agree over the relative merits of the same quarterback, raters of personality tests frequently disagree in their evaluations of the same individual. Interviews and observations also involve unnatural settings, and as we saw in Chapter 1, the very presence of an observer can alter the behavior that is being studied.

- *Objective tests.* Tests like the MMPI-2 provide specific, objective information about a broad range of personality traits in a relatively short period of time; however, accuracy largely depends on cooperative and truthful respondents. Thus, objective, self-report inventories are subject to three major criticisms:

1. *Deliberate deception and social desirability bias.* Some items on self-report inventories are easy to "see through," so respondents may intentionally, or unintentionally, fake particular personality traits. In addition, some respondents want to look good and will answer questions in ways that they perceive as *socially desirable*.

2. *Diagnostic difficulties.* When self-report inventories are used for diagnosis, overlapping items sometimes make it difficult to pinpoint a diagnosis (Graham, 1991). In addition, clients with severe disorders sometimes score within the normal range, and normal clients may score within the elevated range (Cronbach, 1990).

---

critical thinking ▶▶▶▶▶▶▶▶▶▶▶▶▶▶▶▶▶ **Active Learning**

Why Are Pseudo Personality Tests So Popular?

Throughout this text, we have emphasized the value of critical thinking, which requires that we recognize *our personal biases and analyze data for value and content.* By carefully evaluating the evidence and credibility of the source, critical thinkers recognize appeals to emotions and faulty logic. When we look at the various problems with pseudo personality evaluations like the one in our introductory incident, we can identify at least three different logical fallacies: the Barnum effect, the fallacy of positive instances, and the self-serving bias.

The Barnum Effect
The first reason we often accept pseudo personality descriptions and horoscope predictions is that we think they are accurate. We tend to believe these tests have somehow tapped into our unique selves, when in fact they are ambiguous, broad statements that fit just about anyone. Being so readily disposed to accept such generalizations is known as the *Barnum effect* — after P. T. Barnum, the legendary

circus promoter who said, "Always have a little something for everyone" and "There's a sucker born every minute." Reread the bogus personality profile in the introductory incident. Can you see how "You have a strong need for other people to like you and admire you" fits almost everyone? Do you know anyone who doesn't "at times have serious doubts whether [they've] made the right decision or done the right thing"?

The Fallacy of Positive Instances
Now look again at the personality profile and count the number of times both sides of a personality trait are given ("You have a strong need for other people to like you" and "You pride yourself on being an independent thinker.") According to the *fallacy of positive instances,* we tend to notice and remember events that confirm our expectations and ignore those that are nonconfirming. If we see ourselves as independent thinkers, for example, we ignore the "needing to be liked by others" part. Similarly, horoscope readers easily find "Sagittarius characteristics" in a Sagittarius horoscope but fail to notice when Sagit-

tarius predictions miss or when the same traits appear for Scorpios or Leos.

The Self-Serving Bias
Now check the overall tone of the personality description. Note how the traits are generally positive and flattering — or at least neutral. According to the *self-serving bias,* we tend to prefer information that maintains a positive self-image (Brown & Rogers, 1991; Gifford & Hine, 1997). In fact, research shows that the more favorable a personality description, the more people believe it, and the more likely they are to believe it is unique to themselves (Guastello, Guastello, & Craft, 1989). (The self-serving bias might also explain why people prefer pseudo personality tests to bona fide tests — they're generally more flattering.)

Taken together, these three logical fallacies help explain the belief in "pop psych" personality tests and newspaper horoscopes. They offer "something for everyone" (the Barnum effect); we pay attention only to what confirms our expectations (the fallacy of positive instances); and we like flattering descriptions (the self-serving bias).

3. *Cultural bias and inappropriate use.* Some critics think that the standards for "normalcy" on objective, self-report tests fail to recognize the impact of culture. For example, respondents from Latino cultures, such as Mexican, Puerto Rican, and Argentinian, on average tend to score differently than respondents from majority cultures on the masculinity–femininity scale on the MMPI-2 (Lucio-Gomez, Ampudia-Rueda, Duran-Patino, Gallegos-Mejia, & Leon-Guzman, 1999) The fact that these groups score higher on traditional gender roles reflects their cultural training more than individual personality traits.

• *Projective tests.* Although projective tests are extremely time consuming to administer and interpret, their proponents suggest that because they have no right or wrong answers, respondents are less able to deliberately fake their responses. In addition, because these tests are unstructured, respondents may be more willing to talk about sensitive, anxiety-laden topics. Critics point out, however, that the reliability and validity of projective tests is among the lowest of all tests of personality (Lilienfeld, Wood, & Garb, 2000). If you recall from Chapter 8's discussion of intelligence tests, the two most important measures of a good test are *reliability* (Are the results consistent?) and *validity* (Does the test measure what it's designed to measure?). One problem with the Rorschach, in particular, is that interpreting clients' responses depends in large part on the subjective judgment of the examiner, and some examiners are simply more experienced or skilled than others. Also, there are problems with *interrater reliability.* Two examiners may interpret the same response in very different ways.

As you can see, each of these methods has its limits. However, psychologists typically combine results from various methods to create a full picture of individual personality. Having seen how personality is measured and evaluated, we now turn our attention to the major theories that describe, explain, and predict personality.

Check & Review

PERSONALITY ASSESSMENT

Personality is defined as an individual's relatively stable and enduring pattern of thoughts, emotions, and actions. Psychologists assess, describe, explain, and predict personality according to different theoretical orientations.

Psychologists use four basic methods to measure or assess personality: interviews, observations, objective tests, and projective techniques. Objective tests, such as the **Minnesota Multiphasic Personality Inventory** (MMPI-2), use paper-and-pencil questionnaires or inventories, which provide objective standardized information about a large number of personality traits. However, they are limited by respondents' deliberate deception and social desirability bias, diagnostic difficulties, and inappropriate use.

Projective tests, such as the **Rorschach Inkblot Test** or the **Thematic Apperception Test** (TAT), ask test takers to respond to ambiguous stimuli. Although these tests reportedly provide insight into unconscious elements of personality, they have low reliability and validity.

Questions

1. Match each personality test with its description:

   (a) a projective test using inkblots;

   (b) an objective, self-report, paper-and-pencil personality test;

   (c) a projective test using drawings of ambiguous human situations

   _____ i. MMPI-2

   _____ ii. Rorschach

   _____ iii. TAT

2. Two important criteria for evaluating the usefulness of tests used to assess personality are _____. (a) concurrence and prediction; (b) reliability and validity; (c) consistency and correlation; (d) diagnosis and prognosis

3. Describe the three logical fallacies that encourage acceptance of pseudo personality tests and horoscopes.

Answers to Questions can be found in Appendix B.

RESEARCH HIGHLIGHT

Do Animals Have Personality?

"It was exactly 33 years ago that I first met one of my oldest and dearest friends. To this day, the most outstanding aspect of her personality remains a quality I noticed the very first time I laid eyes on her: She is one of the most caring and compassionate people I know. She's also a chimpanzee" (Fouts, 2000, p. 68).

These are the words of a famous and highly respected comparative psychologist, Dr. Roger Fouts. What do you think? Do animals have personality? Roger Fouts proposes that "like us, chimps are highly intelligent, cooperative and sometimes violent primates who nurture family bonds, adopt orphans, mourn the death of mothers, practice self-medication, struggle for power and wage war. And that only makes sense, because the chimp brain and the human brain both evolved from the same brain — that of our common ape ancestor" (Fouts, 2000, p. 68). Other scientists, however, are generally reluctant to ascribe personality traits, emotions, and cognitions to animals, despite the often-cited statistic that humans have 98.4 percent of the same DNA as chimps.

Noting that previous studies on animal personality were scattered across multiple disciplines and various journals, researchers Samuel Gosling and Oliver John attempted to integrate this fragmented literature and summarize what is known about animal personality. They carefully reviewed 19 factor analytic personality studies of 12 different species: guppies, octopi, rats, dogs, cats, pigs, donkeys, hyenas, vervet monkeys, rhesus monkeys, gorillas, and chimpanzees. To integrate the diverse, multispecies information, Gosling and John used the human five-factor model (FFM) discussed earlier. Interestingly, three human FFM dimensions — extraversion, neuroticism, and agreeableness — showed the strongest cross-

Do animals have personality? Recent research has found that some species of animals demonstrate reliable personality traits similar to the Big 5 factors found in human personality.

species generality. How these personality traits are manifested, however, depends on the species. Although a human who scores low on extraversion "stays at home on Saturday night, or tries to blend into a corner at a large party, the [similarly low scoring] octopus stays in its protective den during feedings and attempts to hide itself by changing color or releasing ink into the water" (Gosling & John, 1999, p. 70).

One nonhuman dimension was also found important for describing animal personality — *dominance*. In adult humans, dominance is part of the extroversion dimension, but it has a wider range of personality implications in animals. Gosling and John explain that unlike most species, humans have multiple dominance hierarchies. The class bully may dominate on the schoolyard, the academically gifted may dominate the classroom, and the artist may win prizes for his or her creations.

Sex differences are another area where cross-species studies provide important information. For example, research on the human FFM consistently shows that women score higher on neuroticism than men (i.e., being more emotional and prone to worry) (Hrebickva, Cermak, & Osecka, 2000; McCrae et al., 1999). However, Gosling and John found a reversal of gen-

der differences among hyenas. It was the male hyenas that were most neurotic — being more high-strung, fearful, and nervous (Figure 13.4). They explain that among hyenas, the female is larger and more dominant than the male, and the hyena clan is matrilineal, with the mother recognized as the head of the family. Thus, it may be that sex differences in personality are related to the *ecological niches* (the place or function within the ecosystem) occupied by the two sexes in a species.

According to Gosling and John, comparative studies of animals not only provide insight into the existence of animal personality but also offer a fresh perspective on the interplay between social and biological forces in human personality. As Roger Fouts suggested, "In the past few decades, scientific evidence on chimps and other nonhuman primates has poured in to support one basic fact: We have much more in common with apes than most people care to believe" (Fouts, 2000, p. 68).

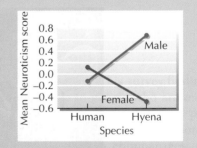

Figure 13.4 *Sex differences in standard (z) scores for neuroticism among humans and hyenas.* The ratings for hyenas are from Gosling (1998); the humans (*n* = 100) were described by peers on the same rating scales used for hyenas.

3. *Situational determinants.* Some personality theorists challenge the entire trait approach on the basis that it cannot be predicted. For example, in a classic study of children's honesty, May, Hartshorne, & Welty (1928) found children might lie at school but not at home, or might cheat on a test but not in an athletic event.

Extending the idea that behavior might be *situational*, in 1968, Walter Mischel published a landmark book in the field of personality, *Personality and Assessment*. Rather than seeing personality as the consistent, internal traits of an individual, Mischel thought that people respond to factors and conditions in the external environment. In other words, behavior — and thus personality — is determined almost entirely by the situations in which people find themselves. People are honest or dishonest, for example, not because of their internal personality but because of external rewards or threats of punishment.

Mischel's research findings were persuasive, and many joined his camp. Others, however, held out for the existence of stable traits that cause individuals to behave consistently in a wide range of settings. For years, a heated debate — known as "trait versus situationism" or the "person–situation controversy" — existed in psychology. After 2 decades of continuing debate and research, the consensus seems to be that situational pressures affect our relatively stable personality traits (Johnson, 1997; Mischel & Shoda, 1999). We will return to this *interactionist* position later in the chapter.

Walter Mischel emphasized the power of the situation, or environment, in determining personality. In other words, honesty depends on the threat of detection or potential reward; it is not an internal personality trait.

Check & Review

TRAIT THEORIES

Trait theorists believe personality consists of relatively stable and consistent characteristics. Early theorists like Gordon Allport, Raymond Cattell, and Hans Eysenck used **factor analysis** to identify the smallest possible number of **traits**. More recently, researchers identified a **five-factor model** (FFM), which can be used to describe most individuals. The Big Five traits are openness, conscientiousness, extraversion, agreeableness, and neuroticism.

General trait theories are subject to three major criticisms: *lack of explanation* (they fail to *explain* why people develop certain traits and why traits sometimes change), *stability versus change* (personality appears stable after age 30, but current theories do not identify which characteristics endure and which are transient), and *situational determinants* (trait theories underestimate the influence of environmental influences).

Questions

1. A relatively stable and consistent characteristic that can be used to describe someone is known as a(n) _____. (a) character; (b) trait; (c) temperament; (d) personality.

2. Match the following personality descriptions with their corresponding Big Five personality factor: (a) openness; (b) conscientiousness; (c) introversion; (d) agreeableness; (e) neuroticism

   _____ i. Tending toward insecurity, anxiety, guilt, worry, and moodiness

   _____ ii. Being imaginative, curious, open to new ideas, and interested in cultural pursuits

   _____ iii. Being responsible, self-disciplined, organized, and high achieving

   _____ iv. Tending to be withdrawn, quiet, passive, and reserved

   _____ v. Being good-natured, warm, gentle, cooperative, trusting, and helpful

3. Trait theories of personality have been criticized for all but one of the following reasons. (a) they fail to explain why people develop their traits; (b) they do not include a large number of central traits; (c) they fail to identify which traits last and which are transient; (d) they fail to consider situational determinants of personality.

Answers to Questions can be found in Appendix B.

PSYCHOANALYTIC/PSYCHODYNAMIC THEORIES

What is Freud's psychoanalytic theory, and how did his followers build on his theory?

In contrast to trait theories that *describe* personality as it exists, psychoanalytic (or *psychodynamic*) theories of personality attempt to *explain* individual differences by examining how unconscious mental forces interplay with thoughts, feelings, and behavior. The founding father of psychoanalytic theory is Sigmund Freud. We will examine Freud's theories in some detail and then briefly discuss three of his most influential followers — Alfred Adler, Carl Jung, and Karen Horney.

Freud's Psychoanalytic Theory: The Power of the Unconscious

Who is the most well known figure in all of psychology? Most people immediately name Sigmund Freud. Even before you studied psychology, you probably came across his name in other courses. Freud's theories have been applied in the fields of anthropology, sociology, religion, medicine, art, and literature. Working from about 1890 until he died in 1939, Freud developed a theory of personality that has been one of the most influential and, at the same time, most controversial, in all of science (Gay, 1999; Taylor, 1999).

In discussing Freud's theory, we will focus on four of his most basic and debatable concepts: levels of consciousness, personality structure, defense mechanisms, and psychosexual stages of development.

Levels of Consciousness

What would you think if you heard a flight attendant say, "It's been a real job serving you ... I mean joy!"? From a Freudian perspective, this little slip of the tongue (known as a *Freudian slip*) reflects the flight attendant's true, unconscious feelings. Freud believed the unconscious is hidden from our personal awareness but still has an enormous impact on our behavior — and reveals itself despite our intentions.

Freud and his famous couch. *Sigmund Freud (1856–1939) is one of the most influential personality theorists. He also developed a major form of therapy (known as psychoanalysis), and treated many patients in the office pictured here.*

"*Good morning, beheaded—uh, I mean beloved.*
Drawing by Dana Fradon © 1979 The New Yorker Magazine, Inc.

Is this an exmple of a Freudian slip?

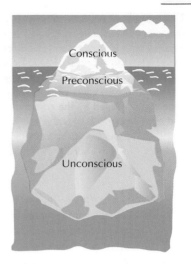

Figure 13.5 Freud's three levels of consciousness. The tip of the iceberg is comparable to the conscious mind, open to easy inspection. Directly below the conscious mind lies the preconscious; its contents can be viewed with a little extra effort. The large base of the iceberg is like the unconscious mind, completely hidden from personal inspection. For example, at this moment your conscious mind is focusing on this text, whereas your preconscious may include feelings of hunger and tiredness and thoughts of where you might go for lunch. Your unconscious might contain feelings of hostility toward your parents, repressed sexual desires, aggressive impulses, and irrational thoughts and feelings.

What exactly is the unconscious? Freud called the mind the *psyche* and believed the unconscious was one of three levels of awareness or consciousness (Figure 13.5). Using the analogy of an iceberg, the first level of awareness, the **conscious**, can be compared to the part of the iceberg above water. This part of the mind consists of all thoughts, feelings, and actions that we are actively aware of at any moment.

Immediately below the conscious realm, and the water's surface, is the somewhat larger **preconscious**. The preconscious includes mental activities not part of our current thoughts but able to be readily brought to mind. The third level, the **unconscious**, lies below the preconscious and forms the bulk of the psyche. According to Freud, the unconscious stores our primitive, instinctual motives, plus anxiety-laden memories and emotions that are prevented from entering the conscious mind.

Just as the enormous mass of iceberg below the surface destroyed the ocean liner *Titanic*, the unconscious may similarly damage our psychological lives. Freud believed most psychological disorders originate from repressed (hidden) memories and instincts (sexual and aggressive) stored in the unconscious.

To treat these disorders, Freud developed *psychoanalysis* — a type of therapy discussed in Chapter 15. As you can imagine, Freud's concepts of the conscious, preconscious, and unconscious mind, as well as his techniques for uncovering hidden, unconscious motives, are difficult to study scientifically. They have, therefore, been the subjects of great debate in psychology.

Personality Structure

In addition to proposing that the mind functions at three levels of awareness, Freud thought personality was composed of three mental structures: *id, ego,* and *superego.* He believed that each resides, fully or partially, in the unconscious (Figure 13.6) and that each accounts for a different aspect of personality. (Keep in mind that the id, ego, and superego are mental concepts — or hypothetical constructs. They are not physical structures you could see if you dissected a human brain.)

Conscious *In Freudian terms, thoughts or information that a person is currently aware of or is remembering*

Preconscious *Freud's term for thoughts or information that one can become aware of easily*

Unconscious *Freud's term for thoughts, motives, impulses, or desires that lie beyond a person's normal awareness but that can be made available through psychoanalysis*

1. Difficult to test. From a scientific point of view, a major problem with psychoanalytic theory is that most of its concepts cannot be empirically tested (Gay, 2000; Lilienfeld, 1999; Macmillan, 1997). How do you conduct an experiment on the id? Or on unconscious conflicts? Scientific standards require testable hypotheses and operational definitions.

2. Overemphasis on biology and unconscious forces. Like many of the neo-Freudians, modern psychologists believe that Freud overemphasized biological determinants and did not give sufficient attention to learning and culture in shaping behavior. In particular, the psychoanalytic belief that "anatomy is destiny" completely ignores the power of culture to create differences between men and women.

3. Inadequate evidence. Freud based his theories almost exclusively on the case histories of his patients. His data, therefore, were all subjective, leading critics today to wonder if Freud saw what he expected to see and ignored the rest. (Do you recognize this as the "fallacy of positive instances" described in this chapter's Critical Thinking/Active Learning exercise?)

Moreover, Freud's patients were almost exclusively upper-class Viennese women who sought his help because they had serious adjustment problems. Such a small and selective sample may mean that his theory describes only disturbed personality development in upper-class Viennese women at the turn of the century.

4. Sexism. Many psychologists reject Freud's theories as misogynistic, or derogatory toward women. First, there is the concept of penis envy, which, as you read earlier, Karen Horney, and others since, have refuted. Second, Freud rejected his patients' reports of childhood sexual abuse when colleagues ridiculed him for taking them seriously. His revised position was that the women were expressing unconscious wishes and fantasies. Given our knowledge now of the high rate of rape and incest throughout history, it's entirely possible that Freud was right in initially trusting his patients and wrong to retreat (Masson, 1984, 1992).

5. Lack of cross-cultural support. The Freudian concepts that ought to be most easily supported empirically — the biological determinants of personality — are generally not borne out by cross-cultural studies (Crews, 1997).

Today there are few Freudian purists left. Modern psychodynamic theorists and psychoanalysts employ only some of his theories and techniques. Instead, they use empirical methods and research findings to reformulate and refine traditional Freudian theories and methods of assessment (Westen, 1998).

There are many legitimate criticisms of Freud. But even so, many psychologists argue that, wrong as he was on many counts, Freud still ranks as one of the giants of psychology (Breger, 2000; Taylor, 1999). He should be credited and remembered for at least four reasons: (1) the emphasis on the unconscious and its influence on behavior; (2) the conflict among the id, ego, and superego and the resulting defense mechanisms; (3) the development of an influential form of therapy, *psychoanalysis*; and (4) the sheer magnitude of his theory.

In reference to this last point, it is hard to overstate Freud's impact on Western intellectual history. He attempted to explain dreams, religion, social groupings, family dynamics, neurosis, psychosis, humor, the arts, and literature. It's easy to criticize Freud if you don't remember that he began his work at the start of the twentieth century and lacked the benefit of modern research findings and technology. To criticize his theory without historical perspective is to criticize the Wright brothers for their crude plane design. We can only imagine how our current theories will look 100 years from now.

Today, Freud's legacy lives on in our thinking and artistic imagination. Often without realizing the source, we talk about unconscious motives, oral fixations, and repression. We accuse people of being anal or egomaniacs. Right or wrong, Freud has a lasting place among the pioneers in psychology.

Freud and his daughter. *Despite criticisms of sexism, psychoanalysis was one of the few areas where women gained prominent positions in the early 20th century. Here Freud is walking with his daughter, Anna Freud (1895–1982), who also became an influential psychoanalyst.*

Check & Review

PSYCHOANALYTIC/PSYCHODYNAMIC THEORIES

Sigmund Freud founded the psychoanalytic approach to personality, which emphasizes the power of the unconscious. The mind (or psyche) reportedly functions on three levels (**conscious**, **preconscious**, and **unconscious**), and the personality has three distinct structures (**id**, **ego**, and **superego**). The ego struggles to meet the demands of the id and superego, and when these demands are in conflict, the ego may resort to defense mechanisms to relieve anxiety. According to Freud, all human beings pass through five **psychosexual stages**: oral, anal, phallic, latency, and genital. How specific conflicts at each of these stages are resolved is important to personality development.

Three influential followers of Freud who broke with him were Alfred Adler, Carl Jung, and Karen Horney. Known as neo-Freudians, they emphasized different issues. Adler emphasized the **inferiority complex** and the compensating *will-to-power*. Jung introduced the **collective unconscious** and **archetypes**. Horney stressed the importance of **basic anxiety** and refuted Freud's idea of *penis envy*, replacing it with *power envy*.

Critics of the psychoanalytic approach, especially Freud's theories, argue that it is difficult to test, overemphasizes biology and unconscious forces, has inadequate empirical support, is sexist, and lacks cross-cultural support. Despite these criticisms, Freud remains a notable pioneer in psychology.

Questions

1. Using the analogy of an iceberg, explain Freud's three levels of consciousness.

2. The _____ operates on the pleasure principle, seeking immediate gratification. The _____ operates on the reality principle, and the _____ contains the conscience and ego-ideal, which provide moral guidance for the ego. (a) psyche, ego, id; (b) id, ego, superego; (c) conscious, preconscious, unconscious; (d) oral stage; anal stage; phallic stage

3. Briefly describe Freud's five psychosexual stages.

4. Match the following concepts with the appropriate theorist, Adler, Jung, or Horney:

   a. inferiority complex: _____

   b. power envy: _____

   c. collective unconscious: _____

   d. basic anxiety: _____

Answers to Questions can be found in Appendix B.

HUMANISTIC THEORIES

Humanistic theories approach the study of personality from the "inside out," emphasizing internal experiences — feelings and thoughts — and the individual's own feelings of basic worth. From a humanistic perspective, people are naturally good (or, at worst, neutral), and they possess a positive drive toward self-fulfillment.

According to this view, each individual's personality is created out of his or her unique way of perceiving and interpreting the world. Behavior is controlled by the individual's perception of reality, not by traits, unconscious impulses, or rewards and punishments. To fully understand another human being you must know how he or she perceives the world. Humanistic psychology was developed largely through the writings of Carl Rogers and Abraham Maslow.

Carl Rogers: The Self-Concept Theory of Personality

To humanistic psychologist Carl Rogers (1902–1987), the most important component of personality is the *self*, the part of experience that a person comes to identify early in life as "I" or "me." Today, Rogerians (followers of Rogers) use the term **self-concept** to refer to all the information and beliefs you have as an individual regarding your own nature, unique qualities, and typical behaviors. Rogers was very concerned with the match between a person's self-concept and his or her actual experiences with life. He believed poor mental health and maladjustment developed from an incongruence or disparity between the self-concept and actual life experiences (Figure 13.8).

What do humanistic theorists believe about personality?

Self-Concept *In Carl Rogers's theory, all the information and beliefs individuals have about their own nature, qualities, and behavior*

Why we help others. *Humanistic approaches to personality emphasize the positive nature of humans and our innate potential for goodness.*

At the same time, humanistic theories have also been criticized. Three of the most important criticisms are:

1. *Naive assumptions.* Critics suggest the humanists are unrealistic, romantic, and even naive about human nature. Are all people as inherently good as they say? Our continuing history of murders, warfare, and other acts of aggression suggests otherwise.

2. *Poor testability and inadequate evidence.* Like many psychoanalytic terms and concepts, humanistic concepts such as unconditional positive regard and self-actualization are difficult to operationally define and scientifically test.

3. *Narrowness.* Like trait theories, humanistic theories have been criticized for merely *describing* personality — rather than *explaining* it. For example, where does the motivation for self-actualization come from? To say that it is an "inborn drive" doesn't satisfy those who favor experimental research and hard data as the way to learn about personality.

Check & Review

HUMANISTIC THEORIES

Humanistic theories emphasize internal experiences, thoughts, and feelings that create the individual's **self-concept**. Carl Rogers emphasized the concepts of *self-esteem* and **unconditional positive regard**. Abraham Maslow emphasized the potential for **self-actualization**. Critics of the humanistic approach argue that these theories are based on naive assumptions and are not scientifically testable or well supported by empirical evidence. In addi-

tion, their focus on description, rather than explanation, makes them narrow.

Questions

1. If you took the _____ approach to personality, you would emphasize internal experiences, like feelings and thoughts, and the basic worth of the individual. (a) humanistic; (b) psychodynamic; (c) personalistic; (d) motivational

2. Rogers thought that _____ is necessary for a child's uniqueness and posi-

tive self-concept to unfold naturally. (a) permissive parenting; (b) a challenging environment; (c) unconditional positive regard; (d) a friendly neighborhood

3. Abraham Maslow's belief that all people are motivated toward personal growth and development is known as _____.

4. What are three major criticisms of humanistic theories?

Answers to Questions can be found in Appendix B.

SOCIAL/COGNITIVE PERSPECTIVE

What is the social/cognitive perspective on personality?

According to the social/cognitive perspective, each of us has a unique personality because of our individual history of interactions with the environment, and because we *think* about the world and interpret what happens to us (Cervone & Shoda, 1999). Furthermore, our interpretations are distinctive because of our previous experiences. Two of the most influential social-cognitive theorists are Albert Bandura and Julian Rotter.

Bandura's and Rotter's Approaches: Social Learning plus Cognitive Processes

Although Albert Bandura is perhaps best known for his work on observational learning or social learning (Chapter 6), he has also played a major role in reintroducing thought processes into personality theory. Cognition is central to his concept of **self-efficacy**, which refers to a person's learned expectation of success (Bandura, 1997, 1999, 2000).

How do you generally perceive your ability to select, influence, and control the circumstances of your life? According to Bandura, if you have a strong sense of self-efficacy, you believe you can generally succeed, regardless of past failures and cur-

Self-Efficacy *According to Albert Bandura, a person's learned beliefs that he or she is capable of producing desired results, such as mastering new skills and achieving personal goals*

rent obstacles. This belief will in turn affect the challenges you accept and the effort you expend in reaching goals.

Doesn't such a belief also affect how others respond to you and thereby affect your chances for success? Precisely! This type of mutual interaction and influence is a core part of another major concept of Bandura's — **reciprocal determinism**. According to Bandura, our cognitions (or thoughts), behaviors, and the environment are interdependent and interactive (Figure 13.9). Thus, a cognition ("I can succeed") will affect behaviors ("I will ask for a promotion"), which in turn will affect the environment ("I can become an executive"), which then affects cognitions ("I am a success"), and so on.

Reciprocal Determinism *Albert Bandura's belief that an individual's cognitions and behaviors and the learning environment interact to produce personality*

Rotter's Locus of Control

Julian Rotter's theory is similar to Bandura's in suggesting that learning creates *cognitive expectancies* that guide behavior and influence the environment (Rotter, 1954, 1990). According to Rotter, your behavior or personality is determined by (1) what you *expect* to happen following a specific action and (2) the *reinforcement value* attached to specific outcomes — that is, the degree to which you prefer one reinforcer to another.

To understand your personality and behavior, for instance, Rotter would want to know your expectancies and what you see as the source of life's rewards and punishments. To secure this information, Rotter would use personality tests that measure your internal versus external *locus of control* (Chapter 3). Rotter's tests ask people to respond "true" or "false" to a series of statements, such as "People get ahead in this world primarily by luck and connections rather than by hard work and perseverance," or "When someone doesn't like you, there is little you can do about it."

As you may suspect, *externals* think environment and external forces have primary control over their lives, whereas *internals* think they can control events in their lives through their own efforts. Numerous studies have found that having an internal locus of control is positively associated with higher psychological functioning and better mental health (Frazier & Waid, 1999; Hans, 2000; Wen, Wang, Zhao, & Sun, 2000).

Evaluating Social/Cognitive Theory: The Pluses and Minuses

The social/cognitive perspective holds several attractions. First, it emphasizes how the environment affects, and is affected by, individuals. Secondly, it meets most standards for scientific research. It offers testable, objective hypotheses and operationally defined terms and relies on empirical data for its basic principles (Lin, 1998; Stajkovic & Luthans, 1998). Critics, however, believe social/cognitive theory is too narrow. It

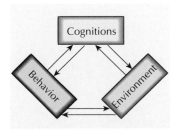

Figure 13.9 *Albert Bandura's theory of reciprocal determinism.* According to Bandura, thoughts (or cognitions), behavior, and the environment all interact to produce personality.

Figure 13.10 *Multiple influences on personality.* Researchers have concluded that personality can be broken down into four major factors: *genetics, inherited traits* (40 to 50 percent); *nonshared environmental factors,* or how each individual's genetic factors react and adjust to his or her particular environment (27 percent); *shared environmental factors,* involving parental patterns and shared family experiences (7 percent); and *error,* unidentified factors or problems with testing (16 to 26 percent) (Bouchard, 1997; Plomin, 1997; Talbot, Duberstein, King, Cox, & Giles, 2000; Wright, 1998).

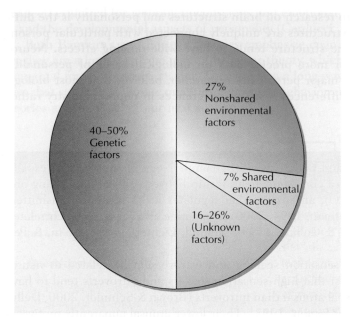

Interactionism: Pulling the Perspectives Together

When it comes to personality, no one theory is more correct than another. Each provides a different perspective and offers different insights into how a person develops the distinctive set of characteristics we call "personality." In fact, instead of adhering to any one theory, many psychologists believe in *interactionism,* the idea that several factors overlap in their contributions to personality (Figure 13.10). Even some psychologists who have done major research in one area of personality theory lean toward interactionism (Cervone & Shoda, 1999; Mischel & Shoda, 1999).

Hans Eysenck (1990), a leading trait theorist and interactionist, believes certain traits (like introversion and extraversion) may reflect inherited patterns of cortical arousal, as well as social learning, cognitive processes, and the environment. Can you see how someone with an introverted personality, and therefore a higher level of cortical arousal, might try to avoid excessive stimulation by seeking friends and jobs with low stimulation levels?

Eysenck's work exemplifies how trait, biological, and social/cognitive theories can be combined to provide better insight into personality. This trend toward integration and interactionism is reflected in a growing number of books and articles, and in decreased polarization on certain issues, such as the "either–or" debate between trait theorists and situational determinists discussed earlier in the chapter.

GENDER & CULTURAL DIVERSITY

Cultural Concepts of Self

Up to this point, we have examined only Western theories of personality. The concept of self is central to each of these theories. Personality is seen as a composition of individual parts (traits and motives), and the self is a bounded individual — separate and autonomous from others (Gardner, Gabriel, & Lee, 1999; Matsumoto, 2000). Can you see how the *conscious, preconscious, unconscious, id, ego, superego, inferiority complex, basic anxiety, self-concept, self-esteem,* and *self-actualization* all assume a unique self composed of discrete traits, motives, and abilities? Our Western perspective reflects an *individualistic* perspective.

In *collectivist* cultures, however, the self is inherently linked to others. For example, in Asia, people are described not by a set of enduring traits but in terms of social relationships (Markus & Kitayama, 1998). The person is defined and understood primarily by looking at his or her place in the social unit. Relatedness, connectedness, and interdependence are valued, as opposed to separateness, independence, and individualism.

If you are North American or Western European, you may find the concept of a self defined in terms of others almost contradictory. A core selfhood seems intuitively obvious to you. Recognizing that this is not the case in collectivist cultures and among some minorities may prevent misunderstanding. For example, North Americans generally define *sincerity* as behaving in accordance with one's inner feelings, whereas Japanese see it as behavior that conforms to a person's role expectations (carrying out one's duties) (Yamada, 1997). Can you see how Japanese behavior might appear insincere to a North American and vice versa?

Understanding how the individualistic perspective differs from that in collectivist cultures may improve global relations. It also points out limits and biases in our current Western personality theories and the need for continued cross-cultural research.

Check & Review

BIOLOGICAL THEORIES

Biological theories emphasize brain structures, neurochemistry, and inherited genetic components of personality. Research on specific traits such as extroversion and sensation seeking support the biological approach. The interactionist approach suggests that the major theories overlap, and each contributes to our understanding of personality. Most theories of personality are biased toward Western, individualistic cultures and their perception of the "self." Recognizing and understanding this bias helps keep our study of personality in perspective.

Questions

1. _____ theories emphasize the importance of genetics in the development of personality. (a) Evolutionary; (b) Phenomenological; (c) Genological; (d) Biological

2. What concerns people about genetic explanations for personality?

3. The _____ approach represents a blending of several theories of personality. (a) unification; (b) association; (c) interactionist; (d) phenomenological

4. Explain how the Western concept of the self reflects an individualistic culture versus a collectivist culture.

Answers to Questions can be found in Appendix B.

KEY TERMS

personality (p. 448)
Personality Assessment
Minnesota Multiphasic Personality Inventory (MMPI-2) (p. 449)
projective tests (p. 450)
Rorschach [ROAR-shock] Inkblot Test (p. 451)
Thematic Apperception Test (TAT) (p. 451)
Trait Theories
factor analysis (p. 454)
Five-Factor Model (FFM) (p. 454)
trait (p. 454)

Psychoanalytic/Psychodynamic Theories
archetypes (p. 468)
basic anxiety (p. 469)
collective unconscious (p. 468)
conscious (p. 461)
ego (p. 462)
id (p. 462)
inferiority complex (p. 468)
Oedipus [ED-uh-puss] complex (p. 465)
pleasure principle (p. 462)
preconscious (p. 461)

psychosexual stages (p. 463)
reality principle (p. 462)
repression (p. 463)
superego (p. 462)
unconscious (p. 461)
Humanistic Theories
self-actualization (p. 473)
self-concept (p. 471)
unconditional positive regard (p. 472)
Social/Cognitive Perspective
reciprocal determinism (p. 475)
self-efficacy (p. 474)

Visual Summary for Chapter 13 ----

Personality Personality: Unique, relatively stable pattern of thoughts, emotions, and actions.

Personality Assessment Psychologists use four methods to measure personality:

Interviews: Can be either structured or unstructured.

Observations: Psychologist uses direct behavioral observation with set of evaluation guidelines.

Objective Tests (such as the **MMPI-2**) ask test-takers to self-report on paper-and-pencil questionnaires or inventories. These tests provide objective standardized information about a large number of personality traits, but they have their limits, including deliberate deception, social desirability bias, diagnostic difficulties and inappropriate use.

Projective Tests [such as the **Rorschach "inkblot"** or **Thematic Apperception Test (TAT)**] ask test-takers to respond to ambiguous stimuli. Though these tests are said to provide insight into unconsious elements of the personality, they are not very reliable or valid.

Reliability and **validity** are the major criteria for evaluating the accuracy of personality tests.

Major Personality Theories and Assessment Techniques

Theorists and Key Concepts	Determinants of Personality	Methods of Assessment
Trait *Early theorists* • Allport: Arranged **traits** in hierarchy. • Cattell (16PF) and Eysenck (Personality Questionnaire): Used **factor analysis** to reduce number of traits. *Modern theory* • **Five-factor model** (FFM): Openness, conscientiousness, extraversion, agreeableness, and neuroticism.	Heredity and environment combine to create personality traits.	Objective (self-report) inventories (e.g., MMPI), observation.

Major Personality Theories and Assessment Techniques (cont.)

Theorist and Key Concepts	Determinants of Personality	Methods of Assessment
Psychoanalytic/Psychodynamic *Freud* • Levels of Consciousness—**conscious, preconscious,** and **unconscious.** • Personality Structure—**id (pleasure principle), ego (reality principle), superego** (morality principle). • Defense Mechanisms—**repression** and others. • **Psychosexual Stages**—oral, anal, phallic (**Oedipus complex**), latency, and genital. *NeoFreudians* • Adler—individual psychology, **inferiority complex**, and will-to-power. • Jung—analytical psychology, **collective unconscious,** and **archetypes.** • Horney—power envy vs. penis envy and **basic anxiety.**	Unconscious conflicts between id, ego and superego lead to defense mechanisms.	Interviews and projective tests: Rorschach inkblot test, Thematic Apperception Test (TAT).
Humanistic *Phenomenological perspective* • Rogers—**self-concept**, self-esteem, and **unconditional positive regard.** • Maslow—**self-actualization.**	Individual's subjective experience of reality.	Interviews, objective (self-report) inventories.
Social/Cognitive • Bandura—**self-efficacy** and **reciprocal determinism.** • Rotter—cognitive expectancies and locus of control.	Interaction between cognition and environment.	Observation, objective (self-report) inventories.
Biological • Brain structures like the frontal lobes may play a role. • Neurochemistry (dopamine, MAO, and others) may play a role. • Genetic factors also contribute to personality.	Brain, neurochemistry, genetics.	Animal studies and biological techniques

Interactionism: Major theories overlap and each contributes to our understanding of personality. Cultural comparisons find most theories biased toward Western, individualistic cultures that emphasize the "self."

14 Psychological Disorders

ary's troubles first began in adolescence. She began to miss curfew, was frequently truant, and her grades declined sharply. During family counseling sessions, it was discovered that Mary also had been promiscuous and had prostituted herself several times to get drug money. She revealed a history of drug abuse, including "everything I can get my hands on." Mary also had ongoing problems with her peers. She quickly fell in love and overly idealized new friends. But when they quickly (and inevitably) disappointed her, she would angrily cast them aside. This pattern of poor grades, cutting classes, and unstable relationships continued throughout high school, two years of college, and a series of clerical jobs. Mary's problems, coupled with a preoccupation with inflicting pain on herself (by cutting and burning) and persistent thoughts of suicide, eventually led to her admittance to a psychiatric hospital at age 26.
Davison & Neale, 2001, p. 358

Jim is a third-year medical student. Over the last few weeks he has been noticing that older men appear to be frightened of him when he passes them on the street. Recently, he has become convinced that he is actually the director of the Central Intelligence Agency and that these men are secret agents of a hostile nation. Jim has found confirmatory evidence for his idea in the fact that a helicopter flies over his house every day at 8:00 A.M. and at 4:30 P.M. Surely, this surveillance is part of the plot to assassinate him.
Bernheim & Lewine, 1979, p. 4

Ken Bianchi, the "Hillside Strangler," terrorized the Los Angeles area for more than a year. Working with his cousin, Angelo Buono, Bianchi used phony police badges to lure victims into his car or home where they were later raped, systematically tortured, and then murdered. Bianchi and Buono killed 10 women aged 12 to 28. Bianchi killed two more after moving to Washington State. After one of the longest trials in Los Angeles history, Bianchi was sentenced to life in prison. Presiding Judge Ronald M. George stated: "If ever there was a case where the death penalty was appropriate, this is that case. Angelo Buono and Kenneth Bianchi ... abducted children and young women, torturing, raping and, finally, depriving their family and friends of them forever as they slowly squeezed out of their victims their last breath of air and their promise of a future life. And for what? The momentary, sadistic thrill of enjoying a brief perverted sexual satisfaction and the venting of their hatred of women."
Magid & McKelvey, 1987, pp. 15–18

Each of these individuals has a severe psychological problem, and each case raises interesting questions. What caused Mary's unstable relationships and suicidal thoughts, Jim's paranoia, and Ken's cold-blooded murders? Was there something in their early backgrounds to explain their later behaviors? Is there something medically wrong with them?

What about less severe forms of abnormal behavior? Is a person who dreams of airplane crashes and refuses to fly mentally ill? Does a compulsively neat student who types all his lecture notes and refuses to write in any textbook need a psychiatric examination? What is the difference between being eccentric and disordered?

In answer to these and other questions, this chapter begins with a look at ways psychological disorders are identified, explained, and classified. Then we explore five main categories of psychological disorders (anxiety, schizophrenia, mood disorders, dissociative disorders, and personality disorders). This chapter focuses on describing and explaining the causes of abnormal behavior; Chapter 15 explores their treatment.

Before we begin, we'd like to warn you about a common problem associated with studying psychological disorders. Reading about abnormal behavior and symptoms of mental disorders can sometimes result in a psychological version of *medical student's disease*, the tendency that medical students have to see in themselves the symptoms of whatever disease they are currently studying.

TRY THIS
Yourself

Not only do some students worry unnecessarily about their own mental health but many also have unwarranted fears about the general topic of abnormal behavior. To test your own misconceptions, answer *true* or *false* to the following statements:

_____1. People with psychological disorders act in bizarre ways and are very different from normal people.

_____2. Mental disorders are a sign of personal weakness.

_____3. Mentally ill people are often violent and dangerous.

_____4. A person who has been mentally ill can never be normal.

_____5. Most mentally ill individuals can work at only low-level jobs.

Each of these five statements is a myth. The facts are provided below and discussed further in this chapter.

1. **Fact:** This is true for only a small minority of individuals and during a relatively small portion of their lives. In fact, sometimes even mental health professionals find it difficult to distinguish normal from abnormal individuals without formal screening.

2. **Fact:** Psychological disorders are a function of many factors, such as exposure to stress, genetic disposition, family background, and so on. Mentally disturbed individuals can't be blamed for their problems any more than people who develop Alzheimer's or other physical illnesses.

3. **Fact:** Only a few disorders, such as some paranoid and antisocial personalities, are associated with violence. The stereotype that connects mental illness and violence persists because of prejudice and selective media attention.

4. **Fact:** The vast majority of people who are diagnosed as mentally ill eventually improve and lead normal productive lives. Moreover, mental disorders are generally only temporary. A person may have an episode that lasts for days, weeks, or months and then may go for years — even a lifetime — without further difficulty.

5. **Fact:** Mentally disturbed people are individuals. As such, their career potentials depend on their particular talents, abilities, experience, and motivation, as well as their current state of physical and mental health. Some of the most creative and distinguished people have suffered serious mental disorders, including author Virginia Woolf, composer Robert Schumann, and statesman Winston Churchill.

Sources: Dinan, 2000; Citrome & Volavka, 1999; Steadman et al., 1998; Tardiff, 1999.

While reading about anxiety disorders, for example, you may think about how you felt when you had to give a speech in class. Or you may recall "blanking out" when introduced to an attractive stranger and may wonder if you have a *social phobia*. You focus on these isolated events and forget the rest of the picture — those times when you didn't behave this way and the fact that most people have similar experiences. On the other hand, psychological disorders are widespread, and most of us will encounter one or more of these disorders in our lifetime — either personally or with our family or friends. If you have serious concerns about yourself or others, we encourage you to talk to your instructor or a counselor.

STUDYING PSYCHOLOGICAL DISORDERS

As the introductory cases show, mental disorders vary from person to person and in their severity. Also, like personality, consciousness, and intelligence, *abnormal behavior* is difficult to define. In this section, we will explore how psychologists attempt to identify, explain, and classify abnormal behavior.

Identifying Abnormal Behavior: Four Basic Standards

One widely accepted definition of **abnormal behavior** is patterns of emotion, thought, and action considered pathological (diseased or disordered) for one or more of the following reasons: statistical infrequency, disability or dysfunction, personal distress, or violation of norms (adapted from Davison & Neale, 2001). As we will see, each criterion has merit and captures some part of what might be the full definition. However, keep in mind that no *single* criterion is adequate for identifying abnormal behavior.

1. **Statistical infrequency.** One way to judge whether a person's behavior is abnormal is to compare the *frequency* of his or her behavior to that of others. Believing that others are plotting against you is statistically abnormal and is usually diagnosed as a *delusion of persecution*. However, as you read in Chapter 8, intelligence is believed to be distributed along a normal, bell-shaped curve, and individuals with an intelligence quotient (IQ) above 132 are statistically infrequent, or "abnormal." Yet having great intelligence — or great athletic ability or artistic skill — is *not* classified as abnormal by the public (or by psychologists). All in all, then, we cannot use statistical frequency as the sole criterion in determining what is normal versus abnormal (Figure 14.1).

2. **Disability or dysfunction.** An alternative to the statistical infrequency model is the disability or dysfunction model. According to this view, people are considered abnormal if their emotions, thoughts, or actions interfere with their ability to function in their own lives and within society. Disability or dysfunction is the primary criterion for identifying abnormal drug use. If the use of alcohol (or any other drug) interferes with a person's normal social or occupational functioning, the person may be diagnosed with a *substance-related disorder*.

3. **Personal distress.** Rather than rely on objective statistical measures or evidence of disability, for some disorders mental health professionals prefer to use an individual's own judgment of his or her level of functioning. For example, someone who drinks heavily every day may realize it is unhealthy and wish to stop. Thus, the personal distress model would help identify this behavior as abnormal. On the other hand, many people with true *alcohol-dependence disorders* deny they have a problem. Also, some serious psychological disorders cause little or no emotional discomfort. A serial killer, for instance, can torture someone without feeling remorse or guilt. The personal distress model by itself, then, is not sufficient for identifying all forms of abnormal behavior.

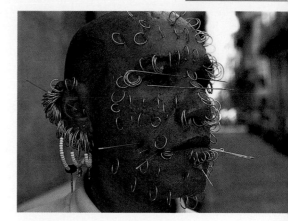

Would this behavior be considered abnormal? Although it is not statistically "normal" to be such a collector and lover of piercing, the term abnormal behavior is generally restricted to behavior that is considered pathological (diseased or disordered).

How do psychologists identify, explain, and classify abnormal behavior?

Abnormal Behavior *Patterns of emotion, thought, and action considered pathological (diseased or disordered) for one or more of these reasons: statistical infrequency, disability or dysfunction, personal distress, or violation of norms*

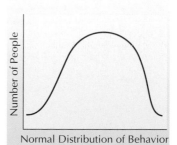

Figure 14.1 *Normal distribution.* When psychologists study behaviors such as intelligence, they often find that people are distributed along a "bell-shaped" curve. That is, a small number of people are found at the two ends of the curve, whereas most people cluster around the center.

4. *Violation of norms*. The fourth approach to identifying abnormal behavior is based on *social norms*, cultural rules that guide behavior in particular situations. Behavior that violates social norms and threatens others can be considered abnormal. Being in such a highly excited state that you forget to pay the rent but pass out $20 bills to strangers is a violation of norms. This type of behavior is common among individuals who are diagnosed with *bipolar disorder*.

A major problem with this criterion, however, is that cultural diversity can affect what people consider a *violation* of norms (Lopez & Guarnaccia, 2000). The impact of culture on behavior is an important issue we have addressed throughout this text. As for culture and abnormal behavior, consider this: During the early years of marriage, the Lepcha of the southeastern Himalayas normally have sex five to nine times a night. Dani newlyweds of New Guinea, on the other hand, wait an average of 2 years before they have sex (cited in Crooks & Baur, 1999; Laumann, Paik, & Rosen, 1999). A Dani couple in New Guinea who behaved like most Americans and a married couple in the United States who waited 2 years before they had sex might be judged abnormal by their respective cultures.

Thus, abnormal behavior is often *culturally relative* — understandable only in terms of the culture in which it occurs. In addition, there are also *culture-bound* disorders that are unique and found only in particular cultures, and *culture-general* symptoms that are found in all cultures (Green, 1999; Lopez & Guarnaccia, 2000). These terms are discussed in the next section.

GENDER & CULTURAL DIVERSITY

A Cultural Look at Disorders

Among the Chippewa, Cree, and Montagnais-Naskapi Indians in Canada, there is a disorder called *windigo* — or *wiitiko* — *psychosis*, which is characterized by delusions (irrational beliefs) and cannibalistic impulses. Believing the spirit of a *windigo*, or cannibal giant with heart and entrails of ice, has possessed them, victims become severely depressed (Barnouw, 1985). As the malady begins, the individual typically experiences loss of appetite, diarrhea, vomiting, and insomnia and may see the people around him or her turning into beavers or other edible animals.

In later stages, the victim becomes obsessed with cannibalistic thoughts. Family members often seek help from a shaman, a folk healer who uses special incantations and ceremonies to remove the spell of the *windigo* spirit. If they fail to seek help in time, the victim may attack and kill loved ones in order to devour their flesh (Berreman, 1971). As Table 14.1 shows, *windigo* psychosis is only one of many unique — or culture-bound — mental disorders that have been reported around the world.

Why do cultures develop such unique problems?

In the case of *windigo* psychosis, one explanation is that the disorder developed after fur trade competition depleted game that the Canadian tribes used for food, leading to widespread famine (Bishop, 1974). Facing starvation could have led to cannibalism and the subsequent "creation" of a *windigo* spirit. Belief in spirit possession is a common feature of many cultures, and in this case, people may have used it to explain a socially and psychologically abhorrent behavior, cannibalism (Faddiman, 1997).

Some researchers question the famine explanation for *windigo* psychosis and even the idea of culture-bound disorders (Dana, 1998; Hoek, Van Harten, Van

TABLE 14.1 EXAMPLES OF CULTURE-BOUND DISORDERS

Culture	Disorder	Symptoms
Puerto Rican and other Latin cultures	*Ataque de nervios* ("attack of nerves")	Trembling, heart palpitations, and seizurelike episodes often associated with the death of a loved one, accidents, or family conflict
Southeast Asian, Malaysian, Indonesian, Thai	Running amok	Wild, out-of-control, aggressive behaviors and attempts to injure or kill others
West Africa	Brain fog	"Brain tiredness," a mental and physical response to the challenges of schooling
Ethiopia	Possession by the "Zar"	Involuntary movements, mutism, and incomprehensible language
South Chinese and Vietnamese	*Koro*	Belief that the penis is retracting into the abdomen and that when it is fully retracted, death will result; attempts to prevent the supposed retraction may lead to severe physical damage
Westerners	Anorexia nervosa	Occurs primarily among young women; preoccupied with thinness, they exercise excessively and refuse to eat; death can result

Sources: Davison & Neale, 2001; *Diagnostic and Statistical Manual of Mental Disorders*, 4th ed., 2000; Guarnaccia & Rogler, 1999; Matsumoto, 2000.

Hoeken, & Susser, 1998). However, there is little doubt that some mental disorders are at least somewhat culture-bound (Guarnaccia & Rogler, 1999; Helms & Cook, 1999; Lopez & Guarnaccia, 2000).

Robert Nishimoto (1988) has found several culture-bound and culture-general symptoms that are useful in diagnosing disorders. Using the Langer (1962) index of psychiatric symptoms, Nishimoto gathered data from three diverse groups, Anglo-Americans in Nebraska, Vietnamese Chinese in Hong Kong, and Mexicans living in Texas and Mexico. (The Langer index is a screening instrument widely used to identify psychological disorders that disrupt everyday functioning but do not require institutionalization). When asked to think about their lives, respondents who needed professional help all named one or more of the same 12 symptoms (Table 14.2).

In addition to the culture-general symptoms (such as "nervousness" or "trouble sleeping"), Nishimoto also found culture-bound symptoms. For example, the Vietnamese Chinese reported "fullness in head," the Mexican respondents had "problems with my memory," and the Anglo-Americans reported "shortness of breath" and "headaches." Apparently people *learn* to express their problems in ways acceptable

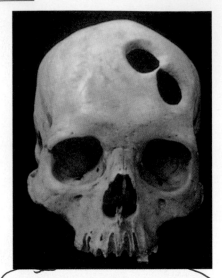

TABLE 14.2 TWELVE CULTURE-GENERAL SYMPTOMS OF MENTAL HEALTH DIFFICULTIES

Nervous	Trouble sleeping	Low spirits
Weak all over	Personal worries	Restless
Feel apart, alone	Can't get along	Hot all over
Worry all the time	Can't do anything worthwhile	Nothing turns out right

Source: Adapted from Brislin, 1993, 2000.

An early "treatment" for abnormal behavior? *During the Stone Age, many believed that demon possession was a primary cause of mental disorders, and one treatment was to bore holes in the skull to allow evil spirits to escape.*

Medical Model *Perspective that assumes diseases have physical causes that can be diagnosed, treated, and possibly cured; using this perspective, abnormal behaviors also have physical causes that can be diagnosed by their symptoms and treated and cured through therapy, including drugs and hospitalization*

to others in the same culture (Brislin, 1997, 2000; Widiger & Sankis, 2000). In other words, most Americans learn that headaches are a common response to stress, whereas Mexicans learn that others will understand their complaints about memory. As you may imagine, it is very important that mental health professionals who work with culturally diverse populations understand that culturally general and culturally bound symptoms exist and what these are for any population.

Culture obviously affects definitions of abnormality, but our concept of what is abnormal also changes over time. Our next section examines historical views of abnormality.

Explaining Abnormality: From Superstition to Science

Over the ages, popular views of the causes of abnormal behavior have changed. In prehistoric times, people believed both good and evil spirits made them see strange things and behave in unusual ways. During the Stone Age, for example, it was believed that demons could *possess* a person's body and soul and that the only treatment was *trephining*. In this operation, stone instruments were used to bore a hole in the skull to allow the evil spirit to escape.

The *demonological model* of abnormality persisted until the fourth century B.C., when the Greek physician Hippocrates suggested a physical basis for behavior disorders. According to this early **medical model**, problems such as epilepsy and depression were seen not as punishments from angry spirits but as results of disease of the brain or body.

The Middle Ages

During the Middle Ages (from about the fifth to the fifteenth century A.D.), supernatural explanations for abnormal behavior again dominated. This time, the Devil

Witchcraft or mental illness? *During the 15th century, some people who may have been suffering from mental disorders were accused of witchcraft and tortured or hung.*

was the evil spirit believed to possess people, and the afflicted person was treated with a religious practice known as *exorcism*. Exorcism involved prayer, fasting, noise-making, beating, and drinking terrible-tasting brews. The idea was to make the body so uncomfortable it would be uninhabitable by the Devil.

During the fifteenth century, people became even more obsessed with the Devil. Not only could you be possessed but you could also *choose* to consort with the Devil. These "willing people" (usually women) were called witches and were tortured, imprisoned for life, or executed. A church manual published in 1484 called *Malleus Maleficarum* ("The Witches' Hammer") described the characteristics of witches, which included sudden loss of reason, delusions, and hallucinations. Given these symptoms, some of the accused witches might have been mentally disturbed.

Asylums

As the Middle Ages ended, advances were made in the treatment of mental disorders. By the fifteenth and sixteenth centuries, specialized hospitals, or asylums, began to appear in Europe. Initially designed to provide quiet retreats from the world and to "protect" society (Alexander & Selesnick, 1966), the asylums unfortunately became overcrowded, inhumane "jails."

Improvement came in 1792 when Philippe Pinel, a French physician, was put in charge of a Parisian asylum where the inmates were shackled to the walls of unlighted and unheated cells. Pinel removed inmates from the dungeons and insisted they be treated humanely. Many inmates improved so dramatically they could be released. Pinel's belief that abnormal behavior was caused by "sick" minds soon became the accepted way of viewing people who had previously been feared and punished for their abnormality. Thus, his idea that disturbed individuals had an underlying *physical illness* resurrected the medical model first conceptualized by Hippocrates.

Modern Times

Pinel's medical model eventually gave rise to the modern specialty of **psychiatry**, in which disorders are diagnosed as physical illnesses and treatments are prescribed. Unfortunately, when we assume that a mental "disease" exists and label people "mentally ill," we sometimes increase rather than alleviate their problems. One of the most outspoken critics of the medical model is psychiatrist Thomas Szasz (1960, 1987, 1995). Szasz believes the medical model encourages people to believe they have no responsibility for their actions and that they can find solutions in drugs, hospitalization, or surgery. He contends that mental illness is a "myth" used to label individuals who are peculiar or offensive to others. The medical model does not acknowledge that labels are created in a particular social and cultural context. Furthermore, labels can become self-perpetuating; that is, the person begins behaving according to the diagnosed disorder.

A famous study done by David Rosenhan of Stanford University illustrates problems with diagnostic labels (Rosenhan, 1973). Rosenhan and several colleagues presented themselves to a local mental hospital and complained of hearing voices (a classic symptom of schizophrenia). Although they had no other complaints, they were admitted to the hospital with a diagnosis of schizophrenia. After admission, they stopped their claims of hearing voices and behaved in their normal fashion. The purpose? Rosenhan wanted to see how long it would take the doctors and hospital staff to recognize they were not mentally ill. Surprisingly, none of the pseudopatients was ever recognized as a phony. Once they were inside a mental ward with a label of "schizophrenia," staff members saw only what they expected to see. Interestingly, real patients were not so easily fooled. They were the first to realize that the psychologists were not really mentally ill.

An early "Catch 22." In the Middle Ages, "dunking tests" were used to determine whether people who behaved abnormally were possessed by demons. Individuals who did not drown while being dunked were believed to be guilty of possession and then punished (usually by hanging). Those who did drown were judged to be innocent.

Psychiatry *The specialized branch of medicine dealing with the diagnosis, treatment, and prevention of mental disorder*

TABLE 14.3 FIVE MAJOR PSYCHOLOGICAL PERSPECTIVES ON ABNORMAL BEHAVIOR

Perspective	General Explanation for Abnormal Behavior
Psychoanalytic	Unconscious conflicts
Humanistic	Blocked personal growth
Learning	Inappropriate conditioning or modeling
Cognitive	Faulty thinking
Biological	Problems with neurotransmitters, genes, or brain

Rosenhan's study offers important insights into problems with labeling mental illness (Hock, 1998). But as you remember from Chapter 1, the scientific method requires operational definitions, control groups, single- and double-blind procedures, and replication. Unfortunately, none of these standards were met in the Rosenhan study. Despite its limits, the study does increase our awareness of the dangers of diagnostic labels in mental illness.

Today, the medical model remains a founding principle of psychiatry, and diagnosis and treatment of mental disorders continue to be based on the concept of mental *illness*. In contrast, psychology offers a multifaceted approach to explaining abnormal behavior. Each of the five major perspectives in psychology — psychoanalytic, learning, humanistic, cognitive, and biological — offers alternative explanations. Table 14.3 summarizes these perspectives.

Classifying Abnormal Behaviors: The *Diagnostic and Statistical Manual IV-TR*

Now that we have *identified* and *explained* abnormal behavior from a historical standpoint, we also need a clear and reliable system for *classifying* the wide range of disorders. Just as physicians need agreed-on terms for identifying one set of signs and symptoms as cancer and another as heart disease, psychologists and psychiatrists need agreed-on terms for distinguishing Mary's disruptive behaviors and broken relationships, as described in the opening vignette, from Jim's paranoia. Without a uniform system for classifying and clearly describing psychological disorders, scientific research on them would be almost impossible and communication among mental health professionals would be seriously impaired. Fortunately, mental health specialists do share a uniform classification system, the *Diagnostic and Statistical Manual of Mental Disorders*, fourth edition, text revision (*DSM-IV-TR*) (American Psychiatric Association, 2000), which was developed in coordination with the tenth edition of the World Health Organization's *International Classification of Diseases (ICD-10)*.

Published by the American Psychiatric Association, the *DSM-IV-TR* is much more than a professional reference book for mental health professionals. It has an extraordinary impact on what we learn, diagnose, and treat in the mental health field. For example, the *DSM-IV-TR* serves as the information base for textbooks in psychiatry, psychology, and other mental health fields. In addition, health professionals are often required to use its diagnostic numbers (that match disorders) to get paid by insurance companies. Now, let's examine this *DSM-IV-TR* more closely.

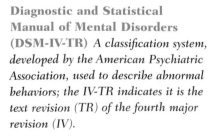

Diagnostic and Statistical Manual of Mental Disorders (DSM-IV-TR) *A classification system, developed by the American Psychiatric Association, used to describe abnormal behaviors; the IV-TR indicates it is the text revision (TR) of the fourth major revision (IV).*

Understanding the DSM

The *DSM-IV-TR* categorizes abnormal behaviors according to major similarities and differences in the way disturbed people behave. For example, the category *mood dis-*

orders includes problems of emotional disturbance (such as depression) and lists the common symptoms associated with subcategories like *major depressive disorders* and *bipolar disorders.*

The *DSM-IV-TR* also carefully describes each disorder, including typical patterns of behavior, thought, and emotion; typical age of onset; predisposing factors; prevalence of the disorder; and cultural issues that help therapists make a diagnosis. This manual does not attempt to explain the causes of disorders or their treatment. It is strictly *descriptive.*

The first edition of the *Diagnostic and Statistical Manual,* now known as *DSM-I,* was published in 1952, the second edition in 1968, and the third edition, *DSM-III,* in 1980. A revised version of *DSM-III* (*DSM-III-R*) was published in 1987. The fourth edition, *DSM-IV,* was published in 1994. A special revised fourth edition, *DSM-IV-TR,* was published in 2000.

Why do they need to keep changing the manual? The major reason for the *DSM* revisions is to incorporate the large volume of new scientific information since the previous edition. Generally, each revision has expanded the list of disorders and changed the descriptions and categories to reflect both the latest in scientific research and changes in the way abnormal behaviors are viewed within our social context (Coolidge & Segal, 1998; Smart & Smart, 1997). For example, the use of the terms **neurosis** and **psychosis** as categories of disorders was significantly revised in *DSM-IV.* In previous editions, *neurosis* was used to describe Freud's idea of the causes of anxiety disorders. He believed anxiety could be felt and expressed directly (through phobias, obsessions, compulsions) or that the unconscious could convert it into bodily complaints (somatoform disorders). But one way or another, all neurotic conditions were believed to reflect repressed anxiety.

Mental health professionals came to feel that Freud's emphasis on unconscious processes was too limiting and the category too large to be maximally useful. In the *DSM-IV,* conditions previously grouped under neurosis were redistributed as anxiety disorders, somatoform disorders, and dissociative disorders. Despite these changes, the term *neurosis* continues as a part of everyday language, and clinicians still use it occasionally when discussing disordered behavior presumed to be due to underlying anxiety.

As with neurosis, the conditions grouped under *psychosis* have been redistributed. Individuals with a psychosis suffer extreme mental disruption and loss of contact with reality. They often have trouble meeting ordinary demands of life, making hospitalization necessary. Schizophrenia, some mood disorders, and some disorders due to medical conditions are recognized as psychoses. Though these disorders are now listed as separate categories, the term *psychosis* is still listed in the *DSM-IV-TR* because it is useful in distinguishing between the most severe mental disorders, where the individual loses contact with reality, and the less disruptive disorders.

What about the term insanity? Where does it fit in? **Insanity** is a legal term indicating that a person cannot be held responsible for his or her actions because of mental illness (Slovenko, 1995). In a criminal case, when a defendant is found not guilty by reason of insanity, that person is considered not responsible for the criminal conduct because a judge or jury determined that mental illness made the defendant unable to appreciate the criminality of the act. In a civil case, a person judged insane is believed to be incapable of conducting his or her affairs in a competent manner. In both criminal and civil cases, the individual may under certain circumstances be involuntarily committed to treatment facilities. The standards and problems of forced treatment and commitment are discussed at the end of Chapter 15. Keep in mind, however, that despite the enormous amount of attention given to the

Neurosis *A large group of disorders characterized by unrealistic anxiety and other associated problems*

Psychosis *Serious mental disorders characterized by loss of contact with reality and extreme mental disruption; because daily functioning is often impaired, psychotic individuals are more likely to need hospitalization*

Insanity *A legal term for people with a mental disorder that implies a lack of responsibility for their behavior and an inability to manage their affairs*

TABLE 14.4 FIVE AXES OF *DSM-IV-TR*[A]

Axis	Description
Axis I: clinical disorders	Symptoms that cause distress or significantly impair social or occupational functioning (such as anxiety disorders, depression)
Axis II: personality disorders and mental retardation	Chronic and enduring problems that generally persist throughout life and impair interpersonal or occupational functioning
Axis III: general medical condition	Physical disorders that may be relevant to understanding or treating a psychological disorder
Axis IV: psychosocial and environmental problems	Problems (such as interpersonal stressors and negative life events) that may affect the diagnosis, treatment, and prognosis of psychological disorders
Axis V: global assessment of functioning	The individual's overall level of functioning in social, occupational, and leisure activities

[a] *Diagnostic Manual of Mental Disorders,* fourth edition, text revision.

Source: Adapted from *DSM-IV-TR,* American Psychiatric Association, Washington, D.C., 2000.

insanity plea, it is pleaded in less than 1 percent of all cases that reach trial and is rarely successful (Silver, 1995).

The DSM-IV-TR *and Modern Times*

As a result of continuing scientific research and clinical practice, the current *DSM-IV-TR* is organized according to five major dimensions, called *axes,* which serve as guidelines for making decisions about symptoms (Table 14.4). Disorders are *diagnosed* along Axis I and II. Axis I describes *state disorders* (the patient's current condition, or "state"), whereas Axis II describes *trait disorders* (enduring problems that seem to be an integral part of the self, rather than something a person acquires). Examples of Axis I disorders are anxiety, substance abuse, and depression. Axis II lists long-running personality disturbances (like antisocial personality disorder) and mental retardation.

The other three axes are used to record important supplemental information. Axis III lists medical conditions that may be important to the person's psychopathology (such as diabetes or hypothyroidism, which can affect mood). Axis IV is reserved for psychosocial and environmental stressors that could be contributing to emotional problems (such as job or housing troubles or the death of a family member). Axis V evaluates a person's overall level of functioning, on a scale from 1 (serious attempt at suicide or complete inability to take care of oneself) to 100 (happy, productive, with many interests).

The current *DSM-IV-TR* also contains descriptions of hundreds of disorders grouped into 17 major categories (Table 14.5). Owing to space limitations, in this chapter we focus on only 5 of the 17 categories. We discuss three of the most common categories — anxiety disorders, mood disorders, and schizophrenia. We also explore the less common, but fascinating, dissociative and personality disorders. Before going on, it is important to note that the *DSM-IV-TR* classifies disorders that people have, *not the people themselves.* To reflect this important distinction, this text (like the *DSM-IV-TR*) avoids the use of terms such as *schizophrenic.* Instead, we use the term *a person with schizophrenia.*

TABLE 14.5 MAIN CATEGORIES OF MENTAL DISORDERS AND THEIR DESCRIPTIONS IN *DSM-IV-TR*[A]

1. Disorders usually first diagnosed in infancy, childhood, or early adolescence: mental retardation, bedwetting, etc.
2. Delirium, dementia, amnestic and other cognitive disorders: problems caused by Alzheimer's, human immunodeficiency virus (acquired immunodeficiency syndrome), Parkinson's, etc.
3. Mental disorders due to a general medical condition not elsewhere classified: problems caused by physical deterioration of the brain due to disease, drugs, etc.

4. Substance-related disorders: problems caused by dependence on alcohol, cocaine, tobacco, and so forth
5. Schizophrenia and other psychotic disorders: a group of disorders characterized by major disturbances in perception, language and thought, emotion, and behavior[b]
6. Mood disorders: problems associated with severe disturbances of mood, such as depression, mania, or alternating episodes of both[b]
7. Anxiety disorders: problems associated with severe anxiety, such as phobias, obsessive-compulsive disorder, and post-traumatic stress disorder[b]

8. Somatoform disorders: problems related to unusual preoccupation with physical health or physical symptoms with no physical cause
9. Factitious disorders: disorders that the individual adopts to satisfy some economic or psychological need

10. Dissociative disorders: disorders in which the normal integration of consciousness, memory, or identity is suddenly and temporarily altered, such as amnesia and dissociative identity disorder[b]

11. Sexual and gender identity disorders: problems related to unsatisfactory sexual activity, finding unusual objects or situations arousing, gender identity problems, and so forth
12. Eating disorders: problems related to food, such as anorexia nervosa, bulimia nervosa, and so forth
13. Sleep disorders: serious disturbances of sleep, such as insomnia, sleep terrors, or hypersomnia
14. Impulse control disorders not elsewhere classified: problems related to kleptomania, pathological gambling, pyromania, and so forth
15. Adjustment disorders: problems related to specific stressors such as divorce, family discord, economic concerns, and so forth

16. Personality disorders: problems related to lifelong behavior patterns such as self-centeredness, overdependency, and antisocial behaviors[b]

17. Other conditions that may be a focus of clinical attention: problems related to physical or sexual abuse, relational problems, occupational problems, and so forth

[a] *Diagnostic Manual of Mental Disorders,* fourth edition, text revision.

[b] Disorders discussed in this chapter.

Source: American Psychiatric Association, 2000.

substance-related disorders

mood disorders

anxiety disorders

Evaluating the DSM-IV-TR

The *DSM-IV* has been praised for carefully and completely describing symptoms, standardizing diagnosis and treatment, facilitating communication among professionals and between professionals and patients, and serving as a valuable educational tool. Critics, on the other hand, suggest it relies too heavily on the medical model and unfairly labels people (Dana, 1998; Roelcke, 1997; Sarbin, 1997). The *DSM-IV* has also been criticized for its possible culture bias. Although it does provide a culture-specific section and a glossary of culture-bound syndromes, the classification of most disorders still reflects a Western European and American perspective (Dana, 1998; Matsumoto, 2000; Smart & Smart, 1997). (Although the 2000 version, *DSM-IV-TR*, is too new for full evaluation, the praise and criticisms of *DSM-IV* should also apply because its changes were confined primarily to updated research.)

Despite its faults, many consider this fourth revision of the *DSM* the most advanced, scientifically based classification system ever developed (Barlow & Durand, 2001; First, Pincus, & Frances, 1999; Nathan & Langenbucher, 1999). As Winston Churchill said about democracy, it is "the worst system devised by the wit of man, except for all the others."

Check & Review

STUDYING PSYCHOLOGICAL DISORDERS

Abnormal behavior refers to patterns of emotion, thought, and action considered pathological for one or more of these reasons: statistical infrequency, disability or dysfunction, personal distress, or violation of norms.

In ancient times, people commonly believed that demons were the cause of abnormal behavior. The **medical model**, which emphasizes diseases and illness, later replaced this demonological model. During the Middle Ages, demonology returned and exorcisms were used to treat abnormal behavior. Toward the close of the Middle Ages, the medical model returned in the form of hospitals known as asylums. Although the medical model still dominates modern times, critics suggest it overlooks the importance of psychological fac-

tors, such as unconscious conflicts, inappropriate learning, faulty cognitive processes, and negative self-concepts. The ***Diagnostic and Statistical Manual of Mental Disorders (DSM-IV-TR)*** categorizes disorders according to major similarities and differences in the way disturbed people behave. *DSM-IV-TR* classification provides detailed descriptions of symptoms, which in turn allow standardized diagnosis and treatment, and improved communication among professionals and between professionals and patients.

The *DSM* has been criticized for not paying sufficient attention to cultural factors, for continuing to support the medical model, and for labeling people. Misdiagnosis also occurs, and the label *mentally ill* can lead to social and economic discrimination.

Questions

1. What are the four major standards for identifying abnormal behavior?

2. In early treatment of abnormal behavior, _____ was used to allow evil spirits to escape, whereas _____ was designed to make the body so uncomfortable it would be uninhabitable by the devil. (a) purging, fasting; (b) trephining, exorcism; (c) demonology, hydrotherapy; (d) the medical model, the dunking test

3. Briefly define *neurosis*, *psychosis*, and *insanity*.

4. What are the chief advantages and disadvantages of the *DSM* system of classifying mental disorders?

Answers to Questions can be found in Appendix B.

ANXIETY DISORDERS

What are anxiety disorders and what causes them?

Maria, A 25-year-old legal secretary, was about to leave her office one evening when she was suddenly overwhelmed by intense feelings of anxiety. Believing that something dreadful was going to happen to her, she became flushed and found it difficult to breathe — almost as though she were choking. She stumbled outside for some fresh air and the feelings gradually subsided. As Maria later described her terror, "It could not be worse if I were hanging by my fingertips from the wing of a plane in flight. The feeling of impending doom was just as real and frightening."

Fishman & Sheehan, 1985; p. 26

Maria and other people with an **anxiety disorder** share one central defining characteristic — unreasonable, often paralyzing, anxiety or fear. They feel threatened, ineffective, unhappy, and insecure in a world that seems dangerous and hostile. Anxiety disorders are the most frequently occurring category of mental disorders in the general population, and they are found about twice as often in women as men (Margolis & Swartz, 2001; National Institute of Mental Health, 1999).

Anxiety Disorder *Type of abnormal behavior characterized by unrealistic, irrational fear*

Unreasonable Anxiety: Five Major Anxiety Disorders

Symptoms of anxiety, such as rapid breathing, dry mouth, and increased heart rate, plague all of us during final exams, first dates, and visits to the dentist. But some people experience unreasonable anxiety that is so intense and chronic it seriously disrupts their lives. We will consider five major types of anxiety disorders: *generalized anxiety disorder*, *panic disorder* (Maria's diagnosis), *phobia*, *obsessive-compulsive disorder*, and *post-traumatic stress disorder*. Although we discuss these disorders separately, it is important to remember that people with one anxiety disorder often have others (Barlow, Esler, & Vitali, 1998).

Generalized Anxiety Disorder

Generalized anxiety disorder is a common chronic problem that affects twice as many women as men and leads to considerable impairment (Brawman-Mintzer & Lydiard, 1996, 1997). As the name implies, **generalized anxiety disorder** is characterized by long-lasting anxiety that is not focused on any particular object or situation. In other words, it is *unspecific* or *free-floating*. People with this disorder feel afraid of *something* but are unable to articulate the specific fear. They fret constantly and have a hard time controlling their worries. Because of persistent muscle tension and autonomic fear reactions, they may develop headaches, heart palpitations, dizziness, and insomnia. These physical complaints, combined with the intense, long-term anxiety, make it difficult to cope with normal daily activities.

Generalized Anxiety Disorder *Type of anxiety disorder characterized by chronic, uncontrollable, and excessive worry; the anxiety is not focused on any particular object or situation*

Panic Disorder

Panic disorder is even more troubling than generalized anxiety disorder. In **panic disorder**, the person suffers sudden but brief *attacks* of intense apprehension that cause trembling and shaking, dizziness, and difficulty breathing. Maria's sense of being "suddenly overwhelmed by intense feelings of anxiety" and feeling like she was choking are characteristic of panic attacks. The American Psychiatric Association (2000) defines a *panic attack* as fear or discomfort that arises abruptly and peaks in 10 minutes or less. Although panic attacks seem to occur out of nowhere, they generally happen after frightening experiences, prolonged stress, and even exercise. Many people who have occasional panic attacks interpret them correctly—as a result of a passing crisis or stress. Unfortunately, others begin to worry excessively and some may even quit jobs or refuse to leave home to avoid future attacks. It is labeled *panic disorder* when several apparently spontaneous panic attacks lead to a persistent concern about future attacks. A common complication of panic disorder is *agoraphobia*—anxiety about being in a place or situation where escape is difficult or embarrassing (Craske, 2000; Gorman, 2000). Phobias are the topic of our next section.

Panic Disorder *Type of anxiety disorder characterized by sudden and inexplicable attacks of intense fear; symptoms include difficulty breathing, heart palpitations, dizziness, trembling, terror, and feelings of impending doom*

Phobia

Phobias involve a strong, irrational fear and avoidance of an object or situation. The person knows the fear is irrational, yet the anxiety remains. Phobic disorders differ from generalized anxiety disorders and panic disorders because there is a specific stimulus or situation that elicits the strong fear response. Imagine how it would feel to be so frightened by a spider that you would try to jump out of a speeding car to get away from it. This is how a person suffering from phobia might feel.

Phobia *Type of anxiety disorder characterized by intense, irrational fear and avoidance of a specific object or situation*

People with phobias have especially powerful imaginations, so they vividly anticipate terrifying consequences from encountering such feared objects as knives, bridges, blood, enclosed places, or certain animals. These individuals recognize their fears are excessive and unreasonable but are generally unable to control their anxiety.

In addition to *specific phobias*, such as fears of knives, rats, or spiders, there is another category of phobias known as *social phobias*. Individuals with this disorder experience intense fear of being negatively evaluated by others or of being publicly embarrassed because of impulsive acts. Almost everyone experiences "stage fright" when speaking or performing in front of a group. But people with social phobias become so anxious that performance is out of the question. In fact, their fear of public scrutiny and potential humiliation becomes so pervasive that normal life is impossible (den Boer, 2000; Margolis & Swartz, 2001).

A related Japanese social phobia is *taijin kyofusho* (TKS), which loosely translates as "fear of people." But it is not a fear that people will criticize you, as in the American disorder. The Japanese disorder is a morbid dread that you will do something to embarrass others. TKS does not exist in Western cultures (Kleinknecht, Dinnel, & Kleinknecht, 1997). In the United States, "we don't think of the fear of embarrassing other people as a psychological syndrome" (cited in Goleman, 1995, p. C-3). But it is so common in Japan that TKS treatment centers, like weight clinics in the United States, are on almost every corner. The difference between Western social phobias and TKS exemplifies again how individualist cultures (like ours) emphasize the individual, whereas collectivist cultures (like Japan) focus on others.

Obsessive-Compulsive Disorder

Do you remember the movie As Good As It Gets? The main character, portrayed by Jack Nicholson, was endlessly counting, checking locks, and repeatedly washing his hands in a seemingly senseless, ritualistic pattern. What's drives this behavior? The answer is **obsessive-compulsive disorder** (OCD), which involves persistent, unwanted thoughts (*obsessions*), irresistible urges to perform an act or repeated ritual (*compulsions*), or both. In adults, this disorder is equally common in men and women, however it is more prevalent among boys when the onset is in childhood (American Psychiatric Association, 2000).

Consider the case of billionaire Howard Hughes:

> Due to his unreasonable fear of germs, he made people who worked with him wear white gloves, sometimes several pairs, when handling documents he would later touch. When newspapers were brought to him, they had to be in stacks of three so he could slide the middle one out by grasping it with Kleenex. To escape contamination by dust, he ordered that masking tape be put around the doors and windows of his cars and houses.
>
> FOWLER (1986)

I sometimes find myself worrying about germs and what others might have touched. Would this be considered an obsessive-compulsive disorder? Many people have obsessive thoughts or find they occasionally check stove burners, count steps, or clean their homes and offices past the point of normal standards. People even casually refer to this as "being OC" or "anal." The difference between an OCD and milder forms of obsession and compulsion is that with OCD the repetitive thoughts and ritualistic actions become *uncontrollable* and seriously interfere with a person's life.

For example, a woman with OCD who worries obsessively about germs might compulsively wash her hands hundreds of times a day until they are raw and bleed-

Obsessive-Compulsive Disorder
Type of anxiety disorder characterized by intrusive thoughts (obsessions), urges to perform repetitive, ritualistic behaviors (compulsions), or both

As good as it gets. In this film, Jack Nicholson portrays a character struggling with obsessive-compulsive disorder.

ing. A man might each night check the lights, locks, oven, and furnace 10 times in a ritualistic pattern before he can go to sleep. Most sufferers of OCD do not enjoy these rituals and realize that their actions are senseless. But when they try to stop the behavior, they experience mounting anxiety that is relieved only by giving in to the urges. They simply cannot stop themselves.

Concerned family and friends generally understand that the person cannot stop their obsessions and compulsions, but they also may feel irritated, confused, and resentful. As with other psychological disorders, therapists may recommend family counseling as well as individual therapies (see Chapter 15).

Post-traumatic Stress Disorder

The essential feature of **post-traumatic stress disorder** (PTSD) is severe anxiety that develops after experiencing a traumatic event (such as rape, natural disaster, war), learning about a violent or unexpected death of a family member, or even being a witness or bystander to violence (American Psychiatric Association, 2000; Brewin, Andrews, Rose, & Kirk, 1999). Symptoms include feelings of terror and helplessness during the trauma and recurrent flashbacks, nightmares, impaired concentration, and/or emotional numbing afterward. Symptoms may continue for years after the event itself.

Although PTSD has received much attention, there is considerable controversy over its prevalence and diagnosis (Keane, Taylor, & Penk, 1997). Some experts believe the largest single group of PTSD sufferers is female sexual assault and abuse victims (New & Berliner, 2000; Seedat & Stein, 2000). Kilpatrick et al. (1985) surveyed more than 2,000 adult women who had experienced various traumas, such as rape, sexual molestation, robbery, and aggravated assault. The women were asked if they had thought about suicide after the trauma, attempted suicide, or had a nervous breakdown. (*Nervous breakdown* is a lay term for severe psychological upset, but it has no official clinical meaning.) The crime with the

Post-traumatic Stress Disorder (PTSD) *Type of anxiety disorder following exposure to a life-threatening or other extreme event that evoked great horror or helplessness; it is characterized by flashbacks, nightmares, and impaired functioning*

most significant emotional impact was rape. Forty-four percent of rape victims reported suicidal thoughts, and 19.2 percent had attempted suicide.

Causes of Anxiety Disorders: Multiple Roots

The causes of anxiety disorders is a matter of considerable debate, but recent research has focused primarily on the roles of learning, biology, and cognitive processes.

Learning

The learning perspective on anxiety disorders suggests that phobias and other reactions are the result of conditioning (both classical and operant conditioning) and social learning (both modeling and imitation) (Chorpita & Barlow, 1998; King, Clowes-Hollins, & Ollendick, 1997). (See Chapter 6 for a review of these terms.)

During classical conditioning, for example, a stimulus that is originally neutral (e.g., the office building in Maria's case) becomes paired with a frightening event (the sudden panic attack) so that it becomes a conditioned stimulus that elicits anxiety. After this kind of classical conditioning, the phobia is typically maintained through operant conditioning. Maria begins to avoid the anxiety-producing stimulus (her office) because avoiding the stimulus reduces the unpleasant feelings of anxiety (a process known as negative reinforcement) (Figure 14.2).

Social-learning theorists propose that some phobias are the result of modeling and imitation. Vulnerability for PTSD, for example, tends to increase when an immediate family member suffers from depression (American Psychiatric Association, 2000). Also, can you see how overprotective, fearful parents may make their children more prone to developing phobias and other anxiety disorders? Howard Hughes's mother, for instance, was extremely protective and worried constantly about his physical health.

Phobias may also develop vicariously (in an indirect, secondhand way). For example, one research team showed videotapes to four groups of rhesus monkeys (Cook & Mineka, 1989). The tapes were spliced together in a special way to show

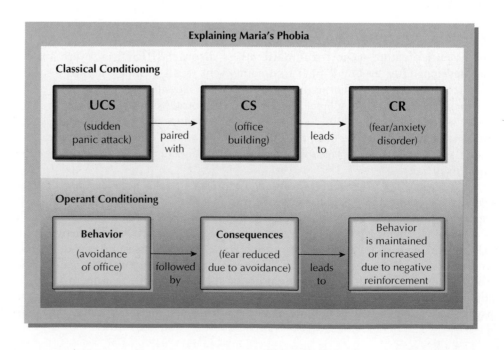

Figure 14.2 *Explaining Maria's phobia.* According to the learning perspective, Maria's phobia (described in the introduction) developed as a result of classical and operant conditioning. In classical conditioning terms, the initial panic attack was paired with the office building where she worked, and a conditioned response (CR) of fear and anxiety developed. Maria's phobia was maintained through operant conditioning — avoiding the office led to reduced fear, which in turn reinforced her phobia. CS-conditioned stimulus; UCS-unconditioned stimulus.

another monkey apparently experiencing extreme fear of a toy snake, a toy rabbit, a toy crocodile, and flowers. The "viewing" monkeys were later afraid of the toy snake and crocodile but not of the toy rabbit or flowers, which suggests that phobias have both a learned and biological component.

Biology

The fact that the rhesus monkeys selectively learned their phobias may mean that we have an evolutionary predisposition to fear what was dangerous to our ancestors, such as snakes and crocodiles (Cartwright, 2000). Recent studies show that anxiety disorders may also have a genetic predisposition or may result from disrupted biochemistry or unusual brain activity (American Psychiatric Association, 2000; Bryant & Harvey, 1998; Fones, Manfro, & Pollack, 1998). For example, twin and family studies shows that some individuals with panic disorder seem to be genetically predisposed toward an overreaction of the autonomic nervous system (Kendler, Karkowski, & Prescott, 1999; Schmidt, Lerew, & Jackson, 1999). These people apparently respond more quickly and intensely to stressful stimuli than others. Stress and arousal also seems to play a role in panic attacks. For example, drugs such as caffeine or nicotine or even hyperventilation (breathing deeper and faster than normal) can trigger an attack, which also suggests a biochemical disturbance (Breslau & Klein, 1999; Yudolfsky & Silver, 1987).

Cognitive Processes

Cognitive approaches to anxiety disorders focus on the distored thinking that causes people to magnify ordinary threats and failures. Most people are anxious in a public speaking situation, but those who are socially phobic are excessively concerned about others' evaluation, hypersensitive to any criticism, and obsessively worried about potential mistakes. This intense self-preoccupation not only intensifies the social anxiety but also leads socially phobic people to think they have failed — even when they have been successful. As you will see in Chapter 16, changing the thinking patterns of anxious people can greatly lessen their fears (Margolis & Swartz, 2001).

Vicarious phobias. Monkeys who watch artificially created videotapes of other monkeys being afraid of either a toy snake, toy rabbit, toy crocodile, or flowers will develop their own set of phobias. The fact that the viewing monkeys only develop fears of snakes and crocodiles demonstrates that phobias are both learned and biological.

Check & Review

ANXIETY DISORDERS

People with **anxiety disorders** have persistent feelings of threat in facing everyday problems. **Phobias** are exaggerated fears of specific objects or situations, such as agoraphobia, a fear of being in open spaces. In **generalized anxiety disorders**, there is a persistent free-floating anxiety. In **panic disorder**, anxiety is concentrated into brief or lengthy episodes of panic attacks. In **obsessive-compulsive disorder**, persistent anxiety-arousing thoughts (obsessions) are relieved by ritualistic actions (compulsions) such as hand washing. In **post-traumatic stress disorder** (PTSD), a person who has experienced an overwhelming trauma, such as rape, has recurrent maladaptive emotional reactions, such as exaggerated startle responses, sleep disturbances, and flashbacks.

Three common explanations for anxiety disorders are learning, biology, and cognitive processes. Learning theorists suggest anxiety disorders result from classical and operant conditioning, as well as modeling and imitation, whereas the biological perspective emphasizes genetic predisposition, brain abnormalities, and biochemistry. The cognitive approach proposes that distorted thinking causes an amplification of ordinary threats.

Questions

1. Match the descriptions below with the following specific forms of anxiety disorder: (a) generalized anxiety disorder; (b) panic disorder; (c) phobia; (d) obsessive-compulsive disorder (OCD); (e) post-traumatic stress disorder (PTSD)

_____ i. Develops from an overwhelming, traumatic event

_____ ii. Characterized by severe attacks of extreme anxiety

_____ iii. Long-term anxiety that is not focused on any particular object or situation

_____ iv. Characterized by irrational fear of an object or situation

_____ v. Characterized by intrusive thoughts and urges to perform repetitive, ritualistic behaviors

2. How do learning theorists and social-learning theorists explain anxiety disorders?

3. Researchers believe that anxiety disorders are probably due to some combination of _____.

Answers to Review Questions can be found in Appendix B.

MOOD DISORDERS

When do disturbances in mood become abnormal?

Ann had been divorced for eight months when she called a psychologist for an emergency appointment. Although her husband had verbally and physically abused her for years, she had had mixed feelings about staying in the marriage. She had anticipated feeling good after the divorce, but she became increasingly depressed. She had trouble sleeping, had little appetite, felt very fatigued, and showed no interest in her usual activities. She stayed home from work for two days because she "just didn't feel like going in." Late one afternoon she went straight to bed, leaving her two small children to fend for themselves. Then, the night before calling for an emergency therapy appointment, she took five sleeping tablets and a couple of stiff drinks. As she said, "I don't think I wanted to kill myself; I just wanted to forget everything for a while."

Meyer & Salmon, 1988; p. 312

Ann's case is a good example of a *mood disorder* (also known as an *affective disorder*). This category encompasses not only excessive sadness like Ann's but also unreasonable elation and hyperactivity.

Understanding Mood Disorders: Major Depressive Disorder and Bipolar Disorder

As the name implies, mood disorders are characterized by extreme disturbances in emotional states. There are two main types of mood disorders — *major depressive disorder* and *bipolar disorder*.

Major Depressive Disorder

Depression has been recorded as far back as ancient Egypt, when the condition was called melancholia and was treated by priests. Most everyone feels "blue" sometimes, especially following the loss of a job, end of a relationship, or death of a loved one. People suffering from **major depressive disorder**, however, may experience a lasting and continuously depressed mood without a clear trigger or precipitating event. In addition, their sadness is far more intense, interfering with their basic ability to function, feel pleasure, or maintain interest in life (Margolis & Swartz, 2001).

Clinically depressed people are so deeply sad and discouraged that they often have trouble sleeping, are likely to lose (or gain) weight, and may feel so fatigued that they cannot go to work or school or even comb their hair and brush their teeth. They may sleep both day and night, have problems concentrating, and feel so profoundly sad and guilty that they consider suicide. These feelings are without apparent cause and may be so severe that the individual loses contact with reality. As in the case of Ann, depressed individuals have a hard time thinking clearly or recog-

Major Depressive Disorder *A diagnostic term, from the Diagnostic and Statistical Manual of Mental Disorders, fourth edition, text revision, for individuals experiencing a long-lasting depressed mood that interferes with the ability to function, feel pleasure, or maintain interest in life; the feelings are without apparent cause and excessive to the given situation*

nizing their own problems, but family or friends who recognize the symptoms can encourage them to seek professional help.

Bipolar Disorder

When depression ends, most people return to a "normal" emotional level. Some people, however, rebound to the opposite state, known as *mania*. In **bipolar disorder**, the person experiences periods of depression, *mania* (an excessive and unreasonable state of over-excitement and impulsive behavior), and normal moods (Figure 14.3).

During a manic episode, the person is overly excited, extremely active, and distractible. The person exhibits an unrealistically high self-esteem and an inflated sense of importance or even delusions of grandeur. He or she often makes elaborate plans for becoming rich and famous. The individual is hyperactive and may not sleep for days at a time yet does not become fatigued. Thinking is speeded up and can change abruptly to new topics, showing "rapid flight of ideas." Speech is also rapid ("pressured speech"), and it is difficult to get a word in edgewise. Poor judgment is common: A person may give away valuable possessions or go on wild spending sprees.

Manic episodes may last a few days to a few months and generally end abruptly. The person's previous manic mood, rapid thinking and speaking style, and hyperactivity are reversed, and the following depressive episode generally lasts three times as long as the manic episode. The lifetime risk for bipolar disorder is low — somewhere between 0.5 and 1.6 percent — but it can be one of the most debilitating and lethal disorders, with a suicide rate between 10 and 20 percent (Goodwin & Ghaemi, 1998; MacKinnon, Jamison, & DePaulo, 1997).

Causes of Mood Disorders: Biological versus Psychosocial Factors

Numerous studies and theories attempt to explain major depressive disorder and bipolar disorder. Most can be categorized as either biological or psychosocial.

Biological Factors

Biological factors play a significant role in both major depression and bipolar disorder. Recent research shows the left frontal lobe, which is active during positive emotions, is inactive during depressive episodes (Davidson, 1999). Other research has identified a small area in the prefrontal cortex that may trigger both the sadness of depression and the mania of bipolar disorders (Liotti & Mayberg, 2001; Steffens & Krishnan, 1998).

Several lines of research also suggest that depression and mania may be caused by imbalances of the neurotransmitters norepinephrine and serotonin (Bellivier et al., 1998; Mann et al., 2000). This makes sense because these same neurotransmitters are involved in the capacity to be aroused or energized and in the control of other functions affected by depression such as sleep cycles and hunger. Moreover, drugs that alter the activity of these neurotransmitters also decrease the symptoms of depression (and hence are called *antidepressants*). The drug *lithium* reduces or prevents manic episodes by preventing norepinephrine and serotonin sensitive neurons from being overstimulated (Chuang, 1998).

There also is evidence that major depressive disorders, as well as bipolar disorders, may be inherited (Dubovsky & Buzan, 1999; Meltzer, 2000). For example, when one identical twin has a mood disorder, there is about a 50 percent chance that the other twin will also develop the illness (Margolis & Swartz, 2001). It is important to remember, however, that relatives generally have similar environments, as well as similar genes.

Bipolar Disorder *A diagnostic term in the DSM-IV-TR, for individuals who experience episodes of mania or of both mania and depression; excessive and unreasonable elation and hyperactivity characterize manic episodes*

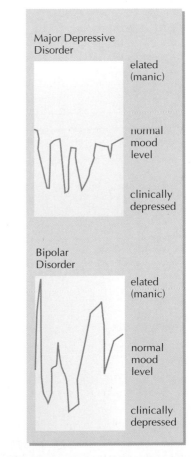

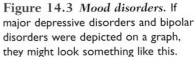

Figure 14.3 *Mood disorders.* If major depressive disorders and bipolar disorders were depicted on a graph, they might look something like this.

Psychosocial Theories

Psychosocial theories of depression focus on disturbances in the person's interpersonal relationships, thought processes, self-concept, and learning history (Agid et al., 1999; Rice & Mirzadeh, 2000). The psychoanalytic explanation sees depression as anger turned inward against oneself when an important relationship or attachment is lost. Anger is assumed to come from feelings of rejection or withdrawal of affection, especially when a loved one dies. The humanistic school says depression results when a person's self-concept is overly demanding or when positive growth is blocked.

The **learned helplessness** theory of depression, developed by Martin Seligman (1975, 1994), is an outgrowth of research on avoidance learning in animals (Chapter 6). Seligman has demonstrated that when animals or humans are subjected to pain that they cannot escape; they develop a sense of helplessness or resignation and thereafter do not attempt to escape painful experiences. In other words, the perception that one is unable to change things for the better leads to depression. Seligman also suggests that our general societal emphasis on individualism and diminished involvement with others makes us particularly vulnerable to depression.

The learned helplessness theory may also involve a cognitive element, known as *attribution*, or the explanations people assign to their own and other's behavior. Once someone perceives that his or her behaviors are unrelated to outcomes (learned helplessness), depression is likely to occur. This is particularly true if the person attributes failure to causes that are *internal* ("my own weakness"), *stable* ("this weakness is long-standing and unchanging"), and *global* ("this weakness is a problem in lots of settings") (Barlow, 1999; Gotlieb & Abramson, 1999).

Learned Helplessness *In Martin Seligman's theory, a state of helplessness or resignation in which people or animals learn that escape from something painful is impossible and depression results*

GENDER & CULTURAL DIVERSITY

Gender, Culture, and Depression

Research shows certain symptoms of depression seem to exist across cultures: (1) frequent and intense sad affect, (2) decreased enjoyment, (3) anxiety, (4) difficulty in concentrating, and (5) lack of energy (Green, 1999; World Health Organization, 2000). On the other hand, there is evidence of some culture-specific symptoms. For example, feelings of guilt are found more often in North America and Europe. In China, *somatization* (converting depression into bodily complaints) is more frequent than in other parts of the world (Helms & Cook, 1999).

Not only does culture have an impact on depression but so does gender. It is widely accepted that women are more likely than men to suffer depressive symptoms. In North America, the rate of clinical (or severe) depression for women is two to three times the rate for men, and this ratio holds true in several other countries as well (Desai & Jann, 2000; Nolen-Hoeksema, Larson, & Grayson, 2000).

Why Are Women More Depressed?

Studies suggest the higher rate of female depression may be due to both biological factors (hormones and genes) and environmental stressors (poverty, discrimination, unhappy marriages, and sexual or physical abuse) (Culbertson, 1997; Desai & Jann, 2000; Schmidt, Fava, Robinson, & Judge, 2000). Other researchers suggest that thinking patterns and socialization processes for men and women reinforce certain behaviors that predispose women toward depression (Alloy et al., 1999; Nolen-Hoeksema, Larson, & Grayson, 2000). Women are encouraged toward passivity, dependence, and emotional sensitivity, whereas men are socialized toward activity, independence, and suppression of emotions. Because depression is related to lack of activity, low energy, and feelings of helplessness, it is not surprising that women may be more depressed than men. The greater degree of aggression found in men may also mean that they act out their depression rather than withdrawing or blaming themselves. Finally, the higher level of substance abuse among men may also mask underlying depression.

Suicide: Ending Your Own Life

Whatever the causes of depression, one of the major dangers associated with it is the increased risk of suicide. Severely depressed people often become suicidal because they feel hopeless and helpless.

TRY THIS
Yourself

Decide whether each of the following is true or false:

1. People who talk about suicide are not likely to commit suicide.
2. Suicide usually takes place with little or no warning.
3. Suicidal people are fully intent on dying.
4. Children of parents who attempt suicide are at greater risk of committing suicide.
5. Suicidal people remain so forever.
6. Men are more likely than women to actually kill themselves by suicide.
7. When a suicidal person has been severely depressed and seems to be "snapping out of it," the danger of suicide decreases substantially.
8. Only depressed people commit suicide.
9. Thinking about suicide is rare.
10. Asking a depressed person about suicide will push him or her over the edge and cause a suicidal act that would not otherwise have occurred.

Now let's look at the experts' answers to these questions (Bostwick & Pankratz, 2000; Davison & Neale, 2001; Garland & Zigler, 1999; Jamison & Baldessarini, 1999; Oquendo & Mann, 2000):

1.*and* 2. **False.** About 90 percent of people who are suicidal talk about their intentions. They may say, "If something happens to me, I want you to…" or "Life just isn't worth living." They also leave behavioral clues, such as giving away valued possessions, withdrawing from family and friends, and losing interest in favorite activities.

3. **False.** Only about 3 to 5 percent of suicidal people truly intend to die. Most are just unsure about how to go on living. They cannot see their problems objectively enough to realize that they have alternative courses of action. They often gamble with death, arranging it so that fate or others will save them. Moreover, once the suicidal crisis passes, they are generally grateful to be alive.

4. **True.** Children of parents who attempt or commit suicide are at much greater risk of following in their footsteps. As Schneidman (1969) puts it, "The person who commits suicide puts his psychological skeleton in the survivor's emotional closet" (p. 22).

5. **False.** People who want to kill themselves are usually suicidal only for a limited period.

6. **True.** Although women are much more likely to attempt suicide, men are more likely to actually commit suicide. Men are more likely to use stronger methods, such as guns versus pills.

7. **False.** When people are first coming out of a depression, they are actually at greater risk because they now have the energy to actually commit suicide.

(continues)

8. **False.** Although suicide rates are highest for people with major depressive disorders, suicide is also the leading cause of premature death in people who suffer from schizophrenia. Suicide is also a major cause of death in people with anxiety disorders and alcohol and other substance-related disorders. Suicide is not limited to people with depression. Poor physical health, serious illness, substance abuse (particularly alcohol), loneliness, unemployment, and even natural disasters may push many over the edge.

9. **False.** Estimates from various studies find that 40 to 80 percent of the general public has thought about committing suicide at least once in their lives.

10. **False.** Because society often considers suicide a terrible, shameful act, asking directly about it can give the person permission to talk. In fact, *not asking* might lead to further isolation and depression.

How can you tell if someone is suicidal? If you believe someone is contemplating suicide, act on your beliefs. Stay with the person if there is any immediate danger, and encourage him or her to talk to you rather than withdraw. Show the person that you care, but do not give false reassurances that "everything will be okay." This type of response makes the suicidal person feel *more* alienated. Instead, openly ask if the person is feeling hopeless and suicidal. Do not be afraid to discuss suicide with people who feel depressed or hopeless, fearing that you will just put ideas into their heads. The reality is that people who are left alone or who are told they can't be serious about suicide often attempt it.

If you suspect someone is suicidal, it is vitally important that you help the person obtain counseling. Most cities have suicide prevention centers with 24-hour hotlines or walk-in centers that provide emergency counseling. Also, share your suspicions with parents, friends, or others who can help in a suicidal crisis. To save a life, you may have to betray a secret when someone confides in you.

More than 2,000 American teens will end their life this year (Time, May 15, 2000, Vol.155, No. 20)

Warning Signs

- •**Significant changes in a teen's eating or sleeping patterns**

- •**Decline in school performance**

- •**Dramatic change in personality or appearance**

- •**Drug or alcohol abuse**

- •**Obsession with death**

- •**Withdrawal from friends, family and regular activities**

- •**Profound guilt or hopelessness**

- •**"Cleaning house" by giving away favorite possessions**

Check & Review

MOOD DISORDERS

Mood disorders are disturbances of affect (emotion) that may include psychotic distortions of reality. In **major depressive disorder**, individuals experience a long-lasting depressed mood, feelings of worthlessness, and loss of interest in most activities. The feelings are without apparent cause and the individual may lose contact with reality. In **bipolar disorder**, episodes of mania and depression alternate with normal periods. During the manic episode, speech and thinking are rapid, and the person may experience delusions of grandeur and act impulsively.

Biological theories of mood disorders emphasize disruptions in neurotransmitters (especially dopamine and serotonin).

There is also evidence of a genetic predisposition for both major depression and bipolar disorder.

Psychosocial theories of mood disorders emphasize disturbed interpersonal relationships, faulty thinking, poor self-concept, and maladaptive learning. **Learned helplessness** theory suggests that depression results from repeatedly failing to escape from a source of stress. Suicide is a serious problem associated with depression, but we can reduce the risk by becoming involved and showing concern.

Questions

1. The two main types of mood disorders are _____. (a) major depression, bipolar disorder; (b) mania, depression; (c) SAD, MAD; (d) learned helplessness, suicide

2. A major difference between major depressive disorder and bipolar disorder is that only in bipolar disorders do people have _____. (a) hallucinations or delusions; (b) depression; (c) manic episodes; (d) a biochemical imbalance

3. What is Martin Seligman's learned helplessness theory of depression?

4. Briefly explain why women are diagnosed with depression more often than men are.

Answers to Questions can be found in Appendix B.

SCHIZOPHRENIA

Imagine for the moment that your daughter has just left for college and you hear voices inside your head shouting, "You'll never see her again! You have been a bad mother! She'll die." Or what if you saw dinosaurs on the street and live animals in your refrigerator? These are actual experiences that have plagued Mrs. T for almost 3 decades (Gershon & Rieder, 1993).

Mrs. T suffers from **schizophrenia**, a disorder characterized by major disturbances in perception, language, thought, emotion, and behavior. All the disorders we have considered so far cause considerable distress, but most sufferers can still function in daily life. Schizophrenia, however, is a form of *psychosis*, a term describing general lack of contact with reality. People with schizophrenia have serious problems caring for themselves, relating to others, and holding a job. In extreme cases, because they lack contact with reality, people with schizophrenia may require institutional or custodial care. To make matters worse, substance abuse rates are very high, perhaps reflecting an attempt to self-medicate (Batel, 2000; Green, 2000).

Schizophrenia is generally considered the most serious and severe form of mental disturbance. According to statistics, 1 of every 100 people develops schizophrenia and approximately half of all people admitted to mental hospitals are diagnosed with schizophrenia (Gottesman, 1991; Kendler, Gallagher, Abelson, & Kessler, 1996; Regier et al., 1993). The disorder usually emerges between the late teens and the mid-thirties and only rarely prior to adolescence or after age 45 (American Psychiatric Association, 2000).

Is schizophrenia the same as "split personality?" No. Schizophrenia means "split mind," but when Eugen Bleuler coined the term in 1911, he was referring to the fragmenting of thought processes and emotions found in schizophrenic disorders (Neale, Oltmanns, & Winters, 1983). Unfortunately, "split mind" and "split per-

What are the symptoms and causes of schizophrenia?

Schizophrenia *Group of psychotic disorders involving major disturbances in perception, language, thought, emotion, and behavior; the individual withdraws from people and reality, often into a fantasy life of delusions and hallucinations*

sonality" are often confused by the general public. One study of college freshmen found that 64 percent thought having multiple personalities was a common symptom of schizophrenia (Torrey, 1998). But as you will read later, *multiple personality disorder* (now known as *dissociative identity disorder*) is the rare condition of having more than one distinct personality. Schizophrenia is a much more common — and altogether different — type of psychological disorder. What are the symptoms of schizophrenia? What are its causes? And how does it differ cross-culturally?

Symptoms of Schizophrenia: Five Areas of Disturbance

Schizophrenia is characterized by psychological disturbances in five areas: perception, language, thought, affect (or emotions), and behavior.

Perceptual Symptoms

The senses of people with schizophrenia may be either enhanced (as in the case of Mrs. T) or blunted. The filtering and selection processes that allow most people to concentrate on whatever they choose are impaired, and sensory stimulation is jumbled and distorted. One patient reported:

> When people are talking, I just get scraps of it. If it is just one person who is speaking, that's not so bad, but if others join in then I can't pick it up at all. I just can't get in tune with the conversation. It makes me feel all open — as if things are closing in on me and I have lost control.
>
> McGhie and Chapman, 1961, p. 106

Hallucinations *Sensory perceptions that occur without an external stimulus*

People with schizophrenia also experience **hallucinations** — they perceive things without external stimuli. Hallucinations can occur in any of the senses (visual, tactile, olfactory), but auditory hallucinations (hearing voices and sounds) are most common in schizophrenia. As with Mrs. T, people with schizophrenia often hear voices speaking their thoughts aloud, commenting on their behavior, or telling them what to do. The voices seem to come from inside their own heads or from an external source such as an animal, telephone wires, or a TV set.

On rare occasions, people with schizophrenia will hurt others in response to their distorted internal experiences or the voices they hear. Unfortunately, these cases receive undue media attention and create exaggerated fears of "mental

Symptoms of schizophrenia? Disorganized thoughts, emotions, and perceptions are sometimes reflected in the artwork of people suffereing from schizophrenia.

TABLE 14.6 LANGUAGE VARIATIONS IN SCHIZOPHRENIA

Language Variation	Examples
Word salad	"The same children are sent of a rose, sweet-smelling perfume that gives us peace and parts and whole." "The sad, kind, and peaceful valleys of the mind come beckoning under rivers."
Neologisms	"Splisters" (combination of *splinters* and *blisters*) "Smever" (combination of *smart* and *clever*)

patients." In reality, a person with schizophrenia is most likely self-destructive and at greater risk of suicide than of violence toward others.

Language and Thought Disturbances

For people with schizophrenia, words lose their usual meanings and associations, logic is impaired, and thoughts are disorganized and bizarre. For example, a patient with schizophrenia gave this explanation for the meaning of the proverb "People who live in glass houses shouldn't throw stones":

> People who live in glass houses shouldn't forget people who live in stone houses and shouldn't throw glass.

When language and thought disturbances are mild, an individual with schizophrenia jumps from topic to topic. In more severe disturbances, phrases and words are jumbled together (referred to as *word salad*), and the person creates artificial words (*neologisms*). Table 14.6 presents examples of these language variations.

The most common thought disturbances experienced by people with schizophrenia are distorted beliefs called **delusions**. In contrast to mistaken beliefs that we all experience from time to time, such as thoughts that a friend is trying to avoid us or that our parents' divorce was our fault, delusions are mistaken beliefs maintained in spite of strong evidence to the contrary.

Mrs. T held the *paranoid delusion* that others were talking about her. In *delusions of grandeur*, people believe they are someone very important, perhaps Jesus Christ or the queen of England. In *delusions of persecution*, individuals believe they are the target of a plot to harm them, as was the case with Jim in our introduction, who believed secret agents were trying to assassinate him. In *delusions of reference*, unrelated events are given special significance, as when a person believes a radio program or newspaper article is giving him or her a special message.

Delusions *Mistaken beliefs maintained in spite of strong evidence to the contrary*

Emotional Disturbances

Changes in emotion, or affect, usually occur in schizophrenia. In some cases, emotions are exaggerated and fluctuate rapidly in inappropriate ways. For example, a person may become extremely fearful, guilty, or euphoric for no reason. In other cases, emotions may become blunted or decreased in intensity. Some people with schizophrenia have *flattened affect* — almost no emotional response of any kind.

Behavioral Disturbances

Disturbances in behavior may take the form of unusual actions that have special meaning. One patient shook his head rhythmically from side to side to try to shake the excess thoughts out of his mind. Another massaged his head repeatedly "to help clear it" of unwanted thoughts. In other cases, the affected person may grimace and display unusual mannerisms. These movements, however, may also be side effects of the medication used to treat the disorder (Chapter 15).

People with schizophrenia may become *cataleptic* and assume an uncomfortable, nearly immobile stance for an extended period. A few people with schizophrenia also have a symptom called *waxy flexibility*, a tendency to maintain whatever posture is imposed on them.

The abnormal behaviors of individuals with schizophrenia are often related to disturbances in their perceptions, thoughts, and feelings. For example, experiencing a flood of sensory stimuli or overwhelming confusion, a person with schizophrenia will often withdraw from social contacts and refuse to communicate.

Types of Schizophrenia: Recent Methods of Classification

For many years, researchers divided schizophrenia into *paranoid*, *catatonic*, *disorganized*, *undifferentiated*, and *residual* subtypes (Table 14.7). Although these terms are still used in the *DSM-IV-TR* (and sometimes by the public), critics say that they have little value in clinical practice and research. They contend that this classification does not differentiate in terms of prognosis (prediction for recovery), etiology (cause), or response to treatment, and that the undifferentiated type is a catchall for difficult diagnostic cases (American Psychiatric Association, 2000).

For all these reasons, Nancy Andreasen and others (Andreasen, 2000; Andreasen, Flaum, Swayze, Tyrrell, & Arndt, 1990; Toomey, Faraone, Simpson, & Tsuang, 1998) propose an alternative classification system of two groups instead of four:

1. *Positive symptoms* involve *additions* or exaggerations of normal thought processes and behaviors, including bizarre delusions, hallucinations, and disorganized speech

2. *Negative symptoms* involve the *loss* or absence of normal thought processes and behaviors, including impaired attention, limited or toneless speech, flattened emotions, and social withdrawal

(Study tip: If you're having difficulty understanding the distinction between positive and negative symptoms of schizophrenia, think back to what you learned in Chapter 5 regarding positive and negative reinforcement and punishment. *Positive* means "the addition of," whereas *negative* refers to the "removal or loss of.")

"That's the doctor who is treating me for paranoia. I don't trust him."

T A B L E   1 4 . 7 SUBTYPES OF SCHIZPHRENIA

Paranoid	Dominated by delusions (persecution and grandeur) and hallucinations (hearing voices)
Catatonic	Marked by motor disturbances (immobility or wild activity) and echo speech (repeating the speech of others)
Disorganized	Characterized by incoherent speech, flat or exaggerated emotions, and social withdrawal.
Undifferentiated	Meets the criteria for schizophrenia but is not any of the above subtypes
Residual	No longer meets the full criteria for schizophrenia but still shows some symptoms

In addition to these two groups, the latest *DSM-IV-TR* suggests adding another dimension to reflect *disorganization of behavior*. One advantage of either a two- or three-dimension model is that they both acknowledge that schizophrenia is more than one disorder and that it has multiple causes.

Causes of Schizophrenia: Nature and Nurture Theories

There are several theories that attempt to explain schizophrenia. Biological theories emphasize physical changes in the nervous system based on abnormal brain functioning or inherited predisposition. Psychosocial theories focus on stressful experiences and disturbed family interactions.

Biological Theories

An enormous amount of scientific research exists concerning possible biological factors in schizophrenia. Most of this research is in three areas: genetics, neurotransmitters, and brain function:

1. *Genetics.* Genetics undoubtedly plays a primary role in the development of schizophrenia. Although researchers are beginning to identify specific genes related to schizophrenia, most genetic studies have focused on twin and adoption research (Bailer et al., 2000; Gershon et al., 1998; Petronis, 2000). By most estimates, heritability is around 50 percent. However, one study of both identical and fraternal twins found an estimated heritability of 83 percent (Cannon, Kaprio, Lonnquvist, Huttunen, & Koskenvuo, 1998). Figure 14.4 (page 510) shows the risk of developing schizophrenia in people with differing degrees of relatedness to a person with schizophrenia. As expected, the risk increases with genetic similarity; that is, people who share more genes are more likely to develop the disorder. For example, if one identical twin develops schizophrenia, the other twin has a 48 to 83 percent chance of also developing schizophrenia (Berrettini, 2000; Cannon, Kaprio, Lonnqvist, Huttunen, & Koskenvuo, 1998). But if one sibling develops schizophrenia, the chances of the other sibling developing it are only 9 percent. If you compare these percentages with the risk for the general population (which is around 1 percent), you can appreciate the role of genetics in schizophrenia.

2. *Neurotransmitters.* Precisely how genetic inheritance produces schizophrenia is unclear. The most widely held view implicates a dopamine imbalance (Gelman, 1999; Schwartz, Diaz, Pilon, & Sokoloff, 2000). According to the **dopamine hypothesis**, an overactivity of certain dopamine neurons in the brain causes schizophrenia. This hypothesis is based on two important observations:

Dopamine Hypothesis *A theory suggesting that schizophrenia is caused by an overactivity of dopamine neurons in a specific region of the brain*

RESEARCH HIGHLIGHT

Alcohol Problems and Comorbidity

Alcohol use disorders (AUDs), which include alcohol abuse and alcohol dependence, may be the Western world's most serious drug problem. In addition to creating massive social and personal difficulties (Chapters 3 and 5), AUDs also overlap with almost all other mental disorders — including anxiety disorders, mood disorders, schizophrenia, and personality disorders (Green, 2000; Kirchner, Owen, Nordquist, & Fischer, 1998; Sher, 2000). This combination of disorders is known as **comorbidity**, or *dual diagnosis*.

What Causes This Type of Overlap Between Disorders?

Perhaps the most influential hypothesis is that of self-medication — individuals drink to reduce their symptoms (Batel, 2000; Green, 2000). Research also shows a high genetic correlation between AUDs and other conditions (Heath, 2000). On the other hand, several environmental variables also predict AUDs and comorbid conditions in adolescence, including reduced parental monitoring, distance from teachers, selective socialization with deviant peers, and disaffiliation with peers (Costello, 2000). Although it may seem contradictory to have both genetic and environmental explanations, we see once again that nature and nurture interact. Researchers suggest that the interaction might result from an alcohol-abusing youth's tendency to seek out deviant peers or that the same genes that contribute to a mother's lax monitoring might also contribute to her child's early experimentation with alcohol (Sher, 2000).

The high cost of alcohol abuse. Children of alcoholic parents are at much greater risk of also abusing alcohol and developing related disorders. Is this because of a genetic predisposition, modeling by the parents, or the emotional devastation of growing up with an alcoholic parent?

Regardless of the causes or correlates of AUDs and comorbid conditions, it is critical that patients, family members, and clinicians recognize and deal with comorbidity if treatment is to be effective. For example, AUDs often accompany serious depression, and simply stopping drinking is not the only solution (though certainly an important first step). Similarly, people suffering from schizophrenia are far more likely to relapse into psychosis, require hospitalization, neglect their medications, commit acts of violence, and kill themselves when they also suffer from AUDs (Batel, 2000; Green, 2000). Recognizing this pattern and potential danger, many individual and group programs that treat schizophrenia now also include methods used in drug abuse treatment.

To sum up, people who suffer from AUDs are at great risk of also experiencing at least one or more other mental disorders. Understanding this *comorbidity* is of great importance to the suffering individual and his or her family. It is also important from a broad social perspective. The pain and destruction experienced by so many people results in enormous costs to society. But as you will see in the next chapter, there are many forms of successful therapy that offer hope for everyone.

Comorbidity *The co-occurrence of two or more disorders in the same person at the same time, as when a person suffers from both depression and alcoholism*

Testing Your Knowledge of Abnormal Behavior

Applying abstract terminology is an important component of critical thinking. Test your understanding of the six major diagnostic cate-gories of psychological disorders by matching the disorders on the left with the diagnostic categories on the right.

Answers can be found in Appendix B.

Description of Disorder

1. Julie mistakenly believes she has lots of money and is making plans to take all her friends on a trip around the world. She has not slept for days. Last month, she could not get out of bed and talked of suicide.
2. Steve is exceptionally charming and impulsive and apparently feels no remorse or guilt when he causes great harm to others.
3. Chris believes he is president of the United States and hears voices saying the world is ending.
4. Each day, Kelly repeatedly checks and rechecks all stove burners and locks throughout her house and washes her hands hundreds of times.
5. Lee has repeated bouts of uncontrollable drinking, frequently misses his Monday-morning college classes, and was recently fired for drinking on the job.
6. Susan wandered off and was later found living under a new name, with no memory of her previous life.

Possible Diagnosis

a. Anxiety disorder

b. Schizophrenia

c. Mood disorder

d. Dissociative disorder

e. Personality disorder

f. Substance-related disorder

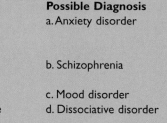

Check & Review

OTHER DISORDERS

In **dissociative disorders**, critical elements of personality split apart. This split is manifested in failing to recall or identify past experiences (*dissociative amnesia*), by leaving home and wandering off (*dissociative fugue*), or by developing completely separate personalities (**dissociative identity disorder** [DID]). Environmental variables are the primary cause of dissociative disorders (e.g., a history of extreme trauma like sexual abuse).

Personality disorders involve inflexible, maladaptive personality traits. The best-known type is the **antisocial personality**, characterized by egocentrism, lack of guilt, impulsivity, and superficial charm. Research suggests this disorder may be related to defects in brain waves, genetic inheritance, or disturbed family relationships. **Borderline personality disorder** (BPD) is the most commonly diagnosed personality disorder. It is characterized by impulsivity and instability in mood, relationships, and self-image.

Questions

1. The major underlying problem for all dissociative disorders is the psychological need to escape from _____.

2. What is DID?

3. A *sociopath* or a *psychopath* would be diagnosed as a(n) _____ personality in the *Diagnostic and Statistical Manual of Mental Disorders*, fourth edition, text revision.

4. One possible biological cause of BPD is _____. (a) childhood history of neglect; (b) emotional deprivation; (c) impaired functioning of the frontal lobes; (d) all of these options.

Answers to Questions can be found in Appendix B.

KEY TERMS

Studying Psychological Disorders
abnormal behavior (p. 485)
Diagnostic and Statistical Manual of Mental Disorders (DSM-IV-TR) (p. 490)
insanity (p. 491)
medical model (p. 488)
neurosis (p. 491)
psychiatry (p. 489)
psychosis (p. 491)
Anxiety Disorders
anxiety disorder (p. 495)
generalized anxiety disorder (p. 495)

obsessive-compulsive disorder (OCD) (p. 496)
panic disorder (p. 495)
phobia (p. 495)
post-traumatic stress disorder (PTSD) (p. 497)
Mood Disorders
bipolar disorder (p. 501)
learned helplessness (p. 502)
major depressive disorder (p. 500)
Schizophrenia
delusions (p. 507)
dopamine hypothesis (p. 509)

hallucinations (p. 506)
schizophrenia (p. 505)
Other Disorders
antisocial personality (p. 516)
borderline personality disorder (BPD) (p. 517)
comorbidity (p. 518)
dissociative disorder (p. 514)
dissociative identity disorder (DID) (p. 514)
personality disorders (p. 516)

Visual Summary for Chapter 14

Studying Psychological Disorders

Identifying Abnormal Behavior

Abnormal behavior: Pattern of emotion, thought, and action considered pathological for one of four reasons (statistical infrequency, disability or dysfunction, personal distress, or violation of norms).

Explaining Abnormality

| Prehistoric—demon model; treated with *trephining* in the Stone Ages. | → | 4th century B.C.—**medical model;** Hippocrates suggests physical causes. | → | Middle Ages—demon model; treated with exorcism, torture, imprisonment, execution. | → | 18th century—Pinel reintroduces medical model and humane asylums. | → | Modern times—medical model persists (e.g., **psychiatry**). |

Classifying Abnormal Behavior

The Diagnostic and Statistical Manual of Mental Disorders (DSM–IV–TR) categorizes disorders according to major similarities and differences and provides detailed descriptions of symptoms.
- Benefits: Standardized diagnosis and treatment, improved communication among professionals and between professionals and patients.
- Problems: Insufficient attention to cultural factors, supports medical model, and labels. Misdiagnosis also occurs, and labeling someone "mentally ill" can lead to social and economic discrimination.

Major Categories of Psychological Disorders

General Description, Examples, and Symptoms

Anxiety Disorders
Anxiety disorders: persistent feelings of threat in facing everyday problems.
- **Phobias:** Exaggerated fears of specific objects or situations.
- **Generalized anxiety disorder:** Persistent free-floating anxiety.
- **Panic disorder:** Anxiety concentrated into brief or lengthy episodes of panic attacks.
- **Obsessive-compulsive disorder (OCD):** Persistent anxiety arousing thoughts (obsessions) are relieved by ritualistic actions (compulsions) such as hand washing.
- **Post-traumatic stress disorder (PTSD):** After a traumatic event (rape, war), a person experiences flashbacks, sleep disturbances, an exaggerated startle response, etc. that may last for years.

Possible Causes

Learning theorists: Classical and operant conditioning, as well as modeling and imitation.

Biological perspective: Genetic predisposition, brain abnormalities, and biochemistry.

The cognitive approach: Distorted thinking that amplifies ordinary threats.

Major Categories of Psychological Disorders (cont.)

General Description, Examples, and Symptoms

Possible Causes

Mood Disorders
Mood disorders are disturbances of affect (emotion) that may include psychotic distortions of reality. Two types:

↓   ↓

• **Major depressive disorder:** Long-lasting depressed mood, feelings of worthlessness, and loss of interest in most activities. Feelings are without apparent cause and person may lose contact with reality.

• **Bipolar disorder:** Episodes of mania and depression alternate with normal periods. During manic episode, speech and thinking are rapid, and the person may experience delusions of grandeur and act impulsively.

• *Depression* involves several culture-general symptoms, such as feelings of sadness and loss of enjoyment in daily activities.
• Women more likely than men to suffer depressive symptoms in many countries.
• Suicide is a serious problem associated with depression, but risk can be reduced by others showing concern.

Biological theories: Neurotransmitters (especially dopamine and serotonin) and genetic predisposition for both major depression and bipolar disorder.

Psychological theories: Disturbed interpersonal relationships, faulty thinking, poor self-concept, and maladaptive learning. **Learned helplessness** theory suggests depression results from repeatedly failing to escape from a source of stress.

Schizophrenia
Schizophrenia: serious psychotic mental disorder afflicting approximately one out of every 100 people.
Five major symptoms: Disturbances in
1) Perception (impaired filtering and selection, **hallucinations**).
2) Language (word salad, neologisms).
3) Thought (impaired logic, **delusions**).
4) Emotion (either exaggerated or blunted emotions).
5) Behavior (social withdrawal, bizarre mannerisms, catalepsy, waxy flexibility).
Two-type classification system:

↓   ↓

Positive symptoms—distorted or excessive mental activity (e.g., delusions and hallucinations).

Negative symptoms—behavioral deficits (e.g., toneless voice, flattened emotions).

Culture: Schizophrenia is the world's most culturally universal mental disorder with many symptoms culturally general (such as delusions). However, significant differences exist in prevalence, form, onset, and prognosis.

Biological theories: Genetics (people inherit a predisposition), disruptions in neurotransmitters (**dopamine hypothesis**) and brain function (such as enlarged ventricles and lower levels of activity in the frontal and temporal lobes).

Psychosocial theories: Stress and disturbed family communication.

Other Disorders
Dissociative disorders: Critical parts of personality split apart. This split is manifested in failing to recall or identify past experiences (dissociative amnesia), by leaving home and wandering off (dissociative fugue), or by developing completely separate personalities (**dissociative identity disorder [DID]** or multiple-personality disorder). Although DID is believed to be rare, a few well-publicized cases (like Sybil) have drawn attention to it.

Environmental variables are the primary cause, little or no biological or genetic influence. Major problem: Need to escape. A history of extreme trauma, usually sexual abuse, found in nearly all cases.

Personality disorders involve inflexible, maladaptive personality traits.
• **Antisocial personality**, the best-known example, is characterized by egocentrism, lack of guilt, impulsivity, and superficial charm.
• **Borderline personality disorders (BPD)**, the most commonly diagnosed personality disorder, is characterized by impulsivity and instability in mood, relationships, and self-image.

Defects in brain waves, genetic inheritance, or disturbed family relationships.

15

Therapy

Did you see the latest version of the movie *The House on Haunted Hill*? Do you remember the gruesome "therapy" scenes in the dark asylum? The movie begins with rapid-fire shots of doctors performing surgery without anesthesia, men and women screaming, and mass hysteria as the inmates revolt against the doctors and nurses. A fire starts amid the chaos, and the sadistic director of the asylum pulls a switch, locking down the entire building so that everyone inside, including himself, burns to death. "A sanitarium of horrors, overseen by a surgeon gone mad" is how the fake newsreel footage of the events describes the scene.

Anthony Hopkins starring in Silence of the Lambs.

Consider, too, how mentally ill people themselves are generally portrayed: They are either cruel, sociopathic criminals (Hannibal Lecter, played by Anthony Hopkins, in Silence of the Lambs) or helpless victims who will never be believed again after being labeled insane (Sarah Connor in Terminator 2, Bruce Willis in Twelve Monkeys, Jack Nicholson in One Flew Over the Cuckoo's Nest, and Winona Ryder in Girl Interrupted). And all of them are inescapably trapped in dark, horror-filled asylums or cold, clinical hospitals.

Since the beginning of the movie age, from The Cabinet of Dr. Caligari to Terminator 2, from Silence of the Lambs to Amadeus, mentally ill people and their treatment have set the mood for some of Hollywood's most popular and influential films. The mad doctor, the brutal treatment of mentally ill patients, and the bizarre methods and machinery used to implement the "cures" perfectly suit the needs of Hollywood directors hoping to boost ticket sales (adapted from Koenig, 2000).

Compare this dimly lit, overcrowded insane asylum with the painfully bright, clinical-looking, high-tech mental facility in Terminator 2: Judgment Day. The leading character, played by Sarah Connor, is trapped inside and desperate to be released. When her case comes up for review, she tries (unsuccessfully) to convince the doctor that she is cured. She says that a nuclear holocaust is not forthcoming and that she no longer believes that cyborgs from the future have been sent back in time to kill her son John. (Of course, everyone who has seen the first film knows that what she is denying is true.)

Winona Ryder starring in Girl Interrupted.

hat's wrong with these films? Are they only "harmless entertainment," or do they perpetuate harmful stereotypes? According to the Surgeon General's Report on Mental Health released in December 1999, the shame and embarrassment caused by the stigma that surrounds a diagnosis of mental illness is the "most formidable obstacle to future progress in the arena of mental illness and health." Remarking on the film industry's distorted and largely negative portrayal of mental illness and its treatment, the Surgeon General also stated: "We want to help overcome the stereotypes, and help people realize that, just as things go wrong with the heart, the liver and the kidney, things can go wrong with the brain, and there should be no shame in that" (Adams, 2000).

The Surgeon General's report also found that nearly two-thirds of all people who have mental disorders avoid seeking treatment because of financial problems, limited access, lack of awareness, and other situations. At least a part of their resistance to therapy also may be due to Hollywood's negative and one-sided portrayals. This is unfortunate. As you will see in this chapter, modern therapy can be very effective and prevent much needless suffering (Kopta, Lueger, Saunders, & Howard, 1999). In our coverage of modern forms of therapy, we hope to offset what you might have "learned" from Hollywood films with a balanced, factual presentation of the latest research. To begin, it's important to emphasize that not everyone who seeks professional help is suffering from mental illness. Although psychological disorders are much more prevalent than most people realize (Chapter 14), for a large number of people the major goal of therapy is to help with everyday problems in living, such as parent–child conflicts, unhappy marriages, death of a loved one, or adjustment to retirement. In addition, some people enter therapy for greater self-knowledge or personal fulfillment.

Numerous forms of therapy exist to serve varying needs. According to one expert (Kazdin, 1994), there may be over 400 approaches to treatment. To organize our discussion of these treatments, we will focus on two major approaches: (1) **biomedical therapies** that act directly on the patient's brain and nervous system and involve the use of drugs, electroconvulsive therapy (ECT), or psychosurgery, and (2) **psychotherapy**, a collection of various *psychological* therapeutic techniques employed to improve psychological functioning and promote adjustment to life. (*Therapy* is a general term including both biomedical therapies and psychotherapies.) The chapter concludes by exploring several issues in therapy: the ethics of forced institutionalization, effectiveness of therapy, therapy in the electronic age, and women and minorities as clients.

Biomedical Therapy *Therapy involving physiological interventions (drugs, electroconvulsive therapy, and psychosurgery) to reduce symptoms associated with psychological disorders*

Psychotherapy *A collection of various psychological techniques employed to improve psychological functioning and promote adjustment to life through understanding one's problems and modifying troubling feelings, behaviors, or relationships*

THERAPY ESSENTIALS

In its strictest sense, *therapy* refers only to techniques used by professionals (e.g., behavior modification, client-centered therapy, group therapy, and psychoanalysis). The professionals who do therapy include not only psychologists who specialize in mental disorders but also psychiatrists, psychiatric nurses, social workers, counselors, and members of the clergy with special training in pastoral counseling.

Here we will focus on the therapies used primarily by psychologists. The one exception is our discussion of *biomedical therapies* (drug treatments, ECT, and psychosurgery). Although psychiatrists and other medical professionals are generally the only ones who can prescribe biomedical techniques, they often work with psychologists to design the best treatment for their clients. It is also becoming clear that general psychotherapy and biomedical therapies overlap. When successful, they both alter brain functions (Gabbard, 1999). All major forms of therapy are designed to help the client in five specific areas (Figure 15.1). Depending on the individual

What do all therapies have in common?

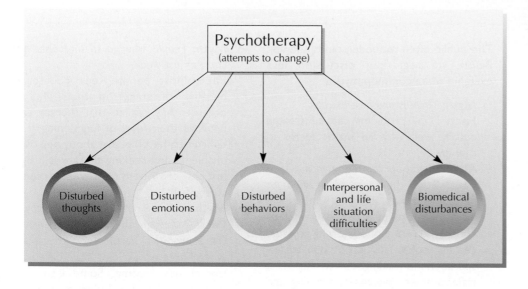

Figure 15.1 *The five most common goals of therapy.* Most therapies focus on one or more of these five goals. As you read about each therapy, see if you can identify which goal(s) would be of most interest to a psychoanalyst, a cognitive therapist, a behaviorist, a psychiatrist, and so on. It will help you differentiate between the approaches to therapy — and it might even help you on an exam on this chapter.

therapist's training and the client's needs, one or more of these five areas may be emphasized more than the others.

1. *Disturbed thoughts.* Troubled individuals typically suffer some degree of confusion, destructive thought patterns, or blocked understanding of their problems. Therapists work to change these thoughts, provide new ideas or information, and guide individuals toward finding their own solutions to problems.

2. *Disturbed emotions.* People who seek therapy generally suffer from extreme emotional discomfort. By encouraging free expression of feelings and by providing a supportive environment, therapists help their clients replace feelings of despair or incompetence with hope and self-confidence.

3. *Disturbed behaviors.* Troubled individuals usually exhibit problem behaviors. Therapists help their clients eliminate troublesome behaviors and guide them toward lives that are more effective.

4. *Interpersonal and life situation difficulties.* Therapists help clients improve their relationships with family, friends, and coworkers. They also help them avoid or minimize sources of stress in their lives, such as job demands or family conflicts.

5. *Biomedical disturbances.* Troubled individuals sometimes suffer biological disruptions that directly cause or contribute to psychological difficulties (e.g., chemical imbalances that lead to depression). Therapists help relieve these problems primarily with drugs.

Although most therapists work with clients in several of these areas, the emphasis varies according to the therapist's training. Psychoanalysts and psychodynamic therapists, for example, generally emphasize unconscious thoughts and emotions. Cognitive therapists focus on their client's faulty thinking and belief patterns, whereas humanistic therapists attempt to alter the client's negative emotional responses. Behaviorists, as the name implies, focus on changing maladaptive behaviors. Therapists who use biomedical techniques attempt to change biological disorders.

It is important to note, however, that if you go to a counseling service seeking a "behaviorist" or "cognitive therapist," you will not find such a listing. These items simply refer to the theoretical background and framework that guide a clinician's thinking. Just as Democrats and Republicans approach political matters in different ways, behaviorists and cognitive therapists approach therapy differently. At the same time, just as Democrats and Republicans borrow ideas from one another, clinicians from different perspectives also share ideas and techniques.

The public often misunderstands therapy. Before we begin our discussion, let's examine some common myths:

- *Myth: There is one best therapy.*
  Fact: Many problems can be treated equally well with all major forms of therapy.
- *Myth: Therapists can read minds.*
  Fact: Good therapists often seem to have an uncanny ability to understand how their clients are feeling and to know when someone is trying to avoid certain topics. This is not due to any special mind-reading ability; rather, it reflects their specialized training and daily experience working with troubled people.

- *Myth: People who go to therapists are crazy or just weak.*
  Fact: Most people seek counseling because of stress in their life or because they realize that therapy can improve their level of functioning. It is difficult to be objective about our own problems, and seeking therapy is a sign not only of wisdom but also of personal strength.
- *Myth: Only the rich can afford therapy.*
  Fact: Although therapy is expensive, there are many clinics and therapists who charge on a sliding scale based on the client's income. Some insurance plans also cover psychological services.

Eclectic Approach *An approach to therapy in which the therapist combines techniques from various theories to find the appropriate treatment for the client*

Clinicians who regularly borrow freely from various theories are said to take an **eclectic approach** (Kopta, Lueger, Saunders, & Howard, 1999). Now, although you won't find a listing for behaviorists, you will find listings for psychologists, psychiatrists, social workers, and sometimes psychoanalysts and counselors. Therapists also usually list the degrees they hold, which generally indicate their professional training (Table 15.1).

TABLE 15.1 MAJOR TYPES OF THERAPISTS

1. **Clinical or counseling psychologists** are therapists who have an advanced degree such as a Ph.D. (doctor of philosophy), a Psy.D. (doctor of psychology), or Ed.D. (doctor of education). They have usually had 4 or more years of graduate education, including a supervised internship.

2. **Psychiatrists** are physicians (M.D.) who specialize in psychiatry after graduation from medical school and completing a year of internship. The 3-year residency program in psychiatry includes supervised practice in therapy techniques and training in the biological treatment of disorders. Because only psychiatrists are physicians, they tend to emphasize biomedical therapies.

3. **Psychoanalysts** are almost always psychiatrists with additional specialized training in the techniques of psychoanalysis. (The exceptions are people trained in analysis after completing other graduate education, such as social work.) During the specialized training period, students must themselves undergo psychoanalysis.

4. **Social workers** have obtained at least a master's degree in social work (MSW). During their graduate education, they are supervised in the treatment of clients in hospitals and outpatient settings. Social workers can also obtain a doctorate (DSW or Ph.D.) or specialize in specific types of therapy, becoming certified to practice as a licensed marriage, family, and child counselor (MFCC) or a licensed clinical social worker (LCSW).

5. **Counselors** specialize in problems related to marriage, family, and child relations (MFT). They also deal with everyday adjustment problems, substance abuse, and career issues. They have obtained at least a master's degree in counseling (M.A.) and have had 2 or more years of graduate training.

Check & Review

THERAPY ESSENTIALS

Therapy is a general term for both biological and psychological treatments for mental disorders. There are numerous forms of therapy, but they all focus treatment on five basic areas of disturbance — thoughts, emotions, behaviors, interpersonal and life situations, and biomedical problems.

Questions

1. Using therapeutic techniques to improve psychological functioning and promote adjustment to life is known as _____. (a) eclectic therapy; (b) psychoanalysis/psychodynamic therapy; (c) psychotherapy; (d) counseling

2. Match the following therapists with their primary emphasis:

   ____ psychoanalysts   (a) faulty thinking and belief patterns
   ____ behaviorists   (b) unconscious thoughts and patterns
   ____ humanistic therapists   (c) biological disorders
   ____ biomedical therapists   (d) negative emotions
   ____ cognitive therapists   (e) maladaptive behaviors

3. What are the five major categories of therapists?

Answers to Questions can be found in Appendix B.

BIOMEDICAL THERAPIES

Biomedical therapies are based on the premise that problem behaviors are caused, at least in part, by chemical imbalances or disturbed nervous system functioning. A physician rather than a psychologist must prescribe biomedical therapies, but psychologists work with patients receiving biomedical therapies and are frequently involved in research programs to evaluate their effectiveness. Despite Hollywood's persistent linking of mental illness with asylums and hospitals, today only people with the most severe and intractable disturbances are institutionalized and abuses like those portrayed in most films are virtually nonexistent. Most people with psychological disorders can be helped with drugs, psychotherapy, or a combination of the two. In this section, we will discuss three types of biomedical therapies, including drugs, ECT, and psychosurgery.

What are the major biomedical therapies?

Drug Therapy: The Pharmacological Revolution

Since the 1950s, drug companies have developed an amazing variety of chemicals to treat abnormal behaviors. In some cases, **drug therapy** corrects a chemical imbalance. In these instances, using a drug is similar to administering insulin to people with diabetes, whose own bodies fail to manufacture enough. In other cases, drugs are used to relieve or suppress the symptoms of psychological disturbances even if the underlying cause is not thought to be biological. Psychiatric drugs are classified into four major categories: antianxiety, antipsychotic, mood stabilizer, and antidepressant. Table 15.2 gives examples of drugs in each category.

Drug Therapy *Use of chemicals (drugs) to treat physical and psychological disorders*

Antianxiety Drugs

Antianxiety drugs (also known as "minor tranquilizers") create feelings of tranquility and calmness in addition to relieving muscle tension. These drugs have replaced sedatives (which had side effects of drowsiness and sleepiness) in the treatment of anxiety disorders. Antianxiety drugs, such as Valium and Xanax, lower the sympathetic activity of the brain — the crisis mode of operation — so that anxiety responses are diminished or prevented (Margolis & Swartz, 2001; Pollack, 2000).

Antianxiety Drugs *Medications used to treat anxiety disorders*

TABLE 15.2 DRUG THERAPY

Type of Drug	Psychological Disorder	Chemical Group	Generic Name	Brand Name
Antidepressant drug	Severe depression (with suicidal tendencies)	Tricyclic antidepressants	Imipramine Amitriptyline	Tofranil Elavil
		Monoamine oxidase inhibitors (MAOIs)	Phenelzine	Nardil
		Second-generation antidepressants	Tranylcypromine Fluoxetine	Parnate Prozac
Antianxiety drugs	Anxiety disorders	Benzodiazepines	Chlordiazepoxide Diazepam	Librium Valium
		Glycerol derivatives	Meprobamate	Miltown Equanil
Antipsychotic drugs	Schizophrenia	Phenothiazines	Chlorpromazine Fluphenazine Thioridazine	Thorazine Prolixin Mellaril
		Butyrophenones	Haloperidol	Haldol
		Dibenzodiazepine	Clozapine	Clozaril
Mood-stabilizer drugs	Bipolar disorder	Antimanic	Lithium carbonate	Lithonate Lithane Eskalith

Antipsychotic Drugs *Chemicals administered to diminish or eliminate hallucinations, delusions, withdrawal, and other symptoms of psychosis; also known as neuroleptics or major tranquilizers*

Antipsychotic Drugs

The medications used to treat schizophrenia and other acute psychotic states are called **antipsychotic drugs**, or *neuroleptics*. They are often referred to as "major tranquilizers," creating the impression they invariably have a strong calming or sedating effect. Some antipsychotic drugs, such as Haldol or Navane, do reduce hallucinations and delusions. But other antipsychotic drugs, such as Clozaril, energize and animate patients. The main effect of antipsychotic drugs is to diminish or eliminate psychotic symptoms, including hallucinations, delusions, withdrawal, and apathy. They are not designed to sedate the patient.

How do these drugs work? The traditional antipsychotics, like Thorazine, appear to decrease activity at the dopamine synapses, which further supports the theory that excessive dopamine contributes to schizophrenia (Chapter 14). Given the multiple types of dopamine receptors in different parts of the brain, the newer *atypical antipsychotics*, like Clozaril, may be more effective because they target specific dopamine receptors (as well as serotonin receptors) and avoid interfering with others (Roth, Willins, Kristiansen, & Kroeze, 1999).

Mood Stabilizer and Antidepressant Drugs

For people suffering from bipolar disorders, *mood-stabilizer* drugs such as lithium can help manic episodes and depression. Because lithium acts relatively slowly — it can be 3 or 4 weeks before it takes effect — its primary use is in preventing *future* episodes and helping to break the manic–depressive cycle. Lithium also has potentially serious side effects, but recent research also shows that it increases the volume of gray matter (the so-called thinking part of the brain) (Manji, Husseini, Moore, & Chen, 2000; Webb, Solomon, & Ryan, 2001).

Antidepressant Drugs *Drugs prescribed to treat depression, some anxiety disorders, and certain eating disorders (such as bulimia)*

People with severe depression are usually treated with one of four types of **antidepressant drugs:**

1. *Tricyclics* (named for their chemical structure that contains three rings), such as imipramine, act on multiple neurochemical pathways in the brain, including serotonin and catecholamines.

2. *Monoamine oxidase inhibitors* (MAOIs), such as phenelzine, block the enzyme *monoamine oxidase*. Because this enzyme inactivates serotonin and catecholamines, blocking it increases the availability of these helpful neurochemicals.

3. *Selective serotonin reuptake inhibitors* (SSRIs), such as Prozac or Zoloft, *work* like the tricyclics, but they *selectively* affect only serotonin. They are by far the most commonly prescribed antidepressants.

4. *Atypical antidepressants*, such as Wellbutrin, are a miscellaneous group of drugs used for patients who fail to respond to the other drugs or for people who experience certain side effects (like decreased sexual function) that are common to other antidepressants.

Electroconvulsive Therapy and Psychosurgery: Promising or Perilous?

In **electroconvulsive therapy** (ECT), also known as *electroshock therapy* (EST), a current of moderate intensity is passed through the brain between two electrodes placed on the outside of the head (Figure 15.2). The electrical current is applied for less than a second, but it triggers widespread firing of neurons, also known as convulsions. The convulsions produce many changes in the central and peripheral nervous systems, including activation of the autonomic nervous system, increased secretion of various hormones and neurotransmitters, and changes in the blood–brain barrier.

During the early years of ECT, some patients received hundreds of treatments (Fink, 1999), but today most receive 12 or fewer treatments. Sometimes the electrical current is applied only to the right hemisphere, which causes less interference with verbal memories and left hemisphere functioning. Modern ECT is used only as a last resort because it produces major brain seizures and may cause varying degrees of memory loss. However, it also can be very effective in the treatment of severe depression when drug therapy has failed, and it is sometimes recommended for sui-

Electroconvulsive Therapy (ECT)
A biomedical therapy based on passing electrical current through the brain; it is used almost exclusively to treat serious depression when drug therapy does not work

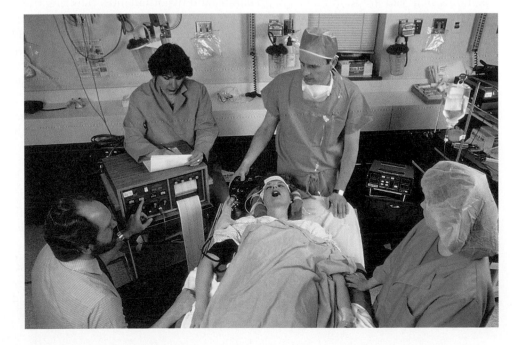

Figure 15.2 *Electroconvulsive therapy (ECT)*. During ECT, electrodes on the forehead apply electric current to the brain, creating a brief cortical seizure. Although ECT is controversial and may seem barbaric to you, for some severely depressed people it is the only hope and often very effective.

One Flew Over the Cuckoo's Nest.
In this film, the lead character, McMurphy (played by Jack Nicholson) is a persistent problem for the hospital staff. To punish and control him, the staff first used drug therapy, then ECT, and finally psychosurgery — a prefrontal lobotomy. Although this was a popular movie, it also deepened public fear and misconceptions about biomedical therapy.

Psychosurgery *Operative procedures on the brain designed to relieve severe mental symptoms that have not responded to other forms of treatment*

Lobotomy *A brain operation in which the nerve pathways between the frontal lobes and the thalamus and hypothalamus are cut in hopes of treating psychological disorders*

cidal patients because it works faster than antidepressant drugs (Cloud, 2001; Prudic & Sackheim, 1999; Sylvester et al., 2000).

The most extreme, and least used, biomedical therapy is **psychosurgery**, brain surgery to reduce psychological symptoms. (It is important to note that psychosurgery is *not* the same as brain surgery used to remove physical problems, such as a tumor or blood clot.) Attempts to change disturbed thinking and behavior by altering the brain have a long history. In Roman times, for example, it was believed that a sword wound to the head could relieve insanity. In 1936, a Portuguese neurologist, Egaz Moniz, treated uncontrollable psychotics by cutting the nerve fibers between the frontal lobes (where association areas for monitoring and planning behavior are found) and the thalamus and hypothalamus. Severing these connections decreases emotional response and the patient accepts frustrating circumstances with a "philosophical calm." Moniz was awarded the Nobel Prize in medicine in 1949 for developing this technique, called a **lobotomy** (Pressman, 1998; Valenstein, 1998).

In the mid-1950s, when antipsychotic drugs came into use, psychosurgery virtually stopped. Recently, however, psychiatrists have been experimenting with a much more limited surgical procedure, called *cingulotomy*, where small, specific target areas are destroyed. On rare occasions, it is used in the treatment of severely debilitating cases of obsessive-compulsive disorder (OCD), depression, and anxiety (Da Costa, 1997; Fenton, 1998).

Evaluating Biomedical Therapies

Like all forms of therapy, the biomedical therapies have both proponents and critics. We will summarize the research in this area:

1. Drug therapies. There are several potential problems with drug therapy. First, although drugs may provide relief of symptoms, they seldom provide "cures" or long-term solutions. Researchers also are still learning about the long-term effects and potential interactions. Furthermore, not all patients are helped by these drugs, and some show only modest improvement. Some patients also develop tolerance to the drugs and become physically dependent. Withdrawal symptoms (such as convulsions and hallucinations) can occur if they suddenly stop taking the drugs. Overdosing with psychotherapeutic drugs intentionally (to get a stronger effect) or unintentionally (by combining them with other drugs, such as alcohol) can be fatal.

Controlling negative side effects is also an important issue with drug therapy. For example, reactions to antipsychotic drugs range from reduced alertness and drowsiness to symptoms similar to Parkinson's disease, including muscle rigidity, tremors, and an unusual shuffling gate (Butler, Joel, & Jeffries, 2000; Drummond, 2000). Recall from Chapter 5 that Parkinson's disease is related to a deficit in dopamine, and that the drug L-dopa (levodopa) increases dopamine and reduces the symptoms of Parkinson's. Because antipsychotic drugs work by reducing excess dopamine, you can see how prolonged use could eventually produce Parkinson-like symptoms. Anti-parkinsonian medications can reduce the side effects of antipsychotic drugs, but they have their own side effects, and their use is controversial.

One of the most serious side effects of antipsychotic drugs is a movement disorder called *tardive dyskinesia*, which develops in 15 to 20 percent of the patients. The symptoms generally appear after prolonged use (hence the term *tardive*, from the Latin root for "slow"). They include involuntary movements of the trunk and limbs (*dyskinesia*, meaning "disorder of movement") that can be severely disabling. Perhaps more characteristic are the facial and tongue motor disturbances. When students see films about schizophrenia, they often confuse the patient's sucking and smacking of their lips or lateral jaw movements as signs of the disorder rather than signs of tardive dyskinesia.

Like antipsychotic medications, mood-stabilizer and antidepressant drugs also have major and minor side effects. Antidepressants may cause dry mouth, fatigue, sexual dysfunction, weight gain, and memory difficulties, whereas mood-stabilizer drugs, such as lithium, can impair memory and cause weight gain. In excessive dosages, lithium can be fatal. Thus, as with other drug therapies, it is important to carefully monitor dosage level and patient reactions (Butler, Joel, & Jeffries, 2000).

What about herbal remedies like St.-John's-wort to treat depression? Recent controlled studies of herbal treatments, such as St.-John's-wort, kava, ginkgo, and valerian, suggest they may be effective and may have fewer side effects than traditional prescription medications (Woelk, 2000). Although these drugs are considered "natural" and therefore "safe," they can produce a number of potentially serious side effects. The quality and amounts of active ingredients vary according to the manufacturer, and the U.S. Food and Drug Administration (US FDA) does not regulate them. For all these reasons, researchers advise a wait-and-see approach (Beaubrun & Gray, 2000).

Despite the problems associated with psychotherapeutic drugs, they have led to revolutionary changes in mental health. Before the use of drugs, some patients were destined for a lifetime in psychiatric institutions. Today, most improve enough to return to their homes if they continue to take their medication to prevent relapse (Conley, Love, Kelly, & Bartko, 1999).

In sum, medication is an effective and often the most appropriate treatment for many psychological disorders. However, the fact that it is also cost-effective and *generally* fast acting has led to its overuse in some cases. For example, one report found that antidepressants are now prescribed roughly 50 percent of the time a patient walks into a psychiatrist's office (Olfson et al., 1998). Although this reflects in part the increased efficacy of the new medications, it also reflects the economics of health care. Because a psychiatrist can see five or six medication patients in an hour, versus the one person per hour generally seen by a psychotherapist, there is considerable financial incentive to favor drugs over therapy. Yet, most studies that have compared medication alone versus medication plus therapy have found the combination more effective (e.g., Pollack, 2000).

2. *ECT and Psychosurgery.* After nearly half a century of use of ECT, we do not fully understand why an ECT-induced convulsion alleviates depression. Partly because we cannot explain how it works, but also because it seems barbaric, ECT is a controversial treatment (Baldwin & Oxlad, 2000; Cloud, 2001). Unlike ECT portrayals in movies like *One Flew Over the Cuckoo's Nest* and *The Snake Pit*, patients show few, if any, visible reactions to the treatment, owing to modern muscle-relaxant drugs, which dramatically reduce muscle contractions during the seizure. Although most ECT patients are given an anesthetic such as sodium pentothal to block their memory of the treatment, some patients report that they find the treatment extremely aversive (Johnstone, 1999). However, many others find it life-saving.

Problems with ECT may become obsolete thanks to a recently developed similar treatment known as *repetitive transcranial magnetic stimulation* (rTMS). Unlike ECT, which passes a strong electric current directly through the brain, rTMS delivers a brief but powerful electric current through a coil of wire placed on the head. The coil creates a strong magnetic field which is applied to certain areas in the brain. When used to treat depression, the coil is usually placed over the prefrontal cortex, a region linked to deeper parts of the brain that regulate mood. Treatment with rTMS appears to be almost as effective as ECT, but it has fewer side effects and does not require anesthesia (George et al., 2000; Klein et al. 1999).

Because all forms of psychosurgery have potentially serious or fatal side effects and complications, some critics suggest it should be banned altogether. Furthermore, the consequences are irreversible. For these reasons, psychosurgery is considered experimental and remains a highly controversial treatment.

We now turn our attention to those forms of therapy most commonly conducted by psychologists — *psychotherapy.*

Check & Review

BIOMEDICAL THERAPIES

Biomedical therapies use biological techniques to relieve psychological disorders. **Drug therapy** is the most common form by far. **Antianxiety drugs** (Valium, Xanax) are used to treat anxiety disorders, **antipsychotic drugs** (Haldol, Navane) treat the symptoms of schizophrenia, **antidepressants** (Prozac, Zoloft) treat depression, and mood stabilizers (lithium) can stabilize bipolar disorders. Although drug therapy has been responsible for major improvements in many disorders, there are also problems with dosage levels, side effects, and patient cooperation.

Electroconvulsive therapy (ECT) is used primarily to relieve serious depression when medication has not worked, but it is risky and considered a treatment of last resort. **Psychosurgeries**, such as a **lobotomy**, have been used in the past but are rarely used today.

Questions

1. The dramatic reduction in numbers of hospitalized patients today, as compared with past decades, is primarily attributable to _____. (a) biomedical therapy; (b) psychoanalysis; (c) psychosurgery; (d) drug therapy

2. What are the four major categories of psychiatric drugs?

3. The effectiveness of antipsychotic drugs is thought to result primarily from blockage of _____ receptors. (a) serotonin; (b) dopamine; (c) acetycholine; (d) epinephrine

4. ECT is used primarily to treat _____. (a) phobias; (b) conduct disorders; (c) depression; (d) schizophrenia

Answers to Questions can be found in Appendix B.

PSYCHOTHERAPY

What do you think of when you hear the word *therapy*? When we ask our students this question, they usually describe a small, cluttered office with a sofa where patients recline and tell their secrets to a male therapist with a beard. Does this description match the one in your own mind? If so, it's probably due once again to Hollywood films. In most films, "therapy" is biomedical (drugs, ECT, and psychosurgery). When they do portray "talk therapy," they focus almost exclusively on a Freudian model, with a bearded therapist listening to a patient reclining on a couch (Figure 15.3). This stereotype has little to do with the realities of modern therapy, however. We begin our discussion of "real" therapy with traditional psychoanalysis (which does use a couch) and its modern counterpart, psychodynamic therapy. Then we explore cognitive, humanistic, and behavior therapies. We conclude with a look at group and family therapies.

Psychoanalysis/Psychodynamic Therapies: A Focus on the Unconscious

Why do psychoanalysts use couches in their form of therapy? Freud believed that the unconscious was more accessible when the patient reclined on a couch with only the ceiling to look at. He also felt the therapist should sit out of sight behind the patient. Freud wanted his patients to feel relaxed and nondefensive, almost as if they were talking to themselves rather than revealing information to another person. Traditional psychoanalysts still use a couch, but most modern forms of psychoanalysis do not.

The use of a couch is only one aspect of Freud's original therapy. Why not relax and recline on your own couch for the moment, and we'll describe the major goals and methods of psychoanalysis.

What is Freudian psychoanalysis? Are there more modern forms of this therapy?

Figure 15.3 *Stereotypes of therapy.* Movies often portray a simplistic view of Freudian style therapy. The patient reclines on a sofa and complains to a therapist who offers little or no direct intervention. In Antz, for example, the main character (Woody Allen) presents a lengthy, whining complaint about his boring ant life, while reclining on a sofa made of leaves. Can you see how these repeated, stereotypical portrayals could prejudice people against seeking therapy in real life? Unlike movie portrayals of therapy, most therapists conduct their sessions with both the therapist and client seated upright in chairs and facing one another, as you can see in the photo on the right.

Judging Effectiveness

Scientifically evaluating the effectiveness of therapy can be tricky. How can you trust the perception and self-report of clients or clinicians? Both have biases and a need to justify the time, effort, and expense of therapy.

To avoid these problems, psychologists use controlled research studies. Clients are randomly assigned to different forms of therapy or to control groups who receive no treatment. After therapy, clients are independently evaluated, and reports from friends and family members are collected. Until recently, these studies were simply compared. But with a new statistical technique called *meta-analysis*, years of such studies and similar research can be averaged together to produce a comprehensive report.

The good news, for both consumers and therapists, is that after years of controlled research and meta-analysis we have fairly clear evidence that therapy does work! Forty to 90 percent of people who receive treatment are better off than people who do not, and short-term treatments can be as effective as long-term (Kopta, Lueger, Saunders, & Howard, 1999; Kotkin, Daviet, & Gurin, 1996; Sanderson, 1995). Some therapies are more effective than others for specific problems. For example, phobias seem to respond best to systematic desensitization, and OCD can be significantly relieved with cognitive-behavior therapy accompanied by medication (see Seligman, 1994, for a review).

Control groups and random assignment are the standard scientific approach to measuring the effectiveness of therapy. However, a large-scale survey conducted by the popular magazine *Consumer Reports* (1995, November) may have added a new yardstick for measuring effectiveness. During its annual questionnaire on appliances and services, the magazine asked its 180,000 readers to fill out a separate mental health section if they had sought help (from friends, relatives, family doctor, clergy, support groups, or mental health professionals) in the previous 3 years. Approximately 7,000 of the respondents answered the mental health questions.

The *Consumer Reports* survey is important for at least two reasons: First, it provides interesting contradictions to the controlled studies research mentioned previously. For instance, the magazine study reported that no specific type of therapy, and therapy combined with medication, did better than any other for any disorder, and long-term therapy produced more improvement than did short-term treatments (Figure 15.7). Second, the study offers a legitimate research alternative. Surveys have certainly been done before now, but the *Consumer Reports* study had an unusually large sample and was developed in consultation with mental health experts.

As expected, the *Consumer Reports* study has been scientifically criticized for its lack of control groups, random assignment, and so on (e.g., Brock, Green, & Reich, 1998). In a type of catch-22, controlled studies are also questioned because they *do* have a control group. Is it ethical to assign troubled people to control groups in which they will receive either no treatment or restricted treatment?

Perhaps the most important finding of both the *Consumer Reports* study and previous controlled studies is that therapy does work. Most people get a lot better. Given that you might currently or someday be interested in therapy, this should be reassuring. A final helpful note from the *Consumer Reports* study is that active clients did better in treatment than passive recipients (Seligman, 1995). It was their idea to seek treatment, they checked around for therapists, they asked questions of the therapist, and they tried to be as open and cooperative as possible during therapy — doing their homework, keeping appointments, and asking for explanations and clarification.

Finding a Therapist

If you have time (and the money) to explore options, it is important to "shop around" for a therapist best suited to your specific goals. Consulting your psychology instruc-

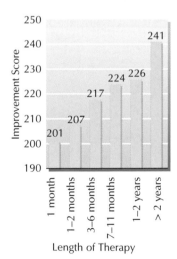

Figure 15.7 *Duration of therapy.* In its 1995 annual survey, *Consumer Reports* magazine included a mental health section for the first time. According to the 7,000 respondents, long-term therapy (more than 2 years) is most effective. Effectiveness was based on (1) specific improvement (i.e., how much treatment helped with the problems that led to therapy), (2) satisfaction with the therapist, and (3) global improvement (i.e., how respondents felt at the time of the survey compared to when they began treatment).

tor or college counseling system for referrals can be an important first step. However, if you are in a crisis — suicidal thoughts, failing grades, or the victim of abuse — get help fast (Beutler, Shurkin, Bongar, & Gray, 2000; First, Pincus, Frances, 1999). Most communities have telephone hotlines that provide counseling on a 24-hour basis, and most colleges and universities have counseling centers that provide immediate, short-term therapy to students free of charge.

If you are encouraging someone to get therapy, you might offer to help locate a therapist and to go with them for their first visit. If he or she refuses help and the problem affects you, it is often a good idea to seek therapy yourself. You will gain insights and skills that will help you deal with the situation more effectively.

RESEARCH HIGHLIGHT

Therapy in the Electronic Age

I never think of the future. It comes soon enough.

Albert Einstein

As we've just seen in the previous section, research psychologists and therapists have been hard at work evaluating and improving current forms of traditional therapy, and, like Einstein, they may not have thought much about the future. But like it or not, the electronic age has arrived.

Today millions of people seek advice and "therapy" from radio call-in programs, telephone services with 900 numbers, and, now, websites for online therapy. The newest mental health therapy, called telehealth, has approximately 200 websites and between 350 and 1,000 online counselors offering counseling, group support chats, e-mail correspondence, private instant messages, and videoconferencing therapy (Davison, Pennebaker, & Dickerson, 2000; Kicklighter, 2000; Segal, 2000). These on-line counselors are psychologists, psychiatrists, social workers, licensed counselors, nonlicensed "helpers," and outright "quacks." Together, they treat an estimated 10,000 clients each week (Kicklighter, 2000).

As you might expect, many qualified therapists and academic institutions are concerned about this new form of therapy. They fear, among other things, that without

a governing body to regulate this type of therapy, there are no checks and balances to protect the client from unethical and unsavory practices. However, many of these concerns were recently addressed by the formulation of 10 Interdisciplinary Principles for Professional Practice in Telehealth. According to these principles, psychologists would be required to follow the basic ethical policies of confidentiality, informed consent, and integrity as prescribed by the APA (American Psychological Association) Ethics Code (Reed, McLaughlin, & Milholland, 2000). Questions remain regarding interstate and international licensing conflicts for psychologists and the lack of consumer protection against those practicing without any license at all.

Why Would Anyone Want to Use an Online Counselor?

The Internet and other electronic forms of therapy may sometimes be more effective than traditional therapy. For example, Enid M. Hunkeler and her colleagues (2000) found that depressed patients who received standard care as well as weekly phone calls from health professionals were significantly more likely to show improvement in their depressive symptoms than were patients who did not receive such calls. In another study, Andrew Winzelberg and his colleagues (2000) evaluated an Internet-based program designed for college students with eating disorders and found a significant improvement in body

image and a decrease in drive for thinness.

Studies have long shown that success rates for both physical and mental health are improved with increased contact between patients and their health care providers. Electronic forms of therapy may be the easiest and most cost-effective way of increasing this contact (Schopp, Johnstone, & Merrell, 2000). Online clients appreciate having increased access to their therapist, especially during times of crisis. Clients also tend to feel safer discussing sensitive topics in the privacy of their own homes.

On the other hand, critics claim that online therapy is a contradiction in terms — an oxymoron. They say psychotherapy is based on both verbal and nonverbal communication, and it's impossible for online therapists to adequately give therapeutic advice to clients without face-to-face contact. Others are concerned about sending private and confidential thoughts into unsecured cyberspace to a person who may not be a qualified therapist (e.g., Bloom, 1998). David Nickelson, director of technology policy and projects for the American Psychological Association (APA), advises people to first seek face-to-face therapy. "We still need research," Nickelson says, "and it may find that there are just some things therapists and their patients can't do over the Internet" (http://www.apa.org/practice/pf/aug97/tele-heal.html).

Visual Summary for Chapter 15 ••••

Major Forms of Psychotherapy

- **Psychotherapy:** Various approaches to improving psychological functioning and promoting adjustment to life.
- **Therapy essentials:** Five basic areas of disturbance -thoughts, emotions, behaviors, interpersonal and life situations, and biomedical.
- **Eclectic approach:** Borrows from all forms of therapy.

Description/ Major Goals	Techniques/Methods	Evaluation/Criticisms
Biomedical therapies: Use biological techniques to relieve psychological disorders.	**Drug therapy** is most common biomedical treatment. • **Antianxiety drugs** (Valium, Xanax) are used to treat anxiety disorders. • **Antipsychotic drugs** (Haldol, Navane) relieve symptoms of schizophrenia. • **Antidepressants** (Zoloft, Prozac) used to treat depression. • **Mood stabilizers** (lithium) help stabilize bipolar disorders. **Electroconvulsive therapy (ECT)** used primarily to relieve serious depression, when medication fails. **Psychosurgeries,** such as a **lobotomy,** are seldom used today.	• Drug therapy improves many disorders, but dosage levels, patient cooperation, and side effects, like tardive dyskinesia (a serious motor disturbance) are serious problems. • ECT and psychosurgery have been successful in treating certain disorders, but they're risky and considered a last resort.
Psychoanalysis/ psychodynamic therapies: Bring unconscious conflicts into conscious awareness.	Five major techniques: **Free association, dream analysis, resistance, transference,** and **interpretation.**	• Limited availability, time-consuming, expensive, unsuitable for many, and lack of scientific credibility. • Modern psychodynamic therapies overcome some of these limits.
Cognitive therapies: Analyze faulty thought processes, beliefs, and negative **self-talk,** and change these destructive thoughts with **cognitive restructuring.**	Ellis's **rational-emotive therapy (RET)** replaces irrational beliefs with rational beliefs and accurate perceptions of the world. Beck's **cognitive-behavior therapy** emphasizes change is necessary in both thought processes and behavior.	• Ellis has had success with a variety of disorders. Beck's procedures are particularly effective for relieving depression. • Criticized for ignoring unconscious processes and client's history, and success may be due to behavioral techniques.
Humanistic therapies: Work to facilitate personal growth.	Rogers' **client-centered therapy** offers **empathy, unconditional positive regard, genuineness,** and **active listening** to facilitate personal growth.	Difficult to evaluate scientifically, and research has had mixed results.

Major Forms of Psychotherapy (cont).

Description/Major Goals	Techniques/Methods	Evaluation/Criticisms
Behavior therapies: Use learning principles to eliminate maladaptive behaviors and substitute healthy ones.	Classical conditioning techniques include **systematic desensitization** (client replaces anxiety with relaxation) and **aversion therapy** (an aversive stimulus is paired with a maladaptive behavior). Operant conditioning techniques include shaping, reinforcement, punishment, extinction, and **modeling therapy** (clients watch and imitate positive role models).	• Behavior therapies are successful with a number of psychological disorders. • Criticized for lack of generalizability, symptom substitution, and questionable ethics of controlling behavior.
Group therapies: Several clients meet with one or more therapists to resolve personal problems.	Provide group support, feedback, information, and opportunities for behavior rehearsal. **Self-help groups** (like Alcoholics Anonymous) are sometimes considered group therapy, but professional therapists do not conduct them.	Less expensive and more available than individual therapy.
Family therapies: Work to change maladaptive family interaction patterns.	Sees family as a system of interdependent parts, therefore treats all members.	Less expensive and more available than individual therapy.

Issues in Therapy

Institutionalization

- People believed to be mentally ill and dangerous to themselves or others can be involuntarily committed to mental hospitals for diagnosis and treatment.
- Abuses of involuntary commitments and other problems led to **deinstitutionalization** — discharging as many patients as possible and discouraging admissions.
- Community services such as Community Mental Health (CMH) centers offset some problems of deinstitutionalization.

Seeking Therapy	Cultural Issues	Gender Issues
• Forty to 80 percent of those who receive treatment are better off than those who do not. • Take time to "shop around," but a crisis requires immediate help. • If others' problems affect you, get help yourself.	• Common features of therapy in all cultures: naming a problem, qualities of the therapist, establishing credibility, placing the problems in a familiar framework, applying techniques to bring relief, and a special time and place. • Differences in therapy between cultures: Individualistic cultures emphasize the "self" and control over one's life. Therapies in collectivist cultures, like Japan's Naikan therapy, emphasize interdependence.	Higher rate of diagnosis and treatment of mental disorders, stresses of poverty, stresses of multiple roles, stresses of aging, and violence against women.

16 Social Psychology

Imagine you are one of several people responding to this ad. As you arrive at the Yale University laboratory, you are introduced to the experimenter and another participant in the study. The experimenter explains he is studying the effects of punishment on learning and memory. One of you will play the role of the learner and the other will be the teacher. You draw lots, and on your paper is written teacher. The experimenter leads you into a room where he straps the other participant — the "learner" — into an "electric chair" apparatus that looks escape-proof. The experimenter then applies electrode paste to the learner's wrist "to avoid blisters and burns" and attaches an electrode that is connected to a shock generator.

You, the "teacher," are shown into an adjacent room and asked to sit in front of this same shock generator, which is wired through the wall to the chair of the learner. As you can see in Figure 16.1, the shock machine consists of 30 switches representing successively higher levels of shock in 15-volt increments. Written labels appear below each group of levers, ranging from Slight Shock to Danger: Severe Shock, all the way to XXX. The experimenter explains it is your job to teach the learner a list of word pairs and to punish any errors by administering a shock. With each wrong answer, you are to give a shock one level higher on the shock generator. For example, at the first wrong response, you give a shock of 15 volts; at the second wrong response, 30 volts; and so on.

As the study begins, the learner seems to be having problems with the task. The responses are often wrong. Before long, you are inflicting shocks that must be extremely painful. Indeed, after you administer 150 volts, the learner begins to protest and demands, "Get me out of here. . . . I refuse to go on."

You hesitate and wonder what to do. The experimenter asks you to continue. He insists that even if the learner refuses, you must keep increasing the shock levels. But the other person is obviously in pain. What should you do?

Actual participants in this series of studies suffered real conflict and distress when confronted with this problem. The following dialogue took place between the experimenter and one of the teachers (Milgram, 1974, pp. 73–74):

TEACHER: I can't stand it. I'm not going to kill that man in there. You hear him hollering?

EXPERIMENTER: As I told you before, the shocks may be painful, but [there is no permanent tissue damage].

LEARNER (screaming): Let me out of here, you have no right to keep me here. Let me out of here, let me out, my heart's starting to bother me, let me out! (Teacher shakes head, pats the table nervously.)

TEACHER: You see, he's hollering. Hear that? Gee, I don't know.

EXPERIMENTER: The experiment requires…

TEACHER (interrupting): I know it does, sir, but I mean — huh! He don't know what he's getting in for. He's up to 195 volts!

(Following this exchange, the teacher continues through 210 volts, 225 volts, 240 volts, 255 volts, and 270 volts, at which point the teacher, with evident relief, runs out of word-pair questions.)

EXPERIMENTER: You'll have to go back to the beginning of that page and go through them again until he's learned them all correctly.

TEACHER: Aw, no, I'm not going to kill that man. You mean I've got to keep going up with the scale? No, sir. He's hollering in there. I'm not going to give him 450 volts.

Figure 16.1 *Milgram's shock generator.* Research participants were told to give increasing levels of shocks to someone they had watched being strapped down and connected to this machine. Note how the shock levels are clearly labeled, starting with *Slight Shock,* moving to *Very Strong Shock, Danger: Severe Shock,* and ultimately, *XXX.* How would you respond? Would you refuse from the beginning, or would you stop after a few shocks and complaints from the recipient? Would you go all the way to 450 volts?

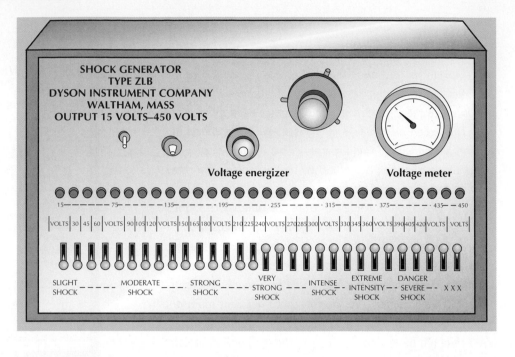

What do you think happened? Did the man continue? This particular teacher continued giving shocks — in spite of the learner's strong protests. He even continued after the learner refused to give any more answers.

As you might have guessed, this was not a study of punishment and learning. The psychologist who designed the study, Stanley Milgram, was actually investigating *obedience to authority.* Would participants see the experimenter as an authority figure and obey his prompts and commands to shock another human being?

Would you, or others you know, have followed the experimenter's demands in this same situation? In Milgram's public survey, less than 25 percent thought they would go beyond 150 volts. And not one respondent predicted they would go past the 300-volt level. Surprisingly, a full 65 *percent* of the teacher-participants obeyed completely — going all the way to the end of the scale. Even Milgram was surprised.

It is important to recognize that *no* participant-learner ever received an actual shock. The "learner" was an accomplice of the experimenter and simply *pretended* to be shocked. However, the "teachers" were true participants. They believed they were administering real shocks, and they sweated, trembled, stuttered, laughed nervously, and repeatedly protested that they did not want to hurt the learner. They were clearly upset. *But still they obeyed.*

Keep in mind that deception is an important part of some research projects, but Milgram's study could never be replicated today, owing to ethical concerns for the rights of participants. Although most participants *were* visibly upset by the experience, Milgram carefully debriefed everyone after the study and followed up with the participants for several months. Most "teachers" reported the experience as being personally informative and valuable.

Setting aside ethical concerns, one lasting benefit from Milgram's research might be its invaluable insight into human social behavior. Although many believe only "monsters" would have followed Hitler's commands to torture and kill millions of Jews during World War II, Milgram's research suggests otherwise. As philosopher Hannah Arendt has suggested, the horrifying, thing about the Nazis was not that they were so deviant but that they were so "terrifyingly normal."

Before we begin, test your understanding of social psychology and how it operates in everyday life by answering *true* or *false* to the following statements. Answers are at the end of this activity and expanded explanations are found throughout the chapter.

1. Groups generally make more conservative decisions than a single individual does.
2. Most people judge others more harshly than they judge themselves.
3. Looks are the primary factor in our initial feelings of attraction, liking, and romantic love.
4. Opposites attract.
5. Romantic love rarely lasts longer than 1 or 2 years.
6. The most effective way to change behavior is to first change the attitude.
7. Prejudice is the same as discrimination.
8. There are positive as well as negative forms of prejudice.
9. Watching a violent sports match or punching a pillow is a good way to release steam and reduce aggression.
10. People are more likely to help another individual when they are alone than when they are in a group.

Answers: 1. False 2. True 3. True 4. False 5. True 6. False 7. False 8. True 9. False 10. True

Our combination of confusion and fascination over social behaviors like those in Milgram's study is what draws many students and researchers to the field of **social psychology**. Social psychologists study how other people influence an individual's behavior (thoughts, feelings, and actions). They explore both the bizarre and the ordinary, from the mindless obedience of religious cults to prejudice, aggression, and attraction. Using the tools of science (experiments, surveys, case studies, self-report, and so on), they seek scientific answers to *social* questions.

Because almost everything we do is *social*, the subject matter is enormous and varied. We will therefore approach our study by looking at each component of the definition in turn. We begin by exploring topics related to *our thoughts about others* (attribution and attitudes). Next, we examine *our feelings toward others* by looking at prejudice, discrimination, and interpersonal attraction. (Prejudice and discrimination could also be discussed under thoughts or actions. But we consider it under feelings because negative emotions are the central defining characteristic of prejudice.) We conclude with a look at *our actions toward others* (social influence, group processes, aggression, and altruism).

Social Psychology *The branch of psychology that studies how other people influence an individual's behavior (thoughts, feelings, and actions)*

OUR THOUGHTS ABOUT OTHERS

How could a mother brutalize and torture her child? Why would someone run into a burning building to rescue a stranger? Why did Chris stop going out with me? Trying to understand the world around us often means trying to understand other people's behavior. We look for reasons and explanations for others' behavior (the process of attribution). We also develop thoughts and beliefs (attitudes) about others.

How do our thoughts affect how we explain and judge others?

Attribution: Explaining Other's Behavior

How do we explain people's obedience in Milgram's study? When we offer an explanation for behavior, we *attribute* it to something — "the participants were weak-

Social psychology in action. Can you imagine how Western television programs might affect the thoughts, feelings, and actions of these viewers?

Attribution *The principles people follow in making judgments about the causes of events, others' behavior, and their own behavior*

willed," "the experimenter was intimidating," and so on. Psychologists use the term **attribution** to describe statements explaining why people do what they do.

After studying how people explain others' behavior, Fritz Heider (1958) noted that most people begin with a basic question: Does the behavior stem mainly from internal *dispositions* or external *situations*? If you concluded that participants in Milgram's study acted because of their own personal characteristics, motives, and intentions, you would be making a *dispositional attribution*. On the other hand, if you decided they responded to situational demands and environmental pressures, you would be making a *situational attribution*.

The choice between disposition and situation is central to accurate judgments of why people do what they do. Unfortunately, our attributions are frequently marred by two major errors: the *fundamental attribution error* and the *self-serving bias*.

1. *The fundamental attribution error — judging the behavior of others.* When we recognize and take into account environmental influences on behavior, we generally make accurate attributions. However, given that people have enduring personality traits (Chapter 13) and a tendency to take cognitive shortcuts (Chapter 8), we more often choose dispositional attributions — we blame the person. This bias toward personal, dispositional factors rather than environmental factors is so common in individualistic cultures that it is called the **fundamental attribution error** (FAE) (Nisbett, Peng, Choi, & Norenzayan, 2000; Susskind, Maurer, Thakkar, Hamilton, & Sherman, 1999).

Fundamental attribution error (FAE) *Misjudging the causes of others' behavior because of overestimating internal personal factors and underestimating external situational influences*

Noting that your instructor seems relaxed and talkative in front of the class, you would probably decide that he or she is an extroverted and outgoing person — a *dispositional attribution*. However, outside of class you may be surprised to find him or her shy and awkward on a one-on-one basis or at a party. Similarly, most students think participants in the Milgram study were "weak-willed" and that they would never act like that in the same situation. They blame the person (dispositional attribution) and overlook and underestimate the power of the environment (situational attribution).

Why do we tend to jump to internal, personal explanations? There are several possible explanations for why we tend to make dispositional rather than situational attributions. The most important reason may be that human personalities and behaviors are more salient (or noticeable) than situational factors. This **saliency bias** helps explain why we focus on participants in Milgram's study versus the situation itself. It also explains why people often blame welfare recipients for their job-

Saliency Bias *The tendency to focus on the most noticeable (salient) factors when explaining the causes of behavior*

PEANUTS; drawings by Charles Schulz; 1989 United Features Syndicate, Inc. Reprinted by permission of UFS, Inc.

Psychology in action. Can you see why this is an example of both the fundamental attribution error and the self-serving bias?

lessness. This type of *blaming the victim* also reflects the fact that large situational factors leading to poverty and joblessness generally are not concrete and conspicuous.

2. The self-serving bias — judging our own behavior. When we judge others' behavior, we tend to emphasize internal personality factors over external situational causes. But when we explain our own behavior, we favor internal personal attributions for our *successes* and external environmental attributions for our *failures*. This **self-serving bias** is motivated by a desire to maintain our self-esteem, as well as a desire to look good to others (Campbell & Sedikides, 1999; Higgins & Bhatt, 2001; Louie, Curren, & Harich, 2000).

Students who do well on an exam, for instance, often take personal credit ("I really studied" or "I'm smart"). If they fail the test, however, they tend to blame the instructor, the textbook, or the "tricky" questions. Similarly, studies find both partners in divorced couples are more likely to see themselves as the victim, to rate

Self-Serving Bias *A way of maintaining a positive self-image by taking credit for one's successes and emphasizing external causes for one's failures*

TRY THIS
Yourself

One of the five individuals pictured below is a murderer who killed two people with a pickaxe, one is a rapist and serial killer, and another is an author of this text. Can you tell who is which? If you're in your critical thinking mode right now, you might be resisting this obvious setup and would argue that you can't make such judgments solely on the basis of appearance. However,

research shows that we often do make such snap decisions about people — and that when we do, we rely on individual attitudes that reflect our specific life experiences and personal stereotypes (Stewart, Doan, Gingrich, & Smith, 1998). (If you want to check your guesses regarding the five photos, the answers are provided at the top of the following page).

Are you a good judge of character and personality? Which of these five individuals is a vicious serial killer, a murderer who died by lethal injection, or an author of this text? The answers appear on the following page.

themselves less responsible for the breakup, and as being more willing to reconcile (Gray & Silver, 1990).

Culture and Attributional Biases

Both the FAE and the self-serving bias may depend in part on cultural factors (Matsumoto, 2000). In most Western nations, people are more likely to make the FAE because of the cultural belief that individuals are responsible for their own actions. The FAE is much harder to demonstrate with Asian populations. In most Eastern countries, people are more group oriented and tend to be more aware of situational constraints on behavior (Nisbett, Peng, Choi, & Norenzayan, 2000; Norenzayan & Nisbett, 2000). If you were watching a baseball game in China and the umpire made a bad call, as a Westerner you would probably make a personality attribution ("He's a lousy umpire"), whereas a Chinese spectator would tend to make a situational attribution ("He's under pressure").

Like the FAE, the self-serving bias is also much less common in Eastern nations, where people do not define themselves as much in terms of their individual accomplishments. Self-esteem is not related to doing better than others. Rather, fitting in and not standing out from the group is stressed. As the Japanese proverb says, "The nail that sticks up gets pounded down."

This emphasis on group relations in Asian cultures is also true of many Native Americans in North America. For example, when the Wintun Native Americans originally described being with a close relation or intimate friend, they would not say, for example, "Linda and I," but rather, "Linda we" (Lee, 1950). This importance attached to community relations instead of individual *selfhood* often seems strange to contemporary Western, individualist societies. But it remains common in collectivist cultures (Markus & Kitayama, 1998).

Attitudes: Our Learned Predisposition Toward Others

Attitude *A learned predisposition to respond cognitively, affectively, and behaviorally to a particular object*

An **attitude** is a learned predisposition to respond cognitively, affectively, and behaviorally to a particular object in a particular way. The object can be anything from pizza to people, from diseases to drugs, from abortion to psychology.

Components of Attitudes

Social psychologists generally agree that an attitude has three components (Figure 16.2): cognitive, affective, and behavioral. The *cognitive component* consists of thoughts and beliefs, such as "Marijuana is a relatively safe drug" or "The dangers

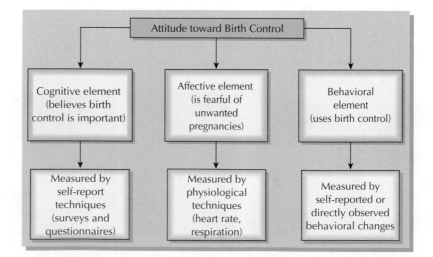

Figure 16.2 *Three components of all attitudes.* When social psychologists study attitudes, they measure each of the three components — cognitive, affective, and behavioral.

of marijuana are greatly underestimated." The *affective*, or *emotional*, *component* involves feelings, such as frustration that our legal system has not legalized marijuana yet or, conversely, that it seems to even consider legalization.

The *behavioral component* consists of a *predisposition* to act in certain ways toward an attitude object. For example, someone who held a positive attitude toward marijuana might write to textbook authors and publishers complaining that we are too critical in our discussion of drugs in Chapter 5. Someone with a negative attitude, on the other hand, might write to complain that even the use of marijuana as an example could encourage its use. (Yes, we are speaking from experience. People do write just this type of letter, and we are glad to get the feedback.)

Attitude Change Through Cognitive Dissonance

You are not born with your attitudes — they are learned. From earliest childhood, you began forming your attitudes through direct experience (eating pizza) and through indirect observation (listening to your parents discuss social issues). Although attitudes begin in early childhood, they are not permanent. Politicians spend millions of dollars on campaigns because they know attitudes can be shaped and manipulated throughout the entire life span.

Although attitude change often involves deliberate efforts at persuasion, one of the most efficient methods is brought about by cognitive dissonance, a perceived discrepancy between an attitude and a behavior or between an attitude and a new piece of information (Albarracin & Wyer, 2000; Cook, 2000; Harmon-Jones, 2000; Shultz, Leveille, & Lepper, 1999). According to Leon Festinger (1957), who developed **cognitive dissonance theory**, this discrepancy leads to a state of psychological tension similar to anxiety. The tension, in turn, motivates the individual to change the attitude, the behavior, or the perception of the inconsistent information to eliminate the discrepancy and the accompanying tension (Figure 16.3).

Picture yourself in this situation. You, as an individual who strongly objects to racist and sexist remarks, must give a speech in favor of the Ku Klux Klan (KKK). How do you think this would affect your attitudes? Do you think you would feel more or less favorable toward the KKK afterward?

This is the type of question that led to a classic experiment conducted by Leon Festinger and J. Merrill Carlsmith (1959). Students selected as participants were given excruciatingly boring tasks for an hour. The experimenters told them that the aim of this procedure was to test their performance, but the actual purpose was to create a negative attitude toward the task. After finishing the task, participants were approached by the experimenter and asked for a favor. The experimenter asked if they would serve as research assistants and tell the next "participant" (who was really a confederate of the experiment) that the task was "very enjoyable" and "fun." Sometimes the person was offered $1 for helping and sometimes $20. After the person lied to the incoming participant and was paid, he or she was led to another room and asked about his or her true feelings toward the experimental tasks.

Cognitive dissonance and the military. *The more grueling and difficult the initiation or training, the more these recruits will come to like and appreciate the military life. Can you explain this according to cognitive dissonance theory?*

Cognitive Dissonance Theory
Leon Festinger's theory that tension results whenever people discover inconsistencies between their attitudes or between their attitudes and their behaviors; this tension drives people to make attitudinal changes that will restore harmony or consistency

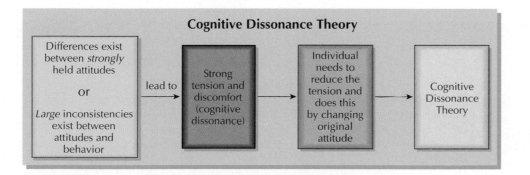

Cognitive Dissonance Theory

Differences exist between *strongly* held attitudes

or

Large inconsistencies exist between attitudes and behavior

→ lead to →

Strong tension and discomfort (cognitive dissonance)

→

Individual needs to reduce the tension and does this by changing original attitude

→

Cognitive Dissonance Theory

Figure 16.3 *Cognitive dissonance theory.* When differences exist between our strongly held attitudes, or when there are large inconsistencies between our attitudes and behavior, we experience discomfort (*dissonance*) and a need to change either the attitude or behavior.

What happens when someone is coaxed into doing something (lying) that is inconsistent with his or her actual experience and attitude? You might expect that people who received $20 for lying would feel more positive toward the task than would those paid $1. In fact, just the reverse occurred.

Can you explain this? Cognitive dissonance theory is essentially a *drive-reduction theory* (Chapter 12), where an attitude change is reinforced by reduction of an uncomfortable emotional state (a drive). People have a strong need to feel that their attitudes are in sync with one another and that their attitudes and behavior are consistent. When this harmony is disrupted, people feel distressed. Festinger believed that this distress (*dissonance*), like the feeling of hunger, is unpleasant and that people are strongly motivated to reduce or eliminate it. To relieve the distress and restore balance, we must change either our attitude or behavior.

In the boring task experiment, participants faced a mismatch between their attitude toward the experiment ("That was boring") and their behavior ("I told another participant it was interesting"). To relieve the resulting tension, they changed their original attitude from boredom to "I enjoyed the task."

The reason that the "$1 participants" showed more attitude change was because they experienced a greater amount of cognitive dissonance than did the "$20 participants." Participants who received only $1 either had to change their attitude toward the task or acknowledge they had lied rather cheaply. Because they could not deny they had lied, they changed their attitude.

In contrast, participants who were paid $20 did not need to change their attitude as much because they could readily explain their behavior in terms of the payment ($20 was a considerable amount in the late 1950s). Being paid well for their actions helped relieve the logical inconsistency (the cognitive dissonance) between what they truly believed about the boring task and what they told others. In contrast, the participants who received $1 had *insufficient justification* for lying to another participant and had more motivation to change their attitude to "The task wasn't so boring after all."

Culture and Dissonance

The experience of cognitive dissonance may not be the same in other cultures. It may presume a particular way of thinking about and evaluating the self that is distinctively Western. As noted in earlier chapters, North Americans are highly individualistic and independent. Making a bad choice or decision has strong, negative effects on self-esteem and a greater motivation for attitude change.

Asians, on the other hand, tend to be much more collectivist and interdependent. Consequently, they feel more tension over a potential loss of connection with others than with a threat to their individual self-esteem. Research comparing Japanese and other Asian samples with Canadian and U.S. participants supports this position (Choi & Nisbett, 2000; Markus & Kitayama, 1998).

Check & Review

OUR THOUGHTS ABOUT OTHERS

We explain people's behavior (make **attributions**) by determining whether their actions resulted from internal factors (their own traits and motives) or external factors (the situation). Attribution is subject to several forms of error and bias. **Fundamental attribution error** is the tendency to overestimate internal personality influences when judging the behavior of others. When we explain our own behavior, however, we tend to attribute positive outcomes to internal factors and negative outcomes to external causes (**self-serving bias**).

Attitudes are learned predispositions toward a particular object. Three components of all attitudes are the cognitive responses (thoughts and beliefs), affective responses (feelings), and behavioral tendencies (predispositions to actions). We sometimes change our attitudes because of **cognitive dissonance**, a state of tension or anxiety we feel when two or more attitudes contradict each other or when our attitudes do not match our behaviors. This mismatch and resulting tension motivate us to change our attitude to restore balance.

Questions

1. The principles people follow in making judgments about the causes of events, others' behavior, and their own behavior are known as _____. (a) impression management; (b) stereotaxic determination; (c) attribution; (d) person perception
2. What is the fundamental attribution error?
3. After hearing about the "shocking" behavior of participants in Stanley Milgram's experiment, most people strongly believe they would have acted differently and easily remember instances in which they have refused to obey others. This may be an example of _____. (a) cognitive dissonance; (b) groupthink; (c) the illusion of invulnerability; (d) the self-serving bias
4. According to _____ theory, people are motivated to change their attitudes because of tension created by a mismatch between two or more competing attitudes or between their attitudes and behavior.

Answers to Questions can be found in Appendix B.

OUR FEELINGS ABOUT OTHERS

Having explored our thoughts about others (attribution and attitudes), we now turn our attention to our feelings about others. We begin by examining the negative feelings (and thoughts and actions) associated with *prejudice* and *discrimination*. We will then explore the generally positive feelings of *interpersonal attraction*.

> What feelings are most important in our social interactions?

Prejudice and Discrimination: It's the Feeling That Counts

Prejudice, which literally means *prejudgment*, is a generally *negative* attitude directed toward specific people solely because of their membership in an identified group. Positive forms of prejudice do exist, such as "all women love babies" or "African Americans are natural athletes."

However, most research and definitions of prejudice usually focus on the negative forms. (It is also interesting to note that even positive forms of prejudice harm the victims. For example, women might think there must be something wrong with them if they don't like being around babies, or African Americans might see athletics as their major way to achieve success.)

Prejudice is prejudgment of others on the basis of limited knowledge and limited contact. It biases us against others and limits our ability to accurately process information. Like all attitudes, prejudice is composed of three elements: (1) a *cognitive component* or **stereotype**, thoughts and beliefs held about people strictly because of their membership in a group; (2) an *affective component*, consisting of feelings and emotions associated with objects of prejudice; and (3) a *behavioral component*, consisting of predispositions to act in certain ways toward members of the group (discrimination).

Although the terms *prejudice* and *discrimination* are often used interchangeably, there is an important difference between them. *Prejudice* refers to an *attitude*, whereas **discrimination** refers to a *behavior* (Fiske, 1998). Discrimination often results from prejudice, but not always (Figure 16.4). People do not always act on their prejudices.

Major Sources of Prejudice and Discrimination

How do prejudice and discrimination originate? Why do they persist? As we explore these questions, you may find your values and beliefs challenged. Use this opportu-

Prejudice *A generally negative attitude directed toward others because of their membership in a specific group; like all attitudes, prejudice involves cognitions (thoughts), affect (feelings), and behavioral tendencies*

Stereotype *A set of beliefs about the characteristics of people in a group that is generalized to all group members; also, the cognitive component of prejudice*

Discrimination *Negative behaviors directed at members of a group*

Figure 16.4 *Prejudice and discrimination.* Note how prejudice can exist without discrimination and vice versa. The only condition in this example without prejudice or discrimination is where someone is given a job simply because he or she is the best candidate.

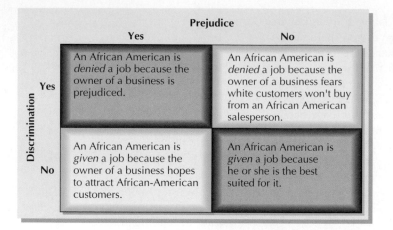

nity to apply your highest critical thinking skills to evaluate your attitudes. We begin with a look at the four most commonly cited sources of prejudice: learning, cognitive processes, economic and political competition, and displaced aggression.

1. *Learning* People learn prejudice in the same ways they learn their attitudes toward abortion, divorce, or pizza — through classical and operant conditioning and social learning (Chapter 6). When children watch TV and movies and read books and magazines that portray minorities and women in demeaning and stereotypical roles, they learn that such images must be acceptable. When children hear their parents, friends, and teachers expressing prejudice, they imitate them. Exposure of this kind initiates and reinforces the learning of prejudice (Dovidio, Brigham, Johnson, & Gaertner, 1995).

People also learn their prejudices through direct experience. They derogate others and experience a rise in their own self-esteem (Fein & Spencer, 1997). They receive attention and sometimes approval for expressing racist or sexist remarks. Also, they may have a single negative experience with a specific member of a group that they then generalize and apply to all members of the group (Vidmar, 1997).

2. *Cognitive processes.* According to some researchers, prejudice develops as a result of normal cognitive processes and everyday attempts to explain a complex social world (Devine & Monteith, 1999; Sherman & Bessenoff, 1999). Stereotypes (the cognitive component of prejudice) are a byproduct of how we cognitively simplify the world through categorization. Stereotyping allows people to make quick judgments about others, thus freeing their mental resources for other activities.

Just as a biologist classifies all living things into categories and mental health professionals classify mental disorders in the *DSM-IV-TR* (*Diagnostic and Statistical Manual of Mental Disorders,* fourth edition, revised; see Chapter 14), people use stereotypes to classify others by membership in a specific group ("jocks," "Mexicans," "chicks," and so on). Given that people generally classify themselves as part of the preferred group, they also create ingroups and outgroups.

An *ingroup* is any category that people see themselves belonging to, whereas an *outgroup* consists of all others. People tend to see ingroup members as being more attractive, having better personalities, and engaging in more socially accepted forms of behavior than outgroup members. In other words, cognitively, they practice **ingroup favoritism** (Mohr & Larsen, 1998; Perreault & Bourhis, 1999).

In addition to ingroup favoritism, people also tend to see more diversity among members of their own ingroup and less among the outgroup (Bartsch, Judd, Louw, Park, & Ryan, 1997; Hilton & Von Hippel, 1996). This "they all look alike to me" tendency is termed the **outgroup homogeneity effect**.

Ingroup Favoritism *A cognitive process in prejudice whereby members of an ingroup are viewed in more favorable terms than members of an outgroup*

Outgroup Homogeneity Effect *A cognitive process in prejudice whereby members of the outgroup are judged as less individual, or diverse, than members of the ingroup*

This outgroup homogeneity bias can be particularly dangerous. When members of minority groups are not perceived as varied and complex individuals who have the same needs and feelings as the dominant group, it is easier to perceive them as faceless objects and treat them in discriminatory ways. During the Vietnam War, for example, Asians were labeled "gooks" for whom "life is cheap." Facelessness made it easier to kill large numbers of Vietnamese civilians (Johnson, 1999).

3. *Economic and political competition* Still other theorists think prejudice develops out of competition for limited resources and is maintained because it offers significant economic and political advantages to the dominant group (Hughes & Dodge, 1997; Pettigrew, 1998). The competition for resources idea is supported by findings showing lower-class whites in the United States having more racist attitudes than higher-class whites. It may be that the upper class can afford to be less prejudiced because minorities represent less threat to their employment, status, and income. In addition, prejudice is maintained because it serves a function — protecting the interests of the dominant class. The stereotype that blacks are inferior to whites, for example, helps justify a social order in the United States where whites hold disproportionate power.

4. *Displaced aggression.* Have you ever wondered why lower-class groups tend to blame each other rather than the upper class or the class system itself? As you will see in the section on aggression, frustration often leads people to attack the source of frustration. But when the source is bigger and capable of retaliating, or when the cause of the frustration is ambiguous, people often displace their aggression on an alternative, nonthreatening target. The innocent victim of displaced aggression is known as a *scapegoat*. There is strong historical evidence for the power of scapegoating (Eilenberg & Wyman, 1998; Miller, 1998; Sidel, 1996). During the Great Depression of the 1930s, Hitler used Jews as scapegoats Germans could blame for their economic troubles. If it is true that a picture is worth a thousand words, then the photos in Figure 16.5 may serve as a small reminder of the atrocities resulting from prejudice and discrimination.

Reducing Prejudice and Discrimination

> Let's go hand in hand, not one before another.
>
> William Shakespeare

What can be done to combat prejudice? We will look at five approaches: cooperation, superordinate goals, increased contact, cognitive retraining, and cognitive dissonance.

Figure 16.5 *The price of prejudice.* Here are only a few examples of the atrocities associated with prejudice: (a) the Holocaust, when millions of Jews were exterminated by the Nazis; (b) slavery in the United States, where Africans were bought and sold as slaves; and (c) the relocation of Native Americans to reservations, which led to almost complete extermination. Can you think of other examples?

(a)   (b)   (c)

1 and **2. *Cooperation and superordinate goals.*** Research shows that one of the best ways to combat prejudice is to encourage *cooperation* rather than *competition* (Brewer, 1996; Walker & Crogan, 1998). Muzafer Sherif and his colleagues (1966, 1998) conducted an ingenious study to show the role of competition in promoting prejudice. The researchers created strong feelings of ingroup and outgroup identification in a group of 11- and 12-year-old boys at a summer camp by physically separating the boys in different cabins and assigning different projects to each group, such as building a diving board or cooking out in the woods.

Once each group developed strong feelings of group identity and allegiance, the researchers set up a series of competitive games, including tug-of-war and touch football, and awarded desirable prizes to the winning teams. Because of this treatment, the groups began to pick fights, call each other names, and raid each other's camps — behaviors the researchers pointed to as evidence of the research-produced prejudice.

After using competition to create prejudice between the two groups, the researchers demonstrated how cooperation could be successfully used to eliminate it. They created "minicrises" and tasks that required expertise, labor, and cooperation from both groups, and prizes were awarded to all. The hostilities and prejudice between groups slowly began to dissipate, and by the end of the camp, the boys voted to return home in the same bus, and the self-chosen seating did not reflect the earlier camp divisions. Sherif's study showed not only the importance of cooperation as opposed to competition but also the importance of *superordinate goals* (the minicrises) in reducing prejudice (Der-Karabetian, Stephenson, & Poggi, 1996).

3. *Increased contact.* A third approach to reducing prejudice is *increasing contact between groups.* By interacting with members of other groups, prejudice can be reduced (Brewer & Brown, 1998; Dovidio, Gaertner, & Bachman, 2001; Pettigrew, 1998). But as you just discovered with Sherif's study of the boys at the summer camp, contact can sometimes increase prejudice. It works under only certain conditions: (1) close interaction (if minority students are "tracked" into vocational education courses and white students are primarily in college prep courses, they seldom interact and prejudice is increased), (2) interdependence (both groups must be involved in superordinate goals that require cooperation), and (3) equal status (everyone must be at the same level). Once people have positive experiences with a group, they tend to generalize to other groups (Pettigrew, 1998).

4. *Cognitive retraining.* One of the most recent strategies in prejudice reduction requires taking another's perspective or undoing associations of negative stereotypical traits (Galinsky & Moskowitz, 2000; Kawakami, Dovidio, Moll, Hermsen, & Russin, 2000). For example, in a computer training session, Kawakami and colleagues (2000) instructed participants to *try not to* think of cultural associations when they saw a photograph of an elderly person and to press a *no* button when they saw a photograph of an elderly person with a trait stereotypically associated (e.g., slow, weak) with elderly people. Conversely, they were instructed to press a *yes* button when they saw a photograph of an elderly person with a trait not normally associated with the elderly. After a number of trials, their response times became faster and faster, indicating they were undoing negative associations and learning positive ones. After the training, participants were less likely to activate any negative stereotype of elderly people in another activity, compared with others who did not participate in the training exercise.

People can also learn to be nonprejudiced if they are taught to selectively pay attention to *similarities* as opposed to *differences* (Phillips & Ziller, 1997). When we focus on how "black voters feel about affirmative action" or how Jewish people feel about "a Jewish candidate for vice president of the United States," we are indirectly encouraging stereotypes and ingroups versus outgroups. Can you see how this might also apply to gender? By emphasizing gender differences (*Men Are from Mars, Women Are from Venus*), we may be perpetuating gender stereotypes (Powlishta, 1999).

5. *Cognitive dissonance.* As mentioned earlier, prejudice is a type of attitude that has three basic components — affective (feelings), behavioral tendencies, and cognitive (thoughts). And one of the most efficient methods to change an attitude is through *cognitive dissonance*, a perceived discrepancy between an attitude and a behavior or between an attitude and a new piece of information (Albarracin & Wyer, 2000; Cook, 2000). As a critical thinker, can you see how recent social changes, such as school busing, integrated housing, and increased civil rights legislation, might create cognitive dissonance and a subsequent reduction in prejudice? Moreover, do you recognize how the four methods of reducing prejudice we just described also involve cognitive dissonance? Cooperation and superordinate goals, increased contact, and cognitive retraining all create discrepancy in the prejudiced person, which leads to tension that motivates them to change their attitudes — and prejudice.

Interpersonal Attraction: Liking and Loving Others

Stop for a moment and think about someone you like very much. Now picture someone you really dislike. Can you explain your feelings? Social psychologists use the term **interpersonal attraction** to refer to the degree of positive or negative feelings toward another. Attraction accounts for a variety of social experiences — admiration, liking, friendship, intimacy, lust, and love. In this section, we will discuss several factors that explain interpersonal attraction.

Interpersonal Attraction *The degree of positive or negative feelings toward another*

Three Key Factors in Attraction: Physical Attractiveness, Proximity, and Similarity

Social psychologists have found three compelling factors in interpersonal attraction — *physical attractiveness*, *proximity*, and *similarity*. Although physical attractiveness and proximity are more influential in the beginning stages of relationships, similarity is the single most important factor in maintaining a long-term relationship.

Physical Attractiveness. Can you remember what first attracted you to your best friend or romantic partner? Was it his or her warm personality, sharp intelligence, or great sense of humor? Or was it looks? Research consistently shows that *physical attractiveness* (size, shape, facial characteristics, and manner of dress) is one of the most important factors in our initial liking or loving of others (Frederick & Morrison, 1999; Langlois et al., 2000).

Like it or not, attractive individuals are seen by both men and women as more poised, interesting, cooperative, achieving, sociable, independent, intelligent, healthy, and sexually warm (Langlois et al., 2000; Mulford, Orbell, Shatto, & Stockard, 1998, Watkins & Johnston, 2000).

GENDER & CULTURAL DIVERSITY

Physical Attractiveness Across Cultures

If you found the previous list of advantages of physical attractiveness unnerving, you'll be even more surprised to know that some research also shows that judgments of attractiveness appear consistent across cultures, and that in 37 cultures around the world, women are judged more beautiful if they are youthful in appearance

Culture and attaction. Which of these women do you find most attractive? Can you see how your cultural background would train you to prefer one look over the others?

(Buss, 1989, 1994, 1999; Cartwright, 2000; Cunningham, Roberts, Barbee, Druen, & Wu, 1995; Langlois et al., 2000). For men, on the other hand, maturity and financial resources seem to be more important than appearance in attracting a mate. According to Buss (1994), "Men prefer to mate with beautiful young women, whereas women prefer to mate with men who have resources and social status" (p. 239).

How can this be so universally true? Evolutionary psychologists would suggest that this cross-cultural similarity in judgment of attractiveness reflects the fact that good looks generally indicate good health, sound genes, and high fertility. For example, facial and body symmetry appear to be key elements in attractiveness (Rhodes, Sumich, & Byatt, 1999; Zajonc, 1998) and symmetry seems to be correlated with genetic health. The fact that women prefer men with resources and social status also supports the evolutionary position. Because the responsibility of rearing and nurturing children more often falls on women's shoulders, men with greater resources will have more to invest in children.

In contrast to this seeming universal agreement on standards of attractiveness, there also is evidence that beauty is in "the eye of the beholder." What we judge as beautiful varies somewhat from era to era and culture to culture. For example, the Chinese once practiced foot binding because small feet were considered beautiful in women. All the toes except the big one were bent under a young girl's foot and into the sole. The physical distortion made it almost impossible for her to walk, and she suffered excruciating pain, chronic bleeding, and frequent infections throughout her life (Dworkin, 1974). Even in modern times, cultural demands for attractiveness encourage an increasing number of women (and men) to undergo expensive and often painful surgery to *increase* the size of their eyes, breasts, lips, chest, and penis and *decrease* the size of their nose, ears, chin, stomach, hips, and thighs (Atkins, 2000; Etcoff, 1999).

Given that only a small percentage of people are as attractive as Cameron Diaz or Denzel Washington or have the money (or inclination) for extensive cosmetic surgery, how do the rest of us ever find mates? The good news is that what people judge as "ideally attractive" may be quite different than what they eventually choose for a mate (Regan, 1998). According to the *matching hypothesis,* men and women of approximately equal physical attractiveness tend to select each other as partners. What people judge as "ideally attractive" may be quite different than what they ultimately choose for a mate (Reagan, 1998).

Proximity Attraction also depends on people being in the same place at the same time, making **proximity**, or geographic nearness, another major factor in attraction. A study of friendship in college dormitories found that the person next door was more often liked than the person two doors away, the person two doors

Proximity *A key factor in attraction involving geographic, residential, and other forms of physical closeness*

Exposure and liking. According to the "mere exposure effect," this model would prefer the reversed photo on the left because this is the version she sees in the mirror. However, most people prefer the "normal" photo on the right because this is what is most familiar to the audience.

away was liked more than someone three doors away, and so on (Priest & Sawyer, 1967).

Proximity promotes attraction largely because of *mere exposure*. Just as familiar people become more physically attractive over time, repeated exposure also increases overall liking (Seamon, McKenna, & Binder, 1998; Zajonc, 1998). This makes sense from an evolutionary point of view. Things we have seen before are less likely to pose a threat than novel stimuli. It also explains why modern advertisers tend to run highly redundant ad campaigns, with familiar faces and jingles (Zajonc, 1968, 1998). Repeated exposure increases our liking — and purchases.

We even like *ourselves* better when we see ourselves in a familiar way. When researchers showed college students pictures of themselves or reversed photos (the mirror image), students strongly preferred the reversed photos — that is, the image they were used to seeing in the mirror. Close friends of the same students preferred the true photos of their friend. They were used to seeing this image (Mita, Dermer, & Knight, 1977). (Can you see why people often complain that photos of themselves "never really look like" them?)

One caution. Repeated exposure to a *negative* stimulus can *decrease* attraction, as evidenced by the high number of negative political ads. Politicians have learned that repeatedly running an attack ad associating an opposing candidate with negative cues (like increased taxes) decreases the viewers' liking of the opponent. On the other hand, running ads showing themselves in a positive light (kissing babies, helping flood victims) helps builds positive associations and increased liking.

Similarity. Once we've had repeated opportunity to get to know someone through simple physical proximity, and assuming we find him or her attractive, we then need something to hold the relationship together over time. The major cementing factor for long-term relationships, whether liking or loving, is *similarity*. We tend to prefer, and stay with, people who are most like us, those who share our ethnic background, social class, interests, and attitudes (Akers, Jones, & Coyl, 1998; Herman, 1998). In other words, "Birds of a feather flock together."

What about the old saying "Opposites attract"? Although it does seem that these two pieces of common folklore are contradictory, the term *opposites* here probably refers to personality traits rather than to social background or values. An attraction to a seemingly opposite person is more often based on the recognition that in one or two important areas that person offers us something we lack (Dryer & Horowitz, 1997). If you are a talkative and outgoing person, for example, your friendship with a quiet and reserved individual may endure because each of you provides important resources for the other. Psychologists refer to this as **need complementarity**, as compared with the **need compatibility** represented by similarity.

Need Complementarity *The tendency to seek out and be attracted to people whose qualities we admire but personally lack*

Need Compatibility *A sharing of similar needs*

Opposites attract or similarity?
Research shows that similarity is the single best predictor for long-term relationships. As shown here, however, many people ignore dissimilarities and hope that their chosen partner will change over time.

Reprinted with special permission of King Features Syndicate.

Loving Others

To complete our discussion of interpersonal attraction, we will explore three perspectives on the mystery of love: liking versus loving, romantic love, and companionate love.

Liking versus loving Because love relationships often develop from friendships and initial feelings of liking for one another, Zick Rubin (1970, 1992) developed two paper-and-pencil tests to explore the relationship between liking and loving (Table 16.1).

In spite of the apparent simplicity of Rubin's scales, they have proven to be useful indicators of both liking and loving. For example, Rubin hypothesized that "strong love" couples would spend more time gazing into one another's eyes than "weak love" couples. To test his hypothesis, while the couples were waiting for the experiment to begin, Rubin and his assistants secretly recorded the actual amount of eye contact between all couples. As predicted, couples who scored highest on the love scale also spent more time looking into one another's eyes. In addition, Rubin found that although both partners tended to match each other on their love scores, women liked their dating partners significantly more than they were liked in return.

How does love differ from liking on Rubin's scales? Rubin found that liking involves a favorable evaluation of another, as reflected in greater feelings of admiration and respect. He found not only that love is more intense than liking but also that love is composed of three basic elements:

- *Caring*, the desire to help the other person, particularly when help is needed
- *Attachment*, the need to be with the other person
- *Intimacy*, a sense of empathy and trust that comes from close communication and self-disclosure from another

TABLE 16.1 SAMPLE ITEMS FROM RUBIN'S LIKING AND LOVING TEST

Love Scale
1. I feel that I can confide in _____ about virtually everything.
2. I would do almost anything for _____.
3. If I could never be with _____, I would feel miserable.

Liking Scale
1. I think that _____ is unusually well adjusted.
2. I would highly recommend _____ for a responsible job.
3. In my opinion, _____ is an exceptionally mature person.

Source: Rubin, Z. (1970). "Measurement of romantic love," *Journal of Personality and Social Psychology, 16,* 265–273. Copyright © 1970 by the American Psychological Association. Reprinted by permission of the author.

Romantic Love When you think of romantic love, do you think of falling in love, a magical experience that puts you on cloud nine? **Romantic love**, also called *passionate love* or *limerence*, has been defined as "any intense attraction that involves the idealization of the other, within an erotic context, with the expectation of enduring for some time in the future" (Jankowiak, 1997, p. 8).

Romantic love has intrigued people throughout history, and its intense joys and sorrows have inspired countless poems, novels, movies, and songs around the world. A cross-cultural study by anthropologists William Jankowiak and Edward Fischer found romantic love in 147 of the 166 societies they studied. The researchers concluded that "romantic love constitutes a human universal, or at the least a near universal" (1992, p. 154).

Problems with Romantic Love Romantic love may be almost universal, but that hardly means it is problem free. First, romantic love is typically short lived. Even in the most devoted couples, the intense attraction and excitement generally begin to fade after 6 to 30 months (Hatfield & Rapson, 1996; Livingston, 1999). Although this research finding may disappoint you, as a critical thinker do you really think any emotion of this intensity could last forever? What would happen if other intense emotions, such as anger or joy, were eternal? Moreover, given the time consuming nature of romantic love, what would happen to other parts of our lives, such as school, career, and family?

Another major problem with romantic love is that it is largely based on mystery and fantasy. People fall in love with others not necessarily as they are but as they want them to be (Fletcher & Simpson, 2000; Levine & Markman, 2001). What happens to these illusions when we are faced with everyday interactions and long-term

Romantic Love *An intense feeling of attraction to another person, within an erotic context and with future expectations*

Romantic love in the media. *Do you remember the story of Snow White? After fleeing from a wicked stepmother and being rescued by seven dwarfs, she apparently dies from a poisoned apple and the dwarfs place her in a glass coffin in the middle of the forest. Prince Charming happens by on a horse, falls in love with her dead body, and is surprised when his kiss brings her back to life. The story ends as they ride off into the sunset to live "happily ever after." The rescuing of a damsel in distress followed by lifelong happiness is a common theme in childhood stories, as well as in modern day romance novels, movies, and love songs. Is this simple entertainment? Or could these early childhood stories and ongoing romantic messages create unrealistic expectations of real life and adult relationships?*

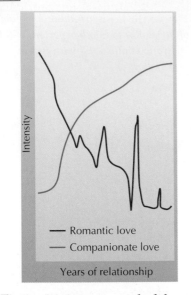

Figure 16.6 *Love over the life span.* Romantic love is high in the beginning of a relationship but tends to diminish over time, with periodic resurgences or "spikes." Companionate love usually increases over time.

Companionate Love *A strong feeling of attraction to another person characterized by trust, caring, tolerance, and friendship; it is believed to provide an enduring basis for long-term relationships*

exposure? Our "beautiful princess" isn't supposed to snore, and our "knight in shining armor" doesn't look very knightly flossing his teeth. And, of course, no princess or knight would ever notice our shortcomings, let alone comment on them.

Is there any way to keep love alive? If you mean romantic love, one of the best ways to fan the flames is through interference, or some form of frustration that keeps you from fulfilling your desire for the presence of your love. Researchers have found that interference (for example, the parents in Shakespeare's *Romeo and Juliet*) apparently increases the feelings of love (Driscoll, Davis, & Lipetz, 1972).

Because romantic love depends on uncertainty and fantasy, it can also be kept alive by situations in which we never really get to know the other person. This may explain why computer chat room romances or old high school flings have such a tug on our emotions. Because we never really get to test these relationships, we can always fantasize about what might have been.

One of the most constructive ways of keeping romantic love alive is to recognize its fragile nature and nurture it with carefully planned surprises, flirting and flattery, and special dinners and celebrations. In the long run, however, romantic love's most important function might be to keep us attached long enough to move on to companionate love.

Companionate Love. **Companionate love** is based on admiration and respect, combined with deep feelings of caring for the person and commitment to the relationship. Studies of close friendships show that satisfaction grows with time as we come to recognize the value of companionship and of having an intimate confidante (Kiraly, 2000; & Hazan, 1991). Companionate love, unlike romantic love, which is very short lived, seems to grow stronger with time and often lasts a lifetime (Figure 16.6).

Companionate love is what we feel for our best friends, and it can be the basis for a strong and lasting marriage. But finding and keeping a long-term relationship is no easy task. Many of our expectations for love are based on romantic fantasies and unconscious programming from fairy tales and TV shows in which everyone lives happily ever after. Therefore, we are often ill equipped to deal with the hassles and boredom that come with any long-term relationship. One tip for maintaining companionate love is to *overlook each other's faults.* Studies of both dating and married couples find that people report greater satisfaction with — and stay longer in — relationships where they have a somewhat idealized or unrealistically positive perception of their partner (Fletcher & Simpson, 2000; Murray & Holmes, 1997). This makes sense in light of research on cognitive dissonance (discussed

Companionate versus romantic love. This couple just celebrated their 60th wedding anniversary. Unlike romantic love, which rarely lasts longer than 6 to 30 months, companionate love can last a lifetime.

earlier). Idealizing our mates allows us to believe we have a good deal — and hence avoids the cognitive dissonance that might naturally arise every time we saw an attractive alternative. As Benjamin Franklin put it, "Keep your eyes wide open before marriage, half shut afterwards."

Check & Review

OUR FEELINGS ABOUT OTHERS

Prejudice is a generally negative attitude directed toward specific people solely because of their membership in a specific group. It contains all three components of attitudes (cognitive, affective, and behavioral). **Discrimination** is not the same as prejudice. It refers to the actual negative behavior directed at members of a group. People do not always act on their prejudices.

The four major sources of prejudice are learning (classical and operant conditioning and social learning), cognitive processes (categorization), economic and political competition, and displaced aggression (scapegoating). Cooperation, superordinate goals, increased contact, cognitive retraining, and cognitive dissonance reduction are five methods for reducing prejudice and discrimination.

Physical attractiveness is very important to **interpersonal attraction**. Physically attractive people are often perceived as more intelligent, sociable, and interesting than less attractive people. Standards for physical attractiveness vary across cultures and time. Physical **proximity** also increases one's attractiveness. If you live near someone or work alongside someone, you are more likely to like that person. Although people commonly believe that "opposites attract" (**need complementarity**), research shows that similarity (**need compatibility**) is a much more important factor in attraction.

Love can be defined in terms of caring, attachment, and intimacy. **Romantic love** is highly valued in our society, but because it is based on mystery and fantasy, it is hard to sustain. **Companionate love** relies on mutual trust, respect, and friendship and seems to grow stronger with time.

Questions

1. Explain how prejudice differs from discrimination.

2. Saying that members of another ethnic group "all look alike to me" may be an example of _____. (a) ingroup favoritism; (b) the outgroup homogeneity effect; (c) outgroup negativism; (d) ingroup bias

3. Cross-cultural research on physical attractiveness has found all but one of the following. (a) the Chinese once practiced foot binding because small feet were considered attractive in women; (b) in most male dominated societies, physical beauty is the most important attribute in a potential wife; (c) in most Eastern cultures, men prefer women with power and financial status over beauty; (d) for men, maturity and financial resources are more important than appearance in their ability to attract a mate

4. Compare the dangers associated with romantic love with the benefits of companionate love.

Answers to Questions can be found in Appendix B.

OUR ACTIONS TOWARD OTHERS

Having just completed our whirlwind examination of how our thoughts and emotions influence others — and vice versa — we turn to topics associated with actions toward others. We begin with a look at social influence (conformity and obedience), and then continue with group processes (membership and decision making). We conclude by exploring two opposite kinds of behavior — aggression and altruism.

How do our actions toward others affect their lives and our own?

Social Influence: Conformity and Obedience

The society and culture into which we are born influence us from the moment of birth until the moment of death. Our culture teaches us to believe certain things, feel certain ways, and act in accordance with these beliefs and feelings. These influences are so strong and so much a part of who we are that we rarely recognize them.

© Sidney Harris

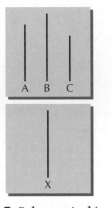

Figure 16.7 *Solomon Asch's study of conformity.* Participants were shown four lines such as these and then asked which line (A, B, or C) was most similar to the one on the bottom (X).

Conformity *A type of social influence in which individuals change their behavior as a result of real or imagined group pressure*

Normative Social Influence *Conforming to group pressure out of a need for acceptance and approval*

Norm *Cultural rule of behavior that prescribes what is acceptable in a given situation*

Just as a fish doesn't know it's in water, we are largely unaware of the strong impact cultural and social factors have on all our behaviors. In this section, we will discuss two kinds of *social influence*: conformity and obedience.

Conformity — Going Along with Others

Imagine for a moment that you have volunteered for a psychology experiment on perception. You find yourself seated around a table with six other students. You are all shown a card with three lines labeled A, B, and C, as in Figure 16.7. You are then asked to select the line that is closest in length to a fourth line, X. Each of you is asked to state your choice out loud, in order, around the table. At first, everyone agrees on the correct line, and the experiment seems pretty boring. On the third trial, however, the first participant gives what is obviously a wrong answer. You know that line B is correct, but he says line A. When the second, third, fourth, and fifth participants also say line A, you really start to wonder: "What's going on here? Are they blind? Or am I?"

What do you think you would do at this point in the experiment? Would you stick with your convictions and say line B, regardless of what the others have answered? Or would you go along with the group? In the original version of this experiment, conducted by Solomon Asch (1951), six participants were actually confederates of the experimenter, and seating was arranged so that the one participant who was the real subject was always in the next-to-last position. The six confederates had been instructed to respond incorrectly on the third trial and selected later trials as a way of testing the participant's degree of **conformity**, or changing one's behavior as a result of real or imagined group pressure.

How did Asch's participants respond? More than one-third conformed and agreed with the group's obviously incorrect choice. This level of conformity is particularly intriguing when it is compared with responses in the control group, which experienced no group pressure and chose correctly virtually 100 percent of the time.

Why would so many people conform? To the onlooker, conformity is often difficult to understand, and even the conformer sometimes has a hard time explaining his or her behavior. We can better understand Asch's participants and our own forms of conformity if we look at three factors: (1) *normative social influence*, (2) *informational social influence*, and (3) the role of *reference groups*.

Normative social influence. The first factor, **normative social influence**, refers to conformity to group pressure out of a need for approval and acceptance by the group. A **norm** is an expected behavior that is adhered to by members of the group. Norms are society's definition of how we "should" behave. They are some-

If you want to personally experience the power of social norms, approach a fellow student on campus and ask for directions to the bookstore, library, or some other landmark. As you are talking, move toward the person until you invade his or her personal space. You should be close enough to almost touch toes. How does the person respond? How do you feel? Now repeat the process with another student, but this time try standing 5 to 6 feet away while asking directions. Which procedure was most difficult for you? Although most people think this will be a fun assignment, they often find it extremely difficult to willingly break our culture's unwritten norms for personal space.

---

times explicit, but most often, norms are quite subtle and implicit. Have you ever asked what others are wearing to the party or watched your neighbor's table manners to be sure you pick up the right fork? Such behavior reflects your desire to conform and the power of normative social influence.

An important norm in every culture has to do with *personal space* (Axtell, 1998; Hall, 1966, 1983; Sommer, 1969). If someone invades the invisible "personal bubble" that we like to maintain around our bodies, we generally feel very uncomfortable. Imagine yourself as the typical American traveling in several Middle Eastern countries. How would you respond when a local citizen answers your question while standing close enough to feel your breath? Most Americans, Canadians, and Northern Europeans feel very uncomfortable at this distance (unless talking with a lover), but most Middle Easterners like to be close enough to "read" one another's eyes. If you "naturally" back away during the conversation, the Middle Easterner might think you are cold and standoffish at the same time that you might consider him or her rude and intrusive.

Why do some people like to stand closer than others do? There are a number of possible explanations. First, culture and socialization have a lot to do with personal space. For reasons unknown, people from Mediterranean, Moslem, and Latin American countries tend to maintain smaller interpersonal distances than do North Americans and Northern Europeans (Axtell, 1998; Steinhart, 1986). Children also tend to stand very close to others until they are socialized to recognize and maintain a greater personal distance. Second, certain relationships, situations, and personalities affect interpersonal distances. Friends stand closer than strangers, women tend to stand closer than men, and violent prisoners prefer approximately three times the personal space of nonviolent prisoners (Axtell, 1998; Gilmour & Walkey, 1981; Roques, Lambin, Jeunier, & Strayer, 1997).

Informational Social Influence Have you ever bought a specific brand of ski equipment or automobile simply because of a friend's recommendation? You conform not to gain their approval (normative social influence) but because you assume they have more information than you do. Conforming to group pressure out of a need for direction and information is considered the result of **informational social influence**. Participants in Asch's experiment might also have conformed for similar reasons. Totalitarian governments recognize the importance of information in social influence and generally maintain strict control over books and news reports within their country.

Reference groups The third major factor in conformity is the power of **reference groups** — those people we most admire, like, and want to resemble.

Informational Social Influence *Conforming to group pressure out of a need for direction and information*

Reference Groups *People to whom we conform (or with whom we go along) because we like and admire them and want to be like them*

Would You Have Obeyed Milgram's Experimenters?

One common intellectual illusion that hinders critical thinking about obedience is the belief that only evil people do evil things or that evil announces itself. For example, the experimenter in Stanley Milgram's study looked and acted like a reasonable person who was simply carrying out a research project. Because he was not seen as personally corrupt and evil, the participants' normal moral guard was down and obedience was maximized.

This relaxed moral guard might also explain obedience to a highly respected military officer or the leader of a religious cult. One of the most infamous cult leaders, Jim Jones, was well known and highly revered for his kindness and "good works" — at least in the beginning. Perhaps because of their relaxed moral guard (combined with the five factors discussed earlier), in 1978 over 900 members of the People's Temple in Guyana committed mass suicide on Jones's order. People who resisted were murdered, but the vast majority took their lives willingly by drinking cyanide-laced Kool-Aid.

In addition, the gradual nature of many obedience situations may explain why so many people were willing to give the maximum shocks in Milgram's study. The initial

The foot-in-the door technique. If this homeowner allows the salesperson to give him a small gift (a "foot-in-the-door" technique), he's more likely to agree to buy something. Can you explain why?

mild level of shocks may have worked as a **foot-in-the-door technique**, in which a first, small request is used as a setup for later, larger requests. Once Milgram's participants complied with the initial request, they might have felt obligated to continue (Chartrand, Pinckert, & Burger, 1999; Sabini & Silver, 1993).

Take this opportunity to think critically about extreme forms of destructive obedience and the everyday examples that we encounter. Rank the following by placing a 1 next to the situation you believe is the

most ethical act of obedience and a 3 next to the least ethical.

_____ Jane is 19 and wants to become a commercial artist. She is offered a scholarship to a good art school, but her parents strongly object to her career choice. After considerable pressure, she gives in and enrolls at the same engineering school her father attended.

_____ Tom is 45 and having serious doubts about his employer's shady business practices, such as double-billing the clients. Although he believes his boss is dishonest and unethical, he cooperates because he really needs the job.

_____ Mary is 20 and a senior in college. She desperately wants to get into a graduate program at a very prestigious school but is failing an important class. The instructor has suggested she could have an A in his course if she would sexually "cooperate." She agrees.

Having analyzed Jane's, Tom's, and Mary's responses, think of a situation in your own life in which you were unethically persuaded. Can you use what you have learned in this chapter about conformity and obedience to clarify why you were persuaded — and perhaps prevent future problems?

Foot-in-the-Door Technique *A social influence technique in which a first, small request is used as a setup for later requests*

Check & Review

SOCIAL INFLUENCE

The process of social influence teaches important cultural values and behaviors that are essential to successful social living. Two of the most important forms of social influence are conformity and obedience.

Conformity refers to changes in behavior in response to real or imagined pressure from others. People conform for approval and acceptance (**normative social influence**), out of a need for

more information (**informational social influence**), and to match the behavior of those they admire and feel similar to (their **reference group**). People also conform because it is often adaptive to do so.

Obedience involves giving in to a command from others. Stanley Milgram's study showed that a surprisingly large number of people would obey orders even when another human being is physically threat-

ened. At least four factors increase or decrease obedience: the power of authority, distance between teacher and learner, assignment of responsibility, and modeling/imitation.

Questions

1. Explain how conformity differs from obedience.

2. A social influence technique in which a first, small request is used as a setup

for later requests is known as_____.
(a) the lowball technique; (b) the foot-in-the-door technique; (c) infiltration technique; (d) ingratiation

3. Milgram's participants thought they were participating in an experiment designed to study the effect of_____. (a) obedience to authority; (b) arousal on memory; (c) punishment on learning; (d) electric shock on brain-wave activity

4. What are the four factors that increase or decrease obedience?

Answers to Questions can be found in Appendix B.

Group Processes: Membership and Decision Making

Psychologists define a *group* as "two or more persons interacting with one another in such a manner that each person influences and is influenced by each other person" (Shaw, 1981, p. 8). In other words, a group consists of any collection of people who have some mutually recognized relationship with one another. A couple on their first date, a family, a class in psychology, and a basketball team are all considered groups. On the other hand, people riding together in an elevator are not a group.

Group Membership

Have you ever been with friends and found yourself doing something that you might not have done alone? Or have you noticed that you behave differently with your friends than with your parents or with your employer or roommates? In each situation, your behavior is largely the result of your group membership. Although we seldom recognize the power of such membership, social psychologists have identified several important ways that groups affect us. In this section we will explore, first, how the roles we assume influence behavior and, next, how group membership sometimes leads to deindividuation.

Roles in groups. Every person in a group is expected to play one or more *roles* — a set of behavioral patterns connected with particular social positions. Some roles are very specifically spelled out and regulated (police officer), whereas others are assumed through informal learning and inference (father). Have you ever wondered how these roles affect behavior? This question fascinated social psychologist Philip Zimbardo. In his famous study at Stanford University, 20 carefully screened, well-adjusted young college men were paid $15 a day for participating in a simulation of prison life (Haney, Banks, & Zimbardo, 1978; Zimbardo, 1993).

TRY THIS
Yourself

To appreciate Philip Zimbardo's prison study, pretend you are one of the 20 college students who volunteered to be a participant and that you were randomly assigned to play the role of "prisoner." You're watching TV at home when you unexpectedly hear a loud knock. When you open the door, several uniformed police officers take you outside, spread-eagle you against the police car, frisk you, and inform you that you are being arrested. At the police station, you are photographed, fingerprinted, and booked. You are then blindfolded and driven to your final destination — the "Stanford Prison." Here you are given an ID number in place of your name; deloused, and issued a shapeless gown to wear, a tight nylon cap to conceal your hair, and no underwear. All prisoners are in similar prisoner clothes; whereas participants who were assigned to be "guards" are outfitted with official-looking uniforms, billy clubs, and whistles. You and the other prisoners are locked in your cells, and the guards are given complete control. What do you think happens next?

Check & Review

GROUP PROCESSES

Groups differ from mere collections of people because group members share a mutually recognized relationship with one another. Group membership affects us through the roles we play. The importance of roles in determining and controlling behavior was dramatically demonstrated in Philip Zimbardo's Stanford Prison Study.

Group membership can also lead to **deindividuation**, in which a person becomes so caught up in the group's identity that individual self-awareness and responsibility are temporarily suspended.

Group polarization research shows that if most group members initially tend toward an extreme idea, the entire group will polarize in that direction. This is because the other, like-minded, members reinforce the dominant tendency. **Groupthink** is a dangerous type of thinking that occurs when a group's desire for agreement overrules its desire to critically evaluate information.

Questions

1. Zimbardo stopped his prison study before the end of the scheduled 2 weeks because _____.

2. The critical factor in deindividuation is _____. (a) loss of self-esteem; (b) anonymity; (c) identity diffusion; (d) group cohesiveness

3. What are the major symptoms of groupthink?

4. In a groupthink situation, the person who takes responsibility for seeing that dissenting opinions are not expressed is called the _____. (a) censor; (b) mindguard; (c) monitor; (d) whip

Answers to Questions can be found in Appendix B.

Aggression: Explaining and Controlling It

Aggression is any form of behavior intended to harm or injure another living being that is motivated to avoid such treatment (Baron, 2000). Why do people act aggressively? We will explore a number of possible explanations for aggression — both *biological* and *psychosocial*. Then we will look at how aggression can be controlled or reduced.

Aggression *Any behavior that is intended to harm someone*

Biological Factors in Aggression

1. Instincts. Because aggression has such a long history and is found among all cultures, many theorists believe humans are instinctively aggressive. After personally witnessing the massive death and destruction that occurred during World War I, Sigmund Freud stated that aggressive impulses are inborn. He argued that the drive for violence arises from a basic instinct and that, therefore, human aggression cannot be eliminated (Gay, 1999, 2000; Rohrlich, 1998).

Evolutionary psychologists and ethologists (scientists who study animal behavior) propose another instinct theory. They believe that aggression evolved because it contributes to survival of the fittest. Whereas Freud saw aggression as destructive and disruptive, ethologists believe aggression prevents overcrowding and allows the strongest animals to win mates and reproduce the species (Cartwright, 2000; Dabbs & Dabbs, 2000; Lorenz, 1981). Most social psychologists, however, reject both Freud's and the ethologists' view of instinct as the source of aggression.

2. Genes. Twin studies suggest that some individuals are genetically predisposed to have hostile, irritable temperaments and to engage in aggressive acts (Miles & Carey, 1997; Segal & Bouchard, 2000; Wasserman & Wachbroit, 2000.) Remember from Chapter 1, however, this does *not* mean that these people are doomed to behave aggressively. Aggression develops from a complex interaction of biology, social experience, and each individual's behavior.

3. The brain and nervous system. Electrical stimulation or severing specific parts of an animal's brain has a direct effect on aggression (Delgado, 1960; Delville, Mansour, & Ferris, 1996; Roberts & Nagel, 1996). Research with brain injuries and organic disorders has also identified possible aggression circuits in the brain — in particular, the hypothalamus, amygdala, and other parts of the brain (Davidson, Putnam, & Larson, 2000; Raine et al., 1998).

4. *Substance abuse and other mental disorders.* Substance abuse (particularly alcohol) within the general public is a major factor in most forms of aggression — child abuse, spousal assault, robberies, murders, stabbings, and so on (Casswell & Zhang, 1998; Goodwin, 2000; Shuntich, Loh, & Katz, 1998). Homicide rates are also higher among men with schizophrenia and antisocial disorders, particularly if they also abuse alcohol (Raesaenen et al., 1998; Tiihonen, Isohanni, Rasanen, Koiranen, & Moring, 1997).

5. *Hormones and neurotransmitters.* Several studies have linked the male gonadal hormone testosterone to aggressive behavior (Boyd, 2000; Dabbs & Dabbs, 2000; Sanchez-Martin et al., 2000). However, the relationship between human aggression and testosterone is complex. Testosterone seems to increase aggression and dominance, but dominance itself increases testosterone (Mazur & Booth, 1998). Violent behavior has also been linked with low levels of the neurotransmitters serotonin and GABA (gamma-aminobutyric acid) (Bernhardt, 1997; Brady, Myrick, & McElroy, 1998; LeMarquand et al., 1998; Manuck et al., 1998).

Psychosocial Factors in Aggression

1. *Aversive stimuli.* Research shows that aversive stimuli such as noise, heat, pain, insults, and foul odors can increase aggression (Anderson, Anderson, Dorr, DeNeve, & Flanagan, 2000; Berkowitz, 1990). Traffic congestion (road rage), cramped airlines (airplane rage), and excessive demands at work (office rage) all reflect another aversive stimuli — *frustration*. Being blocked short of a goal increases aggressive tendencies.

John Dollard and his colleagues (1939) noted this relationship between frustration and aggression more than half a century ago. According to the **frustration-aggression hypothesis**, frustration creates anger, which for some may lead to aggression. This does not mean that if you get mad at your boss, you necessarily punch him or her in the nose. You may displace your aggression and take out your anger on your family when you get home. Or you may turn your aggression toward yourself, becoming self-destructive or withdrawing, giving up, and getting depressed.

Frustration-Aggression Hypothesis *The idea that frustration — the blocking of a desired goal — creates anger, which may lead to aggression*

2. *Culture and learning.* As we discovered in Chapter 6, observational or social learning theory suggests that we learn by watching others. Thus, people raised in a culture with aggressive models will learn aggressive responses (Matsumoto, 2000). In Japan, for example, children are taught very early to value social harmony, and Japan has one of the lowest rates of violence in all industrialized nations (Nisbett, Peng, Choi, & Norenzayan, 2000; Zahn-Waxler, Friedman, Cole, Mizuta, & Himura, 1996). In contrast, the United States is one of the most violent nations, and our children grow up with numerous models for aggression, which they tend to imitate.

3. *Media and video games.* Despite protestations that violence in movies, TV, and video games is only entertainment, considerable evidence exists that the media can contribute to aggression in both children and adults (Anderson & Dill, 2000; Gilligan, 2000; Hogben, 1998; Zillman & Weaver, 1999). For example, the latest video games, such as *Doom*, *Mortal Kombat*, *Resident Evil*, and *Half-Life*, all feature realistic sound effects and gory depictions of "lifelike" violence, which may teach children that violence is exciting and acceptable. Obviously, most children who play violent video games and watch violent movies and TV shows do not go on to become dangerous killers. However, children do imitate what they see on TV [and, presumably, video games] and seem to internalize as a value that violence is acceptable behavior.

RESEARCH HIGHLIGHT

America's "Anger Epidemic"

Two supermarket shoppers get in a fist-fight over who should be first in a newly opened checkout lane.

A Continental Airlines flight returns to the Anchorage airport after a passenger allegedly throws a can of beer at a flight attendant and bites a pilot.

A father beats another father to death in an argument over rough play at their sons' hockey practice.

What do you think of these media reports? According to some experts, our nation is in the middle of an "anger epidemic," ranging from tantrums in supermarkets and on airplanes to deadly fights over a child's hockey practice (Gilligan, 2000; Peterson, 2000). Perhaps most disturbing is the increase in teen violence (Zanigel & Ressner, 2001).

One of the most dramatic examples of teen violence occurred on Tuesday, April 20, 1999, in Littelton, Colorado. On that infamous day, Eric Harris and Dylan Klebold shot and killed 12 fellow Columbine High School students and 1 teacher, wounded many others, and then turned the guns on themselves and committed suicide. Armed with a semiautomatic rifle, two sawed-off shotguns, a semiautomatic handgun, and dozens of homemade bombs, these two young men joined a growing list of recent school shootings in the United States.

Although juvenile massacres are still an aberration, the slaughter at Columbine High "opened a sad national conversation about what turns two boys' souls into poison" (Gibbs, 1999, p. 25). What causes kids to gun down other kids? Can we identify high-risk children at early ages? Is aggressiveness a personality trait that is easily malleable or highly resistant to change?

These are the kinds of questions addressed by researchers Rolf Loeber and Magda Stouthamer-Loeber (1998) of the University of Pittsburgh. Noting that the numbers of juvenile perpetrators and victims have gradually increased over the past decades, these researchers also cite research demonstrating that highly aggressive children are at risk for adult crime, alcoholism, drug abuse, unemployment, divorce, and mental illness.

Research on juvenile antisocial behavior is voluminous, yet Loeber and Stouthamer-Loeber identify five major misconceptions and controversies that block our understanding of the problem and future research.

The Columbine Effect
- Inside the mind of the California teen killer
- Confronting the classroom code of silence
- Why some kids snap—and others don't

1. *Stability of childhood aggression.* Correlation studies give the impression that aggression is highly stable from childhood to adulthood (a review of the literature shows coefficients range from .63 to .92 — very high). In other

---

Could it be that aggressive children just tend to prefer violent television and videogames? Research suggests it is a two-way street. Laboratory studies, correlational research, and cross-cultural studies among children in five different countries (Australia, Finland, Israel, Poland, and the United States) have all found that exposure to TV violence did increase aggressiveness and that aggressive children tend to seek out violent programs (Aluja-Fabregat & Torrubia-Beltri, 1998; Singer, Slovak, Frierson, & York, 1998).

Controlling or Eliminating Aggression

Some therapists advise people to release aggressive impulses by engaging in harmless forms of aggression, such as vigorous exercise, punching a pillow, and watching competitive sports. But studies suggest that "draining the aggression reservoir" doesn't

words, individuals who are aggressive as children are likely to be aggressive as adults. However, Loeber and Stouthamer-Loeber think we are stopping short of the real challenge, researching why some children *don't* go on to become aggressive adults. They cite studies showing that preschool boys commonly show aggressive behaviors and that aggression decreases from preschool to elementary school and from adolescence to adulthood. Knowing why some individuals outgrow aggression could greatly help mental health professionals intervene in high-risk cases.

2. *All serious aggression begins in early childhood.* Loeber and Stouthamer-Loeber suggest we need additional research into violent individuals without a history of early aggression. They go on to suggest three developmental types of aggressive individuals: (a) a life-course type (characterized by aggression in childhood that persists and worsens into adulthood), (b) a limited-duration type (individuals who outgrow aggression), and (c) a late-onset type (individuals without a history of aggression). This three-type classification could be more helpful to clinicians, probation officers, and others working with children.

3. *Controversy over single or multiple pathways.* Loeber and Stouthamer-Loeber suggest researchers should spend less time debating whether a single pathway or multiple pathways lead to antisocial behavior and violence. (By "pathways," they mean causes such as genes, culture, learning, or any of the other possible causes discussed at the beginning of this section). Instead, we should research multiple pathways because "casting a wide net" is more likely to produce results than looking at each possibility one at a time.

4. *Simple versus complex causes of aggression.* Loeber and Stouthamer-Loeber looked at three possible causes of aggression in children — family factors, physiology, and genetics. They report that a more complex relationship exists than was previously thought.

Studies of family factors, for example, show a relationship exists between children who live with aggressive parents in a conflictual home atmosphere and children who commit personal or violent crimes, but not children who commit property crimes. Similarly, physiological studies link certain hormones (such as testosterone) and neurotransmitters (such as serotonin) to juvenile aggression, but not to property crimes. Genetic studies have produced conflicting results.

5. *Male and female aggression is not the same.* Loeber and Stouthamer-Loeber say the assumption that violence develops in much the same way in women and men is erroneous. Although few gender differences have been recorded in toddlerhood, beginning in preschool and throughout adulthood boys show more personal and physical aggression. Furthermore, several investigators have documented that women tend to use more indirect and verbal aggression and relational aggression (gossip and excluding peers) and are less likely to participate in group fighting, gang fighting, aggravated assault, sexual violence, and homicide. For these reasons, Loeber and Stouthamer-Loeber believe major gender differences exist in aggression, but at the same time, they stress that these variations are pieces of the bigger puzzle that must be addressed by future research.

Following the Columbine massacre, the media offered standard and all-too-familiar answers (violence on TV and in the movies, availability of guns, divorce, and "no-parent" households). But as Loeber and Stouthamer-Loeber document in their analysis of juvenile research studies, the problem is complex and we are a long way from answers.

really help (Bushman, Baumeister, & Stack, 1999). In fact, as we pointed out in Chapter 10, expressing an emotion, anger or otherwise, tends to intensify the feeling rather than reduce it.

A second approach, which does seem to effectively reduce or control aggression, is to introduce incompatible responses. Because certain emotional responses, such as empathy and humor, are incompatible with aggression, purposely making a joke or showing some sympathy for the other person's point of view can reduce anger and frustration (Harvey & Miceli, 1999; Kaukianen et al., 1999; Oshima, 2000).

A third approach to controlling aggression is to improve social and communication skills. Studies show that people with the most deficient communication skills account for a disproportionate share of the violence in society (Trump, 2000; Vance, Fernandez, & Biber, 1998). Unfortunately, little effort is made in our schools or families to teach basic communication skills or techniques for conflict resolution.

Visual Summary for Chapter 16

Our Thoughts about Others

Social Psychology: Studies how other people influence an individual's behavior (thoughts, feelings, and actions).

Attribution

Attribution: Explaining others' behavior by deciding that their actions resulted from internal factors (their own traits and motives) or external factors (the situation).

Problems:

Fundamental attribution error: Tendency to overestimate internal personality influences and underestimate situational factors when judging behavior of others. Why? May be **saliency bias**, focusing on most noticeable (salient) factors.

Self-serving bias: Tendency to explain our own behavior by attributing positive outcomes to internal factors and negative outcomes to external causes.

Attitudes

Attitudes: Learned predispositions toward a particular object.

Three components of all attitudes:

Cognitive: thoughts and beliefs

Affective: feelings

Behavioral tendencies: predispositions to action

Cognitive dissonance theory: A state of tension experienced when people discover inconsistencies between their attitudes or between their attitudes and their behavior. This mismatch and resulting tension motivate attitude change to restore balance.

Our Feelings about Others

Prejudice and Discrimination

Prejudice: Generally negative attitude directed toward people solely because of their membership in a specific group. Contains all three components of attitudes—cognitive **(stereotype)**, affective, and behavioral (discrimination).
Discrimination: Refers to the actual negative behavior directed at members of a group. People do not always act on their prejudices.

Four major sources of prejudice:

Learning: Classical and operant conditioning and social learning

Cognitive processes: **Ingroup favoritism, outgroup homogeneity effect**

Economic and political competition

Displaced aggression: Scapegoating

Five methods for reducing prejudice and discrimination:
• Cooperation
• **Superordinate goals**
• Increased contact
• Cognitive retraining
• Cognitive dissonance

Our Feelings about Others (cont).

Interpersonal attraction: Degree of positive or negative feelings toward another. Three key factors:

Physical attractiveness is important to initial attraction, more important to men than women, yet standards of beauty vary across cultures and historically. Physically attractive people generally are considered more intelligent, sociable, and interesting.

Physical **proximity** increases attraction largely due to the *mere exposure effect*.

Although people commonly believe that "opposites attract" **(need complementarity)**, research shows **similarity (need compatibility)** is much more important.

- *Love:* Rubin defines it in terms of caring, attachment, and intimacy.
- **Romantic love** highly valued in our society, but it's based on mystery and fantasy; thus, hard to sustain.
- **Companionate love** relies on mutual trust, respect, and friendship and grows stronger with time.

Our Actions toward Others

Social Influence

Conformity: Changes in behavior in response to real or imagined pressure from others.

Four reasons we conform:

For approval and acceptance **(normative social influence).**

Need for more information **(informational social influence).**

To match behavior of those we admire and feel similar to **(reference group).**

We also conform because it is often adaptive to do so.

Obedience: Going along with a direct command. Milgram's experiment showed a large number of people will obey orders. Why?

Power of authority

Distance between teacher and learner

Assignment of responsibility

Modeling/ imitation

Aggression

Aggression: Deliberate attempt to harm another living being who is motivated to avoid such treatment.
- *Biological causes:* Instincts, genes, the brain and nervous system, substance abuse and other mental disorders, hormones, and neurotransmitters.
- *Psychosocial causes:* Aversive stimuli, learning, media, and videogames.
- *Treatment:* Incompatible responses (like humor), social skills, and improved communication help reduce aggression, but releasing aggressive feeling through violent acts or watching violence are not helpful.

Group Processes

Groups are two or more people interacting and influencing one another's behavior.
- *Group membership* affects us through the roles we play, as demonstrated in Zimbardo's Stanford Prison Study, or through **deindividuation** (immersion in group identity leads to decreased self-awareness and personal responsibility).
- *Group decision making* is affected by two key factors:

Group polarization: If most group members initially tend toward an extreme idea, the entire group will move toward that extreme. Why? "Like-minded" members exposed to persuasive arguments that reinforce the dominant tendency.

Groupthink: Dangerous type of decision making where group's desire for agreement overrules its desire to critically evaluate information.

Altruism

Altruism: Actions designed to help others with no obvious benefit to oneself.
Why do we help?
- Evolutionary theorists believe altruism is innate and has survival value.
- Psychological explanations suggest helping is motivated by anticipated gain (**egoistic model**), or when helper feels empathy for the victim (**empathy-altruism hypothesis**).
Why don't we help?
- It depends on a series of interconnected events, starting with noticing the problem and ending with a decision to help.
- Many emergency situations are ambiguous.
- We assume others will respond (**diffusion of responsibility**).
How do we increase altruism?
- Reduce ambiguity by giving clear directions observers.
- Increase the rewards, while decreasing the costs.

study to determine whether the sex of the debater influences the outcome of a debate. In this study, one group of subjects watches a videotape of a debate between a male arguing the "pro" side and a female arguing the "con"; another group watches the same debate, but with the pro and con roles reversed. In such a study, the form of the presentation viewed by each group (whether "pro" is argued by a male or a female) is the independent variable because the experimenter manipulates the form of presentation seen by each group. Another example might be a study to determine whether a particular drug has any effect on a manual dexterity task. To study this question, we would administer the drug to one group and no drug to another. The independent variable would be the amount of drug given (some or none). The independent variable is particularly important when using **inferential statistics,** which we will discuss later.

The **dependent variable** is a factor that results from, or depends on, the independent variable. It is a measure of some outcome or, most commonly, a measure of the subjects' behavior. In the debate example, each subject's choice of the winner of the debate would be the dependent variable. In the drug experiment, the dependent variable would be each subject's score on the manual dexterity task.

Frequency Distributions

After conducting a study and obtaining measures of the variable(s) being studied, psychologists need to organize the data in a meaningful way. Table A.1 presents test scores from a statistics aptitude test collected from 50 college students. This information is called **raw data** because there is no order to the numbers. They are presented as they were collected and are therefore "raw."

The lack of order in raw data makes them difficult to study. Thus, the first step in understanding the results of an experiment is to impose some order on the raw data. There are several ways to do this. One of the simplest is to create a **frequency distribution,** which shows the number of times a score or event occurs. Although frequency distributions are helpful in several ways, the major advantages are that they allow us to see the data in an organized manner and they make it easier to represent the data on a graph.

The simplest way to make a frequency distribution is to list all the possible test scores, then tally the number of people (N) who received those scores. Table A.2 presents a frequency

distribution using the raw data from Table A.1. As you can see, the data are now easier to read. From looking at the frequency distribution, you can see that most of the test scores lie in the middle with only a few at the very high or very low end. This was not at all evident from looking at the raw data.

This type of frequency distribution is practical when the number of possible scores is 20 or fewer. However, when there are more than 20 possible scores it can be even harder to make sense out of the frequency distribution than the raw data. This can be seen in Table A.3, which presents the Scholastic Aptitude Test scores for 50 students. Even though there are only 50 actual scores in this table, the number of possible scores ranges from a high of 1390 to a low of 400. If we included zero

TABLE A.2 FREQUENCY DISTRIBUTION OF 50 STUDENTS ON STATISTICS APTITUDE TEST

Score	Frequency
73	2
72	3
71	0
70	1
69	0
68	5
67	1
66	2
65	3
64	2
63	5
62	5
61	2
60	2
59	5
58	2
57	3
56	1
55	0
54	1
53	0
52	2
51	1
50	3
Total	50

TABLE A.1 STATISTICS APTITUDE TEST SCORES FOR 50 COLLEGE STUDENTS

73	57	63	59	50
72	66	50	67	51
63	59	65	62	65
62	72	64	73	66
61	68	62	68	63
59	61	72	63	52
59	58	57	68	57
64	56	65	59	60
50	62	68	54	63
52	62	70	60	68

TABLE A.3 SCHOLASTIC APTITUDE TEST SCORES FOR 50 COLLEGE STUDENTS

1350	750	530	540	750
1120	410	788	1020	430
720	1080	1110	770	610
1130	620	510	1160	630
640	1220	920	650	870
930	660	480	940	670
1070	950	680	450	990
690	1010	800	660	500
860	520	540	880	1090
580	730	570	560	740

TABLE A.4 GROUP FREQUENCY DISTRIBUTION OF SCHOLASTIC APTITUDE TEST SCORES FOR 50 COLLEGE STUDENTS

Class Interval	Frequency
1300–1399	1
1200–1299	1
1100–1199	4
1000–1099	5
900–999	5
800–899	4
700–799	7
600–699	10
500–599	9
400–499	4
Total	50

frequencies there would be 991 entries in a frequency distribution of this data, making the frequency distribution much more difficult to understand than the raw data. If there are more than 20 possible scores, therefore, a **group** frequency distribution is normally used.

In a **group frequency distribution,** individual scores are represented as members of a group of scores or as a range of scores (see Table A.4). These groups are called **class intervals.** Grouping these scores makes it much easier to make sense out of the distribution, as you can see from the relative ease in understanding Table A.4 as compared to Table A.3. Group frequency distributions are easier to represent on a graph.

When graphing data from frequency distributions, the class intervals are represented along the **abscissa** (the horizontal or *x* axis), whereas the frequency is represented along the **ordinate** (the vertical or *y* axis). Information can be graphed in the form of a bar graph, called a **histogram,** or in the form of a point or line graph, called a **polygon.** Figure A.1 shows a histogram presenting the data from Table A.4. Note that the class intervals are represented along the bottom line of the graph (the *x* axis) and the height of the bars indicates the frequency in each class interval. Now look at Figure A.2. The information presented here is exactly the same as that in Figure A.1 but is represented in the form of a polygon rather than a histogram. Can you see how both graphs illustrate the

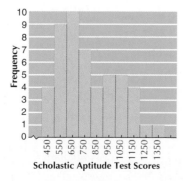

Figure A.1 A histogram illustrating the information found in Table A.4.

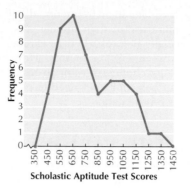

Figure A.2 A polygon illustrating the information found in Table A.4.

same information? Even though reading information from a graph is simple, we have found that many students have never learned to read graphs. In the next section we will explain how to read a graph.

How to Read a Graph

Every graph has several major parts. The most important are the labels, the axes (the vertical and horizontal lines), and the points, lines, or bars. Find these parts in Figure A.1.

The first thing you should notice when reading a graph are the labels because they tell what data are portrayed. Usually the data consist of the descriptive statistics, or the numbers used to measure the dependent variables. For example, in Figure A.1 the horizontal axis is labeled "Scholastic Aptitude Test Scores," which is the dependent variable measure; the vertical axis is labeled "Frequency," which means the number of occurrences. If a graph is not labeled, as we sometimes see in TV commercials or magazine ads, it is useless and should be ignored. Even when a graph *is* labeled, the labels can be misleading. For example, if graph designers want to distort the information, they can elongate one of the axes. Thus, it is important to pay careful attention to the numbers as well as the words in graph labels.

Next, you should focus your attention on the bars, points, or lines on the graph. In the case of histograms like the one in Figure A.1, each bar represents the class interval. The width of the bar stands for the width of the class interval, whereas the height of the bar stands for the frequency in that interval. Look at the third bar from the left in Figure A.1. This bar represents the interval "600 to 699 SAT Scores," which has a frequency of 10. You can see that this directly corresponds to the same class interval in Table A.4, since graphs and tables are both merely alternate ways of illustrating information.

Reading point or line graphs is the same as reading a histogram. In a point graph, each point represents two numbers, one found along the horizontal axis and the other found along the vertical axis. A polygon is identical to a point graph except that it has lines connecting the points. Figure A.2 is an example of a polygon, where each point represents a class interval and is placed at the center of the interval and at the height corresponding to the frequency of that interval. To make the graph easier to read, the points are connected by straight lines.

Displaying the data in a frequency distribution or in a graph is much more useful than merely presenting raw data and can be especially helpful when researchers are trying to find relations between certain factors. However, as we explained earlier, if psychologists want to make predictions or explanations about behavior, they need to perform mathematical computations on the data.

USES OF THE VARIOUS STATISTICS

The statistics psychologists use in a study depend on whether they are trying to describe and predict behavior or explain it. When they use statistics to describe behavior, as in reporting the average score on the Scholastic Aptitude Test, they are using **descriptive statistics.** When they use them to explain behavior, as Bandura did in his study of children modeling aggressive behavior seen on TV, they are using **inferential statistics.**

Descriptive Statistics

Descriptive statistics are the numbers used to describe the dependent variable. They can be used to describe characteristics of a **population** (an entire group, such as all people living in the United States) or a **sample** (a part of a group, such as a randomly selected group of 25 students from Cornell University). The major descriptive statistics include measures of central tendency (mean, median, and mode), measures of variation (variance and standard deviation), and correlation.

Measures of Central Tendency

Statistics indicating the center of the distribution are called **measures of central tendency** and include the mean, median, and mode. They are all scores that are typical of the center of the distribution. The **mean** is what most of us think of when we hear the word "average." The **median** is the middle score. The **mode** is the score that occurs most often.

Mean What is your average golf score? What is the average yearly rainfall in your part of the country? What is the average reading test score in your city? When these questions ask for the average, they are really asking for the "mean." The arithmetic **mean** is the weighted average of all the raw scores, which is computed by totaling all the raw scores and then dividing that total by the number of scores added together. In statistical computation, the mean is represented by an "X" with a bar above it ($\overline{X}$, pronounced "X bar"), each individual raw score by an "X," and the total number of scores by an "N." For example, if we wanted to compute the $\overline{X}$ of the raw statistics test scores in Table A.1, we would sum all the X's (ΣX, with Σ meaning sum) and divide by N (number of scores). In Table A.1, the sum of all the scores is equal to 3,100 and there are 50 scores. Therefore, the mean of these scores is

TABLE A.5 COMPUTATION OF THE MEAN FOR 10 IQ SCORES

IQ Scores X
143
127
116
98
85
107
106
98
104
116
$\Sigma X = 1,100$

$$\text{Mean} = \overline{X} = \frac{\Sigma X}{N} = \frac{1,100}{10} = 110$$

$$\overline{X} = \frac{3,100}{50} = 62$$

Table A.5 illustrates how to calculate the mean for 10 IQ scores.

Median The **median** is the middle score in the distribution once all the scores have been arranged in rank order. If N (the number of scores) is odd, then there actually is a middle score and that middle score is the median. When N is even, there are two middle scores and the median is the mean of those two scores. Table A.6 shows the computation of the median for two different sets of scores, one set with 15 scores and one with 10.

TABLE A.6 COMPUTATION OF MEDIAN FOR ODD AND EVEN NUMBERS OF IQ SCORES

IQ	IQ
139	137
130	135
121	121
116	116
107	108 ← middle score
101	106 ← middle score
98	105
96 ← middle score	101
84	98
83	97
82	N = 10
75	N is even
75	
65	Median $= \dfrac{106 + 108}{2} = \dfrac{107}{62}$
N = 15	
N is odd	

T A B L E A . 7 FINDING THE MODE FOR TWO DIFFERENT DISTRIBUTIONS

IQ	IQ
139	139
138	138
125	125
116 ←	116 ←
116 ←	116 ←
116 ←	116 ←
107	107
100	98 ←
98	98 ←
98	98 ←
Mode = most frequent score	Mode = 116 and 98
Mode = 116	

Mode Of all the measures of central tendency, the easiest to compute is the **mode,** which is merely the most frequent score. It is computed by finding the score that occurs most often. Whereas there is always only one mean and only one median for each distribution, there can be more than one mode. Table A.7 shows how to find the mode in a distribution with one mode (unimodal) and in a distribution with two modes (bimodal).

There are several advantages to each of these measures of central tendency, but in psychological research the mean is used most often. A book solely covering psychological statistics will provide a more thorough discussion of the relative values of these measures.

Measures of Variation

When describing a distribution, it is not sufficient merely to give the central tendency; it is also necessary to give a **measure of variation,** which is a measure of the spread of the scores. By examining the spread, we can determine whether the scores are bunched around the middle or tend to extend away from the middle. Figure A.3 shows three different distributions, all with the same mean but with different spreads of scores. You can see from this figure that, in order to describe these different distributions accurately, there must be some measures of the variation in their spread. The most widely used measure of variation is the standard deviation, which is represented by a lowercase *s.* The standard deviation is a stan-

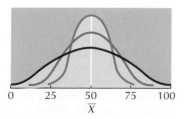

Figure A.3 Three distributions having the same mean but a different variability.

dard measurement of how much the scores in a distribution deviate from the mean. The formula for the standard deviation is

$$s = \sqrt{\frac{\Sigma(X - \overline{X})^2}{N}}$$

Table A.8 illustrates how to compute the standard deviation.

Most distributions of psychological data are bell-shaped. That is, most of the scores are grouped around the mean, and the farther the scores are from the mean in either direction, the fewer the scores. Notice the bell shape of the distribution in Figure A.4. Distributions such as this are called **normal** distributions. In normal distributions, as shown in Figure A.4, approximately two-thirds of the scores fall within a range that is one standard deviation below the mean to one standard deviation above the mean. For example, the Wechsler IQ tests (see Chapter 7) have a mean of 100 and a standard deviation of 15.

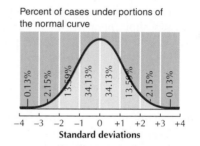

Percent of cases under portions of the normal curve

Figure A.4 *The normal distribution forms a bell-shaped curve.* In a normal distribution, two-thirds of the scores lie between one standard deviation above and one standard deviation below the mean.

T A B L E A . 8 COMPUTATION OF THE STANDARD DEVIATION FOR 10 IQ SCORES

IQ Scores X	$X - \overline{X}$	$(X - \overline{X})^2$
143	33	1089
127	17	289
116	6	36
98	−12	144
85	−25	625
107	−3	9
106	−4	16
98	−12	144
104	−6	36
116	6	36
$\Sigma X = 1100$		$\Sigma(X - \overline{X})^2 = 2424$

Standard Deviation = s

$$= \sqrt{\frac{\Sigma(X - \overline{X})^2}{N}} = \sqrt{\frac{224}{10}}$$

$$= \sqrt{22.4} = 15.569$$

This means that approximately two-thirds of the people taking these tests will have scores between 85 and 115.

Correlation

Suppose for a moment that you are sitting in the student union with a friend. To pass the time, you and your friend decide to play a game in which you try to guess the height of the next male who enters the union. The winner, the one whose guess is closest to the person's actual height, gets a piece of pie paid for by the loser. When it is your turn, what do you guess? If you are like most people, you will probably try to estimate the mean of all the males in the union and use that as your guess. The mean is always your best guess if you have no other information.

Now let's change the game a little and add a friend who stands outside the union and weighs the next male to enter the union. Before the male enters the union, your friend says "125 pounds." Given this new information, will you still guess the mean height? Probably not — you will probably predict *below* the mean. Why? Because there is a **correlation,** a relationship, between height and weight, with tall people usually weighing more than short people. Since 125 pounds is less than the average weight for males, you will probably guess a less-than-average height. The statistic used to measure this type of relationship between two variables is called a correlation coefficient.

Correlation Coefficient   A **correlation coefficient** measures the relationship between two variables, such as height and weight or IQ and SAT scores. Given any two variables, there are three possible relationships between them: **positive, negative,** and **zero** (no relationship). A positive relationship exists when the two variables vary in the same direction (e.g., as height increases, weight normally also increases). A negative relationship occurs when the two variables vary in opposite directions (e.g., as temperatures go up, hot chocolate sales go down). There is no relationship when the two variables vary totally independently of one another (e.g., there is no relationship between peoples' height and the color of their toothbrushes). Figure A.5 illustrates these three types of correlations.

The computation and the formula for a correlation coefficient (correlation coefficient is delineated by the letter "*r*") are shown in Table A.9. The correlation coefficient (*r*) always has a value between +1 and −1 (it is never greater than +1 and it is never smaller than −1). When *r* is close to +1, it signifies a high positive relationship between the two variables (as one variable goes up, the other variable also goes up). When *r* is close to −1, it signifies a high negative relationship between the two variables (as one variable goes up, the other variable goes down). When *r* is 0, there is no linear relationship between the two variables being measured.

Correlation coefficients can be quite helpful in making predictions. Bear in mind, however, that predictions are just that: *predictions*. They will have some error as long as the correlation coefficients on which they are based are not perfect (+1 or −1). Also, correlations cannot reveal any information regarding causation. Merely because two factors are cor-

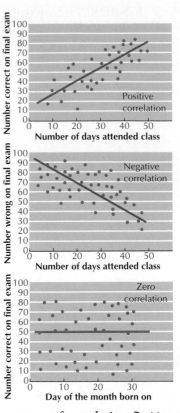

Figure A.5 *Three types of correlation.* Positive correlation (top): As the number of days of class attendance increases, so does the number of correct exam items. Negative correlation (middle): As the number of days of class attendance increases, the number of incorrect exam items decreases. Zero correlation (bottom): The day of the month on which one is born has no relationship to the number of exam items correct.

related, it does not mean that one factor causes the other. Consider, for example, ice cream consumption and swimming pool use. These two variables are positively correlated with one another, in that as ice cream consumption increases, so does swimming pool use. But nobody would suggest that eating ice cream *causes* swimming, or vice versa. Similarly, just because Michael Jordan eats Wheaties and can do a slam dunk it does not mean that you will be able to do one if you eat the same breakfast. The only way to determine the cause of behavior is to conduct an experiment and analyze the results by using inferential statistics.

Inferential Statistics

Knowing the descriptive statistics associated with different distributions, such as the mean and standard deviation, can enable us to make comparisons between various distributions. By making these comparisons, we may be able to observe whether one variable is related to another or whether one variable has a causal effect on another. When we design an experiment specifically to measure causal effects between two or more variables, we use **inferential statistics** to analyze the

TABLE A.9 COMPUTATION OF CORRELATION COEFFICIENT BETWEEN HEIGHT AND WEIGHT FOR 10 MALES

Height (inches) X	X^2	Weight (pounds) Y	Y^2	XY
73	5,329	210	44,100	15,330
64	4,096	133	17,689	8,512
65	4,225	128	16,384	8,320
70	4,900	156	24,336	10,920
74	5,476	189	35,721	13,986
68	4,624	145	21,025	9,860
67	4,489	145	21,025	9,715
72	5,184	166	27,556	11,952
76	5,776	199	37,601	15,124
71	5,041	159	25,281	11,289
700	49,140	1,630	272,718	115,008

$$r = \frac{N \cdot \Sigma XY - \Sigma X \cdot \Sigma Y}{\sqrt{[N \cdot \Sigma X^2 - (\Sigma X)^2]}\sqrt{[N \cdot \Sigma Y^2 - (\Sigma Y)^2]}}$$

$$r = \frac{10 \cdot 115,008 - 700 \cdot 1,630}{\sqrt{[10 \cdot 49,140 - 700^2]}\sqrt{[10 \cdot 272,718 - 1,630^2]}}$$

$$r = 0.92$$

TABLE A.10 REACTION TIMES IN MILLISECONDS (MSEC) FOR SUBJECTS IN ALCOHOL AND NO ALCOHOL CONDITIONS AND COMPUTATION OF T

RT (msec) Alcohol X_1	RT (msec) No Alcohol X_2
200	143
210	137
140	179
160	184
180	156
187	132
196	176
198	148
140	125
159	120
$SX_1 = 1,770$	$SX_2 = 1,500$
$N_1 = 10$	$N_2 = 10$
$\overline{X}_1 = 177$	$\overline{X}_2 = 150$
$s_1 = 24.25$	$s_2 = 21.86$

$$S_{\overline{X}_1} = \frac{s}{\sqrt{N_1 - 1}} = 8.08 \qquad S_{\overline{X}_2} = \frac{s}{\sqrt{N_2 - 1}} = 7.29$$

$$S_{\overline{X}_1 - \overline{X}_2} = \sqrt{S_{\overline{X}_1}^2 + S_{\overline{X}_2}^2} = \sqrt{8.08^2 + 7.29^2} = 10.88$$

$$t = \frac{X_1 - X_2}{S_{\overline{X}_1 - \overline{X}_2}} = \frac{177 - 150}{10.88} = 2.48$$

$$t = 2.48, \; p < .05$$

data collected. Although there are many inferential statistics, the onc we will discuss is the *t*-test, since it is the simplest.

t-Test   Suppose we believe that drinking alcohol causes a person's reaction time to slow down. To test this hypothesis, we recruit 20 participants and separate them into two groups. We ask the participants in one group to drink a large glass of orange juice with one ounce of alcohol for every 100 pounds of body weight (e.g., a person weighing 150 pounds would get 1.5 ounces of alcohol). We ask the control group to drink an equivalent amount of orange juice with no alcohol added. Fifteen minutes after the drinks, we have each participant perform a reaction time test that consists of pushing a button as soon as a light is flashed. (The reaction time is the time between the onset of the light and the pressing of the button.) Table A.10 shows the data from this hypothetical experiment. It is clear from the data that there is definitely a difference in the reaction times of the two groups: There is an obvious difference between the means. However, it is possible that this difference is due merely to chance. To determine whether the difference is real or due to chance, we can conduct a *t*-test. We have run a sample *t*-test in Table A.10.

The logic behind a *t*-test is relatively simple. In our experiment we have two samples. If each of these samples is from the *same* population (e.g., the population of all people, whether drunk or sober), then any difference between the samples will be due to chance. On the other hand, if the two samples are from *different* populations (e.g., the population of drunk pcople *and* the population of sober people), then the difference is a significant difference and not due to chance.

If there is a significant difference between the two samples, then the independent variable must have caused that difference. In our example, there is a significant difference between the alcohol and the no alcohol groups. We can tell this because *p* (the probability that this *t* value will occur by chance) is less than .05. To obtain the *p*, we need only look up the *t* value in a statistical table, which is found in any statistics book. In our example, because there is a significant difference between the groups, we can reasonably conclude that the alcohol did cause a slower reaction time.

APPENDIX B

Answers to Review Questions, Try This Yourself, and Active Learning Exercises

CHAPTER 1 *Understanding Psychology Page 10* 1. scientific; behavior; mental processes. 2. The process of objectively evaluating, comparing, analyzing, and synthesizing information. Critical thinking has three components: *affective skills* (e.g., empathy and tolerance for ambiguity), *cognitive abilities* (e.g., independent thinking and synthesizing), and *behavioral traits* (e.g., delaying judgment and applying knowledge to new situations). 3. (a). *Description* tells "what" occurred. (b). An *explanation* tells "why" a behavior occurred. (c). *Prediction* specifies the conditions under which a behavior or event is likely to occur. (d). *Change* means applying psychological knowledge to prevent unwanted outcomes or bring about desired goals 4. biopsychology or neuroscience, developmental psychology, cognitive psychology, clinical psychology, industrial/organizational psychology. *Scientific Method and Experiments Page 18* 1. (a). literature review (b). formulating a testable hypothesis, (c). designing the study and collecting the data, (d). analyzing the data and accepting or rejecting the hypothesis, (e). publishing followed by replication and scientific review, and f). building further theory. 2. In an experiment, the experimenter manipulates and controls the variables, which allows them to isolate a single factor and examine the effect of that factor alone on a particular behavior. 3. c. 4. The two problems for researchers are experimenter bias and ethnocentrism, whereas the two problems for participants are sample bias and participant bias. To guard against **experimenter bias,** researchers employ blind observers, single-blind and **double-blind studies,** and **placebos.** To control for **ethnocentrism,** they use cross-cultural sampling. To offset participant problems with **sample bias,** researchers use random/representative sampling and **random assignment.** To control for participant bias, they rely on many of the same controls in place to prevent experimenter bias, such as double-blind studies. They also attempt to assure anonymity, confidentiality, and sometimes use deception. *Nonexperimental Studies/Research and Ethical Problems Page 26* 1. **Naturalistic observation** studies and describes behavior in its natural habitat, surveys use interviews or questionnaires to obtain information on a sample of participants, and individual case studies conduct in-depth studies of a participant. 2. d. 3. b. 4. c. *Schools of Psychology Page 34* 1. experimental. 2. functionalists. 3. Freud's theories are controversial because of his nonscientific approach, emphasis on sexual and aggressive impulses, and possible sexist bias in his writings and theories. 4. a.

CHAPTER 2 *An Overview of the Nervous System Page 50* 1. central; peripheral. 2. d. 3. d. 4. The sympathetic nervous system arouses the body and mobilizes energy stores to deal with emergencies, whereas the parasympathetic nervous system calms the body and conserves the energy stores. *Neurons, Neural Communication, and Chemical Messengers Page 58* 1. Check your diagram with Figure 2.2. 2. c. 3. b. 4. Neurotransmitters and endorphins are manufactured and released at the synapse, where the messages are picked up and relayed by neighboring neurons. Hormones are released from glands in the endocrine system directly into the bloodstream. *Tools for Exploration and Lower-Level Brain Structures Page 65* 1. Electrical recording techniques implant electrodes into the brain or on its surface to study the brain's electrical activity, whereas electrical stimulation of the brain uses a weak electric current to stimulate specific areas or structures of the brain and then observe the response. 2. CT, PET, MRI, fMRI. 3. cerebellum. 4. b. *The Cerebral Cortex and Hemispheric Specialization Page 74* 1. cerebral cortex. 2. occipital; temporal; frontal; parietal. 3. a. 4. c. *Genetics and Evolutionary Psychology Page 83* 1. c. 2. Behavioral geneticists use twin studies, adoption studies, family studies, and genetic abnormalities. 3. Because natural selection favors animals whose concern for kin is proportional to their degree of biological relatedness, most people will devote more resources, protection, love and concern to close relatives, which helps ensure their genetic survival. 4. One possible answer is that in ancient societies men were the "hunters" and women "gatherers." The man's superiority on many spatial relationships and target-directed motor skills, may reflect demands of hunting, whereas activities such as gathering, child-rearing, and domestic tool construction and manipulation may have contributed to the woman's language superiority.

CHAPTER 3 *What Health Psychologists Do and Smoking Page 92* 1. It is the study of the relationship between psychological behavior and physical health and illness, with an emphasis on wellness and the prevention of illness. 2. contagious; noncontagious. 3. In addition to social pressures that encourage smoking, nicotine is a powerfully addictive drug and smokers learn to associate positive things with smoking. 4. d. *Binge Drinking and Chronic Pain Page 95* 1. When a man consumes five or more alcoholic drinks in a row and a woman consumes four or more alcoholic drinks in a row. 2. Binge drinkers are just average drinkers — make it clear that binge drinking is not the norm; Binge drinking is harmless — binge drinking causes loss of control that can lead to injury, death, and exposure to sexually transmitted diseases; Okay to binge drink because administration ignores it — administrators must enforce rules; Binge drinking is just part of fraternity or sorority life — colleges must work within the Greek System to decrease binge drinking; Students see alumni drinking at sports and alumni events — all drinking rules must also apply to alumni. 3. chronic. 4. a. ***Sources of Stress Page 101*** 1. a. 2. a. 3. a blocked goal; conflict. 4. Choosing between apple pie or pumpkin pie is an example of an approach-approach conflict. Choosing between early morning or evening classes normally is an approach-avoidance conflict. Taking an exam when you're underprepared or not taking the exam and receiving an automatic F is an example of an avoidance-avoidance conflict. ***Results of Stress Page 104*** 1. The sympathetic branch of the autonomic nervous system is activated, thereby increasing heart rate, blood pressure, etc. The parasympathetic branch of the autonomic nervous system is activated during low-stress conditions and it lowers heart rate and blood pressure, while increasing activity in the stomach and intestines. 2. alarm; resistance; exhaustion. 3. c. 4. They have probably experienced a lot of stress, and stress can suppress the immune system, making them vulnerable to cold and flu viruses. ***Stress and Serious Illness Page 107*** 1. epinephrine; cortisol. 2. b. 3. shotgun, target behavior. Answers will vary, but alternatives include a shotgun approach because it will change my whole Type A personality, or a target behavior approach because it will change only the behaviors that lead to a hostile attitude. 4. A hardy personality is based on three qualities: a commitment to personal goals, control over life, and viewing change as a challenge rather than a threat. ***Coping with Stress Page 113*** 1. emotion-focused, problem focused. 2. Rationalization and denial. Defense mechanisms alleviate anxiety but distort reality. 3. internal. 4. The six resources are health and energy, positive beliefs, social skills, social support, material resources, and personal control. Answers will vary depending on personality and individual life style.

CHAPTER 4 ***Experiencing Sensations Page 122*** 1. c. 2. absolute threshold. 3. The sensory receptors for smell adapt and send fewer messages to the brain. 4. b. ***How We See and Hear Page 130*** 1. Compare your diagram to Figure 4.4.2. thinning and flattening, thickening and bulging, accommodation. 3. Compare your diagram to figure 4.8. 4. Place theory explains how we hear higher-pitched sounds, whereas frequency theory explains how we hear lower-pitched sounds. ***Our Other Senses Page 134*** 1. b. 2. d. 3. kinesthetic. 4. d. ***Selection Page 137*** 1. Illusions are false impressions of the physical world produced by actual physical distortions, hallucinations are sensory perceptions that occur without an external stimulus, and delusions are false beliefs. 2. feature detectors. 3. "Horizontal cats" reared in a horizontal world failed to develop potential feature detectors for vertical lines or objects. 4. c. ***Organization — Form and Constancies Page 143*** 1. proximity, continuity, closure. 2. size constancy. 3. brightness constancy. 4. c. ***Organization — Depth and Color Page 148*** 1. c. 2. b. 3. color aftereffects, green rectangle. 4. The trichromatic system operates at the level of the retina, whereas the opponent-process system occurs at the level of the brain. ***Interpretation and ESP Page 152*** 1. a. 2. a. 3. telepathy, clairvoyance, precognition, telekinesis. 4. usually cannot be replicated.

CHAPTER 5 ***Understanding Consciousness Page 160*** 1. b. 2. They considered it too unscientific and not the proper focus of psychology. 3. focused, minimal. 4. d. ***Circadian Rhythms and Stages of Sleep Page 167*** 1. d. 2. b. 3. electroencephalograph (EEG). 4. a. ***Theories of Sleep and Dreaming Page 171*** 1. Repair/restoration theory suggests we sleep to physically restore our mind and body, whereas evolutionary/circadian theory says that sleep evolved because it helped conserve energy and provided protection from predators. 2. Both men and women have dreams that reflect important life events, but women are more likely to dream of familiar people, household objects, and indoor events, whereas men dream about strangers, violence, sex, achievement, and outdoor events. All cultures dream about basic human needs and fears, but the Yir Yoront men dream of aggression from their mother's brother. Also, Americans dream of being naked in public, whereas cultures wearing few clothes do not dream of being naked. 3. d. 4. c. ***Sleep Disorders Page 175*** 1. insomnia. 2. sleep apnea. 3. night terrors. 4. narcolepsy. ***Drugs and Consciousness Page 187*** 1. c. 2. d. 3. Physical dependence refers to changes in the bodily processes that require continued use of the drug to prevent withdrawal symptoms, whereas psychological dependence refers to the mental desire or craving to achieve the effects produced by the drug. 4. Psychoactive drugs can alter the production, affect storage or release, alter the reception, and block the inactivation of neurotransmitters. ***Additional Routes to Alternate States Page 193*** 1. They may feel guilty or negative because they do not make a distinction between thought and behavior–thinking is not the same as doing. 2. Hypnosis requires the subject to make a conscious decision to relinquish some personal control of his or her consciousness. 3. d. 4. As a part of sacred rituals, for social interactions, and for individual rewards.

CHAPTER 6 ***Understanding Classical Conditioning Page 203*** 1. b. 2. conditioned stimulus, conditioned response. 3. d. 4. c. ***Principles and Applications of Classical Conditioning Page 208*** 1. You no longer respond to the sound of the fire alarm because your response has been extinguished, which occurs when the UCS is repeatedly withheld, and the association between the CS and the UCS is broken. 2. d. 3. higher-order conditioning. 4. c. ***Operant Conditioning Page 222*** 1. Operant conditioning occurs when organisms learn by the consequences of their responses, whereas in classical conditioning organisms learn by pairing up associations. Operant conditioning is voluntary, whereas classical conditioning is involuntary. 2. c. 3. resistant. 4. Marshall's superstition may be wearing the same necklace to every exam because he believes it is helpful to his performance, although in reality wearing the necklace and previous good luck on exams were only accidentally related. ***Cognitive-Social Learning Page 227*** 1. c. 2. latent learning. 3. cognitive maps. 4. b. ***Neuroscience and Evolution Page 231*** 1. d. 2. Garcia and his colleagues laced freshly killed sheep with a chemical that caused nausea and vomiting in coyotes. After the coyotes ate the tainted meat and became ill, they avoided all sheep. 3. Biological preparedness refers to the fact that organisms are innately predisposed to form associations between certain stimuli and responses. 4. Instinctive drift.

CHAPTER 7 ***Three-Stage Memory Model and Encoding, Storage, and Retrieval Page 243*** 1. c. 2. a. 3. Encoding is comparable to typing on a keyboard, storage compares to the hard drive of the computer, and retrieval is analogous to the computer's retrieval of information and its display on the monitor. 4. According to the Parallel Distributed Processing (PDP), or *connectionist*, model, memory resembles a vast number of interconnected units and modules distributed throughout a huge network, all operating in parallel — simultaneously. ***Integration Model and Biological Perspective Page 254*** 1. Semantic memory involves remembering facts and how they relate to one another, whereas episodic memory involves remembering where and when an event happened. 2. recognition, recall. 3. a. 4. Repeated stimulation of a synapse can strengthen the synapse by stimulating the dendrites to grow more spines, and the ability of a particular neuron to release its neurotransmitters can be increased or decreased. *Why Do We Forget? Page 260* 1. d. 2. Using distributed practice, you would space your study time into many learning periods with rest periods in between; using massed practice, you would "cram" all your learning into long, unbroken periods. 3. Retrieval failure theory, decay theory, motivated forgetting theory. *Problems with Memory Page 267* 1. amnesia. 2. d. 3. Source amnesia occurs when the true source of the memory is forgotten. The sleeper effect refers to the initial tendency to discount information from an unreliable source, but later consider it more trustworthy because the source is forgotten. The misinformation effect results from incorporating outside information into one's own memory of an event. 4. Research shows that it is unreliable. *Improving Memory Page 272* 1. Given that the duration of short-term memory is about 30 seconds, to lengthen this time use *maintenance rehearsal*, which involves continuously repeating the material. To effectively encode memory into long-term memory, use *elaborative rehearsal*, which involves thinking about the material and relating it to other information that has already been stored. 2. Because we tend to remember information that falls at the beginning or end of a sequence, be sure to spend extra time with information in the middle of the chapter. 3. organization. 4. Peg-word system, method of loci, method of word associations, substitute word system.

CHAPTER 8 *Try This Yourself page 279* The figures in b are not the same. To solve this problem, mentally rotate one of the objects and then compare the rotated image with the other object to see whether they matched or not. The figures in b were more difficult to solve because they required a greater degree of mental rotation. This is also true of real objects in physical space. It takes more time and energy to turn a cup 20 degrees to the right, than to turn it 150 degrees. *The Thinking Brain and Cognitive Building Blocks Page 282* 1. c. 2. There are at least three methods — artificial concepts, natural concepts, and hierarchies. 3. prototype. 4. b. *Solving Problems Page 287* 1. Preparation, in which we identify the facts, determine which ones are relevant, and define the goal; production, in which we propose possible solutions, or hypotheses; and evaluation, in which we determine whether the solutions meet the goal. 2. b. 3. d. 4. mental sets, functional fixedness, and confirmation bias. Incubation allows a "time out," which helps overcome each of these barriers. *Creativity Page 290* 1. c. 2. divergent, convergent, divergent. 3. intellectual ability, knowledge, thinking style, personality, motivation, and environment. 4. Probably not because people tend to be less creative when they are working for extrinsic rewards. *Language Page 296* 1. phonemes, morphemes. 2. The surface structure refers to the words in a sentence, whereas the deep structure is the actual meaning of the sentence. 3. Language shapes thought. 4. a. *The Nature of Intelligence and Test Construction Page 302* 1. b. 2. Fluid intelligence refers to reasoning abilities, memory, and speed of information processing, whereas crystallized intelligence refers to knowledge and skills gained through experience and education. 3. Sternberg proposed three aspects of intelligence — analytic, creative, and practical. 4. reliability, validity, standardization. *Assessing Intelligence/Explaining Differences in Intelligence Page 312* 1. No, an IQ test merely measures verbal and quantitative abilities and predicts school success. 2. The Stanford–Binet is a single test con-

sisting of several sets of various age-level items, whereas the Wechsler consists of three separate tests; also the Stanford–Binet primarily measures verbal abilities, while the Wechsler measures both verbal and performance abilities. 3. d. 4. Both heredity and environment are important, interacting influences.

CHAPTER 9 *Studying Development Page 323* 1. Developmental psychology studies age-related changes in behaviors and abilities from conception to death. 2. nature or nurture, continuity or stages, stability or change. 3. d. 4. c. *Physical Development Page 332* 1. The three major stages are the germinal period, the embryonic period, and the fetal period. 2. b. 3. c. 4. Primary aging is defined as the inevitable age-related biological changes in physical and mental processes, whereas secondary aging results from abuse, neglect, disuse, or disease. *Language Development Page 334* 1. Cooing is only vowel sounds ("eee"), while babbling adds consonants ("dadada"). 2. d. 3. b. 4. Nativists suggest language is inborn and develops primarily from maturation, while nurturists emphasize the environment and the role of rewards, punishments, and imitation of models. *Social-Emotional Development Page 339* 1. b. 2. Securely attached, anxious-avoidant, and anxious-ambivalent; 3. 1a, 2c, 3b. 4. Authoritarian parents value unquestioning obedience and mature responsibility from their children. Permissive parents either set few limts and provide little attention (the permissive-indifferent), or they're highly involved but few demands (the permissive-indulgent). Authoritative parents are caring and sensitive, but also set firm limits and enforce them. *Active Learning Exercise Page 345* 1. The child is upset because he thinks he now has MORE of the disliked food since the mother spread it around to cool it. He is in the preoperational stage and cannot conserve. 2. Janie has acquired object permanence. She is still in the sensorimotor stage. 3. Tom is upset because of his intense idealism and adolescent egocentrism. He is in the beginning part of the formal operational stage. 4. The older child is in the concrete operational (or formal operational) stage. The younger child is preoperational and cannot conserve, which allows him to be happy with one cookie broken into two pieces — he thinks he has "two cookies." *Cognitive development Page 348–349* 1. c. 2. d. 3. 1b, 2a, 3d, 4c, 5d. 4. Memory problems for older adults are primarily problems of encoding, taking more time to store the information, and retrieval, taking more time to find the information.

Chapter 10 *Moral Development Page 358* 1. Preconventional, postconventional, conventional. 2. c. 3. b. 4. Kohlberg's theory is culturally biased toward individualism versus community and interpersonal relationships. His theory is gender biased because it supposedly favors the male's justice perspective over the female's care perspective. *Personality Development Over the Life Span Page 363.* 1. c. 2. Thomas and Chess describe three categories of temperament — easy, difficult, and slow-to-warm-up — that seem to correlate with stable personality differences. 3. trust versus mistrust, identity versus role confusion, initiative versus guilt, ego integrity versus despair. 4. Research shows that beliefs about adolescent storm and stress, the midlife crisis, and the empty nest syndrome may be exaggerated accounts of a few people's experiences and not those of most people. *Additional Influences on Development Page 370* 1. c. 2. activity; disengagement. 3. c. 4. The social support may help reduce the losses that accompany aging. *Bereavement and Death Pages 374* 1. Preschool children only understand the permanence of death, they do not yet comprehend the nonfunctionality or universality of death. 2. d. 3. a bargaining, b denial, c resolution, d anger, e despair. 4. d.

CHAPTER 11   *Sex and Gender Pages 388* 1. Chromosomal sex b, gender identity d, gonadal sex a, gender role I, hormonal sex c, secondary sex characteristics e, external genitals g, sexual orientation h, internal accessory organs f. 2. d. 3. Social learning theory emphasizes learning through rewards, punishments, and imitation, while cognitive-developmental theory focuses on the active, thinking processes of the individual. 4. d. ***The Study of Human Sexuality Page 393*** 1. b. 2. Ellis based his research on personal diaries; Masters and Johnson pioneered the use of direct observation and measurement of bodily responses during sexual activities; Kinsey popularized the use of the survey method. 3. Cultural comparisons put sex in a broader perspective and help counteract ethnocentrism. 4. d. ***Sexual Behavior Page 397*** 1. Masters and Johnson identified a four-stage sexual response cycle (excitement, plateau, orgasm, and resolution) that acknowledged both similarities and differences between the sexes. However differences are the focus of most research. 2. According to the evolutionary perspective, males engage in more sexual behaviors with more sexual partners because it helps the species survive. The social role perspective suggests this difference reflects a double standard, which subtly encourages male sexuality while discouraging female sexuality. 3. c. 4. d. ***Answers to Active Learning Exercise Page 406 Gender role conditioning*** — A main part of traditional gender conditioning is the belief that women should be the "gatekeepers" for sexuality and men should be the "pursuers." This leads to the myth that male sexuality is overpowering and women are responsible for controlling the situation. ***Double standard*** — Female gender role also encourages passivity, and women are not taught how to aggressively defend themselves. People who believe the myth that women cannot be raped against their will generally overlook the fact that the female gender role encourages passivity and women are not taught how to aggressively defend themselves. ***Media portrayals*** — Novels and films typically portray a woman resisting her attacker and then melting into passionate responsiveness. This helps perpetuate the myth that women secretly want to be raped and the myth that she might as well "relax and enjoy it." ***Lack of information*** — The myth that women cannot be raped against their will overlooks the fact that most men are much stronger and much faster than most women, and a woman's clothing and shoes further hinder her ability to escape. The myth that women cannot rape men ignores the fact that men can have erections despite negative emotions while being raped. Furthermore, an erection is unnecessary, since many rapists (either male or female) often use foreign objects to rape their victims. The myth that all women secretly want to be raped overlooks the fact that if a woman fantasizes about being raped she remains in complete control, whereas in an actual rape she is completely powerless. Also, fantasies contain no threat of physical harm, while rape does.

Tips for Rape Prevention Sex educators and researchers suggest the following techniques for reducing stranger rape (the rape of a person by an unknown assailant) and acquaintance (or date) rape (committed by someone who is known to the victim) (Crooks & Baur, 1999; Denny & Quadagno, 1998). To avoid stranger rape: 1. Follow commonsense advice for avoiding all forms of crime: lock your car, park in lighted areas, install dead-bolt locks on your doors, don't open your door to strangers, don't hitchhike, etc. 2. Make yourself as strong as possible. Take a self-defense course,

carry a loud whistle with you, and demonstrate self-confidence with your body language. Research shows that rapists tend to select women who appear passive and weak (Richards et al., 1991). 3. During an attack, run away if you can, talk to the rapist as a way to stall, and/or attempt to alert others by screaming ("Help, rape, call the police") (Shotland & Stebbins, 1980). When all else fails, women should actively resist an attack, according to current research (Fischhoff, 1992; Furby & Fischhoff, 1992). Loud shouting, fighting back, and causing a scene may deter an attack. To prevent acquaintance rape: 1. Be careful on first dates — date in groups and in public places; avoid alcohol and other drugs (Gross & Billingham, 1998). 2. Be assertive and clear in your communication — say what you want and what you don't want. Accept a partner's refusal. If sexual coercion escalates, match the assailant's behavior with your own form of escalation — begin with firm refusals, get louder, threaten to call the police, begin shouting and use strong physical resistance. Don't be afraid to make a scene! ***Sexual Problems Page 407*** 1. The parasympathetic branch of the autonomic nervous system dominates during sexual arousal, whereas the sympathetic branch dominates during ejaculation and orgasm. 2. c. 3. Relationship focus, integration of physiological and psychosocial factors, emphasis on cognitive factors, emphasis on specific behavioral techniques. 4. Remain abstinent or have sex with one mutually faithful, uninfected partner. Do not use IV drugs or have sex with someone who does. If you do use IV drugs, sterilize or don't share equipment. Avoid contact with blood, vaginal secretions, and semen. Avoid anal intercourse. Don't have sex if you or partner is impaired by drugs.

CHAPTER 12   *Understanding Motivation Page 424* 1. Although these two terms often overlap and interact to influence behavior, motivation refers to internal factors that energize and direct behavior, whereas emotion refers to feelings or affective responses. 2. The major internal factors are the stomach, blood chemistry, and the brain; while the major external factors are cultural conditioning and visual stimuli. 3. d. 4. c. ***General Theories of Motivation Page 428*** 1. An instinct is an unlearned, behavioral pattern that is uniform in expression and universal in a species. Homeostasis is the state of balance or stability in the body's internal environment. 2. a2, b3, c5, d4, e1. 3. d. 4.c. ***Understanding Emotion Page 436*** 1. a3, b1, c2 and c4 2. sympathetic, autonomic. 3. a. 4. b. ***General Theories of Emotion Page 442*** 1. According to the **James-Lange theory**, emotions are based on physical sensations, such as increased heart rate and trembling, whereas the **Cannon-Bard theory** suggests feelings are created from independent and simultaneous stimulation of both the cortex and the autonomic nervous system. The **facial feedback hypothesis** suggests facial movements elicit specific emotions, **Schacter's two-factor theory** proposes that emotions depend on physical arousal and a cognitive labeling of the arousal. 2. a. 3. d. 4. simultaneously.

CHAPTER 13   *Personality Assessment Page 453* 1. a2, b1, c3. 2. b. 3. 4. People accept pseudopersonality tests because they offer generalized statements that apply to almost everyone (Barnum effect), they notice and remember events that confirm predictions and ignore the misses (fallacy of positive instances), and they prefer information that maintains a positive self-image (self-serving bias). ***Trait Theories Page 459*** 1. b. 2. a2, b3, c4, d5, e1. 3. b. ***Psychoanalytic/Psychodynamic Page 471*** 1. The conscious is the tip of the iceberg and the highest level of awareness; the preconscious is just below the surface but can readily be brought to awareness; the unconscious is the large base of the iceberg and operates below the level of awareness. 2. b. 3. Freud believed an individual's adult personality reflected his or her resolution of the specific crisis presented in each psychosexual stage (oral, anal, phallic, latency, and genital). 4. Adler, Horney, Jung, Horney. *Humanistic Theories Page 474* 1. a. 2. c. 3. self-actualization. 4. Humanistic theories are criticized for their naive assumptions, poor testability and inadequate evidence, and narrowness in merely describing, not explaining, behavior. *Social/Cognitive Perspective Page 476* 1. How each individual thinks about the world and interprets experiences. 2. a. 3. c. 4. external locus of control, internal locus of control. *Biological Theories Page 479* 1. d. 2. Some researchers emphasize the importance of the unshared environment, while others fear that genetic determinism could be misused to "prove" certain ethnic groups are inferior, male dominance is natural, or that social progress is impossible. 3. c. 4. Western theories emphasize the "self" as separate and autonomous from others, while collectivist cultures see the self as inherently linked to others.

CHAPTER 14 *Studying Psychological Disorders Page 494* 1. Statistical infrequency, disability or dysfunction, personal distress, and violation of norms. 2. b. 3. Early versions of the DSM used neurosis to refer to mental disorders related to anxiety, while psychosis is currently used to describe disorders characterized by loss of contact with reality and extreme mental disruption. Insanity is a legal term for people with a mental disorder that implies a lack of responsibility for behavior and an inability to manage their own affairs. 4. The chief advantages of the DSM is that it provides detailed descriptions of symptoms, which in turn allows standardized diagnosis and treatment, and improved communication among professionals and between professionals and patients. The major disadvantage is that the label "mental illness" can lead to social and economic discrimination. *Anxiety Disorders Page 500* 1. a3, b2, c4, d5, e1. 2. Learning theorists most often believe anxiety disorders result from classical and operant conditioning, while social learning theorists argue that imitation and modeling are the cause. 3. Learning and biology. *Mood Disorders Page 505* 1. a. 2. c. 3. Seligman believes the individual becomes resigned to pain and sadness and feels unable to change, which leads to depression. It may be due to biological causes (hormones and genes) as well as environmental stressors (poverty, discrimination, unhappy marriages, and sexual or physical abuse). *Schizophrenia Page 513* 1. c. 2. psychosis, 3. a. 4. Three biological causes might be malfunctioning neurotransmitters, brain abnormalities, and genetic predisposition. Two possible psychosocial causes of schizophrenia may be stress and family communication problems. *Other Disorders Pages 519* 1. Stress. 2. Dissociative identity disorder (DID) refers to a dissociative disorder characterized by the presence of two or more distinct personality systems within the same individual. 3. Antisocial personality. 4. d. *Answers to Active Learning Exercise Page 519* 1. c. 2. e. 3. b. 4. a. 5. f. 6. d.

CHAPTER 15 *Therapy Essentials Pages 527* 1. c. 2. b psychoanalysts, e behaviorists, d humanistic therapists, c biomedical therapists, a cognitive therapists. 3. clinical or counseling psychologists, psychiatrists, psychoanalysts, social workers, and counselors. *Biomedical Therapies Page 532* 1. d. 2. antianxiety, antipsychotic, antidepressant, and mood stabilizer. 3. b. 4. c. *Try This Yourself Page 537* The clearest technique being used in this

example is resistance. *Psychoanalysis/Psychodynamic Therapies Page 537* 1. c. 2. Mary is exhibiting transference, reacting to her therapist as she apparently did to someone earlier in her life. John is exhibiting resistance, arriving late because he fears what his unconscious might reveal. 3. Limited applicability, lack of scientific credibility. 4. Psychodynamic therapy is briefer, face-to-face, more directive, and emphasizes current problems and conscious processes. *Cognitive and Humanistic Therapies Page 543* 1. a. 2. The activating event, the belief system, the emotional consequence. 3. Magnification, all-or-nothing thinking. 4. Empathy, genuineness, unconditional positive regard. *Try This Yourself Page 542* All four techniques are shown in this example: empathy ("they scare the hell out of me too"), unconditional positive regard (therapist's acceptance and nonjudgmental attitude and caring about not wanting to do "anything that is upsetting" to the client), genuineness (the therapist's ability to laugh and make a joke at his or her own expense); and active listening (therapist demonstrated genuine interest in what the client was saying). *Behavior Therapies Page 549* 1. behavior therapy. 2. c. 3. By rewarding successive approximations of a target behavior, the patient is "shaped" toward more adaptive behaviors. 4. Behavior therapy is criticized for lack of generalizability, symptom substitution, and questionable ethics. *Group and Family Therapies Page 551* 1. c. 2. Group support, feedback and information, behavioral rehearsal. 3. Self-help groups are recommended as a supplement to individual therapy. 4. d. *Issues in Therapy Page 558* 1. d. 2. Naming the problem, qualities of the therapist, establishment of credibility, placing the problem in a familiar framework, applying techniques to bring relief, a special time and place. 3. c. 4. Rates of diagnosis and treatment of mental disorders, stresses of poverty, stresses of multiple roles, stresses of aging, violence against women.

CHAPTER 16 *Our Thoughts About Others Page 571* 1. c. 2. When judging the causes of others' behaviors, a tendency to overestimate internal personality factors and underestimate external situational factors. 3. d. 4. Cognitive dissonance. *Our Feelings About Others Page 581* 1. Prejudice is an attitude with behavioral tendencies that may or may not be activated, whereas discrimination is actual negative behavior directed at members of an outgroup. 2. b. 3. c. 4. Romantic love is short lived (6 to 30 months) and largely based on mystery and fantasy, which leads to inevitable disappointment. Companionate love is long lasting and grows stronger with time. *Social Influence Page 586* 1. Conformity involves changing behavior in response to real or imagined pressure from others, whereas obedience involves giving in to a command from others. 2. b. 3. c. 4. the power of authority, distance between teacher and learner, assignment of responsibility, and modeling/imitation. *Group Processes Page 592* 1. Guards and prisoners were abusing their roles. 2. b. 3. illusion of invulnerability, belief in the morality of the group, collective rationalizations, stereotypes of the outgroup, self-censorship of doubts and dissenting opinions, illusion of unanimity, and direct pressure on dissenters. 4. b. *Aggression and Altruism Page 598* 1. The five major biological factors are instincts, genes, brain and nervous system, substance use and other mental disorders, hormones and neurotransmitters. The tree key psychosocial factors aversive stimuli, culture and learning, and media and video games. 2. a. 3. According to evolutionary theorists, altruism evolved because it favored overall genetic survival. The egoistic model says helping is motivated by anticipated gain for the helper, while the empathy–altruism hypothesis suggests helping is activated when the helper feels empathy for the victim. 4. d.

CHAPTER 17 *Development of I/O Psychology Page 611* 1. A5Munsterberg, b5Taylor, c5Scott. 2. b. 3. c. 4. The Civil Rights Act of 1964 forced I/O psychologists to make tests and procedures valid for all workers, not just the white majority. *Human Factors Psychology Page 616* 1. b. 2. Human-machine system. 3. Displays are devices such as gauges that form the machine output in the human-machine system, while controls are devices such as wheels and levers that provide the input to the machine. 4. d. *Recruiting, Selecting, and Training Employees Page 621* 1. D. 2. Interview. 3. Friendliness, eagerness, and assertiveness. 4. a. *Evaluating Workers, Sexual Harassment Page 625* 1. a. 2. Pro-

vide feedback to the employee on his/her performance; identify training or development needs. 3. The tendency to rate individuals either too high or too low on the basis of one outstanding trait. 4. An expression of power. *Organizational Psychology Page 632* 1. Participative decision making is a decision-making model where the people involved in implementing a decision are also involved in making it. Most quality circles have been discontinued in the U.S.A. because management and employees tend to be more adversarial than loyal and trusting. 2. Goal setting, expectancy, equity. 3. Less resignations and absenteeism and improved overall productivity; less stress, better health, and improved overall quality of life. 4. d.

Glossary

abnormal behavior Patterns of emotion, thought, and action considered pathological (diseased or disordered) for one or more of these reasons statistical infrequency, disability or dysfunction, personal distress, or violation of norms. *Page 485*

absolute threshold The smallest magnitude of a certain stimulus energy that can be detected. *Page 120*

accommodation In vision, the process by which the lens changes shape to focus light on the retina. The lens thins and flattens to focus on distant objects and thickens and bulges to focus a nearby object. *Page 125*
In cognition, the process of adjusting existing ways of thinking (reworking schemas) to encompass new information, ideas, or objects. *Page 340*

achievement motivation (nAch) The need for success, for doing better than others, and for mastering challenging tasks; the desire to excel, especially in competition with others. *Page 419*

acquired immunodeficiency syndrome See AIDS (acquired immunodeficiency syndrome). *Page 404*

action potential An electro-chemical impulse that carries information along the axon of a neuron. The action potential is generated when positively charged ions move in and out of channels in the axon's membrane. *Page 52*

activation–synthesis hypothesis The idea that dreams are by-products of random stimulation of brain cells. The brain attempts to combine (or synthesize) this spontaneous activity into coherent patterns, known as dreams. *Page 170*

active listening According to Carl Rogers, the ability to listen with total attention to what another is saying. This involves reflecting, paraphrasing, and clarifying what the person says and means. *Page 542*

activity theory A theory of aging that suggests successful adjustment is fostered by a full and active commitment to life. *Page 368*

ageism Prejudice against people on the basis of their age. *Page 369*

aggression Any behavior that is intended to harm someone. *Page 592*

agonist A chemical (or drug) that mimics the action of a specific neurotransmitter. *Page 183*

AIDS (acquired immunodeficiency syndrome) A catastrophic illness in which human immunodeficiency viruses destroy the immune system's ability to fight disease, leaving the body vulnerable to a variety of opportunistic infections and cancers. *Page 404*

algorithm A problem-solving strategy that guarantees a solution if correctly applied; it involves a step-by-step procedure, and as such, is particularly suited to use by a computer for math problems. *Page 283*

alternate states of consciousness (ASCs) A mental state other than ordinary waking consciousness, found during sleep, dreaming, use of psychoactive drugs, hypnosis, and so on. During ASCs, distinct changes typically occur in perception, emotion, memory, time sense, thinking, self-control, and suggestibility. *Page 158*

altruism Actions designed to help others, with no obvious benefit to the helper. *Page 596*

Alzheimer's [ALLS-high-merz] disease (AD) A progressive mental deterioration that occurs most commonly in old age. It is characterized by severe memory loss. *Page 261*

amplitude The height of a light or sound wave; pertaining to light, it refers to brightness. *Page 123*

amygdala [uh-MIG-dull-uh] An almond-shaped lower-level brain structure that is part of the limbic system and involved in emotion. *Page 65*

androgyny [an-DRAW-juh-nee] Combining characteristics considered typically male (e.g., assertive, athletic) with characteristics considered typically female (e.g., yielding, nurturant); from the Greek andro, meaning "male," and gyn, meaning "female." *Page 386*

anorexia nervosa An eating disorder, seen mostly in adolescent and young adult females, in which a severe loss of weight results from an obsessive fear of obesity and self-imposed starvation. *Page 415*

antagonist A chemical (or drug) that opposes or blocks the action of a neurotransmitter. *Page 183*

anterograde amnesia The inability to form new memories. *Page 261*

antianxiety drugs Medications used to treat anxiety disorders. *Page 527*

antidepressant drugs Drugs prescribed to treat depression, some anxiety disorders, and certain eating disorders (such as bulimia). *Page 528*

antipsychotic drugs Chemicals administered to diminish or terminate hallucinations, delusions, withdrawal, and other symptoms of psychosis; also known as neuroleptics or major tranquilizers. *Page 528*

antisocial personality Personality disorder characterized by egocentrism, lack of conscience, impulsive behavior, and manipulation of others. *Page 516*

anxiety disorder Type of abnormal behavior characterized by unrealistic, irrational fear. *Page 495*

applied research Research that uses the principles and discoveries of psychology for practical purposes, to solve real-world problems. *Page 7*

approach–approach conflict Conflict in which a person must choose between two or more alternatives that will lead to desirable results. *Page 99*

approach–avoidance conflict Conflict in which a person must choose between two or more alternatives that will lead to both desirable and undesirable results. *Page 99*

archetypes According to Carl Jung, the images or patterns of thoughts, feelings, and behavior that reside in the collective unconscious. *Page 468*

assimilation The process of responding to a new situation in the same manner that is used in a familiar situation. *Page 340*

association areas So-called quiet areas in the cerebral cortex involved in interpreting, integrating, and acting on information processed by other parts of the brain. *Page 70*

attachment An active, intense emotional relationship between two people that endures over time. *Page 335*

attitude A learned predisposition to respond cognitively, affectively, and behaviorally to a particular object. *Page 568*

attribution The principles people follow in making judgments about the causes of events, others' behavior, and their own behavior. *Page 566*

audition The sense of hearing. *Page 127*

automatic processes Mental activities requiring minimal attention; other ongoing activities are generally not affected. *Page 160*

autonomic nervous system (ANS) Subdivision of the peripheral nervous system that controls involuntary functions, such as heart rate and digestion. It is further subdivided into the sympathetic nervous system, which arouses, and the parasympathetic nervous system, which calms. *Page 48*

aversion therapy Behavior therapy technique that pairs an aversive (unpleasant) stimulus with a maladaptive behavior. *Page 546*

avoidance–avoidance conflict Conflict in which a person must choose between two or more alternatives that will each lead to undesirable results. *Page 99*

axon A long, tubelike structure that conveys impulses away from the neuron's cell body toward other neurons or to muscles or glands. *Page 51*

babbling Vowel–consonant combinations that infants begin to produce at about age 4 months. *Page 333*

basic anxiety According to Karen Horney, the feelings of helplessness and insecurity that adults experience because as children they felt alone and isolated in a hostile environment. *Page 469*

basic research Research conducted to study theoretical questions without trying to solve a specific problem. *Page 6*

behavior therapy A group of techniques based on learning principles that are used to change maladaptive behaviors. *Page 543*

behavioral genetics A new field that combines genetics and psychology to study genetic and environmental influences on behavior. *Page 77*

binocular cues Visual input from two eyes that allows perception of depth or distance. *Page 144*

biofeedback A procedure for electronically recording, amplifying, and feeding back information about internal bodily changes that would normally be imperceptible (such as blood pressure); aids voluntary regulation of these changes. *Page 219*

biological preparedness The idea that an organism is innately predisposed to form associations between certain stimuli. *Page 229*

biomedical therapy Therapy involving physiological interventions (drugs, electroconvulsive therapy, and psychosurgery) to reduce symptoms associated with psychological disorders. *Page 524*

bipolar disorder A diagnostic term in DSM-IV-TR (Diagnostic and Statistical Manual of Mental Disorders, fourth edition, text revision) for individuals who experience episodes of mania or of both mania and depression. Excessive and unreasonable elation and hyperactivity characterize manic episodes. *Page 501*

borderline personality disorder (BPD) A personality disorder characterized by impulsivity and instability in mood, relationships, and self-image. *Page 517*

bottom-up processing Information processing that begins "at the bottom" with raw sensory data that feed "up" to the brain; perceptual analysis that emphasizes characteristics of the stimulus itself rather than internal, cognitive processes. *Page 118*

brainstem An area at the base of the brain, in front of the cerebellum, that is responsible for automatic, survival functions. *Page 63*

bulimia nervosa An eating disorder involving consumption of enormous quantities of food (binges), followed by purging through vomiting or taking laxatives. *Page 415*

burnout A state of physical, emotional, and mental exhaustion attributable to long-term involvement in emotionally demanding situations. *Page 98*

Cannon–Bard theory The theory that the thalamus responds to emotion-arousing stimuli by sending messages simultaneously to the cerebral cortex and the autonomic nervous system. In this view, all emotions are physiologically similar. *Page 437*

care perspective Carol Gilligan's term for an approach to moral reasoning that emphasizes interpersonal responsibility and interconnectedness with others. *Page 357*

case study An in-depth study of a single research participant. *Page 20*

catharsis In psychoanalytic theory, the release of tension and anxiety through the reliving of a traumatic incident. *Page 534*

cell body The part of the neuron that contains the cell nucleus, as well as other structures that help the neuron carry out its functions. *Page 51*

central nervous system (CNS) The brain and spinal cord. *Page 46*

cerebellum [sehr-uh-BELL-um] Structure at the base of the brain, behind the brainstem, responsible for maintaining smooth movement, balance, and some aspects of perception and cognition. *Page 63*

cerebral cortex The bumpy, convoluted area on the outside surface of the two cerebral hemispheres that regulates most complex behavior, including receiving sensations, motor control, and higher mental processes. *Page 66*

chromosome Threadlike strands of DNA (deoxyribonucleic acid) molecules that carry genetic information. *Page 77*

chronic pain Continuous or recurrent pain over a period of 6 months or more. *Page 94*

chunking The process of grouping information into units to store more information in short-term memory. *Page 239*

circadian [ser-KAY-dee-an] rhythms Biological changes that occur on a 24-hour cycle; from circa, meaning "about," and dies, meaning "day." *Page 162*

classical conditioning A basic form of learning in which an organism involuntarily learns to associate stimuli. A previously neutral stimulus is paired with an unconditioned stimulus to elicit a conditioned response that is identical or very similar to the unconditioned response. (Also known as respondent or Pavlovian conditioning.) *Page 200*

client-centered therapy A type of psychotherapy developed by Carl Rogers that emphasizes the client's natural tendency to become healthy and productive; techniques include empathy, unconditional positive regard, genuineness, and active listening. *Page 541*

cochlea (KOK-lee-uh) The three-chambered, snail-shaped structure in the inner ear that contains the receptors for hearing. *Page 128*

coding The three-part process that converts a particular sensory input into a specific sensation. *Page 119*

cognition The mental activities involved in acquiring, storing, retrieving, and using knowledge. *Page 278*

cognitive-behavior therapy Aaron Beck's therapy that works to change not only destructive thoughts and beliefs but the associated behaviors as well. *Page 539*

cognitive dissonance theory Leon Festinger's theory that tension results whenever people discover inconsistencies among their attitudes or between their attitudes and their behaviors. This tension drives people to make attitudinal changes that will restore harmony or consistency. *Page 569*

cognitive-social theory A theory of learning that emphasizes the role of thought and social learning in behavior. *Page 222*

cognitive map A mental image of a three-dimensional space that a person or animal has navigated. *Page 223*

cognitive restructuring The process in cognitive therapy by which the therapist and client work to change destructive ways of thinking. *Page 537*

cognitive therapy Therapy that focuses on faulty thought processes and beliefs to treat problem behaviors. *Page 537*

collective unconscious Carl Jung's concept of an inherited unconscious that all humans share. *Page 468*

comorbidity The co-occurrence of two or more disorders in the same person at the same time, as when a person has both depression and alcoholism. *Page 518*

companionate love A strong feeling of attraction to another person characterized by trust, caring, tolerance, and friendship. It is believed to provide an enduring basis for long-term relationships. *Page 580*

concept A mental category that groups objects, events, activities, or ideas that share similar characteristics. For example, the concept of river groups together the Nile, Amazon, and Mississippi because they share the common characteristic of being a large stream of water that empties into an ocean or lake. *Page 280*

concrete operational stage The third of Jean Piaget's stages of cognitive development (roughly ages 7 to 11 years). The child can perform mental operations on concrete objects and understand reversibility and conservation. *Page 343*

conditioned emotional response (CER) Any classically conditioned emotional response to a previously neutral stimulus. *Page 202*

conditioned response (CR) A learned response to a previously neutral stimulus that has been associated with the stimulus. *Page 200*

conditioned stimulus (CS) A previously neutral stimulus that, through conditioning, now causes a classically conditioned response. *Page 200*

cones Visual receptors concentrated near the center of the retina that are responsible for color vision and fine detail. They are most sensitive in brightly lit conditions. *Page 125*

confirmation bias The tendency to seek out and pay attention to information that confirms existing positions or beliefs while ignoring or not considering contradictory information. *Page 286*

conflict A negative emotional state caused by having to choose between two or more incompatible goals or impulses. *Page 99*

conformity A type of social influence in which individuals change their behavior as a result of real or imagined group pressure. *Page 582*

conscious In Freudian terms, thoughts or information that a person is currently aware of or is remembering. *Page 461*

consciousness An organism's awareness of its own self and surroundings, according to Damasio. Consciousness is always about something. It concerns perceptions (of objects and events), thoughts (including verbal thought and mental images, such as dreams and daydreams), feelings, and actions, according to Farthing. *Page 158*

conservation The ability to recognize that a given quantity, weight, or volume remains constant despite changes in shape, length, or position. *Page 343*

consolidation A hypothetical process explaining the gradual conversion of information into long-term memories. *Page 250*

constructive processes The active organizing and shaping of information as we encode and retrieve it, which can result in errors and distortions. *Page 263*

continuous reinforcement Reinforcement in which every correct response is reinforced. *Page 212*

control group In a controlled experiment, the group of participants that receives a zero level of the independent variable and that is used to assess the effects of the independent variable or treatment. *Page 15*

controlled processes Mental activities found at one extreme of the continuum of awareness; they require focused attention and generally interfere with other ongoing activities. *Page 160*

conventional level Lawrence Kohlberg's second level of moral development, where moral judgments are based on compliance with the rules and values of society. *Page 356*

convergence A binocular depth cue in which the closer the object, the more the eyes converge, or turn inward. *Page 144*

convergent thinking Conventional thinking; thinking directed toward a single correct answer (e.g., standard academic tests generally require convergent thinking). *Page 288*

cooing Vowel-like sounds infants produce beginning at about age 2 months. *Page 333*

corpus callosum [**CORE-puss**] [**cah-LOW-sum**] Bundle of nerve fibers connecting the brain's left and right hemispheres. *Page 70*

correlational study A form of research that studies relationships between variables without the ability to infer causal relationships. Correlational studies describe how strongly two variables are related and whether they are positively, negatively, or not at all (zero) correlated. *Page 21*

creativity The generation of ideas that are original, novel, and useful. *Page 288*

critical period A period of special sensitivity to specific types of learning that shapes the capacity for future development. *Page 319*

critical thinking The process of objectively evaluating, comparing, analyzing, and synthesizing information. Critical thinking has three components affective skills (e.g., empathy and tolerance for ambiguity), cognitive abilities (e.g., independent thinking and synthesizing), and behavioral traits (e.g., delaying judgment and applying knowledge to new situations). *Page 4*

cross-sectional method A technique of data collection that measures individuals of various ages at one point in time and gives information about age differences. *Page 319*

crystallized intelligence Knowledge and skills gained through experience and education that tend to increase over the life span. *Page 297*

dark adaptation The process by which the eyes' rods and cones adjust to allow vision in dim light. *Page 126*

debriefing A necessary and important aspect of deception research in which the participants are informed after the research about the purpose of the study, the nature of the anticipated results, and any deceptions used. *Page 23*

defense mechanisms Unconscious strategies used to distort reality and relieve anxiety and guilt. *Page 108*

deindividuation The increased arousal and reduced self-consciousness, inhibition, and personal responsibility that can occur when a person is part of a group, particularly when the members feel anonymous. *Page 589*

deinstitutionalization The policy of discharging as many people as possible from state hospitals and discouraging admissions. *Page 553*

delusions Mistaken beliefs maintained in spite of strong evidence to the contrary. *Page 507*

dendrites Branching neuron structures that receive neural impulses from other neurons and convey impulses toward the cell body. *Page 51*

dependent variable (DV) The variable that is observed and measured for change in an experiment; thought to be affected by (or dependent on) the manipulation of the independent variable. *Page 14*

depressants Psychoactive drugs that act on the central nervous system to suppress or slow bodily processes and reduce overall responsiveness. *Page 177*

depth perception The process by which we organize perception in three dimensions — even though the images that strike the retina are two-dimensional — so that we can perceive distance. *Page 143*

designer drugs Illicitly manufactured variations on known recreational drugs. *Page 187*

developmental psychology The branch of psychology that describes, explains, predicts, and sometimes aims to modify age-related behaviors from conception to death. This field emphasizes maturation, early experiences, and various stages in development. *Page 318*

Diagnostic and Statistical Manual of Mental Disorders, fourth edition, text revision (DSM-IV-TR) A classification system, developed by the American Psychiatric Association, used to describe abnormal behaviors; the IV-TR indicates it is the text revision (TR) of the fourth major edition (IV). *Page 490*

difference threshold The smallest magnitude of difference in stimulus energy that a person can detect; also called the just-noticeable difference. *Page 120*

diffusion of responsibility In groups of two or more, people tend to take less individual responsibility because they assume someone else will take action (or responsibility). *Page 597*

discrimination Negative behaviors directed at members of a group. *Page 571*

discriminative stimulus A cue that signals when a particular response is likely to be followed by a certain type of consequence. *Page 217*

disengagement theory A theory of aging suggesting that both the individual and society gradually and naturally pull away from each other in preparation for the individual's death. *Page 369*

dissociative disorder Stress-related disorder characterized by amnesia, fugue, or multiple personality. In all cases, though, the person is trying to escape from the memory of a painful experience. *Page 514*

dissociative identity disorder (DID) A dissociative disorder characterized by the presence of two or more distinct personality systems in the same individual; previously known as multiple personality disorder. *Page 514*

distress Unpleasant, objectionable stress. *Page 96*

distributed practice A learning technique in which practice sessions are interspersed with rest periods. *Page 255*

divergent thinking Thinking that produces many alternatives or ideas; a major element of creativity (e.g., finding as many uses as possible for a paper clip). *Page 288*

dopamine hypothesis A theory suggesting that schizophrenia is caused by an overactivity of dopamine neurons in a specific region of the brain. *Page 509*

double-blind study A study in which neither the participant nor the experimenter knows which treatment is being given to the participant or to which group the participant has been assigned. *Page 16*

double standard The beliefs, values, and norms that subtly encourage male sexuality and discourage female sexuality. *Page 400*

drive-reduction theory The theory that motivation begins with a physiological need (a lack or deficiency) that elicits a psychological energy or drive directed toward behavior that will satisfy the original need. Once the need is met, a state of balance (homeostasis) is restored and motivation decreases. *Page 425*

drug abuse Drug taking that causes emotional or physical harm to the drug user or others. *Page 176*

drug therapy Use of chemicals (drugs) to treat physical and psychological disorders. *Page 527*

eclectic approach An approach to therapy in which the therapist combines techniques from various theories to find the appropriate treatment for the client. *Page 526*

ego In Sigmund Freud's theory, the rational part of the psyche that deals with reality and attempts to control the impulses of the id while also satisfying the social approval and self-esteem needs of the superego. *Page 462*

egocentrism The inability to consider another's point of view, which Jean Piaget considered a hallmark of the preoperational stage. *Page 342*

egoistic model The proposal that helping behavior is motivated by anticipated gain — later reciprocation, increased self-esteem, or avoidance of guilt and distress. *Page 596*

elaborative rehearsal An encoding technique of associating new information with already-stored knowledge in long-term memory. Also known as deeper levels of processing. *Page 245*

electroconvulsive therapy (ECT) A biomedical therapy based on passing electrical current through the brain. It is used almost exclusively to treat serious depression when drug therapy does not work. *Page 529*

embryonic period The second stage of pregnancy (from uterine implantation through the eighth week), characterized by development of major body organs and systems. *Page 324*

emotion-focused forms of coping Coping strategies based on changing one's perceptions of stressful situations. *Page 108*

emotion An individual's feelings or affective responses that include cognitions (thoughts, beliefs, and expectations), physiological arousal (heart pounding), and behavioral expressions (frowns, smiles, running, etc.). *Page 412*

emotional intelligence According to Daniel Goleman, the ability to know and manage one's emotions, empathize with others, and maintain satisfying relationships. *Page 436*

empathy In Rogerian terms, an insightful awareness and ability to share another person's inner experience. *Page 541*

empathy–altruism hypothesis The proposal that altruistic behavior is motivated by empathy for someone in need of help. *Page 596*

encoding The process of translating information into neural codes (language) that will be retained in memory. *Page 242*

encoding specificity principle The principle that retrieval of information is improved when conditions of recovery are similar to the conditions when information was encoded. *Page 249*

endocrine [EN-doh-krin] system A system of glands located throughout the body that secrete hormones into the bloodstream. *Page 57*

endorphins [en-DOR-fins] Chemical substances in the nervous system that are similar in structure and action to opiates and are involved in pain control, pleasure, and memory. *Page 57*

episodic memory The subpart of explicit/declarative memory that stores memories of personally experienced events; a mental diary of a person's life. *Page 247*

ethnocentrism The belief that behavior in your culture is typical of all cultures. Also, viewing one's own ethnic group (or culture) as central and "correct" and then judging the rest of the world according to this standard. *Page 16*

eustress Pleasant, desirable stress. *Page 96*

evolutionary psychology A branch of psychology that studies evolutionary principles, like natural selection and genetic mutations, which affect adaptation to the environment and help explain commonalities in behavior. *Page 80*

evolutionary/circadian theory The theory that sleep is a part of circadian rhythms and evolved as a means of conserving energy and protecting individuals from predators. *Page 168*

excitement phase First stage of the sexual response cycle, characterized by increasing levels of arousal and increased engorgement of the genitals. *Page 393*

experiment A carefully controlled scientific procedure conducted to determine whether certain variables manipulated by the experimenter have a causal effect on other variables. *Page 13*

experimental group In a controlled experiment, the group of participants that receives the independent variable. *Page 15*

experimenter bias The tendency of experimenters to influence the results of a research study in the expected direction. *Page 16*

explicit/declarative memory The subsystem within long-term memory that stores facts, information, and personal life experiences; also called explicit memory or declarative memory. *Page 247*

extinction The gradual suppression of a behavior or a response that occurs when a conditioned stimulus is repeatedly presented without the unconditioned stimulus with which it had been previously associated. *Page 204*

extraneous variables Variables that are not directly related to the hypothesis under study and that the experimenter does not actively attempt to control (e.g., time of day and heating of room). *Page 15*

extrasensory perception (ESP) Perceptual, or "psychic," abilities that supposedly go beyond the known senses, including telepathy, clairvoyance, precognition, and psychokinesis. *Page 151*

extrinsic motivation Motivation based on obvious external rewards or threats of punishment rather than on factors within the individual or the behavior itself. *Page 420*

facial feedback hypothesis The proposal that movements of the facial muscles produce or intensify emotional reactions. *Page 438*

factor analysis A statistical procedure used to determine the most basic units or factors in a large array of data. *Page 454*

family therapy A psychological treatment that attempts to change maladaptive interaction patterns among members of a family. *Page 550*

farsightedness (hyperopia) A visual acuity problem that results when the cornea and lens focus an image behind the retina. *Page 125*

feature detectors Specialized cells in the brain that respond only to certain sensory information. *Page 136*

fetal alcohol syndrome (FAS) A combination of birth defects, including organ deformities and mental, motor, and/or growth retardation, that results from maternal alcohol abuse. *Page 325*

fetal period The third, and final, stage of prenatal development (8 weeks to birth), characterized by rapid weight gain in the fetus and the fine detailing of fetal body organs and systems. *Page 325*

figure and ground A Gestalt law of perceptual organization stating that our perceptions consist of two aspects the figure, which stands out and has a definite contour or shape, and the ground, which is less distinct. *Page 138*

five-factor model (FFM) A trait theory that explains personality in terms of a "Big Five" model — openness, conscientiousness, extraversion, agreeableness, and neuroticism. *Page 454*

fixed-interval schedule A schedule of reinforcement in which a participant is reinforced for the first response after a specific period of time has elapsed. *Page 213*

fixed-ratio schedule A partial schedule of reinforcement in which a participant must make a certain number of responses before being reinforced. *Page 213*

fluid intelligence Aspects of intelligence, including reasoning abilities, memory, and speed of information processing, that tend to decline slowly as people age. *Page 297*

foot-in-the-door technique A social influence technique in which a first, small request is used as a "setup" for later requests. *Page 586*

formal operational stage Jean Piaget's fourth stage of cognitive development (around age 11 years and beyond) characterized by abstract and hypothetical thinking. *Page 343*

free association In psychoanalysis, reporting whatever comes to mind without monitoring its contents — regardless of how painful, embarrassing, or irrelevant it may seem. Sigmund Freud believed that the first thing to come to a patient's mind was often an important clue to what the unconscious mind wants to conceal. *Page 534*

frequency How often a light wave or sound wave cycles; that is, the number of complete wavelengths that pass a point in a given time (e.g., per second). *Page 123*

frequency theory Theory that explains how we hear lower-pitched sounds; hair cells on the basilar membrane of the cochlea bend and fire action potentials at the same rate as the frequency of the low sound. *Page 128*

frontal lobes Cortical lobes in the front of the brain, which govern motor control, speech production, and higher functions, such as thinking, personality, emotion, and memory. *Page 66*

frustration An unpleasant state of tension, anxiety, and heightened sympathetic activity resulting from a blocked goal. *Page 99*

frustration-aggression hypothesis The idea that frustration — the blocking of a desired goal — creates anger, which may lead to aggression. *Page 593*

functional fixedness A barrier to problem solving that occurs when people are unable to recognize novel uses for an object because they are so familiar with its common use. *Page 285*

fundamental attribution error (FAE) Misjudging the causes of others' behavior because of overestimating internal, personal factors and underestimating external, situational influences. *Page 566*

gate-control theory of pain The idea that pain sensations are processed and altered by mechanisms within the spinal cord. *Page 121*

gender The psychological and sociocultural meanings added to biological maleness or femaleness. *Page 381*

gender identity How one psychologically perceives oneself as either male or female. *Page 381*

gender role The societal expectations for normal and appropriate male and female behavior. When these expectations are based on exaggerated and biased beliefs about differences between the sexes and are rigidly applied to all members of each sex, they are known as gender role stereotypes. *Page 383*

gene A segment of DNA (deoxyribonucleic acid) that occupies a specific place on a particular chromosome and carries the code for hereditary transmission. *Page 77*

general adaptation syndrome (GAS) As described by Hans Selye, a generalized physiological reaction to severe stressors consisting of three phases the

alarm reaction, the resistance phase, and the exhaustion phase. *Page 102*

generalized anxiety disorder Type of anxiety disorder characterized by chronic, uncontrollable, and excessive worry. The anxiety is not focused on any particular object or situation. *Page 495*

genuineness In Rogerian terms, authenticity or congruence; the awareness of one's true inner thoughts and feelings and being able to share them honestly with others. *Page 542*

germinal period The first stage of pregnancy (conception to 2 weeks) characterized by rapid cell division. *Page 324*

glial cells Nervous system cells that provide structural, nutritional, and other support for the neuron; also called glia or neuroglia. *Page 51*

grammar The rules of a language that specify how phonemes, morphemes, words, and phrases should be combined to meaningfully express thoughts. *Page 291*

group polarization A group's movement toward either riskier or more conservative behavior, depending on the members' initial dominant tendency. *Page 590*

group therapy Treatment method in which multiple people meet together to work toward therapeutic goals. *Page 549*

groupthink A condition that results when a highly cohesive group strives for agreement to the point of avoiding inconsistent information; the result is faulty decision making. *Page 590*

gustation The sense of taste. *Page 132*

habituation The tendency of the brain to ignore environmental factors that remain constant. *Page 137*

hallucinations Sensory perceptions that occur without an external stimulus. *Page 506*

hallucinogens [hal-LU-sin-oh-jenz] Drugs that produce sensory distortions or perceptual distortions. *Page 181*

hardiness A resilient personality characteristic based on three qualities a commitment to personal goals, control over life, and viewing change as a challenge rather than a threat. *Page 107*

hassles Little problems of daily living that are not significant in themselves, but they accumulate and sometimes become a major source of stress. *Page 98*

health psychology The study of the relationship between psychological

behavior and physical health and illness, with an emphasis on wellness and the prevention of illness. *Page 88*

heritability The proportion of observed variance in a particular trait (such as intelligence) that can be attributed to inherited genetic factors in contrast to environmental ones. *Page 79*

heuristic Problem-solving strategies, or "rules of thumb," used as shortcuts to complex solutions, which generally, but not always, lead to a solution. *Page 283*

hierarchy of needs Abraham Maslow's theory of motivation that some motives (such as physiological and safety needs) have to be satisfied before an individual can attend to higher needs (such as belonging and self-actualization). *Page 427*

higher-order conditioning In classical conditioning, a procedure in which a neutral stimulus (NS) becomes a conditioned stimulus through association with an already established conditioned stimulus (CS); a NS is paired with a previous CS (CS1), which then becomes a secondary CS (CS2) and produces the same conditioned response as CS1. *Page 204*

HIV positive Being infected by the human immunodeficiency virus (HIV). *Page 404*

hormones Chemicals manufactured by endocrine glands and circulated in the bloodstream to produce bodily changes or maintain normal bodily functions. *Page 57*

hue The visual dimension seen as a particular color; determined by the length of a light wave. *Page 123*

humanistic therapy Therapy that helps individuals become creative and unique persons through affective restructuring (or emotional readjustment). *Page 541*

hypnosis An alternate state of heightened suggestibility characterized by relaxation and intense focus. *Page 188*

hypothalamus [high-poh-THAL-uh-muss] Small structure beneath the thalamus that maintains homeostasis and regulates emotions and drives, such as hunger, thirst, sex, and aggression. *Page 64*

hypothesis A statement of a predicted relationship between two or more variables. *Page 11*

id According to Sigmund Freud, the source of instinctual energy, which works on the pleasure principle and is concerned with immediate gratification. *Page 462*

identity crisis According to Erik Erikson, a period of inner conflict during which an individual examines his or her life and values and makes decisions about life roles. *Page 361*

illusion A false impression of the environment. *Page 135*

implicit/nondeclarative/procedural memory The subsystem within long-term memory that consists of skills acquired through repetitive practice, habits, and simple classically conditioned responses; also called implicit memory, nondeclarative memory, or procedural memory. *Page 247*

imprinting An innate or instinctual form of learning in which the young of certain species follow and become attached to large moving objects (usually their mothers). *Page 335*

incentive theory The theory that motivation results from environmental stimuli that "pull" the organism in certain directions, as opposed to internal needs that drive or "push" the organism. *Page 426*

incubation A period of time during which active searching for a problem's solution is set aside; this is sometimes necessary for a successful solution of the problem. *Page 287*

independent variable (IV) In an experiment, a variable that is manipulated by the experimenter to determine its causal effect on the dependent variable. *Page 14*

inferiority complex Alfred Adler's idea that feelings of inferiority develop from early childhood experiences of helplessness and incompetence. *Page 468*

informational social influence Conforming to group pressure out of a need for direction and information. *Page 583*

informed consent A participant's agreement to take part in a study after being told what to expect. *Page 23*

ingroup favoritism A cognitive process in prejudice whereby members of an ingroup are viewed in more favorable terms than members of an outgroup. *Page 572*

insanity A legal term for people with a mental disorder that implies a lack of responsibility for their behavior and an inability to manage their affairs. *Page 492*

insight A sudden flash of understanding that occurs during problem solving. *Page 223*

insomnia A sleep disorder in which a person has persistent problems in falling asleep or staying asleep or awakens too early. *Page 172*

instinctive drift A biological constraint that occurs when an animal's learned responses shifts (or drifts) toward innate response patterns. *Page 230*

instincts Behavioral patterns that are (1) unlearned, (2) always expressed in the same way, and (3) universal in a species. *Page 425*

intelligence The general capacity to profit from experience, to acquire knowledge, and adapt to changes in the environment. *Page 296*

intelligence quotient (IQ) A score on a test that is intended to measure verbal and quantitative abilities. *Page 303*

interaction A process in which multiple factors mutually influence the outcome — as in the interaction between heredity and environment. *Page 6*

interpersonal attraction The degree of positive or negative feelings toward another. *Page 575*

interpretation A psychoanalyst's explanation of a patient's free associations, dreams, resistance, and transference; more generally, any statement by a therapist that presents a patient's problem in a new way. *Page 534*

intrinsic motivation Motivation that comes from personal enjoyment of a task or activity, rather than from external rewards or fear of punishment. *Page 420*

James–Lange theory The theory that emotion is the perception of one's own bodily reactions and that each emotion is physiologically distinct. *Page 437*

justice perspective Carol Gilligan's term for an approach to moral reasoning that emphasizes individual rights and views people as differentiated and standing alone. *Page 357*

kinesthesis The sensory system that provides information on body posture and orientation. *Page 134*

language acquisition device (LAD) In Noam Chomsky's view, the child's inborn brain capacity to analyze language and unconsciously understand essential grammatical rules. *Page 334*

latent content The true, unconscious meaning of a dream, according to Freudian dream theory. *Page 170*

latent learning Learning that occurs in the absence of a reward and remains hidden until there is some incentive to demonstrate it. *Page 223*

lateralization Specialization of the left and right hemispheres of the brain for particular operations. *Page 70*

learned helplessness In Martin Seligman's theory, a state of helplessness or resignation in which people or animals learn that escape from something painful is impossible and depression results. *Page 502*

learning A relatively permanent change in behavior or behavioral potential as a result of practice or experience. *Page 198*

limbic system An interconnected group of brain structures involved with the arousal and regulation of emotion, motivation, memory, and learning. *Page 64*

lobotomy A brain operation in which the nerve pathways between the frontal lobes and the thalamus and hypothalamus are cut in hopes of treating psychological disorders. *Page 530*

localization of function Specialization of various parts of the brain for particular functions. *Page 62*

locus of control The belief that life's circumstances are under personal, internal control, or controlled by outside, external factors. *Page 111*

long-term memory (LTM) The third stage of memory that functions as storage of information for long periods of time; its capacity is limitless and its duration is relatively permanent. *Page 240*

long-term potentiation (LTP) A long-lasting increase in the strength of synaptic responsiveness believed to be a biological mechanism for learning and memory. *Page 250*

longitudinal method A data collection technique that measures a single individual or group of individuals over an extended period and gives information about age changes. *Page 319*

maintenance rehearsal The process of repeating the contents of short-term memory (STM) over and over to maintain it in STM. *Page 239*

major depressive disorder A DSM-IV-TR (Diagnostic and Statistical Manual of Mental Disorders, fourth edition, text revision) diagnostic term for individuals experiencing a long-lasting depressed mood that interferes with the ability to function, feel pleasure, or maintain interest in life. The feelings are without apparent cause and excessive to the given situation. *Page 500*

manifest content The surface content of a dream, containing dream symbols that distort and disguise the true meaning of the dream, according to Freudian dream theory. *Page 170*

massed practice A learning technique in which time spent learning is massed into long, unbroken intervals; also known as cramming. *Page 255*

maturation Biological growth processes that enable orderly changes in behavior, relatively uninfluenced by the environment. *Page 318*

medical model Perspective that assumes diseases have physical causes that can be diagnosed, treated, and possibly cured. Using this perspective, abnormal behaviors also have physical causes that can be diagnosed by their symptoms and treated and cured through therapy, including drugs, hospitalization, and so on. *Page 488*

meditation A group of techniques designed to focus attention and produce a heightened state of awareness. *Page 190*

medulla [muh-DULL-uh] Structure at the base of the brain stem responsible for automatic body functions such as breathing and heart rate. *Page 63*

memory An internal record or representation of some prior event or experience; also a set of mental processes that receives, encodes, stores, organizes, alters, and retrieves information over time. *Page 236*

mental images The mind's representation of a sensory experience, including visual, auditory, gustatory, motor, olfactory, or tactile elements (e.g., visualizing a train and hearing its whistle). *Page 279*

mental set A mental barrier to problem solving that occurs when people apply only methods that have worked in the past rather than trying innovative ones. *Page 284*

meta-analysis A statistical procedure for combining and analyzing data from many studies. *Page 13*

Minnesota Multiphasic Personality Inventory (MMPI-2) The most widely researched and clinically used self-report personality test; the revised version is called the MMPI-2. *Page 449*

misinformation effect A memory error that results from incorporating outside information into one's own memory of an event. (Also known as suggestibility.) *Page 263*

mnemonic [nih-MON-ik] device A memory-improvement technique based on encoding items in a special way. *Page 269*

modeling therapy A type of behavior therapy that involves watching and imitating appropriate models that demonstrate desirable behaviors. *Page 548*

monocular cues Visual input from a single eye alone that contributes to perception of depth or distance. *Page 144*

morpheme [MOR-feem] The smallest meaningful unit of language, formed from a combination of phonemes. *Page 291*

motivation Factors within an individual (such as needs, desires, and interests) that activate, maintain, and direct behavior toward a goal. *Page 412*

myelin [MY-uh-lin] sheath A layer of fatty insulation wrapped around the axon of some neurons, which increases the rate at which nerve impulses travel along the axon. *Page 51*

narcolepsy [NAR-co-lep-see] A disease marked by sudden and irresistible onsets of sleep during normal waking hours; from narco, meaning "numbness," and lepsy, meaning "seizure". *Page 174*

natural selection The driving mechanism behind evolution that allows individuals with genetically influenced traits that are adaptive in a particular environment to stay alive and produce offspring. *Page 80*

naturalistic observation The systematic recording of observable behavior in the participant's natural state or habitat with little or no experimenter intervention. *Page 18*

nature–nurture controversy The longstanding dispute over the relative contributions of nature (heredity) and nurture (environment) to the development of behavior and mental processes. *Page 6*

nearsightedness (myopia) A visual acuity problem that occurs when the cornea and lens focus an image in front of the retina. *Page 125*

need compatibility A sharing of similar needs. *Page 577*

need complementarity The tendency to seek out and be attracted to people whose qualities we admire but personally lack. *Page 577*

negative punishment The process of taking away or removing a stimulus that decreases the likelihood of that response occurring again. *Page 214*

negative reinforcement The process of taking away or removing a stimulus that increases the likelihood of that response occurring again. *Page 210*

neurogenesis [new-roh-JEN-uh-sis] The division of nonneuronal cells to produce neurons. *Page 76*

neuron Individual nerve cell responsible for processing, storing, and transmitting information throughout the body. *Page 50*

neuroplasticity The brain's ability to reorganize and change its structure and function throughout the life span. *Page 76*

neuroscience An interdisciplinary field studying how biological processes, especially activity in the brain and nervous system, relate to behavior. *Page 46*

neurosis A large group of disorders characterized by unrealistic anxiety and other associated problems. *Page 491*

neurotransmitter Chemicals manufactured and released by neurons that alter activity in other neurons. *Page 53*

night terrors Abrupt awakenings from non-REM (non–rapid-eye-movement sleep accompanied by intense physiological arousal and feelings of panic. *Page 174*

nightmares Anxiety-arousing dreams that generally occur near the end of the sleep cycle, during REM (rapid-eye-movement) sleep. *Page 174*

norm Cultural rule of behavior that prescribes what is acceptable in a given situation. *Page 582*

normative social influence Conforming to group pressure out of a need for acceptance and approval. *Page 582*

obedience A type of social influence in which an individual follows direct commands, usually from someone in a position of authority. *Page 584*

object permanence A Piagetian term for an infant's understanding that objects (or people) continue to exist even when they cannot be directly seen, heard, or touched. *Page 341*

obsessive-compulsive disorder (OCD) Type of anxiety disorder characterized by intrusive thoughts (obsessions) and urges to perform repetitive, ritualistic behaviors (compulsions). *Page 496*

occipital [ahk-SIP-uh-tuhl] lobes Cortical lobes at the back of the brain responsible for vision and visual perception. *Page 68*

Oedipus (ED-uh-puss) complex During the phallic stage, children are sexually attracted to the opposite-sex parent and hostile toward the same-sex parent. *Page 465*

olfaction The sense of smell. *Page 131*

operant conditioning Learning based on consequences. Behavior is strengthened if followed by reinforcement and diminished if followed by punishment. *Page 208*

operational definition A precise description of how the variables in a study will be observed and measured. For example, drug abuse might be defined as "the number of missed work days due to excessive use of an addictive substance." *Page 12*

opiates Drugs that are derived from opium and function as an analgesic or pain reliever. The word opium derives from the Greek word meaning "juice." *Page 181*

opponent-process theory The theory first proposed by Ewald Hering that color perception is based on three systems of color opposites — blue–yellow, red–green, and black–white. *Page 147*

orgasm phase Third stage of the sexual response cycle when pleasurable sensations peak and orgasm occurs. *Page 394*

outgroup homogeneity effect A cognitive process in prejudice whereby members of the outgroup are judged as less individual, or diverse, than members of the ingroup. *Page 572*

overextension A child's tendency to define a word too broadly to include objects that do not fit the word's meaning. *Page 333*

overgeneralize A common error in language acquisition in which the child overuses the basic rules of grammar. The rules for past tense and plurals are extended to irregular forms (e.g., they may say "mans" instead of "men.") *Page 333*

panic disorder Type of anxiety disorder characterized by sudden and inexplicable attacks of intense fear. Symptoms include difficulty breathing, heart palpitations, dizziness, trembling, terror, and feelings of impending doom. *Page 495*

parallel distributed processing (PDP) approach A model of memory in which knowledge is represented as connections among interacting processing units, distributed in a vast network, and all operating in parallel. *Page 242*

parasympathetic nervous system Subdivision of the autonomic nervous system responsible for calming the body. *Page 48*

parietal [puh-RYE-uh-tuhl] lobes Cortical lobes at the top of the brain where bodily sensations are interpreted. *Page 67*

partial (intermittent) reinforcement Reinforcement in which some, but not all, correct responses are reinforced. *Page 212*

perception The process of selecting, organizing, and interpreting sensory data into usable mental representations of the world. *Page 118*

perceptual constancy The tendency for the environment to be perceived as remaining the same even with changes in sensory input. *Page 141*

perceptual set A readiness to perceive in a particular manner on the basis of expectations. *Page 149*

performance anxiety A fear that one will be unable to meet the expectations for sexual "performance" of oneself or one's partner. *Page 399*

peripheral nervous system (PNS) All nerves and neurons outside the brain and spinal cord. Its major function is to connect the central nervous system to the rest of the body. *Page 48*

personality An individual's relatively stable and enduring pattern of thoughts, feelings, and actions. *Page 448*

personality disorders A DSM-IV-TR (Diagnostic and Statistical Manual of Mental Disorders, fourth edition, revised) category that describes individuals with inflexible, maladaptive personality traits. The best-known type is the antisocial personality. *Page 516*

pheromones (FARE-oh-mones) Airborne chemicals released from one individual that affect another individual's behavior, including recognition of family members, aggression, territorial marking, and sexual mating. *Page 132*

phobia Type of anxiety disorder characterized by intense, irrational fear and avoidance of a specific object or situation. *Page 495*

phoneme [FOH-neem] The most basic unit of speech; an individual speech sound. *Page 291*

physical dependence A condition in which bodily processes have been so modified by repeated use of a drug that continued use is required to prevent withdrawal symptoms. *Page 176*

pitch The highness or lowness of tones or sounds, depending on their frequency. *Page 127*

place theory Theory that explains how we hear higher-pitched sounds; different high-pitched sounds bend the basilar membrane hair cells at different locations in the cochlea. *Page 128*

placebo [pluh-SEE-boh] An inactive substance or fake treatment used as a control technique, usually in drug research, or given by a medical practitioner to a patient. *Page 16*

plateau phase Second stage of the sexual response cycle, characterized by a leveling off of high arousal. *Page 393*

pleasure principle In Freudian theory, the principle on which the id operates — that immediate pleasure is the sole motivation for behavior. *Page 462*

polygraph Instrument that measures emotional arousal through heart rate, respiration rate, blood pressure, and skin conductivity. These measurements are taken while a participant is asked questions designed to determine his or her credibility. *Page 434*

pons Structure at the top of the brainstem involved in respiration, movement, waking, sleep, and dreaming. *Page 63*

positive punishment The process of adding or presenting a stimulus that decreases the likelihood of that response occurring again. *Page 214*

positive reinforcement The process of adding or presenting a stimulus that increases the likelihood of that response occurring again. *Page 210*

postconventional level Lawrence Kohlberg's highest level of moral development, which occurs when individuals develop personal standards for right and wrong. *Page 356*

post-traumatic stress disorder (PTSD) Type of anxiety disorder following exposure to a life-threatening or other extreme event that evoked great horror or helplessness; it is characterized by flashbacks, nightmares, and impaired functioning. *Page 497*

preconscious Sigmund Freud's term for thoughts or information that one can become aware of easily. *Page 461*

preconventional level Lawrence Kohlberg's first level of moral development, characterized by moral judgments based on fear of punishment or desire for pleasure. *Page 354*

prejudice A generally negative attitude directed toward others because of their membership in a specific group. Like all attitudes, prejudice involves cognitions (thoughts), affect (feelings), and behavioral tendencies. *Page 571*

Premack principle Using a response that has a high probability of occurrence to reinforce a response that has a lower probability of occurrence. *Page 211*

preoperational stage The second of Jean Piaget's stages (roughly ages 2 to 7 years) characterized by the ability to employ significant language and to think symbolically. But the child lacks operations (reversible mental processes), and thinking is egocentric and animistic. *Page 341*

primary reinforcers Stimuli that increase the probability of a response because they satisfy a biological need, such as food, water, and sex. *Page 210*

priming The process by which an earlier encounter with a stimulus (such as a word or picture) increases the likelihood of that stimulus or a related stimulus being remembered at a later time. *Page 248*

proactive interference Forgetting in which old information interferes with remembering new information; forward-acting memory interference. *Page 258*

problem-focused forms of coping Coping strategies based on using problem-solving strategies to decrease or eliminate the source of stress. *Page 108*

projective tests Psychological tests using ambiguous stimuli, such as inkblots or drawings. The ambiguity of the stimuli reportedly allows the test taker to project his or her true unconscious conflicts, motives, psychological defenses, and personality traits onto the test material. *Page 450*

prototype A typical, highly representative example that serves as a model on which other examples are based or judged (e.g., baseball is a prototype of the concept of sports). *Page 280*

proximity A key factor in attraction involving geographic, residential, and other forms of physical closeness. *Page 576*

psychiatry The specialized branch of medicine dealing with the diagnosis, treatment, and prevention of mental disorder. *Page 489*

psychoactive drugs Chemicals that affect the nervous system and cause a change in behavior, mental processes, and conscious experience. *Page 175*

psychoanalysis A system of therapy developed by Sigmund Freud that seeks to bring unconscious conflicts, which usually date back to early childhood experiences, into consciousness. Psychoanalysis is also Freud's theoretical school of thought, which emphasizes the study of unconscious processes. *Page 534*

psychodynamic therapy A form of psychotherapy that emphasizes internal conflicts, motives, and unconscious forces. *Page 536*

psychological dependence A desire or craving to achieve the effects produced by a drug. *Page 176*

psychology The scientific study of behavior and mental processes. *Page 4*

psychoneuroimmunology [**sigh-koh-NEW-ro-IM-you-NOLL-oh-gee**] An interdisciplinary field that studies the effects of psychological factors on the immune system. *Page 103*

psychophysics The branch of psychology that studies the relation between attributes of the physical world and our psychological experience of them. *Page 120*

psychosexual stages In psychoanalytic theory, five developmental periods during which particular kinds of pleasures must be gratified if personality development is to proceed normally. *Page 463*

psychosis Serious mental disorders characterized by loss of contact with reality and extreme mental disruption. Because daily functioning is often impaired, psychotic individuals are more likely to need hospitalization. *Page 492*

psychosocial stages Erik Erikson's theory that individuals pass through eight developmental stages and that adult personality reflects how the distinct challenges or crises at each stage are resolved. *Page 359*

psychosurgery Operative procedures on the brain designed to relieve severe mental symptoms that have not responded to other forms of treatment. *Page 530*

psychotherapy A collection of various psychological techniques employed to improve psychological functioning and promote adjustment to life through understanding one's problems and modifying troubling feelings, behaviors, or relationships. *Page 524*

puberty The period in life when sex organs mature and sexual reproduction becomes possible. Puberty generally begins for girls between the ages of 10 and 12 years and for boys about 2 years later. *Page 329*

punishment Any action or event that decreases the likelihood that a response will be repeated. *Page 209*

random assignment Occurs when participant's chances of being assigned to each group in an experiment are equal, thereby ensuring that any later differences between people in the experimental and control conditions must be the result of the treatment. *Page 17*

rapid-eye-movement (REM) sleep A stage of sleep marked by rapid eye movements, high-frequency brain waves, and dreaming. *Page 166*

rational-emotive therapy (RET) Cognitive therapy system developed by Albert Ellis that attempts to eliminate self-defeating beliefs through rational examination. *Page 538*

reality principle According to Sigmund Freud, the principle on which the conscious ego operates as it tries to meet the demands of the unconscious id and the realities of the environment. *Page 462*

recall Process of using a very general retrieval cue to search the contents of long-term memory. *Page 248*

reciprocal determinism Albert Bandura's belief that an individual's cognitions and behaviors and the learning environment interact to produce personality. *Page 475*

recognition Process of matching a specific retrieval cue to an appropriate item in long-term memory. *Page 248*

reference groups People to whom we conform (or with whom we go along) because we like and admire them and want to be like them. *Page 583*

refractory period Phase following orgasm during which further orgasm is considered physiologically impossible. *Page 394*

reinforcement Any action or event that increases the probability that a response will be repeated. *Page 209*

relearning Learning material a second time, which usually takes less time than original learning; also called the savings method. *Page 255*

reliability A measure of the consistency and stability of test scores when the test is readministered. *Page 301*

repair/restoration theory The theory that sleep serves a recuperative function, allowing organisms to repair or replenish key factors in the brain or body that are depleted during daytime activities. *Page 168*

repression Sigmund Freud's first and most basic defense mechanism that blocks unacceptable impulses from coming into awareness. *Page 463*

resilience A term referring to a child's good developmental outcome, sustained competence under stress, and recovery from trauma despite high-risk status. *Page 367*

resistance A stage in psychoanalysis when the patient avoids (resists) the analyst's attempts to bring threatening unconscious material to conscious awareness. *Page 534*

resolution phase Final stage of the sexual response cycle when the body returns to its unaroused state. *Page 394*

reticular formation (RF) A diffuse set of neurons in the core of the brain stem that screen incoming information and arouses the cortex. *Page 63*

retina The light-sensitive inner surface of the back of the eye, which contains the receptor rods and cones plus other neurons that help in processing visual information. *Page 125*

retinal disparity A binocular cue to distance in which the separation of the eyes causes different images to fall on each retina. *Page 144*

retrieval The process of recovering information from memory storage. *Page 242*

retrieval cue A clue or prompt that helps stimulate recall and retrieval of a stored piece of information from long-term memory. *Page 248*

retroactive interference Forgetting in which new information interferes with remembering old information; backward-acting interference. *Page 258*

retrograde amnesia Difficulty in remembering previously learned material. *Page 261*

rods Visual receptors in the retina that detect black, white, and gray and are responsible for peripheral vision. They are most sensitive in dim light. *Page 125*

romantic love An intense feeling of attraction to another person, within an erotic context and with future expectations. *Page 579*

Rorschach [ROAR-shock] Inkblot Test A projective test that presents a set of 10 cards with symmetrical abstract patterns, known as inkblots, and respondents describe what they "see" in the image. Their response is thought to be a projection of unconscious processes. *Page 451*

saliency bias The tendency to focus on the most noticeable (salient) factors when explaining the causes of behavior. *Page 566*

sample bias The tendency for the sample of participants in a research study to be atypical of a larger population. *Page 16*

Schachter's two-factor theory The theory that emotional experience results from physical arousal and cognitive labeling (or interpretation) of that arousal. *Page 440*

schema Cognitive structures or patterns consisting of a number of organized ideas that grow and differentiate with experience. *Page 340*

schizophrenia Group of psychotic disorders involving major disturbances in perception, language, thought, emotion, and behavior. The individual withdraws from people and reality, often into a fantasy life of delusions and hallucinations. *Page 505*

secondary reinforcers Stimuli that increase the probability of a response because of their learned value, such as money and material possessions. *Page 210*

selective attention The process whereby the brain sorts out and attends to only the important messages from the senses. *Page 136*

self-actualization According to Abraham Maslow, an innate tendency toward growth that motivates all human behavior and results in the full realization of a person's highest potential. *Page 473*

self-concept In Rogerian theory, all the information and beliefs individuals have about their own nature, qualities, and behavior. *Page 471*

self-efficacy According to Albert Bandura, a person's learned beliefs that he or she is capable of producing desired results, such as mastering new skills and achieving personal goals. *Page 474*

self-help group Groups that are leaderless or guided by a nonprofessional, in which members assist each other in coping with a specific problem, as in Alcoholics Anonymous. *Page 550*

self-serving bias A way of maintaining a positive self-image by taking credit for one's successes and emphasizing external causes for one's failures. *Page 567*

self-talk Internal dialogue; the things people say to themselves when they interpret events. *Page 537*

semantic memory The subpart of explicit/declarative memory that stores general knowledge; a mental encyclopedia or dictionary. *Page 247*

semantics Meaning or the study of meaning derived from morphemes, words, and sentences. *Page 292*

semicircular canals Three arching structures in the inner ear that contain hair receptors that respond to head movements to provide information on balance. *Page 133*

sensation The process of receiving, translating, and transmitting raw sensory data from the external and internal environments to the brain. *Page 118*

sensorimotor stage The first of Jean Piaget's stages (birth to approximately age 2 years), in which cognitive development takes place by exploring the world via sensory perceptions and motor skills. *Page 341*

sensory adaptation A sensory phenomenon in which the perceived intensity of a repeated stimulus decreases over time. *Page 120*

sensory memory The first stage of memory, in which a relatively exact image of each sensory experience is held briefly until it can be further processed; its capacity is relatively large but its duration is restricted to a few seconds. *Page 238*

sensory reduction The process of filtering and analyzing incoming sensations that occur before a neural impulse is sent to the cortex. *Page 119*

serial position effect The phenomenon of remembering the material at the beginning and the end of a list better than the material in the middle. *Page 255*

set point An organism's personal homeostatic level for a particular body weight that results from factors such as early feeding experiences and heredity. *Page 414*

sex Biological maleness and femaleness, including chromosomal sex, gonadal sex, hormonal sex, external genitals, and internal accessory organs. Also, activities related to sexual behaviors, such as masturbation and intercourse. *Page 381*

sexual dysfunction Impairment of the normal physiological processes of arousal and orgasm. *Page 398*

sexual orientation An individual's primary erotic attraction can be toward members of the same sex (homosexual or gay or lesbian), both sexes (bisexual), or other sex (heterosexual). *Page 382*

sexual prejudice Negative attitudes toward an individual because of his or her sexual orientation. *Page 397*

sexual response cycle William Masters and Virginia Johnson's description of the bodily response to sexual arousal. The four stages are excitement, plateau, orgasm, and resolution. *Page 393*

sexual scripts Socially dictated descriptions of the sequences of behavior that are considered appropriate in sexual interactions. *Page 400*

shaping A procedure in which reinforcement is delivered for successive approximations of the desired response. *Page 214*

short-term memory (STM) The second stage of memory that contains information a person is consciously thinking about or working with; its capacity is limited to five to nine items and its duration is about 30 seconds. *Page 238*

sleep apnea A temporary cessation of breathing during sleep; one of the suspected causes of snoring, sudden infant death syndrome (SIDS), high blood pressure, and heart damage. *Page 173*

sleeper effect The initial tendency to discount information from an unreliable source but to later consider it more trustworthy because the source is forgotten. *Page 263*

social psychology The branch of psychology that studies how other people influence an individual's behavior (thoughts, feelings, and actions). *Page 565*

somatic nervous system (SNS) A subdivision of the peripheral nervous system that connects to sensory receptors and controls skeletal muscles. *Page 48*

source amnesia Attributing to a wrong source an event that we have experienced, heard about, read about, or imagined; also called source confusion or source misattribution. *Page 263*

split-brain A surgical separation of the brain's two hemispheres used medically to treat severe epilepsy. Split-brain patients provide data on the functions of the two hemispheres. *Page 70*

spontaneous recovery The reappearance of a previously extinguished response after a period of time without exposure to the conditioned stimulus. *Page 204*

standardization The process of establishing the norms and uniform procedures for giving and scoring a test. *Page 301*

stem cell Precursor (immature) cells that produce new specialized cells. A stem cell holds all the information it needs to make bone, blood, brain — any part of a human body — and can also copy itself to maintain a stock of stem cells. *Page 76*

stereotype (1) A set of beliefs about the characteristics of people in a group that is generalized to all group members or (2) the cognitive component of prejudice. *Page 571*

stereotype threat A psychological predicament in which a person experiences doubt about his or her performance, owing to negative stereotypes about his or her group's abilities. *Page 311*

stimulants Drugs that act on the brain and nervous system to increase their overall activity and general responsiveness. *Page 179*

stimulus discrimination The occurrence of a learned response to a specific stimulus but not to other, similar stimuli. *Page 204*

stimulus generalization The occurrence of a learned response not only to the original stimulus but also to other similar stimuli. *Page 203*

storage The process of retaining neural coded information over time. *Page 242*

stress A nonspecific response of the body to any demand made on it; the arousal, both physical and mental, to situations or events that we perceive as threatening or challenging. *Page 96*

subliminal Pertaining to any stimulus presented below the threshold of conscious awareness. *Page 150*

superego In psychoanalytic theory, the part of the personality that incorporates parental and societal standards for morality. *Page 462*

survey Nonexperimental research technique that assesses behaviors and attitudes of a sample or population. *Page 19*

sympathetic nervous system Subdivision of the autonomic nervous system responsible for arousing the body and mobilizing its energy during times of stress; also called the fight-or-flight system. *Page 48*

synapse [SIN-aps] The junction between the axon tip of the sending neuron and the dendrite or cell body of the receiving neuron. *Page 53*

syntax The grammatical rules that specify in what order the words and phrases should be arranged in a sentence to convey meaning. *Page 291*

systematic desensitization In behavior therapy, a gradual process of extinguishing a learned fear (or phobia) by associating a hierarchy of fear-evoking stimuli with deep relaxation. *Page 544*

telegraphic speech The two- or three-word sentences of young children that contain only the most necessary words. *Page 333*

temperament A basic, inborn disposition that appears shortly after birth and characterizes an individual's style of approaching people and situations. *Page 358*

temporal lobes Cortical lobes above the ears involved in audition (hearing), language comprehension, memory, and some emotional control. *Page 68*

teratogen [TER-ah-toe-jen] An external, environmental agent that can cross the placental barrier and disrupt development, causing minor or severe birth defects; from the Greek word teras, meaning "malformation." *Page 325*

thalamus [THAL-uh-muss] A brain structure at the top of the brainstem that relays sensory messages to the cerebral cortex. *Page 64*

thanatology [THAN-uh-tall-uh-jee] The study of death and dying. The term comes from Thanatos, the Greek name for a mythical personification of death, and was borrowed by Sigmund Freud to represent the death instinct. *Page 374*

Thematic Apperception Test (TAT) A projective test that shows a series of ambiguous black-and-white pictures and asking the test taker to create a story related to each. The responses presumably reflect a projection of unconscious processes. *Page 451*

theory A system of interrelated, accumulated research findings used to explain a set of observations and generate testable hypotheses. *Page 11*

tip-of-the-tongue (TOT) phenomenon A retrieval failure that involves a sensation of knowing that specific information is stored in long-term memory but being temporarily unable to retrieve it. *Page 260*

tolerance A decreased sensitivity to a drug brought about by its continuous use. *Page 176*

top-down processing Processing that starts "at the top" with the observer's thoughts, expectations, and knowledge and works down; perceptual analysis that emphasizes the perceiver's internal cognitive processes rather than being driven by characteristics of the outside stimuli. *Page 118*

trait A relatively stable and consistent characteristic that can be used to describe someone. *Page 454*

transduction The process by which a stimulus to a receptor is converted into neural impulses. *Page 119*

transference In psychoanalysis, the patient may displace (or transfer) thoughts, feelings, fears, wishes, and conflicts from past relationships, particularly from childhood, onto new relationships, especially with the therapist. *Page 535*

trichromatic theory The theory, first proposed by Thomas Young, stating that color perception results from mixing three distinct color systems — red, green, and blue. *Page 147*

type A personality Set of behavior characteristics that includes intense ambition, competition, drive, constant preoccupation with responsibilities, exaggerated time urgency, and a cynical, hostile outlook. *Page 106*

type B personality Set of behavior characteristics consistent with a calm, patient, relaxed attitude toward life. *Page 106*

unconditional positive regard According to Carl Rogers, the nonjudgmental attitude and genuine caring that the therapist should express toward the client to increase his or her self-esteem. *Page 472,542*

unconditioned response (UCR) The reflex response evoked by a stimulus without any learning required. *Page 200*

unconditioned stimulus (UCS) Any stimulus that causes a reflex or emotional response without any learning or conditioning. *Page 200*

unconscious Sigmund Freud's term for thoughts, motives, impulses, or desires that lie beyond a person's normal awareness but that can be made available through psychoanalysis. *Page 461*

validity The ability of a test to measure what it was designed to measure. *Page 301*

variable-interval schedule A schedule of reinforcement in which the participant is reinforced for the first response after a period of time has elapsed. This period of time varies from one reinforcement to the next. *Page 213*

variable-ratio schedule A schedule of reinforcement in which the participant is reinforced, on the average, for making a specific number of responses, but the number of required responses between reinforcements is varied. *Page 213*

wavelength The length of a light wave or sound wave, measured from the crest of one wave to the crest of the next. *Page 123*

withdrawal Discomfort and distress, including physical pain and intense cravings, experienced after stopping the use of addictive drugs. *Page 176*

Zeigarnik effect Process whereby interupted tasks are better recalled than completed tasks. *Page 250*

References

Aarons, L. (1976). Evoked sleep-talking. *Perceptual and Motor Skills, 31,* 27–40.

Abadinsky, H. (2001). *Drugs: An introduction* (4th ed.). Stamford, CT: Thomson Learning.

Abi-Dargham, A. (1998). Increased striatal dopamine transmission in schizophrenia. *American Journal of Psychiatry, 155,* 761–767.

Abusharaf, R. (1998, March/April). Unmasking tradition. *The Sciences,* 22–27.

Achenbaum, W. A., & Bengtson, V. L. (1994). Re-engaging the disengagement theory of aging: On the history and assessment of theory development in gerontology. *Gerontologist, 34,* 756–763.

Acklin, M. W. (1999). Behavioral science foundations of the Rorschach Test: Research and clinical applications. *Assessment, 6*(4), 319–326.

Adamopoulos, J., & Kashima, Y. (1999). *Social psychology and cultural context.* Thousand Oaks, CA: Sage.

Adelman, P. K., & Zajonc, R. B. (1989). Facial efference and the experience of emotion. In M. R. Rosenzweig & L. W. Porter (Eds.), *Annual review of psychology* (pp. 249–280). Palo Alto, CA: Annual Reviews Inc.

Adler, A. (1964). The individual psychology of Alfred Adler. In H. L. Ansbacher & R. R. Ansbacher (Eds.), *The individual psychology of Alfred Adler.* New York: Harper & Row.

Adler, A. (1998). *Understanding human nature.* Center City: MN: Hazelden Information Education.

Adler, N. E., Boyce, T., Chesney, M. A., Cohen, S., Folkman, S., Kahn, R. L., & Syme, L. (1994). Socioeconomic status and health: The challenge of the gradient. *American Psychologist, 49,* 15–24.

Adolphs, R., Tranel, D., & Damasio, A. R. (1998). The human amygdala in social judgment. *Nature, 393,* 470–474.

Affleck, G., Tennen, H., & Apter, A. (2001). Optimism, pessimism, and daily life with chronic illness. In E. C. Chang (Ed), *Optimism & pessimism: Implications for theory, research, and practice* (pp. 147–168). Washington, DC: American Psychological Association.

Agid, O., Shapira, B., Zislin, J., Ritsner, M., Hanin, B., Murad, H., Troudart, T., Bloch, M., Heresco-Levy, U., & Lerer, B. (1999). Environment and vulnerability to major psychiatric illness: A case control study of early parental loss in major depression, bipolar disorder, and schizophrenia. *Molecular Psychiatry, 4,* 163–172.

Agras, W. S., & Berkowitz, R. I. (1999). Behavior therapies. In R. E. Hales, S. C. Yudofsky, & J. A. Talbott (Eds.), *American Psychiatric Press textbook of psychiatry.* Washington, DC: American Psychiatric Press.

Akan, G. E., & Grilo, C. M. (1995). Sociocultural influences on eating attitudes and behaviors, body image, and psychological functioning: A comparison of African American, Asian American, and Caucasian college women. *International Journal of Eating Disorders, 18,* 181–187.

Akers, J. F., Jones, R. M., & Coyl, D. D. (1998). Adolescent friendship pairs: Similarities in identity status development, behaviors, attitudes, and intentions. *Journal of Adolescent Research, 13,* 178–201.

Ahijevych, K., Yerardi, R., & Nedilsky, N. (2000). Descriptive outcomes of the American Lung Association of Ohio hypnotherapy smoking cessation program. *International Journal of Clinical & Experimental Hypnosis, 48*(4), 374–387.

Ainsworth, M. D. S. (1967). *Infancy in Uganda: Infant care and the growth of love.* Baltimore: Johns Hopkins University Press.

Ainsworth, M. D. S., Blehar, M., Waters, E., & Wall, S. (1978). *Patterns of attachment: Observations in the strange situation and at home.* Hillsdale, NJ: Erlbaum.

Albarracin, D., & Wyer, R. S., Jr. (2000). The cognitive impact of past behavior: Influences on beliefs, attitudes, and future behavioral decisions. *Journal of Personality & Social Psychology, 79*(1), 5–22.

Alden, L. E., & Wallace, S. T. (1995). Social phobia and social appraisal in successful and unsuccessful social interactions. *Behaviour Research and Therapy, 33*(5), 497–505.

Alexander, F. G., & Selesnick, S. T. (1966). *The history of psychiatry.* New York: Harper & Row.

Alexander, M., & Hegarty, J. R. (2000). Measuring staff burnout in a community home. *British Journal of Developmental Disabilities, 46,* 51–62.

Allen, J. P., Philiber, S., Herrling, S., & Kupermine, G. P. (1997). Preventing teen pregnancy and academic failure: Experimental evaluation of a developmentally based approach. *Child Development, 64,* 729–742.

Allen, P. L. (2000). *The wages of sin: Sex and disease, past and present.* Chicago: University of Chicago Press.

Allen, R. P., & Mirabile, J. (1997, June 18). Cited in E. Woo, How to get A's, not Zzz's. *Los Angeles Times,* p. 34.

Allgeier, E. R., & Allgeier, A. R. (2000). *Sexual interactions* (5th ed.). New York: Houghton Mifflin.

Alloy, L. B., & Clements, C. M. (1998). Hopelessness theory of depression. *Cognitive Therapy and Research, 22,* 303–335.

Alloy, L. B., Abramson, L. Y., Whitehouse, W. G., Hogan, M. E., Tashman, N. A., Steinberg, D. L., Rose, D. T., & Donovan, P. (1999). Depressogenic cognitive styles: Predictive validity, information processing and personality characteristics, and developmental origins. *Behaviour Research and Therapy, 37,* 503–531.

Allport, G. (1937). *Personality: A psychological interpretation.* New York: Holt, Rinehart and Winston.

Allport, G. W., & Odbert, H. S. (1936). Trait-names: A psycho-lexical study. *Psychological Monographs: General and Applied, 47,* 1–21.

Almeida, D. M., & Kessler, R. C. (1998). Everyday stressors and gender differences in daily distress. *Journal of Personality and Social Psychology, 75,* 670–680.

Aluja-Fabregat, A., & Torrubia-Beltri, R. (1998). Viewing of mass media violence, perception of violence, personality and academic achievement. *Personality and Individual Differences, 25,* 973–989.

Amabile, T. (2000). *Creativity in context.* Boulder, CO: Westview.

American Cancer Society. (2000). Pregnant women may have ample motivation to quit smoking, but few have access to smoking cessation programs tailored to their maternal condition. Available: http://www2.cancer.org/zine/index.cfm?fn=001_110319 98_0

American Heart Association. (2000). Heart Patient Information. Available: http://americanheart.org/Patient_Information/hindex.html

American Psychiatric Association Work Group on Alzheimer's Disease & Related Dementias. (1997). Practice guideline for the treatment of patients with Alzheimer's disease and other dementias of late life. *American Journal of Psychiatry, 154(5,* Suppl), 1–39.

American Psychiatric Association. (2000). *Diagnostic and statistical manual of mental disorders* (4th ed. TR). Washington, DC: American Psychiatric Press.

Amunts, K., Jaencke, L., Mohlberg, H., Steinmetz, H., & Zilles, K. (2000). Interhemispheric asymmetry of the human motor cortex related to handedness and gender. *Neuropsychologia, 38(3),* 304–312.

Anastasio, P. A., Rose, K. C., & Chapman, J. (1999). Can the media create public opinion? A social-identity approach. *Current Directions in Psychological Science, 8(5),* 152–155.

Andersen, B. L. (1998). Psychology's science in responding to the challenge of cancer. *Psychological Science Agenda, 11(1),* 14–15.

Anderson, A. K., & Phelps, E. A. (2000). Expression without recognition: Contributions of the human amygdala to emotional communication. *Psychological Science, 11(2),* 106–111.

Anderson, C. A., & Dill, K. E. (2000). Video games and aggressive thoughts, feelings, and behavior in the laboratory and in life. *Journal of Personality and Social Psychology, 78,* 772–790.

Anderson, C. A., Anderson, K. B., Dorr, N., DeNeve, K. M., & Flanagan, M. (2000). Temperature and aggression. *Advances in Experimental Social Psychology, 32,* 63–133.

Anderson, M. C., Bjork, R. A. & Bjork, E. L. (1994). Remembering can cause forgetting: Retrieval dynamics in long-term mem-

ory. *Journal of Experimental Psychology: Learning, Memory, and Cognition, 20,* 1063–1087.

Anderson, S. W., Bechara, A., Damasio, H., Tranel, D., & Damasio, A. R. (1999). Impairment of social and moral behavior related to early damage in human prefrontal cortex. *Nature Neuroscience, 2,* 1032–1037.

Andreasen, J. (2000). Meditation meets behavioural medicine: The story of experimental research on meditation. *Journal of Consciousness Studies,7(11–12),* 17–73.

Andreasen, N. C. (1997). The role of the thalamus in schizophrenia. Canadian *Journal of Psychiatry, 155,* 1784–1786.

Andreasen, N. C. (1999). Understanding the causes of schizophrenia. *New England Journal of Medicine, 340(8),* 645–647.

Andreasen, N. C. (2000). Schizophrenia: The fundamental questions. *Brain Research Reviews, 31,* 106–112.

Andreasen, N. C., Flaum, M., Swayze, V. O., Alliger, R., Cohen, G., Ehrhardt, J., & Yuh, W. T. (1993). Intelligence and brain structure in normal individuals. *American Journal of Psychiatry, 150,* 130–134.

Andreasen, N. C., Flaum, M., Swayze, V. W., Tyrrell, G., & Arndt, S. (1990). Positive and negative symptoms in schizophrenia. *Archives of General Psychiatry, 47,* 615–621.

Andreasen, N. C., Flaum, M., Swayze, V. W., Tyrrell, G., & Arndt, S. (1990). Positive and negative symptoms in schizophrenia. *Archives of General Psychiatry, 47,* 615–621.

Anooshian, L. J. (1997). Distinctions between implicit and explicit memory: Significance for understanding cognitive development. *International Journal of Behavioral Development, 21,* 453–478.

Apkarian, A. V., Darbar, A., Kraus, B. R., Gelnar, P. A., & Szeverenyi, N. M. (1999). Differentiating cortical areas related to pain perception from stimulus identification: Temporal analysis of fMRI activity. *Journal of Neurophysiology, 81,* 2956–2963.

Aries, P. (1981). *The hour of our death.* (H. Weaver, Trans.). New York: Knopf.

Arnsten, A. F. (1998). The biology of being frazzled. *Science, 280,*1711–1712.

Aronson, E., Wilson, T. D., & Akert, R. A. (1999). *Social psychology: The heart and the mind* (3rd ed.). New York: Freeman.

Arthur, W., Bennett, W., Stanush, P. L., McNelly, T. L. (1998). Factors that influence skill decay and retention: A quantita-

tive review and analysis. *Human Performance, 11,* 57–101.

Arthur, W., Jr., Bennett, W., Jr., Stanush, P. L., & McNelly, T. L. (1998). Factors that influence skill decay and retention: A quantitative review and analysis. *Human Performance, 11,* 57–101.

Arvey, R. D., et al. (1994, December 13). Mainstream science on intelligence. *The Wall Street Journal,* p. A18.

Asch, S. E. (1951). Effects of group pressure upon the modification and distortion of judgment. In H. Guetzkow (Ed.), *Groups, leadership, and men.* Pittsburgh: Carnegie Press.

Aspinall, S. Y. (1996). Educating children to cope with death: A preventive model. *Psychology in the Schools, 33,* 341–349.

Atchley, P., & Kramer, A. F. (2000). Age related changes in the control of attention in depth. *Psychology & Aging, 15(1),* 78–87.

Atchley, R. C. (1997). *Social forces and aging* (8th ed.). Belmont, CA: Wadsworth.

Atkinson, R. C., & Shiffrin, R. M. (1968). Human memory: A proposed system and its control processes. In K. W. Spence & J. T. Spence (Eds.), *The psychology of learning and motivation* (Vol. 2). New York: Academic Press.

Axtell, R. E. (1998). *Gestures: The do's and taboos of body language around the world, revised and expanded ed.* New York: Wiley.

Bacciagaluppi, M. (1998). Recent advances in evolutionary psychology and psychiatry. *Journal of the American Academy of Psychoanalysis, 26,* 5–13.

Bachman, G., & Zakahi, W. R. (2000). Adult attachment and strategic relational communcation: Love schemas and affinity-seeking. *Communication Reports, 13(1),* 11–19.

Backstrom, J. R., Chang, M. S., Chu, H., Niswender, C. M., & Sanders–Bush, E. (1999). Agonist-directed signaling of serotonin 5-HT-sub(2C) receptors: Differences between serotonin and lysergic acid diethylamide (LSD). *Neuropsychopharmacology, 21*(Supl, 2), 77S–81S.

Baddeley, A. (1998). Recent developments in working memory. *Current Opinion in Neurobiology, 8,* 234–238.

Baddeley, A. D. (1992). Working Memory. *Science, 255,* 556–559.

Baddeley, A. D. (2000). Short-term and working memory. In E. Tulving, F. I. M. Craik, et al. (Eds.), *The Oxford handbook of memory.* New York: Oxford University Press.

Baer, J. (1994). Divergent thinking is not a general trait: A multi-domain training experiment. *Creativity Research Journal, 7,* 35–36.

Bagby, R. M., Rogers, R., & Buis, T. (1994). Detecting malingered and defensive responding on the MMPI–2 in a forensic inpatient sample. *Journal of Personality Assessment, 62,* 191–203.

Bagemihl, B. (1999). *Biological exuberance: Animal homosexuality and natural diversity.* New York: St Martins Press.

Bailer, U., Leisch, F., Meszaros, K., Lenzinger, E., Willinger, U., Strobl, R., Gebhardt, C., Gerhard, E., Fuchs, K., Sieghart, W., Kasper, S., Hornik, K., & Aschauer, H. N. (2000). Genomes scan for susceptibility loci for schizophrenia. *Neuropsychobiology, 42*(4), 175–182.

Bailey, C. H., & Kandel, E. R. (1995). Molecular and structural mechanisms underlying long-term memory. In M. S. Gazzanig, et al. (Eds.), *The cognitive neurosciences.* Cambridge, MA: MIT Press.

Bailey, J. M., & Shriver, A. (1999). Does childhood sexual abuse cause borderline personality disorder? *Journal of Sex and Marital Therapy, 25,* 45–57.

Bailey, J. M., Dunne, M. P., & Martin, N. G. (2000). Genetic and environmental influences on sexual orientation and its correlates in an Australian twin sample. *Journal of Personality & Social Psychology,* 78(3), 524–536.

Baker, D., Telfer, M., Richardson, C. E., & Clark, G. R. (1970). Chromosome errors in men with antisocial behavior: Comparison of selected men with Klinefelter's syndrome and XYY chromosome pattern. *Journal of the American Medical Association, 214,* 869–878.

Baker, R. A. (1996). *Hidden memories.* New York: Prometheus Books.

Baker, R. A. (1998). A view of hypnosis. *Harvard Mental Health Letter, 14,* 5–6.

Baldwin, N. (2001). *Edison: Inventing the century.* Chicago: University of Chicago Press.

Baldwin, S., & Oxlad, M. (2000). *Electroshock and minors: A fifty year review.* New York: Greenwood Publishing Group.

Balfour, D. J. K., & Ridley, D. L. (2000). The effects of nicotine on neural pathways implicated in depression: A factor in nicotine addiction? *Pharmacology, Biochemistry & Behavior, 66*(1), 79–85.

Baltes, P. B., Staudinger, U. M., & Lindenberger, U. (1999). Lifespan psychology: Theory and application to intellectual functioning. *Annual Reviews of Psychology, 50,* 471–507.

Bandura, A. (1969). *Principles of behavior modification.* New York: Holt, Rinehart and Winston.

Bandura, A. (1986). *Social foundations of thought and action: A social cognitive theory.* Englewood Cliffs, NJ: Prentice Hall.

Bandura, A. (1989). Social cognitive theory. In R. Vasta (Ed.), *Annals of child development* (Vol. 6). Greenwich, CT: JAI Press.

Bandura, A. (1991). Social cognitive theory of moral thought and action. In W. M. Kurtines & J. L. Gewirtz (Eds.), *Handbook of moral behavior and development: Vol. 1. Theory.* Hillsdale, NJ: Erlbaum.

Bandura, A. (1997). *Self-efficacy: The exercise of control.* New York: Freeman.

Bandura, A. (1997, March). Self-efficacy. *Harvard Mental Health Letter, 13*(9), 4–6.

Bandura, A. (1999). Social cognitive theory of personality. In L. A Pervin, & O. P. John (Eds.), *Handbook of personality: Theory and Research.* New York: Guilford Press.

Bandura, A. (2000). Exercise of human agency through collective efficacy. *Current Directions in Psychological Science, 9*(3), 75–83.

Bandura, A., & Walters, R. H. (1963). *Social learning and personality development.* New York: Holt, Rinehart and Winston.

Bandura, A., Blanchard, E. B., & Ritter, B. J. (1969). The relative efficacy of desensitization and modeling therapeutic approaches for inducing behavioral, affective, and attitudinal changes. *Journal of Personality and Social Psychology, 13,* 173–199.

Banks, A., & Gartrell, N. K. (1995). Hormones and sexual orientation: A questionable link. *Journal of Homosexuality, 28*(3–4), 247–268.

Banks, M. S., & Salapatek, P. (1983). Infant visual perception. In M. M. Haith & J. J. Campos (Eds.), *Handbook of child psychology.* New York: Wiley.

Bannon, A. W., Decker, M. W., Kim, D. J. B., Campbell, J. E., & Arneric, S. P. (1998). ABT-594, a novel cholinergic channel modulator, is efficacious in nerve ligation and diabetic neuropathy models of neuropathic pain. *Brain Research, 801,* 158–163.

Bar-On, R. (2000). *The handbook of emotional intelligence.* New York: Jossey-Bass.

Barber, C. E. (1997). Olfactory acuity as a function of age and gender: A comparison of African and American samples. *International Journal of Aging and Human Development, 44,* 317–334.

Barber, N. (2000). On the relationship between country sex ratios and teen pregnancy rates: A replication. *Cross-Cultural Research: The Journal of Comparative Social Science, 34,* 26–37.

Barker, R. A., & Dunnett, S. B. (1999). *Neural repair, transplantation, and rehabilitation.* Hove, England: Psychology Press/Taylor & Francis.

Barber, T. X. (2000). A deeper understanding of hypnosis: Its secrets, its nature, its essence. *American Journal of Clinical Hypnosis, 42*(3–4), 208–272.

Bard, C. (1934). On emotional expression after decortication with some remarks on certain theoretical views. *Psychological Review, 41,* 309–329.

Bargh, J. A. (1999, January 29). The most powerful manipulative messages are hiding in plain sight. *Chronicle of Higher Education,* B6.

Barinaga, M. (1999). Learning visualized, on the double. *Science, 286,* 1661.

Barker, P. (2000). *Basic family therapy.* Malden, MA: Blackwell Science, Inc.

Barley, N. (1997). *Grave matters: A lively history of death around the world.* Austin, TX: Henry Holt & Company.

Barlow, D. H. (1999). *Anxiety and its disorders: The nature and treatment of anxiety and panic* (2nd ed.). New York: Guilford.

Barlow, D. H., & Durand, V. M. (2001). *Abnormal psychology* (2nd ed.). Belmont, CA: Wadsworth.

Barlow, D. H., Esler, J. L., & Vitali, A. E. (1998). Psychosocial treatments for panic disorders, phobias, and generalized anxiety disorder. In P. E. Nathan, J. M. Gorman, et al. (Eds.), *A guide to treatments that work* (pp. 288–318). New York: Oxford University Press.

Barnes, E., Graft, B., Reaves, J. A., & Shannon, E. (2000, March 13). It's all the rave. *Time,* pp. 64–66.

Barnouw, V. (1985). *Culture and personality* (4th ed.). Homewood, IL: Dorsey Press.

Baron, J., Roediger, H. L. III, & Anderson, M.C. (2000). Human factors and the Palm Beach ballot. *APS Observer, 13*(10), 5–7.

Baron, R. (2000). *Social psychology* (7th ed.). Boston: Allyn & Bacon.

Barr, A. (1999). *Drink: A social history of America.* New York: Carroll & Graf.

Barrett–Lennard, G. T. (1999). *Carl Rogers' helping system: Journey and substance.* Thousand Oaks, CA: Corwin Press.

Barstow, D. G. (1999). Female genital mutilation: The penultimate gender abuse. *Child Abuse and Neglect, 23*(5), 501–510.

Bartlett, F. C. (1958). *Thinking.* London: Allen & Unwin.

Bartsch, R. A., Judd, C. M., Louw, D. A., Park, B., & Ryan, C. S. (1997). Cross-national outgroup homogeneity: United States and South African stereotypes. *South African Journal of Psychology, 27*(3), 166–170.

Bashore, T. R., & Rapp, P. E. (1993). Are there alternatives to traditional polygraph procedures? *Psychological Bulletin, 113,* 3–22.

Batel, P. (2000). Addiction and schizophrenia. *European Psychiatry, 15,* 115–122.

Batson, C. D. (1991). *The altruism question: Toward a social-psychological answer.* Hillsdale, NJ: Erlbaum.

Batson, C. D. (1998). Altruism and prosocial behavior. In D. T. Gilbert, S. T. Fiske, and G. Lindzey (Eds.), *The handbook of social psychology, Vol. 2* (4th ed.) (pp. 282–316). Boston, MA: McGraw-Hill.

Batson, C. D., et al. (1999). Two threats to the common good: Self-interested egoism and empathy and empathy-induced altruism. *Personality and Social Psychology Bulletin, 25,* 3–16.

Baum, A., & Posluszny, D. M. (1999). Health psychology: Mapping biobehavioral contributions to health and illness. *Annual Review of Psychology, 50,* 137–163.

Baumeister, R. J. (1998). The self. In D. T. Gilbert, S. T. Fiske, and G. Lindzey (Eds.), *The handbook of social psychology, Vol. 2* (4th ed.) (pp. 680–740). Boston, MA: McGraw-Hill.

Baumrind, D. (1980). New directions in socialization research. *American Psychologist, 35,* 639–652.

Baumrind, D. (1995). *Child maltreatment and optimal caregiving in social contexts.* New York: Garland.

Beach, F. A. (1977). *Human sexuality in four perspectives.* Baltimore: The Johns Hopkins University Press.

Beal, D., & DiGiuseppe, R. (1998). Training supervisors in rational emotive behavior therapy. *Journal of Cognitive Psychotherapy, 12,* 127–137.

Beatty, J. (2001). *The human brain: Essentials of behavioral neuroscience.* Thousand Oaks, CA: Sage Publications.

Beaubrun, G., & Gray, G. E. (2000). A review of herbal medicines for psychiatric disorders. *Psychiatric Services, 51*(9), 1130–1134.

Beaumont, G. (2000). Antipsychotics-The future of schizophrenia treatment. *Current Medical Research and Opinion, 16,* 37–42.

Bechara, A., Damasio, H., Damasio, A. R., & Lee, G. P. (1999). Different contributions of the human amygdala and ventromedial prefrontal cortex to decision-making. *Journal of Neuroscience, 19,* 5473–5481.

Bechara, A., Tranel, D., Damasio, H., & Damasio, A. R. (1996). Failure to respond automatically to anticipated future outcomes following damage to prefrontal cortex. *Cerebral Cortex, 6,* 215–225.

Beck, A. T. (1976). *Cognitive therapy and the emotional disorders.* New York: International Universities Press.

Beck, A. T. (2000). *Prisoners of hate.* New York: Harperperennial.

Beck, A. T., Brown, G. K., Steer, R. A., Kuyken, W., & Grisham, J. (2001). Psychometric properties of the Beck Self-Esteem Scales. *Behaviour Research & Therapy, 39*(1), 115–124.

Beck, J. S. (1995). *Cognitive therapy: Basics and beyond.* New York: Guilford.

Becker, A., Stief, C., Machtens, S., Schult-heiss, D., Hartmann, U., Truss, M., & Jonas, U. (1998). Oral phentolamine as treatment for erectile dysfunction. *Journal of Urology, 159,* 1214–1216.

Beckerman, S., Hardy, S. B., Baker, R. R., Crocker, W. H., Valentine, P., & Hawkes, K. (1999). Partible paternity: Matings with multi-ple men leading to multiple fathers per child. *Meeting of the American Association for the Advancement of Science.* January, Anaheim, CA.

Beeckmans, K., Michiels, K. (1996). Personality, emotions and the temporolimbic system: A neuropsychological approach. *Acta Neurologica Belgica, 96,* 35–42.

Begg, I. M., Needham, D. R., & Bookbinder, M. (1993). Do backward messages unconsciously affect listeners? No. *Canadian Journal of Experimental Psychology, 47,* 1–14.

Begley, S. (2000, January 1). Rewiring your gray matter. *Newsweek,* pp. 63, 65.

Beilin, H. (1992). Piaget's enduring contribution to developmental psychology. *Developmental Psychology, 28,* 191–204.

Bekaroglu, M., Soylu, C., Soylu, N., & Bilici, M. (1997). Bipolar affective disorder associated with Klinefleter's syndrome: A case report. *Israel Journal of Psychiatry & Related Sciences, 34,* 308–310.

Bell, A. P., Weinberg, M. S., & Hammersmith, S. K. (1981). *Sexual preference: Its development in men and women.* Bloomington: Indiana University Press.

Bellivier, F., Leboyer, M., Courtet, P., Buresi, C., Beufils, B., Samolyk, D., et al. (1998). Association between the tryptophan hydroxylase gene and manic-depressive illness. *Archives of General Psychiatry, 55,* 33–37.

Belsky, J., & Cassidy, J. (1994). Attachment: Theory and evidence. In M. Rutter & D. Hay (Eds.), *Development through life: A handbook for clinicians* (pp. 373–402). Oxford, England: Blackwell.

Bem, S. L. (1974). The measurement of psychological androgyny. *Journal of Consulting and Clinical Psychology, 42*(2), 155–162.

Bem, S. L. (1981). Gender schema theory: A cognitive account of sex typing. *Psychological Review, 88,* 354–364.

Bem, S. L. (1993). *The lenses of gender: Transforming the debate on sexual inequality.* New Haven, CT: Yale University Press.

Benes, F. M. (1997). The role of stress and dopamine-GABA interactions in the vulnerability for schizophrenia. *Journal of Psychiatric Research, 31*(2), 257–275.

Benson, H. (1977). Systematic hypertension and the relaxation response. *New England Journal of Medicine, 296,* 1152–1156.

Berger, T. W., & Thompson, R. F. (1982). Hippocampal cellular plasticity during extinction of classically conditioned nictitating membrane behavior. *Behavioural Brain Research, 4*(1), 63–76.

Berkowitz, L. (1990). On the formation and regulation of anger and aggression. *American Psychologist, 45,* 494–503.

Berkowitz, L. (1999). Evil is more than banal: Situationism and the concept of evil. *Personality and Social Psychology Review, 3*(3), 246–253.

Berman, M. E., Tracy, J. I., & Coccaro, E. F. (1997). The serotonin hypothesis of aggression revisited. *Clinical Psychology Review, 17*(6), 651–665.

Bermond, B., Fasotti, L., Nieuwenhuyse, B., & Schuerman, J. (1991). Spinal cord lesions, peripheral feedback, and intensities of emotional feelings. *Cognition and Emotion, 5,* 201–220.

Bernard, L. L. (1924). *Instinct.* New York: Holt.

Bernhardt, P. C. (1997). Influences of serotonin and testosterone in aggression and dominance: Convergence with social psychology. *Current Directions in Psychological Science, 6,* 44–48.

Bernheim, K. F., & Lewine, R. R. J. (1979). *Schizophrenia: Symptoms, causes, and treatments.* New York: Norton.

Berreman, G. (1971). *Anthropology today.* Del Mar, CA: CRM Books.

Berrettini, W. H. (2000). Genetics of psychiatric disease. *Annual Review of Medicine, 51,* 465–479.

Berrettini, W. H. (2000). Susceptibility loci for bipolar disorder: Overlap with inherited vulnerability to schizophrenia. *Biological Psychiatry, 47*(3), 245–251.

Berry, J. W., Poortinga, Y. A., Segall, M. H., & Dasen, P. R. (1992). *Cross-cultural psychology: Research and applications.* New York: Cambridge University Press.

Bertram, K., & Widener, A. (1998). Repressed memories: The real story. *Professional Psychology: Research & Practice, 29,* 482–487.

Bertram, K., & Widener, A. (1999). Repressed memories: Just the facts. *Professional Psychology: Research & Practice, 30,* 625–626.

Best, D. L., & Williams, J. E. (1994). Masculinity/femininity in the self and ideal self-descriptions of university students in fourteen countries. In A. M. Bouvy, F. J. R. van de Vijver, P. Boski, & P. Schmitz (Eds.), *Journeys into cross-cultural psychology* (pp. 297–306). Amsterdam: Swets & Zeitlinger.

Best, J. B. (1999). *Cognitive psychology,* (5th ed.) Belmont, CA: Wadsworth.

Beutler, L. E., Brown, M. T., Crothers, L., Booker, K., et al. (1996). The dilemma of factitious demographic distinctions in psychological research. *Journal of Consulting and Clinical Psychology, 64,* 892–902.

Beutler, L. E., Shurkin, J. N., Bongar, B. M., & Gray, J. (2000). *A consumers guide to psychotherapy.* Oxford: Oxford University Press.

Bhugra, D. (2000). Disturbances in objects of desire: Cross-cultural issues. *Sexual & Relationship Therapy, 15*(1), 67–78.

Bidrose, S., & Goodman, G. S. (2000). Testimony and evidence: A scientific case study of memory for child sexual abuse. *Applied Cognitive Psychology, 14,* 197–213.

Biehl, M., Matsumoto, D., Ekman, P., Hearn, V., Heider, K., Kudoh, T., & Ton, *V.* (1997). Matsumoto and Ekman's Japanese and Caucasian facial expressions of emotion (JACFEE): Reliability data and cross–national differences. *Journal of Nonverbal Behavior, 21,* 3–21.

Biller, H. B. (1993). *Fathers and families: Paternal factors in child development.* Westport, CT: Auburn House.

Binder, J. R., et al. (1997). Human brain language areas identified by functional magnetic resonance imaging. *Journal of Neuroscience, 17,* 353–362.

Bink, M. L., & Marsh, R. L. (2000). Cognitive regularities in creative activity. *Review of General Psychology, 4*(1), 59–78.

Bishop, C. A. (1974). *The northern Objibwa and the fur trade.* Toronto: Holt, Rinehart, and Winston.

Bishop, K. M., & Wahlsten, D. (1997), Sex differences in the human corpus callosum: Myth or reality? *Neuroscience and Biobehavioral Reviews, 21,* 581–601.

Bjorklund, D. F. (1995). Children's thinking: Developmental function and individual differences. Pacific Grove, CA: Brooks/Cole.

Bjorkqvist, K. (1994). Sex differences in physical, verbal, and indirect aggression: A review of recent research. *Sex Roles, 30,* 177–188.

Blagrove, M., & Akehurst, L. (2000). Effects of sleep loss on confidence accuracy relationships for reasoning and eyewitness memory. *Journal of Experimental Psychology: Applied, 6,* 59–73.

Blakemore, C., & Cooper, G. F. (1970). Development of the brain depends on the visual environment. *Nature, 228,* 477–478.

Blanchard, J. J., Squires, D., Henry, T., Horan, W. P. Bogenschutz, M., et al., (1999). Examining an affect regulation model of substance abuse in schizophrenia: The role of traits and coping. *Journal of Nervous and Mental Disease, 187,* 72–79.

Blanton, C. K. (2000). "They cannot master abstractions, but they can often be made efficient workers": Race and class in the intelligence testing of Mexican Americans and African Americans in Texas during the 1920s. *Social Science Quarterly, 81*(4), 1014–1026.

Blass, T. (1999). The Milgram Paradigm after 35 years: Some things we now know about obedience to authority. *Journal of Applied Social Psychology, 29*(5), 955–978.

Bliwise, D. L. (1997). Sleep and aging. In M. R. Pressman & W. C. Orr (Eds.), *Understanding sleep: The evaluation and treat-* *ment of sleep disorders.* Washington, DC: American Psychological Association.

Bloom, F. E., & Lazerson, A. (1988). Brain, mind, and behavior (2nd ed.). New York: W. H. Freeman.

Bloom, J. W. (1998). The ethical practice of Web-Counseling. *British Journal of Guidance & Counseling, 26*(1), 53–59.

Blum, K., Braverman, E. R., Holder, J. M., Lubar, J. F., Monastra, V. J., Miller, D., Lubar, J. O., Chen, T. J. H., & Comings, D. E. (2000). Reward deficiency syndrome: A biogenetic model for the diagnosis and treatment of impulsive, addictive, and compulsive behaviors. *Journal of Psychoactive Drugs, 32*(Suppl), 1–68.

Blum, K., Cull, J. G., Braverman, E. R., & Comings, D. E. (1996). Reward deficiency syndrome. *American Scientist, 84,* 132–145.

Bobak, M., McKee, M., Rose, R., & Marmot, M. (1999). Alcohol consumption in a national sample of the Russian population. *Addiction, 94*(6), 857–866.

Bock, G. R., & Goode, J. A. (Eds.) (1996). *Genetics of criminal and antisocial behavior.* Chichester, England: Wiley.

Boden, M. A. (2000). State of the art: Computer models of creativity. *Psychologist, 13*(2), 72–76.

Bohart, A. C., O'Hara, M., & Leitner, L. M. (1998). Empirically violated treatments: Disenfranchisement of humanistic and other psychotherapies. *Psychotherapy Research, 8,* 141–157.

Boivin, D. B., Czeisler, C. A., & Waterhouse, J. W. (1997). Complex interaction of the sleep-wake cycle and circadian phase modulates mood in healthy subjects. *Archives of General Psychiatry, 54,* 145.

Bolles, R. C. (1970). Species–specific defense reactions and avoidance learning. *Psychological Review, 77,* 32–48.

Bolles, R. C. (1975). Theory of motivation (2nd ed.). New York: Harper & Row.

Bond, F. W., & Bunce, D. (2000). Mediators of change in emotion-focused and problem-focused worksite stress management intervention. *Journal of Occupational Health Psychology, 5,* 153–163.

Bonder, B. R., Zadorzny, C., & Martin, R. J. (1998). Dressing in Alzheimer's disease: Executive function and procedural memory. *Clinical Gerontologist, 19,* 88–92.

Book, H. E., & Luborsky, L. (1998). *Brief psychodynamic psychotherapy.* Washington, DC: American Psychological Association.

Borba, M. (2001). *Building moral intelligence: The seven essential virtues that teach kids to do the right thing.* New York: Jossey-Bass.

Borbely, A. A. (1982). Circadian and sleep-dependent processes in sleep regulation. In J. Aschoff, S. Daan, & G. A. Groos (Eds.), *Vertebrate circadian rhythms* (pp. 237–242). Berlin: Springer/Verlag.

Borkenau, P., Riemann, R., Angleitner, A., & Spinath, F. M. (2001). Genetic and environmental influences on observed personality: Evidence from the German Observational Study of Adult Twins. *Journal of Personality & Social Psychology, 80*(4), 655–668.

Born, J. Lange, T., Hansen, K., Molle, M., & Fehm, H. L. (1997). Effects of sleep and circadian rhythm on human circulating immune cells. *Journal of Immunology, 158,* 4454–4464.

Bostwick, J. M., & Pankratz, V. S. (2000). Affective disorders and suicide risk: A reexamination. *American Journal of Psychiatry, 157*(12), 1925–1932.

Bouchard, C. (1996). Can obesity be prevented? *Nutrition Reviews, 54,* S125–S130.

Bouchard, C. (1997). Human variation in body mass: Evidence for a role of the genes. *Nutrition Reviews, 55,* S21–S30.

Bouchard, T. J., Jr. (1994). Genes, environment, and personality. *Science, 264,* 1700–1701.

Bouchard, T. J. Jr. (1997). The genetics of personality. In K. Blum & E. P. Noble (Eds.), *Handbook of psychiatric genetics.* Boca Raton, FL: CRC Press.

Bouchard, T. J., Jr. (1999). The search for intelligence. *Science, 284,* 922–923.

Bouchard, T. J., Jr., & Hur, Y. (1998). Genetic and environmental influences on the continuous scales of the Myers-Briggs Type Indicator: An analysis based on twins reared apart. *Journal of Personality, 66,* 135–149.

Bouchard, T. J., Jr., Mcgue, M., Hur, Y., & Horn, J. M. (1998). A genetic and environmental analysis of the California Psychological Inventory using adult twins reared apart and together. *European Journal of Personality, 12,* 307–320.

Bourguignon, E. (1973). Introduction: A framework for the comparative study of altered states of consciousness. In E. Bourguignon (Ed.), *Religion, altered states of consciousness and social change.* Columbus: Ohio State University Press.

Bourne, L. E., Dominowski, R. L., & Loftus, E. F. (1979). *Cognitive processes.* Englewood Cliffs, NJ: Prentice Hall.

Bouton, M. E. (1994). Context, ambiguity, and classical conditioning. *Current Directions in Psychological Science, 2,* 49–53.

Bower, B. (1999). Criminal links to prenatal smoking. *Science News, 155,* 203.

Bower, B. (2000). Cooperative strangers turn a mutual profit. *Science News, 157,* 231.

Bower, G. H., Thompson-Schill, S. & Tulving, E. (1994). Reducing retroactive interference: An interference analysis. *Journal of Experimental Psychology: Learning, Memory, and Cognition, 20,* 51–66.

Bower, H. (2001). The gender identity disorder in the DSM-IV classification: A critical evaluation. *Australian & New Zealand Journal of Psychiatry, 35*(1), 1–8.

Bowers, K. S., & Woody, E. Z. (1996). Hypnotic amnesia and the paradox of intentional forgetting. *Journal of Abnormal Psychology, 105,* 381–390.

Bowlby, J. (1969). *Attachment and loss, Vol. I: Attachment.* New York: Basic Books.

Bowlby, J. (1973). *Attachment and loss, Vol. II: Separation and anxiety.* New York: Basic Books.

Bowlby, J. (1979). *The making and breaking of affectional bonds.* London, England: Tavistock.

Bowlby, J. (1982). Attachment and loss: Retrospect and prospect. *American Journal of Orthopsychiatry, 52,* 664–678.

Bowlby, J. (1989). *Secure attachment.* New York: Basic Books.

Bowlby, J. (2000). *Attachment.* New York: Basic Books.

Bowling, A. C., & Mackenzie, B. D. (1996). The relationship between speed of information processing and cognitive ability. *Personality & Individual Differences, 20*(6), 775–800.

Boyce, N. (2001, February 19). Aids is far from over. *U.S. News & World Report,* p. 56.

Boyd, N. (2000). *The beast within: Why men are violent.* London: Greystone Books, Ltd.

Brady, K. T., Myrick, H., & McElroy, S. (1998). The relationship between substance use disorders, impulse control disorders, and pathological aggression. *American Journal on Addictions, 7*(3), 221–230.

Bragdon, A. D., & Gamon, D. (1999). *Building left-brain power: Left-brain condi-tioning exercises and tips to strengthen language, math, and uniquely human skills.* Thousand Oaks, CA: Brainwaves Books.

Brandon, T. H., Collins, B. N., Juliano, L. M., & Lazev, A. B. (2000). Preventing relapse among former smokers: A comparison of minimal interventions through telephone and mail. *Journal of Consulting and Clinical Psychology, 68*(1), 103–113.

Brannigan, A. (1997). Self control, social control and evolutionary psychology: Towards an integrated perspective on crime. *Canadian Journal of Criminology, 39,* 403–431.

Brannigan, G. C., Allgeier, E. R., & Allgeier, A. R. (1998). *The sex scientists.* New York: Longman.

Bransford, J. D. (1979). *Human cognition.* Belmont, CA: Wadsworth.

Brawman-Mintzer, O., & Lydiard, R. B. (1996). Generalized anxiety disorder: Issues in epidemiology. *Journal of Clinical Psychiatry, 57,* 3–8.

Brawman-Mintzer, O., & Lydiard, R. B. (1997). Biological basis of generalized anxiety disorder. *Journal of Clinical Psychiatry, 58,* 16–25.

Bredeson, C. (2000). *John Glenn returns to orbit: Life on the space shuttle.* New York: Enslow Publishers.

Breedlove, S. M. (1997). Sex on the brain. *Nature, 389,* 801–804.

Breger, L. (2000). *Freud: Darkness in the midst of vision.* New York: Wiley.

Breland, K., & Breland, M. (1961). The misbehavior of organisms. *American Psychologist, 16,* 681–684.

Breslau, N., & Klein, D. F. (1999). Smoking and panic attacks: An epidemiologic investigation. *Archives of General Psychiatry, 56,* 1141–1147.

Brewer, J. B., Zhao, Z., Desmond, J. E., Glover, G. H., & Gabrieli, J. D. (1998). Making memories: Brain activity that predicts how well visual experience will be remembered. *Science, 281,* 1185–1187.

Brewer, M. B. (1996). When contact is not enough: Social identity and intergroup cooperation. *International Journal of Intercultural Relations, 20*(3–4), 291–303.

Brewer, M. B., & Brown, R. J. (1998). Intergroup relations. In D. T. Gilbert, S. T. Fiske, and G. Lindzey (Eds.), *The handbook of social psychology, Vol. 2* (4th ed.) (pp. 554–594). Boston, MA: McGraw-Hill.

Brewer, W. F., & Pani, J. R. (1996). Reports of mental imagery in retrieval from long-term memory. *Consciousness &*

Cognition: An International Journal, 5, 265–287.

Brewin, C. R., Andrews, B., Rose, S., & Kirk, M. (1999). Acute stress disorder and posttraumatic stress disorder in victims of violent crime. *American Journal of Psychiatry, 156,* 360–366.

Brewster, K. L., Billy, J. O. G., & Grady, W. R. (1993). Social context and adolescent behavior: The impact of community on the transition to sexual activity. *Social Forces, 71,* 713–740.

Briggs, F., & Hawkins, R. M. F. (1999). The importance of parent participation in child protection curricula. In L. E. Berk, *Landscapes of development* (pp. 323–338). Belmont, CA: Wadsworth.

Brislin, R. B. (2000). *Understanding culture's influence on behavior.* Ft. Worth, TX: Harcourt.

Brislin, R. W. (1993). *Understanding culture's influence on behavior.* Orlando, FL: Harcourt Brace Jovanovich.

Brislin, R. W. (1997). *Understanding culture's influence on behavior.* San Diego: Harcourt Brace.

Brock, T. C., Green, M. C., & Reich, D. A. (1998). New evidence of flaws in the Consumer Reports study of psychotherapy. *American Psychologist, 53,* 62–63.

Brody, N. (1992). *Intelligence* (2nd ed.). San Diego, CA: Academic Press.

Brook, J. S., Richter, L., & Whiteman, M. (2000). Effects of parent personality, upbringing, and marijuana use on the parent–child attachment relationship. *Journal of the American Academy of Child & Adolescent Psychiatry, 39*(2), 240–248.

Brooks, C., Taylor, R. D., Hardy, C., & Lass, T. (2000). Proneness to eating disorders: Weightlifters compared to exercisers. *Perceptual & Motor Skills, 90*(3, Pt1), 906.

Brown, D., Scheflin, A. W., & Hammond, D. C. (1997). *Memory, trauma treatment and the law.* New York: Norton.

Brown, E, Deffenbacher, K., & Sturgill, K. (1977). Memory for faces and the circumstances of encounter. *Journal of Applied Psychology, 62,* 311–318.

Brown, J. D. (1991). Accuracy and bias in self-knowledge. In C. R. Snyder & D. F. Forsyth (Eds.), *Handbook of social and clinical psychology: The health perspective.* New York: Pergamon Press.

Brown, J. D., & Rogers, R. J. (1991). Self-serving attributions: The role of physiological arousal. *Personality and Social Psychology Bulletin, 17,* 501–506.

Brown, L. S., & Burman, E. (1997). Editor's introduction: The delayed memory debate: Why feminist voices matters. *Feminism and Psychology, 7,* 7–16.

Brown, R. P., & Josephs, R. A. (1999). A burden of proof: Stereotype relevance and gender differences in math performance. *Journal of Personality and Social Psychology, 76*(2), 246–257.

Brown, R., & Kulik, J. (1977). Flashbulb memories. *Cognition, 5,* 73–99.

Brown, R., & McNeill, D. (1966). The "tip of the tongue" phenomenon. *Journal of Verbal Learning and Verbal Behavior, 5,* 325–337.

Brownell, K. D., & Rodin, J. (1994b). The dieting maelstrom: Is it possible and advisable to lose weight? *American Psychologist, 49,* 781–791.

Bruggeman, E. L., & Hart, K. J. (1996). Cheating, lying, and moral reasoning by religious and secular high school students. *Journal of Educational Research, 89,* 340–344.

Brundin, P., Pogarell, O., Hagell, P., Piccini, P., Widner, H., Schrag, A., Kupsch, A., Crabb, L., Odin, P., Gustavii, B., Bjoerklund, A., Brooks, D. J., Marsden, C. D., Oertel, W. H., Quinn, N. P., Rehncrona, S., & Lindvall, O. (2000). Bilateral caudate and putamen grafts of embryonic mesencephalic tissue treated with lazaroids in Parkinson's disease. *Brain, 123*(7), 1380–1390.

Bryant, R. A., & Harvey, A. G. (1998). Relationship between acute stress disorder and posttraumatic stress disorder following mild traumatic brain injury. *American Journal of Psychiatry, 155,* 625–629.

Buchanan, R. W., Vlader, K., Barta, P. E., & Pearlson, G. D. (1998). Structural evaluation of the prefrontal cortex in schizoprenia. *American Journal of Psychiatry, 155,* 1049–1055.

Buchsbaum, M. S., & Hazlett, E. A. (1998). Positron emission tomography studies of abnormal glucose metabolism in schizophrenia. *Schizophrenia Bulletin, 24,* 343–364.

Buck, R. (1984). *The communication of emotion.* New York: Guilford Press.

Buckley, K. W. (1982). The selling of a psychologist: John Broadus Watson and the application of behavioral techniques to advertising. *Journal of the History of the Behavioral Sciences, 18,* 207–221.

Buckley, K. W. (1989). *Mechanical man: John Broadhus Watson and the beginnings of behaviorism.* New York: Guilford Press.

Bugental, B. B., & Goodnow, J. J. (1998). Socialization process. In W. Damon & N. Eisenberg (Eds.), *Handbook of child psychology* (5th ed.). New York: John Wiley & Sons.

Bugental, D. B., & Johnston, C. (2000). Parental and child cognitions in the context of the family. *Annual Review of Psychology, 51,* 315–344.

Buka, S. L., Goldstein, J. M., Seidman, L. J., Zornberg, G., Donatelli, J. A., Denny, L. R., & Tsuang, M. T. (1999). Prenatal complications, genetic vulnerability, and schizophrenia: The New England longitudinal studies of schizophrenia. *Psychiatric Annals, 29,* 151–156.

Bullough, B., & Bullough, V. (1997). Are transvestites necessarily heterosexual? *Archives of Sexual Behavior, 26,* 1–12.

Burg, M. W. (1995). Anger, hostility, and coronary heart disease: A review. *Mind/Body Medicine, 1,* 159–172.

Burgdorf, J., Knutson, B., & Panksepp, J. (2000). Anticipation of rewarding electrical brain stimulation evokes ultrasonic vocalization in rats. *Behavioural Neuroscience, 114*(2), 320–327.

Burgess, C., O'Donohoe, A., & Gill, M. (2000). Agony and ecstasy: A review of MDMA effects and toxicity. *European Psychiatry, 15*(5), 287–294.

Burke, R. J., & Greenglass, E. R. (2000). Hospital restructuring and nursing staff well-being: The role of coping. *International Journal of Stress Management, 7,* 49–59.

Burns, D. M. (2000). Cigarette smoking among the elderly: Disease consequences and the benefits of cessation. *American Journal of Health Promotion, 14*(6), 357–361.

Burns, N. R., Nettelbeck, T., & Cooper, C. J. (2000). Event-related potential correlates of some human cognitive ability constructs. *Personality & Individual Differences, 29*(1), 157–168.

Bursik, K. (1998). Moving beyond gender differences: Gender role comparisons of manifest dream content. *Sex Roles, 38,* 203–214.

Bushman, B. J., Baumeister, R. F., & Stack, A. D. (1999). Catharsis, aggression, and persuasive influence: Self-fulfilling or self-defeating prophecies? *Journal of Personality and Social Psychology, 76,* 367–376.

Buss, D. H. (1999). *Evolutionary Psychology: The new science of the mind.* Boston: Allyn & Bacon.

Buss, D. M. (1989). Sex differences in human mate preferences: Evolutionary hypotheses tested in 37 cultures. *Behavioral and Brain Sciences, 12,* 1–49.

Buss, D. M. (1991). Evolutionary personality psychology. *Annual Review of Psychology, 42,* 459–491.

Buss, D. M. (1994). The strategies of human mating. *American Scientist, 82,* 238–249.

Buss, D. M. (2000). *The dangerous passion: Why jealousy is as necessary as love and sex.* New York: Free Press.

Buss, D. M. and 40 colleagues. (1990). International preferences in selecting mates: A study of 37 cultures. *Journal of Cross-Cultural Psychology, 21,* 5–47.

Buss, D. M., Shackelford, T. K., Choe, J., Buunk, B. P., Dijkstra, P. (2000). Distress about mating rivals. *Personal Relationships, 7*(3), 235–243.

Butcher, J. N. (2000). Revising psychological tests: Lessons learned from the revision of the MMPI. *Psychological Assessment, 12*(3), 263–271.

Butcher, J. N., & Rouse, S. V. (1996). Personality: Individual differences and clinical assessment. *Annual Review of Psychology, 47,* 87–111.

Butler, K. Joel, J. C., & Jeffries, M. (2000). *Clinical handbook of psychotropic drugs.* New York: Wiley.

Butler, R. A. (1954, February). Curiosity in monkeys. *Scientific American, 190,* 70–75.

Butterworth, B. (1999). A head for figures. *Science, 284,* 928–929.

Butzlaff, R. L., & Hooley, J. M. (1998). Expressed emotion and psychiatric relapse. *Archives of General Psychiatry, 55,* 547–552.

Byrne, R. S., & Fone, B. (2000). *Homophobia: A history.* New York: Metropolitan Books.

Cacioppo, J. T., & Gardner, W. L. (1999). Emotion. *Annual Review of Psychology, 50,* 191–214.

Cadoret, R. J., Leve, L. D., & Devor, E. (1997). Genetics of aggressive and violent behavior. *Psychiatric Clinics of North America, 20,* 301–322.

Cagnacci, A., Kraeuchi, K., Wirz-Justice, A., & Volpe, A. (1997). Homeostatic versus circadian effects of melatonin on core body temperature in humans. *Journal of Biological Rhythms, 12,* 509–617.

Cahill, L, & McGaugh, J. L. (1998). Mechanisms of emotional arousal and lasting declarative memory. *Trends in Neuroscience, 21,* 294–299.

Cahill, L., Vazdarjanova, A., & Setlow, B. (2000). The basolateral amygdala complex is involved with, but is not necessary for, rapid acquisition of Pavlovian "fear conditioning." *European Journal of Neuroscience, 12*(8), 3044–3050.

Cairns, D., & Pasino, J. A. (1977). Comparison of verbal reinforcement and feedback in the operant treatment of disability due to chronic back pain. *Behavior Therapy, 8*(4), 621–630.

Campbell, W. K., & Sedikides, C. (1999). Self-threat magnifies the self-serving bias: A meta-analytic integration. *Review of General Psychology, 3,* 23–43.

Campfield, L. A., Smith, F. J., Rosenbaum, M., & Hirsch, J. (1996). Human eating: Evidence for a physiological basis using a modified paradigm. *Neuroscience and Biobehavioral Reviews, 20,* 133–137.

Cannon, T. D., Kaprio, J., Lonnqvist, J., Huttunen, M., & Koskenvuo, M. (1998). The genetic epidemiology of schizophrenia in a Finnish twin cohort. *Archives of General Psychiatry, 55,* 67–74.

Cannon, T. D., Rosso, I. M., Hollister, J., Megginson, B., Carrie, E., Sanchez, L. E., & Hadley, T. (2000). A prospective cohort study of genetic and perinatal influences in the etiology of schizophrenia. *Schizophrenia Bulletin, 26,* 351–366.

Cannon, W. B. (1927). The James-Lange theory of emotions: A critical examination and an alternative theory. *American Journal of Psychology, 39,* 106–124.

Cannon, W. B., & Washburn, A. (1912). An explanation of hunger. *American Journal of Physiology, 29,* 441–454.

Cannon, W. B., Lewis, J. T., & Britton, S. W. (1927). The dispensability of the sympathetic division of the autonomic nervous system. *Boston Medical Surgery Journal, 197,* 514.

Cantor, J., & Engle, R. (1993). Working-memory capacity as long-term memory activation: An individual differences approach. *Journal of Experimental Psychology: Learning, memory, and Cognition, 19*(5), 1101–1114.

Carbone, J. (2000). *From partners to parents: 2nd revolution in family law.* New York: Columbia University Press.

Carboni, E., Borone, L., Giua, C. & Di Chiara, G. (2000). Dissociation of physical abstinence signs from changes in extra-cellular dopamine in the nucleus accumbens and in the prefrontal cortex of nicotine dependent rats. *Drug and Alcohol Dependence, 58*(1–2), 93–102.

Carducci, B. J. (1998). *The psychology of personality: Viewpoints, research, and applications.* Pacific Grove, CA: Brooks/Cole.

Carducci, B. J. (2000). *Shyness: A bold new approach.* New York: Harperperennial.

Carlson, N. R. (1998). *Physiology of behavior* (6th ed.). Boston: Allyn and Bacon.

Caron, S. L. (1998). *Cross-cultural perspectives on human sexuality.* Boston: Allyn and Bacon.

Carr, A. (2000). *Family therapy: Concepts, process, and practice.* New York: Wiley.

Carrere, S., Buehlman, K. T., Gottman, J. M., Coan, J. A., & Ruckstuhl, L. (2000). Predicting marital stability and divorce in newlywed couples. *Journal of Family Psychology, 14*(1), 42–58.

Carstensen, L. L. (1995). Evidence for a life-span theory of socioemotional selectivity. *Current Directions in Psychological Science, 4*(5), 151–156.

Carton, J. S. (1996). The differential effects of tangible rewards and praise on intrinsic motivation: A comparison of cognitive evaluation theory and operant theory. *Behavior Analyst, 19,* 237–255.

Cartwright, J. (2000). *Evolution and human behavior.* Harvard, MA: MIT Press.

Caspi, A. (2000). The child is father of the man: Personality continuities from childhood to adulthood. *Journal of Personality and Social Psychology, 78*(1), 158–172.

Casswell, S. & Zhang, J. F. (1998). Impact of liking for advertising and brand allegiance on drinking and alcohol-related aggression: A longitudinal study. *Addiction, 93*(8), 1209–1217.

Casti, J. L. (2000). *Paradigms regained: A further exploration of the mysteries of modern science.* New York: Morrow.

Castillo, R. J. (1997). *Culture and mental illness: A client-centered approach.* Pacific Grove, CA: Brooks/Cole.

Castle, D. J. (2000). Sex differences in brain development, organization and degeneration: Are they relevant to sex differences in schizophrenia? In D.J. Castle & J. McGrath, et al. (Eds.), *Women and schizophrenia* (pp. 5–18). New York: Cambridge University Press.

Cattell, R. B. (1950). *Personality: A systematic, theoretical, and factual study.* New York: McGraw-Hill.

Cattell, R. B. (1963). Theory of fluid and crystallized intelligence: A critical experiment. *Journal of Educational Psychology, 54*, 1–22.

Cattell, R. B. (1965). *The scientific analysis of personality.* Baltimore: Penguin.

Cattell, R. B. (1971). *Abilities: Their structure, growth, and action.* Boston, MA: Houghton Mifflin.

Cattell, R. B. (1990). Advances in Cattellian personality theory. In L. A. Pervin (Ed.), *Handbook of personality: Theory and research.* New York: Guilford Press.

Ceci, S. J., & Bjork, R. A. (2000). Psychological science in the public interest: The case for juried analyses. *Psychological Science, 11*(3), 177–178.

Ceci, S. J., Rosenblum, T., deBruyn, & Lee, D. Y. (1997). A bio-ecological model of intellectual development: Moving beyond h2. In R. J. Sternberg & E. L. Grigorenko (Eds.), *Intelligence, heredity, & environment.* New York: Cambridge University Press.

Centers for Disease Control. (1999). Trends in the HIV & AIDS Epidemic. Available: http://www.cdc.gov/hiv/stats/trends98.pdf

Centers for Disease Control. (2000). Tracking the Hidden Epidemics: Trends in STDs in the United States, 2000. Available: http://www.cdc.gov/nchstp/dstd/Stats_Trends/Trends2000.pdf

Centers for Disease Control. (2001). Heart disease still main cause of death in US. *Morbidity and Mortality Weekly Report, 50*, 90–93.

Centers for Disease Control. (2001). *Women and Smoking: A Report of the Surgeon General – 2001.* Available: http://www.cdc.gov/tobacco/sgr/sgr_forwomen/ataglance.htm#Health_Consequences

Cervone, D., & Shoda, Y. (1999). Beyond traits in the study of personality coherence. *Current Directions in Psychological Science, 8*(1), 27–32.

Cesaro, P, & Ollat, H. (1997). Pain and its treatments. *European Neurology, 38*, 209–215.

Chaban, M. (2000). *The life work of Dr. Elisabeth Kubler-Ross and its impact on the death awareness movement.* Baltimore: Edwin Mellen Press.

Challem, J., Berkson, B., Smith, M. D., & Berkson, B. (2000). *Syndrome X: The complete program to prevent and reverse insulin resistance.* New York: Wiley.

Charland, W. A. (1992, January). Nightshift narcosis. *The Rotarian, 160*, 16–19.

Chartrand, T., Pinckert, S., & Burger, J. M. (1999). When manipulation backfires: The effects of time delay and requester on the foot-in-the-door technique. *Journal of Applied Social Psychology, 29*, 211–221.

Chase, W. G., & Simon, H. A. (1973). The mind's eye in chess. In W. Chase (Ed.), *Visual information processing.* New York: Academic Press.

Chaves, J. F. (2000). Hypnosis in the management of anxiety associated with medical conditions and their treatment. In D. I. Mostofsky & D. H. Barlow (Eds.), *The management of stress and anxiety in medical disorders* (pp. 119–142). Needham Heights, MA: Allyn & Bacon.

Chi, I., & Chou, K. (1999). Financial strain and depressive symptoms among Hong Kong Chinese elderly: A longitudinal study. *Journal of Gerontological Social Work, 32*, 41–60.

Chi, M. T. H., & Glaser, R. (1985). Problem solving ability. In R. J. Sternberg (Ed.), *Human abilities: An information processing approach* (pp. 227–251). New York: Freeman.

Chin, G. (2000). Memory maps in the brain. *Science, 287*, 13.

Choi, I., & Nisbett, R. E. (2000). Cultural psychology of surprise: Holistic theories and recognition of contradiction. *Journal of Personality & Social Psychology, 79*(6), 890–905.

Chomsky, N. (1957). Syntactical structures. The Hague: Mouton.

Chomsky, N. (1965). *Aspects of the theory of syntax.* Cambridge, MA: MIT Press.

Chomsky, N. (1968). *Language and mind.* New York: Harcourt, Brace, World.

Chomsky, N. (1980). *Rules and representations.* New York: Columbia University Press.

Chorpita, B. F., & Barlow, D. H. (1998). The development of anxiety: The role of control in the early environment. *Psychological Bulletin, 124*, 3–21.

Christensen, D. (2000). Is snoring a dizzease? Nighttime snoring may serve as a wake-up call for future illness. *Science News, 157*, 172–173.

Christensen, D. (2001). Making sense of centenarians. *Science News, 159*, 156–157.

Chromiak, W., Barber, T. A., & Kyler, K. J. (2000). Selective associations in day-old chicks: When do CS traces become available for sickness-conditioned learning? *Behavioral Neuroscience, 114*(1), 117–124.

Chuang, D. (1998). Cited in J. Travis, Stimulating clue hints how lithium works. *Science News, 153*, 165.

Church, R. M., & Kirkpatrick, K. (2001). Theories of conditioning and timing. In R. R. Mowere, S. B. Klein (Eds.), *Handbook of contemporary learning theories.* Mahwah, NJ: Lawrence Erlbaum.

Cialdini, R. (1993). *Influence: Science and practice* (3rd ed.). New York: HarperCollins.

Cialdini, R. B. (2001). The science of persuasion. *Scientific American, 284*(2), 76–81.

Cicchetti, D., & Toth, S. L. (1998). Perspectives on research and practice in developmental psychopathology. In W. Damon, I. E. Siegel, & K. A. Renninger (Eds.), *Handbook of child psychology* (5th ed.) (pp. 479–584). New York: Wiley.

Clark, K. B., & Clark, M. P. (1939). The development of consciousness of self and the emergence of racial identification in Negro preschool children. *Journal of Social Psychology, 10*, 591–599.

Clarke-Stewart, K. A., Fitzpatrick, M. J., Allhusen, V. D., & Goldberg, W. A. (2000). Measuring difficult temperament the easy way. *Journal of Developmental and Behavioral Pediatrics, 21*(3), 207–220.

Clarke-Stewart, K. A., Vandell, D. L., McCartney, K., Owen, M. T., & Booth, C. (2000). Effects of parental separation and divorce on very young children. *Journal of Family Psychology, 14*(2), 304–326.

Classen, C., Koopman, C., Hales, R., & Spiegel, D. (1998). Acute stress disorder as a predictor of posttraumatic stress symptoms. *American Journal of Psychiatry, 155*, 620–624.

Cloud, J. (2001, February 26). New sparks over electroshock. Time, 60–62.

Cockerill, I. M., & Riddington, M. E. (1996). Exercise dependence and associated disorders: A review. *Counseling Psychology Quarterly, 9*, 119–129.

Cohen, A. (1997, September 8). Battle of the binge. *Time*, pp. 54–56.

Cohen, B., Novick, D., & Rubinstein, M. (1996). Modulation of insulin activities by leptin. *Science, 274*, 1185–1188.

Cohen, D. B. (1999). *Stranger in the nest: Do parents really shape their child's personality, intelligence, or character?* New York: Wiley.

Cohen, S., & Herbert, T. B. (1996). Health psychology: Psychological factors and physical disease from the prespective of human psychoneuroimmunology. *Annual Review of Psychology, 47,* 113–142.

Cohen, S., & Williamson, G. M. (1991). Stress and infectious disease in humans. *Psychological Bulletin, 109,* 5–24.

Cohen, S., Doyle, W. J., & Skoner, D. P. (1999). Psychological stress, cytokine production, and severity of upper respiratory illness. *Psychosomatic Medicine, 61,* 175–180.

Cohen, S., Frank, E., Doyle, W. J., et al. (1998). Types of stressors that increase susceptibility to the common cold in healthy adults. *Health Psychology, 17,* 214–223.

Cohen, S., Frank, E., Doyle, W. J., Skoner, D. P., Rabin, B. S., & Gawltney, J. M., Jr. (1998). Types of stressors that increase susceptibility to the common cold in healthy adults. *Health Psychology, 17,* 214–223.

Colapinto, J. (2000). *As nature made him: The boy that was raised as a girl.* New York: HarperCollins.

Cole, D. L. (1982). Psychology as a liberating art. *Teaching of Psychology, 9,* 23–26.

Cole, M., Gray, J., Glick, J. A., & Sharp, D. W. (1971). *The cultural context of learning and thinking.* New York: Basic Books.

Cole, M. D. (2000). *John Glenn: Astronaut and senator.* New York: Enslow Publishers.

Coley, R. L., & Chase-Lansdale, P. L. (1998). Adolescent pregnancy and parenthood: Recent evidence and future directions. *American Psychologist, 53*(2), 152–166.

Collette, F., Van der Linden, M., & Salmon, E. (1999). Executive dysfunction in Alzheimer's disease. *Cortex, 35,* 57–72.

Collins, W. A., Maccoby, E. E., Steinberg, L., Hetherington, E. M., & Bornstein, M. H. (2000). Contemporary research on parenting: The case for nature and nurture. *American Psychologist, 55*(2), 218–232.

Conley, R. R., Love, R. C., Kelly, D. L., & Bartko, J. J. (1999). Rehospitalization rates of patients recently discharged on a regimen of risperidone or clozapine. *American Journal of Psychiatry, 156,* 863–868.

Connolly, S. (2000). *LSD (just the facts).* Baltimore: Heinemann Library.

Consumer Reports (1995, November). Mental health: Does therapy help? *Consumer Reports,* pp. 734–739.

Contrada, R. J., Ashmore, R. D., Gary, M. L., Coups, E., Egeth, J. D., Sewell, A., Ewell, K., Goyal, T. M., & Chasse, V. (2000). Ethnicity-related sources of stress and their effects on well-being. *Current*

Directions in Psychological Science, 9(4), 136–139.

Converging PET findings in depression and normal sadness. *American Journal of Psychiatry, 156,* 675–682.

Convay, M. A., & Pleydell-Pearce, C. W. (2000). The construction of autobiographical memories in the self-memory system. *Psychological Review, 107,* 261–288.

Conyne, R. K. (1999). *Failures in group work.* Thousand Oaks, CA: Sage.

Cook M., & Mineka, S. (1989). Observational conditioning of fear to fear-relevant versus fear-irrelevant stimuli in rhesus monkeys. *Journal of Abnormal Psychology, 98,* 448–459.

Cook, A. S., & Dworkin, D. S. (1992). *Helping the bereaved: Therapeutic interventions for children, adolescents, and adults.* New York: Basic Books.

Cook, E. W., Hodes, R. L., & Lang, P. J. (1986). Preparedness and phobia: Effects of stimulus content on human visceral conditioning. *Journal of Abnormal Psychology, 95,* 195–207.

Cook, P. F. (2000). Effects of counselors' etiology attributions on college students' procrastination. *Journal of Counseling Psychology, 47*(3), 352–361.

Coolidge, F., & Segal, D. (1998). Evolution of personality disorder diagnosis in the Diagnostic and Statistical Manual of Mental Disorders. *Clinical Psychology Review, 18,* 585–599.

Cooper, E. E. (2000). Spatial-temporal intelligence: Original thinking processes of gifted inventors. *Journal for the Education of the Gifted, 24*(2), 170–193.

Cooper, M. L., Shaver, P. R., & Collins, N. L. (1998). Attachment styles, emotion regulation, and adjustment in adolescence. *Journal of Personality and Social Psychology, 74*(5), 1380–1397.

Corballis, M. C. (1998). Sperry and the Age of Aquarius: Science, values and the split brain. *Neuropsychologia, 36,* 1083–1087.

Coren, S. (1996). *Sleep thieves: An eye-opening exploration into the science and mysteries of sleep.* New York: Freeman.

Corey, G. (2001a). *Case approach to counseling and psychotherapy.* Belmont, CA: Wadsworth.

Corey, G. (2001b). *The art of integrative counseling.* Belmont, CA: Wadsworth.

Costa, L., Bauer, L., Kuperman, S., Porjesz, B., O'Connor, S., Hesselbrock, V., Rohrbaugh, J., & Begleiter, H. (2000). Frontal P300 decrements: Alcohol

dependence, and antisocial personality disorder. *Biological Psychiatry, 47*(12), 1064–1071.

Cote, S. (1999). Affect and performance in organizational settings. *Current Directions in Psychological Science, 8*(2), 65–68.

Courage, M. L., & Adams, R. J. (1990). Visual acuity assessment from birth to three years using the acuity card procedures: Cross-sectional and longitudinal samples. *Optometry and Vision Science, 67,* 713–718.

Courtenay, W. H. (2000). Engendering health: A social constructionist examination of men's health beliefs and behaviors. *Psychology of Men and Masculinity, 1*(1), 4–15.

Courtney, S. M., Ungerleider, L. G., Keil, K., & Hazby, J. V. (1998). Object and spatial visual working memory activate separate neural systems in human cortex. *Cerebral Cortex, 6,* 39–49.

Couzin, J. (1999, September 13). A good trend spoiled. *U. S. News & World Report,* p. 55.

Covington, M. V. (1999). Caring about learning: The nature and nurturing of subject matter appreciation. *Educational Researcher, 34,* 127–136.

Covington, M. V. (2000). Intrinsic versus extrinsic motivation in schools: A reconciliation. *Current Directions in Psychological Science, 9*(1), 22–25.

Cowley, G. (2000, January 31). Alzheimer's unlocking the mystery. *Newsweek,* 46–51.

Craig, A. D., & Bushnell, M. C. (1994). The thermal grill illusion: Unmasking the burn of cold pain. *Science, 265,* 252–255.

Craik, F. I. M., & Lockhart, R. S. (1972). Levels of processing: A framework for memory research. *Journal of Verbal Learning and Verbal Behavior, 11,* 671–684.

Craik, F. I. M., Moroz, T. M., Moscovitch, M., Stuss, D. T., Winocur, G., Tulving, E., & Kapur, S. (1999). In search of the self: A positron emission tomography study. *Psychological Science, 10,* 26–34.

Crair, M. C., Gillespie, D. C., & Stryker, M. P. (1998). The role of visual experience in the development of columns in cat visual cortex. *Science, 279,* 566–570.

Crandall, C. S., & Martinez, R. (1996). Culture, ideology, and antifat attitudes. *Personality and Social Psychology Bulletin, 22,* 1165–1176.

Craske, B. (1977). Perception of impossible limb positions induced by tendon vibration. *Science, 196*(4285), 71–73.

Craske, M. (2000). *Mastery of your anxiety and panic: Therapist guide* (3rd ed.). New York: Academic Press.

Crews, F. (1997). The verdict on Freud. *Psychological Science, 7*(2), 63–68.

Crick, N. R. (1996). The role of overt aggression, relational aggression, and prosocial behavior in the prediction of children's future social adjustment. *Child Development, 67,* 2317–2327.

Cristofalo, V. J. (1996). Ten years later: What have we learned about human aging from studies of cell cultures? *Gerontologist, 36,* 737–741.

Croizet, J., & Claire, T. (1998). Extending the concept of stereotype threat to social class: The intellectual underperformance of students from low socioeconomic backgrounds. *Personality and Social Psychology Bulletin, 24,* 588–594.

Cronbach, L. (1990). *Essentials of psychological testing.* New York: Harper & Row.

Crooks, R., & Baur, K. (1999). *Our sexuality* (7th ed.). Pacific Grove: Brooks/Cole.

Crosson, B. (1999). Subcortical mechanisms in language: Lexical-semantic mechanisms and the Thalamus. *Brain & Cognition, 40,* 414–438.

Crosson, B., Sadek, J. R., Maron, L., Goekcay, D., Mohr, C. M., Auerbach, E. J., Freeman, A. J., Leonard, C. M., & Briggs, R. W. (2001). Relative shift in activity from medial to lateral frontal cortex during internally versus externally guided word generation. *Journal of Cognitive Neuroscience, 13*(2), 272–283.

Crowder, R. G. (1976). *Principles of learning and memory.* Hillsdale, NJ: Erlbaum.

Culbertson, F. M. (1997). Depression and gender. *American Psychologist, 52,* 25–31.

Cunningham, M. R., Roberts, A. R., Barbee, A. P. Druen, P. B., & Wu, C. (1995). "Their ideas of beauty are on the whole, the same as ours": Consistency and variability in the cross-cultural perception of female physical attractiveness. *Journal of Personality and Social Psychology, 68,* 261–279.

Curtiss, S. (1977). *Genie: A psycholinguistic study of a modern-day "wild child."* New York: Academic Press.

Cutler, W. B., (1999). Human sex-attractant hormones: Discovery, research, development, and application in sex therapy. *Psychiatric Annals, 29,* 54–59.

Cutler, W. B., Friedmann, E., & Mc Coy, N. L. (1998). Pheromonal influences on sociosexual behavior in men. *Archives of Sexual Behavior, 27,* 1–13.

D'Imperio, R. L., Dubow, E. F., & Ippolito, M. F. (2000). Resilent and stress-affected adolescents in an urban setting. *Journal of Clinical and Child Psychology, 29,* 129–142.

Da Costa, D. A. (1997). The role of psychosurgery in the treatment of selected cases of refractory schizophrenia: A reappraisal. *Schizophrenia Research, 28,* 223–230.

Dabbs, J. M., & Dabbs, M. G. (2000). *Heroes, rogues, and lovers: Testosterone and behavior.* New York: McGraw-Hill.

Dadds, M. R., Bovbjerg, D. H., Redd, W. H., & Cutmore, T. R. H. (1997). Imagery in human classical conditioning. *Psychological Bulletin, 122,* 89–103.

Dager, S. R., et al. (1999). Human brain metabolic response to caffeine and the effects of tolerance. *American Journal of Psychiatry, 156,* 229–237.

Dalenberg, C. J. (2000). *Countertransference and the treatment of trauma.* Washington, DC: American Psychological Association.

Daley, S. E., Burge, D., & Hammen, C. (2000). Borderline personality disorder symptoms as predictors of 4-year romantic relationship dysfunction in young women: Addresing issues of specificity. *Journal of Abnormal Psychology, 109*(3), 451–460.

Daly, M. P. (1999). Diagnosis and management of Alzheimer disease. *Journal of the American Board of Family Practice, 5,* 375–385.

Damasio, A. R. (1994). *Descartes' error.* New York: Putnam's Sons.

Damasio, A. R. (1999). *The feeling of what happens: Body and emotion in the making of consciousness.* New York: Harcourt Brace.

Damasio, H., Grabowski, T., Frank, R., Galaburda, A. M., & Damasio, A. R. (1994). The return of Phineas Gage: Clues about the brain from the skull of a famous patient. *Science, 264,* 1102–1105.

Dana, R. H. (1998). Cultural identity assessment of culturally diverse groups: 1997. *Journal of Personality Assessment, 70,* 1–16.

Dansky, B. S., Brewerton, T. D., & Kilpatrick, D. G. (2000). Comorbidity of bulimia nervosa and alcohol use disorders: Results from the National Women's Study. *International Journal of Eating Disorders, 27*(2), 180–190.

Darwin, C. (1859). *On the origin of species.* London: Murray.

Darwin, C. R. (1872). *The expression of the emotions in man and animals.* London: John Murray.

Davidson, K., MacGregor, M. W., Stuhr, J., Dixon, K., & MacLean, D. (2000). Constructive anger verbal behavior predicts blood pressure in a population-based sample. *Health Psychology, 19,* 55–64.

Davidson, R. (1999, April). Cited in Ruksnis, E. (1999). The emotional brain and the emergence of affective neuroscience. *APS Observer, 13.*

Davidson, R. J. (1992). Emotion and affective style: Hemispheric substrates. *Psychological Science, 3,* 39–43.

Davidson, R. J. (2000). Affective style, psychopathology, and resilience: Brain mechanisms and plasticity. *American Psychologist, 55*(11), 1196–1214.

Davidson, R. J., Putnam, K. M., Larson, C. L. (2000). Dysfunction in the neural circuitry of emotion regulation—a possible prelude to violence. *Science, 289*(5479), 591–594.

Davies, I. (1998). A study of colour grouping in three languages: A test of the linguistic relativity hypothesis. *British Journal of Psychology, 89,* 433–452.

Davies, J. M. (1996). Dissociation, repression and reality testing in the countertransference: the controversey over memory and false memory in the psychoanalytic treatment of adult survivors of childhood sexual abuse. *Psychoanalytic Dialogues, 6,* 189–218.

Davies, P. T., & Cummings, E. M. (1998). Exploring children's emotional security as a mediator of the link between marital relations and child adjustment. *Child Development, 69,* 124–139.

Davila, J., Burge, D., & Hammen, C. (1997). Why does attachment style change? *Journal of Personality and Social Psychology, 73,* 826–838.

Davis, C. G., Nolen-Hoeksema, S., & Larson, J. (1998). Making sense of loss and benefiting from the experience: Two construals of meaning. *Journal of Personality and Social Psychology, 75*(2), 561–574.

Davis, C., Dionne, M., & Shuster, B. (2001). Physical and psychological correlates of appearance orientation. *Personality & Individual Differences, 30*(1), 21–30.

Davis, K. D., Kiss, Z. H., Luo, L. et al. (1998). Phantom sensations generated by thalamic microstimulation. *Nature, 391,* 385–387.

Davis, M. (1999). Oral contraceptive use and hemodynamic, lipid, and fibrinogen Responses to smoking and stress in women. *Health Psychology, 18,* 122–130.

Davison, G. C., & Neale, J. M. (2001). Abnormal psychology (8th ed.). New York: Wiley.

Davison, K. P., Pennebaker, J. W., & Dickerson, S. S. (2000). Who talks? The social psychology of illness support groups. *American Psychologist, 55*(2), 205–217.

Day, N. L., Richardson, G. A., Goldschmidt, L., & Cornelius, M. D. (2000). Effects of prenatal tobacco exposure on preschoolers' behavior. *Journal of Developmental & Behavioral Pediatrics, 21*(3), 180–188.

Day, N. L., Zuo, Y., Richardson, G. A., Goldschmidt, L., Larkby, C. A., & Cornelius, M. D. (1999). Prenatal alcohol use and offspring size at 10 years of age. *Alcoholism: Clinical & Experimental Research, 23*(5), 863–869.

De Brabander, B., Hellemans, J., boon, C., & Gerits, P. (1996). Locus of control, sensation seeking, and stress. *Psychological Reports, 79,* 1307–1312.

de Charms, R., & Moeller, G. H. (1962). Values expressed in American children's readers: 1800–1950. *Journal of Abnormal and Social Psychology, 64*(2), 136–142.

de Roiste, A., & Bushnell, L. W. R. (1996). Tactile stimulation: Short-and long-term benefits for pre-term infants. *British Journal of Developmental Psychology, 14,* 41–53.

De Vries, G. J., & Boyle, P. A. (1998). Double duty for sex differences in the brain. *Behavioural Brain Research, 92,* 205–213.

Deary, I. J., & Stough, C. (1996). Intelligence and inspection time: Achievements, prospects, and problems. *American Psychologist, 51,* 599–608.

Deary, I. J., & Stough, C. (1997). Looking down on human intelligence. *American Psychologist, 52,* 1148–1149.

DeCasper, A. J., & Fifer, W. D. (1980). Of human bonding: Newborns prefer their mother's voices. *Science, 208,* 1174–1176.

DeCasper, A. J., & Spence, M. J. (1986). Prenatal maternal speech influences newborn's perception of speech sounds. *Infant Behavior and Development, 9,* 133–150.

Deci, E. L. (1995). Why we do what we do: The dynamics of personal autonomy. New York: Putnam's Sons.

Deffenbacher, K. A. (1980). Eyewitness accuracy and confidence: Can we infer anything about their relationship? *Law and Human Behavior, 4,* 243–260.

Dehaene, S., Spelke, E., Pinel, P., Stanescu, R., & Tsivkin, S. (1999). Sources of mathematical thinking: Behavioral and brain-imaging evidence. *Science, 284,* 970–974.

Dehue, T. (2000). From deception trials to control reagents: The introduction of the control group about a century ago. *American Psychologist, 55,* 264–268.

Delahanty, D. L., Liegey Dougall, A., Hayward, M., Forlenza, M., Hawk, L. W. & Baum, A. (2000). Gender differences in cardiovascular and natural killer cell reactivity to acute stress following a hassling task. *International Journal of Behavioral Medicine, 7,* 19–27.

Delgado, J. M. R. (1960). Emotional behavior in animals and humans. *Psychiatric Research Report, 12,* 259–271.

Delgado-Gaitan, C. (1994). Socializing young children in Mexican-American families: An intergenerational perspective. In P. M. Greenfield & R. R. Cocking (Eds.), *Cross-cultural roots of minority child development* (pp. 55–86). Hillsdale, NJ: Erlbaum.

Dellu, F., Mayo, W., Piazza, P. V., LeMoal, M., & Simon, H. (1993). Individual differences in behavioral responses to novelty in rats: Possible relationship with the sensation-seeking trait in man. *Personality and Individual Differences, 14,* 411–418.

Delville, Y., Mansour, K. M., & Ferris. C. F. (1996). Testosterone facilitates aggression by modulating vasopressin receptors in the hypothalamus. *Physiology and Behavior, 60,* 25–29.

Dement, W. C. (1992, March). The sleepwatchers. *Stanford,* pp. 55–59.

Dement, W. C., & Vaughan, C. (1999). *The promise of sleep.* New York: Delacorte Press.

Dement, W. C., & Wolpert, E. (1958). The relation of eye movements, bodily motility, and external stimuli to dream content. *Journal of Experimental Psychology, 53,* 543–553.

Demo, D. H. (1992). Parent–child relations: Assessing recent changes. *Journal of Marriage and the Family, 54,* 104–117.

DeMoranville, B.M., Jackson, I., Ader, R., Madden, K. S., Felten, D. L., Bellinger, D. L., & Schiffer, R.B. (2000). Endocrine and immune systems. In B. S. Schiffer, & R. B. Schiffer, et al. (Eds), *Synopsis of neuropsychiatry* (pp. 133–153). Philadelphia: Lippincott Williams & Wilkins Publishers.

den Boer, J. A. (2000). Social anxiety disorder/social phobia: Epidemiology, diagnosis, neurobiology, and treatment. *Comprehensive Psychiatry, 41*(6), 405–415.

Denney, N. W., & Quadagno, D. (1998). *Human sexuality* (4th ed.). St. Louis, MS: Mosby.

Dennis, W., & Dennis, M. G. (1940). Cradles and cradling customs of the Pueblo Indians. *American Anthropologist, 42,* 107–115.

Denoyelle, F., et al. (1997). Prelingual deafness: high prevalence of a 30delG mutation in the connexin 26 gene. *Human Molecular Genetics, 6,* 2173–2177.

Depue, R. A., & Collins, P. F. (1999). Neurobiology of the structure of personality: Dopamine, facilitation of incentive motivation, and extraversion. *Behavioral & Brain Sciences, 22*(3), 491–569.

Der-Karabetian, A., Stephenson, K., & Poggi, T. (1996). Environmental risk perception, activism and world-mindedness among samples of British and U. S. College students. *Perceptual and Motor Skills, 83*(2), 451–462.

Desai, H. D., & Jann, M. W. (2000). Major depression in women: A review of the literature. *Journal of the American Pharmaceutical Association, 40,* 525–537.

DeValois, R. L. (1965). Behavioral and electrophysiological studies of primate vision. In W. D. Neff (Ed.), *Contributions to sensory physiology* (Vol. 1). New York: Academic Press.

Devine, P. G., & Monteith, M. J. (1999). Automaticity and control in stereotyping. In S. Chaiken, Y. Trope, et al. (Eds.), *Dual-process theories in social psychology,* pp. 339–360. New York: Guilford Press.

Diamond, M. (2000). Sex and gender: Same or different? *Feminism & Psychology, 10,* 46–54.

Diamond, M., & Hopson, J. (1998). *Magic trees of the mind: How to nurture your child's intelligence, creativity, and healthy emotions from birth through adolescence.* New York: Dutton.

Diamond, M., & Sigmundson, H. K. (1997). Sex reassignment at birth: Long-term review and clinical implications. *Archives of Pediatrics and Adolescent Medicine, 151,* 298–304.

Diana, E. M., & Webb, J. M. (1997). Using geographic maps in classrooms: The conjoint influence of individual differences and dual coding on learning facts. *Learning & Individual Differences, 9,* 195–214.

DiChiara, G. (1997). Alcohol and dopamine. *Alcohol Health & Research World, 21,* 108–114.

Dickinson, L. M., deGruy, F. V., Dickinson, W. P., & Candib, L. M. (1999). Health related quality of life and symptom profiles of female survivors of sexual abuse. *Archives of Family Medicine, 8,* 35–43.

Diederich, N. J., & Goetz, C. G. (2000). Neuropsychological and behavioral aspects of transplants in Parkinson's disease and Huntington's disease. *Brain & Cognition, 42*(2), 294–306.

Diener, E., & Diener, C. (1996). Most people are happy. *Psychological Science, 7,* 181–185.

Dietz, T. L. (1998). An examination of violence and gender role portrayals in video games. *Sex Roles, 38,* 425–442.

Digman, J. M. (1997). Higher-order factors of the Big Five. *Journal of Personality and Social Psychology, 73,* 1246–1256.

DiLalla, D. L., Carey, G., Gottesman, I. I., & Bouchard, T. J., Jr. (1996). Heritability of MMPI personality indicators of psychopathology in twins reared apart. *Journal of Abnormal Psychology, 105,* 491–499.

Dimberg, U., & Thunberg, M. (1998). Rapid facial reactions to emotion facial expressions. *Scandinavian Journal of Psychology, 39*(1), 39–46.

Dimberg, U., Thunberg, M., & Elmehed, K. (2000). Unconscious facial reactions to emotional facial expressions. *Psychological Science, 11*(1), 86–89.

Dimoff, T. A. (2000). *How to recognize substance abuse.* New York: CSS Publishing.

Dinan, T. G. (2000). Antidepressants and violence: Cause for concern or media hype? *Human Psychopharmacology Clinical & Experimental, 15*(6), iii–iv.

Doby, V., & Caplan, R. D. (1995). Organizational stress as threat to reputation: Effects on anxiety at work and at home. *Academy of Management Journal, 38,* 1105–1123.

Doghramji, K. (2000, December). Sleepless in America: Diagnosing and treating insomnia. [On-line serial]. Available: http://psychiatry. medscape. com/Medscape/psychiatry/ClinicalMgmt/CM. v02/public/index-CM. v02. html

Dollard, J., Doob, L., Miller, N., Mowrer, O. H., & Sears, R. R. (1939). *Frustration and aggression.* New Haven, CT: Yale University Press.

Dols, M., Willems, B., van den Hout, M., & Bittoun, R. (2000). Smokers can learn to influence their urge to smoke. *Addictive Behaviors, 25*(1), 103–108.

Domhoff, G. (1996). *Finding meaning in dreams: A quantitative approach.* New York: Plenum.

Domhoff, G. W. (1999). New directions in the study of dream content using the Hall and Van de Castle coding system. *Dreaming, 9,* 115–137.

Domhoff, G. W. (2001). A new neurocognitive theory of dreams. *Dreaming, 11*(1), 13–33.

Domino, G., & Morales, A. (2000). Reliability and validity of the D-48 with Mexican American college students. *Hispanic Journal of Behavioral Sciences, 22*(3), 382–389.

Donovan, J. J., & Radosevich, D. J. (1999). A meta-analytic review of the distribution of practice effect: Now you see it, now you don't. *Journal of Applied Psychology, 84,* 795–805.

Dorion, A. A., Chantome, M., Hasboun, D., Zouaoui, A., Marsault, C., Capron, C., & Duyme, M. (2000). Hemispheric asymmetry and corpus callosum morphometry: A magnetic resonance imaging study. *Neuroscience Research, 36*(1), 9–13.

Dovidio, J. F., Brigham, J. C., Johnson, B. T., & Gaertner, S. L. (1995). Stereotyping, prejudice, and discrimination: Another look. In N. Macrae, M. Hewstone, & C. Stangor (Eds.), *Foundations of stereotypes and stereotyping.* New York: Guilford.

Dovidio, J. F., Gaertner, S. L., Bachman, B. A. (2001). Racial bias in organizations: The role of group processes in its causes and cures. In M. E. Turner (Ed.),*Groups at work: Theory and research* (pp. 415–444). Mahwah, NJ: Erlbaum.

Doweiko, H. E. (1999). *Concepts of chemical dependency.* Pacific Grove, CA: Brooks/Cole.

Draijer, N., & Langeland, W. (1999). Childhood trauma and perceived parental dysfunction in the etiology of dissociative symptoms in psychiatric inpatients. *American Journal of Psychiatry, 156,* 379–385.

Dresser, N. (1996). *Multicultural manners: New rules of etiquette for a changing society.* New York: Wiley.

Drieschner, K., & Lange, A. (1999). A review of cognitive factors in the etiology of rape: Theories, empirical studies, and implications. *Clinical Psychology Review, 19,* 57–77.

Driscoll, R., Davis, K. E., & Lipetz, M. E. (1972). Parental interference and romantic love: The Romeo and Juliet effect. *Journal of Personality and Social Psychology, 24,* 1–10.

Druckman, D., & Bjork, R. A. (Eds.) (1994). *Learning, remembering, believing: Enhancing human performance.* Washington, DC: National Academy Press.

Druckman, D., & Swets, J. A. (1988). *Enhancing human performance: Issues, theories, and techniques.* Washington, DC: National Academy Press.

Drummond, E. (2000). *The complete guide to psychiatric drugs.* New York: Wiley.

Drummond, T. (1998, July 27). Touch early and often. *Time,* p. 54.

Dryer, D. C., & Horowitz, L. M. (1997). When do opposites attract? Interpersonal complementarity versus similarity. *Journal of Personality and Social Psychology, 72,* 592–603.

Dubovsky, S. L., & Buzan, R. (1999). Mood disorders. In R. E. Hales, S. C. Yudofsky, & J. A. Talbott (Eds.), *American psychiatric press textbook of psychiatry.* Washington, DC: American Psychiatric Press.

Duckworth, K., & Borus, J. F. (1999). Population-based psychiatry in the public sector and managed care. In A. M. Nicholi (Ed.), *The Harvard guide to psychiatry.* Cambridge, MA: Harvard University Press.

Dukes Conrad, S., & Stevens Morrow, R. (2000). Borderline personality organization, dissociation, and willingness to use force in intimate relationships. *Psychology of Men & Masculinity, 1*(1), 37–48.

Duncan, J., & Owen, A. M. (2000). Common regions of the human frontal lobe recruited by diverse cognitive demands. *Trends in Neurosciences, 23*(10), 475–483.

Duncker, K. (1945). On problem-solving. *Psychological Monographs, 58,* 361–362.

Dunlap, J. (1998). Circadian rhythms: An end in the beginning. *Science, 280,* 1548–1549.

Dunn, M. (2000). *Good death guide: Everything you wanted to know but were afraid to ask.* New York: How to Books.

Durham, M. D., & Dane, F. C. (1999). Juror knowledge of eyewitness behavior: Evidence for the necessity of expert testimony. *Journal of Social Behavior & Personality, 14,* 299–308.

Dworkin, A. (1974). *Woman hating.* New York: E. P. Dutton.

Dworkin, B. R., & Miller, N. E. (1986). Failure to replicate visceral learning in the acute curarized rat preparation. *Behavioral Neuroscience, 100,* 299–314.

Eagly, A. H. (1997). Sex differences in social behavior: Comparing social role theory and evolutionary psychology. *American Psycholo-gist, 52,* 1303–1382.

Eagly, A. H., & Wood, W. (1999). The origins of sex differences in human behavior: Evolved dispositions versus social roles. *American Psychologist, 54,* 408–423.

Eccles, J. S., Buchanan, C. M., Flanagan, C., Fuligni, A., Midgley, C., & Yee, D. (1999). Control versus autonomy during early adolescence. In L. E. Berk, *Landscapes of development* (pp. 393–406). Belmont, CA: Wadsworth.

Eckhardt, L., Woodruff, S. I., & Elder, J. P. (1997). Relative effectiveness of continued, lapsed, and delayed smoking prevention intervention in senior high school students. *American Journal of Health Promotion, 11*(6), 418–421.

Edwards, B. (1999). The new drawing on the right side of the brain. Baltimore: J P Tarcher.

Ehlers, A. & Steil, R. (1995). Maintenance of intrusive memories in posttraumatic stress disorder: A cognitive approach. *Behavioral & Cognitive Psychotherapy, 23,* 217–249.

Eibl-Eibesfeldt, I. (1980b). Strategies of social interaction. In R. Plutchik & H. Kelerman (Eds.), Emotion: Theory, research, and experience. New York: Academic Press.

Eichenbaum, H. (1999a). Conscious awareness, memory and the hippocampus. *Nature Neuroscience, 2,* 775–776.

Eichenbaum, H. (1999b). The hippocampus and the mechanisms of declarative memory. *Behavioral Brain Research, 103,* 123–133.

Eilenberg, M. E., & Wyman, S. E. (1998). Scapegoating in an early adolescent girls group. *Journal of Child and Adolescent Group Therapy, 8*(1), 3–11.

Eisenberg, N. (2000). Emotion, regulation, and moral development. *Annual Review of Psychology, 51,* 665–697.

Eisenberger, R., & Armeli, S. (1997). Can salient reward increase creative performance without reducing intrinsic creative interest? *Journal of Personality and Social Psychology, 72,* 652–663.

Eisenberger, R., & Cameron, J. (1996). De-trimental effects of reward: Reality or myth? *American Psychologist, 51,* 1153–1166.

Ekelund, J., Lichtermann, D., Jarvelin, M., & Peltonen, L. (1999). Association between novelty seeking and the type 4 dopamine receptor gene in a large Finnish cohort sample. *American Journal of Psychiatry, 156,* 1453–1455.

Ekman, P. (1993). Facial expression and emotion. *American Psychologist, 48,* 384–392.

Ekman, P., & Friesen, W. V. (1971). Constants across cultures in the face and emotion. *Journal of Personality and Social Psychology, 17,* 124–129.

Ekman, P., & Keltner, D. (1997). Universal facial expressions of emotion: An old controversy and new findings. In U. C. Segerstrale & P. Molnar (Eds.), *Nonverbal communication: Where nature meets culture.* Mahwah, NJ: Erlbaum.

Elder, G. (1998). The life course as developmental theory. *Current Directions in Psychological Science, 69,* 1–12.

Elkind, D. (1967). Egocentrism in adolescence. *Child Development, 38,* 1025–1034.

Elkind, D. (1981). *The hurried child.* Reading, MA: Addison-Wesley.

Elkind, D. (1998). *Reinventing childhood: Raising and educating children in a changing world.* New York: Modern Learning.

Elkind, D. (1999). Authority of the brain. *Journal of Developmental & Behavioral Pediatrics, 20*(6), 432–433.

Elkind, D. (2000). A quixotic approach to issues in early childhood education. *Human Development, 43*(4–5), 279–283.

Elkins, R. L. (1991). An appraisal of chemical aversion (emetic therapy) approaches to alcoholism treatment. *Behaviour Research & Therapy, 29*(5), 387–413.

Ellis, A. (1961). *A guide to rational living.* Englewood Cliffs, NJ: Prentice-Hall.

Ellis, A. (1996). Better, deeper, and more enduring brief therapy. New York: Institute for Rational Emotive Therapy.

Ellis, A. (1997). Using Rational Emotive Behavior Therapy techniques to cope with disability. *Professional Psychology: Research and Practice, 28,* 17–22.

Ellis, A. (2000). *How to control your anxiety before it controls you.* Charleston, SC: Citadel Press.

Ellis, J. L., et al. (1999). Development of muscarine analgesics derived from epibatidine: Role of the M-sub-4 receptor subtype. *Journal of Pharmacology & Experimental Therapeutics, 288,* 1143–1150.

Ellman, S. J., Spielman, A. J., Luck, D., Steiner, S. S., & Halperin, R. (1991). REM deprivation: A review. In S. A. Ellman & J. S. Antrobus (Eds.), *The mind in sleep: Psychology and psychophysiology* (2nd ed., pp. 329–368). New York: Wiley.

Emery, R. E. (1999). *Marriage, divorce, and children's adjustment* (2nd ed). Thousand Oaks, CA: Sage.

Emery, R. E., & Laumann-Billings, L. (1998). An overview of the nature, causes, and consequences of abusive family relationships: Toward differentiating maltreatment and violence. *American Psychologist, 53*(2), 121–135.

Endersbe, J. (2000). *Teen pregnancy: Tough choices.* New York: Life Matters.

Endersbe, J. (2000). *Teen sex: Risks and consequences.* New York: Life Matters.

Ennis, N. E., Hobfoll, S. E., Schroeder, K. E. E. (2000). Money doesn't talk, it swears: How economic stress and resistance resources impact inner-city women's depressive mood. *American Journal of Community Psychology, 28,* 149–173.

Epstein, M. (1998). *Going to pieces without falling apart.* New York: Broadway Books.

Eriksson, P. S., Perfilieva, E., Bjork-Eriksson, T., Alborn, A. M., Nordborg, C., Peterson, D. A., & Gage, F. H. (1998). Neurogenesis in the adult human hippocampus. *Nature Medicine, 4*(11), 1313–1317.

Espin, O. M. (1993). Feminist theory: Not for or by white women only. *Counseling Psychologist, 21,* 103–108.

Esposito, S., Prange, A. J., & Golden, R. N. (1998). The thyroid axis and mood disorders: Overview and future prospects. *Psychopharmacology Bulletin, 33,* 205–217.

Esser, J. K. (1998). Alive and well after 25 years: A review of groupthink research. *Organizational Behavior and Human Decision Processes, 73,* 116–141.

Etcoff, N. (1999). *Survival of the prettiest: The science of beauty.* New York: Doubleday.

Ethical Principles of Psychologists and Code of Conduct. (1992). *American Psychologist, 47,* 1597–1611.

European School Survey Project on Alcohol and Other Drugs (ESPAD) (2001). Substance abuse increasing among European adolescents. *Reuters Medical News for the Professional* [On-line]. Available: psychiatry.medscape.com/reuters/prof/2001/02/02.21

Evans, G. W., Hygge, S., & Bullinger, M. (1995). Chronic noise and psychological stress. *Psychological Science, 6*(6), 333–338.

Evans, R. B. E., & Rilling, M. (2000). How the challenge of explaining learning influenced the origins and development of John B. Watson's behaviorism. *American Journal of Psychology, 113*(2), 275–301.

Everett, C., & Everett, S. V. (1994). *Healthy divorce.* San Francisco: Jossey-Bass.

Ewart, C. K., & Fitzgerald, S. T. (1994). Changing behaviour and promoting well-being after heart attack: A social action theory approach. *Irish Journal of Psychology, 15*(1), 219–241.

Ewart, C. K., & Kolodner, K. B. (1994). Negative affect, gender, and expressive style predict elevated ambulatory blood pressure in adolescents. *Journal of Personality and Social Psychology, 66,* 596–605.

Exner, J. E., Jr. (1997). The future of Rorschach in personality assessment. *Journal of Personality Assessment, 68*(1), 37–46.

Eyler, F., Behnke, M., Conlon, M., Woods, N., & Wobie, K. (1998). Birth outcome from a prospective, matched study of prenatal crack cocaine use: I. Interactive and dose effects on health and growth. *Pediatrics, 101,* 229–237.

Eysenck, H. J. (1967). *The biological basis of personality.* Springfield, IL: Charles C Thomas.

Eysenck, H. J. (1982). *Personality, genetics, and behavior: Selected papers.* New York: Prager.

Eysenck, H. J. (1990). Biological dimensions of personality. In L. A. Pervin (Ed.), *Handbook of personality: Theory and research.* New York: Guilford Press.

Eysenck, H. J. (1991). *Smoking, personality, and stress: Psychosocial factors in the prevention of cancer and coronary heart disease.* New York: Springer-Verlag.

Fackelmann, K. (1997). Marijuana on trial: Is marijuana a dangerous drug or a valu-able medicine? *Science News, 151,* 178–179, 183.

Facon, B., & Facon-Bollengier, T. (1999). Chronological age and crystallized intelligence of people with intellectual disability. *Journal of Intellectual Disability Research, 43*(6), 489–496.

Faddiman, A. (1997). *The spirit catches you and you fall down.* New York: Straus & Giroux.

Faigman, D. L., Kaye, D., Saks, M. J., & Sanders, J. (1997). *Modern scientific evidence: The law and science of expert testimony.* St. Paul, MN: West.

Fantuzzo, J. W., & Mohr, W. K. (1999). Prevalence and effects of child exposure to domestic violence. *Future of Children, 9*(3), 21–32.

Fantz, R. L. (1956). A method for studying early visual development. *Perceptual and Motor Skills, 6,* 13–15.

Fantz, R. L. (1963). Pattern vision in newborn infants. *Science, 140,* 296–297.

Fanz, E. A., Waldie, K. E., & Smith, M. J. (2000). The effect of callostomy on novel versus familiar bimanual actions: A neural dissociation between controlled and automatic processes. *Psychological Science, 11*(1), 82–85.

Farber, P. L. (2000). *Finding order in nature: The naturalist tradition from Linnaeus to E. O. Wilson.* Baltimore: Johns Hopkins Univ. Press.

Farrington, D. P. (2000). Psychosocial predictors of adult antisocial personality and adult convictions. *Behavioral Sciences & the Law, 18*(5), 605–622.

Farthing, W. G. (1992). *The psychology of consciousness.* Englewood Cliffs, NJ: Prentice Hall.

Fava, G. A., et al. (1998). Prevention of recurrent depression with cognitive behavioral therapy. *Archives of General Psychiatry, 55*(9), 816–820.

Fehr, C., Grintschuk, N., Szegedi, A., Anghelescu, I., Klawe, C., Singer, P., Hiemke, C., & Dahmen, N. (2000). The HTR1B 861G > C receptor polymorphism among patients suffering from alcoholism, major depression, anxiety disorders and narcolepsy. *Psychiatry Research, 97*(1), 1–10.

Fein, S., & Spencer, S. J. (1997). Prejudice as self-image maintenance: Affirming the self through derogating others. *Journal of Personality and Social Psychology, 73*(1), 31–44.

Feldman, R. S. (1982). *Development of nonverbal behavior in children.* Seacaucus, NJ: Springer-Verlag.

Fenton, G. W. (1998). Neurosurgery for mental disorder. *Irish Journal of Psychological Medicine, 15,* 45–48.

Fernandez, G., et al. (1999). Real-time tracking of memory formation in the human rhinal cortex and hippocampus. *Science, 285,* 1582–1585.

Fernandez, G., Hufnagel, A., Helmstaedter, C., Zetner, J., Elger, C. E. (1996). Memory function during low intensity hippocampal electrical stimulation in patients with temporal lobe epilepsy. *European Journal of Neurology, 3,* 335–344.

Fernandez, G., Weyerts, H., Schrader-Boelsche, M., Tendolkar, I., Smid, H. G. O. M., Tempelmann, C., Hinrichs, H., Scheich, H., Elger, C. E., Mangun, G. R., & Heinze, H- J. (1998). Successful verbal encoding into episodic memory engages the posterior hippocampus: A parametrically analyzed functional magnetic resonance imaging study. *Journal of Neuroscience, 18*(5), 1841–1847.

Fernandez-Ruiz, J., & Diaz, R. (1999). Prism adaptation and aftereffect: Specifying the properties of a procedural memory system. *Learning & Memory, 6,* 47–53.

Fernendez, G., et al. (1998). Successful verbal encoding into episodic memory engages the posterior hippocampus: A parametrically analyzed functional magnetic resonance imaging study. *Journal of Neuroscience, 18,* 1841–1847.

Ferry, B., Roozendaal, B., & McGaugh, J. L. (1999). Involvement of alpha 1-adrenoceptors in the basolateral amygdala in modulation of memory storage. *European Journal of Pharmacology, 372,* 9–16.

Festinger, L. A. (1957). *A theory of cognitive dissonance.* Evanston, IL: Row, Peterson.

Festinger, L. A., & Carlsmith, L. M. (1959). Cognitive consequences of forced compliance. *Journal of Abnormal and Social Psychology, 58,* 203–210.

Field, K. M., Woodson, R., Greenberg, R., & Cohen, D. (1982). Discrimination and imitation of facial expressions by neonates. *Science, 218,* 179–181.

Finch, C. E., & Tanzi, R. E. (1997). Genetics of aging. *Science, 278,* 407–411.

Fink, M. (1999). *Electroshock: Restoring the mind.* London: Oxford University Press.

Finkel, D., & Pedersen, N. L. (2000). Contribution of age, genes, and environment to the relationship between perceptual speed and cognitive ability. *Psychology & Aging, 15*(1), 56–64.

Finley, W. H., McDanal, C. E., Finley, S. C., & Rosecrans, C. J. (1973). Prison survey for the XYY karyotype in tall inmates. *Behavior Genetics, 3,* 97–100.

Fiore, M. C. (2000). A clinical practice guideline for treating tobacco use and dependence: A US Public Health Service Report. *Journal of the American Medical Association, 283*(24), 3244–3254.

First, M. B., Pincus, H. A., & Frances, A. (1999). Another perspective on "Putting DSM-IV in perspective." *American Journal of Psychiatry, 156*(3), 499–500.

Firth, C. D., & Firth, U. (1999). Interacting minds—A biological basis. *Science, 286,* 1692–1695.

Fischman, J. (2000, February 7). Why we fall in love. *U. S. News & World Report*, pp. 42–48.

Fisher, S. E., Vargha-Khadem, F., Watkins, K. E., et al. (1998). Localisation of a gene implicated in a severe speech and language disorder. *Nature Genetics, 18,* 168–170.

Fisher, S., & Greenberg, R. P. (1996). *Freud scientifically reappraised: Testing the theories and therapy.* New York: Wiley.

Fishman, S. M., & Sheehan, D. V. (1985, April). Anxiety and panic: Their cause and treatment. *Psychology Today,* pp. 26–32.

Fiske, S. T. (1998). Stereotyping, prejudice, and discrimination. In D. T. Gilbert, S. T. Fiske, and G. Lindzey (Eds.), *The handbook of social psychology,* Vol. 2 (4th ed.) (pp. 357–411). Boston, MA: McGraw-Hill.

Flavell, J. H. (1999). Cognitive development: Children's knowledge about the mind. *Annual Reviews of Psychology, 50,* 21–45.

Fletcher, G. J. O., & Simpson, J. A. (2000). Ideal standards in close relationships: Their structure and functions. *Current Directions in Psychological Science,* 9(3), 102–105.

Flexser, A. J., & Tulving, E. (1978). Retrieval independence in recognition and recall. *Psychological Review, 85,* 153–171.

Flexser, A. J., & Tulving, E. (1982). Priming and recognition failure. *Journal of Verbal Learning and Verbal Behavior, 21,* 237–248.

Flora, M. E. (2000). *Meditation: Key to spiritual awakening.* New York: CDM Publications.

Flynn, J. R. (1987). Massive IQ gains in 14 nations: What IQ tests really measure. *Psychological Bulletin, 101,* 171–191.

Flynn, J. R. (1998). IQ gains over time: Toward finding the causes. In U. Neisser (Ed.), *The rising curve: Long-term gains in IQ and related measures.* Washington, DC: American Psychological Association.

Flynn, J. R. (1999). Searching for justice: The discovery of IQ gains over time. *American Psychologist, 54,* 5–20.

Flynn, J. R. (2000). The hidden history of IQ and special education: Can the problems be solved? *Psychology, Public Policy, & Law,* 6(1), 191–198.

Flynn, J. R. (2000). IQ gains and fluid g. *American Psychologist,* 55(5), 543.

Foa, E. B., Franklin, M. E., Perry, K. J., & Herbert, J. D. (1996). Cognitive biases in generalized social phobia. *Journal of Abnormal Psychology,* 105(3), 433–439.

Fold, M. A., & Friedman, S. (2000). Cadet basic training: an ethnographic study of stress and coping. *Military Medicine, 165,* 147–152.

Folk, C. L., & Remington, R. W. (1998). Selectivity in distraction by irrelevant featural singletons: Evidence for two forms of attentional capture. *Journal of Experimental Psychology: Human Perception and Performance, 24,* 1–12.

Folkman, S., Lazarus, R. S., Gruen, R. J., & DeLongis, A. (1986). Appraisal, coping, health-status, and psychological symptoms. *Journal of Personality and Social Psychology, 50,* 571–579.

Foltin, R. W., & Haney, M. (2000). Conditioned effects of environmental stimuli paired with smoked cocaine in humans. *Psychopharmacology,* 149(1), 24–33.

Fone, B. R. S. (2000). *Homophobia: A history.* New York: Metropolitan Books.

Fones, C. S., Manfro, G. G., & Pollack, M. H. (1998). Social phobia: An update. *Harvard Review of Psychiatry, 5,* 247–259.

Foulkes, D. (1982). *Children's Dreams.* New York: Wiley.

Foulkes, D. (1993). Children's dreaming. In D. Foulkes & C. Cavallero (Eds.), *Dreaming as cognition,* pp. 114–132. New York: Harvester Wheatsheaf.

Fowler, I. L., Carr, V. J., Carter, N. T., & Lewin, T. J. (1998). Patterns of current and lifetime substance use in schizophrenia. *Schizophrenia Bulletin, 24,* 443–455.

Fowler, J. S., Volkow, N. D., Wang, G. J., Pappas, N., Logan, J., MacGregor, R., Alexoff, D., Shea, C., Shyler, D., Wolf, A. P., Warner, D., Zazulkova, I., & Cilento, R. (1996). Inhibition of monoamine oxidase B in the brains of smokers. *Nature, 379,* 733–736.

Fowler, R. D. (1986, May). Howard Hughes: A psychological autopsy. *Psychology Today,* pp. 22–33.

Fowles, D. C. (1992). Schizophrenia: Diathesis-stress revisited. *Annual Review of Psychology, 43,* 303–336.

Fraley, R. C., & Shaver, P. R. (1997). Adult attachment and the suppression of unwanted thoughts. *Journal of Personality and Social Psychology, 73,* 1080–1091.

Frances, A., & First, M. B. (1998). Your mental health: A layman's guide to the psychiatrist's bible. New York: Scribners.

Franken, R. E. (1998). *Human motivation* (4th ed.). Pacific Grove, CA: Brooks/Cole.

Franz, E. A., Waldie, K. E., & Smith, M. J. (2000). The effect of callostomy on novel versus familiar bimanual actions: A neural dissociation between controlled and automatic processes? *Psychological Science, 11* (1), 82–85.

Frazier, L. (2000). Coping with disease-related stressors in Parkinson's disease. *Gerontologist, 2000, 40,* 53–63.

Frazier, L. D., & Waid, L. D. (1999). Influences on anxiety in later life: The role of health status, health perceptions, and health locus of control. *Aging & Mental Health,* 3(3), 213–220.

Frederick, C. M., & Morrison, C. S. (1999). Date selection choices in college students: Making a potential love connection. *North American Journal of Psychology,* 1(1), 41–50.

Fredrickson, M., Wik, G., Fischer, H., & Andersson, J. (1995). Affective and attentive neural networks in humans: A PET study of Pavlovian conditioning. *Neuroreport: An International Journal for the Rapid Communication of Research in Neuroscience,* 7(1), 97–101.

Fredrikson, M., Wik, G., & Fischer, H. (1999). Higher hypothalamic and hippocampal neural activity in type A than type B women. *Personality & Individual Differences, 26,* 265–270.

Frensch, P. A., & Sternberg, R. J. (1990). Intelligence and cognition. In M. W. Eysenck (Ed.), Cognitive psychology: An international review. (pp. 57–103). New York: Wiley.

Freud, S. (1900/1953). The interpretation of dreams. In J. Stratchey (Ed. and Trans.), *The standard edition of the complete psychological works of Sigmund Freud* (Vols. 4 and 5). London: Hogarth Press. (Original work published 1900).

Freud, S. (1961). The ego and the id. In J. Stratchey (Ed. and Trans.), *The standard edition of the complete psychological works of Sigmund Freud* (Vol. 19). London: Hogarth Press. (Original work published 1923).

Friedman, H. S., Hawley, P. H., & Tucker, J. S. (1994). Personality, health, and longevity. *Current Directions in Psychological Science,* 4(2), 37–41.

Friedman, L. J., & Coles, R. (1999). *Identity's architect: A biography of Erik H. Erikson.* New York: Simon & Schuster.

Friedman, M., & Rosenman, R. H. (1959). Association of specific overt behavior patterns with blood and cardiovascular findings: Blood cholesterol level, blood clotting time, incidence of arcus senilis and clinical coronary artery disease. *Journal of the American Medical Association, 169,* 1286–1296.

Friedman, M., Thoresen, C. E., Gill, J. J., Ulmer, D., Powell, L. H., Price, V. A., Brown, B., Thompson, L., Rabin, D. D., Breall, W. S., Bourg, E., Levy, R., & Dixon, T. (1986). Alteration of Type A behavior and its effect on cardiac recurrences in past myocardial infarction patients: Summary results of the Recurrent Coronary Prevention Project. *American Heart Journal, 112,* 653–665.

Friedman, N. P., & Miyake, A. (2000). Differential roles for visuospatial and verbal working memory in situation model construction. *Journal of Experimental Psychology, 129,* 61–83.

Friend, T. (1997, February 5). Heroin spreads across the USA. *USA Today,* p. 2, 4.

Fritz, G. K., & McQuaid, E. L. (2000). Chronic medical conditions: Impact on development. In A. J. Sameroff, & M. Lewis, et al., (Eds.), *Handbook of developmental psychopathology* (2nd ed.) (pp. 277–289). New York: Kluwer Academic/Plenum Publishers.

Fruehwald, S., Loffler, H., Eher, R., Saletu, B., & Baumhackl, U. (2001). Relationship between depression, anxiety, and quality of life: A study of stroke patients compared to chronic low back pain and myocardial ischemia patients. *Psychopathology, 34*(1), 50–56.

Fry, C. L. (1985). Culture, behavior, and aging in the comparative perspective. In J. E. Birren, K. W. Schaie, et al. (Eds.), *Handbook of the psychology of aging* (2nd ed.), pp, 216–244. New York: Van Nostrand Reinhold Co.

Frye, R. E., Schwartz, B. S., & Doty, R. L. (1990). Dose-related effects of cigarette smoking on olfactory function. *Journal of the American Medical Association, 263,* 1233–1236.

Fuchs, E., & Segre, J. A. (2000). Stem Cells: A New Lease on Life. *Cell, 100*(1), 143–155.

Fullerton, D. (1997). A review of approaches to teenage pregnancy. *Nursing Times, 93,* 48–49.

Fulton, S., Woodside, B., & Shizgal, P. (2000). Modulation of brain reward circuitry by leptin. *Science, 287,* 125–128.

Furman, E. (1990, November). Plant a potato learn about life (and death). *Young Children, 46*(1), 15–20.

Furmark, T., Fischer, H., Wik, G., Larsson, M., & Fredrikson, M. (1997). The amygdala and individual differences in human fear conditioning. *Neuroreport: An International Journal for the Rapid Communication of Research in Neuroscience, 8*(18), 3957–3960.

Gabbard, G. O. (1999). Psychodynamic therapy in an age of neuroscience. *Harvard Mental Health Letter, 15*(7), 4–5.

Gabrieli, J. D., Brewer, J. B., & Poldrack, R. A. (1998). Images of medial temporal lobe functions in human learning and memory. *Neurobiology of Learning & Memory, 70,* 275–283.

Gaensbauer, T. J., & Hiatt, S. (1984). Facial communication of emotion in early infancy. In N. Fox & R. Davidson (Eds.), *The psychobiology of affective development* (pp. 207–230). Hillsdale, NJ: Erlbaum.

Gaertner, S. L., Dovidio, J. F., Rust, M. C., Nier, J. A., Banker, B. S., Ward, C. M., Mottola, G. R., & Houlette, M. (1999). Reducing intergroup bias: Elements of intergroup cooperation. *Journal of Personality and Social Psychology, 76*(3), 388–402.

Gaetz, M., Weinberg, H. Rzempoluck, E., & Jantzen, K. J. (1998). Neural network classifications and correlational analysis of EEG and MEG activity accompanying spontaneous reversals of the Necker Cube. *Cognitive Brain Research, 6,* 335–346.

Gage, F. H. (2000). Mammalian neural stem cells. *Science, 287,* 1433–1438.

Gagnon, J. H. (1990). The explicit and implicit use of the scripting perspective in sex research. *Annual Review of Sex Research, 1,* 1–43.

Galinsky, A. D., & Moskowitz, G. B. (2000). Perspective-taking: Decreasing stereotype expression, stereotype accessibility, and in-group favoritism. *Journal of Personality & Social Psychology, 78*(4), 708–724.

Gallagher, A. M., De Lisi, R., Holst, P. C., McGillicuddy-De Lisi, A. V., Morely, M., Cahalan, C. (2000). Gender differences in advanced mathematical problem solving. *Journal of Experimental Child Psychology, 75*(3), 165–190.

Gallistel, C. R., & Gibbon, J. (2000). Time, rate, and conditioning. *Psychological Review, 107*(2), 289–344.

Galloway, J. L. (1999, March 8). Into the heart of darkness. *U. S. News and World Report,* pp. 25–32.

Garcia, G. M., & Stafford, M. E. (2000). Prediction of reading by Ga and Gc specific cognitive abilities for low-SES White and Hispanic English-speaking children. *Psychology in the Schools, 37*(3), 227–235.

Garcia, J., Ervin, F. R., & Koelling, R. A. (1966). Learning with prolonged delay of reinforcement. *Psychonomic Science, 5*(3), 121–122.

Garcia, S. D., & Khersonsky, D. (1997). 'They are a lovely couple': Further examination of perceptions of couple attractiveness. *Journal of Social Behavior and Personality, 12,* 367–380.

Gardner, B. T., & Gardner, R. A. (1971). Two-way communication with an infant chimpanzee. In A. M. Schrier & F. Stollnitz (Eds.), *Behavior of nonhuman primates* (Vol. 4). New York: Academic Press.

Gardner, H. (1983). *Frames of mind.* New York: Basic Books.

Gardner, H. (1986). From testing intelligence to assessing competencies. A pluralistic view of intellect. *Roeper Review, 8*(3), 147–150.

Gardner, H. (1988). Creativity: An interdisciplinary perspective. *Creativity Research Jour-nal, 1,* 8–26.

Gardner, H. (1991). *The unschooled mind: How children think & how schools should teach.* New York: Basic Books.

Gardner, H. (1998). A multipliciaty of intelligences. *Scientific American Presents Exploring Intelligence, 9,* 18–23.

Gardner, H. (1999, February). Who owns intelligence? *Atlantic Monthly,* pp. 67–76.

Gardner, R. A., & Gardner, B. T. (1969). Teaching sign language to a chimpanzee. *Science, 165,* 664–672.

Gardner, W. L., Gabriel, S., & Lee, A. Y. (1999). "I" value freedom, but "we" value relationships: Self-construal priming mirrors cultural differences in judgment. *Psychological Science, 10*(4), 321–326.

Garland, A. F., & Zigler, E. (1999). Adolescent suicide prevention: Current research and social policy implications. In L. E. Berk, *Landscapes of development* (pp. 407–426). Belmont, CA: Wadsworth.

Garnefski, N. (2000). *Journal of the American Academy of Child and Adolescent Psychiatry, 39,* 1175–1181.

Gathercole, S. E., & Pickering, S. J. (2000). Working memory deficits in children with low achievements in the national curriculum at 7 years of age. *British Journal of Educational Psychology, 70,* 177–194.

Gay, P. (1983). *The bourgeois experience: Victoria to Freud. Vol. 1: Education of the senses.* New York: Oxford University Press.

Gay, P. (1999, March 29). Psychoanalyst Sigmund Freud. *Time,* 65–69.

Gay, P. (2000). *Freud for historians.* Replica Books.

Gazzaniga (Ed.), The cognitive neurosciences. Cambridge, MA: MIT Press.

Gazzaniga, M. S. (1970). *The bisected brain.* New York: Appleton-Century-Crofts.

Gazzaniga, M. S. (1995). Consciousness and the cerebral hemispheres. In M. S.

Gazzaniga, M. S. (2000). *The mind's past.* University California Press.

Geller, L. (1982). The failure of self-actualization theory: A critique of Carl Rogers and Abraham Maslow. *Journal of Humanistic Psychology, 22,* 56–73.

Gelman, S. (1999). *Schizophrenia and medication: A history.* New York: Rutgers University Press.

Gemignani, A., Santarcangelo, E., Sebastiani, L., Marchese, C., Mammoliti, R., Simoni, A., & Ghelarducci, B. (2000). Changes in autonomic and EEG patterns induced by hypnotic imagination of aversive stimuli in man. *Brain Research Bulletin, 53*(1), 105–111.

George, M. S., Sackeim, H. A., Rush, A. J., Marangell, L. B., Nahas, Z., Husain, M. M., Lisanby, S., Burt, T., Goldman, J., & Ballenger, J. C. (2000). Vagus nerve stimulation: A new tool for brain research and therapy. *Biological Psychiatry, 47*(4), 287–295.

Gershon, E. S. et al., (1998). Closing in on genes for manic-depressive illness and schizophrenia. *Neuropsychopharmacology, 18,* 233–242.

Gershon, E. S., & Rieder, R. O. (1993). Major disorders of mind and brain. Mind and brain: *Readings from Scientific American magazine* (pp. 91–100). New York, NY: Freeman.

Geschwind, N. (1979). Specialization of the human brain. *Scientific American, 241,* 180–199.

Gianakos, I. (2000). Gender roles and coping with work stress. *Sex Roles, 42,* 1059–1079.

Giancola, P. R. (2000). Temperament and antisocial behavior in preadolescent boys with or without a family history of a substance use disorder. *Psychology of Addictive Behaviors, 14*(1), 56–68.

Gibbs, N. (1995, October 2). The EQ factor. *Time,* pp. 60–68.

Gibbs, N. (1999, May 3). Crime: The Littleton massacre. *Time,* 20–36.

Gibbs, W. W. (1995). Seeking the criminal element. *Scientific American,* pp. 100–107.

Gibson, E. J., & Walk, R. D. (1960). The visual cliff. *Scientific American, 202*(2), 67–71.

Gifford, R., & Hine, D. W. (1997). "I'm cooperative, but you're greedy": Some cognitive tendencies in a commons dilemma. *Canadian Journal of Behavioural Science, 29*(4), 257–265.

Gilbert, A. N., & Wysocki, C. J. (1987). The smell survey results. *National Geographic, 172,* 514–525.

Gilbert, L., & Alexander, L. (1998). A profile of sexual health behaviors among college women. *Psychological Reports, 82,* 107–116.

Gilligan, C. (1977). In a different voice: Women's conception of morality. *Harvard Educational Review, 47*(4), 481–517.

Gilligan, C. (1990). Teaching Shakespeare's sister. In C. Gilligan, N. Lyons, & T. Hanmer (Eds.), *Mapping the moral domain* (pp. 73–86). Cambridge, MA: Harvard University Press.

Gilligan, C. (1993). Adolescent development reconsidered. In A. Garrod (Ed.), *Approaches to moral development: New research and emerging themes.* New York: Teachers College Press.

Gilligan, C., & Attanucci, J. (1988). Two moral orientations. In C. Gilligan, J. V. Ward, et al. (Eds.), *Mapping the moral domain: A contribution of women's thinking to psychological theory and education,* (pp. 73–86). Cambridge, MA: Harvard University Press.

Gilligan, J. (2000). *Violence: Reflections on a Western epidemic.* London: Jessica Kingsley.

Gilmour, D. R., & Walkey, F. H. (1981). Identifying violent offenders using a video measure of interpersonal distance. *Journal of Consulting and Clinical Psychology, 49,* 287–291.

Giovagnoli, A. R. (2001). Relation of sorting impairment to hippocampal damage in temporal lobe epilepsy. *Neuropsychologia, 39*(2), 140–150.

Giros, B., Jaber, M., Jones, S. R., Wightman, R. M., & Caron, M. G. (1996). Hyperlocomotion and indifference to cocaine and amphetamine in mice lacking the dopamine transporter. *Nature, 379,* 606–612.

Glassman, A. H., & Shapiro, P. A. (1998). Depression and the course of coronary artery disease. *American Journal of Psychiatry, 155,* 4–11.

Glassman, R. B. (1999). A working memory "theory or relativity": Elasticity in temporal, spatial, and modality dimensions conserves item capacity in radial maze, verbal tasks and other cognition. *Brain Research Bulletin, 48,* 475–489.

Gleaves, D. H. (1996). The sociocognitive model of dissociative identity disorder: A reexamination of the evidence. *Psychological Bulletin, 120,* 42–59.

Gluck, M. A., & Myers, C. E. (1997). Psychobiological models of hippocampal function in learning and memory. *Annual Review of Psychology, 48,* 481–514.

Gobert, F. (1998). Expert memory: A comparison of four theories. *Cognition, 66,* 115–152.

God, M. A., & Friedman, B., (2000). Cadet basic training: An ethnographic study of stress and coping. *Military Science, 165,* 147–152.

Goddard, A. W., et al. (1996). Plasma levels of gamma-aminobutyric acid and panic disorder. *Psychiatry Research, 63,* 223–225.

Godden, D. R., & Baddeley, A. D. (1975). Context-dependent memory in two natural environments: On land and underwater. *British Journal of Psychology, 66,* 325–331.

Goebel, M. U., & Mills, P. J. (2000). Acute psychological stress and exercise and changes in peripheral leukocyte adhesion molecule expression and density. *Psychosomatic Medicine, 62*(5), 664–670.

Goertz, J. (2000). Creativity: An essential component for effective leadership in today's schools. *Roeper Review, 22*(3), 158–162.

Gold, M. A., & Friedman, S. B. (2000). Cadet basic training: An ethnographic study of stress and coping. *Military Medicine, 165*(2), 147–152.

Goldberg, S. (2000). *Attachment and development.* New York: Edward Arnold.

Goldberger, L., & Breznitz, S. (1993). *Handbook of stress.* New York: Free Press.

Golden, G., & Lemonick, M. D. (2000, July 3). The race is over. *Time,* pp. 18–23.

Goldman, J., Nahas, Z., & George, M. S. (2000). What is transcranial magnetic stimulation? *Harvard Mental Health Letter, 17*(5), 8.

Goldstein, B. (1976). *Introduction to human sexuality.* New York: McGraw-Hill.

Goleman, D. (1980, February). 1,528 little geniuses and how they grew. *Psychology Today,* pp. 28–53.

Goleman, D. (1995). *Emotional intelligence: Why it can matter more than IQ.* New York: Bantam.

Goleman, D. (1995, December 5). Making room on the couch for culture. *New York Times*, C1–C3, C4.

Goleman, D. P. (2000). *Working with emotional intelligence.* New York: Bantam Doubleday.

Golombok, S., & Tasker, F. (1996). Do parents influence the sexual orientation of their children? Findings from a longitudinal study of lesbian families. *Developmental Psychology, 32,* 3–11.

Gong, J., Chen, F., Jiang, Z., Chen, M., & Guo, X. (2000). 1 /Investigation of goiter incidence and intelligence level in children in light-iodine-deficient areas. *Chinese Journal of Clinical Psychology,* 8(2), 107–108, 110.

Goodall, J. (1971). *Tiwi wives.* Seattle, WA: University of Washington Press.

Goode, E. E., Schrof, J. M., & Burke, S. (1991, June 24). Where emotions come from. *U. S. News and World Report*, pp. 54–60.

Goodwin, D. W. (2000). *Alcoholism: The facts.* London: Oxford University Press.

Goodwin, F. K., & Ghaemi, S. N. (1998). Understanding manic-depressive illness. *Archives of General Psychiatry, 55,* 23–25.

Gordon, R. A. (2000). *Eating disorders: Anatomy of a social epidemic* (2nd ed.). Malden, MA: Blackwell Publishers Inc.

Gordon, T. (1975). *Parent effectiveness training.* New York: Plume.

Gordon, W. C. (1989). *Learning and memory.* Pacific Grove, CA: Brooks/Cole.

Gorman, C. (2001, February 5). Repairing the damage. *Time,* 53–58.

Gorman, J. (1999, January). The 11-year-old debunker. *Discover, 20,* 62–63.

Gorman, J. (2000). Neuroanatomical hypothesis of panic disorder revised. *American Journal of Psychiatry, 57,* 493–505.

Gosling, S. D. (1998). Personality dimensions in spotted hyenas (Crocuta crocuta). *Journal of Comparative Psychology, 112,* 107–118.

Gosling, S. D., & John, O. P. (1999). Personality dimensions in nonhuman animals: A cross-species review. *Current Directions in Psychological Science,* 8(3), 69–75.

Gotlieb, I. H., & Abramson, L. Y. (1999). Attributional theories of emotion. In T. Dalgleish & M. Power (Eds.), *Handbook of cognition and emotion.* New York: Wiley.

Gottesman, I. I. (1991). *Schizophrenia genesis: The origins of madness.* New York: Freeman.

Gottlieb, G. (2000). Environmental and behavioral influences on gene activity. *Current Directions in Psychological Science,* 9(3), 93–97.

Gottman, J. M. (1998). Psychology and the study of marital processes. *Annual Review of Psychology, 49,* 169–197.

Gottman, J. M., Coan, J., Carrere, S., & Swanson, C. (1998). Predicting happiness and stability from newlywed interactions. *Journal of Marriage and the Family, 60,* 42–48.

Gould, E., Reeves, A. J., Graziano, M. S. A., & Gross, C. G. (1999). Neurogenesis in the neocortex of adult primates. *Science, 286,* 548–552.

Gould, E., Reeves, A. J., Graziano, M. S., & Gross, C. G. (1999). Neurogenesis in the neocortex of adult primates. *Science, 286,* 548–552.

Gould, E., Tanapat, P., Hastings, N. B., & Shors, T. J. (1999). Neurogenesis in adulthood: a possible role in learning. *Trends in Cognitive Science,* 3(5), 186–1992.

Gould, R. L. (1975, August). Adult life stages: Growth toward self-tolerance. *Psychology Today,* pp. 74–78.

Graf, P. (1990). Life-span changes in implicit and explicit memory. *Bulletin of the Psychonomic Society, 28,* 353–358.

Graham, J. R. (1991). Comments on Duck-worth's review of the Minnesota Multiphasic Personality Inventory-2. *Journal of Counseling and Development, 69,* 570–571.

Grant, S., et al. (1996). Activation of memory circuits during the cue-elicited cocaine craving. *Proceedings of the National Academy of Sciences, 93,* 12040.

Gray, J. D., & Silver, R. C. (1990). Opposite sides of the same coin: Former spouses' divergent perspectives in coping with their divorce. *Journal of Personality & Social Psychology,* 59(6), 1180–1191.

Green, A. I. (2000). What is the relationship between schizophrenia and substance abuse? *Harvard Mental Health Letter,* 17(4), 8.

Green, D. P., Glaser, J., Rich, A. (1998). From lynching to gay bashing: The elusive connection between economic conditions and hate crime. *Journal of Personality and Social Psychology, 75,* 82–92.

Green, J. W. (1999). *Cultural awareness in the human services: A multi-ethnic approach.* Needham Heights, MA: Allyn & Bacon.

Green, J. T., & Woodruff-Pak, D. S. (2000). Eyeblink classical conditioning: Hippocampal formation is for neutral stimulus associations as cerebellum is for association-response. *Psychological Bulletin,* 126(1), 138–158.

Greenberg, J., Pyszcynski, T., Solomon, S., Pinel, E., et al., (1993). Effects of self-esteem on vulnerability-denying defensive distortions: Further evidence of an anxiety-buffering function of self-esteem. *Journal of Experimental Social Psychology,* 29(3), 229–251.

Greene, K., Rubin, D. L., Hale, J. L., & Walters, L. H. (1996). The utility of understanding adolescent egocentrism in designing health promotion messages. *Health Communication, 8,* 131–152.

Greenfield, P. M. (1984). A theory of the teacher in the learning activities of everyday life. In B. Rogoff & J. Lave (Eds.), *Everyday Cognition* (pp. 117–138). Cambridge, MA: Harvard University Press.

Greenfield, P. M. (1994). *Cross-cultural roots of minority child development.* Hillsdale, NJ: Erlbaum.

Greenfield, P. M. (1997). You can't take it with you: Why ability assessments don't cross cultures. *American Psychologist, 52,* 1115–1124.

Greenfield, P. M. (2000). Three approaches to the psychology of culture: Where do they come from? Where can they go? *Asian Journal of Social Psychology,* 3(33), 223–240.

Greenfield, P. M., Maynard, A., E., & Childs, C. P. (2000). History, culture, learning, and development. Cross-Cultural Research: *The Journal of Comparative Social Science,* 34(4), 351–374.

Greeno, C. G., Wing, R. R., & Shiffman, S. (2000). Binge antecedents in obese women with and without binge eating disorder. *Journal of Consulting & Clinical Psychology,* 68(1), 95–102.

Greenwald, A. G., & Banaji, M. R. (1995). Implicit social cognition: Attitudes, self-esteem, and stereotypes. *Psychological Review, 102,* 4–27.

Greenwald, A. G., & Banaji, M. R. (1995). Implicit social cognition: Attitudes, self-esteem, and stereotypes. *Psychological Review, 102,* 4–27.

Gregory, R. L. (1969). Apparatus for investigating visual perception. *American Psychol-ogist,* 24(3), 219–225.

Griffith, M. A., & Dubow, E. F., & Ippolito, M. F. (2000). Developmental and cross-situational differences in adolescents' coping strategies. *Journal of Youth and Adolescence, 29,* 183–204.

Griffiths, A. W. (1971). Prisoners of XYY constitution: Psychological aspects. *British Journal of Psychiatry, 119,* 193–194.

Grigorenko (Eds.), *Intelligence, heredity, and environment.* New York: Cambridge University Press.

Grodzinsky, Y. (2000). The neurology of syntax: Language use without Broca's area. *Behavioral & Brain Sciences, 23*(1), 1–71.

Groth-Marnat, G. (1990). *Handbook of psychological assessment* (2nd ed.). New York: Wiley.

Gruber, E., & Machamer, A. M. (2000). Risk of school failure as an early indicator of other health risk behaviour in American high school students. *Health, Risk & Society, 2*(1), 59–68.

Grunberg, L., Moore, S., Anderson-Connolly, R., & Greenberg, E. (1999). Work stress and self-reported alcohol use: The moderating role of escapist reasons for drinking. *Journal of Occupational Health Psychology, 4,* 29–36.

Guarnaccia, P. J., & Rogler, L. H. (1999). Research on culture-bound syndromes: New directions. *American Journal of Psychiatry, 156*(9), 1322–1327.

Guarnaccia, P. J., & Rogler, L. H. (1999). Research on culture-bound syndromes: New directions. *American Journal of Psychiatry, 156,* 1322–1327.

Guastello, S. J., Guastello, D. D., & Craft, L. L. (1989). Assessment of the Barnum effect in computer-based test interpretations. *Journal of Psychology, 123,* 477–484.

Guidelines for the treatment of animals in behavioural research and teaching. (2000). *Animal Behaviour, 59* (1), 253–257.

Guilford, J. P. (1967). *The nature of human intelligence.* New York: McGraw-Hill.

Guinard, J., et al. (1996). Does consumption of beer, alcohol, and bitter substances affect bitterness perception? *Physiology & Behavior, 49,* 625–631.

Gur, R. C., et al. (1999). Sex differences in brain gray and white matter in healthy young adults: Correlations with cognitive performance. *Journal of Neuroscience, 19,* 4065–4072.

Gur, R., Mozley, L., Mozley, P., Resnick, S., Karp, J., Alavi, A., Arnold, S., & Gur, R. (1995). Sex differences in regional cerebral glucose metabolism during a resting state. *Science, 267,* 528–531.

Gur, R., Mozley, P., Resnick, S., Karp, J., Alavi, A., Arnold, S., & Gur, R. (1995). Sex differences in regional cerebral glucose metabolism during a resting state. *Science, 267,* 528–531.

Gurevich, E. V., Bordelon, Y., Shapiro, R. M., Arnold, S. E., Gur, R. E., & Joyce, J. N. (1997). Mesolimbic dopamine D3 receptors and use of antipsychotics in patients with schizophrenia. *Archives of General Psychiatry, 54,* 225–232.

Gustavson, C. R., & Garcia, J. (1974, August). Pulling a gag on the wily coyote. *Psychology Today,* pp. 68–72.

Gustavson, C. R., Kelly, D. J., Sweeney, M., & Garcia, J. (1976). Prey-lithium aversions: I. Coyotes and wolves. *Behavioral Biology, 17,* 61–72.

Guthrie, R. V. (1998). *Even the rat was white.* Boston: Allyn & Bacon.

Gutkin, J. (1989). A study of "flashbulb" memories for the moment of the explosion of the space shuttle Challenger. *Unpublished manuscript,* Emory University, Atlanta.

Haaga, D. A. F., Rabois, D., & Brody, C. (1999). Cognitive behavior therapy. In M. Hersen & A. S. Bellack (Eds.), *Handbook of comparative treatments for adult disorders.* New York: Wiley.

Haerenstam, A., Theorell, T., & Kaijser, L. (2000). Coping with anger-provoking situations, psychosocial working conditions, and ECG-detected signs of coronary heart disease. *Journal of Occupational Health Psychology, 5*(1), 191–203.

Hagarty, P. (1997). Materializing the hypothalamus: A performative account of the "gay brain." *Feminism & Psychology, 7,* 355–372.

Hagerty, M. R. (2000). Social comparisons of income in one's community: Evidence from national surveys of income and happiness. *Journal of Personality & Social Psychology, 78*(4), 764–771.

Haier, R. J. (1993). Cerebral glucose metabolism and intelligence. In P. A. Vernon (Ed.), *Biological approaches to the study of human intelligence.* Norwood, NJ: Ablex.

Haier, R. J., Chueh, D., Touchette, P., Lott, I., Buchsbaum, M. S., MacMillan, D., Sandman, C., LaCasse, L., & Sosa, E. (1995). Brain size and cerebral glucose metabolic rate in non-specific mental retardation and Down Syndrome. *Intelligence, 20,* 191–210.

Haier, R. J., Siegel, B. V., Jr., Nuechterlein, K. H., Hazlett, E., Wu, J. C., Peak, J., Browning, H., & Buchsbaum, M. S. (1988). Cortical glucose metabolic rate correlates of abstract reasoning and attention studied with positron emission tomography. *Intelligence, 12,* 199–217.

Haith, M. M., & Benson, J. B. (1998). Infant cognition. In W. Damon & R. M. Lerner (Eds.), *Handbook of child psychology* (Vol. 1). New York: John Wiley & Sons.

Hall, C. S., & Van de Castle, R. L. (1966). *The content analysis of dreams.* New York: Appleton-Century-Crofts.

Hall, C., Domhoff, G. W., Blick, K. A., & Weesner, K. E. (1982). The dreams of college men and women in the 1950 and 1980: A comparison of dream contents and sex differences. *Sleep, 5,* 188–194.

Hall, E. T. (1966). *The hidden dimension.* New York: Doubleday.

Hall, E. T. (1983, June). A conversation with Erik Erikson. *Psychology Today,* pp. 22–30.

Hall, G., & Barongan, C. (1997). Prevention of sexual aggression: Sociocultural risk and protective factors. *American Psychologist, 52,* 5–14.

Hall, W. G., Arnold, H. M., & Myers, K. P. (2000). The acquisition of an appetite. *Psychological Science, 11*(2), 101–105.

Hall, W. G., Moore, A., & Myers, K. P. (2000). The acquisition of an appetite. *Psychological Science, 11*(2), 101–105.

Halpern, D. F. (1997). Sex differences in intelligence: Implications for education. *American Psychologist, 52,* 1091–1102.

Halpern, D. F. (1997). Sex differences in intelligence: Implications for education. *American Psychologist, 52,* 1091–1102.

Halpern, D. F. (1998). Teaching critical thinking for transfer across domains. *American Psychologist, 53,* 449–455.

Halpern, D. F. (2000). *Sex differences in cognitive abilities.* Hillsdale, NJ: Erlbaum.

Hamer, D. H., & Copeland, P. (1999). *Living with our genes: Why they matter more than you think.*

Hamid, P. N., & Chan, W. T. (1998). Locus of control and occupational stress in Chinese professionals. *Psychological Reports, 82,* 75–79.

Hamilton, V. L. (1978). Obedience and responsibility: A jury simulation. *Journal of Personality and Social Psychology, 36,* 126–146.

Hammer, R. P., Egilmez, Y., & Emmett-Oglesby, M. W. (1997). Neural mechanisms of tolerance to the effects of cocaine. *Behavioural Brain Research, 84,* 225–239.

Hampson, E., Rovet, J. F., & Altmann, D. (1998). Spatial reasoning in children with congenital adrenal hyperplasia due to 21–hydroxylase deficiency. *Developmental Neuropsychology, 14*(2–3), 299–320.

Haney, C., Banks, C., & Zimbardo, P. (1978). Interpersonal dynamics in a stimulated prison. *International Journal of Criminology and Penology, 1,* 69–97.

Hanna, S. M., & Brown, J. H. (1999). *The practice of family therapy: Key elements across models* (2nd ed.). Belmont, CA: Brooks/Cole.

Hans, T. A. (2000). A meta-analysis of the effects of adventure programming on locus of control. *Journal of Contemporary Psychotherapy, 30*(1), 33–60.

Hanson, G., Venturelli, P. J., & Fleckenstein, A. E. (2000). *Drugs and society* (6th ed.). New York: Jones & Bartlett.

Hardy, J. B., & Zabin, L. S. (1991). *Adolescent pregnancy in an urban environment: Issues, programs, and evaluation.* Baltimore: Urban and Schwarzenberg.

Hare, R. D. (1993). *Without conscience: The disturbing world of the psychopaths among us.* New York: Pocket Books.

Harkness, S., & Super, C. M. (1996). *Parents' cultural belief systems: Their origins, expressions, and consequences.* New York: Guilford Press.

Harlow, H. F., & Harlow, M. K. (1966). Learning to love. *American Scientist, 54,* 244–272.

Harlow, H. F., & Zimmerman, R. R. (1959). Affectional responses in the infant monkey. *Science, 130,* 421–432.

Harlow, H. F., Harlow, M. K., & Meyer, D. R. (1950). Learning motivated by a manipulation drive. *Journal of Experimental Psychology, 40,* 228–234.

Harlow, J. (1868). Recovery from the passage of an iron bar through the head. *Publications of the Massachusetts Medical Society, 2,* 237–246.

Harlow, J. M. (1848). Passage of an iron rod through the head. *Boston Medical and Surgical Journal, 39,* 389–393.

Harmon, R. J., Bender, B. G., Linden, M. G., & Robinson, A. (1998). Transition from adolescence to early adulthood: Adaptation and psychiatric status of women with 47, XXX. *Journal of the American Academy of Child & Adolescent Psychiatry, 37,* 286–291.

Harmon-Jones, E. (2000). Cognitive dissonance and experienced negative affect: Evidence that dissonance increases experienced negative affect even in the absence of aversive consequences. *Personality & Social Psychology Bulletin, 26*(12), 1490–1501.

Harris, A. C. (1996). African American and Anglo American gender identities: An empirical study. *Journal of Black Psychology, 22,* 182–194.

Harris, J. C. (1995). *Developmental neuropsychiatry Vol. 1.* New York: Oxford University Press.

Harris, R., & Harris, C. (2000). *20–minute retreats.* Thousand Oaks, CA: Owl books.

Harrison, L., & Gardiner, E. (1999). Do the rich really die young? Alcohol-related mortality and social class in Great Britain, 1988–94. *Addiction, 94*(12), 1871–1880.

Hartup, W. W., & van Lieshout, C. F. M. (1995). Personality development in social context. In J. T. Spence, J. M. Darley, & D. J. Foss (Eds.), *Annual review of psychology, 46,* 655–687.

Harvey, A. G., & McGuire, B.E. (2000). Suppressing and attending to pain-related thoughts in chronic pain patients. *Behaviour Research & Therapy, 38*(11), 1117–1124.

Harvey, M. G., & Miceli, N. (1999). Antisocial behavior and the continuing itragedy of the commons. *Journal of Applied Social Psychology, 29,* 109–138.

Hata, Y., & Stryker, M. P. (1994). Control of thalamocortical afferent rearrangement by postsynaptic activity in developing visual cortex. *Science, 265,* 1732–1735.

Hatfield, E., & Rapson, R. L. (1996). *Love and Sex: Cross-cultural perspectives.* Needham Heights, MA: Allyn & Bacon.

Hay, D. F. (1994). Prosocial development. *Journal of Child Psychology and Psychiatry, 35,* 29–71.

Hayashi, S., Kuno, T., Morotomi, Y., Osawa, M., Shimizu, M., & Suetake, Y. (1998). Client-centered therapy in Japan: Fujio Tomoda and taoism. *Journal of Humanistic Psychology, 38,* 103–124.

Hayflick, L. (1977). The cellular basis for biological aging. In C. E. Finch & L. Hayflick (Eds.), *Handbook of the biology of aging* (pp. 159–186). New York: Van Nostrand Reinhold.

Hayflick, L. (1996). *How and why we age.* New York: Ballantine Books.

Hayne, H., Boniface, J., & Barr, R. (2000). The development of declarative memory in human infants: Age-related changes in deferred imitation. *Behavioral Neuroscience, 114*(1), 77–83.

Hayward, M. D., Friedman, S., & Chen, H. (1998). Career trajectories and older men's retirement. *Journal of Gerontology: Social Sciences, 53,* S91–S103.

Hazan, C., & Shaver, P. (1987). Romantic love conceptualized as an attachment process. *Journal of Personality and Social Psychology, 52,* 511–524.

Hazan, C., & Shaver, P. R. (1994). Attachment as an organizational framework for research on close relationships. *Psychological Inquiry, 5,* 1–22.

Hazan, C., & Zeifman, D. (1994). Sex and the psychological tether. In K. Bartholomew & D. Perlman (Eds.), *Attachment processes in adulthood. Advances in personal relationships* (Vol. 5) (pp. 151–178). London: Jessica Kingsley.

Hazeltine, E., Grafton, S. T., & Ivry, R. (1997). Attention and stimulus characteristics determine the locus of motor-sequence encoding. A PET study. *Brain, 40,* 123.

Hazlett, E. A., Buchbaum, M. S., Byne, W., Wei, T-C., Spiegel-Cohen, J., Geneve, C., Kinderlehrer, R., Haznedar, M. M., Shihabuddin, L., & Siever, L. J. (1999). Three-dimensional analysis with MRI and PET of the size, shape, and function of the thalamus in the schizophrenia spectrum. *American Journal of Psychiatry, 156*(8), 1190–1199.

Healy, A. F., & McNamara, D. S. (1996). Verbal learning and memory: Does the modal model still work? *Annual Review of Psychology, 47,* 143–172.

Hebb, D. O. (1949). *The organization of behavior.* New York: Wiley.

Hebb, D. O. (1955). Drive and the CNS (central nervous system). *Psychological Review, 62,* 243–254.

Hebb, D. O. (1966). *A textbook of psychology* (2nd ed.) Philadelphia: Saunders.

Heider, F. (1958). *The psychology of interpersonal relations.* New York: Wiley.

Heimann, M., & Meltzoff, A. N. (1996). Deferred imitation in 9- and 14-month-old infants. *British Journal of Developmental Psychology, 14,* 55–64.

Heine, S. J., & Lehman, D. R. (1997). Culture, dissonance, and self-affirmation. *Personality and Social Psychology Bulletin, 23,* 389–400.

Hejmadi, S., Davidson, R. J., & Rozin, P. (2000). Exploring Hindu Indian emotion expressions: Evidence for accurate recognition by Americans and Indians. *Psychological Science, 11*, 183–187.

Helms, J. E. (1992). Why is there no study of cultural equivalence in standardized cognitive ability testing? *American Psychologist, 47*, 1083–1101.

Helms, J. E., & Cook, D. A. (1999). *Using race and culture in counseling and psychotherapy: Theory and process.* Boston: Allyn & Bacon.

Hennessey, B. A., & Amabile, T. M. (1998). Reward, intrinsic motivation, and creativity. *American Psychologist, 53*, 674–675.

Hennevin, E., Hars, B., Maho, C., & Bloch, V. (1995). Processing of learned information in paradoxical sleep: Relevance for memory. *Behavioral Brain Research, 69*, 125–135.

Henrich, J., & Boyd, R. (1998). The evolution of conformist transmission and the emergence of between group differences. *Evolution and Human Behavior, 19*, 215–241.

Hensch, T. K., & Stryker, M. P. (1996). Ocular dominance plasticity under metabotropic glutamate receptor blockade. *Science, 272*, 554–557.

Henshaw, S. K. (1998). Unintended pregnancy in the United States. *Family Planning Perspectives, 30*, 24–29, 46.

Herman, B. H., & O'Brien, C. P. (1997). Clinical medications development for opiate addiction: Focus on nonopiods and opiod antagonists for the amelioration of opiate withdrawal symptoms and relapse prevention. *Seminars in Neuroscience, 9*, 158.

Herbst, J. H., Zonderman, A. B., McCrae, R. R., & Costa, P. T., Jr. (2000). Do the dimensions of the Temperament and Character Inventory map a simple genetic architecture? Evidence from molecular genetics and factor analysis. *American Journal of Psychiatry, 157*(8), 1285–1290.

Herdt, G. H. (1981). *Guardians of the flutes: Idioms of masculinity.* New York: McGraw-Hill.

Herek, G. (2000). The psychology of prejudice. *Current Directions in Psychological Science, 9*(1), 19–22.

Herkenham, M. (1992). Cannabinoid receptor localization in brain: Relationship to motor and reward systems. *Annals of the New York Academy of Sciences, 654*, 19–32.

Herman, L. M., Richards, D. G., & Woltz, J. P. (1984). Comprehension of sentences by bottlenosed dolphins. *Cognition, 16*, 129–139.

Herman, S. M. (1998). The relationship between therapist-client modality similarity and psychotherapy outcome. *Journal of Psychotherapy Practice and Research, 7*, 56–64.

Herrnstein, R. J., & Murray, C. (1994). *The bell curve: Intelligence and class structure in American life.* New York: Free Press.

Hershberger, S. L. (1997). A twin registry study of male and female sexual orientation. *Journal of Sex Research, 34*, 212–223.

Hetherington, E. M., & Stanley-Hagan, M. (1999). The adjustment of children with divorced parents: A risk and resiliency perspective. *Journal of Child Psychology & Psychiatry & Allied Disciplines, 40*(1), 129–140.

Hetherington, E. M., Bridges, M., & Insabella, G. M. (1998). What matters? What does not?: Five perspectives on the association between marital transitions and children's adjustment. *American Psychologist, 53*(2), 167–184.

Hewitt, J. K. (1997). The genetics of obesity: What have genetic studies told us about the environment? *Behavior Genetics, 27*, 353–358.

Hewitt, P. L., Coren, S., & Steel, G. D. (2001). Death from anorexia nervosa: Age span and sex differences. *Aging & Mental Health, 5*(1), 41–46.

Hewlett, B. S. (1992). Introduction. In B. S. Hewlett (Ed.), *Father-child relations: Cultural and biosocial contexts.* New York: Aldine de Gruyter.

Higgins, E. T. (1997). Beyond pleasure and pain. *American Psychologist, 52*, 1280–1300.

Higgins, N. C., & Bhatt, G. (2001). Culture moderates the self-serving bias: Etic and emic features of casual attributions in India and in Canada. *Social Behavior & Personality, 29*(1), 49–61.

Hikosaka, O., Miyashita, K., Miyachi, S., Sakai, K., & Lu, X. (1998). Differential roles of the forntal cortex, basal ganglia, and cerebellum in visuomotor sequence learning. *Neurobiology of Learning & Memory, 70*, 137–149.

Hilgard, E. R. (1978). Hypnosis and consciousness. *Human Nature, 1*, 42–51.

Hilgard, E. R. (1986). *Divided consciousness: Multiple controls in human thought and action* (expanded ed.). New York: Wiley-Interscience.

Hilgard, E. R. (1992). Divided consciousness and dissociation. *Consciousness and Cognition, 1*, 16–31.

Hill, C. E., Diemer, R. A., & Heaton, K. J. (1997). Dream interpretation sessions: Who volunteers, who benefits, and what volunteer clients view as most and least helpful. *Journal of Counseling Psychology, 44*, 53–62.

Hill, J. O., & Peters, J. C. (1998). Environmental contributions to the obesity epidemic. *Science, 280*, 1371–1374.

Hilton, J. L., & von Hippel, W. (1996). Stereotypes. In J. T. Spence, J. M. Darley, & D. J. Foss (Eds.), *Annual Review of Psychology, 47* (pp. 237–271). Palo Alto, CA: Annual Review.

Hinshaw, S. P., Zupan, B. A., Simmel, C., Nigg, J. T., & Melnick, S. (1997). Peer status in boys with and without attention-deficit hyperactivity disorder: Predictions from overt and covert antisocial behavior, social isolation, and authoritative parenting beliefs. *Child Development, 68*, 880–896.

Hirono, N., et al. (1997). Procedural memory in patients with mild Alzheimer's disease. *Dementia & Geriatric Cognitive Disorders, 8*, 210–216.

Hirshkowitz, M., Moore, C. A., & Minhoto, G. (1997). The basics of sleep. In M. R. Pressman & W. C. Orr (Eds.), *Understanding sleep: The evaluation and treatment of sleep disorders.* Washington, DC: American Psychological Association.

Hobson, J. A. (1988). *The dreaming brain.* New York: Basic Books.

Hobson, J. A. (1999). *Dreaming as delirium: How the brain goes out of its mind.* Cambridge, MA: MIT Press.

Hobson, J. A., & McCarley, R. W. (1977). The brain as a dream state generator: An activation-synthesis hypothesis of the dream process. *American Journal of Psychiatry, 134*, 1335–1348.

Hobson, J. A., & Silvestri, L. (1999). Para-somnias. *The Harvard Mental Health Letter, 15*(8), 3–5.

Hock, R. (1998). *Forty studies that changed psychology: Explorations into the history of psychological research.* Englewood Cliffs, NJ: Prentice Hall.

Hoek, H. W., Van Harten, P. N., Van Hoeken, D., & Susser, E. (1998). Lack of relation between culture and anorexia nervosa: Results of an incidence study on Curacao. *New England Journal of Medicine, 338*, 1231–1232.

Hoffman, A. M., & Summers, R. W. (2000). *Teen violence: A global view.* New York: Greenwood Publishing Group.

Hoffman, M. L. (1993). Empathy, social cognition, and moral education. In A. Garrod (Ed.), *Approaches to moral develop-*

ment: *New research and emerging themes.* New York: Teachers College Press.

Hoffman, M. I. (2000). Empathy and moral development: Implications for caring and justice. New York: Cambridge University Press.

Hoffman, P. (1997). The endorphin hypothesis. In W. P. Morgan, et al., (Eds.), *Physical activity and mental health. Series in health psychology and behavioral medicine* (pp. 163–177). Washington, DC: Taylor & Francis.

Hofman, A. (1968). Psychotomimetic agents. In A. Burger (Ed.), *Drugs affecting the central nervous system* (Vol. 2). New York: Dekker.

Hogben, M. (1998). Factors moderating the effect of televised aggression on viewer behavior. *Communication Research, 25,* 220–247.

Holden, C. (1980). Identical twins reared apart. *Science, 207,* 1323–1325.

Holland, B. (1998, March). The long good-bye. *Smithsonian,* pp. 87–93.

Holmes, T. H., & Rahe, R. H. (1967). The social readjustment rating scale. *Journal of Psychosomatic Research, 11,* 213–218.

Holtzworth-Munroe, A. (2000). A typology of men who are violent toward their female partners: Making sense of the heterogeneity in husband violence. *Current Directions in Psychological Science, 9*(4), 140–143.

Hooley, J. M., & Gotlib, I. H. (2000). A diathesis-stress conceptualization of expressed emotion and clinical outcome. *Applied & Preventive Psychology, 9*(3), 135–151.

Hooley, J. M., & Hiller, J. B. (2000). Personality and expressed emotion. *Journal of Abnormal Psychology, 109,* 40–44.

Hong, S. (2000). Exercise and psychoneuroimmunology. *International Journal of Sport Psychology, 31*(2), 204–227.

Horney, K. (1939). *New ways in psychoanalysis.* New York: International Universities Press.

Horney, K. (1945). *Our inner conflicts: A constructive theory of neurosis.* New York: Norton.

Horowitz, J. M. (1999, March 29). Good news. *Time,* p. 19.

Hovland, C. I. (1937). The generalization of conditioned responses: II. The sensory generalization of conditioned responses with varying intensities of tone. *Journal of Genetic Psychology, 51,* 279–291.

Howe, M. L., & O'Sullivan, J. T. (1997). What children's memories tell us about recalling our childhoods: A review of storage and retrieval processes in the development of long-term retention. *Developmental Review, 17,* 148–204.

Horton-Ausknecht, J. R., Mitzdorf, U., & Melchart, D. (2000). The effect of hypnosis therapy on the symptoms and disease activity in Rheumatoid Arthritis. *Psychology & Health, 14*(6), 1089–1104.

House, R. D., & McIntosh, E. G. (2000). The Zeigarnik effect in a sample of mentally retarded persons. *Perceptual & Motor Skills, 90*(2), 702.

Hoyert, D. L., & Rosenberg, H. M. (1999). Mortality from Alzheimer's disease: an update. *National Vital Statistics Report, 47*(20), 1–8.

Hrebickva, M., Cermak, I., & Osecka, L. (2000). Development of personality structure from adolescence to old age: Preliminary findings. *Studia Psychologica, 42*(3), 163–166.

Huang, L. N., & Ying, Y. (1989). Japanese children and adolescents. In J. T. Gibbs & Ln N. Huang (Eds.), *Children of color.* San Francisco: Jossey-Bass.

Huang, M., & Hauser, R. M. (1998). Trends in Black–White test-score differentials: II. The WORDSUM Vocabulary Test. In U. Neisser (Ed.), *The rising curve: Long-term gains in IQ and related measures* (pp. 303–334). Washington, DC: American Psychological Association.

Hubel, D. H. (1963). The visual cortex of the brain. *Scientific American, 209,* 54–62.

Hubel, D. H., & Wiesel, T. N. (1965). Receptive fields and the functional architecture in two nonstriate visual areas (18 and 19) of the cat. *Journal of Neurophysiology, 28,* 229–289.

Hubel, D. H., & Wiesel, T. N. (1979). Brain mechanisms of vision. *Scientific American, 241,* 150–162.

Huesmann, L. R., & Moise, J. (1996, June). Media violence: A demonstrated public health threat to children. *Harvard Mental Health Letter,* pp. 5–7.

Hugdahl, K. (1998). Cortical control of human classical conditioning: Autonomic and positron emission tomography data. *Psychophysiology, 35,* 170–178.

Hughes, D., & Dodge, M. A. (1997). African American women in the workplace: Relation-ships between job conditions, racial bias at work, and perceived job quality. *American Journal of Community Psychology, 25*(5), 581–599.

Hull, C. (1952). *A behavior system.* New Haven, CT: Yale University Press.

Hulme, C., et al. (1997). Word-frequency effects on short-term memory tasks: Evidence for a redintegration process in immediate serial recall. *Journal of Experimental Psychology: Learning, Memory, & Cognition, 23,* 1217–1232.

Hulme, C., Newton, P., Cowan, N., Stuart, G., & Brown, G. (1999). Think before you speak: Pauses, memory search, and trace redintegration processes in verbal memory span. *Journal of Experimental Psychology: Learning, Memory, & Cognition, 25,* 447–463.

Humphreys, G. W., & Muller, H. (2000). A search asymmetry reversed by figure-ground assignment. *Psychological Science, 11*(3), 196–201.

Hunkeler, N. et al. (2000). Efficacy of nurse telehealth care and peer support in augmenting treatment of depression in primary care. *Archives of Family Medicine, 9,* 700–708.

Hunsley, J., & Bailey, J. M. (1999). The clinical utility of the Rorschach: Unfulfilled promises and an uncertain future. *Psychological Assessment, 11*(3), 266–277.

Hunt, M. (1993). *The story of psychology.* New York: Doubleday.

Hur, Y., Bouchard, T. J., Jr., & Eckert, E. (1998). Genetic and environmental influences on self-reported diet: A reared-apart twin study. *Physiology & Behavior, 64,* 629–636.

Hyde, J. S., & Linn, M. C. (1988). *The psychology of gender: Advances through meta-analysis.* Baltimore: The Johns Hopkins University Press.

Hyde, J., Fenneman, E., & Lamon, S. (1990). Gender differences in mathematics performance: A meta-analysis. *Psychological Bulletin, 107,* 139–155.

Hyman, I. E., & Kleinknecht, E. E. (1999). False childhood memories: Research, theory, and applications. In L. M. Williams, & V. L. Banyard (Eds.), *Trauma and memory.* Thousand Oaks, CA: Sage.

Hyman, I. E., & Loftus, E. F. (1998). Errors in autobiographical memory. *Clinical Psychology Review, 18,* 933–947.

Hyman, R. (1981). Cold reading: How to convince strangers that you know all about them. In K. Fraizer (Ed.), *Paranormal borderlands of science* (pp. 232–244). Buffalo, NY: Prometheus.

Hyman, R. (1996). The evidence for psychic functioning: Claims vs. reality. *Skeptical Inquirer, 20,* 24–26.

Iacono, W. G., & Lykken, D. T. (1997). The validity of the lie detector: Two surveys of scientific opinion. *Journal of Applied Psychology, 82*(3), 426–433.

Ikonomidou, C., Bittigau, P., Ishimaru, M. J., Wozniak, D. F., Koch, C., Genz, K., Price, M. T., Stefovska, V., Horster, F., Tenkova, T., Dikranian, K., & Olney, J. W. (2000). Ethanol-induced apoptotic neurodegeneration and fetal alcohol syndrome. *Science, 287,* 1056–1060.

Ince, S. (1995). *Sleep disturbance.* Boston, MA: Harvard Medical School.

International Human Genome Sequencing Consortium (IHGSC). (2001). Initial sequencing and analysis of the human genome. *Nature, 409,* 860–921.

Inzlicht, M., & Ben-Zeev, T. (2000). A threatening intellectual environment: Why females are susceptible to experiencing problem-solving deficits in the presence of males. *Psychological Science, 11*(5), 365–371.

Irwin, M., Mascovich, A., Gillin, J. C., Willoughby, R., et al. (1994). Partial sleep deprivation reduced natural killer cell activity in humans. *Psychosomatic Medicine, 56*(6), 493–498.

Israel, P. (1998). *Edison: A Life of Invention.* New York: Wiley.

Itakura, S. (1992). Symbolic association between individuals and objects by a chimpanzee as an initiation of ownership. *Psychological Reports, 70,* 539–544.

Iyer, P. (2001). *The global soul: Jet lag, shopping malls, and the search for home.* London: Vintage Books.

Jablensky, A. (1999). Schizophrenia: Epidemiology. *Current Opinion in Psychiatry, 12,* 19–28.

Jackson, C. J., Furnham, A., Forder, L., & Cotter, T. (2000). The structure of the Eysenck Personality Profiler. *British Journal of Psychology, 91,* 233–239.

Jacobs, G. D. (1999). *Say good night to insomnia.* Austin, TX: Henry Holt & Company.

Jacobsen, T., & Hofmann, V. (1997). Chil-dren's attachment representations: Longitu-dinal relations to school behavior and aca-demic competency in middle childhood and adolescence. *Developmental Psychology, 33,* 703–710.

Jacoby, L. L., Levy, B. A., & Steinbach, K. (1992). Episodic transfer and automaticity: Integration of data-driven and conceptu-ally-driven processing in rereading. *Journal of Experimental Psychology: Learning, Memory, & Cognition, 18*(1), 15–24.

Jaffee, S., & Hyde, J. S. (2000). Gender differences in moral orientation: A meta-analysis. *Psychological Bulletin, 126*(5), 703–726.

James, J. W., & Friedman, R. (1998). *The grief recovery handbook: The action program for moving beyond death, divorce, and other losses.* New York: Harpercollins.

James, W. (1890). *The principles of psychology* (Vol. 2). New York: Holt.

Jamison, K. R., & Baldessarini, R. J. (1999). Effects of medical interventions on suicidal behavior. *Journal of Clinical Psychiatry, 69,* 4–6.

Jang, K. L., McCrae, R. R., Angleitner, A., Riemann, R., & Livesley, W. J. (1998). Heritability of facet-level traits in a cross-culture twin sample: Support for a hierarchical model of personality. *Journal of Personality and Social Psychology, 74*(6), 1556–1565.

Jang, K. L., Vernon, P. A., & Livesley, W. J. (2000). Personality disorder traits, family environment, and alcohol misuse: A multivaritate behavioural genetic analysis. *Addiction, 95,* 873–888.

Janis, I. L. (1972). *Victims of groupthink: A psychological study of foreign-policy decisions and fiascoes.* Boston: Houghton Mifflin.

Janis, I. L. (1989). *Crucial decisions: Leadership in policymaking and crisis management.* New York: Free Press.

Jankowiak, W. (1997). *Romantic passion: A universal experience.* New York: Columbia University Press.

Jankowiak, W., & Fischer, E. (1992). Cross-cultural perspective on romantic love. *Ethnology, 31,* 149–155.

Jansen, A. S. P., Nguyen, X. V., Karpitskiy, V., Mettenleiter, T. C., & Loewy, A. D. (1995). Central command neurons of the sympathetic nervous system: Basis of the fight-or-flight response. *Science, 270,* 644–646.

Jansen, L. M. C., Wied, C. C. G., & Kahn, R. S. (2000). Selective impairment in the stress response in schizophrenic patients. *Psychopharmacology, 149,* 319–325.

Janus, S. S., & Janus, C. L. (1993). *The Janus report on sexual behavior.* New York: Wiley.

Jaroff, L. (2001, March 5). Talking to the dead. *Time, 52.*

Jausovec, N., & Jausovec, K. (2000). Correlations between ERP parameters and intelligence: A reconsideration. *Biological Psychology, 55*(2), 137–154.

Jegalian, K., & Lahn, B. T. (2001, February). Why the Y is so weird. *Scientific American,* 56–61.

Jennings, L., & Skovholt, T. M. (1999). The cognitive, emotional, and relational characteristics of master therapists. *Journal of Counseling Psychology, 46*(1), 3–11.

Jerome, L. W., DeLeon, P. H., James, L. C., Folen, R., Earles, J., & Gedney, J. J. (2000). The coming of age of telecommunications in psychological research and practice. *American Psychologist, 55*(4), 407–421.

Jiang, Y., Olson, I. R., & Chun, M. M. (2000). Organization of visual short-term memory. *Journal of Experimental Psychology: Learning, memory, and cognition, 26,* 683–702.

Jog, M. S., Kubota, Y., Connolly, C. I., Hillegaart, V., & Graybiel, A. M. (1999). Building neural representations of habits, *Science, 286,* 1745–1749.

Jog, M. S., Kubota, Y., Connolly, C. I., Hillegaart, V., & Graybiel, A. M. (1999). Building neural representations of habits. *Science, 286,* 1745–1749.

Johnson, D. (1991). Animal rights and human lives: Time for scientists to right the balance. *Psychological Science, 1,* 213–214.

Johnson, H. M., & Seifert, C. M. (1994). Sources of the continued influence effect: When misinformation in memory affects later inferences. *Journal of Experimental Psychology: Learning, Memory, and Cognition, 20,* 1420–1436.

Johnson, J. A. (1997). Units of analysis for the description and explanation of personality. In R. Hogan, J. Johnson, & S. Briggs (Eds.), *Handbook of personality psychology.* New York: Academic Press.

Johnson, J. G., Cohen, P., Brown, J., Smailes, E. M., & Bernstein, D. P. (1999). Childhood maltreatment increases risks for personality disorders during early adulthood. *Archives of General Psychiatry, 56,* 600–606.

Johnson, J., Smailes, E., Cohen, P., Brown, J., & Bernstein, D. (2000). Associations between four types of childhood neglect and personality disorder symptoms during adolescence and early adulthood: Findings of a community-based longitudinal study. *Journal of Personality Disorders, 14,* 171–187.

Johnson, M. D., & Ojemann, G. A. (2000). The role of the human thalamus in language and memory: Evidence from electrophysiological studies. *Brain & Cognition, 42,* 218–230.

Johnson, M. H. (1997). *Developmental cognitive neuroscience: An introduction.* Cambridge, MA: Blackwell.

Johnson, T. J., & Cropsey, K. L. (2000). Sensation seeking and drinking game participation in heavy-drinking college students. *Addictive Behaviors, 25*(1), 109–116.

Johnston, J. J. (1978). Answer-changing behavior and grades. *Teaching of Psychology, 5* (1), 44–45.

Johnstone, L. (1999). Adverse psychological effects of ECT. *Journal of Mental Health (UK), 8*(1), 69–85.

Jones, P. B., Rantakallio, P., Hartikainen, A., Isohanni, M., & Sipila, P. (1998). Schizophrenia as a long-term outcome of pregnancy, delivery, and perinatal complications: A 28-year follow-up of the 1966 North Finland General Population Birth Cohort. *American Journal of Psychiatry, 155,* 355–364.

Jones, T., & Roediger, H. L. (1995). The experiential basis of serial position effects. *European Journal of Cognitive Psychology, 7,* 65–80.

Joseph, R. (2000). The evolution of sex differences in language, sexuality, and visual-spatial skills. *Archives of Sexual Behavior, 29*(1), 35–66.

Jouvet, M. (1999). Sleep and Serotonin: An unfinished story. *Neuropsychopharmacology, 21*(Suppl, 2), 24S–27S.

Joyce, C. A., Paller, K. A., McIsaac, H. K., & Kutas, M. (1998). Memory changes with normal aging: Behavioral and electrophysiological measures. *Psychophysiology, 35,* 669–678.

Julien, R. M. (2000). *A primer of drug action: A concise, nontechnical guide to the actions, uses, and side effects of psychoactive drugs.* New York: Freeman.

Jung, C. (1969). The concept of the collective unconscious. In *Collected works* (Vol. 9, Part 1). Princeton, NJ: Princeton University Press. (Original work published 1936).

Jung, C. G. (1946). *Psychological types.* New York: Harcourt Brace.

Jung, C. G. (1959). The archetypes and the collective unconscious. In H. Read, M. Fordham, & G. Adler (Eds.), *The collected works of C. G. Jung,* Vol. 9. New York: Pantheon.

Kagan, J. (1998). Biology and the child. In W. Damon & R. M. Lerner (Eds.), *Handbook of child psychology* (Vol. 1). New York: John Wiley & Sons.

Kahne, J. (1999). Personalized philanthropy: Can it support youth and build civic commitments? *Youth and Society, 30,* 367–387.

Kalat, J. W. (1985). Taste-aversion learning in ecological perspective. In T. D. Johnston & A. T. Pietrewicz (Eds.), *Issues in the ecological study of learning.* Hillsdale, NJ: Erlbaum.

Kamii, C., & Housman, L. B. (1999). *Young children reinvent arithmetic: Implications of Piaget's theory.* New York: Teachers College Press.

Kandel, E. R., & Schwartz, J. H. (1982). Molecular biology of learning: Modification of transmitter release. *Science, 218,* 433–442.

Kandel, E. R., & Schwartz, J. H. (1982). Molecular biology of learning: Modulation of transmitter release. *Science, 218,* 433–442.

Kandel, E., & Schwartz, J. H. (1982). Molecular biology of learning: Modulation or transmitter release. *Science, 218,* 433–442.

Kandel, E., Abel, T. (1995). Neuropeptides, adenylyl cyclase, and memory storage. *Science, 268,* 825–826.

Kanner, A. D., Coyne, J. C., Schaefer, C., & Lazarus, R. S. (1981). Comparison of two modes of stress management: Daily hassles and uplifts versus major life events. *Journal of Behavioral Medicine, 4,* 1–39.

Karni, A., Tanne, D., Rubenstein, B. S., Askenasy, J. J. M., & Sagi, D. (1994, July 29). Dependence on REM sleep of overnight improvement in perceptual skill. *Science, 265,* 679–682.

Kasser, T., & Sharma, Y. S. (1999). Reproductive freedom, educational equality, and females' preference for resource-acquisition characteristics in mates. *Psychological Science, 10*(4), 374–377.

Kastenbaum, R. (1999). Dying and bereavement. In J. C. Cavanaugh & S. K. Whitbourne (Eds.), *Gerontology: An interdisciplinary perspective.* New York: Oxford University Press.

Katula, J. A., Blissmer, B. J., McAuley, E. (1999). Exercise and self-efficacy effects on anxiety reduction in healthy, older adults. *Journal of Behavioral Medicine, 22*(3), 233–247.

Katz, M., Marsella, A., Dube, K., Olatawura, M., et al. (1988). On the expression of psychosis in different cultures: Schizophrenia in an Indian and in a Nigerian community. *Culture, Medicine, and Psychiatry, 12,* 331–355.

Kaukiainen, A., Bjoerkqvist, K., Lagerspetz, K., Oesterman, K., Salmivalli, C. et al. (1999). The relationship between social intelligence, empathy, and three types of aggression. *Aggressive Behavior, 25,* 81–89.

Kavanau, J. L. (2000). Sleep, memory maintenance, and mental disorders. *Journal of Neuropsychiatry & Clinical Neurosciences, 12*(2), 199–208.

Kawakami, K., Dovidio, J. F., Moll, J., Hermsen, S., & Russin, A. (2000). Just say no (to stereotyping): Effects of training in the negation of stereotypic associations on stereotype activation. *Journal of Personality & Social Psychology, 78*(5), 871–888.

Kazdin, A. E. (1994). Methodology, design, and evaluation in psychotherapy research. In A. E. Bergin & S. L. Garfield (Eds.), *Handbook of psychotherapy and behavior change* (4th ed.). New York: Wiley.

Keane, T. M., Taylor, K. L., & Penk, W. E. (1997). Differentiating posttraumatic stress disorder (PTSD) from major depression (MDD) and generalized anxiety disorder (GAD). *Journal of Anxiety Disorders, 11,* 317–328.

Keating, C. F., Mazur, A., Segall, M. H., Cysneiros, P. G., DiVale, W. T., Kilbride, J. E., Komin, S., Leahy, P., Thurman, B., & Wirsing, R. (1981). Culture and the perception of social dominance from facial expression. *Journal of Personality and Social Psychology, 40,* 601–614.

Keating, C. R. (1994). World without words: Messages from face and body. In W. J. Lonner & R. Malpass (Eds.), *Psychology and culture* (pp. 175–182). Boston: Allyn & Bacon.

Keats, D. M. (1982). Cultural bases of concepts of intelligence: A Chinese versus Australian comparison. In P. Sukontasarp, N. Yongsiri, P. Intasuwan, N. Jotiban, & C. Suvannathat (Eds.), *Proceedings of the Second Asian Workshop on Child and Adolescent Development* (pp. 67–75). Bangkok: Burapasilpa Press.

Keller, H. (1962). Quoted in R. Harrity & R. G. Martin, *The three lives of Helen Keller* (p. 23). Garden City, NY: Doubleday.

Keller, H., & Greenfield, P. M. (2000). History and future of development in cross-cultural psychology. *Journal of Cross-Cultural Psychology, 31*(1), 52–62.

Kellogg, W. N., & Kellogg, L. A. (1933). *The ape and the child.* New York: McGraw-Hill.

Kelly, I. W. (1998). Why astrology doesn't work. *Psychological Reports, 82,* 527–546.

Kelly, I. W. (1999, November/December). Debunking the debunkers: A response to an astrologer's debunking of skeptics. Skeptical Inquirer, 37–43.

Keltner, D., & Bonanno, G. A. (1997). A study of laughter and dissociation: The distinct correlates of laughter and smiling during bereavement. *Journal of Personality and Social Psychology, 73,* 687–702.

Keltner, D., Kring, A. M., & Bonanno, G. A. (1999). Fleeting signs of the course of life: Facial expression and personal adjustment. *Current Directions in Psychological Science, 8*(1), 18–22.

Kempermann, G., & Gage, F. H. (1999, May). New nerve cells for the adult brain. *Scientific American,* pp. 48–53.

Kendler, K. S. (1996). Parenting: A genetic-epidemiologic perspective. *The American Journal of Psychiatry, 153,* 11–20.

Kendler, K. S., Gallagher, T. J., Abelson, J. M., & Kessler, R. C. (1996). Lifetime prevalence, demographic risk factors, and diagnostic validity of nonaffective psychosis as assessed in a U. S. community sample. *Archives of General Psychiatry, 53,* 1022–1031.

Kendler, K. S., Gardner, C. O., & Prescott, C. A. (1997). Religion, psychopathology, and substance use and abuse: A multimeasure, genetic-epidemiologic study. *American Journal of Psychiatry, 154,* 322–329.

Kendler, K. S., Karkowski, L. M., & Prescott, C. A. (1999). Fears and phobias: Reliability and heritability. *Psychological Medicine, 29,* 539–553.

Kendler, K. S., Neale, M., Kessler, R. C., Heath, A., & Eaves, L. (1992). The genetic epidemiology of phobias in women: The interrelationship of agoraphobia, social phobia, situational phobia, and simple phobia. *Archives of General Psychiatry, 49,* 273–281.

Kenealy, P. M. (1997). Mood-state-dependent retrieval: The effects of induced mood on memory reconsidered. *Quarterly Journal of Experimental Psychology: Human Experimental Psychology, 50A,* 290–317.

Kerfoot, P., Sakoulas, G., & Hyman, S. E. (1996). Cocaine. In L. S. Friedman, N. F. Fleming, D. H. Roberts, & S. E. Hyman (Eds.), *Source book of substance abuse and addiction.* Baltimore: Williams & Wilkins.

Kessler, R. C., Zhao, S., Katz, S. J., Kouzis, A. C., Frank, R. G., Edlund, M., & Leaf, P. (1999). Past year use of outpatient services for psychiatric problems in the National Comorbidity Survey. *American Journal of Psychiatry, 156,* 115–123.

Kiecolt-Glaser, J. K., & Glaser, R. (2001). Stress and immunity: Age enhances the risk. *Current Directions in Psychological Science, 10*(1), 18–21.

Kihlstrom, J. F. (1997). Memory, abuse, and science. *American Psychologist, 52,* 994–995.

Kikusui, T., Aoyagi, A., & Kaneko, T. (2000). Spatial working memory is independent of hippocampal CA1 long-term potentiation in rats. *Behavioral Neuroscience, 114,* 700–706.

Killen, J. D., Fortmann, S. P., Schatzberg, A. F., Hayward, C. S., Sussman, L.,Rothman, M., Strausberg, L. & Varady, A. Nicotine patch and paroxetine for smoking cessation. (2000). *Journal of Consulting & Clinical Psychology, 68*(5), 883–889.

Killen, M., & Hart, D. (1999). *Morality in everyday life: Developmental perspectives.* New York: Cambridge University Press.

Kilpatrick, D. G., Best, C. L., Vernonen, L. J., Amick, A. E., Villeponteaux, L. A., Ruff, G. A. (1985). Mental health correlates of criminal victimization: A random community survey. *Journal of Consulting and Clinical Psychology, 53,* 866–873.

Kim, K. H. S., Relkin, N. R., Lee, K-M., & Hirsch, J. (1997). Distinct cortical areas associated with native and second languages. *Nature, 388,* 171–174.

Kimmel, M. S. (2000). *The gendered society.* London: Oxford University Press.

King, N. J., Clowes-Hollins, V., & Ollendick, T. H. (1997). The etiology of childhood dog phobia. *Behaviour Research and Therapy, 35,* 77.

Kingree, J. B., Braithwaite, R., & Woodring, T. (2000). Unprotected sex as a function of alcohol and marijuana use among adolescent detainees. *Journal of Adolescent Health, 27*(3), 179–185.

Kinney, H. C., Korein, J., Panigrahy, A., Dikkes, P., & Goode, R. (1994). Neuropatho-logical findings in the brain of Karen Ann Quinlan: The role of the thalamus in the persistent vegetative state. *New England Journal of Medicine, 330,* 1469–1475.

Kinsbourne, M. (1972). Eye and head turning indicates cerebral lateralization. *Science, 176,* 539–541.

Kinsey, A. C., Pomeroy, W. B., & Martin, C. E. (1948). *Sexual behavior in the human male.* Philadelphia: Saunders.

Kinsey, A. C., Pomeroy, W. B., Martin, C. E., & Gebhard, P. H. (1953). *Sexual behavior in the human female.* Philadelphia: Saunders.

Kiraly, Z. (2000). The relationship between emotional self-disclosure of male and female adolescents' friendship. (gender differences, ninth-grade). *Dissertation Abstracts International: Section B: The Sciences & Engineering, 60*(7–B), 3619.

Kirchner, J. E., Owen, R. R., Nordquist, C., & Fischer, E. P. (1998). Diagnosis and management of substance use disorders among inpatients with schizophrenia. *Psychiatric Services, 49,* 82–85.

Kirk, K. M., Bailey, J. M., Dunne, M. P., & Martin, N. G. (2000). Measurement models for sexual orientation in a community twin sample. *Behavior Genetics, 30*(4), 345–356.

Kirsch, I., & Lynn, S. J. (1995). The altered state of hypnosis: Changes in the theoretical landscape. *American Psychologist, 50,* 846–858.

Kitamura, T., Nakamura, M., Miura, I., & Fujinawa, A. (1997). Symptoms of neuroses: Profile patterns and factor structure of clinic attenders with non-psychotic functional psychiatric disorders. *Psychopathology, 30,* 191–199.

Kitayama, S. (2000). Collective construction of the self and social relationships: A rejoinder and some extensions. *Child Development, 71*(5), 1143–1146.

Kitayama, S., Markus, H. R., & Kurokawa, M. (2000). Culture, emotion, and well-being: Good feelings in Japan and the United States. *Cognition & Emotion, 14*(1), 93–124.

Klass, D. (2000). Response to Colin Murray Parkes' comments on my article "Developing a cross-cultural model of grief." *Omega: Journal of Death & Dying, 41*(4), 327–330.

Klatzky, R. L. (1984). *Memory and awareness.* New York: Freeman.

Klein, E., Kreinin, I., Chistyakov, A., Koren, D., Mecz, L. Marmur, S., Sen-Shachar, D., & Feinsod, M. (1999). Therapeutic efficacy of right prefrontal slow repetitive transcranial magnetic stimulation in major depression. *Archives of General Psychiatry, 56*(4), 315–320.

Klein, L. L. (2000). *The support group sourcebook: What they are, how you can find one, and how they can help you.* New York: Wiley.

Kleinknecht, R. A., Dinnel, D., & Kleinknecht, E. E. (1997). Cultural factors in social anxiety: A comparison of social phobia symptoms and taijin kyofusho. *Journal of Anxiety Disorders, 11,* 157–177.

Kleinman, A., & Cohen, A. (1997, March). Psychiatry's global challenge. *Scientific American,* 86–89.

Klimes-Dougan, B., & Kistner, J. (1990). Physically abused preschoolers' responses to peers' distress. *Developmental Psychology, 26,* 599–602.

Klinger, E. (1987, October). The power of daydreams. *Psychology Today,* pp. 37–44.

Klohnen, E. C., & Bera, S. (1998). Behavioral and experiential patterns of avoidantly and securely attached women across adulthood: A 31-year longitudinal perspective. *Journal of Personality and Social Psychology, 74*(1), 211–223.

Knight, B. G., Silverstein, M., McCallum, t. J., & Fox, L. S. (2000). A Socioculturals. Stress and coping model for mental health outcomes among African American caregivers in Southern California. *Journals of Gerontology: Series B: Psychological Sciences & Social Sciences, 55B,* 142–150.

Knoll, L., & Abrams, J. (1998). Evaluation of penile ultrasonic velocitometry versus penile duplex ultrasonography to assess penile arte-rial hemodynamics. *Urology, 51,* 89–93.

Kobak, R. R., & Hazan, C. (1991). Attachment in marriage: Effects of security and accuracy of working models. *Journal of Personality & Social Psychology, 60*(6), 861–869.

Kobasa, S. (1979). Stressful life events, personality, and health: An inquiry into hardiness. *Journal of Personality and Social Psychology, 37,* 1–11.

Kobasa, S. (1990). Stress-resistant personality. In R. E. Ornstein, C. Swencionis, et al. (Eds.), *The healing brain: A scientific reader.* New York: Guilford Press.

Kobasa, S., Maddi, S., & Kahn, S. (1982). Hardiness and health: A prospective study. *Journal of Personality and Social Psychology, 42,* 168–177.

Kobun, K., & Reyes, O. (2000). A descriptive study of urban Mexican American adolescents' perceived stress and coping. *Hispanic Journal of Behavioral Sciences, 22,* 163–178.

Koechlin, E., Basso, G., Pietrini, P., Panzer, S., & Grafman, J. (1999). The roll of the anterior prefrontal cortex in human cognition. *Nature, 399,* 148–151.

Koenig, S. (2000). The inmates and the asylum: How Hollywood depicts mental hospitals.

Kohlberg, L. (1964). Development of moral character and moral behavior. In L. W. Hoffman & M. L. Hoffman (Eds.), *Review of child development research* (Vol. 1). New York: Sage.

Kohlberg, L. (1966). A cognitive-developmental analysis of children's sex-role concepts and attitudes. In E. E. Maccoby (Ed.), *The development of sex differences.* Stanford, CA: Stanford University Press.

Kohlberg, L. (1969). Stage and sequence: The cognitive-developmental approach to socialization. In D. A. Goslin (Ed.), *Handbook of socialization theory and research.* Chicago: Rand McNally.

Kohlberg, L. (1981). *The meaning and measurement of moral development.* Worcester, MA: Clark University Press.

Kohlberg, L. (1984). *The psychology of moral development: Essays on moral development* (Vol. II). San Francisco: Harper & Row.

Kohler, W. (1925). *The mentality of apes.* New York: Harcourt, Brace.

Kohn, A. (2000). *Punished by rewards: The trouble with gold stars, incentive plans, A's, and other bribes.* New York: Houghton Mifflin.

Kole-Snijders, A. M., Vlaeyen, J. W., Goossens, M. E., Rutten-van Moelken, M. P., & Breukelen, G., & von Eek, H. (1999). Chronic low-back pain: What does cognitive coping skills training add to operant behavioral treatment? Results of a randomized clinical trial. *Journal of Consulting & Clinical Psychology, 67,* 931–944.

Komiya, N., Good, G. E., & Sherrod, N. B. (2000). Emotional openness as a predictor of college students' attitudes toward seeking psychological help. *Journal of Counseling Psychology, 47*(1), 138–143.

Koob, G. F., & Nestler, E. J. (1997). Neuro-biology of drug addiction. *Journal of Neuropsychiatry and Clinical Neuroscience, 9*(3), 482–497.

Koppel, J. (2000). *Good/Grief.* New York: Harperperennial.

Kopta, S. M., Lueger, R. J., Saunders, S. M., & Howard, K. I. (1999). Individual psychotherapy outcome and process research: Challenges leading to a greater turmoil or a positive transition? *Annual Review of Psychology, 50,* 441–469.

Kosslyn, S. M. (1987). Seeing and imagining in the cerebral hemispheres: A computational approach. *Psychological Review, 94,* 148–175.

Kotkin, M., Daviet, C., & Gurin, J. (1996). The Consumer Reports mental health survey. *American Psychologist, 51*(10), 1080–1082.

Kottler, J. A., & Brown, R. W. (1999). *Introduction to therapeutic counseling.* Monterey, CA: Brooks/Cole.

Koulack, D. (1997). Recognition memory, circadian rhythms, and sleep. *Perceptual & Motor Skills, 85,* 99–104.

Kouri, E. M., Lukas, S. E., Pope, H. G. Jr., & Olivia, P. S. (1998). ?Increased aggressive responding in male volunteers following administration of gradually increased doses of testosterone cypionate?: Erratum. *Drug and Alcohol Dependence, 50,* 255.

Kramer, A. F., Hahn, S., Irwin, D. E., & Theeuwes, J. (2000). Age differences in the control of looking behavior. *Psychological Science, 11*(3), 210–217.

Krantz, D. S., Gruenberg, N. E., & Baum, A. (1985). Health psychology. *Annual Review of Psychology, 36,* 349–383.

Krishna, G. (1999). *The dawn of a new science.* Los Angeles: Institute for Consciousness Research.

Kropp, P., et al. (1997). Behavioral treatment in migraine. *Functional Neurology, 12*(1), 17–24.

Krug, E. G., Kresnow, M., Peddicord, J., Dahlberg, L. Powell, K. E., Crosby, A. E., & Annest, J. L. (1998). Suicide after natural disasters. *New England Journal of Medicine, 338,* 373–378.

Krupa, D. J., & Thompson, R. F. (1997). Reversible inactivation of the cerebellar interpositus nucleus completely prevents acquisition of the classically conditioned eye-blink response. *Learning and Memory, 3*(6), 545–556.

Krupa, D. J., Thompson, J. K., Thompson, R. F. (1993). Localization of a memory trace in the mammalian brain. *Science, 260,* 989–991.

Kryger, M. H., Roth, T., & Dement, W. C. (2000). *Principles and practice of sleep medicine* (3rd ed.). New York: W. B. Saunders.

Kubler-Ross, E. (1983). *On children and death.* New York: Macmillan.

Kubler-Ross, E. (1997). *Death: The final stage of growth.* New York: Simon & Schuster.

Kubler-Ross, E. (1999). *On death and dying.* New York: Simon & Schuster.

Kuebli, J. (1999). Young children's understanding of everyday emotions. In L. E. Berk, *Landscapes of development* (pp. 123–136). Belmont, CA: Wadsworth.

Kuffer, D. J., & Reynolds, C. R. (1997). Management of insomnia. *New England Journal of Medicine, 336,* 341–346.

Kushner, S. A., Dewey, S. L., & Kornetsky, C. (1999). The irreversible gamma-aminobutyric acid (GABA) transminase inhibitor gamma-vinyl-GABA blocks cocaine self-administration in rats. *Journal of Pharmacology & Experimental Therapeutics, 290,* 797–802.

Lace, W. W. (1999). *Tiger Woods: Star golfer.* New York: Enslow.

Laird, J. D., & Bressler, C. (1992). The process of emotional experience: A self-perception theory. In M. S. Clark (Ed.), *Review of personality and social psychology* (pp. 213–234). Newbury Park, CA: Sage.

Lakein, A. (1998). *Give me a moment and I'll change your life: Tools for moment management.* New York: Andrews McMeel Publishing.

Lal, S. K. L., et al. (1998). Effect of feedback signal and psychological characteristics on blood pressure self-manipulation capability. *Psychophysiology, 35(4),* 405–412.

Lamb, H. R., & Weinberger, L. E. (2000). Commentary: A major advance in the laws pertaining to community treatment for persons with severe mental illness. *Journal of the American Academy of Psychiatry & the Law, 28(2),* 149–153.

Lamb, M. E. (1996). *The role of the father in child development* (3rd ed.). New York: Wiley.

Lamberg, L. (1998). Gay is okay with APA-Forum honors landmark 1973 events. *Journal of the American Medical Association, 280,* 497–499.

Lamberts, S. W. J., van den Beld, A. W., & van der Lely, A. (1997). The endocrinology of aging. *Science, 278,* 419–424.

Landen, M., Walinder, J., & Lundstrom, B. (1998). Clinical characteristics of a total cohort of female and male applicants for sex reassignment: A descriptive study. *Acta Psychiatrica Scandinavia, 97,* 189–194.

Landry, D. W. (1997). Immunotherapy for cocaine addiction. *Scientific American, 276,* 42–45.

Lane, R. D., Reiman, E. M., Ahern, G. L., & Schwartz, G. E. (1997). Neuroanatomical correlates of happiness, sadness, and disgust. *American Journal of Psychiatry, 154,* 926–933.

Langella, M., Colarieti, L., Ambrosini, M. V., & Giuditta, A. (1992). The sequential hypothesis of sleep function: A correlative analysis of sleep variables in learning and nonlearning rats. *Physiology and Behavior, 51(2),* 227–238.

Langer, T. (1962). A twenty-two item screening score of psychiatric symptoms indicating impairment. *Journal of Health and Human Behavior, 3,* 269–276.

Langlois, J. H., Kalakanis, L., Rubenstein, A. J., Larson, A., Hallam, M., & Smoot, M. (2000). Maxims or myths of beauty? A meta-analytic and theoretical review. *Psychological Bulletin, 126(3),* 390–423.

Lannon, C. M., Bailey, A. G. D., Fleischman, A. R., Kaplan, G. W., Shoemaker, C. T., Swanson, G. T., & Couston, A. (1999). Circumcision policy statement. *Pediatrics, 103,* 686–693.

Lanyon, R. I., & Goodstein, L. D. (1997). *Personality assessment.* New York: Wiley.

Lapsley, D. K. (1996). *Moral psychology.* Boulder, CO: Westview.

Laruelle, M., Abi-Dargham, A., Gil, R., Kegeles, L., & Inis, R. (1999). Increased dopamine transmission in schizophrenia: Relationship to illness phases. *Biological Psychiatry, 46 (1),* 56–72.

Larzelere, R. E., & Johnson, B. (1999). Evaluations of the effects of Sweden's spanking ban on physical child abuse rates: A literature review. *Psychological Reports, 85(2),* 381–392.

Lashley, K. (1929). *Brain mechanisms and intelligence.* Chicago: University of Chicago Press.

Lashley, K. (1950). In search of the engram. *Symposia of the Society of Experimental Biology, 4,* 454–482.

Latane, B., & Darley, J. M. (1970). *The unresponsive bystander: Why doesn't he help?* New York: Appleton-Century-Crofts.

Laumann, E. O., Paik, A., & Rosen, R. C. (1999). Sexual dysfunction in the United States. *Journal of the American Medical Association, 281,* 537–544.

Laumann, E., Gagnon, J., Michael, R., & Michaels, S. (1994). *The social organization of sexuality: Sexual practices in the United States.* Chicago: University of Chicago Press.

Laurelle, M., Abi-dargham, A., Gil, R., Kegeles, L., & Innis, R. (1999). Increased dopamine transmission in schizophrenia: Relationship to illness phases. *Biological Psychiatry, 46,* 56–72.

Lazarus, A. A. (1971). *Behavior therapy and beyond.* New York: McGraw-Hill.

Lazarus, R. S. (1999). Stress and emotion: A new synthesis. New York: Springer.

Lazarus, R. S., & Folkman, S. (1984). *Stress appraisal and coping.* New York: Springer.

Lazev, A. B., Herzog, T. A., & Brandon, T. H. (1999). Classical conditioning of environmental cues to cigarette smoking. *Experimental & Clinical Psychopharmacology, 7(1),* 56–63.

Leahy, T. H., & Harris, R. J. (1997). *Learning and cognition* (4th ed.). Englewood Cliffs, NJ: Prentice Hall.

Leaper, C. (2000). Gender, affiliation, assertion, and the interactive context of parent–child play. *Developmental Psychology, 36(3),* 381–393.

Leaper, C., Anderson, K., & Sanders, P. (1998). Moderators of gender effects on parents' talk to their children: A meta-analysis. *Developmental Psychology, 34,* 3–27.

Lebow, J. L., & Gurman, A. S. (1995). Research assessing couple and family therapy. In J. T. Spence, J. M. Darley, & D. F. Foss (Eds.), *Annual Review of Psychology, 46* (pp. 27–57). Palo Alto, CA: Annual Review.

Leclerk, G., Lefrancois, R., Dube, M., Hebert, R., & Gaulin, P. (1998). The self-actualization concept: A content validation. *Journal of Social Behavior & Personality, 11,* 69–84.

LeDoux, J. (1996). *The emotional brain: The mysterious underpinnings of emotional life.* New York: Simon & Schuster.

LeDoux, J. E. (1992). Systems and synapses of emotional memory. In L. R. Squire, N. M. Weinberger, G. Lynch, & J. L. McGuagh (Eds.), *Memory: Organization and locus of change.* New York: Oxford University Press.

LeDoux, J. E. (1996). Sensory systems and emotion: A model of affective processing. *Integrative Psychiatry, 4,* 237–243.

Lee, D. (1950). The conception of the self among the Wintu Indians. In D. Lee (Ed.), *Freedom and culture.* Englewood Cliffs, NJ: Prentice-Hall.

Lee, L., et al. (1999). Are reporting errors due to encoding limitations or retrieval failure? Surveys of child vaccination as a case study. *Applied Cognitive Psychology, 13,* 43–63.

Leeper, R. W. (1935). A study of a neglected portion of the field of learning: The development of sensory organization. *Journal of Genetic Psychology, 46,* 41–75.

Lefebvre, K. A. (1997). Performing a sexual evaluation on the person with disability or illness. In M. Sipski & C. Alexander (Eds.), *Sexual function in people with disability and chronic illness.* Gaithersburg, MD: Aspen Publishers.

Lefley, H. P. (2000). Cultural perspectives on families, mental illness, and the law. *International Journal of Law and Psychiatry, 23,* 229–243.

Lehrman, S. (1995). U. S. stalls over tests of marijuana to treat AIDS patients. *Nature, 374,* 7–8.

Leibowitz, S. F., & Alexandr, J. T. (1998). Hypothalamic serotonin in control of eating behavior, meal size, and body weight. *Biological Psychiatry, 44,* 851–864.

Leichtman, M. D., & Ceci, S. J. (1995). The effects of stereotypes and suggestions on preschoolers' reports. *Developmental Psychology, 31,* 568–578.

Leitenberg, H., & Henning, K. (1995). Sexual fantasy. *Psychological Bulletin, 117,* 469–496.

Leland, J. (1996, August 26). The fear of heroin is shooting up. *Newsweek,* pp. 55–56.

LeMarquand, D. G., Pihl, R. O., Young, S. N., Tremblay, R. E., Seguin, J. R., Palmour, R. M., & Benkelfat, C. (1998). Tryptophan depletion, executive functions, and disinhibition in aggressive, adolescent males. *Neuropsychopharmacology, 19*(4), 333–341.

Lemery, K. S., Goldsmith, H. H., Klinnert, M. D., & Mrazek, D. A. (1999). Developmental models of infant and childhood temperament. *Developmental Psychology, 35,* 189–204.

Lemonick, M. D. (1998, April 13). Emily's little experiment. *Time,* p. 67.

Lemonick, M. D. (2000, July 3). The genome is mapped. Now what? *Time,* pp. 24–29.

Lengua, L. J., Wolchik, S. A., Sandler, I. N., & West, S. G. (2000). The additive and interactive effects of parenting and temperament in predicting problems of children of divorce. *Journal of Clinical Child Psychology, 29*(2), 232–244.

Lenhart, R. S., & Ashby, J. S. (1996). Cog-nitive coping strategies and coping modes in relation to chronic pain disability. *Journal of Applied Rehabilitation Counseling, 27,* 15–18.

Lenne, M. G., Triggs, T. J., Redman, J. R. (1998). Interactive effects of sleep deprivation, time of day, and driving experience on a driving task. *Sleep, 21*(1), 38–44.

Leo, S. (2000, December 6). Verbal judo for beginners. *Time,* p. 6.

Leonard, B. E. (1996). Serotonin receptors and their function in sleep, anxiety disorders and depression. *Psychotherapy & Psychosomatics, 65,* 66–75.

Leonard, B. E. (2000). Stress, depression, and the immune system. *Stress Medicine, 16*(3), 133–137.

Lepore, S. J., Ragan, J. D., & Jones, S. (2000). Talking facilitates cognitive-emotional processes of adaptation to an acute stressor. *Journal of Personality and Social Psychology, 78*(3), 499–508.

Lepper, M. R., Greene, D., & Nisbett, R. E. (1973). Undermining children's intrinsic interest with extrinsic rewards: A test of the overjustification hypothesis. *Journal of Personality and Social Psychology, 28,* 129–137.

Lerner, R. M., & Galambos, N. L. (1998). Adolescent development: Challenges and opportunities for research, programs, and policies. *Annual Review of Psychology, 49,* 413–446.

Leserman, J., Petitto, J. M., Golden, R. N., Gaynes, B. N., Gu, H., Perkins, D. O., Silva, S. G., Folds, J. D., & Evans, D. L. (2000). Impact of stressful life events, depression, social support, coping, and cortisol on progression to AIDS. *American Journal of Psychiatry, 157*(8), 1221–1228.

Leslie, M. (2000). The Vexing Legacy of Lewis Terman. Stanford Magazine, Available: http://www.stanfordalumni.org/jg/mig/news_magazine/magazine/julaug00/index.html

Lettvin, J. Y., Maturana, H. R., McCulloch, W. S., & Pitts, W. H. (1959). What the frog's eye tells the frog's brain. *Proceedings of the Institute of Radio Engineers, 47,* 1940–1951.

LeVay, S. (1991). A difference in hypothalimic structure between heterosexual and homosexual men. *Science, 253,* 1034–1038.

LeVay, S. (1996). *Queer science: The use and abuse of research into homosexuality.* Cambridge, MA: MIT Press.

Levenson, R. W. (1992). Autonomic nervous system differences among emotions. *Psychological Science, 3,* 23–27.

Leveroni, C. L., & Berenbaum, S. A. (1998). Early androgen effects on interest in infants: Evidence from children with congenital adrenal hyperplasia. *Developmental Neuropsychology, 14,* 321–340.

Levin, E. D., Torry, D., Christopher, N. C., Yu, X., Einstein, G, & Schartz-Bloom, R. D. (1997). Is binding to nicotinic acetylcholine and dopamine receptors related to working memory in rats? *Brain Research Bulletin, 43,* 295–304.

Levine, J. R. (2001). *Why do fools fall in love: Experiencing the magic, mystery, and meaning of succeful relationships.* New York: Jossey-Bass.

Levinson, D. J. (1977). The mid-life transition, *Psychiatry, 40,* 99–112.

Levinson, D. J. (1996). *The seasons of a woman's life.* New York: Knopf.

Lewis, D. O., Yeager, C. A., Swica, Y., Pincus, J. H., & Lewis, M. (1997). Objective documentation of child abuse and dissociation in 12 murderers with dissociative identity disorder. *American Journal of Psychiatry, 154,* 1703–1710.

Lewis, D. O., Yeager, C. A., Swica, Y., Pincus, J. H., & Lewis, M. (1997). Objective documentation of child abuse and dissociation in 12 murderers with dissociative identity disorder. *American Journal of Psychiatry, 154,* 1703–1710.

Lewis, S. (1963). *Dear Shari.* New York: Stein & Day.

Liben, L. S., & Signorella, M. L. (1993). Gender-schematic processing in children: The role of initial interpretations of stimuli. *Developmental Psychology, 29,* 141–149.

Libkuman, T. M., Nichols-whitehead, P., Griffith, J., & Thomas, R. (1999). Source of arousal and memory for detail. *Memory & Cognition, 27,* 166–190.

Liggett, D. R. (2000). Enhancing imagery through hypnosis: A performance aid for athletes. *American Journal of Clinical Hypnosis, 43*(2), 149–157.

Lilienfeld, L. R., Kaye, W. H., Greeno, C. G., Merikangas, K. R., Plotnicov, K., et al. (1999). Psychiatric disorders in women with bulimia nervosa and their first-degree relatives: Effects of comorbid substance dependence. *International Journal of Eating Disorders, 22,* 253–264.

Lilienfeld. S. O. (1999). Projective measures of personality and psychopathology: How well do they work? *Skeptical Inquirer, 23,* 32–39.

Lilienfeld, S. O., Wood, J. M., & Howard, N. G. (2000). The scientific status of projective techniques. *Psychological Science in the Public Interest, 1*(2), 27–66.

Lillard, A. (1998). Ethnopsychologies: Cultural variations in theories of mind. *Psychological Bulletin, 123,* 3–32.

Lin, C. (1998). Comparison of the effects of perceived self-efficacy on coping with chronic cancer pain and coping with chronic low back pain. *Clinical Journal of Pain, 14,* 303–310.

Lin, J. S., Hou, Y., Sakai, K., & Jouvet, M. (1996). Histaminergic descending inputs to the mesopontine tegmentum and their role in the control of cortical activation and wakefulness in the cat. *Journal of Neuroscience, 16,* 1523–1537.

Lindsay, D. S. (1998). Depolarizing views on recovered memory experiences. In S. J. Lynn & K. M. McConkey (Eds.), *Truth in memory.* New York: Guilford Press.

Links, P. S., Heslegrave, R., & van Reekum, R. (1998). Prospective follow-up of borderline personality disorder: Prognosis, prediction outcome, and Axis II comorbidity. *Canadian Journal of Psychiatry, 43,* 265–270.

Linszen, D. H., et al. (1997). Patient attributes and expressed emotion as risk factors for psychotic relapse. *Schizophrenia Bulletin, 23,* 119–130.

Liotti, M., & Mayberg, H. S. (2001). The role of functional neuroimaging in the neuropsychology of depression. *Journal of Clinical & Experimental Neuropsychology, 23*(1), 121–136.

Liu, H., Mantyh, P., & Basbaum, A. I. (1997). NMDA-receptor regulation of substance P release from promary afferent nociceptors. *Nature, 386,* 721–724.

Liu, J. H., & Latane, B. (1998). Extremitiza-tion of attitudes: Does thought-and discussion-induced polarization cumulate? *Basic and Applied Social Psychology, 20,* 103–110.

Livingston, J. A. (1999). Something old and something new: Love, creativity, and the enduring relationship. *Bulletin of the Menninger Clinic, 63,* 40–52.

Loay, D., & Loay, M. D. (2000). *Sexually-Transmitted diseases.* Baltimore: Merit Publishing International.

Lobel, T. E. (1994). Sex typing and the social perception of gender stereotypic and nonstereotypic behavior: The uniqueness of feminine males. *Journal of Personality and Social Psychology, 66,* 379–385.

Lock, J., & Steiner, H. (1999). Gay, lesbian, and bisexual youth risks for emotional, physical, and social problems: Results from a community-based survey.

Journal of the American Academy of Child & Adolescent Psychiatry, 38(3), 297–304.

Loeber, R., & Stouthamer-Loeber, M. (1998). Development of juvenile aggression and violence: Some common misconceptions and controversies. *American Psychologist, 53,* 242–259.

Loehlin, J. C., McCrae, R. R., Costa, P. T., & John, O. (1998). Heritabilities of common and measure-specific components of the Big Five personality factors. *Journal of Research in Personality, 32,* 431–453.

Loftus, E. (1993). Psychologists in the eyewitness world. *American Psychologist, 48,* 550–552.

Loftus, E. E., & Ketcham, K. (1994). *The myth of repressed memories: False memories and allegations of sexual abuse.* New York: St. Martin's Press.

Loftus, E. F. (1982). Memory and its distortions. In A. G. Kraut (Ed.), *The G. Stanley Hall Lecture Series* (Vol. 2, pp. 123–154). Washington, DC: American Psychological Association.

Loftus, E. F. (1993). The reality of repressed memories. *American Psychologist, 48,* 518–537.

Loftus, E. F. (1997). Memory for a past that never was. *Current Directions in Psychological Science, 6*(3), 60–65.

Loftus, E. F. (2000). Remembering what never happened. In E. Tulving, et al. (Eds.), *Memory, consciousness, and the brain: The Tallinn Conference,* pp. 106–118. Philadelphia, PA: Psychology Press/Taylor & Francis.

Loftus, E. F., & Polage, D. C. (1999). Repressed memories: When are they real? When are they false? *Psychiatric Clinics of North America, 22,* 61–70.

Lohman, J., & Jarvis, P. A. (2000). Adolescent stressors, coping strategies, and psychological health studied in the family context. *Journal of Youth & Adolescence, 29,* 15–43.

Loo, R., & Thorpe, K. (1998). Attitudes toward women's roles in society. *Sex Roles, 39,* 903–912.

Lopez, F. G., Melendez, M. C., & Rice, K. G. (2000). Parental divorce, parent–child bonds, and adult attachment orientations among college students: A comparison of three racial/ethnic groups. *Journal of Counseling Psychology, 47*(2), 177–186.

Lopez, S. R., & Guarnaccia, P. J. J. (2000). Cultural psychopathology: Uncovering the social world of mental illness. *Annual Review of Psychology, 51,* 571–598.

Lorenz, K. (1937). The companion in the bird's world. *Auk, 54,* 245–273.

Lorenz, K. Z. (1981). *The foundations of ethology.* New York: Springer-Verlag.

Lott, D. A. (2000). *The new flirting game.* London: Sage.

Louie, T. A., Curren, M. T., & Harich, K. R. (2000). "I knew we would win": Hindsight bias for favorable and unfavorable team decision outcomes. *Journal of Applied Psychology, 85*(2), 264–272.

Low, B. S. (2000). *Why sex matters: A Darwininan look at human behavior.* Princeton, NJ: Princeton University Press.

Lu, L., Kao, S-F., Cooper, C. L., & Spector, P. E. (2000). Managerial stress, locus of control, and job strain in Taiwan and UK: A comparative study. *International Journal of Stress Management, 7*(3), 209–226.

Lu, Z. L., Williamson, S. J., & Kaufman, L. (1992). Behavioral lifetime of human auditory sensory memory predicted by physiological measures. *Science, 258,* 1668–1670.

Lubinski, D., & Benbow, C. P. (2000). States of excellence. *American Psychologist, 55*(1), 137–150.

Lubinski, D., & Dawis, R. V. (1992). Aptitudes, skills, and proficiencies. In M. D. Dunnette & L. M. Hough (Eds.), *The handbook of industrial/organizational psychology* (pp. 1–59). Palo Alto, CA: Consulting Psychologists Press.

Lucio-Gomez, E., Ampudia-Rueda, A., Duran-Patino, C., Gallegos-Mejia, L., & Leon-Guzman, I. (1999). La nueva version del Inventario Multifasico de la Personalidad de Minnesota para adolescentes Mexicanos. /The new version of the Minnesota Multiphasic Personality Inventory for Mexican adolescents. *Revista Mexicana de Psicologia, 16*(2), 217–226.

Luft, A., Skalej, M., Stefanou, A., Klose, U., & Voight, K. (1998). Comparing motion-and imagery-related activation in the human cerebellum: A functional MRI study. *Human Brain Mapping, 6*(2), 105–113.

Luker, K. (1996). *Dubious conceptions: The politics of teenage pregnancy.* Cambridge, MA: Harvard University Press.

Luria, A. R. (1976). *Cognitive development: Its cultural and social foundations.* Cambridge, MA: Harvard University Press.

Luthar, S. S. (1999). *Poverty and children's adjustment.* Thousand Oaks, CA: Sage.

Lykken, D. T. (1984). Polygraphic interrogation. *Nature*, 307, 681–684.

Lykken, D. T. (1988). The case against polygraph testing. In A. Gale (Ed.), *The polygraph test: Lies, truth, and science*. London: Sage.

Lykken, D. T. (1998). *A tremor in the blood: Uses and abuses of the lie detector*. New York: Plenum Press.

Lynch, E. D., Lee, M. K., Morrow, J. E., Welcsh, P. L., LeÛn, P. E., & King, M. (1997). Nonsyndromic deafness DFNA1 associated with mutation of a human homolog of the Drosophila gene diaphanous. *Science*, 278, 1315–1318.

Lynn, R. (1995). Cross-cultural differences in intelligence and personality. In D. H. Saklofske & M. Zeidner (Eds.), *International handbook of personality and intelligence*. New York: Plenum.

Lynn, S. J. (1997). Automaticity and hypnosis: A sociocognitive account. *International Journal of Clinical and Experimental Hypnosis*, 45, 239–250.

Lyons, M. J., et al. (1998). A registry-based twin study of depression in men. *Archives of General Psychiatry*, 55, 468–472.

Maas, J. B. (1999). *Power sleep*. New York: HarperPerennial.

Maccoby, E. E. (2000). Parenting and its effects on children: On reading and misreading behavior genetics. *Annual Review of Psychology*, 51, 1–27.

MacDonald, K. (1998). Evolution, culture, and the five-factor model. *Journal of Cross-Cultural Psychology*, 29(1), 119–149.

Mackay, D. G., Stewart, R., & Burke, D. M. (1998a). H. M. 's language production deficits: Implications fro relations between memory, semantic binding, and the hippocampal system. *Journal of Memory & Language*, 38, 28–69.

Mackay, D. G., Stewart, R., & Burke, D. M. (1998b). H. M. revisited: Relations between language comprehension, memory, and the hippocampal system. *Journal of Cognitive Neuroscience*, 10, 377–394.

Mackay, J. (2001). Global sex: Sexuality and sexual practices around the world. *Sexual & Relationship Therapy*, 16(1), 71–82.

Mackey, R. A., & O'Brien, B. A. (1998). Marital conflict management: Gender and ethnic differences. *Social Work*, 43(2), 128–141.

MacKinnon, D. F., Jamison, K. R., & DePaulo, J. R. (1997). Genetics of manic-depressive illness. *Annual Review of Neuroscience*, 10, 355–373.

MacMillan, H. L. (2000). Child maltreatment: What we know in the year 2000. *Canadian Journal of Psychiatry*, 45(8), 702–709.

Macmillan, M. (1997). *Freud evaluated*. Cambridge, MA: MIT Press.

Macmillan, M. B. (1986). A wonderful journey through skull and brains: The travels of Mr. Gage's tamping iron. *Brain and Cognition*, 5, 67–107.

Macmillan, M. B. (2000). *An odd kind of fame: Stories of Phineas Gage*. Cambridge, MA: MIT Press.

Maddock, R. J., & Buonocore, M. H. (1997). Activation of left posterior cingulate gyrus by the auditory presentation of threat-related words: An fMRI study. *Psychiatry Research: Neuroimaging*, 75, 1–14.

Maeda, H. (1977). Septum and aggression: A review. *Kyushu Neuropsychiatry*, 23(1), 7–16.

Maehr, M. L., & Urdan, T. C. (2000). *Advances in motivation and achievement: The role of context*. Greewich, CT: JAI Press.

Magid, K., & McKelvey, C. A. (1987). *High risk: Children without a conscience*. New York: Bantam.

Main, M., & George, C. (1985). Responses of abused and disadvantaged toddlers todistress in agemates: A study in the day care setting. *Developmental Psychology*, 21, 407–412.

Malnic, B., Hirono, J., & Buck, L. B. (1999). Combinatorial receptor codes for odors. *Cell*, 96, 713–715.

Manji, H. K., & Lenox, R. H. (1998). Lithium: A molecular transducer of mood-stabilization in the treatment of bipolar disorders. *Neuropsychopharmacology*, 19, 161–166.

Manji, H. K., Moore, G. J., & Chen, G. (2000). Clinical and preclinical evidence for the neurotrophic effects of mood stabilizers: Implications for the pathophysiology and treatment of manic-depressive illness. *Biological Psychiatry*, 48(8), 740–754.

Mann, A. (1998, April 6). Cross-gender sex pill. *Time*, p. 62.

Mann, J. J., Huang, Y., Underwood, M. D., Kassir, S. A., Oppenheim, S., Kelly, T. M., Dwork, A. J., & Arango, V. (2000). A serotonin transporter gene promoter polymorphism (5-HTTLPR) and prefrontal cortical binding in major depression and suicide. *Archives of General Psychiatry*, 57(8), 729–738.

Manoach, D. S., Gollub, R. L., Benson, E. S., ; Searl, M., Goff, D. C., Halpern, E., Saper, C., & Rauch, S. L. (2000). Schizophenia subjects show aberrant fMRI activation of dorsolateral prefrontal cortex and basal ganglia during working memory performance. *Biological Psychiatry*, 48, 99–109.

Manuck, S. B., Flory, J. D., McCaffery, J. M., Matthews, K. A., Mann, J. J., & Muldoon, M. F. (1998). Aggression, impulsivity, and central nervous system serotonergic responsivity in a nonpatient sample. *Neuropsychopharmacology*, 19(4), 287–299.

Maquet, P., et al. (1997). Functional neuroanatomy of human slow wave sleep. *Journal of Neuroscience*, 17, 2807–2812.

Marcus, D., Scharff, L., & Turk, D. C. (1995). Nonpharmacological management of headaches during pregnancy. *Psychosomatic Medicine*, 57, 527–535.

Maren, S. (1999). Long-term potentiation in the amygdala: A mechanism for emotional learning and memory. *Trends in Neurosciences*, 22, 561–567.

Margolis, S., & Swartz, K. L. (2001). *Depression and anxiety. Johns Hopkins White Papers*. Baltimore: Johns Hopkins Medical Institutions.

Markides, K. S. (1995). Aging and ethnicity. *The Gerontologist*, 35, 276–277.

Marks, D. F. (1990). Comprehensive commentary, insightful criticism. *Skeptical Inquirer*, 14, 413–418.

Markus, H. R., & Kitayama, S. (1998). The cultural psychology of personality. *Journal of Cross-Cultural Psychology*, 29, 63–87.

Marmot, M. G., & Wilkinson, R. G. (1999). *Social determinants of health*. Oxford: Oxford University Press.

Marshall, D. S. (1971). Sexual behavior in Mangaia. In D. S. Marshall & R. C. Suggs (Eds.), *Human sexual behavior* (pp. 103–162). Englewood Cliffs, NJ: Prentice Hall.

Martinez, J. L., & Derrick, B. E. (1996). Long-term potentiation and learning. *Annual Review of Psychology*, 47, 173–203.

Martire, L. M., Stephens, M. A. P., & Townsend, A. L. (2000). Centrality of women's multiple roles: Beneficial and detrimental consequences for psychological well-being. *Psychology & Aging*, 15(1), 148–156.

Maslach, C. (1982). *Burnout: The cost of caring.* Englewood Cliffs, NJ: Prentice Hall.

Maslow, A. H. (1954). *Motivation and personality.* New York: Harper & Row.

Maslow, A. H. (1970). Motivation and personality (2nd ed.). New York: Harper & Row.

Maslow, A. H. (1999). *Toward a psychology of being* (3rd ed.). New York: Wiley.

Mason, P. T., & Kreger, R. (1998). Stop walking on eggshells: Taking your life back when someone you care about has borderline personality disorder. New York: New Harbinger Publishers.

Masson, J. M. (1992). The assault on truth: Freud's suppression of the seduction theory. New York: Harper Perennial.

Masten A. S., & Coatsworth, J. D. (1998). The development of competence in favorable and unfavorable environments. *American Psychologist, 53*(2), 205–220.

Masten, A. S. (1998). Resilience comes of age: Reflections on the past and outlook for the next generation of research. In M. D. Glantz, J. Johnson, & L. Huffman (Eds.), *Resilience and development: Positive life adaptations.* New York: Plenum.

Masters, W. H., & Johnson, V. E. (1966). *Human sexual response.* Boston: Little, Brown.

Masters, W. H., & Johnson, V. E. (1970). Human sexual inadequacy. Boston: Little, Brown.

Masters, W., & Johnson, V. (1961). Orgasm, anatomy of the female. In A. Ellis & A. Abarbonel (Eds.). *Encyclopedia of Sexual Behavior,* Vol. 2. New York: Hawthorn.

Matlin, M. W., & Foley, H. J. (1997). *Sensation and perception* (4th ed.). Boston: Allyn and Bacon.

Matsumoto, D. (1992). More evidence for the universality of a contempt expression. *Motivation and Emotion, 16,* 363–368.

Matsumoto, D. (2000). *Culture and psychology: People around the world.* Belmont, CA: Wadsworth.

Mattila, K. M., Forsell, C., Pirttilae, T., Rinne, J. O., Lehtimaeki, T., Roeyttae, M., Lilius, L., Eerola, A., St George-Hyslop, P. H., Frey, H., & Lannfelt, L. (1998). The Glu318Gly mutation of the presenilin-1 gene does not necessarily cause Alzheimer's disease. *Annals of Neurology, 44,* 965–967.

Matusov, E., & Hayes, R. (2000). Sociocultural critique of Piaget and Vygotsky. *New Ideas in Psychology, 18*(2–3), 215–239.

Matuszek, P. A. C. (2000). A biofeedback-enhanced stress management program for the fire service. *Dissertation Abstracts International: Section B: The Sciences & Engineering, 60*(7–B), 3212.

May, M. A., Hartshorne, H., & Welty, R. E. (1928). Personality and character tests. *Psychological Bulletin, 25,* 422–443.

Mayberg, H. S., Liotti, M., Brannan, S. K., McGinnis, S., Mahurin, R. K., Jerabek, P. A., Silva, J. A., Tekell, J. L., Martin, C. C., Lancaster, J. L., & Fox, P. T. (1999). Reciprocal limbic-cortical function and negative mood. *American Journal of Psychiatry, 156,* 675–682.

Mayer, J. D., & Salovey, P. (1997). What is emotional intelligence? In P. Salovey & D. Sluyter (Eds.), *Emotional development, emotional literacy, and emotional intelligence.* New York: Basic Books.

Mayford, M., Barzilai, A., Keller, F., Schachter, S., & Kandel, E. R. (1992). Modulation of an NCAM-related adhesion molecule with long-term synaptic plasticity in aplysia. *Science, 256,* 638–644.

Mayr, U., & Kliegl, R. (2000). Complex semantic processing in old age: Does it stay or does it go? *Psychology & Aging, 15*(1), 29–43.

Mazur, A., & Booth, A. (1998). Testosterone and dominance in men. *Behavioral and Brain Sciences, 21,* 353–363.

McAndrew, F. T., Akande, A., Turner, S., & Sharma, Y. (1998). A cross-cultural ranking of stressful life events in Germany, India, South Africa, and the United States. *Journal of Cross-Cultural Psychology, 29,* 717–727.

McArthur, L. Z., & Berry, D. S. (1987). Cross-cultural agreement in perceptions of baby-faced adults. *Journal of Cross-Cultural Psychology, 18,* 165–192.

McCall, M. (1997). The effects of physical attractiveness on gaining access to alcohol: When social policy meets social decision making. *Addiction, 92,* 597–600.

McCall, R. B. (1994). Academic underachievers. *Current Directions in Psychological Science, 3,* 15–19.

McCartt, A. T., Rohrbaugh, J. W., Hammer, M. C., & Fuller, S. Z. (2000). Factors associated with falling asleep at the wheel among long-distance truck drivers. *Accident Analysis and Prevention, 32*(4), 493–504.

McClelland, D. C. (1958). Risk-taking in children with high and low need for achievement. In J. W. Atkinson (Ed.), *Motives in fantasy, action, and society.* Princeton, NJ: Van Nostrand.

McClelland, D. C. (1987). Characteristics of successful entrepreneurs. *Journal of Creative Behavior, 3,* 219–233.

McClelland, D. C. (1993). Intelligence is not the best predictor of job performance. *Current Directions in Psychological Science, 2,* 5–6.

McClelland, J. L. (1995). Constructive memory and memory distortions: A parallel-distributed processing approach. In D. L. Schachter (Ed.), *Memory distortions: How minds, brains, and societies reconstruct the past* (pp. 69–90). Cambridge: Harvard University Press.

McClintock, J. (2000, February). Let sleeping dogs arise. *Discover,* pp. 76–81.

McCloskey, L. A., & Bailey, J. A. (2000). The intergenerational transmission of risk for child sexual abuse. *Journal of Interpersonal Violence, 15*(10), 1019–1035.

McConkey, K. M. (1995). Hypnosis, memory, and the ethics of uncertainty. *Australian Psychologist, 30,* 1–10.

McConville, B. (1998). A bloody tradition. *Nursing Times, 94*(3), 34–36.

McCrae, R. E., & Costa, P. T. Jr. (1990). *Personality in adulthood.* New York: Guilford Press.

McCrae, R. R., & Costa, P. T. (1997). Personality trait structure as a human universal. *American Psychologist, 52,* 509–516.

McCrae, R. R., & Costa, P. T. Jr. (1999). A five-factor theory of personality. In L. A. Pervin, & O. P. John (Eds.), *Handbook of personality: Theory and research.* New York: Guilford Press.

McCrae, R. R., & Costa, P. T. Jr., de Lirna, M. P., Simoes, A., Ostendorf, F., Angleitner, A., Marusic, I., Bratko, D., Caprara, G. V., Barbaranelli, C., Chae, J. H., & Piedmont, R. L. (1999). Age differences in personality across the adult life span: Parallels in five cultures. *Developmental Psychology, 35,* 466–477.

McCrae, R. R., Costa, P. T., Jr., Ostendorf, F., Angleitner, A., Hrebickova, M., Avia, M. D., Sanz, J., Sanchez-Bernardos, M. L., Kusdil, M. E., Woodfield, R., Saunders, P. R., & Smith, P. B. (2000). Nature over nurture: Temperament, personality, and life span development. *Journal of Personality & Social Psychology, 78*(1), 173–186.

McDonald, C., & Murray, R. M. (2000). Early and late environmental risk factors for schizophrenia. *Brain Research Reviews*, *31*, 130–137.

McDonald, J. W., Liu, X. Z., Qu, Y., Liu, S., Mickey, S. K., Turetsky, D., Gottlieb, D. I., & Choi, D. W. (1999). Transplanted embryonic stem cells survive, differentiate, and promote recovery in injured rat spinal cord. *Nature & Medicine*, *5*, 1410–1412.

McDonald, M. (2001, January 8). Psst! Want a hot tip? Try a crystal ball. *U.S. News & World Report*, 34.

McDougall, W. (1908). *Social psychology*. New York: Putnam's Sons.

McEntee, D. J., & Halgin, R. P. (1999). Cognitive group therapy and aerobic exercise in the treatment of anxiety. *Journal of College Student Psychotherapy*, *13*(3), 37–55.

McGaugh, J. L. (1989). Modulation of memory storage processes. In P. R. Soloman, G. R. Goethals, C. M. Kelley, & B. R. Stephens (Eds.), *Memory: Interdisciplinary approaches*. New York: Springer-Verlag.

McGaugh, J. L. (1990). Significance and remembrance: The role of neuromodulatory systems. *Psychological Science*, *1*, 15–25.

McGaugh, J. L. (1992). Hormones and memory. In L. R. Squire (Ed.), *Encyclopedia of learning and memory*. New York: MacMillian.

McGaugh, J. L. (2000). Memory—a century of consolidation. *Science*, *287*, 248–251.

McGaughy, J., Decker, M. W., Sarter, M. (1999). Enhancement of sustained attention performance by the nicotine acetycholine receptor agonist ABT-418 in intact but not basal forebrain-lesioned rats. *Psychopharmacology*, *144*(2), 175–182.

McGaughy, J., et al. (1997). Lack of effects of lesins of the dorsal norandrenergic bundle on behavioral vigilance. *Behavioral Neuroscience*, *111*, 646–652.

McGeoch, J. A. (1942). *The psychology of human learning*. New York: Longmans, Green.

McGhie, A., & Chapman, H. (1961). Disorders of attention and perception in early schizophrenia. *British Journal of Medical Psychology*, *34*, 103–116.

McGraw, D. (1999, March 1). Justice delayed. U. S. *News and World Report*, pp. 76–79.

McIlduff, E., & Coghlan, D. (2000). Reflections: Understanding and contending with passive-aggressive behaviour in teams and organizations. *Journal of Managerial Psychology*, *15*(7–8), 716–732.

McKee, M. G. (1991). Contributions of psychophysiologic monitoring to diagnosis and treatment of headache pain: A case study. *Headache Quarterly*, *2*, 327–330.

McKellar, P. (1972). Imagery from the standpoint of introspection. In P. W. Sheehan (Ed.), *The function and nature of imagery*. New York: Academic Press.

McKnight, J. D., & Glass, D. C. (1995). Perceptions of control, burnout, and depressive symptomatology. *Journal of Consulting and Clinical Psychology*, *63*, 490–494.

McLoyd, V. C. (1998). Socio-economic disadvantage and child development. *American Psychologist*, *53*, 185–204.

McMillan, T. M., Robertson, I, H., & Wilson, B. A. (1999). Neurogesesis after brain injury: Implications for neurorehabilitation. *Neuropsychological Rehabilitation*, *9*, 129–133.

McMullin, R. E. (2000). *The new handbook of cognitive therapy techniques*. New York: W. W. Norton & Company.

Medina, J. J. (1996). *The clock of ages: Why we age*. Cambridge, MA: Cambridge University Press.

Meisenzahl, E. M., Dresel, S., F. T., Schmitt, G. J. E., Preuss, U. W., Rossmueller, B., Tatsch, K., Mager, T., Hahn, K., & Moeller, H. J. (2000). D-sub-2 receptor occupancy under recommended and high doses of olanzapine: An iodine-123-iodobenzamide SPECT study. *Journal of Psychopharmacology*, *14*(4), 364–370.

Melamed, S., Ugarten, U., Shirom, A., Kahana, L., Lerman, Y., & Froom, P. (1999). Chronic burnout, somatic arousal, and elevated salivary cortisol levels. *Journal of Psychosomatic Research*, *46*, 591–598.

Melchert, T. P. (2000). Clarifying the effects of parental substance abuse, child sexual abuse, and parental caregiving on adult adjustment. *Professional Psychology: Research & Practice*, *31*(1), 64–69.

Meloy, J. R., Acklin, M. W., Gacono, C. B., Murray, J. F., & Peterson, C. A. (Eds.) (1997). Contemporary Rorschach interpretation. Mahwah, NJ: Erlbaum.

Meltzer, H. Y. (2000). Genetics and etiology of schizophrenia and bipolar disorder. *Biological Psychiatry*, *47*, 171–173.

Meltzoff, A. N., & Moore, M. K. (1977). Imitation of facial and manual gestures by human neonates. *Science*, *198*, 75–78.

Meltzoff, A. N., & Moore, M. K. (1985). Cognitive foundations and social functions of imitation and intermodal representation in infancy. In J. Mehler & R. Fox (Eds.),

Neonate cognition: Beyond the blooming buzzing confusion. Hillsdale, NJ: Erlbaum.

Meltzoff, A. N., & Moore, M. K. (1994). Imitation, memory, and the representation of persons. *Infant Behavior and Development*, *17*, 83–99.

Melzack, R. (1999). Pain and stress: A new perspective. In R. J. Gatchel & D. C. Turk (Eds.), *Psychosocial factors in pain: Critical perspectives*. New York: Guilford Press.

Melzack, R., & Wall, P. D. (1965). Pain mechanisms: A new theory. *Science*, *150*, 971–979.

Melzack, R., Israel, R., Lacroix, R., & Schultz, G. (1997). Phantom limbs in people with congenital limb deficiency or amputation in early childhood. *Brain*, *120*, 1603–1620.

Merckelbach, H., Arntz, A., Arrindell, W. A., & DeJong, P. J. (1992). Pathways to spider phobia. *Behviour Research and Therapy*, *30*, 543–546.

Merckelbach, H., de Jong, P. J., Muris, P., & van den Hout, M. A. (1996). The etiology of specific phobias: A review. *Clinical Psychology Review*, *16*, 337–361.

Merikle, P. M., & Skanes, H. E. (1992). Subliminal self-help audiotapes: A search for placebo effects. *Journal of Applied Psychology*, *77*, 772–776.

Merlin, M., Lebot, V., & Lindstrom, L. (1992). *Kava: The Pacific drug*. New Haven, CT: Yale University Press.

Meschke, L. L., Bartholomae, S., & Zentall, S. R. (2000). Adolescent sexuality and parent-adolescent processes: Promoting healthy teen choices. Family Relations: Interdisciplinary Journal of Applied Family Studies, *49*(2), 143–154.

Meston, C. M., & Frohlich, P. F. (2000). The neurobiology of sexual function. *Archives of General Psychiatry*, *57*(11), 1012–1030.

Metcalf, P., & Huntington, R. (1991). *Celebrations of death: The anthropology of mortuary ritual* (2nd ed.). Cambridge, England: Cambridge University Press.

Meyer, R. G., & Salmon, P. (1988). *Abnormal psychology* (2nd ed.). Boston: Allyn & Bacon.

Michael, R., Gagnon, J., Laumann, E., & Kolata, G. (1994). *Sex in America*. Boston: Little, Brown.

Migliore, M. (2000). *The hunger within: A twelve-week self-guided journey from compulsive eating to recovery*. New York: Main Street Books.

Migueles, M, & Garcia-Bajos, E. (1999). Recall, recognition, and confidence patterns in eyewitness testimony. *Applied Cognitive Psychology, 13,* 257–268.

Miles, C., & Hardman, E. (1998). State-dependent memory produced by aerobic exercise. *Ergonomics, 41,* 20–28.

Miles, D. R., & Carey, G. (1997). Genetic and environmental architecture on human aggression. *Journal of Personality and Social Psychology, 72,* 207–217.

Milgram, S. (1963). Behavioral study of obedience. *Journal of Abnormal and Social Psychology, 67,* 371–378.

Milgram, S. (1974). *Obedience to authority: An experimental view.* New York: Harper & Row.

Miller, B., & Coyl, D. D. (2000). Adolescent pregnancy and childbearing in relation to infant adoption in the United States. *Adoption Quarterly, 1 4*(1), 3–25.

Miller, F. A. (1998). Strategic culture change: The door to achieving high performance and inclusion. *Public Personnel Management, 27*(2), 151–160.

Miller, G. A. (1956). The magical number seven, plus or minus two: Some limits on our capacity for processing information. *Psychological Review, 63,* 81–97.

Miller, G. E., & Cohen, S. (2001). Psychological interventions and the immune system: A meta-analytic review and critique. *Health Psychology, 20*(1), 47–63.

Miller, J. (1998). The enemy inside: An exploration of the defensive processes of introjecting and identifying with the aggressor. *Psychodynamic Counseling, 4*(1), 55–70.

Miller, J. G., & Bersoff, D. M. (1998). The role of liking in perceptions of the moral responsibility to help: A cultural perspective. *Journal of Experimental Social Psychology, 34,* 443–469.

Miller, L. C., & Fishkin, S. A. (1997). On the dynamics of human bonding and reproductive success: Seeking windows on the adapted-for-human-environmental interface. In J. A. Simpson & D. T. Kenrick (Eds.). *Evolutionary social psychology* (pp. 197–236). Mahwah, NJ: Erlbaum.

Miller, L. T., & Vernon, P. A. (1997). Developmental changes in speed of information processing in young children. *Developmental Psychology, 33,* 549–554.

Miller, M. A., & Rahe, R. H. (1997). Life changes scaling for the 1990s. *Journal of Psychosomatic Research, 43,* 279–292.

Miller, M., & Kantrowitz, B. (1999, January 25). Unmasking Sybil: A reexamination of the most famous psychiatric patient in history. *Newsweek,* pp. 11–16.

Miller, N. E. (1991). Commentary on Ulrich: Need to check truthfulness of statements by opponents of animal research. *Psychological Science, 2,* 422–424.

Miller, N. E., & DiCara, L. (1967). Instru-mental learning of heart rate changes in curarized rats: Shaping and specificity to discriminative stimulus. *Journal of Comparative and Physiological Psychology, 63,* 12–19.

Miller, T. O., Smith, T. W., Turner, C. W., Guijarro, M. L., & Hallet, A. J. (1996). A meta-analytic review of research on hostility and physical health. *Psychological Bulletin, 119,* 322–348.

Milton, J., & Wiseman, R. (1999). Does psi exist? Lack of replication of an anomalous process of information transfer. *Psychological Bulletin, 125,* 387–391.

Mischel, W., & Shoda, Y. (1999). Integrating dispositions and processing dynamics within a unified theory of personality: The cognitive-affective personality system. In L. A. Pervin, & O. P. John (Eds.), *Handbook of personality: Theory and research.* New York: Guilford Press.

Mita, T. H., Dermer, M., & Knight, J. (1977). Reversed facial images and the mere-exposure hypothesis. *Journal of Personality & Social Psychology, 35*(8), 597–601.

Mitchell, E., Sachs, A., Tu, J. I-Chin (1997, September 29). Teaching feelings 101. *Time,* p. 62.

Mohr, P. B., & Larsen, K. (1998). Ingroup favoritism in umpiring decisions in Australian football. *Journal of Social Psychology, 138*(4), 495–504.

Money, J. (1985a). Sexual reformation and counter-reformation in law and medicine. *Medicine and Law, 4,* 479–488.

Money, J., & Ehrhardt, A. A. (1972). *Man and woman, boy and girl.* Baltimore: The Johns Hopkins University Press.

Money, J., Prakasam, K. S., & Joshi, V. N. (1991). Semen-conservation doctrine from ancient Ayurvedic to modern sexological theory. *American Journal of Psychotherapy, 45,* 9–13.

Monk, T. H. (1997). Shift work. In M. R. Pressman and W. C. Orr (Eds.), *Understanding sleep: The evaluation and treatment of sleep disorders. Application and practice in health psychology* (pp. 249–266). Washington, DC: American Psychological Association.

Moore, M. M. (1998). The science of sexual signaling. In G. C. Brannigan, E. R. All-geier, & A. R. Allgeier (Eds.), *The sex scientists* (pp. 61–75). New York: Longman.

Moore, R. Y. (1997). Circadian rhythms: Basic neurobiology and clinical applications. *Annual Review of Medicine, 48,* 253–266.

Moore, T. E. (1995). Subliminal self-help auditory tapes: An empirical test of perceptual consequences. *Canadian Journal of Behavioral Science, 27,* 9–20.

Moran, C. C., & Massam, M. M. (1999). Differential influences of coping humor and humor bias on mood. *Behavioral Medicine, 25*(1), 36–42.

Morelli, G. A., Oppenheim, D., Rogoff, B., & Goldsmith, D. (1992). Cultural variations in infant sleeping arrangements: Questions of independence. *Developmental Psychology, 28,* 604–613.

Morelli, G. A., Rogoff, B., Oppenheim, D., & Goldsmith, D. (1999). Cultural variations in infants' sleeping arrangements: Questions of independence. In L. E. Berk, *Landscapes of development* (pp. 65–80). Belmont, CA: Wadsworth.

Morgenstern, J., Labouvie, E., McCrady, S., Kahler, C. W., & Frey, R. M. (1997). Affiliation with Alcoholics Anonymous after treatment: A study of the therapeutic effects and mechanisms of action. *Journal of Consulting and Clinical Psychology, 65,* 768–777.

Morgenstern, J., Langenbucher, J., Labouvie, E., & Miller, K. J. (1997). The comorbidity of alcoholism and personality disorders in a clinical population: Prevalence rates and relation to alcohol typology variables. *Journal of Abnormal Psychology, 106,* 74–84.

Mori, E., Ikeda, M., Hirono, N., Kitagaki, H., Imamura, T., & Shimomura, T. (1999). Amygdalar volume and emotional memory in Alzheimer's disease. *American Journal of Psychiatry, 156,* 216–222.

Morris, J. S., Frith, C. D., Perrett, D. L., Rowland, D., Young, A. W., Calder, A. J., & Dolan, R. J. (1996). A differential neural response in the human amygdala to fearful and happy expressions. *Nature, 383,* 812–815.

Morrison, M. F., & Tweedy, K. (2000). Effects of estrogen on mood and cognition in aging women. *Psychiatric Annals, 30*(2), 113–119.

Moss, A. J., Allen, K. f., Gioviano, G. A., & Mills, S. L. (1992). *Recent trends in adolescent smoking, smoking-update correlates, and expectations about the future. Advance Data No. 221* (from Vital and

Health Statistics of the Centers for Disease Control and Prevention p. 537).

Mueller, C. M., & Dweck, C. S. (1998). Praise for intelligence can undermine children's motivation and performance. *Journal of Personality & Social Psychology, 75,* 33–52.

Muente, T. F. (1997). Event-related brain potentials to unfamiliar faces in explicit and implicit memory tasks. *Neuroscience Research, 28,* 223–233.

Mui, A. C. (1992). Caregiver strain among black and white daughter caregivers: A role theory perspective. *The Gerontologist, 32,* 203–212.

Muir, G. D., & Steeves, J. D. (1997). Sensorimotor stimulation to improve locomotor recovery after spinal cord injury. *Trends in Neurosciences, 20,* 72–77.

Mulford, M., Orbell, J., Shatto, C., & Stockard, J. (1998). Physical attractiveness, opportunity, and success in everyday ex-change. *American Journal of Sociology, 103,* 1565–1592.

Munroe, R. L., & Gauvain, M. (2001). Why the paraphilias? Domesticating strange sex. *Cross-Cultural Research: The Journal of Comparative Social Science, 35*(1), 44–64.

Muris, P., Merckelbach, H., Gadet, B., & Moulaert, V. (2000). Fears, worries, and scary dreams in 4– to 12–year-old children: Their content, developmental pattern, and origins. *Journal of Clinical Child Psychology, 29*(1), 43–52.

Murphy, C. M., & O'Farrell, T. J. (1996). Marital violence among alcoholics. *Current Directions in Psychological Science, 5*(6), 183–186.

Murphy, S. T., & Zajonc, R. (1993). Affect, cognition, and awareness: Affective priming with optimal and suboptimal stimulus exposures. *Journal of Personality and Social Psychology, 64,* 723–739.

Murray, B. (1995, October). Americans dream about food, Brazilians dream about sex. *APA Monitor,* p. 30.

Murray, H. A. (1938). *Explorations in personality.* New York: Oxford University Press.

Murray, S. L., & Holmes, J. G. (1997). A leap of faith? Positive illusions in romantic relationships. *Personality and Social Psychology Bulletin, 23,* 586–604.

Myerson, J., Rank, M. R., Raines, F. Q., & Schnitzler, M. A. (1998). Race and general cognitive ability: The myth of diminishing returns to education. *Psychological Science, 9,* 139–142.

Nadon, R., Hoyt, I. P., Register, P. A., & Kihlstrom, J. F. (1991). Absorption and hypnotizability: Context effects reexamined. *Journal of Personality and Social Psychology, 60,* 144–153.

Naglieri, J. A., & Ronning, M. E. (2000). Comparison of White, African American, Hispanic, and Asian children on the Naglieri Nonverbal Ability Test. *Psychological Assessment, 12*(3), 328–334.

Nakao, M., Nomura, S., Shimosawa, T., Yoshiuchi, K., Kuboki, T., et al. (1997). Clinical effects of blood pressure biofeedback treatment on hypertension by autoshaping. *Psychosomatic Medicine, 59,* 331–338.

Napolitane, C. (1997). *Living and loving after divorce.* New York: Signet.

Narduzzi, K. J., & Jackson, T. (2000). Personality differences between eating-disordered women and a nonclinical comparison sample: A discriminant classification analysis. *Journal of Clinical Psychology, 56*(6) 699–710.

Nass, R., & Baker, S. (1991). Learning disabilities in children with congenital adrenal hyperplasia. *Journal of Child Neurology, 6* (4), 306–312.

Nathan, P. E., & Langenbucher, J. W. (1999). Psychopathology. *Annual Review of Psychology, 50,* 79–107.

National Center for Health Statistics. (2001). Trends in Causes of Death Among the Elderly. *Centers for Disese Control,* Available: http://navigation.helper.realnames.com/framer/1/112/default.asp?realname=National+Center+for+Health+Statistics&url=http%3A%2F%2Fwww%2Ecdc%2Egov%2Fnchswww%2F&frameid=1&providerid=112&uid=30011018

National Institute of Mental Health. (1999). *Facts about anxiety disorders.* Available: http://www.nimh.nih.gov/anxiety/adfacts.cfm

Neale, J. M., Oltmanns, T. F., & Winters, K. C. (1983). Recent developments in the assessment and conceptualization of schizophrenia. *Behavioral Assessment, 5,* 33–54.

Neher, A. (1991). Maslow's theory of motivation: A critique. *Journal of Humanistic Psy-chology, 31,* 89–112.

Neisser, U. (1967). *Cognitive psychology.* New York: Appleton-Century-Crofts.

Neisser, U. (1998). Introduction: Rising test scores and what they mean. In U. Neisser (Ed.), *The rising curve: Long-term gains in IQ and related measures.* Washington, DC: American Psychological Association.

Neisser, U., & Harsch, N. (1992). Phantom flashbulbs: False recollections of hearing the news about Challenger. In E. Winograd, & U. Neisser (Eds.), *Affect and accuracy in recall: Studies of "flashbulb" memories.* New York: Cambridge University Press.

Neisser, U., Boodoo, G., Bouchard, T. J., Jr., Boykin, A. W., Brody, N., Ceci, S. J., Halpern, D. F., Loehlin, J. C., Perloff, R., Sternberg, R. J., & Urbina, S. (1996). Intelligence: Knowns and unknowns. *American Psychologist, 51,* 77–101.

Nesbitt, M. N., & Penn, N. E. (2000). Gender stereotypes after thirty years: A replication of Rosenkrantz, et al. (1968). *Psychological Reports, 87,* 493–511.

Nestler, E. J., & Landsman, D. (2001).Learning about addiction from the genome. *Nature, 409*(6822), 834–835.

Neuringer, A., Deiss, C., & Olson, G. (2000). Reinforced variability and operant learning. *Journal of Experimental Psychology: Animal Behavior Processes, 26*(1), 98–111.

New, M., & Berliner, L. (2000). Mental health service utilization by victims of crime. *Journal of Traumatic Stress, 13*(4), 693–707.

Newman, J. (1997). Putting the puzzle together: II. Towards a general theory of the neural correlates of consciousness. *Journal of Consciousness Studies, 4,* 100–121.

Newman, L. S., Duff, K., & Baumeister, R. (1997). A new look at defensive projection: Thought suppression, accessibility, and biased person perception. *Journal of Personality and Social Psychology, 72,* 980–1001.

Newton-John, T. O., Spence, S. H., & Schotte, D. (1995). Cognitive-behavioral therapy versus EMG biofeedback in the treatment of chronic low back pain. *Behaviour Research & Therapy, 33,* 691–697.

NIAAA. (2000). Research on Relationships Between Alcohol and Violence. *National Institute on Alcohol Abuse and Alcoholism,* Available: http://www.niaaa.nih.gov/extramural/relation.htm

Nicholson, N. (1997). Evolutionary psychology: Toward a new view of human nature and organizational society. *Human Relations, 50,* 1053–1078.

Nickell, J. (1996, May/June). A study of fantasy proneness in the thirteen cases of alleged encounters in John Mack's Abduction. *Skeptical Inquirer, 54,* 18–20.

Nickerson, R. (1998). Confirmation bias: A ubiquitous phenomenon in many guises. *Review of General Psychology, 2,* 175–220.

Nickerson, R. S., & Adams, M. J. (1979). Long-term memory for a common object. *Cognitive Psychology, 11,* 287–307.

Nicolson, R., Bhalerao, S., & Solman, L. (1998). 47, XYY karyotypes and pervasive developmental disorders. *Canadian Journal of Psychiatry, 43,* 619–622.

Niehoff, D. (1999). *The biology of violence: How understanding the brain, behavior, and environment can break the vicious cycle of aggression.* New York: Free Press.

Niemann, Y. F. (2001). Stereotypes about Chicanas and Chicanos: Implications for counseling. *Counseling Psychologist, 29*(1), 55–90.

Nigg, J. T., & Goldsmith, H. H. (1994). Genetics of personality disorders: Perspectives from personality and psychopathology research. *Psychological Bulletin, 115,* 346–380.

Nisbett, R. E., Peng, K., Choi, L., & Norenzayan, A. (2000). Culture and systems of thought: Holistic vs. analytic cognition. *Psychological Review, 21,* 34–45.

Nishimoto, R. (1988). A cross-cultural analysis of psychiatric symptom expression using Langer's twenty-two item index. *Journal of Sociology and Social Welfare, 15,* 45–62.

Nishimura, H., et al. (1999). Sign language "heard" in the auditory cortex. *Nature, 397,* 116.

Noble, E. P. (2000). Addiction and its reward process through polymorphisms of the D-sub-2 dopamine receptor gene: A review. *European Psychiatry, 15*(2), 79–89.

Nolen-Hoeksema, S., Larson, J., & Grayson, C. (2000). Explaining the gender difference in depressive symptoms. *Journal of Personality and Social Psychology, 77,* 1061–1072.

Norenzayan, A., & Nisbett, R. E. (2000). Culture and causal cognition. *Current Directions in Psychological Science, 9*(4), 132–135.

O'Connor, F. L. (1998). The role of serotinin and dopamine in schizophrenia. *Journal of the American Psychiatric Nurses Association, 4,* S30–S34.

O'Leary, D. S., Block, R. I., Flaum, M., Schultz, S. K., Ponto, L. L. Boles, Watkins, G. L., Hurtig, R. R., Andreasen, N. C., Hichwa, R. D. (2000). Acute marijuana effects on rCBF and cognition: A PET study. *Neuroreport: For Rapid Communication of Neuroscience Research, 11*(17), 3835–3841.

O'Scalaidhe, S. P., Wilson, F. A. W., & Goldman-Rakic, P. S. (1997). A real segregation of face-processing neurons in prefrontal cortex. *Science, 278,* 1135–1138.

Ogilvie, R. D., Wilkinson, R. T., & Allison, S. (1989). The detection of sleep onset: Behavioral, physiological, and subjective convergence. *Sleep, 12*(5), 458–474.

Ohayon, M. M. (1997). Prevalence of DSM-IV diagnostic criteria of insomnia: Distin-guishing insomnia related to mental disorders from sleep disorders. *Journal of Psychiatric Research, 31,* 333–346.

Okazaki, S., & Sue, S. (2000). Implications of test revisions for assessment with Asian Americans. *Psychological Assessment, 12*(3), 272–280.

Olds, J., & Milner, P. M. (1954). Positive reinforcement produced by electrical stimulation of septal area and other regions of rat brains. *Journal of Comparative and Physiological Psychology, 47,* 419–427.

Olfson, M., Marcus, S., Pincus, H. A., Zito, J. M., Thompson, J. W., & Zarin, D. A. (1998). Antidepressant prescribing practices of outpatient psychiatrists. *Archives of General Psychiatry, 55,* 310, 316.

Omori, M., Murata, T., Kimura, H., Koshimoto, Y., Kado, H., Ishimori, Y., Ito, H., & Wada, Y. (2000). Thalamic abnormalities in patients with schizophrenia revealed by proton magnetic resonance spectroscopy. *Psychiatry Research: Neuroimaging, 98* (3), 155–162.

Opinion Archive. (2001). One Million Dollar Paranormal Challenge. *James Randi Educational Foundation,* Available: http://www.randi.org/research/index.html

Oquendo, M. A., & Mann, J. J. (2000). The biology of impulsivity and suicidality. *Psychiatric Clinics of North America, 23*(1), 11–25.

Orth-Gomer, K., et al. (1994). Lipid lowering through work stress reduction. *International Journal of Behavioral Medicine, 1,* 204–214.

Ortiz, E. (1998). Female genital mutilation and public health: Lessons from the British experience. *Health Care for Women International, 19,* 119–129.

Orubuloye, I., Caldwell, J., & Caldwell, P. (1997). Perceived male sexual needs and male sexual behavior in southwest Nigeria. *Social Science and Medicine, 44,* 1195–1207.

Orzack, M. H. (1999). Computer addiction: Is it real or virtual. *The Harvard Mental Health Letter, 15*(7), 8.

Oshima, K. (2000). Ethnic jokes and social function in Hawaii. *Humor: International Journal of Humor Research, 13*(1), 41–57.

Oshiro, Y. Fuijita, N., Tanaka, H., Hirabuki, N., Nakamura, H., Yoshiya, I. (1998). Functional mapping of pain-related activation with echo-planar MRI: Significance of the SII-insular region. *Neuroreport: An International Journal for the Rapid Communication of Research in Neuroscience, 9,* 2285–2289.

Otero, G. A., Aguirre, D. M., Porcayo, R., & Fernandez, T. (1999). Psychological and electroencephalographic study in school children with iron deficiency. *International Journal of Neuroscience, 99*(1–4), 113–121.

Ozinga, J. A. (2000). *Altruism.* New York: Praeger Pub.

Page, T. L. (1994). Time is the essence: Molecular analysis of the biological clock. *Science, 263,* 1570–1572.

Pahlavan, F., Bonnet, P., & Duda, D. (2000). Human motor responses to simultaneous aversive stimulation and failure on a valued task. *Psychological Reports, 86,* 232–242.

Palfai, T. P., Monti, P. M., Ostafin, B., & Hutchinson, K. (2000). Effects of nicotine deprivation on alcohol-related information processing and drinking behavior. *Journal of Abnormal Psychology, 109,* 96–105.

Pakaslahti, L., & Keltikangas-Jaervinen, L. (2000). Comparison of peer, teacher and self-assessments on adolescent direct and indirect aggression. *Educational Psychology, 20*(2), 177–190.

Paniagua, F. A. (1998). *Assessing and treating culturally diverse clients: A practical guide* (2nd ed.). London: Sage.

Papert, S. (1999, March 29). *Child psychologist Jean Piaget. Time,* 105–107.

Parasuraman, S., & Purohit, Y. S. (2000). Distress and boredom among orchestra musicians: The two faces of stress. *Journal of Occupation Health Psychology, 5*(1), 74–83.

Paris, J. (1998). Does childhood trauma cause personality disorders in adults? *Canadian Journal of Psychiatry, 43,* 148–153.

Paris, J. (2000). Childhood precursors of personality disorder. *Psychiatric Clinics of North America, 23,* 77–88.

Park, A. (2000, August 7). Neurobiology: Old brains, new tricks. *Time,* p. 70.

Park, R. (2000). *Voodoo science: The road from foolishness to fraud.* Oxford University Press.

Parke, R. D., & Buriel, R. (1998). Socialization in the family: Ethnic and ecological perspectives. In W. Damon (Ed.), *Handbook of child psychology* (Vol. 3). New York: Wiley.

Parker, W. D., (1998). Birth order effects in the academically talented. *Gifted Child Quarterly, 42,* 29–36.

Parkes, C. M. (1972). *Bereavement: Studies of grief in adult life.* New York: International Universities Press.

Parkes, C. M. (1991). Attachment, bonding, and psychiatric problems after bereavement in adult life. In C. M. Parkes, J. Stevenson-Hinde, & P. Marris (Eds.), *Attachment across the life cycle.* London: Tavistock/Routledge.

Parkes, M., & White, K. (2000). Glucose attenuation of memory impairments. *Behavioral Neuroscience, 114,* 307–319.

Parkinson, J. A., Willoughby, P. J., Robbins, T. W., & Everitt, B. J. (2000). Disconnection of the anterior cingulated cortex and nucleus accumbens core impairs Pavlovian approach behavior: Further evidence for limbic cortical-ventral striatopallidal systems. *Behavioral Neuroscience, 114*(1), 42–63.

Parks, C. A. (1998). Lesbian parenthood: A review of the literature. *American Journal of Orthopsychiatry, 68,* 376–389.

Patten, C. A. (2000). A critical evaluation of nicotine replacement therapy for teenage smokers. *Journal of Child & Adolescent Substance Abuse, 9*(4), 51–75.

Patterson, D. R., & Ptacek, J. T. (1997). Baseline pain as a moderator of hypnoticanalgesia for burn injury treatment. *Journal of Consulting and Clinical Psychology, 65,* 60–67.

Patterson, F., & Linden, E. (1981). *The education of Koko.* New York: Holt, Rinehart and Winston.

Paul, D. B., & Blumenthal, A. L. (1989). On the trail of little Albert. *The Psychological Record, 39,* 547–553.

Paulhus, D. L., Trapnell, P. D., & Chen, D. (1999). *Psychological Science, 10*(6), 482–488.

Paunonen, S. V., & Ashton, M. C. (1998). The structured assessment of personality across cultures. *Journal of Cross-Cultural Psychology, 29,* 150–170.

Pelaez-Nogueras, M., Gewirtz, J. L., Field, T., & Cigales, M. (1996). Infants' preference for touch stimulation in face-to-face interactions. *Journal of Applied Developmental Psychology, 17,* 199–213.

Penev, P. D., Zee, P. C., & Turek, F. W. (1997). Serotonin in the spotlight. *Nature, 385,* 123.

Penfield, W. (1958). Functional localization in temporal and deep Sylvian area. *Research Publications of the Association for Research in Nervous & Mental Disease, 36,* 210–226.

Penfield, W. (1975). *The mystery of the mind.* Princeton, NJ: Princeton University Press.

Pengilly, J. W., & Dowd, E. T. (2000). Hardiness and social support as moderators of stress. *Journal of Clinical Psychology, 56,* 813–820.

Pennisi, E. (1997). The architecture of hearing. *Science,* 1223–1224.

Peppard, P. E., Young, T., Palta, M., & Skatrud, J. (2000). Prospective study of the association between sleep-disordered breathing and hypertension. *New England Journal of Medicine, 342*(19), 1378–1384.

Perez, L. A., Peynircioglu, Z. F., & Blaxton, T. A. (1998). Developmental differences in implicit and explicit memory performance. *Journal of Experimental Psychology: Learning, Memory, & Cognition, 25,* 644–663.

Perez, R. L. (2000). Fiesta as tradition, fiesta as change: Ritual, alcohol, and violence in a Mexican community. *Addiction, 95*(3), 365–373.

Perkins, K. A., Levine, M., Marcus, M., Shiffman, S., D'Amico, Miller, A., Keina, A., Ashcom, J., & Broge, M. (2000). Tobacco withdrawl in women and menstrual cycle phase. *Journal of Counseling and Clinical Psychology, 68,* 176–180.

Perreault, S., & Bourhis, R. Y. (1999). Ethnocentrism, social identification, and discrimination. *Personality & Social Psychology Bulletin, 25*(1), 92–103.

Perry, C. (1997). Admissability and per se ex-clusion of hypnotically elicited recall in American courts of law. *International Journal of Clinical and Experimental Hypnosis, 45,* 266–279.

Perry, R. J., & Hodges, J. R. (1999). Attention and executive deficits in Alzheimer's disease: A critical review. *Brain, 122,* 383–404.

Persons, J. B., Davidson, J., & Tompkins, M. A. (2000). *Essential components of cognitive-behavior therapy for depression.* Washington, DC: American Psychological Association.

Pert, C. B., & Snyder, S. H. (1973). The opiate receptor: Demonstration in nervous tissue. *Science, 179,* 1011–1014.

Pert, C. B., Snowman, A. M., & Snyder, S. H. (1974). Localization of opiate receptor binding in presynaptic membranes of rat brain. *Brain Research, 70,* 184–188.

Peskind, E. R. (1998). Pharmacologic approaches to cognitive deficits in Alzheimer's disease. *Journal of Clinical Psychiatry, 59,* 22–27.

Peters, E. P., & Day, R. R. (2000). Fatherhood: Research, interventions and policies. Baltimore: Haworth Press.

Peterson, A. L. & Halstead, T. S. (1998). Group cognitive behavior therapy for depression in a community setting: A clinical replication series. *Behavior Therapy, 29,* 3–18.

Peto, R., Lopez, A. D., Boreham, J., Thun, M., & Hath, C., Jr. (1992). Mortality from tobacco in developed countries: Indirect estimates from national vital statistics. *Lancet, 339,* 1268–1278 (p. 536).

Petronis, A. (2000). The genes for major psychosis: Aberrant sequence or regulation? *Neuropsychopharmacology, 23,* 1–12.

Pettigrew, T. F. (1998). Reactions towards the new minorities of Western Europe. *Annual Review of Sociology, 24,* 77–103.

Pfaffmann, C. (1982). Taste: A model of incentive motivation. In D. W. Pfaff (Ed.), *The physiological mechanisms of motivation.* New York: Springer-Verlag.

Phelps, J. A., Davis, J. O., & Schartz, K. M. (1997). Nature, nurture, and twin research strategies. *Current Directions in Psychological Science, 6,* 117–120.

Phillips, S. T., & Ziller, R. C. (1997). Toward a theory and measure of the nature of nonprejudice. *Journal of Personality and Social Psychology, 72,* 420–434.

Piaget, J. (1951). *Play, dreams, and imitation in childhood.* New York: Norton.

Picciotto, M. R. (1998). Common aspects of the action of nicotine and other drugs of abuse. *Drug and Alcohol Dependence, 51,* 165–172.

Pich, E. M., Chiamulera, C., & Caarboni, L. (1999). Molecular mechanisms of the positive reinforcing effect of nicotine. *Behavioural Pharmacology, 10*(6–7), 587–596.

Pich, E. M., Pagliusi, S. R., Tessari, M., Talabot-Ayer, D., Van Huijsduijnen, R. H., & Chiamulera, C. (1997). Common neural substrates for the addictive properties of nicotine and cocaine. *Science, 275,* 83–86.

Pietromonaco, P. R., & Carnelley, K. B. (1994). Gender and working models of attachment: Consequences for perception of self and romantic relationships. *Personal Relationships, 1,* 3–26.

Pihl, R. O., Lau, M. L., & Assaad, J-M. (1997). Aggressive disposition, alcohol, and aggression. *Aggressive Behavior, 23,* 11–18.

Pilcher, J. J., & Huffcutt, A. I. (1996). Effects of sleep deprivation on performance: A meta-analysis. *Sleep, 19,* 318–326.

Pillard, R. C., & Bailey, M. J. (1995). A biological perspective on sexual orientation. *The Psychiatric Clinics of North America, 18,* 71–84.

Pines, A. M. (1993). Burnout. In L. Goldberger & S. Breznitz (Eds.), *Handbook of stress: Theoretical and clinical aspects.* New York: Free Press.

Pinto, C., Dhavale, H., Nair, S., Patil, B., & Dewan, M. (2000). Borderline personality disorder exists in India. *Journal of Nervous & Mental Disease, 188,* 386–388.

Plihal, W., & Born, J. (1999). Effects of early and late nocturnal sleep on priming and spatial memory. *Psychophysiology, 36,* 571–582.

Plomin, R. (1990). The role of inheritance in behavior. *Science, 248,* 183–188.

Plomin, R. (1997, May). Cited in B. Azar, Nature, nurture: Not mutually exclusive. *APA Monitor,* p. 32.

Plomin, R. (1999). Genetics and general cognitive ability. *Nature, 402,* C25–C29.

Plomin, R. (1999). Genetics of chidhood disorders: III. Genetics and intelligence. *Journal of the American Academy of Child & Adolescent Psychiatry, 38,* 786–788.

Plomin, R., & Caspi, A. (1999). Behavioral genetics and personality. In L. A. Pervin, & O. P. John (Eds.), *Handbook of personality: Theory and research.* New York: Guilford Press.

Plomin, R., & Crabbe, J. (2000). DNA. *Psychological Bulletin, 126,* 806–828..

Plomin, R., & Dale, P. S. (2000). Genetics and early language development: A UK study of twins. In D. V. M. Bishop & L. B. Leonard (Eds.), *Speech and language impairments in children: Causes, characteristics, intervention, and outcome.* Oxford: Oxford University Press.

Plomin, R., & DeFries, J. C. (1998, May). The genetics of cognitive abilities and disabilities. *Scientific American, 278,* 62–69.

Plomin, R., & Petrill, S. A. (1997). Genetics and Intelligence: What's new? *Intelligence, 24,* 53–77.

Plomin, R., & Rutter, M. (1998). Child development, molecular genetics and what to do with genes once they are found. *Child Development, 69,* 68–71.

Plomin, R., DeFries, J. C., McClearn, G. E., & Rutter, M. (1997). *Behavioral genetics* (3rd ed.). New York: Freeman.

Plous, S. (1991). An attitude survey of animal rights activists. *Psychological Science, 2,* 194–196.

Plous, S. (1998). Signs of change within the animal rights movement: Results from a follow-up survey of activists. *Journal of Comparative Psychology, 112,* 48–54.

Plutchik, R. (1984). Emotions: A general psychoevolutionary theory. In K. R. Scherer, & P. Ekman (Eds), *Approaches to emotion.* Hillsdale, NJ: Erlbaum.

Plutchik, R. (1994). *The psychology and biology of emotion.* New York: HarperCollins.

Plutchik, R. (2000). *Emotions in the practice of psychotherapy: Clinical implications of affect theories.* Washington, DC: American Psychological Association.

Pollack, M. H. (2000). What are the current treatments for panic disorder. *Harvard Mental Health Letter, 16*(11), 8.

Pollak, S. D., Cicchetti, D., Klorman R., & Brumaghim, J. T. (1997). Cognitive brain event-related potentials and emotion processing in maltreated children. *Child Development, 68,* 773–787.

Pollard, I. (2000). Substance abuse and parenthood: Biological mechanisms-bioethical challenges. *Women & Health, 30*(3), 1–24.

Pontieri, F. E., Tanda, G., Orzi, F., & DiChiara, G. (1996). Effects of nicotine on the nucleus accumbens and similarity to those of addictive drugs. *Nature, 382,* 255–257.

Poole, D. A. & Lindsay, D. S. (1995). Interviewing preschoolers: Effects of non-suggestive techniques, parental coaching and leading questions on reports of nonexperienced events. *Journal of Experimental Child Psychology, 60,* 129–154.

Pope, K. S. (1997). Science as careful questioning: Are claims of a false memory syndrome epidemic based on empirical evidence? *American Psychologist, 52,* 997–1006.

Powell, D. H. (1998). *The nine myths of aging: Maximizing the quality of later life.* San Francisco: Freeman.

Powell, R. A., & Gee, T. L. (1999). The effects of hypnosis on dissociative identity disorder: A reexamination of the evidence. *Canadian Journal of Psychiatry, 44,* 914–916.

Powell-Hopson, D., & Hopson, D. S. (1988). Implications of doll color preferences among Black preschool children and White preschool children. *Journal of Black Psychology, 14,* 57–63.

Powlishta, K. K. (1999). Gender segregation among children: Understanding the "cootie phenomenon." In L. E. Berk, (Ed.), *Landscapes of development* (pp. 281–294). Belmont, CA: Wadsworth.

Prall, R. C. (2000). *The rights of children in separation and divorce: The essential handbook for parents.* Austin, TX: Landmark Editions.

Pratt, L. A., Ford, D. E., Crum, R. M., Armenian, H. K., Gallo, J. J., & Eaton, W. W. (1996). Depression, psychotropic medication, and risk of myocardial infarction: Prospective data from Baltimore ECA follow-up. *Archives of Internal Medicine, 94,* 3123–3129.

Premack, D. (1976). Language and intelligence in ape and man. *American Scientist, 64*(6), 674–683.

Pressman, J. D. (1998). *Last resort psychosurgery and the limits of medicine.* Cambridge, MA: Cambridge University Press.

Pressman, M. R., & Orr, W. C. (Eds.) 1997). *Understanding sleep: The evaluation and treatment of sleep disorders.* Washington, DC: American Psychological Association.

Price, R. H., & Crapo, R. H. (1999). *Cross-cultural perspectives in introductory psychology.* Belmont, CA: Wadsworth.

Priest, R. F., & Sawyer, J. (1967). Proximity and peership: Bases of balance in interpersonal attraction. *American Journal of Sociology, 72,* 633–649.

Primavera, L. H., & Herron, W. G. (1996). The effect of viewing television violence on aggression. *International Journal of Instructional Media, 23,* 91–104.

Prudic, J., & Sackheim, H. A. (1999). Electroconvulsive therapy and suicide risk. *Journal of Clinical Psychiatry, 60,* 104–110.

Pullum, G. K. (1991). *The great Eskimo vocabulary hoax and other irreverent essays on the study of language.* Chicago: University of Chicago Press.

Purdy, J. E., Markham, M. R., Schwartz, B. L., & Gordon, W. C. (2001). *Learning and memory* (2nd ed.). Belmont, CA: Wadsworth.

Putnam, F. W. (1992). Altered states: Peeling away the layers of multiple personality. *Science, 32*(6), 30–36.

Quattrocki, E., Baird, A., & Yurgelun-Todd, D. (2000). Biological aspects of the link between smoking and depression. *Harvard Review of Psychiatry*, 8(3), 99–110.

Quinn, J. F., & Strelkauskas, A. J. (1993). Psycho immunologic effects of Therapeutic Touch on practitioners and recently bereaved recipients: A pilot study. *ANS Advanced Nursing Science*, 15(4), 13–26.

Raesaenen, P. M., Tiihonen, J., Isohanni, M., Rantakallio, P., Lehtonen, J., & Moring, J. (1998). Schizophrenia, alcohol abuse, and violent behavior: A 26-year follow up study of an unselected birth cohort. *Schizophrenia Bulletin*, 24, 437–441.

Raesaenen, S., Pakaslahti, A., Syvaelahti, E., Jones, P. B., & Isohanni, M. (2000). Sex differences in schizophrenia: A review. *Nordic Journal of Psychiatry*, 54, 37–45.

Rafferty, F. T. (1999). Evolutionary psychology. *Journal of the American Academy of Child & Adolescent Psychiatry*, 38, 641–642.

Ragavan, C. (2001, February 5). Cracking down on ecstasy. *U.S. News & World Report*, pp. 14–17.

Raine, A., Lencz, T., Bihrle, S., LaCasse, L., & Colletti, P. (2000). Reduced prefrontal gray matter volume and reduced autonomic activity in antisocial personality disorder. *Archives of General Psychiatry*, 57, 119–127.

Raine, A., Meloy, J. R., Bihrle, S., Stoddard, J., LaCasse, L., & Buchsbaum, M. S. (1998). Reduced prefrontal and increased subcortical brain functioning assessed using positron emission tomography in predatory and affective murderers. *Behavioral Sciences & the Law*, 16(3), 319–332.

Rainnie, D. G., Grunze, H. C. R., McCarley, R. W., & Greene, R. W. (1994). Adenosine inhibition of mesopontine cholinergic neurons: Implications for EEG arousal. *Science*, 263, 689–692.

Raloff, J. (1999). Common pollutants undermine masculinity. *Science News*, 155, 213.

Ramachandran, V. S., & Blakeslee, S. (1998). *Phantoms in the brain*. New York: William Morrow.

Ramirez, G., Zemba, D., & Geiselman, R. E. (1996). Judges' cautionary instructions on eyewitness testimony. *American Journal of Forensic Psychology*, 14, 31–66.

Ramus, F., Hauser, M. D., Miller, C., Morris, D., & Mehler, J. (2000). Language discrimination by human newborns and by cotton-top tamarin monkeys. *Science*, 288(5464), 349–351.

Randi, J. (1997). *An encyclopedia of claims, frauds, and hoaxes of the occult and supernatural: James Randi's decidedly skeptical definitions of alternate realities.* New York: St Martin's Press.

Raven, B. H. (1998). Groupthink: Bay of Pigs and Watergate reconsidered. *Organizational Behavior and Human Decision Processes*, 73, 352–361.

Ray, W. J. (2000). *Methods: Toward a science of behavior and experience.* Wadsworth: Belmont, CA.

Read, J. D., & Bruce, D. (1982). Longitudinal tracking of difficult memory retrievals. *Cognitive Psychology*, 14, 280–300.

Reagan, N., & Reagan, R. (2000). *I love you, Ronnie.* New York: Random House.

Rechtschaffen, A. (1997, August). Cited in T. Geier, What is sleep for? *U. S. News and World Report*, pp. 17–21.

Rechtschaffen, A., & Bergmann, B. M. (1995). Sleep deprivation in the rat by the disk-over-water method. *Behavioural Brain Research*, 69, 55–63.

Reed, G. M., McLaughlin, C. J., & Milholland, K. (2000). Ten interdisciplinary principles for professional practice in telehealth: Implications for psychology. *Professional Psychology: Research and Practice*, 31(2), 170–178.

Reed, T., & Brown, M. (2001). The expression of care in the rough and tumble play of boys. *Journal of Research in Childhood Education*, 15(1), 104–116.

Regan, P. C. (1998). What if you can't get what you want? Willingness to compromise ideal mate selection standards as a function of sex, mate value, and relationship context. *Personality & Social Psychology Bulletin*, 24(12), 1294–1303.

Regan, P. C. (2000). The role of sexual desire and sexual activity in dating relationships. *Social Behavior & Personality*, 28(1), 51–60.

Regier, D. A., Narrow, W. E., Rae, D. S., Mander-scheid, R. W., Locke, B. Z., & Goodwin, F. K. (1993). The de facto US mental and addictive disorders service system. *Archives of General Psychiatry*, 50, 85–93.

Reifman, A. (2000). Revisiting the Bell Curve. *Psychology*, 11, 21–29.

Reiner, W. (1997). To be male or female-that is the question. *Archives of Pediatric and Adolescent Medicine*, 151, 224–225.

Renaud, C. A., & Byers, E. S. (1999). Exploring the frequency, diversity and content of university students' positive and negative sexual cognitions. *Canadian Journal of Human Sexuality*, 8(1), 17–30.

Renner, M. J., & Mackin, R. S. (1998). A life stress instrument for classroom use. *Teaching of Psychology*, 25, 46–48.

Repetti, R. L. (1993). Short-term effects of occupational stressors on daily mood and health complaints. *Health Psychology*, 12, 125–131.

Reppucci, N. D., Woolard, J. L., & Fried, C. S. (1999). Social, community, and preventive interventions. *Annual Review of Psychology*, 50, 387–418.

Rest, J., Narvaez, D., Bebeau, M., & Thoma, S. (1999). A neo-Kohlbergian approach: The DIT and schema theory. *Educational Psychology Review*, 11(4), 291–324.

Rest, J., Thoma, S., & Edwards, L. (1997). Designing and validating a measure of moral judgment: Stage preference and stage consistency approaches. *Journal of Educational Psychology*, 89, 5–28.

Rest, J. R., Turiel, E., & Kohlberg, L. (1969). Relations between level of moral judgment and preference and comprehension of the moral judgments of others. *Journal of Personality*, 37, 225–252.

Reutens, D. C., Savard, G., Andermann, F., Dubeau, F., & Olivier, A. (1997). Results of surgical treatment in temporal lobe epilepsy with chronic psychosis. *Brain*, 120, 1929–1936.

Reynolds, G. P. (1999). Dopamine receptors, antipsychotic action and schizophrenia. *Journal of Psychopharmacology*, 13, 202–203.

Rhodenizer, L., Bowers, C. A., & Bergondy, M. (1998). Team practice schedules: What do we know? *Perceptual & Motor Skills*, 87, 31–34.

Rhodes, G., Sumich, A., & Byatt, G. (1999). Are average facial configurations attractive only because of their symmetry? *Psychological Science*, 10(1), 52–58.

Rice, K. G., & Mirzadeh, S. A. (2000). Perfectionism, attachment, and adjustment. *Journal of Counseling Psychology*, 47(2), 238–250.

Rice, M. E. (1997). Violent offender research and implications for the criminal justice system. *American Psychologist*, 52, 414–423.

Richards, J. E. (1997). Effects of attention on infant's preference for briefly exposed visual stimuli in the paired-comparison recognition-memory paradigm. *Developmental Psychology, 32,* 22–31.

Richardson, D. R., & Green, L. R. (1999). Social sanction and threat explanations of gender effects on direct and indirect aggression. *Aggressive Behavior, 25*(6), 425–434.

Richter, J. S. (2001). Eating disorders and sexuality. In J. J. Robert-McComb (Ed), *Eating disorders in women and children: Prevention, stress management, and treatment* (pp. 201–208). Boca Raton, FL: CRC Press.

Robbins, S. P. (1996). *Organizational behavior: Concepts, controversies, and applications.* Englewood Cliffs, NJ: Prentice Hall.

Robbins, T. W. (1997). Arousal systems and attentional processes. *Biological Psychology, 45,* 57–71.

Robert-McComb, J. J. (2001). Eating disorders. In J. J. Robert-McComb (Ed), *Eating disorders in women and children: Prevention, stress management, and treatment* (pp. 3–37). Boca Raton, FL: CRC Press.

Roberts, W. W., & Nagel, J. (1996). First-order projections activated by stimulation of hypothalamic sites eliciting attack and flight in rats. *Behavioral Neuroscience, 110,* 509–527.

Robertson, D. A., Gernsbacher, M. A., Guidotti, S. J., Robertson, R. R. W., Irwin, W., Mock, B. J., & Campana, M. E. (2000). Functional neuroanatomy of the cognitive process of mapping during discourse comprehension. *Psychological Science, 11*(3), 255–260.

Robicsek, F. (1992, Sept./Oct.). Sacred smoke. *Utne Reader,* pp. 90–91.

Robins, L. N., & Regier, D. A. (1991). *Psychiatric disorders in America: The epidemiological catchment area.* New York: The Free Press.

Rodgers, J. L., Cleveland, H. H., van den Oord, E., & Rowe, D. C. (2000). Resolving the debate over birth order, family size, and intelligence. *American Psychologist,* 55(6), 599–612.

Roelcke, V. (1997). Biologizing social facts: An early 20th century debate on Kraepelin's concepts of culture, neurasthenia, and degeneration. *Culture, Medicine, and Psychiatry, 21,* 383–403.

Rogers, C. R. (1961). *On becoming a person.* Boston: Houghton Mifflin.

Rogers, C. R. (1980). A way of being. Boston: Houghton Mifflin.

Rogosch, F. A., Cicchetti, D., & Aber, J. L. (1995). The role of child maltreatment in early deviations in cognitive and affective processing abilities and later peer relationship problems. *Development and Psychopathology, 7,* 591–609.

Rohner, R. (1986). The warmth dimension. Newbury Par, CA: Sage.

Rohrlich, J. B. (1998). The meanings of aggression. *Psychiatric Annals,* 28, 246–249.

Rolnick, A., & Lubow, R. E. (1991). Why is the driver rarely motion sick? The role of controllability in motion sickness. *Ergonomics, 34*(7), 867–879.

Romo, R., Brody, C. D., Hernandez, A., & Lemus, L. (1999). Neuronal correlates of parametric working memory in the prefrontal cortex. *Nature, 399,* 470–473.

Roozendaal, B., & McGaugh, J. L. (1999). Role of norepinephrine in mediating stress hormone regulation of long-term memory storage: a critical involvement of the amygdala. *Biological Psychiatry, 46,* 1140–1152.

Roques, P. Lambin, M., Jeunier, B., Strayer, F. (1997). Multivariate analysis of personal space in a primary school classroom. *Enfance, 4,* 451–468.

Rosa, L., Rosa, E., Sarner, L., Barrett, S. (1998). A close look at therapeutic touch. *Journal of the American Medical Association, 279,* 1005–1010.

Rosaforte, T. (2000). *Raising the bar: The championship years of Tiger Woods.* New York: St. Martin's Press.

Rosch, E. (1978). Principles of organization. In E. Rosch & H. L. Lloyd (Eds.), *Cognition and categorization.* Hillsdale, NJ: Erlbaum.

Rosch, E. H. (1973). Natural categories. *Cognitive Psychology, 4,* 328–350.

Rose, S. A., & Feldman, J. F. (1997). Memory and speed: Their role in the relation of infant information processing to later IQ. *Child Development, 68,* 630–641.

Rosenblatt, R. (1999, October 25). The way we look at giants. *Time,* p. 142.

Rosenhan, D. (1973). On being sane in insane places. *Science, 197,* 250–258.

Rosenheck, R., Cramer, J., Allan, E., Erdos, J., Frisman, J. et al. (1999). Cost-effectiveness of clozapine in patients with high and low levels of hospital use. *Archives of General Psychiatry, 56,* 565–572.

Rosenthal, M. K., & Roer-Strier, D. (2001). Cultural differences in mothers' developmental goals and ethnotheories.

International Journal of Psychology, 36(1), 20–31.

Rosenthal, N. E. (1998). *Winter blues: Seasonal affective disorder.* New York: Guilford.

Rosenzweig, M. R., Bennet, E. L., & Diamond, M. C. (1972). Brain changes in response to experience. *Scientific American, 226,* 22–29.

Rosenzweig, M. R., Leiman, A. L., & Breedlove, S. M. (1999). *Biological psychology: An introduction to behavioral, cognitive, and clinical neuroscience.* Sunderland, MA: Sinauer Associates.

Ross, B. M., & Millson, C. (1970). Repeated memory of oral prose in Ghana and New York. *International Journal of Psychology, 5,* 173–181.

Roth, B. L., Willins, D. L., Kristiansen, K., & Kroeze, W. K. (1999). Activation is hallucinogenic and antagonism is therapeutic: Role of 5-HT 2A receptors in atypical antipsychotic drug actions. *Neuroscientist, 5,* 254–262.

Rotter, J. B. (1954). *Social learning and clinical psychology.* Englewood Cliffs, NJ: Pren-tice Hall.

Rotter, J. B. (1990). Internal versus external control of reinforcement: A case history of a variable. *American Psychologist, 45,* 489–493.

Rottnek, M. (2000). *Sissies and tomboys: Gender nonconformity and homosexual childhood.* New York: New York University Press.

Rovee-Collier, C. (1999). The development of infant memory. *Current Directions in Psychological Science, 8,* 80–85.

Rowan, J. (1998). Maslow amended. *Journal of Humanistic Psychology, 38,* 81–92.

Rowe, D. C. (1997). Genetics, temperament, and personality. In R. Hogan, J. Johnson, & S. Briggs (Eds.), *Handbook of personality psychology.* New York: Academic Press.

Royce, R., Sena, A., Cates, W., & Cohen, M. (1997). Sexual transmission of HIV. *New England Journal of Medicine, 336,* 1072–1078.

Roye, C., & Balk, S. (1997). Evaluation of an intergenerational program for pregnant and parenting adolescents. *Maternal-Child Nursing Journal, 24,* 32–36.

Rozin, P. (1996). Towards a psychology of food and eating: From motivation to module to model to marker, morality, meaning, and metaphor. *Current Directions in Psychological Science, 5,* 18–24.

Rubin, L. B. (1992). The empty nest. In J. M. Henslin (Ed.), *Marriage and family in a changing society* (4th ed., pp. 261–270). New York: Free Press.

Rubin, Z. (1970). Measurement of romantic love. *Journal of Personality and Social Psychology, 16,* 265–273.

Ruble, D. N., & Martin, C. L. (1998). Gender development. In W. Damon & R. M. Lerner (Eds.), *Handbook of child psychology (Vol. 1).* New York: Wiley.

Rudd, M. D., Ellis, T. E., Rajab, M. H., & Wehrly, T. (2000). Personality types and suicidal behavior: An exploratory study. *Suicide & Life-Threatening Behavior, 30(3),* 199–212.

Ruffin, C. L. (1993). Stress and health-little hassles vs. major life events. *Australian Psychologist, 28,* 201–208.

Rug, M. D., et al. (1998). Dissociation of the neural correlates of implicit and explicit memory. *Nature, 392,* 595–598.

Rumbaugh, D. M., et al. (1974). Lana (chimpanzee) learning language: A progress report. *Brain & Language, 1(2),* 205–212.

Rushton, J. P., & Ankney, C. D. (1996). Brain size and cognitive ability: Correlations with age, sex, social class, and race. *Psychonomic Bulletin & Review, 3,* 21–36.

Rushton, J. P., & Ankney, C. D. (2000). Size matters: A review and new analyses of racial differences in cranial capacity and intelligence that refute Kamin and Omari. *Personality & Individual Differences, 29(4),* 591–620.

Russell, J., Baur, L. A., Beumont, P. J. V., Byrnes, S., Gross, G., Touyz, S., Abraham, S., & Zipfel, S. (2001). Altered energy metabolism in anorexia nervosa. *Psychoneuroendocrinology, 26(1),* 51–63.

Rutan, J. S., & Stone, W. N. (2000). *Psychodynamic group psychotherapy* (3rd ed.). New York: Guilford Press.

Rutler, M. L. (1997). Nature–nurture integration: The example of antisocial behavior. *American Psychologist, 52,* 390–398.

Ruzovsky, F. A. (1984). *Consent to treatment: A practical guide.* Boston: Little, Brown.

Ryan, R. M., & Deci, E. L. (2000). Self-determination theory and the facilitation of intrinsic motivation, social development, and well-being. *American Psychologist, 55(1),* 68–78.

Rybacki, J. J., & Long, J. W. (1999). *The essential guide to prescription drugs 1999.* New York: Harper/Perennial.

Rybash, J. M. (2000). *Adult development and aging.* Columbus, OH: Brown and Benchmark.

Rye, D. B. (1997). Contributions of the pedunculopontine region to normal and altered REM sleep. *Sleep, 20,* 757–788.

Rymer, R. (1993). *Genie: An abused child's first flight from silence.* New York: Harper-Collins.

Saarinen, T. F. (1987). *Centering of mental maps of the world.* Discussion paper. Tucson, AZ: University of Arizona, Department of Geography and Regional Development.

Sabini, J., & Silver, M. (1993). Critical thinking and obedience to authority. In J. Chaffee (Ed.), *Critical thinking* (2nd ed.) (pp. 367–376). Palo Alto, CA: Houghton Mifflin.

Sachs, J. S. (1967). Recognition memory for syntactic and semantic aspects of connected discourse. *Perception and Psychophysics, 2,* 437–442.

Saenger, P. (1996). Current concepts: Turner's syndrome. *New England Journal of Medicine, 335,* 1749–1754.

Sahelian, R. (1998). *Kava: The miracle antianxiety herb.* New York: St Martins.

Salgado, J. F. (1997). The five factor model of personality and job performance in the European community. *Journal of Applied Psychology, 82,* 30–43.

Salisbury, D. F., et al. (1998). First-episode schizophrenic psychosis differs from first-episode affective psychosis and controls in P300 amplitude over left temporal lobe. *Archives of General Psychiatry, 55,* 173–180.

Salmon, D. P., Butters, N., & Chan, A. S. (1999). The deterioration of semantic memory in Alzheimer's disease. *Canadian Journal of Experimental Psychology, 53,* 108–116.

Saltus, R. (2000, June 22). Brain cells are coaxed into repair duty. *Boston Globe,* A18.

Sanchez-Martin, J. R., Fano, E., Ahedo, L., Cardas, J., Brain, P. F., & Azpiroz, A. (2000). Relating testosterone levels and free play social behavior in male and female preschool children. *Psychoneuroendocrinology, 25(8),* 773–783.

Sanderson, W. C. (1995, March). Which therapies are proven effective? *APA Monitor,* p. 4.

Sano, M., Stern, Y., Cote, L., Williams, J. B., & Mayeux, R. (1990). Depression in Parkinson's disease: A biochemical model. *Archives of Neurology, 48,* 1052–154.

Sapolsky, R. (1999, March). Stress and your shrinking brain. *Discover,* pp. 116–120.

Sapolsky, R. M. (1994). *Why zebras don't get ulcers: A guide to stress, stress related diseases, and coping.* New York: Freeman.

Sapolsky, R. M. (1996a). Stress, glucocorticoids, and damage to the nervous system: The current state of confusion. Stress: *The International Journal on the Biology of Stress, 1,* 1–19.

Sapolsky, R. M. (1996b). Why stress is bad for your brain. *Science, 273,* 749–750.

Sarafino, E. P. (1998). *Health psychology: Biopsychosocial interactions* (3rd ed.). New York: Wiley.

Sarafino, E. P. (2000). *Behavior modification: Understanding principles of behavior change.* Mayfield.

Sarbin, T. R. (1997). On the futility of psychiatric diagnostic manuals (DSMs) and the return of personal agency. *Applied and Preventive Psychology, 6,* 233–243.

Sarkar, P., Rathee, S. P., & Neera, N. (1999). Comparative efficacy of pharmacotherapy and biofeedback among cases of generalized anxiety disorder. *Journal of Projective Psychology & Mental Health, 6,* 69–77.

Sartori, G., & Umilta, C. (2000). The additive factor method in brain imaging. *Brain & Cognition, 42,* 68–71.

Saudino, K. J. (1997). Moving beyond the heritability question: New directions in behavioral genetic studies of personality. *Current Directions in Psychological Science, 6,* 86–90.

Savage-Rumbaugh, E. S. (1990). Language acquisition in a nonhuman species: Implications for the innateness debate. *Developmental Psychobiology, 23,* 599–620.

Savitsky, K., Medvec, V. H., & Gilovich, T. (1997). Remembering and regretting: The Zeigarnik effect and the cognitive availability of regrettable actions and inactions. *Personality & Social Psychology Bulletin, 23,* 248–257.

Saxe, L., & Ben-Shakhar, G. (1999). Admissibility of polygraph tests: The application of scientific standards post-Daubert. *Psychology, Public Policy, & Law, 5(1),* 203–223.

Scanlan, J. M., Vitaliano, P. P., Ochs, H., Savage, M. V., & Borson, S. (1998). CD4 and CD8 counts are associated with interactions of gender and psychosocial stress. *Psychosomatic Medicine, 60,* 644–653.

Schachter, S., & Singer, J. E. (1962). Cog-nitive, social, and physiological determinants of emotional state. *Psychological Review, 69,* 379–399.

Schacter, D. L. (1999). The seven sins of memory: Insights from psychology and cognitive neuroscience. *American Psychologist, 54,* 182–203.

Schafe, G. E., Fitts, D. A., Thiele, T. E., LeDoux, J. E., & Bernstein, I. L. (2000). The induction of c-Fos in the NTS after taste aversion learning is not correlated with measures of conditioned fear. *Behavioral Neuroscience, 114*(1), 99–106.

Schaie, K. W. (1993). The Seattle longitudinal studies of intelligence. *Current Directions in Psychological Science, 2,* 171–175.

Schaie, K. W. (1994). The course of adult intellectual development. *American Psychologist, 49,* 304–313.

Schaie, K. W. (1994). The life course of adult intellectual abilities. *American Psychologist, 49,* 304–313.

Schapira, A. H. V. (1999). Clinical review: Parkinson's disease. *British Medical Journal, 318*(3), 311–314.

Scheiber, B., & Selby, C. (2000). *Therapeutic touch.* Buffalo, NY: Prometheus Books.

Scherer, K. R., & Wallbott, H. G. (1994). Evidence for universal and cultural variation of differential emotion response patterning. *Journal of Personality and Social Psychology, 66*(2), 310–328.

Schiffer, F, Zaidel, E, Bogen, J, & Chasan-Taber, S. (1998). Different psychological status in the two hemispheres of two split-brain patients. *Neuropsychiatry, Neuropsychology, & Behavioral Neurology, 11,* 151–156.

Schmajuk, N. A., & DiCarlo, J J. (1991). A neural network approach to hippocampal function in classical conditioning. *Behavioral Neuroscience, 105*(1), 82–110.

Schmidt, L. A. (1999). Frontal brain electrical activity in shyness and sociability. *Psychological Science, 10*(4), 316–320.

Schmidt, M. E., Fava, M., Robinson, J. M., & Judge, R. (2000). The efficacy and safety of a new enteric-coated formulation of fluoxetine given once weekly during the continuation treatment of major depressive disorder. *Journal of Clinical Psychiatry, 61*(11), 851–857.

Schmidt, N. B., Lerew, D. R., & Jackson, R. J. (1999). Prospective evaluation of anxiety sensitivity in the pathogenesis of panic: Replication and extension. *Journal of Abnormal Psychology, 108,* 532–537.

Schmolck, H., Buffalo, E. A., & Squire, L. R. (2000). Memory distortions develop over time: Recollections of the O. J. Simpson trial verdict after 15 and 32 months. *Psychological Science, 11,* 39–45.

Schmolck, H., & Squire, L. R. (2001). Impaired perception of facial emotions following bilateral damage to the anterior temporal lobe. *Neuropsychology, 15*(1), 30–38.

Schneider, D. M., & Sharp, L. (1969). *The dream life of a primitive people: The dreams of the Yir Yoront of Australia.* Ann Arbor, MI: University of Michigan.

Schneidman, E. S. (1981). Suicide. *Suicide and Life-Threatening Behavior, 11*(4), 198–220.

Schofield, W. (1964). *Psychotherapy: The purchase of friendship.* Englewood Cliffs, NJ: Prentice Hall.

Scholnick, E. K. et al. (1999). *Conceptual development: Piaget's legacy.* Mahwah, NJ: Erlbaum.

Schooler, N. R. et al. (1997). Relapse and rehospitalization during maintenance treatment of schizophrenia: The effects of dose reduction and family treatment. *Archives of General Psychiatry, 54,* 453–463.

Schopp, L., Johnstone, B., & Merrell, D. (2000). Telehealth and neuropsychological assessment: New opportunities for psychologists. *Professional Psychology: Research & Practice, 31*(2), 179–183.

Schreurs, B. G., Shi, T., Pineda, S. III, & Buck, D. L. (2000). Conditioning the unconditioned response: Modification of the rabbit's (Oryctolagus cuniculus) unconditioned nictitating membrane response. *Journal of Experimental Psychology: Animal Behavior Processes, 26*(2), 144–156.

Schuh, K. J., & Griffiths, R. R. (1997). Caffeine reinforcement: The role of withdrawal. *Psychopharmacology, 130,* 320–326.

Schulz, R. & Heckhausen, J. (1996). A life-span model of successful aging. *American Psychologist, 51,* 702–714.

Schwartz, J-C., Diaz, J., Pilon, C., & Sokoloff, P. (2000). Possible implications of the dopamine D-sub-3 receptor in schizophrenia and in antipsychotic drug actions. *Brain Research Reviews, 31,* 277–287.

Scribner, S. (1977). Modes of thinking and ways of speaking: Culture and logic reconsidered. In P. N. Johnson-Laird & P. C. Wason (Eds.), *Thinking: Readings in cognitive science* (pp. 324–339). New York: Cambridge University Press.

Scribner, S. (1979). Modes of thinking and ways of speaking: Culture and logic reconsidered. In I. O. Freedle (Ed.), *New directions in discourse processing* (pp. 223–243). Norwood, NJ: Able.

Scroppo, J. C., Drob, S. L., Weinberger, J., & Eagle, P. (1998). Identifying dissociative identity disorder: A self-report and projective study. *Journal of Psychology, 107,* 272–284.

Seager, S. B. (1998). *Street crazy: The tragedy of the homeless mentally ill.* New York: Westcom Press.

Seamon, J. G., McKenna, P. A., & Binder, N. (1998). The mere exposure effect is differentially sensitive to different judgment tasks. *Consciousness and Cognition: An International Journal, 7,* 85–102.

Sears, S., & Urizar, G. G., & Evans, G. D. (2000). Examining a stress-coping model of burnout and depression in extension agents. *International Journal of Stress Management, 7,* 49–59.

Seedat, S., & Stein, D. J. (2000). Trauma and post-traumatic stress disorder in women: A review. *International Clinical Psychopharmacology, 15*(Supp3), S25–S33.

Segal, N. L. (2000). Virtual twins: New findings on within-family environmental influences on intelligence. *Journal of Educational Psychology, 92*(3), 442–448.

Segal, N. L., & Bouchard, T. J. (2000). *Entwined lives: Twins and what they tell us about human behavior.* New York: Plumsock.

Segal, N. L., Topolski, T. D., Wilson, S. M., Brown, K. W., et al. (1995). Twin analysis of odor identification and perception. *Physiology and Behavior, 57,* 605–609.

Segall, M. H., Dasen, P. R., Berry, J. W., & Portinga, Y. H. (1990). *Human behavior in global perspective: An introduction to cross-cultural psychology.* Elmsford, NY: Pergamon Press.

Segerstrale, U. (2000). *Defenders of the truth: The battle for science in the sociobiology debate and beyond.* London: Oxford University Press.

Sejnowski, T. J. (1997). The year of the dendrite. *Science, 275,* 178–179.

Self, T., Aahony, M., Fleming, J., Walsh, J., Brown, S. D., & Steel, K. P. (1998). Shaker-1 mutations reveal roles for myosin VIIA in both development and function of cochlear hair cells. *Development, 125,* 557–566.

Seligman, M. E. P. (1975) *Helplessness: On depression, development, and death.* San Francisco: Freeman.

Seligman, M. E. P. (1994). *What you can change and what you can't.* New York: Alfred A. Knopf.

Seligman, M. E. P. (1995). The effectiveness of psychotherapy: The Consumer Reports study. *American Psychologist, 50,* 965–974.

Selye, H. (1936). A syndrome produced by diverse nocuous agents. *Nature, 138,* 32.

Selye, H. (1974). *Stress without distress.* New York: Harper & Row.

Seppa, N. (2000). Silencing a gene slows breast-tumor fighter. *Science News, 157,* 407.

Seppa, N. (2001). Sedentary off-hours link to Alzheimer's. *Science News, 159,* 148.

Shafer, A. B. (2000). Relation of the Big Five to Biodata and aspects of the self. *Personality & Individual Differences, 28,* 1017–1035.

Shaver, P., R., & Hazan, C. (1994). Attachment. In A. L. Weber & J. H. Harvey (Eds.), *Perspectives on close relationships* (pp. 110–130). Boston: Allyn & Bacon.

Shaw, M. E. (1981). *Group dynamics: The psychology of small group behavior* (3rd ed.). New York: McGraw-Hill.

Shaywitz, B. A., Bennett, A., Shaywitz, S. E., Pugh, K. R., Constable, R. T., et al. (1995). Sex differences in the functional organization of the brain for language. *Nature, 373,* 607–609.

Shaywitz, S. E., Shaywitz, B. A., Pugh, K. R., Fulbright, R. K., Skudlarski, P., Mencl, W. E., Constable, R. T., Naftolin, F., Palter, S. F., Marchione, K. E., Katz, L., Shankweiler, D. P., Fletcher, J. M., Lacadie, C., Keltz, M., & Gore, J. C. (1999). Effect of estrogen on brain activation patterns in postmenopausal women during working memory tasks. *Journal of the American Medical Association, 28,* 1197–1202.

Shea, S. C. (1988). *Psychiatric interviewing: The art of understanding.* Philadelphia: Saunders.

Sheehy, G. (1976). *Passages: Predictable crises of adult life.* New York: Dutton.

Sher, L. (2000). Psychological factors, immunity, and heart disease. *Psychosomatics, 41,* 372–373.

Sherif, M. (1966). *In common predicament: Social psychology of intergroup conflict and cooperation.* Boston: Houghton Mifflin.

Sherif, M. (1998). Experiments in group conflict. In J. M. Jenkins, K. Oatley et al.(Eds.), *Human emotions: A reader* (pp. 245–252). Malden, MA: Blackwell Publishers Inc.

Sherman, J. W., & Bessenoff, G. R. (1999). Stereotypes as source-monitoring cues: On the interaction between episodic and semantic memory. *Psychological Science, 10*(2), 106–110.

Sherman, R. A., Davis, G. D., & Wong, M. F. (1997). Behavioral treatment of exercise-induced urinary incontinence among female soldiers. *Military Medicine, 162,* 690–694.

Sherrid, P. (2001, February 26). After the breakthrough. *U.S. News & World Report,* p. 48.

Shiraev, E., & Levy, D. (2000). *Introduction to cross-cultural psychology: Critical thinking and contemporary applications.* Boston: Allyn & Bacon.

Shultz, T. R., Leveille, E., & Lepper, M. R. (1999). Free choice and cognitive dissonance revisited: Choosing 'lesser evils' versus 'greater goods.' *Personality and Social Psychology Bulletin, 25,* 40–48.

Shum, M. S. (1998). The role of temporal landmarks in autobiographical memory processes. *Psychological Bulletin, 124,* 423–442.

Shuntich, R. J., Loh, D., & Katz, D. (1998). Some relationships among affection, aggression and alcohol abuse in the family setting. *Perceptual and Motor Skills, 86,* 1051–1060.

Sidel, R. (1996). The enemy within: A commentary on the demonization of difference. *American Journal of Orthopsychiatry, 66*(4), 490–495.

Siegel, A., & Brutus, M. (1990). Neural substrates of aggression and range in the cat. *Progress in Psychobiology and Physiological Psychology, 14,* 135–143.

Sigelman, C. K. (1999). *Life-span human development* (3rd ed.). Pacific Grove, CA: Brooks/Cole.

Silver, E. (1995). Punishment or treatment? Comparing the lengths of confinement of successful and unsuccessful insanity defendants. *Law & Human Behavior, 19*(4), 375–388.

Silverman, I., & Phillips, K. (1998). The evolutionary psychology of spatial sex differences. In C. Crawford, & D. L. Krebs (Eds.), *Handbook of evolutionary psychology: Ideas, issues, and applications.* Mahwah, NJ: Erlbaum.

Simon, C. W., & Emmons, W. H. (1956). Responses to material presented during various stages of sleep. *Journal of Experimental Psychology, 51,* 89–97.

Simon, G. E. (1998). Management of somatoform and factitious disorders. In P. E. Nathan & J. M. Gorman (Eds.), *A guide to treatments that work* (pp. 408–422). New York: Oxford University Press.

Singer, M. I., Slovak, K., Frierson, T., & York, P. (1998). Viewing preferences, symptoms of psychological trauma, and violent behaviors among children who watch television. *Journal of the American Academy of Child and Adolescent Psychiatry, 37,* 1041–1048.

Skinner, B. F. (1948). Superstition in the pigeon. *Journal of Experimental Psychology, 38,* 168–172.

Skinner, B. F. (1953). *Science and human behavior.* New York: Macmillan.

Skinner, B. F. (1992). "Superstition" in the pigeon. *Journal of Experimental Psychology: General, 121*(3), 273–274.

Skodol, A. E., Oldham, J. M., & Gallaher, P. E. (1999). Axis II comorbidity of substance use disorders among patients referred for treatment of personality disorders. *American Journal of Psychiatry, 156,* 733–738.

Skuse, et al. (1997). Evidence from Turner's syndrome of an imprinted X-linked locus affecting cognitive function. *Nature, 387,* 705–708.

Slade, J. (1999). Nicotine. In B. S. McCrady, & E. E. Epstein (Eds). *Addictions: A comprehensive guidebook* (pp. 162–170). New York: Oxford University Press.

Sloan, L., Edmond, T., Rubin, A., & Doughty, M. (1998). Social workers' knowledge of and experience with sexual exploitation by psychotherapists. *Journal of the National Association of Social Workers, 43,* 43–53.

Slovenko, R. (1995). *Psychiatry and criminal culpability.* New York: Wiley.

Smart, D. W., & Smart, J. F. (1997). DSM-IV and culturally sensitive diagnosis: Some observations for counselors. *Journal of Counseling and Development, 75,* 392–398.

Smart, R., & Peterson, C. (1997). Super's career stages and the decision to change careers. *Journal of Vocational Behavior, 51,* 358–374.

Smith, A. (1982). *Powers of mind.* New York: Summit.

Smith, C. A., & Kirby, L. D. (2001). Affect and cognitive appraisal processes. In J. P. Forgas (Ed.), *Handbook of affect and* *social cognition*, pp. 75–92. Mahwah, NJ: Lawrence Erlbaum.

Smith, D. C., & Smith, D. (1997). *Caregiving: Hospice-proven techniques for healing body and soul.* New York: Macmillan Press.

Smith, E. E. (1995). Concepts and categorization. In E. E. Smith, D. N. Osherson, et al. (Eds.), *Thinking: An invitation to cognitive science*, Vol. 3 (2nd ed.), (pp. 3–33). Cambridge: MIT Press.

Smith, P. B., Dugan, S., & Trompenaars, F. (1997). Locus of control and affectivity by gender and occupational status: A 14-nation study. *Sex Roles, 36,* 51–77.

Smuts, B. (1995). The evolutionary origins of patriarchy. *Human Nature, 6,* 1–32.

Snarey, J. R. (1985). Cross-cultural universality of social-moral development: A critical review of Kohlbergian research. *Psychological Bulletin, 97,* 202–233.

Snarey, J. R. (1995). In communitarian voice: The sociological expansion of Kohlbergian theory, research, and practice. In W. M. Kurtines & J. L. Gerwirtz (Eds.), *Moral development: An introduction* (pp. 109–134). Boston: Allyn & Bacon.

Snow-Turek, A. L., Norris, M. P., & Tan, G. (1996). Active and passive coping strategies in chronic pain patients. *Pain, 64,* 445–462.

Sobel, D. S., & Ornstein, R. (1996). Rx: Healthy Thinking. *Mental Medicine Update, 4,* 3–6.

Sobieski, D. J. (2000, July 24). Letters. *Time,* p. 3.

Solms, M. (1997). *The neuropsychology of dreams.* Mahwah, NJ: Lawrence Erlbaum.

Soloff, P. H., Lynch, K. G., Kelly, T. M., Malone, K. M., & Mann, J. (2000). Characteristics of suicide attempts of patients with major depressive episode and borderline personality disorder: A comparative study. *American Journal of Psychiatry, 157,* 601–608.

Solomon, M. (2000). The fruits of their labor: A longitudinal exploration of parent personality and adjustment in their adult children. *Journal of Personality, 68(2),* 281–308.

Solomon, M., & Englis, B. G. (1994). Observations: The big picture: Product complementarity and integrated communications. *Journal of Advertising Research, 34(1),* 57–63.

Sommer, R. (1969). *Personal space.* Englewood Cliffs, NJ: Prentice Hall.

Son, L. K., & Metcalfe, J. (2000). Metacognitive and control strategies in study-time allocation. *Journal of Experimental Psychology: Learning, Memory, & Cognition, 26(1),* 204–221.

Spanis, C. W., Bianchin, M. M., Izquierdo, I, & McGaugh, J. L. (1999). Excitotoxic basolateral amygdala lesions potentiate the memory impairment effect of muscimol injected into the medial septal area. *Brain Research, 816,* 329–326.

Spearman, C. (1923). *The nature of "intelligence" and the principles of cognition.* London: Macmillan.

Spencer, P., & Vanden-Boom, E. (1999). Year after the death of Michigan State U. Student, family advocates sensible drinking. Lansing, MI: University Wire.

Sperling, G. (1960). The information available in brief visual presentations. *Psychological Monographs, 74* (Whole No. 498).

Spiegel, D. (1995). Hypnosis and suggestion. In D. L. Schachter (Ed.), *Memory distortion: How minds, brains, and societies reconstruct the past.* Cambridge, MA: Harvard University Press.

Spiegel, D. (1999). An altered state. *Mind/Body Health Newsletter, 8(1),* 3–5.

Spiegel, D., & Maldonado, J. R. (1999). Dissociative disorders. In R. E. Hales, S. C. Yudofsky, & J. C. Talbott (Eds.), *American psychiatric press textbook of psychiatry.* Washington, DC: American Psychiatric Press.

Spinweber, C. L. (1993). Randy Gardner. In M. A. Carskadon (Ed.), *Encyclopedia of sleep and dreaming.* New York: Macmillan.

Spitz, R. A., & Wolf, K. M. (1946). The smiling response: A contribution to the ontogenesis of social relations. *Genetic Psychology Monographs, 34,* 57–123.

Springer, S. P., & Deutsch, G. (1998). *Left brain, right brain.* New York: Freeman.

Squier, L. H., & Domhoff, G. W. (1998). The presentation of dreaming and dreams in introductory psychology textbooks: A critical examination. *Dreaming, 10,* 21–26.

Squire, L. R., & Zola, S. M. (1998). Episodic memory, semantic memory, and amnesia. *Hippocampus, 8,* 205–211.

Squire, L. R., Knowlton, B., & Musen, G. (1993). The structure and organization of memory. *Annual Review of Psychology, 44,* 453–495.

Sroufe, L. A. (1979). Socioemotional development. In J. Osofsky (Ed.), *Handbook of infant development* (pp. 462–516). New York: Wiley.

Stahl, S. M. (1997). Mental illness may be damaging to your brain. *Journal of Clinical Psychiatry, 58,* 289–290.

Stajkovic, A. D., & Luthans, F. (1998). Self-efficacy and work-related performance: A meta-analysis. *Psychological Bulletin, 124,* 240–261.

Stake, J. E. (1997). Integrating expressiveness and instrumentality in real-life settings: A new perspective on the benefits of androgyny. *Sex Roles, 37,* 541–564.

Steadman, H. J., McGreevy, M. A. Morrissey, J. P., Callahan, L. A., Robbins, P. C., & Cirincione, C. (1993). *Before and after Hinckley: Evaluating insanity defense reform.* New York: Guilford.

Steele, C. M. (1992, April). Race and the schooling of black Americans. *The Atlantic Monthly,* pp. 68–78.

Steele, C. M. (1997). A threat in the air: How stereotypes shape intellectual identity and performance. *American Psychologist, 52,* 613–629.

Steele, C. M., & Aronson, J. (1995). Stereotype threat and the intellectual test performance of African Americans. *Journal of Personality and Social Psychology, 69,* 797–811.

Steffens, D. C., & Krishnan, K. R. R. (1998). Strutural neuroimaging and mood disorders: Recent findings, implications for classification, and future directions. *Biological Psychiatry, 43,* 705–712.

Steinhart, P. (1986, March). Personal boundaries. *Audubon,* pp. 8–11.

Steinmetz, J. E. (1998). The localization of a simple type of learning and memory: The cerebellum and classical eyeblink conditioning. *Current Directions in Psychological Science, 7,* 72–77.

Steinmetz, J. E. (2000). Brain substrates of classical eyeblink conditioning: A highly localized but also distributed system. *Behavioural Brain Research, 110(1–2),* 13–24.

Stella, N., Schweitzer, P., & Piomelli, D. (1997). A second endogenous cannabinoid that modulates long-term potentiation. *Nature, 382,* 677–678.

Stephan, W., Berscheid, E., & Walster, E. (1971). Sexual arousal and heterosexual perception. *Journal of Personality and Social Psychology, 20(1),* 93–101.

Stepkoe, A., Cropley, M. & Joekes, K. (2000). Task demands and the pressures of everyday life: Associations between cardiovascular reactivity and work blood pressure and hearth rate. *Health Psychology, 19,* 46–54.

Sterman, M. B. (1996). Physiological origins and functional correlates of EEG rhythmic activities: Implications for self-regulation. *Biofeedback and Self Regulation, 21,* 3–33.

Stern, K., & McClintock, M. K. (1998). Regulation of ovulation by human pheromones. *Nature, 392,* 177–179.

Sternberg, R. J. (1985). *Beyond IQ: A triarchic theory of human intelligence.* New York: Cambridge University Press.

Sternberg, R. J. (1998). Principles of teaching for successful intelligence. *Educational Psychologist, 33,* 65–72.

Sternberg, R. J. (1999). The theory of successful intelligence. *Review of General Psychology, 3,* 292–316.

Sternberg, R. J., & Kaufman, J. C. (1998). Human abilities. *Annual Review of Psychology, 49,* 479–502.

Sternberg, R. J., & Lubart, T. I. (1992). Buy low and sell high: An investment approach to creativity. *Current Directions in Psychological Science, 1*(1), 1–5.

Stevenson, H. L., & Stigler, J. (1992). *The learning gap: Why our schools are failing and what we can learn from Japanese and Chinese education.* New York: Summit Books.

Stewart, A. J., & Ostrove, J. M. (1998). Women's personality in middle age: Gender, history, and midcourse corrections. *American Psychologist, 53*(11), 1185–1194.

Stewart, R. (1997). Female circumcision: Implications for North American nurses. *Journal of Psychosocial Nursing, 35,* 35–39.

Stewart, T., Doan, K. A., Gingrich, B. E., & Smith, E. (1998). The actor as context for social judgments: Effects of prior impressions and stereotypes. *Journal of Personality and Social Psychology, 75,* 1132–1154.

Stip, E. (2000). Novel antipsychotics: Issues and controversies. Typicality of atypical antipsychotics. *Journal of Psychiatry & Neuroscience, 25,* 137–153.

Stockhorst, U., Spennes-Saleh, S., Koerholz, D., Goebel, U., Schneider, M. E., Steingrueber, H-J., & Klosterhalfen, S. (2000). Anticipatory symptoms and anticipatory immune responses in pediatric cancer patients receiving chemotherapy: Features of a classically conditioned response? *Brain, Behavior & Immunity, 14*(3), 198–218.

Stolerman, I. P., & Jarvis, M. J. (1995). The scientific case that nicotine is addictive. *Psychopharmacology, 117,* 2–10.

Stoner, J. A. (1961). A comparison of individual and group decisions involving risk. *Unpublished master's thesis,* School of Industrial Management, MIT, Cambridge, MA.

Stormshak, E. A., Bierman, K. L., McMahon, R. J., & Lengua, L. J., Conduct Problems Prevention Research Group. (2000). Parenting practices and child disruptive behavior problems in early elementary school. *Journal of Clinical Child Psychology, 29*(1), 17–29.

Strack, F., Martin, L. L., & Stepper, S. (1988). Inhibiting and facilitating conditions of the human smile: A nonobstrusive test of the facial feedback hypothesis. *Journal of Personality and Social Psychology, 54,* 768–777.

Stratton, G. M. (1897). Vision without inversion of the retinal image. *Psychological Review, 4*(4), 341–360.

Sturges, J. W., & Sturges, L. V. (1998). In vivo systematic desensitization in a single-session treatment of an 11-year-old girl's elevator phobia. *Child & Family Behavior Therapy, 20*(4), 55–62.

Sue, D. W., & Sue, D. (1999). *Counseling the culturally different.* New York: Wiley.

Sullivan, M. J. L., Tripp, D. A., & Santor, D. (1998). Gender differences in pain and pain behavior: The role of catastrophizing. Paper presented at the annual meeting of the American Psychological Association, San Francisco.

Sulloway, F. J. (2000). Birth order, sibling competition, and human behavior. In P. C. Davies & H. R. Holcombs (Eds.), The evolution of minds: Psychological and philosophical perspectives. Boston: Kluwer Academic.

Susskind, J., Maurer, K. Thakkar, V., Hamilton, D. L., & Sherman, J. W. (1999). Perceiving individuals and groups: Expectan-cies, dispositional inferences, and causal attributions. *Journal of Personality and Social Psychology, 76,* 181–191.

Sutherland, G. R., & McNaughton, B. (2000). Memory trace reactivation in hippocampal and neocortical neuronal ensembles. *Current Opinion in Neurobiology, 10,* 180–186.

Suzuki, L. A., & Valencia, R. R. (1997). Race-ethnicity and measured intelligence: Educational implications. *American Psychologist, 52,* 11–3–1114.

Swets, J. A., Dawes, R. M., & Monahan, J. (2000). Psychological science can improve diagnostic decisions. *Psychological Science in the Public Interest, 1,* 1–26.

Sylvester, A. P., Mulsant, B. H., Chengappa, K. N. R., Sandman, A. R., & Haskett, R. F. (2000). Use of electroconvulsive therapy in a state hospital: A 10–year review. *Journal of Clinical Psychiatry, 61,* 534–544.

Szasz, T. (1995, May/June). Idleness and lawlessness in the therapeutic state. *Society,* pp. 30–35.

Szasz, T. S. (1960). The myth of mental illness. *American Psychologist, 15,* 113–118.

Szasz, T. S. (1987). *Insanity: The idea and its consequences.* New York: Wiley.

Takeshita, T., & Morimoto, K. (1999). Self-reported alcohol-associated symptoms and drinking behavior in three ALDH2 genotypes among Japanese University students. *Alcoholism: Clinical & Experimental Research, 23*(6), 1065–1069.

Talbot, N. L., Duberstein, P. R., King, D. A., Cox, C., & Giles, D. E. (2000). Personality traits of women with a history of childhood sexual abuse. *Comprehensive Psychiatry, 41,* 130–136.

Tanda, G., Pontieri, F. E., & Di Chiara, G. (1997). Cannabinoid and heroin activation of mesolimbic dopamine transmission by a common 1 opioid receptor mechanism. *Science, 276,* 2048–2050.

Tang, Y-P., Shimizu, E., Dube, G. R., Rampon, C., Kerchner, G. A., Zhuo, M., Liu, G., & Tsien, J. Z. (1999). Genetic enhancement of learning and memory in mice. *Nature, 401,* 63–69.

Tanner, B. L. (1992). Mental disorders, psychiatric patients and suicide. In R. W. Marls, A. L. Berman, J. T. Maltsberger, & R. I. Yufit (Eds.), *Assessment and prediction of suicide* (pp. 227–320).

Tanner-Halverson, P., Burden, T., & Sabers, D. (1993). WISC-III normative data for Tohono O'odham Native-American children. In B. A. Bracken & R. S. McCallum (Eds.), *Journal of Psychoeducational Assessment Monograph Series, Advances in Psychoeducational Assessment: Wechsler Intelligence Scale for Children–Third Edition* (pp. 125–133). Germantown, TN: Psychoeducational Corporation.

Taraban, R., Maki, W. S., & Rynearson, K. (1999). Measuring study time distributions: Implications for designing computer-based courses. *Behavior Research Methods, Instruments & Computers, 31,* 263–269.

Tardiff, K. (1999). Violence. In R. E. Hales, S. C. Yudofsky, & J. A. Talbott (Eds.), *American psychiatric press textbook of psychiatry*. Washington, DC: American Psychiatric Press.

Tart, C. T. (1986). Consciousness, altered states, and worlds of experience. *Journal of Transpersonal Psychology, 18,* 159–170.

Tattersall, C. (2000). *Date rape drugs*. Thousand Oaks, CA: Rosen Publishers.

Taub, E., & Uswatte, G. (2000). Constraint-induced movement therapy based on behavioral neuroscience. In R. G. Frank, T. R. Elliott, et al. (Eds.), *Handbook of rehabilitation psychology* (Vol. 14). Washington, DC: American Psychological Association.

Taub, E., Crago, J. E., & Uswatte, G. (1998). Constraint-induced movement therapy: A new approach in physical rehabilitation. *Rehabilitation Psychology, 43* (2), 152–170.

Tauscher, J., Pirker, W., de Zwann, M., Asenbaum, S., Bruecke, T., & Kasper, S. (1999). In vivo visualization of serotonin transporters in the human brain during fluoxetine treatment. *European Neuropsychopharmacology, 9,* 117–179.

Taylor, E. (1999). William James and Sigmund Freud: "The future of psychology belongs to your work." *Psychological Science, 10*(6), 465–469.

Taylor, M. J. (2000). The influence of self-efficacy on alcohol use among American Indians. *Cultural Diversity and Ethnic Minority Psychology, 6,* 152–167.

Taylor, R. C., Harris, N. A., Singleton, E. G., Moolchan, E. T., & Heishman, S. J. (2000). Tobacco craving: Intensity-relate effects of imagery scripts in drug abusers. *Experimental and Clinical Psychopharmacology, 8*(1), 75–87.

Taylor, R. D., & Wang, M. C. (2000). *Resilience across contexts: Family, work, culture, and community*.

Taylor, S. E., & Armor, D. A. (1996). Positive illusions and coping with adversity. *Journal of Personality, 64,* 873–898.

Tedlock, B. (1992). Zuni and Quiche dream sharing and interpreting. In B. Tedlock (Ed.), *Dreaming: Anthropological and psychological interpretations*. Santa Fe, NM: School of American Research Press.

Tein, J-Y, Sandler, I. N., Zautra, A. J. (2000). Stressful life events, psychological distress, coping, and parenting of divorced mothers longitudinal study. *Journal of Family Psychology, 14*(1), 27–42.

Tellegen, A. (1985). Structures of mood and personality and their relevance to assessing anxiety with an emphasis on self-report. In A. H. Tuma & J. D. Maser (Eds.), *Anxiety and the anxiety disorders* (pp. 681–706). Hillsdale, NJ: Erlbaum.

Teller, D. Y., Peeples, D. R., & Sekel, M. (1978). Discrimination of chromatic from white light by two-month-old human infants. *Vision research, 18*(1), 41–48.

Temple, C. M., & Marriott, A. J. (1998). Arithmetical ability and disability in Turner's syndrome: A cognitive neuropsychological analysis. *Developmental Neuropsychology, 14,* 47–67.

Tennant, C. (1999). Life stress, social support, and coronary heart disease. *Australian & New Zealand Journal of Psychiatry, 33,* 636–641.

Terman, L. M. (1916). The measurement of intelligence. Boston: Houghton Mifflin.

Terman, L. M. (1954). Scientists and non-scientists in a group of 800 gifted men. *Psychological Monographs, 68*(7), 1–44.

Terrace, H. S. (1979, November). How Nim Chimpsky changed my mind. *Psychology Today,* pp. 65–76.

Thomas, A., & Chess, S. (1977). *Temperament and development*. New York: Brunner/Mazel.

Thomas, A., & Chess, S. (1987). Roundtable: What is temperament: Four approaches. *Child Development,* 58, 505–529.

Thomas, A., & Chess, S. (1991). Temperament in adolescence and its functional significance. In R. M. Lerner, A. C. Petersen, & J. Brooks-Gunn (Eds.), *Encyclopedia of adolescence* (Vol. 2). New York: Garland.

Thompson, C. P., Cowan, T. M., & Frieman, J. (1993). *Memory search by a mnemonist*. Hillsdale, NJ: Erlbaum.

Thompson, D. (1997, March 24). A boy without a penis. *Time,* 83.

Thompson, M., & Kaslow, N. J. (2000). Childhood maltreatment, PTSD, and suicidal behavior among African American females. *Journal of Interpersonal Violence,* 15, 3–16.

Thompson, R. A. (1998). Early sociopersonality development. In W. Damon & R. M. Lerner (Eds.), *Handbook of child psychology* (Vol. 1). New York: John Wiley & Sons.

Thompson, R. F. (1986). The neurobiology of learning and memory. *Science, 233,* 941–947.

Thompson, R. F. (1989). A model system approach to memory. In P. R. Solomon, G.

R. Goethals, C. M. Kelley, & B. R. Stephens (Eds.), *Memory: Interdisciplinary approaches*. New York: Springer-Verlag.

Thompson, R. F. (1992). Memory. *Current Opinion in Neurobiology, 2,* 203–208.

Thompson, V. A., & Paivio, A. (1994). Memory for pictures and sounds: Independence of auditory and visual codes. *Canadian Journal of Experimental Psychology,* 48, 380–398.

Thorndike, E. L. (1898). Animal intelligence. *Psychological Review Monograph,* 2(8).

Thorndike, E. L. (1911). *Animal intelligence*. New York: Macmilan.

Thunberg, M., & Dimberg, U. (2000). Gender differences in facial reactions to fear-relevant stimuli. *Journal of Nonverbal Behavior, 24*(1), 45–51.

Thurstone, L. L. (1938). *Primary mental abilities*. Chicago: University of Chicago Press.

Tice, D. M., & Baumeister, R. F. (1997). Longitudinal study of procrastination, performance, stress, and health: The costs and benefits of dawdling. *Psychological Science,* 8, 454–458.

Tien, J. Y., Sandler, I. N., & Zautra, A. J. (2000). Stressful life events, psychological distress, coping, and parenting of divorced mothers longitudinal study. *Journal of Family Psychology, 14*(1), 27–41.

Tierney, M. C., Varga, M., Hosey, L., Grafman, J., & Braun, A. (2001). PET evaluation of bilingual language compensation following early childhood brain damage. *Neuropsychologia, 39*(2), 114–121.

Tiffany, S. T., Sanderson, L., & Flash, C. A. (2000). Effects of transdermal nicotine patches on abstinence-induced and cue-induced craving in cigarette smokers. *Journal of Consulting and Clinical Psychology,* 68, 233–240.

Tiihonen, J., Isohanni, M., Rasanen, P., Koiranen, M., & Moring, J. (1997). Specific major mental disorders and criminality: A 26-year prospective study of the 1966 northern Finland birth cohort. *American Journal of Psychiatry, 154,* 840–845.

Tobin, D. L. (2000). *Coping strategies therapy for bulimia nervosa*. Washington, DC: American Psychological Association.

Tolman, E. C., & Honzik, C. H. (1930). Introduction and removal of reward and maze performance in rats. *University of California Publications in Psychology, 4,* 257–275.

Tolman, E. C., Ritchie, B. F., & Kalish, D. (1946). Studies in spatial learning: II.

Place learning versus response learning. *Journal of Experimental Psychology, 36,* 221–229.

Tolosa, E., Marti, M. J., Valldeoriola, F., & Molinuevo, J. L. (1998). History of levodopa and dopamine agonists in Parkinson's disease treatment. *Neurology, 50*(6, Suppl 6), S2–S10.

Toomey, R., Faraone, S. V., Simpson, J. C., & Tsuang, M. T. (1998). Negative, positive, and disorganized symptom dimensions in schizophrenia, major depression, and bipolar disorder. *Journal of Nervous and Mental Disease, 186,* 470–476.

Torgersen, S. (2000). Genetics of patients with borderline personality disorder. *Psychiatric Clinics of North America, 23,* 1–9.

Torrey, E. F. (1998). *Out of the shadows: Confronting America's mental illness crisis.* New York: Wiley.

Torrey, E. F., & Yolken, R. H. (1998). Is household crowding a risk factor for schizophrenia and bipolar disorder? *Schizophrenia Bulletin, 24,* 321–324.

Torrey, E. F., & Yolken, R. H. (2000). Familial and genetic mechanisms in schizophrenia. *Brain Research Reviews, 31,* 113–117.

Toth, J. P., & Reingold, E. M. (1996). *Beyond perception: Conceptual contributions to unconscious influences of memory.* Oxford, England: Oxford University Press.

Tracy, J. A., Thompson, J. K., Krupa, D. J., & Thompson, R. F. (1998). Evidence of plasticity in the pontocerebellar condition stimulus pathway during classical conditioning of the eyeblink response in the rabbit. *Behavioral Neuroscience, 112,* 267–285.

Trappey, C. (1996). A meta-analysis of consumer choice and subliminal advertising. *Psychology and Marketing, 13,* 517–530.

Travis, J. (2000). Brain heal thyself. *Science News, 158,* 63.

Travis, J. (2000). Human genome work reaches milestone. *Science News, 158,* 4.

Travis, J. (2000). Nerve connections come ready to assemble. *Science News, 157,* 262.

Troll, S. J., Miller, J., & Atchley, R. C. (1979). *Families in later life.* Belmont, CA: Wadsworth.

Trotter, R. J. (1987, January). The play's the thing. *Psychology Today,* pp. 27–34.

Truchlicka, M., McLaughlin, T. F., & Swain, J. C. (1998). Effects of token reinforcement and response cost on the accuracy of spelling performance with middle-school special education students with behavior disorders. *Behavioral Interventions, 13*(1), 1–10.

Trull, T., Sher, K. J., Minks-Brown, C., Durbin, J., & Burr, R. (2000). Borderline personality disorder and substance use disorders: A review and integration. *Clinical Psychology Review, 20,* 235–253.

Trump, K. S. (2000). *Classroom killers? Hallway hostages? How schools can prevent and manage school crises.* Thousand Oaks, CA: Sage.

Tu, G-C., & Israel, Y. (1995). Alcohol consumption by Orient in North America is predicted largely by a single gene. *Behavior Genetics, 25*(1), 59–65.

Tulving, E, & Markowitsch, H. J. (1998). Episodic and declarative memory: Role of hippocampus. *Hippocampus, 8,* 198–204.

Tulving, E. (1985). How many memory systems are there? *American Psychologist, 40*(4), 385–398.

Tulving, E., & Thompson, D. M. (1973). Encoding specificity and retrieval processes in episodic memory. *Psychological Review, 80,* 352–373.

Turk, D. C. (1994). Perspectives on chronic pain: The role of psychological factors. *Cur-rent Directions in Psychological Science, 3,* 45–48.

Turnbull, C. M. (1961). Some observations regarding the experiences and behavior of the Bamputi pygmies. *American Journal of Psychology, 74,* 304–308.

Udry, J. R. (1998). Doing sex research on adolescents. In G. G. Brannigan, E. R. Allgeier, & A. R. Allgeier (Eds.), *The sex scientists* (pp. 49–60). New York: Longman.

Uecker, A. (1997). Neuroanatomical correlates of implicit and explicit memory for structurally possible and impossible visual objects. *Learning & Memory, 4,* 337–355.

Ulfberg, J., Carter, N., & Edling, C. (2000). Sleep-disorder breathing and occupational accidents. *Scandinavian Journal of Work, Environment, & Health, 26*(3), 237–242.

Ulrich, R. E., Stachnik, T. J., & Stainton, N. R. (1963). Student acceptance of generalized personality interpretations. *Psychological Reports, 13,* 831–834.

Underwood, J., & Pezdek, K. (1998). Memory suggestibility as an example of the sleeper effect. *Psychonomic Bulletin & Review, 5,* 449–453.

U.S. Bureau of the Census. (1999). *Historical Poverty Tables.* Available: http://www.census.gov/hhes/poverty/histpov/hstpov3.html

Unni, L. K. (1998). Beyond Tarcine: Recently developed cholinesterase inhibitors for the treatment of Alzheimer's disease. *CNS Drugs, 10,* 447–460.

Vaillant, G. E. (2000). Adaptive mental mechanisms: Their role in a positive psychology. *American Psychologist, 55*(1), 89–98.

Valenstein, E. S. (1998). *Blaming the brain: The truth about drugs and mental health.* New York: Free Press.

Valsiner, J. (2000). *Culture and human development.* Thousand Oaks, CA: Sage.

Van de Carr, F. R., & Lehrer, M. (1997). *While you are expecting: Your own prenatal classroom.* New York: Humanics Publishing.

Van de Castle, R. L. (1995). *Our dreaming mind.* New York: Ballantine Books.

van IJzendoorn, M. H., & De Wolff, M. S. (1997). In search of the absent father: Meta-analyses of infant-father attachment: A rejoinder to our discussants. *Child Development, 68,* 604–609.

Van Reekum, R., Conway, C. A., Gansler, D., & White, R. (1993). Neurobehavioral study of borderline personality disorder. *Journal of Psychiatry and Neuroscience, 18,* 121–129.

Vanable, P. A., Ostrow, D. G., McKirnan, D. J., Taywaditep, K. J., & Hope, B. A. (2000). Impact of combination therapies on HIV risk perceptions and sexual risk among HIV-Positive and HIV-Negative gay and bisexual men. *Health Psychology, 19*(2), 134–145.

Vance, J. E., Fernandez, G., & Biber, M. (1998). Educational progress in a population of youth with aggression and emotional disturbance: The role of risk and protective factors. *Journal of Emotional and Behavioral Disorders, 6,* 214–221.

Vaughan, C. (1996). *How life begins: The science of life in the womb.* New York: Times Books.

Vaughn, D. (1996). *The Challenger launch decision: Risky technology, culture, and deviance at NASA.* Chicago: University of Chicago Press.

Veatch, T. C. (1998). A theory of humor. *Humor: International Journal of Humor Research, 11,* 161–215.

Venter, C. et al., (2001). The sequence of the human genome. *Science, 291,* 1304–1323.

Ventura, S. J., Martin, J. A., Curtin, S. C., & Mathews, T. J. (1997). Report of final natality statistics, 1995. *Monthly Vital Statistics Report, 45*(11, Suppl. 2).

Hyattsville, MD: National Center for Health.

Vermeulen, R. J., Drukarch, B, Wolters, E. C., & Stoof, J. C. (1999). Dopamine D-sub(1) receptor agonists: The way forward for the treatment of Parkinson's disease. *CNS Drugs, 11,* 83–91.

Vertosick, F. T. (2000). *Why we hurt: The natural history of pain.* New York: Harcourt, Inc.

Vickers, J. C., et al. (2000). The cause of neuronal degeneration in Alzheimer's disease. *Progress in Neurobiology, 60,* 139–165.

Vidmar, N. (1997). Generic prejudice and the presumption of guilt in sex abuse trials. *Law and Human Behavior, 21*(1), 5–25.

Vogel, G. (2000). Death triggers regrowth of zebra finch neurons. *Science, 287,* 1381.

Volavka, J. (1990). Aggression, electroencephalography, and evoked potentials: A critical review. *Neuropsychiatry, Neuropsychology, and Behavioral Neurology, 3,* 249–259.

Volavka, J. (1999). The neurobiology of violence: An update. *Journal of Neuropsychiatry & Clinical Neurosciences, 11,*(3) 307–314.

Voyer, D., Voyer, S., & Bryden, M. (1995). Magnitude of sex differences in spatial abilities: A meta-analysis and consideration of critical variables. *Psychological Bulletin, 117,* 250–270.

Vuilleumier, P., Reverdin, A., & Landis, T. (1997). Four legs: Illusory reduplication of the lower limbs after bilateral parietal lobe damage. *Archives of Neurology, 54,* 1534–1547.

Wadden, T. S., Vogt, R. A., Anderson, R. E., Bartlett, S. J., Foster, G. D., Kuehnel, R. H., Wilk, J., Weinstock, R., Buckenmeyer, P., Berkowitz, R. I., & Steen, S. N. (1997). Exer-cise in the treatment of obesity: Effects of four interventions on body composition, resting energy expenditure, appetite, and mood. *Journal of Consulting and Clinical Psychology, 65,* 269–277.

Wade, T. D., Bulik, C. M., Sullivan, P. F., Neale, M. C., & Kendler, K. S. (2000). The relation between risk factors for binge eating and bulimia nervosa: A population-based female twin study. *Health Psychology, 19*(2), 115–123.

Wade, T. J., & Abez, H. (1997). Social cognition and evolutionary psychology: Physical attractiveness and contrast effects on women's self-perceived body image. *International Journal of Psychology, 32,* 35–42.

Wagner, A. D., Schacter, D. L., Rotte, M., Koustaal, W., Maril, A., Dale, A. M., Rosen, B. R., & Buckner, R. L. (1998). Building memories: Remembering and forgetting of verbal experiences as predicted by brain activity. *Science, 281,* 1188–1191.

Wagner, D. A. (1982). Ontogeny in the study of culture and cognition. In D. A. Wagner & H. W. Stevenson (Eds.), *Cultural perspectives on child development* (pp. 105–123). San Francisco: Freeman.

Walker, E. F., & Diforio, D. (1997). Schizo-phrenia: A neural diathesis-stress model. *Psychological Review, 104,* 667–685.

Walker, I., & Crogan, M. (1998). Academic performance, prejudice, and the Jigsaw classroom: New pieces to the puzzle. *Journal of Community and Applied Social Psychology, 8,* 381–393.

Wallace, A. F. C. (1958). Dreams and wishes of the soul: A type of psychoanalytic theory among the seventeenth century Iroquois. *American Anthropologist, 60,* 234–248.

Wallace, D. C. (1997, August). Mitochondrial DNA in aging and disease. *Scientific American,* 40–47.

Waller, N. G., & Ross, C. A. (1997). The prevalence and biometric structure of pathological dissociation in the general population: Taxometric and behavior genetics findings. *Journal of Abnormal Psychology, 106,* 499–510.

Wallerstein, J. S., & Lewis, J. (1998). The long-term impact of divorce on children: A first report from a 25-year study. *Family & Conciliation Courts Review, 36*(3), 368–383.

Walsh, J. K., & Lindblom, S. S. (1997). Psychophysiology of sleep deprivation and disruption. In M. R. Pressman, W. C. Orr, et al. (Eds.), *Understanding sleep: The evaluation and treatment of sleep disorders. Application and practice in health psychology* (pp. 73–110). Washington, DC: American Psychological Association.

Walton, B. (2000, May 29). Basketball's tarnished knight. Time, p. 96.

Wang, A., Laing, Y., Fridell, R. A., Probst, F. J., Wilcox, E. R., Touchman, J. W., Morton, C. C., Morell, R. J., Noben-Trauth, K., Camper, S. A., & Friedman, T. B. (1998). Association of unconventional myosin MY015 mutations with human nonsyndromic deafness DFNB3. *Science, 280,* 1447–1451.

Wang, D. L. (1999). Object selection based on oscillatory correlation. *Neural Networks, 12,* 579–592.

Wang, D. L., & Terman, D. (1997). Image segmentation based on oscillatory correlation. *Neural Computation, 9,* 805–836.

Wang, M., Irwin, R., & Hautus, M. J. (1998). Discriminability in length of lines in the Müller-Lyer figure. *Perception & Psycho-physics, 60,* 511–517.

Wang, S., Mason, J., Charney, D., & Yehuda, R. (1997). Relationships between hormonal profile and novelty seeking in combat-related posttraumatic stress disorder. *Biological Psychiatry, 41,* 145–151.

Ward, I. (2000). *Introducing psychoanalysis.* Thousand Oaks, CA: Totem Books.

Wark, G. R., & Krebs, D. L. (1996). Gender and dilemma differences in real-life moral judgment. *Developmental Psychology, 32,* 220–230.

Wartik, N. (1996). Learning to mourn. *American Health, 15*(4), 76–79, 96.

Wasserman, D., & Wachbroit, R. S. (2000). *Genetics and criminal behavior.* Cambridge, MA: Cambridge University Press.

Wason, P. C. (1968). Reasoning about a rule. *Quarterly Journal of Experimental Psychology, 20*(3), 273–281.

Watkins, L. M., & Johnston, L. (2000). Screening job applicants: The impact of physical attractiveness and application quality. *International Journal of Selection & Assessment, 8*(2), 76–84.

Watkins, L. R., & Maier, S. F. (2000). The pain of being sick: Implications of immune-to-brain communication for understanding pain. *Annual Review of Psychology, 51,* 29–57.

Watson, J. (1913). Psychology as the behaviorist views it. *Psychological Review, 20,* 158–177.

Watson, J. (2000, July 3). The double helix revisited. *Time,* p. 30.

Watson, J. B., & Rayner, R. (1920). Conditioned emotional reactions. *Journal of Experimental Psychology, 3,* 1–14.

Watson, J. B., & Rayner, R. (2000). Conditioned emotional reactions. *American Psychologist, 55*(3), 313–317.

Watson, J. B., Mednick, S. A.; Huttunen, M., Wang, X. (1999). Prenatal teratogens and the development of adult mental illness. *Development & Psychopathology, 11*(3), 457–466.

Weaver, C. A., & Kelemen, W. L. (1997). Judgments of learning at delays: Shifts in response patterns or increased metamemory accuracy? *Psychological Science, 8,* 318–321.

Webb, A. L., Solomon, D. A., & Ryan, C. A. (2001). Lithium levels and toxicity among hospitalized patients. *Psychiatric Services, 52*(2), 229–231.

Webb, W. B. (1992). *Sleep the gentle tyrant* (2nd ed.). Bolton, MA: Anker.

Wechsler, H., Dowdall, G. W., Maenner, G., Gledhill-Hoyt, J., & Lee, H. (1998). Changes in binge drinking and related problems among American college students between 1993 and 1997: Results of the Harvard School of Public Health College Alcohol Study. *Journal of American College Health, 47,* 57–68.

Wechsler, H., Lee, J. E., Kuo, M., & Lee, H. (2000). College binge drinking in the 1990's: A continuing problem: Results of the Harvard School of Public Health 1999 College Alcohol Study. *Journal of American College Health, 48,* 199–210.

Wechsler, H., Rigotti, N. A., Gledhill-Hoyt, J., & Lee, H. (1998). Increased levels of cigarette use among college students: A cause for national concern. *Journal of the American Medical Association, 280*(19), 1673–1678.

Wegerer, V., Moll, H., Bagli, M., Rothenberger, A., Ruether, E., & Huether, G. (1999). Persistently increased density of serotonin transporters in the frontal cortex of rats treated with fluoxetine during early juvenile life. *Journal of Child & Adolescent Psychopharmacology, 9*(1), 13–24.

Wehrle, T., Kaiser, S., Schmidt, S., & Scherer, K. R. (2000). Studying the dynamics of emotional expression using synthesized facial muscle movements. *Journal of Personality and Social Psychology, 78*(1), 105–119.

Weil, A., & Rosen, W. (1993). *From chocolate to morphine: Everyday mind-altering drugs.* Boston: Houghton Mifflin.

Weil, M. M., & Rosen, L. D. (1997). Coping with technology @work @home @play. New York: Wiley.

Weiner, B. (1972). *Theories of motivation.* Chicago: Rand-McNally.

Weiner, B. (1982). The emotional consequences of causal attributions. In M. S. Clark & S. T. Fiske (Eds.), *Affect and cognition.* Hillsdale, NJ: Erlbaum.

Weingardt, K. R., Baer, J. S., Kivlahan, D. R., Roberts, L. J., Miller, E. T., & Marlatt, G. A. (1998). Episodic heavy drinking among college students: Methodological issues and longitudinal perspectives. *Psy-*

chology of Addictive Behaviors, 12(3), 155–161.

Weisberg, R. W. (1993). *Creativity: Beyond the myth of genius.* New York: W. H. Freeman.

Welch-Ross, M. K., & Schmidt, C. R. (1996). Gender-schema development and children's constructive story memory: Evidence for a developmental model. *Child Development, 67,* 820–835.

Welchman, K. (2000). *Erik Erikson: His life, work, and significance.* London: Oxford University Press.

Wells, G. L., Malpass, R. S., Lindsay, R. C. L., Fisher, R. P., Turtle, J. W., & Fulero, S. M. (2000). From the lab to the police station: A successful application of eyewitness research. *American Psychologist, 55,* 581–598.

Wen, W., Wang, Y., Zhao, G., & Sun, J. (2000). 1/Research on the relationship between social support and psychological control and mental health. *Chinese Mental Health Journal, 14*(4), 258–260.

Werner, E. E. (1993). Risk resiliency and recovery: Perspectives from the Kauai Longitudinal Study. *Development and Psychopathology, 5,* 503–515.

Werner, E. E. (1995). Resilience in development. *Current Directions in Psychological Science, 5,* 112–116.

Werner, E. E. (1999). Risk, resilience, and recovery: Perspectives from the Kauai Longi-tudinal Study. In L. E. Berk, *Landscapes of development* (pp. 445–460). Belmont, CA: Wadsworth.

Werner, J. S., & Wooten, B. R. (1979). Human infant color vision and color perception. *Infant Behavior and Development, 2*(3), 241–273.

Wertz, F. J. (1998). The role of the humanistic movement in the history of psychology. *Journal of Humanistic Psychology, 38,* 42–70.

Westen, D. (1998). Unconscious thought, feeling, and motivation: The end of a century-long debate. In R. F. Bornstein & J. M. Masling (Eds.), *Empirical perspectives on the psychoanalytic unconscious.* Washington, DC: American Psychological Association.

Wetter, D. W., Fiore, M. C., Gritz, E. R., Lando, H. A., Stitzer, M. L., Hasselblad, V., & Baker, T. B. (1998). The Agency for Health Care Policy and Research Smoking Cessation Clinical Practice Guideline: Findings and implications for psychologists. *American Psychologist, 53*(6), 657–669.

Whelan, T. A., & Kirkby, R. J. (2000). Parent adjustment to a child's hospitalization. *Journal of Family Studies, 6,* 46–64.

Whitbourne, S. (2000). *Adult development and aging: Biopsychosocial perspectives.* New York: Wiley.

White, J. R., & Freeman, A. S. (2000). *Cognitive-behavioral group therapy for specific problems and populations.* Washington, DC: American Psychological Association.

White, L. K., & Rogers, S. J. (1997). Strong support but uneasy relationships: Coresidence and adult children's relationships with their parents. *Journal of Marriage and the Family, 59,* 62–76.

White, N. M., & Milner, P. M. (1992). The psychobiology of reinforcers. *Annual Review of Psychology, 43,* 443–471.

White, W. F. (1997). Why students can't remember: The problem of forgetting. *Journal of Instructional Psychology, 24,* 140–143.

Whiteside, M. F., & Becker, B. J. (2000). Parental factors and the young child's postdivorce adjustment: A meta-analysis with implications for parenting arrangements. *Journal of Family Psychology, 14*(1), 5–26.

Whorf, B. L. (1956). Science and linguistics. In J. B. Carroll (Ed.), *Language, thought and reality.* Cambridge, MA: MIT Press.

Whyte, M. K., (1992, March-April). Choosing mates – the American way. *Society,* pp. 71–77.

Wickelgren, I. (1998). Teaching the brain to take drugs. *Science, 280,* 2045–2047.

Wickelgren, I. (1999). Rat spinal cord function partially restored. *Science, 286,* 1826–1827.

Widiger, T. A., & Sankis, L. M. (2000). Adult psychopathology. *Annual Review of Psychology, 51,* 377–404.

Wigfield, A., & Eccles, J. S. (2000). Expectancy-value of achievement motivation. *Contemporary Educational Psychology, 25*(1), 68–81.

Williams, A. L., Haber, D., Weaver, G. D., & Freeman, J. L. (1998). Altruistic activity: Does it make a difference in the senior center? *Activities, Adaptation and Aging, 22*(4), 31–39.

Williams, D. E., & Page, M. M. (1989). A multi-dimensional measure of Maslow's hierarchy of needs. *Journal of Research in Person-ality, 23,* 192–213.

Williams, J. E., & Best, D. L. (1990). *Sex and psyche: Gender and self viewed cross-culturally.* Newbury Park, CA: Sage.

Williams, T. J., Pepitone, M. E., Christensen, S.E., Cooke, B. M., Huberman, S. D., Breedlove, N. J., Breedlove, T. J., Jordan, C. I., & Breedlove, M. (2000). Finger length patterns and human sexual orientation. *Nature, 404*(6777),455–456.

Williams, W. M., & Ceci, S. J. (1997). Are Americans becoming more or less alike? Trends in race, class, and ability differences in intelligence. *American Psychologist, 52,* 1126–1235.

Williamson, M. (1997). Circumcision anesthesia: A study of nursing implication for dorsal penile nerve block. *Pediatric Nursing, 23,* 59–63.

Willner, P. (1997). The dopamine hypothesis of schizophrenia: current status, future prospects. *International Clinical Psychopharmacology, 12,* 297–308.

Wilson, C. (1967). Existential psychology: A novelist's approach. In J. F. T. Bugental (Ed.), *Challenges of humanistic psychology.* New York: McGraw-Hill.

Wilson, E. O. (1975). *Sociobiology: The new synthesis.* Cambridge, MA: Harvard University Press.

Wilson, E. O. (1978). *On human nature.* Cambridge, MA: Harvard University Press.

Wilson, R. S., Gilley, D. W., Bennett, D. A., Beckett, L. A., & Evans, D. A. (2000). Person-specific paths of cognitive decline in Alzeimer's disease and their relation to age. *Psychology & Aging, 15*(1), 18–28.

Windle, M. (1999). *Alcohol use among adolescents.* Thousand Oaks, CA: Sage.

Winnubst, J. A. M., Buunk, B. P., & Marcelissen, F. H. G. (1988). Social support and stress: Perspectives and processes. In S. Fisher & J. Reason (Eds.), *Handbook of life stress, cognition and health.* New York: Wiley.

Winzelberg, A., Eppstein, D., Eldredge, K. L., Wilfley, D., Dasmahpatra, R., Taylor, C. B., & Dev, P. E. (2000). Effectiveness of an Internet-based program for reducing risk factors for eating disorders. *Journal of consulting and Clinical Psychology, 68*(2), 346–350.

Wirshing, D. A., Marshall, B. D., Green, M. F., Mintz, J. et al. (1999). Risperidone in treatment-refractory schizophrenia. *American Journal of Psychiatry, 156,* 1374–1379.

Wise, R. A., & Rompre, P. P. (1989). Brain dopamine and reward. *Annual Review of Psychology, 40,* 191–225.

Wisniewski, A. B. (1998). Sexually-dimorphic patterns of cortical asymmetry, and the role for sex steroid hormones in determining cortical patterns of lateralization. *Psychoneuroendocrinology, 23,* 519–547.

Witelson, S. F., Glazer, I. I., & Kigar, D. I. (1994). Sex differences in numerical density of neurons in human auditory association cortex. *Society for Neuroscience Abstracts, 30,* (Abstract No. 582. 12).

Witelson, S. F., Kigar, D. L., & Harvey, T. (1999). The exceptional brain of Albert Einstein. *The Lancet, 353,* 2149–2153.

Witt, S. D. (1997). Parental influences on children's socialization to gender roles. *Adolescence, 32,* 253–259.

Woelk, H. (2000). Comparison of St. John's wort and imipramine for treating depression: Randomised controlled trial. BMJ: *British Medical Journal, 321*(7260), 536–539.

Wolfe, D. A. (1999). *Child abuse: Implications for child development and psychopathology* (2nd ed). Thousand Oaks, CA: Sage.

Wolff, P. (1969). The natural history of crying and vocalization in early infancy. In B. M. Foss (Ed.), *Determinants of infant behavior* (Vol. IV). London: Methuen.

Wolpe, J. (1997). Thirty years of behavior therapy. *Behavior Therapy, 28,* 633–635.

Wolpe, J., & Plaud, J. J. (1997). Pavlov's contributions to behavior therapy. *American Psychologist, 52*(9), 966–972.

Wong, J., & Checkland, D. (2000). *Teen pregnancy and parenting: Social and ethical issues.* Toronto: University of Toronto Press.

Wood, D., Bruner, J. S., & Ross, G. (1976). The role of tutoring in problem solving. *Journal of Child Psychology & Psychiatry & Allied Disciplines, 17*(2), 89–100.

Wood, W., Christensen, P. N., Hebl, M. R., & Rothgerber, H. (1997). Conformity to sex-typed norms, affect, and the self-concept. *Journal of Personality and Social Psychology, 73,* 523–535.

Woods, E. R., Lin, Y. G., Middleman, A., Beckford, P., Chase, L., & DuRant, R. H. (1997). The associations of suicide attempts in adolescents. *Pediatrics, 99,* 791–796.

Woods, S. C., & Ramsay, D. S. (2000). Pavlovian influences over food and drug intake. *Behavioural Brain Research, 110*(1–2), 175–182.

Woods, S. C., Schwartz, M. W., Baskin, D. G., & Seeley, R. J. (2000). Food intake and the regulation of body weight. *Annual Review of Psychology, 51,* 255–277.

Woods, S. C., Seeley, R. J., Porte, D., & Schwartz, M. W. (1998). Signals that regulate food intake and energy homeostasis. *Science, 280,* 1378–1383.

Wootton, J. M., Frick, P. J., Shelton, K. K., & Silverthorn, P. (1997). Ineffective parenting and childhood conduct problems: The moderating role of callous-unemotional traits. *Journal of Consulting and Clinical Psychology, 65,* 301–308.

Worden, J. K., Flynn, B. S., Solomon, L. J., & Secker-Walker, R. H. (1996). Using mass media to prevent cigarette smoking among adolescent girls. *Health Education Quarterly, 23*(4), 453–468.

World Health Organization. (2000). *Epidemiology of Mental Disorders and Psychosocial Problems.* Available: http://www.who.int/dsa/cat98/men8.htm

Wright, D. B., Self, G., & Justice, C. (2000). Memory conformity: Exploring misinformation effects when presented by another person. *British Journal of Psychology, 91,* 189–202.

Wright, J. H., & Beck, A. T. (1999). Cognitive therapies. In R. E. Hales, S. C. Yudofsky, & J. A. Talbott (Eds.), *American Psychiatric Press textbook of psychiatry.* Washington, DC: American Psychiatric Press.

Wright, M. O., & Masten, A. S. (1997). Vulnerability and resilience in young children. In J. D. Noshpita (Series Ed.) & S. Greenspan, S. Weider, & J. Osofsky (Vol. Eds.), *Handbook of child and adolescent psychiatry: Vol. 1. Infants and preschoolers: Development and syndromes* (pp. 202–224). New York: Wiley.

Wright, W. (1998). *Born that way: Genes, behavior, personality.* New York: Knopf.

Wu, W., Yamaura, T., Murakami, K., Murata, J., Matsumoto, K., Watanabe, H., & Saiki, I. (2000). Social isolation stress enhanced liver metastasis of murine colon 26–L5 carcinoma cells by suppressing immune responses in mice. *Life Sciences, 66*(19),1827–1838.

Wyatt, J. K., & Bootzin, R. R. (1994). Cognitive processing and sleep: Implications for enhancing job performance. *Human Performance, 7,* 119–139.

Wysocki, C. J., & Preti, G. (1998). Pheromonal influences. *Archives of Sexual Behavior, 27,* 627–629.

Yamada, H. (1997). *Different games, different rules: Why Americans and Japanese misunderstand each other.* London: Oxford University Press.

Yee, A. H., Fairchild, H. H., Weizmann, F., & Wyatt, G. E. (1993). Addressing psychology's problem with race. *American Psychologist, 48,* 1132–1140.

Yehuda, R., Schmeidler, J., Wainberg, M., Binder-Brynes, K, & Duvdevani, T. (1998). Vulnerability to posttraumatic stress dis-order in adult offspring of Holocaust survivors. *American Journal of Psychiatry, 155,* 1163–1171.

Yeung, R. R. (1996). The acute effects of exercise on mood state. *Journal of Psychosomatic Research, 40,* 123–141.

Yonkers, K. A., Zlotnick, C., Allsworth, J., Warshaw, M., Shea, T., & Keller, M. B. (1998). Is the course of panic disorder the same in women and men? *American Journal of Psychiatry, 155,* 596–602.

Yoo, S. H., & Sung, K. (1997). Elderly Koreans' tendency to live independently from their adult children: Adaptation to cultural differences in America. *Journal of Cross-Cultural Gerontology, 12*(3), 225–244.

Young, T. (1802). Color vision. *Philosophical Transactions of the Royal Society,* p. 12.

Yudolfsky, S., & Silver, J. (1987). Treating performance anxiety. *The Harvard Mental Health Letter, 4*(6), 8.

Zahn-Waxler, C., Friedman, R. J., Cole, P. M., Mizuta, I., & Himura, N. (1996). Japanese and United States preschool children's responses to conflict and distress. *Child Development, 67,* 2462–2477.

Zajonc, R. B. (1968). The attitudinal effects of mere exposure. *Journal of Personality and Social Psychology, 9,* 1–27.

Zajonc, R. B. (1998). Emotions. In D. T. Gilbert, S. T. Fiske, & G. Lindzey (Eds.), *The handbook of social psychology,* Vol. 2 (4th ed.) (pp. 591–632). Boston, MA: McGraw-Hill.

Zaidel, D. W. (1985). Hemifield tachistoscopic presentations and hemispheric spe-cialization in normal subjects. In D. F. Benson, E. Zaidel, et al. (Eds.), *The dual brain: Hemispheric specialization in humans* (Vol. 18). New York: Guilford Press.

Zaidel, E. (1998). Stereognosis in the chronic split brain: Hemispheric differences, ipsilateral control and sensory integration across the midline. *Neuropsychologia, 36* (10), 1033–1047.

Zanarini, M. C., Williams, A. A., Lewis, R. E., Reich, R. B., Vera, S. C., et al. (1997). Reported pathological childhood experiences associated with the development of borderline personality disorder. *American Journal of Psychiatry, 154,* 1101–1106.

Zanigel, R., & Ressner, J. (2001). The copycat? Did Columbine inspire a new plot—or a fantasy? *Time,* p. 73.

Zeanah, C. H. (2000). Disturbances of attachment in young children adopted from institutions. *Journal of Developmental & Behavioral Pediatrics, 21*(3), 230–236.

Zelinski, E. M., & Stewart, S. T. (1998). Individual differences in 16-year memory changes. *Psychology & Aging, 13,* 622–630.

Zhou, J., Hofman, M., Gooren, L., & Swaab, D. (1995). A sex difference in the human brain and its relation to transsexuality. *Nature, 378,* 68–70.

Ziegler, J. M., Gustavson, C. R., Holzer, G. A., & Gruber, D. (1983). Anthelmintic-based taste aversions in wolves (Canis lupus). *Applied Animal Ethology, 3-sup-4,* 373–377.

Zillman, D., & Weaver, J. B. (1999). Effects of prolonged exposure to gratuitous media violence on provoked and unprovoked hostile behavior. *Journal of Applied Social Psychology, 29,* 145–165.

Zimbardo, P. (1993). Stanford prison experiment: A 20-year retrospective. *Invited presentation at the meeting of the Western Psycho-logical Association,* Phoenix, AZ.

Zimbardo, P. G. (1970). The human choice: Individuation, reason, and order versus deindividuation, impulse, and chaoe. In W. J. Arnold & D. Levine (Eds.), *Nebraska symposium on motivation.* Lincoln: University of Nebraska Press.

Zimbardo, P. G., Ebbeson, E. B., & Maslach, C. (1977). *Influencing attitudes and changing behavior.* Reading, MA: Addison-Wesley.

Zipursky, R. B., Lambe, E. K., Kapur, S., & Mikulis, D. J. (1998). Cerebral gray matter volume deficits in first episode psychosis. *Archives of General Psychiatry, 55,* 540–546.

Zuckerman, M. (1979). *Sensation seeking: Beyond the optimal level of arousal.* Hillsdale, NJ: Erlbaum.

Zuckerman, M. (1994). *Behavioral expressions and biosocial bases of sensation seeking.* New York: Cambridge University Press.

Zuckerman, M. (1995). Good and bad humors: Biochemical bases of personality and its disorders. *Psychological Science, 5,* 325–332.

Zuckerman, M. (1996). Item revisions in the Sensation Seeking Scale Form V (SS-V). *EDRA: Environmental Design Research Association, 20*(4), 515.

Zuckerman, M., & Kuhlman, D. M. (2000). Personality and risk-taking: Common biosocial factors. *Journal of Personality, 68*(6), 999–1029.

Zurbriggen, E. L. (2000). Social motives and cognitive power-sex associations: Predictors of aggressive sexual behavior. *Journal of Personality & Social Psychology, 78*(3), 559–581.

Photo Credits

Text and Illustration Credits

Name Index

Subject Index